WITHDRAWN

HANDBOOK OF
LATIN AMERICAN STUDIES:
No. 67

A Selective and Annotated Guide to Recent Publications
in Anthropology, Geography, Government and Politics,
International Relations, Political Economy, and Sociology

VOLUME 68 WILL BE DEVOTED TO THE HUMANITIES:
ART, HISTORY, LITERATURE, MUSIC, AND PHILOSOPHY

EDITORIAL NOTE: Comments concerning the *Handbook of Latin American Studies* should be sent directly to the Humanities or Social Sciences Editor, *Handbook of Latin American Studies*, Hispanic Division, Library of Congress, Washington, D.C. 20540-4851.

HANDBOOK OF LATIN AMERICAN STUDIES: NO. 67

SOCIAL SCIENCES

Prepared by a Number of Scholars
for the Hispanic Division of The Library of Congress

TRACY NORTH, *Social Sciences Editor*
KATHERINE D. McCANN, *Humanities Editor*

2012

UNIVERSITY OF TEXAS PRESS   *Austin*

International Standard Book Number: 978-0-292-73737-2
International Standard Serial Number: 0072-9833
Library of Congress Catalog Card Number: 36-32633

First Edition, 2012

The paper used in the publication meets the minimum requirements of American
National Standard for Information Sciences—Permanence of Paper for Printed
Library Materials, ANSI z39.48-1984. ∞

CONTRIBUTING EDITORS

SOCIAL SCIENCES

Benigno E. Aguirre-López, *University of Delaware*, SOCIOLOGY
Enrique Desmond Arias, *The City University of New York (CUNY)*, GOVERNMENT
AND POLITICS
Melissa H. Birch, *University of Kansas*, POLITICAL ECONOMY
Federico Bossert, *Universidad de Buenos Aires, Argentina*, ANTHROPOLOGY
Christian Brannstrom, *Texas A&M University*, GEOGRAPHY
Jacqueline Anne Braveboy-Wagner, *The City University of New York (CUNY)*,
INTERNATIONAL RELATIONS
Charles D. Brockett, *Sewanee: The University of the South*, GOVERNMENT AND
POLITICS
Roderic A. Camp, *Claremont-McKenna College*, GOVERNMENT AND POLITICS
William L. Canak, *Middle Tennessee State University*, SOCIOLOGY
María Esperanza Casullo, *Universidad Torcuato Di Tella, Argentina*, SOCIOLOGY
Jennifer N. Collins, *University of Wisconsin-Stevens Point*, GOVERNMENT AND
POLITICS
Thomaz Guedes Da Costa, *National Defense University*, INTERNATIONAL
RELATIONS
Bartholomew Dean, *University of Kansas*, ANTHROPOLOGY
Meredith Dudley, *Tulane University*, SOCIOLOGY
Duncan Earle, *Marymount College*, ANTHROPOLOGY
Scott M. Fitzpatrick, *North Carolina State University*, ANTHROPOLOGY
Mario A. González-Corzo, *The City University of New York (CUNY)*, POLITICAL
ECONOMY
Clifford E. Griffin, *North Carolina State University*, GOVERNMENT AND POLITICS
Daniel Hellinger, *Webster University*, POLITICAL ECONOMY
John Henderson, *Cornell University*, ANTHROPOLOGY
Peter H. Herlihy, *University of Kansas*, GEOGRAPHY
Eric Hershberg, *American University*, POLITICAL ECONOMY
Daniel Hilliard, *Zoo Conservation Outreach Group*, SOCIOLOGY
Silvia María Hirsch, *Universidad Nacional de San Martín, Argentina*,
ANTHROPOLOGY
Jonathan Hiskey, *Vanderbilt University*, POLITICAL ECONOMY
Keith Jamtgaard, *University of Missouri*, SOCIOLOGY
Arthur A. Joyce, *University of Colorado at Boulder*, ANTHROPOLOGY
Peter Klepeis, *Colgate University*, GEOGRAPHY
Daniel Klooster, *University of Redlands*, GEOGRAPHY
Gregory W. Knapp, *The University of Texas at Austin*, GEOGRAPHY
Xela Korda, *Tulane University*, SOCIOLOGY

Barbara Kotschwar, *Georgetown University*, POLITICAL ECONOMY
José Antonio Lucero, *University of Washington, Seattle*, GOVERNMENT AND
   POLITICS
Markos J. Mamalakis, *University of Wisconsin-Milwaukee*, POLITICAL ECONOMY
Ana Margheritis, *University of Florida, Gainesville*, POLITICAL ECONOMY
Daniel Masís-Iverson, *American University*, POLITICAL ECONOMY
Kent Mathewson, *Louisiana State University*, GEOGRAPHY
Philip Mauceri, *University of Northern Iowa*, GOVERNMENT AND POLITICS
Betty J. Meggers, *Smithsonian Institution*, ANTHROPOLOGY
Cecilia Menjívar, *Arizona State University*, SOCIOLOGY
Mary K. Meyer McAleese, *Eckerd College*, INTERNATIONAL RELATIONS
Donna J. Nash, *University of North Carolina at Greensboro*, ANTHROPOLOGY
Andrew Orta, *University of Illinois at Urbana-Champaign*, ANTHROPOLOGY
Enrique Pumar, *Catholic University*, SOCIOLOGY
Laura Randall, *Hunter College, City University of New York*, POLITICAL ECONOMY
Nicholas Rattray, *University of Arizona*, SOCIOLOGY
René Salgado, *Independent Consultant*, GOVERNMENT AND POLITICS
Joseph Leonard Scarpaci, Jr., *Virginia Polytechnic Institute*, GEOGRAPHY
Jörn Seeman, *Universidade Regional do Cariri, Brazil*, GEOGRAPHY
Andrew D. Selee, *Woodrow Wilson International Center for Scholars*,
   INTERNATIONAL RELATIONS
Peter M. Siavelis, *Wake Forest University*, GOVERNMENT AND POLITICS
Russell E. Smith, *Washburn University*, POLITICAL ECONOMY
Steven L. Taylor, *Troy University*, GOVERNMENT AND POLITICS
Brian Turner, *Randolph-Macon College*, GOVERNMENT AND POLITICS
Antonio Ugalde, *The University of Texas at Austin*, SOCIOLOGY
Aldo C. Vacs, *Skidmore College*, INTERNATIONAL RELATIONS
Robin M. Wright, *University of Florida, Gainesville*, ANTHROPOLOGY

HUMANITIES

Maureen Ahern, *Ohio State University*, TRANSLATIONS
Diana Alvarez-Amell, *Seton Hall University*, LITERATURE
Severino J. Albuquerque, *University of Wisconsin-Madison*, LITERATURE
Félix Ángel, *Inter-American Development Bank*, ART
Leslie Bayers, *St. Mary's College of Maryland*, LITERATURE
Dain Borges, *University of Chicago*, HISTORY
Dário Borim, *University of Massachusetts, Dartmouth*, LITERATURE
John Britton, *Francis Marion University*, HISTORY
Francisco Cabanillas, *Bowling Green State University*, LITERATURE
José Cardona-López, *Texas A&M International University*, LITERATURE
Matt Childs, *University of South Carolina*, HISTORY
Don M. Coerver, *Texas Christian University*, HISTORY
Jerry W. Cooney, *Professor Emeritus, University of Louisville*, HISTORY
Édgar Cota-Torres, *University of Colorado, Colorado Springs*, LITERATURE
Edward L. Cox, *Rice University*, HISTORY

Sandra Cypess, *University of Maryland, College Park*, LITERATURE
Paula De Vos, *San Diego State University*, HISTORY
Juan Duschesne-Winter, *Pittsburgh University*, LITERATURE
César Ferreira, *University of Wisconsin-Milwaukee*, LITERATURE
Myrna García-Calderón, *Syracuse University*, LITERATURE
John D. Garrigus, *University of Texas at Arlington*, HISTORY
Janet Gold, *University of New Hampshire*, LITERATURE
Luis A. González, *Indiana University, Bloomington*, HISTORY
Lolita Gutiérrez Brockington, *North Carolina Central University*, HISTORY
Paola Hernández, *University of Wisconsin-Madison*, LITERATURE
Regina Igel, *University of Maryland, College Park*, LITERATURE
Clara Jalif de Bertranou, *Universidad Nacional de Cuyo, Mendoza, Argentina*,
     PHILOSOPHY
Héctor Jaimes, *North Carolina State University*, LITERATURE
Jill S. Kuhnheim, *University of Kansas*, LITERATURE
Erick D. Langer, *Georgetown University*, HISTORY
Hal Langfur, *The State University of New York at Buffalo*, HISTORY
Dana Leibsohn, *Smith College*, ART
Alfred E. Lemmon, *Historic New Orleans Collection*, MUSIC
Peter S. Linder, *New Mexico Highlands University*, HISTORY
Maria Angélica Guimarães Lopes, *Professor Emerita, University of South Carolina*,
     LITERATURE
Laura Loustau, *Chapman University*, LITERATURE
Cristina Magaldi, *Towson University*, MUSIC
Carol Maier, *Kent State University*, TRANSLATIONS
María N. Marsilli, *John Carroll University*, HISTORY
Claire Emilie Martin, *California State University, Long Beach*, LITERATURE
Daniel Masterson, *United States Naval Academy, Annapolis*, HISTORY
Frank D. McCann, *Professor Emeritus, University of New Hampshire*, HISTORY
Karen Melvin, *Bates College*, HISTORY
Elizabeth Monasterios, *University of Pittsburgh*, LITERATURE
José M. Neistein, *Independent Scholar, Washington DC*, ART
Suzanne B. Pasztor, *Humboldt State University*, HISTORY
Daphne Patai, *University of Massachusetts, Amherst*, TRANSLATIONS
Valentina Peguero, *University of Wisconsin, Stevens-Point*, HISTORY
Charles A. Perrone, *University of Florida*, LITERATURE
Bianca Premo, *Florida International University*, HISTORY
José Promis, *University of Arizona*, LITERATURE
Susan E. Ramírez, *Texas Christian University*, HISTORY
Jane M. Rausch, *University of Massachusetts-Amherst*, HISTORY
Jonathan Ritter, *University of California, Riverside*, MUSIC
Humberto Rodríguez-Camilloni, *Virginia Polytechnic Institute*, ART
Oscar D. Sarmiento, *State University of New York, Potsdam*, LITERATURE
William F. Sater, *Professor Emeritus, California State University, Long Beach*,
     HISTORY
Jacobo Sefamí, *University of California, Irvine*, LITERATURE
Lisa Sousa, *Occidental College*, HISTORY
Peter Szok, *Texas Christian University*, HISTORY
Barbara A. Tenenbaum, *Hispanic Division, Library of Congress*, HISTORY

CONTENTS

GEOGRAPHY

INTERNATIONAL RELATIONS

POLITICAL ECONOMY

SOCIOLOGY

INDEX

EDITOR'S NOTE

I. GENERAL AND REGIONAL TRENDS

Several trends in the literature observed in *HLAS 65* are evident during the biennium under review for *HLAS 67*. Most notably, scholars continue to examine the role of Latin America's indigenous peoples in the political sphere. At the macro level of analysis, the lack of political legitimacy and a weakening of state capacity underpin much of the scholarly literature. Specifically, democratic consolidation is being challenged throughout Latin America, from Central America to Peru and as far south as Argentina. Violence, insecurity, and ever-present corruption combine to threaten the progress toward democratization that has occurred in the region over the past several decades (notwithstanding a major political scandal in 2006, Brazil may be the region's only exception, given the relative political stability the country has experienced over the past 20 years).

Research related to crime and security has surged in recent years. Violence continues as a main theme in the literature throughout the region. In Colombia, current publications consider the role of paramilitary groups and discuss their legacy as either terrorists or legitimate political actors. With violence continuing unabated, Colombian democracy remains tenuous. The policies of President Álvaro Uribe—including the 2003 electoral reforms, the political party system and the Uribe coalitions, and attempts at quelling the violence by ushering in a peace process—are under the microscope. A similar situation exists in Peru, where democratic stability encountered a test during the 2006 presidential election run-off in which supporters of Ollanta Humala and eventual winner Alan García clashed on multiple occasions. That same year was a momentous one for Peru's neighbor to the south. While on house arrest for egregious human rights crimes committed during his infamous 15-year reign, Chilean dictator General Augusto Pinochet suffered a heart attack and died a few days later. Many observers of Chile's political situation saw this event as the official end of the country's transition to democracy. Subsequently, in 2010 the Concertación coalition relinquished power after 20 years in a leadership position when Sebastián Piñera, the first democratically elected president of the right in over 50 years, took office. Several works examine the role of the coalition in bolstering economic performance and political stability in the country. It is worth mentioning that the Concertación was set to lose power four years earlier but for the brilliant candidacy of Michelle Bachelet, who became the first female president of Chile. Studies of Bachelet's four-year term range from political biography (item **1408**) to analyses of the turmoil that besieged her administration from the outset (items **1390** and **1401**, among others).

Returning to the noted theme of indigenous peoples, Todd Eisenstadt has continued his line of research on *usos y costumbres* ("traditions and customs") in Mexico, comparing electoral participation among indigenous communities who rely on traditional political processes and those who adapt to the country's party politics (item **1064**). In a similar vein, a monograph on feminism and indigenous women in Mexico looks at the power that indigenous women yield in the political sphere and the challenges they face in attempting to transform society and political identity as a result of long-standing *usos y costumbres* (item **465**). Duncan Earle describes the transformation of indigenous peoples in the eyes of state power "from being viewed as an obstacle to full national development, to being recognized as an aggrieved stakeholder in the uneven ongoing multicultural national project (items **481** and **512**)" (p. 70). This topic is the touchstone of the political debate about the role of the state and the limits of its power over the citizenry, especially those of different histories and ethnicities. As many of the publications included in this volume indicate, one thing is clear: rather than living on the fringes of mainstream society, indigenous peoples are now at the center of political discourse as a result of successful cultural and social movements.

Given that much of the research and many of the publications included in this *HLAS* volume take up the case of indigenous peoples, it is significant to mention a monograph that introduces the reader to the Cavineños peoples of the Bolivian Amazon. The auto-ethnography encompasses a lifetime of research and describes encounters with non-indigenous peoples, including missionization and exploitation by rubber companies, and the resulting new forms of social organization and changes in religious beliefs (item **609**). With the increase in development, discovery of uncontacted groups has become a true rarity.

Identity politics is a major theme, from Brazil to the Andean region. Andrew Orta describes indigenous political participation as "not merely reactive to the circumstances of external threats, but rather a generative of new meanings and social forms" (p. 119–120). Scholars examine how ethnicity and identity relate to political participation. For Ecuador in particular, "the indigenous movement continues to be a central focus of scholarly attention" (Collins, p. 247). Not surprisingly, the 2009 landslide re-election of Bolivia's first indigenous president, Evo Morales, has drawn significant attention. Morales and his Movimiento al Socialismo (MAS) political party are at the center of several scholarly examinations, most of which go beyond indigeneity and ethnic identity to analyze economic reforms and development policies.

Taking the discussion a step further, Bartholomew Dean describes the political anthropology of Lowland Western Amazonia and questions the extent to which indigenous leaders' "subjectivity shaping" initiatives have been influenced by interactions with the state and NGOs. Furthermore, he highlights local conceptions of status, leadership, and citizenship as factors in determining ethnic political identity (p. 99–100 and item **578**).

Another topic that arises in the literature on Lowland Amazonia is the role of ethnobotany in the lives of indigenous peoples. While shamanism is not a new subject of scholarly debate, a specific hallucinogen, ayahuasca, has captured the attention of the field of ethnology, where the role of plants in spiritual healing is examined. Works on shamanism also appear for the Caribbean (item **243**) as well as for Colombia and Argentina (Nash, p. 45). Studies from the related field of ethnobiology also appear in the scholarly literature (Hirsch, p. 102).

Several works on Archeology reveal an unfortunate situation. Cases of looting of archeological sites and forging within the antiquities market have brought archeological ethics into question (items **40** and **163**). Worse, looting has contributed to the deterioration of archeological sites throughout Latin America (item **373**). Indeed, it is important to note that natural processes along with local political decisions, such as opening the sites to tourism, contribute to destruction. Even some well-intentioned restoration projects have been plagued by poor management and planning, resulting in further degradation to archeological sites (see, for example, item **365** for Chile).

On a more inspiring note, artifact-based studies of pottery uncovered during archeological excavations have resulted in rich interpretations and reconstructions of iconographic symbolism and exchange routes. One fascinating publication describes the work of Jorge Yázpik, a contemporary Mexican architect and sculptor who utilizes the same type of stone as prehispanic artisans (item **218**). An exciting advancement in archeological research is the publication of three additional volumes containing the field notebooks of Julio C. Tello (1880–1947), the founder of Peruvian archeology. One hopes these original documents will spur future study and investigation of archeological sites in Peru and throughout the region. The notebooks contain transcriptions of texts and sketches, along with photographs of crews working. Perhaps most enticing of all, an accompanying CD-ROM contains digital images of the materials (items **396–398**).

The field of Geography is showing signs of a new level of maturity. While both natural and social catastrophes have wracked Latin America throughout time, research from geographers has not been at the forefront of the discussion. In a noticeable shift, we are seeing geographers question the assumptions of the "nature/culture" divide. Kent Mathewson and Jörn Seemann note several examples and point to this reconsideration as an emerging trend. Leading the way is *Aftershocks: Earthquakes and Popular Politics in Latin America*, the edited collection on the impact of natural disasters on political, social, and cultural conditions (item **661**). The historical and contemporary case studies of earthquakes throughout the region ably demonstrate that dramatic political upheaval inevitably ensued, and in some cases was accompanied by redistribution of land.

In Haiti, where recovery from the devastating 2010 earthquake is painstakingly slow, political stability remains elusive. A significant emerging research area is the tense interaction among international aid organizations, international financial institutions, NGOs, the military, and local politicians and agrarian leaders; while the ultimate mission of these disparate actors is the same, their strategies are vastly different. Clifford Griffin offers a useful overview of contemporary political conditions in Haiti in his introduction to the Caribbean Government and Politics section (p. 226–228). One article in particular argues for the need to shift rebuilding efforts from donor-driven decision-making to user-driven design (item **731**).

In line with the active global interest in climate change, analyses of climatic fluctuations and the El Niño events continue to appear. Rising to the top among several studies is an article by Dull *et al.* that "offers a brilliant riposte to the climate change/global warming deniers' obdurate refusal to comprehend current realities" (p. 132 and item **675**). The implications of climate change for local communities are analyzed specifically for the Andean region (items **830** and **884**). One approach to studying climate change taken by several geographers uses a historical perspective to understand events; this creative effort to revisit the past has contributed to a boom in interest in both historical cartography and historical geography throughout the region.

Following the theme of indigenous identity and representation, race and identity are explored using the scholarly apparatus of trained geographers. In reference to the scholarship on Central America, Peter Herlihy describes the use of repeat geography as an emerging methodology (p. 146–147). Multiple examples of recent publications take up existing field notes, photographs, maps, and other rich primary sources to reconsider past observations. One remarkable effort is Maurício Abreu's two-volume historical geography of Rio de Janeiro (item **971**) for which the author made use of several hundred *livros de notas* housed in the Arquivo Nacional documenting land-ownership transactions—in addition to spending several years scouring archives in both Europe and Brazil. Another relatively recent methodology, participatory mapping, continues, although two publications highlight potential problems of this map-making method for indigenous groups in Belize and Nicaragua (item **749**) and Honduras (item **764**). Looking north to Mexico, an article on the PROCEDE government program suggests that this important land certification initiative has led to mixed results for indigenous communities, including the undesired effect of fragmentation of indigenous lands (item **804**).

Much of the scholarly discourse on international relations reflects the ongoing trend of regional integration initiatives throughout Latin America, but a fundamental shift has occurred. The focus is now on Brazil's efforts to position itself in the international system, specifically within subregional or South-South relationships. Many of the contributions are from Latin American and European scholars, who are re-examining the role of the US vis-à-vis South-South integration and relations between the US and Latin America, which have not been a focal point for US foreign policy since the post-9/11 War on Terror began. From the Latin American perspective, several issues continue to be of importance for Latin America-US relations: trade, migration, security, and social inequality and poverty. Some academics have argued that the lack of attention to Latin America ultimately will have political costs for the US. An Aspen Institute conference summary sheds light on contemporary political and economic concerns within the realm of Latin America-US relations (item **1573**). Members of the US Congress who attended the conference heard from academic practitioners and policy experts on Latin America who highlighted key issues, policy implications, and future challenges for the relationship.

Shedding new light on the history of the relationship between Latin America and the US, Helen Delpar's welcome monograph on the historiography and development of the field of Latin American area studies in the US from 1850–1975 should be read by anyone interested in the trajectory of the field (item **1538**). In particular, Delpar has approached the narrative based on domestic concerns within the US, mostly regarding economic, military, and social policy, but also with an eye toward specific trends in academia throughout the time period under review. It is hoped that others will follow the example set by Delpar to evaluate and scrutinize the ever-important connection between Latin America and the US, long considered to be the regional hegemonic power.

Within the boundaries of Latin America, recent publications on regional integration have employed several approaches to explore the reasons for integration. Echoing recurring themes in the literature, the principal incentives include "development, security, and autonomy" (Meyer, p. 306). Studies look at the history of integration efforts, the impact of integration on public policy, the debate about deeper integration, public opinion about economic integration, and analysis of the results of recent initiatives amid growing socioeconomic inequality.

Turning to state-level analysis, several findings have come to light in recent years. For Mexico, Andrew Selee notes a number of groundbreaking studies on foreign policy that appeared during this review period. Two contributions in particular address Mexico's relationship with the US in the 20th century. The first describes events surrounding Mexican expropriation of land belonging to US companies in the 1930s (item **1590**). The author's original analysis shows that the weaker government in an asymmetrical relationship can win a series of difficult negotiations. The second looks at the Mexico-US relationship during and after WWII and focuses on military cooperation during the war, a commercial treaty, and the Bracero program (item **1581**). Once again, the findings indicate important lessons vis-à-vis Mexico's asymmetrical relationship with the US; Mexico was able to exploit factors such as timing and comparative advantage to achieve its desired goals. A reconsideration of historical episodes in which Mexico successfully negotiated with the US should inform contemporary challenges in the relationship between the two countries.

Cuba follows closely behind Mexico in terms of level of US interest and attention. In this regard, two contributions in *HLAS 67* stand out. One is a thought-provoking article on the legalities of the leasing arrangement for Guantánamo (item **1679**) and the other is Lars Schoultz's definitive tome on Cuba-US policy (item **1677**). On the opposite side of the spectrum of US interest level, a unique English-language study of Paraguay-US relations was published by two prominent scholars, Frank O. Mora and Jerry W. Cooney (item **1746**).

In terms of extrahemispheric relations, the European Union is a focal point given that it has pursued bilateral and multilateral arrangements with Latin American countries. Spain in particular ramped up foreign investment in recent years. However, even before the spectacular economic downturn suffered by Spain, frustration on the part of Latin American partners dampened the fervor; while preferential trade relationships can create economic advantages, it appears that many of the Latin America-EU agreements are merely empty rhetoric.

Its presence now firmly established in the region, China shows every sign of continuing to increase its participation in Latin American development, in what one contributor refers to as a "meteoric rise of relations" (Costa, p. 355). Apart from immigration of foreign nationals, China, Japan, and other Asian countries have continued to pursue bilateral trade agreements with individual Latin American countries. In the case of Brazil, Chinese demand for Brazilian primary agricultural and mineral exports resulted in an international trade surplus for the first time since 1975 (Birch and Smith, p. 453). Evidence of Asia's presence is also noted in diplomatic relations with entire regions such as Central America and with subregional entities such as Mercosur and the Andean Community. The EU and Asian nations are not the only global trade partners for Latin America; studies have been published on bilateral relations between Latin American countries and such nontraditional, extraregional partners as South Korea, the Netherlands, Italy, South Africa, and the Middle East. In a similar vein, the role of individual Latin American countries in the UN and its peacekeeping missions is explored for Brazil (item **1771**), Chile (item **1722**), and Argentina and Uruguay (item **1472**).

The global financial crisis of 2008–2009 presented an opportunity for Latin America to test its resolve in maintaining political and economic stability. Among other factors, ties to the Asian markets and a renewed emphasis on primary exports assisted in a generally benign outcome (with some significant exceptions) and even positive economic growth for a handful of countries in the region during this challenging period (Hiskey, p. 363–365). Based on the indications of the works reviewed in *HLAS 67*, one could argue that Latin America is in a post-neoliberal stage of development in which the region's economies have moved past the crisis-driven model of the late 20th century. One analysis of the post-neoliberal model by Jean Grugel and Pía Riggirozzi examines the role of the state in driving economic growth and social stability in Argentina (item **2105**). As more empirical data on economic reform becomes available, we will enter into "an exciting period in research . . . that will offer a more balanced and accurate sense of the challenges and opportunities the region's economies will face moving forward" (Hiskey, p. 365).

Some of the scholarship on political economy continues to rely on opinion and overused rhetoric rather than evidence-based arguments. In the case of Venezuela, many of the assessments of the policies of President Hugo Chávez are polemical; however, one notable exception is the monograph by Leslie C. Gates in which she invokes empirical research and an innovative methodology to present a complex picture of Chávez's electoral success in the country (item **1981**). Regarding Venezuela's neighbor to the west, a similar story has unfolded in Colombia. Profound differences in theoretical approach by a range of policy analysts (both public and NGO-based), academics, and activists has resulted in a wide disparity among conclusions about the country's economic and political performance (Hershberg, p. 405).

One of the main themes in the literature on Peru is the redistribution of wealth. The election of President Ollanta Humala in 2011 represents the electoral expression of popular dissatisfaction with the status quo. Despite healthy economic growth, voters have protested neoliberal reforms (Kotschwar, p. 421). Humala capitalized on this sentiment by campaigning against unequal distribution of wealth during his successful bid for the presidency. More broadly, Enrique Pumar confirms that some of the principal topics in the Sociology literature are social inequality, politics and economics, and crime and security (p. 469). He points to the "stubborn legacy" of social inequality that persists in the region despite advances in democratization and economic performance.

Finally, I would be remiss if I did not join those drawing attention to the ongoing drug-related violence in Mexico. Since 2006, when President Felipe Calderón mobilized the military to assist in combating drug violence, organized crime has retaliated harshly. Rival cartels inflict evermore horrific and appalling reprisals, counter-reprisals, warnings, and punishments against each other, the military, the police force, and anyone unfortunate enough to venture too close to the brutal battle for control of the nearly 50 billion dollar industry. Several works included in this volume discuss "Mexico's number one problem" (Ugalde, p. 483). However, doubts about the reliability of data due to inconsistencies have hampered serious scholarship. On a related note, Daniel Klooster notes that the Mexico-US border is a focus of geographical research. One article he highlights examines geo-techniques for measuring infrastructure needs of informal settlements, assessments of environmental activism, and evaluations of adaptive potential to climate change (item **820**). Similarly, an environmental assessment of the border wall between Mexico and the US underlines the many factors at play as Mexico and the US grapple with the social, political, economic, and ecological issues of the border region (item **786**). With scholars of all disciplinary persuasions focused on issues of social inequality, security, and political stability, we can anticipate thought-provoking research and recommendations for future policies that will continue to foster development throughout the region.

II. CLOSING DATE

Most of the publications under review for this volume were published between 2006–2009. With some exceptions, the closing date for works annotated in this volume was 2010. Publications received and cataloged at the Library of Congress after that date will be annotated in the next Social Sciences volume, *HLAS 69*. In consultation with the *HLAS* Advisory Board, in recent years the *Handbook* has begun to pay closer attention to publication dates of materials considered for review. We are more stringent about including works from only the previous five years.

III. ELECTRONIC ACCESS TO THE *HANDBOOK*

Web Site

The *Handbook's* web site, *HLAS Online*, continues to offer, free of charge, all bibliographic records corresponding to *HLAS* volumes 1–67. Records that did not appear in a print volume may or may not be annotated, and newer records are in a preliminary editorial stage. The web site also includes a list of *HLAS* subject headings, a list of journal titles and the corresponding journal abbreviations found in *HLAS* records, tables of contents for volumes 50–65 and linked introductory essays for volumes 50–61 (*http://www.loc.gov/hlas/contents.html*), as well as introductory essays for volumes 1–49, which are searchable in the database by using the phrase "general statement." The web address for *HLAS Online* is *http://www.loc .gov/hlas/*. The interface for the site is trilingual (English, Spanish, and Portuguese) and the data is updated weekly. *HLAS Online* is an OpenURL source, allowing seamless linking from *HLAS* entries to related electronic resources available at your institution.

HLAS biographic records from volumes 50 onward may be searched through *HLAS Web*. Searches may be refined by language, publication date, place of publication, and/or type of material (book or journal article). The address for *HLAS Web* is *http://hlasopac.loc.gov/*. In addition, selected bibliographic records in the Library of Congress online catalog (*http://catalog.loc.gov/*) contain *HLAS* annotations.

In 2011, the Library formed the *HLAS* Conversion Project Working Group to explore the possibility of combining the two *HLAS* web interfaces into one system. The level of detail that is required for a data project such as this one is truly amazing. The challenge is a welcome one for the team as we believe it will pay long-lasting dividends for our users.

CD-ROM

Volumes 1–55 (1935–96) of the *Handbook* are available on the *Handbook of Latin American Studies: CD-ROM: HLAS/CD (v. 2.0)*. This retrospective version is produced by the Fundación Histórica TAVERA (Madrid) and distributed for them by DIGIBIS. For ordering information, contact DIGIBIS:

DIGIBIS Producciones Digitales
Calle Claudio Coello, 123, 4a planta
28006 Madrid SPAIN
Tel. 00 34 91 581 20 01
Fax. 00 34 91 581 47 36
http://www.digibis.com/

IV. CHANGES FROM THE PREVIOUS SOCIAL SCIENCES VOLUME

Geography

Several of the sections in the Geography chapter are now under new leadership. Daniel Klooster, University of Redlands, has sole responsibility for selecting and annotating publications on Mexico. Gregory W. Knapp, University of Texas, Austin, has agreed to canvass and review materials for the Andean region. And works on the Southern Cone countries are ably covered by Peter Klepeis, Colgate University.

Government and Politics

It is thrilling to report that, after several years of not including publications on Ecuador in the *HLAS* Government and Politics chapter, the section is now being prepared by Jennifer N. Collins, University of Wisconsin-Stevens Point.

Political Economy

Laura Randall, Professor Emerita at Hunter College of the City University of New York, stepped in to review the materials on Mexican political economy while Pamela Starr was on hiatus to focus on a book project. It has been a pleasure to work with Dr. Randall and we appreciate her time and effort on this valuable endeavor.

Sociology

We were pleased to welcome three new contributing editors to the *HLAS* team of sociologists. Enrique Pumar, Catholic University, has taken over the General section from Benigno Aguirre-López. We are thankful that Dr. Pumar is local to the Washington, DC area; we've enjoyed his presence in the Hispanic Reading Room as he prepared his section. Dr. Aguirre did continue his long-standing relationship with *HLAS* as he prepared the Caribbean section for this volume. Cecilia Menjívar, Arizona State University, is well-positioned to canvass and annotate the literature on Central America. With the whole-hearted endorsement of our outgoing contributor for Ecuador, Jason Pribilsky, that section for vol. 67 was reviewed and annotated by Nicholas Rattray, University of Arizona. We in the *HLAS* office look forward to a long, fruitful relationship with our new contributing editors.

Tracy North, *Social Sciences Editor*

ANTHROPOLOGY

ARCHEOLOGY
Mesoamerica

JOHN HENDERSON, *Professor of Anthropology, Cornell University*
ARTHUR A. JOYCE, *Professor of Anthropology, University of Colorado at Boulder*

TEN YEARS AFTER THE TURN OF THE 21st CENTURY, Mesoamericanists have again turned their attention to reviewing and assessing topical themes, approaches, and general theoretical perspectives that have been popular in Mesoamerican studies in the last decade (items 7, 10, 11, 14, 16, 21, 38, 39, 42, 64, 71, 73, 76, and 80). There are several major contributions to the history of anthropology and archeology in the countries that comprise Mesoamerica as well (items 15 and 70).

Reconstructing social dimensions of ancient Maya societies, especially everyday practices, continues to be popular in Maya archeology, and results are increasingly framed with explicit reference to theoretical perspectives favored in social anthropology. Interpreting the social relations of exchange and craft production is an increasingly common focus (items 74, 85, 88, 98, 103, 120, 121, 138, 162, 187, 205, 214, and *HLAS 65:9*). Other foci in social archeology include spatial organization (items 22, 101, 126, 141, and 145); identity (items 101, 145, 151, 166, 168, 185, and 212); gender roles (items 145 and 168); and social memory (items 141 and *HLAS 65:102*).

Mayanists, especially those trained in Mexico and Central America, have not abandoned descriptive work (items 97, 112, 116, 152, 154, 182, and 203). In this vein, empirically oriented reports of the findings of field and laboratory investigations are very well represented in the literature: studies of ancient artifacts, technology and sources of raw material (items 89, 112, 117, and 192); excavation projects (items 15, 86, 114, 119, 123, 147, 152, 189, and 198); settlement pattern studies (items 15, 52, 87, 111, 113, 154, 160, 179, 203, and 207); and especially analyses of ancient environments, agriculture, and ecology (items 48, 63, 75, 130, 155, 156, 160, 167, 173, 204, and 216). Historical archeology is increasingly popular in the Maya world (items 26, 87, 107, 108, 124, and 200).

Traditional concerns in Maya studies persist: ancient Maya political geography (items 107, 123, 130, 138, 151, and 235); royal courts and institutions (items 35, 111, and 155); the ideology of politics, militarism and warfare (items 14, 25, 28, 57, 64, 67, 84, 95, 125, 171, 190, and 191); collapse, termination, and transformation (items 49, 91, 92, 137, 156, 167, 200, and *HLAS 65:102*) ritual and belief (items 79, 124, 148, 173, and 186); and archeoastronomy (items 206, 219, and 220).

Bioarcheology, especially of mortuary treatment, continues to expand (items 99, 115, 122, 169, 177, 178, 210, 216, 217, and *HLAS 65:185*). Analyses of ancient Maya hieroglyphic texts continue to reflect traditional emphases on political organization and dynastic history (items **84, 123, 125,** and **235**) and traditional approaches to interpretation of meaning in imagery and text (items **17, 24, 43, 57, 68, 100, 114, 140,** and **144**) are common. At the same time, the trajectory of increasingly nuanced perspectives on grammar and syntax (items **219, 224, 233,** and **239**) continues as well. The Maya calendar has re-emerged as a focus, both in terms of bringing new understandings of grammar and syntax to bear on calendar recording and in terms of its political uses (items **30, 220, 226, 227,** and **230**).

Recognition of the importance of archeological remains and of archeological research and writing for living peoples, and collaborations between archeologists and descendant communities are less rare than they were a few years ago (items **22** and **81**). Considerations of looting, collecting, the antiquities market, and archeological ethics appear in the literature with slowly increasing frequency (items **40, 112,** and **163**). [JSH]

NORTHERN MESOAMERICA

Important themes in recent publications on the archeology of northern Mesoamerica include research on religion, ideology, and politics; landscape, place, and settlement; interregional interaction; economy and subsistence; and artifact-based studies, as well as more general regional and site-based syntheses.

University presses continue to be important publication venues for the archeology of northern Mesoamerica. The presses that publish extensively on northern Mesoamerican archeology include the University Press of Colorado, the University of Texas Press, the University of Utah Press, Cotsen Institute of Archaeology Press, and the Mexican Instituto Nacional de Antropología e Historia (INAH). Important monograph series are published by the Cotsen Institute of Archaeology at the University of California at Los Angeles, the University of Pittsburgh, and the University of Michigan. In Mexico, the *Colección Científica* of the INAH publishes many important field reports and monographs. Important professional journals focusing on Mesoamerican archeology are *Latin American Antiquity, Ancient Mesoamerica, Arqueología,* and *Mexicon. Arqueología Mexicana* publishes short accessible articles on Mexican archeology for a more popular audience.

Recent general works on the archeology of northern Mesoamerica include syntheses of the archeology of the states of Querétaro (item **45**) and Tamaulipas (item **65**). Regional and site-based studies include works with a focus on West Mexico (item **34**), the Tuxtlas region of Veracruz (item **72**); Mexicaltzingo, D.F. (item **90**); La Laguna, Tlaxcala (item **102**); Cuthá, Puebla (item **104**); the Mixteca region of Oaxaca (item **236**); San Dieguito, Nayarit (item **128**); Maltrata, Veracruz (item **159**); the Costa Grande region of Guerrero (item **44**); the Mezcala region of Guerrero (item **66**); Chiepetlán, Guerrero (item **221**); Caballito Blanco, Oaxaca (item **199**); Cuauhtémoc, Chiapas (item **195**); the site of Santa Cruz Axitapán, México (item **131**), and early formative Soconusco (item **157**). Books on the archeology of Oaxaca include Joyce's (item **37**) major synthesis of the Mixtec, Zapotec, and Chatino regions as well as Robles García's (item **51**) far ranging edited volume from the Mesa Redonda de Monte Albán. Studies of major prehispanic cities focus on Teotihuacan (item **46**) and El Tajín (item **55**). An edited volume by Jiménez López (item **78**) considers debates over the peopling of the Americas and the implications for understanding the earliest inhabitants of the basin of Mexico. González and Winter (item **134**) examine the early formative site of Barrio de los Tepalcates on the Isthmus of Tehuantepec, Oaxaca. Kepecs and Alexander (item **61**) edited an important volume on the postclassic to colonial era transition and Salas Contreras (item **197**) presented the results of excavations in the ex-Convento de la Encarnación in Mexico City. Several works deal with issues of preservation, patrimony, and the role of archeology in contemporary society (items **50** and **211**) including a volume in honor of Gustavo Vargas (item **56**). Riusech and Kamel (item **36**) consider the method and theory of interdisciplinary research in archeology.

The journal *Ancient Mesoamerica* dedicated an entire issue to major review articles marking the 20 year anniversary of the journal. The articles review the history of archeological research in Mesoamerica with a focus on the past 20 years and consider future directions. Topics deal with landscape archeology (item **10**), ethnohistory (item **11**), states and empires (item **16**), urbanism (item **38**), historical linguistics (item **39**), visual culture (item **42**), Aztec studies (item **54**), the Olmec (item **60**), sustainability (item **73**), geoarcheology (item **76**), and bioarcheology (item **80**).

A diversity of publications examines issues of religion, ideology, and politics based on archeology, archeoastronomy, ethnohistory, epigraphy, and iconography. Major themes include Aztec religion and ritual (items **17, 222,** and **225**), mortuary ritual (items **18, 19, 96, 135,** and **136**), rock art (items **8, 9, 82,** and **161**), and the relationship between warfare, religion, and politics (items **14, 77,** and **118**). Studies also examined prehispanic religion among the Mixteca (items **142** and **240**), the religious significance of metallurgy in Michoacan (item **237**), the political organization of Tlaxcalla (item **23**), and early colonial period political relations among the Mixteca (item **238**). Two general edited volumes on archeoastronomy include several chapters on northern Mesoamerica (items **223** and **241**). Lind and Urcid (item **158**) examine the political evolution of the Valley of Oaxaca from the perspective of the important late classic center of Lambityeco. Fash and López Luján (item **64**) edit a volume examining the political significance of architecture and imagery with chapters that discuss the sites of Chalcatzingo, Monte Albán, Cholula, Teotihuacan, El Tajín, and Tula. Jones (item **1**) edits a volume in honor of Elizabeth P. Benson with several chapters discussing religion and ritual in northern Mesoamerica. Olmec political organization and interaction among polities in the Gulf Coast are examined by Pool and colleagues (item **183**), while Mora-Marín (items **232** and **234**) critically considers work on early Olmec writing.

Landscape, space, and settlement studies over the past few years declined relative to previous periods. Publications include regional settlement studies (items **164** and **196**), human ecology in the lower Río Verde Valley of Oaxaca (item **132**), and the use of geophysical techniques to examine architecture at the site of Teotepec (item **209**). An edited volume on cultural landscapes (item **4**) includes a chapter on the life history of place of Monte Albán. Landscape change in the Pátzcuaro basin was discussed in two chapters of an edited volume on landscapes of early states (item **59**).

Interregional interaction also declined somewhat as a major focus of publication. Important topics are exchange and other forms of long-distance interaction involving the early/middle formative period Olmec (items **13, 109, 110,** and **149**) and the exchange of obsidian artifacts (items **20** and **150**). A major regional synthesis examines production and exchange in central and southern Mexico (item **2**). Lead isotope analysis is used to show that Mexico was the point of origin of early colonial period Romita pottery (item **146**). An edited volume on commercial and productive relationships within the greater Southwest includes several chapters discussing interaction with northern Mesoamerica (item **5**).

Works dealing with economics and subsistence continue as a major focus of publication for northern Mesoamerica. Major themes cover prehispanic market systems (items **3, 29, 53, 143,** and **176**), Archaic and formative period agriculture (items **6, 41,** and **201**), and craft production (item **31**) including obsidian (items **139, 175, 180, 181,** and **188**), pottery (item **62**), copper (item **165**), and ornamental shell (item **208**). Water management systems are examined including the Purrón Dam Complex in the Tehuacán Valley (item **83**) as well as a broad synthesis of the technological, economic, and symbolic dimensions of water systems throughout prehispanic Mexico (item **69**). The relationship between maize agriculture and broader economic and political relations is discussed for postclasssic Xaltocan in the basin of Mexico (item **172**). Rodríguez-Alegría (item **193**) challenges the dominate narrative that stone tool technologies were rapidly abandoned after the Spanish conquest also with evidence from the site of Xaltocan. Political economy is the topic of a wide-ranging edited volume that includes chapters dealing with the Olmecs, Zapotecs, and Teotihuacan (item **58**). Williams discusses the production of a variety of prestige goods in West Mexico (item **12**) and considers the role of aquatic resources at Late Cuitzeo, Michoacán (item **215**). Domestic economy is addressed for the early formative Olmec site of El Remolino (item **213**).

Publication of artifact-based studies has increased over the past few years with major themes including ceramic typologies for the postclassic and early colonial period basin of Mexico (item **129**), early colonial period Oaxaca (item **133**), and the formative to postclassic at the site of Xochitécatl (item **202**). Cervera Obregón (item **105**) presents a broad study of prehispanic armaments with a focus on the Aztec, Muñoz Espinosa (item **174**) analyzes pottery from the Sierra Gordo region of Querétaro, Rojas Martínez Garcida (item **194**) explores the iconography and symbolism of Silvia polychrome pottery from Cholula, and Yázpik (item **218**) considers the relationship between modern sculptures and prehispanic stone working. Ladrón de Guevara (item **153**) examines the late classic reutilization of preclassic Olmec monuments. The conservation of an Aztec monolith is discussed by Barajas and colleagues (items **93** and **94**).

I would like to thank Morgan Koukopoulos for assistance with the annotated bibliography. [AAJ]

GENERAL

1 Adventures in Pre-Columbian studies: essays in honor of Elizabeth P. Benson. Edited by Julie Jones. Washington, D.C.: Pre-Columbian Society of Washington, D.C., 2010. 209 p.: bibl., ill. (chiefly col.).

Edited volume of essays in honor of Elizabeth P. Benson on assorted topics in the precolumbian Americas. Esther Pasztory discusses sacrifice as reciprocity in Mesoamerica and the Andes. Alana Cordy-Collins traces the sacred deer complex throughout the Americas. [AAJ]

2 Alvarez, Luis Rodrigo. Las rutas, los productos y el comercio prehispánicos en el sur y sureste de Mesoamerica: un enfoque arqueológico. Oaxaca, Mexico: Instituto de Investigaciones Sociológicas de la Univ. Autónoma "Benito Juárez" de Oaxaca: Proveedora Escolar, 2006. 374 p.: bibl., ill.

Describes exchange routes of many products within south and southeastern Mesoamerica. Sections on Morelos, the Gulf Coast, the Valley of Tlaxcalteca, the Valley of Tehuacán, Tlaxcala, coastal Guerrero and its sea routes, and Oaxaca. Products include live animals, meat, skins, feathers, fish, honey and wax, vegetables, textiles, woods, obsidian, metals, and shell. [AAJ]

3 Archaeological approaches to market exchange in ancient societies. Edited by Christopher P. Garraty and Barbara L. Stark. Boulder: Univ. Press of Colorado, 2010. 322 p.: bibl., index.

Edited volume on market exchange containing theoretical approaches, case studies, and comparative chapters. Topics include the markets of Oaxaca covered by Gary M. Feinman and Linda M. Nicholas; South-Central Veracruz covered by Barbara L. Stark and Alanna Ossa, and Morelos markets covered by Michael E. Smith. [AAJ]

4 The archaeology of meaningful places. Edited by Brenda J. Bowser and María Nieves Zedeño. Salt Lake City: Univ. of Utah Press, 2009. 222 p.: bibl., ill., index, maps. (Foundations of archaeological inquiry)
Edited volume focusing on the significance of places and their roles within the societies that constructed them. Arthur Joyce discusses the life history of Monte Albán's main plaza as its significance changes over its 2,500 year history. [AAJ]

5 Archaeology without borders: contact, commerce, and change in the U.S. Southwest and northwestern Mexico. Edited by Laurie D. Webster, Maxine E. McBrinn, and Eduardo Gamboa Carrera. Boulder: Univ. Press of Colorado; Chihuahua, Mexico: Conaculta/INAH, 2008. 420 p.: bibl., ill., index, maps.
Edited volume focusing on the commercial and productive relationships within and between regions of the southwest US and Northern Mexico. Pt. 3 focuses on research from Chihuahua, Durango, Zacatecas, Michoacán, Coahuila, and Nuevo León. [AAJ]

6 Arnold, Philip J. Settlement and subsistence among the Early Formative Gulf Olmec. (*J. Anthropol. Archaeol.*, 28:4, Dec. 2009, p. 397–411)
Argues that floodplain resources were the first economic factor that gave rise to early formative centers. Agriculture stimulated increasing complexity in the middle formative, but became a factor only after early centers had already been established. This contrasts with traditional models that describe agriculture as the key factor from the beginning. [AAJ]

7 Arqueología y complejidad social. Coordinación de Patricia Fournier García, Walburga Wiesheu Forster y Thomas H. Charlton. México: Escuela Nacional de Antropología e Historia: Instituto Nacional de Antropología e Historia, 2007. 308 p.: ill., maps.

Collection of papers on economic, social, and political complexity in Mesoamerican city-states from a session at the 2006 International Congress of Americanists in Seville. Includes an essay on the *altepetl*, the political institution at the core of Mesoamerican city-states, along with a series of case studies on territoriality, economic organization, social organization, and architecture: coastal Guerrero, Cacaxtla, Monte Albán, Pátzcuaro, Dzibanché, Teotihuacan, colonial Mexico City and El Salvador, and 19th-century Sonora. [JSH]

8 Arte rupestre del noreste: historia. Compilación de William Breen Murray. Monterrey, Mexico: Fondo Editorial de Nuevo León, 2007. 316 p.: bibl., ill., maps. (Col. La historia en la ciudad del conocimiento)
Edited volume about rock art in northeast Mexico. Chapters present data from recent investigations and connect rock art to landscapes, sacred spaces, and the cultural role of specific places. [AAJ]

9 El arte rupestre en México: ensayos 1990–2004. Compilación de María del Pilar Casado López. Coordinación de Lorena Mirambell. México: Instituto Nacional de Antropología e Historia, 2006. 574 p.: bibl., ill. (Col. Obra Diversa)
Edited volume on recent rock art studies in Mexico. Chapters include summaries of research from various regions of Mexico and parts of the American Southwest. [AAJ]

10 Ashmore, Wendy. Mesoamerican landscape archaeologies. (*Anc. Mesoam.*, 20:2, Fall 2009, p. 183–187)
Review of recent work on landscape archeology in Mesoamerica. Identifies key conceptual developments and likely future trends in landscape interpretations rooted in ecology; social history and social identity; ritual and pilgrimage; and cosmology and symbolic meaning. [JSH]

11 Berdan, Frances F. Mesoamerican ethnohistory. (*Anc. Mesoam.*, 20:2, Fall 2009, p. 211–215)
Assessment of the current state of the field of ethnohistory in Mesoamerica. Identifies more nuanced analysis of precolumbian pictorial books in terms of their cultural and historical contexts; the shift in focus in post-invasion studies, acknowl-

edging continuing cultural diversity and emphasizing indigenous adaptations to colonial institutions; and a more critical approach to projecting from well-known contexts to poorly known regions and to earlier periods are particularly important recent research trends. [JSH]

12 Bienes estratégicos del antiguo occidente de México: producción e intercambio. Edición de Eduardo Williams. Zamora, Mexico: El Colegio de Michoacán, 2004. 379 p.: bibl., ill., index, maps. (Col. Occidente)

Edited volume describing the organization and production of resources within western Mexico. Includes chapters on salt, obsidian, shell, pottery, feathers, and metals in different areas and precontact time periods. [AAJ]

13 Blomster, Jeffrey P. Complexity, interaction, and epistemology: Mixtecs, Zapotecs, and Olmecs in early formative Mesoamerica. (*Anc. Mesoam.*, 21:1, Spring 2010, p. 135–149)

Challenges the dominant neoevolutionary models of interaction between Gulf Coast Olmecs and other early formative regions in Mesoamerica. Neutron activation analysis of pottery suggests an unequal relationship in which Gulf Coast Olmecs exported to Mixtecs and Zapotecs in Oaxaca. Author uses an agency perspective to describe the relationships among Mixtec, Zapotec, and Olmec groups. [AAJ]

14 Blood and beauty: organized violence in the art and archaeology of Mesoamerica and Central America. Edited by Heather S. Orr and Rex Koontz. Los Angeles, Calif.: Cotsen Institute of Archaeology Press, 2009. 370 p.: bibl., index. (Ideas, debates and perspectives; 4)

Edited volume on the art and archeology of politically organized violence within Mesoamerica and Central America. Four broad themes are warfare, ball games and boxing, trophy-head taking, and pain and healing. Includes articles by Workinger and Joyce on formative period warfare in Oaxaca and by Koontz on El Tajín. [AAJ]

15 The Carnegie Maya II: Carnegie Institution of Washington current reports, 1952–1957. Compiled and with an introduction by John M. Weeks. Boulder: Univ. Press of Colorado, 2009. 672 p.: bibl., ill., index, maps, photos, tables.

Reprints the entire series of Carnegie Institution of Washington Current Reports, originally published between 1952 and 1957. The series was established for rapid reporting of the findings of investigations of the late Maya city of Mayapan in northern Yucatán, the final Carnegie project in Mesoamerican archeology. Includes a CD containing the Current Reports as well as the Year Books reprinted in the first Carnegie Maya volume. The original publications are difficult to find and cumbersome to search, so the reprint is important for the contemporary archeological research as well as for the history of Maya archeology. [JSH]

16 Chase, Arlen F.; Diane Z. Chase; and Michael E. Smith. States and empires in ancient Mesoamerica. (*Anc. Mesoam.*, 20:2, Fall 2009, p. 175–182)

Review of recent work on complex political systems in precolumbian Mesoamerica. Emphasizes variability among ancient "states" and "empires" in the region, but concludes that belief and ritual were always integral to political processes and that most Mesoamerican polities were hegemonic, without tightly centralized control of extensive territories. [JSH]

17 Chinchilla Mazariegos, Oswaldo. Of birds and insects: the hummingbird myth in ancient Mesoamerica. (*Anc. Mesoam.*, 21:1, Spring 2010, p. 45–61)

Analysis of the theme of seduction/ abduction of a maiden by a disguised deity, widely distributed in origin myths throughout Mesoamerica. Argues that homologous elements can be identified in precolumbian imagery and in post-invasion narratives and performance, and that they can be used together to reconstruct an ancient Mesoamerican myth. Relies heavily on looted objects without archeological provenience. [JSH]

18 Clayton, Sarah C. Gender and mortuary ritual at ancient Teotihuacan, Mexico: a study of intrasocietal diversity. (*Camb. Archaeol. J.*, 21:1, Feb. 2011, p. 31–52)

Argues that investigation of gender can be better understood through a multiscalar approach. A case study describes the differing performances of mortuary ritual in four residential areas of classic Teotihuacan. [AAJ]

19   Darras, Véronique and **Brigitte Fau-géres.** Chupicuaro and the preclassic shaft tomb tradition. (*Mexicon/Germany,* 32:1/2, 2010, p. 22–30)

Describes the construction methods of shaft tombs at Chupicuaro, on the border of Guanajuato and Michoacán. Connects shaft tombs at Chupicuaro to similar traditions in western Mexico and proposes links between the two areas. [AAJ]

20   De León, Jason P.; Kenn Hirth; and **David M. Carballo.** Exploring formative period obsidian blade trade: three distribution models. (*Anc. Mesoam.,* 20:1, Spring 2009, p. 113–128)

Analysis of obsidian blade trading in Mesoamerica during the early and middle formative periods. Authors describe three models: whole-blade trade, processed-blade trade, and local-blade production and find that the trade of blades took different forms at different times and places. [AAJ]

21   Demarest, Arthur Andrew. Maya archaeology for the twenty-first century: the progress, the perils, and the promise. (*Anc. Mesoam.,* 20:2, Fall 2009, p. 253–263)

Reviews recent trends in Maya archeology, highlighting the more detailed and more nuanced understandings of ancient ecologies, economies, and political systems made possible by the development of more sophisticated analytical tools. Emphasizes the need for continued basic research, including chronology-building and artifact classification, in poorly studied regions and periods and especially for research designs that bring all available tools to bear on well-formulated research questions. [JSH]

22   Diásporas, migraciones y exilios en el mundo maya. Edición de Mario Humberto Ruz, Joan García Targa y Andrés Ciudad Ruiz. Madrid: Sociedad Española de Estudios Mayas; Mérida, Mexico: UNAM, 2009. 369 p.: bibl., ill., maps. (Monografías; 8)

Collection of papers focusing on population mobility in the Maya world in precolumbian, colonial, and recent times. Includes papers on migrations in Maya myth and history; the role of deities in con-

cepts of territoriality; archeological, architectural, and linguistic evidence for precolumbian population movements; the effect of colonial policies on population mobility; migration and tourism; and the recent international diaspora of Maya people. [JSH]

Domestic life in prehispanic capitals: a study of specialization, hierarchy, and ethnicity. See item **288.**

Dreiss, Meredith L. and **Sharon Greenhill.** Chocolate: pathway to the gods. See *HLAS 66:217.*

23   Fargher, Lane F.; Richard E. Blanton; and **Verenice Y. Heredia Espinoza.** Egalitarian ideology and political power in prehispanic Central Mexico: the case of Tlaxcallan. (*Lat. Am. Antiq.,* 21:3, Sept. 2010, p. 227–251)

Argues that Tlaxcallans' successful resistance against the Aztec Empire was in part the result of their corporate form of rulership that involved government by a council that included commoners. Uses collective action theory. [AAJ]

24   Fiery pool: the Maya and the mythic sea. Edited by Daniel Finamore and Stephen D. Houston. Salem, Mass.: Peabody Essex Museum; New Haven, Conn.: Yale Univ. Press, 2010. 328 p.: bibl., ill. (chiefly col.), index, col. maps.

Catalog of 2010–11 exhibition of Maya imagery relating to water, and the sea in particular. Color plates and commentary on exhibited objects are interspersed among brief essays on water and the natural environments of the Maya world, water management in Maya cities, seafaring, trade, water and related symbols in Maya belief systems, and the iconography of water in Maya art. [JSH]

25   Fitzsimmons, James L. Death and the classic Maya kings. Austin: Univ. of Texas Press, 2009. 281 p.: bibl., ill. (some col.), index, map. (The Linda Schele series in Maya and pre-columbian studies)

Review of archeological and epigraphic evidence of death, funerary rituals, and burial of aristocrats, especially royals in classic period (AD 300–900) lowland Maya cities. Interpretation emphasizes the political functions for successors of funerary activity and memorials to the royal dead. [JSH]

Flint, Richard. No settlement, no conquest: a history of the Coronado Entrada. See *HLAS 66:705.*

26 **Fowler, William R.** Historical archaeology in Yucatan and Central America. (*in* International Handbook of Historical Archaeology. Edited by Teresita Majewski and David Gaimster. New York, N.Y.: Springer, 2009, p. 429–447)

Overview of the archeology of the post-invasion period in the Maya world and lower Central America. Summarizes recent results and highlights key themes and conceptual approaches, including settlement archeology; rural landscapes; hacienda archeology, especially in the context of the Caste War in Yucatán; city layouts; and archeology of the Church. [JSH]

27 **Gamio, Manuel.** Forjando patria: pro-nacionalismo. Translated and with an introduction by Fernando Armstrong-Fumero. Boulder: Univ. Press of Colorado, 2010. 176 p.: bibl., index.

Gamio, a key figure in the emergence of anthropology and archeology as distinct academic enterprises in Mexico, wrote *Forjando patria* just before and during the Mexican Revolution, a critical moment in nation-building and emerging national identity. This is the first English translation of a work that was influential in establishing the relevance of Mexico's indigenous and mestizo cultures and its archeological heritage—central concerns in anthropology and archeology—to issues of national identity. [JSH]

28 **García Barrios, Ana.** El aspecto bélico de Chaahk, el dios de la lluvia, en el Periodo Clásico maya. (*Rev. Esp. Antropol. Am.*, 39:1, 2009, p. 7–29, bibl., ill., photos)

Argues that Chaahk—best known as a deity of rain, thunder, and lightning—was also intimately connected with warfare during the classic period (AD 250–1000), perhaps in part as a reflection of influence from western Mesoamerica where Tlaloc had the same set of associations. Interprets imagery of deities with protruding upper lips or noses in association with prisoners and in royal military costume after about AD 700 as representations of Chaahk. [JSH]

29 **Garraty, Christopher P.** Evaluating the distributional approach to inferring marketplace exchange: a test case from

the Mexican Gulf lowlands. (*Lat. Am. Antiq.*, 20:1, March 2009, p. 157–174)

Applies Kenneth Hirth's "distributional approach" of identifying the existence of markets in archeological context using the middle postclassic Lower Blanco region of Veracruz as a test case. Statistical analysis of sherd collections over a large area is compared to a similar analysis at Teotihuacan, which is known to have a market system. Determines that this area of Veracruz likely had a market system centered on the town of El Sauce. [AAJ]

30 **González, Gaspar Pedro.** 13 B'aktun: Mayan visions of 2012 and beyond. Berkeley, Calif.: North Atlantic Books, 2010. 141 p.: bibl., ill.

Reflections of a Q'anjob'al Maya writer on Maya concepts of time, creation, and history and their meaning for Maya people today. [JSH]

Hernández, Patricia. La regulación del crecimiento de la población en el México prehispánico. See *HLAS 66:223.*

31 **Housework: craft production and domestic economy in ancient Mesoamerica.** Edited by Kenn Hirth. Hobenken, N.J.: Wiley, 2009. 251 p.: bibl., ill., maps. (Archeological papers of the American Anthropological Association, 19)

Edited volume on production and economy at the household level of Mesoamerica. Split into sections about utilitarian and wealth goods. Covers diverse crafting skills and production of resources such as bitumen, salt, obsidian, pottery, adhesives, and metallurgy. [AAJ]

32 **Houston, Stephen D.** and **Takeshi Inomata.** The classic Maya. New York, N.Y.: Cambridge Univ. Press, 2009. 383 p.: bibl., ill., index, maps. (Cambridge world archaeology)

Overview of Maya civilization, focusing on the period of maximum diversity and complexity in the first millennium CE. Discussions of the history of Maya studies and conceptual perspectives for understanding Maya archeology are followed by a review of the history of the development of Maya civilization and consideration of the social groups that made up Maya societies (royals, nobles, craftsmen, traders, farmers) and the supernatural forces that defined their universe. A final chapter considers the decline of Maya kingdoms in the 9th and 10th centuries. [JSH]

33 **In the maw of the earth monster: Mesoamerican ritual cave use.** Edited by James E. Brady and Keith M. Prufer. Austin: Univ. of Texas Press, 2005. 438 p.: bibl., ill., index, maps. (The Linda Schele series in Maya and pre-Columbian studies)
Edited volume with chapters that use archeological, ethnohistoric, and ethnographic data to examine prehispanic, colonial period, and contemporary cave rituals. Includes chapters on central Mexico, northern Veracruz, and Oaxaca, including studies from Acatzingo Viejo, Blade Cave, and the Colossal Natural Bridge in the Coixtlahuaca basin. [AAJ]

34 **Introducción a la arqueología del occidente de México.** Compilación de Beatriz Braniff C. Colima, Mexico: Univ. de Colima; México: CONACULTA·INAH, 2004. 542 p.: bibl., ill. (some folded), maps. (Col. Orígenes)
Introductory text to the archeology of western Mexico. Covers the motivations behind investigations, economic and political structures, and revitalization of native heritage. [AAJ]

35 **Jackson, Sarah E.** Imagining courtly communities: an exploration of Classic Maya experiences of status and identity through painted ceramic vessels. (*Anc. Mesoam.*, 20:1, Spring 2009, p. 71–85)
Analysis of depictions of royal courts painted on late classic period (AD 600–900) Maya ceramic vessels, emphasizing representation of identity and status. Relies heavily on looted objects without archeological provenience. For art historian's comment, see *HLAS 66:7.* [JSH]

36 **Jornadas de Arqueología (Mexico), *Escuela Nacional de Antropología e Historia.*** Investigación, docencia y patrimonio: memorias. Coordinación de Ivonne Schönleber Riusech y Alberto Villa Kamel. México: CONACULTA-INAH, Escuela Nacional de Antropología e Historia, 2006. 204 p.: bibl., ill., maps.
Edited volume on interdisciplinary work between archeology and numerous other disciplines. Theory and method are considered in areas such as lithic analysis,

site excavation, chronology, survey, agricultural production, religion, and heritage. [AAJ]

37 **Joyce, Arthur A.** Mixtecs, Zapotecs, and Chatinos: the ancient peoples of southern Mexico. Malden, Mass.: Wiley-Blackwell, 2010. 351 p.: bibl., ill., index. (The Peoples of America)
Overview of the precolumbian history of the region that is now the state of Oaxaca in southern Mexico from 1500 BC through the Spanish invasion. Makes effective use of precolumbian texts and imagery, and invasion-period documents in reconstructing the history of Zapotec, Mixtec, and Chatino civilizations. Using recent social theory as a framework, addresses issues like the development of complex societies and the ideological underpinnings of political power. [JSH]

38 **Joyce, Arthur A.** Theorizing urbanism in ancient Mesoamerica. (*Anc. Mesoam.*, 20:2, Fall 2009, p. 189–196)
Review and assessment of recent research on urbanism in precolumbian Mesoamerica. Argues that functionalism, cultural evolution, and an emphasis on elites constrain Mesoamericanists' thinking about urbanism. Draws on examples from Oaxaca to suggest that newer theoretical frameworks, particularly perspectives focusing on practice and social negotiation, can produce more nuanced understandings. [JSH]

39 **Kaufman, Terrence** and **John Justeson.** Historical linguistics and pre-Columbian Mesoamerica. (*Anc. Mesoam.*, 20:2, Fall 2009, p. 221–231)
Summarizes the authors' perspectives on combining the data and perspectives of historical linguistics, epigraphy, and archeology to reconstruct Mesoamerican cultures and their histories. Addresses the development of agriculture, migrations, interaction between Mesoamerica and North America, the roles of Nahua and Otomanguean speakers in Mesoamerican history, and the potential for refining glottochronology. [JSH]

40 **Kelker, Nancy L.** and **Karen Olsen Bruhns.** Faking ancient Mesoamerica. Walnut Creek, Calif.: Left Coast Press, 2010. 256 p.: bibl., index.
Analysis of fake and forged precolumbian Mesoamerican objects from the 19th

century to the present day. Based on first-hand study of the activities of forgers as well as on the published literature. Convincingly shows that a high proportion of purportedly ancient pieces in public and private collections are recent fakes. [JSH]

41 Kennett, Douglas J. et al. Pre-pottery farmers on the Pacific coast of southern Mexico. (*J. Archaeol. Sci.*, 37:12, Dec. 2010, p. 3401–3411)

Suggests a model of subsistence for Archaic period populations along the Pacific coast of Mesoamerica based on slash-and-burn farming. This model is an alternative to the theory that Archaic period groups were foragers who seasonally exploited coastal and estuarine resources before the development of pottery and the adoption of sedentary village life. [AAJ]

42 Koontz, Rex. Visual culture studies in Mesoamerica. (*Anc. Mesoam.*, 20:2, Fall 2009, p. 217–220)

Reviews recent thinking about Meso-american material culture that falls in the domain of visual culture studies, which embraces all kinds of objects, not just those usually classed as fine art, and pays close attention to their economic dimensions. Identifies world-systems approaches with an emphasis on Maya royal courts and symbolic dimensions of architecture and urban layouts as important trends in Meso-american research that foster visual culture studies. [JSH]

43 Looper, Matthew George. To be like gods: dance in ancient Maya civilization. Austin: Univ. of Texas Press, 2009. 276 p.: bibl., ill., index. (The Linda Schele series in Maya and pre-Columbian studies)

Describes and analyzes evidence for dance—hieroglyphic texts, imagery, and possible architectural settings—in classic period (AD 250–1000) cities in the Maya lowlands. Focuses on the iconography of dance imagery and on interpretation of dance as ritual and political performance. [JSH]

44 Manzanilla López, Rubén. La región arqueológica de la Costa Grande de Guerrero: su definición a través de la organización social y territorialidad prehispánicas. México: Instituto Nacional de Antropología e Historia, 2008. 165 p.: bibl., ill., maps. (Col. científica, Serie Arqueología; 526)

Combines document sources and archeological investigation to describe the social and spatial organization of the Costa Grande of Guerrero. Begins by outlining the geographical context of Guerrero's coast and the limits of historical sources. The second half describes the archeological evidence and its correlation to the documentary evidence. [AAJ]

Márquez Morfín, Lourdes and **Patricia Hernández Espinoza.** Salud y sociedad en el México prehispánico y colonial. See *HLAS 66:741*.

45 Martínez Ruiz, Héctor. Historia de la arqueología en Querétaro. Santiago de Querétaro, Mexico: Gobierno del Estado de Querétaro: Univ. Autónoma de Querétaro, 2006. 220 p.: bibl., ill. (some col.), maps. (Serie Humanidades)

History of archeology in the state of Querétaro organized by time period. Begins during the colonial period and ends in the latest century of work. Within each time period highlights individuals who contributed to the archeology of Querétaro. [AAJ]

46 Matos Moctezuma, Eduardo. Teoti-huacan. México: Fondo de Cultura Económica: El Colegio de México, Fideicomiso Historia de las Américas, 2009. 154 p.: bibl., ill. (Col. Historia-Fideicomiso Historia de las Américas. Serie Ciudades)

Summary and introduction to Teoti-huacan. Topics include precursors to Teoti-huacan, its development, social and political organization, religion, art, funerary practices, and the decline of the city. [AAJ]

47 Maya worldviews at conquest. Edited by Leslie G. Cecil and Timothy W. Pugh. Boulder: Univ. Press of Colorado, 2009. 426 p.: bibl., index. (Mesoamerican worlds)

Collection of essays drawing on archeological, ethnohistorical, and ethnographic data to reconstruct worldview, sacred landscapes, and ritual in various parts of the Maya world in the last centuries of the precolumbian period and since the Spanish invasion. Emphasizes Maya responses to the European presence. [JSH]

48 McAnany, Patricia Ann. Ancestral Maya economies in archaeological perspective. Cambridge, England; New

York, N.Y.: Cambridge Univ. Press, 2010. 373 p.: bibl., ill., index, maps.

Broad interpretive treatment of ancient Maya economies, using material remains and hieroglyphic texts, ethnohistorical documents, and ethnographic accounts. Explores relationships among various aspects of Maya economies and the links among economic institutions and ecology; social organization, especially gender, social distinction, and identity; and political power. [JSH]

49   McAnany, Patricia Ann and **Tomás Gallareta Negrón.** Bellicose rulers and climatological peril?: retrofitting twenty-first century woes on eighth-century Maya society. (*in* Questioning collapse: human resilience, ecological vulnerability, and the aftermath of empire. Edited by Patricia A. McAnany and Normal Yoffee. New York, N.Y.: Cambridge Univ. Press, 2010, p. 142–175)

Critique of orthodox approaches to explaining the transformation of Maya societies in the terminal classic period (AD 800–1000) as oversimplifications that inappropriately generalize one or a few of a diverse array of contributing factors, in part as a projection of contemporary concerns onto the past. Suggests that the process should be conceptualized as one of change, rather than collapse. [JSH]

50   Memoria del registro arqueológico en México: treinta años. Coordinación de Silvia Mesa Dávila *et al.* México: Instituto Nacional de Antropología e Historia, 2009. 849 p.: bibl., ill., maps. (Col. científica; 548. Serie Arqueología)

Edited volume that covers a variety of themes in Mexican archeology over the past 30 years. Includes essays on the legal framework of archeological patrimony, changes in archeology between 1972 and 1996, the INAH-Procede program, the establishment of archeological boundaries, interdisciplinary efforts to protect archeological areas and the role of archeological patrimony in contemporary society. [AAJ]

51   Mesa Redonda de Monte Albán, 4th, Oaxaca, Mexico, 2004. Bases de la complejidad social en Oaxaca: memoria de la Cuarta Mesa Redonda de Monte Albán. Edición de Nelly M. Robles García. México:

Instituto Nacional de Antropología e Historia, 2009. 673 p.: bibl., ill., maps.

Presents a variety of papers from the 2004 Mesa Redonda de Monte Albán focusing on the theme of social complexity. Themes include the domestic unit and units of production, strategies of trade, economic organization, and social and religious development. [AAJ]

52   Mesa Redonda de Palenque, 5th, Palenque, Mexico, 2004. El territorio maya: memoria de la Quinta Mesa Redonda de Palenque. Coordinación de Rodrigo Liendo Stuardo. México: Instituto Nacional de Antropología e Historia, 2008. 492 p.: bibl., ill., maps.

Collection of papers focusing on territoriality, settlement patterns, political systems and divisions, and frontiers in the Maya world, mainly during the classic period (AD 250–1000). Also includes papers on demography, health and nutrition, exchange, language, ethnicity, and the impact of Teotihuacan. [JSH]

53   Minc, Leah D. Style and substance: evidence for regionalism within the Aztec market system. (*Lat. Am. Antiq.,* 20:2, June 2009, p. 343–374)

Argues that the rise of the Triple Alliance in the basin of Mexico did not lead to the formation of a single, basin-wide exchange system. Uses stylistic, compositional, and spatial analysis of Aztec redware to show that economic divisions existed and that they can be mapped for a large portion of the valley. [AAJ]

54   Nichols, Deborah L. and **Susan Toby Evans.** Aztec studies. (*Anc. Mesoam.,* 20:2, Fall 2009, p. 265–270)

Describes Aztec culture as a gateway to Mesoamerican studies because of its connecting role between the prehispanic and the present. Reviews major trends in Aztec scholarship. [AAJ]

55   Pascual Soto, Arturo. El Tajín: en busca de los orígenes de una civilización. México: CONACULTA, INAH: UNAM, Instituto de Investigaciones Estéticas, 2006. 409 p.: bibl., ill. (some col.), indexes.

Describes the site of El Tajín and its outliers in Veracruz during the early and late classic period. Discusses the ceramic assemblage at Morgadal Grande, and outlines elite status during the early classic. Extensive appendices include methodology, stratigraphic information, ceramic profiles, and radiocarbon dates. [AAJ]

56 Perspectivas de la investigación arqueologica II: homenaje a Gustavo Vargas. Coordinación de Cristina Corona, Patricia Fournier García y Alejandro Villalobos-Figueroa. México: INAH, CONACULTA, 2006. 292 p.: bibl., ill., maps.

Edited volume in honor of Gustavo Vargas on a variety of topics surrounding conservation and archeology's presence within modern societies. Chapters include the preservation of sites within Mexico City, urbanization around Monte Albán, and the selling of pottery outside Teotihuacan. [AAJ]

57 The place of stone monuments: context, use, and meaning in Mesoamerica's preclassic transition. Edited by Julia Guernsey, John E. Clark, and Bárbara Arroyo. Washington, D.C.: Dumbarton Oaks Research Library and Collection; Cambridge, Mass.: Harvard Univ. Press, 2010. 358 p.: bibl., index. (Dumbarton Oaks pre-Columbian symposia and colloquia)

Collection of papers focusing on the archeological contexts, imagery, and iconography of monumental stone sculpture displayed in various Mesoamerican cities during the middle and late formative periods (800 BC–AD 250). Emphasizes late Olmec and Isthmian sculptures from central Mexico, the Gulf coast, and the highlands, Pacific slope and coast of Guatemala. [JSH]

58 The political economy of ancient Mesoamerica: transformations during the formative and classic periods. Edited by Vernon L. Scarborough and John E. Clark. Albuquerque: Univ. of New Mexico Press, 2007. 228 p.: bibl., ill., index, maps.

Edited volume on political economy of Mesoamerican societies in a variety of times and locations before Spanish contact. Includes chapters on the Olmecs, Zapotecs, and Teotihuacan as well as broader chapters on the state in Mesoamerica, the relationship of the local village to larger-scale political economy, and the role of wetlands in Mesoamerican economies. [AAJ]

59 Polities and power: archaeological perspectives on the landscapes of early states. Edited by Steven E. Falconer and Charles L. Redman. Tucson: Univ. of Arizona Press, 2009. 277 p.: bibl., ill., index, maps.

Edited volume on the investigation of state organization and power through landscape. Chapters are followed by commentary from another author. Chris Fisher investigates landscape in the Tarascan state through an ecodynamics approach. Arthur Joyce's commentary on Fisher's chapter places ecodynamics within the history of Americanist archeological traditions and discusses its role in landscape archeology's future. [AAJ]

60 Pool, Christopher A. Asking more and better questions: Olmec archaeology for the next Katun. (*Anc. Mesoam.*, 20:2, Fall 2009, p. 241–252)

Review of the last 20 years of work in Olmec studies and suggestions for new research goals. [AAJ]

61 The postclassic to Spanish-era transition in Mesoamerica: archaeological perspectives. Edited by Susan Kepecs and Rani T. Alexander. Albuquerque: Univ. of New Mexico Press, 2005. 260 p.: bibl., ill., index, maps.

Edited volume on a variety of topics centered on the theme of indigenous culture through the transition into the colonial period. Articles span the American Southwest to Guatemala. Topics include consumption in colonial Mexico City, the Mápa de México de 1550, the archeology of the basin of Mexico, and the political changes in the Lake Pátzcuaro basin. [AAJ]

62 Pottery economics in Mesoamerica. Edited by Christopher A. Pool and George J. Bey. Tucson: Univ. of Arizona Press, 2007. 322 p.: bibl., index.

Edited volume on the production, distribution, and consumption of pottery in Mesoamerica. Time periods range from early formative to modern ethnoarcheological studies. Gary Feinman and Linda Nicholas discuss household production in classic period Oaxaca; Barabara Stark discusses production and distribution in the Gulf lowlands; and Thomas Charlton *et al.* focus on production, distribution, and consumption at Aztec Otumba. [AAJ]

63 Pre-Columbian foodways: interdisciplinary approaches to food, culture, and markets in ancient Mesoamerica. Edited by John E. Staller and Michael Carrasco. New York, N.Y.: Springer, 2010. 691 p.: bibl., ill., index, maps.

Collection of papers on the archeology, epigraphy, ethnohistory, ethnography, and linguistics of food in Mesoamerica. Includes discussions of food production, food preparation, feasting, exchange of subsistence items, and the ritual uses and symbolic meanings of food. [JSH]

64 Pre-Columbian Symposium, Dumbarton Oaks, *Museo del Templo Mayor*, Mexico City, 2005. The art of urbanism: how Mesoamerican kingdoms represented themselves in architecture and imagery. Edited by William Leonard Fash and Leonardo López Luján. Washington, D.C.: Dumbarton Oaks Research Library and Collection; Cambridge, Mass.; Harvard Univ. Press, 2009. 480 p.: bibl., ill. (some col.), index, maps (some col.). (Dumbarton Oaks Pre-Columbian symposia and colloquia)

Discusses how architecture and imagery were used in monumental centers. Chapters deal with Chalcatzingo, Monte Albán, Cholula, Teotihuacán, El Tajín, Tula, and Tenochtitlán. [AAJ]

Prufer, Keith M. and **W. Jeffrey Hurst.** Chocolate in the underworld space of death: cacao seeds from an early classic mortuary cave. See *HLAS 66:248.*

65 Ramírez Castilla, Gustavo A. Panorama arqueológico de Tamaulipas. Ciudad Victoria, Mexico: Programa de Estímulo a la Creación y al Desarrollo Artístico de Tamaulipas, 2007. 298 p.: bibl., ill. (some col.).

Synthesizes the environmental and cultural features of archeological work in the state of Tamaulipas. Organizes groups into the people of the plain, people of the Laguna Madre, the Huaxtecs, and the people from the Valley of Tula. [AAJ]

Reyes Landa, María Luisa and **Arturo Guevara Sánchez.** En el viejo camino a Chiguagua: avances en el estudio de la cultura de tobosos y grupos afines. See item **515.**

66 Reyna-Robles, Rosa María. La cultura arqueológica Mezcala. México: Instituto Nacional de Antropología e Historia, 2006. 248 p.: bibl., ill., maps. (Col. Científica; 487. Serie Arqueología)

Summarizes past archeological work within the Mezcala region of Guerrero from the 19th century to recent investigations. Discusses different aspects of Mezcala culture and its role as an archeological region. [AAJ]

67 Rice, Prudence M. On Classic Maya political economies. (*J. Anthropol. Archaeol.*, 28:1, March 2009, p. 70–84)

Argues that esoteric knowledge and the claim of control over time were fundamental to the differential distribution of wealth and power in classic period (AD 300–1000) Maya societies. Envisions palace economies focusing on control of luxury goods and the creation of social distinction through mechanisms such as feasting and performances emphasizing elite privilege. [JSH]

68 Rivera Dorado, Miguel. Dragones y dioses: el arte y los símbolos de la civilización maya. Madrid: Editorial Trotta, 2010. 324 p.: bibl., ill., index. (Paradigmas; 45)

Study of imagery that blends features of crocodiles, snakes, and centipedes in the art of the ancient Maya. Includes analysis of reptiles in Maya belief as reflected in post-invasion myth, legend, and folktales, along with a comparative discussion of dragons in other artistic traditions. [JSH]

69 Rojas Rabiela, Teresa; José Luis Martínez Ruiz; and **Daniel Murillo Licea.** Cultura hidráulica y simbolismo mesoamericano del agua en el México prehispánico. Progreso, Mexico: IMTA; México: CIESAS, 2009. 298 p.: bibl., ill. (some col.), index, maps (some col.). (Papeles de la Casa Chata)

Description of water systems and water symbolism in Mesoamerica. Part one outlines domestic, agricultural, wetland, and drainage uses of water in various locations around Mesoamerica. Part two connects hydraulic traditions with their symbolic contexts for cultures of Mesoamerica including the Olmecs, Mixtecs, Zapotecs, and the Valley of Mexico. [AAJ]

70 Rutsch, Mechthild. Entre el campo y el gabinete: nacionales y extranjeros en la profesionalización de la antropología mexicana, 1877–1920. México: Instituto Nacional de Antropología e Historia: UNAM, Instituto de Investigaciones Antropológicas, 2007. 454 p.: bibl., ill., index, ports.

Analysis of the history of the emergence of anthropology and archeology as professional disciplines in late 19th- and early 20th-century Mexico, with special attention to the complementary roles of Mexicans and foreign anthropologists. Particular focus on the national museum and various institutions involved in the teaching of anthropology. [JSH]

71 El sacrificio humano en la tradición religiosa mesoamericana. Coordinación de Leonardo López Luján y Guilhem Olivier. México: Instituto Nacional de Antropología e Historia: UNAM, Instituto de Investigaciones Históricas, 2010. 597 p.: bibl., ill. (some col.), maps.

Collection of papers on human sacrifice in precolumbian Mesoamerica. Focus is on the Aztecs and their Toltec and Chichimec ancestors, with considerations of the Maya, Oaxaca, Gulf coast, Teotihuacan, and Michoacán. Includes a paper on human sacrifice in the Moche culture of precolumbian Peru and three ethnographic accounts of other forms of sacrifice in contemporary Mexico. [JSH]

72 Santley, Robert S. The prehistory of the Tuxtlas. Albuquerque: Univ. of New Mexico Press, 2007. 258 p.: bibl., ill., index, maps.

Discusses the history of the Tuxtlas as a culture group, focusing on the classic period. Covers environmental and cultural history; the production and distribution of ceramics; relationships between Teotihuacan, Matacapan, and the Tuxtlas; political economy and origins and fall of complex society. [AAJ]

73 Scarborough, Vernon L. The archaeology of sustainability: Mesoamerica. (*Anc. Mesoam.*, 20:2, Fall 2009, p. 197–203)

Author discusses the human ecology of Mesoamerica and some directions that appear in recent literature, within and outside of archeology: ecological risk and resilience, economic organization, and trajectories of complexity. Emphasizes the unique structure of the Mesoamerican environment in comparison to that of the Old World. [AAJ]

74 Scarborough, Vernon L. and Fred Valdez. An alternative order: the dualistic economies of the ancient Maya. (*Lat. Am. Antiq.*, 20:1, March 2009, p. 207–227)

Analyzes settlement and economic organization of sites in the Programme for Belize ecological-archeological reserve in northwestern Belize, focusing on relationships among communities of various sizes to complement the emphasis on the economic roles of large political centers in orthodox Maya archeology. Argues that multiple economic relationships based on local economic specializations represent an important dimension of regional economies that was largely independent of the major political centers. [JSH]

75 Scarborough, Vernon L. and William R. Burnside. Complexity and sustainability: perspectives from the ancient Maya and the modern Balinese. (*Am. Antiq.*, 75:2, April 2010, p. 327–363)

Interprets the roles of technology and labor organization in agricultural ecology and the modification and maintenance of landscapes in the Maya lowlands. Argues that "labortasking"—emphasizing skilled labor, often not hierarchically organized, in adaptation to tropical ecology—was especially important in the development of complex political and economic organization in the Maya world. Includes a brief complementary case study of modern Bali. [JSH]

76 Sheets, Payson D. Contributions of geoarchaeology to Mesoamerican studies. (*Anc. Mesoam.*, 20:2, Fall 2009, p. 205–209)

Reviews recent geoarcheological work in Mesoamerica. Argues that research designs that go beyond physical science paradigms to include aspects of social theory, such as agency and practice, represent a trend with great potential for future development of the field. Praises the more interdisciplinary efforts and argues that Mesoamerican humanity cannot be cleanly split into Western disciplinary categories. [JSH/AAJ]

77   Sherman, Jason *et al.* Expansionary dynamics of the nascent Monte Albán state. (*J. Anthropol. Archaeol.*, 29:3, Sept. 2010, p. 278–301)

Authors propose a model of the emergence of the Monte Albán state as the result of territorial expansion for resource control. The expansion of Monte Albán is a result of the competitive sociopolitical environment of Oaxaca. Authors use excavations, survey, GIS modeling, and cross-cultural comparison to support their theory. [AAJ]

78   Simposio Internacional "El Hombre Temprano en América y Sus Implicaciones en el Poblamiento de la Cuenca de México", 1st, México, 2002. El hombre temprano en América y sus implicaciones en el poblamiento de la cuenca de México: Primer Simposio Internacional. Coordinación de José Concepción Jiménez López *et al.* México: Instituto Nacional de Antropología e Historia, 2006. 274 p.: bibl., ill. (Col. Científica; 500. Serie Antropología física)

Edited volume discussing investigations about the earliest inhabitants of the Valley of Mexico. Covers osteological, genetic, archeological evidence for the origins of these early inhabitants. [AAJ]

79   Simposio Internacional Ritual Público y Ritual Privado en el Mundo Maya, *Granada, Spain and Santafé, Spain, 2009.* El ritual en el mundo maya: de lo privado a lo público. Edición de Andrés Ciudad Ruiz, María Josefa Iglesias Ponce de León y Miguel Sorroche Cuerva. Madrid: Sociedad Española de Estudios Mayas; Granada, Spain: Grupo de Investigación Andalucía-América, Patrimonio Cultural y Relaciones Artísticas; Mérida, Mexico: Centro Peninsular en Humanidades y Ciencias Sociales, UNAM, 2010. 487 p.: bibl., ill., maps. (Publicaciones de la S.E.E.M.; 9)

Collection of papers focusing on Maya ritual and ceremony, in the domestic sphere and especially in public contexts, mainly during early precolumbian times.

Includes papers on caches, offerings, burials, sacrifices, and other archeological evidence for rituals, along with evidence of shamanism and other ceremonial activity in precolumbian imagery, hieroglyphic texts, and colonial documents. For ethnologist's comment, see item **525**. [JSH]

80   Spence, Michael W. and Christine D. White. Mesoamerican bioarchaeology: past and future. (*Anc. Mesoam.*, 20:2, Fall 2009, p. 233–240)

Reviews recent bioarcheological investigations in Mesoamerica with an emphasis on their contributions to analytical themes including age, gender, identity, diet, health, and mobility. Argues that fuller participation of bioarcheologists in research design will produce much more nuanced perspectives on these and other issues. [JSH]

81   Taracena Arriola, Arturo. La civilización maya y sus herederos: un debate negacionista en la historiografía moderna guatemalteca. (*Estud. Cult. Maya*, 27, 2006, p. 43–55, bibl.)

Reviews Guatemalan historians' argument that there was no continuity between the indigenous Maya cultural tradition and modern Guatemalan society. Concludes that this allegation inappropriately denies Maya peoples a role in the formation of Guatemalan national identity; discontinuity is more apparent than real, reflecting selective use of an incomplete historical and archeological record. [JSH]

82   Viramontes, Carlos. Gráfica rupestre y paisaje ritual: la cosmovisión de los recolectores-cazadores de Querétaro. México: Instituto Nacional de Antropología e Historia, 2005. 301 p.: bibl., ill.

Describes rock art and sacred landscapes with a case study in Querétaro. Discusses different rock art traditions, the role of shamanism in rock art, the rock art tradition in Querétaro, and how rock art relates to the sacred landscape of hunter-gatherers. [AAJ]

FIELDWORK AND ARTIFACTS

83   Aiuvalasit, Michael J.; James A. Neely; and **Mark D. Bateman.** New radiometric dating of water management features at the prehistoric Purrón

Dam Complex, Tehuacán Valley, Puebla, México. (*J. Archaeol. Sci.*, 37:6, June 2010, p. 1207–1213)

Applies new dating techniques to the Purrón Dam Complex of the Tehuacán Valley. Their results are more accurate but confirm that the dam complex dates to the formative period. [AAJ]

84   **Aldana y Villalobos, Gerardo.** The apotheosis of Janaab' Pakal: science, history, and religion at classic Maya Palenque. Boulder: Univ. Press of Colorado, 2007. 230 p.: bibl., ill., index, maps. (Mesoamerican worlds)

Extended analysis of a long hieroglyphic text in the mortuary temple of the great 7th-century king of the classic Maya city in Chiapas, Mexico. Argues that the complex dates in the text reflect a program of calendar ritual designed by Pakal and his successor to reestablish the supernatural underpinnings of the city's legitimacy in the aftermath of a devastating military defeat at the hands of Calakmul. Includes an interpretation of the significance of the mysterious 819-day cycle. For ethnohistorian's comment, see *HLAS 64:188.* [JSH]

85   **Anderson, J.H.** and **Kenn Hirth.** Obsidian blade production for craft consumption at Kaminaljuyú. (*Anc. Mesoam.*, 20:1, Spring 2009, p. 163–172)

Analysis of early classic period (AD 200–400) obsidian flakes and blades from workshop refuse at the Maya city in the highlands of Guatemala. The low frequency of fine blades suggests that they, or finished cores, were used elsewhere. Indications of use on irregular blades that are by-products of the production of obsidian cores point to craft production activities in the same context. [JSH]

86   **Andres, Christopher R.; Gabriel D. Wrobel;** and **Shawn G. Morton.** Tipan Chen Uitz, "fortress mountain well": a major "new" Maya center in the Cayo District, Belize. (*Mexicon/Germany*, 32:4, 2010, p. 88–94)

Reports on mapping and excavation at the newly discovered city in central Belize, arguing that the site's location, in an upland zone between drainages, reflects its importance in settlement systems in both. Sinkholes within the center were the locus of ritual activity, suggesting that its residents may have been responsible for the ritual activity documented in caves in the region. [JSH]

87   **Andrews, Anthony P.** and **Fernando Robles C.** La arqueología histórica del noroeste de Yucatán. (*in* En Arqueología colonial latinoamericana: modelos de estudio. Edición de Juan García Targa y Patricia Fournier García. Oxford, England: British Archaeological Reports, 2009, p. 115–131)

Analysis of archeological evidence of settlement patterns in northwestern Yucatán since the colonial period. Relates changes in settlement distributions in the historic period to shifting economic trends, especially extraction of forest products (notably Campeche dyewood) and cultivation of henequen. [JSH]

88   **Ardren, Traci** *et al.* Cloth production and economic intensification in the area surrounding Chichén Itzá. (*Lat. Am. Antiq.*, 21:3, Sept. 2010, p. 274–289)

Describes the collection of spindle whorls from excavations in residential contexts at the small Maya settlement of Xuenkal in northern Yucatán. Argues that the increase in density of spindle whorls in the terminal classic period (AD 900–1000) reflects intensified spinning and weaving in response to tribute demands by the emerging political center at Chichén Itzá. [JSH]

89   **Arnold, Dean E.** *et al.* The first direct evidence of the production of Maya Blue: rediscovery of a technology. (*Antiquity/Cambridge*, 82:315, 2008, p. 151–164)

Reports identification of palygorskite and indigo, the components of a striking blue pigment, mixed with copal incense in an offering bowl dredged from the main cenote at the Maya city of Chichén Itzá in Yucatán. Suggests that this reflects pigment production in a ritual context, since the burning incense would provide the sustained low heat required to produce the stable Maya Blue pigment. [JSH]

90   **Avila López, Raúl.** Mexicaltzingo: arqueología de un reino culhua-mexica. México: Instituto Nacional de Antropología e Historia, 2006. 2 v. (Col. Obra Diversa)

First volume in a two-volume set describes the investigation of Mexicaltzingo in the south of the basin of Mexico. Covers chronology from the first settlement to Spanish conquest and describes the results of excavations and surveys in the area. Second volume describes the investigation of Mexicaltzingo. Presents the analysis of ceramics found at Mexicaltzingo. [AAJ]

91 Bachand, Bruce R. Onset of the early classic period in the southern Maya lowlands: new evidence from Punta de Chimino, Guatemala. (*Anc. Mesoam.*, 21:1, Spring 2010, p. 31–44)

Reports on transformations of the central public sector of the small Maya city in the southwestern region of the Petén lowlands that suggest self-conscious ritual termination and abandonment about AD 400. The timing of these events, coincident with abandonment of Ceibal and other nearby cities, along with the appearance of foreign elements, suggest that these changes were part of a process in which Tikal, and perhaps its Central Mexican allies, had an increasing impact on the Petexbatun region. [JSH]

92 Bachand, Bruce R. The pre-classic ceramic sequence of Punta de Chimino, Petén, Guatemala. (*Mayab/Madrid*, 19, 2007, p. 5–26, bibl., ill., maps)

Describes pottery of the middle formative through early classic periods (800 BC–AD 600) from the small city in Lake Petexbatun in the southern Petén lowlands of Guatemala. Ritual destruction of the city's main civic structures about AD 400 along with discontinuities in pottery styles point to a disruption in the region's political geography. [JSH]

93 Barajas, María et al. Effect of organic and inorganic consolidation agents on Tlaltechuhtli monolith. (*J. Archaeol. Sci.*, 36:10, Oct. 2009, p. 2244–2252)

Compares the effectiveness of organic and inorganic consolidants in an attempt to preserve an Aztec monolith representing Tlaltecuhtli, a female representation of the Earth that ingests the dead and then gives them new life through birth. See also item **94**. [AAJ]

94 Barajas, María et al. Stabilization of the Tlaltecuhtli monolith pigments. (*J. Archaeol. Sci.*, 37:11, Nov. 2010, p. 2881–2886)

Article discusses research to improve the preservation of resins used on a painted monolith depicting Tlaltecuhtli, a female representation of the Earth that ingests the dead and then gives them new life through birth. See also item **93**. [AAJ]

95 Baudez, Claude F. and Nicolas Latsanopoulos. Political structure, military training, and ideology at Chichén Itzá. (*Anc. Mesoam.*, 21:1, Spring 2010, p. 1–20)

Analysis of iconography at the powerful 10th-century city in northern Yucatán in terms of its implications for political and military organization. Imagery from the Temple of the Wall panels portrays members of a jaguar warrior order in ways that suggest concepts shared with central Mexican societies. [JSH]

96 Bautista Martínez, Josefina and Albertina Ortega Palma. Catálogo de los cráneos aislados de la Colección Solórzano. México: Instituto Nacional de Antropología e Historia, 2005. 183 p.: bibl., ill. (Col. Científica; 483. Serie Antropología física)

Catalog of skulls from the collection of Feredico A. Solórzano Barréto. Their provenience is uncertain and they are all isolated skulls. Study includes diagrams and measurements for all skulls. [AAJ]

97 Blanco Padilla, Alicia; Bernardo Rodríguez Galicia; and Raúl Valadez Azúa. Estudio de los cánidos arqueológicos del México prehispánico. México: Instituto Nacional de Antropología e Historia: UNAM, Instituto de Investigaciones Antropológicas, 2009. 269 p.: bibl., ill. (Textos básicos y manuales)

Comprehensive review of skeletal characteristics of domestic dogs, coyotes, and wolves, identification of races of dogs in precolumbian Mesoamerica, and case studies analyzing canid remains from Teotihuacán, Tula, and Tenochtitlán. [JSH]

98 Boucher, Sylviane and Lucía Quiñones. Entre mercados, ferias y festines: los murales de la Sub 1–4 de Chiik Nahb, Calakmul. (*Mayab/Madrid*, 19, 2007, p. 27–50, bibl., ill., photos, tables)

Summarizes the archeological context and imagery of mural paintings that cover a buried platform at the classic period (AD 250–1000) Maya city in Campeche.

Dates the paintings to the 7th century and interprets them as representations of a feast rather than a market or ceremony. [JSH]

99 Braswell, Geoffrey E. and Megan R. Pitcavage. The cultural modification of teeth by the ancient Maya: a unique example from the Pusilha, Belize. (*Mexicon/ Germany,* 31:1, 2009, p. 24–27)

Reports the excavation of an eighth-century child burial at the Maya city in southern Belize. The presence of jade decoration in the child's deciduous teeth is unique in Mesoamerica. Speculates that placement of the inlays may have been post-mortem since the enamel of deciduous teeth is very thin. [JSH]

100 Bruhns, Karen Olsen and Paul Ama-roli. Yacatecuhtli in El Salvador. (*Mexicon/Germany,* 31:4, 2009, p. 89–90)

Identifies the image of a long-nosed being on a sherd from an early postclassic palace at Cihuatán in El Salvador as a representation of Yacatecuhtli, a deity associated with merchants and warfare in Aztec belief. This motif adds to the evidence for relationships between communities in the region and central Mexico, and for their participation in the Mixteca-Puebla interaction sphere. [JSH]

101 Canuto, Marcello A.; James P. Charton; and Ellen E. Bell. Let no space go to waste: comparing the uses of space between two late classic centers in the El Paraíso Valley, Copan, Honduras. (*J. Archaeol. Sci.,* 37:1, Jan. 2010, p. 30–41)

Reports on an analysis of phosphorus from floors at two late classic period (AD 600–850) sites in northwestern Honduras. The results indicate very different uses of space for public and domestic activities, which may reflect the cultural preferences of different ethnic groups. [JSH]

102 Carballo, David M. Household and status in formative Central Mexico: domestic structures, assemblages, and practices at La Laguna, Tlaxcala. (*Lat. Am. Antiq.,* 20:3, Sept. 2009, p. 473–501)

Uses residential structures, assemblages, and practices to compare two terminal formative domestic areas of La Laguna, Tlaxcala for status differences. Situates analysis within previous frameworks for examining household status. [AAJ]

103 Carrasco Vargas, Ramón; Verónica A. Vázquez López; and Simon Martin. Daily life of the ancient Maya recorded on murals at Calakmul, Mexico. (*Proc. Natl. Acad. Sci. U.S.A.,* 106:46, Nov. 2009, p. 19245–19249)

Analysis of 7th-century murals painted on the exterior of a terraced platform at the major Maya city in southern Yucatán. The imagery—depicting people with food and other goods—and accompanying hieroglyphic texts referring to the participants and the items they are exchanging provide rare insights into pre-columbian Maya social and economic life. [JSH]

104 Castellón Huerta, Blas Román. Cuthá, el cerro de la máscara: arqueología y etnicidad en el sur de Puebla. México: Instituto Nacional de Antropología e Historia, 2006. 329 p.: bibl., ill., maps. (Col. Científica. Serie Arqueología)

Describes the archeology and ethnography of Cuthá, Puebla. Covers previous archeological, geographical, ethnohistorical, and ethnographical work in the area. Also presents chronology and the results of investigations surrounding prehispanic ceramics and architecture. [AAJ]

105 Cervera Obregón, Marco Antonio. El armamento entre los mexicas. Madrid: Consejo Superior de Investigaciones Científicas: Instituto Histórico Hoffmeyer: Instituto de Historia: Ediciones Polifemo, 2007. 201 p.: bibl., ill., maps. (Anejos de Gladius; 11)

Describes armaments in various areas of Mesoamerica by location and period and then focuses on the Mexica. Discusses the relationship between weapons and religion and the representation of warfare and arms in the art of the Mexica. [AAJ]

106 Chávez Balderas, Ximena. Rituales funerarios en el Templo Mayor de Tenochtitlan. México: Instituto Nacional de Antropología e Historia, 2007. 375 p.: bibl., ill. (Premios INAH)

Reviews ethnohistorical and ethnographic information on Mesoamerican funerary rituals and beliefs about death. Uses these data to interpret material remains of death rituals from excavations at the principal temple of the Aztecs. [JSH]

107   Chávez Jiménez, Ulises. Potonchán
y Santa María de la victoria: una
propuesta geomorfológico/arqueológica a un
problema histórico. (*Estud. Cult. Maya*, 29,
2007, p. 103–139, bibl., maps, photos)

Reviews documentary data relevant
to the location of the invasion-period
trading port of Potonchán and the Spanish
town established in the same location in
the 16th century. Summarizes geological
processes active in the relevant part of the
coast of Tabasco and suggests that known
archeological sites in the area represent
surviving parts of both communities.
[JSH]

108   Cheek, Charles D. Arqueología de los
negros caribes en la Costa Caribe de
Honduras. (*Yaxkin/Tegucigalpa*, 25:1, 2009,
p. 7–22)

Analysis of three sites on the northeast coast of Honduras occupied by the
Garífuna ("Black Caribs") in late 18th and
early 19th centuries after the English de-
ported them from St. Vincent. Interprets
the high proportion of mass-produced
English wares at these sites as part of the
Garífuna strategy of asserting a distinct
identity. [JSH]

109   Cheetham, David. Cultural imperatives in clay: early Olmec carved
pottery from San Lorenzo and Cantón Corralito. (*Anc. Mesoam.*, 21:1, Spring 2010,
p. 165–185)

"Olmec style" pottery objects are
known to have been exported from the Gulf
Coast Olmec, especially the large center
of San Lorenzo, to several other regions of
Mesoamerica. Quality of locally produced
imitations in these regions can inform
about the relationship of local potters to
Olmec centers. San Lorenzo pottery is compared to local products from Cantón Corralito, Chiapas as a test case. [AAJ]

110   Cheetham, David *et al.* Petrographic
analyses of early formative Olmec
carved pottery. (*Mexicon/Germany*, 31:3,
2009, p. 69–72)

Discusses the distribution of a type
of Olmec-style pottery called Calzadas
Carved. Past studies are discussed and the
results of new work using petrography and
x-ray diffraction are presented and summa-
rized. [AAJ]

**111   Classic Maya provincial politics:
Xunantunich and its hinterlands.**
Edited by Lisa J. LeCount and Jason Yaeger.
Tucson: Univ. of Arizona Press, 2010. 451 p.:
bibl., ill., index, maps.

Collection of papers drawing on
archeological data recovered in long-
term investigation of the classic period
(AD 300–1000) Maya center in western
Belize. Includes discussion of settlement
patterns in Xunantunich's hinterland, public architecture and carved monuments,
roads, craft production, pottery, and stone
tools. Interpretation focuses on the political
organization and changing relations among
settlements in the upper Belize Valley, and
between them and the major city of Na-
ranjo, on the eve of the transformation of
the Maya lowlands at the end of the classic
period. [JSH]

**112   Conservación de bienes culturales:
acciones y reflexiones.** Coordinación
de Luis Fernando Guerrero Baca. México:
Instituto Nacional de Antropología e
Historia, 2009. 370 p.: bibl., ill., maps.
(Divulgación)

Collection of papers on preservation,
conservation, and protection of archeological, historical, and ethnographic materials.
Includes essays on Olmec cave paintings in
Guerrero, stucco reliefs and mural painting at Maya centers, funerary bundles from
Calakmul, colonial period documents and
religious art, ethnographic materials, relations with local communities, conservation
issues raised by travelling exhibits, and the
problem of theft of Mexico's cultural heritage. [JSH]

113   Cruz Castillo, Oscar Neil and **Ranferi Juárez Silva.** Patrónes de asentamiento en la cuenca del Río Cangrejal,
sus afluentes y la llanura costera. (*Yaxkin/
Tegucigalpa*, 25:1, 2009, p. 93–118)

Describes an archeological survey in
the lower drainage of the Río Cangrejal on
the central Caribbean coast of Honduras.
Reports the documentation of nine sites,
three of them with monumental public
structures. Surface artifacts were insufficient to date the sites. [JSH]

114   Cuevas García, Martha. Los incen-
sarios efigie de Palenque: deidades y
rituales mayas. México: UNAM: Instituto

Nacional de Antropología e Historia, 2007.
350 p.: bibl., ill. (some col.), maps. (Serie
Testimonios y materiales arqueológicos para
el estudio de la cultura maya. Instituto de
Investigaciones Filológicas, Centro de Estudios Mayas: 1)

Description and analysis of effigy
incense burners excavated in the temples
of the Cross Group in the classic period
(AD 300–800) Maya city in Chiapas, Mexico. Interprets the anthropomorphic figures
as representations of aspects of deities
closely associated with the city's dynasty,
two of the so-called "Palenque Triad." [JSH]

115 Danforth, Marie E. et al. Juvenile
age estimation using diaphyseal long
bone lengths among ancient Maya populations. (*Lat. Am. Antiq.*, 20:1, March 2009,
p. 3–13)

Analysis of skeletal indicators of age
in a sample of 96 juvenile burials from the
early colonial Maya town of Tipú in western
Belize. Finds that long bone shaft length—
often the only available data—correlates well
with dental age markers, and provides a standard of comparison for use in determining
age of juvenile skeletal remains from other
Mesoamerican skeletal populations. [JSH]

116 Delvendahl, Kai. Calakmul in sight:
history and archaeology of an ancient
Maya city. Mérida, Mexico: Unas Letras
Industria Editorial, 2008. 197 p.: bibl., ill.,
maps.

Description of the large Maya city in
central Yucatán, Mexico, with summary of
its precolumbian history during the formative and classic periods (200 BC–AD 1000).
Delvendahl, who participated in the investigations, intends the volume to make the
project's findings accessible to the general
public. [JSH]

Desmond, Lawrence Gustave. Yucatán
through her eyes: Alice Dixon Le Plongeon:
writer and expeditionary photographer. See
HLAS 66:822.

117 Doonan, William F. The artifacts of a
royal residence: group 10L-2, Copan,
Honduras. New Orleans, La.: Middle American Research Institute, Tulane Univ., 2010.
167 p.: bibl., ill. (Copan Acropolis Archaeological Project, Tulane Univ. excavations in
group 10L-2; 1)

Describes artifacts from Tulane University excavations in an elite residential
group adjacent to the royal palace complex
at the Maya city in western Honduras.
Includes consideration of chipped stone,
ground and polished stone, bone, shell, and
miscellaneous ceramic objects. [JSH]

118 Duncan, William N. et al. A human
maxilla trophy from Cerro Tilcajete,
Oaxaca, Mexico. (*Mexicon/Germany*, 31:5,
2009, p. 108–113)

Discusses a human maxilla trophy recovered from a secondary context at the site
of Cerro Tilcajete. Argues that the Tilcajete
maxilla resembles those from Teotihuacan's
Feathered Serpent Pyramid and considers
the political implications of the discovery.
[AAJ]

119 Eberl, Markus et al. El asentamiento
preclásico del sitio arqueológico Dos
Ceibas en la región del Petexbatún, Guatemala. (*Mexicon/Germany*, 31:6, 2009,
p. 134–141)

Reports excavations at the Maya town
in the lowlands of the southwestern Petén
region in Guatemala that document late formative (400 BC–AD 300) remains beneath
classic period buildings in the central sector
of the site. The late formative town at Dos
Ceibas had at least two plazas, with public
and domestic structures at its core. [JSH]

120 Emery, Kitty F. Aprovechamiento
de la fauna en Piedras Negras: dieta,
ritual y artesanía del periodo clásico maya.
(*Mayab/Madrid*, 19, 2007, p. 51–69, bibl.,
graphs, map, tables)

Summarizes archeological remains
of fauna from excavations at the classic
period (AD 250–1000) city on the Río Usumacinta in the northern Petén lowlands of
Guatemala. Animals were used in ritual,
for medicine, and in craft production as
well as for food. Analysis of the distribution of animal bone indicates that exotic
animals and desirable cuts of meat were not
restricted to the elite, but the production of
both utilitarian and luxury goods from animal products took place in elite residential
contexts. [JSH]

121 Emery, Kitty F. Perspectives on
ancient Maya bone crafting from a
classic period bone-artifact manufacturing

assemblage. (*J. Anthropol. Archaeol.*, 28:1, March 2009, p. 458–470)

Analyzes evidence of production of utilitarian bone awls, needles, and pins in a small residence on the edge of the public center of the Maya city of Dos Pilas in the Petexbatun region of northern Guatemala. Argues that the scale of production implies distribution beyond the household—probably for the nearby palace in the late classic period (AD 600–800) and for a broader constituency in the terminal classic (AD 800–1000). [JSH]

122   Escuela Nacional de Antropología e Historia (Mexico). Cuerpo Académico "Sociedad y Salud en Poblaciones Antiguas."Congreso. 2nd, 2008. Los niños, actores sociales ignorados: levantando el velo, una mirada al pasado. Coordinación de Lourdes Márquez Morfín. México: Escuela Nacional de Antropología e Historia, Instituto Nacional de Antropología e Historia, 2010. 359 p.: bibl., ill. (Investigación. Proa)

Collection of papers on the lives and social roles of children in precolumbian and colonial Mexico. Focuses on interpretations based on an early colonial skeletal population of juveniles from Xochimilco, with discussions of child sacrifice and analyses of comparative data from Teotihuacan, Monte Albán, El Zapotal, El Faisán, Chichén Itzá, and the Aztec Templo Mayor. [JSH]

123   Estrada-Belli, Francisco et al. A Maya palace at Holmul, Peten, Guatemala and the Teotihuacan "entrada": evidence from murals 7 and 9. (*Lat. Am. Antiq.*, 20:1, March 2009, p. 228–259)

Reports the excavation of early classic period (AD 300–600) murals at the Maya city of Holmul in the eastern lowlands of the Petén region. Associated architecture and material remains have both Teotihuacan and Maya features, and a hieroglyphic text in one of the murals celebrates the arrival of individuals associated with Teotihuacan at Tikal. Interpretation focuses on the role of Tikal and its Teotihuacan connections in the affairs of smaller cities in the Petén. [JSH]

124   Fernández Souza, Lilia et al. Morir al filo del tiempo: un entierro infantil colonial en urna en Sihó, Yucatán. (*Mexicon/Germany*, 32:4, 2010, p. 82–87)

Reports the discovery of the skeletal remains of a child buried in the colonial period in a large ceramic vessel in an abandoned precolumbian building in northern Yucatán. The location and style of the burial suggest that it represents a conscious rejection of Christian ritual and belief: a form of resistance by the Maya against their European overlords. [JSH]

125   Fitzsimmons, James L.; Laura Gámez; and Mélanie Forné. Monuments, caches, and the lords of Jaguar Hill: creating the sacred from the mundane. (*Mexicon/Germany*, 31:2, 2009, p. 43–49)

Reports on investigation of carved stone monuments in the center of the late classic (AD 600–800) Maya city of Zapote Bobal (Hix Witz, or "jaguar hill" in hieroglyphic texts) in the northwestern Petén lowlands of Guatemala. Excavated caches associated with the stelae are part of the dedication ritual that accompanied their erection. [JSH]

126   Folan, William J. et al. Coba, Quintana Roo, Mexico: a recent analysis of the social, economic and political organization of a major Maya urban center. (*Anc. Mesoam.*, 20:1, Spring 2009, p. 59–70)

Analysis of the distribution of high-status architecture (measured by estimated labor cost) at the major classic period Maya city in northern Yucatán. Argues that elite compounds were concentrated at the core of the community, in contrast to the more scattered distribution of high-cost buildings at Tikal. [JSH]

127   French, Kirk D. and Christopher J. Duffy. Prehispanic water pressure: a New World first. (*J. Archaeol. Sci.*, 37:5, May 2010, p. 301–306)

Describes a buried water channel at the Maya city of Palenque in eastern Mexico that brought water from a small spring to a downslope residential complex. The closed conduit, reduced in size near the outlet, creates a pressure system—the only documented example in the precolumbian Americas. [JSH]

128   García Moreno, Cristina. El complejo San Dieguito en el noroeste de México. México: Instituto Nacional de Antropología e Historia, 2008. 323 p.: bibl., ill., maps. (Premios INAH)

Investigation of the San Dieguito complex near the town of Acaponeta, Nayarit, Mexico. Describes excavations and lithic analysis at the site. [AAJ]

129 **Garraty, Christopher P.** Attribute-based seriation of postclassic and early colonial sherd collections from the Basin of Mexico. (*J. Field Archaeol.*, 34:2, Summer 2009, p. 153–170)

Seriation study of ceramic collections based on individual attributes instead of types to increase resolution. Develops a five-phase sequence for middle-late postclassic and early colonial period collections from the basin of Mexico. [AAJ]

130 **Garrison, Thomas G.** and **Nicholas P. Dunning.** Settlement, environment, and politics in the San Bartolo-Xultun territory, El Peten, Guatemala. (*Lat. Am. Antiq.*, 20:4, Dec. 2009, p. 525–552)

Analysis of settlement organization and cultural ecology of a region of the Maya lowlands in northeastern Petén from 1000 BC to 1100 AD. Interprets the area as a coherent political unit, with Xultun replacing San Bartolo as the dominant political center about AD 300. [JSH]

131 **La gente de la ciénaga en tiempos antiguos: la historia de Santa Cruz Atizapán.** Coordinación de Yoko Sugiura Yamamoto. Zinacantepec, Mexico: Colegio Mexiquense; México: UNAM, Instituto de Investigaciones Antropológicas, DGAPA, 2009. 316 p.: bibl., ill. (some col.), maps (some col.). (Publicaciones)

Edited volume on the site of Santa Cruz Azitapán in the state of Mexico. Includes essays on genetics, architecture, geology, botany, ceramics, obsidian, and furnaces found at the site. [AAJ]

132 **Goman, Michelle** *et al.* Multiproxy paleoecological reconstruction of prehistoric land-use history in the western region of the lower Río Verde Valley, Oaxaca, Mexico. (*Holocene/Sevenoaks*, 20:5, Aug. 2010, p. 761–772)

Fine-grained analysis of human/land interactions over the past 3000 years based on paleoecological archives and archeological evidence in the western Lower Río Verde Valley. [AAJ]

133 **Gómez Serafín, Susana** and **Enrique Fernández Dávila.** Las cerámicas coloniales del ex convento de Santo Domingo de Oaxaca: pasado y presente de una tradición. México: Instituto Nacional de Antropología e Historia, 2007. 342 p.: bibl., ill. (Col. científica; 496. Serie Arqueología)

Outlines the typology of colonial ceramics in the ex-convent of Santo Domingo in Oaxaca. Presents quantitative interpretations, analysis of whole vessels, and the effect of introduced ceramics on the regional ceramic trade. [AAJ]

134 **González, Liliana Carla Reyes** and **Marcus Winter.** The early formative period in the southern isthmus: excavations at Barrio Tepalcate, Ixtepec, Oaxaca. (*Anc. Mesoam.*, 21:1, Spring 2010, p. 151–163)

Excavations at Barrio Tepalcate, Ixtepec, Oaxaca reveal an early formative village along the Los Perros River. Relationship to the immediate settlement hierarchy and the Olmec style horizon are discussed. [AAJ]

135 **González Miranda, Luis Alfonso.** Entierros de Teotihuacan explorados de 1980 a 1982. México: Instituto Nacional de Antropología e Historia, 2009. 284 p.: bibl., ill. (Catálogos)

Describes the background to excavations of burials at Teotihuacan between 1980 and 1982. Presents the burial data with illustrations and field notes. [AAJ]

136 **González Zozaya, Fernando.** Un espacio para la muerte: arqueología funeraria en San Juan del Río, Querétaro. México: Instituto Nacional de Antropología e Historia, 2009. 130 p.: bibl., ill., maps. (Col. Científica; 540. Serie Arqueología)

Presents archeological interpretations of funerary practices at San Juan del Río, Querétaro. Discusses theory and method, conceptions of natural space, the archeological work at the site, the archeological view of the funerary context, and reconstructed funerary practices. [AAJ]

137 **Guderjan, Thomas H.** *et al.* New information about the demise of a Maya city: fieldwork at Blue Creek, Belize, 2006 and 2007. (*Mexicon/Germany*, 32:1/2, 2010, p. 15–22)

Excavations carried out as part of long-term investigation of the Maya city in northwestern Belize indicate that outlying elite residential groups continued to function with new political connections during the terminal classic period (AD 800–1000) when the public structures and residences in the city center were being abandoned. In the early postclassic period (AD 1000–1200) a very small group occupied part of the old settlement and continued to use the ancient agricultural fields and water channels. [JSH]

138 Halperin, Christina T. and **Antonia E. Foias.** Pottery politics: late classic Maya palace production at Motul de San José, Petén, Guatemala. (*J. Anthropol. Archaeol.*, 29:3, Sept. 2010, p. 392–411)

Describes evidence of production of polychrome pottery in a palace context in the late classic period (AD 600–900) at the Maya city in the Petén region. Interprets the distinctive polychrome pottery as a reflection of the political and economic networks of the Motul state, called Ik' in hieroglyphic inscriptions. [JSH]

139 Healan, Dan M. Ground platform preparation and the "banalization" of the prismatic blade in western Mesoamerica. (*Anc. Mesoam.*, 20:1, Spring 2009, p. 103–111)

Examines causes for the shift of prismatic obsidian blades from scarce items of possible prestige value to ubiquitous tools in Mesoamerica. Discusses a contemporaneous shift in core preparation technique as a commonly cited causal factor, but argues that it was increases in blade makers's skills that spurred the wider availability of the blades. [AAJ]

140 Helmke, Christophe. The transferral and inheritance of ritual privileges: a classic Maya case from Yaxchilan, Mexico. (*Wayeb Notes*, 35, 2010, p. 1–14, bibl., ill., photos, table)

Interprets dance and costume imagery on the late classic period (AD 600–800) lintels from the Maya city on the Usumacinta River in terms of specific ritual performances, particularly dances, and the regalia used in performing them. Draws analogies with systems of rights and privileges involving ritual practices and regalia widely docu-

mented ethnographically in the Americas. [JSH]

141 Hendon, Julia A. Houses in a landscape: memory and everyday life in Mesoamerica. Durham, N.C.: Duke Univ. Press, 2010. 292 p.: bibl., index. (Material worlds)

Exploration of material remains of daily life, drawing on facets of social theory holding that social practice constitutes the cultural framework in which people live. Interpretations draw extensively on data from Hendon's excavations in late classic period (AD 600–1000) archeological sites in Honduras: the Maya city of Copán, Cerro Palenque in the Lower Ulúa valley, and the Cuyamapa valley. [JSH]

142 Hernández Sánchez, Gilda. Vessels for ceremony: the pictography of codex-style Mixteca-Puebla vessels from central and south Mexico. (*Lat. Am. Antiq.*, 21:3, Sept. 2010, p. 252–273)

Describes the imagery on a large sample of late postclassic codex-style polychrome vessels from central and southern Mexico. The imagery is confirmed as part of the broader Mixteca-Puebla artistic style and is related to the ceremonial activities in which the vessels were used. [AAJ]

143 Hirth, Kenn. Craft production in a central Mexican marketplace. (*Anc. Mesoam.*, 20:1, Spring 2009, p. 89–102)

Explores the possibility of identifying marketplaces through evidence of craft production in primary contexts. Uses the site of Xochicalco, Morelos, Mexico as a case study and concludes that debitage can be a useful indicator of markets in the right context. [AAJ]

144 Houston, Stephen D. and **Karl Taube.** Meaning in early Maya imagery. (*in* Iconography without texts. Edited by Paul Taylor. London: Warburg Institute, 2008, p. 127–144)

Analysis of early (ca. 300 BC–AD 300) imagery from Maya Mesoamerica, suggesting that interpretation of meaning is possible even in the absence of texts because of strong continuities that permit analogies based on later imagery with better established meanings. [JSH]

145 Hutson, Scott R. Dwelling, identity, and the Maya: relational archaeology at Chunchucmil. Lanham, Md.: AltaMira Press, 2010. 239 p.: bibl., index. (Archaeology in society series)

Analysis of archeological data—especially from individual households—from the early classic period (AD 300–600) Maya town and its hinterland in northern Yucatán. Interpretation of the material remains is thoroughly embedded in a discussion of social groups, identity, gender, age, social status, agency, and daily practice in terms of social theory. [JSH]

146 Iñañez, Javier G. et al. Romita pottery revisited: a reassessment of the provenance of ceramics from colonial Mexico by LA-MC-ICP-MS and INAA. (*J. Archaeol. Sci.*, 37:11, Nov. 2010, p. 2698–2704)

Concerning the debate over the origin of Romita pottery in colonial Mexico, new lead isotope analysis suggests that Romita pottery was manufactured in Mexico by indigenous craftsmen imitating a Spanish style and was not imported from Spain. [AAJ]

147 Inomata, Takeshi. Settlements and fortifications of Aguateca: archaeological maps of a Petexbatun center. Nashville: Vanderbilt Univ. Press, 2007. 1 v.: bibl. (Vanderbilt Institute of Mesoamerican archaeology series; 4)

Results of a survey and mapping of the precolumbian city in the Maya lowlands of northern Guatemala. Includes a map of the Aguateca region, a map of the entire site core, and nine detailed plans of sectors of the central part of the city, along with a discussion of mapping procedures and conventions. A CD contains digital files of data on structures and artifacts from intensive excavation of structures in the site center. These data are discussed in Vol. 3 of the series, in connection with an interpretation of social and political disruption in the terminal classic period (AD 800–1000), a major focus of the Vanderbilt University project. [JSH]

148 Ishihara, Reiko. Rising clouds, blowing winds: late classic Maya rain rituals in the Main Chasm, Aguateca, Guatemala. (World Archaeol., 40:2, June 2008, p. 169–189)

Reports on evidence of ritual activity recovered in excavations in a deep chasm that runs through the late classic period (AD 600–900) Maya city in the Petexbatun region of northern Guatemala. A concentration of fragments of pottery and bone musical instruments in a part of the chasm that experiences unusual clouds and wind phenomena suggests ceremonies relating to rain. [JSH]

149 Jaime-Riverón, Olaf. Olmec greenstone in early formative Mesoamerica: exchange and process of production. (*Anc. Mesoam.*, 21:1, Spring 2010, p. 123–133)

Inter-regional trade of Olmec greenstone is one way that asymmetry developed between Olmec sites and across Mesoamerica. Examines this asymmetry through the distribution of technological traits in greenstone objects. [AAJ]

150 Knight, Charles L.F. and **Michael D. Glascock.** The terminal formative to classic period obsidian assemblage at Palo Errado, Veracruz, Mexico. (*Lat. Am. Antiq.*, 20:4, Dec. 2009, p. 507–524)

Uses neutron activation analysis on obsidian artifacts from the terminal formative to early late classic period site of Palo Errado, Veracruz, Mexico. Consumers at Palo Errado had access to obsidian from Zaragoza-Oyamales, but also procured obsidian from other areas of Central Mexico through exchange networks. [AAJ]

151 The Kowoj: identity, migration, and geopolitics in late postclassic Petén, Guatemala. Edited by Prudence M. Rice and Don S. Rice. Boulder: Univ. Press of Colorado, 2009. 458 p.: bibl., ill., index, maps, photos. (MesoAmerican worlds)

Collection of papers focusing on the Kowoj Maya of lowland northern Guatemala, who were in contention with the Itzá for political and economic power during the last centuries of the precolumbian era and the early part of the colonial period. Includes summaries and assessments of ethnohistorical sources and linguistic data, but focuses on the archeological record of Zacpetén, the Kowoj center on Lake Salpetén. [JSH]

152 La Blanca y su entorno: cuadernos de arquitectura y arqueología maya. Edición de Cristina Vidal Lorenzo y Gaspar Muñoz Cosme. Valencia, Spain: Univ. Politécnica de Valencia, 2007. 201 p.: bibl., col. ill.

Report on archeological investigations at the late and terminal classic (AD 600–1000) Maya city in the Río Mopán drainage of Guatemala. Includes papers on mapping of buildings, palace excavations, burials, pottery, stone tools, conservation, and public education, along with four papers on investigations of contemporary sites in the Petén region. [JSH]

153 Ladrón de Guevara, Sara. Reutilización de monumentos olmecas en tiempos del clásico. (*Anc. Mesoam.*, 21:1, Spring 2010, p. 63–68)

Examines the reutilization of preclassic period Olmec monuments at sites in southern Veracruz during the late classic period. [AAJ]

154 Laporte, Juan Pedro. *et al.* Las sabanas del centro de Petén, Guatemala: un panorama sobre el asentamiento arqueológico. (*Mexicon/Germany*, 31:3, 2009, p. 61–69)

Reports archeological survey in the savanna environment of the central Petén region of the Maya lowlands. Identifies nine major centers and 25 subordinate sites in the region, indicating that settlement was denser than previously thought. Argues that the savanna environment is natural, not an effect of forest clearance and farming. [JSH]

155 LeCount, Lisa J. Maya palace kitchens: suprahousehold food preparation at the Late and Terminal Classic site of Xunantunich, Belize. (*in* Inside ancient kitchens: new directions in the study of daily meals and feasts. Edited by Elizabeth A. Klarich. Boulder, Colo.: Univ. of Colorado Press, 2010, p. 133–160, bibl., ill., maps, tables)

Discussion of food production and consumption in the precolumbian Maya world, particularly in the context of royal courts and elite residences. Draws on extensive excavation data from the late and terminal classic Maya center in western Belize to identify material correlates of feasts and associated activities. [JSH]

156 Lentz, David L. and **Brian Hockaday.** Tikal timbers and temples: ancient Maya agroforestry and the end of time. (*J. Archaeol. Sci.*, 36:7, July 2009, p. 1342–1353)

Reports on an analysis of wood samples from construction timbers of the major late classic period (AD 600–900) temples and palaces at the Maya city of Tikal in northern Guatemala. Early preference for large upland trees gave way to an increasing reliance on seasonal wetland species beginning in the 8th century, as lintel size decreased. Argues that this is a reflection of widespread deforestation in the Maya lowlands. [JSH]

157 Lesure, Richard G. Settlement and subsistence in early formative Soconusco: El Varal and the problem of inter-site assemblage variation. Los Angeles, Calif.: Cotsen Institute of Archaeology Press, 2009. 292 p.

Describes the archeology at El Varal in the Soconusco focusing on settlement and subsistence. Pt. 1 describes the archeological data from El Varal. Pt. 2 discusses the analysis of the data. Pt. 3 extends the analysis to describe settlement, subsistence, and community within the region. [AAJ]

158 Lind, Michael and **Javier Urcid.** The lords of Lambityeco: political evolution in the Valley of Oaxaca during the Xoo phase, 650–850 CE. Boulder: Univ. Press of Colorado, 2009. 412 p.: bibl., index. (Mesoamerican worlds)

Summary of research at the Zapotec site of Lambityeco in the Valley of Oaxaca, Mexico. Late classic period Xoo phase investigations are highlighted. Concludes with a discussion of the political evolution of the valley and the collapse of Monte Albán. [AAJ]

159 Lira López, Yamile. Arqueología del valle de Maltrata, Veracruz: resultados preliminares. Colaboración de Agustín García Márquez. México: UNAM, Instituto de Investigaciones Antropológicas; Xalapa, Mexico: Univ. Veracruzana, Instituto de Antropología, 2004. 184 p.: bibl., ill., maps.

Presents preliminary results of excavations in the Valley of Maltrata. Describes project goals, methodology, previous fieldwork, project results, and history of occupation in the valley from the formative to contact periods. [AAJ]

160 **Lohse, Jon C.** Archaic origins of the Lowland Maya. (*Lat. Am. Antiq.*, 21:3, Sept. 2010, p. 312–352)

Reviews data on late early formative period (1100–900 BC) sites in the Maya lowlands, the earliest known settled village communities in the region, along with evidence for preceding preceramic occupations. Suggests that the orthodox focus on the features that characterize later complex Maya societies, combined with the destruction of evidence of the period of transition to settled life by the construction of the early settled communities, has obscured continuities from the Archaic period to later societies. [JSH]

161 **López Wario, Luis Alberto.** Lenguaje en piedra: manifestaciones gráfico rupestres registradas por la Dirección de Salvamento Arqueológico. México: Instituto Nacional de Antropología e Historia, 2008. 230 p.: bibl., ill., map. (Col. Científica; 528. Serie Arqueología)

Catalogs all rock carvings that have been documented from the Dirección de Salvamiento Arqueológico project. Discusses new methods for standardizing the registry and study of rock carvings. [AAJ]

162 **Luke, Christina.** Ulua marble vessels abroad: contextualizing social networks between the Maya world and lower Central America. (*in* Trade and exchange: archaeological studies from history and prehistory. Edited by Carolyn D. Dillian and Carolyn L. White. New York, N.Y.: Springer, 2010, p. 37–58)

Reviews evidence for the production of Ulúa-style carved marble vessels in the Lower Ulúa valley of northern Honduras. Interprets their distribution to the Guanacaste region of Costa Rica and Nicaragua, and to the southern Maya lowlands of Guatemala and Belize, in terms of evolving late classic period (AD 600–800) social networks linking communities in these regions. [JSH]

163 **Luke, Christina** and **John S. Henderson.** El saqueo del Valle del Ulúa, Honduras y un análisis del mercado para sus antigüedades. (*Yaxkin/Tegucigalpa*, 25:1, 2009, p. 23–52)

Analysis of the destruction of archeological sites in northern Honduras by looters. Places the region's looting in the context of the operation of the international antiquities market and in the context of Honduran and foreign legislation that attempts to protect the cultural heritage. [JSH]

164 **Macías Quintero, Juan Ignacio.** La arqueología de Aguascalientes: nuevas aportaciones a la historia prehispánica regional. Aguascalientes, Mexico: Instituto Cultural de Aguascalientes, 2007. 76 p.: bibl., ill., maps. (Col. Primer libro)

Overview of archeological survey in the southwest portion of the Mexican state of Aguascalientes. Describes lithics, ceramics, and shell artifacts as well as settlement patterns. [AAJ]

165 **Maldonado, Blanca E.** and **Thilo Rehren.** Early copper smelting at Itziparátzico, Mexico. (*J. Archaeol. Sci.*, 36:9, Sept. 2009, p. 1998–2006)

Analysis of the copper smelting site of Itziparátzico. Itziparátzico served as part of a system of mining, smelting, and processing locations that produced copper products for the Tarascan state. [AAJ]

166 **Manahan, T. Kam** and **Marcello A. Canuto.** Bracketing the Copán dynasty: late preclassic and early postclassic settlements at Copán, Honduras. (*Lat. Am. Antiq.*, 20:4, Dec. 2009, p. 553–580)

Summarizes information from recent investigations on the periods preceding and following the florescence (AD 300–800) of the Copán region in northwestern Honduras. Suggests that similarities in architecture and settlement organization with open, easily accessible public spaces reflects regional continuity that was masked during the classic period by the foreign features of lowland Maya political art and architecture. [JSH]

167 **McNeil, Cameron L.; David A. Burney;** and **Lida P. Burney.** Evidence disputing deforestation as the cause for the collapse of the ancient Maya polity of Copán, Honduras. (*Proc. Natl. Acad. Sci. U.S.A.*, 107:3, Jan. 2010, p. 1017–1022)

Reports analysis of a pollen core from the Copán region in western Honduras. Episodes of forest clearance at about 900 BC and AD 400 may correlate with adoption of agriculture in the region and with the onset of large-scale public construction, but there is no indication of heavy forest clearance during the late classic period (AD 600–800). Earlier claims that environmental degradation was a major contributor to the societal decline that began in the 9th century are therefore cast into doubt. [JSH]

168   Mesoamerican figurines: small-scale indices of large-scale social phenomena. Edited by Christina T. Halperin *et al.* Gainesville: Univ. Press of Florida, 2009. 440 p.: bibl., ill., index, maps.

Collection of essays on ceramic figurines from various regions of Mesoamerica from before 1000 BC to the Spanish invasion. Approaches include stylistic analysis, interpretation of ritual and political symbolic meanings, and figurines as reflections of age, gender, and identity. [JSH]

169   Metcalfe, Jessica Z. *et al.* Isotopic evidence for diet at Chau Hiix, Belize: testing regional models of hierarchy and heterarchy. (*Lat. Am. Antiq.*, 20:1, March 2009, p. 15–36)

Analysis of carbon and nitrogen in skeletal remains from the Maya city dating to the period from about AD 300 through the historic period following the European invasion. Results indicate no consistent differences between the diets of men and women, but children ate more maize than adults, and high status individuals ate more maize and marine foods during the classic period (AD 300–1000). Comparison with nearby cities of Lamanai and Altun Ha indicate that elites also had diets that differed from those of ordinary people, but in different ways. An increase in marine protein after AD 1000 suggests closer ties with coastal settlements. [JSH]

170   Metz, Brent E.; Cameron L. McNeil; and Kerry M. Hull. The Ch'orti' Maya area: past and present. Gainesville: Univ. Press of Florida, 2009. 346 p.: bibl., ill., index, maps.

Collection of papers dealing with the Chorti Maya and their history from pre-columbian times through the present. Uses archeological, epigraphic, ethnohistorical, and ethnographic data to address a variety of problems, including the relationship of Chorti language to ancient Maya hieroglyphic inscriptions, how Chorti identity is reflected in material remains, and the current situation of Chorti peoples in Honduras and Guatemala. For ethnologist's comment, see item **493**. [JSH]

171   Milbrath, Susan and **Carlos Peraza Lope.** Survival and revival of Terminal Classic traditions at Postclassic Mayapan. (*Lat. Am. Antiq.*, 20:4, Dec. 2009, p. 581–606)

Analysis of architectural, sculpture, and construction history at the late postclassic period (AD 1200–1500) Maya city in northern Yucatán in relation to the changing political fortunes of the Xiu and Cocom, the two dominant groups. Interprets revivals of earlier styles and building programs based on Uxmal and other Puuc cities on the one hand, and Chichén Itzá on the other, as aspects of the political programs of the Xiu and Cocom respectively. [JSH]

172   Morehart, Christopher T. and **Dan T.A. Eisenberg.** Prosperity, power, and change: modeling maize at Postclassic Xaltocan, Mexico. (*J. Anthropol. Archaeol.*, 29:1, March 2010, p. 94–112)

Through the examination of the maize economy at Xaltocán, a site in the northern basin of Mexico, the authors identify factors that affect the relationship between agriculture, politics, and the wider economy. Situates the maize economy within its wider context and describes the effects of factors like tribute and conflict. Wider conclusions are drawn based on the relationship of different groups that interact at the local level, like the state and farmers. [AAJ]

173   Moyes, Holley *et al.* The ancient Maya drought cult: late classic cave use in Belize. (*Lat. Am. Antiq.*, 20:1, March 2009, p. 175–206)

Analyzes classic period (AD 300–900) ritual activity in Chechem Ha cave in western Belize in relation to climatic reconstructions using data from stalagmites. Interprets intensified ritual use of the cave about AD 600 as a response to a drying climate, and its cessation toward the end of the period as a reflection of an ancient perception that culturally prescribed responses had failed. This same mindset may have played a larger role in the failure of Maya states at the end of the classic period. [JSH]

174 Muñoz Espinosa, María Teresa.
Cultura e historia de la Sierra Gorda de Querétaro. México: CONACYT: Plaza y Valdés, 2007. 216 p.: bibl., ill., maps. (Antropología)

Describes the collection and analysis of ceramic material from the Sierra Gorda in Querétaro. Discusses previous work in the area, the provenance of the ceramic material, and then presents the analysis. [AAJ]

175 Nelson, Zachary. Obsidian biface production at Teotihuacan: reexamining a Coyotlatelco phase workshop from Hacienda Metepec. (*Anc. Mesoam.*, 20:1, Spring 2009, p. 149–162)

Reexamines a biface workshop first excavated by Evelyn Rattray in 1979. Argues that a single craftperson produced points over a several year period. [AAJ]

176 Nichols, Deborah L. *et al.* Chiconautla, Mexico: a crossroads of Aztec trade and politics. (*Lat. Am. Antiq.*, 20:3, Sept. 2009, p. 443–472)

Presents analysis of ceramics from Chiconautla in the Teotihuacan Valley and relates the findings with past excavations at the site. Uses the ceramic analysis, excavation data, and early colonial documents to describe Chiconautla role as a crossroads of trade routes within the Valley of Mexico and beyond. [AAJ]

177 Ortega Muñoz, Allan. Los mayas prehispánicos de El Meco: la vida, la muerte y la salud en la costa oriental de la península de Yucatán. México: Instituto Nacional de Antropología e Historia, 2007. 95 p.: bibl., ill., maps. (Col. científica. Serie antropología; 520)

Study of human skeletal remains of the late postclassic period (AD 1200–1550) excavated in the small Maya city on the east coast of Yucatán. Focuses on analysis of indications of age at death, nutritional stress, and disease and their implications for the demography and health status of the population. [JSH]

178 Paradigmas y retos de la bioarqueología mexicana. Coordinación de Ernesto González Licón y Lourdes Márquez Morfín. México: Escuela Nacional de Antropología e Historia: Instituto Nacional de Antropología e Historia, 2009. 309 p.: bibl., ill. (Investigación/Proa)

Collection of papers on the human biology of precolumbian and colonial Mexico, emphasizing skeletal remains, especially those of infants and juveniles. Includes analyses of individual variability, health and disease status, social and occupational differences, body imagery, and funerary contexts at Xochimilco, Monte Albán, and El Rey (Cancún). [JSH]

179 Parcak, Sarah H. Satellite remote sensing for archaeology. London; New York, N.Y.: Routledge, 2009. 286 p.: bibl., ill., index, maps.

Includes a brief summary of remote sensing in the Petén region of the Maya lowlands in northern Guatemala. Describes the identification and analysis of archeological sites, buildings, canals, reservoirs, and other features within them, along with features of the natural environment, and their roles in interpreting regional settlement patterns and subsistence systems. [JSH]

180 Pastrana, Alejandro. La distribución de la obsidiana de la Triple Alianza en la Cuenca de México. México: Instituto Nacional de Antropología e Historia, 2007. 210 p.: bibl., ill., maps. (Col. Científica. Serie Arqueología; 517)

Description of the role and uses of obsidian within the basin of Mexico under the Triple Alliance. Covers obsidian procurement, distribution, crafting, and use within the basin of Mexico. Discusses the domestic, artistic, and military spheres of obsidian use. [AAJ]

181 Pastrana, Alejandro and Silvia Domínguez. Cambios en la estrategia de la explotación de la obsidiana de Pachuca: Teotihuacan, Tula y la Triple Alianza. (*Anc. Mesoam.*, 20:1, Spring 2009, p. 129–148)

Pachuca obsidian exploitation by the Aztecs, Toltecs, and people of Teotihuacan. Connects obsidian with its economic, military, religious, and state functions. Discusses manufacture and changes in procurement strategies through time. [AAJ]

182 Perrot Minnot, Sébastien and Philippe Costa. Arte rupestre y asentamientos: el caso de la Piedra Sellada en el Parque Nacional El Imposible, El Salvador. (*Mexicon/Germany*, 31:4, 2009, p. 90–95)

Reports more than 100 geometric and representational petroglyphs carved on a large basalt boulder in western El Salvador. Occupation in the region began at least as early as the 3rd or 4th century B.C. and continued through the Spanish invasion in the 16th century AD. Late classic (A.D. 600–900) sherds found in the vicinity of the boulder may date the petroglyphs. [JSH]

183 Pool, Christopher A. et al. The early horizon at Tres Zapotes: implications for Olmec interaction. (Anc. Mesoam., 21:1, Spring 2010, p. 95–105)

In an effort to better understand Gulf Coast Olmec communities and their relationships with each other and with other regions, the authors compare pottery, figurines, and obsidian from an isolated early formative find at Tres Zapotes with contemporaneous collections from San Lorenzo and Macayal. Their analysis points to a sociopolitical network between heterogeneous polities that engaged in alliance, competition, and interaction. [AAJ]

184 Price, T. Douglas et al. Kings and commoners at Copan: isotopic evidence for origins and movement in the Classic Maya period. (J. Anthropol. Archaeol., 29:1, March 2010, p. 15–32)

Analysis of strontium and oxygen isotope ratios from the bones and teeth of individuals, elite and nonelite, buried at the Maya city in northwestern Honduras. Chemical evidence, combined with associated material remains, are consistent with the interpretation that the individual in the Hunal tomb is Yax K'uk' Mo'o, the dynastic founder, who came from the Petén region to the north. The woman in the nearby Margarita tomb, who spent her childhood in the Copán region, may have been his wife. The occupant of the "sub-jaguar" tomb, likely the 8th ruler in the dynasty, has a slightly different bone chemistry and may have spent his childhood at the nearby subordinate city of Quiriguá, where many of the ceramic vessels buried with him were manufactured. [JSH]

185 Pugh, Timothy W. Contagion and alterity: Kowoj Maya appropriations of European objects. (Am. Anthropol., 111:3, Sept. 2009, p. 373–386)

Analysis of colonial period artifacts from the 16th- and 17th-century Kowoj capital at Zacpetén in northern Guatemala. Argues that the ceremonial contexts in which the foreign objects were found indicates that they were incorporated into ritual because they were seen as sources of supernatural power attributed to Europeans. [JSH]

186 Purfer, Keith M. and **Peter S. Dunham.** A shaman's burial from an early classic cave in the Maya mountains of Belize, Central America. (World Archaeol., 41:2, June 2009, p. 295–320)

Reports the recovery of the skeletal remains of a decapitated male buried in a walled enclosure within a cave in southern Belize. The burial location, along with associated artifacts—notably a wooden stool and painted pottery with death and bundle imagery—suggest that the individual may have been a religious specialist. [JSH]

187 Pyburn, K. Anne. Pomp and circumstance before Belize: ancient Maya commerce and the New River conurbation. (in Ancient city: new perspectives on urbanism in the old and new world. Edited by Joyce Marcus and Jeremy A. Sabloff. Santa Fe, N.M.: School for Advanced Research Press, 2008, p. 247–272)

Argues that understanding cities in the precolumbian Maya world requires attention to land ownership, production, consumption, and exchange, and to the roles of elites and commoners in these aspects of regional economies. Author illustrates her interpretation with data drawn from Lamanai, Altun Ha, and Chau Hiix in northern Belize, which she sees as part of a single political and economic sphere. [JSH]

188 Rebnegger, Karin J. Obsidian production and changing consumption in the Lake Patzcuaro Basin, Michoacan, Mexico. (Anc. Mesoam., 21:1, Spring 2010, p. 79–89)

Analysis of the consumption and production of obsidian items at Urichu and Erongaricuaro within the Lake Pátzcuaro basin indicates differences in site function and the shifting climate of obsidian production in the late postclassic period. Author concludes that not all obsidian was controlled by elites in the capital, and that craft production took place outside the capital at the site of Erongaricuaro. [AAJ]

189 Rich, Michelle et al. An Olmec style figurine from El Perú-Waka', Petén, Guatemala: a preliminary report. (Mexicon/ Germany, 32:5, 2010, p. 115–122)

Reports the discovery of an Olmec-style greenstone figurine in the tomb of a late classic ruler of the Maya city in the northern lowlands of Guatemala. Indications of wear on the figurine suggest that it was an heirloom rather than an archaizing piece. [JSH]

190 Ringle, William M. The art of war: imagery of the Upper Temple of the Jaguars, Chichén Itzá. (*Anc. Mesoam.*, 20:1, Spring 2009, p. 15–44)

Presents a new assessment of the painting and architecture of a terminal classic period (AD 800–1000) temple attached to the great ball court at the major Maya city in northern Yucatán, making use of newly available digital photographs of the interior murals. Interprets the imagery of the murals as representations of specific historical conflicts, with investiture as a major theme. Identifies close analogues in central Mexican architecture and imagery. For art historian's comment, see *HLAS 66:11*. [JSH]

191 Rivera Dorado, Miguel. Geometría monumental del poder maya: el caso de Oxkintok. (*Rev. Esp. Antropol. Am.*, 37:2, 2007, p. 7–21, bibl.)

Analyzes the symbolic dimensions of the layout of monumental public architecture in the core of the classic period (AD 400–800) city in western Yucatán. Argues that the geometry of public buildings and their orientations reflect fundamental Maya concepts of state symbolism, particularly the association of kingship with the sun. [JSH]

192 Rivero Torres, Sonia E. Figurillas antropomorfas y zoomorfas del Juego de Pelota de Lagartero, Chiapas. Tuxtla Gutiérrez, Mexico: Univ. de Ciencias y Artes de Chiapas, 2002. 121 p.: bibl., ill., maps. (Serie Ciencias sociales y humanidades)

Classification and description of figurines excavated in the ball court complex of the early classic period (AD 200–600) Maya city in eastern Mexico. [JSH]

193 Rodríguez-Alegría, Enrique. Narratives of conquest, colonialism, and cutting-edge technology. (*Am. Anthropol.*, 110:1, March 2008, p. 33–43)

Argues against the dominant narrative in the Americas that says that stone tool technologies were abandoned shortly after Spanish contact in favor of steel knives. Uses Xaltocán, Mexico as an example of increased stone-tool use after contact based on access to means of production. Invites a rewriting of the narrative of postcolonial technological change that does not assume rapid replacement of indigenous tools and technologies. [AAJ]

194 Rojas Martínez Garcida, Araceli. Las vasijas polícromo tipo Silvia de Cholula con el glifo de ofrenda. (*Mexicon/ Germany*, 31:1, 2009, p. 18–24)

Discusses the design attributes and symbolism of middle postclassic Silvia polychrome ceramics from Cholula. Argues that they were relatively abundant in the archeological record and could have held ceremonial offerings. [AAJ]

195 Rosenwig, Robert M. Early Mesoamerican garbage: ceramic and daub discard patterns from Cuauhtémoc, Soconusco, Mexico. (*J. Archaeol. Method Theory*, 16:1, March 2009, p. 1–32)

Addresses the formation processes of the site of Cuauhtémoc, Chiapas, Mexico through an analysis of refuse disposal patterns. Middens and trash pits are examined from before, during, and after the establishment of Cuauhtémoc, spanning 1600–800 B.C. [AAJ]

196 Rosenwig, Robert M. Prehispanic settlement in the Cuauhtémoc region of the Soconusco, Chiapas, Mexico. (*J. Field Archaeol.*, 33:4, Winter 2008, p. 389–411)

Presents a full coverage settlement survey in the Cuauhtémoc region of the Soconusco in southern Chiapas, Mexico. Detailed descriptions of survey methods and the results of 80 new recorded sites are included. Documents occupation from approximately 1900 cal B.C. to late postclassic settlements in the early 16th century A.D. and relates the results to adjacent coastal areas in southern Chiapas and northern Guatemala. [AAJ]

197 Salas Contreras, Carlos. Arqueología del ex Convento de la Encarnación de le Ciudad de México: edificio sede de la Secretaría de Educación Pública. México:

Instituto Nacional de Antropología e Historia, 2006. 245 p.: bibl., ill. (Col. cientifíca; 493. Seríe arqueología)

Results of excavations at the ex-Convento de la Encarnación investigating domestic life. Identifies work, living, and dining areas within the complex; establishes the crafts carried out at the convent; and describes architectural features and preservation. Also covers chronology and excavation data. [AAJ]

198 Sanchez, Carleen D. Monumental architecture and preclassic occupation at La Unión in western Honduras. (*Mexicon/Germany*, 32:5, 2010, p. 109–114)

Reports on investigations at the Maya city in western Honduras indicating that a monumental center had emerged there in the late formative period (400 BC–AD 200). Usulután pottery reflects participation in external interaction spheres. [JSH]

199 Schávelzon, Daniel. Caballito Blanco, Oaxaca, un estudio del sitio y de su observatorio. (*Mexicon/Germany*, 32:6, 2010, p. 154–158)

Detailed description of Building O from the site of Caballito Blanco, which closely resembles Building J at Monte Albán. Describes other structures at the site originally excavated by John Paddock and calls for additional research and preservation. [AAJ]

200 Schwarz, Kevin R. Eckixil: understanding the classic to postclassic survival and transformation of a Peten Maya village. (*Lat. Am. Antiq.*, 20:3, Sept. 2009, p. 413–441)

Analysis of the occupation of small islands in Lake Quexil in the central Petén region of the Maya lowlands from AD 800 through the early colonial period. Comparison of changing architectural styles in Quexil sites and their contemporaries elsewhere in the lakes region illustrates considerable variability in the process of transformation that affected the Maya world in the terminal classic (AD 800–1000) and in the nature of later societies. When the region was brought under colonial control at the end of the 17th century, the area was part of the Itzá state centered at Tayasal in Lake Petén Itzá. [JSH]

201 Seinfeld, Daniel M.; Christopher von Nagy; and Mary D. Pohl. Determining Olmec maize use through bulk stable carbon isotope analysis. (*J. Archaeol. Sci.*, 36:11, Nov. 2009, p. 2560–2565)

Article describes the possibilities of using bulk stable carbon isotope analysis of ceramics to describe maize-use patterns. The Olmec site of San Andres, Tabasco, Mexico is used as a case study, and luxury beverage wares are compared against utilitarian vessels. [AAJ]

202 Serra Puche, Mari Carmen; Jesús Carlos Lazcano Arce; and Manuel de la Torre Mendoza. Cerámica de Xochitécatl. México: UNAM, Instituto de Investigaciones Antropológicas, 2004. 229 p.: bibl., ill. (some col.), maps.

Outlines the ceramic typology for Xochitécatl from the formative to the postclassic and discusses foreign pottery in each time period. [AAJ]

203 Sharer, Robert J.; David W. Sedat; and Alessandro Pezzati. Sitios arqueológicos en la Costa Norte de Honduras. (*Yaxkin/Tegucigalpa*, 25:1, 2009, p. 73–91)

Describes archeological survey of the Caribbean coast of Honduras undertaken to determine whether the coastal zone had a significant formative period (1500 BC–AD 200) occupation. Reports the discovery of 17 new sites, 11 of which could be placed in the classic (AD 200–1000) or postclassic (AD 1000–1525) periods. [JSH]

204 Silverstein, Jay E. et al. Rethinking the great earthwork of Tikal: a hydraulic hypothesis for the classic Maya polity. (*Anc. Mesoam.*, 20:1, Spring 2009, p. 45–58)

Reports on new investigation of ditch and embankment constructions at the classic period (AD 300–900) Maya city in northern Guatemala. Rejects the orthodox interpretation of the earthworks as defensive installations or boundary markers, interpreting them instead as filtration trenches for collection of water for dry season use. [JSH]

205 Speal, C.S. The economic geography of chert lithic production in the southern Maya lowlands: a comparative examination of early-stage reduction debris. (*Lat. Am. Antiq.*, 20:1, March 2009, p. 91–119)

Analysis of evidence for chert production at precolumbian lowland Maya communities, suggesting that production of different kinds of chert artifacts (traded elite and ritual items, standardized utilitarian tools, and informal tools) were produced in different contexts and distributed through different mechanisms. Argues for more standardization in categories and methods to facilitate this kind of comparative analysis. [JSH]

206 Šprajc, Ivan; Carlos Morales-Aguilar; and Richard D. Hansen. Early Maya astronomy and urban planning at El Mirador, Peten, Guatemala. (*Anthropol. Noteb.*, 15:3, 2009, p. 79–101, bibl., maps, tables)

Reports analysis of building orientations from the late formative period (300 BC–AD 200) Maya city in northern Guatemala in relation to calendar systems and astronomical observations. Identifies several important sunrise/sunset alignments, including a group clustering around 17 degrees, an orientation popular at many later cities, especially in central Mexico. [JSH]

207 Šprajc, Ivan et al. Archaeological reconnaissance in south-eastern Campeche, Mexico: summary of the 2007 field season. (*Mexicon/Germany*, 32:6, 2010, p. 148–154)

Report on the seventh season of an archeological survey in the Calakmul region of the central Maya lowlands. Sites documented cover the middle formative through terminal classic periods (ca. 800 BC–AD 1000) and include large cities, two of which have defensive walls enclosing the civic core, as well as smaller centers, towns, and villages. [JSH]

208 Suárez Diez, Lourdes. Conchas y caracoles: ese universo maravilloso. Fotografía de Martha Alicia López Díaz. 2. ed. México: Instituto Nacional de Antropología e Historia, 2007. 235 p.: bibl., col. ill.

Describes the role of marine shells in Mesoamerican societies. Covers how shell is procured, distributed, used in craft production, and its roles within Mesoamerica. Explores the relationships between shells and music, color, religion and magic, writing, and art. [AAJ]

209 Thompson, Victor D.; Philip J. Arnold; and Amber M. VanDerwarker. Geophysical investigations at Teotepec, Mexico, 1000 B.C.–A.D. 1000. (*J. Field Archaeol.*, 34:4, Winter 2009, p. 439–455)

Investigation of socioeconomic conditions at the site of Teotepec in Southern Veracruz, Mexico during the middle formative through late classic (1000 BC–AD 1000) focusing on the form and function of a distinctive architectural configuration, the Long Plaza Group. Geophysical survey defines the Long Plaza Group and shows that Teotepec architecture incorporated natural features. The site's significant time depth and different mound construction techniques highlight the importance of Teotepec within the region throughout these time periods. [AAJ]

210 Tiesler, Vera. "Olmec" head shapes among the preclassic period Maya and cultural meanings. (*Lat. Am. Antiq.*, 21:3, Sept. 2010, p. 290–311)

Analyzes 10 skulls from the Maya world that were artificially shaped in infancy by wrapping the child's head against a cradleboard. Argues that this form of cranial modification, found in formative period contexts (before AD 250) reflects continuity from the earlier formative Olmec culture, and that the intent may have been to identify with the maize deity, whose head has the same form in early Maya imagery. [JSH]

211 Villaseñor Alonso, María Isabel. La fachada poniente del templo de Quetzalcóatl: estudio del deterioro y consideraciones para su conservación. México: Instituto Nacional de Antropología e Historia, 2006. 187 p.: ill., maps. (Obra diversa)

Describes the temple of Quetzalcóatl at Teotihuacán and possible courses of action to conserve the west face. Covers the archeology of the temple itself, the surrounding city, and the materials used in construction. [AAJ]

212 Von Schwerin, Jennifer. The problem of the "Copan style" and political identity: the architectural sculpture of El Paraíso, Honduras in a regional context. (*Mexicon/Germany*, 32:3, 2010, p. 56–66)

Analysis of architectural sculpture in the region to the east of the Maya city of Copán in western Honduras indicating that

El Paraíso and other regional centers share political symbolism with the larger city during the late classic period (AD 600–800). Argues that the shared elements do not constitute a distinctive Copán style and that they reflect diverse political relationships and identities rather than a political sphere dominated by Copán. [JSH]

213 **Wendt, Carl J.** A San Lorenzo phase household assemblage from El Remolino, Veracruz. (*Anc. Mesoam.*, 21:1, Spring 2010, p. 107–122)

Assemblages from El Remolino, a nonelite settlement within the San Lorenzo Olmec region, are analyzed to develop a baseline of the Olmec domestic assemblage. Author finds that aside from its location, El Remolino does not qualify as an Olmec site using the current accepted criteria. Argues that models of Olmec influence across Mesoamerica are biased due to the current poor understanding of variation within the Gulf Coast region itself. [AAJ]

214 **Whittaker, John C. *et al.*** Lithic industry in a Maya center: an axe workshop at El Pilar, Belize. (*Lat. Am. Antiq.*, 20:1, March 2009, p. 134–156)

Describes excavation of a workshop on the outskirts of the classic Maya city in western Belize where chert tools, mainly axes, were manufactured. Proximity to the civic precinct may imply that chert tool production was organized and controlled by the state, but there is no direct evidence for this. [JSH]

215 **Williams, Eduardo.** The exploitation of aquatic resources at Lake Cuitzeo, Michoacán, Mexico: an ethnoarchaeological study. (*Lat. Am. Antiq.*, 20:4, Dec. 2009, p. 607–627)

Combines ethnohistorical sources, archeological evidence, and ethnographic study to better describe the exploitation of marine resources at Lake Cuitzeo, Michoacán. Although archeological evidence of resource exploitation focuses on obsidian and salt, other resources that do not preserve as well, such as water fowl, wild plants, and fish, could have been as important to the local economy. [AAJ]

216 **Williams, Jocelyn S.; Christine D. White; and Fred J. Longstaffe.** Maya marine subsistence: isotopic evidence from Marco Gonzalez and San Pedro, Belize. (*Lat. Am. Antiq.*, 20:1, March 2009, p. 37–56)

Analysis of carbon and nitrogen in postclassic and early historic (AD 900–1650) skeletal remains from two communities on the Cayes off the coast of Belize. Results indicate that inhabitants of Marco Gonzalez, a town with ties to the inland city of Lamanai, ate more maize and terrestrial animals than did their contemporaries in the fishing village of San Pedro. [JSH]

217 **Wright, Lori E. *et al.*** The children of Kaminaljuyu: isotopic insight into diet and long distance interaction in Mesoamerica. (*J. Anthropol. Archaeol.*, 29:2, June 2010, p. 155–178)

Reports chemical analysis of skeletal remains from the Maya city in the highlands of Guatemala. Results indicate that consumption of maize declined after about AD 200, when Lake Miraflores, which had watered agricultural fields, began to dry up. Many of the individuals buried in elite tombs were juveniles; the bone chemistry of principal burials suggest locals, while several of the accompanying individuals spent their early lives in other areas, notably the Maya lowlands. Only two individuals show indications of a possible connection with Teotihuacan. [JSH]

218 **Yázpik, Jorge; Alejandra Pastrana; and Felipe R. Solís Olguín.** Piedras sagradas: El México precolombino y la mirada de Jorge Yázpik. México: Instituto Nacional de Antropología e Historia: Museo Nacional de Antropología, 2008. 63 p.: bibl., ill.

Presents the work of Jorge Yázpik, a modern sculptor who works with the same stone as prehispanic artisans. Essays discuss the relationship of modern artisans to prehispanic artisans and the importance of lithics to modern conceptions of the past. [AAJ]

NATIVE SOURCES AND EPIGRAPHY

219 **Astronomers, scribes, and priests: intellectual interchange between the northern Maya lowlands and highland Mexico in the late postclassic period.** Edited by Gabrielle Vail and Christine L. Hernández. Washington, D.C.: Dumbarton Oaks, 2010. 431 p.: bibl., index.

Collection of essays focusing on aspects of worldview, belief, astronomy, and ritual practice shared by societies in western Mesoamerica and the Maya world in the last centuries of the precolumbian period. Includes consideration of a variety of material remains, but focuses on style and iconography, and precolumbian and post-invasion texts. [JSH]

220 **Aveni, Anthony F.** The end of time: the Maya mystery of 2012. Boulder, Colo.: Univ. Press of Colorado, 2009. 190 p.: bibl., index.

Explores popular scenarios that envision the end of the world at the end of the Maya calendar cycle in 2012, and puts them in the context of Maya concepts of time, calendars, and astronomy. Includes a consideration of end-of-the-world scenarios in other cultures and an analysis of their popular appeal. [JSH]

221 **Chiepetlán un pueblo en la Montaña: más de 520 años de historia.** Compilación de Mario O. Martínez Rescalvo. Textos de Joaquín Galarza *et al.* Chilpancingo, Mexico: Univ. Autónoma de Guerrero, 2010. 238 p.: bibl., ill., maps.

Edited volume on the history of Chiepetlán in the mountains of Guerrero during both the pre- and postcontact periods. Chapters discuss town identity, the *Lienzos* of Chiepetlán, the *Relación* de Chiepetlán, the movement of Nahuas into Guerrero, the synthesis of archeology and ethnohistory in Chiepetlán, preservation and development of local heritage, the shaman of Chiepetlán, and Chiepetlán's local legends. [AAJ]

222 **DiCesare, Catherine R.** Sweeping the way: divine transformation in the Aztec festival of Ochpaniztli. Boulder: Univ. Press of Colorado, 2009. 208 p.: bibl., ill., index, photos. (Mesoamerican worlds: from the Olmecs to the danzantes)

Examines the Aztec festival of Ochpaniztli through Spanish colonial documents. Discusses the texts used by previous studies and the current one; the sacred images used in the Ochpanztli festival; how the festival promoted renewal and purification; and the colonial interpretation of the principal deity of the festival, Tlazolteotl. For historian's comment, see *HLAS 66:5.* [AAJ]

223 **Foundations of new world cultural astronomy: a reader with commentary.** Edited by Anthony F. Aveni. Boulder: Univ. Press of Colorado, 2008. 826 p.: ill., index, maps, photos.

An extensive reader covering method, cultural context, assorted topics of ethnoastronomy across the globe. Chapters include Michael D. Coe's overview of Mesoamerican astronomy; Ivan Šprajc's discussion of the alignment of the Templo Mayor of Tenochtitlan, Mexico; discussion of the Temple of the Sun by Mendes *et al.*; and Miguel León-Portilla's description of the Mesoamerican ethos. [AAJ]

224 **Gronemeyer, Sven** and **Barbara Mac-Leod.** What could happen in 2012: a re-analysis of the 13-Bak'tun prophecy on Tortuguero Monument 6. (*Wayeb Notes,* 34, 2010, p. 1–68, bibl., ill., tables)

Analysis of the hieroglyphic text from the Maya city in Chiapas, one of a very few that refers to the end of the current Great Cycle of the Long Count on the December solstice in 2012. Argues that, while the nuanced meaning of the text is uncertain, the gist of the relevant clause is a prophecy that a deity will undergo investiture. [JSH]

225 **Henderson, Lucia.** Producer of the living, eater of the dead: revealing Tlaltecuhtli, the two-faced Aztec Earth. Oxford, England: Archaeopress, 2007. 71 p.: bibl., ill. (BAR international series; 1649)

Discusses the importance of Tlaltecuhtli in the Aztec worldview. Focuses on dismemberment and rebirth, the sun and the earth, and dualities and triads. Outlines different variants of Tlaltecuhtli iconography. [AAJ]

226 **Hull, Kerry M.; Michael Carrasco;** and **Robert Wald.** The first-person singular independent pronoun in classic Ch'olan. (*Mexicon/Germany,* 31:2, 2009, p. 36–43)

Argues that the first-person singular pronoun can be identified in lowland Maya hieroglyphic texts of the late classic period (AD 600–800). This points to unappreciated diversity in ancient texts, most of which are third-person narratives. Unfortunately most of the texts used in the analysis are painted on unprovenienced ceramic vessels. [JSH]

227 Klokocník, J. et al. Correlation between the Mayan calendar and ours: astronomy helps to answer why the most popular correlation GMT is wrong. (*Astron. Nachr.*, 329:4, April 2008, p. 426–436)

Assesses the current status of the problem of correlating the Maya Long Count with the Christian calendar. Uses astronomical records in the *Dresden Codex*, painted in northern Yucatán in the last centuries before the Spanish invasion, to argue that the "GMT" correlation favored by most Mayanists should be rejected in favor of one proposed by B. and V. Böhm that would make Maya dates about 100 years more recent. [JSH]

228 Knowlton, Timothy W. Maya creation myths: words and worlds of the Chilam Balam. Boulder, Colo.: Univ. Press of Colorado, 2010. 231 p.: bibl., index. (Mesoamerican worlds: from the Olmecs to the Danzantes)

New translations of Maya myths of creation recorded in the Yucatán in the colonial period, emphasizing their diversity. Interpretive commentary approaches the texts as part of the Mayas' responses to European attempts to suppress their beliefs, rather than as survivals of precolumbian beliefs. For ethnologist's comment, see item **476**. [JSH]

229 Lejarazu, Manuel Hermann. Códice de Yucunama: edición facsimilar, interpretación y análisis. Mexico: CIESAS, 2009. 92 p.: bibl., facsim., ill. (some col.), maps (some col.).

First detailed description of the Mixtec book, written in precolumbian style in the 2nd half of the 16th century; includes a foldout color facsimile, along with analysis of the imagery and signs, in the context of the Mixtec tradition of writing. The book, one of the very few such books still in the possession of the descendants of its authors, includes information about land holdings, economic production, and genealogy of local elites. [JSH]

Martínez González, Roberto. Sobre la función social del buen *nahualli*. See *HLAS* 66:230.

230 Maya daykeeping: three calendars from highland Guatemala. Textos de John M. Weeks, Frauke Sachse, and Chris-

tian M. Prager. Boulder, Colo.: Univ. Press of Colorado, 2009. 387 p.: bibl., index, maps, photos. (Mesoamerican worlds)

Presents three divinatory calendars recorded in the Maya highlands in the 17th, 18th and 19th centuries with parallel K'iche or Kaqchikel texts and English translations. Includes a general consideration of Maya calendars and divinatory practice. [JSH]

231 Monterrosa Desruelles, Hervé and **Edgar Pineda Santa Cruz.** Estudio de los topónimos Tenanco Texocpalco Tepopolla y Acxotlan Calnáhuac Cochtocan: un *Altepetl* y un *Tlayacatl* de la región de Chalco-Amaquemecan. (*Estud. Cult. Náhuatl*, 37, 2006, 139–167, bibl., ill., maps, photo, table)

Analyzes two place names recorded in indigenous and European scripts in early colonial period documents from the southern Valley of Mexico. Identifies the names with modern communities in the region. For ethnohistorian's comment, see *HLAS 64:265*. [JSH]

232 Mora-Marín, David F. Early Olmec writing: reading format and reading order. (*Lat. Am. Antiq.*, 20:3, Sept. 2009, p. 395–412)

Analyzes the reading format and order of the Cascajal Block, which has an Olmec-style inscription. Argues that the block should be read left-to-right and top-to-bottom like later Mesoamerican scripts, contradicting Rodríguez Martínez *et al.* (2006) and arguing that a 90-degree rotation allows this reading format. Also identifies several patterns that may show linguistic structuring. [AAJ]

233 Mora-Marín, David F. A note on a glyph from the San Bartolo murals: a possible rebus based on *aj 'reed' for *7aj+ 'male/large/occupation proclitic.' (*Wayeb Notes*, 33, 2010, p. 1–5, bibl., ill.)

Proposes that a sign appearing in late formative and early classic period Mayan texts has the sound value aj r ja, based on its pictorial origin depicting a reed (aj in many Mayan languages). [JSH]

234 Mora-Marín, David F. A review of recent work on the decipherment of epi-Olmec hieroglyphic writing. (*Mexicon/Germany*, 32:1/2, 2010, p. 31–36)

A review of published material on epi-Olmec hieroglyphic writing that examines the methodology used by researchers. Also examines the coherence of results, both orthographically and in relation to other researcher's efforts. [AAJ]

235 Munson, Jessica L. and **Martha J. Macri.** Sociopolitical network interactions: a case study of the classic Maya. (*J. Anthropol. Archaeol.*, 28:4, Dec. 2009, p. 424–438)

Analyzes relationships among classic period (AD 300–600) Maya cities as reflected in references to warfare, alliance, marriage, subordination, and other kinds of interactions in hieroglyphic texts. Uses techniques of social network analysis to characterize the political geography of the Maya lowlands and interpret changes in it. [JSH]

236 Pasado y presente de la cultura mixteca. Recopilación de Reina Ortiz Escamilla y Ignacio Ortiz Castro. Huajuapan de León, Mexico: Univ. Tecnológica de la Mixteca, 2005. 321 p.: bibl., ill. (some col.), maps.

Edited volume combining archeological and ethnographic work in the Mixteca. Themes include archeology and the codices, culture and religion, modern migration, and gender in the Mixteca. For ethnohistorian's comment, see *HLAS 66:243*. [AAJ]

237 Roskamp, Hans. God of metals: Tlatlauhqui Tezcatlipoca and the sacred symbolism of metallurgy in Michoacan, West Mexico. (*Anc. Mesoam.*, 21:1, Spring 2010, p. 69–78)

Article explores the sacred aspects of metal and the metalworking process through indigenous narratives and documents from 16th-century western Mexico. The god Tlatlauhqui Tezcatlipoca has a crucial role in the symbolism of metallurgy. [AAJ]

238 Ruiz Medrano, Ethelia. Mixteca Alta, un lugar llamado Santa María Cuquila y el códice Egerton. (*Mexicon/Germany*, 31:5, 2009, p. 113–118)

Uses unpublished archival data to demonstrate matrimonial ties between the Mixteca Alta community of Santa María Cuquila and the Mixteca Baja community of Tepejillo dating back to the early colonial and perhaps the prehispanic eras. Argues that the provenance of the *Codex Egerton* is Santa María Cuquila. [AAJ]

239 Sanz González, Mariano. Apuntes y reflexiones sobre la categoría de tiempo en las inscripciones mayas. (*Mayab/Madrid*, 19, 2007, p. 123–138, bibl., ill., tables)

Analyzes the reflection of tense and aspect in classic period (AD 250–1000) hieroglyphic texts in relation to the ways these linguistic categories work in modern languages of the Cholan and Yucatecan branches of the Mayan family. [JSH]

240 El significado de los sueños y otros temas Mixtecos. Edición de Reina Ortiz Escamilla. México: Univ. Tecnológica de la Mixteca, 2009. 190 p.: bibl., ill. (some col.), maps.

Edited volume covering diverse themes within Mixtec culture. Includes essays on murals, sexuality, toponyms, oral history, and the role of the Internet in modern Mixtec culture. [AAJ]

241 Skywatching in the ancient world: new perspectives in cultural astronomy studies in honor of Anthony F. Aveni. Edited by Clive L.N. Ruggles and Gary Urton. Boulder: Univ. Press of Colorado, 2007. 390 p.: bibl., index. (Mesoamerican worlds)

Edited volume describing work in cultural astronomy's recent development as a subdiscipline. Topics include the correlation of the Zapotec and Gregorian calendars, a re-examination of Paul Kirchhoff's work on the *Codex Borbonicus*, and two chapters on the *Dresden Codex*. [AAJ]

Caribbean Area

SCOTT M. FITZPATRICK, *Associate Professor of Archaeology, North Carolina State University*

THERE CONTINUES TO BE A STEADY INCREASE in published works related to the archeology of the Caribbean islands and surrounding mainlands. In the past two years, numerous books and edited volumes have been released, many of which continue to focus on islands in the Greater Antilles and northern Lesser Antilles as well several dealing with rock art, shamanism, and religion. These include books on Cuba (item **246**) and Puerto Rico (item **272**), two volumes on rock art in the Caribbean (items **265** and **270**), a review of ritual objects known as cemis (see *HLAS 65:280*), two dealing with Taíno mythology (items **253** and **276**), and an edited volume on the colonization and settlement of the Caribbean (item **259**). A steady stream of journal articles continues to highlight the importance of the Caribbean in understanding a host of issues in world prehistory, including island adaptations and interaction spheres. Of particular note is the continued effort by Caribbean scholars to publish in more widely disseminated journals accessible to a larger readership. This remains an encouraging sign as it should help attract a future generation of scholars dedicated to the study of precolumbian peoples and the effects of European contact.

RECENT DOCTORAL DISSERTATIONS

Bright, Alistair J. "Blood is thicker than water. Amerindian intra-and inter-insular relations and social organization in the pre-Colonial Windward Islands." Univ. of Leiden, 2011.

Kaye, Quetta. "Ritual drug use, material culture, and the social context of power among the indigenous peoples of the Caribbean using ethnographic, ethnohistoric and archaeological data." Univ. College London, 2010.

Samson, Alice. "Renewing the house: trajectories of social life in the yucayeque (community) of El Cabo, Higüey, Dominican Republic, AD 800 to 1504?" Univ. of Leiden, 2010.

LOWER CENTRAL AMERICA

242 Erquicia, José Heriberto. Proyecto de registro y reconocimiento de sitios arqueológicos históricos de El Salvador, PAHES-UTEC: fase I. San Salvador: Univ. Tecnológica de El Salvador, Escuela de Antropología, Facultad de Ciencias Sociales, 2008. 67 p.: bibl., ill., photos, tables.

The first phase of an attempt to document historic archeological sites in El Salvador. A brief description of the investigations done to date, along with a justification and methodological scheme for doing so. A commendable first start in developing a tabular and spatial database of sites, including simple schematic drawings and photographs of various historic ruins.

243 Stone, Rebecca. The jaguar within: shamanic trance in ancient Central and South American art. Austin: Univ. of Texas Press, 2011. 229 p.: bibl., ill., index, photos. (The Linda Schele series in Maya and Pre-Columbian studies)

A review of Central and South American indigenous shamanism based on ethnographic and ethnohistorical accounts. Shamanism, in which an individual through various means attempts to experience visions in an attempt to gain important knowledge for divining, healing, etc., was an important facet of many early societies. Examination of the characteristics of trance visions, such as flying, enhanced senses, undulating sensations, and bodily distortions, and how they are depicted in art, especially those of the Moche in Peru.

CARIBBEAN ISLANDS

244 Baisre, Julio A. Setting a baseline for Caribbean fisheries. (*J. Island Coastal Archaeol.*, 5:1, 2010, p. 120–147, bibl., maps, photos, tables)

Examining whether peoples had impacts on island environments, and the degree to which they may have affected local flora and fauna, is a major topic in archeological research. Part of a major forum piece responded to by other scholars, the article argues that many, if not all, of the impacts to fisheries have occurred historically and in modern times, and that native peoples would not have had the population density or technology to do so. Responses from archeologists and biologists counter and contextualize Baisre's arguments.

245 Barse, William P. The Early Ronquin paleosol and the Orinocan ceramic sequence. (*Bull. Peabody Mus. Nat. Hist.*, 50:1, 2009, p. 85–98)

Suggests revision of an earlier interpretation by Jose Cruxent and Irving Rouse (1958) that the lower portion of the Ronquin site, termed "Early Ronquin," may simply be a single occupation dating to ca. AD 500.

246 Beyond the blockade: new currents in Cuban archaeology. Edited by Susan Kepecs, L. Antonio Curet, and Gabino La Rosa Corzo. Chapters by Cuban authors translated from Spanish by Susan Kepecs. Tuscaloosa: Univ. of Alabama Press, 2010. 206 p.: bibl., ill., index, maps, photos, tables. (Caribbean archaeology and ethnohistory)

For various economic, social, and political reasons, Cuban archeology has remained out of the spotlight. The chapters contained within help fill this void, and speak to a long intellectual tradition by Cubans that was at one time influenced greatly by North Americans, but has waned over time. Updates on current archeological investigations being conducted in Cuba by both local and foreign scholars demonstrate the importance of Cuba in understanding

the broader realm of Caribbean island prehistory along with issues related to urban historical archeology and architectural restorative measures.

247 Boomert, Arie. Between the mainland and the islands: the Amerindian cultural geography of Trinidad. (*Bull. Peabody Mus. Nat. Hist.*, 50:1, 2009, p. 63–73)

A discussion of how Trinidad shares many similarities geographically, culturally, and ethnohistorically with the South American mainland and can be seen in a sense as a continuation of the Orinoco River Valley and delta. The island also featured prominently in subsequent patterns of prehistoric population movement and interaction.

248 Carlson, Lisabeth A. and **David W. Steadman.** Examining temporal differences in faunal exploitation at two Ceramic Age sites in Puerto Rico. (*J. Island Coastal Archaeol.*, 4:2, 2009, p. 207–222)

Examination of two inland prehistoric sites on Puerto Rico—AR-39 and AR-38—which are relatively close to each other, but date to different time periods (AD 400–800 and AD 1100–1500, respectively). The sites offer a unique perspective on changing subsistence strategies over time, with the earlier site showing evidence of heavy exploitation of marine fishes along with the presence of dog and hutia, and the later site having no marine fish remains, but with two different translocated species (guinea pig and hutia). Authors argue that the differences seen are a reflection of native groups impacting terrestrial vertebrates and then moving toward localized foraging strategies.

249 Cooper, Jago and **Matthew Peros.** The archaeology of climate change in the Caribbean. (*J. Archaeol. Sci.*, 37:6, June 2010, p. 1226–1232, bibl., ill., maps, photos)

Advances in climate science have spurred archeologists to investigate in more detail the influence that various climatic changes or anomalies may have had on ancient cultures. Authors provide an outline for investigating these issues in the Caribbean, focusing on three phenomena: relative sea-level rise, variation in precipitation, and variation in the frequency and intensity of hurricane activity and how it may have impacted settlement location, food procurement strategies, and household architecture. While this type of research in the Caribbean is still in its infancy, authors stress that continued research on the subject should pay dividends when attempting to decipher the underlying reasons behind prehistoric social behaviors.

250 Curet, L. Antonio and **William J. Pestle.** Identifying high-status foods in the archaeological record. (*J. Anthropol. Archaeol.*, 29:4, Dec. 2010, p. 413–431, bibl., ill., maps, tables)

Food is not just part of a basic human requirement, but is endowed with special meaning and social significance. Using the Caribbean as an example, and the site of Tibes on Puerto Rico as a case study, authors attempt to develop criteria such as abundance, labor investment, acquisition, preparation, scarcity, place of origin, and so on to determine whether high-status foods can in fact be recognized in the archeological record. While they rely solely on faunal taxa in their examination, the authors argue that prestige and high-valued foods can be recognized and used to develop more refined models of human consumption and how it relates to cultural evolution.

251 Drewett, Peter. Above sweet waters: cultural and natural change at Port St. Charles, Barbados, c. 1750 BC–AD 1850. Pottery reports by Mary Hill Harris. London: Archetype Publications for the Barbados Museum and Historical Society, 2007. 87 p.: bibl., ill., maps, tables.

Based on research conducted at the Port St. Charles site (formerly known as Heywoods) over several field seasons, Drewett reports on what might rightly be considered the most impressive and important prehistoric archeological site on Barbados. Detailed description of the finds recovered in excavation, most of which had to be done under the guise of a salvage project due to the development of a marina, demonstrates that the island may have been settled around 4000 years ago by Archaic peoples with later occupation during the Ceramic Age. The unexpected discovery of beautifully preserved ceramic pot stacks for lining wells and wooden posts with adze marks are just a few of the impressive finds from the site.

252 Fitzpatrick, Scott M. *et al.* Precolumbian settlements on Carriacou, West Indies. (*J. Field Archaeol.*, 34:3, Fall 2009, p. 247–266, bibl., ill., maps, photos, tables)

The island of Carriacou in the southern Grenadines has been the focus of intensive archeological investigations since 2003. The island, first colonized around AD 380, holds important clues as to how peoples settled and adapted to smaller island environments in the Caribbean. Research focusing primarily at the Grand Bay site demonstrates that people lived continuously on the site for about 1,000 years, built longhouses, discarded refuse in larger middens outside the living areas, and buried their dead in pits or beneath houses. Interestingly, much of the pottery appears to have been made with nonlocal materials or imported. Analysis of faunal remains reveals a reliance on near-shore fisheries for subsistence.

253 Gannier, Odile. Les derniers indiens des Caraïbes: image, mythe et réalité. Matoury, French Guiana: Ibis rouge éditions, 2003. 516 p.: bibl., ill., indexes, maps.

In this tome entitled *Last Indians of the Caribbean: Image, Myth, and Reality,* Gannier describes how many of the cultural behaviors of native Amerindians have been wrongly homogenized and misinterpreted by both Europeans at contact and scholars over the years. The author seeks to highlight the vast array of ethnic differences present in the Caribbean and dispel some of the mythical behaviors which have been perpetuated by historians and other academics.

254 García-Casco, Antonio *et al.* A new jadeitite jade locality, Sierra del Convento, Cuba: first report and some petrological and archaeological implications. (*Contrib. Mineral. Petrol.*, 158, 2009, p. 1–16, bibl., ill., maps, table)

Increased discussion about the extent to which prehistoric Amerindian groups in the Caribbean islands interacted with one another and with other societies in mainland areas have led to a stronger emphasis on provenance study of artifacts. A lingering question in Caribbean archeology regionally has been the origin of various jade (jadeite and jadeitite) objects. While earlier mineralogical analysis suggested that jade found in the region may have come from Guatemala as no Caribbean sources were known, this study finds evidence for similar outcrops in Hispaniola and Cuba, indicating that peoples may have alternatively acquired this resource through local channels.

255 Gillott, Alan. Infant burials in Puerto Rico associated with pottery "baby bowls" or urns excavated by Froelich Rainey in 1934. (*Bull. Peabody Mus. Nat. Hist.*, 50:1, 2009, p. 187–197)

Reports on the unusual practice of interring infants in ceramic vessels based on research conducted by Froelich Rainey in the Virgin Islands. The urns are placed within a wider context in the Caribbean, noting that only a few other examples have been found.

256 Giovannetti, Jorge L. Historia visual y etnohistoria en Cuba: inmigración antillana e identidad en *Los hijos de Baraguá*. (Caribb. Stud., 30:2, July/Dec. 2002, p. 216–252, bibl., photos, tables)

A critique of a documentary made by cinematographer Gloria Rolando which portrays the descendents of Caribbean immigrants in Cuba and compares it to the author's own ethnographic research, showing how disparities are created when two distinct methods of creating history are compared.

257 Giovas, Christina M. The shell game: analytic problems in archaeological mollusc quantification. (J. Archaeol. Sci., 36:7, July 2009, p. 1557–1564, bibl., ill., maps)

Analysis of shellfish recovered from the Grand Bay site on the island of Carriacou (southern Grenadines) is used to test different approaches to estimating the minimum number of individuals (MNI) in zooarcheological analysis. Results indicate that using nonrepetitive elements (NREs) may be unreliable and hinder integration with other invertebrate and vertebrate remains.

258 Hofman, Corinne Lisette and **Eithne B. Carlin.** The ever-dynamic Caribbean: exploring new approaches to unraveling social networks in the pre-colonial and early colonist periods. (*in* Linguistics and archaeology in the Americas: the historization of language and society. Edited by Eithne B.

Carlin and Simon van de Kerke. Leiden, The Netherlands: Brill, 2010, p. 107–122)

Illustrates the importance of examining migration events to islands in the Caribbean from a perspective that harnesses both archeology and linguistics. While earlier notions of colonization focused on cultural historical models based almost exclusively on ceramic typologies, this chapter recognizes that settlement patterns were more complex and that boundaries of movement were fluid as networks of interaction were renegotiated.

259 Island shores, distant pasts: archaeological and biological approaches to the pre-Columbian settlement of the Caribbean. Edited by Scott M. Fitzpatrick and Ann H. Ross. Foreword by Clark Spencer Larsen. Gainesville: Univ. Press of Florida, 2010. 246 p.: bibl., ill., index, maps, photos. (Bioarchaeological interpretations of the human past)

This volume derives from a special session of papers presented at the 2006 Society for American Archaeology conference in San Juan, Puerto Rico. Includes an introduction, nine chapters, and an epilogue focusing on when and how precolumbian peoples settled the Caribbean islands beginning over 6,000 years ago. Papers from some of the leading authors in their respective fields highlight the utility of using a multidisciplinary approach to answering these questions, ranging from discussion of radiocarbon dating, stable isotopes, seafaring simulations, DNA analysis, and craniometric techniques.

260 *Journal of Caribbean Archaeology.* Vol. 3, special issue, 2010, Mobility and exchange from a Pan-Caribbean perspective. Edited by Corinne Lisette Hofman and Alistair J. Bright. Gainesville: Univ. of Florida, Florida Museum of Natural History.

This compilation of 10 papers is an effort to synthesize much of the current research regarding how precolumbian societies in the Antilles interacted over time. Examines the role that circum-Caribbean regions such as South and Central America may have had in influencing societal development. Emphasis is placed on how scholars should view the Caribbean islands—not as a group of insular and bounded entities—

but as nodes within a larger interactive network.

261 Kaye, Quetta *et al.* Beyond Time Team: archaeological investigations at Coconut Walk, Nevis, West Indies, 1st July–4th August, 2010. (*Pap. Inst. Archaeol.*, 20, 2011, p. 137–147, bibl., ill., maps, photos, tables)

Presents one of the few concerted efforts since the 1980s to archeologically investigate a precolumbian site on the island of Nevis. Previously excavated by the Time Team television show in the late 1990s, the site of Coconut Walk on the southeast part of the island now provides a clearer picture of Late Ceramic Age occupation dating to between ca. AD 850–1170. Geophysical data collected here and at the Indian Castle site show several anomalies to be the focus of future fieldwork. A public exhibition at the local museum showcases many of the more interesting finds recovered at Coconut Walk.

262 Keegan, William F. and **Lisabeth A. Carlson.** Talking Taino: Caribbean natural history from a native perspective. Tuscaloosa: Univ. of Alabama Press, 2008. 208 p.: bibl., ill., index, map. (Caribbean archaeology and ethnohistory)

Drawing on decades of their own personal archeological experiences and fieldwork, the authors provide an easy-to-read guide to Caribbean plants and animals through the eyes of native islanders who inhabited the Antilles for thousands of years.

263 Lammers-Keijsers, Yvonne Marie Jacqueline. Tracing traces from present to past: a functional analysis of pre-Columbian shell and stone artefacts from Anse à la Gourde and Morel, Guadeloupe, FWI. Leiden, The Netherlands: Leiden Univ. Press, 2008. 181 p.: ill., maps, photos, tables.

Detailed analysis of a variety of shell and stone artifacts recovered from two sites on Guadeloupe. Focuses on a basic description of the vast range of objects produced from these mediums, including beads, figurines, ornaments, vomit spatulas, and pendants.

264 LeFebvre, Michelle J. and **Christina M. Giovas.** The zooarchaeology of islands: towards synergy and synthesis. (*J. Island Coastal Archaeol.*, 4:2, 2009, p. 141–150, bibl.)

Although not explicitly devoted to Caribbean studies, this article, written by two doctoral students specializing in Caribbean archeology, discusses the importance that zooarcheological studies on islands have played in directing this field of study. As the lead-off paper to a special section in the *Journal of Island and Coastal Archaeology* devoted to the topic, the authors argue that "that cross-regional collaborations such as this special issue are fundamental to advancing research and investigative goals of island-and coastal-based zooarchaeology."

265 López Belando, Adolfo. El arte en la penumbra: pictografías y petroglifos en las cavernas del Parque Nacional del Este, República Dominicana = Art in the shadows: pictographs and petroglyphs in the caves of the National Park of the East, Dominican Republic. Santo Domingo: Grupo BHD, 2003. 358 p.: bibl., ill. (chiefly col.), maps.

Documents the impressive array of precolumbian rock art found in the National Park of the East in the Dominican Republic. Useful introductory discussion of the natural history is followed by detailed maps, photos, and descriptions of the caves and the pictographs and petroglyphs found within. A necessary companion for those interested in comparing and contrasting Taíno art in this medium with the many other examples recorded around the Caribbean.

266 Lovén, Sven. Origins of the Tainan culture, West Indies. Preface by L. Antonio Curet. Tuscaloosa: Univ. of Alabama Press, 2010. 696 p.: bibl., ill., map, plates. (Caribbean archaeology and ethnohistory)

Originally published in German in 1924 and later in English in 1935, this classic book was one of the first to synthesize what was known ethnohistorically, ethnographically, and archeologically about ancient Amerindians in the Caribbean. While there is a focus on cultures of the Greater Antilles, Lovén necessarily weaves together a narrative that includes the broader circum-Caribbean region. Chapters organized by immigration and origin of Caribbean peoples, artifacts and technology, social organization, funerary customs, and religion. For a review of 1935 English edition, see *HLAS 2:102.*

267 **Martinique. Direction Régionale des Affaires Culturelles.** Bilan scientifique de la région Martinique, 2003. Fort-de-France: Direction Regionale des Affaires Culturelles, 2006. 27 p.: bibl.

Annual report of archeological research conducted by the Regional Service of Archaeology on the island of Martinique. Includes brief descriptions of research at colonial Fort-de-France, Le Lorrain (Séguineau), Sainte-Anne (Grande Anse des Salines), Sainte-Luce (Les Côteaux), and research focused on how Neolithic sites on Martinique fit within the wider context of the Antillean chain of islands.

268 **Martinique. Direction Régionale des Affaires Culturelles.** Bilan scientifique de la région Martinique, 2004. Fort-de-France: Direction Regionale des Affaires Culturelles, 2006. 27 p.: bibl.

Annual report of archeological research conducted by the Regional Service of Archaeology on the island of Martinique. Includes brief descriptions of research at precolumbian sites in Le Carbet (Boutbois, Godinot) and three colonial sites at Saint-Pierre (Rue Victor-Hugo) and Trois-Ilets (Anse Mitan, Habitation Vatable). Continued research led by Benoît Bérard on precolumbian (Neolithic) sites in Martinique and how it fits within other Antillean research is also discussed.

269 **Price, Charles Reavis.** "Cleave to the black": expressions of Ethiopianism in Jamaica. (*NWIG*, 77:1/2, 2003, p. 31–64, bibl.)

The development of many pro-black and pro-African groups has its roots in Jamaica where, incidentally, "Ethiopianism" became well established and provided the foundation for social and economic inequalities. Using historical and ethnographic information, Reavis traces the roots of these black movements in Jamaica, including early Rastafarianism, and the ideologies that developed between the late 1700s up through the early 1900s.

270 **Rock art of the Caribbean.** Edited by Michele H. Hayward, Lesley-Gail Atkinson, and Michael A. Cinquino. Tuscaloosa: Univ. of Alabama Press, 2009. 285 p.: bibl., ill., index, maps. (Caribbean archaeology and ethnohistory)

This compilation of papers illustrates the rich and distinctive tradition of rock art in the Caribbean, ranging from petroglyphs produced from pecking, grinding, abrasion, or scratching to pictographs done with a variety of colors on a host of different mediums (e.g., limestone and granite). Commonalities across the islands include a predominance of rock art in locations near water (rivers, oceans). Chapters also deal with various legal and conservation issues associated with rock art investigation and preservation along with new analytical advances.

271 **Rodríguez Ramos, Reniel.** From the Guanahatabey to the Archaic of Puerto Rico: the nonevident evidence. (*Ethnohistory/Columbus*, 55:3, Summer 2008, p. 393–415, bibl.)

The Guanahatabey, also known as the Ciboney, are a group of people who were reported to have occupied the westernmost part of Cuba and southwestern Haiti. They are often described by scholars as having lived a more hunting and gathering lifestyle (akin to that observed during the Archaic period) at European contact, while Taíno groups were much more complex. Misconceptions about who these people were are addressed, as well as implications that early accounts had for understanding the archeological record.

272 **Rodríguez Ramos, Reniel.** Rethinking Puerto Rican precolonial history. Tuscaloosa: Univ. of Alabama Press, 2010. 267 p.: bibl., index. (Caribbean archaeology and ethnohistory)

Based on the author's PhD dissertation at the University of Florida, Rodríguez Ramos argues for a new paradigm in Puerto Rican archeology in which past colonialist practices (theoretical, methodological, structural) are reevaluated to establish an alternate framework for archeological inquiry. The author suggests that previous cultural-historical models mask the true complexity of the island's past inhabitants. An excellent review of the archeology of Puerto Rico to date, with discussion of many of the major artifact types.

273 **Rodríguez Suárez, Roberto** and **Jaime R. Pagán Jiménez.** Primeras evidencias directas del uso de plantas en la

dieta de los grupos agroalfareros del oriente de Cuba. (*Catauro/Habana*, 8:14, 2006, p. 100–120, bibl., map, photos)

Analysis of starch granules found on a buren (disk-shaped implement) at the site of Macambo II in Guantanamo province, Cuba. Study reveals evidence of consumption of four different plants and differs from what was reported by early chroniclers to the region.

274 Samson Alice and **Bridget Waller.** Not growling but smiling: new interpretations of the bared-teeth motif in the precolumbian Caribbean. (*Curr. Anthropol.*, 51:3, June 2010, p. 425–433)

Examination of the "bared-teeth motif" (BTM) which is seen in artifacts from the Caribbean typically dating post-AD 1000. The BTM is usually found on decorative objects used for adorning the body and associated with shamanism and ritual activities. The motif has often been considered by scholars to represent aggression, death, or the shamanic trance, but not as anything more benign or positive. Using an evolutionary biological approach, the authors argues that the BTM could have served as a communicative signal in various social interactions. For art specialist's comment, see *HLAS 66:16*.

275 Siegel, Peter E. Continuity and change in the evolution of religion and political organization on pre-Columbian Puerto Rico. (*J. Anthropol. Archaeol.*, 29:3, Sept. 2010, p. 302–326, bibl., ill., maps, photos)

The author provides a model of cultural evolution for precolumbian peoples in Puerto Rico. Argues that the cosmological belief system of Taíno peoples was rooted in ancestral linkages with groups who ventured to the islands from South America earlier in time. Archeological data suggest an egalitarian social structure during the Saladoid period (beginning ca. 500 BC), but one which was also intimately connected to the cosmos in terms of village planning, certain artifacts, and household organization and that became increasingly complex over time.

276 Stevens Arroyo, Antonio M. Cave of the Jagua: the mythological world of the Taínos. 2nd ed. Scranton, Pa.: Univ. of Scranton Press, 2006. 294 p.: bibl., ill., index, maps, photos, tables.

A robust and interesting view of the complex mythologies found with extinct Taíno peoples in the northern Antilles of the Caribbean, the first to be contacted by Columbus. The author notes that the Taíno have often been relegated to the backwater of historical studies, but that they have much to offer in terms of understanding native viewpoints and their influence on Spanish culture and language. Reviews of past historical works by Pané, among other early chroniclers, give rise to a more nuanced understanding of the Taíno creation myth, hero myth, and their cosmos.

277 Sued Badillo, Jalil. Guadalupe: ¿caribe o taína? La isla de Guadalupe y su cuestionable identidad caribe en la época pre-colombina: una revisión etnohistórica y arqueológica preliminar. (*Caribb. Stud.*, 35:1, Jan./June 2007, p. 37–85, bibl.)

Argues that it is crucial for scholars to reread and be critical of past ethnohistorical and ethnographic data in detail if we are to adequately interpret the Caribbean's archeological record. Author uses Guadeloupe as a case study to investigate Carib identity and possible "Taíno" affiliations.

278 Tibes: people, power, and ritual at the center of the cosmos. Edited by L. Antonio Curet and Lisa M. Stringer. Tuscaloosa: Univ. of Alabama Press, 2010. 329 p.: bibl., ill., index, maps, photos, tables. (Caribbean archaeology and ethnohistory)

A comprehensive review of archeological, zooarcheological, paleoethnobotanical, bioarcheological, and geophysical research conducted at the 2000 year old site of Tibes, a civic-ceremonial site in southern Puerto Rico. The multidisciplinary project from which this research derives focuses on trying to understand the sociopolitical changes that occurred through time as societies became increasingly more complex. Also looks at how this information can be teased out of the archeological record by combining multiple types and stages of analysis.

279 Van den Bel, Martijn and **Thomas Romon.** A Troumassoid site at Trois-Rivières, Guadeloupe FWI: funerary practices and house patterns at La Pointe de Grande Anse. (*J. Caribb. Archaeol.*, 9, 2010, p. 1–17, bibl., ill., maps, tables)

Discusses findings from a newly discovered Late Ceramic Age site on the island of Guadeloupe. Similar to Troumassoid sites found on other islands, the site of La Pointe de Grand Anse, Trois-Rivières revealed postholes and burials, but discrepancies in the ages of the houses and human interments (ca. 500 years apart) suggest that peoples occupying the site later used earlier portions of the site as cemeteries.

South America

BETTY J. MEGGERS, *Research Associate, Department of Anthropology, National Museum of Natural History, Smithsonian Institution*
DONNA J. NASH, *Assistant Professor of Anthropology, University of North Carolina, Greensboro*

SOUTH AMERICA

RESEARCHERS IN THE ANDEAN countries of South America are looking back to earlier eras of archeological scholarship to examine historical developments (items **286, 294, 305, 365,** and **416**). In Peru, Julio C. Tello's field notebooks have been published (items **396, 397,** and **398**) along with photos, some of which reveal the rapid deterioration of archeological sites. This process may be attributed in part to natural processes, but also has occurred as the result of looting (item **373**). Surprisingly, some of the recent destruction to archeological sites is the result of decisions by local authorities to develop sites to garner tourist dollars. Unfortunately, restoration projects are sometimes poorly engineered and can accelerate damage to the site, such as the recent wall collapses at Sacsayhuamán. Archeology has become a discipline caught up in political agendas and archeological sites have become capital assets where economic outcomes overshadow academic pursuits to understand the past (item **365**). Archeologists must now become actively involved in such developments to ensure the long-term preservation of cultural resources (items **289, 295,** and **403**).

Fortunately, scholars conducting archeological research in South America are coming together and sharing their results across political borders. New textbooks are available in Spanish that introduce World Prehistory with a focus on Latin America (items **280** and **296**). The published proceedings of international conferences demonstrate a growing number of collaborations and a shared interest in particular themes, such as diet, subsistence, the development of social inequality, and the rise of urbanism (items **281, 286, 288,** and **289**).

Perhaps the topic that has garnered the most international appeal is rock art (item **295**), not just as isolated phenomena but also in relation to other styles of material culture (items **302** and **306**) or using several attributes to create chronological typologies (item **372**). In northern Chile, rock art has been an important line of evidence for delineating routes of movement between Tarapacá and the Loa drainage-San Pedro de Atacama region (item **369**) in addition to the appearance of hybrid artifacts, whereas in Patagonia the variation of rock art has been used, among other lines of evidence, to demonstrate little interaction between coastal and inland groups (item **300**). In general rock art is viewed as a medium of public communication (item **369**), however Jamin (item **414**), working in Manú National Park, has gone a step farther by associating the petroglyphs of Pusharo with the

Inka incursion of the region, equating the figures with *tocapu*, and describing both as ideograms (a form of writing). Jackson also examines the possibility that symbols held specific meanings for the Moche (item **413**).

In Andean South America one topic of research that unites scholarly interest is the Inka Empire. Given that both archeological remains and ethnohistorical records are available, Inka research touches on a diverse range of themes. Because Spanish chroniclers recorded details of Inka ideology, it is one of the few societies for which links can be made between iconography and meaning (items **405**, **409**, and **420**), and cosmological perspectives pertaining to the landscape and built environment can be explored (items **282**, **292**, **370**, and **412**). In a more tangible way, many prehistoric regional development sequences end with the Inka occupation (item **302**), which provide examples of the diverse ways in which the Inka impacted local societies and converted local institutions to serve the imperial agenda (items **308** and **400**). The ongoing Qhapaqñan project, focused on the Inka Road network, continues to provide a wealth of data about the empire itself but also about the diverse ecologies and local groups that were connected over a vast territory in late prehistory (item **423**). Nevertheless, the Inka road system was not the first to connect groups through the movement of goods over long distances and many segments of the Inka road appear to overlay much older trade routes (item **287**).

A growing database of published artifact styles and new technologies have advanced research of trade relations and other forms of interaction between groups. In many cases, trade is presumed to have taken place through the use of caravans (item **293**), but evidence recovered from a burial located in the Atacama between the coast and highlands suggests that some goods were carried by people during the formative period (item **366**). It appears that long-lived exchange networks in the region may have resulted in growing similarities between groups (item **369**).

Sourcing data using geochemical techniques is also revealing that patterns of exchange cannot be predicted using modern economic principles. For instance, in northwest Argentina obsidian distributions from two sources at 20 different sites suggest that existing social networks were more important than proximity or material quality (see *HLAS 65:308*). It has also been presumed that large scale trade enterprises are driven by state-level administered exchanges in the Andes because of the apparent absence of markets; however, more nuanced programs of research, such as those focused on spondylus bead production in Ecuador (item **385**), suggest that production for long distance exchange could take place in modest domestic contexts rather than centrally controlled production locales.

Some scholars view long distance exchange and increasing trade and interaction as a catalyst for increasing complexity (items **293**, **297**, and **383**); however, other recent syntheses—particularly in Colombia—take a landscape perspective and focus on the role of shamanism and mortuary monuments (items **373**, **374**, **377**, **378**, **379**, and **380**). In Argentina shamanism is also viewed as significant for the Santa Mariana (item **303**) and a landscape approach is also being applied (item **292**). Other scholars emphasize the importance of feasting and the production of prestige goods (items **383**, **387**, and **424**).

These factors may have also played a role in the development of Moche society. Several volumes represent the recent surge in Moche research and include results from multiple valleys (items **404**, **413**, and **419**) or focus on a key site (items **399** and **408**). Long thought to precede Moche emergence, Millaire's compilation on Gallinazo (item **410**) is a valuable complement to understanding formative developments on the North Coast of Peru. Several other works also describe the "formative period" (which employs a wide array of terminology throughout South America), and the associated power struggles as social inequality takes hold, including early monuments built in the Norte Chico of Peru (items **403** and **422**), Chavín (item **402**), and Ecuador (items **381, 382,** and **384**).

Lumbreras (item **416**) reconsiders the "Neolithic" (Late Archaic) and formative periods (Cotton Preceramic) for North and Central Peru. Lavallée (item **290**) also re-evaluates data for early domesticates, sedentism, and other "Neolithic" developments in South America. This interest in subsistence strategies (item **281**) and hunter-gatherer lifeways is widespread with many publications focusing exclusively on the Archaic (items **298, 299, 300, 304, 371, 401,** and **415**) or with regional sequences spanning from Archaic to Inka (items **282, 287, 395,** and **399**). In fact, systematic survey and horizontal excavations are coming together into many synthetic presentations of regional developments (items **367, 377,** and **380**); however, few such reports provide comprehensive details about site features and artifact types, and with a few exceptions (item **417**) the Andean region in general is lacking monographs that can serve as reference texts needed to identify exotics imported via long-distance trade networks, population migrations, and imperial expansions. Perhaps the publication of Tello's detailed field notebooks will inspire a new generation of researchers and show them that culture history can be of great value when testing anthropological theories with archeological data. [DJN]

BRAZIL AND THE GUIANAS

Distribution of archeological information via the internet in Brazil has increased substantially during recent years. In addition to journal articles, most dissertations are now available on line, adding significantly to the amount and geographical distribution of data, particularly by students and amateurs. In assembling this section, only published contributions are considered.

Two topics have dominated in Amazonia. One is the origin and use of "terra preta," a fertile black soil that dominates in habitation sites throughout the lowlands. Although soil experts consider it to be the product of the disintegration of organic habitation refuse and archeologists correlate its distribution with semi-sedentary settlement behavior, the dominant view is now that it was created for permanent cultivation and permitted dense long-term occupation. Two significant publications challenge this finding: one examines the use of *terra preta* by modern caboclos on the middle Madeira (item **327**) and the other compares refuse disposal by the modern Kuikuru on the upper Xingu with its composition in recently abandoned archeological sites and finds the composition of the *terra preta* to be the same (item **357**). The other topic is the discovery by satellite photography of massive circular and square ditches over 250 km on the border of southern Brazil and Bolivia (items **307, 309, 311, 341,** and **354**). Except in Acre, speculation exceeds evidence in explaining their purpose (item **307**).

Two multi-authored contributions summarize detailed results of long-term fieldwork in Minas Gerais (item **314**) and regional summaries along the Brazilian coast (item **321**). The most important resource, however, is *Arqueologia Amazônica*, the two-volume publication of articles from the Encuentro Internacional de Arqueologia Amazônica in Belem in 2008 (item **285**). Topics cover all parts of Brazil, as well as the Guianas, and provide an overview of current research in regions previously unknown. [BJM]

GENERAL

280 **Alcina Franch, José.** Las culturas precolombinas de América. Madrid: Alianza Editorial, 2009. 259 p.: bibl., maps.

Textbook describes a sampling of societies that once occupied areas of Latin America including Mesoamerica, the Intermediate Area and the Andes, with a brief general introduction to early hunter-gatherers. Also includes a glossary of terms. For review of first edition, see *HLAS 60:659*. [DJN]

281 **La alimentación en la América precolombina y colonial: una aproximación interdisciplinaria.** Coordinación de Aylen Capparelli, Alexandre Chevalier y Raquel Piqué. Madrid: Consejo Superior de Investigaciones Científicas, 2009. 184 p.: bibl., ill. (Treballs d'Etnoarqueologia)

Edited volume describes a number of different datasets to assess diet and the use of animal and plant resources in Latin America. Chapters examine the Southern Cone region, northwest Argentina, Buenos Aires, Brazil, Colombia, Peru, and Oaxaca, Mexico. Authors evaluate health and lifeways of hunter-gatherers, prehistoric chiefdoms, the Chimu and Inca empires, colonial and recent urban populations. [DJN]

282 *Anales de Arqueología y Etnología.* Vol. 61/62, 2006/2007. Mendoza, Argentina: Univ. Nacional de Cuyo, Facultad de Filosofía y Letras.

This volume was published in honor of Humberto Lagiglia and includes a tribute to his career. The other contributions cover a wide range of regions, time frames, and themes from the lithic tool technologies used by hunter-gatherers to the details of an Inca-era mummy found on Cerro Aconcagua. [DJN]

283 **Andean civilization: a tribute to Michael E. Moseley.** Edited by Joyce Marcus and Patrick Ryan Williams. Los Angeles: Cotsen Institute of Archaeology, Univ. of California, 2009. 419 p.: bibl., index. (UCLA Cotsen Institute of Archaeology Press monographs; 63)

The edited volume contains chapters on a variety of topics from the peopling of South America to the production of wine during the early colonial period. In general, the regional and topical coverage mirrors the career of Moseley, who worked both on the North Coast and Southern highlands of Peru. It also includes a retrospective on the contributions of Moseley to climate and maritime studies. [DJN]

284 **Arnold, Denise Y.** and **Christine Ann Hastorf.** Heads of state: icons, power, and politics in the ancient and modern Andes. Walnut Creek, Calif.: Left Coast Press, 2008. 293 p.: bibl., ill., index.

The authors explore the multiple shades of meaning centered on human heads in the Andes. They focus on modern and prehistoric literature and evidence to describe symbolic meaning, concepts linking heads to fertility and regeneration, violence, politics, value, and both group and individual identity. [DJN]

285 **Arqueologia amazônica.** Organização de Edithe Pereira e Vera Guapindaia. Belém, Brazil: Museu Paraense Emílio Goeldi, 2010. 2 v., 1110 p.: bibl., ill., maps.

Proceedings of the Encontro Internacional de Arqueologia Amazônica held in Belém, 2–5 Sept. 2008. In addition to coverage of Amazonia and coastal Brazil, there are chapters on eastern Peru, Colombia, Venezuela, and French Guiana, providing a comprehensive overview of current archeological research. [BJM]

286 **Asociación Latinoamericana de Antropología Biólogica. Congreso.** *7th, México, 2002.* Memoria del VII Congreso de la Asociación Latinoamericana de Antropología Biológica. Coordinación de Patricia Hernández, Carlos Serrano Sánchez y José Francisco Ortiz Pedraza. México: Instituto Nacional de Antropología e Historia, 2006. 293 p.: bibl., ill., maps. (Col. científica; 507. Serie antropología física)

Conference proceedings include articles covering a number of themes: ancient populations, forensic anthropology, demography, population genetics, contemporary populations, and the history of physical anthropology. The works cover areas in Mesoamerica and South America with a few drawing from all of Latin America. Several articles specifically examine women—prehistoric or contemporary. [DJN]

287 Avilés Loayza, Sonia Victoria.
Qhapaqñan: caminos sagrados de los inkas. La Paz: Producciones Cima Editores, 2008. 323 p.: bibl., ill., maps (some col.).

The author examines the segment of the Inca road that runs from La Paz to Coroico via Chucura in Bolivia to assess who used the route before the Inca. Studies how use of this route impacted the societies and their development from the road's first establishment through the Inca period. [DJN]

Dillehay, Tom D. and **Ramiro Matos.** History, memory and knowledge in Andean visual imagery: the intersection of art, architecture, and landscape. See *HLAS 66:310.*

288 **Domestic life in prehispanic capitals: a study of specialization, hierarchy, and ethnicity.** Edited by Linda R. Manzanilla and Claude Chapdelaine. Ann Arbor: Univ. of Michigan, Museum of Anthropology, 2009. 266 p.: bibl., ill., maps. (Memoirs of the Museum of Anthropology/University of Michigan; 46 Studies in Latin American ethnohistory & archaeology; 7)

The volume profiles domestic life in ancient capitals from a number of perspectives for both Mesoamerican and Andean prehispanic polities. The capitals of Monte Albán (Oaxaca), Teotihuacán (central Mexico), Xochicalco (Morelos, Mexico), Tula (Hidalgo, Mexico), Tikal (lowland Maya), Copan (Honduras), and Chac-Sayil (Yucatán) are considered for the Mesoamerican region, and Tiwanaku (Andean Region), Moche (northern Peru), Huari (central Andes), Chan Chan (Peru), and Cuzco (Peru) are examined in the Andean region. [DJN]

Ethnicity in ancient Amazonia: reconstructing past identities from archaeology, linguistics, and ethnohistory. See item **543.**

Historias sumergidas: hacia la protección del patrimonio cultural subacuático en Latinoamérica. See *HLAS 66:427.*

289 **Jornadas de Investigadores en Arqueología y Etnohistoria del Centro-oeste del País, 5th, Río Cuarto, Argentina, 2003.** Debates actuales en arqueología y etnohistoria: publicación de las V y VI Jornadas de Investigadores en Arqueología y Etnohistoria del Centro-oeste del País. Foro de Pueblos Originarios-Arqueólogos. Compilación de Ernesto Olmedo y Flavio Ribero. Río Cuarto, Argentina: Univ. Nacional de Río Cuarto, 2007. 361 p.: bibl., ill., maps.

Conference proceedings that include articles about several regions of South America and cover both prehistoric and historic archeology, as well as ethnohistory. Many papers examine the theme of frontiers both theoretically and from specific datasets. There is also a cluster of papers that consider conservation of sites, presentation of the past to the public, and related ethical issues. [DJN]

290 **Lavallée, Danièle.** Secuencias y consecuencias de algunos procesos de neolitización en los Andes Centrales. (*Estud. Atacameños*, 32:1, 2006, p. 35–41, bibl.)

Author examines the Neolithic in the Central Andes area and suggests that, similar to the Near East, there were sedentary communities before agriculture and pastoralism on the Andean coast. Nevertheless, hunter-gatherer communities did start the process of plant domestication before the end of the Pleistocene. Dating of early domesticates are being re-evaluated. New data for domesticated animals suggests the process was initiated in several areas. [DJN]

291 **Meggers, Betty J.** Prehistoric America: an ecological perspective. 3rd expanded. New Brunswick, N.J.: Aldine-Transaction, 2010. 201 p.: bibl., index.

Author compares indigenous groups based on their occupation of eight general environmental zones. She suggests that the agricultural potential of the landscape was the primary determining factor in the degree of cultural developments, but emphasizes that access to compatible groups, with which ideas and technologies could be exchanged, also played a crucial role in some settings. [DJN]

292 **Procesos sociales prehispánicos en el sur andino: la vivienda, la comunidad y el territorio.** Compilación de Axel E. Nielsen *et al.* Córdoba, Argentina: Editorial Brujas, 2007. 410 p.: bibl., ill. (Col. historia social precolombina; 1)

Authors in the volume consider recent theoretical trends to examine the use of space and the impact of the built environment on social organization at the household and community scale. The volume covers sites in Argentina and Chile ranging from those occupied by hunter-gatherers to sites with public architecture during the Regional Development and Inca Periods. [DJN]

293 Producción y circulación prehispánicas de bienes en el sur andino. Compilación de Axel E. Nielsen *et al.* Córdoba, Argentina: Editorial Brujas, 2007. 442 p.: bibl., ill., maps. (Col. historia social precolombina; 2)

Authors in this volume examine the movement of goods in the southern Andes (Northwest Argentina, Bolivia, and Chile) and consider how production of goods for exchange, movement of people, things, and ideas, the management of herd animals and caravans, and shifting trade routes impacted sociopolitical developments in the region. [DJN]

294 Seminario Internacional de Arqueología Uniandes, 1st, Bogotá, 2005. Arqueología en Latinoamérica: historias, formación académica y perspectivas temáticas: memorias del Primer Seminario Internacional de Arqueología Uniandes. Compilación de Luis Gonzalo Jaramillo E. Bogotá: Univ. de los Andes, Facultad de Ciencias Sociales, Depto. de Antropología, Centro de Estudios Socioculturales e Internacionales-CESO: Ediciones Uniandes, 2008. 273 p.: bibl., ill., maps, port.

This volume examines the historical developments of archeology as a profession in Latin America. Chapters focus on the growth of the discipline in specific countries such as El Salvador, Costa Rica, Colombia, Venezuela, Ecuador, and Peru, with a comparative overview authored by the editor. [DJN]

295 Simposio Nacional de Arte Rupestre, 1st, Cusco, Peru, 2004. Actas del Primer Simposio Nacional de Arte Rupestre Cusco, noviembre 2004. Edición de Rainer Hostnig, Matthias Strecker y J. Guffroy. Lima: Instituto Francés de Estudios Andinos: Institut de recherche pour le développement: Embajada de la República Federal de Alemania, Lima, 2007. 473 p.: bibl., ill., maps. (Actes & mémoires; 12)

This volume of conference proceedings includes papers that cover the north, central, and southern regions of Peru—with additional contributions describing rock art from Bolivia, Chile, Argentina, Ecuador, and North America. Authors address a variety of themes and look at rock art at individual sites, in surveys of entire regions, and also at issues of conserving geoglyphs and rock art in areas being developed for tourism. [DJN]

296 Sulca, Olga. De la banda carroñera a la jefaturas prehispánicas: manual de prehistoria. Tucumán, Argentina: Manuales Humanitas, 2007. 336 p.: bibl., ill.

The textbook covers basic introductory topics for archeology and chronologically presents prehistory in the Americas. Starts with the environment and human evolution, addresses human radiation out of Africa, the Paleolithic, peopling of the New World, and then examines cultural developments in Latin America from Paleo-Indian to the Aztec and Inca empires. [DJN]

297 Taller Internacional de Arqueología del NOA y Andes Centro Sur, Buenos Aires, 2004. Sociedades precolombinas surandinas: temporalidad, interacción y dinámica cultural del NOA en el ámbito de los Andes centro-sur. Edición de Verónica Isabel Williams *et al.* Buenos Aires: Artes Gráficas Busch, 2007. 419 p.: bibl., ill., maps.

The volume of conference proceedings presents articles on the southern Andes grouped into the following themes: economic, political, and ideological aspects of interaction; chronological markers in northwest Argentina; and notions of complexity in the archeology of the south-central Andes. The articles have excellent maps, photos, and illustrations of value to scholars working in the region. [DJN]

Young-Sánchez, Margaret. Tiwanaku: ancestors of the Inca. See *HLAS 66:21.*

ARGENTINA

298 Babot, María del Pilar. El papel de la molienda en la transición hacia la producción agropastoril: un análisis desde la Puna Meridional argentina. (*Estud. Atacameños,* 32:1, 2006, p. 75–92, bibl., graphs, tables)

Author describes 39 grinding tools drawn from Puna sites. She describes the transition from hunting and gathering to agropastoralism as a gradual process and links the intensification of grinding from 6500 to 1100 BP to changes in mobility, which allow for larger tools and results in specialized grinding areas. [DJN]

299   Barberena, Ramiro. Arqueología y biogeografía humana en Patagonia meridional. Buenos Aires: Sociedad Argentina de Antropología, 2008. 395 p.: bibl., ill. (some col.), maps (some col.). (Col. Tesis doctorales)

The author examines subsistence patterns, mobility, and use of the landscape in the Campo Volcanico de Pali Aike. He considers these topics within a biogeographic framework using landscape ecology, sedimentology, isotope analysis of human remains, faunal remains, and lithic materials to explore change. Data was collected through surface survey and excavation. [DJN]

300   Bellelli, Cristina; Vivian Scheinsohn; and M. Mercedes Podestá. Arqueología de pasos cordilleranos: un caso de estudio en Patagonia norte durante el holoceno tardío. (*Bol. Mus. Chil. Arte Precolomb.*, 13:2, 2008, p. 37–55, bibl., ill., maps, photos)

Report examines circulation between different ecological zones in Patagonia of Argentina and Chile (between 41°30′ and 43°40′ south latitude). They compare data from the Epuyén and Manso drainages with published reports from other zones, specifically comparing rock art, decorated artifacts, and obsidian. They conclude that there is no evidence that those groups utilizing the forest and steppe had contact with coastal groups. [DJN]

301   Congreso Argentino de Americanistas, 6th, Buenos Aires, 2008. VI Congreso Argentino de Americanistas: año 2008. Buenos Aires: Sociedad Argentina de Americanistas, 2009. 3 v.: bibl., ill., maps.

This compilation of articles covers a wide range of themes, times (historic and prehistoric), and places. The volume includes 21 articles on archeology, one on the works of Ismael Quiles S.J., and one on music of the Americas. Archeological contributions describe survey results, excavation findings, materials analysis (e.g., lithic, ceramic, metal, shell), and explore theoretical topics. [DJN]

302   Entrelazando ciencias: sociedad y ambiente antes de la conquista española. Compilación de Norma Ratto. Textos de Norma Ratto *et al.* Buenos Aires: Eudeba, 2009. 219 p.: bibl., ill., maps. (Temas/arqueología)

This edited volume reports on collaborative research conducted in western Tinogasta, Catamarca, of the period from AD 500 to Inca intrusion. Researchers consider environmental variation and complementarity, rock art, domestic remains, production and distribution of goods, and how volcanic events and the volcanoes themselves had an impact on populations in the region through time. [DJN]

303   Nastri, Javier. La figura de las largas cejas de la iconografía santamariana: chamanismo, sacrificio y cosmovisión calchaquí. (*Bol. Mus. Chil. Arte Precolomb.*, 13:1, 2008, p. 9–34, ill., map, photos)

Article considers 756 complete vessels from the Santa Mariana tradition of Northwest Argentina. Focusing on examples representing the figure of long eyebrows, the author considers how changes in the associated imagery through time might be related to the social and political organization and the extent religious practices (e.g., form of shamanism). [DJN]

304   Prates, Luciano. Los indigenas del Río Negro: un enfoque arqueológico. Buenos Aires: Sociedad Argentina de Antropología, 2008. 323 p.: bibl., ill., maps. (Col. Tesis doctorales)

Presents results from a survey of the northern middle valley of the Río Negro in Patagonia during the late Holocene where hunter-gatherers were generalized foragers that lived near bodies of water but used the larger landscape to obtain a diverse array of resources. The author describes the environmental context, settlement patterns, activities, and stone tool technology. [DJN]

305   Ramundo, Paola Silvia. Estudio historiográfico de las investigaciones sobre cerámica arqueológica en el noroeste argentino. Oxford, England: Archaeopress, 2008. 365 p.: bibl., ill., maps. (BAR international series; 1840)

This work considers the historical development of the archeological research of ceramics in Northwest Argentina from the earliest beginnings to the present day, examining the broader trends of the discipline and their social context. It contains an extensive bibliography on the subject including many types of publications. [DJN]

306 Ruiz, Marta Susana and **Domingo Chorolque.** Arte rupestre del Pukara de Rinconada: una larga historia visual. San Salvador de Jujuy, Argentina: CREA-UNJu, 2007. 161 p.: bibl., ill. (some col.), col. maps.

The authors interpret the corpus of rock art, both petroglyphs and pictographs, at sites in the province of Jujuy, northwest Argentina: Mesada o Pukara Chico, Mesada de las Pinturas, Quebrada y Mesada de Chacuñayoc, and Peñón del Puma. They associate styles with different time periods and link these representations to memory, ethnicity, and power. [DJN]

BOLIVIA

307 Erickson, Clark L. The transformation of environment into landscape: the historical ecology of monumental earthwork construction in the Bolivian Amazon. (*Diversity/Basel*, 2, 2010, p. 618–652, bibl., ill., tables)

Erickson elaborates his previous arguments for the prehistoric existence of monumental earthworks and dense populations in the Baures region with estimates of the amount of labor that would have been required for clearing forest, digging ditches, constructing palisades, and other activities, but confesses that "pottery, other artifacts, and occupation midden in ring ditch sites are rare." [BJM]

308 El Inkario en los valles del Sur Andino Boliviano: los yamparas entre la arqueología y etnohistoria. Edición de Sonia Alconini Mujica. Oxford, England: John and Erica Hedges Ltd., 2008. 144 p.: bibl., ill., maps. (BAR international series; 1868. South American archaeology series; 5)

The volume pulls together recent research in the Chuquisaca Valley to examine the nature of the Yampara, which ethnohistory places in the region before and

during the Inca occupation. Authors address the challenge of reconciling archeological remains with ethnohistoric accounts and discuss the problems with ceramic typology, cultural affiliation, and interpretation, among other important topics. [DJN]

309 Lombardo, Umberto and **Heiko Prümers.** Pre-columbian human occupation patterns in the eastern plains of the Llanos de Moxos, Bolivian Amazonia. (*J. Archaeol. Sci.*, 37:8, Aug. 2010, p. 1875–1885, bibl., ill., maps)

An area approximately 4500 km square east of Trinidad was mapped using remote sensing and analyzed to identify connections between 113 mounds, 273 forest islands, and 957 km of canals and causeways. Drained fields were not encountered. The archeological evidence indicates the mounds were densely inhabited and communities were organized hierarchically, but it is not clear how such large and permanent settlements were maintained. [BJM]

310 Lombardo, Umberto *et al.* Raised fields in the Bolivian Amazonia: a prehistoric green revolution or a flood risk mitigation strategy? (*J. Archaeol. Sci.*, 38:3, March 2011, p. 502–512, bibl., ill., table)

Raised fields were built on the Llanos de Moxos only where no alternatives for agriculture existed because of intense and frequent flooding. They do not coincide with the regions where precolumbian societies reached high levels of social complexity. [BJM]

311 Saunaluoma, Sanna. Pre-columbian earthworks in the Riberalta region of the Bolivian Amazon. (*Amazôn. Rev. Antropol.*, 2:1, 2010, p. 86–115, bibl., ill., map, table)

Survey along the Beni adjacent to the border with Brazil identified 11 habitation sites, seven associated with ring ditches, straight ditches, and small mounds. Multiple stratigraphic excavations were made in most of the sites and rare pottery was tempered with cariapé and decorated with incision. Eighteen radiocarbon dates cluster into two periods: 100 BC–AD 400 and AD 1260-European contact, but what happened before and between them is unknown. The function of the ditches is uncertain and Sauna-luoma argues that the purpose of these was more symbolic than practical. [BJM]

BRAZIL

312   Albuquerque, Marcos and Veleda
      Lucena. Arqueologia amazônica: o potencial arqueológico dos assentamentos e fortificações de diferentes bandeiras. (in Arqueologia amazônica. Organização de Edithe Pereira e Vera Guapindaia. Belém, Brazil: Museu Paraense Emílio Goeldi, 2010, v. 2, p. 968–1019, bibl., ill., maps)
      Reviews the cartographic and archival evidence for early European contact and settlement at the mouth of the Amazon and contact with indigenous populations preliminary to describing archeological investigations at the Forte de Obidos, the Fortaleza São José de Macapá, and Mazagão Velho. Abundant illustrations demonstrate the contribution that archeology can make to interpretation of the historical documents and restoration of the original architecture of colonial sites. [BJM]

313   Amazonian dark earths: Wim Som-
      broek's vision. Edited by William I. Woods et al. New York, N.Y.: Springer Dordrecht, 2008. 502 p.
      Twenty-eight chapters by 73 authors provide detailed chemical, physical, and biological analyses of samples of terra preta from a variety of locations in Brazil, as well as the southern US and Africa. The archeologists included are Eduardo Neves, Denise Schaan, and Michael Heckenberger, who discuss evidence from sites in peripheral Amazonian locations. All assume that the prehistoric soils were created for agricultural exploitation, but base their interpretations on the behavior of modern farmers, whose methods and motivations are distinct from those of the prehistoric inhabitants. For geographer's comment, see item 974. [BJM]

314   Arqueologia do vale do rio Peruaçu e
      adjacências-Minas Gerais. Edição de André Prous e Maria Jacqueline Rodet. Belo Horizonte, Brazil: Arquivos do Museu de História Natural, 2009. 1 v., 533 p.: bibl., ill. (some color), maps, tables.
      Decades of fieldwork in the valley of the Peruaçu, a tributary of the São Fran-cisco in southern Minas Gerais, are summarized in 22 chapters describing aspects of the geology, geomorphology, palynology, vegetation, vertebrates, history of Portuguese settlement, human skeletal remains, archeobotany, rock art, lithics, and pottery. [BJM]

315   Arqueologia interpretativa: o método
      quantitativo para estabelecimento de sequências cerâmicas: estudos de caso. Organização de Betty J. Meggers. Textos de Marcos Aurélio Camara Zimmerman et al. Porto Nacional, Brazil: UNITINS, 2009. 129 p.: bibl., ill., maps.
      In Sept. 2002, the Núcleo Tocanti-nense de Arqueologia sponsored a symposium on the quantitative method for classifying pottery and constructing cultural chronologies attended by four Brazilian, one Argentine, and one Venezuelan archeologist. Meggers explains the theoretical basis and analytic procedures and the participants provide case studies from their fieldwork. The texts are accompanied by maps and seriated sequences that illustrate the results, making this an important resource for anyone interested in applying the method. [BJM]

316   Arroyo-Kalin, Manuel. The Amazo-
      nian formative: crop domestication and anthropogenic soils. (Diversity/Basel, 2, 2010, p. 473–504, bibl., ill., maps)
      Argues that the existence of terra preta implies a sedentary lifestyle that stimulated the domestication of manioc, and accounts for the emergence of the Amazonian formative during the first millennium AD. [BJM]

317   Arroyo-Kalin, Manuel. Steps towards
      an ecology of landscape: the pedostratigraphy of anthropogenic dark earths. (in Amazonian dark earths: Wim Som-broek's vision. Edited by William I. Woods et al. New York, N.Y.: Springer Dordrecht, 2008, p. 33–83, bibl., ill., map, tables)
      Provides a detailed description of the spatial and chronological composition of the microstratigraphy of terra preta sediments in the Hatahara and Lago Grande sites in central Amazonia, but the uniqueness of the occupations makes the applicability of the author's interpretations to other regions doubtful. [BJM]

318 **Bandeira, Arkley.** Ocupações pré-históricas de pescadores-coletores-caçadores e ceramistas no litoral equatorial amazônico: a antiguidade cerâmica em foto. (*in* Arqueologia amazônica. Organização de Edithe Pereira e Vera Guapindaia. Belém, Brazil: Museu Paraense Emílio Goeldi, 2010, v. 2, p. 655–680, bibl., ill., maps, tables)

Describes stratigraphic excavations in the Bacanga sambaqui on the coast of Maranhão with seven radiocarbon dates from shell and eight from pottery extending from 5600–2100 BP. Lithics are rare but bone artifacts are common. Detailed comparison with artifacts from radiocarbon-dated shell middens on the coast of Pará, Lower Xingu, and Lower Amazon indicates that this subsistence adaptation occurred earlier on the coast than in the interior. [BJM]

319 **Buc, Natacha.** Explorando la variabilidad de la tecnología ósea a lo largo de la Cuenca inferior del rio Paraná. (*Pesqui. Antropol.*, 68, 2010, p. 133–166, bibl., ill., map, tables)

Classifies bone projectile points into nine morphofunctional types and compares their distributions with ecological differences in the environment. [BJM]

320 **Bueno, Lucas.** A Amazônia brasileira no holoceno inicial: tecnologia lítica, cronologia e processos de ocupação. (*in* Arqueologia amazônica. Organização de Edithe Pereira e Vera Guapindaia. Belém, Brazil: Museu Paraense Emílio Goeldi, 2010, v. 2, p. 545–560, bibl., map, table)

Brief descriptions are accompanied by a list of sites with radiocarbon dates prior to 7000 BP. [BJM]

321 **Cenários regionais em arqueologia brasileira.** Organização de Walter Fagundes Morales e Flavia Prado Moi. São Paulo: Annablume; Porto Seguro, Brazil: ACERVO-Centro de Referência em Patrimônio e Pesquisa, 2009. 339 p.: bibl., ill. (some col.), maps (some col.).

Six chapters provide syntheses of archeological investigations during the past two decades in Rio Grande do Sul, Sergipe, Pantanal, Rio Grande do Norte, Espírito Santo, and Mato Grosso. Six others discuss rock art, burial patterns, social complexity, and historical archeology. All have useful

bibliographies. Two chapters are reviewed separately in items 329 and 347. [BJM]

322 **A cerâmica guarani e guarani missioneira.** Cuidados de Cecilia Santinelli. Roma, Italy: Instituto Italo-Latino Americano, Serviço de Cooperação, 2006. 175 p.: bibl., ill. (some col.). (Cadernos IILA. Série Cooperação; 29)

Descriptions of the characteristics of prehistoric Guarani pottery and changes made by Jesuits and a glossary of terms precede copies of forms and illustrations accompanying vessels restored by participants in the Curso de Restauração da cerâmica sul-americana São Miguel das Missões, RS, Brasil, in 2005. [BJM]

Os ceramistas tupiguarani. See item 552.

323 **Chmyz, Igor et al.** A arqueologia da área da Mina Dois Irmãos, em São Mateus do Sul, Paraná. (*Arqueologia/ Curitiba*, 6, número especial, 2009, p. 1–147, bibl., ill.)

Describes field methods, laboratory procedures, and artifacts obtained from salvage excavations at 11 sites of the Itararé and Tupiguarani traditions. Radiocarbon dates for Itararé extend from 1150 to 920 BP and those for Tupiguarani from 490 to 440 BP. [BJM]

324 **Fátima Rossetti, Dilce; Ana Maria Góes; and Peter Mann de Toledo.** Archaeological mounds in Marajó Island in northern Brazil: a geological perspective integrating remote sensing and sedimentology. (*Geoarchaeology/New York*, 24:1, Jan./ Feb. 2009, p. 22–41, bibl., ill., maps, photos, table)

Sedimentological and geomorphological investigations east of Lago Araré and radiocarbon dates indicate that the largest mounds on Marajó are natural features created by late Pleistocene and early Holocene fluvial and tidal-influenced paleochannels and paleobars, rather than artificial constructions, with significant implications for traditional interpretations of the social complexity of Marajoara culture. Five radiocarbon dates from the upper 2.6 m range from 6130–3500 BP. [BJM]

325 **Feathers, James et al.** How old is Luzia?: liminescence dating and stratigraphic integrity at Lapa Vermelha,

Lagoa Santa, Brazil. (*Geoarchaeology/New York*, 25:4, July/Aug. 2010, p. 295–436, bibl., ill., map, tables)

Lapa Vermelha contains the largest number of prehistoric human skeletons from a single location in the Americas, but their scattered stratigraphic distribution has led to uncertainty of their antiquity. A detailed description of the stratigraphy, sediment, chemical composition, and micromorphology by strata precedes explanation of the luminescence procedures applied to nine sediment samples. Dates of 12.7–16 ka support the radiocarbon range of 11.4–16.4 ka. [BJM]

326 Fonseca, João Aires da. As estatuetas líticas do baixo amazonas. (*in* Arqueologia amazônica. Organização de Edithe Pereira e Vera Guapindaia. Belém, Brazil: Museu Paraense Emílio Goeldi, 2010, v. 1, p. 235–257, bibl., ill., map)

Illustrates 20 carved and polished stone images of unknown origin, the majority exotic human-animal combinations, that have been found during the past 150 years. [BJM]

327 Fraser, James A. and **Charles Roland Clement.** Dark earths and manioc cultivation in central Amazonia: a window on pre-columbian agricultural systems? (*Bol. Mus. Para. Emílio Goeldi Sér. Ciênc. Hum.*, 3:2, maio/agôsto 2008, p. 1–21, bibl., ill., map, tables)

In an effort to establish the suitability of anthropogenic black soil (*terra preta*) for manioc cultivation, the agricultural behavior of contemporary farmers in Barro Alto, a caboclo settlement on the middle Madeira, was selected for systematic evaluation. Four types of soils were identified: *terra preta, terra mulata*, oxisol, and utisol. Detailed records were kept on 52 farmers, including what they planted, where it was planted, frequency of plantings, productivity of harvest, and length of fallow, as well as their observations. The authors warn against applying these data to the interpretation of prehistoric behavior, and recommend additional similar systematic examinations conducted elsewhere for comparison. [BJM]

328 Giannini, Paulo César *et al.* Interações entre evolução sedimentar e ocupação humana pré-histórica na costa centro-sul de Santa Catarina, Brasil. (*Bol.*

Mus. Para. Emílio Goeldi Sér. Ciênc. Hum., 5:1, jan./abril 2010, p. 105–128, bibl., ill., maps, table)

Seventy-six sambaquis (shell middens) were mapped and tested stratigraphically, and 48 were radiocarbon dated, providing 130 dates. Four phases of construction were defined based on sedimentary context, stratigraphy, composition, and age, the earliest dating to 7500–5500 BP and the most recent to less than 1700 BP. Differences in their spatial distributions and faunal content imply changes in the composition and elevation of the sediments in which they occur. [BJM]

329 Gomes, Denise Maria Cavalcante. Os Tapajó e os outros. (*in* Cenários regionais em arqueologia brasileira. Organização de Walter Fagundes Morales and Flavia Prado Moi. São Paulo: Annablume; Porto Seguro, Brazil: ACERVO-Centro de Referência em Patrimônio e Pesquisa, 2009, p. 239–260, bibl., ill., map)

After summarizing the results of recent excavations in the vicinity of Parauá, 100 km south of Santarem on the Tapajós, which do not support the presence of Santarem influence, Gomes describes fieldwork in the Aldeia region of Santarem. Her evidence indicates that the extensive *terra preta* is the product of successive multiple occupations by small villages rather than a large permanent settlement with a stratified social organization, as is generally assumed. For review of full volume, see item **321**. [BJM]

330 Gonzalez, Manoel. Rei dos mares, Deus na terra: cenários da pré-história brasileira. Santos, Brazil: Editora Comunnicar, 2009. 342 p.: bibl., ill.

Part I provides an exhaustive description of the biology, systematics, geographical distribution, and global exploitation of sharks and rays; a detailed synthesis of the distribution of the species on the Brazilian coast; and their significance in Africa, Oceania, and North, Central, and South America. Part II documents their occurrence in sambaquis on the coast of São Paulo in minute detail. [BJM]

331 Heckenberger, Michael J. and **Eduardo Góes Neves.** Amazonian archaeology. (*Annu. Rev. Anthropol.*, 38, 2009, p. 251–266, bibl.)

This synthesis of changes in the interpretation of Amazonian prehistory during the past two decades is biased by the long-term investigations of the authors in the Upper Xingu and on the central Amazon and the southern borderlands, all of which have atypical environments and atypical cultural remains. They claim that early expressions of sociopolitical complexity appeared in several other parts of the Amazon between 2500 and 1500 BC, but give no examples. They argue that "politically independent, permanent villages may have periodically joined into larger, regional confederations" or "more centralized and hierarchical regional societies were integrated through ritual and elite exchange," but the only examples they provide are the Marajoara on Marajó, the Central Amazon, and the Llanos de Mojos. They believe that there was a town at Santarém that rivaled Cahokia and Chan Chan, again citing no evidence except the extent of the *terra preta*, but conceding that whether it was a large, centralized polity or smaller, integrated polities within a regional peer-polity remains unclear. They accept the current view that Amazonia is a domesticated landscape, although none of the proponents are anthropologists and the literature documenting natural environmental change is immense. They conclude that "it is an exciting, challenging, and important time to be engaged with Amazonian archeologies," which is true, but not for the reasons they provide. [BJM]

332 López Mazz, José Maria. Aldeas Matis y paleoaldeas de las Tierras Bajas. (*in* Arqueologia amazônica. Organização de Edithe Pereira e Vera Guapindaia. Belém, Brazil: Museu Paraense Emílio Goeldi, 2010, v. 2, p. 825–851, bibl., ill., map)

Comparison of the settlement behavior in a contemporary Panoan community in the Javari valley, northwest Brazil, with the interpretation of archeological sites composed of groups of mounds indicates that the latter are only "ventanas" and not necessarily reliable reconstructions of past behavior. [BJM]

333 Milheira, Rafael Guedes; Carlos Roberto Appoloni; and Paulo Sérgio Parreira. Arqueometria em cerâmicas Guarani no sul do Brasil: um estudo de caso. (*Rev. Mus. Arqueol. Etnol.*, 19, 2009, p. 355–364, bibl., ill.)

X-ray fluorescence analysis of black crust up to five cm thick on the exterior surface of Guarani sherds from sites on the southwest side of the Laguna dos Patos in Rio Grande do Sul identifies them as natural accumulations deposited by water from the lagoon. [BJM]

334 Miller, Eurico Theofilo. A cultura cerâmica do tronco tupí no alto Ji-Paraná, Rondônia, Brasil: algumas reflexões teóricas, hipotéticas e conclusiva. (*Rev. Bras. Linguíst. Antropol.*, 1:1, 2009, p. 35–136, bibl., ill., maps)

Compares the distributions of languages considered to be affiliated with Tupi-Guarani and ceramics of the Irapuã phase of the Tupiguarani Painted subtradition with painted and corrugated decoration from sites in the Ji-Parana, where they are best documented, to southeastern Brazil and the south coast, where their antiquity is speculative. The author's extensive discussion provides much food for thought. [BJM]

335 Muito além dos campos: arqueologia e história na Amazônia Marajoara. Organização de Denise Pahl Schaan e Cristine Pires Martins. Belém, Brazil: GKNORONHA, 2010. 201 p.: bibl., ill. (some col.), maps, tables.

Survey of six municipalities in western Marajó identified 169 habitation sites, 86 percent prehistoric consisting of 145 with pottery, nine with pottery and lithics, and three with shell middens. The remaining 14 percent had indigenous pottery associated with colonial objects. Survey conducted in the municipality of Santa Cruz do Arari northeast of Chaves identified 15 sites, all affiliated with the Marajoara Fase. In addition to providing the first overview of the prehistoric occupation of western Marajó, this publication establishes the failure of the Marajoara to expand west of the savanna. [BJM]

336 Neves, Eduardo Góes. A arqueologia da Amazônia Central e as classificações na arqueologia amazônica. (*in* Arqueologia amazônica. Organização de Edithe Pereira e Vera Guapindaia. Belém, Brazil: Museu Paraense Emílio Goeldi, 2010, v. 2, p. 560–579, bibl., ill., maps, table)

Neves created the Central Amazon Project in 1995 to reconstruct prehistoric settlement and social organization in the region west of the Negro and north of the Solimões. He does not accept the standardized criteria for the classification of pottery and the creation of seriated sequences adopted elsewhere in Brazil to define prehistoric communities (phases), but considers the Manacapuru, Paredão, and Guarita phases recognized by earlier archeologists to be "extremely satisfactory." Decorated pottery from the numerous trenches excavated across the region was classified into these phases and more than 100 radiocarbon dates were obtained and used to create the chronological sequence. They are also the basis for identifying groups of mounds dominated by Paredão and Manacapuru pottery as ring villages. Guarita Phase sites are shallower than those of the earlier phases and more numerous and Neves compares their distribution to those of the contemporary Tupinamba culture on the Brazilian coast. He cites the descriptions of Orellano and other earlier travelers on the Amazon of the existence of dense sedentary populations in support of his archeological interpretations. [BJM]

337   **Neves, Eduardo Góes.** Warfare in precolonial central Amazonia: when Carneiro meets Clastres. (*in* Warfare in cultural context: practice, agency, and the archaeology of violence. Edited by Axel E. Nielsen and William H. Walker. Tucson: Univ. of Arizona Press, 2009, p. 139–164, ill., maps)

Although warfare is generally assumed to be fundamental to the emergence of centralized political organization and mounds, causeways, and other kinds of major construction to imply the existence of chiefdoms, the rare occurrence of ditches and moats in archeological sites in the central Amazon, the Upper Xingu, and northwestern Amazonia does not support a defensive purpose. In spite of the absence of archeological evidence for warfare, Neves assumes that it existed and that the political differences and rewards associated with the emergence and maintenance of chiefdoms were intangible. [BJM]

338   **Oliveira, Jorge Eremites de.** Arqueologia pantaneira: história e historiografia, 1875–2000. Dourados, Brazil: Editora UFGD, 2008. 222 p.: bibl., ill., maps.

A detailed and objective synthesis of the history of archeological research and interpretation in the Pantanal of Mato Grosso prior to and subsequent to the professionalization of archeology in Brazil in 1980, including conflicts among proponents of different theoretical perspectives. [BJM]

339   **Oliveira, Jorge Eremites de** and **Levi Marques Pereira.** Ñande Ru Marangatu: laudo antropológico e histórico sobre uma terra kaiowa na fronteira do Brasil com o Paraguai, município de Antônio João, Mato Grosso do Sul. Dourados, Brazil: Editora UFGD, 2009. 282 p.: bibl., ill., maps.

Provides a case study of the evidence required for evaluating the claim of the Kaiowa indigenous community to ancestral lands on the southern frontier of Mato Grosso do Sul. Gives answers to the questions from the Indian Service and the Federal Public Ministry, and the authors provide detailed cultural, social, biological, and ideological evidence for the claim. [BJM]

340   **Oliveira, Kelly de.** A cerâmica pintada da tradição tupiguarani: estudando o a coleção Itapiranga, SC. (*Arqueol. Rio Gd. Sul*, 11, 2009, p. 5–88, bibl., ill., map, tables)

The motifs in the painted decoration on 334 sherds from a massive surface collection were classified into three groups: straight lines, curved and sinuous lines, and straight and sinuous lines, and subjected to a detailed comparison. Abundant illustrations are provided. [BJM]

341   **Pärssinen, Martti; Denise Pahl Schaan; and Alceu Ranzi.** Pre-Columbian geometric earthworks in the upper Pur'us: a complex society in western Amazonia. (*Antiquity/Cambridge*, 83:322, 2009, p. 1084–1095, bibl., ill., map)

Brief descriptions are provided for some of the several dozen circular and rectangular geoglyphs identified in eastern Acre, which are typical of those distributed for 200 km to the east. A charcoal sample produced a radiocarbon date of 750 ± 35 BP. Although the function of the ditches is unknown, the amount of labor required for their construction implies a population of at least 300 per geoglyph and a level of social complexity that "will certainly contribute significantly to the rewriting of the history of cultural development in the tropical lowlands." [BJM]

342 Pereira, Edithe. Arte rupestre e cultural material na Amazônia brasileira. (*in* Arqueologia amazônica. Organização de Edithe Pereira e Vera Guapindaia. Belém, Brazil: Museu Paraense Emílio Goeldi, 2010, v. 1, p. 259–283, bibl., ill.)

Compares depictions on rock art from Monte Alegre and Prainha with similar elements on Santarém pottery, among them anthropomorphic figures—eyes, mouths, facial expressions, nose connected with eyebrows, and animals—but does not consider this finding proves the two are related. [BJM]

343 Pereira, Edithe. O Museu Goeldi e a pesquisa arqueológica: um panorama dos últimos deszessete anos, 1991–2008. (*Bol. Mus. Para. Emílio Goeldi Sér. Ciênc. Hum.*, 4:1, jan./abril 2009, p. 171–190)

Provides a synthesis of the changes in the staff, administration, functions, research, educational role, conservation, and other activities of the archeological section of the Museu Goeldi during the past 17 years. [BJM]

344 Prehistory of Brazil. Organized by Bia Hetzel and Silvia Negreiros. Coordinated by Maria Dulce Gaspar. Translated by Hugo Moss. Photographs by Bernardo Magalhães *et al.* Rio de Janeiro: Manati Produções Editoriais, 2007. 270 p.: bibl., ill. (chiefly col.), col. maps, photos.

This English-language translation of the original Portuguese *Pré-história do Brasil* provides a general summary of Brazilian prehistory from Paleo-Indian to present and is accompanied by 136 pages of color illustrations of rock art organized by state of occurrence. [BJM]

345 Prous, André. Arte pré-histórica no Brasil. Orientações pedagógicas de Lucia Gouvêa Pimentel. Belo Horizonte, Brazil: Editora C/Arte, 2007. 127 p.: bibl., ill. (some col.), col. map. (Col. Didática. Historiando a arte brasileira; 1)

Summarizes the composition and distribution of three types of prehistoric art: painting on rock surfaces, sculpture in stone and bone, and decoration on pottery. All are well illustrated. [BJM]

346 Rambelli, Gilson. Arqueologia subaquática na Amazônia brasileira. (*in* Arqueologia amazônica. Organização de Edithe Pereira e Vera Guapindaia. Belém, Brazil: Museu Paraense Emílio Goeldi, 2010, v. 1, p. 469–488, bibl., ill.)

Describes the discovery of underwater petroglyphs in the Trombetas, submerged pottery vessels in the Anajás on Marajó, and a dugout canoe associated with potsherds on the Pedreira in Amapá, indicating the potential of such investigations. [BJM]

347 Ribeiro, Loredana *et al.* Os Tupiguarani do sul do Espírito Santo usavam muito a pedra, além do barro: a indústria lítica na pré-história tardia (e depois). (*in* Cenários regionais em arqueologia brasileira. Organização de Walter Fagundes Morales and Flavia Prado Moi. São Paulo: Annablume; Porto Seguro, Brazil: ACERVO-Centro de Referência em Patrimônio e Pesquisa, 2009, p. 151–187, bibl., ill., maps)

Detailed analysis of archeological evidence from seven sites reveals significant differences in the presence, abundance, composition, use, and discard of lithics within and between sites, and correlations with their location (shore and inland) and age (preceramic, Tupi-Guarani, colonial). Seven TL dates from four sites extend from 680 ± 110 to 370 ± 60 BP. Brief descriptions of the sites are followed by detailed analysis of the lithics and their distributions. Polished tools provide more information on behavior than do either chipped stones or pottery. For review of full volume, see item **321**. [BJM]

348 Rodet, Maria Jacqueline; Vera Guapindaia; and Amauri Matos. Análise tecnológica e cadeia operatória: uma nova proposta para a indústria lítica lascada das culturas ceramistas da Amazônia. (*in* Arqueologia amazônica. Organização de Edithe Pereira e Vera Guapindaia. Belém, Brazil: Museu Paraense Emílio Goeldi, 2010, v. 2, p. 681–711, bibl., ill., map, tables)

Thirteen stratigraphic excavations in the Boa Vista site on the rio Trombetas identified two consecutive occupations, the first by the Poco phase and the second by the Konduri phase. Radiocarbon dates for

Poco extend from 360 BC to AD 410; those for Konduri from AD 1000 to 1420. Describes the differences in the distributions and compositions of three classes of lithics in the two complexes. [BJM]

349 Rogge, Jairo Henrique and Pedro Ignácio Schmitz. Projeto Arroio do Sal: a ocupação indígena pré-histórica no litoral norte do RS. (*Pesqui. Antropol.*, 68, 2010, p. 167–225, bibl., ill., maps, tables)

Describes 61 sites on the north coast of Rio Grande do Sul identified as preceramic shell middens and ceramic habitations representing the Taquara and Tupiguarani traditions occupied from 3600 BP to the European arrival during the 18th century. [BJM]

350 Roosevelt, Anna Curtenius et al.
Early hunter-gatherers in the *terra firme* rainforest: stemmed projectile points from the Curuá goldmines. (*Amazôn. Rev. Antropol.*, 1:2, 2009, p. 442–483, bibl., ill., map)

Review of the distribution of stone projectile points in Amazonia reveals an association between lithic artifacts, food remains, and wooden tools in the goldbearing sediments of the Curuá River, a tributary of the Upper Xingu. This article provides a rambling account of efforts to enlist the cooperation of the divers to obtain more evidence of their diversity and antiquity. [BJM]

351 Scatamacchia, Maria Cristina Mineiro and Gilson Rambelli. Na terra e na água o resgate dos vestígos da antiga aldeia Toca do Bugio. (*Rev. Arqueol. Am./ México*, 26, 2008, p. 173–195, bibl., ill., maps, photos)

Salvage excavations were conducted in a habitation site of the Tupiguarani tradition on the coast of São Paulo destroyed by bulldozing and flooding. Provides descriptions of the terrestrial and underwater field procedures, the latter the first in the region, as well as the cultural remains, especially the ceramics. [BJM]

352 Schaan, Denise Pahl. Cultura marajoara. Ed. trilíngüe. Rio de Janeiro: Senac Editoras; Belém, Brazil: Federação de Comércio do Estado do Pará, Centro do Comércio do Pará, 2009. 399 p.: bibl., col. ill., maps.

Schaan, one of the archeologists who has excavated in Marajoara sites, provides a detailed history of the previous investigations beginning with the first visitors, summarizes their fieldwork and interpretations, reconstructs the history and social organization of the Marajoara, and speculates on why they declined prior to European contact. [BJM]

353 Schaan, Denise Pahl. Long-term human induced impacts on Marajó Island landscapes, Amazon estuary. (*Diversity/ Basel*, 2, 2010, p. 182–206, bibl., ill., map)

The locations and characteristics of sites, composition of subsistence resources, and other kinds of archeological evidence indicate that the Marajoara tradition achieved a sustainable exploitation of environmental resources sufficient to maintain a dense population for two millennia, in contrast to the degradation of soils and vegetation being inflicted by the dominance of cattle raising today. [BJM]

354 Schaan, Denise Pahl; Alceu Ranzi; and Antonia Damasceno Barbosa.
Geoglifos: paisagens da Amazônia ocidental. Rio Branco, Brazil: Gknoronha, 2010. 99 p.: bibl., ill. (some col.), maps.

Provides 89 pages of color illustrations of aerial views of isolated or adjacent circular and square geoglyphs, either single or concentric. A brief introduction gives details on construction and dimensions. Their function is unknown. [BJM]

355 Schaan, Denise Pahl; D.P. Kern; and F.J.L. Frazão. An assessment of the cultural practices behind the formation, or not, of Amazonian dark earths in Marajo Island archaeological sites. (*in* Amazonian dark earths: Wim Sombroek's vision. Edited by William I. Woods et al. New York, N.Y.: Springer Dordrecht, 2008, p. 127–141, bibl., ill., map)

Comparison of stratigraphic differences in the frequency of P2 03, Mn and Zn in habitation sites PA-JO-50, PA-JO-55, and Camutins in central Marajó reveals otherwise invisible evidence of vertical and horizontal differences in behavior, settlement size, and spatial organization within and between the sites, and indicates that the presence of *terra preta* alone is not a reliable indicator of settlement behavior. [BJM]

356 Scheel-Ybert, Rita et al. Estudos de paleoetnobotânica, paleoambiente e paisagem na Amazônia Central e o exemplo do sudeste-sul de Brasil. (Arqueologia amazônica. Organização de Edithe Pereira e Vera Guapindaia. Belém, Brazil: Museu Paraense Emílio Goeldi, 2010, v. 2, p. 909–935, bibl., ill.)

Provides analysis of paleobotanical evidence from excavations at eight sambaquis and two Tupi-Guarani sites on the coast of Rio de Janeiro and two sambaquis on the coast of Santa Catarina to illustrate the potential of applying similar methods for reconstructing prehistoric climate change and subsistence in Amazonia. [BJM]

357 Schmidt, Morgan J. Historical landscapes in the neotropics: a model for prehistoric anthrosol terra preta formation in the upper Xingu. (in Arqueologia amazônica. Organização de Edithe Pereira e Vera Guapindaia. Belém, Brazil: Museu Paraense Emílio Goeldi, 2010, v. 2, p. 853–878, bibl., ill., map, tables)

Comparison of soil pH and organic carbon levels in the upper 5 cm of occupied and abandoned Kuirkuru villages indicates that the current practices are producing soils similar to the prehistoric anthrosols, refuting the interpretation that the latter were intentionally produced for cultivation. Observations also demonstrate that the assumption that prehistoric slash-and-burn agriculture was not possible because stone axes were not capable of clearing forest is invalid. [BJM]

358 Schmidt, Morgan J. and M.J. Heckenberger. Amerindian anthrosols: Amazonian dark earth formation in the upper Xingu. (in Amazonian dark earths: Wim Sombroek's vision. Edited by William I. Woods et al. New York, N.Y.: Springer Dordrecht, 2008, p. 163–191, bibl., ill., map, tables)

Soil samples collected from 743 locations in current and former villages occupied by the Kuikuru, prehistoric sites, current forest, secondary forest, and grassland were subjected to detailed chemical analysis. The frequencies of PH and organic C in nine activity areas in current and former villages show that the Kuikuru modify the soil in different parts of the house, village, and surroundings unintentionally with different results and that the locations of the activity areas shift constantly. Comparison of the frequencies of pH and organic carbon in samples from 237 locations in four houses show marked differences from those in forest soils. This detailed evidence is the first of its kind and provides a useful model for similar observations in other indigenous communities elsewhere in the lowlands. It also supports the interpretation that prehistoric *terra preta* is the product of settlement behavior and was not produced intentionally for agriculture. [BJM]

359 Schmitz, Pedro Ignácio. Caçadores antigos no vale do rio Caí, RS. (Pesqui. Antropol., 68, 2010, p. 79–108, bibl., ill., map, tables)

Describes excavations in a rock shelter on the Brazilian planalto occupied during the preceramic Umbu tradition, with abundant projectile points, bifaces, and scrapers, and a radiocarbon date of 7800 BP. [BJM]

360 Schmitz, Pedro Ignácio and Jairo Henrique Rogge. Um sítio da tradição cerâmica Aratu em Apucarana, PR = A site of the Aratu ceramic tradition in Apucarana, PR. (Rev. Mus. Arqueol. Etnol., 18, 2008, p. 47–68, bibl., ill, map, table)

Describes pottery and lithics from the southernmost habitation site of the Aratu tradition with a radiocarbon date of 590 ± 40 BP. [BJM]

361 Schmitz, Pedro Ignácio et al. Casas subterrâneas no planalto de Santa Catarina: São José do Cerrito. (Pesqui. Antropol., 68, 2010, p. 7–78, bibl., ill., maps)

Describes excavations, pottery, and lithics from 17 sites with one to 18 pit houses dating from 830 to 317 BP and a single open site dating 2460 BP. [BJM]

362 Silveira, Maura Imazio da and Denise Pahl Schaan. A vida nos manguezais: a ocupação humana da costa atlântica amazônica durante o Holoceno. (in Arqueologia amazônica. Organização de Edithe Pereira e Vera Guapindaia. Belém, Brazil: Museu Paraense Emílio Goeldi, 2010, v. 1, p. 35–48, bibl., table)

Summarizes the distribution of

53 shell middens on the Lower Amazon, Marajó, and the coast of Pará and Maranhão, and provides 68 radiocarbon and TL dates extending from 7090 ± 80 to 545 ± 70 BP. [BJM]

363 Simão, Lucieni de Menezes. Elos do patrimônio: Luiz de Castro Faria e a preservação dos monumentos arqueológicos no Brasil. (*Bol. Mus. Para. Emílio Goeldi Sér. Ciênc. Hum.*, 4:3, set./dez. 2009, p. 421–435, bibl., ill.)

Provides a detailed history of the significant role of Luiz de Castro Faria in the preservation of shell middens and in the formulation and implementation of legislation for the recognition, documentation, and excavation of archeological sites before and after becoming director of the Museu Nacional. [BJM]

364 Stenborg, Per. Points of convergence—routes of divergence: some considerations based on Curt Nimuendajú's archaeological work in the Santarem-Trombetas area and at Amapá. (*in* Anthropologies of Guayana: cultural spaces in northeastern Amazonia. Edited by Neil L. Whitehead and Stephanie W. Aleman. Tucson: Univ. of Arizona Press, 2009, p. 55–73, ill., maps)

Provides a useful summary of the pioneering investigations by Curt Nimuendajú during the 1920s on behalf of the Göteborg Museum and his acute observations, including the cultural origin of *terra preta*. For review of entire volume, see item **388**. [BJM]

CHILE

365 Ayala Rocabado, Patricia. Políticas del pasado: indígenas, arqueólogos y Estado en Atacama. Prólogo de Cristóbal Gnecco. San Pedro de Atacama, Chile: Línea Editorial IIAM, 2008. 231 p.: bibl., ill., map.

This book examines the historical development of the relations between Atacameños, archeologists, and the state in Chile, and how power has shifted to the Atacameños who now use symbols and other elements of their past described by archeologists as economic and political resources to reinvent their identities and make demands with regards to their cultural patrimony. [DJN]

366 Cases, Bárbara *et al.* Sugerencias, desde un contexto funerario en un "espacio vacío" del desierto de Atacama. (*Bol. Mus. Chil. Arte Precolomb.*, 13:1, 2008, p. 51–70, map, photos, table)

Describes the burial of a male individual, pathologies of the skeleton, faunal remains, textiles, and the route along which the body was found. Authors examine the features in the context of the late formative period and suggest that the person participated in moving goods between the coast and uplands without a caravan. [DJN]

Mason, Peter. Siete maneras de ser moai. See *HLAS 66:20*.

367 Núñez A., Lautaro. Vida y cultura en el oasis de San Pedro de Atacama. Santiago: Editorial Univ., 2007. 300 p.: bibl., ill., maps. (Imagen de Chile)

Reprinted edition of "Cultura y conflicto en los oasis de San Pedro de Atacama" (see *HLAS 55:607*) describes historical developments in the San Pedro de Atacama region of Chile from its earliest occupation, ~9000 BC, through the 20th century. The book is well illustrated with maps, photos, and drawings, with an additional bibliography of recent publications on the area. [DJN]

368 Núñez A., Lautaro; Martín Grosjean; and Isabel Cartajena. Ocupaciones humanas y paleoambientes en la puna de Atacama. San Pedro de Atacama, Chile: Instituto de Investigaciones Arqueologicas y Museo, Univ. Católica del Norte-Taraxacum, 2005. 480 p.: bibl., ill., maps.

This volume pulls together a number of previously published works, some of which were revised, to present a complete picture of climate change, settlement patterns, and related social dynamics in the Puna de Atacama, Chile. Chapters examine different periods and human adaptations and responses to different ecological conditions through time. [DJN]

369 Pimentel, Gonzalo E. and Indira Montt S. Tarapacá en Atacama: arte rupestre y relaciones intersocietales entre el 900 y 1450 DC. (*Bol. Mus. Chil. Arte Precolomb.*, 13:1, 2008, p. 35–50, map, photos)

Authors discuss the distribution of materials and the rock art associated with the Pica-Tarapacá complex and Loa-San

Pedro (Atacameño) during the Late Intermediate Period. They identify changes through time in the presence of both styles at settlement and cemetery sites, noting the presence of hybrid artifacts. They emphasize the communicative role of rock art located along trade routes. [DJN]

370   **Sanhueza Tohá, Cecilia.** Territorios, prácticas rituales y demarcación del espacio en Tarapacá en el siglo XVI. (*Bol. Mus. Chil. Arte Precolomb.*, 13:2, 2008, p. 57–75, bibl., maps, photos)
      Article considers the cultural logic used to delimit space in the Inca period by reviewing documentary and archeological evidence from the Inca era and colonial period through Toledan reform. The author suggests that groups are defined by jurisdiction not territory, even though archeological evidence shows that boundary markers were in use; more symbolic notions of the landscape also played a role. [DJN]

371   **Torres, Jimena; Claudia Silva;** and **Marcela Lucero.** El rol de la pesca en la intensificación de las ocupaciones costeras durante el Holoceno Medio-Tardío, Bahía de concepción, región del Bío-Bío, Chile. (*Magallania/Punta Arenas*, 35:1, 2007, p. 71–93, bibl., graph, map, photos, tables)
      Authors describe stratified deposits from the Playa Negra 9 site and present the results from faunal and lithic analysis to discuss changes in resource use in the littoral during the Middle Holocene. They conclude that occupants of the site are coastal specialists with technology and ritual focused on the coastal environment. [DJN]

372   **Troncoso, Andrés et al.** Arte rupestre en el Valle el Encanto, Ovalle, región de Coquimbo: hacia una revaluación del sitio-tipo del estilo Limarí. (*Bol. Mus. Chil. Arte Precolomb.*, 13:2, 2008, p. 9–36, bibl., ill., maps, photos)
      The authors re-evaluate the corpus of rock art at the Calle el Encanto site and subdivide the representations into three groupings that can be associated with the Late Archaic, Alfarero Temprano, and Late Intermediate Period/Late Horizon periods. They consider the production technologies, design elements, and location within the site and suggest some correlations with contemporaneous cultural complexes. [DJN]

COLOMBIA

373   **Aguas arriba y aguas abajo: de la arqueología en las márgenes del río Cauca, curso medio.** Compilación de Luis Gonzalo Jaramillo E. Textos de Darío Echeverry Messa *et al.* Bogotá: Univ. de los Andes, Facultad de Ciencias Sociales-CESO, Depto. de Antropología, 2008. 157 p.: bibl., ill., maps.
      This edited volume presents results from recent studies in the middle Cauca valley focused on several themes. A few papers examine chronological issues through ceramics, cultural changes at the long occupied site of Tesorito (100–1500 CE), and the implications of funerary remains. The final paper of the collection considers the present practice of looting and its related sociopolitics. [DJN]

374   **Antiguos pobladores en el valle del Magdalena Tolimense, Espinal-Colombia.** Textos de Héctor Salgado López *et al.* Ibagué, Colombia: Univ. del Tolima, 2006. 373 p.: bibl., ill. (some col.), maps. (Col. Universidad del Tolima 50 años; 9)
      Reports on results from the excavation of five sites in the dept. of Tolima west of the Magdalena River. Using landscape archeology as a theoretical framework, the authors examine patterns of land use, subsistence, the production and distribution of goods, and funerary practices to examine how ideas about the landscape changed through time. [DJN]

375   **Pineda Camacho, Roberto.** The spirit of ancient Colombian gold = El espíritu del oro antiguo de Colombia. Texts by Roberto Pineda Camacho and María Alicia Uribe. Edited by Sarah Crusin. Washington, D.C.: Smithsonian National Museum of Natural History, 2006. 95 p.: bibl., ill.
      Exhibit catalog with written works in English and Spanish describes the sociopolitical significance of gold in ancient Colombian societies. Three articles discuss the ideological meaning of gold, how it was used in different contexts, the history of metallurgy, and the political formations that the Spanish encountered upon contact. [DJN]

376   **Ramos, Elizabeth** and **Sonia Archila.** Arqueología y subsistencia en Tubará, siglos IX–XVI D.C. Bogotá: Univ. de los

Andes, Facultad de Ciencias Sociales-CESO, Depto. de Antropología, 2008. 190 p.: bibl., ill., maps.

Authors report on the first phase of investigation in Tubará, dept. of the Atlantic, Colombia, where they conducted a survey of 20 km² and four test excavations. Materials from surface collection and excavations are analyzed to establish a regional chronology. Examines changing patterns of subsistence in order to test models of developing sociopolitical complexity. [DJN]

377 **Rodríguez, Carlos Armando.** Diversidad humana y sociocultural antigua en la región geohistórica del Magdalena Medio. Cali, Colombia: Programa Editorial, Univ. del Valle, 2008. 188 p.: bibl., ill., maps.

The author presents a synthesis of current knowledge about prehispanic societies through time in the Middle Magdalena. He systematically describes landscape, climate, population, subsistence patterns, sociopolitical organization, craft production, ritual, and mortuary practices from the late Pleistocene to the contact period chiefdoms in the region. [DJN]

378 **Sánchez, Carlos Augusto.** Economía y sociedad prehispánica: el uso de la tierra en el Alto Magdalena. Bogotá: Fundación de Investigaciones Arqueológicas Nacionales, Banco de la República, 2007. 120 p.: bibl., ill. (some col.), maps.

The author models the development of chiefly power with relation to the control of resources by examining the influence that soil conditions and their productivity had on the situation and growth of settlements in the Upper Magdalena. Survey results are coupled with detailed studies of field drainage systems to understand the importance of landscape to increasing complexity in the region. [DJN]

379 **Simposio Economía y Política en las Sociedades Precapitalistas,** *Popayán, Colombia, 2004.* Economía, prestigio y poder: perspectivas desde la arqueología. Edición de Carlos Augusto Sánchez. Bogotá: Instituto Colombiano de Antropología e Historia, 2009. 386 p.: bibl., ill., maps. (Col. Perspectivas arqueológicas)

Edited volume examines the basis of social inequality and the sources of power in chiefdoms of Colombia and Venezuela, and explores the relationship between economic activity and politics. Chapters focus on themes such as the political economy, feasting, craft production, long distance exchange, and the role of ideology. [DJN]

380 **Territorio ancestral, rituales funerarios y chamanismo en Palmira prehispánica, Valle del Cauca.** Edición de José Vicente Rodríguez Cuenca. Bogotá: Univ. Nacional de Colombia, Facultad de Ciencias Humanas, Depto. de Antropología, 2007. 189 p.: bibl., ill. (some col.), folded col. map.

The volume describes results from research in the municipality of Palmira in the Cauca valley of Colombia. The authors examine prehistoric remains—preceramic through European contact—using ethnographic insights with regard to cosmology in an effort to understand the meaning of the landscape, community, house, and funerary ritual in the region. [DJN]

ECUADOR

381 **Bischof, Henning** and **Julio Viteri Gamboa.** Entre Vegas y Valdivia: la fase San Pedro en el suroeste del Ecuador. (*Bull. Inst. fr. étud. andin.*, 35:3, 2006, p. 361–376, bibl., maps)

Report describes a pre-Valdivia pottery style called San Pedro identified through excavations at the Valdivia type site. Although this style has been encountered at other sites in the region, the authors suggest that its origin remains unknown but likely is outside the region. [DJN]

382 **Bouchard, Jean-François; Franklin Fuentes;** and **Telmo López.** Aldeas y pueblos prehispánicos en la costa de Manabí: Chirije y Japoto. (*Bull. Inst. fr. étud. andin.*, 35:3, 2006, p. 243–256, bibl., photos)

Report introduces the sites of Chirije and Japoto located in Manabí between the Chone and Porto Viejo rivers. Chirije, a hamlet, and Japoto, a larger settlement with more than 60 mounds, were both occupied during the Regional Development period. Settlements are considered based on available resources and archeological remains. Also describes mound construction. [DJN]

383 **Cordero Ramos, María Auxiliadora.** El cacicazgo cayambi: trayectoria hacia la complejidad social en los Andes

septentrionales. Quito: Abya Yala, Univ. Politécnica Salesiana, 2009. 157 p.: bibl., ill., maps.

The author examines the changes in elite strategies during the Integration Period in the region of Caranqui to the northeast of Quito. Using vessel form and the frequency of imported ceramics drawn from two sites, Puntiachíl and Hacienda La Remonta near Cayambe, she assesses whether inter-regional exchange and feasting played a significant role. [DJN]

384 **Grieder, Terence** *et al.* The art and archaeology of Challuabamba, Ecuador. Austin: Univ. of Texas Press, 2008. 221 p.: bibl., ill., index, photos.

Authors consider remains from the formative period (2300–1700 BCE) Challuabamba site located in modern-day Cuenca. Ceramics are considered for their form, decoration, fabric, and production. Other chapters examine figurines, seals, lithics, shells, burial remains, and fauna. The authors outline lifeways for occupants of the site and make connections with other regions in the area. [DJN]

385 **Guinea, Mercedes.** Un sistema de producción artesanal de cuentas de concha en un contexto doméstico manteño: Japoto, provincia de Manabí, Ecuador. (*Bull. Inst. fr. étud. andin.*, 35:3, 2006, p. 299–312, bibl., photos)

Report describes a shell bead production context uncovered at the site of Japoto dating to the Integration Period (AD 800–1435). The author suggests that the beads were produced in a domestic structure and outlines the production process, possibly identifying different producers. She concludes that bead production was a part-time domestic activity rather than the effort of specialists. [DJN]

386 **Klein, Daniel** and **Iván Cruz Cevallos.** Ecuador: el arte secreto del Ecuador precolombino. Textos de Miguel Angel Cabodevilla Iribarren *et al.* Fotografía de Pierre-Yves Dhinaut. Quito: Casa del Alabado: Museo de Arte Precolombino; Milan, Italy: 5 Continentes, 2007. 359 p.: bibl., ill. (chiefly col.), maps (some col.).

Exhibition on the art of Ecuador shows many pieces of stone, wood, ceramic, and metal in color photos. Many are figu-rines, busts, or vessels that depict people, some in elaborate costumes. Cultural traditions include: Valdivia, Machalilla, Chorrera, Tolita, Jama-Coaque, Bahía, Guangala, Manteño, Capulí, Carchi, Piartal, Panzaleo, Cotocollao, Puruhá, Inca, Napo, Mayo Chinchipe. Chapters have a special focus on ceramic production and metallurgy. [DJN]

387 **Stothert, Karen E.** La cerámica de etiqueta de las tolas de Japoto, costa de Ecuador. (*Bull. Inst. fr. étud. andin.*, 35:3, 2006, p. 265–283, bibl., photos)

Author outlines a model of developing social complexity based on "great houses" or corporate groups that constructed tola mounds. During the early Manteño period there appears to have been interaction between different groups, or at least those of high rank, because a tradition of "etiquette ware" that is fairly similar over a wide area emerges. The early Manteño style is described and linked to commensal politics. [DJN]

THE GUIANAS

388 **Anthropologies of Guayana: cultural spaces in northeastern Amazonia.** Edited by Neil L. Whitehead and Stephanie W. Alemán. Tucson: University of Arizona Press, 2009. 300 p.: bibl., index. (Native peoples of the Americas)

Thirteen chapters by different authors discuss aspects of indigenous society, history, language, ethnopolitics and identity, and the validity of anthropological interpretations of indigenous behavior. Three provide brief summaries of prehistoric cultures on the Guiana coast, the north side of the Amazon, and coastal Amapá. [BJM]

389 **Meggers, Betty J.** Revisiting the Upper Essequibo: new perspectives on the Taruma Phase. (*Archaeol. Anthropol.*, 16:2, 2010, p. 1–28, bibl., ill., maps, table)

Reseriating the ceramic sequence constructed for the Upper Essequibo in 1960 using new criteria for identifying social organization suggests the existence of consecutive pre-Taruma and Taruma communities, both divided into two matrilocal moieties that occupied and reoccupied different locations within the same territory prior to European contact. [BJM]

390 **Migeon, Gérald.** La Guayana Francesa y sus relaciones con las regiones vecinas en los tiempos pre-cabralianos. (in Arqueologia amazônica. Organização de Edithe Pereira e Vera Guapindaia. Belém, Brazil: Museu Paraense Emílio Goeldi, 2010, v. 2, p. 713–739, bibl., ill., map)

Disputes the interpretations by Rostain of the western origin of the ceramic traditions along the coast of the Guianas and describes recent investigations at habitation sites along the Oyapock with pottery related to coastal Brazil. Extensive excavations along the Lower Sinnamary on the central coast provide a detailed sequence from early preceramic to late ceramic occupations. Radiocarbon dates on the wooden hafts of 15 stone axes found by divers in the Approuague River extend from cal 488–640 to cal 1429–1515 AD. [BJM]

391 **Plew, Mark G.** Pleistocene-early Holocene environmental change: implications for human adaptive responses in the Guianas. (in Anthropologies of Guayana: cultural spaces in northeastern Amazonia. Edited by Neil L. Whitehead and Stephanie W. Aleman. Tucson: Univ. of Arizona Press, 2009, p. 23–35, maps)

Summarizes evidence for Paleo-Indian and Archaic occupations prior to 6000 BP and associated environmental change. For review of entire volume, see item **388**. [BJM]

392 **Plew, Mark G. and Gerard Pereira.** Report on an archaeological survey in the vicinity of Shea village, south Rupununi savannah. (Archaeol. Anthropol., 16:2, 2010, p. 43–54, bibl., ill., map)

Describes stone alignments, a lithic workshop, and an urn cemetery in a rock shelter with red pictographs and relates them to the distributions of other cultural features in the region. [BJM]

393 **Rostain, Stéphen.** Cacicazgos guyanenses: mito o realidad? (in Arqueologia amazônica. Organização de Edithe Pereira e Vera Guapindaia. Belém, Brazil: Museu Paraense Emílio Goeldi, 2010, v. 1, p. 168–192, bibl., ill., maps)

Argues that the existence of ridged fields associated with Araquinoid sites implies intensification of agricultural productivity, permitting increased population density and associated sociocultural complexity. [BJM]

394 **Van den Bel, Martijn.** A Koriabo site on the lower Maroni river: results of the preventive archaeological excavation at Crique Sparouine, French Guiana. (in Arqueologia amazônica. Organização de Edithe Pereira e Vera Guapindaia. Belém, Brazil: Museu Paraense Emílio Goeldi, 2010, v. 1, p. 61–93, bibl., ill., map, tables)

Describes excavations, lithics, and ceramics, suggesting the existence of two occupations at a site on the western coast. Four radiocarbon dates extend from 1045 to 583 BP. [BJM]

PERU

395 **Arqueología de la costa centro sur peruana.** Compilación de Omar Pinedo y Henry Tantaleán. Lima: Avqi Ediciones, 2008. 503 p.: bibl., ill. (some col.), maps (some col.). (Investigaciones; 1)

Edited volume presents results from recent investigations along the south-central coast of Peru and honors the memory of Carlos Williams in the final chapter. Authors discuss time periods from Paiján to Inca and examine architectural traditions, artifact styles, and ethnohistory to answer diverse research questions. [DJN]

396 **Arqueología de Pachacamac: excavaciones en el Templo de la Luna y cuarteles, 1940–1941.** Edición de Víctor Paredes Castro. Lima: Museo de Arqueología y Antropología, Univ. Nacional Mayor de San Marcos, 2009. 404 p.: ill. (some col.), maps (some col.). (Cuadernos de investigación del Archivo Tello; 6)

The volume is the sixth in a series publishing the field notebooks of Julio C. Tello, which includes transcriptions of the text and sketches, many of which were created in colored pencil and are reproduced in color. The drawings illustrate details recovered during excavations, profiles, reconstructions, building plans, and artifacts. There are also a number of excavation photos showing crews working and in situ discoveries. [DJN]

397 **Arqueología de Pachacamac: excavaciones en Urpi Kocha y Urpi Wachak.** Lima: Museo de Arqueología y Antropología, Univ. Nacional Mayor de San Marcos, 2007. 183 p.: bibl., ill. (some col.), maps

(some col.). (Cuadernos de investigación del Archivo Tello; 5)

The volume is the fifth in a series publishing the field notebooks of Julio C. Tello. Transcriptions of original notes and sketches are accompanied by comments from Luisa Díaz Arriola and Izumi Shimada. The drawings illustrate details recovered during excavations, profiles, reconstructions, building plans, and artifacts, some are reproduced in color. Excavation photos have been integrated and demonstrate the precision of Tello's work. [DJN]

398 Arqueología del valle de Nepeña: excavaciones en Cerro Blanco y Punkurí. Transcripción y edición de Víctor Paredes Castro y Wilbert Salas Egúsquiza. Lima: Museo de Arqueología y Antropología, Univ. Nacional Mayor de San Marcos, 2005. 184 p.: bibl., ill., maps, 1 CD-ROM (4 3/4 in.). (Cuadernos de investigación del Archivo Tello; 4)

The volume is the fourth in a series publishing the field notebooks of Julio C. Tello with transcriptions of the text and sketches. Includes a number of excavation photos showing crews working and *in situ* discoveries. These images are also available on an accompanying CD-ROM, a wonderful resource for teaching. Vega-Centeno introduces the work and provides historical context. [DJN]

399 El Brujo: Huaca Cao, centro ceremonial Moche en e Valla de Chicama. Textos de Elías Mujica B. *et al.* Fotografías de Eduardo Hirose Maio. Lima: Fundación Wiese, 2007. 339 p.: bibl., ill., maps, plates.

The volume presents more than a decade of research at Huaca Cao Viejo and the surrounding region in both English and Spanish with brilliant color photographs, maps, illustrations, and 3D reconstructions. Authors describe the regional ecology and occupation of the area from archaic Paiján to the colonial period; the spectacular Moche temples, associated murals, interments, and material remains are the major focus of the work. [DJN]

400 Cavero Palomino, Yuri Igor. Ushnus y santuario inka en Lucanas y Huancasancos, Ayacucho. Ayacucho, Peru: Univ. Nacional de San Cristobal de Huamanga, 2009. 139 p.: bibl., ill., maps.

Examines the role of Osqonta as a religious center during the Late Intermediate Period and Late Horizon and presents the results of a survey in the surrounding Puna region of Ayacucho. Based on surface collection and some excavation, the author suggests that Osqonta was a local center in the LIP that was converted to the principle Inca sanctuary in the region with others below it in some form of hierarchical system. [DJN]

401 Chauchat, Claude. Prehistoria de la costa norte del Perú: el Paijanense de Cupisnique. Colaboración de Elizabeth Wing *et al.* Traducción de Santiago Uceda. Lima: Instituto Francés de Estudios Andinos; Trujillo, Peru: Patronato Huacas del Valle de Moche, 2006. 413 p.: bibl., ill. (Travaux de l'Institut français d'études andines; 211)

The volume details the remains of Paiján material culture recovered in the Cupisnique region, the desert coast between the Chicama and Jequetepeque rivers, and includes illustrations of the lithics recovered. In addition, maps depict settlement patterns and artifact distributions; also includes descriptions of the associated faunal and human remains. [DJN]

402 Chavín: art, architecture, and culture. Edited by William J. Conklin and Jeffrey Quilter. Los Angeles: Cotsen Institute of Archaeology, Univ. of California, 2008. 336 p.: bibl., ill. (some col.), index, maps. (Cotsen Institute of Archaeology at UCLA monographs; 61)

Edited volume presents recent interpretations of the Chavín cultural complex and related coastal and highland societies of Peru. Authors describe recent excavation and mapping data along with reconsiderations of elaborate art objects to discuss the nature of the Chavín phenomenon based on archeological remains and iconographic content. [DJN]

403 Chu Barrera, Alejandro. Bandurria: arena, mar y humedal en el surgimiento de la civilización andina. Huacho, Peru: Proyecto Arqueológico Bandurria, 2008. 185 p.: bibl., ill., maps.

The author describes the research history of the coastal area just north of Lima (Norte Chico), presenting competing interpretations of early monumental centers. Recent excavations at Bandurria shed light on the domestic and ceremonial structures, the economy, and developing cosmology, which may be linked to early social inequality. The book also includes a section on Bandurria's recent development for tourism. [DJN]

404 Congreso Internacional de Jóvenes Investigadores de la Cultura Mochica, 1st, Lima, 2004. Arqueología mochica: nuevos enfoques: actas del primer Congreso Internacional de Jóvenes Investigadores de la Cultura Mochica, Lima 4 y 5 de agosto de 2004. Edición de Luis Jaime Castillo Butters *et al.* Lima: Fondo Editorial, Pontificia Univ. Católica del Perú, 2008. 470 p.: bibl., ill. (1 col.), maps.

The volume highlights the recent work of young scholars working on different themes, time frames, and regions of the north coast of Peru. The authors examine craft production, ritual, funeral treatments, human sacrifice, ideology, chicha consumption, inter-regional interaction, the use of space (both residential and ceremonial), botanical remains, ceramics, metal, textiles, and human remains. [DJN]

405 Cornejo Guerrero, Miguel Antonio. El rombo escalonado: un símbolo de poder inka. (*Rev. Arqueol. Am./México,* 24, 2006, p. 125–141, bibl., ill., photos, tables)

Author discusses the stepped rhombus motif as a symbol of Inca power represented in modified natural rocks, architecture, and portable art. The symbol of the rhombus has three forms: a complete rhombus, half rhombus, or quarter rhombus. Although the symbol has antecedents, it appears the Inca coopted it to use on monuments and sacred locales in Cuzco and many provinces of the empire. [DJN]

406 Dalen Luna, Pieter Dennis van. Los ecosistemas arqueológicos en la cuenca baja del río Chancay, Huaral: su importancia para el desarrollo de las formaciones sociales prehispánicas. Lima: Juan Gutemberg Editores-Impresores, 2008. 192 p.: ill. (some col.), maps (some col.).

Author examines the components of the ecosystem in the Chancay Valley of the central coast of Peru. He describes through time the resources available to occupants of the valley and the interaction between groups and their environment. He suggests

that environmental decline started at Spanish contact and accelerated during the Republican period. [DJN]

407 Dean, Carolyn S. Aculture of stone: Inka perspectives on rock. Durham, N.C.: Duke Univ. Press, 2010. 297 p.: bibl., index, photos.

Argues that the Incas viewed rocks very differently than we do and attempts to explain how they distinguished between sacred and mundane examples and the consequences of this distinction. [BJM]

408 Donnan, Christopher B. Moche tombs at Dos Cabezas. Los Angeles: Cotsen Institute of Archaeology at UCLA, 2007. 241 p.: bibl., ill. (some col.), index, col. maps. (Monograph; 59)

The author describes five elaborate tombs from the Moche site of Dos Cabezas located on the south bank of the Jequetepeque River. Details of each tomb are discussed with regard to architecture, position of the body, grave goods, and elements of costume. Descriptions are accompanied by schematics, reconstructions, illustrations, and color photos. An appendix reports on the faunal remains. [DJN]

409 Echevarría López, Gori Tumi. Choquequirao: un estudio arqueológico de su arte figurativo. Lima: Hipocampo Editores, 2008. 70 p.: bibl., ill. (some col.), maps. (Col. Escuela latinoamericana; 1)

Report examines the decoration present in terrace walls elaborated through masonry techniques at Choquequirao in order to link motifs to ideology and in an effort to examine their chronology. The site is situated near the Apurimac River in Cuzco and was part of an Inca imperial estate. The study includes drawings and color photographs. [DJN]

410 Gallinazo: an early cultural tradition on the Peruvian north coast. Edited by Jean-François Millaire with Magali Morlion. Los Angeles, Calif.: Cotsen Institute of Archaeology Press, 2009. 253 p.: bibl., index. (Monograph; 66)

The edited volume brings together authors working in different valleys on the north coast of Peru to examine the nature of Gallinazo material culture and the relationship of the people who made and used this ceramic style with those that used Moche, Vicús, Virú, and Salinar. Evidence suggests that Gallinazo was a widely shared cultural tradition that does not correspond to a polity. [DJN]

411   González Carré, Enrique. Historia prehispánica de Ayacucho. 3. ed. Lima: Lluvia Editores, 2007. 138 p.: bibl., ill., map.

Author presents a synthetic culture history based on current archeological knowledge for the Ayacucho region of Peru. He describes the earliest human occupation in the lithic period, early communities, the formative period, Huarpa, Wari, Chanka, Inca, and the early colonial period. For review of 2nd ed., see *HLAS 55:676*. [DJN]

412   Gudemos, Mónica L. *Taqui Qosqo Sayhua*: espacio, sonido y ritmo astronómico en la concepción simbólica del Cusco incaico. (*Rev. Esp. Antropol. Am.*, 38:1, 2008, p. 115–138, bibl., maps)

The author examines how scenery, sound, movement, and rhythm were important elements of Inca ritual. In particular she explores the importance of astronomical phenomena and the positioning of sacred mountain peaks and other natural features in the landscape surrounding Cuzco and highlights how some natural settings could be used to stage ceremonial rituals to great effect. [DJN]

413   Jackson, Margaret Ann. Moche art and visual culture in ancient Peru. Albuquerque: Univ. of New Mexico Press, 2008. 232 p.: ill. (some col.), index, map, plates.

The author describes the communicative aspects of Moche art with an emphasis on murals and ceramic vessels. To assess how Moche art may have worked as a visual notation system, she discusses its sociopolitical context, its production (specifically at Cerro Mayal), and attributes of the Muchic language. [DJN]

414   Jamin, Thierry. Pusharo: la memoria recobrada de los incas. Prefacio de Nicole and Herbert Cartagena. Traducción del francés al español de Nicole de Cartagena. Lima: Estudio de Impresiones S.A., 2007. 258 p.: bibl., ill. (some col.), maps (some col.), plates.

Author describes the petroglyphs of Pusharo in Parque Nacional Manú. The

book includes many color photographs and line drawings. He suggests they are affiliated with Inca incursion into the region and compares elements with Inca tocapus and other design elements. Considers the rock carvings to be ideographs. [DJN]

415   Kasapata and the Archaic period of the Cuzco Valley. Edited by Brian S. Bauer. Los Angeles, Calif.: Cotsen Institute of Archaeology at UCLA, 2007. 142 p.: bibl., index. (Monograph; 57)

This report details excavation and analysis results from the site of Kasapata within the regional context of systematic survey results. It includes descriptions of excavated features and materials analyses (stone, human remains, fauna, and obsidian sourcing) accompanied by interpretive models to understand the poorly documented Archaic period. [DJN]

416   Lumbreras, Luis Guillermo. Un formativo sin cerámica y cerámica preformativa. (*Estud. Atacameños*, 32:1, 2006, p. 11–34, bibl.)

Lumbreras briefly reviews the trajectory of thought in anthropology with regards to the development of "civilization." He evaluates the association of pottery with the Neolithic revolution and summarizes the current data for the Northern and Central Andes for the Cotton Preceramic (Late Archaic) through to the Early Horizon (ca. 3000–1500 BC). [DJN]

417   Marcus, Joyce. Excavations at Cerro Azul, Peru: the architecture and pottery. Los Angeles: Cotsen Institute of Archaeology, Univ. of California, 2008. 332 p.: bibl., index. (Cotsen Institute of Archaeology monographs; 62)

The monograph is an excellent, detailed site report (of which more are needed in the Andean region) presenting excavation and analysis results from work at the Late Intermediate site of Cerro Azul. Using ethnohistoric insights, the author describes architecture, ceramic assemblages, and the ways in which variations in pottery can be used to sketch a prehistoric polity and its regional affiliations. [DJN]

418   Mould de Pease, Mariana. Machu Picchu: antes y después de Hiram Bingham: entre el saqueo de "antigüedades" y el estudio científico. Edición de Martín H.

Romero Pacheco. Perú: Biblioteca del Centro de Estudios Históricos Luis E. Valcárcel, 2008. 66 p.: bibl., ill., maps. (Col. Franklin Pease G.Y. para la historia andina del Perú)

Book records one Peruvian's perspective on the conflict between Yale University and Peruvian authorities over Bingham's work at Machu Picchu and the associated collections. The author takes a critical perspective and discusses how international relations and tourism may be having a negative effect on the conservation of the site and its scientific investigation. [DJN]

419 New perspectives on Moche political organization. Edited by Jeffrey Quilter and Luis Jaime Castillo B. Washington, D.C.: Dumbarton Oaks Research Library and Collection, Trustees for Harvard Univ., 2010. 388 p.: bibl., index.

Chapters in this edited volume use new evidence emerging from recent intensive research on the Moche in multiple valleys of the north coast of Peru to model the sociopolitical organization, power relations, ideology, expansion, and economic foundations of polities during the Early Intermediate Period. [DJN]

420 Ramos Gómez, Luis Javier. La escena del "Brindis con el Sol" en los queros o vasos de madera andinos de época colonial. (*Rev. Esp. Antropol. Am.*, 38:1, 2008, p. 139–166, bibl., photo)

Author reviews interpretations for a series of colonial painted cups themed "Toast with the Sun." Scenes from the wooden vessels are examined along with their variations. He postulates that early examples correspond to the mythical meeting between the Incas and Collas, however later iterations may have disguised the practice of mountain worship that also included toasts. [DJN]

421 Ruiz Estrada, Arturo. La alfarería de Kuelap: tradición y cambio. Lima: Avqi Ediciones, 2009. 172 p.: bibl., ill. (some col.), map. (Tesis; 4)

Report describes ceramics recovered from Kuelap located near the Utcubamba tributary of the Maroñon in Amazonas, Peru. The site was occupied during all periods from the Early Intermediate to the Late Horizon. Based on ceramic associations, it appears the fortress was constructed in the

Kuelap phase, which spans the Late Middle Horizon to the early part of the Late Intermediate Period. [DJN]

422 Ruiz Rubio, Alvaro A.; Winifred Creamer; and Jonathan Haas. Investigaciones arqueológicas en los sitios del Arcaico Tardío (3000 a 1800 años a. C.) del Valle de Pativilca, Perú. Barranca, Peru: Instituto Cultural del Norte Chico, 2007. 129 p.: bibl., ill., maps.

Authors report on results of research in the Lower Pativilca Valley, Peru. They focus on the dating of Late Archaic monuments (~3000–1800 BC) and present a map, photos, a brief description, profile drawings, and radiocarbon dates for each of nine sites. The report is a Spanish reprint of a work with the same title published in English in the journal *Fieldiana—Anthropology*, vol. 1546, 2007. [DJN]

423 Sistema vial Qollasuyu: avances de investigación. Lima: Instituto Nacional de Cultura, Dirección de Registro y Estudio de la Cultura en el Perú Contemporáneo, 2007. 236 p.: bibl., ill., col. maps.

Report describes findings from the Qhapaq Ñan (royal road) project in Qollasuyu, the southern quarter of the Inca Empire and details the borders of Qollasuyu, the major and secondary roads, bridges, and ways stations (*tambo*). The volume also describes general information about climate, ecology, geography, settlement history through the colonial period, and cultural features of modern communities. [DJN]

424 Vaughn, Kevin J. The ancient Andean village: Marcaya in prehispanic Nasca. Tuson: Univ. of Arizona Press, 2009. 210 p.: bibl., index.

Vaughn describes findings from excavation of a Nazca village—Maracaya. He presents a synthetic view of Nazca society based on current evidence and suggests Nazca villages were integrated through interactions at Cahuachi from which polychrome pottery was distributed as part of ritual feasting and ceremony. [DJN]

URUGUAY

425 Lezama, Antonio. Investigaciones arqueológicas sobre la vida rural en el siglo XVIII: la "guardia del Rosario," departamento de Colonia, Uruguay. Montevideo: Univ. de la República, Depto. de Arqueología, Facultad de Humanidades y Ciencias de la Educación, Depto. de Publicaciones, 2008. 1 v.: bibl., ill. (some col.), maps. (Col. "Carlos Vaz Ferreira"; 4)

Report describes what archeological investigations can reveal about the 18th-century occupation of the Guardia de Rosario and associated estancias. Excavation results from two sites—Cerros and Reboleda de Talas—supplement historical documents to reveal some aspects of the rural occupation on the frontier of Montevideo in this era of conflict. [DJN]

VENEZUELA

426   Catalogo de piezas arqueológicas. Textos de Jacqueline Clarac de Bricenño *et al.* Mérida, Venezuela: Museo Arqueológico "Gonzalo Rincón Gutiérrez," Univ. de Los Andes, 2006. 120 p.: bibl., col. ill.

This catalog features a selection of museum pieces (lithic, shell, and pottery) in full color and is accompanied by written works that describe the cultural and chronological context of the artifacts using ethno-historic and archeological information, techniques of manufacture, and aspects of the museum collection's conservation. [DJN]

ETHNOLOGY
Middle America

DUNCAN EARLE, *Professor of Anthropology and Director of Global Studies, Marymount College*

END OF PERIOD MARKERS: Mesoamerica Old and New

Many years ago, as a young graduate student eager to engage in the subjects of the day, I chased down senior anthropologist Sol Tax at a professional meeting to inquire about his most unexpected field experience—what most surprised him or stumped him in his many years of work. He answered that in his early work, the older, traditional peoples of a Maya village he was studying lamented that they would be the last generation to keep the old ways, and that the young were lost to them. Then a generation later, their children, now grown, were carrying out the same culturally prescribed tasks, and saying the same thing of the new generation, that *they* were the last traditionalists in a changed world, a cycle he was later able to see repeat into a third generation. He was always amazed that while changing, adapting, and appropriating the armatures of a history of dominators (item **473**), the Mayas remained somehow fundamentally unchanged, unconquered by conquest, and followed the same underlying cultural logic for new conditions, new innovations, and new adaptations (see items **436**, **437**, **472**, and **527**). In fact, some say the Maya are re-inventing themselves as traditional today, thanks in part to Mesoamerican scholarship accessible to literate indigenous peoples, and their avatars, in Spanish translation (items **474** and **494**).

What I gained from that long past encounter with a now passed Mesoamericanist elder resonates with the selections we have visited in this *Handbook* volume. Mesoamerican indigenousness is alive and well (item **493**)—changing, maintaining (item **531**), adapting (item **483**), adopting (items **452**, **470**, and **521**), resisting (items **477** and **488**), contesting (item **538**) and expanding—despite the many challenges to indigenous peoples inside nations run on different, typically ethnocentric cultural templates. Indigenous peoples face old and new challenges, but there remains a strong political (item **457**) and cultural force and heritage (item **459**), with multiple viable permutations throughout the social and immaterial landscapes that they still inhabit today (item **528**). Far from melding into rural and peri-urban culturally generalized mestizo poverty, the new impetus of cultural rights and identity politics in Mexico (items **454, 499,** and **507**) and, in a different key in Guatemala (items **440, 467,** and **536**) and other parts of Central America (items **438** and **519**) and beyond (item **496**), has transformed the indigenous in the eyes of state power—from being viewed as an obstacle to full national development, to being recognized as an aggrieved stakeholder in the uneven ongoing multicultural national project (items **481** and **512**). Dignity in cultural difference is in vogue (item **466**). This momentous shift in the national imaginary of countries like Mexico and Guatemala has begun to mature and percolate into research and writings (item **455**), and more than a fad or trend (and in fact there are many trends in the literature), it is now the touchstone of political debate about the state—and the limits of its power over citizenry, especially those of different histories and ethnicities.

For some scholars across the region, the status of indigenous peoples has fundamentally changed; it is now at the center of political discourse—no longer at the hidden edges studied by foreign anthropologists with esoteric writings (although these still appear, as in item **531**), but central to the nature of the state and its relations with ethnicity and polity (items **462** and **494**). This development, in turn, fuels a special civil rights movement, confronting the ultimate contradiction of the Americas, the real dark legend: invasion and expropriation. Others find the indigenous peoples' appeal to autonomy disturbing (item **513**) and contradictory to notions of equal rights under the law, and worry about a tyranny of traditions— especially feminist voices. Other writers suspect that cultural politics may come to serve power (item **536**) in the way that the state may begin to keep material concerns off the table to preserve its privileges (with some exceptions, such as in item **465**). Indigenous status is debated by others who see in the new indigenous cultural rights movements a medium for politics that include material issues such as land reform and local control of resources, and reinforces a popular countervalence to the power of the state. The growing attention in the region to indigenous legal status, conjoined with the recent UN declaration on indigenous rights, and new UN attention to statelessness, chasing the *fin de siècle* shift in national perceptions of indigenous people and their concerns globally, are reflections of a new and distinct imaginary from the one that dominated the past. In fact, the new global views on traditional, stateless peoples indicate a political maturing at a global level.

Not only does this change in perspective depart from the 20th-century acculturative/deculturative project, it departs also from the liberal-conservative and left-right political pendulum swings of an elite political class, which has been the principle political dynamic for much of Latin America since independence. Suddenly *el indio* is in the salon, cutting to the core of cultural and power critiques of the status quo, illuminating the holograph of racism, speaking with a voice legitimized after five centuries of silencing and unjust death (item **490**). No more Mesoamerica without the living Mesoamericans (and their dead, such as in item **466**). The days of anthropologists reducing indigenous culture to imposed colonial trauma and current peoples to rural proletarians has passed (items **489** and **518**). Their languages must be respected (no more calling them "dialects"), their forms of governance, their religious beliefs and practices (item **494**), their sacred landscapes, their locally demanded and UN-recognized rights (item **526**), must be recognized and valued by all. The politics of this shift is tremendous and complex (items **457, 475, 499, 512,** and **513**). This huge shift raises many questions about the relationship between ethnic groups and states.

While indigenousness is ascendant in all of Latin America, the Meso-american piece of it is remarkable and truly the trendsetter (e.g., Zapatistas), the *Middle World* again expressing its sentiments about power and resistance, about a New World point of view on how to live and how to approach the world. The Mesoamerican inhabitants push the political envelop for indigenous people because they, like their ancestors, keep to core concepts running deeply in Meso-american latitudes, with periodic renovations and revolts. A number of scholars juxtapose these steadfast tendencies to the unevenness of change in the wake of globalization—invented traditions, mutual syncretisms, the contestability of indigenous identity, the creative appropriations of the past under the alien yolks of church and state, and ultimately of an alien epistemology—an invading way of arranging thought itself. If contact began as a war of conquest, then one of reloca-tion, imperfect conversion, labor extraction, and finally, acculturation, these low intensity wars remain today in a multitude of configurations—*la conquista está vigente.* Sometimes so insidiously internalized is the slow invasion that some indigenous people fight for it against their own traditions and traditional people (item **442**), while others cling to their invented traditions against new waves of faux traditionalisms and imagined indianesses (item **520**). Nowhere is there the pristine, bona fide, and entirely unconquered Mesoamerica, yet everyone every-where insists on authenticity—a concept which is itself laden with invader episte-mological baggage (item **433**). So while some struggle for authenticity, others never lost it, and the cycles of sociability reproduce.

Many more topics appear in this collection: some traditional ethnographies, quite a few collections that run from archeology through ethnohistory and up to the present, others that examine regionally several towns or sites—with con-trolled comparisons to bring out continuities, differences, and creativity, and a good number of works about the colonial period and indigenous adaptation to it. Through almost all the contributions, both the continuities and the creative inno-vations of Mesoamericans are interwoven, and in most contemporary cases, there is a renewed call for considering indigenous voices in the imagining of nations, or at least contemplating the implications of doing so. These old and new perspec-tives and debates have many years before them—as does an emerging political indigenousness in the Americas, renewed by a new global recognition and local determination. This is an old story, just begun.

427 After the coup: an ethnographic reframing of Guatemala, 1954. Edited by Timothy J. Smith and Abigail E. Adams. Urbana: Univ. of Illinois Press, 2010. 167 p.: index.

This collection explores the dimen-sions of the 1954 US-backed coup, the previous 10 years of Guatemala's aborted revolution, and the impact of these political events on the nation's indigenous peoples, including articles by June Nash on restoring peace and by Richard Adams on ethnicity in Guatemala in the second half of the 20th century. Ethnographically grounded in the impact of the coup on local communities, the essays provide a nuanced view of the political players leading up to and following the coup, and moves away from the common use of the coup as historical bookend, or reducing it to the interests of the CIA. For those interested in the historical roots of later violence, the evolving role of the Catholic Church and Protestantism, and early efforts at bilingual education and other social planning for indigenous "development," this volume fills a gap in Guatemalan scholarship.

428 Alpuche Garcés, Óscar. El cuezcomate de Morelos: simbolismo de una troje tradicional. México: Casa Juan Pablos: Univ. Autónoma del Estado de Morelos: Instituto de Cultura de Morelos, 2008. 253 p.: bibl., ill., maps. (Ediciones mínimas. Agropecuarias; 1)

Two traditional villages in Morelos state are studied in regard to a once-common and very ancient architectural part of rural daily life, a maize-storage troje. Traditionally designed with a thatch roof and bulging sides with a reduced base, like a light bulb with a hat on, the *cuezcomate* carries with its simple function complex symbolism, full of meanings now increasingly in danger of being lost. Built by master builders trained in the significance of the structures, it has serves as a repository and generator of indigenous meanings often not appreciated in the manner of public ceremonies or shamanic ritual. The author goes to great scholarly lengths to link the granary with the cosmic tree of origin and other basic concepts of Mesoamerica, including the myths that parallel maize production, the importance of circular platforms, conical caps, the symbolic navel, and other architectonic features, and the primordial hill cave where the first corn is discovered. As the guardian of the source of life, and as symbolic uterus, the granary carries a significance unnoticed by most Mesoamericanists, the author maintains.

429 América indígena ante el siglo XXI. Edición de Julián López García y Manuel Gutiérrez Estévez. Textos de Manuel Gutiérrez Estévez *et al.* Madrid: Fundación Carolina: Siglo XXI de España Editores, 2009. 505 p.: bibl., ill.

Brings together 16 articles (six on Mesoamerica) and an introduction by the editors on the subject of indigenous peoples and their re-emergence into the political

spotlight at the end of the 20th century. Many of the papers are informed by extensive interviews with indigenous peoples holding political office throughout the Americas. Analyzes the role of civil society in assisting indigenous groups to organize and present their political platforms or community development trajectories, and describes the new and distinct ways in which indigenous groups operate in relation to the state.

430 Anderson, Mark David. Black and indigenous: Garifuna activism and consumer culture in Honduras. Minneapolis: Univ. of Minnesota Press, 2009. 290 p.: bibl., index.

Explores the politics of race, diaspora, and indigenous culture as woven into the active relations among consumption, neoliberalism, and multiculturalism—based on ethnography of the Garifuna, who cross-cut categories of difference often deployed about them—and sometimes by them. Identity instability, overlap, and contestability provide a field in the flux in situated affiliations, negotiated resistances, and identity politics, as the subjects of this study existentially confront discrete categorization as African, transnational, locally rooted, and Amerindians—all within the Honduran context—and demand their rights to difference, land, and respect. Challenges the facile use of many terms and labels of identity.

Andrews, Abigail. Constructing mutuality: the Zapatistas transformation of transnational activist power dynamics. See *HLAS 66:900.*

431 Antropoenfermería, salud, migración y multiculturalidad en América Latina. Textos de Patricia Casasa *et al.* México: ENEO: Miguel Ángel Porrúa, 2010. 214 p.: bibl. (Antropología y etnología serie)

A collection of 17 articles from UNAM exploring the intersection between anthropology and nursing, as a sort of interdisciplinary encounter between medical anthropology and the nursing profession, and as seen through different health challenges in Mexico associated with migration, ethnic and cultural variation, and health rights for indigenous communities. Also explores the historical role of sickness and illness behavior and medicinal plants and bioethics. Includes four articles associated with migrants and Chicanos in the US, ranging from traditional medicine to psychotherapy for alienated youth. The studies are more oriented toward a lack of adequate financial resources and professional skills than toward efforts to decentralize medical knowledge or an examination of the political economy of medicine in Mexico. The articles are based on a nursing/hospital orientation rather than a fieldwork from below. Identifies many of the obstacles to health among poor rural and urban Mexicans.

432 Arrecillas Casas, Alejandro. Hegemonía y educación bilingüe-bicultural en la Sierra Tarahumara. Chihuahua, Mexico: Instituto Chihuahuense de la cultura, 2008. 156 p.: bibl., ill., maps. (Solar col. Serie: ensayos)

As the title suggests, this study examines the bilingual education system set up by the government for the Tarahumara (Raramuri) in the community of Munérachi, with an eye toward how the educational system serves as a hegemonic arm of the state and Mexican society. Assesses many of the sociocultural elements of the indigenous community, with special attention to cultural and linguistic conflicts that have arisen due to the implementation of bilingual education. Approaches the government program as a form of forced acculturation and hegemony based on the teaching of Castillian to displace indigenous languages and to further undermine the authority and value they have in society.

433 Astor-Aguilera, Miguel Angel. The Maya world of communicating objects: quadripartite crosses, trees, and stones. Albuquerque: Univ. of New Mexico Press, 2010. 330 p.: bibl., ill., index, photos.

Takes to task scholars forcing experiential Mesoamerican cosmology and practice into Western dual categories of religion (à la Eliade). Views the sacred/profane dichotomy as alien to the epistemology of the invaded. Nonhuman personalities populate this world, and social relations with them are a central area of ritual activity and personal concern, implemented by ties between object and spirit/owners, with most powers emanating from ethnonature or ancestors. Cleaves to the minority view valorizing

rural daily life, as lived by maize farmers, sees their lives as the source of a worldview containing ancient urban elite symbols and rituals of power and legitimization—a worldview still much alive in rural Mesoamerica. Claims that rereadings of ancient artifacts and iconography flow from this epistemological reform, as well as a closer understanding of the ethnographic record and current ritual practice.

434 Ávila Chi, Rubentino. Andando bajo el monte, picando chicle, cazando lagartos, tumbando palos y haciendo milpa: una autobiografía. Edición de José A. Hernández Trujeque, Leticia de los Ángeles Caballero Mass y William J. Folan. México: Consejo Nacional para la Cultura y las Artes, 2009. 270 p.: bibl. (Memoria Histórica)

An edited autobiography of a Maya from Campeche who lived a long and active life in the jungles of southeast Mexico (Lacandon) as a chicle collector, wood cutter, farmer, and alligator hunter. His many rural adventures are captured in this book in the form of dialogues. Reveals much about the socioeconomic conditions in an area not well studied.

435 Babb, Florence E. The tourism encounter: fashioning Latin American nations and histories. Stanford, Calif.: Stanford Univ. Press, 2010. 243 p.: bibl., index, photos.

A bittersweet journey through tourist zones of Latin America (Cuba, Mexico, Nicaragua, Peru), as they shift from selling utopian landscapes to creative revolutionary nostalgic imaginaries. Unlike the accounts in Nicaragua and Peru, the Zapatista Chiapas tourism chapter describes tourism in the midst of an actual social revolution, the one case of the book that is both nostalgic and contemporary at once. The narrative runs along the colorful surfaces of many tourism trails with first-person accounts and a travelogue discourse that is accessible and personable, demonstrating that like the Maya of Chiapas, both revolution and ethnic exotica sell well as authenticated encounter.

436 Báez Cubero, Lourdes. El juego de las alternancias: la vida y la muerte: rituales del ciclo vital entre los nahuas de la Sierra de Puebla. México: Ediciones del Programa de Desarrollo Cultural de la

Huasteca, 2005. 205 p.: bibl., ill. (some col.), maps.

Study of Naupan, a Nahua municipality bordering on and sharing traditions with the Huasteca and the Sierra Norte de Puebla, whose cosmovision continues to serve as a guide to their accommodations to the outside. Introduces the spiritual universe, the social webs of relations, and the specialists who oversee life cycle rituals. Follows the life cycle rituals and practices that define community life and the sense of self identity. Shows how these rites of passage have both a cosmic and a social dimension at the same time, reproducing social relations and relations with the nonordinary realms.

437 Bartolomé, Miguel Alberto. La tierra plural: sistemas interculturales en Oaxaca. México: Instituto Nacional de Antropología e Historia, 2008. 328 p.: bibl., ill. (Col. Etnografía de los pueblos indígenas de México. Serie Estudios monográficos)

This masterful work integrates ethnographic and environmental material across multiple ethnic groups speaking two dozen languages and adapted to diverse ethnoecologies in the Mexican state of Oaxaca. After an archeological summary and a small colonial section, the author introduces a comparative regional inter-ethnic social analysis in current times, including the indigenous people in the capital city of the state. This discussion is followed by coverage of indigenous cosmovisions, kinship, arts and crafts, and finally indigenous intellectuals and their writings.

438 Bataillon, Gilles. Enquête sur une guérilla: Nicaragua, 1982–2007. Paris: Félin, 2009. 330 p.: bibl., maps. (Marches du temps)

In this inquiry into the civil/contra war in the Miskitu territory of Nicaragua, the author interviews 100 combatants in an effort to tease out a discursive position that led many Miskitu to join the US-backed Contras, and fight against the Sandinistas. By exploring their habitués—cultural, religious, and political—the author helps us understand how the conflict was understood by Miskitu in the historical context of the time, and how these perceptions evolved over time. Intimate access to the field sites and careful accounting of events before, during, and after the war frame the local context from which these indigenous soldiers emerged.

439 Border crossings: transnational Americanist anthropology. Edited and with an introduction by Kathleen Sue Fine-Dare and Steven Rubenstein. Lincoln: Univ. of Nebraska Press, 2009. 369 p.: bibl., index.

Adopts a border metaphor to follow the lead of indigenous continental solidarity of identity imaginary, calling for a "Transnational Americanist Anthroplogy"— "novel forms of Pan-American association and understanding. . ." (p. xvii) that are both true to their localism and connected to regional and global forces and understandings. The collection of 12 contributions and an afterword combines a first section examining general insights on border crossing and reflection, with a second section of cases, and a third delineating the effects on scholars of transborder experiences—the dualistic burdens that arise for those biculturals living in two places at once. Seeks to revisit Area Studies critiques, calling for more interconnections within the Americas that reflect transnational identities of recent massive inter-American migration.

440 B'otz'onik: el rostro maya en la administración del Presidente Álvaro Colom: informe situacional: análisis y reflexión acerca del rostro maya en la presente administración. Ciudad de Guatemala: Tob'nel Tinamit, 2009. 100 p.

Report on the political efforts to bring the "Maya face" proposal to fruition under the administration of Álvaro Colom in Guatemala. Explores the efforts at inclusion by a political party and organization that ultimately used indigenous identity politically, without substantive reform of ethnic prejudice against the Maya. Lays out various avenues of legal rights to challenge discrimination, and insists that more investment be made in concrete expenditures in indigenous communities and development programs. Economic analysis of inter-ethnic inequality in Guatemala is parallel to the historical asymmetries in the nation. Impressive for its free political speech, and laudable clamor for greater authentic participation in Guatemala's government along with more government commitment to real aid for indigenous communities. Lends insight into the racial dynamics of social tensions created by the appearance of Maya in the halls of national power.

441 Caminando por la Pimería Baja: O'ob pajlobguim: territorio e identidad. Textos de Alejandro Aguilar Zeleny *et al.* Hermosillo, Mexico: Gobierno del Estado de Sonora: Comisión para la Atención de los Pueblos Indígenas de Sonora, 2009. 374 p.: bibl., ill., maps.

A collection of articles focused on the archeology and history of the Pima (O'ob) indigenous group in central and eastern Sonora, and to some extent in the state of Chihuahua, based on a mix of primary and secondary sources. Addresses a great range of subjects, from architecture to chronicles and legends. Outlines the continued marginality of these oppressed rural people who, in addition to the colonial-like relations they have experienced for centuries, now confront the invasions of their remote lands by drug cartels who force Pimas to work without pay, increase the already elevated levels of alcoholism and substance abuse, and operate with virtual impunity in areas outside the control of the state.

442 Carlsen, Robert Stanley. The war for the heart & soul of a highland Maya town. New preface, new final chapter, and contribution by Martín Prechtel. Foreword by Davíd Carrasco. Rev. ed. Austin: Univ. of Texas Press, 2011. 227 p.: bibl., ill., index, maps.

Updated classic ethnography of a traditional Highland Maya village under siege from national and global forces, including military, and factional in its internal make up, socially and spiritually—with extreme yet incomplete erosion of prior religious tradition. Demonstrates the intersection of cult conversion and low-intensity political violence with tourism and other globalizations, as the Guatemalan security state fades and fractures—embodied in the dark figure of Atitlán's Maximon. For review of earlier edition, see *HLAS 59:750.*

443 Casasa, Patricia. Una visión antropológica de la enfermería en México. México: UNAM: M.Á. Porrúa, 2009. 211 p.: bibl., ill. (Antropología y etnología serie)

Applies an anthropological perspective to nursing in Mexico, providing some historical and social context for the development of the Western nursing tradition in urban, hospital settings, an institution within the Western medical paradigm that the author champions. The first half of the text follows this European tradition from its roots in the Middle East and India through early Europe; the second half devotes only three pages to indigenous medicine before discussing the epidemics of the conquest, early hospitals, and health in the colonial and post-independence periods. The last section follows the nursing profession, what the author terms a subaltern profession in medicine, to contemporary times in urban Mexico.

444 Castillo Farreras, Víctor M. Los conceptos nahuas en su formación social: el proceso de nombrar. México: UNAM, 2010. 143 p.: bibl. (Serie de cultura náhuatl. Monografías; 32)

Close examination of the colonial use of the Nahuatl language by early missionaries, and the borders of what could be communicated and what was lost in translation, written by a Mexican historian. Most of the book breaks down specific words, suffixes, roots, and other language elements in classical Nahuatl, to show the limitations of the early grammatical studies—obstacles to current readings of these historical texts.

445 Castillo Hernández, Mario Alberto. Mismo mexicano pero diferente idioma: identidades y actitudes lingüísticas en los maseualmej de Cuetzalan. México: Instituto Nacional de Antropología e Historia: UNAM, Instituto de Investigaciones Antropológicas, 2007. 287 p.: bibl., ill., maps.

A psychosociolinguistic assessment of inter-ethnic communication between Nahuas and both Totonacs and mestizos. Explores situated bilingualism and the social uses of different languages, with an eye towards language maintenance and community identity. Detailed study of language use and how language mediates and reflects social relations.

446 Coloquio Carl Lumholtz de Antropología e Historia del Norte de México, 1st, Chihuahua, Mexico, 2005. Retos de la antropología en el norte de México: I Coloquio Carl Lumholtz: en el aniversario de la ENAH Chihuahua. Compilación y edición de Juan Luis Sariego Rodríguez. México: Instituto Nacional de Antropología e Historia, 2008. 399 p.: bibl., ill. (Col. ENAH Chihuahua; 1)

Interdisciplinary study with perspectives from archeology, ethnohistory, and ethnography, this collection by 14 authors follows the anthropology of northern Mexico (especially Chihuahua) from its early horizons of habitation through the colonial missions and revolts, up to current concerns of rights, cosmovision, and political ecology—as well as narcoculture and other current social and political topics. Furthers the study and circulation of analysis of this part of Mexico, and covers a long period of time from before agriculture to recent party politics of the state of Chihuahua.

447 Coloquio Internacional Patrimonio Inmaterial y Pueblos Indígenas de América, Querétaro, Mexico, 2007. Memoria, 6 al 8 de diciembre de 2007, Querétaro, México. Edición de Mirza Mendoza Rico y Francisco Vidargas. Santiago de Querétaro, Mexico: Instituto de Estudios Constitucionales del Estado de Querétaro; México: Instituto Nacional de Antropología e Historia, 2008. 181 p.: bibl., ill.

A collection of articles on intangible patrimony, derived from a conference in Querétaro, following a General Convention of UNESCO campaign giving importance to documentation and preservation of cultural patrimony in the areas of the symbolic—belief, ritual, and traditions. The convention shows the movement from material patrimony, monuments, and great buildings to a concern for the intangible aspects of culture. In this vision, the mandates of cultural diversity imply the importance of providing support for cultural survival, for a sort of rescue anthropology that provides people with access to their own heritage. Some articles are general; others are focused on a single country, group, or area; and all take up the subject of intangible cultural patrimony and how it can be protected and preserved.

Coloquio México-Guatemala. Estado y Ciudadanía, San Cristóbal de Las Casas, Mexico, 2005. México y Guatemala: entre el liberalismo y la democracia multicultural:

azares de una transición política inconclusa. See item **1156**.

448 Cruz, Víctor de la. Mapas genealógicos del Istmo oaxaqueño. Oaxaca, Mexico: Consejo Nacional para la Cultura y las Artes: Gobierno del Estado de Oaxaca: Fundación Alfredo Harp Helú Oaxaca, AC: Centro de Investigaciones y Estudios Superiores en Antropología Social, 2008. 126 p.: bibl., ill., maps (some col.), plates. (Col. Diálogos, pueblos originarios de Oaxaca. Serie Veredas)

Part of a larger project on recovery and composition of Zapotec (diidxaza') history of writing, this book focuses on surviving maps and *lienzos* (drawn on cloth), contact period graphics showing kinship and descent, as they were laid out in symbols on spaces. Unfortunately the graphics are poorly reproduced and difficult to see. The book covers two *lienzos* and two maps; the Lienzo de Guevea and the Lienzo de Huamelula y Astata; the geneological map of Guibixi o Huilotepec, and finally the map of Zanatepec. Copious commentary accompanies the documents.

449 Cruz Burguete, Jorge Luis; Gabriela Robledo Hernández; and Carlos Uriel del Carpio Penagos. Las migraciones internas de los pueblos indígenas de Chiapas. Tapachula, Mexico: ECOSUR; San Cristóbal de Las Casas, Mexico: Univ. Intercultural de Chiapas, 2007. 194 p.: bibl., maps.

A collection of five articles, framed in an introduction by Andrés Fábrigas Puig, examining indigenous migration patterns and their histories within the state of Chiapas as an important antecedent to the recent swell of out-migration from the state to the US. Breaks down into an overview of a history of movements, a look at border movements, a discussion of rural-urban migration, an analysis of the impacts of the Zapatista uprising and consequent militarization, and follows some Maya colonies far from their home communities, but still within the state. Militarization is tied to prostitution that impacts indigenous communities, and often leads to the eventual urban migration of women and girls. Religious and political fragmentation also generate conflicts that often lead to displacement and migration, as does increased contact with successful migrants returning from abroad. Useful examination of the recent processes of displacement as part of global impacts and local responses. Gives new context to the Zapatista uprising.

450 Cuesta Avila, Rafael. Crónicas de Yucatán: tres experiencias etnográficas en el sur de México. Granada, Spain: Univ. de Granada, 2008. 330 p.: bibl., ill., maps. (Biblioteca de humanidades/antropología. Monográfica; 12)

An ethnographic journey through housing, the general cemetery, and their complex and varied meanings in Mérida, Yucatán, as well as the small nearby town of Acanceh, which has become industrialized. Rich depictions of the reflections and connections between the cemetery and the rest of Mérida's built space, of tying home types to socioeconomic status and other social and cultural factors, and an applied anthropology account of a rural Maya community facing the changes of globalization in the form of a maquila factory. The final section on planning from above and from below demonstrates an engagement with, and commitment to, the people and the applied topic.

451 Cultural tourism in Latin America: the politics of space and imagery. Edited by Michiel Baud and Johanna Louisa Ypeij. Leiden, The Netherlands; Boston, Mass.: Brill, 2009. 323 p.: bibl., ill., index, maps. (CEDLA Latin America studies; 96)

Collection on Latin American cultural tourism with five articles located in Mesoamerica—Yucatán (Vargas-Cetina, Breglia, Castañeda), Oaxaca (Feinberg), and Antigua, Guatemala (Little). The book arose from a 2007 conference at the Centre for Latin American Research and Documentation (Netherlands) focused on cultural heritage site management, identity discourses, national belonging, and development possibilities associated with cultural tourism. Papers explore local consequences of global tourism trends and impacts in indigenous regions of Central America and the Andean highlands, and tie these to national and international imaginaries about heritage, experiential authenticity, and the circula-

tion of identities. Contributions look at local sustainable tourism alternatives to international company domination, and analyze the cultural but also social and political implications of this asymmetrical encounter in the "touristic border zone," locating tourism in the larger context of globalization and its many facets. Theorizes the nation-building patrimony/heritage role of ancient places and authentic (nonmodern, past) exotic peoples, and its tension with global touristic imaginaries and regional governmental and private sector efforts to capture and control cultural heritage as resources—often in conflict with local indigenous interests.

452 DeHart, Monica Christine. Ethnic entrepreneurs: identity and development politics in Latin America. Stanford, Calif.: Stanford Univ. Press, 2010. 192 p.: bibl., index.

To the contested sites of development we must include ethnic entrepreneurs—as both subjects of and agents in market penetration, as the global reaches into the local in Latin America, and as ethnicity becomes a market value in neoliberal times (and places). The book takes up this topic, with special reference to indigenous Guatemala, and specifically Totonicapan, but also other ethnicities, including transnational Latinos and cases of migration and remittances. The study charts the perennial problems that arise from the model of ethnic capitalism as development: the most privileged and capable are rewarded in ways not shared with the whole community, thereby serving as an axis of localized global corporate interests while factionalizing at the local level, and appropriating ethnic discourses of legitimacy for micropolitical ends.

453 Díaz, Floriberto. Escrito: comunalidad, energía viva del pensamiento mixe = Ayuujktsënää'yën—ayuujkwënmää'ny—ayuujk mëk'äjtën. Compilación de Sofía Robles Hernández y Rafael Cardoso Jiménez. México: UNAM, 2007. 435 p.: bibl., ill. (Col. La pluralidad cultural en México; 14. Voces indígenas)

Part of a series called Voces indígenas, this volume champions the posthumous work of indigenous anthropologist Floriberto Díaz Gomes, of Mixe linguistic origin (Oaxaca state), and his concerns with Mixe language longevity through primary and secondary education. Díaz's *revindicación* position speaks toward a postcolonial language regarding indigenous views between each other and before the state—including autonomy. The subjects are framed in an energetic struggle for Mixe and Mexican indigenous rights, moving between the autobiographical, to the organizational and case study, conjoined with advocacy. His double position as academic and member of the Mixe indigenous group have led his studies to advocacy action.

454 Díaz Meléndez, Adela. Migración indígena y apropiación del espacio público en Monterrey: el caso de la Alameda. Monterrey, Mexico: Centro de Estudios Históricos UDEM, Univ. de Monterrey: Univ. Autónoma de Nuevo León, Facultad de Filosofía y Letras; México: Centro de Investigaciones y Estudios Superiores en Antropología Social, 2009. 231 p.: bibl., ill., index, maps.

A new addition to migration studies in Mexico, this work focuses on indigenous women migrants from the Huasteca with a long tradition into urban Monterrey, and how they have come to occupy a public park as a ground zero for their collective presence in the city—a presence often tied to domestic labor opportunities. The author studies social spaces and how the indigenous appropriation of these spaces relates to social network building and maintenance, ties to identity in the face of social stigma (el indio), and ethnic urban geography. A central theme of the book describes a scenario in which men and women in typically nuclear families who emerge from many different indigenous towns begin to interact in this appropriated social space, and when they find themselves in similar straits, suffering similar stigmas and marginalization, they create new social structures of mutual support.

455 Durand Alcántara, Carlos. La autonomía regional en el marco del desarrollo de los pueblos indios: estudio de caso, la etnia náhuatl del estado de Oaxaca, Santa María Teopoxco. México: Estados Unidos Mexicanos, Cámara de Diputados, LX Legislatura, Consejo Editorial: Miguel Angel Porrúa, 2009. 429 p.: bibl., ill., maps. (Antropología y etnología serie) (Conocer para decidir)

Ambitious study of a Nahuatl township in Oaxaca state, weaving together natural history, historical memory, socioeconomic structures and relations, and culture. The objective is to make a sufficiently integrated and proactive research project whose end is to construct a sustainable development proposal to help the people from Santa María confront the structural poverty of the region. Based on teamwork, the book connects archeology and ethnohistory with the current situation and provides a historical basis for their project, as well as contextualized insights about the future threats to and potential of the township.

Eisenstadt, Todd A. *Usos y Costumbres* and postelectoral conflicts in Oaxaca, Mexico, 1995–2004: an empirical and normative assessment. See item **1064**.

456 Ekern, Stener. Chuwi meq'en ja' = Comunidad y liderazgo en la Guatemala K'iche'. Traducción al idioma español de Sara Martínez Juan. Guatemala: CHOLSAMAJ, 2010. 285 p.: bibl., ill.

A quality study of the Totonicapán region of Guatemala. A Norwegian anthropologist (in the early 2000s) focused on indigenous leadership, legitimacy, and local politics in this prosperous part of the western highlands. Presented here is a careful examination of the rituals and practices associated with the annual traditional transfer of power from one village-level official to the next, suggesting a parallel pattern of legitimization of indigenous autonomy and legitimate control of space and place as it is carried out at a national level by the state. Detailed elaboration of the roles and responsibilities of different types of leadership and authority, both traditional and constitutional, as well as a historical foundation of their origins and evolution through time.

457 Engle, Karen. The elusive promise of indigenous development: rights, culture, strategy. Durham, N.C.: Duke Univ. Press, 2010. 400 p.: bibl., index.

Documents indigenous social and cultural movements since the 1970s in Latin America and their interaction with domestic and international law. Discusses how their cultural rights victories also have a downside associated with the reification of indigenous culture, and sometimes decreased opportunity for political autonomy and equitable development. The hegemony of NGO-sponsored "indigenous conferences" and their pan-indigenous networks, the struggle with constraints imposed by biased legal regimes, and the unevenness between collective and individual cultural rights and politically less feasible efforts at self-determination—the book ultimately assesses the comparative benefits of different strategies dealing with these approaches and their tensions in a very encompassing and critical account.

458   Entre textos e imágenes: representaciones antropológicas de la América indígena. Edición de Fermín del Pino, Pascal Riviale y Juan José R. Villarías Robles. Madrid: Consejo Superior de Investigaciones Científicas, 2009. 276 p.: bibl., ill. (De acá y de allá. Fuentes etnográficas; 5)

Franco-Spanish collaboration exploring the representations—narrative and iconographic of many sorts—made by humanists and scientists from the 16th century to the present, to show an imaginary of indigenous peoples in Latin America, a narrative always embedded in the sociopolitical context of the times. Seventeen contributions are grouped into three sections, the first linking ethnohistorical archival work and fieldwork, the second looking at graphics depicting indigenous peoples in the colonial era, and a third bringing indigenous representational schema up to the recent past and modern present. Excellent gallery of color illustrations, mostly idealized representations of indigenous people and ruins.

459   Erickson, Kirstin C. Yaqui homeland and homeplace: the everyday production of ethnic identity. Tucson: Univ. of Arizona Press, 2008. 186 p.: bibl., ill., index, map.

Erickson describes the creation of a sense of Yaqui identity and belonging, community maintenance and struggle against poverty, prejudice, and social decomposition in the wake of changes that have remade their world. Narratives of place and belonging, and discussions of the role of women in the maintenance and reproduction of culture and identity comprise the body of the book. Rich source of description for linking material culture to the arrangements of household space and the changes in that space and its meaning due to well-described external and internal forces.

460   Escalona Victoria, José Luis. Política en el Chiapas rural contemporáneo: una aproximación etnográfica al poder. México: UNAM, 2009. 420 p.: bibl. (Col. La pluralidad cultural en México; 19 Cuadernos de la Cátedra Interinstitucional Arturo Warman)

This ethnographically based study of political power in Chiapas looks at the localized popular exercise of collective power by examining a case study of a Tojolabal ejido settlement in eastern Chiapas. The study makes linkages between the concerns of daily life and political demands made to their elected leaders, which are embodied in protests, road blocks, occupations of offices, expulsions, public denouncements, etc.—many popular methods of pressing political claims against authorities. The central thesis is the link between mass political expression and the daily conflicts between proximate groups and the conclusion that both reflect a Maya ordering of power along lines of hierarchy, ranking, and rupture—the contradictions between micro-clashes and macro-solidarity in the face of persistent power asymmetry.

461   Escuela y proceso cultural: ensayos sobre el sistema de educación formal dirigido a los mayas. Coordinación de Jesús Lizama Quijano. México: CIESAS, 2008. 251 p.: bibl. (Col. Peninsular archipiélago)

Eight articles focused on indigenous education in Yucatán, Mexico, assessing the disjuncture between the culture of primary and secondary education that the Mayas of Yucatán attend and the local Maya culture within the family and community—and how these disjunctures impact educational achievement. The conclusions indicate the need for a collaborative effort to completely restructure education to accommodate the Maya culture, requiring funding and collaboration between civil society and government.

462   Estados plurales: los retos de la diversidad y la diferencia. Coordinación de Laura R. Valladares de la Cruz, Maya Lorena Pérez-Ruiz y Margarita Zárate Vidal.

México: Univ. Autónoma Metropolitana, Unidad Iztapalapa: Juan Pablos, 2009. 471 p. (Biblioteca de Alteridades; 10)

Collection of 14 articles and an introduction wrestling with the tensions and contradictions between the contemporary issue of cultural diversity and empowering ethnic identity on one hand, and class, inequality, and structural analysis on the other. Some authors are concerned that the emphasis on indigenous and ethnic identity and rights obscures relations determined by asymmetries other than race and culture. Others see ethnic identity and autonomy movements as politically reinvigorating social movements and action, and addressing an embodied colonial reality obscured by traditional class analysis—ignoring indigenous culture, rights, and agency. The contributions struggle to situate the themes of multicultural politics into historical context, and to examine how they relate to the state.

463 Estrada Martínez, Rosa Isabel. Indígenas de San Cristóbal de las Casas, Chiapas: de dónde vienen, cómo viven, cómo se ven y cómo son vistos. Guadalajara, Mexico: Producción Groppe, 2009. 180 p.: bibl.

Chronicles the transformation of San Cristóbal from a mostly mestizo (ladino) colonial heritage town to one with an immigrant Maya majority with ascendant political aspirations. Provides thorough description of current immigrant life—various religions, indigenous organizations, typical labor patterns—and maps out new "exile" Maya neighborhoods surrounding the city. Serves as a handbook for urban inter-ethnic relations in San Cristóbal and explains how they have changed. Offers a remarkable description of Muslim Mayas. Sorts out the complex social landscape of a city transformed by Maya immigration and agrarian strife.

464 Etnografía de los confines: andanzas de Anne Chapman. Coordinación de Andrés Medina y Angel Ochoa. México: Instituto Nacional de Antropología e Historia: Centro de Estudios Mexicanos y Centroamericanos: UNAM-Instituto de Investigaciones Antropológicas, 2007. 300 p.: bibl., ill. (Col. Científica; 514. Serie Antropología)

Thirteen essays in four sections honoring the person and the intellectual contributions to Mesoamerican and other anthropological, archeological, and historical scholarship of Anne Chapman. One section specifically addresses her conception of Mesoamerican long-distance trade as part of the political economy of a culture area and the ethno-economic borders between those groups within it—taking Chapman's ideas further along with new data and analysis. Other sections discuss historical and current ethnographic concerns, such as Yolotl González's piece on comparative ethnography of maize, and Carlos Navarrete's piece on the recently modernized pilgrimage shrine of Esquipulas, Honduras, and a final section with articles related to Argentina. Gives a robust sense of Chapman's contributions to Mesoamerican studies and Mexican anthropology.

465 Etnografías e historias de resistencia: mujeres indígenas, procesos organizativos y nuevas identidades políticas. Edición de Rosalva Aída Hernández Castillo. México: Centro de Investigaciones y Estudios Superiores en Antropología Social: UNAM, Programa Univ. de Estudios de Género, 2008. 514 p.: bibl., ill., maps. (Publicaciones de la Casa Chata Antropologías)

An introductory essay on decentering feminism is followed by 10 chapter articles, some specific cases like that of Zapatista women, some more comparative in terms of indigenous women's struggles. The focus is on Mexico, with Puebla, Oaxaca, Guerrero, Veracruz, and Chiapas states all represented, the last by three pieces. Demonstrates the faults of the dichotomy of old and new social movements when applied to indigenous women, who typically are pushing for both material and cultural rights and opportunities at once. Cases outline how feminist analysis assists in bringing class and cultural issues together, and uniting practical and strategic interests, as women transform their society and their political identity through participation in NGOs. Presents important studies of women's power in social and political transformative change, working against the new hegemony of patriarchal traditions found in some *usos y costumbres.*

466 **Flores Martos, Juan Antonio** and **Luisa Abad González.** Etnografías de la muerte y las culturas en América Latina. Cuenca, Spain: Univ. de Castilla La Mancha; Spain: Ministerio de Asuntos Exteriores; Agencia Española de Cooperación Internacional, 2007. 488 p.: bibl., ill. (Coediciones; 64)

Twenty anthropologists, historians, and sociologists from 10 European and American countries present perspectives on death in the Americas. Typical is Brandes' chapter, "Mexican Visions of the Dead," where Mexican's contradictory relationships with death are unearthed from scarce ethnographic description and analysis, showing strong emotions of immediate family mediated by community members set on distracting mourners with ceremony and celebration (which in many indigenous cultures derives from social concern that excessive mourning may inhibit the departure of the defunct soul, who may pause to take one or more of the most aggrieved along for company). In contrast to intimate indigenous ethnography, the nationalist, artistic, and touristic fascination with death imagery becomes another subject of discussion. Humberto Ruz captures the depth of Maya understandings for the idea that the dead share time with the living, but not space, creating a discontinuously continuous community where the dead are nowhere and ever-present. This other presence has real impacts on life, just as all of the nonordinary often impinges on the quotidian in this worldview. Death and the dead are distinct. For the individual there is disconsolation, but for the community, a delicate rite of passage placating the newly dead to assure the fecund seeds of future children and plants. The imbrications of life and death domains make this eclectic collection come alive in its treatment of diverse times, peoples, and locations in the Americas.

467 **French, Brigittine M.** Maya ethnolinguistic identity: violence, cultural rights, and modernity in highland Guatemala. Tucson: The Univ. of Arizona Press, 2010. 161 p.: bibl., index.

Critical theory approach to social meanings of language politics in Guatemala, with a focus on K'iche' and Kaqchikel. Decries the state's essentially nationalist project of multiculturalism, and how language and identity labeling serve the interests of power. Shows how acculturation to urban settlements dovetails with ideological notions of modernity and backwardness, past and present, and other dichotomies that reduce and obscure ethnic heterogeneity, both an ongoing national project and ironically, a project of pan-Mayanist revitalization by an educated minority. The latter have lost touch with *municipio* community identity, historically the unit of both identity and resistance to the state, and have been caught up in modernist ("linguistic science") projects conflating homogenized language with imagined collective identity.

468 **Galinier, Jacques.** El espejo otomí: de la etnografía a la antropología psicoanalítica. México: Centro de Estudios Mexicanos y Centroamericanos: Comisión Nacional para el Desarrollo de los Pueblos Indígenas: Instituto Nacional de Antropología e Historia, 2009. 214 p.: bibl., ill., map. (Col. Etnografía de los pueblos indígenas de México. Serie Estudios monográficos)

Based on over 40 years of ethnographic inquiry among the Otomi of the southern Huasteca, this book approaches the Otomi by way of perceptions and conceptions of the body, expressed in internal and external dimensions of ritual practice. The anthropologist utilizes Freud in contrast with Otomi epistemology, and identifies a level of Mesoamerican logic behind the many changes in social affiliation and economic arrangements of the globalized era the Otomi live at the edge of today. The evidence of fieldwork shows in the depth of local understanding and analysis. He discovers that the Otomis, like many Mesoamericans, entertain a certainty of a larger unseen world for which dreams provide entry and "signposts"—making their relationship to dreams distinct from western psychotherapeutic ones, and clashing with the epistemic claims to an empirical normal waking state as "the real."

469 **García Vettorazzi, María Victoria.** Escala y territorios del comercio k'iche': una mirada desde San Francisco El Alto, Totonicapán, 1930–1970. Ciudad de

Guatemala: AVANCSO, 2009. 84 p.: bibl., ill., maps (some col.). (Textos para debate; 22)

A study of the commercial activities of a K'iche' town in Guatemala, San Francisco El Alto, which, by contrast with most adjacent Maya villages, is not made of peasant agriculturalists, but those engaged in small and large scale commerce, some international in scope. The region, which has a comparatively high level of commercial activity and strong indigenous control of local politics, also suffered far less political violence during the 1980s than other areas. This small book explores the notion of scale to suggest that the region has established a sufficient sociogeographic space to resist the impositions of alien systems of power and commerce.

470 **Goldin, Liliana R.** Global Maya: work and ideology in rural Guatemala. Tucson: Univ. of Arizona Press, 2009. 242 p.: bibl., ill., index.

Based on four revealing case studies of forms of work (cottage garment production, direct marketing and export production of vegetables, and factory wage-labor) Golden's careful study elucidates the linkages between local highland Maya communities and global economic forces, both the economic data and the evolving ideologies and local values that arise in distinct economic roles, and across age and gender differences. A vital contribution to understanding class formation and how it creates shifts in attitude, identity, and social distribution. A compelling case for identity chasing work.

471 **González Martínez, Joaquín Roberto.** La historia vivida en las representaciones espaciales: la conformación del espacio Tzeltal-Tzotzil: ensayo de aproximación geoetnográfica. Veracruz, Mexico: Instituto Veracruzano de la Cultura, 2008. 223 p.: bibl., ill. (some col.), maps, plates. (Col. Atarazanas)

Based on work done in the early 1970s, and part of a geography doctoral thesis completed in 1992, the author weaves together Borgia Group codices, ethnohistoric sources, and ethnographic material from Tzotzils and Tzeltals collected by US anthropologists 30–40 years ago, to outline a thesis about the layout of Mesoamerican sacred space and its significance. The book contains imagery and analysis of these sources. Focuses on duality, four-sided spaces with a central axis, and other spatial patterns that typify Mesoamerica.

472 **Guzmán Mejía, Rafael and María del Carmen Anaya Corona.** Cultura de maíz-peyote-venado: sustentabilidad del pueblo wixarika. Tepatitlán de Morelos, Mexico: Univ. de Guadalajara, Centro Univ. de Los Altos, 2007. 448 p.: bibl., ill. (1 col.), maps.

The book condenses 10 years of study and five of field ethnography by the authors among the Wixarika, better known as the well-studied Huichol of west-central Mexico (Jalisco). As the title suggests, maize, the deer, and peyote, representing their subsistence farming, their history as hunters, and their pilgrimage of psycho-spiritual self-discovery and cultural intensification, provide the conceptual trinity of their identity. Guzmán grew up in rural coastal Jalisco, and the authors take up and critique previous scholars' work and provide their insights and corrections. Integrates cultural ecology, gender analysis, questions of sustainability, and personal and collective identity, as well as numerous explorations into spiritual practices, landscapes, and beliefs.

473 **Hanks, William F.** Converting words: Maya in the age of the cross. Berkeley: Univ. of California Press, 2010. 439 p.: bibl., ill., index. (The anthropology of Christianity; 6)

A deep exploration of a colonial religious project with the Yucatec Maya, especially *reducción*, to chart its contribution to speaking, text-making, and spiritual verbal practice today. Hanks combines linguistics, ethnohistory, and participatory ethnography to show the profound colonial roots of the current indigenous language-expressed culture of Yucatán—and thus serves as a historical interrogation of syncretism. Hanks attempts to clarify the complexities of this strategic melding, as the early language transformations of Franciscan and other Church and governmental efforts (appropriating the Maya language) in turn led to a reappropriation of the enemy by the Maya themselves, a creativity far from notions of idols behind altars. Much as there is a novel recent appropriation of anthropological texts by "spiritual" Guatemalan Maya to legitimate and empower their cultural resistance, likewise earlier centuries of Maya in Yucatán made similar creative hybrids, often later mistaken for a more frozen authenticity. Hanks' control of early religious and other texts—dictionaries, language *artes*, prayer texts, catechisms, and the later Maya texts like the Chilam Balam—is prodigious, and we can hope, as he does, that scholars will look at Yucatec Spanish for its side of this language co-evolution.

474 Hart, Thomas. The ancient spirituality of the modern Maya. Albuquerque: Univ. of New Mexico Press, 2008. 270 p.: bibl., ill., index, plates.

A faithful effort to represent a cross-section of practitioners in the western highland Guatemalan indigenous calendar divining tradition, and generalizations about their worldview—one that has come to be known in recent years as "Maya spirituality"—by a lay author with personal experience and involvement. Hart arranges numerous Maya texts in emergent categories of mostly K'iche' and Mam theology, regarding such areas of spiritual concern as concepts of the holy, time, healing and curing, sacred spaces, earth spirits, dreams, animal signs, and death. Attempts to place the growing priestly Maya movement in the context of recent and ancient history, and less so with the pre-1980s period, before most day-keeper Mayas were literate, and their tradition impacted by exposure to the Popol Vuh and anthropological writings. Ideal holistic introduction to this complex system of faith and worldview, and valuable corpus of texts (only in translation, however) that will speak beyond the presented analysis for current and future scholars.

475 Jung, Courtney. The moral force of indigenous politics: critical liberalism and the Zapatistas. Cambridge, England; New York, N.Y.: Cambridge Univ. Press, 2008. 350 p.: bibl., ill., index, maps. (Contemporary political theory)

Discusses the turn from class towards indigenousness as a moral and politically tenable basis of rural demands on the state in parts of Latin America, and especially Mexico, in the wake of the Zapatista uprising and its morphing to indigenous rights

champion. Notes that the uprising had a major impact on the state and the continent in terms of legislated rights and incipient recognition of land claims and autonomy. Debates whether indigenous rights turn on the status of class and the ability of the state to manage and control indigenous cultural rights claims without a threat to power or advancement of claims to redistributive justice. Jung deepens this discussion by recognizing a power in indigenous politics, despite its contradictions and vulnerabilities. Author believes the ultimate test of cultural rights would be to challenge neoliberalism in response to its proposed Plan Puebla-Panamá, a huge commercial and factory corridor.

476 Knowlton, Timothy W. Maya creation myths: words and worlds of the Chilam Balam. Boulder: Univ. Press of Colorado, 2010. 231 p.: bibl., index. (Mesoamerican worlds: from the Olmecs to the Danzantes)

Grounded in a dialogical theory of language in approaching the Chilam Balam corpus, this work offers a close reading of the 17th-century iterations of ancient Maya myths of creation. The Chilam Balam reflects the strong influences of Christianity and puts forth strong Maya counterpoints. The basic premise is that documents like the Chilam Balam of Chumayel must be read as intense theological dialog with the invading culture and its religious missionaries, with intent to create a synthesis that ultimately preserves Maya intellectual culture within the medium of colonial Yucatec society. Envisions Mesoamerican and Maya metaphysics in terms of correlative monism (coordinating calendars) and complementary dualism (unities composed of contrastive pairs, or "diphrastic kenning"), which the author oddly views as new to Maya interpretation, but which has appeared for decades in the work of Carmack, Earle, and others, in ethnohistory and ethnography. These two concepts frame his fresh readings of these difficult texts. For archeologist's comment, see item **228**.

477 Konefal, Betsy. For every indio who falls: a history of Maya activism in Guatemala, 1960–1990. Albuquerque: Univ. of New Mexico Press, 2010. 247 p.: bibl., index.

Important contribution to our understanding of the 40-year evolution of Maya social movements, bridging the borderlands between pre- and postgenocidal Guatemala, and drawing linkages between the agrarian and indigenous organizational struggles that arose in the 1970s and the more recent cultural rights movement. Captures the complexity of positions toward state repression as selective killings of community, labor, and cooperative leaders shifted to massive, village-wide ones. Attention given to armed resistance, the role of the activist Catholic Church in promoting pan-Mayanism over village traditions, and the military counterinsurgency strategy motivated by threats of alliance between armed left and indigenous rights groups. Exacting detailing of guerrilla groups and less-studied Maya-only revolutionaries and their struggles with ethnicity and class, respectively—foreshadowing Maya cultural (but not class) movement.

478   Kraemer Bayer, Gabriela. Autonomía de los zapotecos del Istmo: relaciones de poder y cultura política. Chapingo, Mexico: Univ. Autónoma Chapingo: Consejo Nacional de Ciencia y Tecnología: Plaza y Valdés, 2008. 224 p.: bibl., ill.

Retrospective on Isthmus Zapotec movement COCEI, that took power in the region over three decades ago, and which has since lost strength and is now in decline. The Isthmus of Tehuantepec is a strategic and complex zone, and this study explains the trajectory of the Zapotec sociopolitical movement in terms of changing political forces and trends. Offers interesting contrasts with more recent, explicitly indigenous rights movements; the author is concerned with the issue of political and cultural autonomy of indigenous peoples and their evolving relations to the state. A vital window into the complexity of indigenous appropriations of politics and the responses of the region and state, as well as how this dynamic has evolved.

479   Lastra de Suárez, Yolanda; Dina Sherzer; and **Joel Sherzer.** Adoring the saints: fiestas in central Mexico. Austin: Univ. of Texas Press, 2009. 211 p.: bibl., index. (The William & Bettye Nowlin series in art, history, and culture of the Western hemisphere)

Explores in depth the patron saint festivals in two ethnically distinct but historically linked towns near San Miguel de Allende, Mexico. Attention is given to performance—". . . the dynamism and creativity of patron saint fiestas, their visual, aural, kinetic and verbal features. . ." (p. 3)—so as to bring readers close to the action and to the meanings generated, and tie the activities to their larger social and cultural significance. Good exposure to multiple scholarly perspectives on patron saint festivals and the complexity of the subject; an excellent guide for interpreting many typical fiesta practices in a comparative, contextualized light.

480   Lenkersdorf, Carlos. Aprender a escuchar: enseñanzas maya-tojolabales. México: Plaza y Valdés, 2008. 165 p.: bibl.

Approaches differences in social interaction based on a linguistic assessment of the language of interaction in Tojolabal, Maya, as spoken in Chiapas, Mexico. The "I said, you listened" or I-thou understanding embedded in the language is contrasted with "I tell you" constructions of occidental languages to access understandings of Tojolabal ways of being and thinking, which the author claims are more dialogical. Provides a crosscultural comparison of approaches to listening. Especially moving is the discussion of listening to nature and the land and its relevance to current issues of land, free trade, and national agricultural economics, as raised by the Chiapas rebellion of 1994, and as relates to subjectivities in the linkages of land and identity.

481   Liffman, Paul M. Huichol territory and the Mexican nation: indigenous ritual, land conflict, and sovereignty claims. Tucson: Univ. of Arizona Press, 2011. 278 p.: bibl., ill., index, maps, photos.

Author studies the Huichol to learn and document "cultural grounds for territorial claims" and discovers how hierarchies of rituals across large spaces result in an ideological basis for confronting the state over land and agrarian/indigenous rights. Taking a multiperspective approach provided by fieldwork, the author frames Huichol knowledge about their perceived territory in relation to ritual, violence, the state, and global forces. Each chapter has local, national, and global armatures, from ranchos and forest fires to narcoviolence to indigeneity; the book serves as a toolkit for a critique of conventional land rights and a rethinking of native sense of place.

482 Lizama Quijano, Jesús. Estar en el mundo: procesos culturales, estrategias económicas y dinámicas identitarias entre los mayas yucatecos. México: Centro de Investigaciones y Estudios Superiores en Antropología Social: Miguel Angel Porrúa, 2007. 212 p.: bibl., ill. (Col. Peninsular. Serie Estudios)

Ethnography of Yucatec Mayas, their traditions, identity, daily life, and cultural recreations, in the shadow of globalizing forces and pressures of contemporary Mexico. Maintains that the Yucatec Mayas' historical need to accommodate prior invasions and alien work regimes contribute to their abilities to adjust to new conditions today. The study looks at three Maya villages for rich controlled comparisons.

483 Lyon, Sarah. Coffee and community: Maya farmers and fair-trade markets. Boulder: Univ. Press of Colorado, 2010. 266 p.: bibl., index, photos.

Critical ethnographic examination of fair trade coffee production and marketing in San Juan La Laguna. Looks at commodity chains, concluding that the fair trade approach is often flawed, and provides insights into how to fix the process. Explores added value of fair trade just production in theory and application, noting many problems with certification processes. Points out the structural substitution of imagined fair production sites with real relationships of solidarity with equitable conditions, financial outcomes, and distribution of opportunity. Insightful case study of cultural, social, and other challenges of global fair trade marketing.

484 Mace, Carroll Edward. Los negritos de Rabinal y el juego del tun. Guatemala: Academia de Geografía e Historia de Guatemala, 2008. 352 p.: bibl., ill., index, maps. (Publicación Especial; 44)

Revisits the ethnographic work of Mace from 1957–85 in Rabinal, an Achi/K'iche' municipality in the department of Baja Verapaz, Guatemala, with a strong focus on their dance traditions. Studies of this period, from the 1950s to the start of the violence of the 1980s, are of great value due to the tremendous change since then, and the renewed, post-peace accords interest in cultural recuperation by activist Mayas. This book represents information, most of it heretofore unpublished, that documents the work of an ethnographer's lifetime, evidenced by his deep knowledge of the subject and his comparative understandings based in wide-ranging Mesoamerican scholarship. Enhanced by entire librettos of dances and their analysis and the comparisons made over more than a generation of cultural evolution. For historian's comment, see *HLAS 66:3339.*

485 Martín, Kathleen Rock. Discarded pages: Araceli Cab Cumí, Maya poet and politician. Albuquerque: Univ. of New Mexico Press, 2007. 312 p.: bibl., ill., index.

A biography of a complex politician, poet, and essayist arising from Maxcanu', Yucatán, as chronicled by the author with extensive texts from Cab Cumi. Well known locally as the first Maya woman state senator; less known are her more creative writings, indexed here. Of special interest regarding rights and voices of indigenous women, connecting political action with organic feminist poetic expression. For literature specialist's comment, see *HLAS 66:3225.*

486 Martínez Casas, Regina. Vivir invisibles: la resignificación cultural entre los otomíes urbanos de Guadalajara. México: CIESAS, 2007. 290 p.: bibl., ill., maps. (Publicaciones de la Casa Chata)

This sociolinguistic ethnographic study captures the complexities of relations between the urban Otomi peoples (in Guadalajara, Mexico) and their rural homeland community, as migrant urban adaptations require both maintenance and modifications of home culture, which in turn impact the sending *municipio.* The author elaborates an Otomi moral space that distributes necessarily across geography with migration, creating "resignifications" in new settings, but also remaining part of the Otomi resistant identity. Shows how anchor communities provide identity lifelines for the challenges of intercultural asymmetries of their urban migrants.

487 Martínez Veloz, Jaime. Chiapas: la paz inconclusa: —había una vez una COCOPA. México: Gernika, 2007. 295 p.: bibl., ill.

Insider chronicle of COCOPA, the Mexican organization mediating a peace accord between the Mexican government and the Zapatistas. As the San Andrés accords ratification broke down, the COCOPA disbanded. Takes the position that Mexico still needs the work initiated by COCOPA to resolve smoldering problems that were shelved when the accords language was undermined, for example, to establish legislation agreeable to the movement, and to solidify a mutually binding accord. Without these developments, the author maintains, there will never be peace in Chiapas.

488 Masferrer Kan, Elio. Los dueños del tiempo: los tutunakú (totonacos) de la Sierra Norte de Puebla. México: Fundación Juan Rulfo, AC, 2009. 319 p.: bibl., ill., maps.

A synthesis of 30 years of research on the Tutunakú (Totonac) of the Sierra Norte in the state of Puebla, Mexico, the work places this large ethnic group in regional context in Aztec times, then brings them through the colonial era, ending with an in-depth ethnographic rendering of the current indigenous people and their larger socioeconomic and political context, both with urban society and with neighbor Otomis and Nahuas. The author's approach to ethnicity and ethnic identity involves examining past and present relations with other ethnic groups. Compares coffee and maize to other rural agricultural production, and demonstrates how the control of agricultural commercialization is a basic political issue up to recent times. Charts the growing engagement by rural indigenous farmers in labor/producer organizations and migration, and describes the political shifts up to current times.

489 Masson, Sabine *et al.* Tzome Ixuk: una historia de mujeres tojolabales en lucha: etnografía de una cooperativa en el contexto de los movimientos sociales en Chiapas. México: Plaza y Valdés, 2008. 214 p.: bibl. (Ciencias Sociales)

Study of Las Margaritas, Chiapas, indigenous Tojolabal Maya women's cooperative. Offers an important contribution to understanding the sociopolitical space opened up by the Zapatista uprising for new, empowered forms of indigenous and women's organizing, as exemplified by the women's cooperative and, later, a center for battered women. The book follows the experiences of the women of the entire Tojolabal community in four temporal stages: life on the old fincas, life as a migrant to a small town urban barrio, the making of the cooperative (the focus of the book), and finally the women's center. Shows the impact of Catholic social organizing and feminist and indigenous rights ideas in the wake of national, regional, and global responses to Chiapas' indigenous peoples' plight, revolt, and demands. Good case study for the larger trend in indigenous empowerment through organization and faith.

490 Memorias rebeldes contra el olvido = Paasantzila txumb'al ti' sotzeb' al k'u'l. Investigación de Rosalinda Hernández Alarcón *et al.* Guatemala: Cuerda: Plataforma Agraria: AVANCSO, Associación para el Avance de las Ciencias Sociales en Guatemala, 2008. 122 p.: bibl., col. ill., col. maps.

A touching and earnest account by Ixil Maya women who were for a time part of the Guatemalan armed rebels in northern Quiche province. These ex-combantant indigenous women suffered greatly in multiple dimensions, first because they did not have adequate support with the EGP guerrillas, and their efforts to get food from the local Ixil led the military to forcibly displace them, and then because they were not included during the demobilization process. Already marginalized by their status as indigenous, rural, and female, they were not informed about the demobilization supports of the Peace Accords, and many remained out of sight for years. Finally in 1999, 600 women formed an organization to share their experiences and this effort, with the help of AVANSCO, led to this publication. Heartrending tales of remembrance that revivify indigenous women's desire to maintain a critical perspective and "imagine another reality" in their collective future.

491 Mendoza Castelán, Guillermo. Medicina tradicional y plantas medicinales en México. Chapingo, Mexico: Univ.

Autónoma Chapingo, Depto. de Fitotecnia, Programa Univ. de Medicina Tradicional y Terapéutica Naturista, 2007. 640 p.: bibl.

A large and thorough treatment of the subject of traditional medical practices in indigenous and mestizo communities, especially as tied to curative plants. Begins with pre-European period and what is known about healers and plants from that time, then weaves in European influences and their diseases, how 20th-century traditional healers are trained, specializations of some indigenous healers (Nahua, Maya, Huichol, Raramuri), division of healing labors (spiritual curing, midwifery, bone setting, pulsing, rubbing, etc.), nahualism and the use of psychotropics, use of the sweat bath, minerals, maize, animals, and most important, a cornucopia of plants, including a section on the therapeutic bases of many medicinal plants, and the variations in nature that effect their potency.

492 Merino Rascón, Miguel. Consejo Supremo Tarahumara: organización y resistencia indígena, 1939–2005. Chihuahua, Mexico: Doble Hélice Ediciones: Culturas Populares e Indígenas, Unidad Regional, Chihuahua: Instituto Chihuahuense de la Cultura, 2007. 140 p.: ill. (Col. Chihuahua y sus regiones. Serie Historiografía)

Indigenous author chronicles the life and struggles of the Council of the Tarahumara (Raramuri), a political organization representing indigenous interests (with reference to similar organizations for the Pima, Tepehuano, and Guarojio groups of northern Mexico). Provides fascinating early accounts of the founding and functioning of the council in the 1930s, a second epoch in the 1950s, and a third in the 1960s and 70s. The book outlines the council's decline when it shifted to a PRI-sponsored national organization in the late 1980s, as part of the state's effort to control indigenous organizations, and its revival efforts in the 1990s. Insider account of 65 years of efforts at indigenous organizing and political action.

493 Metz, Brent E.; Cameron L. McNeil; and **Kerry M. Hull.** The Ch'orti' Maya area: past and present. Gainesville: Univ. Press of Florida, 2009. 346 p.: bibl., ill., index, maps.

A benchmark collection of articles capturing Chorti culture, language, and history, in some cases integrating archeological, linguistic, and ethnographic analysis, exploring numerous dimensions of this neglected and vitally important side of the Maya family. Timely, in conjunction with Chorti revitalization emerging adjacent to Copán ruins, and synergistic balance of information and focus—from their central role in the rise of the Classic Maya (most glyphs are in Ch'olti'an), their migration to Copán, Camotán, and Zapotitlán; the insights in ethnographic analogy for evolution in the colonial period, ancient identity, and art; to their current efforts to retake their identity. Coyote and Rabbit tales, dual-gendered supernaturals, plant lore keepers, health behavior, tourism and Copán, and indigenous resistance to a famine in 2001 are among the topics covered. Clear prose, extensive citations and references, and solid editing. Includes a fascinating, ethnographically grounded discussion of identity, modernization, language loss and retention, and the relationship of culture to types of indigenousness. For archeologist's comment, see item **170**.

494 Morales Sic, José Roberto. Religión y política: el proceso de institucionalización de la espiritualidad en el movimiento maya guatemalteco. Guatemala: Postgrado Centroamericano, FLACSO: Editorial de Ciencias Sociales, 2007. 148 p.: bibl., ill. (Col. Cuadernos de maestría)

Guatemalan study addressing the Maya resistance practices of appropriating and transforming imposed Catholic religion by cloaking their older tradition with new garments over centuries of conquest and resistance. Maya religious "costumbre," once largely clandestine or hidden within public rituals—with an opaque Catholic veneer—was not seen in public spheres beyond the centers of remote Maya towns. Since the Peace Accords have given rights to Maya religion by statute, an emergent movement of Maya religion that has departed from the prior hidden tradition has flourished, and has purged its liturgy of Christian references to creatively repopulate it with Popol Vuh characters and those of archeologists' and cultural anthropologists' writings—a more urbanized revitalization movement seeking authenticity and fidelity to imagined ancient Mayas. This movement, distinct from the traditionalist one that continues on in older people and more remote communities, and alien to Catholic community-based movements, is based more on literacy and inter-ethnic encounters and the political implications for the nation-state of indigenous multiculturalism, and has emerged as a new political player on the Guatemalan social landscape. The members of the movement perform sanctifying rituals at major archeological tourist sites, making their voices heard in national dialog about educational and other social policies. Other efforts at promotion of a politics of Maya culture in Guatemala and globally have borne fruit, while raising many contradictions.

495 Navarrete, Carlos. Rosario Castellanos: su presencia en la antropología mexicana. México: UNAM, Instituto de Investigaciones Antropológicas; San Cristóbal de las Casas, Mexico: PROIMMSE, Programa de Investigaciones Multidisciplinarios sobre Mesoamérica y el Sureste, 2007. 191 p.: bibl., ill.

Publication of versions of works first presented in 1986 and 1987 by Navarrete, reflecting on the involvement of the famous Mexican writer in a Chiapas project (1955–58) as a promoter and designer of cultural activities for the Instituto de Artes y Ciencias de Chiapas, and as an education program coordinator for the INI in San Cristóbal, introduced there by Dr. Alfonso Caso, then its director, to the Centro Coordinador Indigenista Tzeltal-Tzotzil. There Castellanos developed a popular puppet theater (*guinol*), with an indigenous "star" whose clothing and dialect shifted with the village, and with plots based in local hierarchies and issues. The book presents an anthology of these puppet shows, combining messages about development, education, and sanitation with historical and mythic content, even a representation of a tourist, along with some other writings that situate Castellanos in her time and anthropological surroundings.

496 New world of indigenous resistance: Noam Chomsky and voices from North, South, and Central America. Edited by Lois Meyer and Benjamín Maldonado Alvarado. San Francisco, Calif.: City Lights Books, 2010. 416 p.: bibl., index. (Open media series)

Creative effort to publish a conversation in book format, based on several interviews with Noam Chomsky, followed by commentaries by eight Mexican, three Guatemalans, a Panamanian, two Ecuadorians, two Peruvians, two Bolivians, an Argentinian, a Uruguayan, and one voice from the US (both specialists and activists) with a follow-up interview with Chomsky and two more commentaries. Examines the political significance of indigenous movements and voices and views in the hemisphere. Discusses learning and knowledge formation as a critique of occidental education-as-domination. Zapatista epistemic and political critique weaves through many contributions, calling for a world in which many worlds fit.

497 Noh Cuxim, Israel et al. — y me lo contó mi abuelita: identidad y cultura popular e indígena. Coordinación de Marco Antonio Anaya Pérez et al. Chapingo, Mexico: Univ. Autónoma Chapingo, 2004. 206 p.: bibl., ill. (Identidad y Cultura Popular e Indígena; 2)

Broad collection of 18 articles gathered by the Universidad Autónoma Chapingo, written by students about their own communities, indigenous and mestizo. Sections include traditional technologies and cultivars, traditional medicine, medicinal plants, the steam bath (*temazcal*), daily life and customs, traditional fiestas, myths and legends, historical memory, and traditions and daily life of Chapingo. Other regions represented include Yucatán, Oaxaca, Hidalgo, Veracruz, México state, Puebla, and Michoacán, with Oaxaca having the most entries.

498 Noyola, Antonio. En busca del jícuri: el peyote en la Tarahumara. México: Consejo Nacional para la Cultura y las Artes: Ceiba Arte Editorial, 2008. 145 p.: bibl. (Col. Crónicas de viajeros)

Cinematographer's narrative of his movement through social and sacred space in the land of the Raramuri (in the Sierra Tarahumara of the state of Chihuahua, Mexico). Wonderfully written descriptions of place and scene. Some of his encounters with the Raramuri (significantly he calls them by their old name of Tarahumaras) are difficult for trained ethnographers to read given that he demonstrates the unself-conscious sort of ethnocentric interactions with marked insensitivity to local patterns of behavior. Nevertheless the text allows the reader to take a fascinating ride into the Sierra in search of the sacred medicine, peyote.

499 Núñez Rodríguez, Carlos Juan. La marcha de la dignidad indígena como búsqueda de la autonomía. México: Plaza y Valdés, 2008. 239 p.: bibl.

Using the Zapatista communiques and their 2001 march to the capital as central sources of analysis, this work engages an ethico-hermeneutic analysis of the texts associated with the march to outline a different sort of politics, based in dignity, respect, autonomy, and concepts of indigeneity, and placed in powerful symbolic webs of Mexican history. Part of a large corpus of work dedicated to assessing the contributions of Zapatista political concepts and discourse to political and social theory. Much of it is metatheoretical considerations of Marcos' understandings of this total social movement, reflecting numerous indigenous concepts that locate and decenter power and decry Mexico's history of prejudice in ways unlike the discourses of the West.

500 Olavarría, María Eugenia; Cristina Aguilar Rivas; and Erica Merino. El cuerpo flor: etnografía de una noción yoeme. México: Univ. Autónoma Metropolitana, Unidad Iztapalapa: M.Á. Porrúa, 2009. 249 p.: bibl., ill. (Las Ciencias Sociales. Tercera Década)

An ethnographic exploration into the Yaqui (Yoeme) culture by way of the body and its principle metaphor and symbol, the flower. The book elaborates an anthropologist's interpretation of the Yaqui theory of the body, disease, and wellness, tied to healing arts and curanderos, and then brings Yaqui voices into the text. Six chapters start with an emic description of the yoeme body, its parts and functions, ties it to myth and notions of gender and the hot/cold dyad. This section is followed by a discussion of

their view of body, the soul, and in some, the "body flower", and a chapter on the life cycle. The therapeutic discourse of the curer, linking the reciprocal obligations accruing to the calling (Don), is also mentioned. The next section looks at witchcraft, via look, feel, language, food, contact, more. The final section compares the Yaqui system and allopathic healing to grasp the dynamic of inter-ethnic dialog.

501 Palerm, Angel. Agua y agricultura: Ángel Palerm, la discusión con Karl Wittfogel sobre el modo asiático de producción y la construcción de un modelo para el estudio de Mesoamérica. Prólogo de Juan Maestre Alfonso. Estudio introductorio y notas de Alba González Jácome. México: Univ. Iberoamericana: Agencia Española de Cooperación Internacional, Dirección General de Relaciones Culturales y Científicas, 2007. 135 p.: bibl.

The subtitle of this collection sums up its intent. With a prologue and an introduction to set up the texts, the book presents four related pieces collectively called, "A Defense of the Asiatic Mode of Production according to Marx and Wittfogel" by the late Dr. Palerm, an influential scholar on the rise of states and hydraulic systems of agriculture. His work informs some models of the rise of states in precontact Mesoamerica.

502 Pérez Lugo, Luis. Tridimensión cósmica otomí: aportes al conocimiento de su cultura. Chapingo, Mexico: Univ. Autónoma de Chapingo/Plaza y Valdés, S.A. de C.V., 2007. 173 p.: bibl.

An ethnographic study to challenge the hegemony of cultural interpretation of Mesoamericans derived from the dualism of the Aztecs, maintaining that Otomi cultures are better understood in the frame of triads, not dualities. These triads are exemplified by mother-father-child, sun-fire-lightning, hot-cold-cool, cosmos-Earth-humanity, among others. Also elaborates other central ideas, such as the skin being like the earth surface, the body as a model for/of the earth, maize, and the tree, where the symbolizing of the material world is also clustered in threes. Presents an Otomi cultural logic that contrasts robustly with other systems of thinking from the West.

503 Pitarch Ramón, Pedro. The jaguar and the priest: an ethnography of Tzeltal souls. Austin: Univ. of Texas Press, 2010. 251 p.: bibl., index. (The Linda Schele series in Maya and pre-Columbian studies)

A lasting Chiapas ethnography explores the complex, multifaceted Tzeltal (Cancuc) soul, as a window into Maya views of history, culture, and community, identity and identities of others in their social landscape. The study touches on shamanism, sacred geography, politics, cosmology, kinship, religion, and other subjects to rethink many Mesoamerican concepts and approaches to ethnographic scholarship. The detailed rendering and interpretation of healing chants, a complex analysis of saints, and many other elements in traditional Tzeltal life, along with the author's mastery of the subtleties of the language, enrich the work.

504 Portal, María Ana and Xóchitl Ramírez. Alteridad e identidad: un recorrido por la historia de la antropología en México. México: Univ. Autónoma Metropolitana, Unidad Iztapalapa: Juan Pablos Editor, 2010. 291 p.: bibl. (Biblioteca de alteridades; 13)

This book serves as a textbook to teach university-level students about the history of the field of anthropology in Mexico and what Mexican anthropologists and others have contributed to our understandings of Mexico. It also serves a theoretical function to reflect on the historical construction of a national identity, with the indigenous subaltern as a central and contradictory element in this construct, reviewing specifically the role of anthropology in this nationalist project. Explores the decline of Marxist analysis in the face of new interest in identity and the political implications of indigenous movements like the Zapatistas, and the rise in recent years of team-based, regional, and interdisciplinary studies. For philosophy specialist's comment on an earlier version of this work, see *HLAS 58:5096.*

505 Presencia de José Lameiras en la antropología mexicana. Edición de José Eduardo Zárate Hernández. Zamora, Mexico: Colegio de Michoacán, 2008. 154 p.: bibl., ill., index, ports. (Col. Testimonios)

Collection of nine articles (plus one by Lameiras, a biography, and bibliography) focused on the anthropological contributions of Pepe Lameiras, teacher of generations of anthropologists in Mexico, passionate scholar, and an early proponent of the importance of identity as a social concept. These contributions suggest, however, that Lameiras was above all else an anthropologist of Mexican anthropology itself. Consistent with Mexican notions of applying anthropology, he applied himself to building an architecture and culture of Mexican anthropology and documenting it as a project for the group he most identified with—anthropologists.

506 El pueblo nahua de Ayotitlán: pasado, presente y perspectiva. Textos de Carlos Lucio *et al.* Guadalajara, Mexico: Univ. de Guadalajara: Unidad de Apoyo a las Comunidades Indígenas: Taller Editorial La Casa del Mago, 2008. 113 p.: bibl., ill., maps. (Col. El revés de la trama)

Brings together six articles about the Nahua-speaking indigenous community of Ayotitlán, located on the border between the Mexican states of Colima and Jalisco. Documents the multigenerational struggle in which there are, as outside players in the story, an agrarian reform petition from 1921 that is still clouded and contested—and delayed for decades to accommodate illegal logging; a general seeking to take away a large tract of protected land for lumber exploitation; a transnational mining company and its nefarious agents grabbing copper deposits; a biospheric reserve imposed by the Mexican government; and internal strife between traditional and constitutional authorities. The backdrop for this activity is the Nahua community which continues to carry on its ceremonies, its mayordomia cargos, and its culture (which itself is contested).

507 Los pueblos indígenas de Chiapas: atlas etnográfico. Coordinación de Margarita Nolasco Armas *et al.* México: Instituto Nacional de Antropología e Historia, 2008. 421 p.: bibl., ill. (some col.), col. maps.

With some 50 different articles coordinated into themes, this is one of a series of ethnographic atlases produced by Mexico in recent years. The themes include basic history and current conditions, "Man, Land and Environment," social organization, indigenous social movements, cosmovisions, art, health and illness, religious diversity, indigenous normative systems (such as rights), and migration—to, from, and within Chiapas—as there have been many displaced groups due to religious and political conflicts. Richly illustrated with photographs (current and archival), maps, charts, and other graphics of high quality and attractive layout.

508 Los pueblos indígenas de Chiapas: la respuesta está en el aire, y los avatares del siglo XXI la guiarán: Margarita Nolasco, un homenaje. Coordinación de Javier Gutiérrez Sánchez y Hadlyyn Cuadriello Olivos. Tlapan, Mexico: Escuela Nacional de Antropología e Historia; México: Instituto Nacional de Antropología e Historia, 2010. 241 p.: bibl. (Investigación/Proa)

Posthumous publication of the two final major articles by noted Mexican anthropologist Nolasco, along with contributions from five members of her southern borderlands research team. Nolasco's first piece summarizes the state of indigenous peoples of Mexico, tracing their history of labor exploitation to their political re-emergence, especially after the Zapatista uprising, undoing the assimilationist national project. Using demographic analysis she shows indigenous populations growing and moving and one that mirrors the population at contact. She also interrogates rights claims between individuals and groups and underlines Zapatista right to dignity, an individual right not considered by the state. The second contribution along with the others cover typical Chiapas topics, such as work, women, identity, Liberation Theology as locally adopted, and organic coffee raising in the Soconusco.

509 Los pueblos indígenas de Puebla: atlas etnográfico. Coordinación de Elio Masferrer Kan, Jaime Mondragón y Georgina Vences. Puebla de Zaragoza, Mexico: Gobierno del Estado de Puebla; México: Instituto Nacional de Antropología e Historia, 2010. 470 p.: bibl., ill. (some col.), col. maps. (Divulgación)

Lush atlas of the Mexican state of Puebla, organized into sections, each with 2–5 articles addressing loosely related subjects including ethnohistory, ethnography, religious practice and belief, languages and education, social organization, migration, healing, music, and craft production. A multitude of maps, graphics, and charts decorate the book, covering ethnicity, language, agrosystems and production, types of vegetation, education, socioeconomic status, and much more. Archival b/w photographs complement the current photography and graphics, and the text engages the reader. Graphics such as the calendar of Puebla state festivals and their village locations are invaluable to those wishing to visit the area.

510 Los pueblos indígenas de Veracruz: atlas etnográfico. Coordinación de Enrique Hugo García Valencia y Iván Romero Redondo. Jalapa Enríquez, Mexico: Gobierno del Estado de Veracruz; México: Instituto Nacional de Antropología e Historia, 2009. 335 p.: bibl., ill. (some col.), col. maps. (Divulgación)

Nearly 50 articles and section introductions are complemented by lavish geographic, ethnic, linguistic, social maps (even an indigenous festivity map), of Veracruz state in Mexico, with active and descriptive photography, clear facsimile codices and lienzos, and charts cross-referencing town and ethnic groups with percentages of different religious affiliations. Includes sharp graphics of relative access to education, access by gender, maps of distribution of political party, historical revolts, etc. Good coverage of indigenous groups including Huastec, Nahua, Otomi, Totonac, Popoluca, Tepehua, Tlalpaneco, and more. A veritable anthropological travelog though the peoples, places, and cultures of Veracruz—highly accessible to the visually oriented, alongside vivid textual accounts.

511 Ramírez González, Irma. Perfiles indígenas en el Estado de México. Toluca, Mexico: Univ. Autónoma del Estado de México, 2009. 182 p.: bibl., ill. (Cuadernos de investigación; 55)

With a focus on the state of Mexico, surrounding the Mexican capital, and indigenous people in this state, the author finds conditions not untypical of far more remote locations in the republic, such as low levels of literacy, high fertility, high infant mortality as compared with national statistics, high levels of preventable diseases, malnourishment of various degrees for 65 percent of the indigenous population, poor agricultural capacity, inferior housing, and lack of labor alternatives—along with deficiencies in public social services such as potable water, clinics, and schools. These conditions aid in generating migration, which in turn shifts increasing responsibilities to those who remain, especially women and the elderly. Despite these stresses, the author notes the continued maintenance of identity and community through religious ceremonies, festivals, cargos, and community assemblies of governance.

512 Recondo, David. La démocratie mexicaine en terres indiennes. Paris: Karthala, 2009. 452 p.: bibl. (Recherches internationales / CERI)

Explores the energetic contradiction between the long-standing Mexican state which homogenizes the political agenda and the recent laws (responding to the Zapatista uprising) which recognize customary indigenous practices as an alternative basis of governance, examined in detail in indigenous regions of Oaxaca. The debate pits those who champion autonomy and self-governance for indigenous peoples against those insisting separate laws create segregated communities and encourage intercommunity conflicts, leaving open the legal door to deciding who is indigenous for the purposes of other forms of rights not available to all citizens. The study follows these debates into the field to see them play out in hotly contested rural Oaxaca.

513 El regreso de lo indígena: retos, problemas y perspectivas. Edición de Valérie Robin Azevedo y Carmen Salazar-Soler. Lima: Instituto Francés de Estudios Andinos; Cuzco, Peru: Centro de Estudios Regionales Andinos Bartolomé de Las Casas, CBC; Paris: Mondes américains, societés, circulations, pouvoirs XVe–XXIe siécle; Toulouse: France, LISST, Centre d'anthropologie sociale; Lima: Cooperación Regional para los Países Andinos, Embajada de Francia en el Perú, 2009. 292 p.: bibl. (Actes & mémoires; 26) (Estudios y debates regionales andinos; 3109)

Bringing together 10 authors and

articles, plus an introduction, the book addresses the shift in the last two decades from class-based social analysis to one involving ethnicity and indigenous rights. Questions how critically this shift has been assessed by scholars concerned with issues of power and equity. The internal colonialism that marked the contradiction between national equality under the law and the reality of exploitation and marginalization broke open in the 1990s with legislation in many Latin American countries recognizing ethnic and cultural differences and rights. Concerns include a renewed segregation and a populism that shifts analysis from structural injustice to cultural celebration of difference—and not all difference with equal attention or approbation.

514 Los retos de la diferencia: los actores de la multiculturalidad entre México y Colombia. Edición de Odile Hoffmann y María Teresa Rodríguez. México: Centro de Investigaciones y Estudios Superiores en Antropología Social, 2007. 551 p.: bibl., ill., index, maps. (Publicaciones de la Casa Chata) (Antropologías)

The 16 articles in this volume deal with various aspects of the struggle to maintain ethnic identities in Mexico and Colombia. The book is divided in five sections; the first one studies the role of the state and politics assisting or promoting the integration of ethnic minorities into the national culture. The second part examines the impact that the war on violence and migration has had in transforming identities. The Colombian Constitution of 1991 opened the way to ethnic black and Amerindian populations to reaffirm their distinctiveness from the rest of the country, while in Mexico, three studies in Veracruz offer examples of reconstruction of identity. In the fourth part, two chapters look at how differences can help unite or separate ethnic groups. The final section examines the ways in which religion and festivities contribute to manifest or strengthen identities. [A. Ugalde]

515 Reyes Landa, María Luisa and **Arturo Guevara Sánchez.** En el viejo camino a Chiguagua: avances en el estudio de la cultura de tobosos y grupos afines. Chihuahua, Mexico: Programa Editorial de Gobierno del

Estado: Instituto Chihuahuense de la Cultura, 2008. 319 p.: ill., maps.

Study of former foraging-to-incipient agricultural peoples of arid southeast Chihuahua, western Coahuila, and northern Durango, with emphasis on the Tobosco—based largely in ethnohistoric data and detailed archeology. Fierce and adamant opponents to the European invasion of their homelands, these indigenous populations were overcome by a confluence of violence, land displacement, and the arrival of Apaches and Comanches from the north, also in conflict. Rock-painted pictographs and associated landscapes are of particular interest for this little-known area and epoch, with some symbols clearly associated with Southwest US "rock art" tradition.

516 Rincón García, Luis Antonio. Comunicación y cultura en Zinacantán: un acercamiento a los procesos comunicacionales. Tuxtla Gutiérrez, Mexico: Centro Estatal de Lenguas, Arte y Literatura Indígenas, Gobierno del Estado de Chiapas, 2007. 191 p.: bibl. (Col. Hechos en palabras) (Ts'ib-jaye)

A study of culture and communication in the Tzotzil township of Zinacantán, in the highlands of Chiapas, Mexico, with an emphasis on the dynamics of communicative performance across gender, generation, and local political debates, as well as in the context of interactions with non-indigenous, such as tourists and mestizos (Ladinos). Provides a close look at women working in crafts cooperatives, youth dealing with change and cultural maintenance, and village political personalities dealing with each other and outsiders and managing their understanding of heritage and indigenous identity.

517 Ritos de paso. Coordinación de Patricia Fournier García, Carlos Mondragón y Walburga Wiesheu Forster. México: Instituto Nacional de Antropología e Historia: Escuela Nacional de Antropología e Historia: Consejo Nacional para la Cultura y las Artes: Programa de Mejoramiento del Profesorado, 2009. 307 p.: bibl., ill. (Arqueología y antropología de las religiones; 3)

A collection of 14 articles addressing rites of passage, of which four are largely about prehispanic Mesoamerica, and one, in part about contemporary Otomi del Valle de Mesquital. This article suggests that the pilgrimages to the four images (placed in their locations by the original, foundational Otomi couple), and especially the sojourn to Chalma (a major destination for pilgrimages in central Mexico) constitutes a rite of passage. The piece traces the three stages of separation, liminal state, and reintegration in the Chalma case.

518 Robledo Hernández, Gabriela. Identidades femeninas en transformación: religión y género entre la población indígena urbana en el altiplano chiapaneco. México: CIESAS, 2009. 242 p.: bibl., ill., map. (Publicaciones de la Casa Chata)

Describes the complex impacts on women and identity when displaced indigenous families form religious communities within an alien urban setting (San Cristóbal de Las Casas), and women enter into new forms of labor, new inter-ethnic relations, and evolving social roles far from their original socialization. Focuses on two exiled evangelical communities, and shows how the changing familial relations in the context of the new religion favor more responsibilities and more social vehicles for social interaction and action beyond the domestic unit and nets of kin. These cults serve as springboards for empowering women in ways not available to them inside their prior Maya gender relations. Like the gender role renovations of the Zapatista movement, new social and religious movements in Chiapas have given women new avenues to find their voice and empower their views into action. The study shows how these newly urban Mayas appropriate foreign dogmas and social organizations for their own ends, and how women have benefitted from appropriations of new ways to enact being Maya.

519 Rojas Conejo, Daniel. Dilema e identidad del pueblo Bribri. San José: Editorial UCR, 2009. 260 p.: bibl., ill. (Col. Identidad cultural)

Looks at Costa Rica's largest indigenous group, the tensions between traditional and modern influences in the construction of identity, how identity is tied to (three) foundational myths, as well as tensions between forms of Christianity (and Baha'i) and shamanism, and the concept of harmony and balance, presented as existentially fundamental. Shows creative reappropriation of culture for identity revitalization, cross-cutting other social identities, in the Costa Rican context.

520 Rostas, Susanna. Carrying the word: the Concheros dance in Mexico City. Boulder: Univ. Press of Colorado, 2009. 303 p.: bibl., index.

This easy-to-read contribution goes beyond previous Conchero research in theory (identity/performance/ritual) and method (participatory) as well as frame, or "invented ethnicity." Rostas provides ample evidence of how Mesoamerica swims below the surface of a Catholic devotional—one now in competitive dialog with more recent danzante groups. These centuries-old dance traditions that are central to Mexican urban imaginary use their performance as key to the embodiment of group meanings. The author's extensive dance participation provides the framework for the study, based in the impacts of dance-induced reverie on membership, and she compares them with other dance groups. This ethnography brings new and old together creatively, clearly, and authoritatively.

521 Samson, C. Mathews. Re-enchanting the world: Maya Protestantism in the Guatemalan highlands. Tuscaloosa: Univ. of Alabama Press, 2007. 197 p.: bibl., ill., index, maps. (Contemporary American Indian studies)

Following work by David Scotchmer, the Presbyterian author explores accommodations between Protestant sects (especially Presbyterians) and Maya culture (Mam, Kaqchikel) and community dynamics in highland Guatemalan Mayan townships. His conclusions are mixed as to the degree and nature of the integration of Protestant sects in indigenous communities, and to the role of the religion in creating community-level conflicts and revitalizing/remaking of Maya identity. Setting aside the "crisis-solace" theory of the growth of evangelical sects during the violence, this study provides a more syncretic vision of variation and pluralism, looking at cases where religion and ethnicity mobilized people around

development, human rights, and cultural activism. The author sees this conversion as a "re-enchantment" alternative to rational secularization in a globalizing nation. His reading of Maya evangelicalism, regardless of origins and divisiveness, is as part of a universalizing process locally lived.

522 Sánchez González, José. Los rancheros de la Sierra del Tigre, 1800–1920: estudio etnográfico. Zapopan, Mexico: Centro Univ. de Ciencias Biológicas y Agropecuarias, Univ. de Guadalajara, 2004. 249 p.: bibl., ill. (some col.).

A study of wealthy ranching families who become established in the Sierra de Tigre area, south of Lake Chapala and between the regions of Colima and the Tarascans, in the Central Mesa of Mexico, at the start of the 19th century—after the fall of the haciendas—with a focus on three important families. Includes many historical pictures of the people discussed, and many recent images of ethnographic artifacts of the day, as well as extensive genealogies (and trees) and numerous family history facts.

523 Sariego Rodríguez, Juan Luis. La Sierra Tarahumara: travesías y pensares. México: Instituto Nacional de Antropología e Historia, 2008. 280 p.: bibl., col. ill., col. map. (Col. ENAH Chihuahua; 9)

Series of timely essays regarding aspects of anthropology among the Tarahumara (Raramuri) and related groups (Wariji, 'Odame, O'oba). Raramuri are the most studied of the Chihuahua region indigenous groups on the Mesoamerican periphery, and the book includes useful summaries of European, US, and Mexican ethnographic studies in the 19th and 20th centuries, as well as colonial era sources. Sariego arranges studies and students of the region into charts of contrasting categories of perspective. Continental idealized notions of native cultures unstained by Western thought and urban society are contrasted with Mexican indigenismo notions of unilineal national integration, with applied educational anthropology as a tool. Approaches the region with a geographical component; discusses forestry, land tenure, and legal rights; explores ideological elements in outsider development efforts; provides a history and political economy context; and introduces indigenous concepts and interpretations of the world—especially social notions of community and family-unit dispersion as adaptations to invasion, and the imposition of alien communitarianism as a contested government policy of control, following a colonial pattern Raramuri continue to resist.

524 El señuelo del norte: migración indígena contemporánea en Chiapas. Coordinación de Graciela Freyermuth Enciso, Sergio Meneses Navarro y Germán Martínez Velasco. San Cristóbal de las Casas, Mexico: Gobierno de Chiapas, COESPO Chiapas: UNFPA, 2007. 223 p.: bibl., ill.

Original collection of articles discussing migration within Mexico and beyond, primarily in the state of Chiapas but also Guerrero, covering themes such as sexually transmitted diseases in migrant Chamulas, migrant transit and the burgeoning sex trade in the state capital, and rural indigenous women who migrate to Acapulco for work. Shows the ties between failed internal migration efforts seeking economic betterment and the flow of migration to the US.

525 Simposio Internacional Ritual Público y Ritual Privado en el Mundo Maya, *Granada, Spain and Santafé, Spain, 2009.* El ritual en el mundo maya: de lo privado a lo público. Edición de Andrés Ciudad Ruiz, María Josefa Iglesias Ponce de León y Miguel Sorroche Cuerva. Madrid: Sociedad Española de Estudios Mayas; Granada, Spain: Grupo de Investigación Andalucía-América, Patrimonio Cultural y Relaciones Artísticas; Mérida, Mexico: Centro Peninsular en Humanidades y Ciencias Sociales, UNAM, 2010. 487 p.: bibl., ill., maps. (Publicaciones de la S.E.E.M.; 9)

Collection of articles concentrating on Maya ritual from the archeological and epigraphic past, with some cases from the ethnohistoric and historical record, and a few ethnographic cases embedded in articles, focused on the common theme of public versus private rituals. Most of the historical and ethnographic references work towards analogy to illuminate the precontact past, in what is mostly an archeological tome. Shows the often facile appropriation of bits of current ethnography to illuminate the past. For archeologist's comment, see item **79**.

526 Speed, Shannon. Rights in rebellion: indigenous struggle and human rights in Chiapas. Stanford, Calif.: Stanford Univ. Press, 2008. 244 p.: bibl., ill., index.

Valuable and insightful discussion of how the evolution of the Zapatista rebellion in Chiapas challenges prior notions of human rights and indigenous peoples' legal relations to the state. Follows closely the *red de defensores comunitarios*, a network of paralegals utilizing the law to defend the rights of indigenous communities, to show their strategic application of human rights law to the cause. Takes up the thorny issue of using the laws legitimating the state to resist it, and demonstrates how the Zapatistas shift from lobbying the state (San Andrés accords) to gaining authority for their rights based in exercising them (as they formed their civilian governance structure). Raises issues of indigenousness, gender, local appropriation, resistance to the "neoliberal global order," and the complexities of activism in scholarship.

527 Stephen, Lynn. Transborder lives: indigenous Oaxacans in Mexico, California, and Oregon. Durham, N.C.: Duke Univ. Press, 2007. 375 p.: bibl., ill., index, maps.

Another solid study of indigenous Mexicans who, as a result of a multigenerational pattern of migration to the US, have established a binational, transborder life, oscillating between their place of ethnic origin and one or more US sites—as an adaptation to the harsh structural conditions imposed on rural Mexico in the last 30 years, and sustained US low-end labor demand. Based on years of fieldwork in Oaxaca state with Zapotec weavers, the author's relocation to Oregon and involvement with indigenous migrants to the West Coast brings her work into a controlled comparative perspective, closely examining differences in migratory experiences related to village histories, and discovering the borders of prejudice found at multiple sites. Central to the tragic drama is the US border crossing, which has become deadly in the last 15 years, especially for the more vulnerable, less experienced crossers. "The disappeared," once a term in Latin America reserved for those taken away permanently for political reasons, now is employed by transborder communities to refer to those who have not been heard from since they attempted to make their way through the deserts of the Southwest—the primary method of gaining unauthorized entry. Weaving together personal histories and structural constraints, Stephen highlights the creative responses to these conditions by men and especially women who are changed by—and transform—their communities as a result of a challenging transborder lifeway.

528 Stresser-Péan, Guy. The sun god and the savior: the christianization of the Nahua and Totonac of the Sierra Norte de Puebla, Mexico. Boulder: Univ. Press of Colorado, 2008. 627 p.: bibl., ill., index, maps, photos (some col.), tables. (Mesoamerican worlds: from the Olmecs to the Danzantes)

A sound translation (from the French-*Soleil-dieu et le Christ: la christianisation des Indiens du Mexique vue de la sierra de Puebla*, 2005) of the noted continental Mesoamericanist's extensive opus on the Sierra people he spent a generation studying. This book lays out a panoramic view across history and across the small variables between closely tied and generally similar people. It turns a comparative gaze on cultural performance (i.e., traditional dances) and syncretic religious creativity and variation, with its accommodation and appropriations, sorting out, in a classic cultural history approach, the syncretic and nonsyncretic regional religions and their historical transformations, across villages and languages, though practices and histories. Excellent sections on conversion efforts by the colonial Church, daily life in later periods up to the present, and on public ceremonial activities of the annual calendar round, both more and less Christianized, and on a variety of public dance theater traditions such as the Volador and Moors/Christians, and a dozen more. Stresser-Péan discusses indigenous views on "end of world" prophesy, human diversity, cosmology, supernatural beings, and the nature of the soul. Ethnographic data is well integrated into understandings of larger and ancient Mesoamerica, in the manner of

symbolic lines of continuity and change of Mesoamerican fundamentals.

529 Taller Internacional Mujeres Indígenas y Violencia Doméstica: del Silencio Privado a las Agendas Públicas, *San Cristóbal de Las Casas, Mexico, 2005.* Memoria. México: Comisión Nacional de Derechos Humanos, 2007. 136 p.: bibl.

Proceedings of an international workshop on human rights, specifically the rights of indigenous women. Lays out an ambitious agenda for improving the legal, social, and political position of indigenous women, including sweeping calls for legislation, support for women vis-à-vis domestic violence, but also increasing women's access to training in rights, health, family planning, information access, organizations of support, leadership, and community-based participatory development. Includes remarks by specialists on women's rights and their objective conditions; also includes a few indigenous women's voices (from Chiapas communities), as well as the words of political appointees who, in the wake of the indigenous rights awakening instigated by the Zapatista uprising, are trying to catch up.

530 Taylor, Analisa. Indigeneity in the Mexican cultural imagination: thresholds of belonging. Tucson: Univ. of Arizona Press, 2009. 143 p.: bibl., ill., index.

This comprehensive examination looks at the contradictory ways in which indigenous peoples have been represented in Mexican culture over time; romanticism, prejudice and denigration, appeals to modernize, marginalization, and erasure characterize this ambivalence. Explores indigenismo as a suspect project of the state, seeking assimilation as a means of incorporation in the corporatist party, the rise of resistance to this imagining, especially focusing on women and their emergent voices, and traces this struggle to the contemporary dilemma of "whether indigenous reformulation of national belonging as a pluralistic, even dialogic endeavor will find effective avenues of expression within the neoliberal model of market-driven governance and cultural production." Examining issues of ethics and violence, the author includes a section on Zapatismo approaches to retaking indigenousness from urban cultural production, and explores testimonials as a transitional literary form of the subaltern voice, juxtaposed to canonical mestizo representations of the indigenous in literature, film, or social science.

531 Tedlock, Dennis. 2000 years of Mayan literature. Berkeley: Univ. of California Press, 2010. 465 p.: bibl., ill., index, maps.

Masterful convocation of Maya forms of literary expression based in precolumbian, colonial, and ethnographic sources, extensively illustrated in keeping with the subject, following the long trail of surviving Maya texts beginning with fragments in 400 B.C.E., and moving forward through the classic and postclassic and on to Maya appropriations of alphabetic writing under Christians, from early documents like the Popol Vuh and the books of Chilam Balam, to later dance-drama texts like the Rabinal Achi, still performed today. In weaving together the subjects of these texts, Tedlock covers immense ground—glyph readings, astronomy, dynastic politics, history, myth, and social relations—always with an eye to the contrast between occidental notions of literary arrangements and those of the Maya, based in semantic and sound parallelism, and tracing Maya expressive patterns over broad ranges of time and medium. He decenters writing in relation to other expressive media, clarifies misconceptions, and provides a clear heuristic exposition of Maya writing, calendar, and number system. Written in poetic style that itself reflects the book's subject.

532 Temas y contextos: investigación social. Coordinación de Manuel Buenrostro Alba y Antonio Higuera Bonfil. Chetumal, Mexico: Univ. de Quintana Roo; s.l.: C.A. Investigación Aplicada al Fortalecimiento de la Cultura e Identidad; México: Plaza y Valdés Editores, 2009. 186 p.: bibl., ill.

An introduction and eight articles loosely gathered around indigenous themes in Mexico, some of them covering the present and past Maya. Subjects include how town fiestas link transnational migrants to their home culture, the workings of an urban fiesta, ancient Maya ceremonial centers and their expressive significance, religious freedom in indigenous Mexico, southern border violence (Mexico-Belize), commerce and "subjectivities," as well as an article on historic preservation and urban planning in Barcelona. No overarching theme holds the collection together.

533 Temó, Pedro Cholotío. The dog who spoke and more Mayan folktales = El perro que hablá y más cuentos mayas. Translated and edited by James D. Sexton and Fredy Rodríguez-Mejía. Stories told in Spanish by Pedro Cholotío Temó and Alberto Barreno. Norman: Univ. of Oklahoma Press, 2010. 261 p.: bibl.

James Sexton and his team again show the ability to deliver Maya voices from Lake Atitlán in this tome of stories from Sexton's richly erudite Maya collaborators, in an edition enhanced by texts in both Spanish and English. With 34 pages of detailed context and setting provided by Sexton, and 33 tales both more and less traditional in form and content, this volume serves as a rich source of contemporary Tzutuhil oral tradition and as a contribution to Maya oral literature. Bilingual renderings provide accessibility for those teaching Spanish or bilingual education and seeking non-Western literature.

534 Teratol, Romin; Antzelmo Peres; and Robert M. Laughlin. Jxanviletik ta namal balamil = Los viajeros al otro mundo. Traducción de tsotsil a español de Mariano Reynaldo Vázquez López. Compilación de Carol Karasik. Tuxtla Gutiérrez, Mexico: Gobierno del Estado de Chiapas, 2006. 215 p.: ill. (Biblioteca popular de Chiapas; 127. Estudios antropología)

A contribution to bilingual publications (Spanish-Tzotzil) and an homage to the transparent and candid relationship between a long-term ethnographer and the indigenous peoples of southern Mexico. Ethnographer Robert Laughlin arranged two trips to the US for the two Maya authors, Romin Teratol and Antzelmo Péres, in 1963 and 1967. After many years, he convinced them to provide an account of their journeys, the historic events they witnessed, the celebrities they met, and the elements of daily life in the US that shocked, stunned, and amused them. The result is an erudite and highly accessible narrative of daily life in a time now passed, in Chiapas as well as in the US. The back-and-forth ethnography between the Maya authors and Laughlin provides context for Laughlin's Tzotzil dictionary opus. For review of English-language translation, see item **535**.

535 Torre, Domingo de la; Romin Teratol; and Antzelmo Péres. Travelers to the other world: a Maya view of North America. Translated and coordinated by Robert M. Laughlin. Edited by Carol Karasik. Albuquerque: Univ. of New Mexico Press, 2010. 255 p.

Ethnographer Robert Laughlin arranged two trips to the US for the two Maya authors, in 1963 and 1967. After many years, he convinced them to provide a written account of their journeys, the historic events they witnessed, the celebrities they met, and the elements of daily life in the US that shocked, stunned, and amused them. The result is an erudite and highly accessible narrative of daily life in a time now passed, in Chiapas as well as in the US. The back-and-forth ethnography between the Maya authors and Laughlin provides context for Laughlin's Tzotzil dictionary opus. Includes a guide to pronunciation and a forward by travel writer veteran Peter Canby. For review of Spanish-language translation, see item **534**.

536 Valle Escalante, Emilio del. Nacionalismos mayas y desafíos postcoloniales en Guatemala: colonialidad, modernidad y políticas de la identidad cultural. Guatemala: FLACSO Guatemala: Editorial de Ciencias Sociales, 2008. 238 p.: bibl. (Col. Lecturas de ciencias sociales; 4)

An exploration of social theory with the Guatemalan Maya subaltern political project, beyond and outside of the "intercultural" propositions of a state embracing it to legitimate the monoethnic position of power. The author discusses the writings of Luis de Lión (1940–84) who critiqued the representations of Mayas in Miguel Ángel Asturias' writings and problematized the idea that the indigenous are the factor holding back the nation from modernity implicit in these and other writings by nonindigenous Guatemalan writers. His claim is

that in order to understand the "Maya Movement" and other indigenous struggles in Guatemala, it is necessary to put these findings in dialog with the nonindigenous writers who claim authority to write about the indigenous world. This dialog is best perceived in the context of the "colonialism of power" and various current versions of "interculturality" including the "cosmovision Maya" approach of Lión and Rigoberta Menchú, and the mestizaje alternative. Valle Escalante interrogates the post-peace accords efforts at multicultural and multilinguistic education to assess its relations to the state's hegemonic interests.

537 Vázquez Estrada, Alejandro. Cruz a cuestas: identidad y territorio entre los chichimeca otomíes del semidesierto queretano. México: Instituto Nacional de Antropología e Historia, 2009. 123 p.: bibl., ill., maps. (Etnografía de las regiones indígenas de Querétaro)

Explores how Otomi pilgrimages to mountains (tracking two main cases) serve as ritual condensation of group identity and reiterate boundary. The study is placed in the context of general Mesoamerican cosmology; explores identity and territory, examines the socioreligious nexus of pilgrimage; and describes how this plays out in several ethnographic settings. Sensitive to the interplay between ancient Mesoamerican substrate and recent transformations and tensions, the work captures the way perceptions of Chichimeca-ness move through history to the present. The detailed descriptions of pilgrimages, interspersed with interpretation, allow the reader to see the relationship between the actions observed and the author's view of their significance; an ethnographic transparency combined with a persuasive perspective.

538 Velásquez Nimatuj, Irma Alicia. Pueblos indígenas, estado y lucha por tierra en Guatemala: estrategias de sobrevivencia y negociación ante la desigualdad globalizada. Ciudad de Guatemala: AVANCSO, Asociación para el Avance de las Ciencias Sociales en Guatemala, 2008. 319 p.: bibl., ill. (Autores invitados; 17)

One of a growing number of indigenous Maya writers (K'iche') with advanced academic degrees (PhD, University of Texas at Austin, Anthropology) writing about indigenous conditions of life, in this case three Mam communities impacted by the coffee crisis of the first decade of the century. The author places emphasis on the triple oppression of rural, indigenous women, and moves from the micro-conditions of her communities to the macro-conditions of Guatemala's complex political and social history and the impact of globalization. The work explores the evolution of pro-campesino, returned refugee, and other rural indigenous organizations and their relations with each other and the armed revolutionary left (CUC, EGP), and with theoretical sophistication masterfully integrates questions of class, race, and ethnicity. A rare and refreshing integration of controlled, comparative ethnography, and in-depth regional, national, and global analysis.

539   Williams García, Roberto. Danzas y andanzas: etnología. Prólogo de Félix Báez-Jorge. 2. ed. corr. y aúm. Veracruz, Mexico: Gobierno del Estado de Veracruz de Ignacio de la Llave, 2007. 2 v.: bibl., ill., index, map. (Col. Investigaciones)

A collection of 30 of the many articles by veteran Mexican ethnographer Williams García, with a prologue and introductory sections by Báez-Jorge and Alberto Beltrán. His ethnographic writings are grouped into sections covering southern Veracruz, the Totonac area, and northern Veracruz. The dance reference in the title includes his analysis of the Dance of the Tigre (tiger, cat), which he believes to be a surviving cultural artifact of the Olmec "mother culture." He is a strong supporter of ethnographic analogy, often bringing together precolumbian and current data for comparison.

South America
Lowlands

FEDERICO BOSSERT, *Researcher, CONICET, Universidad de Buenos Aires, Argentina*
BARTHOLOMEW DEAN, *Associate Professor, Department of Anthropology, University of Kansas and Director de Antropología, Museo Regional-Universidad Nacional de San Martín, Tarapoto, Peru*
SILVIA MARÍA HIRSCH, *Professor, Instituto de Altos Estudios Sociales, Universidad Nacional de San Martín, Argentina*
ROBIN WRIGHT, *Associate Professor of Religion, University of Florida, Gainesville*

WESTERN AMAZONIA

Despite regional ecological crises, political turmoil, and social strife, study of the western flanks of Lowland South America continues to flourish. The theoretical sophistication of recent scholarship on western Amazonia—as reflected in a number of novel studies on native cosmology, ritual power, and social organization (see, for instance, item **540**)—is matched by the study of deeply consequential issues in the ethnology of Lowland South America. This body of work includes sustained analyses of Amazonian ethnogenesis; critical review of the sociolinguistic implications of language contact; study of the region's diverse ecosystems including understanding the challenges facing the vulnerable Amazonian floodplain or várzea; and ethnographic documentation of various permutations of shamanism.

Contemporary ethnological research on Lowland South America has been particularly rich in the realm of political anthropology, including study of the extent to which indigenous leaders' "subjectivity-shaping" initiatives have been influenced by associations with the state and NGOs, as well as local conceptions of status, leadership, and citizenship (see for instance item **578**). A number of ethnographies of western Amazonia have brilliantly chronicled challenging historical legacies that shape current local realities. For instance, Richard Kernaghan's *Coca's Gone* explores the legacy of violence in the social topography of Peru's Upper Huallaga Valley (item **580**), while María Clemencia Ramírez's *Between the Guerrillas and the State* is a systematic study of rebels, drug trafficking, paramilitarism, and the *cocalero* movement in the Putumayo region of the Colombian Amazon (item **574**).

The qualitative study of western Lowland South America is equaled by a growing body of rigorous, empirically driven studies oriented to documenting the factors driving social and ecological change, such as determining the extent to which ethnobotanical skills are linked to rates of deforestation, as noted among Tsimane' communities of Bolivia (item **606**). Political ecology continues to shape the intellectual proclivities of the ethnology of Lowland South America. Study of the prominent role plants have played in the lives of Lowland South American peoples remains a central concern of scholarship, as noted in the robust investigations of the roles that a diverse range of plants (from rubber, to ayahuasca, to coca) have played within the cosmology, history, and political economies of Amazonia. [BD]

BRAZIL

The material on Brazilian ethnology covers six categories of research and knowledge production, as follows: 1) history of Brazilian ethnology and archeology; 2) perspectivist ethnographies, theory, and applications to well-known themes such as personhood in Lowland South American ethnology; 3) identity politics in Amazonia; 4) political ecology, the mobility of Amazonian peoples, and its implications; 5) territoriality and cosmovision, particularly in reference to the Guarani peoples of southern Brazil; and 6) Afro-Brazilian religious traditions.

Five outstanding works frame the period under consideration (2007–2009): (1) Turner's article on "The Crisis of Late Structuralism, Perspectivism and Animisim: Rethinking Culture, Nature, Bodiliness and Spirit," published in the journal *Tipiti*, of the Society for the Anthropology of Lowland South America (item **570**); (2) the collection of articles edited by Hutchins and Wilson, titled *Editing Eden* (item **554**) on identity, politics, and place in Amazonia; (3) the collection of articles in *Native Christians: Modes and Effects of Christianity among Indigenous Peoples of the Americas*, edited by Aparecida Vilaça and Robin M. Wright (item **545**); (4) the collection of articles in the special issue edited by Wright on "The Religious Lives of Amazonian Plants," published in the *Journal of the Society for the Study of Religion, Nature and Culture* (2009); and (5) a collection of articles, edited by Fernando Santos-Granero, titled *The Occult Life of Things: Amazonian Notions of Personhood and Materiality* (item **565**). Another strong collection of articles perhaps related to Hutchins and Wilson''s collection is Alexiades'' volume focusing on the theme of mobility and migration from the perspective of "ethno-ecology" in indigenous "folk" Amazonia (item **544**).

These five works well illustrate some of the principal theoretical tendencies with regard to indigenous peoples in Lowland South America, and the theoretical sophistication which the field of Ethnology has reached. In the first, Turner assesses the legacy of Levi-Straussian structuralism for Amazonian Ethnology. He discusses the two main derivative theories that emerged in response to the "crisis" in which late structuralism became embedded: the "new Animism" as developed by Philippe Descola, and the "perspectivism" developed by Eduardo Viveiros de Castro and his colleagues at the Museu Nacional in Brazil. Both vertents develop new insights on indigenous "modes of thought" in relation to other-than-human beings. Both scholars revitalized and reshaped old ideas about the "spirit" of indigenous peoples and its omnipresence in the world, ideas about the "non-human otherness" of the animals, which point to a reformulation of the categories of "nature" and "culture". A constructive critique of perspectivism, in particular, leads to Turner's positive assessment of the nature/culture dichotomy reformulated to include productive activities. Among the ethnographies reviewed, those by Oscar Calavia on the Yaminawa (item **551**) and Pissolato on the Mbya-Guarani notion of personhood (item **566**) best exemplify the "perspectivist" school with its analysis of social categories and their inter-relations, narratives, and ritual.

Along lines that are based in South American Ethnology"s longtime research on the notion of personhood among native Amazonians, Fernando Santos-Granero of the Smithsonian Institution has organized a stimulating collection on the also-well-known concept that native Amazonians consider "objects" to be imbued with "life and spirit" (item **565**). Thus, we cannot call any "tool" or "artwork" an "object"; rather, many are imbued with subjectivity, and in some cases, agentivity, independently of their "owner". The authors in this collection examine the relations between body and artifact, e.g., the sacred flutes of the Northwest Amazon, body ornaments, hammocks and bowls; the transformation of fabricated materials into animate beings which may display modalities of existence that differ from humans; and finally, indigenous theories of the status of materialized subjectivities, as in the occult nature of sacred flutes, the power of objects to do things.

Wright's edited special issue of the *Journal for the Study of Religion, Nature and Culture* on "The Religious Lives of Amazonian Plants" contributes to this discussion insofar as the articles—written by ethnologists and religious studies scholars—together seek to explore how plants are imbued with agency and subjectivity (items **572, 576, 582,** and **584**). With regard to the plants selected for study, many do not share the qualities of predation that Viveiros de Castro finds necessary for his theory. Rather, plants are considered to be primordial sources in the fabrication of humanity (consistent with many of the ideas in Santos-Granero's collection). They are treated today as kinds of other-than-human beings, which has implications for such activities as gardening practices. Plants considered to be sacred, such as ayahuasca and parika, have powers that go far beyond providing sustenance, powers related to healing, shamanic soul voyaging, and transformation. As sources of musical instruments and edible fruits, Amazonian palm trees present particularly potent images of connections between the ancestral world and descendants, as in the image of an umbilical cord.

A second edited volume focuses on the much-debated notion of "conversion to Christianity" (item **545**). The novelty in Vilaça and Wright's collection is, first of all, that it contributes to the growing field of the Anthropology of Christianity. For scholars of religion, the book has value insofar as it focuses primarily on how Christianity is conceived, received, and experienced by indigenous peoples across North America and especially South America. New insights are offered into both the discontinuities and continuities of Catholic and Protestant forms of Christian faith as these are culturally, theologically, and practically adapted by indigenous Americans amidst the forces of modernization and even globalization.

The publications thus far discussed are connected by a common thread of the theoretical modes of conceptualizing indigenous Amazonians' understanding of the "nature/culture" (Western) dichotomy which clearly involves the ontological and cosmological status of objects and plants, as well as continuities and discontinuities in indigenous spirituality vis-à-vis different forms of Christianity.

The collections by Hutchins and Wilson (item **554**) and Alexiades (item **544**) concentrate, we could say, far more on ethnic politics and social and political dynamics of mobility and migration. In the first, Amazonia is seen as an "object of the imagination" replete with preconceived notions of indigeneity; as a "frontier zone" generating ideas of liminality and marginality; and as a "field" in which the ideologies of the West still confront the cosmologies of native peoples. Alexiades' organized collection seeks to conjugate etic and emic perspectives on mobility and migrations of Amazonian native peoples in four countries by using an ethnoecological approach to ethnobotany, resource management, and mobility—analytically conceptualized through the key concepts of "circulation" (mobility, subsistence practices) and "transfrontiers" (place-making, knowledge, and identity). A clear-cut example of the issues raised in the latter volume is that of the Guarani of southern Brazil, studied by Maria Inês Ladeira in several exceptionally well-done ethnographies which devote special attention to Guarani notions of space, territory, and identity (items **553** and **559**).

A wide diversity of other themes characterize the literature for this period: the history of Brazilian anthropology and the Brazilian Anthropological Association (item **558**), archeology (Paulo Brochado and his connections with Donald Lathrop, item **552**), museology and major ethnological museums, such as the Museu Paraense Emílio Goeldi (item **569**), the Museu Rondon (item **563**), indigenist praxis (item **561**), physical anthropology (E. Roquette-Pinto, item **549**), the sociology of race (by its best-known exponent, the medical doctor Nina Rodrigues, item **550**), Afro-Brazilian studies of Umbanda (item **557**), and the legal status of *mocambos* (communities of descendants of runaway African slaves, item **562**). Other topics include indigenous identity, as emergent (the Tupinambá of Olivença, item **571**), as multiplex (Eliane Potiguara, item **567**); non-indigenous local traditions ("capixaba," item **564**); indigenous education (among the Palikur, item **568**); indigenous narratives (the Gavião of Rondônia state, item **553**); and struggles over land rights and demarcations of indigenous territories in the Peruvian Amazon (item **541**).

Finally, several works focus on developing methods and theory in the anthropological study of ritual in such forms as the festival of the Divine Holy Spirit and the popular festival "Bumba-meu-Boi" (item **556**); fieldwork methods in relation to gender research and field diaries by women ethnographers (item **555**); and debates over the existence of so-called partible paternity (item **546**), which finds that in some Amazonian societies, it is believed that a child is the product of sexual relations between its mother and a number of "fathers," each of whom contributes a part of the new child's being. The author of this work defends a well-grounded critique of primitivist thought in which this idea was originally proposed. [RMW]

ARGENTINA, BOLIVIA, AND PARAGUAY

The publications reviewed for this volume can be grouped in the following themes: examinations of ethnobiology, territorial land claims, political and ethnic mobilizations, religious missions, and war and historical processes.

Ethnobiological studies have contributed works that explore classification of plants and animals and their language correlation (items **586**, **591**, and **600**). Ethnographic data included in these works provides an in-depth understanding of indigenous knowledge about the environment, the use of natural resources, and religious beliefs. Furthermore, these studies are methodologically associated with linguistics and provide invaluable data on lexicon and typologies.

Indigenous peoples throughout Argentina, Bolivia, and Paraguay continue to demand their territorial rights, and several works account for this process (items **590** and **604**) and for the legislative changes at the local and national level (item **597**). Furthermore, indigenous peoples have undergone processes of ethnic re-emergence and political mobilization leading to their visibility in the political arena and to the public presence of groups considered extinct (item **604**). Hence, the emergence of these new groups sheds light on the politics of ethnicity in the last decade in Lowland South America. Territorial claims have been grounded in experiences based on the elaboration of maps which create oral histories of the processes of mobility and sedentarization of Chaco groups (item **608**).

The demand of indigenous peoples for intercultural and bilingual education has also been at the center of indigenous' rights claims. The volume edited by Hirsch and Serrudo provides an overview of experiences in bilingual intercultural education in Argentina and addresses the difficulties of carrying out educational programs which take into consideration the specific demands of indigenous peoples (item **595**). This publication is representative of an emerging field of research (see also item **587**).

The impact on indigenous communities of development projects carried out by NGOs and state agencies is analyzed in terms of how globalization affects local-level processes. In this venue, state agencies and projects have helped create indigenous political organizations and fostered the emergence of new forms of leadership (items **588** and **610**). Hence, internal power conflicts between different types of leaders are exacerbated as a result of intervention by external actors and institutions (items **588** and **596**). Some studies focus on the impact of this interference on religious beliefs and social representations (items **589**, **601**, and *HLAS 63:875*).

The quantity of ethnohistorical works continues to grow; a new series of publications based on primary sources is being developed in Bolivia (Scripta Authoctona) focusing mainly on Lowland groups of that country. Combès' book on the Zamucos sheds light on the complex configuration of ethnic names of several groups of the northern Chaco region from the 16th century to the present (item **593**). Furthermore, another work of this series delves into the "Southern Pano" of Amazonian Bolivia (Pacaguara, Chacobo, and Caripuna) (item **611**). These works contribute to the analysis of ethnonyms and inter-ethnic relations, and to the social and political formation of indigenous groups, setting a new methodological perspective for the region. The importance of the above-mentioned publications lies at the core of ethnological and ethnohistorical inquiry and sheds light on how these groups received and created ethnic names.

Continuing with the historical trend of examining the impact of wars and religious institutions on Lowland groups, a second volume on the Chaco War published in France and Bolivia contributes an insightful analysis on the impact of that conflict on Chacoan indigenous peoples, incorporating oral history (item **598**).

The influence of missions has been of longtime interest in academic production, in particular among the diverse Guarani groups. Wilde's work on the

Guarani missions inserts an anthropological perspective on the relations between missions and political and religious Guarani institutions (item **612**). Furthermore, Langer's work on the Bolivian Chiriguano focuses on the economic basis for the development and decay of Franciscan missions from 1830 to the Chaco War (1932–35) (item **598**).

A few works have been published on lesser-known groups in Paraguay and Bolivia. An ethnography on the Cavineños, written by a native scholar, brings to light an understudied group which has undergone intense contact, missionization, and displacement, and has developed new forms of social organization and religious beliefs (item **609**). [SMH and FB]

GENERAL

540 Burst of breath: indigenous ritual wind instruments in Lowland South America. Edited by Jonathan David Hill and Jean-Pierre Chaumeil. Lincoln: Univ. of Nebraska Press, 2011. 433 p.: bibl., ill., index, maps, photos.

Underscoring novel approaches to understanding the cosmological power and social import of Amazonian wind instruments (flutes, whistles, trumpets, clarinets, and bullroarers), this volume provides a comparative study of the many roles and contexts associated with indigenous musical cultures. The edited collection offers a comprehensive synopsis of the history and symbolic meanings of ritual wind instruments in a number of ethnographic contexts in Lowland South America (northwestern Amazonia, Upper Xingu, Guianas, Orinoco, Mato Grosso). In Amazonia, ritual use of wind instruments facilitates human communication with, or impersonations of, mythic creatures or spirits, particularly the so-called spirit-owners (*madres*) of the forest's animals and plants. In native Lowland South America, wind instruments are frequently associated with natural species, while the sounds they make are linked to the various behaviors of forest animals. Drawing insight from approaches from anthropology, ethnomusicology, ethnolinguistics, and museum studies, contributors to this pioneering volume explore how ritual wind instruments (aerophones) introduce "natural" sounds into social contexts, and in so doing transgress the boundaries between verbal and nonverbal communication. Contributors assess how the ritualized use of wind instruments is an integral aspect of native Amazonian social life—shaping the very nature of gender relations, familial organization, affinity, and the ways in which indigenous societies interact with outsiders. For instance, the adoption of "Inca" aerophones among the Marubo is a marker of alterity intimately tied to purportedly "authentic" or "true" Marubo cultural practices. [BD]

541 Chirif, Alberto and **Pedro García Hierro.** Marcando territorio: progresos y limitaciones de la titulación de territorios indígenas en la Amazonía. Copenhagen: IWGIA, Grupo Internacional de Trabajo sobre Asuntos Indígenas, 2007. 340 p.: bibl., col. maps.

Peruvian anthropologist Alberto Chirif and lawyer Pedro García review the advances and set backs made in processes of land recognition in various countries of Amazonia, based on direct knowledge of these different situations. This comparative view serves as a guide for a very detailed examination of the origin of "native communities" in the Peruvian Amazon. The result of processes of territorial loss and reduction of the indigenous populations since colonial times, the creation of these "communities" has consequently deprived the indigenous population of control over their territories, making them ever more dependent on state assistance. The authors recount in detail various initiatives for indigenous land titling; the problem of indigenous territories in relation to natural areas protected by the state; and finally, the pressures that various extractivist agencies have exercised on indigenous territories. [RMW]

542 Dobkin de Rios, Marlene and **Róger Rumrrill.** A hallucinogenic tea, laced with controversy: ayahuasca in the Amazon and the United States. Westport, Conn.: Praeger, 2008. 162 p.: bibl., index.

This book explores the preparation and consumption of the entheogen ayahuasca, which the authors translate as "spirit vine." In many indigenous cultures of Lowland South America, this hallucinogenic brew is considered a sacrosanct and enlightening curative concoction. While providing a useful history of indigenous Amazonian use of ayahuasca, the authors explore the controversy surrounding its consumption in non-Amazonian contexts, particularly in the US, where its use has prompted legal battles in the Supreme Court. Some US-based religious groups have struggled for government approval of their ritual use of the entheogen. The authors note how ayahuasca has attracted "drug tourists" to South America. Yet the authors caution tourists who they warn may be duped by charlatans who are not "authentic" shamans, but rather profiteers. This book includes useful text from the UN Convention on Psychotropic Substances as well as interviews with Amazonian shamans. [BD]

543 Ethnicity in ancient Amazonia: reconstructing past identities from archaeology, linguistics, and ethnohistory. Edited by Alf Hornborg and Jonathan David Hill. Boulder: Univ. Press of Colorado, 2011. 408 p.: bibl., ill., index, maps, tables.

Stemming from a series of meetings (two in Lund, one in Washington, D.C.) addressing various aspects of long-term ethnogenesis, this volume contains an interdisciplinary collection of essays by a distinguished group of ethnologists, linguists, and archeologists that traces the development, expansion, and decline of various indigenous cultural identities in ancient Amazonia. Editors Hornborg and Hill note that essentialist notions of ethnic identities linking language, culture, and biology have obfuscated the actual distribution of ethnic groups and languages in Amazonia. In contrast, contributors to this innovative volume on the nature of Amazonian ethnolinguistic diversity underscore the fluid, dialectic relationship among ethnic identity, language, genetics, and geography. The editors note that study of Amazonian ethnolinguistic distribution patterns has fortunately

moved away from a fixation with migrating "peoples" simply hauling their cultural baggage across Lowland South America to contemporary concerns with ethnogenetic processes within regional systems of exchange. Study of different ethnic markers such as pottery styles or language use, for instance, demonstrates how collective identity formation in Amazonia has always been a dynamic process. Of special note in this regard are the outstanding contributions on Amazonian ethnogenesis (see, for instance, Meredith Dudley's chapter on ethnogenesis in the Piedmont Region of Bolivia, and Norman Whitten's essay on ethnogenesis and interculturality among the Canelos of Ecuador). [BD]

544 Mobility and migration in indigenous Amazonia: contemporary ethnoecological perspectives. Edited by Miguel N. Alexiades. New York, N.Y.: Berghahn Books, 2009. 310 p.: bibl., ill., index, maps. (Studies in environmental anthropology and ethnobiology; 11)

An important collection of articles on the theme of mobility and migration from the perspective of ethnoecology in indigenous "folk" Amazonia. Articles discuss the Huaorani of Ecuador, the Piaroa of the middle Orinoco, and the Ese Eje of Peru and Bolivia. Themes include: ethnobotany, resource management, and mobility; domestication of plants—all of which are organized around two overarching areas the editors call "circulation" (mobility, subsistence, and the environment) and "transfrontiers" (knowledge, identity, place-making, and domestication of nature). This collection makes a significant contribution to the literature on historical and political ecology of Amazonia. [RMW]

545 Native Christians: modes and effects of Christianity among indigenous peoples of the Americas. Edited by Aparecida Vilaça and Robin M. Wright. Aldershot, England; Burlington, Vt.: Ashgate, 2009. 252 p.: bibl., ill., index, maps. (Vitality of indigenous religions series)

Native Christians reflects on the modes and effects of Christianity among indigenous peoples of the Americas drawing on comparative analysis of ethnographic and historical cases. Christianity in this region has been part of the process of conquest and domination, through the association usually made between civilizing and converting. While Catholic missions have emphasized the "civilizing" process, teaching the Indians the skills which they were expected to exercise within the context of a new societal model, the Protestants have centered their work on promoting a deep internal change, or "conversion," based on the recognition of God's existence. Of the 11 articles in the collection, five discuss native peoples in the Brazilian Amazon, and most others are from South America, two from North America, and interesting comments by Joel Robbins comparing the Americas with Melanesia. [RMW]

546 Shapiro, Warren. Partible paternity and anthropological theory: the construction of an ethnographic fantasy. Lanham, Md.: Univ. Press of America, 2009. 67 p.: bibl.

This book seeks to debunk the argument originally proposed by S. Beckerman and P. Valentine of a "partible paternity" in Amazonian native societies in which a child is the product of sexual relations between its mother and a number of "fathers"—each of whom constructs a portion of the child's body and/or soul. The source of this idea is L.H. Morgan's theory of "group marriage," the "primitivist" notions held by Engels, and more contemporary theorists who seek to explain this phenomenon through evolutionary psychology and cognitive science. The author's argument is a well-founded critique of the essentialism in primitivist thought among Western intellectuals and scholars. [RMW]

BRAZIL

Aikhenvald, Alexandra Y. Language contact in Amazonia. See item **573**.

547 The Amazon várzea: the decade past and the decade ahead. Edited by Miguel Pinedo-Vasquez *et al.* Dordrecht, Netherlands; New York, N.Y.: Springer, 2011. 362 p.: bibl., ill. (some col.), index, maps (some col.).

A valuable multidisciplinary retrospective on the current state of research on the vulnerable ecosystems of the Amazon floodplain or várzea. Dedicated to the memory of José Márcio Ayres, a renowned scholar of the Amazonian floodplains, this collection explores future trends shaping the ecological and human communities of the várzea. Of particular note are contributions by Richard Chase Smith on human adaptations to contextual uncertainties in the Amazonian estuary, and Miguel Pinedo-Vasquez and Robin Sears' study of conservation and várzea biodiversity. [BD]

548 Amazonien: Weltregion und Welt-theater. Edited by Willi Bolle, Marcel Vejmelka, and Edna Castro. Berlin: Trafo, 2010. 317 p.: bibl., ill., maps. (Reihe Latein-amerika-Studien; 1)

Multidisciplinary conference proceedings (Vienna, 2007) about Amazonia from ethnographic history to actual living conditions. A parallel edition is available in Portuguese (São Paulo, Editora Globo, 2010). [F. Obermeier]

549 Antropologia brasiliana: ciência e educação na obra de Edgard Roquette-Pinto. Organização de Nísia Trindade Lima e Dominichi Miranda de Sá. Belo Horizonte, Brazil: Editora UFMG; Rio de Janeiro: Editora Fiocruz, 2008. 327 p.: bibl., ill., maps. (Humanitas)

This book evaluates the contributions made to physical anthropology by one of Brazil's best-known exponents, who also was director of the Museu Nacional at the beginning of the 20th century. Roquette-Pinto's research included anthropometric measurements of military recruits on duty in Rio de Janeiro, seeking to determine whether "mixed-bloods" were a "degenerated" peoples. But Roquette-Pinto was also an ethnographer and followed in the wake of Rondon's opening of the western frontier to study with the Pareci Indians. He was a pioneer in the making of educational films. The chapters in this collection cover his relation to the project of the creation of a Brazilian nation and the relation of his research to the positivism dominant in Brazilian social science at the time. Though Roquette-Pinto is not well-known outside of Brazil, his writings are relevant to the formation of the Brazilian nation. [RMW]

550 Associação Brasileira de História das Religiões. Simpósio. 8th, *São Luís do Maranhão, Brazil, 2006*. Religião, raça e identidade: Colóquio do Centenário da Morte de Nina Rodrigues. Organização de Adroaldo J.S. Almeida, Lyndon de A. Santos e Sergio Figueiredo Ferretti. São Paulo: Paulinas: Edições ABHR, 2009. 191 p.: bibl. (Col. Estudos da ABHR; 6)

Brings together a collection of articles from the centenary of Nina Rodrigues' work. He was a controversial late 19th-century medical doctor who is generally credited with having founded the anthropological study of the Afro-Brazilian population, being the first Brazilian anthropologist to deal with racial themes. His theories generally situated Afro-Brazilians within a social evolutionary context; his theory of religion thus characterizes it as "animist fetiches," an idea that became influential in the formation of religious ethnographies. Notable contributions to this collection are by Lilia Moritz Schwarcz, who analyzes Rodrigues' views on criminal anthropology; and a series of essays that show the influences of Rodrigues' views on religious pluralism, change in Afro-Brazilian religions, and the understanding of ethnic identity in the contemporary context. [RMW]

551 Calavia Sáez, Oscar. O nome e o tempo dos Yaminawa: etnologia e história dos Yaminawa do rio Acre. São Paulo: Editora Unesp: Instituto Socioambiental; Rio de Janeiro: Núcleo Transformações Indígenas, 2006. 479 p.: bibl., ill., indexes, maps.

One of several works produced over the past decade by ethnologists affiliated with the "perspectivist" school of Brazilian anthropologist Eduardo Viveiros de Castro and colleagues at the Museu Nacional in Rio de Janeiro. This poststructuralist "school" analyzes indigenous worldviews and modes of thought based on the categories which, to the researcher, seem to be central to the indigenous point of view. The dichotomy of kin and affines is a key part of the indigenous perspective. Calavia's ethnography of the Yaminawa, a Panoan-speaking people, begins with the structure of their kinship system, showing the categories in action, especially in the ritual field. Historical analysis seeks to show how these categories have transformed yet are still present in peoples' memories. Finally, the monograph analyzes sacred stories to dis-

cover the logic of thought and the meaning of society in time. An extensive collection of sacred stories is included. [RMW]

552 Os ceramistas tupiguarani. Vol. 1, Sinteses regionais. Edição de André Prous e Tania Andrade Lima. Brasília: Instituto do Patrimônio Histórico e Artístico Nacional, 2008. 1 v.: bibl., ill. (some col.), maps (some col.).

This is an important evaluation of the state of the art of archeological studies of Tupi-Guarani ceramics, organized by one of the leading Brazilian archeologists and an ethnologist known for her contribution to the theory of perspectivism in indigenous ethnology. The volume includes a global picture of Tupi-Guarani ceramic traditions in Amazonia, the Northeast, Southeast, and South. An introductory essay concentrates on the important work done by José Proenza Brochado, whose collaboration with North American archeologist Donald Lathrap defined one of the principal directions in Brazilian ethnology of the 1980s. For archeologist's comment, see *HLAS 65:341*. [RMW]

553 Couro dos espíritos: namoro, pajés e cura entre os índios Gavião-Ikolen de Rondônia. Textos de Betty Mindlin *et al.* Colaboração de Mauro Leonel. São Paulo: Terceiro Nome: Editora Senac São Paulo, 2001. 251 p.: bibl., ill. (some col.).

Couro dos espíritos ("Flesh of the Spirits") is a collection of stories from the Gavião-Ikolen Indians of Rondônia. Organized and edited by the anthropologist Betty Mindlin, this work is the latest in a series of books on traditions of the Indians of Rondônia by her and her husband Mauro Leonel. Indigenous narrators are listed as co-authors. The collection is organized around several themes but without any clear connection except that of enticing potential readers ("Love," "Here, the Beyond"). The final section by Leonel relates some of the historical context which has transfigured the Gavião in recent years; it also discusses the role of NGOs in supporting the rights of the Gavião. There is a quasi-prophetic message at the end by a great shaman who for many years skillfully led a dual life as shaman and evangelical pastor. [RMW]

554 Editing Eden: a reconsideration of identity, politics, and place in Amazonia. Edited by Frank Hutchins and Patrick C. Wilson. Lincoln: Univ. of Nebraska Press, 2010. 273 p.: bibl., index.

This is an outstanding collection of highly relevant articles focusing on inter-ethnic relations between indigenous and non-indigenous populations in contemporary Amazonia, the complexity of those relations, especially with regard to identity construction, and representations of place. Amazonia is seen as an "object of the imagination" replete with preconceived notions of indigeneity; as a "frontier zone" generating ideas of liminality, marginality; and as a "field" in which the ideologies of the West still confront the cosmologies of native peoples. An outstanding essay by Beth Conklin presents an insightful interpretation of Western and indigenous Wari' expectations in the contact situation. [RMW]

555 Entre saias justas e jogos de cintura. Organização de Alinne Bonetti e Soraya Resende Fleischer. Ilha de Santa Catarina, Brazil: Editora Mulheres: EDUNISC, 2007. 370 p.: bibl.

A collection of field diaries by women ethnographers whose research centered on questions of gender and fieldwork; sexuality and fieldwork; women among men talking about their masculinity and reproductive decisions; and research among lesbians. Various theoretical issues are raised having to do with power; Brazilian rituals of coming-of-age in non-indigenous contexts. There is no recipe proposed for doing a good ethnography; however, sharing experiences and putting oneself in the other's place are useful for further research. Above all, the organizers focus on how attributes of gender and generation have influenced "tight skirts" and the "jogos de cintura" found in the field. [RMW]

556 As festas e os dias: ritos e sociabilidades festivas. Organização de Maria Laura Viveiros de Castro Cavalcanti e José Reginaldo Santos Gonçalves. Textos de Els Lagrou *et al.* Rio de Janeiro: Contra Capa, 2009. 269 p.: bibl., ill.

This collection of articles focuses on ritual theory, including several contributions by the new generation of anthropologists seeking to enhance understanding of ritual forms in diverse contexts: the Festival of the Divine Holy Spirit among immigrants in Rio de Janeiro; urban socialities, time, and narrative in the popular festival "bumba-meu-boi" (a cowboy rite that has become symbolic of the lifestyle and carnavalesque vision of rural Brazilians); laughter, the smile, and performance; ritual disguises and human sociability; and ritual in ethnographic film. The product is a stimulating set of new perspectives on the nature and esthetics of ritual, ultimately leading to a theory of culture. [RMW]

557 Hale, Lindsay. Hearing the mermaid's song: the Umbanda religion in Rio de Janeiro. Albuquerque: Univ. of New Mexico Press, 2009. 192 p.: bibl., index.

This ethnographic study examines Umbanda in Rio de Janeiro, an Afro-Brazilian religion, the specialists of which are mediums who speak in the voices of the deities while in a trance-like state. Based on many years of research on Umbanda, the author places the religion in its historical and cultural context. He demonstrates how its popularity has grown significantly over the past few decades, attracting not only those who seek the assistance of spirits in solving the problems in their lives, but also those in pursuit of a path to a rich spiritual life and a fellowship of faith and service. For comment by sociologist, see item **2599.** [RMW]

558 Homenagens: Associação Brasileira de Antropologia: 50 anos. Organização de Cornelia Eckert e Emília Pietrafesa de Godoi. Florianópolis, Brazil: Nova Letra Gráfica & Editora, 2006. 408 p.: bibl., ill.

This notable collection of statements celebrates the 50th anniversary of the Associação Brasileira de Antropologia. The contributions are written by several of the association's most outstanding past presidents—Roberto Cardoso de Oliveira, Antonio Arantes, Mariza Correa (all from the Universidade Estadual de Campinas). Each pays homage to the association and its directions, its activities relevant to political and social demands, and theoretical questions that have shaped contemporary Brazilian anthropology. A series of events took place in various parts of the country on the occasion of the association's 50th anniversary. [RMW]

559   Ladeira, Maria Inês. O caminhar sob a luz: território mbya à beira do oceano. São Paulo: Editora UNESP, 2007. 199 p.: bibl., ill., maps.

This book, by one of the most knowledgeable social scientists to have worked with the Guarani of southern Brazil, is one of the best introductions to the culture of these peoples, who are undoubtedly the largest indigenous population of the Southern Cone to have survived the conquest and for the longest duration of time. Ladeira's MA thesis (originally written in 1992) dispels the stereotype of the Guarani as "nomads" based on observations of their mobility, connecting their dynamic mobility with their cosmovision that provides a structure for their symbolic imaginary and philosophy of life. Kinship ties, the constant search for a better space, and a near-untouched land in the 21st century are the fundamental elements of a people's millenarian search for a place where they can live their way of life (tekoha). [RMW]

560   Ladeira, Maria Inês. Espaço geográfico Guarani-Mbya: significado, constituição e uso. Maringá, Brazil: Eduem; São Paulo: Edusp, 2008. 228 p.: bibl., ill. (some col.), col. maps.

This is a pioneering contribution based on decades of fieldwork with the Guarani Indians in the south of Brazil. It provides an astonishingly rich study of their worldview. Among its implications are that development projects involving territorial organization should not consider nature and its dynamics as merely "resources" for indigenous peoples who perceive nature as a totality. This is a prime book for understanding Guarani views on their migrations. It provides an excellent study of the Guarani Indians' notions of space and their movement in it, throughout a vast territory they know and experience throughout their lives. For the Guarani, according to the author, what fixes the earthly world in space—and configures it as a territory—is what moves through it. This movement, taking care of the territory, is practiced with perseverance, even under the most adverse conditions for all the beings that interact in various spheres of the Mbya world. [RMW]

561   Lasmar, Denise Portugal. O acervo imagético da Comissão Rondon: no Museu do Índio, 1890–1938. Rio de Janeiro: Museu do Índio, FUNAI, 2008. 262 p.: bibl., ill., col. maps. (Publicação avulsa do Museu do Índio; 3)

This important collection includes reproductions of photos and documents from the Rondon Telegraph Commission around the turn of the 20th century. A brief history of the Commission is followed by a discussion of the production of photographic and microfilm documents; these introduce a spectacular collection of photos of peoples such as the Pareci and others with whom the Commission made contact, in some cases for the first time. [RMW]

562   Laudos periciais antropológicos em debate. Organização de Ilka Boaventura Leite. Textos de Ilka Boaventura Leite et al. Florianópolis, Brazil: ABA: NUER/ UFSC, 2005. 281 p.: bibl., ill.

A significant collection of articles focusing on the question of "expert testimony" in the cases of land demarcation for indigenous peoples and communities of descendants of African slaves (mocambos). The articles offer significant reflections on the ethics of this type of applied work, its implications for the peoples whom the testimony is intended to benefit, the difficult question of "ethnic identity and traditional territories"—i.e., how boundaries are to be determined, and the limitations of anthropological understanding of indigenous notions of territory. The case studies cover nearly all of Brazil, but especially the Northeast and South. Key documents from the Associação Brasileira de Antropologia on "expert testimony" are included. [RMW]

563   Machado, Maria Fátima Roberto. Museu Rondon: antropologia & indigenismo na Universidade da Selva. Cuiabá, Brazil: Entrelinhas, 2009. 334 p.: bibl., ill. (some col.), map.

This carefully constructed history of the Museu Rondon, published by the Associação Brasileira de Antropologia, appears along with several other books commemorating the Columbus Quincentenary. Its goal is to reflect on the relation between Anthropology and Indigenism in the museum's history. The museum, located in the state of Mato Grosso, is a part of the Universidade Federal de Mato Grosso. Broader questions regarding Anthropology and museums are discussed with ideas on the future of museums as institutions engaged in the production of knowledge for the benefit of the public-at-large. [RMW]

564   Neves, Guilherme Santos. Coletânea de estudos e registros do folclore capixaba, 1944–1982. Edição de Reinaldo Santos Neves. Vitória, Brazil: Centro Cultural de Estudos e Pesquisas do Espírito Santo, 2008. 2 v.: bibl., ill.

This collection is the result of the editor's long-term research on the popular traditions from the state of Espirito Santo called "Capixaba Folklore 1944–82" published in 2 volumes. Around 250 studies and records of a wide variety of capixaba folklore are listed—ranging from oral traditions to beliefs and "superstitions," festivals, popular recipes, music, and popular dramatizations. The volume was financed by Petrobras, valorizing local traditions and identities. [RMW]

565   The occult life of things: native Amazonian theories of materiality and personhood. Edited by Fernando Santos-Granero. Tucson: Univ. of Arizona Press, 2009. 256 p.: bibl., index.

In this collection, 10 authors reflect on the place and role of objects in human social life, exploring how various indigenous Amazonian peoples envision the lives of material objects: the "occult," or extraordinary lives of things, whose "personae" are not normally visible to people. Among the native societies included in this collection are the Eastern Tukanoans, the Nambikwara, Wauja, Kayapo, Matis, and Cashinahua. [RMW]

Oliveira, Jorge Eremites de and **Levi Marques Pereira.** Ñande Ru Marangatu: laudo antropológico e histórico sobre uma terra kaiowa na fronteira do Brasil com o Paraguai, município de Antônio João, Mato Grosso do Sul. See item **339.**

566   Pissolato, Elizabeth. A duração da pessoa: mobilidade, parentesco e xamanismo mbya guarani. São Paulo: Editora UNESP: Instituto Socioambiental; Rio de Janeiro: Núcleo Transformações Indígenas, 2007. 445 p.: bibl., ill.

"The Duration of the Person" is the author's PhD dissertation on the Mbya Guarani of the old reserve of Parati-mirim in the state of Rio de Janeiro. Its focus is the notion of the person—a well-worked theme in Brazilian ethnology—but the author offers a slightly different twist to the previous French structuralist-influenced studies by presenting Guarani "personhood" as constituted by relations, and the mobility of the Guarani in search of ideal social relations. The author analyzes rich and captivating material on the Guarani notion of "transformation" as well. [RMW]

567   Potiguara, Eliane. Metade cara, metade máscara. São Paulo: Global Editora: Instituto Indígena Brasileiro para Propriedade Intelectual, 2004. 138 p.: bibl., ill. (Serie Visões indígenas)

"Half Face, Half Mask," as the title suggests, concerns the identity of the indigenous peoples of the Americas who have been dislodged from their territories and robbed of their cultures and lands; the "village-less" peoples, the products of 500 years of colonization. While the book is about the author's specific life-experiences, it could easily be abstracted to refer to all displaced indigenous peoples. Inspired by Fanon's *Wretched of the Earth*, Potiguara (whose people, a Tupian-speaking group, were from the Northeast coast) bares her soul through poetry, vignettes, and her life story with all its sufferings, pride, courage, and intense political spontaneity. [RMW]

568   Rebolledo, Nicanor. Cultura, escolarización y etnografía: los palikur en el Amazonas brasileño del Bajo Uaça. México: Univ. Iberoamericana, 2009. 333 p.: bibl., ill., maps. (Col. Trabajos destacados de titulación de posgrado)

Besides offering an ethnography of primary school education among the Palikur Indians of the Uaçá River region, the author seeks to make a more extensive reflection on methods in the ethnography of education. First, he offers an introduction to the field of the Anthropology of education; second, an anthropological reading of indigenous school education; and third, reflections on fieldwork by non-indigenous schoolteachers working in indigenous schools. In one chapter, the author combines indigenous interpretations with ethnographic descriptions and details the Palikur way of life, especially the importance of religious questions, indigenous cosmovision, myths, and rituals central to their education. [RMW]

569 Simpósio Internacional Amazônia 500 Anos, 2000. Amazônia: além dos 500 anos. Organização de Louis Carlos Forline, Rui Murrieta e Ima Célia Guimarães Vieira. Belém, Brazil: Museu Paraense Emílio Goeldi, 2006. 566 p.: bibl., ill., maps.

Proceedings of a conference held in April 2000, on the occasion of the Quincentenary. Brings together an excellent collection of texts by a group of 22 well-known scholars from a variety of disciplines, all associated with the Museu Paraense Emilio Goeldi in Belém do Pará. The collection offers a reflection on the situation of indigenous peoples and what the non-indigenous societies have learned from them. Authors re-evaluate processes of colonization and their implications for the emergence of a distinctly Amazonian society, as well as "modernization" policies for the region and their implications for its future. [RMW]

570 Turner, Terence. The crisis of late structuralism: perspectivism and animism: rethinking culture, nature, bodiliness, and spirit. (*Tipití*, 7:1, June 2009, p. 3–42)

This article's point of departure is an assessment of the achievements and limitations of structuralism as exemplified by the work of Claude Levi-Strauss, with particular attention to its applications for Amazonian ethnographic data. The author suggests how recent development in Amazonianist Anthropology, notably the rethinking of animism by Philippe Descola and the development of perspectivism by Eduardo Viveiros de Castro, can be understood as attempts to avoid or transcend the "crisis" of late structuralism by reformulating some of its key theoretical assumptions, beginning with the relation of nature and culture. The article concludes with a positive assessment of the reformulation of nature and culture rooted in the fundamental role of productive activity. [RMW]

571 Viegas, Susana de Matos. Terra calada: os Tupinambá na Mata Atlântica do Sul da Bahia. Rio de Janeiro: 7Letras; Coimbra, Brazil: Almedina, 2007. 339 p.: bibl., ill. (some col.), maps (some col.).

The author presents testimony of the existence of a rural population near Ilheus, Bahia, who have traditionally been known as "caboclos" but who assumed their indigenous identity as "Tupinambá" when they became aware of Brazilian history. Today, they are known as the "Tupinambá of Olivença." The ethnography takes an interpretivist, perspectivist approach to understanding the peoples' notions of person, kinship, and social units. It contributes to the "anthropology of sentiments" in discussing affect, family tensions, fantasies, and conciliations between men and women. The ethnography is historical, providing a basis for the anthropological certification of the community's indigenous identity and hence the demarcation of a land reserve. In view of the land conflicts the community faces, the ethnography is an important document. [RMW]

572 Wright, Robin M. The fruit of knowledge and the body of the gods: religious meanings of plants among the Baniwa. (*J. Stud. Relig. Nat. Cult.*, 3:1, 2009, p. 126–153)

This article focuses on the sacrificial acts of divinities and other primal beings whose bodies became cultivated and wild plants; and plants as forms of gifts and other types of exchange from the deities to humanity among the Baniwa peoples of the Northwest Amazon. It seeks to reflect on Viveiros de Castro's ideas on Amerindian "perspectivism" (1996, 2002) to evaluate their "fit" to Baniwa spiritual ethnobotany. Initially, the author argues that there is a major difference between the perspectivism and agentivity of animal and fish-people, which is very common amongst all Arawak and Tukanoan-speaking peoples, and the plants which derive more often from a divinity that has been sacrificed, dismembered, transformed, and divided into many distinct plants. The predator-prey relation between animals, fish, and humans is secondary when compared to sacrifice and gifting relations between plants and humans, which seem to have more to do with the peaceful development of chiefly and priestly societies. [RMW]

COLOMBIA, VENEZUELA, AND THE GUIANAS

573 **Aikhenvald, Alexandra Y.** Language contact in Amazonia. Oxford, England: Oxford Univ. Press, 2010. 363 p.: bibl., ill., indexes, map, plates. (Oxford linguistics)

One of the most comprehensive studies on the consequences of language contact in Lowland South America, this book provides insight into the sociolinguistic consequences of contact with Portuguese and English, as well as the scale of areal diffusion and its implications for grammatical categorization. Replete with careful linguistic analysis, the volume explores contact between Arawak and Tucanoan languages spoken in the Vaupés River basin of northwest Amazonia. In this region that spans Colombia and Brazil, language is an important mark of collective identity, and perhaps not surprisingly, language mixing is opposed on ideological grounds. For review of 1st edition, see *HLAS 61:706*. [BD]

Mejía Ochoa, William. Presencia embera en el Área Metropolitana Centro Occidente. See item 2473.

574 **Ramírez, María Clemencia.** Between the guerrillas and the state: the cocalero movement, citizenship, and identity in the Colombian Amazon. Translated by Andy Klatt. Durham, N.C.: Duke Univ. Press, 2011. 311 p.: bibl., ill., index, maps.

This compelling ethnographic account of Colombia's *cocalero* social movement explores how the movement emerged in the "lawless" department of Putumayo, a region long subjected to the de facto rule of rebel and paramilitary armed forces. Colombia's national government has characterized the Putumayo as an uncivilized and disorderly place, and as such refused to view the coca growers as anything but criminals. The text chronicles how the *cocaleros* have in effect demanded that the state acknowledge campesinos as citizens, offer basic social services, and assist them to make the shift from coca growing to sustainable, legal livelihoods. For sociologist's review of the first edition (in Spanish), see *HLAS 61:3579*. [BD]

575 **Sandoval Forero, Eduardo.** La guardia indígena nasa y el arte de la resistencia pacífica. Bogotá: Fundación Hemera, 2008. 142 p.: bibl., ill. (Col. Étnica)

Exploration of nonviolence as a medium for struggle by the indigenous people of Colombia, especially the Nasa. Contributes to the general literature on the subject. [D. Earle]

576 **Zent, Egleé L.** "We come from trees": the poetics of plants among the Jotï of the Venezuelan Guayana. (*J. Stud. Relig. Nat. Cult.*, 3:1, 2009, p. 9–35)

Study of the prominent role plants play in the daily lives of the Jotï peoples, an indigenous society from the Venezuelan Guayana. Article reveals how plants are constitutive agents in Jotï biological, cultural, and cosmological production and reproduction. In addition to establishing the centrality of plants in the creation of humanity, the essay explores Jotï ethnobotany in terms of "the symbolic economy of alterity." [BD]

PERU AND ECUADOR

577 **Beyer, Stephan V.** Singing to the plants: a guide to mestizo shamanism in the upper Amazon. Albuquerque: Univ. of New Mexico Press, 2009. 530 p.: bibl., ill., index.

Emphasizing the eclectic and syncretic nature of Upper Amazonian mestizo shamanism, this work seeks to understand shamanism, in its own locally conceived categories as well as in terms of the "new global economy." The book provides a detailed description of mestizo shamanism in Peruvian Amazonia. The text chronicles ayahuasca healing ceremonies, describes how shamans establish spiritual ties with plant spirits, and discusses how botanical preparations are used in curing rituals, love potions, and sorcery. [BD]

578 **Erazo, Juliet.** Constructing indigenous subjectivities: economic collectivism and identity in the Ecuadorian Amazon. (*Dev. Change/Oxford*, 41:6, Nov. 2010, p. 1017–1039)

Essay embraces a governmentality analytic in an effort to understand how indigenous representatives from the Ecuadorian Amazon have fostered collective engagement in market-driven pursuits. A detailed assessment of one indigenous organization highlights the extent to which leaders' "subjectivity-shaping" initiatives have been shaped by associations with the state and NGOs, as well as local conceptions of status, leadership, and authority. The author notes that leaders frequently employ collaborative economic projects as a means for forging new types of indigenous citizenship. Underscoring the agentive aspects of the new senses of citizenship, the essay asserts that indigenous leaders are not simply agents for the state and international development groups' subjectivity-shaping projects; nor are they merely acting in their own interest. Instead they both "constitute and regulate new types of citizens" as a means of ensuring the viability of their organizations political agenda. [BD]

Greene, Shane. Customizing indigeneity: paths to a visionary politics in Peru. See item **651**.

579   Jernigan, Kevin A. Dietary restrictions in healing among speakers of Iquito, an endangered language of the Peruvian Amazon. (*J. Ethnobiol. Ethnomed.*, 7:20, July 2011, p. 1–10, bibl., map, photo, tables)

Presents the results of a study of customary prohibitions among the Iquito, a Zaparoan speaking indigenous society of Peruvian Amazonia. For the Iquito the practice of "dieting" (siyan++ni) is central to rites of healing. Iquito restrictions involve dietary prohibitions and prohibition of activities thought to exacerbate illness, such as contact with environmental influences that clash with some healing methods (e.g., enemas or steam baths). The study reveals that restrictions found among the Iquito correspond to some aspect of illness explanatory models. To wit, 35 percent correspond with specific illness etiologies; 53 percent correspond to specific pathophysiologies; 18 percent correspond with overall seriousness of the illness; while 18 percent are only associated with particular forms of treatment. This study of Iquito ethnomedicine concludes that diets predicated on personalistic reasoning have a considerably higher than average number of restrictions than those associated with naturalistic reasoning. A

number of the specific restrictions reported among the Iquito do correlate with patterns seen in other Amazonian societies, especially those connected to sympathetic reasoning and the spiritual uses of plants. [BD]

580   Kernaghan, Richard. Coca's gone: of might and right in the Huallaga postboom. Stanford, Calif.: Stanford Univ. Press, 2009. 308 p.: bibl., index.

Emphasizing collective memory, this volume explores the legacy of violence in the social topography of Peru's Upper Huallaga Valley following a 20-year cocaine boom and bloody civil war. This deeply compelling ethnography lucidly conveys the texture of lived experience for those whose daily existence coincided with a time of fear and state-sanctioned brutality. The author skillfully recounts stories of social trauma while providing a haunting meditation on the difficult inter-relationships between violence, law, and time. [BD]

581   Lu, Flora E. and **Ciara Wirth.** Conservation perceptions, common property, and cultural polarization among the Waorani of Ecuador's Amazon. (*Hum. Organ.*, 70:3, Fall 2011, p. 233–243)

Study of the change in perceptions of resource scarcity, levels of social cohesion, and involvement in biodiversity conservation among the Waorani of northeastern Ecuador. While local perceptions of resource scarcity are more apparent today than they were a decade ago, the authors contend that the primary risks to ensuring environmentally responsible resource stewardship among the Waorani are increased strains resulting from the increased juxtaposition of individual rights with collective duties on the one hand, and changing ideas of territorial boundaries on the other hand. [BD]

582   Madera, Lisa Maria. Visions of Christ in the Amazon: the gospel according to ayahuasca and Santo Daime. (*J. Stud. Relig. Nat. Cult.*, 3:1, 2009, p. 66–98)

Comparative study of the influence of ayahuasca and "eco-revolutionary" Christian visions in Amazonia. Essay explores the "Gospel" as told by the Ecuadorian Quichua Aguarico Runa and then assesses local understanding of the Gospel according to Santo Daime, a Christian sect devoted to the ritualized consumption of ayahuasca. [BD]

583 Salisbury, David S.; José Borgo López; and Jorge W. Vela Alvarado. Transboundary political ecology in Amazonia: history, culture, and conflicts of the borderland Ashaninka. (*J. Cult. Geogr.*, 28:1, Feb. 2011, p. 147–177)

Embracing a "transboundary political ecology framework," this useful account assesses the scramble for natural resources in the context of Peru and Brazil's border dispute over the Ucayali and Jurua watersheds, the customary homelands of the Ashaninka. Authors note that global resource demand has shaped the boundary formation and resulted in indigenous labor migration. [BD]

584 Swanson, Tod Dillon. Singing to estranged lovers: Runa relations to plants in the Ecuadorian Amazon. (*J. Stud. Relig. Nat. Cult.*, 3:1, 2009, p. 36–65)

Study of the relationship between Runa peoples and plants in the Ecuadorian Amazon. Provides a nuanced analysis of ritual plant songs and gardening practices, and persuasively shows how plants are likened to dangerous lovers or demand ing children. Analysis of Quichua and Shuar language accounts of the origins of different plant species reveals that plant species are thought to have emerged from a previously human state in which the plants were once lovers or children who eventually became estranged. Over time, emotional estrangement in the physical transformation has given rise to a novel species. Essay concludes by noting that the treatment of plants as "high maintenance lovers" gives rise to elaborate and time-consuming gardening practices. [BD]

585 Wylie, Lesley. Rare models: Roger Casement, the Amazon, and the ethnographic picturesque. (*Ir. Stud. Rev.*, 18:3, Aug. 2010, p. 315–330, bibl., photos)

Essay recounts the history of Omarino and Ricudo, two indigenous Amazonian young men who arrived in Britain in the summer of 1911 at the behest of Roger Casement, who had been dispatched the previous year to the Putumayo by the British government to investigate the alleged

human rights abuses of the Peruvian Amazon Company. Wylie explores the degree to which Omarino and Ricudo were treated as human "exhibits" by Casement, who in addition to introducing them to prominent members of the British establishment, arranged for them to be painted and photographed according to the prevailing ethnographic conventions of the time. [BD]

PARAGUAY, ARGENTINA, AND BOLIVIA

586 Arenas, Pastor and Gustavo Porini. Las aves en la vida de los tobas del oeste de Formosa, Argentina. Asunción: Editorial Tiempo de Historia, 2009. 299 p.: bibl., ill., index, map.

Ethno-ornithological research among Toba groups of northern Argentina. Offers a meticulous description of the relation between the Toba and birds: religious representations, classification systems, and usage of birds as food, medicine, equipment, or shamanic tools. Provides a detailed account of both material culture and social use. Includes a listing of species. Contributes valuable ethnographic information. [SMH]

587 Bigot, Margot. Los aborígenes Qom en Rosario: contacto lingüístico-cultural, bilingüismo, diglosia y vitalidad etnolingüística en grupos de aborígenes "qom" (tobas) asentados en Rosario (Empalme Graneros y Los Pumitas). Rosario, Argentina: Univ. Nacional de Rosario, 2007. 255 p.: bibl.

Ethnolinguistic and anthropological study of language vitality and use among the Qom of Rosario (Argentina). Study analyzes the impact of diverse factors including migration of the Qom from rural areas to urban settlements and sociolinguistic representations of the language. Contribution to the analysis of language and ethnicity among an urbanized indigenous group. [SMH]

588 Blaser, Mario. Storytelling globalization from the Chaco and beyond. Durham, N.C.: Duke Univ. Press, 2010. 292 p.: bibl., ill., index, maps. (New ecologies for the twenty-first century)

Author provides a critical and theoretically grounded analysis of the interplay of globalization and development projects among the Yshiro Indians of the Chaco region of Paraguay. Examines the ways in which pro-Indian (indigenista) development discourses and projects influence representations and imaginings of who the Yshiro are and how they want to live, and the contentious struggle for the emergence of a pan-Indian Yshiro organization. Contributes an engaging storytelling of the entangled penetration of globalization, development projects, and politics, and how these are contested and experienced by the Yshiro. [SMH]

589 Braunstein, José. Les Maká: tradition et tourisme. (Indiens des frontières coloniales. Amérique australe, XVIe siècle-temps présent. Textes par Jimena Paz Obregón Iturra, Luc Capdevila et Nicolás Richard. Rennes, France: Presses Univ. de Rennes, 2011, p. 217–232)

This article explores the relationship between the Maká (Paraguayan Chaco) and Russian Gen. Jean Belaieff. Focuses on the dual material culture of the Maká: one for internal use, the other for tourist trade. The author traces—through myth and oral history—the origins of this second material culture as an outcome of a traditionalist reaction to Christian messianic ideas. [SMH]

590 Carrasco, Morita. Tierras duras: historias, organización y lucha por el territorio en el Chaco argentino. Buenos Aires: IWGIA, 2009. 430 p.

Book traces two decades of history of Lhaka Honhat, a large multi-ethnic indigenous organization of Argentina's Chaco. Provides valuable insights into problems of access to land, the organization of indigenous movements, and the interference of Protestant churches and NGOs. [SMH]

591 Cebolla Badie, Marilyn. Una etnografía sobre la miel en la cultura Mbya-Guaraní. Quito: Abya-Yala: Univ. Politécnica Salesiana, 2009. 147 p.: bibl., ill., maps.

Ethnography of the use and knowledge of bees and honey among the Mbya Guaraní Indians of Argentina. Contributes to the understanding of the classification system of the Guaraní, the link of honey

and bees to the mythical world, and ritual. [SMH]

592 Combès, Isabelle. Los fugitivos escondidos: acerca del enigma tapiete. (Bull. Inst. fr. étud. andin., 37:3, 2008, p. 511–533, bibl., map)

The ethnic origin of the Tapiete has long been of interest in Lowland studies. Based on ethnographic and secondary sources, Combès proposes the hypothesis that this group took on a Guarani identity in two different historic periods, in one case under the influence of the Chané—a people who had been "guaranized" earlier. [SMH]

593 Combès, Isabelle. Zamucos. Cochabamba, Bolivia: Instituto Latinoamericano de Misiología, 2009. 318 p.: bibl., ill., indexes, maps. (Col. Scripta autochtona; 1)

Considered an "isolated" people until the middle of the 20th century, the history of Zamuco-speaking groups has been largely neglected. Combès gathers diverse historical sources and analyzes the many ethnic names found in documents written by early explorers, Jesuits, and others between the 16th and 20th centuries. Reconstructs the social transformation endured by Zamuco speakers in the missions in the 18th century and the emergence of more encompassing ethnic groups after the Chaco War. Includes a collection of unpublished documents. [SMH]

594 Combès, Isabelle; Diego Villar; and **Kathleen Lowrey.** Comparative studies and the South American Gran Chaco. (Tipití, 7:1, June 2009, p. 69–102)

Article offers a thorough review of ethnohistorical and ethnographic work in Gran Chaco (Argentina, Paraguay, Bolivia), surveying types of historical sources, schools of thought and main trends in Chaco literature. Authors suggest that the academically marginal place of this region, next to the Andes and Amazonia, as well as the cultural hybridity of its peoples, has led to heterogeneous theoretical approaches. Finally, they point out the usefulness of a comparative study between Chaco and North America Great Plains. [SMH]

595 La educación intercultural bilingüe en Argentina: identidades, lenguas y protagonistas. Compilación de Silvia María Hirsch y Adriana Serrudo. Buenos Aires: Noveduc, 2010. 358 p.: bibl.

Collection of 13 articles which describe and analyze intercultural bilingual education programs in schools with indigenous students in Argentina. Introductory essay by Hirsch and Serrudo provides a historical account of the development of education in indigenous communities and the emergence of the intercultural approach. Contributes to a growing field of interest related to indigenous education, formation of bilingual indigenous teachers, and language revitalization. [SMH]

596 Gordillo, Gastón. The clientelization of ethnicity: party hegemony and indigenous political subjectivities. (*J. Lat. Am. Cult. Stud.*, 17:3, Dec. 2008, p. 335–348)

Focuses on the immersion of indigenous actors within national political parties—the "clientelization of ethnicity." Critiques Argentina's mass-media representation of indigenous peoples as passive victims of clientelism and political violence. Through a description of two political conflicts, the article illustrates the interaction between ethnic and political divisions. [SMH]

597 Hacia una nueva carta étnica del Gran Chaco VII. Las Lomitas, Argentina: Centro del Hombre Antiguo Chaqueño, 2010. 207 p.

Collection of articles written by anthropologists and lawyers about legal cases in indigenous communities. Includes articles ranging from theoretical essays about cultural diversity and the relation between punitive systems and criminal law to studies on particular legal cases which include reports by anthropological experts. [SMH]

598 Los hombres transparentes: indígenas y militares en la guerra del Chaco, 1932–1935. Textos de Luc Capdevila *et al.* La Paz: Instituto Latinoamericano de Misionología, U.C.B.: Itinerarios: CERHIO, 2010. 230 p.: bibl., ill., maps. (Col. Scripta autochtona; 5)

The sequel to *Mala Guerra: los indígenas en la Guerra del Chaco, 1932–35* (see *HLAS 65:624*), this book has the same general goal: to offer an account of the Chaco War (1932–35) from the indigenous perspective. The five articles focus on different ethnic groups involved in the war. Arguably, the most interesting contributions of the volume are those by Combès, which includes a comprehensive account of Col. Ángel Ayoroa's little-known explorations to the Chaco, and P. Barbosa/N. Richard, whose contribution is based on a survey conducted among the Nivaclé of Paraguay about their memories of the war and provides a sound reconstruction of Nivaclé recent history from the indigenous point of view. [SMH]

599 Langer, Erick D. Expecting pears from an elm tree: Franciscan missions on the Chiriguano frontier in the heart of South America, 1830–1949. Durham, N.C.: Duke Univ. Press, 2009. 375 p.: bibl., ill., index.

Comprehensive history of the Franciscan missions among the Chiriguano in southeastern Bolivia during the republican period, from their establishment until their secularization after the Chaco War. Langer depicts life inside the missions as a long negotiation between Indians and friars, endeavoring to show their rationale and intentions. Excellent account on the destruction of missions by soldiers during and after the Chaco War. For historian's comment, see *HLAS 66:1780.* [SMH]

600 Léxico y categorización etnobiológica en grupos indígenas del Gran Chaco. Compilación de Cristina Messineo, Gustavo F. Scarpa y Florencia Tola. Santa Rosa, Argentina: Univ. Nacional de La Pampa, 2010. 296 p.

Multidisciplinary collection of articles that examine different problems of nominal classification among the Toba, Mocoví, Chorote, Wichí, and Maká Indians. Mainly in the fields of zoonomy and phytonomy, but also including illness and kinship. Most articles are meticulous and richly detailed, including large lists of indigenous terms. [SMH]

601 Lowrey, Kathleen. Salamanca and the city: culture credits, nature credits, and the modern moral economic of indigenous Bolivia. (*J. Royal Anthropol. Inst.*, 12:2, June 2006, p. 275–292)

Suggestive article focusing on representations of Isoso indigenous peoples beliefs' on "Salamanca," a traditional source of shamanic power recently applied to the city of Santa Cruz. Author shows that Salamanca discourses are an effective way of conceptualizing the new relations between the local communities and the state, and— given the morally ambivalent status of this place—the role played by their own political organization as mediator. [SMH]

602 Masferrer-Dodasa, Elena; Luis Rico-Garcia; and Tomás Huanca. Consumption of market goods and wellbeing in small-scale societies: an empirical test among the Tsimane' in the Bolivian Amazon. (*Ecol. Econ./Amsterdam*, Sept. 2011, http://dx.doi.org/10.1016/j.ecolecon.2011.08.009)

Article evalutes the association between human well-being and the consumption of market goods among the Tsimane' of the Bolivian Amazon. Multivariate analyses suggest that the consumption of market goods is not necessarily coupled with enhanced personal or communal well-being. [BD]

603 Montani, Rodrigo. La etnicidad de las cosas entre los wichís del Gran Chaco, provincia de Salta, Argentina. (*Indiana/Berlin*, 25, 2008, p. 117–142)

Article examines the production and distribution of objects made by Wichí women in Argentina. It explores material culture as a semantic system used to understand and interact with others. It successfully demonstrates a relation between the Wichí morphological classification of objects and ethnic categories applied to other groups. Includes detailed ethnographical data and makes thorough use of ethnolinguistic techniques. [SMH]

604 Movilizaciones indígenas e identidades en disputa en la Argentina. Compilación de Gastón Gordillo y Silvia María Hirsch. Argentina: FLACSO Argentina: La Crujía, 2010. 285 p.: bibl., ill., map.

Collection of 10 articles that analyze the process of ethnic emergence among indigenous groups of Argentina. Based on fieldwork carried out by Argentine anthropologists among indigenous groups, the articles address the interplay of political factors, legislative changes, and ethnic recognition to illustrate the emerging processes of

ethnic politics among native peoples at the community, regional, and national level. An introductory article by Gordillo and Hirsch provides an overview of the relations between the state and indigenous peoples. [SMH]

605 Reunión Anual de Etnología. Serie Anales de la Reunión Anual de Etnología: 22 al 25 de agosto, 2007. La Paz: MUSEF, 2007. 2 v.: ill., maps.

Two volumes of the proceedings of the Reunión Anual de Etnología of Bolivia. First volume contains papers on archeology, historical anthropology, and linguistic and bilingual intercultural education. Vol. 2 includes contributions on gender, health, politics, and identity. Both volumes cover current studies conducted among Highlands and Lowlands groups. [SMH]

606 Reyes-García, Victoria *et al.* The role of ethnobotanical skills and agricultural labor in forest clearance: evidence from the Bolivian Amazon. (*Ambio/Stockholm*, 40:3, May 2011, p. 310–321)

Essay on the research results of a study of local ecological knowledge for conservation. The authors assess whether ethnobotanical skills, which they use as a stand-in for local ecological knowledge, are linked to rates of deforestation noted among Tsimane' communities of Bolivia. The study documents a direct effect of ethnobotanical skills in diminishing the extent of forest cleared in fallow, but not old-growth, forest. The authors contend that the interplay between ethnobotanical skills and labor invested in shifting cultivation has opposite effects depending on whether the clearing is done in fallow or in old-growth forest. [BD]

607 Rodríguez Mir, Javier. Los wichí en las fronteras de la civilización: capitalismo, violencia y shamanismo en el Chaco argentino, una aproximación etnográfica. Quito: Abya-Yala, 2006. 416 p.: bibl., ill., maps.

Based on the author's doctoral dissertation, the book provides an overview of the Wichí groups living in northern Argentina. The author focuses on the various forms of past and present violence, including ethnographic accounts of inter-ethnic war, resistance to forced settlement, suicide, internal conflicts, shamanism, and the economic and symbolic violence imposed by the state and private employers. Offers a valuable overview of the present situation and problems of Wichí communities, as well as some insightful ethnographical data. [SMH]

608 Salamanca, Carlos A. Movilizaciones indígenas, mapas e historias por la propiedad de la tierra en el Chaco argentino: la lucha de las familias tobas por poxoyaxaic alhua. Buenos Aires: IWGIA-FLASCO, 2011. 81 p.

Based on fieldwork in three Toba (Qom) villages of Argentina, this book focuses on indigenous territorial practices, conflicts and political struggles for the land, the often violent harassment suffered by Indians, and most notably, the recent use of cartography as a means for political and legal recognition. Briefly outlines the history of sedentarization of the Toba population in the region and shows the continuance of traditional social organization beyond single "communities." [SMH]

609 Tabo Amapo, Alfredo. El eco de las voces olvidadas: una autoetnografía y etnohistoria de los cavineños de la Amazonía boliviana. Edición de Mickaël Brohan y Enrique Herrera Sarmiento. Copenhagen: Grupo Internacional de Trabajo sobre Asuntos Indígenas, 2008. 309 p.: bibl., ill., maps.

This auto-ethnography is a product of two decades of research by the author, a Cavineño native. Gathers oral traditions aiming to reconstruct the ancient social organization and general history of this people. Offers rich linguistic and ethnographic data, including a large collection of myths. Explores the penetration of evangelic cults, life in Catholic missions, and exploitation of native workers by rubber companies. Profusely annotated edition by anthropologists Brohan and Herrera. [SMH]

610 Villagra Carron, Rodrigo. The two shamans and the owner of the cattle: alterity, storytelling and shamanism amongst the Angaité of the Paraguayan Chaco. (*Supl. Antropol.*, 44:2, dic. 2009, p. 7–386)

Doctoral thesis based on research conducted among the Angaité of the Paraguayan Chaco region. Explores the history of the Angaité, the process of language loss,

and acquisition of the Guarani language. Delves into the oral history and inter-ethnic relations, and analyzes the transformation of shamanism and leadership. Engages in a rich ethnographic and theoretical analysis of notions of exchange and sharing, the process of colonization of the Chaco and how it impinged upon the Angaité, as well as elucidating the ways in which they have been represented by the national society and scholars. [SMH]

611 Villar, Diego; Lorena I. Córdoba; and Isabelle Combès. La reducción imposible: las expediciones del Padre Negrete a los pacaguaras, 1795–1800. Cochabamba, Bolivia: Instituto Latinoamericano de Misionología, U.C.B.; Buenos Aires: Misiones Franciscanas Conventuales, 2009. 262 p.: bibl., ill., map. (Scripta autochtona; 3)

First part of the book presents a detailed history of the ethnic groups known as "Southwestern Panoan" (Chacobo, Pacaguara, and Caripuna, Amazonian Bolivia). Reports on ethnographical data on social organization, Pano languages, kinship, and toponyms. Provides analysis of both published and unpublished documents and concludes that ethnonyms did not designate stables entities, but depended on context and history. Excellent contribution to Amazonian history. The second section includes documents by missionary Padre Negrete on his journeys through the region. [SMH]

612 Wilde, Guillermo. Religión y poder en las misiones de guaraníes. Buenos Aires: Sb, 2009. 509 p.: bibl., ill., maps. (Paradigma indicial. Serie Historia americana)

Comprehensive ethnohistorical and anthropological account based on systematic use of primary sources on the Guarani missions from the 17th to the 19th centuries. Throughout 11 densely documented chapters, Wilde explores the tense relations between Jesuits, leaders, and shamans, the expulsion of the Jesuits, the political and social transformations of the missions, and the emergent relations between the Guarani and the criollo settlers. Excellent contribution to the study of Lowland indigenous peoples and missions. For historian's comment, see *HLAS 66:1572*. [SMH]

Highlands

ANDREW ORTA, *Associate Professor of Anthropology, University of Illinois at Urbana-Champaign*

PUBLICATIONS REVIEWED for this section of *HLAS* 67 represent a robust range of ethnographic scholarship on the Andean Highlands. From offerings to local place deities, to the urban experiences of migrants, to the frontlines of indigenous social movements, to the role of ritual practices in constituting Highlands indigenous communities, the ethnography of the Andean Highlands well reflects the contemporary complexities and challenges facing the peoples of the region.

As has been a trend for a number of years now, a good deal of the regional scholarship is concerned with the politics of indigenous identity. In the context of the ascendance of discourses of indigenous ethnic identity in declarations of the International Labour Organization (ILO) and the UN, in a series of constitutional reforms and related legislation impacting countries across the region, in the work of the World Bank and other multilateral lending institutions and NGOs, and in the political mobilization of a range of indigenous social movements, scholarly attention remains focused on new forms of political participation by indigenous Andeans, and the transforming salience of indigeneity as a basis of local, national, and transnational political action.

Indigenous political action takes a number of forms. Albó and Anderson each offer a survey of indigenous social movements across the region; Albó's discussion sets current developments in historical perspective and examines relevant differences among the core Andean nations (item **613**). Others, as in the case of Anderson, see in current ethnic politics a barometer of the limitations of efforts to democratize and decolonize the region and an index of potentially dangerous political instability (item **614**; see also Fischer, item **616**). Two exemplary contributions (items **615** and **651**) take recent cases of indigenous political mobilization as an opportunity to rethink the categorical distinctions by which indigeneity has been conventionally conceived. Greene does this by recognizing indigeneity as an exogenous idea that is "customized" by indigenous actors in local circumstances. De la Cadena takes up a different sort of challenge, inquiring about the ways indigenous political action, and particularly the invocation of place deities and links to the land, may require a reframing of conventional understandings of "politics" (see, for example, item **624**).

These selections share with other authors an approach to indigenous politics—and to indigenous social forms more broadly—as not merely reactive to the circumstances of external threats, but rather as generative of new meanings and social forms out of the complex circumstances that have long shaped indigenous life in the region (e.g., items **636** and **650**). A related strand of scholarship examines ethnographically the impact of recent constitutional and juridical reforms, detailing new forms of civil society and political participation in national environments shaped by neoliberal reforms and their aftermaths (e.g., items **616, 625, 629, 630,** and **634**). Especially important in this vein are a number of works of more explicitly engaged scholarship, ethnographically documenting local complexities in dialogue with recent policy developments. Examples here include compilations from meetings uniting the experiences of local activists from across the region (items **617** and **623**), histories of local activist organizations (items **635** and **642**), as well as studies that aim to inform policymakers about frictions and gaps between models of indigenous society idealized in policy and the on-the-ground complexities of contemporary campesino life (items **631**, **657**, and **659**).

These discussions are supplemented by work examining the politics of indigeneity from the perspectives of elite and other non-indigenous interactants, discussing the counter-discourses of right-wing activists in Santa Cruz, Bolivia (item **626**), studying elite and state constructions of Mapuche identity in Chile (item **643**), looking at interactions between Yanacona activists and representatives of the Colombian state and UNESCO (*HLAS 65:647*), or between Kichwa shamans and international clients on the entheogen tourist circuit (item **646**).

A number of studies annotated here focus on non-indigenous contexts of Andean life, including Argentine oil field workers dealing with the privatization of their industry (item **621**), and the experiences of Colombian labor activists in the context of the transnational campaign against the Coca-Cola company (item **644**). In addition to signaling a growing ethnographic interest in business and labor settings, these works echo an important theme referenced above: the tensions between transnationally circulated ideals about, say, privatization, or labor solidarity (or indigenous territorial autonomy, see item **631**), and the integration of those ideals in specific contexts with their own local histories and expectations. This is analogous with a more classic theme in Andean ethnography concerning the localization of Christian meanings and practices, evident in various ways in this chapter in works by Citro (item **620**), Orta (item **633**), Spedding (item **638**), Curivil (item **640**), Corr (item **645**), Pacheco (item **655**), Pérez (item **656**), and Vega-Centeno (item **660**).

Gill's work shares with other items in this selection a transnational, and particularly North-South, frame of analysis. In addition to her examination of (principally US-based) transnational and Colombian labor activism, scholars here also address the cultural ideals informing international adoption practices alongside alternative local practices in Cuzco (item **654**), the experiences of Quechua shepherds in Wyoming as part of the US Guest Worker Program (item **653**), the implications of the circulation of a Shuar shrunken head recently repatriated from foreign museums (see *HLAS 65:600*), and a comparative discussion of racial politics of 20th-century lynchings in the US and more contemporary examples of lynching in Ecuador (item **648**).

In an informative convergence with de la Cadena's interest in the significance of "earth beings" in the context of indigenous political movements, a cluster of works in this selection take up strongly place-based themes. Fernández Juárez and Albó (item **627**) and Gil García (item **628**) each take up the deep significance of sacred mountains and other landscape elements for indigenous Andean communities. The studies in Kopp (item **631**) argue that a broader understanding of a community's connection to the land is necessary when managing policies of territorial autonomy. Through a detailed discussion of Mapuche religion, anchored in connections to the land, Curivil (item **640**) argues that this might provide an intercultural framework for dialogue between Mapuche and the dominant Chilean society.

A final theme to be underscored in this volume's selections is childhood in the region. Writing about the Argentine and Peruvian cases respectively, Villalta (item **622**) and Leinaweaver (item **654**) each examine national histories of violent conflict through the lens of adoption policies and practices. Leinaweaver engages as well with local practices of child circulation in Ayacucho as these shape sensibilities of family belonging and moral connection that differ from those apparently driving official adoption policies. A different sort of child circulation is evident in the study by Sinerva and Hill of the prominence of children as a visual cultural spectacle as both the subjects and the ambulatory vendors of postcards marketed to tourists in Cuzco (item **658**).

That such robust variation at the same time distributes across a set of shared thematic and analytic foci surely reflects current trends in the state of ethnography generally. But the partial sample of work annotated here also indicates a number of new and renewed dimensions of regional comparative coherence and points to a rich and necessary future for ethnographic work focused on the Andean region.

GENERAL

613 Albó, Xavier. Movimientos y poder indígena en Bolivia, Ecuador y Perú. La Paz: CIPCA, 2008. 294 p.: bibl. (Cuadernos de Investigación; 71)

A review of indigenous movements in Bolivia, Ecuador, and Peru, with a chapter on each case offering a demographic and geographic overview of each nation, and a condensed but informative review, providing an historical perspective for developments since the 1990s. A concluding chapter addresses key points of difference and commonality across the three Andean cases, suggesting converging challenges for indigenous movements in the early 21st century. For political scientist's comment, see *HLAS 65:1639*.

614 Andersen, Martin Edwin. Peoples of the Earth: ethnonationalism, democracy, and the indigenous challenge in "Latin" America. Lanham, Md.: Lexington Books, 2010. 296 p.: bibl., index.

An ambitious survey of indigenous activism across Latin America, shaped by the analytic frame of ethnonationalism. Andean countries figure prominently in the volume, which begins with a series of chapters posing struggles for indigenous rights as the final challenge of decolonization, a barometer of the limitations of recent steps toward democratization in the region, and a potential risk to regional stability if not dealt with properly. A set of brief country case studies follow, with a concluding discussion looking to US and Canadian Indian policies as exemplary models from which useful lessons might be learned.

615 Cadena, Marisol de la. Indigenous cosmopolitics in the Andes conceptual reflections beyond "politics." (*Cult. Anthropol.*, 25:2, May 2010, p. 334–370)

An important essay engaging the possibility that the intensification of indigenous politics in the Andes opens up a potential reframing of politics, specifically through the indigenous invocation of "earth beings." The introduction of natural elements as sentient beings to be figured in political debate is said to unsettle long-established distinctions between culture and nature, and thus unsettle the framing of the "ethnic" or "cultural" slot into which indigenous political actors might otherwise be assimilated. Based principally around events related to opposition to a mining concession in Peru, the discussion aims to encompass similar developments in Ecuador and Bolivia.

Dobkin de Rios, Marlene and **Róger Rumrrill.** A hallucinogenic tea, laced with controversy: ayahuasca in the Amazon and the United States. See item **542**.

616 Indigenous peoples, civil society, and the neo-liberal state in Latin America. Edited by Edward F. Fischer. New York, N.Y.: Berghahn Books, 2009. 214 p.: bibl., ill., index, maps.

A collection demonstrating the variety of forms of "vernacular" civil society forged in the experiences of indigenous peoples within neoliberal states in Latin America. Four of the eight case studies discuss Andean contexts: Bolivia (D. Goldstein); Ecuador (S. Sawyer and R. Colloredo-Mansfeld); and Colombia (J. Rappaport). Alongside a brief introductory essay by the editor, focused on the concept of civil society, a historical essay (M. Baud) with a focus on the Andean region helpfully places contemporary indigenous social movements in deeper historical perspective.

Native Christians: modes and effects of Christianity among indigenous peoples of the Americas. See item **545.**

617 Seminario Internacional "Bolivia Post-Constituyente: Tierra, Territorio y Autonomías Indígenas", La Paz, 2009. Bolivia post-constituyente: tierra, territorio y autonomías indígenas: memoria del Seminario Internacional, La Paz, 26, 27 y 28 de octubre 2009. Edición de Andrea Urioste E., Carlos Sotomayor y Floriana Soria Galvarro. La Paz: International Land Coalition: Fundación TIERRA, 2009. 170 p.: bibl., ill. (some col.), map.

Summaries of 24 presentations from an international seminar organized in 2009 by the International Land Coalition and Fundación Tierra. Presentations focus on the impact of constitutional reform and decentralization with an emphasis on land rights and access to resources, local political participation, and indigenous autonomy. Although the Bolivian case is the point of departure for the seminar, participants include academics, political leaders, and activists addressing the cases of Brazil, Colombia, Ecuador, Peru, as well as discussions of Latin American more generally.

ARGENTINA

618 Alvarado, Margarita and **Mariana Giordano.** Imágenes de indígenas con pasaporte abierto: del Gran Chaco a Tierra del Fuego. (*Magallania/Punta Arenas*, 35:2, 2007, p. 15–36, bibl., photos)

Comparative examination of photographic representations of indigenous peoples of the Gran Chaco and Tierra del Fuego. The authors identify a representational grammar of poses and argue for a "transhumance iconography" shaping the similar representations of distinct social environments.

619 Barúa, Guadalupe. Un arte delicado: relaciones entre el parentesco, el conflicto y el acontecimiento entre los Wichí del Chaco Central. Buenos Aires: Editorial Dunken, 2007. 278 p.: bibl., ill.

An expansive ethnographic meditation on sociality and alliance focusing on the case of the Wichí (Mataco) of the Argentine/Bolivian Chaco region. Drawing primarily on material previously published (by the author and by other ethnographers), and in dialog with a wide array of classical and contemporary anthropological theorists of kinship and social organization, the author aims to place the Wichí within a broader comparative ethnographic framework.

620 Citro, Silvia V. Memories of the "old aboriginal dances": the Toba and Moví performances in the Argentine Chaco. (*J. Lat. Am. Caribb. Anthropol.*, 15:2, Nov. 2010, p. 363–386)

Comparison of indigenous dance practices in two regions of the Argentinian Chaco, distinguished by the earlier and more recent impact of Christianity and other nonindigenous cultural practices. Drawing upon historical oral interviews describing the different dance practices, the author aims to show that "traditional" cultural forms are dynamic, and that regional differences reflect the ways that dance and similar genres of bodily movement are historically responsive.

621 Shever, Elana. Neoliberal associations: property, company and family in the Argentine oil fields. (*Am. Ethnol./ Washington*, 35:4, Nov. 2008, p. 701–716)

Examines the transition to neoliberal privatization of the state-owned Argentine oil company in the 1990s. In noting the ways that preexisting models of company leadership and family-focused bonds shaped the sentiments and behaviors of newly neoliberal corporate subjects of the new corporations and their newly constituted subcontracting microenterprises, the article documents the limited extent to which such changes produce the purely calculating rational subjects of neoliberal ideology.

622 Villalta, Carla. De los derechos de los adoptantes al derecho a la identidad: los procedimientos de adopción y la apropiación criminal de niños en la Argentina. (*J. Lat. Am. Caribb. Anthropol.*, 15:2, Nov. 2010, p. 338–362)

A genealogy of shifting adoption policies in Argentina, focusing on two periods of reform: in the early 1970s and the late

1990s. The analysis examines the impact of the illegal "adoption" of children during the period of military rule, and the activism of groups such as the Abuelas de Plaza de Mayo as these have shaped the current policies of the state toward kinship, family, and adoption.

BOLIVIA

623   Autonomías indígenas, construcción de nación y fortalecimiento del Estado: estudios de caso en las regiones Norte de Potosí, guaraní del Isoso y kallawaya. Compilación de José Antonio Rocha Torrico. Investigación de Carla María Bazoalto Olmos y Luis Fernando Cuéllar Camargo. La Paz: Programa de Investigación Estratégica en Bolivia; Cochabamba, Bolivia: Centro de Culturas Originarias Kawsay, 2008. 212 p.: bibl., ill. (Investigación)

A needed examination of indigenous autonomy in practice, based upon research in the three regions of Bolivia signaled in the subtitle. Alongside background and contextual descriptions of the three cases, interview data are used to discuss both indigenous autonomy in the light of local community structures as well as shifting understandings of "state" and "nation."

624   Burman, Anders. The strange and the native: ritual and activism in the Aymara quest for decolonization. (*J. Lat. Am. Caribb. Anthropol.*, 15:2, Nov. 2010, p. 457–475)

Interesting juxtaposition of discourses of Aymara healing, focused on spirit loss, and discourses of Aymara activism, which turn on a sense of a challenged or lost native self. The author describes both a correspondence between indigenous ritual healing and activism as well as an intertwining of the two fields. He suggests that greater attention to this relationship will enable a fuller understanding of emerging contemporary indigeneities in the Andes.

625   De Munter, Koen and **Ton Salman.** Extending political participation and citizenship: pluricultural civil practices in contemporary Bolivia. (*J. Lat. Am. Caribb. Anthropol.*, 14:2, Nov. 2009, p. 432–456)

Taking the multiple inaugural acts for President Evo Morales as a point of departure, the authors argue that this is evidence of multiple modes of citizenship in contemporary Bolivia. A review of recent literature on plural citizenship and a sketch of recent Bolivian political history is followed by a summary report on fieldwork with Aymara in El Alto. Report suggests that they are engaged in supplementing inherited and inadequate forms of citizenship and civic participation.

626   Fabricant, Nicole. Performative politics: the Camba countermovement in Eastern Bolivia. (*Am. Ethnol./Washington*, 36:4, Nov. 2009, p. 768–783)

An ethnographic critique of right-wing social movements in Santa Cruz, Bolivia, contextualizing the "Camba" rejection of the administration of Evo Morales, and arguing that Camba activists have adopted a politics of spectacle ranging from appropriations of key signifiers of Lowlands indigenous identity, to performances of violence evident in attacks on indigenous activists and lynchings of effigies of President Morales.

627   Fernández Juárez, Gerardo and **Xavier Albó.** Pachjiri: cerro sagrado del Titicaca. (*Rev. Esp. Antropol. Am.*, 38:1, 2008, p. 239–255, bibl., photos)

A detailed discussion of a powerful mountain deity in the vicinity of Lake Titicaca, including the significance of the mountain as a site for the initiation of Aymara ritual specialists (*yatiris*) and for a variety of offerings linked to the agricultural and political calendars of the region. An intriguing but relatively undeveloped final section notes a series of rumors regarding a human sacrifice conducted at the site in 1995 and suggests that Protestant groups have taken steps to assert their own symbolic control of the mountain altars in response.

628   Gil García, Francisco M. A la sombra de los *mallkus*: tradición oral, ritualidad y ordenamiento del paisaje en una comunidad de Nor Lípez, Potosí, Bolivia. (*Rev. Esp. Antropol. Am.*, 38:1, 2008, p. 217–238, bibl., photos)

Examines the relationship between community members and two sacred mountains that dominate the landscape in the region of Nor Lipez. Data ranging from the orientation of local architecture, to mythical accounts, to ritual offerings, to children's drawings of the landscape are analyzed to discuss the ways that sacred mountains are meaningful for Andean communities.

629 Guiteras Mombiola, Anna. El resurgimiento de la identidad en la defensa de los derechos y el territorio: las marchas indígenas y campesinas de los *Orientes* bolivianos como mecanismo pacífico de cambio político. (*Tiempos Am./Castellón*, 14, 2007, p. 131–142, photo)

An interesting analysis of the impact of the 1990 "March for Territory and Dignity" involving indigenous groups from the eastern Bolivian lowlands marching to the Altiplano city of La Paz. The discussion links the 1990 Bolivian march to similar indigenous mobilizations elsewhere in Latin America, and details the significance of the event as a turning point in the roles played by lowlands indigenous organizations in Bolivian national politics.

630 Hipper, Christine. The politics and practices of constructing development identities in rural Bolivia. (*J. Lat. Am. Caribb. Anthropol.*, 16:1, April 2011, p. 90–113)

Illuminating examination of the ways that discourses of official multiculturalism intersect with ideals of local participatory democracy and development, compelling local residents to negotiate "development identities" as part of their civic participation. Drawing on fieldwork from Huancarani, Cochabamba, the author discusses the differential success of community groups in asserting indigenous identity during their participation in two local development contexts.

631 Kopp, Adalberto and **Alvaro Diez Astete.** Uru Chipaya y Chullpa: soberanía alimentaria y gestión territorial en dos culturas andinas. La Paz: Centro de Servicios Agropecuarios y Socio-Comunitarios: Veterinarios Sin Fronteras: Plural Editores, 2009. 216 p.: bibl., ill. (some col.), maps.

Two ethnographic essays focused on issues of sustainability and food security impacting the Uru Chipaya and Chullpa of Bolivia. The essays are part of an effort to engage with official definitions of territorial autonomy (*Tierras Comunitarias de Origen*) in Bolivia, underscoring a more comprehensive and integrated understanding of a people's connections with landscape and resources.

632 Luqui Lagleyze, Julio Mario. El doctor Dick Edgar Ibarra Grasso y el hallazgo y desciframiento de la escritura indígena andina. (*Temas Hist. Argent. Am.*, 22:12, enero/junio 2008, p. 147–163, bibl., photos)

A brief intellectual biography of the Argentine anthropologist Dick Edgar Ibarra Grasso focused primarily on his research and publications concerning indigenous pictographic writing. Includes a bibliography of his work on the subject.

633 Orta, Andrew. Dusty signs and roots of faith: the limits of Christian meaning in highlands Bolivia. (*in* Limits of meaning: case studies in the anthropology of Christianity. Edited by Matthew Engelke and Matt Tomlinson. New York, N.Y.: Berghahn Books, 2006, p. 165–188)

An ethnography of interactions between Catholic pastoral workers and Aymara examining the limits of Christian meaning in contemporary inculturationist missionary settings. Taking the case of a missionary-embraced Aymara ritual performance that fails to enact fully the intended Christian exegesis, the discussion contrasts the modes of meaning underscored in missionary discourse with other forms of meaning that emerge in the ritual event.

634 Orta, Andrew. Misioneros y municipios: la inculturación y la descentralización política en el altiplano boliviano. (*in* San Juan Diego y la Pachamama: nuevas vías del catolicismo y de la religiosidad indígena en América Latina. Edición de Félix Báez-Jorge y Alessandro Lupo. Xalapa, Mexico: Editora de Gobierno del Estado de Veracruz, 2010, p. 370–422)

Discusses a case of political decentralization and the creation of a new municipality in rural highlands Bolivia, focusing on the career of an Aymara catechist whose service to the Church positioned him as a local adept of the newly decentralized landscape of neoliberal Bolivia.

635 Pati Paco, Pelagio. Desde las mujeres aymaras para naciones originarias: 20 años de formación política e ideológica de las mujeres y pueblo aymara. La Paz: Centro de Desarrollo Integral de la Mujer Aymara "Amuyt'a," 2009. 117 p.: bibl., ill. (chiefly col.).

Part historical report and part manifesto for the Centro de Desarollo Integral de la Mujer Aymara "Amuyt'a," an organization established in 1989 and dedicated to the capacitation of indigenous women and women's organizations in the context of communal indigenous political structures. Chapters include brief testimonies from women and men involved with the organization, as well as a statement summarizing methodological experiences in working with women and youth in rural contexts.

Postero, Nancy Grey. Morales's MAS government: building indigenous popular hegemony in Bolivia. See item **1340**.

Reunión Anual de Etnología. Serie Anales de la Reunión Anual de Etnología: 22 al 25 de agosto, 2007. See item **605**.

636 Rockefeller, Stuart Alexander. Starting from Quirpini: the travels and places of a Bolivian people. Bloomington: Indiana Univ. Press, 2010. 306 p.: bibl., ill., index, maps.

An ethnographic meditation on place, circulation, and mobility. Richly detailed chapters evoke the circuits and practices by which Quirpinis make places. The scope of the chapters expands outward: focusing in turn on households, the inter-household practice of planting and processing corn, the production of community through festivals, the regional and national contexts of Quirpini life, and culminating with the experiences of labor migrants from the area to Buenos Aires.

637 Salazar de la Torre, Cecilia. Pueblo de humanos: metáforas corporales y diferenciación social indígena en Bolivia. (*Anthropol. Dep. Cienc. Soc.*, 24:24, 2006, p. 5–27, photos)

Ambitious discussion joining, on the one hand, something of a genealogy of the idea of education as an engine of modernization producing new social distinctions among indigenous Andeans and, on the other, a review of bodily signs of distinction and bodily metaphors of identity in Bolivia. A series of photographs illustrate this second part of the analysis.

638 Spedding, Alison. Religión en los Andes: extirpación de idolatrías y modernidad de la fe andina. La Paz: Instituto

Superior Ecuménico Andino de Teología (ISEAT), 2008. 200 p.: bibl., ill., map.

An overview of Andean religion, framed as a creative and lived combination of Christian and Andean elements, with a focus primarily on the Altiplano region of Bolivia. Written for Andean readers, the book combines something of a primer on the anthropology of religion with a nuanced treatment of contemporary Andean religious practices. The chapters are punctuated by questions to the reader inviting observations and reflections connecting their day-to-day experiences with the discussions of Andean religion in the text.

639 Van Vleet, Krista E. Narrating violence and negotiating belonging: the politics of self-representation in an Andean *tinkuy* story. (*J. Lat. Am. Caribb. Anthropol.*, 15:1, April 2010, p. 195–221)

An analysis of a narrative account by a man from Pocoata, recounting his first participation in a *tinkuy* battle. Applying a sociolinguistic analysis of narrative as a mode of self-representation, producing and asserting identity in complex circumstance, the discussion focuses on the *tinkuy* narrative as it negotiates multifaceted racial identities and forms of sociopolitical belonging in the Bolivian countryside.

CHILE

640 Curivil Paillavil, Ramón Francisco. La fuerza de la religión de la tierra: una herencia de nuestros antepasados. Santiago: Ediciones Univ. Católica Silva Henríquez, 2007. 117 p.: bibl., ill.

Systematic presentation of contemporary Mapuche religion, building from a discussion of Mapuche connections to the land, and moving through a discussion of ritual practices and conceptions of divinity. The author is interested in proposing a religious dialog between the dominant Chilean society and the intercultural Mapuche religion presented here. Extensive use of interviews with Mapuche spiritual leaders and sketches by Mapuche school children. Glossaries of key Mapuche terms follow each of the main chapters.

641 Haughney, Diane. Neoliberal policies, logging companies, and Mapuche struggle for autonomy in Chile. (*Lat. Am. Caribb. Ethn. Stud.*, 2:2, Sept. 2007, p. 141–160, bibl.)

Taking the case of Mapuche opposition to the work of logging companies in neoliberal Chile, but really focusing on interactions between Mapuche activists and the Chilean state, the author details a number of familiar critiques of neoliberalism as an environment for indigenous social movements. Tensions between an ethos of broad civic participation and claims of collective culturalist rights, and between a legacy of alliances with national political parties and new networks of activists and grassroots organizations raised particular challenges for the Concertación government and, the author argues, strengthened Mapuche ethnic identity and generated new ethnonational political claims.

642 Moyano, Adrián. Crónicas de la resistencia mapuche. San Carlos de Bariloche, Argentina: A. Moyano, 2007. 270 p.: bibl., ill., maps.

An evocative memorial of Mapuche resistance to colonial, national, and transnational domination. Each of the 12 chapters presents a scene from a long history of Mapuche struggle combining commentary by the author with primary texts ranging from oral histories, excerpts from manifestos by Mapuche activists, poems, and interviews.

643 Richards, Patricia. Of Indians and terrorists: how the state and local elites construct the Mapuche in neoliberal multicultural Chile. (*J. Lat. Am. Stud.*, 42:1, Feb. 2010, p. 59–90)

An examination of neoliberal multiculturalism in Chile, focusing on the ways that the transnational set of discourses around multiculturalism takes on new forms in the particular circumstances of the Mapuche in Chile. A review of the history of Mapuche-state relations and official multiculturalism in Chile is supplemented by analysis of interview data with local elites reflecting enduring and emerging constructions of the Mapuche that are at odds with multicultural ideals.

COLOMBIA

644 Gill, Lesley. The limits of solidarity: labor and transnational organizing against Coca-Cola. (*Am. Ethnol./Washington*, 36:4, Nov. 2009, p. 667–680)

An examination of the transnational campaign against the Coca-Cola company, focusing on Colombian workers and US activists and the differing perspectives and expectations they brought to the movement. Interesting reflection on the specificities of the Colombian situation as these may fall outside the framework of transnational labor activism and solidarity.

Los retos de la diferencia: los actores de la multiculturalidad entre México y Colombia. See item **514**.

ECUADOR

645 Corr, Rachel. Ritual and remembrance in the Ecuadorian Andes. Tucson: Univ. of Arizona Press, 2010. 184 p.: bibl., index.

An ethnographically rich discussion, tightly focused on the parish of Salasaca, examining Salasacan religion and ritual in the context of a long history of engagement with and incorporation of missionized Catholicism. Archival and ethnohistorical work on the parish are combined with ethnographic discussions of saints' festivals, mortuary practices, and shamanic healing.

646 Davidov, Veronica M. Shamans and shams: the discursive effects of ethnotourism in Ecuador. (*J. Lat. Am. Caribb. Anthropol.*, 15:2, Nov. 2010, p. 387–410)

Discusses the commodification of shamanism in the context of ethnotourism and, particularly, entheogen tourism focused on the use of psychoactive substances in religious, mystical, or curative rituals. Drawing principally upon interviews with a single Kichwa shaman as well as research with entheogen tourists, the analysis deals with the pressures of tourist demand on Kichwa perceptions of shamanic quality and authenticity.

647 Ferrar, Emilia. *Trueque*: an ethnographic account of barter, trade and money in Andean Ecuador. (*J. Lat. Am. Caribb. Anthropol.*, 16:1, April 2011, p. 168–184)

A contribution to the ethnographic literature on barter through an examination of the case of *trueque*: a negotiated process of exchange of goods, money, or animals for goods offered by itinerant vendors in northern Ecuador. The analysis focuses primarily on two ethnographic elements: the role of money as an item in a barter exchange, and the ways that *trueque* as a category of exchange references specific moral positions of locals and the itinerant transacting "other" with whom they enter into exchange relations.

648 Krupa, Christopher. Histories in red: ways of seeing lynching in Ecuador. (*Am. Ethnol./Washington*, 36:1, Feb. 2009, p. 20–39)

Uses the case of a nationally publicized 2003 lynching in the indigenous community of Cayambe to argue against increasingly common analyses of such events as indigenous campesino reactions to the neoliberal political and security environment. Developing an interesting comparative connection to the rise of lynchings in the US South, and focusing at once on the physical realities of lynching violence and on the ways such events are narrativized in national media, the author argues that lynching narratives are organized around racial systems of knowledge and reflect historical developments that impact those systems.

649 Wibbelsman, Michelle. Ritual encounters: Otavalan modern and mythic community. Urbana: Univ. of Illinois Press, 2009. 208 p.: bibl., ill., index. (Interpretations of culture in the new millennium)

Ethnographically rich discussion of community ritual practices in contemporary Otavalo, examining both the transformations of the rituals in shifting historical circumstances and the functions of the rituals in constituting community out of the complex and far-flung conditions of modern Otavalans. An appendix details an annual calendar of festive rituals in the region.

PERU

650 Dean, Bartholomew. Urarina society, cosmology, and history in Peruvian Amazonia. Gainesville, Fla.: Univ. Press of Florida, 2009. 368 p.: bibl., index.

A rich and nuanced ethnography of the Urarina, focusing on the shaping of Urarina society in the context of their engagement with colonial and postcolonial forces, particularly those related to forest

extraction. Effectively weaves discussions of extractive external economic practices with accounts of local processes for producing value, thereby unsettling any conceptions of the Urarina as isolated from or resistant to national and global processes.

651 Greene, Shane. Customizing indigeneity: paths to a visionary politics in Peru. Stanford, Calif.: Stanford Univ. Press, 2009. 244 p.: bibl., ill., index, maps.

An important and innovative examination of "indigeneity" approached ethnographically through the case of the Aguaruna. Emphasizing the ways that the exotic idea of indigeneity is "customized" by the Aguaruna through locally meaningful actions undertaken in translocally complex circumstances, this book illuminates Aguaruna life, Amazonian cultural and political history, and the position of the Aguaruna in the contemporary Amazonian indigenous movement.

652 Itier, César. El hijo del oso: la literatura oral quechua de la región del Cuzco. Traducción de César Itier. Lima: Instituto Francés de Estudios Andinos: Instituto de Estudios Peruanos: Fondo Editorial, Pontificia Univ. Católica del Perú: Fondo Editorial, Univ. Nacional Mayor de San Marcos, 2007. 225 p.: bibl., ill. (some col.), maps. (Travaux de l'Institut français d'études andines, 252) (Serie Lengua y sociedad, 28)

An excellent presentation of 12 Andean tales recorded between 1994 and 2001 in the vicinity of Cuzco. The material is presented in the original Quechua with side-by-side Spanish translation. Sometimes variants of shorter stories are presented. Each tale is preceded by a summary and an analytic essay that discusses other published versions of the story. Photographs and maps nicely supplement the text, which appeared originally in French in 2004.

653 Krögel, Alison. Quechua sheepherders on the mountain plains of Wyoming. (*J. Lat. Am. Caribb. Anthropol.*, 15:2, Nov. 2010, p. 261–288)

Examination of the situation of Quechua migrants from Peru working as sheepherders under the US Guest Worker Program. In addition to detailing the history of the program and the experiences of the migrants, the article contains the herders' reflections on the differences between herding practices in Peru and in Wyoming.

654 Leinaweaver, Jessaca B. The circulation of children: kinship, adoption, and morality in Andean Peru. Durham, N.C.: Duke Univ. Press, 2008. 225 p.: bibl., ill., index, maps. (Latin America otherwise)

This richly detailed ethnography works productively across two important phenomena in Ayacucho, Peru. One concerns the practices and policies of orphanages and adoption agencies, which have taken on new prominence within the burgeoning field of international adoption and in the wake of the civil war in Peru. Against the internationally circulating ideals of childhood, family, and human rights that inform the field of international adoption, the author examines the longstanding Ayacuchano practice of child circulation, whereby children from one household are sent to live in another, as an opportunity to uncover alternative local sensibilities of childhood, family, and experiences of belonging and moral connection.

655 Pacheco, Karina. Incas, indios y fiestas: reivindicaciones y representaciones en la configuración de la identidad cusqueña. Cusco: Instituto Nacional de Cultura, Dirección Regional de Cultura de Cusco, 2007. 447 p.: bibl., col. ill.

A contemporary cultural history of the city of Cuzco, focused on the mid-19th through the turn of the 21st century, and examining Cuzco as a cradle of indigenismo. Chapters deal with representations of and attitudes toward the Incan past, Spanish colonialism, the rural highlands, and include detailed discussions of contemporary festival practices, monuments, and tourist sites in Cuzco.

656 Pérez, Beatriz. Turismo y representación de la cultura: identidad cultural y resistencia en comunidades andinas del Cusco. (*Anthropol. Dep. Cienc. Soc.*, 24:24, 2006, p. 29–49, bibl.)

An analysis of the participation of indigenous authorities in *Raimis* (festivals) that have become an important tourist event in Pisac, Cuzco. Although there is little description of the festivals themselves, the author takes the phenomena as a point

of departure for interesting reflections on questions of cultural authenticity, ethnic identity, and the longer history of indigenous authorities constituted in complexly negotiated relations with the state.

657 Qué sabemos de las comunidades campesinas? Textos de Pedro Castillo *et al.* Lima: ALLPA, Comunidades y Desarrollo, 2007. 364 p.: bibl.

Aimed at addressing the relative ignorance among Peruvian policy makers of the situations of peasant communities, the volume assembles a set of review essays detailing the juridical condition of peasant communities, current research on political organization and land tenure in the communities, and work on gender relations and ethnic identity. Useful summaries of the state of the literatures, with a particular emphasis upon the legal and political economic questions of land tenure and the juridical standing of rural communities.

658 Sinerva, Aviva and **Michael Hill.** The visual economy of Andean childhood poverty: interpreting postcards in Cusco, Peru. (*J. Lat. Am. Caribb. Anthropol.*, 16:1, April 2011, p. 114–142)

Interesting study of postcards and the way they create a visual cultural spectacle around the lives of poor indigenous children in Peru. In addition to critically examining the photos and accompanying text on selected postcards, the discussion touches upon the production of the photographs, their circulation and sale by ambulant vendors (often children), as well as their reception or consumption by tourists or local Cuzqueños.

659 Suxo Yapuchura, Moisés. La voz de una nación: los aymaras de Lima Metropolitana, caso Unicachi. Lima: Editorial San Marcos, 2008. 246 p.: bibl., ill., maps.

The first and main section of this book focuses on the experiences of Aymara migrants to Lima from the Altiplano community of Unicachi, Department of Puno, and details the role of migrant associations, and community financial and social networks in their lives. The second and third sections of the book contain wide-ranging reflections by the author, himself from Unicachi, on the situation of Aymara in the

Peruvian nation and a proposal for inter- and intra-cultural education.

660 Vega-Centeno B., Imelda. Celebración popular del Viernes Santo en el Cuzco: análisis etnohistórico de una práctica ritual secular. (*Social. Particip.*, 102, enero 2007, p. 135–147, bibl., table)

Drawing upon research conducted in Cuzco in 1995 and 2002, along with previous personal experiences earlier in the 20th century, the author examines changes and continuities in the Good Friday tradition of a popular market for ritual paraphernalia linked to curing. Despite the increasing commercialization of the market as well as the growing role of nongovernmental organizations in this folkloric event, the author argues that an Andean cultural logic shaping experiences of illness and healing remains a central principal of the event.

GEOGRAPHY

GENERAL

KENT MATHEWSON, *Associate Professor, Department of Geography and Anthropology, Louisiana State University*
JÖRN SEEMANN, *Associate Professor, Departamento de Geociências, Universidade Regional do Cariri, Brazil*

THE CATASTROPHIC EVENTS that occurred during the past biennium in Latin America—earthquakes in Haiti and Chile, the inevitable hurricanes in the Caribbean, mudslides in Central America, and the Macondo/Deepwater Horizon oil disaster in the Gulf of Mexico—continue to put a spotlight on human-environment relations as important theaters and sites for geographic research and publication. Though usually local in occurrence and impact, increasingly the implications of these events are viewed at wider scales. Extreme events, whether "natural" or "social," have always been part of the regional imagery and identity of Latin America, though geographers have not always been in the forefront in their reportage or analysis. Recent work at the regional scale, and some at the scale of the Latin America realm, suggests that geographers are joining the front lines. Perhaps even more significantly, geographers are increasingly questioning the ontological legitimacy of the "nature/culture" divide. Work framed at the scale of the Latin America realm as whole has yet to yield many examples of these shifts and reconceptualizations, but this can be forecast as a future trend. In the meantime, we do have some examples pitched at regional scales. Buchenau and Johnson's (item **661**) edited collection on the effects of earthquakes and their political fallouts offers one such set of examples. The editors provide a useful introduction to the theme, while the essay authors revisit earthquakes and their consequences at intervals from Lima 1746, Venezuela 1812, Valparaíso 1906, San Juan (Argentina) 1944, Managua 1972, Guatemala 1976, up to Mexico City 1985. In each instance, the earthquakes also precipitated seismic shifts in the political landscape. Acosta's (item **687**) edited volume on history and disasters in Latin America pursues a complementary set of topics, looking at the social impacts of a variety of disasters including droughts, climatic variations, volcanic eruptions, hurricanes, epidemics, and earthquakes. Both these books and a rising tide—though still short of tsunami intensity—of publications on "natural" disasters suggest that this topic will continue to be a staple theme in Latin Americanist geographical work for the foreseeable future.

While abrupt disruptions in the "normal" flow of socionatural processes, as evidenced by volcanic eruptions, earthquakes, hurricanes, and other extreme events, offer sporadic if predictable research opportunities, the more quotidian deviations of "natural" processes continue to enlist the most geographic scrutiny.

The best example is Veblen, Young, and Orme's edited volume on the physical geography of South America (item **702**) that presents a detailed cross-section of topics and spaces, and could be considered the most authoritative reference work on these issues in the last decades. Other representatives of this line of research are the papers presented in Allan Lavell and Alonso Brenes' (item **678**) edited volume on climatic variability and attendant disaster risks associated with ENSO (El Niño and the Southern Oscillation) phenomena. The volume features case studies from Mexico, Costa Rica, Colombia, Ecuador, and Argentina. All the studies stress the reoccurring nature of the disasters associated with ENSO events and the varying levels of preparedness evident in differing local contexts, pointing out that seemingly capricious "acts of nature" are not so random or so natural. Similarly, Karsh and MacIver's (item **692**) contribution to a collection on climate change, biodiversity, and sustainability (item **670**) in the Americas points to what will more than likely become a stock item in the literature, that is to say, recording and charting the effects of climate change on biodiversity, especially in the equatorial tropics. Climate change should also spawn an increasing number of studies of its effects on hydrologic systems, especially as these changes relate to water resource issues. Moscoso Cavallini, Oakley, and Egocheaga Young's volume (item **662**) on water resource use and sustainability is representative here, as is Esch *et al.*'s volume *La gota de la vida* (item **684**). Both volumes recognize the biophysical underpinnings of water resource questions, while exploring cultural, social, economic, and especially political dimensions of access to these resources. Currently, most of the publications on the impact of climate change seem to focus on present conditions or future projections. Kronik's (item **693**) focus on the vulnerability of indigenous communities to climate change and the perturbations it produces is representative. However, perhaps the most original and potentially important article in this area to be published in this biennial period is historical in scope. Dull *et al.*'s article (item **675**), "The Columbian Encounter and the Little Ice Age," offers a brilliant riposte to the climate change/global warming deniers' obdurate refusal to comprehend current realities. With Dull *et al.*'s compelling suggestion that global cooling occurred in the wake of the post-1492 demographic collapse, which in turn meant massive cessation of forest clearance and corresponding increases in carbon sequestration, we have here possible historical confirmation of the validity of the global warming dynamics that we confront today.

Two excellent volumes on the historical cartography of Latin America point out that Hispanic and Luso-America have not been left out in the general current boom in publications devoted to cartographic history. Mendoza Vargas and Lois' edited volume (item **688**) presents an eclectic but effective selection of case studies and essays on cartographic topics, and should serve as a benchmark. Dym and Offen's (item **697**) edited reader is a milestone. It brings together more than 50 essays on a wide and imaginative array of cartographic topics, questions, and quandaries. The editors and their authors have not only remapped the field of Latin American historical cartography, they have charted a new path for critical map studies. This volume should be seen not only as an innovative venture, but also as an indispensible reference work for Latin Americanist scholars of all callings.

Other work on historical topics includes Sluyter's (item **708**) reconstruction of the "tasajo trail." Sluyter has expanded his earlier work on cattle in colonial Mexico to trace the trail of dry salted beef across its trajectories in the colonial and 19th-century Hispanic Atlantic world. In doing so, he also intersects with the burgeoning interest in Atlantic studies, an inviting arena for Latin Americanist geographers to join. To date, few geographers of any regional specialty have contributed to this increasingly popular enterprise. Not so novel but still popular are studies of travel and tourism from historical perspectives. Driever (item **674**) offers an overview of the intrepid figure of Harry Franck, who by the mid-20th century had brought Latin America into the purview of more Anglophone travel readers than almost any other writer. Zusman, Lois, and Castro's edited collection (item **712**) puts an eye to the contributions of travel accounts and migrations for the construction of place.

Questions of identity, especially race, continue to be favored terrain for geographic exploration. Whereas issues of class, especially conditions of the rural peasantry or infra-proletariat urban dwellers, were formerly center stage, now once-marginalized categories such as race, gender, sexuality, ethnicity, and other expressions of identity have come to the fore. Sundberg (item **710**) puts race at the center of a proposed methodology to redirect concepts of social and environmental relations. Wade (item **713**) provides an historical overview of the ways that race and ethnicity in Latin America have been approached. Yovanovich and Huras' (item **694**) volume brings together a series of interpretive essays on aspects of identity and its formations in Latin America since 1980. Lazzara and Unruh's multidisciplinary work (item **711**) stresses the importance of ruins from the far and recent past as symbolic landscape markers that shape identities in Latin America. The peasantry, however, has not entirely disappeared as evidenced by Welch and Mançano Fernandes' (item **695**) stock-taking volume on the peasantry, past, present, and future. Finally, questions of the identity of geography and its Latin Americanist practitioners, always a stable item in the literature, continue to be a minor staple. Sánchez-Crispín and Liberali's (item **683**) collection is a welcome addition to the literature on geographic pedagogy and practice in Latin America. Similarly Palacio Prieto (item **701**) provides new information on the state of Latin American academic geography, particularly concerning the expansion of programs and the popular perception of the discipline in the region. More specifically, Buzai and Robinson (item **667**) analyze the trends in the relatively young history of geographical information systems (GIS) in Latin American countries. Urquijo Torres and Barrera-Bassols' (item **671**) compilation and publication of papers delivered at the 2005 Conference of Latin Americanist Geographers in Morelia, Mexico, provides an important window on the state of geographic research by Latin American(ist) geographers across a broad spectrum of interests and approaches. Judging from this volume and similar conference proceedings, geography's identity in Latin America is solid and its sphere of influence is expanding.

661 Aftershocks: earthquakes and popular politics in Latin America. Edited by Jürgen Buchenau and Lyman L. Johnson. Albuquerque: Univ. of New Mexico Press, 2009. 230 p.: bibl., ill., index, photos. (Diálogos)

Collection of seven articles on the social, cultural, and political impact of earthquakes. Includes historical and recent case studies from several Latin American countries that permit a comparative analysis of disasters and shed light on the structures, beliefs, and political interests that lie beneath a country's society. For historian's comment, see *HLAS 66:391.*

662 El agua como recurso sustentable y de uso múltiple: políticas para su utilización en zonas urbanas y peri urbana de América Latina y el Caribe. Edición de Julio Moscoso Cavallini, Stewart Oakley y Luis Egocheaga Young. Santiago: RIMISP, Centro Latinoamericano para el Desarrollo Rural: Catalonia; Canada: IDRC-CRDI, 2008. 229 p.: bibl., ill., maps.

Collection of 10 projects and two technical reports that discuss aspects of the use of water resources in Latin America. The case studies discuss themes such as water quality and treatment, environmental education, watershed management, and the access to water in urban and rural settings.

663 Ajedrez ambiental: manejo de recursos naturales, comunidades, conflictos y cooperación. Edición de Joseph S. Weiss y Teodoro Bustamante. Quito: FLACSO Ecuador: Ministerio de Cultura, 2008. 330 p.: bibl., ill., col. maps.

Collection of papers presented at the Congress of Latin American and Caribbean Social Sciences held in Quito, 2007. Topics covered include: indigenous communities and the natural environment: concepts and realities; socioenvironmental conflicts and attendant forms of struggle; local political dynamics; and the growing role of international cooperation.

664 Annals of the American Academy of Political and Social Science. Vol. 630, July 2010, Continental divides: international migration in the Americas. Edited by Katharine M. Donato *et al.* Philadelphia, Penn.: American Academy of Political and Social Science.

Special journal issue on migration patterns in Latin American countries that are juxtaposed to Mexico-US migration flows. The 15 articles cover a wide range of topics from the causes and processes of migrations in the Americas to specific themes such as remittances, gender, undocumented migrants, and occupational mobility.

665 Ballesteros, Aurora García; Beatriz Jiménez Basco; and Ángela Redondo González. La inmigración latinoamericana en España en el siglo XXI. (*Invest. Geogr./ México*, 70, dic. 2009, p. 55-70)

Insightful article that investigates the immigration of Latin Americans to Spain at the turn of the 21st century. Discusses aspects such as age and gender structure, health conditions, legal situation, and the impacts of the migratory process on the countries of origin. Also looks into the spatial distribution of the immigrants.

666 Brothers, Timothy S. *et al.* Jonathan D. Sauer, 1918-2008: perspectives on his life and work in Latin America

and beyond. (*J. Lat. Am. Geogr.*, 8:1, 2009, p. 165-180)

This forum celebrates the life and work of Jonathan Sauer, son of Carl Sauer and accomplished botanist and cultural biogeographer. A standard memoriam-styled accounting of his career is accompanied by personal statements by former students.

667 Buzai, Gustavo D. and David J. Robinson. Geographical information systems (GIS) in Latin America, 1987-2010: a preliminary review. (*J. Lat. Am. Geogr.*, 9:3, 2010, p. 9-31)

Informative review article on the historical development of GIS applications in Latin American countries from 1987 to the present. Reconstructs the use of the technologies in the academic environment through the analysis of the published proceedings of the meetings of the Iberoamerican Conference of Geographical Information Systems.

668 Canaparo, Claudio. Geo-epistemology: Latin America and the location of knowledge. Bern; New York, N.Y.: Peter Lang, 2009. 284 p.: bibl., ill., indexes. (Hispanic studies: culture and ideas, 23)

Overview of epistemological issues in contemporary geography with examples drawn from, and reference to, Latin America.

669 Chapman, Brandon; Douglas Jackson-Smith; and Peggy Petrzelka. Comparative institutions and management resiliency in Latin American small-scale fisheries. (*Soc. Sci. J./New York*, 45:2, June 2008, p. 313-329, bibl.)

Investigates small-scale fishery in Latin America in the light of territorial encroachment by commercial fleets. Presents a comparison of seven case studies from different countries to discuss local management and strategies for resistance.

670 Climate change, biodiversity, and sustainability in the Americas: impacts and adaptations. Edited by Francisco Dallmeier *et al.* Washington, D.C.: Smithsonian Institution Scholarly Press, 2009. 183 p.: bibl., index.

Collection of eight essays on the impacts of human activity and climate change on biodiversity in the Americas. The case studies from North, Central, and South

America discuss regional bird monitoring, plant adaptation to climate change and the effects of native and secondary tree vegetation on biomass. For review of the chapter, "Impacts of Climate Extremes on Biodiversity in the Americas," see item **692** .

671 Conference of Latin Americanist Geographers, *Morelia, Mexico, 2005*. Temas de geografía latinoamericana: Reunión CLAG-Morelia. Coordinación de Pedro Sergio Urquijo Torres y Narciso Barrera-Bassols. Morelia, Mexico: UNAM, Centro de Investigaciones en Geografía Ambiental, 2009. 443 p.: bibl., ill., maps. (Serie Científica)

Collection of papers presented at the 2005 CLAG conference in Morelia, Mexico. Topics include: indigenous territoriality and ethnoecology; historical geography; conservation geography; rural perspectives; and urban geography.

672 Dachary, Alfredo César and Stella Maris Arnaiz Burne. Pueblos originarios y turismo en América Latina: la conquista continua. (*Estud. Perspect. Turismo*, 18:1, enero 2009, p. 69–91)

Sheds light on the tensions between tourism and indigenous populations in Latin America and discusses aspects such as the role of the state, cultural resistance, the tourist gaze, and conflicts that result from the encroachment of tourism into the territories of traditional societies.

673 Diasporische Bewegungen im transatlantischen Raum: diasporic movements-movimientos diaspóricos. Herausgegeben von Stefanie Kron *et al.* Berlin: Edition Tranvía- Verlag Walter Frey, 2010. 308 p.: bibl., ill. (Fragmentierte Moderne in Lateinamerika; 11)

Multilingual collection of 15 essays on the migration of people and knowledge in the transatlantic world. Discusses diasporas and their mobility through the lens of historical narratives and feminist and postcolonial approaches.

674 Driever, Steven L. Geographic narratives in the South American travelogues of Harry A. Franck: 1917–1943. (*J. Lat. Am. Geogr.*, 10:2, 2011, p. 53–69)

Reviews the career and craft of one of the most prolific travel writers of the first half of the 20th century. Franck's writings stand out from the standard items of this period and genre thanks to his intimate and intense engagement with local conditions, landscapes, and people. Largely forgotten now, Franck's dated perspectives and attitudes merit attention nonetheless.

675 Dull, Robert A. *et al.* The Columbian encounter and the Little Ice Age: abrupt land use, change, fire, and greenhouse forcing. (*Ann. Assoc. Am. Geogr.*, 100:4, Oct. 2010, p. 755–771)

Advances the controversial yet compelling argument that the abrupt post-Columbian demographic collapse of New World indigenous populations led to a massive carbon sequestration process through the reforestation of much of the Americas. This reforestation is interpreted as having acted as a primary climate-forcing agent intensifying the Little Ice Age cooling event. With a new round of forest burning and clearance in the Americas and the onset of the Industrial Revolution in Europe in the 18th century, the cooling trend was reversed.

676 Durán, Ricardo Adrián Vergara. La mirada de la geografía en un continente en transformación: las problemáticas urbano-regionales del desarrollo. (*Invest. Desarro./Barranquilla*, 17:2, dic. 2009, p. 230–241)

Presents a regional approach to the Latin American development debate. Argues that the understanding of global structures and the economic and political integration within Latin America could be improved by initially studying territorial questions and planning issues from an urban and regional perspective.

677 Encuentro de Geógrafos de América Latina, *11th, Bogotá, 2007*. Globalización y territorio: reflexiones geográficas en América Latina. Edición de Ovidio Delgado Mahecha y Hellen Cristancho Garrido. Bogotá: Univ. Nacional de Colombia, Facultad de Ciencias Humanas, Depto. de Geografía, 2009. 412 p.: bibl., ill., index. (Biblioteca abierta; 378. Col. General. Serie Geografía)

Selected papers from 11th Encuentro de Geógrafos de América Latina, held in Bogotá in March 2007. Topics include: Latin American geographic discourses, globalization and urban change, transformation of rural spaces, challenges for environmental sustainability, and issues in geographic education.

678 ENOS: variabilidad climática y riesgo de desastre en las Américas: proceso, patrones, gestión. Compilación de Allan Michael Lavell y Alonso Brenes. Textos de Allan Michael Lavell *et al.* San José: Editorial Librería Alma Mater, 2008. 370 p.: bibl., ill. (some col.), maps (some col.).

This collection of papers focuses on climate variability and disaster risk as related to El Niño events. Geographer Allan Lavell provides a cogent overview of the emergent research theaters, especially under the auspices of various research networks that are addressing the topic. Other contributors present research results and projections from Mexico to Argentina.

679 Environmental justice in Latin America: problems, promise, and practice. Edited by David V. Carruthers. Cambridge, Mass.: MIT Press, 2008. 329 p.: bibl., ill., index, map. (Urban and industrial environments)

Collection of 12 essays exploring practices and struggles in environmental justice in Latin America and the Caribbean. Includes case studies on the conflicts between environmental and political and economic interests such as international trade politics, waste and resource management, ecotourism, and land use. (Four of the essays are singled out for individual citation and annotation. See items **699, 710, 715,** and **716.**)

680 Feldmann, Paulo Roberto. A influência da cultura na gestão das empresas latinoamericanas. (*Estud. Av.*, 24:68, 2010, p. 321–334, bibl., table)

Explores the influence of geographical, economic, and cultural factors on the creation and administration of corporations in Latin America. Concludes that the Latin American business culture needs to be reconsidered in order to compete in the world market.

681 Food for the few: neoliberal globalism and biotechnology in Latin America. Edited by Gerardo Otero. Austin: Univ. of Texas Press, 2008. 321 p.: bibl., ill., index.

Examines the socioeconomic and environmental impacts of biotechnologies used in agriculture. The 12 essays present empirical case studies from different Latin American countries. Topics include biosafety, genetically modified crops, and the role of small-scale farmers in the light of neoliberal biotechnology policies that turn agricultural products in "food for the few."

682 Las fronteras de América Latina: dinámica, procesos y elementos para su análisis. Edición de Hudilú Rodríguez Sangroni, Juan Carlos Morales Manzur y Lucrecia Morales García. Maracaibo, Venezuela: Gobernación del Estado Zulia, Acervo Histórico del Estado Zulia, 2006. 301 p.: bibl., ill.

Collection of 12 essays examining the impacts of frontiers in Latin America. Discusses the significance of borders in the light of international migration flows, geopolitical conflicts, and regional economic configurations.

683 La geografía en América Latina: visión por países. Compilación de Álvaro Sánchez Crispín y Ana María Liberali. Buenos Aires: Unión Geográfica de América Latina; México: Sociedad Mexicana de Geografía y Estadística: Instituto de Geografía, UNAM; Caracas: Centro de Estudios Alexander von Humboldt, Red de Estudios Latinoamericanos de la UGI, 2009. 263 p.: bibl.

Collection of essays discussing the state of art of formal geography education in 13 Latin American countries. Analyzes the historical development and recent trends in teacher training, higher education curricula, research agendas, and job market perspectives. Time depth is chiefly limited to the 20th century with an emphasis on recent developments in geography's university institutionalizations.

684 La gota de la vida: hacia una gestión sustentable y democrática del agua. Edición de Sophie Esch *et al.* Textos de Pedro Arrojo *et al.* México: Fundación Heinrich Böll, Oficina Regional para C.A., México y Cuba, 2006. 400 p.: bibl., ill.

Valuable collection of papers authored by European and Latin American activists and academics on water issues. Topics include: the human right to water; visions and realities; water and the challenges of sustainable development; water, democracy, and the construction of citizenship; and efforts toward a democratic management of water.

685 Governing the metropolis: principles and cases. Edited by Eduardo Rojas, Juan R. Cuadrado-Roura, and José Miguel Fernández Güell. Washington, D.C.: Inter-American Development Bank, 2008. 296 p.

Collection of five essays on the governance of metropolitan areas, with a strong emphasis on Latin American cities. Presents examples to discuss directions for the efficient management of urban agglomerations.

686 Graham, Alan. Late Cretaceous and Cenozoic history of Latin American vegetation and terrestrial environments. St. Louis: Missouri Botanical Garden Press, 2009. 617 p. (Monographs in systematic botany from the missouri botanical garden; 113)

Exhaustive paleobotanical study of the plant communities and ecosystems in Latin America from the Cretaceous period to the present. Reconstructs paleoenvironments, lineages, plant migrations, evolution, and adaptation processes. Includes tables and appendices containing details of 10,000 fossil plants according to their geographic location, taxonomy, and age.

687 Historia y desastres en América Latina. v. 3. Coordinación de Virginia García Acosta. Bogotá: La RED/CIESAS: Tercer Mundo Editores, 2008. 1 v.: bibl., ill., maps. (Vol. 3: Publicaciones de la Casa Chata)

Collection of nine essays on the impact of natural disasters in Latin America. Includes historical case studies on extreme events such as drought, climatic variations, volcanoes, hurricanes, earthquakes, and cholera from the 16th century to the present.

688 Historias de la cartografía de Iberoamérica: nuevos caminos, viejos problemas. Coordinación de Héctor Mendoza Vargas y Carla Lois. México: Instituto de Geografía, UNAM; INEGI, 2009. 494 p.: ill., maps. (Col. Geografía para el siglo XXI. Serie Libros de investigación; 4)

Collection of 19 essays on the history

of cartography from a Latin American perspective, presented at the Segundo Simposio Iberoamericano de Historia de la Cartografía in Mexico, 2008. The volume discusses the nature of cartographic representations, their role in shaping and controlling territories, and their contribution to the building of nation-states. Includes case studies from different countries and time periods.

689 Humboldt, Alexander von. Political essay on the island of Cuba: a critical edition. Edited with an introduction by Vera M. Kutzinski and Ottmar Ette. Translated by J. Bradford Anderson, Vera M. Kutzinski, and Anja Becker. Annotations by Tobias Kraft, Anja Becker, and Giorleny D. Altamirano Rayo. Chicago, Ill.; London: Univ. of Chicago Press, 2011. 519 p.: ill., index, maps.

Although primarily concerned with the geography of Cuba, Humboldt characteristically puts his detailed reportage and analysis in much wider contexts. Especially illuminating and valuable is his comparative commentary on Cuba's place in Latin American and Atlantic world contexts. The editors and translators have produced a superb edition, setting a new standard for Humboldt scholarship in translation.

690 Humboldt, Alexander von and **Aimé Bonpland.** Essay on the geography of plants. Edited with an introduction by Stephen T. Jackson. Translated by Sylvie Romanowski. Chicago, Ill.: Univ. of Chicago Press, 2008. 274 p.: bibl., ill., 1 poster (60 × 98 cm., folded to 12 × 19 cm.).

Foundational work in plant geography, previously not available in English translation. Neotropical flora and ecology provide the primary inspiration and exemplars.

691 Inter/secciones urbanas: origen y contexto en América Latina. Coordinación de Jaime Fabián Erazo Espinosa. Quito: FLACSO Ecuador: Ministerio de Cultura, 2009. 430 p.: bibl., ill., maps. (Col. 50 años)

Collection of papers presented at the Congress of Latin American and Caribbean Social Sciences held in Quito, 2007. Topics covered include: vitality and management of city centers; popular habitats and social inclusion; mass transit and urban mobility; and urban management and risk/disaster prevention. Contributions by two geographers and a mix of other social scientists, engineers, and architects.

692   Karsh, Marianne B. and **Don MacIver.** Impacts of climate extremes on biodiversity in the Americas. (*in* Climate change, biodiversity and sustainability in the Americas. Edited by Francisco Dallmeier *et al.* Washington, D.C.: Smithsonian Institution Scholary Press, 2010, p. 53–94, tables)

Review article on the impacts of extreme climate on the diversity or the flora and fauna in the Americas. Contains detailed tables that list a wide range of hazards to biodiversity with regards to their prediction, effects, and geographic distribution. For review of the entire book, see item **670** .

693   Kronik, Jakob and **Dorte Verner.** Indigenous peoples and climate change in Latin America and the Caribbean. Washington, D.C.: World Bank, 2010. 185 p.: bibl., ill. (some col.), index, col. maps. (Directions in development. Environment and sustainable development)

Focuses on the effects and consequences of climate change and variability for indigenous populations in Latin America and the Caribbean. Stresses that these traditional groups are most vulnerable to climatic change and extreme events such as drought or hurricanes, and reflects on how their resilience and adaptability can be improved.

694   Latin American identities after 1980. Edited by Gordana Yovanovich and Amy Huras. Waterloo, Canada: Wilfrid Laurier Univ. Press, 2010. 316 p.: bibl., index.

Interdisciplinary approach to modern and postmodern social and cultural identities in Latin America and their contact with other cultures and nations. Contains 14 essays that explore a wide range of themes from cultural resistance, impacts of globalization, and human rights to collective memory, transculturation of music, and the representation of identities in literature.

695   *Latin American Perspectives*. Vol. 36, No. 4, July 2009, Peasant movements in Latin America: looking back, moving ahead. Edited by Cliff Welch and Bernardo Mançano Fernandes. Thousand Oaks, Calif.: SAGE Publications.

Special journal issue on land reforms and peasant movements in Latin America. Includes case studies that examine the historical dimension, ethnicity, social organization, and conflicts in different countries.

696   *Latin American Perspectives*. Vol. 37, No. 2, March 2010, Globalization, neoliberalism, and the Latin American coffee societies. Edited by Steven Topik, John M. Talbot, and Mario Samper. Thousand Oaks, Calif.: SAGE Publications.

Special journal issue on the central role of coffee in the understanding of economic development in Latin America. The seven essays explore historical aspects, commodity chains, global policies, small-scale production, and conflicts in six different countries.

697   Mapping Latin America: a cartographic reader. Edited by Jordana Dym and Karl H. Offen. Chicago, Ill.; London: Univ. of Chicago Press, 2011. 338 p.: ill., index, maps.

In a single volume featuring 57 succinct yet authoritative chapters, Dym and Offen have not only remapped the field of Latin American historical cartography, but have also charted a new path for critical map studies. More than a millennium's time depth and a continent's expanse are surveyed with fascinating details and composite illumination.

Martín-Merás, Luisa. La expedición hidrográfica del atlas de la América septentrional, 1792–1805. See *HLAS 66:546.*

698   The natural world in Latin American literatures: ecocritical essays on twentieth century writings. Edited by Adrian Taylor Kane. Jefferson, N.C.: McFarland & Co., Publishers, 2010. 244 p.: bibl., ill., index.

Collection of 10 essays that explore the relationship between humans and their environment in Latin American fiction writing. Includes case studies that link the debates on ecological criticism to a wide range of issues such as the perception and representation of nature, travels and landscapes, and gender and race.

699   Newell, Peter. Contesting trade politics in the Americas: the politics of environmental justice. (*in* Environmental justice in Latin America: problems, promise, and practice. Edited by David V. Carruthers. Cambridge, Mass.: MIT Press, 2008, p. 49–73)

Discusses the conflicts between social and environmental movements and official trade politics in Latin America in the light of environmental justice and alternative social and economic assessments. For review of the entire book, see item **679**.

700 Ordóñez, Juan Córdoba and **Cándida Gago García.** Latin American cities and globalisation: change and permanency in the context of development expectations. (*Urban Stud./Harlow*, 47:9, Aug. 2010, p. 2003–2021)

Argues that the study of mobility relations between cities can shed light on the current urbanization processes in Latin America. Analyzes the air transport connections between 1970 and 2008 as an example of these new forms of mobility. The study indicates the coexistence of traditional structures such as centralism and polarization. Also points to new key issues, such as migration and tourism.

701 Palacio Prieto, José Luis. Los estudios de geografía en las universidades de América Latina: desarrollo, situación actual y perspectivas. (*Invest. Geogr./México*, 74, abril 2011, p. 107–124)

Contends that despite contextual constraints, geography programs in Latin America have expanded significantly in recent years. During the past decade, 56 new programs were launched. Changes in public perceptions of the field may stem from new techniques, applications to planning, and university expansions.

702 The physical geography of South America. Edited by Thomas T. Veblen, Kenneth R. Young, and A.R. Orme. Oxford, England; New York, N.Y.: Oxford Univ. Press, 2007. 361 p.: bibl., ill., index, maps (some col.), plates. (Oxford regional environments)

Major reference work on South America's physical geography. The 21 authoritative chapters are divided into three parts: the description of physical aspects of the continent such as tectonics, climates, hydrology, and geology; the presentation of regional environments (the tropical rainforest, the Andean landscapes, etc.); and the

human-nature relations from precolonial times to the present, with an outlook to the future.

703 Recicloscopio: miradas sobre recuperadores urbanos de residuos de América Latina. Compilación de Pablo Javier Schamber y Francisco M. Suárez. Buenos Aires: Ediciones de la UNLa: Univ. Nacional de General Sarmiento: Prometeo Libros, 2007. 324 p.: bibl., ill.

Collection of 18 essays exploring a wide range of aspects of informal urban garbage collection and recycling in South American countries. The articles present insights into living conditions, organizational strategies, and conflict situations in the lives of the collectors.

704 Rethinking the informal city: critical perspectives from Latin America. Edited by Felipe Hernández, Peter William Kellett, and Lea K. Allen. New York, N.Y.: Berghahn Books, 2010. 249 p.: bibl., ill., index. (Remapping cultural history; 11)

Collection of 12 interdisciplinary essays that analyze the phenomenon of urban informality in Latin American cities in the light of sociopolitical contexts. Topics include popular housing projects, urban policies, architectural projects, and informal settlements in different countries.

705 Saavedra, Fernando Estenssoro. Crisis ambiental y cambio climático en la política global: una tema crecientemente complejo para América Latina. (*Universum/Talca*, 25:2, July 2010, p. 57–77)

Analyzes the global environmental crisis, especially climatic changes, in the context of global policies and in relation to Latin America. Discusses the role of international superpowers in the conflict and contends that the global political scenario in the 21st century can be considered as geopolitics of the environment. The ecological debate on the preservation of the Amazon is cited as an empirical example.

706 Sánchez, Darío César. Ética social vs. ética científica: la dicotomía de la geografía actual en América Latina. (*Rev. Geogr./México*, 143, enero/junio 2008, p. 47–95)

Heavily footnoted review article on the recent trends of academic geography in Latin America. Describes in detail the past epistemological tensions between objective and subjective currents in the discipline and proposes a new focus on the dichotomy between scientific ethics and social ethics.

707 Schütte, Anna Ulrike. Ein ferner Kontinent der Abenteuer und der Armut: Lateinamerika in der deutschsprachigen Kinder- und Jugendliteratur der Gegenwart. Frankfurt, Germany: Lang, 2010. 392 p.: bibl., ill. (Kinder- und Jugendkultur, -literatur und -medien, 67)

Studies how the imagination of Latin America is represented in children's and juvenile literature between 1978 and 2003. Selects five thematic aspects for analysis: the colonial history of Latin America, the image of the tropical rainforest, the underdeveloped rural zones, military regimes and resistance, and urban life.

708 Sluyter, Andrew. The Hispanic Atlantic's tasajo trail. (*LARR*, 45:1, 2010, p. 98–120, bibl., graph, map)

Historical geography study of the movement of tasajo (dried salted beef) in the Hispanic Atlantic world during the colonial period and the 19th century. Sluyter effectively demonstrates that the tasajo trade was not only a crucial component of the Atlantic slave system, but that its mostly south-north meridian circuits crosscut and complicated the dominant west-east trade triangulations with a strong Catalan involvement and direction.

709 Sobre Carl Sauer: uma introdução. Editado por Roberto Lobato Corrêa e Zeny Rosendahl. Rio de Janeiro: EdUERJ, 2011. 204 p.

Volume of Portuguese translations of five essays on Carl O. Sauer. Four of the essays (by J.A. May, R. Peet, M. Penn and F. Lukermann, and W.W. Speth) were originally published in *Culture, Land, and Life: Perspectives on Carl O. Sauer and Berkeley School Geography*, edited by Kent Mathewson and Martin Kenzer (Baton Rouge, La.: Geoscience Publications, 2003). An additional essay by Daniel Gade explores the role of curiosity in Sauer's work and thought. The editors provide an introductory essay on Sauer and his relevance to the current generation of Latin American geographers.

710 Sundberg, Juanita. Tracing race: mapping environmental formations in environmental justice research in Latin America. (*in* Environmental justice in Latin America: problems, promise, and practice. Edited by David V. Carruthers. Cambridge, Mass.: MIT Press, 2008, p. 25–47)

Presents the idea of race as a key variable for the unequal organization of social relations and environmental concepts in Latin America. Proposes a methodology to "un-map" or deconstruct commonly accepted ideas of nature, legal frameworks, and political-economic forces. For review of the entire book, see item **679**.

711 Telling ruins in Latin America. Edited by Michael J. Lazzara and Vicky Unruh. New York, N.Y.: Palgrave Macmillan, 2009. 276 p.: bibl., ill., index. (New concepts in Latino American cultures)

Collection of 21 essays on the cultural implications of ruins in Latin America. The authors stress the relations between ruins and story-telling and point out that ruins can be considered an embodiment of change that links past, present, and future. Includes examples from areas such as literature, visual art, architecture, archeology, and geography.

712 Viajes y geografías: exploraciones, turismo y migraciones en la construcción de lugares. Edición de Perla Zusman, Carla Lois y Hortensia Castro. Textos de Hortensia Castro *et al*. Buenos Aires: Prometeo Libros, 2007. 262 p.: bibl., maps.

Collection of 12 essays discussing the relevance of processes of mobility and displacement for the consolidation of places in the past and the present of the Ibero-American world. Case studies, mainly from Argentina, include analyses of historical travel accounts and present-day migration patterns.

713 Wade, Peter. Race and ethnicity in Latin America. 2nd ed. London; New York, N.Y.: Pluto Press; New York, N.Y.: Palgrave Macmillan, 2010. 215 p.: bibl., index. (Anthropology, culture and society)

Revised and updated second edition of a study on indigenous peoples and Afro-descendants in Latin America. Presents a historical approach to the different theoretical perspectives on race and ethnicity that have guided scholarly research.

714 Warf, Barney. Diverse spatialities of the Latin American and Caribbean internet. (*J. Lat. Am. Geogr.*, 8:2, 2009, p. 126–145, bibl., graph, maps, tables)

Discusses the social and spatial dimensions of the internet in Latin America and the Caribbean. Provides details on informational infrastructures, internet users, the digital divide, perspectives of electronic commerce, and governmental censorship. Draws the conclusion that increasing internet use in Latin America may lead to an improved democratization of information and opinion.

715 Wickstrom, Stefanie. Cultural politics and the essence of life: who controls the water? (*in* Environmental justice in Latin America: problems, promise, and practice. Edited by David V. Carruthers. Cambridge, Mass.: MIT Press, 2008, p. 287–319)

Debates questions about the control of water resources in Latin America. Presents case studies of conflicts among government, transnational business, and indigenous communities in Chile, Bolivia, and Mexico. Stresses the importance of indigenous meanings and practices for sustainable and just water use. For review of the entire book, see item **679**.

716 Zebich-Knos, Michele. Ecotourism, park systems, and environmental justice in Latin America. (*in* Environmental justice in Latin America: problems, promise, and practice. Edited by David V. Carruthers. Cambridge, Mass.: MIT Press, 2008, p. 185–211)

Investigates the tensions among ecotourism, national parks, and local communities in Latin America. Case studies from Mexico, Belize, and Panama are used to indicate that sustainable projects with governmental funding and the involvement of the local population and local economic activities at the same time can guarantee responsible forms of ecotourism. For review of the entire book, see item **679**.

THE CARIBBEAN

JOSEPH LEONARD SCARPACI, JR., *Professor Emeritus of Geography, Virginia Tech, Associate Professor of Marketing, Gary E. West College of Business, West Liberty University*

NEARLY HALF OF THE PUBLISHED MATERIALS reviewed here address themes related to the environment and tourism, once again underscoring the Caribbean's fragile island ecologies and their susceptibility to the impacts of mass tourism. Environmental coverage (items **717, 726, 727, 729, 739,** and **741**) addresses mining, watershed, geohazard, and beach erosion subtopics. The extant literature on sustainable tourism (items **718, 721, 735,** and **736**) underscores the paradigm that long-term tourist projects must be sustained economically, environmentally, and socially if both the region and the industry are to move forward in salutary fashion. Cartographic (item **732**) and land-tenure issues (item **730**) received scant coverage in this snapshot of geographic research on the Caribbean. Topics germane to urban development (items **720, 738,** and **743**), population change (items **722** and **928**), and migration (items **723** and **725**) connect well with themes of sustainability and tourism, and highlight the region's long-standing history of intra- and extra-regional flows of labor that respond to broader economic and political forces.

717 Aluminium smelting: health, environment and engineering perspectives. Edited by Mukesh Khare *et al.* Kingston; Miami, Fla.: Ian Randle Publishers, 2008. 228 p.: bibl., ill., maps.

Interdisciplinary assessment of the aluminum industry in the Caribbean that approaches the topic through six perspectives: productivity and economics, industrial and land-use planning, environmental concerns, smelter-emission effects, industrialization impact on ecosystems, and coastal, geotechnical, and oceanographic aspects of reclamation and artificial island development. Contributors' backgrounds include engineering, life sciences, occupational health, veterinary medicine, and planning.

718 Baldwin, Jeff. The contested beach: resistance and resort development in Antigua, West Indies. (*in* Seductions of place: geographical perspectives on globalization and touristed landscapes. Edited by Carolyn Cartier and Alan A. Lew. New York, N.Y.: Routledge, 2005, p. 222–241, maps, table)

A "mature" tourist destination, Antigua's resort development often sets local farmers and residents in opposition to national and international interests. A review of Caribbean- and Antigua-based trends culminates with a Malaysian consortium's unsuccessful efforts to build an "Asian village" with 1,000 rooms and two 18-hole golf courses on nearby Guana Island and adjacent islets.

719 Caballero, Orlando; Alexis Mojica; and Juan Martín-Rincón. Prospecciones geofísicas y arqueológicas para la recuperación de la traza urbana de Panamá La Vieja: el caso de la calle Santo Domingo. (*Rev. Geofís.*, 60, 2004, p. 43–64, maps, photos)

Magnetic soundings and readings of potential subsoil archeological material in the Old City of Panama in Santo Domingo prove an effective way to help pinpoint possible architectural and street ruins from the colonial period. The authors develop a model for interpreting electromagnetic soundings that minimizes the costs of archeological digs while preserving the nation's rich heritage.

720 The Caribbean city. Edited by Rivke Jaffe. Kingston; Miami, Fla.: I. Randle; Leiden, Netherlands: KITLV Press, 2008. 358 p.: bibl., ill., index, maps, tables.

Compilation of papers based on a 2004 workshop held in Leiden, whose authors hail from social sciences and literary criticism backgrounds to discuss developments in Hispanic, Francophone, Dutch, and Anglophone Caribbean cities. Topics covered include violence, housing, urban development, residential perceptions, inequality, and culture and literary criticism.

721 Conway, Dennis and Benjamin F. Timms. Re-branding alternative tourism in the Caribbean: the case for "slow tourism." (*Tour. Hosp. Res.*, 10:4, Oct. 2010, p. 329–344)

Slow tourism provides an alternative practical and conceptual model to mass tourism complexes that prevail throughout the region. The authors argue that slow tourism is appropriate for remote areas of the Caribbean and they present several prototypes. Caribbean expatriates could be key in establishing this rebranding process.

722 Cruz Báez, Ángel David. Perfil socioeconómico de Vieques (Puerto Rico) según el censo poblacional. (*Pap. Geogr.*, 45/46, 2007, p. 39–66, bibl., graphs, tables)

An historical economic and demographic summary of the evolution of the island's population from 1940 until 2002. The cessation of the US naval military and firing maneuvers on three-fourths of the island of Vieques now opens the entire territory for sustainable tourism. Assessing the island's demographic and economic profile with the other counties (*municipios*) in Puerto Rico, the work concludes with a review of tenets derived from the Rio de Janeiro Treaty that are relevant to Vieques.

723 Dilla Alfonso, Haroldo. República Dominicana: la nueva cartografía transfronteriza. (*Caribb. Stud.*, 35:1, Jan./June 2007, p. 181–205, bibl., maps, tables)

The economic and social functions of the DR-Haitian border are analyzed, as are the key corridors of cross-border commodity flows. Border factory production, biweekly markets, legal international commerce, and informal trade dominate the economic activity of this north-south corridor. Future growth will likely create a mestizo (e.g., blended) economic and cultural zone as it takes on greater importance for each country.

724 Dorrejo, Erick; Karina Negrín; and Cesar Pérez. El sistema de transporte colectivo en la articulación del gran Santo Domingo. (*Cienc. Soc./Santo Domingo*, 32:1, enero/marzo 2007, p. 88–121, bibl., graphs, table)

Traces the road infrastructure and nine-fold demographic expansion of Santo Domingo, Dominican Republic, from a base population of around 300,000 in 1960, to 2005. Argues for a much needed policy of integration and "articulation" among disparate public and private organizations to develop a more functional transportation network and reduce the prevalent mode of private automobile travel in the nation's capital.

725 Dynamiques migratoires de la Caraïbe. Coordonné par GEODE Caraïbe, André Calmont et Cédric Audebert. Paris: Karthala: GEODE Caraïbe, 2007. 399 p.: bibl., ill. (chiefly col.). (Terres d'Amérique; 6)

This French volume with Spanish and English summaries examines the Caribbean diaspora as manifested by migration within and beyond the Caribbean basin. Themes organizing the 22 chapters include the spatial migration, socioeconomic insertion, identity, and regional migratory dynamics to and from the Greater and Lesser Antilles. Special attention is given to Canada, Cuba, Dominican Republic, France, French Antilles, Great Britain, Guyana, Jamaica, Martinique, Puerto Rico, and South Florida.

726 The economics of an integrated (watershed) approach to environmental management in small island developing states (SIDS): from ridge to reef. Textos de Dennis A. Pantin *et al.* St. Augustine, Trinidad and Tobago: UWI-SEDU/SIDS, 2008. 156 p.: bibl., ill. (some col.), maps (some col.), tables. (UWI-SEDU—Small & Island Developing States (SIDS) greening policy publication series; 1)

Data- and figure-rich compendium of 10 essays offering cost-benefit, waste management, valuation, forest ecosystem, nearshore valuation and protection, air emission, sewage, tourism, and natural disaster analyses of Caribbean SIDS. National case studies of Trinidad and Tobago, Jamaica, and St. Lucia are included.

727 Enduring geohazards in the Caribbean: moving from the reactive to the proactive. Edited by Serwan M. J. Baban. Kingston: Univ. of the West Indies Press, 2008. 256 p.: bibl., ill., maps.

Fourteen chapters examine causes and preventive measures for landslides, floods, and geohazards broadly defined. The holistic approach to proactive planning entails the development of conceptual frameworks, detailed resource inventories based on mapping strategies, and public awareness programs throughout the region.

728 Fanning, Lucia; Robin Mahon; and Patrick McConney. Towards marine ecosystem-based management in the wider Caribbean. Amsterdam: Amsterdam Univ. Press, 2010. 425 p.: ill. (MARE publications series; 6)

In order to ensure sustainable use of their shared marine resources, the nations of the West Caribbean region must adopt an approach that encompasses both the human and natural dimensions of ecosystems. This volume directly contributes to that vision, bringing together the collective knowledge and experience of scholars and practitioners within the wider Caribbean to assemble a roadmap towards marine ecosystem-based management for the region. [C.E. Griffin]

729 Ferguson, Therese and Elizabeth Thomas-Hope. Environmental education and constructions of sustainable development in Jamaica. (*in* Sustainable development: national aspirations, local implementation. Edited by Jennifer Hill, Alan Terry, and Wendy Woodland. Burlington, Vt.: Ashgate, 2006, p. 91–113, bibl., graphs, tables)

Environmental awareness discourses emerging from the developed North in the 1960s now permeate the "South." Drawing on a survey of 394 pupils, aged 11–14, in four schools in Jamaica, the paper offers a discursive examination of the effect of the National Education Action Plan for Sustainable Development on students' knowledge and perception of nature and human-environment relations. Findings reveal that most (57.4 percent) students' concepts of nature rest on the quality of nature versus the relationship with nature, esthetic or emotive factors, or inner nature.

730 Gaalaas Mullaney, Emma. Carib territory: indigenous access to land in the Commonwealth of Dominica. (*J. Lat. Am. Geogr.*, 8:2, 2009, p. 71–96, bibl., maps, photos)

Proposes land security as the key component in tensions between indigenous groups and the Commonwealth. Primary data indicate that ownership per se is too limited a concept among natives in understanding place-land attachment for the Carib in Dominica.

García-Colón, Ismael. Land reform in Puerto Rico: modernizing the colonial state, 1941–1969. See item **1214**.

731 Hausler, Elizabeth. Building earthquake-resistant houses in Haiti: the homeowner-driven model. (*Innov./Cambridge*, 5:4, Oct. 2010, p. 91–115)

Contending that it is not the earthquake that kills people but the collapse of poorly designed and built structures, this case narrative describes a building model that will work for Haiti and explains why it is critical to use a homeowner-driven model rather than a donor-driven one. [C.E. Griffin]

732 Imágenes insulares: cartografía histórica dominicana. Compilación de José Chez Checo. Santo Domingo: Banco Popular Dominicano, 2008. 418 p.: bibl., ill. (some col.), maps (some col.).

Chronological collection of 391 b/w and color maps of Hispaniola, with emphasis on the eastern half, ranging from late 16th to early 21st centuries. Brief Spanish-language bibliographic notations for each image convey (often estimated) date of creation, brief description, dimensions, and the location of the library or archive where the original map is housed.

733 Julca, Alex and **Oliver Paddison.** Vulnerabilities and migration in Small Island Developing States in the context of climate change. (*Nat. Haz.*, 55:3, Dec. 2010, p. 717–728)

This article sheds light on some of the vulnerabilities that Small Island Developing States (SIDS) face with particular reference to their environmental and economic vulnerabilities. It then highlights the ambiguous role that international migration plays in the recreation of those vulnerabilities. [C.E. Griffin]

734 Les littoraux de la Caraïbe: pratiques sociales et nouvelles dynamiques spatiales. Coordonné par GEODE Caraïbe, Thierry Hartog et Michel Desse. Paris: Karthala; Schoelcher, Martinique: GEODE Caraïbe, 2009. 219 p.: bibl., ill. (some col.), maps, plates. (Terres d'Amérique; 7)

A French volume with Spanish and English summaries brings together chapters that describe the social practices engendered by intra- and inter-regional migration to and from the Caribbean. With a particular focus on port and maritime settings, thematic topics covered include environmental threats, hip-hop, the rum industry, informal economies, as well as several chapters on tourism.

735 Momsen, Janet Henshall. Sustainable food for sustainable tourism in the Caribbean: integrated pest management and changes in the participation of women. (*in* Sustainable development: national aspirations, local implementation. Edited by Jennifer Hill, Alan Terry, and Wendy Woodland. Burlington, Vt.: Ashgate, 2006, p. 159–174, bibl., tables)

Uses secondary data to assess the effectiveness and challenges of pest-management practices by women in selected Caribbean nations. Draws on Agenda 21 principles to determine how women are entering the organic farm markets that cater to local and sustainable tourism. The rise in supplying hotels with local produce has dipped in recent years but could be remedied if forward linkages are made between local farmers and national governments, on one hand, and external funding, on the other hand.

736 Momsen, Janet Henshall. Uncertain images: tourism development and seascapes of the Caribbean. (*in* Seductions of place: geographical perspectives on globalization and touristed landscapes. Edited by Carolyn Cartier and Alan A. Lew. New York, N.Y.: Routledge, 2005, p. 209–221, maps)

A cursory literature review of issues in Caribbean tourism and development with a small focus on the cruise ship industry and a proposal for adding a fourth "s" to the traditional sun, surf, and sand recipe: sex. The rising importance of the most touristed aspect of the travel experience—seascape—rests on the cruise ship where tourists can be coddled and protected, much like the all-inclusive "enclave" resort. The "ship" experience may form a fifth "s" in the traditional mix of the Caribbean tourist experience.

737 Moore, Winston Ricardo. The impact of climate change on Caribbean tourism demand. (*Curr. Issues Tour.*, 13:5, Sept. 2010, p. 495–505, bibl., tables)

Climate change can either positively or negatively impact the attractiveness of a destination. To evaluate the potential effects of these changes for Caribbean destinations, a cross-country tourism demand model is augmented with relative tourism climatic indices to examine the importance of an island's climatic features. The model is estimated using a dynamic panel approach and monthly observations over the period 1977–2006. [C.E. Griffin]

738 Ponce Herrero, Gabino. Crisis, posmodernidad y planificación estratégica en La Habana. (*An. Geogr. Univ. Complut.*, 27:2, 2007, p. 135–150, bibl., maps)

Descriptive summary of recent land-use and economic development plans for the greater metropolitan area of Havana in light of the country's propensity to accommodate international tourism. Traces the evolution of pre- and post-Special Period approaches to metropolitan land-use planning, the latter embracing what the author refers to as postmodern planning.

739 Rodríguez Paneque, Ridel A. and **Elier A. Córdova García.** La erosión en las playas de la región nororiental de Cuba. (*Rev. Geogr./México*, 139, enero/junio 2006, p. 9–26, bibl., graphs, maps, photos, tables)

Nearly 60 percent of 99 sampled beaches in northeastern Cuban provinces, from Holguín (Boca de Bahía de Nuevitas) to Guantánamo (Punta de Quemado), have experienced an average of 0.6 m of annual beach erosion in recent years due to intense storms that originate from cold fronts in the north. Human actions in the form of beach sand removal from berms and dunes for the purposes of building construction exacerbate shoreline erosion.

740 Stricker, Pamela. Toward a culture of nature: environmental policy and sustainable development in Cuba. Lanham, Md.: Lexington Books, 2007. 157 p.: bibl., index.

Accepts the Cuban government's official position on environmental matters and the premise that sustainable development is taking hold in Cuba. Argues that the island offers a much-needed social justice perspective in sustainable development policies that can serve other countries.

741 Terry, Allan; Jennifer Hill; and **Wendy Woodland.** Uniting national aspirations and local implementation in sustainable development: an introduction. (*in* Sustainable development: national aspirations, local implementation. Edited by Jennifer Hill, Alan Terry, and Wendy Woodland. Burlington, Vt.: Ashgate, 2006, p. 1–11, bibl.)

The editors of this book present this introductory chapter outlining the scope of this volume that builds on and applies the "Earth Summit" (Rio de Janeiro) and Millennium Development Goals in many regions, including the Caribbean. Discontinuities between macro- and national-level goals provide metrics against which progress towards sustainability can be determined.

742 Timms, Benjamin F. Development theory and domestic agriculture in the Caribbean: recurring crises and missed opportunities. (*Caribb. Geogr.*, 15:2, Jan. 2008, p. 101–117)

Despite the widely known problems of monocultural production, many Caribbean islands still rely on that model of agriculture. The recent global economic crisis, however, provides a new incentive to diversify agricultural production and to offset the rising costs of food throughout the Caribbean.

743 Tindigarukayo, Jimmy Kazaara. Squatters in Jamaica: a policy assessment. Cave Hill, Barbados: Sir Arthur Lewis Institute of Social and Economic Studies, Univ. of the West Indies, 2005. 84 p.: bibl., ill.

A 2001 national survey of squatters in Jamaica draws on 791 household heads across the island's parishes and characterizes the positive and negative aspects of settlements and policy tools from Operation Pride in addressing them. Recommends that squatters be integrated into the socioeconomic fabric of the island and that good relations between government and squatters be fostered by enlisting the latter's potentially enthusiastic participation in planning and implementation to solve squatter problems.

**744 Turismo, medio ambiente y coopera-
ción internacional en el Caribe: una
aproximación situacional.** Compilación de Rafael Romero Mayo y Juan Carlos Arriaga Rodriguez. Textos de Bonnie Lucía Campos Cámara *et al.* Chetumal, Mexico: Univ. de Quintana Roo, División de Ciencias Políticas y Humanidades; México: Plaza y Valdés, 2007. 221 p.: bibl., ill., maps.

Ten chapters written by scholars from the Universidad de Quintana Roo assess tourist poles and environmental problems, environmental strategies and cooperation in the Caribbean, and environmental impact and social participation. International cooperation to meet tourism challenges is examined through regional foci: the Mexican Caribbean, the Caribbean in general, and separate analyses of Cuba and Barbados, and Latin America.

CENTRAL AMERICA

PETER H. HERLIHY, *Associate Professor of Geography, University of Kansas*

THE GEOGRAPHICAL SCHOLARSHIP ON CENTRAL AMERICA surveyed for this biennium focuses more on the cultural than physical side of the discipline, and more on rural than urban areas. The literature annotated here continues previous research trends, as discussed below, with developing areas on natural disasters research, as well as on the use of repeat geography and participatory mapping methodologies. The selection reflects the existence of a particularly active community of human geographers from the US and Canada doing field, archival, and GIS research on the lands and peoples of the region. Special recognition is given to honor the 2007 passing of Universidad de Panamá's geographer Alberto Arturo McKay.

Of note among the more physical studies is an analysis of the geomorphology of the paleo-lacustrine deposits in the Lake Nicaragua graben (item **774**), as well as a project documenting the earliest paleo-environmental record of the Guatemala Highlands based on sediment pollen and charcoal evidence, showing similarities to the Maya lowlands (item **756**). Human impact mapping of the Mopan and Chiquibul rivers documents the deleterious impacts on the system (item **747**).

Natural disaster studies were particularly important during the period. Geographic research focused on disaster impacts, particularly from the gargantuan Hurricane Mitch in 1998, considering the different types of vulnerability that result from conditions of poverty, migration/displacement, institutional, or physical/environmental (item **757**). Two field studies demonstrate the pervasive impact of Mitch on Honduras, one showing the inadequacies of postdisaster recovery efforts that do not address root causes of vulnerability (item **769**), and the other finding the parallax of "disaster capitalism" when residents of the hardest-hit communities were coerced into leaving the Celaque National Park, ultimately serving park management interests (item **773**). Another case details the impacts

Hurricane Mitch had on the indigenous Tawahka communities in the remote Honduran Mosquitia, showing how residents played it to their advantage to gain more equitable land distribution (item **771**). Looking at seismic vulnerability, natural and constructed weaknesses are distinguished in Costa Rica's Brunca region, likewise showing the impacts of development on the social construction of vulnerability (item **752**).

A strong interest continues in cultural-historical and ethnogeographic research that combines field and archival work, increasingly with GIS analysis. One study looks at the late-19th-century writings and influences of Bishop Thiel on indigenous Maleku communities (item **750**). Others use historic maps to delimit Miskitu territory (item **778**), or look at the imprint of the Moravian Church on the Miskitu settlement landscape, offering another way to verify land claims (item **772**). An excellent essay considers the "cultural preadaption" of the Garífuna communities to their coastal setting (item **770**).

A significant quantity of outstanding geographic scholarship focused on contemporary indigenous and Afro-descendant populations in Central America. Universidad de Costa Rica historian Héctor Pérez Brignoli provides an excellent overview of the demographic dynamic of indigenous populations in the humid tropics of Central America, including outstanding color maps (item **745**). Decades of field and archival study tempered geographer William V. Davidson's outstanding baseline assessment of the ethnic geography of Honduras through his meticulous analysis of the 2001 census—the first to report ethnicity (item **765**). He likewise published *Etnología y etnohistoria de Honduras,* a collection of 20 of his essays on the ethnogeography of Honduras (item **766**).

Geographers show how the hegemonic discourses of terror and mistrust are emblematic in a cultural landscape dotted with "model villages" and clandestine graves in Highland Guatemala (item **758**). Queen's University geographer George Lovell vividly narrates a K'iche' Maya woman's tale of the continued insecurity and lack of justice that permeates Guatemala's indigenous communities (see *HLAS 65:1010*). We celebrate Lovell's retirement from 28 years of dedicated editorship of the premiere journal *Mesoamérica,* and his collaboration with Julio Castellanos Cambranes, Christopher H. Lutz, and Armando J. Alfonzo, in producing the first 50 issues (1980–2008, with *Índice General*) and building this *editorial* into one of the most important scholarly journals on the social sciences of Central America, and likewise becoming an important outlet for geographic scholarship.

An authoritative collection by an interdisciplinary group of researchers focused on the autonomy and territorial rights of Miskitu and other ethnic communities in the settlements, protected areas, and autonomous regions of Nicaragua's Caribbean coast (item **776**). Other studies demonstrated how two large dam projects violated indigenous Emberá, Kuna, and Ngöbe rights in Panama (item **781**), and how carbon offsetting programs in that country can cause harm to indigenous Naso and Ngöbe populations (item **780**).

Critical geographers opened a discourse on the potential dangers of participatory mapping to indigenous peoples (items **749** and **764**), while others continued to develop new applications of the methodology with important results. Participatory research mapping (PRM) was combined with GIS analysis to investigate the spatial patterns of hunting among indigenous Miskitu communities of the Río Plátano Biosphere Reserve (item **767**) and among the Buglé of Panama (item **782**).

Two studies used the developing repeat-geography methodology working with the "vintage" observations geographer Robert C. West made in Honduras during the 1950s: one used his field notes, maps, manuscript, census data, and aerial photographs to detail the changing livelihoods and landscapes of the Lenca communities in Honduras today (item 763); the other viewed present Honduran landscape changes through 100 photos West took throughout the country, focusing especially on indigenous and mining places (item 762).

The geographic literature maintains a focus on the management of forest resources and protected areas, particularly those inhabited by indigenous populations. One thorough study focuses on the dynamics of contemporary ownership, appropriation, and reconcentration of lands among the predominantly q'eqchi' populations in the Guatemalan Alta Verapaz (item 759), with detailed case studies including the Sierra de las Minas Biosphere Reserve. Another study shows how Garífuna uses of marine resources in the Cayos Cochinos reserve are not always harmonious with conservation goals (item 768).

The impacts of globalization are increasingly scrutinized. Research shows how decentralization policies actually bring about more centralized state power over communal forests in Guatemala (item 761), with little autonomous decision-making left to municipal governments in Nicaragua (item 777). Costa Rica changed its import substitution model and now offers contract incentives to bring small farmers into pepper and chayote production (item 753). Today, economic pull replaces the push of political oppression in drawing Nicaraguan migrants to Costa Rica, with greater numbers of women and families coming in search of better opportunities (item 751).

Universidad de Costa Rica geographer Gilbert Vargas characterizes tourism developments in Central America (item 746), showing how tourism has grown since pacification in the late 1980s despite limited implementation of regional accords. Costa Rica is the regional leader in international tourist arrivals and notable for nature tourism, but newly developing medical tourism attracted over 20,000 "tourists" to Costa Rica in 2008 for a wide array of procedures at significant cost savings (item 755). One study focuses on how NGOs and others can provide support for developing community-based tourism (item 754).

Finally, while identifying strong trends and exceptional examples of geographic research on Central America, the literature survey points to the need for promoting research—from both human and physical geographers—on the significant urban and environmental issues facing the region.

GENERAL

745 Pérez Brignoli, Héctor. La dinámica demográfica de las poblaciones indígenas del trópico húmedo en América Central, censos de 2000. (*in* IUSSP XXV International Population Conference, Tours, France, July 18–23, 2005. Demography of indigenous peoples (session 809). http://iussp2005.princeton.edu, p. 1–16, maps)

A concise, authoritative overview of the demography of contemporary indigenous populations of the humid tropics of Central America, excluding Guatemala, primarily focused on those communities along the Caribbean side of the isthmus and in the Darién region. The exceptional maps make the analysis particularly vivid.

746 Vargas Ulate, Gilbert. La actividad turística en América Central: desarrollo y características. (*Anu. Estud. Centroam.*, 32, 2006, p. 9–35, bibl., graphs, maps, photos, tables)

Since the pacification of the isthmus at the end of the 1980s, tourism has grown significantly with Costa Rica as the regional leader in international tourist arrivals, and Nicaragua attractive for "nature tourism," while Guatemala, Honduras, and El Salvador are more appreciated for "cultural tourism." And while political forces create regional institutions and promote tourism throughout Central America, most policies remain largely unimplemented, exacerbated by significant differences in levels of socioeconomic development within each country, limiting the application of regional accords.

BELIZE

747   Karper, Jes and Ed Boles. Human impact mapping of the Mopan and Chiquibul rivers within Guatemala and Belize. (*Belizean Stud.*, 28:1, April 2006, p. 31–41, bibl., maps, tables)
The Mopan River above the confluence with the Chiquibul River shows greater sedimentation, nutrient loading, habitat alteration, thermal alteration, contaminants, and tropic alteration than downriver. A binational effort is reportedly underway to mitigate causes and negative impacts on ecosystem stability.

748   Metcalfe, Sarah E. *et al.* Environmental change in northern Belize since the latest Pleistocene. (*JQS*, 24:6, Sept. 2009, p. 627–641, bibl., graphs, maps, tables)
Diatom and stable isotope analyses from core samples from the New River Lagoon in Belize indicate that the Holocene had moist, stable conditions, with access to freshwater allowing continuous occupation at the Maya site of Lamanai on the shores of the lagoon.

749   Wainwright, Joel and Joe Bryan. Cartography, territory, property: postcolonial reflections on indigenous counter-mapping in Nicaragua and Belize. (*Cult. Geogr./London*, 16:2, April 2009, p. 153–178, bibl., table)
Reflecting on the potential dark powers of "counter-mapping" while discussing two often-mentioned indigenous lands cases of the Maya of Belize and Awas Tingni in Nicaragua, the authors suggest that the correct combination of maps and lawsuits might allow for a just recognition of indigenous geographies. Unfortunately, they do not provide sufficient detail on the all-important mapmaking process—which the authors themselves worked on—for anyone to determine if the research in these projects meets such standards.

COSTA RICA

750   Castillo Vásquez, Roberto. El Obispo Bernardo Augusto Thiel y los indígenas maleku de la zona norte de Costa Rica. (*Rev. Reflex./San José*, 90:2, 2011, p. 53–70, bibl., maps)
Bishop Thiel made valuable geographic and ethnographic observations during his five late-19th-century visits to the Maleku communities. The author uses these observations to show how Thiel helped save the Maleku from extermination at the hands of rubber-tappers, but perhaps paradoxically, he promoted their Christianization, incorporation into Nicaraguan society, and overall "ethnocide."

751   Otterstrom, Samuel M. Nicaraguan migrants in Costa Rica during the 1990s: gender differences and geographic expansion. (*J. Lat. Am. Geogr.*, 7:2, 2008, p. 7–33, maps, tables)
This research analyzes the wave of undocumented migrants in Costa Rica who fled from Nicaragua after its civil war but before Hurricane Mitch primarily for economic reasons, with greater numbers of women and families creating a widespread and less transitory presence.

752   Peraldo Huertas, Giovanni and Mauricio Mora Fernández. Aspectos geográficos relacionados con el aumento de la vulnerabilidad ante sismos en los valles de los ríos Buenavista y Chirripó Pacífico, Costa Rica. (*Rev. Geogr./México*, 142, julio/dic. 2007, p. 51–87, bibl., ill., maps, photos)
Two types of seismic vulnerability, natural and constructed, are distinguished in the study area covering two upland river valleys (307.85 km²) of the Brunca region. The differential transformation from a forested zone at the turn of the 20th century through agricultural colonization and conservation practices created distinct cultural landscapes that demonstrate the impacts of development processes on the social construction of vulnerability.

753 **Ruben, Ruerd** and **Fernando Sáenz.**
Farmers, markets and contracts:
chain integration of smallholder producers
in Costa Rica. (*Rev. Eur. Estud. Latinoam.
Caribe,* 85, Oct. 2008, p. 61–80, bibl., tables)
Costa Rica changed its import-
substitution orientation to incorporate the
agricultural sector into an open-market
economy with limited state interventions.
Under this system, contracts help small
producers establish pepper and chayote
production given the start-up time involved
in their cultivation.

754 **Trejos, Bernardo; Lan-Hung Nora
Chiang;** and **Wen-Chi Huang.** Support networks for community-based tourism
in rural Costa Rica. (*Open Area Stud. J.,* 1,
2008, p. 16–25)
Working with grassroots organizations embedded in support networks, and
sometimes even functioning as tour operators, helps rural inhabitants without essential skills in a market with high development costs and the dominance of mass
tourism operators.

755 **Warf, Barney.** Do you know the way
to San José?: medical tourism in
Costa Rica. (*J. Lat. Am. Geogr.,* 9:1, 2010,
p. 51–66, bibl., ill. (some col.), tables)
Medical tourism in Costa Rica has
grown from an occasional US tourist arriving for low-cost cosmetic surgery in the
1980s to up to 25,000 medical tourists (in
2008) undergoing a wide array of procedures,
especially dental and other surgeries. Costa
Rican health care is appealing for its significant cost savings.

GUATEMALA

756 **Caffrey, Maria A.; Matthew J. Taylor;**
and **Donald G. Sullivan.** A 12,000–
year record of vegetation and climate change
from the Sierra de los Cuchumatanes,
Guatemala. (*J. Lat. Am. Geogr.,* 10:2, 2011,
p. 129–152, bibl., graphs, ill. (some color),
map, tables)
Pollen, charcoal, and geochemical
evidence in the sediment record of the
páramo-like Miqul Meadow (at 3,147 me-
ters) near Huehuetenango in the Sierra de
los Cuchumatanes provides the earliest
paleo-environmental record of highland
Guatemala. The area shows similarity to

the Maya lowlands, with drying about 4750
years ago, even in areas without human
settlements.

757 **Cifuentes Soberanis, María Isabel.**
Territorio y vulnerabilidad en Guatemala. Revisión y edición final de Amanda
Morán Mérida y José Florentín Martínez
López. Ciudad de Guatemala: Univ. de San
Carlos Guatemala, Centro de Estudios Urbanos y Regionales, 2009. 254 p.: bibl., ill.,
maps (some col.). (Serie Territorio y regionalización en Guatemala; 2)
Reviewing fundamental concepts
concerning territory, region, development,
and risk, the author compares the different
types of vulnerability created by poverty,
migration/displacement, institutional impacts, and physical/environmental changes,
that are produced in different regions of the
country. Looks particularly at droughts,
floods, and earthquakes, reviewing the impact of recent disasters, including the 1976
earthquake, Hurricane Mitch in 1998, the
drought of 2001, and Hurricane Stan in 2005.

758 **Clouser, Rebecca.** Remnants of terror: landscapes of fear in post-conflict
Guatemala. (*J. Lat. Am. Geogr.,* 8:2, 2009,
p. 7–22, bibl., maps, photos)
In postconflict Guatemala, state hegemonic discourses of terror and mistrust endure in the cultural landscape in the forms
of model villages, "clandestine" graves, and
the lack of public memorials, creating a
culture of fear that still pervades society.

759 **Hurtado, Laura.** Dinámicas agrarias y
reproducción campesina en la globalización: el caso de Alta Verapaz, 1970–2007.
Ciudad de Guatemala: F&G Editores, 2008.
424 p.: bibl., ill., maps.
The sociologist explains the "principal agrarian dynamics" of contemporary
ownership, appropriation, and reconcentration of lands in the Guatemalan Alta
Verapaz, including outstanding case studies
on the agricultural frontier, the "regularization" of land rights, overlapping land rights,
the production of coffee and cardamom, and
the Sierra de las Minas and Sierra de Chi-
naja biosphere reserves.

760 **Taylor, Matthew J.** *et al.* Burning
for sustainability: biomass energy,
international migration, and the move to
cleaner fuels and cookstoves in Guatemala.

(*Ann. Assoc. Am. Geogr.*, 101:4, July 2011, p. 918–928)

With increased incomes, migrant households in San Cristóbal make rational decisions about their cooking-fuel purchases, using a mix of three-stone fires, wood-burning stoves, and gas stoves. While they can use more-efficient gas for cooking, most continue to use more economical purchased firewood as their primary fuel given their preferred food preparation traditions.

761   Wittman, Hannah and **Charles Geisler.** Negotiating locality: decentralization and communal forest management in the Guatemalan highlands. (*Hum. Organ.*, 64:1, Spring 2005, p. 62–74)

Decentralization policies in Guatemala place administrative power and territorial controls of communal forests at the municipal level. However the authors suggest that these policies actually allow increased centralized state power over local authority and threaten to displace customary law, lands, and even livelihoods by putting communal forests within the reach of state authorities.

HONDURAS

762   Bass, Joby. Learning landscape change in Honduras: repeat photography and discovery. (*in* Repeat photography: methods and applications in the natural sciences. Edited by Robert H. Webb, Diane E. Boyer, and Raymond M. Turner. Washington, D.C.: Island Press, 2010, p. 275–288, bibl., photos)

The geographer demonstrates the complexities of understanding landscape changes throughout Honduras by using repeat photography at 100 sites photographed and studied by geographer Robert C. West during the summer of 1957. The results, testifying to West's great interests in indigenous lands and colonial mining towns, show a much different contemporary landscape that retains strong indigenous and colonial legacies, but has more developed rural and urban economic patterns and associated land uses, with related environmental conditions. Perhaps surprisingly, the study shows increases in vegetation cover throughout, in some places resulting from coffee production, elsewhere from reforesta-

tion and dooryard orchard-gardens. For comment on related study, see item **763**.

763   Brady, Scott. Revisiting a Honduran landscape described by Robert West: an experiment in repeat geography. (*J. Lat. Am. Geogr.*, 8:1, 2009, p. 7–27, bibl., graphs, map)

The repeat geography methodology, without photography, uses the "vintage geographical studies" of geographer West to assess the changing Lenca landscape. Still displaying its picturesque adobe and bajareque-walled houses topped with clay tiles of the past, Lenca now produces cash crops and handicraft production in a context of forest conservation efforts and an urbanizing population. For review of related study, see item **762**.

764   Bryan, Joe. Walking the line: participatory mapping, indigenous rights, and neoliberalism. (*Geoforum/New York*, 42:1, Jan. 2011, p. 951–962)

Well-constructed prose on the potential dangers of participatory mapping belies the fact that these "dangers" have not materialized to any degree in the study area of the Honduran Mosquitia. The author's critical discourse dodges the ill-defined methodology and controversial use of participatory mapping that he and his collaborators used to delimit and map land-claims between the indigenous communities there.

765   Davidson, William V. Ethnic geography of Honduras, 2001: tables and maps based on the National Census. Tegucigalpa: Academia Hondureña de Geografía e Historia, 2011. 333 p.: bibl., maps, photos, tables.

An exhaustive analysis of the country's ethnic geography based on the 2001 National Census that for the first time reported the ethnicity of each individual. Davidson provides a baseline for future ethnicity studies, meticulously distilling the population and settlement characteristics of the country's eight ethnic groups, providing insightful details that refine understandings.

766   Davidson, William V. Etnología y etnohistoria de Honduras: ensayos. Tegucigalpa: Instituto Hondureño de Antropología e Historia, 2009. 351 p.: bibl., ill., maps, plates, tables. (Estudios antropológicos e históricos; 22)

A translation of 20 published and unpublished papers on Honduras by the geographer, with a few coauthored with his graduate students and Honduran anthropologist Fernando Cruz. Resulting from field and archival research, these thorough yet concise essays make important contributions to the cultural history of Honduras, especially as related to the settlement histories, migrations, and place-names of the indigenous populations.

767 Dunn, Marc Andre and Derek A. Smith. The spatial patterns of Miskitu hunting in northeastern Honduras: lessons for wildlife managment in tropical forests. (*J. Lat. Am. Geogr.*, 10:1, 2011, p. 85–109, bibl., maps, tables)

An excellent study of the spatial patterns of hunting in two Miskitu communities along the southeastern rainforest-savanna boundary of the Río Plátano Biosphere Reserve. Results from participatory mapping and field observations showed 58 regular hunters among their total population of 947, who use 242 km² of land that is spatially divided into "garden-hunting" and "day-trip" zones that provide 86 percent of the game caught, and a more distant "multiple-day" zone occurs around agricultural sites, called kiamps. The researchers demonstrate the power and applicability of participatory mapping and its important use in wildlife management programs.

768 Lansing, David. The spaces of social capital: livelihood geographies and marine conservation in the Cayos Cochinos Marine Protected Area, Honduras. (*J. Lat. Am. Geogr.*, 8:1, 2009, p. 29–54, bibl., maps, photos, tables)

The relation between household social capital and the use of marine resources in the Cayos Cochinos Reserve shows how marine resources help Garífuna fishing families build networks of trust and reciprocity, using them in ways that are not always harmonious with conservation goals that could better reflect the socially complex uses of resources.

769 The legacy of Hurricane Mitch: lessons from post-disaster reconstruction in Honduras. Edited by Marisa O. Ensor. Tucson: Univ. of Arizona Press, 2009. 222 p.: bibl., ill., index, maps.

Hurricane Mitch brought about the worst natural disaster ever experienced in Honduras; a decade later, the country is still recovering from the hurricane's pervasive impact. Five anthropologists, a political scientist, and an environmentalist offer a largely field-based analysis of the hurricane's impact and long-term consequences, revealing the inadequacies of postdisaster recovery efforts that do not address the root causes of vulnerability.

770 Mack, Taylor E. Cultural maladaptation and preadaptation in colonial Honduras: Spaniards vs. Black Caribs, 1787–1821. (*J. Lat. Am. Geogr.*, 10:1, 2011, 177–193, bibl., maps, table)

An excellent essay that resurrects the notion of cultural preadaptation to show how two different culture groups who arrived at Trujillo on the north coast of Honduras at the end of the 18th century faired quite differently; the Spanish colonists did poorly being maladapted culturally, while the Black Carib (Garífuna) settlers faired well in the tropical environment.

771 McSweeney, Kendra and Oliver T. Coomes. Climate-related disaster opens a window of opportunity for rural poor in northeastern Honduras. (*Proc. Natl. Acad. Sci. U.S.A.*, 108:13, March 2011, p. 5203–5208, bibl., maps, tables)

Field research results from four different projects during the 1994–2002 period reveal how indigenous Tawahka communities in the heart of the Honduran Mosquitia rainforest corridor were vulnerable to Hurricane Mitch in 1998. However, the disaster led to more equitable land distribution due to the adoption of a questionable practice of claiming forest tracts by cutting paths around parcels, which in turn slowed primary forest conversion through reducing speculative forest clearing.

772 Tillman, Benjamin Farr. Imprints on native lands: the Miskito-Moravian settlement landscape in Honduras. Tucson: Univ. of Arizona Press, 2011. 186 p.: bibl., ill., index, maps. (First peoples: new directions in indigenous studies)

The author combines field research, interviews, and empirical observations with the analysis of texts, maps, photographs, and other archival materials to show the significant impact of Moravians on the settlement landscape of the Honduran Miskitu, further documenting their ethnic landscape and land claims.

773   Timms, Benjamin F. The (mis)use of disaster as opportunity: coerced relocation from Celaque National Park, Honduras. (*Antipode*, 43:4, Sept. 2011, p. 1357–1379, bibl., tables)

Through the lens of "disaster capitalism," this provocative analysis shows how conditional aid helped implement an exclusionary protected area and management plan depopulation goal for the Celaque National Park after Hurricane Mitch caused the dislocation of about half the resident population outside the reserve. Questionnaires administered to 49 of the 61 relocated households show negative consequences on their land uses and income-generating activities, ultimately serving the capitalist interests of international conservation and the agro-export coffee industry.

NICARAGUA

774   Bergoeing, Jean Pierre and **Roberto Protti.** Geomorfología paleo-lacustre del sur del lago de Nicaragua. (*Rev. Geogr./ México*, 139, enero/junio 2006, p. 27–38, bibl., graphs, maps, photos)

Lake Nicaragua is in a tectonic graben that was filled with volcanic deposits in Miocene time, followed by sedimentary deposits in a marine environment with renewed volcanic activity in the Pliocene, then filling with sediments of volcanic origin from the Cordillera de Guanacaste in the Quaternary. The area was covered by the sea until the late Pleistocene.

775   Cupples, Julie. Rethinking electoral geography: spaces and practices of democracy in Nicaragua. (*Trans. Inst. Br. Geogr.*, 34:1, Jan. 2009, p. 110–124, bibl., ill., tables)

Nicaraguans find room to maneuver within a political system characterized by panopticisms where voting is neither resistance nor compliance, but a hybrid action interweaving complex social and political considerations of the voter.

776   Demarcación territorial de la propiedad comunal en la Costa Caribe de Nicaragua. Compilación de Alvaro Rivas y Rikke Broegaard. Managua: MultiGrafic, 2006. 282 p.: bibl., ill., maps.

This landmark collection provides an integrated and interdisciplinary vision of the contemporary history and politics behind the autonomy and territorial rights of the indigenous and other ethnic communities in the settlements, protected areas, and autonomous regions of Nicaragua's Caribbean coast, including significant case studies by anthropologists Galio Gurdián, Charles Hale, Anthony Stocks, and Armstrong Wiggins.

777   Larson, Anne M. Formal decentralization and the imperative of decentralization "from below": a case study of natural resource management in Nicaragua. (*in* Democratic decentralization through a natural resource lens. Edited by Jesse C. Ribot and Anne M. Larson. London; New York, N.Y.: Routledge, 2004, p. 55–70)

Decentralization brought deconcentration and privatization, but vague or contradictory laws and regulations mean the central government releases little control over the management and protection of natural resources with municipal governments ending up with little autonomous decision-making power.

778   Offen, Karl H. El mapeo de la Mosquitia colonial y las prácticas espaciales de los pueblos mosquitos. (*Mesoamérica/ Antigua*, 29:50, 2008, p. 1–36, bibl., ill., maps)

Broadly defining a spatial practice as "any political feat, economic activity, forceful claim, or social performance that asserts and demonstrates authority over people and space," the author presents original interpretations using historic maps showing how indigenous Miskitu defined their own spatial control and territory through their actions and discourses. For historian's comment, see *HLAS 64:875.*

779   Región norte central de Nicaragua: Matagalpa y Jinotega a través de su historia. Coordinación de Jilma Romero. Edición de Virgilio Espinoza y Alfredo Lobato Blanco. Textos de Dolores Alvarez *et al.* Managua: Depto. de Historia de la Univ. Nacional Autónoma de Nicaragua, 2005. 211 p.: bibl., ill. (some col.), maps (some col.).

Resulting from a remarkably interdisciplinary collaboration, this study in regional and local history provides a concise collage of the physical and cultural character of this north-central region of the country.

PANAMA

780 Finley-Brook, Mary and **Curtis Thomas.** Renewable energy and human rights violations: illustrative cases from indigenous territories in Panama. (*Ann. Assoc. Am. Geogr.*, 101:4, July 2011, p. 863–872, bibl., maps, photos, tables)

Green authoritarianism and carbon colonialism are illustrated in the construction of two dams in Naso and Ngöbe villages in western Panama, demonstrating that developers did not follow international standards for informed consent.

781 Finley-Brook, Mary and **Curtis Thomas.** Treatment of displaced indigenous populations in two large hydro-projects in Panama. (*Water Altern.*, 3:2, June 2010, p. 269–290, bibl., map, photo, table)

Two large-scale dam projects in the Bayano and Teribe-Changuinola river valleys violated indigenous Emberá, Kuna, and Ngöbe land rights, while opening dialog about more ethical governance of resource development in indigenous territories and elsewhere.

782 Smith, Derek A. The harvest of rainforest birds by indigenous communities in Panama. (*Geogr. Rev.*, 100:2, April 2010, p. 187–203, bibl., map, tables)

Questionnaire results show 59 households in five neighboring communities in the Buglé area in the Río Caloveborita watershed captured 1,584 game birds from over 125 species over six months, with just four accounting for more than half the harvest that included the most important great curassow, great tinamou, and crested guan; 60 percent of the kill sites were within one kilometer from the house.

MEXICO

DANIEL KLOOSTER, *Professor of Environmental Studies, University of Redlands*

URBAN STUDIES CONTINUED as the major category among works published this biennium. Studies of urbanization, urban economic geography, transportation, hazards, demography, work-residence accessibility studies, and urban form were common. Topics included the geographies of retail commerce and of theft in Mexico City (item **819**) as well as studies of individual cities such as Morelia and Culiacán. Publications in the area of urban form have been especially rich in the border cities, where studies continued to address the morphology of border cities, including the growth of gated communities in Tijuana (item **795**) and the polarization of housing in Guadalajara (item **800**). Migration and environmental impacts of urbanization have also been the focus of publications during this time period. The journal *Economia, Sociedad, y Territorio* is a particularly rich source for urban materials. La Red Mexicana de Ciudades Hacia la Sustentabilidad, centered at El Colegio Mexiquense, A.C. in Zinacantepec, is a forum that brings together academics and government officials, organizes conferences, and facilitates communications and publications on themes of urban problems and policy (item **813**). A network of research in urban observatories contributes to international work in this area (item **807**).

The US-Mexico border has also been the focus of publications in the field, including geo-techniques for measuring infrastructure needs of informal settlements, assessments of environmental activism, and evaluations of adaptive potential to climate change (item **820**). An academic-government collaboration addresses the environmental impacts of the border wall (item **786**).

Many publications addressed environment-development themes. The subtheme of sustainable development was especially rich with work addressing topics such as sustainability indicators and regional studies, including several conventional empirical geographies and a more innovative political-ecological approach to fleshing out the relationships between nature and society (item **808**).

An important body of work addressed conservation strategy, especially in protected areas and strategic regions, including studies of human populations living in and near conservation areas (item **788**). Environmental policy more generally was also the focus of publications, as were questions of environmental history and environmental activism.

Conservation studies integrated attention to historical and legal contexts, the views of nature related to different models of resources use, and a keen interest in actors, social movements, and projects that promote conservation (item **791**). Many of these publications are joint efforts of academics and federal environmental agencies.

Mexico is a center of maize agrodiversity, and several important works addressed the maize sector in the context of the North American Free Trade Agreement (NAFTA), migration, and the declining viability of traditional agriculture (item **809**). The practices of farmer seed exchanges and specialty maize markets (item **803**) play increasing roles in rural livelihood agrodiversity conservation in this context.

Water is a central challenge to sustainable development in Mexico. Regional case studies took a historical and geographical approach to the use and misuse of scarce water resources. National overviews examine water users' willingness to pay and outline the political challenges of collecting fees for water. The overviews also identify the main problems of the current market approach to water regulation, in which a weak state is said to fail to invest in water provision, is unable to attract private investment to the sector, and cannot effectively regulate the nation's water resources (item **783**). Case studies suggest that water provision problems occur because authorities place priority on industrial allocations over domestic needs, or examine the precarious and expensive informal markets that provide water in peripheral urban settlements (item **784**). Other work notes the lack of coordination between environmental policy and water policy, or examines the challenge of water demand in desert coastal tourism areas where desalinization plants might play a role.

Tourism is one of Mexico's major economic activities and a smaller number of publications address the topic. Regional case studies predominate, and much of this work reflects a general interest in sustainable development and rural social actors (item **792**).

Several publications addressed agrarian struggles in specific regions; researchers maintain an interest in the efforts of rural people to retain control over their landscape and natural resources. Garibay's insightful comparative ethnography of forest communities was especially notable in this field (item **797**). An important body of work also addresses the impact of a major land-certification program affecting ejidos and *comunidades agrarias* (item **816**).

Migration drew the attention of researchers as well, with the environmental impacts of migration a significant subtopic (item **796**). Themes addressed include migration, remittances, and community sustainable development projects. A number of works explored the relationship between migration and environmental change. Radel and others continued to shed light on the gender implications of migration in both sending and receiving areas (items **804** and **812**).

Geospatial work using GIS and remote sensing work is not much sampled here, although it is often involved in risk analysis and land-use change studies, and to model human impact on conservation areas (item **788**). GIS is also being used as a tool to assess the impact of land-certification on indigenous peoples (item **804**).

783   Aboites, Luis. La decadencia del agua de la nación: estudio sobre desigualdad social y cambio político en México, segunda mitad del siglo XX. México: Colegio de México, 2009. 145 p.: bibl., ill., index.

This pithy publication describes the development of a market-environmental approach to water management, in which the state reduced its payments in water provision and began to charge for its use. It identifies the weakness of the state compared to business groups and popular protest and describes the recent development of the current federal water management system. The author also discusses problems in data gathering and management of water quality and use. There are no measures to reduce overexploitation of aquifers. Waste water goes untreated. Even as government expenditures in water provisioning have been reduced, private capital has not stepped up. Much water remains unmetered and charges uncollected. The author calls for researchers to pay more attention to power relations in the water sector.

784   Aguilar, Adrián Guillermo and **Flor M. López.** Water insecurity among the urban poor in the peri-urban zone of Xochimilco, Mexico City. (*J. Lat. Am. Geogr.*, 8:2, 2009, p. 98–123, bibl., graph, maps, tables)

This paper examines water access in spontaneous settlements without public water provision and formal urbanizations with insufficient public water provision in southern Mexico City. In both cases, residents rely on private, clandestine, informal markets for water. These arrangements provide expensive, precarious access to water. No public policies exist to address this situation.

785   Antinori, Camille and **Gordon C. Rausser.** Ownership and control in Mexico's community forestry sector. (*Econ. Dev. Cult. Change*, 57:1, Oct. 2008, p. 101–136, appendix, graphs, tables)

The authors use regression analysis and contract theory to examine the transaction costs involved in vertical integration of community forestry enterprises. Where transaction costs are present, ownership assures a greater flow of benefits.

786   Una barrera a nuestro ambiente compartido: el muro fronterizo entre México y Estados Unidos. Coordinación de Ana Córdova y Carlos de la Parra. Colaboración de Luis Fernando Abitia *et al.* México: Secretaría de Medio Ambiente y Recursos Naturales; Instituto Nacional de Ecología, 2007. 214 p.: bibl., ill., map.

Resulting from a 2007 workshop supported by Mexican federal environmental agencies with academic collaborators, this book addresses the environmental impact of the border wall on water, soil, air, species, and ecosystems that do not recognize the US-Mexico border. Sections also address the legal and political context.

Boyer, Christopher R. Revolución y paternalismo ecológico: Miguel Ángel de Quevedo y la política forestal en México, 1926–1940. See *HLAS 66:911.*

787   Brenner, Jacob C. What drives the conversion of native rangeland to buffelgrass (*Pennisetum ciliare*) pasture in Mexico's Sonoran desert?: the social dimensions of a biological invasion. (*Hum. Ecol.*, 38:4, Aug. 2010, p. 495–505)

Brenner examines the direct and indirect social factors associated with ranchers' decisions to convert native rangeland to pastures of an exotic species. He finds ranch size, rotational grazing, buffelgrass seed harvest, and exposure to government research to be the main explanatory factors.

788   Candeau Dufat, Rafael and **Sergio Franco Maass.** Dinámica y condiciones de vida de la población del Parque Nacional Nevado de Toluca (PNNT) en la generación de presión a los ecosistemas circundantes y de impactos ambientales a través de un sistema de información geográfica. (*Invest. Geogr./México*, 62, abril 2007, p. 44–68, bibl., graphs, maps, tables)

Using a GIS model relating social variables to geosystems and environmental degradation, this article examines the social context of conservation in an inhabited protected area.

789 **Chambers, Kimberlee J.** and **Steve B. Brush.** Geographic influences on maize seed exchange in Bajío, Mexico. (*Prof. Geogr.*, 62:3, Aug. 2010, p. 305–322)

Seed exchanges between farmers are important for maintaining crop diversity and social practices. Household survey data in four villages was used to analyze seed exchange. Exchanges are complex, opportunistic, individualistic, and influenced by agroecological conditions. Migration and other globalizing factors also influence the scale and character of seed exchanges.

790 **Confronting the coffee crisis: fair trade, sustainable livelihoods and ecosystems in Mexico and Central America.** Edited by Christopher M. Bacon *et al.* Cambridge, Mass.: MIT Press, 2008. 390 p.: bibl., ill., index. (Food, health, and the environment)

This collection addresses the context of an international coffee crisis and details a variety of policy responses in Mexico and Central America. Specific chapters detail coffee-producer strategies, organizational histories, and experiences with organic and fair trade certification. Smallholder coffee producers diversify, migrate, and attempt to increase income from coffee sales. Alternative coffee markets do not currently provide a solution to the crisis. The certification movement should grow to increase the demand for certified coffee and to bring consumers and producers into closer and more equal relationships. For political economist's comment, see item **1853**.

791 **Del saqueo a la conservación: historia ambiental contemporánea de Baja California Sur, 1940–2003.** Coordinación de Martha Micheline Cariño y Mario Monteforte. México: Secretaría de Medio Ambiente y Recursos Naturales: Instituto Nacional de Ecología: Consejo Nacional de Ciencia y Tecnología; La Paz, Mexico: Univ. Autónoma de Baja California Sur,

2008. 778 p.: bibl., ill. (some col.), maps, plates.

Presents the theoretical, historical, and policy context of natural resource use and conservation in Baja California Sur. This extensive book takes a sectoral approach to resource degradation, and then addresses the politics of conservation through a series of chapters detailing actors and strategies involved in conservation practice. Looting and conservation have been the two main nature-society interactions in Baja California Sur. Each model has its own protagonists with their accompanying views of development and natural resource use.

792 **Desarrollo turístico y sustentabilidad social.** Coordinación de Javier Orozco Alvarado, Patricia Núñez Martínez y Carlos Rogelio Virgen Aguilar. México: Univ. de Guadalajara, Centro Universitario de la Costa: Miguel Ángel Porrúa, 2008. 266 p.: bibl., ill., maps.

One of several publications on the topic from the Universidad de Guadalajara's Centro Universitario de la Costa, this work focuses on rural tourism, arguing for greater participation of rural communities in forms of alternative tourism which spread the economic benefits of tourism beyond established centers.

793 **Duhau, Emilio** and **Angela Giglia.** Nuevas centralidades y prácticas de consumo en la Ciudad de México: del microcomercio al hipermercado. (*EURE/Santiago*, 33:98, abril 2007, p. 77–95, bibl., maps, tables)

Big box retail chains have grown explosively in Mexico City, but informal (street) microcommerce continues to exist. Consumption patterns are linked to mobility, but also to the enhanced informality of labor markets that accompany the expansion of globalized chains. Big box retailers have expanded aggressively by offering low-cost goods to impoverished classes, and have established commercial poles on the outskirts of the city.

794 **Dupuy Rada, Juan Manuel** *et al.* Cambios de cobertura y uso del suelo, 1979–2000, en dos comunidades rurales en el noroeste de Quintana Roo. (*Invest. Geogr./México*, 62, abril 2007, p. 104–124, appendix, bibl., graphs, maps, tables)

The authors use airphoto interpretation, ground-truthing, and social surveys to examine land use change in two communities. In one, the forest area increased following suspension of federal cattle-promotion programs. In the other, forest cover for agriculture decreased slightly. The work shows the value of fine-scaled, land-use change studies using mixed methods.

Endfield, Georgina H. Climate and society in colonial Mexico: a study in vulnerability. See *HLAS 66:700.*

795 Enríquez Acosta, Jesús Ángel. Ciudad de muros: socialización y tipología de las urbanizaciones cerradas en Tijuana. (*Front. Norte*, 19:38, julio/dic. 2007, p. 127–156, bibl., map)

Gated communities have emerged as a principal response to urban insecurity in Tijuana. Walls, guard houses, and private guards regulate access and provide security. These measures provide residents with a false sense of security, however, because crime continues to occur within the gates. The growth of gated communities reduces the diversity of land use, sustainability, connectivity, and social diversity.

796 García-Zamora, Rodolfo et al. Paradojas de la migración internacional y el medio ambiente. (*Econ. Soc. Territ.*, 6:24, mayo/agosto 2007, p. 975–994, bibl.)

Drawing on previous work on migration in Zacatecas, the authors argue that environmental degradation does not cause migration directly. The effects of soil degradation, for example, are filtered through markets influenced by competition with more productive states in Mexico as well as NAFTA. Changes in migration patterns are leading to labor scarcity. However, migration can also lead to transnational migrant organizations (hometown associations), which invest remittances in environmental improvements ranging from trash collection to water treatment to forest protection. Migrants also take up reduced-impact agricultural practices.

797 Garibay Orozco, Claudio. Comunalismos y liberalismos campesinos: identidad comunitaria, empresa social forestal y poder corporado en el México contemporáneo. Zamora, Mexico: El Colegio de Michoacán, 2008. 466 p.: bibl., ill., index, maps. (Col. Investigaciones)

Unlike most rural communities in which the campesino family is the central organizing unit, two to three dozen industrial forestry communities have gone against the grain of neoliberal rural economic policy and established a communitarian social order which disciplines its members and demands their loyalty in exchange for economic security and certainty in the social order. Based on insightful, historical ethnographies, this book compares the processes of establishing communalistic societies in two well-known industrial forestry communities: San Pedro el Alto in Oaxaca and Nuevo San Juan Parangaricutiro in Michoacán.

González Jácome, Alba. Humedales en el suroeste de Tlaxcala: agua y agricultura en el siglo XX. See *HLAS 66:938.*

798 Guerrero Peñuelas, Adriana Guadalupe. El impacto de la migración en el manejo de solares campesinos, caso de estudio La Purísima Concepción Mayorazgo, San Felipe del Progreso, Estado de México. (*Invest. Geogr./México*, 63, agosto 2007, p. 105–124, bibl., graphs, tables)

Based on a review of the international literature, this article develops two general models of the impact of migration on natural resources and then tests the impact of migration on the case of agrodiversity among backyard gardens maintained by indigenous (Mazahua) households. Using questionnaires and semi-structured interviews applied to families with and without migrants, the author finds that diversity is higher in backyard gardens of nonmigrants, although households with migrants also maintain gardens with food plants.

799 Harner, John P. The changing location of trade and services in Guadalajara, Mexico, 1994–2004. (*Geogr. Rev.*, 100:4, Oct. 2010, p. 494–520)

This paper analyzes a number of businesses and employment in retail and services from 1994–2004 in Guadalajara. New suburban shopping centers are competing with the traditional central city for the dominance of commercial businesses. Across this decade, services became more important in the suburbs, but the central city remained a commercial retail hub. Walmarts may harm small commercial stores in adjacent areas, but those shopping centers also spurred growth in other service businesses.

800 **Harner, John P.; Edith Jiménez; and Heriberto Cruz Solís.** Buying development: housing and urban growth in Guadalajara, Mexico. (*Urban Geogr.*, 30:5, July/Aug. 2009, p. 465–489)

One of only a handful of articles co-authored by scholars from both Mexico and the US, this study examines all land development for housing from 1970–2000 in Guadalajara. Housing reforms in Mexico greatly increased the construction and purchase of social-interest housing programs that cater to the middle class, yet at the same time the contrasting extremes of low income self-built houses and elite enclaves also continued to contribute to housing options. The patterns and landscape reflect neoliberal policies towards the privatization of home construction and ownership that have increased housing availability, but largely excluded the urban poor.

801 **Hunter, Richard.** Methodologies for reconstructing a pastoral landscape: land grants in sixteenth-century New Spain. (*Hist. Methods*, 43:1, Jan./March 2010, p. 1–13)

This piece's importance lies in its mapping of early-colonial sheep ranches that show they occupied higher elevations, indicating that the landscape-wide degradation present today was caused by sheep overstocking in the upper elevations and agricultural terrace abandonment in the lower elevations.

802 **Hunter, Richard.** Positionality, perception, and possibility in Mexico's Valle del Mezquital. (*J. Lat. Am. Geogr.*, 8:2, 2009, p. 49–69, bibl., maps, photo)

Why did a prominent geographer and a well-regarded environmental historian have opposing views on the historical causes of soil erosion in highland central Mexico? Hunter moves this debate forward by reading the original land grants for sheep grazing ranches and finding indications that agricultural terrace abandonment following native depopulation caused erosion in some locations. He also examines questions of methodology and positionality affecting the two views. See also item **801**.

803 **Keleman, Alder and Jonathan Hellin.** Specialty maize varieties in Mexico: a case study in market-driven agro-biodiversity conservation. (*J. Lat. Am. Geogr.*, 8:2, 2009, p. 147–174, bibl., ill., maps, tables)

The markets for *pozole* and blue maize varieties in the state of Mexico offer opportunities for small farmers to generate income and conserve local maize varieties *in situ*. The authors discuss the potential role of certification and geographic denomination of origin in expanding these benefits, and see greater possibilities for this in the case of *pozole* than blue maize. Specialty maize value chains could benefit from careful policy interventions.

804 **Kelly, John H.; Peter H. Herlihy; and Derek A. Smith.** Indigenous territoriality at the end of the social property era in Mexico. (*J. Lat. Am. Geogr.*, 9:3, 2010, p. 161–181, bibl., graph, maps, table)

This study uses GIS to link census, land tenure, and agrarian datasets from the Huasteca Potosina region in order to assess the impact of PROCEDE (Programa de Certificación de Derechos Ejidales y Titulación de Solares), a significant national land-certification program. The authors find that the program is leading to a complex mosaic of tenure regimes which are neither fully private nor entirely social. Indigenous ejidos and *comunidades agrarias* are more likely to reject privatization of communal lands than nonindigenous communities; traditional, communal land tenure and resource management is likely to survive in some parts of Mexico well into the future. Nevertheless, PROCEDE implements a modern cadastral system, brings some formerly inalienable communal lands into the marketplace, further fragments an indigenous region, and may threaten indigenous peoples' long term cultural survival as distinct peoples.

805 **Messina, John.** Álamos, Sonora: architecture and urbanism in the dry tropics. Tucson: Univ. of Arizona Press, 2008. 165 p.: bibl., index, maps, photos. (Southwest Center series)

This architectural study looks at the silver-mining town of Álamos, Sonora. It examines 300 years of social and economic history of the town, its urban form, and

architectural styles of an "extremely coherent urban place" (p. 141). The town provides
lessons for urban forms elsewhere, such as
adaptation to existing topography, the use
of appropriate materials, and an adaptable
typology of urban and residential forms.

806 Mitchell, Ross E. El ejercicio de la
democracia en dos comunidades
forestales de la sierra norte de Oaxaca,
México. (*Desacatos*, 27, mayo/agosto 2008,
p. 149–168, bibl., photos, table)

In an examination of two different
community forestry enterprises in Oaxaca,
the author finds that common property
management practices are relatively democratic. They involve electoral processes,
high-quality deliberations, and meaningful
social participation in decision-making. On
the other hand, they also suffer from problems such as gender exclusion.

807 Observatorios urbanos en México:
lecciones, propuestas y desafíos.
Coordinación de Carlos Garrocho y José
Antonio Álvarez Lobato. Zinacantepec,
Mexico: Colegio Mexiquense, 2008. 342 p.:
bibl., ill., maps.

This collection of essays summarizes
current work in Mexican urban observatories. The contributions discuss the need to
establish a common research agenda that is
linked to international agendas, such as the
UN urban observatories; national research
needs related to the Secretaría de Desarrollo
Social, SEDESOL; as well as local research
needs.

808 Perramond, Eric P. Political ecologies of cattle ranching in northern
Mexico: private revolutions. Tucson: Univ.
of Arizona Press, 2010. 259 p.: bibl., index.
(Society, environment, and place)

This book explains the evolution of
ranching in the Rio Sonora Valley, critiquing caricatures of ranchers as a homogenous
class by detailing many different types of
ranchers. It examines labor and management strategies on different size ranches,
considering both cultural and economic motivations for rancher's actions. It details the
political ecologies of resource use and conflict on different ranches and in the region,
including the socioecological implications
of cattle and forage species selection and the
hybrid landscapes they help create.

809 Presente y futuro del sector agrícola
mexicano en el contexto del TLCAN.
Edición de José Antonio Ávila Dorantes,
Alicia Puyana de Palacios y José Antonio
Romero. México: Colegio de México; Cha-
pingo, Estado de México: Univ. Autónoma
Chapingo, 2008. 385 p.: bibl., ill., maps.

NAFTA put Mexican agriculture into
competition with the highly efficient and
heavily subsidized agricultural system of
the US. This book examines the impact of
NAFTA on maize and other key agricultural
sectors. Limited benefits have been seen
in fruits and vegetables, while small and
medium producers of maize, wheat, rice,
and soy lost market share and employment.
Displaced workers have not been absorbed
elsewhere in agriculture, as projected when
the agreement was made more than 10 years
ago, but instead were incorporated into an
informal sector of low wages and no benefits. Many emigrated to the US. Mexico has
seen declining food self-sufficiency following NAFTA.

810 Radel, Claudia and **Birgit Schmook.**
Migration and gender: the case of
a farming ejido en Calakmul, Mexico.
(*Yearb. Assoc. Pac. Coast Geogr.*, 71, 2009,
p. 144–163)

This article examines the effects of
men's migration on the status of the women
remaining behind in a rural community in
the Yucatán. There are some changes in gender roles and responsibilities, but evidence
for women's increased participation in
decision-making is unclear. Findings suggest that gender ideology is defended even as
gender responsibilities change.

811 Radel, Claudia; Birgit Schmook; and
Rinku Roy Chowdhury. Agricul-
tural livelihood transition in the southern
Yucatán region: diverging paths and their
accompanying land changes. (*Reg. Environ.
Change*, 10:3, Sept. 2010, p. 205–218)

Using household-surveys, this article examines agricultural transition and
accompanying land-use changes in southeastern Mexico. Increasing proportions
of households are pursuing two divergent
paths—one of agricultural withdrawal and
one of intensification and commercialization. As smallholders adjust in different
ways to intensified incorporation into global

economies, they produce simultaneous and contradictory land change outcomes.

812 Radel, Claudia; Birgit Schmook; and Susannah McCandless. Environment, transnational labor migration, and gender: case studies from southern Yucatán, Mexico and Vermont, USA. (*Popul. Environ.*, 32:2/3, Dec. 2010, p. 177–197)

The authors juxtapose gender dimensions for a Mexican migrant labor-sending location with those for a US migrant labor-receiving location. In southern Campeche, labor migration alters pasture, maize, and chili production, and gender norms strongly affect household land-use decisions. In Vermont, a largely male migrant labor force helps maintain an idealized, pastoral landscape, with gender deeply embedded in how that labor is constructed and managed.

813 Red Mexicana de Ciudades hacia la Sustentabilidad. *Seminario-Taller Internacional. 10th, Monterrey, Mexico, 2008.* Replanteando la metrópoli: soluciones institucionales al fenómeno metropolitano: memorias del X Seminario-Taller Internacional de la Red Mexicana de Ciudades hacia la Sustentabilidad y del Congreso Nacional para la Reforma Metropolitana. Compilación de Roberto García Ortega y Alfonso X. Iracheta C. Monterrey, Mexico: Gobierno de Nuevo León, DUNL; México: Cámara de Diputados, LX Legislatura; Mexico: Red Mexicana de Ciudades hacia la Sustentabilidad; Zinacantepec, Mexico: Colegio Mexiquense, 2008. 764 p.: bibl., ill., maps.

La Red Mexicana de Ciudades hacia la Sustentabilidad, composed of academics and government officials, centered at El Colegio Mexiquense, A.C. in Zinacantepec, is a forum which organizes conferences and publications on themes of urban problems and policy. This volume of conference proceeding brings together presentations on urban transportation, land use, housing, environment, infrastructure, and regional contexts.

814 Schmook, Birgit and **Claudia Radel.** International labor migration from a tropical development frontier: globalizing households and an incipient forest transition: the southern Yucatán case. (*Hum. Ecol.*, 36:6, Dec. 2008, p. 891–908)

Drawing on a survey of 203 house-

holds, the authors show that migration earnings substitute for agricultural earnings and that migrating households cultivate significantly less farmland, with some forest recovery. They interpret this result in the light of forest transition theory and argue for the need to incorporate globalizing household economies into this theory.

815 Seminario Internacional, "Periferia Urbana, Deterioro Ambiental y Sustentabilidad", *Instituto de Geografía de la UNAM, 2007.* Periferia urbana: deterioro ambiental y reestructuración metropolitana. Coordinación de Adrián Guillermo Aguilar y Irma Escamilla. México: Instituto de Geografía, UNAM: Miguel Ángel Porrúa, 2009. 399 p.: bibl., ill., maps. (Estudios urbanos serie)

Population growth in formerly rural, peri-urban areas around Mexico City and other urban centers is more rapid than urban growth in general. This book of conference proceedings examines the social and environmental implications of this process. Topics studied include water supply, sewage treatment, solid waste disposal, loss of agricultural land, and loss of green spaces. Most chapters address Mexico City peri-urban areas, but Toluca, Monterrey, and Guadalaraja are also represented.

816 Smith, Derek A. *et al.* The certification and privatization of indigenous lands in Mexico. (*J. Lat. Am. Geogr.*, 8:2, 2009, p. 175–207, bibl., ill., maps, tables)

The article examines the PROCEDE (Programa de Certificación de Derechos Ejidales y Titulación de Solares Urbanos) which has surveyed hundreds of thousands of square kilometers of communal lands in Mexico. Researchers examined national datasets and actual implementation in 11 indigenous communities. Surveyed boundaries sometimes differ from boundaries recognized on the ground. Sales and rentals have increased in areas where parcels have been certified, though not at rates as high as originally expected. Where parcels are certified, participation in communal institutions and practices has decreased. Communal lands continue to exist, however; in many cases indigenous peoples have resisted the program by refusing to participate or by requesting certification only of their territorial perimeter, not of individual parcels. The program has not eliminated communal tenure, even in areas where certification has occurred.

817 Toudert, Djamel. Algunos rasgos y particularidades de la polarización territorial de la producción de contenidos Web en México. (*Econ. Soc. Territ.*, 6:23, enero/abril 2007, p. 579–611, bibl., graphs, maps)

The intranational geography of the internet is uneven; it reflects pre-existing uneven geographies. Even when controlled for population density, Mexico City is disproportionately represented in the production of web pages and the proportion of web users. This finding is related to the continuing uneven geographies of globalization and the digital divide.

Urquijo Torres, Pedro Sergio. Humboldt y el Jorullo: historia de una exploración. See *HLAS 66:567.*

818 Velázquez García, Mario Alberto. La construcción de un movimiento ambiental en México: el club de golf en Tepoztlán, Morelos. (*Reg. Soc./Hermosillo*, 20:43, sept./dic. 2008, p. 61–96, bibl.)

Uses social construction theory and social movement theory to examine an environmental movement protesting plans to build a tourism complex. The author argues that the movement started as a land conflict, but generated links to environmental groups and interests, which was then reflected among the discourse and action of local peoples.

819 Vilalta, Carlos. Un modelo descriptivo de la geografía del robo en la zona metropolitana del valle de México. (*J. Lat. Am. Geogr.*, 8:1, 2009, p. 55–78, bibl., ill., maps, tables)

This article reviews literature on crime geography, especially in cities in the developing world; describes and maps the geography of theft in Mexico City; tests a descriptive model; and discusses policy implications.

820 Wilder, Margaret et al. Adapting across boundaries: climate change, social learning, and resilience in the U.S.-Mexico border region. (*Ann. Assoc. Am. Geogr.*, 100:4, Oct. 2010, p. 917–928)

This article examines possibilities for management of and adaptive planning to climate change in the Arizona-New Mexico/Sonora border region. Climate models project reduced rainfall in that region, but binational desalination plans would increase environmental vulnerability in Mexico. Greater adaptive potential comes from transboundary scientist-stakeholder collaboration such as occurs in data sharing and improved information flows for the assessment of shared groundwater resources, such as the US-Mexico Transbounadray Aquifer Assessment Program and the networks of knowledge production surrounding the Border Climate Summary.

WESTERN SOUTH AMERICA

GREGORY W. KNAPP, *Associate Professor, Department of Geography and the Environment, The University of Texas at Austin*

GEOGRAPHICAL RESEARCH ON THE ANDES continues to be international and interdisciplinary, with strong contributions from international organizations and NGOs, as well as academics in universities.

Research on humanistic themes, such as perception, has been especially strong in urban planning and architecture programs. There have been numerous studies of urban public spaces, housing, and symbolic geography. Nina Laurie argued for studies of religious geography (item **826**), Mathewson for the study of non-indigenous regional cultures (item **872**), and Gade for the distinctiveness of places (item **905**). Studies supporting the preservation of rural cultural monuments include Abad Pérez's volume on the Inca Highway (item **879**). Andolina, Laurie, and Radcliffe edited a compelling book on culturally appropriate development (item **822**).

Other geographers have used the techniques of economics and positivistic social science to track the progress of the demographic transition in Bolivia (item **900**), land prices (item **842**), urban transportation (item **846**), the spatial patterns of poverty (item **831**), and the complex impacts of privatization on access to water and communications (item **889**). The Interoceanic Highway has generated support from this literature (item **882** and **890**).

Historical geography includes studies of urban history, cattle ranching (item **858**), and new attempts to model the dynamics of agricultural change and food distribution in the Colca Valley (items **896** and **897**).

A large number of studies look at the interactions of development, conservation, and the environment in the Guiana Highlands (items **832** and **839**), Ecuador (items **862**, **863**, **868**, and **877**), Lowland Peru (items **885**, **891**, and **893**), and Bolivia. Participatory mapping remains a theme (item **902**) and rural sustainability a goal (item **873**). Other studies focus on urban and regional sustainability (items **837**). A large number of studies have looked at irrigation and urban water supplies in cultural, political, and economic contexts (items **827** and **915**). Both long distance migration (item **913**) and short distance migration (items **875**) have been studied in terms of impacts on the environment.

Critical studies have examined violence, drugs, and territorial zoning in Colombia (items **841** and **855**), and the growth of mining (item **880**), hydroelectric development (item **906**), hydrocarbon development (item **828**), tourism (item **883**), agriculture and nontraditional exports (item **914**), and dam projects on the Bolivian-Brazilian border (item **906**).

Human impacts on the environment remain an important theme (item **886**). Climate change has also attracted a great deal of attention, in terms of impacts on conservation policy, and implications for local livelihoods, adaptation, and resilience (items **830** and **884**). Hazards research has grown in strength, and has benefitted from studies of the social dimensions of El Niño (item **888**).

Together, these studies display the tension between empiricism and theory, utopian hopes and tragic histories, and the multiple voices of different interpretive communities. Geography's optic of synthesis, of studying the interaction between otherwise unrelated systems, is particularly suited to facing if not reconciling these contrasts.

GENERAL

821 Agua y servicios ambientales: visiones críticas desde los Andes. Edición de Edgar Isch L. y Ingo Gentes. Quito: Abya Yala, 2006. 254 p.: bibl.

This edited volume includes a series of general reflections on the theme of water and environmental services in the Andes; authors include a variety of NGO personnel and environmentalist faculty from Wageningen (Rutgerd Boelens), Bolivia, Peru, Chile, and Ecuador.

822 Andolina, Robert; Nina Laurie; and Sarah A. Radcliffe. Indigenous development in the Andes: culture, power, and transnationalism. Durham, N.C.: Duke Univ. Press, 2009. 345 p.: bibl., index.

Focused on Bolivia and Ecuador, this coauthored book examines the difficulties involved with designing culturally appropriate development agendas. Although indigenous peoples have made some progress in gaining voice in issues surrounding land, water, identity, and gender, problems of racism, inequality, and dependency remain. For sociologist's comment, see item **2493**.

823   Aubron, Claire *et al.* Labor and its productivity in Andean dairy farming systems: a comparative approach. (*Hum. Ecol.*, 37:4, Aug. 2009, p. 407–419)

Includes data from a Peruvian community as well as a literature review of data from Ecuador, Peru, and Bolivia to outline the characteristics and labor efficiency of dairy farming. Labor efficiency data suggests that smallholder dairy farming can only continue to flourish if (primarily female) labor opportunity costs remain low, synergies with other activities remain high, and the Peruvian free trade agreement is supplemented with policies to protect producers from international competition.

824   Boelens, Rutgerd. The rules of the game and the game of the rules: normalization and resistance in Andean water control. Wageningen, The Netherlands: Wageningen Univ., 2008. 573 p.: bibl., ill., maps.

Numerous examples are adduced to demonstrate the complexity of contemporary water rights and water rules in the Andes as negotiated by different Andean actors and groups in different interpretive communities at different scales. A doctoral dissertation, based on many years of participatory and activist scholarship in the Andes.

825   Knapp, Gregory W. The Andes: personal reflections on cultural change, 1977–2010. (*J. Cult. Geogr.*, 27:3, Oct. 2010, p. 307–316)

A personal retrospective by an Andeanist geographer from the US, assessing the political, economic, cultural, and humanistic dimensions of change.

826   Laurie, Nina. Finding yourself in the archives and doing geographies of religion. (*Geoforum/New York*, 41:2, March 2010, p. 165–167)

Editorial by a Christian scholar doing research on the geography of evangelicals in the Andes. Reflects on the relationship between faith, feminism, and research, and argues for the creation of a safe space for people of faith to speak openly and to do research in geography.

827   Out of the mainstream: water rights, politics and identity. Edited by Rutgerd Boelens, David H. Getches, and Jorge

Armando Guevara Gil. London; Sterling, Va.: Earthscan, 2010. 366 p.: bibl., index.

An important volume that brings together scholars of geography and legal studies, addressing issues of conflict between local water organizations and national and international water policies and programs. Most of the chapters of this edited book deal with recent events in the Andes with an emphasis on indigenous community activism. Topics include overviews of the Andes (by the three editors, and by P.H. Gelles, J. Hendriks, A.J. Hoekema, R. Bustamante, T. Perreault, A. Bebbington, D.H. Bebbington, and J. Bury), plus chapters on cultural identity and water rights in southern Bolivia (A. Zoomers), and central Peru (A. Guevara-Gil).

828   Perreault, Tom and Gabriela Valdivia. Hydrocarbons, popular protest and national imaginaries: Ecuador and Bolivia in comparative context. (*Geoforum/New York*, 41:5, Sept. 2010, p. 689–699)

Compares the Ecuadorian and Bolivian cases to explore the roots of resistance to neoliberal pressures to privatize petroleum and natural gas development. These struggles involving state employees and popular movements invoked ideas of nationalism and identity which went far beyond mere economic motivations.

829   Young, Kenneth R. Andean land use and biodiversity: humanized landscapes in a time of change. (*Ann. Mo. Bot. Gard.*, 96:3, Sept. 2009, p. 492–507)

Provides a conceptual model for how native species, land use, and conservation issues in the Andes might respond spatially to climate change towards warmer and dryer conditions.

830   Young, Kenneth R. and Jennifer K. Lipton. Adaptive governance and climate change in the tropical highlands of western South America. (*Clim. Change*, 78:1, Sept. 2006, p. 63–102)

Uses a case study of the Cordillera Blanca in Peru, plus an extensive review of the literature elsewhere in the Andes, to argue that the natural and cultural systems of the Andes have tended to be resilient, and that adapting to climate change is probably within the capacity of many, unless external socioeconomic and political forces are antagonistic.

VENEZUELA

831 Acosta Torres, Wilfredo David. La dimensión relegada: expresión territorial de la pobreza en Venezuela: período 1981–2006. Caracas: Fondo Editorial de la Facultad de Humanidades y Educación, Univ. Central de Venezuela, 2009. 290 p.: bibl., ill., maps. (Col. Estudios. Geografía)

A statistical study of the spatial distribution of poverty in Venezuela. Between 1981 and 2006 spatial inequalities of income increased. The poorest households are concentrated away from the major cities. Inequality has been exacerbated because social programs have been targeted at the highly visible and accessible poor neighborhoods of big cities.

832 Bilbao, Bibiana A.; Alejandra V. Leal; and Carlos L. Méndez. Indigenous use of fire and forest loss in Canaima National Park, Venezuela: assessment of and tools for alternative strategies of fire management in Pemón indigenous lands. (*Hum. Ecol.*, 38:5, Oct. 2010, p. 663–673)

The authors conducted a fire experiment to suggest the natural fire return interval in the upland savanna is three to four years. They provide arguments for policy changes taking into account both fire ecology and indigenous perceptions and practices.

833 El espacio público entre la universidad y la ciudad. Coordinación de Beatriz Ramírez Boscán. Mérida, Venezuela: Publicaciones Vicerrectorado Académico: CEP, 2006. 320 p.: bibl., ill., maps (some col.). (Col. Ciencias sociales y humanidades)

An edited volume about urban public spaces as cultural landscapes, drawing on examples from around the world but especially focused on the example of Mérida, Venezuela, as a university city.

834 Franceschi, Arturo. Geografía socioeconómica del Estado Bolívar. Ciudad Guayana, Venezuela: Fondo Editorial UNEG, 2006. 262 p.: bibl., ill., maps.

A classical regional geography of the large state of Bolívar in Venezuela, which occupies the southeastern part of the country including much of the Guiana highlands. The author, a geography professor, covers the physical geography, natural resources, historical demography, economic

geography, and urban geography of the region.

835 Hurtado Salazar, Samuel. Ecología, agricultura y comunidad. Caracas: Univ. Central de Venezuela, Ediciones de la Biblioteca-EBUC, 2008. 158 p.: bibl. (Col. Ciencias económicas y sociales; 43)

A field study of agriculture, social relations, and development pathways in the Paria peninsula (Sucre state). The field study took place in 1988; actual publication took 20 years. The useful ethnographic work is based on a distinction between *conuco* (subsistence) and *finca* (commercial) agriculture.

836 Menéndez Prieto, Ricardo. Los modelos de localización a la luz del espacio geográfico: el caso específico de las áreas marginales de Caracas. Caracas: Fundación para la Cultura Urbana, 2009. 231 p.: bibl., ill. (Fundación para la cultura urbana; 70)

This book by Venezuelan geographer and urbanist Ricardo Menéndez Prieto begins with an extended discussion of spatial and location theories since Von Thunen. It then evaluates the Venezuelan-developed free software package, TRANUS, in terms of understanding the localization of low-income people in Caracas.

837 Mérida sostenible: una ciudad para la gente. Coordinación de William Lobo Quintero. Mérida, Venezuela: Vicerrectorado Académico: Academia de Mérida, 2007. 482 p.: bibl., ill., maps. (Col. Ciencias sociales y humanas)

An edited volume with chapters on various aspects of sustainable urban development in Mérida, a moderately sized city in the Venezuelan Andes. Topics include hazards, waste management, health, education, the economy, and politics.

838 Ortigosa Morillo, Eugenia. Habitar la tecnología y los imaginarios del construir en Maracaibo. (*Espac. Abierto*, 16:4, oct./dic. 2007, p. 689–713, bibl., ill., photos)

Summarizes doctoral dissertation research on the phenomenology of houses in Maracaibo. The author examined photographic and newspaper archives, collected oral histories, and interviewed children (who also made drawings). Documents the importance of security, solidity, hygiene, and protection from heat as important factors, along with fashion and aspiration, in the widespread adoption of construction techniques using blocks supported by columns of cement and rebar.

839 Sletto, Bjørn. Conservation planning, boundary-making and border terrains: the desire for forest and order in the Gran Sabana, Venezuela. (*Geoforum/New York*, 42:2, March 2011, p. 197–210)

Outlines the contradictions in fire management practices in the savanna and dry forest landscapes of Canaima National Park, due to divided allegiances and misguided projects of boundary-making in a complex environment.

COLOMBIA

840 Arboleda Guzmán, Elizabeth. La frontera borrosa en la construcción conceptual y fáctica del habitar: relaciones centro-periferia, caso sector San Lorenzo, Medellín. Medellín, Colombia: Maestría en Hábitat, Escuela del Hábitat, Facultad de Arquitectura, Univ. Nacional de Colombia, Sede Medellín, 2007. 188 p.: bibl., ill., maps, plates. (Col. Maestría en Hábitat; 5)

An extended philosophical reflection on boundaries, territories, and habitats, drawing on the ideas of Milton Santos and Canclini, and applied to a wealthy enclave at the heart of the city of Medellín.

841 Asher, Kiran and **Diana Ojeda.** Producing nature and making the state: *ordenamiento territorial* in the Pacific lowlands of Colombia. (*Geoforum/New York*, 40:3, May 2009, p. 292–302)

Discusses state-initiated territorial zoning of the Pacific lowlands of Colombia in terms of Gramscian Marxist theory, as hegemonic material and symbolic processes of the state and capital, which, however, are contested by local activism.

842 Buitrago Bermudez, Oscar. Factores determinantes de los precios de la tierra rural: en los municipios contiguos a Bogotá, D.C. Cali, Colombia: Programa Editorial, Univ. del Valle, 2007. 180 p.: bibl., ill., maps. (Col. Libros de investigación)

The author, a geography professor in Colombia, looks at factors determining land prices in the larger metropolitan area of Bogotá. Accessibility is the most important single factor, but its significance varies by subregion and other factors may dominate. In some areas recreational potential, or access to irrigation water, are more important in determining land value; ownership by entities involved in urban development also contributes to higher land prices.

843 Cauca: características geográficas. Edición de Iván Darío Gómez Guzmán *et al.* Textos de Natalia Gisela Méndez Suárez, Nancy Fabiola Gómez Contreras y Pablo Iglesias Sánchez. Bogotá: República de Colombia, Depto. Administrativo Nacional de Estadística, Instituto Geográfico Agustín Codazzi, 2006. 350 p.: bibl., ill. (some col.), col. maps.

An example of traditional regional geography, in this case of the Department of Cauca in southwestern Colombia. Numerous detailed maps, diagrams, and photographs illustrate the major themes of physical geography, environmental issues, population geography, economic geography, and spatial organization. A product of the Instituto Geográfico Agustín Codazzi.

844 De las ciudades a las regiones: desarrollo regional integrado en Bogotá-Cundinamarca. v. 1, Soporte técnico. v. 2, Estudios y proceso. Bogotá: UNDESA/UNCRD: Mesa de Planificación Regional Bogotá-Cundinamarca, 2005. 2 v.: bibl., ill. (some col.), indexes, maps (some col.).

Produced by the UN Center for Regional Development. Presents the results of activities of the Round Table for Regional Planning of Bogotá-Cundinamarca, which met from 2001 to 2003 to promote the socio-economic integration of the capital and its periphery, in two volumes with numerous maps and diagrams. Three scenarios for occupation of territory were identified, including concentrated, linear, and dispersed settlements. Workshops by various stakeholders unanimously chose the scenario of decentralized development; participants outlined various projects which could help realize this scenario. The study noted problems associated with the absence of reliable data and good empirical studies, and the problems of poorly developed articulation between different stakeholders.

845 Durán Bernal, Carlos Andrés. ¿Es nuestra isla para dos?: conflicto por el desarrollo y la conservación en Islas del

Rosario, Cartagena. Bogotá: Univ. de Los Andes, Facultad de Ciencias Sociales-Ceso, Depto. de Antropología, 2007. 200 p.: bibl., ill. (Col. Prometeo)

An overview of the history of development and conservation in the Rosario islands. Discusses the role of contraband and drug trafficking, tourism, and conservation agendas in the context of local cultures and social movements. Theoretically situated in terms of the ideas of Cronon, Escobar, Foucault, Said, Scott, and Alcida Ramos.

Ecología política en la Amazonia: las profusas y difusas redes de la gobernanza. See item **1240**.

846 Gilbert, Alan. Bus rapid transit: is *Transmilenio* a miracle cure? (*Transp. Rev.*, 28:4, July 2008, p. 439–467)

Analyzes some of the criticisms of Bogotá's highly praised and efficient *Transmilenio* busway rapid transit system. Gilbert's analysis suggests that even highly successful systems can falter if other transportation and political reforms are not pursued.

847 González E., Luis Fernando. Medellín, los orígenes y la transición a la modernidad: crecimiento y modelos urbanos 1775–1932. Medellín, Colombia: Escuela del Hábitat-CEHAP, Facultad de Arquitectura, Univ. Nacional de Colombia, Sede Medellín, 2007. 190 p.: bibl., ill. (Investigaciones; 27)

A brief study by an architect of the growth of Medellín from 1775 to 1932, focusing on ideas, ideologies, and plans. Looks at the limitations of these methods.

848 Gutiérrez Flórez, Felipe. Rutas y el sistema de hábitats de Colombia: la ruta como objeto: epistemología y nuevas cartografías para pensar el hábitat. Medellín, Colombia: Escuela del Hábitat, Facultad de Arquitectura, Univ. Nacional de Colombia, 2007. 178 p.: bibl., ill., maps. (Maestría en hábitat; 1)

The author, an historian, outlines some of the philosophical issues and disciplinary options for the study of "habitat." He looks in particular at the case example of the emergence of New Granada in terms of transportation flows via the Magdalena River. He draws primarily on the Colombian and Latin American literature, including Milton Santos, but also Braudel.

Herrera Ángel, Marta. Ordenar para controlar: ordenamiento espacial y control político en las llanuras del Caribe y en los Andes Centrales Neogranadinos, siglo XVIII. See *HLAS 66:1372*.

849 Mejía Escalante, Mónica Elizabeth. Del discurso de vivienda al espacio de residencia: el caso de vivienda en altura en sistema constructivo de cajón. Medellín, Colombia: Maestría en Hábitat, Escuela del Hábitat, Facultad de Arquitectura, Univ. Nacional de Colombia, Sede Medellín, 2007. 166 p.: bibl., ill., maps. (Col. Maestría en hábitat; 2)

A study of discourses, perceptions, and realities pertaining to high-rise residential complexes in Medellín, based on interviews. The author identifies numerous areas where buildings fail to live up to the needs and preference of purchasers, or to meet the goals of good urban planning.

Nieto Olarte, Mauricio. Orden natural y orden social: ciencia y política en el *Semanario del nuevo reyno de Granada*. See *HLAS 66:1380*.

850 Ortiz Guerrero, César Enrique; Manuel Enrique Pérez Martinez; and Luis Alfredo Muñoz Wilches. Los cambios institucionales y el conflicto ambiental: el caso de los valles del río Sinú y San Jorge. Bogotá: Editorial Pontificia Univ. Javeriana, 2006. 129 p.: bibl., ill., maps. (Col. libros de investigación)

This multidisciplinary study looks at the historical political ecology of the valleys of the San Jorge and Sinú rivers. Processes of global economic integration and social destabilization are linked to problems of water quality, soil erosion, salinization, overfishing, and overhunting.

851 Páramo, Pablo. El significado de los lugares públicos para la gente de Bogotá. Bogotá: Univ. Pedagógica Nacional, 2007. 165 p.: bibl., ill., maps. (Col. Tesis doctorales; 3)

The author, an environmental psychologist, explores the interaction between people and public spaces of Bogotá over time and in the present, using focus groups for part of his data. The book is strongly grounded in the international literature, including the literature in English (e.g., Harvey, Agnew).

852 Pardo, María Fabiola. Territorialidades cívicas: espacio público y cultura urbana en Bogotá. Bogotá: Univ. Externado de Colombia, 2008. 288 p.: bibl., ill.

Analyzes initiatives by public authorities and the citizenry to reclaim the public spaces of Bogotá, after the "culture of fear" and internal migrations of past decades, based in part on interviews. The author, a political scientist, has an especially broad grasp of the literature of urban studies and urban geography in France and English-speaking countries, as well as of the Latin American literature.

853 Paredes Cisneros, Santiago. Algo nuevo, algo viejo, algo prestado: las transformaciones urbanas de Barbacoas entre 1850 y 1930. Bogotá: Univ. Nacional de Colombia, 2009. 235 p.: bibl., ill., maps. (Punto aparte)

A history of a small urban place, Barbacoas, in Nariño province near the Pacific coast of Colombia, focusing on its struggle for identity as a real city rather than just a gold mining town. The study has useful maps and illustrations and a careful analysis of local documents.

854 Pérez Rincón, Mario Alejandro. Comercio internacional y medio ambiente en Colombia: mirada desde la economía ecológica. Prólogo de Joan Martínez Alier. Cali, Colombia: Programa Editorial Univ. del Valle, 2007. 385 p.: bibl., ill., 1 CD-ROM. (Col. Libros de investigación)

An environmental economist and economic historian who specializes in water, the author argues that via international trade rich nations have been able to buy Colombia's natural resources without paying for loss or depreciation of the environmental patrimony. The book looks at the impacts of such traditional export crops as coffee, as well as the expansion of sugarcane and flower production.

Pérez V., Gerson Javier. Dimensión espacial de la pobreza en Colombia. See item **2028.**

855 Reyes Posada, Alejandro. Guerreros y campesinos: el despojo de la tierra en Colombia. Con la colaboración de Liliana Duica Amaya. Buenos Aires: Bogotá: Grupo Editorial Norma, 2009. 378 p.: bibl., maps, tables. (Col. Vitral)

Reyes Posada is a sociologist with extensive experience in government and journalism. This ambitious study examines the failure of the politics of agrarian reform, the expansion of guerrilla warfare, the rise of paramilitary movements, and the spread of drug trafficking in Colombia as they have resulted in the loss of land rights by rural smallholders. The impressive amount of detail, including maps and statistical tables, is not always adequately sourced, but clearly documents the range of impacts on land holdings.

856 Sanín Santamaría, Juan Diego. Hogar en tránsito: apropiaciones domésticas de la vivienda de interés social (vis) y reconfiguraciones del sentido de hogar. (*Antípoda*, 7, julio/dic. 2008, p. 31–61, bibl., ill., photos)

In 2006 the residents of informal self-constructed housing on a mountain of trash in Medellín were relocated to new, modern housing developments. This article, based on semi-structured interviews and photographs, looks at the ways in which the relocated families appropriated the new housing complexes to recreate their traditional sense of home, especially through the physical and symbolic deployment of the ordinary objects of daily life and the society of consumption.

857 Urbanización para el desarrollo humano: políticas para un mundo de ciudades. Dirigida por Fabio Giraldo Isaza *et al.* Bogotá: ONU-HABITAT, 2009. 396 p.: bibl., ill. (some col.), maps.

A product of a UN team project, the book examines urbanization and development in the world, specifically Latin America, Colombia, and Bogotá, in terms of the millennium development goals. The chapters on Bogotá focus on housing, urban growth, social integration and equity, governance, adaptation to climate change, and the global economy.

858 Van Ausdal, Shawn. Pasture, profit, and power: an environmental history of cattle ranching in Colombia, 1850–1950. (*Geoforum/New York*, 40:5, Sept. 2009, p. 707–719)

Shows that substantial deforestation in the Colombian lowlands began in the mid-19th century, promoted by a highly profitable beef ranching sector and the spread of Africanized grasses. Argues against viewing deforestation and pasture establishment as something recent or primarily motivated by noneconomic factors.

859 Zuleta Jaramillo, Luis Alberto and **Lino Jaramillo G.** Cartagena de Indias, impacto económico de la zona histórica. Bogotá: Convenio Andrés Bello, 2006. 184 p.: bibl., col. ill. (Economía & cultura; 13)

The authors conducted interview and survey research to determine the economic impact of the historic zone of Cartagena on the economy of the city. About 60 percent of the employment in the historic zone is related to the historic attractions there, but the impact on employment in the city as a whole is only five percent, and the impact on value added is less than four percent. The authors look at other impacts and evaluate possibilities for improvement.

860 Zuluaga Valencia, Julián Adolfo. La levedad de la memoria: símbolos e imaginarios ambientales urbanos en Popayán, Colombia. Popayán, Colombia: Ediciones Axis Mundi: Univ. del Cauca, 2007. 202 p.: bibl., index. (Ensayo. Estudios urbanos)

This book, written by an architect, presents a brief history of the city of Popayán, followed by a discussion of symbolic and cultural urban landscapes including natural areas, the Molino River, architecture, and religious features.

ECUADOR

861 Andrade, Xavier. "Mas ciudad", menos ciudadanía: renovación urbana y aniquilación del espacio público en Guayaquil. (*Ecuad. Debate*, 68, agosto 2006, p. 161–197)

Critiques the massive urban renewal projects constructed in Guayaquil under Mayors Febres Cordero and Nebot between 1996 and 2004. Argues that the new architecture in places like the Malecón 2000 uses an esthetic language based on a generic global tourism; renewed spaces are largely devoted to commercial purposes; ornamental plant-

ings do not provide sufficient shade or recreational potential; and that the supposedly public spaces are regulated by private security forces. Guayaquil landscapes are increasingly polarized, as exemplified by the gated communities of exclusivity in Samborondón.

Borrero Vega, Ana Luz. Cambios históricos en el paisaje de Cuenca, siglos XIX–XX. See *HLAS 66:1691.*

Cuvi, Nicolás. La institucionalización del conservacionismo en el Ecuador, 1949–1953: Misael Acosta Solis y el Departamento Forestal. See *HLAS 66:1697.*

862 Development with identity: community, culture and sustainability in the Andes. Edited by Robert E. Rhoades. Wallingford, UK; Cambridge, Mass.: CABI Publishing, 2006. 325 p.: bibl., ill. (some col.), index, maps, plates.

Contains many chapters related to a long-term research partnership with Cotacachi county in northern highland Ecuador, a place which has long had an indigenous mayor and population interested in alternative development. This project involved indigenous community participation in research design in such disparate areas as biodiversity conservation, soil and water management, agriculture and food, and development with identity.

863 Farley, Kathleen A. Pathways to forest transition: local case studies from the Ecuadorian Andes. (*J. Lat. Am. Geogr.*, 9:2, 2010, p. 7–26)

Three case examples from the Ecuadorian Andes indicate that forest expansion is not associated with land abandonment, but rather with active tree planting strategies related to perceived advantages and profitability of forests.

864 Las fronteras con Colombia. Edición de Roque Espinosa. Investigación de Milena Almeida, Alicia Granda y Isabel Ramos. Quito: Univ. Andina Simón Bolívar, Sede Ecuador: Corporación Editora Nacional, 2008. 545 p.: bibl., ill., maps (2 col. folded). (Biblioteca de ciencias sociales; 62)

This substantial book presents the results of a team project by the Universidad Andina Simón Bolívar, funded by the Inter-American Development Bank, with fieldwork and interviews conducted in 2005 and 2006. The histories and characteristics of the frontier zones with Colombia are discussed with special attention to the impacts of drug trafficking and the drug war.

865 Galápagos: migraciones, economía, cultura, conflictos y acuerdos.
Edición de Pablo Ospina y Cecilia Falconí. Quito: Corporación Editora Nacional: Univ. Andina Simón Bolívar, 2007. 397 p.: bibl., ill., map. (Biblioteca de ciencias sociales; 57)

Proceedings of an international colloquium held in 2006, this volume contains 24 articles on various challenges facing sustainable development in the Galápagos islands, including migrations, economy, culture, conflicts, and agreements. Includes a 39-page partially annotated bibliography.

866 Gente y ambiente de Páramo: realidades y perspectivas en el Ecuador.
Edición de Juan Sebastián Martínez. Textos de Rodrigo de la Cruz *et al.* Quito: Eco-Ciencia, Proyecto Páramo Andino: Abya-Yala: Condesa: GEF: PNUMA, 2009. 134 p.: bibl., ill.

Most of the papers in this edited volume were presented at a series of conferences in late 2006 in Quito, as brief reflections on the theme of social and environmental aspects of Andean Páramos. Participants included the historian Galo Ramón, and various environmentalists from Ecuadorian universities, government agencies, indigenous groups, and NGOs.

867 Girard, Sabine. Quatre siècles de luttes et d'alliances pour le contrôle de l'eau dans le sillon interandin: du monopole des haciendas sous la colonisation espagnole au récent réveil indien; le cas du versant de Santa Rosa-Pilahuin, Équateur. (*Bull. Inst. fr. étud. andin.*, 37:2, 2008, p. 375–401, bibl., ill., maps, tables)

Continues the strong tradition of French scholarship in the study of Ecuadorian irrigation, in this case, the region of Santa Rosa to the east of Ambato in the central highlands. Argues that the Spanish initiated the construction of vertical canals, with large land holdings. Many more canals, including contour canals, were constructed during republican times along with the emergence of smallhold irrigated farming by mestizos at lower elevations. Recently indigenous communities have used newly acquired water rights to irrigate higher elevation lands. History, geography, and culture combine to make the negotiations of water rights difficult but necessary.

868 Himley, Matthew. Nature conservation, rural livelihoods, and territorial control in Andean Ecuador. (*Geoforum/New York*, 40:5, Sept. 2009, p. 832–842)

Explores conservation encounters with local actors in a community in the south central highlands of Ecuador; argues for attention to power and politics in nature conservation issues, following Sundberg, Bebbington, and Perreault. Among others, Himley worked with Ecuadorian geographer and farmer Stu White.

869 Martínez Flores, Alexandra. Naturaleza y cultura: un debate pendiente en la antropología ecuatoriana. (*Ecuad. Debate*, 72, dic. 2007, p. 135–150, bibl.)

Ecuadorian anthropologist examines environmental theses, articles, and books produced in Ecuador between 1995 and 2005, and concludes that Ecuadorian anthropologists, while producing valuable work on cultural identities, landscapes, and especially ethnoecology and ethnomedicine, have not explicitly challenged the modern paradigm separating nature and society.

870 Martínez Valle, Luciano. Repensando el desarrollo rural en la dimensión del territorio: una reflexión sobre los límites del PROLOCAL en el caso ecuatoriano. (*Rev. Eur. Estud. Latinoam. Caribe*, 87, Oct. 2009, p. 27–45, bibl., graph, map, table)

A sociologist associated with FLACSO in Quito evaluates the World Bank-funded PROLOCAL program for local rural development from 2002 to 2006. The program targeted selected rural zones in the coast and highlands, and prioritized help for small scale agricultural projects. However, the program did not start with an adequate understanding of local economic and social forces, such as plantations, contract farming, town-country relationships, and migration; the lack of social capital and higher level social organizations doomed the projects to irrelevance. The author looks to the new Constitution of 2008 as providing a fresh start for development based on local territorial realities.

871 Martínez Yánez, Esperanza. Yasuní: el tortuoso camino de Kioto a Quito. Quito: Abya Yala, Univ. Politécnica Salesiana: Comité Ecuménico de Proyectos, 2009. 116 p.: bibl., ill., maps.

Looks at the trajectory of the 2005 proposal by Oilwatch to ban oil development in the Yasuní Biosphere Reserve, in terms of actors at a variety of scales, from local to global, through March 2009.

872 Mathewson, Kent. Coastal Ecuador's montubios in ethnographic and historical perspective. (*in* Ethno-historical geographic studies in Latin America: essays honoring William V. Davidson. Edited by Peter H. Herlihy, Kent Mathewson, and Craig S. Revels. Baton Rouge, La.: Geoscience Publications, Dept. of Geography and Anthropology, Louisiana State Univ., 2008, p. 239–262)

An original analysis of coastal Ecuadorian *montubio* culture as exemplified in the vicinity of Samborondón (before its transformation into a site of gated elite communities), including farming, ceramic making, fishing, and canoe-building. Argues for attention to the many groups that are neither European nor indigenous, but have developed their own strong localisms in tropical lowland, riverrine, and savanna environments.

873 Neira, Francisco; Santiago Gómez; and Gloria Pérez. Sostenibilidad de los usos de subsistencia de la biodiversidad en un área protegida de la Amazonía ecuatoriana: un análisis biofísico. (*Ecuad. Debate,* 67, abril 2006, p. 155–163, bibl.)

Brief examination of local Quichua farming, fishing, and hunting in the Limoncocha Biological Reserve in the Ecuadorian Amazon, based on interviews and focus groups conducted in 2004–2005 and concepts drawn from cultural ecology. Current use seems sustainable, and local institutions are strong, but locals report having to exert more effort in hunting and fishing over time, and increased population density is a challenge.

874 ¿Reforma agraria en el Ecuador?: viejos temas, nuevos argumentos. Edición de Frank Brassel, Stalin Herrera, y Michel Laforge. Quito: Sistema de Investigación sobre la Problemática Agraria en el Ecuador, 2008. 248 p.: bibl., ill. (some col.), maps (chiefly col.).

Presents the results of various case studies of the status of land tenure, conducted in 2007 and 2008 with the participation of various national and international NGOs. Case studies include the banana agroindustry in Barbones, sugar plantations in La Troncal, and the flower industry in Ayora. The editors argue for a renewed emphasis on democratization of access to land.

875 Swanson, Kate. Begging as a path to progress: indigenous women and children and the struggle for Ecuador's urban spaces. Athens: Univ. of Georgia Press, 2010. 146 p.: bibl., ill., index, maps. (Geographies of justice and social transformation)

Study of a particular highland village's migrants to the city, their activities in vending and begging, and issues surrounding their constructed image as lazy, sick, and dirty.

876 Terán, Juan Fernando. Las quimeras y sus caminos: la gobernanza del agua y sus dispositivos para la producción de pobreza rural en los Andes ecuatorianos. Buenos Aires: CLACSO, 2007. 263 p.: bibl., maps. (Col. CLACSO-CROP)

The author, a sociologist at the Universidad Andina Simón Bolívar, provides an overview of neoliberal development policy and its arguments for privatization, before turning to a brief look at Cotopaxi province in the central highlands of Ecuador. Relying heavily on the work of historian Galo Ramón, Terán points out that water rights in Cotopaxi have historically been associated with class and ethnic struggles, and that neoliberal development proposes a depoliticization that would harm the càpacity of users to continue to adequately manage their water. Data collected by NGOs such as SIPAE and the UN (CEPAL's 2005 report) in Cotopaxi are used to question the benefit of nontraditional exports (flowers) and to suggest that a free trade agreement would hurt most local farmers.

877 Walsh, Stephen J. *et al.* Community expansion and infrastructure development: implications for human health and environmental quality in the Galápagos Islands of Ecuador. (*J. Lat. Am. Geogr.,* 9:3, 2010, p. 137–160)

Deploys a mixed methods approach including GIS, remote sensing, and interviews to document and map spatial problems in water and wastewater services in a growing settlement in the islands.

878 Yasuní en el siglo XXI: el estado ecuatoriano y la conservación de la Amazonía. Coordinación de Guillaume Fontaine e Iván Narváez Quiñónez. Quito: FLACSO Sede Ecuador; Lima: IFEA; Quito: Abya Yala: Petrobras, Ecuador: Wildlife Conservation Society Ecuador: Centro Ecuatoriano de Derecho Ambiental, 2007. 341 p.: bibl., col. maps. (Foro) (Travaux de l'Institut français d'études andines; 249)

Six chapters by diverse authors examine environmental politics and policy as affecting the Yasuní Biosphere Reserve, including indigenous rights and petroleum policy. The book is a product of an investigation by the FLACSO Socio-Environmental Observatory.

PERU

879 Abad Pérez, César. Apu Pariacaca y el Alto Cañete: estudio de paisaje cultural. Investigación y textos de César Abad Pérez, Josué González Solórzano y Anderson Chamorro García. Lima: Instituto Nacional de Cultura, Programa Qhapaq Ñan, 2009. 312 p.: bibl., ill. (some col.), col. maps (some folded).

Produced as part of the international Qhapaq Ñan project studying the route of the Inca highway. Provides a detailed, illustrated inventory of material culture, including landscape features such as archeological sites and traditional canals, along with descriptions of beliefs and folklore. Includes policy recommendations for preserving the cultural patrimony.

880 Bebbington, Anthony and Jeffrey T. Bury. Institutional challenges for mining and sustainability in Peru. (*Proc. Natl. Acad. Sci. U.S.A.*, 106:41, Oct. 2009, p. 17296–17301)

A good example of the work coming out of the larger joint project of Bebbington and Bury, examining the impact of mining projects in Ecuador, Peru, and Bolivia. This paper looks at two case examples in Peru and concludes that institutional innovations

are essential for resource-based growth to be sustainable, even if conflict is involved.

881 Beraún Chaca, John James and Alan Joe Beraún Chaca. Dinámicas socio-territoriales en espacios neorrurales: la metamorfosis de la comunidad campesina San Pedro de Yanahuanca. (*Investig. Soc./ San Marcos*, 20, agosto 2008, p. 85–102, bibl., graphs, map, tables)

Based on an MA thesis project, this study illustrates patterns of spatial fragmentation and consolidation in a highland community, due to larger processes of neoliberal change since 1980. Models and concepts are developed to understand similar changes elsewhere.

882 Bonifaz, José Luis and Roberto Urrunaga. Beneficios económicos de la carretera Interoceánica. Lima: Univ. del Pacífico, Centro de Investigación, 2008. 166 p.: bibl., ill.

This study was written to promote further state investment in Peru's Interoceanic Highway. Using data from 2007, the author uses macroeconomic methods to suggest the highway contributed over one billion US dollars to the regional and national economy.

883 Bury, Jeffrey. New geographies of tourism in Peru: nature-based tourism and conservation in the Cordillera Huayhuash. (*Tour. Geogr.*, 10:3, Aug. 2008, p. 312–333)

Uses historical research and interview data to analyze changing sources and impacts of tourism in a mountain region of Peru. Nature tourism has been rapidly expanding, alongside large tourism companies. The environmental and social impacts are worrisome.

884 Carey, Mark P. In the shadow of melting glaciers: climate change and Andean society. Oxford, England; New York, N.Y.: Oxford Univ. Press, 2010. 273 p.: bibl., index.

An important historical study of environmental catastrophes in the Cordillera Blanca of Peru. The author suggests that state responses were most vigorous during authoritarian regimes, and that local people have not been powerless in the face of larger economic and political forces. He argues for a greater recognition of the role of positionality in climate change science, technology, and policy.

885 Coomes, Oliver T. Of stakes, stems and cuttings: the importance of local seed systems in traditional Amazonian societies. (*Prof. Geogr.*, 62:3, Aug. 2010, p. 323–334)

Provides observations from the Peruvian Amazon to make the point that agricultural planting materials are critically important for local agriculture as well as for generating social and market linkages.

886 Coomes, Oliver T.; C. Abizaid; and **M. Lapointe.** Human modification of a large meandering Amazonian river: genesis, ecological and economic consequences of the Masisea cutoff on the central Ucayali, Peru. (*Ambio/Stockholm*, 38:3, May 2009, p. 130–134)

A study of how people using simple tools were able to change the course of a major river in the Amazon basin, threatening the viability of a port and the livelihoods of many.

887 Fernández-Maldonado, Ana María. Expanding networks for the urban poor: water and telecommunications services in Lima, Peru. (*Geoforum/New York*, 39:6, Nov. 2008, p. 1884–1896)

Tracks the impact of neoliberal reforms on the provision of telecommunications and water services in Lima. Points out that the provision of these services has always been unequal, and that reforms have on balance led to improvements in provisions to the poor along with continuing and new inequalities. Competition, regulation, investment, and subsidies have played complex roles. Indicates the importance of empirical research and attention to the details of policy in urban geography.

888 Franco Temple, Eduardo. Siempre habrá un Niño en nuestro futuro: aportes de Eduardo Franco al estudio de las respuestas sociales a El Niño y cambio climático. Lima: Rosa Rivero Editora, 2007. 174 p.: bibl.

This book republishes a number of papers and essays by the eminent Peruvian anthropologist and hazards researcher Eduardo Franco (1952–2003). The essays focus on social contexts and impacts of Niño events, including the development of policy and scholarly institutions at a local and global scale.

889 Jiménez Díaz, Luis. Costo de oportunidad y externalidades en el valor económico del agua superficial para uso agrícola en el Valle de Mala. Lima: Asamblea Nacional de Rectores, 2008. 199 p.: bibl., ill., map.

This study by an economist looks at the costs (including externalities and opportunity costs) and benefits of water in the Mala Valley on the coast of Peru. Uses of water include agriculture (apple growing), domestic use, woodlands, shrimp farming, and recreation. The author shows that the least efficient use of water is for agriculture, and argues for the introduction of market mechanisms for water, as well as the reorganization of the irrigation system and a shift to crops that are better adapted to a seasonal irrigation regime.

890 León Cornejo, Daniela and **Paola Mego Canta.** El *cluster* forestal en Madre de Dios: obstáculos y opotunidades para su crecimiento y competitividad. (*Apuntes/Lima*, 60/61, segundo semestre 2007, p. 169–220, bibl., graphs, tables)

Uses economic analysis to argue that the Interoceanic Highway should lead to more profitability for forestry in southeastern Peru, resulting in expansion of the sector. Outlines various scenarios of development which may or may not lead to sustainable forestry; it is important, for example, that international markets diversify their demand for species, inefficient local producers be provided exit strategies, and that more data be acquired on species distributions and status so that overexploitation does not occur.

891 Moreau, Marie-Annick and **Oliver T. Coomes.** Aquarium fish exploitation in western Amazonia: conservation issues in Peru. (*Environ. Conserv./Cambridge*, 34:1, March 2007, p. 12–22, graphs, map, tables)

An important study of the dimensions and characteristics of the wild freshwater fish trade from the Peruvian Amazon to the international aquarium market. The industry is economically important to many rural poor. Government regulations are not well developed, and should include local knowledge to a greater extent.

892 Ocola, Leonidas. Peligro, vulnerabilidad, riesgo y la posibilidad de desastres sísmicos en el Perú. (*Rev. Geofís.*, 61, 2005, p. 81–125, bibl., graphs, maps, photos)

An overview of seismic risks and vulnerabilities in Peru, with many maps. The greatest seismic risks (in terms of probabilities of high seismic accelerations) are in the southern and northern coastal areas, with the lowest risks in the Amazon part of the country. However, taking into account poverty, construction materials, and settlement concentrations, the seismic disaster risk hotspots nationwide are Ica, Lima, Trujillo, Chiclayo, and Piura on the coast, as well as all the major cities in the highlands.

893 Salisbury, David S. *et al.* Fronteras vivas or dead ends?: the impact of military settlement projects in the Amazon borderlands. (*J. Lat. Am. Geogr.*, 9:2, 2010, p. 49–71)

A case study of the resource management, household economics, and political geography of a Peruvian borderland military settlement shows adverse impacts on forests, fauna, and relations with Brazil. Authors argue for the creation of peace parks, *fronteras verdes*, as an alternative to military *fronteras vivas*.

Salisbury, David S.; José Borgo López; and **Jorge W. Vela Alvarado.** Transboundary political ecology in Amazonia: history, culture, and conflicts of the borderland Ashaninka. See item **583**.

894 Salo, Matti and **Aili Pyhälä.** Exploring the gap between conservation science and protected area esablishment in the Allpahuayo-Mishana National Reserve, Peruvian Amazonia. (*Environ. Conserv./ Cambridge*, 34:1, March 2007, p. 23–32, graph, map, tables)

The authors investigate the history of an environmental reserve in the Peruvian Amazon between its establishment in 1999 and its approved management plan in 2005. Although the reserve was originally conceived to conserve biodiversity, its effective establishment was due to a change of emphasis to include the livelihood requirements of local communities and environmental services.

895 Simposio: Organización y Gestión de Recursos en Ecosistemas de Montaña, Lima, 2005. Los Andes y las poblaciones altoandinas en la agenda de la regionalización y la descentralización. Edición de Hilda Araújo. Lima: CONCYTEC: República del Perú, 2008. 2 v.: bibl., ill. (some col.), maps (some col.).

Includes papers presented at a 2005 conference on Peruvian mountain ecosystem resource management, including agriculture, climate change, and tendencies towards decentralized control. Especially noteworthy in these two volumes are papers by Hilda Araújo on climate change and adaptive change by farmers near Lake Titicaca, and John Earls on the resilience of Andean technology and society to cope with climate change.

896 Wernke, Steven A. A reduced landscape: toward a multi-causal understanding of historic period agricultural deintensification in highland Peru. (*J. Lat. Am. Geogr.*, 9:3, 2010, p. 51–84)

Argues that terrace and canal abandonment in the Colca Valley after 1500 was in part due to depopulation, but that the spatial patterning of abandonment can be explained by climatic cooling and the resettlement that increased walking distance to fields. Since privileged households tended to have the closest fields, they abandoned fields primarily due to frost risk; less privileged households were also forced to take distance into account.

897 Wernke, Steven A. and **Thomas M. Whitmore.** Agriculture and inequality in the colonial Andes: a simulation of production and consumption using administrative documents. (*Hum. Ecol.*, 37:4, Aug. 2009, p. 421–440)

Household demographic and landholding declarations from colonial visitas in the Colca Valley are used to model food production and nutritional needs at the household level. The results suggest that although the Colca Valley produced an agricultural surplus as a whole, about 30 percent of households experienced hunger.

898 Yeckting Vilela, Fabiola. Visiones del desarrollo en las comunidades: impactos de tres proyectos de desarrollo agropecuario en las comunidades pastoriles surandinas del Perú durante el período de violencia interna, 1980–1995. Lima: Instituto Francés de Estudios Andinos, UMIFRE 17, CNRS-MAEE: Republique Française, Embajada de Francia: CBC, Centro Bartolomé de las Casas: SER, 2008. 233 p.: bibl., ill., map. (Col. "Travaux de l'Institut français d'études andines"; 265) (Serie "Ecología y desarrollo"; 11)

Examines the "development visions" of three major agricultural projects in southern Andean Peru during the period of internal violence (1980–95). These visions did not always coincide with local visions, and the internal political violence made it difficult for social negotiations to take place.

BOLIVIA

899   Achi Chritèle, Amonah and **Marcelo Delgado.** A la conquista de un lote: estrategias populares de acceso a la tierra urbana. Cochabamba, Bolivia: CESU-UMSS: DICYT-UMSS; La Paz: Fundación PIEB, 2007. 187 p.: bibl., ill., maps. (Investigaciones Cochabamba)

A study of local tactics for gaining access to land for informal settlements on the outskirts of Cochabamba, Bolivia. The authors report on six months of field study, and also provide a wide-ranging commentary on contemporary politics and policy affecting housing.

Bebbington, Denise Humphreys and **Anthony Bebbington.** Anatomy of a regional conflict: Tarija and resource grievances in Morales's Bolivia. See item **1310.**

900   Bolivia: población, territorio y medio ambiente: análisis de situación de la población. Edición de Rubén Vargas y María Eugenia Villalpando. La Paz: Fondo de Población de las Naciones Unidas: Ministerio de Planificación del Desarrollo, 2007. 242 p.: bibl., col. ill., col. maps, 1 CD-ROM (4 3/4 in.).

An overview of the demographic status of Bolivia, the result of a collaboration between the UN Population Fund and the national government. Also includes discussions of migration, geography, and policy. The authors conclude that Bolivia is undergoing major transformations linked to the demographic transition. The strong socioeconomic inequalities in Bolivia sug-

gest that the transition is being experienced differently by different regions, social classes, and ethnic groups. The authors predict a growth in Bolivia's population from 9.8 million in 2007 to 12.4 million in 2020, and population stabilization and reduction after that, with corresponding impacts on dependency ratios. They also call for efforts to combat poverty and inequality.

901   Chilón Camacho, Eduardo. Tecnologías ancestrales y reducción de riesgos del cambio climático: terrazas precolombinas taqanas, quillas y wachus. La Paz: Proyecto de Manejo de Recursos Naturales: Ministerio de Planificación del Desarrollo: IFAD, 2009. 323 p.: bibl., ill. (some col.), maps.

A survey of traditional terracing, raised fields, and water management systems in Bolivia, with numerous diagrams and maps. The book draws primarily on the Spanish-language literature published in Bolivia, but also cites the early works of Murra, Earls, Denevan, and Guillet. Includes abundant details on the location, environmental context, and land use of agricultural landforms, as well as the "software" of production, tools, techniques, and social organization. The author argues for the reutilization of these technologies.

902   Cronkleton, Peter *et al.* Social geomatics: participatory forest mapping to mediate resource conflict in the Bolivian Amazon. (*Hum. Ecol.*, 38:1, Feb. 2010, p. 65–76)

Reports on a participatory mapping project to clarify resource rights to Brazil nut trees and trails, and argues that the effectiveness of such approaches is enhanced if they occur early in the process of rights allocation.

903   Despues de las guerras del agua. Coordinación de Carlos Crespo y Susan Spronk. La Paz: Plural, 2007. 245 p.: bibl.

This edited volume presents various critical perspectives on the privatization of urban water supplies in Bolivia, including contributions by geographers Thomas Perreault and Karen Bakker, as well as articles by political scientists, economists, sociologists, planners, and biologists. Case examples focus on Cochabamba and El Alto.

All of the articles were written prior to the elections of Dec. 2005.

904 El Alto: desde una perspectiva poblacional. Coordinación de Sandra Garfias *et al.* La Paz: Consejo de Población para el Desarrollo Sostenible: Institut de Recherche pour le developpment, 2005. 130 p.: bibl., ill., indexes, maps.

An overview of the human geography of El Alto, the highest major city in the Andes. The book contains numerous useful maps, which are a product of a collaboration with French geographers from the Institut de Recherche pour le developpment (IRD).

905 Gade, Daniel W. Sucre, Bolivia, and the quiddity of place. (*J. Lat. Am. Geogr.*, 9:2, 2010, p. 99–117)

Argues for the indispensability of humanistic, phenomenological approaches to the study of such unique places as Sucre, Bolivia. The market, church, old mental hospital, and cemetery provoke reflections on food supply, beeswax candles, iodine deficiency, cretinism, and burial customs. Sucre remains a unique place.

Kaup, Brent Z. A neoliberal nationalization?: the constraints on natural gas-led development in Bolivia. See item **1323.**

906 El norte amazónico de Bolivia y el complejo del Río Madera. Coordinación de Patricia Molina. Cochabamba, Bolivia: Comisión para la Gestión Integral del Agua en Bolivia; La Paz: FOBOMADE, 2007. 164 p.: bibl., ill. (some col.), maps (some col.).

Presents a series of articles by academics and activists critical of dam projects on the Madera (Madeira) River in northern Bolivia and Brazil. The authors assert that these projects will result in the inundation of Bolivian territory and the export of electricity without adequate safeguards or provisions for Bolivian needs.

907 La otra frontera: usos alternativos de recursos naturales en Bolivia. La Paz: PNUD Bolivia, 2008. 509 p.: bibl., ill. (some col.), maps (some col.), 1 videodisc (4 3/4 in.).

This collaboration between Conservation International and the UNDP critiques traditional economic activities and exports and argues for an alternative economy. Many case examples focus on such products as animal hides, wild cacao, certified wood, organic coffee, sesame, organic onions, quinoa, and maca, as well as integrated park management, ecotourism, and environmental services.

908 Pacheco, Pablo. What lies behind decentralisation?: forest, powers and actors in lowland Bolivia. (*in* Democratic decentralisation through a natural resource lens. Edited by Jesse C. Ribot and Anne M. Larson. London; New York, N.Y.: Routledge, 2004, p. 90–109, bibl.)

Looks at decentralization in lowland Bolivia as part of a package of reforms associated with neoliberalism. In some cases small farmers and indigenous people have been empowered, while in others cattle ranchers and other local elites have benefitted; there is increasing pressure, however, for different groups to negotiate with each other. Municipalities have been empowered to manage forests, but outcomes have been diverse and conservation implications are still unclear.

909 Radhuber, Isabella Margerita. El poder de la tierra: el discurso agrario en Bolivia: un análisis de las ideas sociales, políticas, económicas y de las relaciones de poder. Prefacio de Luis Tapia. La Paz: Embajada de Austria en Lima: Plural Editores, 2008. 197 p.: bibl.

A brief historical and contemporary study of agrarian politics, policies, and discourses in Bolivia, influenced by Murra, Foucault, and Bourdieu. The author, an Austrian scholar, interviewed politicians, government agents, and representatives of social movements, NGOs, and business groups. Conflicts are outlined between the liberal and indigenous cosmovisions, with the latter said to focus on autonomy, subsistence, and community.

910 Ruíz, Sergio Antonio and **Ingo Georg Gentes.** Retos y perspectivas de la gobernanza del agua y gestión integral de recursos hídricos en Bolivia. (*Rev. Eur. Estud. Latinoam. Caribe*, 85, Oct. 2008, p. 41–59, bibl.)

Discusses the events and challenges of water policy and water politics since the "water war" of Cochabamba in 2000, and the election of Evo Morales and the creation of a Ministerio de Agua in 2006. Many problems remain to be solved.

911 Salinas, Elvira. Conflictos ambientales en áreas protegidas de Bolivia. La Paz: Wildlife Conservation Society, 2007. 157 p.: bibl., col. ill., col. maps.

Provides an overview of potential conflicts in Bolivia's National System of Protected Areas, with a particular emphasis on Madidi to the north of La Paz. The study, funded by USAID and the Moore Foundation, looks at demography, including social groups such as indigenous peoples, and such extractive activities as lumbering.

912 Sarmiento Sánchez, Susana Jacqueline. Género y recursos naturales: visión de dos comunidades de Yanacachi. La Paz: Univ. Mayor de San Andrés, Instituto de Ecologia, Centro de Postgrado en Ecología y Conservación: Programa de Investigación Estratégica en Bolivia; Montevideo: Centro Internacional de Investigación para el Desarrollo, 2008. 169 p.: bibl., ill., maps.

The author performed a field study of resource management in Yanacachi in the Department of La Paz, as influenced by the ideas of Murra, Altieri, and Agarwal and the feminist literature. She looks at use of soil, water, and vegetation, and the impact of management strategies on the environment. Agricultural activities include coca and flower cultivation for sale, and the increased use of chemicals, but the absence of irrigation is a severe challenge. Both men and women recognize climate changes (higher temperatures, lower spring flow, bigger storms, and more strongly defined wet and dry seasons). Men are particularly worried about deforestation and pesticide misuse, while women worry about rising subsistence costs. Women remain disempowered due to unequal access to education and social spaces.

913 Yarnall, Kaitlin and **Marie Price.** Migration, development, and a new rurality in the Valle Alto, Bolivia. (*J. Lat. Am. Geogr.*, 9:1, 2010, p. 107–124)

Uses data from interviews, surveys, and field observations to study the remittance economy of Valle Alto near Cochabamba, Bolivia. The development impact on a new rurality can be sustainable when social networks are rich and a strong attachment to place exists.

914 Zimmerer, Karl S. Nature under neoliberalism and beyond in Bolivia: community-based resource management, environmental conservation, and farmer-and-food movements, 1985-present. (*in* Beyond neoliberalism in Latin America?: societies and politics at the crossroads. Edited by John Burdick, Philip Oxhorn, and Kenneth M. Roberts. New York, N.Y.: Palgrave Macmillan, 2009, p. 157–174)

Provides a long-term overview of community agricultural, resource, and food movements in Bolivia, and an assessment of prospects for change under Morales' post-neoliberal leadership. The volume also contains a worthwhile essay on Bolivia's environmental governance by Perreault.

915 Zimmerer, Karl S. Woodlands and agrobiodiversity in irrigation landscapes amidst global change: Bolivia, 1990–2002. (*Prof. Geogr.*, 62:3, Aug. 2010, p. 335–356)

Field study of landscape and agrobiodiversity change near Cochabamba showed that irrigation development coupled with ethnodevelopment can be at least partially consistent with agrobiodiversity conservation.

THE SOUTHERN CONE

PETER KLEPEIS, *Associate Professor of Geography, Colgate University*

RECENT SCHOLARSHIP ON THE SOUTHERN CONE resonates in a vital way with research themes in the discipline of geography as a whole, with select works contributing to areas of critical theoretical and applied importance. The realm of nature-society studies, in particular, includes outstanding research. For example, Newell's analysis of state influence in the growth of the biotechnology sector in Argentina is likely to inform debates about changes in the agrarian sector worldwide (item **938**). Likewise Bellisario (item **954**) and Santana Ulloa (item **966**) have produced seminal studies of the dynamics of agricultural change in Chile.

Representing a growing number of projects on natural hazards, Ríos and Pírez—whose work builds on what now amounts to a considerable body of literature focusing on gated communities in the region—expose the implications of such development for increasing flood events (item **943**). Other potentially influential works on natural resource management and environmental change consider the political ecology of water management policy (item **956**), indigenous land rights and parks (item **961**), and land-cover change analysis in Paraguay's Atlantic Forest ecoregion (item **968**).

Multiple studies of economic and cultural geography also consider rural regions. For example, scholarship on rural change and amenity migration are prominent international areas of scholarship. Connecting to this literature, Craviotti outlines challenges in the decline of primary production and the influx of new landowners with diverse ideas about nature and society (item **931**). Additional research on rural development (item **916**) and Patagonia's part in a global land grab (item **925**) expose not only environment and development tensions, but also raise concerns about social justice.

In the context of weakening emphasis by many governments worldwide on social welfare programs, Bosco weighs the capacity of voluntary systems of caring to fill some of the void (item **927**). Other insightful cultural geography work focuses on gender studies (item **917**), cultural identity (item **920**), and protest spaces (item **945**). In a key trend, the urban geography tradition in the Southern Cone shows signs of growth, with many researchers applying historical perspectives on architecture and urban spaces; among these, Page's study of public spaces in colonial Córdoba stands out (item **939**).

A study by Barton, Gwynne, and Murray exemplifies multiple strong works of economic and resource geography (item **953**). The authors investigate Chile's position in the resource periphery and successfully champion the need for more structuralist-informed political economic analysis. Also considering ways that neoliberalism affects the Southern Cone, Kentor Corby questions conventional wisdom regarding potential negative impacts on wine cooperatives and producers in Argentina (item **936**).

Studies highlighted in this volume, in particular those focusing on urban geography, natural resource management, nature-society studies, and the rural sector, underscore the value of Southern Cone scholarship beyond the region. Unfortunately, there continues to be an imbalance in scholarly coverage on particular subregions, with Uruguay and Paraguay dramatically underrepresented, and the Buenos Aires and Santiago urban regions receiving the bulk of attention. Latin American researchers seem to be speaking primarily to regional scholars, with research that is sometimes thin theoretically. Nonetheless, opportunities exist to make significant contributions to debates in the scholarly community writ large. In addition to contributing to theoretical debates, people in high latitude regions are being exposed to external shocks of many kinds, including market shifts, technological change, and global warming. Research on their vulnerability and capacity for adaptation presents an exciting opportunity for future research and the potential to attract more attention to the broad range of scholarship on southern South America.

GENERAL

916   Ciudadanía, territorio y desarrollo endógeno: resistencias y mediaciones de las políticas locales en las encrucijadas del neoliberalismo. Coordinación de Rubén Zárate y Liliana Artesi. Textos de Liliana Artesi *et al.* Prólogo de Oscar Madoery. Buenos Aires: Editorial Biblos; Río Gallegos, Argentina: IDER Patagonia: Univ. Nacional de la Patagonia Austral, 2007. 422 p.: bibl., ill. (Col. Estado, política y administración pública. Serie Investigaciones)

The privatization of public enterprises, the promotion of natural resource exploitation, and changes in monetary policy have led to rapid social, economic, and institutional change in Patagonia. Thirteen contributors from multidisciplinary backgrounds and extensive experience as development practitioners in the region argue for a new geography of public responsibilities rooted in the heightened agency of local actors.

917   Da Silva, Susana and Diana Lan. Geography and gender studies: the situation in Brazil and Argentina. (*Belgeo/ Leuven*, 3, 2007, p. 371–382, bibl.)

Reviews progress in the development of feminist geography in Latin America. The authors argue that the number of studies of women and gender by regional scholars in Argentina is growing steadily, but that most are largely empirical and lack the kind of theoretical sophistication that would allow scholars to make broader contributions to the literature. The article is likely to interest primarily students of the discipline.

918   Gascón, Margarita. Percepción del desastre natural. Con la colaboración de Natalia Ahumada y Elisa Galdame. Buenos Aires: Editorial Biblos, 2009. 159 p.: bibl., ill. (some col.), maps, photos. (Intertextos)

For those unfamiliar with environmental hazards research, this book draws on international literature and provides a quick introduction to mythical, religious, and scientific perspectives on risk and natural disasters as well as their representations throughout history (e.g., in photos, maps, and paintings). It includes a case study from Gran Mendoza, Argentina.

919   Marenco, Juan José and Adriana H. Narváez. Geografía económica. v. 1, Producciones, redes y medio ambiente.

San Justo, Argentina: Univ. Nacional de La Matanza; Buenos Aires: Prometeo Libros, 2008. 287 p.: bibl., graphs, ill., index, maps, tables.

The first of two volumes presents an overview of concepts in economic geography, brings together basic data on primary production (emphasizing Latin America and Argentina, but covering global patterns as well), and identifies fundamental tensions between economic development and natural resource conservation.

920   McCleary, Kristen. Ethnic identity and elite idyll: a comparison of carnival in Buenos Aires, Argentina and Montevideo, Uruguay, 1900–1920. (*Soc. Identities*, 16:4, July 2010, p. 497–517, bibl.)

The two cities are compared because they share a geography of the River Plate region, and the decline of carnival in Buenos Aires is linked to the movement of the middle and upper classes from Buenos Aires to Montevideo. The transformation of carnival in both cities is analyzed in the context of the commercialization of leisure time, a maturing tourism industry, and the ruling elite's attempts to both promote consumerism and maintain public order.

921   Riffo Rosas, Margarita. Impactos espaciales y socioeconómicos de la vitivinicultura en Chile y Argentina. (*Rev. Geogr./México*, 143, enero/junio 2008, p. 163–209, bibl., maps, photos, tables)

Secondary sources and descriptive statistics underpin an overview of how the wine industry rose to international prominence by the 1990s. Case studies from each country highlight the fragmentation of rural economy and community as wine exports grow and identify regional winners and losers. Many figures in the text are hard to read.

ARGENTINA

922   Abraham, E. *et al.* Overview of the geography of the Monte Desert biome, Argentina. (*J. Arid Environ.*, 73:2, Feb. 2009, p. 144–153, bibl., ill., maps, tables)

This survey of research on the Monte ecoregion emphasizes biophysical conditions, but also describes land use and natural resource management challenges, including land degradation. The authors identify a lack of interdisciplinary socioecological studies, the kind of which are necessary to help identify more sustainable management strategies.

923 Adamo, Susana B. and **Kelley A. Crews-Meyer.** Aridity and desertification: exploring environmental hazards in Jáchal, Argentina. (*Appl. Geogr.*, 26:1, Jan. 2006, p. 61–85, bibl., ill., maps, tables)

Contributing to a vast literature on dryland degradation, the authors use remote-sensing analysis to present the paper's main results: a net decrease in the amount of vegetation between 1971 and 2003, and increasing fragmentation of vegetation classes. Despite the title, however, the authors do not explore carefully the land-use system, nor do they incorporate much of the hazards literature, and they ignore widespread critiques of the desertification concept.

924 Andrade, Maria Isabel and **Olga E. Scarpati.** Recent changes in flood risk in the Gran la Plata, Buenos Aires province, Argentina: causes and management strategy. (*GeoJournal/Boston*, 70:4, Dec. 2007, p. 245–250, bibl., ill., maps, tables)

Reflecting a broad consensus in hazards research, the authors argue that calculating flood risk should go beyond consideration of biophysical factors and include an assessment of social vulnerability as well. Using geospatial analytical techniques, the authors show changing inter-decadal flood patterns in La Plata City from 1971–2000. Increasing flood risk is connected to climate, topography, and urban growth (land-use change).

925 La apropiación y el saqueo de la naturaleza: conflictos ecológicos distributivos en la Argentina del bicentenario. Compilación de Walter A. Pengue. Prólogo de Joan Martínez Alier. Textos de Elsa Bruzzone *et al.* Buenos Aires: Grupo de Ecología del Paisaje y Medio Ambiente, Univ. de Buenos Aires: Fundación Heinrich Böll: Federación Agraria Argentina: Lugar Editorial, 2008. 341 p.: bibl., maps.

In an important contribution to a growing international literature on the foreignization of land, two dozen contributors describe the rapid rise of this phenomenon over the last 20 years in Argentina and its negative social and environmental impacts.

The book is an explicit attempt to pressure government officials to respond to what the authors see as a social and ecological crisis.

926 Benedetti, G. and **A. Campo de Ferreras.** Arbolado de alineación: el mapa verde de un barrio en la ciudad de Bahía Blanca, Argentina. (*Pap. Geogr.*, 45/46, 2007, p. 27–38, bibl., maps, photo)

The authors demonstrate a methodology that they argue should serve as a primary element of natural resource management in urban areas. Using a neighborhood-scale case study, the authors map tree species and indictors of their well being, and consider tree security and functionality as well as neighborhood esthetics in management decisions. The paper suffers from a lack of discussion of the rich use of spatial-analytical tools and approaches in urban planning.

927 Bosco, Fernando J. Hungry children and networks of aid in Argentina: thinking about geographies of responsibility and care. (*Child. Geogr.*, 5:1/2, Feb. 2007, p. 55–76, bibl., ill.)

Contributing to a dynamic emerging literature on geography, ethics, and care, the author assesses the effectiveness of two NGOs that created networks of aid to help needy children during the country's economic crisis. In particular, he identifies both limitations and advantages of internet-based approaches. A thoughtful and important paper that both makes theoretical contributions and addresses a broader set of issues about the role of voluntary systems of caring in the context of a decline in government social welfare programs.

928 Características de la distribución espacial en el Gran San Juan: estadística 2005. Textos de Alberto Papparelli *et al.* San Juan, Argentina: Área Arquitectura Ambiental, Instituto de Estudios en Arquitectura Ambiental, Facultad de Arquitectura, Urbanismo y Diseño, Univ. Nacional de San Juan; Buenos Aires: Nobuko, 2007. 110 p.: bibl., ill., maps, tables.

Part of a series of five-year urban and regional population analyses of the San Juan Metropolitan Area of San Juan, Argentina. Enlists spatial statistics in the form of urban nodes, population density and isolines, distance-decay, and related measures in city center, urban, suburban, and non-urban sectors of the metropolitan area. Uses five-year data from 1900 to 2005 to construct population growth models. [J.L. Scarpaci]

929 Carter, Eric D. State visions, landscapes and disease: discovering malaria in Argentina, 1890–1920. (*Geoforum/New York*, 39:1, Jan. 2008, p. 278–293, bibl., ill., map)

The author positions Argentina's malaria control program within theoretical debates in geography about efforts by states to control their citizens and coordinate economic development through the standardization, transformation, and bureaucratization of space, territory, and landscape.

930 Conocimiento del territorio y cartografía urbana: reflexiones sobre el mapa como producto cultural. Dirección de Bibiana Cicutti. Rosario, Argentina: Facultad de Arquitectura, Planeamiento y Diseño, Univ. Nacional de Rosario; Buenos Aires: Nobuko, 2008. 136 p.: bibl., ill., maps. (Serie Publicaciones de cátedra)

Seven architects from the Universidad Nacional de Rosario contribute to this conventional rumination on cartography as a form of social discourse and as a mechanism for producing regional identity, with particular emphasis on the city of Rosario, Argentina, from 1852 to 1935.

931 Craviotti, Clara. Tensiones entre una ruralidad productiva y otra residencial: el caso del partido de Exaltación de la Cruz, Buenos Aires, Argentina. (*Econ. Soc. Territ.*, 6:23, enero/abril 2007, p. 745–772, bibl., tables)

Since the 1970s, and intensifying in the 1990s, rural spaces are becoming fragmented as part of a postproductivist transition. A large influx of new residents is causing tension with primary producers. An unexpected component of the new rurality is the revitalization of aviculture and an increase in landscape heterogeneity.

932 Encuentro de Geohistoria Regional, 26th, Resistencia, Argentina, 2006. Actas. Coordinación de Hugo Humberto Beck y María Laura Salinas. Resistencia, Argentina: Instituto de Investigaciones Geohistóricas-CONICET: Secretaría General de Extensión Univ.-UNNE, 2007. 585 p.: bibl., ill., maps.

A subset of 65 papers from the proceedings of the annual conference that focuses on northeastern Argentina (Gran Chaco, Santa Fe, and Entre Rios). The dense volume (no index) presents an eclectic mix of topics from the humanities and social sciences.

Gaffney, Christopher Thomas. Temples of the earthbound gods: stadiums in the cultural landscapes of Rio de Janeiro and Buenos Aires. See item **992.**

933 Hocsman, Luis Daniel. Territorialidad campesina y economía de subsistencia. (*Estudios/Córdoba*, 19, primavera 2006, p. 91–102, bibl.)

The forces of capitalism are causing pressures and changes to forms of communal land tenure, agrarian production, and social relations among "Kolla" peasants in the province of Salta. The author draws on secondary literature to argue that there has been a redefinition of use and control of local natural resources, a process he names reterritorialization.

934 Jornadas Interdisciplinarias del Sudoeste Bonaerense, 5th, Bahía Blanca, Argentina, 2008. Ambientes y recursos naturales del sudoeste bonaerense: producción, contaminación y conservación: actas. Edición de Néstor J. Cazzaniga y Hugo M. Arelovich. Bahía Blanca, Argentina: Editorial de la Univ. Nacional del Sur, 2009. 513 p.: bibl., ill., maps.

Thirty-eight papers focus on nature-society relationships in southwestern Buenos Aires province. Representing a subset of a broader 2008 conference on the region, the book is an eclectic collection of brief introductions to natural resource management issues. It lacks an index, however, and does not include a discussion of overarching lessons from the body of work it presents.

935 Kanitscheider, Sigrun. Diferenciación socioespacial en la periferia argentina, el ejemplo de San Salvador de Jujuy. (*Rev. Geogr. Norte Gd.*, 37, junio 2007, p. 23–33, bibl., maps)

Using factor analysis of census data (1960–2000), the author studies the provincial capital in northernmost Argentina and identifies ways in which urban development there differs from common urban structures (e.g., dispersal of commercial centers, rise of gated communities) found in larger Latin American cities. A clear framework for comparative analysis is lacking, however.

936 Kentor Corby, Julia H. For members and markets: neoliberalism and co-operativism in Mendoza's wine industry. (*J. Lat. Am. Geogr.*, 9:2, 2010, p. 27–47)

The Federación de Cooperativas Vitivinícolas Argentinas (FeCoVitA) was formed in 1990 and consists of 3,000 producers. While the cooperative represents a concentration of power in the industry, a potential cause for concern, it has maintained benefits to its members, capitalized on the privatization of Argentine state wineries, and fostered innovation in the wine sector.

937 Miniconi, Renaud and **Sylvain Guyot.** Conflits et coopérations en territoire montagnard Mapuche, Argentine: les cas du Parc National Nahuel Huapi. (*Rev. géogr. alp.*, 98:1, 2010, p. 123–153, bibl., maps, photos)

The potential for comanagement of the Nahuel Huapi National Park may provide opportunities for indigenous groups to achieve legal recognition and land access. Sounding an optimistic tone, and in contrast to the way parks are often characterized for fostering conflict, the paper considers parks as tools that indigenous people may use to achieve greater rights.

938 Newell, Peter. Bio-hegemony: the political economy of agricultural biotechnology in Argentina. (*J. Lat. Am. Stud.*, 41:1, Feb. 2009, p. 27–57)

This important and well-argued paper draws on extensive interviews with state and market actors. Proponents and producers of agricultural biotechnology have ensured an almost total absence of opposition to the technology due to the industry's significant contributions to the state economy and its continued access to, and influence over, state decision-makers and the media.

939 Page, Carlos A. El espacio público en las ciudades hispanoamericanas: el caso de Córdoba, Argentina, siglos XVI a XVIII. Córdoba, Argentina: Junta Provincial de Historia de Córdoba; Santiago: Sociedad Chilena de Historia y Geografía, 2008. 361 p.: bibl., ill., map. (Serie Libros; 28)

The author presents an accessible review of theoretical debates about the role that public spaces play in the social fabric of cities in Latin America, and develops a rich case study of colonial Córdoba. The text is well referenced and nicely complemented by maps, photographs, paintings, and images of historical texts.

940 Pastorino, María Inés; Guillermo Odstrcil; and **Albert Casas.** Estudio gravimétrico preliminar sobre una zona afectada por problemas de subsidencia en la proximidad de El Timbó, Tucumán, Argentina. (*Rev. Geofís.*, 61, 2005, p. 69–79, bibl., graphs, ill., maps, photos)

In a poorly referenced study, the authors describe the after effects of salt mining and associated land subsidence. They argue that the use of a gravity survey is an important, nondestructive technique for the study of subsurface processes, although comparison with alternative methodologies is not clearly presented.

941 Perren, Joaquín. Migraciones y patrones residenciales en el Neuquén aluvional, 1970–1990. (*Estud. Migr. Latinoam.*, 21:63, agosto 2007, p. 331–365, bibl., tables)

Incorporating an analysis of 2,500 marriage certificates, the author (a historian) describes the creation of a distinct pattern of new neighborhoods. He then argues, somewhat loosely, that although these urban spaces were clearly defined by social strata and region of origin they nonetheless served as catalysts for cultural exchange between different groups of people.

942 Región Centro: desarrollo sustentable con equidad. Coordinación del Dr. Juan A. Roccatagliata. Colaboración de la Organización TECHINT. Buenos Aires: Docencia: Fundación Hernandarias, 2006. 3 v., 1425 p.: bibl., ill., maps.

The Centro de Estudios para el Desarrollo Territorial y la Gestión de la Infraestructura is a working group created under the auspices of the Academia Nacional de Geografía and the Fundación Hernandarias to identify strategic planning and development goals for the regions of Argentina. A subset of this larger project, the three volumes here focus on the provinces of Córdoba, Santa Fe, and Entre Ríos. In 30 chapters, two dozen contributors document the social and environmental conditions and problems of the region, emphasizing social welfare, energy, tourism, infrastructure, and natural resource management. They advocate for clear, strategic regional planning and present an agenda guided by key questions, challenges, and goals. Despite the title, a scholarly interpretation of sustainable development does not guide the work. Instead, representing a call to arms, the target audience seems to be, primarily, policy-makers. The quality of the graphics is sometimes poor and the volumes lack an index. See also item **1443**.

943 Ríos, Diego and **Pedro Pírez.** Urbanizaciones cerradas en áreas inundables del municipio de Tigre: ¿producción de espacio urbano de alta calidad ambiental? (*EURE/Santiago*, 34:101, abril 2008, p. 99–119, bibl., maps)

Explores the private production of urban space and the ecology of gated communities. Contrary to the way they are legitimated in public discourse as environmentally sustainable developments, some 3,300 hectares on the floodplain were occupied by gated communities in 2001, which negatively affects ecosystem services and puts the population at risk to flood hazards.

944 Rodríguez, Javier Leonel. Consecuencias económicas de la soja transgénica: Argentina, 1996–2006. Buenos Aires: Ediciones Cooperativas: CLACSO, 2008. 290 p.: bibl., ill.

Well-researched and using two case studies (from the provinces of Chaco and Córdoba), the book critiques the methodology used by the Food and Agriculture Organization (FAO) to evaluate the economic impacts of expanding genetically modified (GM) crop use. The author presents an alternative approach, but fails to justify sidestepping key debates about GM crops, environment, food security, and social justice.

945 Salmenkari, Taru. Geography of protest: places of demonstration in Buenos Aires and Seoul. (*Urban Geogr.*, 30:3, April/May 2009, p. 239–260, bibl., maps)

Demonstrations in Argentina reflect an internationally shared demonstration culture that determines place suitability. In Buenos Aires, most protest locations are chosen to maximize the capacity to communicate with authorities as well as for their public appeal, such as places connected with a grievance or symbolic meaning. The author presents a nuanced discussion of protest geography.

946 Vereda, Marisol. Tierra del Fuego y Antártica: un inventario de recursos turísticos desde la idea de complementariedad de destino. (*Estud. Perspect. Turismo*, 17:3/4, julio/oct. 2008, p. 199–225, bibl., maps)

Tierra del Fuego not only represents a gateway for visitors to Antarctica, but there are material and symbolic connections between the two places that should resonate with tourists. Opportunities abound on the island to consider how geology, flora, cartography, and explorer accounts connect Antarctica's history with that of the southern tip of South America.

Viajes y geografías: exploraciones, turismo y migraciones en la construcción de lugares. See item **712**.

947 Whitson, Rita. "The reality of today has required us to change": negotiating gender through informal work in contemporary Argentina. (*Ann. Assoc. Am. Geogr.*, 100:1, Jan. 2010, p. 159–181, bibl., tables)

Based on interviews conducted in 2002 with informal workers, the author analyzes the practice and effects of informal work on individuals and families during a period of economic crisis. She concludes that these effects require understanding not only socioeconomic class, but also changing gendered norms and performances.

948 Zusman, Perla; Hortensia Castro; and **Mercedes Soto.** Cultural and social geography in Argentina: precedents and recent trends. (*Soc. Cult. Geogr.*, 8:5, Oct. 2007, p. 775–798, bibl.)

The relatively small amount of scholarship in the human geography realm is linked to the periodic disruption of democratic governments in the country. By the 1960s, landscape, forms of human settlement, toponymy, and cultural diversity were important themes under investigation. Today, theoretical-epistemological and empirical approaches are both prominent, with social inequality, feminist geography, environmental change, both rural and urban studies, and tourism receiving considerable attention.

CHILE

949 **Álvarez Rojas, Ana María.** La segmentación socioeconómica del espacio: la comunidad ecológica y la toma de Peñalolén. (*EURE/Santiago*, 34:101, abril 2008, p. 121–136, bibl.)

Using qualitative methods to study citizen declarations communicated via newspapers, the author argues that social identity and distinction fundamentally define the nature and perception of conflict over the location, development, and character of gated communities and public and private spaces.

950 **Arenas, Federico.** El Chile de las regiones: una historia inconclusa. (*Estud. Geogr./Madrid*, 70:266, enero/junio 2009, p. 11–30, bibl.)

In a largely descriptive review of the development of Chile's political regions from the 1820s to the present, the author argues that the process of decentralizing Chile's state institutions is incomplete. There are challenges to overcome, such as top-down decision-making processes that result in antagonism between the central government and regional officials.

951 **Azócar Zamudio, Andrés.** Tompkins: el millonario verde. Santiago: Univ. Diego Portales, Escuela de Periodismo: Copa Rota, 2007. 315 p.: bibl. (Col. tal cual)

Targeting a general audience, this journalist's accessible account of the controversial American and environmentalist, Douglas Tompkins, explores environmental activism and politics in Chile. For those interested in environment and development debates about Patagonia, and the many actors involved, the book is essential reading. Scholars will miss the lack of both a bibliography and an index.

952 **Barton, Jonathan R.; Robert N. Gwynne;** and **Warwick E. Murray.** Competition and co-operation in the semi-periphery: closer economic partnership and sectoral transformations in Chile and New Zealand. (*Geogr. J./London*, 173:3, Sept. 2007, p. 224–241, bibl., ill., maps, tables)

The article analyzes the potential impacts of the strategic economic partnership (the Trans-Pacific SEP or P4, which was signed by Chile, New Zealand, Singapore, and Brunei Darussalam in 2005) on the dairy, wine, and fisheries sectors, export markets that generate limited geopolitical tensions. A thoughtful paper that argues that the P4 may represent the kind of cooperation, rather than competition, periphery economies need to open or maintain competitiveness in international markets.

953 **Barton, Jonathan R.; Robert N. Gwynne;** and **Warwick E. Murray.** Transformations in resource peripheries: an analysis of the Chilean experience. (*Area/London*, 40:1, March 2008, p. 24–33, bibl.)

Uneven development in Chile is fundamentally linked to its status as a resource periphery. Structuralist-informed political-economic analysis is deemed essential to understanding patterns of development, producing more inclusive scholarship in economic geography, and helping to transform legacies of dependency and exploitation into more sustainable development models. A well-argued, compelling call for re-energized scholarship on economic geography in the region.

954 **Bellisario, Antonio.** The Chilean agrarian transformation: agrarian reform and capitalist "partial" counter-agrarian reform, 1964–1980. Part 1, Reformism, socialism and free-market neoliberalism. (*J. Agrarian Change*, 7:1, Jan. 2007, p. 1–34, bibl.)

A superb analysis of the logic employed in three key phases of reform and the impacts that the new policies had on Chile's agrarian structure. Drawing on the recently available archive of the country's Corporación de la Reforma Agraria (the state planning agency for agrarian reform), the author shows clearly how the redistribution of previously expropriated agricultural land led to the creation of a dynamic agricultural sector, albeit one that became highly exclusionary under military rule. Essential reading for scholars of Chilean agricultural policy.

955 **Borsdorf, Axel** and **Rodrigo Hidalgo.** Searching for fresh air, tranquility and rural culture in the mountains: new lifestyle for Chileans? (*Erde/Berlin*, 140, 2009, p. 275–292, bibl., maps, photos, tables)

Part of a special issue on the global phenomenon of amenity migration, the article develops two case studies on the rural outskirts of Santiago, Chile. The authors identify factors driving the development of *parcelas de agrados* (pleasure lots) and, drawing largely on conjecture, evaluate their economic and social benefits and costs.

956 **Budds, Jessica.** Contested H20: science, policy and politics in water resources management in Chile. (*Geoforum/ New York*, 40:3, May 2009, p. 418–430, bibl., graph, map)

A case study on the La Ligua river basin, located in Chile's semi-arid Norte Chico region, exposes how environmental science and technocratic assessments are privileged in water management policy. This excellent article underscores how science is not neutral or apolitical, and promotes the incorporation of the public in decision-making processes.

957 **Calderón Squadrito, Alfonso.** Memorial de la Estación Mapocho. Colaboración de Lila Calderón y Lila Díaz. Santiago: RIL editores, 2005. 222 p.: bibl., ill.

The author presents a history and celebration of Santiago's emblematic terminal, which was closed to trains in the 1980s but that remains a fundamental part of the city's cultural landscape. The lack of an index makes the book somewhat hard to navigate.

958 **Calderón Squadrito, Alfonso.** Memorial de Santiago. Providencia, Chile: RiL Editores, 2005. 294 p.: bibl., ill., maps. (Crónicas)

A breezy reflection on the cultural history of some of Santiago's most celebrated places, such as El Parque Forestal and El Teatro Municipal. The book is best enjoyed by readers familiar with the city who will appreciate the quirky collection of images and affectionate anecdotes about daily life.

959 **Camus, Pablo; Sergio Castro;** and **Fabián Jaksic.** El conejo europeo en Chile: historia de una invasión biológica. (*Historia/Santiago*, 41:2, julio/dic. 2008, p. 305–339, tables)

Rabbits were introduced to central Chile by the mid-18th century where they were celebrated initially for their economic benefits (meat and skins). After their spread to southernmost Chile, concerns about environment and the rural economy led to 20th-century eradication campaigns, which included the use of the virus myxomatosis.

960 **López-Morales, Ernesto José.** Real estate market, state entrepreneurialism and urban policy in the "gentrification by ground rest dispossession" of Santiago de Chile. (*J. Lat. Am. Geogr.*, 9:1, 2010, p. 145–173)

Provides a concise review of theoretical perspectives on gentrification and urban entrepreneurialism. The author develops a new concept to show that neighborhood change and development in Santiago's Urban Renewal Subsidy Area is a product of class monopolization of potential ground rents and other factors not normally captured by conventional narratives of gentrification.

961 **Meza, Laura E.** Mapuche struggles for land and the role of private protected areas in Chile. (*J. Lat. Am. Geogr.*, 8:1, 2009, p. 149–163, bibl., maps)

Nature conservation is used as a political tool by both big landowners and indigenous groups to gain territorial control. The author argues, somewhat loosely, that creating indigenous private parks may advance both indigenous rights and conservation goals.

962 **Olave F., Didima** and **Julia Fawaz.** Calidad de vida rural a inicios del siglo XXI: análisis de caso en comunas de la provincia de Ñuble, región del Bío Bío, Chile. (*Rev. Geogr./México*, 143, enero/junio 2008, p. 29–46, bibl., graphs, map, tables)

A life quality index incorporates 10 variables that include housing and infrastructure, education, economic information, communication, and recreation dimensions. Overall, indicators of well-being show an improving quality of life for people in the three regions studied.

963 Peña Muñoz, Manuel. Chile, memorial de la tierra larga: crónicas. 2. ed. Santiago: RIL, 2008. 397 p.: ill.

Contributing to South America's rich tradition in travel writing, the author celebrates the diversity of Chile's physical and human geography, supplemented with photographs that are primarily his own. In a sentimental personal narrative, he offers his perceptions and descriptions of social life.

964 Raposo Moyano, Alfonso. Estado, ethos social y política de vivienda. Santiago: RiL Editores, 2008. 149 p.: bibl., ill., maps. (Ensayos & estudios)

The author is director of El Centro de Estudios Arquitectónicos, Urbanísticos y del Paisaje at the Universidad Central de Chile. Part of a larger project tracing the history of architecture in Chile, the book provides an overview of the development of the state and housing policy until the year 1976.

965 Sagredo Baeza, Rafael. Geografía y nación: Claudio Gay y la primera representación cartográfica de Chile. (*Estud. Geogr./Madrid*, 70:266, enero/junio 2009, p. 231–267, bibl., maps)

French naturalist Claudio Gay was hired in 1830 by the Chilean government to study the country's territory and resources. As part of the author's overview of Gay's work, he presents an insightful exploration of maps as instruments in nation-building and the formation of regional identities.

966 Santana Ulloa, Roberto. Agricultura chilena en el siglo XX: contextos, actores y espacios agrícolas. Osorno, Chile: Centro de Estudios Regionales, Univ. de los Lagos; Santiago: Centro de Investigaciones Diego Barros Arana, 2006. 338 p.: bibl., ill., maps. (Col. Sociedad y cultura; 43)

The book is a thoughtful contribution to understanding agrarian change. It presents a critical analysis of select elements in the evolution of Chilean agriculture and rural development, and critiques the conventional way in which the agrarian crisis in Chile is characterized. A key theme exposes the social and political exclusion of rural workers and peasants.

967 Tecklin, David; Carl Bauer; and **Manuel Prieto.** Making environmental law for the market: the emergence, character, and implications of Chile's environmental regime. (*Environ. Polit.*, 20:6, Nov. 2011, p. 879–898, bibl.)

In analyzing the growth of environmental policy in Chile, the authors conclude that a primary emphasis on economic neoliberal principles has led to weak regulatory oversight and an environmental regime that expresses a strongly market-enabling quality.

PARAGUAY

968 Huang, Chengquan *et al.* Assessment of Paraguay's forest cover change using Landsat observations. (*Glob. Planet. Change*, 67:1/2, May 2009, p. 1–12, bibl., ill., maps, photos, tables)

Using satellite imagery and aerial photographs, the authors produce a high quality remote sensing analysis of forest cover change from the 1970s to the 2000s. The Atlantic Forest ecoregion experienced a dramatic loss of 73.4 percent cover in the 1970s, dropping to 24.9 percent by the 2000s. The authors also identify driving forces of change and efforts at forest protection.

969 Kleinpenning, J.M.G. Rural Paraguay 1870–1963: a geography of progress, plunder and poverty. Madrid: Iberoamericana; Frankfurt am Main, Germany: Vervuert, 2009. 2 v.: bibl., ill., indexes, maps. (Bibliotheca Ibero-americana)

Devastation in Paraguay at the end of the War of the Triple Alliance in 1870 led to the massive sale of government land to individuals to raise yerba mate, tobacco, cotton, and cattle, and also to exploit quebracho wood. With the aim of repopulating the countryside, the government also opened the door to the establishment of more than 100 ethnic colonies, among them German, Italian, Japanese, and Australian. Fine reconstruction of nearly a century of rural land and life in a country still marked by those two decisions. For comment on earlier publication by J.M.G. Kleinpenning, see *HLAS 61:1849.* For political economist's comment, see item **2127.** [D.W. Gade]

970 Quintana, Jesus and **Stephen Morse.** Social interactions and resource ownership in two private protected areas of Paraguay. (*J. Environ. Manag.*, 77:1, Oct. 2005, p. 64–78, bibl., ill, maps, photos, tables)

A private reserve owned by an NGO is compared with a publicly managed reserve, both located in the Atlantic Forest ecoregion. The authors analyze social interactions between stakeholders in each of the reserve areas and find that inequality in land ownership, which fosters land invasion, is the most significant threat to conservation in both cases.

BRAZIL

CHRISTIAN BRANNSTROM, *Associate Professor of Geography, Texas A&M University*

COLONIAL-ERA RIO DE JANEIRO, urbanism, and land reform were major themes in geographical scholarship, partially eclipsing the Amazonian environment-development theme noted in *HLAS 65*. The single most prominent outstanding work is Maurício Abreu's magnificent two-volume historical geography of Rio de Janeiro from the early 1500s to 1700, situating Guanabara Bay within colonial territorial and commercial processes while detailing urban processes (item **971**). Abreu's study period covers the establishment of Portuguese colonial rule and the development of a Rio de Janeiro that was relatively poor and reliant on sugarcane production. After 1700, Rio became increasingly wealthy through strengthened commercial ties to mineral extraction in Minas Gerais and the importation of African slaves. Abreu's study is strongly empirical, based on 15 years of archival research in Europe and Brazil; especially important is Abreu's work with some 500 *livros de notas*, found in Rio's Arquivo Nacional, which document transactions relating to thousands of land-based assets. The high production quality of the volumes' illustrations (maps, sketches, photographs, and documents) is noteworthy.

Brazil's urban geography was the focus of two major works, one on soccer stadiums by Christopher Gaffney (item **992**), and the other an edited collection of essays on several Brazilian cities (item **981**). Gaffney's book looks at Rio de Janeiro and Buenos Aires. In the part devoted to Rio, he studies four of the city's stadiums, proposing that soccer offers a glimpse into Brazilian urbanism and the globalization process. Gaffney shows how soccer went from an elite to a popular practice and how stadiums became part of a network of urban social spaces. *Contemporary Urbanism in Brazil: Beyond Brasília* (item **981**), a beautifully illustrated work, is another important contribution to Brazilian urbanism. This collection of essays, covering Brasília, Curitiba, Palmas, Rio de Janeiro, Salvador, and São Paulo, is concerned with architectural styles, the origin and development of urban revitalization projects, and various social inclusion policies designed for cities. The book invites readers to think of Brazilian urban planning throughout the country and to consider the many lessons that the cases offer to urban planning and urban geography more broadly. Other important urban geographical work focused on Fortaleza, the site of Linda Maria Gondim's impressive study of the Dragão do Mar center (item **996**) and Jeff Garmany's work on state-society relations in a slum area (items **993** and **994**).

Land reform was the subject of Wendy Wolford's book (item **1037**) on Brazil's landless movement, the Movimento dos Trabalhadores Rurais Sem Terra (MST).

The MST grew from isolated land occupations in the late 1970s and early 1980s to emerge as Latin America's largest social movement by the late 1990s, enjoying the increasing support of Brazil's middle classes while playing a major role in pro-peasant international networks against neoliberal policies. Wolford's ethnographic account of the MST focuses on sites in Santa Catarina and Pernambuco states. She argues that the MST has obtained limited success in organizing production and maintaining peasants as MST members. Particularly important is Wolford's con-trast between the agrarian populism promoted by the MST and the on-the-ground reality of rural settlements, as well as her insight into how land itself has variable meaning depending on the political and moral economies of settlements.

Another impressive study joined Wolford's book in contributing to agrar-ian studies: Cynthia Simmons and colleagues studied direct-action land reform (DLAR)—in which the MST is a key player, but certainly not the only organiza-tion involved—using a household survey in Amazonian settlements (item **1024**). They distinguished between DLAR led by social movement organizations (SMOs) and the "spontaneous" DLAR. An SMO-led DLAR is more likely to occur on pri-vate land, obtain assistance from the state, and practice improved cropping strate-gies, while a spontaneous DLAR is more likely to occupy forest land and obtain relatively little from the state. Other important work in agrarian issues includes an edited volume dedicated to geographer Ariovaldo Umbelino de Oliveira (item **995**) and Ben Selwyn's scholarship on the Petrolina-Juazeiro export-oriented irri-gated agriculture (items **1019**, **1020**, **1021**, and **1022**).

Major contributions to the Amazon environment-development theme include a high-profile paper by Robert Walker and colleagues (item **1033**) argu-ing that a "climate-tipping point" could be prevented by policies that maintain Amazonia's protected areas, which cover approximately one-fourth of the legal Amazon's land area. Britaldo Soares-Filho and colleagues (item **1025**) published a similarly important paper, arguing that Amazonian protected areas are poten-tially useful for maintaining forest cover, but they emphasized the importance of finding economic incentives to counter the potential lost income due to forest preservation. Scholars also devote attention to the intersection between liveli-hoods and resource conflicts (items **973**, **1002**, **1013**, and **1029**) and the dramatic increase in the size of the Amazon cattle herd (item **1034**). Finally, an edited collection focuses the impacts of hydroelectric projects in the Xingu River ba-sin added substantially to the Amazonian environment-development theme (item **1027**).

971 Abreu, Maurício de Almeida. Geo-grafia histórica do Rio de Janeiro: 1502–1700. Rio de Janeiro: Andrea Jakobsson Estúdio Editorial Ltda., 2010. 2 v.: ill.

Study of early colonial Rio de Ja-neiro and Guanabara Bay, focusing on co-lonial territorial, commercial, and urban processes. Uses wide-ranging empirical sources and includes very high quality illustrations.

972 Ab'Sáber, Aziz Nacib. Brasil, paisa-gens de exceção: o litoral e o Pantanal Mato-Grossense, patrimônios básicos. São Paulo: Ateliê Editorial, 2006. 182 p.: bibl., ill. (some col.), maps. (Textos básicos)

Study by Brazil's pre-eminent physi-cal geographer on the geomorphology of Pantanal and coastal regions.

973 Almeida, Alfredo Wagner Berno de; Joaquim Shiraishi Neto; and Cynthia Carvalho Martins. Guerra ecológica nos babaçuais: o processo de devastação do pal-meirais, a elevação do preço de *commodities* e o aquecimento do mercado de terras na Amazônia. São Luís, Brazil: MIQCB/Balaios Typ., 2005. 186 p.: bibl., ill.

Study of issues arising from the babaçu economy in Maranhão, Pará, Piauí, and Tocantins states, with emphasis to the appropriation of babaçu lands by ranchers, soy farmers, paper-pulp firms, and charcoal producers. Argues that these competing land uses are destroying babaçu lands and causing negative impacts on livelihoods. Analysis of "social cartography" focuses on case studies of conflict zones.

The Amazon várzea: the decade past and the decade ahead. See item **547**.

974 Amazonian dark earths: Wim Sombroek's vision. Edited by William I. Woods *et al.* New York, N.Y.: Springer Dordrecht, 2008. 502 p.

Multidisciplinary essays covering several academic disciplines regarding Amazonian Dark Earth (ADE), such as the development of academic inquiry on ADE, implications of ADE for knowledge of pre-European settlement in the Amazon, and cultural processes that may have created ADE. For archeologist's comment, see item **313**.

975 Arnauld de Sartre, Xavier and **Romain Taravella.** National sovereignty vs. sustainable development lessons from the narrative on the internationalization of the Brazilian Amazon. (*Polit. Geogr.*, 28:7, Sept. 2009, p. 406–415)

Analysis of internationalization discourses relating to the Amazon. Outlines the history of anti-internationalization and explores uses of anti-internationalization through a case in the eastern Amazon during the mid-2000s, when landowners' groups contested the creation of a protected area.

976 Azevedo, Genoveva Chagas de. Representações sociais de meio ambiente: a Reserva Florestal Adolpho Ducke. Manaus, Brazil: Fundação de Amparo à Pesquisa do Estado de Amazonas: Editora da Univ. Federal do Amazonas: Editora INPA, 2007. 210 p.: bibl., ill., maps. (Biblioteca científica da Amazônia)

Analysis of perceptions of the Adolpho Ducke Forest Reserve, north of Manaus, contrasting a sample of researchers from the Instituto Nacional de Pesquisas na Amazônia and residents from the Cidade de Deus district bordering the reserve. Residents

from Cidade de Deus, which began as a squatter settlement but has been upgraded, have significantly different views of the reserve compared to Amazonian researchers, who use the reserve for scientific study.

977 Barberia, Lorena G. and **Ciro Biderman.** Local economic development: theory, evidence, and implications for policy in Brazil. (*Geoforum/New York*, 41:6, Nov. 2010, p. 951–962)

Studies municipal-scale economic development policies, with concern for fiscal mechanisms and intended outcomes, such as industrial clusters.

978 Brannstrom, Christian. Forests for cotton: institutions and organizations in Brazil's mid-twentieth century cotton boom. (*J. Hist. Geogr.*, 36:2, 2010, p. 169–182)

Argues that cotton expansion in São Paulo state during the 1930s and 1940s responded to institutional and organizational reforms. Cotton expanded at the expense of forested lands, or a "forest rent," and relied on share-tenant social relations.

979 Brannstrom, Christian. South America's neoliberal agricultural frontiers: places of environmental sacrifice or conservation opportunity? (*Ambio/ Stockholm*, 38:3, May 2009, p. 141–149)

Analysis of land-use and land-cover change in western Bahia state from 1979 to 2005, emphasizing how Cerrado conversion to agriculture increased during a period of increased attention to environmental impacts of Cerrado clearance.

980 Cabral, Diogo de Carvalho. Floresta, política e trabalho: a exploração das madeiras-de-lei no Recôncavo da Guanabara, 1760–1820. (*Rev. Bras. Hist./São Paulo*, 28:55, jan./junho 2008, p. 217–241)

Analyzes the timber industry for naval shipbuilding around Rio de Janeiro using varied archival sources, mainly to reconstruct labor relations between workers and landowners.

981 Contemporary urbanism in Brazil: beyond Brasília. Edited by Vicente del Rio and William J. Siembieda. Foreword by Jon Lang. Gainesville: Univ. Press of Florida, 2009. 331 p.: bibl., ill., index, maps.

Collection of essays on Brasília, Curitiba, Palmas, Rio de Janeiro, Salvador, and

São Paulo relating to themes of late modernism, revitalization projects, and social inclusion policies. High-quality illustrations contribute to the analysis of urban processes and policies, such as the program to revitalize Salvador's Pelourinho, processes of verticalization, and São Paulo's shopping malls.

982 Coriolano, Luzia Neide Menêzes Teixeira and **Fábio Perdigão Vasconcelos.** O turismo e a relação sociedade-natureza: realidades, conflitos e resistências. Fortaleza, Brazil: EdUECE, 2007. 439 p.: bibl., ill., maps.

Essays cover a wide range of geographical aspects of tourism, with a special focus on cultural and environmental impacts on Brazil's northeast coast. Noteworthy chapters discuss Fortaleza's tourism economy and Ceará's policy for tourism development.

983 Cunha, Alexandre Mendes. No sertão, o lugar das minas: reflexões sobre a formação do espaço central das Minas Gerais no começo do século XVIII. (*Estud. Hist./Rio de Janeiro,* 40, julho/dez. 2007, p. 25–45, bibl.)

Studies early 18th-century notions of space and territory in Minas Gerais, arguing for the importance of cities in mediating society and nature relations.

984 Da Cunha, José Marcos P. *et al.* Social segregation and academic achievement in state-run elementary schools in the municipality of Campinas, Brazil. (*Geoforum/New York,* 40:5, Sept. 2009, p. 873–883)

Analysis of effects of segregation on school performance, comparing different regions of a large metropolitan area on the basis of poverty and wealth. Reports significant differences in test performance based on school location.

985 Dantas, Aldo. Pierre Monbeig: um marco de geografia brasileira. Porto Alegre, Brazil: Editora Sulina, 2005. 142 p.: bibl.

Concise intellectual biography of French geographer Pierre Monbeig, who exerted a major role in the development of the study of geography at the Universidade de São Paulo. Discusses Monbeig's idea of the "pioneer fringe" and subsequent critiques. Includes reprinted articles and a 1979 interview with a reporter for *Estado de São Paulo* newspaper.

986 Encontro Nacional da ANPEGE, 6th, Fortaleza, Brazil, 2005. Panorama da geografia brasileira. Organização de José Borzacchiello da Silva, Luiz Cruz Lima e Denise Elias. São Paulo: Annablume: Associação Nacional de Pós-Graduação e Pesquisa em Geografia, 2006. 2 v.: bibl., ill., maps.

Collection of essays covering a wide range of topics studied by Brazilian geographers, including tourism, urban processes, human-environment issues, agricultural dynamics, use of geographic information, and geography education.

987 Encontro Nacional de Turismo com Base Local, 10th, João Pessoa, Paraíba, Brazil, 2007. Turismo de base local: identidade cultural e desenvolvimento regional. Organização de Giovanni Seabra. João Pessoa, Brazil: Editora Universitária, 2007. 356 p.: bibl.

Collection of essays showing critical perspectives on tourism development with respect to place-based concerns. Essays cover the use of Candomblé in the marketing of Salvador and municipal-level tourism planning.

988 Extrativismo da Samambaia-Preta no Rio Grande do Sul. Organização de Gabriela Coelho de Souza, Rumi Regina Kubo e Lovois de Andrade Miguel. Textos de Adelar Mantovani *et al.* Porto Alegre, Brazil: UFRGS Editora, 2008. 263 p.: bibl., ill., maps. (Série Estudos e pesquisas—IEPE)

Collection of essays covers aspects of the ornamental plant known as seven-weeks-fern (samambaia-preta) obtained from southern Brazil's Atlantic Forest. Legal, ecological, and livelihood issues are topics of chapters. Argues that proper management of extraction could lead to positive outcomes for conservation of the Atlantic Forest.

989 Fernandes, Bernardo Mançano; Clifford Andrew Welch; and **Elienaí Constantino Gonçalves.** Agrofuel policies in Brazil: paradigmatic and territorial disputes. (*J. Peasant Stud.,* 37:4, Oct. 2010, p. 793–819)

Analysis of land conflicts between agrarian reform settlements and biofuel projects in the Pontal do Paranapanema region in São Paulo state, indicating that social movements have tried to create their own biofuels programs.

990 Freire-Medeiros, Bianca. The favela and its touristic transits. (*Geoforum*/ New York, 40:4, July 2009, p. 580–588)

Analysis of favela tourism focusing on the Rocinha area of Rio de Janeiro. Interprets favela tourism as a process that transforms poverty into a commodity and as a site that encourages multiple representations.

991 Gaffney, Christopher Thomas. Mega-events and socio-spatial dynamics in Rio de Janeiro, 1919–2016. (*J. Lat. Am. Geogr.*, 9:1, 2010, p. 7–29)

Comparison of the ideologies that underpin large international sporting events in Rio de Janeiro, changing from social inclusion to neoliberal orientations.

992 Gaffney, Christopher Thomas. Temples of the earthbound gods: stadiums in the cultural landscapes of Rio de Janeiro and Buenos Aires. Austin: Univ. of Texas Press, 2008. 259 p.: bibl., ill., index.

Study of soccer stadiums in Rio de Janeiro and Buenos Aires as social spaces. For Rio, Gaffney traces the history of soccer in Brazil and the development of four stadiums during the 20th century.

993 Garmany, Jeff. The embodied state: governmentality in a Brazilian favela. (*Soc. Cult. Geogr.*, 10:7, Nov. 2009, p. 721–739)

Study of the reach of the state in a favela in Fortaleza, based on ethnographic research and informed by Foucault's notion of governmentality. Concern is with how everyday practices of favela residents change in spaces associated with the state.

994 Garmany, Jeff. Religion and governmentality: understanding governance in urban Brazil. (*Geoforum*/New York, 41:6, Nov. 2010, p. 908–918)

Focuses on how spaces of religion and churches help create new forms of subjectivity among favela residents of Fortaleza.

995 Geografia agrária: teoria e poder. Organização de Bernardo Mançano Fernandes, Marta Inez Medeiros Marques e Julio Cesar Suzuki. São Paulo: Expressão Popular, 2007. 382 p.: bibl., ill. (Geografia em movimento)

Collection of essays on agrarian geography dedicated to Ariovaldo Umbelino de Oliveira, a prominent scholar. Essays focus on Oliveira's intellectual trajectory and policies and challenges for family farming.

996 Gondim, Linda Maria de Pontes. O Dragão do Mar e a Fortaleza pós-moderna: cultura, patrimônio e imagem da cidade. São Paulo: Annablume, 2006. 240 p.: bibl., ill.

Study of urban processes beginning in the late 1970s in Fortaleza, which aimed to make the city a tourist destination. Special attention is given to the Dragão do Mar cultural center, which was the focus of redevelopment efforts. Study also considers the visitors to the Dragão do Mar in terms of demographic characteristics and experience at the center.

997 História ambiental paulista: temas, fontes e métodos. Organização de Paulo Henrique Martinez. São Paulo: Editora Senac São Paulo, 2007. 304 p.: bibl., ill.

Essays on the environmental history of São Paulo state cover topics ranging from domestic gardens, public water supply, and coffee to hydroelectricity and clay.

998 Ioris, Antonio A.R. The political nexus between water and economics in Brazil: a critique of recent policy reforms. (*Rev. Radic. Polit. Econ.*, 42:2, June 2010, p. 231–250)

Critical review of water reforms, arguing that reforms have neither prevented water conflicts nor avoided degradation of water resources. Indicates that use of the market in several aspects is the main cause for poor outcomes of reforms.

999 Ioris, Antonio A.R. Water reforms in Brazil: opportunities and constraints. (*J. Environ. Plann. Manag.*, 52:6, Sept. 2009, p. 813–832)

Case study of the Paraíba do Sul basin, showing how the prioritization of water pricing policies undermined other aspects of water reforms, with negative consequences for water management.

1000 Jepson, Wendy E.; Christian Brannstrom; and Anthony M. Filippi. Access regimes and regional land change in the

Brazilian Cerrado, 1972–2002. (*Ann. Assoc. Am. Geogr.*, 100:1, Jan. 2010, p. 87–111)

Patterns and processes of land-cover and land-use change are explained with reference to eastern Mato Grosso state. Stresses the influence of meso-scale institutions in determining land-use outcomes.

1001 Jorge, Janes. Tietê, o rio que a cidade perdeu: São Paulo, 1890–1940. São Paulo: Alameda, 2006. 232 p.: bibl., ill., maps.

Historical-geographical study of the Tietê River, which flows through São Paulo, during the 20th century. Special attention is paid to the transformation of the wetlands surrounding the river. Reconstructs the ways in which inhabitants used the river's resources and responded to hazards presented by the Tietê.

1002 Le Torneau, François-Michel and Anne Greissing. A quest for sustainability: Brazil nut gatherers of São Francisco do Iratapuru and the Natura Corporation. (*Geogr. J./London*, 176:4, Dec. 2010, p. 334–349)

Studies Brazil nut cultivation between a village in the eastern Amazon using a nature reserve and Natura, a cosmetics firm. Argues that this type of relationship could be used elsewhere in the Amazon basin.

1003 Leandro, José Augusto. A roda, a prensa, o forno, o tacho: cultura material e farinha de mandioca no litoral do Paraná. (*Rev. Bras. Hist./São Paulo*, 27:54, dez. 2007, p. 261–278)

Uses postmortem judicial proceedings to analyze the importance of manioc flour in feeding workers in 19th-century Paranaguá on the coast of Paraná state. Argues for the ubiquitous presence of cassava flour and implements for producing the staple food.

1004 Maia, João Marcelo Ehlert. Governadores de ruínas: os relatos de viagem de Couto de Magalhães e Leite Moraes. (*Estud. Hist./Rio de Janeiro*, 40, julho/dez. 2007, p. 3–23, bibl.)

Analyzes the spatial references in the writings of Couto de Magalhães and Leite Moraes regarding their travels on the Araguaia River.

1005 Marcovitch, Jacques. Para mudar o futuro: mudanças climáticas, políticas públicas e estratégias empresariais. São Paulo: Editora Saraiva: EDUSP, 2006. 366 p.: bibl., index.

Presents the results of a climate change policy survey of major firms, such as Sadia and Petrobrás. Shows verbatim results of the firms' responses to areas such as participation in the Clean Development Mechanism and development of carbon-emission policies.

1006 Marcus, Alan P. Brazilian immigration to the United States and the geographical imagination. (*Geogr. Rev.*, 99:4, Oct. 2009, p. 481–498)

Study of Brazilian immigration with attention to place perceptions, experiences of place, and social networks. Argues that economic or financial explanations are only partial, suggesting instead the importance of factors such as family influence and education.

1007 Marcus, Alan P. (Re)creating places and spaces in two countries: Brazilian transnational migration processes. (*J. Cult. Geogr.*, 26:2, June 2009, p. 173–198)

Study of Brazilian immigration to the US, focusing on Marietta, Ga., and Framingham, Mass., with concern for place-making practices of immigrants and impacts on sending communities in Goiás and Minas Gerais.

1008 Martins, Luciana. Illusions of power: vision, technology and the geographical exploration of the Amazon, 1924–1925. (*J. Lat. Am. Cult. Stud.*, 16:3, Dec. 2007, p. 285–307, photos)

Studies the production of images, films, and maps by 20th-century explorers, focusing on the work of Alexander Hamilton Rice and his expeditions to the Amazon. Argues that Brazilians were influential in the images that resulted from the expeditions.

1009 Mendes Pereira, João Márcio. The World Bank's "market-assisted" land reform as a political issue: evidence from Brazil, 1997–2006. (*Rev. Eur. Estud. Latinoam. Caribe*, 82, April 2007, p. 21–49, bibl., table)

Studies the implementation and

development of market-oriented land-reform policies introduced with World Bank funding. Considers the changes between policies under the Cardoso and Lula administrations.

1010 Moraes, Antonio Carlos Robert. Geografia histórica do Brasil: cinco ensaios, uma proposta e uma crítica. São Paulo: Annablume, 2009. 150 p.: bibl. (Geografias e adjacências)

Concise text synthesizes the author's earlier work on Brazil's historical geography around themes of colonial geopolitics, state formation, and the sertão as geographical "other." Argues that Brazil's historical development is inseparable from territorial expansion.

1011 Múltiplos olhares sobre o semi-árido nordestino: sociedade, desenvolvimento, políticas públicas. Organização de Tânia Elias da Silva e Eliano Sérgio Azevedo Lopes. Aracaju, Brazil: Fundação de Amparo à Pesquisa do Estado de Sergipe: Univ. Federal de Sergipe, 2003. 329 p.: bibl., ill., maps.

Semi-arid northeastern region is studied with multidisciplinary approaches covering topics ranging from rural rebellions to irrigation and agrarian reform. Useful contrast provided for Sergipe state between large-scale, state-funded irrigation projects and small-scale loans distributed as municipal scales of government.

1012 Novo, Andre et al. Biofuel, dairy production and beef in Brazil: competing claims on land use in São Paulo state. (*J. Peasant Stud.*, 37:4, Oct. 2010, p. 769–792)

Indicates the effects of sugarcane ethanol on dairy and beef production in São Paulo, showing the historical development of the three sectors. Concludes that biofuel expansion is not the only reason for the decline in beef and dairy production.

1013 Pacheco, Pablo. Smallholder livelihoods, wealth and deforestation in the eastern Amazon. (*Hum. Ecol.*, 37:1, Jan. 2009, p. 27–41)

Study links wealth and deforestation processes in a case study of Uruará and Redenção in Pará state. Uses cluster analysis to identify farm system types. Argues that cattle are a major factor in wealth among households. Deforestation is explained by

the hiring of day laborers, time on land parcels, and distance between parcel and market.

1014 Resistência & integração: 100 anos de imigração japonesa no Brasil. Rio de Janeiro: IBGE, 2008. 29 p.: bibl., ill. (some col.), col. maps.

Beautifully produced collection of essays on Japanese immigration to Brazil. Notable chapters survey the demographic and geographic evolution of Japanese immigrants since 1920 and their presence in São Paulo and Paraná states.

1015 Saes, Alexandre Macchione. Modernização e concentração do transporte urbano em Salvador, 1849–1930. (*Rev. Bras. Hist./São Paulo*, 27:54, dez. 2007, p. 219–238)

Studies tramway development in Salvador as a modernization process involving foreign investment. Considers competition between a Brazilian firm and the Canada-based Light for Salvador's market.

1016 Salazar, Admilton Pinheiro. Amazônia: globalização e sustentabilidade. Manaus, Brazil: Valer Editora, 2004. 396 p.: bibl., ill.

Reviews development of capitalism in the Amazon, focusing on industrialization policies for Manaus. Traces the origin of the free-trade zone in Manaus, established to motivate industries, with special attention to fiscal incentives, industrial sectors attracted, and implications for Brazil's foreign trade policies.

1017 Sanjad, Nelson. Emílio Goeldi, 1859–1917: a ventura de um naturalista entre a Europa e o Brasil. Rio de Janeiro: EMC Edições, 2009. 232 p.: bibl., ill. (some col.), maps.

Beautifully illustrated intellectual biography of the Swiss zoologist Emílio Goeldi, hired first by the Museu Nacional in Rio and later by the Museu Paraense in the Amazon region. Study considers Goeldi's work in understanding a variety of physical and human processes.

1018 Secreto, María Verónica. A ocupação dos "espaços vazios" no governo Vargas: do "Discurso do rio Amazonas" à saga dos soldados da borracha. (*Estud. Hist./Rio de Janeiro*, 40, julho/dez. 2007, p. 115–135, bibl.)

Studies the policies for westward migration espoused by Cassiano Ricardo and Getúlio Vargas during the late 1930s and early 1940s, centering on the Amazon region as destination for northeasterners. Discusses propaganda methods used by the Vargas regime to recruit "rubber soldiers" who tapped natural rubber during WWII.

1019 Selwyn, Ben. Gender wage work and development in north east Brazil. (*Bull. Lat. Am. Res.*, 29:1, Jan. 2010, p. 51–70)

Studies changes in gender divisions of labor in export-oriented production in the Petrolina-Juazeiro region, emphasizing how market demands influence farm labor tasks and patterns. Conditions for women have diverged, with some workers witnessing improvements, while other female workers face worse conditions.

1020 Selwyn, Ben. Globalized horticulture: the formation and global integration of export grape production in north east Brazil. (*J. Agrarian Change*, 10:4, Oct. 2010, p. 537–563)

Focuses on the processing leading to the organization of export grape producers in the Petrolina-Juazeiro region. Emphasizes how producer organizations interacted with and benefitted from state agencies, creating spaces for small- and medium-sized grape exporters.

1021 Selwyn, Ben. Institutions, upgrading and development: evidence from northeast Brazilian export horticulture. (*Compet. Change*, 12:4, Dec. 2008, p. 377–396)

Studies the role of state agencies in encouraging strong export performance for high-value crops in the Petrolina-Juazeiro district. Argues that the state provided a critical role in assisting growers.

1022 Selwyn, Ben. Labour flexibility in export horticulture: a case study of northeast Brazilian grape production. (*J. Peasant Stud.*, 36:4, Oct. 2009, p. 761–782)

Analyzes the flexible labor regimes that harvest cycles, quality demands, and trade unions helped to create in the Petrolina-Juazeiro region. Special attention is focused on labor recruitment strategies, which are local and regional, seeking to avoid demands of trade unions. See also item **1020.**

1023 Sills, Erin O. and **Jill L. Caviglia-Harris.** Evolution of the Amazonian frontier: land values in Rondônia, Brazil. (*Land Use Policy*, 26:1, Jan. 2009, p. 55–67)

Analysis of determinants of land values obtained by surveys of land users in the Ouro Preto d'Oeste region of central Rondônia. Location, farm improvements, and soil degradation are determinants of land value variability.

1024 Simmons, Cynthia S. et al. Doing it for themselves: direct action land reform in the Brazilian Amazon. (*World Dev.*, 38:3, March 2010, p. 429–444)

Study of more than 700 households participating in contentious or "direct action" land reform (DLAR) in Pará and Rondônia states. Tests several hypotheses. Shows commonalities and differences between spontaneous DLAR and social-movement-led DLAR, arguing that these are legitimate providers of improved livelihood for Brazil's rural poor.

1025 Soares-Filho, Britaldo et al. Role of Brazilian Amazon protected areas in climate change mitigation. (*Proc. Natl. Acad. Sci. U.S.A.*, 107:24, June 2010, p. 10821–10826)

Argues that protected areas are effective in conserving the Brazilian Amazon's remaining forests. Indicates the need for financial support to counter the profit and investment forgone in the interests of forest conservation.

1026 Sorrensen, Cynthia. Potential hazards of land policy: conservation, rural development and fire use in the Brazilian Amazon. (*Land Use Policy*, 26:3, July 2009, p. 782–791)

Argues that fire policy has not effectively addressed the main causes of fire in the Amazon. Indicates that land-tenure issues are the main cause of fire use among smallholders.

1027 Tenotã-Mõ: alertas sobre as conseqüências dos projetos hidreléctricos no rio Xingu. Organização de A. Oswaldo Sevá Filho. Editado por Glenn Switkes. São Paulo: International Rivers Network, 2005. 344 p.: bibl., ill., maps (1 col. folded).

Edited volume highly critical of hydroelectric projects planned for the Xingu

River in the Amazon region. Special focus is on indigenous peoples and the Brazilian government's energy and mining policies.

1028 Urbanizador Social: da informalidade à parceria. Textos de Ana Lúcia Fialho *et al.* Organização de Cláudia Damasio. Porto Alegre, Brazil: Livraria do Arquiteto, 2006. 234 p.: bibl., ill., maps.

Surveys results of Porto Alegre's Urbanizador Social program, implemented in the early 2000s to formalize the informal land market and regularize squatter settlements. Chapters consider how the policy worked within Porto Alegre's urban processes and provide useful case-study information on particular neighborhoods within the city.

1029 Vadjunec, Jacqueline; Carlos Valerio A. Gomez; and Thomas Ludewigs. Land-use/land-cover change among rubber tappers in the Chico Mendes Extractive Reserve, Acre, Brazil. (*J. Land Use Sci.*, 4:4, Oct. 2009, p. 249–274)

Uses household surveys and remote sensing analysis to demonstrate the increasing deforestation of the Chico Mendes Reserve and decreasing importance of rubber tapping for livelihoods.

1030 Valentim, Luís Sérgio Ozório. Requalificação urbana, contaminação do solo e riscos à saúde: um caso na cidade de São Paulo. São Paulo: Annablume: FAPESP, 2007. 159 p.: bibl., ill., col. maps.

Study of the rehabilitation process of sites contaminated by industrial pollution in São Paulo. Examines public policies, especially the interaction between the state environmental agency and the judiciary. Examples of rehabilitated sites are presented as models for future work.

1031 Vianna, Lucila Pinsard. De invisíveis a protagonistas: populações tradicionais e unidades de conservação. São Paulo: Annablume, 2008. 339 p.: bibl., ill., maps.

Study of the traditional uses of the Juatinga protected area in Paraty, a coastal city of Rio de Janeiro state. Surveys the legal construction of Juatinga. Provides an ethnographic study of inhabitants of the reserve and resource uses, aiming to contribute to the debate on the presence of the "traditional use" of protected areas.

1032 Vicentini, Yara. Cidade e história na Amazônia. Curitiba, Brazil: Editora UFPR, 2004. 287 p.: bibl., ill., maps. (Pesquisa)

Historical-geographical study of urbanization in the Amazon, focusing on the second half of the 1900s. Analyzes a network of Amazonian cities as an "urban frontier" while providing useful maps of several urban centers. Considers cities as both fragile settlements and critical nodes of territorial and resource control over the Amazon.

1033 Walker, Robert T. *et al.* Protecting the Amazon with protected areas. (*Proc. Natl. Acad. Sci. U.S.A.*, 106:26, June 2009, p. 10582–10586)

Uses regional climate model and spatial data on various types of conservation areas to predict that policy enforcement and conservation management could avoid drying in southern Amazonian areas.

1034 Walker, Robert T. *et al.* Ranching and the new global range: Amazônia in the 21st century. (*Geoforum/New York*, 40:5, Sept. 2009, p. 733–745, map)

Explains the strong increase in the Amazonian cattle herd as a result of various policies, such as sanitary controls and export promotion. Considers the impact of increased cattle numbers on forest cover and other land-cover and land-use changes. Includes a cattle density map that is particularly useful.

1035 Wilkinson, John and Selena Herrera. Biofuels in Brazil: debates and impacts. (*J. Peasant Stud.*, 37:4, Oct. 2010, p. 749–768)

Overview of the multifaceted debate regarding the expansion of ethanol and biodiesel. Reviews critiques of the rapid increase in biofuels.

1036 Wolford, Wendy. Participatory democracy by default: land reform, social movements and the state in Brazil. (*J. Peasant Stud.*, 37:1, Jan. 2010, p. 91–109)

Studies relations between the Movimento dos Trabalhadores Rurais Sem Terra (MST) and the Instituto Nacional de Colonização e Reforma Agrária (INCRA) with regard to access to institutional resources in Paraíba state. Focuses on the negotiations between individuals associated with the organizations. Finds that the MST has encouraged better performance from INCRA officials.

1037 Wolford, Wendy. This land is ours now: social mobilization and the meanings of land in Brazil. Durham, N.C.: Duke Univ. Press, 2010. 281 p.: bibl., index. (New ecologies for the twenty-first century)

Ethnographic account of the Movimento dos Trabalhadores Rurais Sem Terra (MST) in Santa Catarina and Pernambuco states. Contrasts agrarian populism promoted by the MST and actual settlements. Special attention is given to the variable meaning of land, contingent on political and moral economies of the particular settlements.

GOVERNMENT AND POLITICS

GENERAL

América indígena ante el siglo XXI.
See item **429**.

Ameringer, Charles D. The socialist impulse: Latin America in the twentieth century. See *HLAS 66:575*.

Archenti, Nélida and **María Inés Tula.**
Cuotas de género y tipo de lista en América Latina. See item **1422**.

Cloos, Patrick. Health inequalities in the Caribbean: increasing opportunities and resources. See item **1179**.

1038 Córdova, Abby and **Mitchell A. Seligson.** Economic shocks and democratic vulnerabilities in Latin America and the Caribbean. (*Lat. Am. Polit. Soc.*, 52:2, Summer 2010, p. 1–35, bibl., graphs, tables)

What economic conditions are most threatening, and how might they weaken consolidating democracies? This article uses the AmericasBarometer conducted by the Latin American Public Opinion Project (LAPOP) to answer these questions by focusing on core attitudes for the consolidation of democracy. The study finds that conditions of low levels of economic development, low economic growth, and high levels of income inequality increase those vulnerabilities substantially, but the effects are not uniform across individuals. Some groups, especially the young and the poor, are particularly vulnerable to some antidemocratic appeals. [C.E. Griffin]

Emerson, R. Guy. Radical neglect?: the "War on Terror" and Latin America. See item **1540**.

Garzón Vergara, Juan Carlos. Mafia & Co.: the criminal networks in Mexico, Brazil, and Colombia. See item **2237**.

1039 Glassman, Amanda *et al.* Confronting the chronic disease burden in Latin America and the Caribbean. (*Health Aff.*, 29:12, Dec. 2010, p. 2142–2148)

While much remains to be done to cope with the emerging public health and fiscal threat to Latin America and the Caribbean posed by increases in chronic illnesses, a set of studies sponsored by the Inter-American Development Bank brings good news on potentially cost-effective strategies to improve medical coverage and outcomes. [C.E. Griffin]

Malamud, Carlos. Perón y su vigencia en los populismos latinoamericanos actuales. See item **1455**.

Mansilla, H.C.F. La crisis de la identidad nacional y la cultura política: aproximaciones a una teoría crítica de la modernización. See item **1329**.

1040 Mazzolari, Francisco. Dual citizenship rights: do they make more and richer citizens? (*Demography/Washington*, 46:1, Feb. 2009, p. 169–191)

In the 1990s, Colombia, the Dominican Republic, Ecuador, Costa Rica, and Brazil passed dual citizenship laws granting their expatriates the right to naturalize in the receiving country without losing their nationality of origin. This article estimates the effects of these new laws on naturalization rates and labor market outcomes in the US and concludes—based on data from the 1990 and 2000 US censuses—that the effects of dual citizenship on improved economic performance, if mediated through naturalization, are consistent with American citizenship conferring greater economic opportunities. [C.E. Griffin]

**1041 Populisten, Revolutionäre, Staats-
männer: Politiker in Lateinamerika.**
Edited by Nikolaus Werz. Frankfurt am
Main: Vervuert, 2010. 616 p.: bibl., ill. (Bibliotheca ibero-americana; 129)

   Presenting the various types of politicians in Latin America from the 19th century onwards (including representatives for
populism and caudillismo), this collection
of articles tries to show the range of political approaches to politics in Latin America
centered on their main agents. The book is
divided into biographies with short evaluations of their importance and an annotated
bibliography. [F. Obermeier]

1042 Rodríguez, Ileana. Liberalism at
   its limits: crime and terror in the
Latin American cultural text. Pittsburgh,
Pa.: Univ. of Pittsburgh Press, 2009. 235 p.:
index. (Illuminations—cultural formations
of the Americas)

   Ambitious work of political philosophy aimed at the purported flaws of

liberalism, written from the perspective of
humanities critical theory and centered on
three case studies: Rigoberta Menchú in
Guatemala, "La Violencia" in Colombia,
and feminicido in Juárez, Mexico. Highlights Menchú's identification of Maya not
as a peripheral minority but as a millenarian culture deserving respect for *derecho de
gentes.* [C. Brockett]

**Seminario Internacional: Políticas Pú-
blicas, Derechos y Trabajo Social en el
MERCOSUR, 1st, *Universidad Nacional
de Córdoba, 2007.*** Políticas públicas, derechos, y trabajo social en el Mercosur. See
item **1470.**

**La sociedad de la opinión: reflexiones sobre
encuestas y cambio político en democracia.**
See item **1414.**

Vargas Llosa, Mario. Sables y utopías: visiones de América Latina. See item **1375.**

**Which way Latin America?: hemispheric
politics meets globalization.** See item **1845.**

MEXICO

RODERIC A. CAMP, *Professor of Government, Claremont-McKenna College*

OVER THE LAST DECADE, especially after the benchmark 2000 presidential
election, an interesting shift in emphasis on topics related to elections and voting is apparent, especially among Mexican scholars. In this respect, little change
in focus has occurred in this volume compared to *HLAS 61, 63,* and *65.* Moreover, the same topics largely continue to be neglected, ranging from the impact
of religion generally—and the Catholic Church specifically—on politics, to the
importance of gender at all levels of politics and in the voting process specifically.
Not surprisingly, however, some important topics have emerged in the scholarly
discussion on Mexico, and will surely increase their presence in future volumes.
Naturally, the most noteworthy of these topics is public security and the influence
of drug trafficking organizations in Mexico.

   The issue of public security, as drug-related violence has increased significantly, is explored from a variety of angles. A prominent historian, Wil Pansters,
and his co-author, Héctor Castillo Berthier, examine criminality in Mexico City
prior to 2000; they provide a valuable empirical basis for comparison between
recent levels of insecurity and those prior to democratic consolidation (item **1102**).
One perspective which has formed the basis for significant policy proposals from
both Mexican and American officials in addressing public security is reforming
the judicial system and the civilian police force. One of the most comprehensive
books to date on this topic is Niels Uidriks' thorough analysis, *Mexico's Unrule of*

Law: Implementing Human Rights in Police and Judicial Reform under Democratization (item **1125**). This outstanding work offers an original analysis of the topic based on the author's personal observations, interviews with police, and survey research. A different approach emphasizing the relationship between ordinary Mexicans and their political institutions rather than legal reforms, and focusing on local governments, can be found in José María Ramos García's *Inseguridad pública en México: una propuesta de gestión de política estratégica en gobiernos locales* (item **1109**). Finally, Raúl Benitez Manaut, who has explored national security topics for decades (notably the role of the armed forces), offers insights into the difficulties that the Fox administration faced in this arena, and analyzes the obstacles to conceptualizing national security in Mexico (item **1047**).

One of the neglected topics in years past has generated slightly more interest among scholars. Mexico's Comisión Nacional de los Derechos Humanos has produced a valuable volume on women's participation in Mexican politics (item **1103**). The work provides extensive data and up-to-date observations on women's involvement in politics, as well as one of the most comprehensive investigations of indigenous female involvement in local politics. Another work which adds to the growing serious analyses of women is Nancy García Vázquez's attempt to identify the extent to which women influence the legislative agenda in Congress, in her *Legislar para todos: mujeres en la Cámara de Diputados (1997–2003)* (item **1072**). This study is largely based on quantitative data. Lisa Baldez, who has played a major role in emphasizing original research in Mexico on women and politics, specifically on the impact of quota systems in increasing female representation in the Chamber of Deputies, reports on the disconcerting finding that a number of women have won recent seats in Congress, only to resign and be replaced by their male alternates (item **1046**).

Some of the most important political actors, including the armed forces, the Catholic Church, and political parties, continue to receive little serious scholarly attention. Among these potential topics, one significant contribution stands out: Alejandro Díaz Domínguez, a former official of the Electoral Court of the Federal District, analyzes many specific allegations of Church involvement in politics, and follows the specific allegations through the legal process (**1063**).

Political culture continues to attract modest scholarly attention. The most unique work on this topic is Sara Sefchovich's frank analysis, *País de mentiras: la distancia entre el discurso y la realidad en la cultura mexicana,* which explores what public officials say compared to the actual reality of the topic they are discussing (item **1118**). She examines the impact of such lies on the political culture and on Mexican behavior. The Mexican government itself continues to contribute to the wealth of information on citizen attitudes and values in the results of the Third National Study of Political Culture (2005) (item **1053**). The report on this survey provides comparisons with previous government studies as well as with similar research from Latin America. Pursuing an institutional focus on culture, Stephen Morris updates his classic work on corruption in *Political Corruption in Mexico: The Impact of Democratization,* arguing that the Mexican state remains weak and that culture may continue to be a significant variable in explaining political change and corruption (item **1099**).

As has been the case for a decade, all facets of electoral studies dominate the literature. The best general analyses, examining national elections, can be found in the edited work, *Consolidating Mexico's Democracy: The 2006 Presidential Campaign in Comparative Perspective* (item **1056**), which builds on the editors' previous book on the 2000 presidential race, funded by the National Science Foundation. As was the case with the earlier volume, the contributors rely on an original panel survey conducted at various phases of the electoral campaign. A counterpart effort by some of Mexico's leading scholars is available in the well-researched collection *Rumbo a los Pinos en el 2006: los candidatos y los partidos en el espacio público* (item **1114**). Using data from both of the NSF-funded projects, Alejandro Moreno, who directs *Reforma's* polling, identifies important voter attitudes and their consequences for presidential elections (item **1095**). From an historical perspective, thoroughly established in the theoretical literature, Beatriz Magaloni analyzes why Mexico's PRI survived for so many decades and why it was defeated in 2000, using sophisticated statistical models in her award-winning book to explain autocratic governance (item **1088**). Two additional studies on the 2006 presidential election are equally original and valuable analyses. José Antonio Crespo provides one of the most judicious, critical evaluations of the electoral results, arguing that the Instituto Federal Electoral data does not accurately reflect the vote totals (item **1058**). A shorter work by Allyson Lucinda Benton explores, for the first time, how economic markets reacted to the possibility of Andrés Manuel López Obrador winning the election, discovering that as his voter support changed, the market's volatility was affected—but not its returns (item **1048**). Finally, an analysis of the electoral literature for this volume suggests an increasing focus on local electoral participation; four notable studies are included in this section. Todd Eisenstadt, who has provided much original scholarship on the topic, uses his essay on "*Usos y costumbres* and Postelectoral Conflicts in Oaxaca" to compare communities which have chosen to rely on traditional, indigenous practices with party-based electoral participation (item **1064**). Following this same emphasis, Jorge Hernández Díaz and Anabel López Sánchez use a case study of one municipality, suggesting the importance of increased revenues on local governance (item **1079**). The third study, by Carlos Moreno-Jaimes, examines the direct relationship between competitive elections and improved governance at the local level in the decade from 1990 to 2000 (item **1097**). Moreno-Jaimes discovers, surprisingly, that such elections were not a significant variable in improving municipal services in that decade, and instead, in spite of literacy rates, socioeconomic status, and level of participation producing consequences on governance, it was likely that continued clientelism affected the performance levels of various municipalities. The fourth work explores the corporatist relationship between labor and the three major political parties in Chihuahua. The author, Aldo Muñoz Armenta, argues that many traditional organizations continue their relationship with PRI because PRD and PAN are limited institutionally from performing this task (item **1100**).

One of the complementary interests of scholars focusing on elections and participation is research on civil society and NGOs. Ilan Bizberg concludes that in Mexico after the 2000 election, most of the civic organizations failed to transform into influential actors, and that numerous enclaves of authoritarian practices continued unabated (item **1049**). Daniel Sabet devotes an extensive case study to one of the most critical policy issues in Mexico, that of water usage, and the efforts of NGOs to affect water policy, in his *Nonprofits and Their Networks: Cleaning the Waters along Mexico's Northern Border* (item **1116**). He shares observations similar to those of Bizberg. In another excellent book-length study based on extensive field research, Jon Shefner examines a popular organization in Guadalajara to evaluate changes in its behavior since the advent of both neoliberal economic changes and democratization, and also looks at their impact on clientelism (item **1119**). For years, Jonathan Fox has followed civic organizations with a particular focus on rural citizens. In his *Accountability Politics: Power and Voice in Rural Mexico*, he argues that the rural poor have benefitted more from increased associations than from democratic elections (item **1069**). Finally, Martha Singer Sochet has edited an excellent collection on indigenous political participation, exploring the impact of democratization on political involvement (item **1091**).

The rising influence of new institutional actors, such as the legislative and the judicial branches, have received some, if not adequate attention. A rare comparative work based on nearly 200 interviews, *Comportamiento electoral y parlamentario en México y España: una experiencia estadual,* contrasts state legislators from Guerrero, Sinaloa, and México state with those of Castilla and León in Spain, providing numerous worthwhile insights (item **1055**). This may be the first comparative study with another country ever published on Mexican state legislators. The Supreme Court receives even less attention than the legislative branch. Nevertheless, an interesting analysis by Julio Ríos-Figueroa offers a historical picture of how court leadership altered its behavior toward the executive branch after Vicente Fox's 2000 victory (item **1113**). Ríos-Figueroa makes the unusual argument that the justices' altered behavior toward the Chamber of Deputies, not the important legal reforms introduced by President Ernesto Zedillo in 1994, were essential in changing the court's relationship to the executive branch.

Most of the studies in public administration, which typically examine some aspect of the federal bureaucracy, rarely offer fresh perspectives affecting Mexican governance. A notable exception is José Luis Méndez's essay in *Foro Internacional,* which for the first time examines the impact of presidential staffs in Mexico and the US and their respective presidents (item **1090**). He argues that such staffs in Mexico are weaker than their US counterparts because Mexican presidents rely heavily on confidants in the cabinet. A second study, edited by María del Carmen Pardo and Ernesto Velasco Sánchez, also is comparative, but includes Canada, Mexico, and the US, providing an analysis of policy-making in all three countries (item **1074**).

Scholars in both Mexico and the US have focused on regional administrative relationships. Rogelio Hernández Rodríguez, who continues his helpful work on state governors, examines their potential impact on federal government fiscal policies, highlighting the collaborative effort of governors and the legislative branch to achieve their goals (item **1080**). Horacio Sobarzo, in one of Mexico's leading economic journals, carefully examines the impact of the federal government's decentralization policy in terms of fiscal management, shedding light on the effectiveness of such a strategy and describing its limitations at the local level (item **1121**).

Alarcón Olguín, Víctor. Realineamiento electoral en México: 2000–2006. See item **2270**.

1043 Arzuaga, Javier; Orlando Espinosa-Santiago; and José Javier Niño-Martínez. Élites, alternancia y partidos políticos en el estado de México: entre la pluralidad, la búsqueda del voto y el debilitamiento institucional. (*Econ. Soc. Territ.,* 7:25, sept./dic. 2007, p. 129–156, bibl., graph, tables)

The authors explore the behavior and impact of influential political leaders in México state, the most influential state politically and economically. Despite the increased electoral competition, the expansion of both the PAN and the PRD, and the level of economic development in the state, the PRI remains in control of state politics. This pattern is attributed to the intensity of competition for party nominations, the institutional structure of the parties, and the level of elite cohesion nationally and locally, among other variables.

1044 Aziz Nassif, Alberto. El retorno del conflicto: elecciones y polarización política en México. (*Desacatos*, 24, mayo/agosto 2007, p. 13–54, bibl., photos, tables)

Aziz Nassif, who has made important contributions to understanding Mexican politics, examines the many familiar controversies of the 2006 presidential election, highlighting the composition of the Instituto Federal Electoral (IFE), the federal campaign finance law, the involvement of business groups in the campaign, and presidential intervention. He concludes pessimistically that Mexico has reached a stage in its democracy where there exists a radical separation between the governors and the governed, and that this new model has returned Mexico to political conflict.

1045 Aziz Nassif, Alberto and **Ernesto Isunza Vera.** La crisis del modelo electoral mexicano: financiamento, medios, instituciones y política social. (*Foro Int./México*, 47:4, oct./dic. 2007, p. 740–784, bibl., tables)

Based on an analysis of the cost of public financing for political parties and the expenditures on media coverage during political campaigns from 1997 to 2006, the authors identify numerous weaknesses which plague the electoral process. In spite of reforms introduced in 2007, they remain critical of the level of public spending to support a democratic political process.

1046 Baldez, Lisa. Primaries vs. quotas: gender and candidate nominations in Mexico, 2003. (*Lat. Am. Polit. Soc.*, 49:3, Fall 2007, p. 69–96, graphs, tables)

Lisa Baldez is a leading voice in analyzing the changing role of women in Mexican legislative politics. Much of her work has focused on gender quotas and nominations for legislative seats. She concludes that the legal enforcement of such laws, and the Instituto Federal Electoral's interpretation of the law, can and did affect the extent of its impact. Indeed, as the 2009 congressional elections revealed, many women who actually won their seats resigned after the election to be replaced by their male alternates, thus emasculating the intent of the quota system.

1047 Benítez Manaut, Raúl. La seguridad nacional en la indefinida transición: mitos y realidades del sexenio de Vicente Fox. (*Foro Int./México*, 48:1/2, enero/junio 2008, p. 184–208, tables)

One of the few Mexican scholars who has examined Mexico's evolving national security policy and the role of the armed forces in that policy provides useful insights into the issues confronting the Fox administration, and the difficulties in conceptualizing national security within the Mexican context.

1048 Benton, Allyson Lucinda. ¿Quién está preocupado por López Obrador?: las respuestas del mercado a las tendencias electorales durante la campaña presidencial mexicana del 2006. (*Colomb. Int.*, 64, julio/dic. 2006, p. 68–95, bibl., graphs, tables)

This essay is one of the most original analyses of the 2006 presidential election. Using a highly sophisticated model, the author examines the reaction of economic markets to the possibility of Andrés Manuel López Obrador's election, and presents evidence which suggests that changing levels of support for the candidate did not affect market returns but did affects its volatility, and that investors may have accepted the likelihood of a López Obrador victory but not the instability which occurred after the election.

1049 Bizberg, Ilán. La sociedad civil en el nuevo régimen político. (*Foro Int./México*, 47:4, oct./dic. 2007, p. 785–816, table)

Bizberg provides a thoughtful and insightful exploration of the failure of civil society and the civil organizations that spawned the democratization of Mexican politics to emerge successfully from the 2000 election and expand their influence. He identifies numerous explanations for their lack of success and points to numerous "enclaves" where authoritarian practices are entrenched and continue unabated.

1050 Blas López, Cuauhtémoc. Oaxaca, ínsula de rezagos: crítica a sus gobiernos de razón y de costumbre. Mexico: Editorial Siembra, 2007. 279 p.: bibl., ill.

The traditional-customary institutions and contemporary political institutions of Oaxaca have attracted more attention than those of any other state among all the research and publications on Mexico. Here the topic is examined critically and carefully by the author, who argues that the political system in Oaxaca is on the verge of collapse and its economic future is in doubt.

1051 Calvo Barrera, Raúl. Proceso electoral y alternancia en Guerrero. México: Porrúa, Miguel Ángel, 2007. 139 p.: bibl., ill., maps.

Although Mexican scholars have produced numerous works on state electoral politics, most of those contributions have been edited collections. This short volume on Guerrero, one of the states most characterized by political conflict, and now drug violence, is a careful study of the 2004–2005 gubernatorial election, including detailed background information on the previous political setting.

Camp, Roderic Ai. Exercising political influence: religion, democracy, and the Mexican 2006 presidential race. See *HLAS 66:916.*

Camp, Roderic Ai. The metamorphosis of leadership in a democratic Mexico. See *HLAS 66:917.*

1052 Candados y contrapesos: la protección de los programas, políticas y derechos sociales en México y América Latina. Coordinación de David Gómez Álvarez. Textos de John M. Ackerman *et al.* México: PNUD; Guadalajara, Mexico: ITESO, Univ. Jesuita de Guadalajara; Guatemala: Univ. Rafael Landívar; Córdoba, Argentina: Asociación Civil Editorial Univ. Católica de Córdoba; Montevideo: Univ. Católica del Uruguay; Caracas: Univ. Católica Andrés Bello; Santiago: Univ. Alberto Hurtado; Bogotá: Pontificia Univ. Javeriana, 2009. 347 p.: bibl., ill.

A wide-ranging collection of leading policy recommendations and analysis based on a conference on non-Mexican and Mexican experts sponsored by the UNDP in 2007 focusing on social programs. Some of these essays are based on extensive scholarly research and others are best described as based on thoughtful expertise.

1053 Coloquio Cultura Política y Participación Ciudadana en México, Antes y Después del 2006, *Distrito Federal, Mexico, 2006.* Cultura política y participación ciu-

dadana en México antes y después del 2006. México: SEGOB, Secretaría de Gobernación, 2007. 312 p.: bibl., ill., tables.

Anyone interested in Mexican political culture will want to read this work which reports the results of the Third National Study of Political Culture in Dec. 2005 and the analysis from leading survey researchers and Mexican political scientists participating in a workshop that same year. The book includes numerous tables with comparative data from the first two studies as well as comparisons with survey research from Latin America.

1054 Coloquio de Estado y Movimientos Sociales, *12th, Univ. Autónoma Metropolitana, Unidad Iztapalapa, 2006.* Balance del sexenio foxista y perspectivas para los movimientos sociales. Coordinación de Ana Alicia Solís de Alba *et al.* México: Editorial Ítaca, 2007. 358 p.: bibl., ill.

This collection, which focuses exclusively on the Fox administration, is composed of political tracts and some serious essays with a decidedly critical view of his social and economic policies.

1055 Comportamiento electoral y parlamentario en México y España: una experiencia estadual. Coordinación de Margarita Jiménez Badillo. México: Estados Unidos Mexicanos, Cámara de Diputados, LX Legislatura, Consejo Editorial: Instituto Electoral del Estado de México: Miguel Ángel Porrúa, 2009. 259 p.: bibl., ill., maps. (Serie Las ciencias sociales) (Conocer para decidir)

This is a valuable and rare comparative work between Spain and Mexico which is based on extensive interviews (nearly 200) with the Guerrero state legislators 2002–2005, the Sinaloa legislators 2004–2007, the Mexico state legislators of 2003–2006, and the regional legislators of Castilla and León (2003–2007) in Spain.

1056 Consolidating Mexico's democracy: the 2006 presidential campaign in comparative perspective. Edited by Jorge I. Domínguez, Chappell Lawson, and Alejandro Moreno. Baltimore, Md.: John Hopkins Univ. Press, 2009. 366 p.: bibl., ill., index.

This collection, funded by a grant from the National Science Foundation, is the most original published work on the

2006 presidential campaign, and in part complements an earlier book edited by Domínguez and Lawson on the pathbreaking 2000 presidential election (*Mexico's Pivotal Democratic Election: Candidates, Voters, and the Presidential Campaign of 2000*, 2004). This work relies on original data from a panel survey that identifies changing behavior among Mexican voters at various stages of the campaign and suggests which variables were most important in altering voter choices that determined the electoral outcome.

1057 Construcción democrática de ciudadanía: diálogos con las organizaciones de la sociedad civil. Coordinación de Griselda Gutiérrez Castañeda. México: UNAM: Plaza y Valdés, 2008. 329 p.: bibl., ill. (Ciudadanía y cultura política)

Although more attention needs to be paid to civic organizations in Mexican political scholarship, most of the studies in this collection tend to be administrative and institutional descriptions rather than detailed case studies of civic organizations processes and their influence on governmental agencies.

1058 Crespo, José Antonio. 2006—hablan las actas: las debilidades en la autoridad electoral mexicana. México: Debate, 2008. 232 p.: bibl., ill.

José Antonio Crespo, one of Mexico's leading political scientists, explores the controversial 2006 election results carefully and mathematically, concluding that the Instituto Federal Electoral's data does not accurately reflect electoral results, and that the reported results are not conclusive as to the outcome. Anyone interested in the balloting and the controversy surrounding the outcome should read this work, and especially review Crespo's point-by-point conclusions.

1059 Dellacioppa, Kara Zugman. This bridge called Zapatismo: building alternative political cultures in Mexico City, Los Angeles, and beyond. Lanham, Md.: Lexington Books, 2009. 207 p.: bibl., index.

This interesting work seeks to develop the broader consequences of the Zapatista movement on political culture and discourse, not only in Mexico but in Los

Angeles and elsewhere. The author provides evidence to support her argument that those involved in the movement did add to or redefine important concepts such as the individual, the nation, and democracy, and perhaps their view of the individual is most important.

1060 Deloya Cobián, Guillermo. El México pendiente: agenda para la gobernabilidad. México: M.A. Porrúa, 2008. 242 p.: bibl., ill., maps.

This collection brings together a group of essays recommending policy reforms in their respective areas ranging from democratic governance to public security. The chapter on public security provides a particularly useful overview of numerous relevant components of this agenda.

1061 Democracia y exclusión: caminos encontrados en la Ciudad de México. Coordinación de Lucía Álvarez Enríquez, Carlos San Juan Victoria, y Cristina Sánchez Mejorada. México: UNAM, Centro de Investigaciones Interdisciplinarias en Ciencias y Humanidades: Univ. Autónoma Metropolitana-Azcapotzalco: Univ. Autónoma de la Ciudad de México: Instituto Nacional de Antropología e Historia: Plaza y Valdés, 2006. 527 p.: bibl., ill., maps. (México y democracia)

This collection, focused on the theme of the impact of democratization on citizens in Mexico City seven years after Fox's electoral victory, covers a wide range of topics, with largely critical assessments of the degree to which democratic consequences have reached ordinary Mexicans.

1062 La deuda de la democracia: ensayos sobre la (problemática) consolidación de un nuevo régimen político en México. Coordinación de Rubén Ibarra Reyes. Textos de José A. Turriza Zapata et al. Zacatecas, Mexico: Univ. Autónoma de Zacatecas: Ayuntamiento Zacatecas: Instituto Zacatecano de Cultura Ramón López Velarde, 2007. 185 p.: bibl., ill. (Col. Contraimperio)

The contributors to this volume focus on the failure of democratic politics during the Fox administration to represent the interests of many Mexicans and, from the editor's perspective, to eliminate authoritarian governance.

1063 Díaz Domínguez, Alejandro. La regulación religiosa en materia electoral mexicana: una explicación alternativa sobre sus diferencias. (*Econ. Soc. Territ.*, 6:22, sept./dic. 2006, p. 431–456, bibl., tables)

Díaz Domínguez, who was the secretary of the president of the Electoral Court of the Federal District when he authored this essay, adds some original information to our knowledge about the relationship between religion and politics in the Mexican electoral arena. He examines a number of specific allegations about Church involvement in politics to demonstrate that each allegation has been handled by the electoral courts on an individual basis and based on local conditions, and that parties have been punished, where appropriate, if the laws have been violated.

1064 Eisenstadt, Todd A. *Usos y costumbres* and postelectoral conflicts in Oaxaca, Mexico, 1995–2004: an empirical and normative assessment. (*LARR*, 42:1, 2007, p. 52–77, bibl., tables)

Eisenstadt, who has offered some of the most original work on legal norms and local electoral conflicts in Mexican politics, provides a fascinating analysis of municipal elections, contrasting those characterized by party-based elections with those communities using accepted traditional modes of appointive leadership. He concludes that a definitive evaluation of the impact of the traditional approach cannot yet be ascertained based on his case studies of Oaxaca.

1065 Espino, Germán. El nuevo escenario de las campañas presidenciales: la transformación de la comunicación política en el sistema político mexicano. México: La Jornada; Mexico: Univ. Autónoma de Querétaro: Instituto Electoral de Querétaro: Instituto Queretano de la Cultura y las Artes: Instituto Nacional de Antropología e Historia, 2006. 400 p. (Nuestro tiempo)

Although this work omits some essential contributions to the literature on the media in presidential campaigns, it provides useful insights into the 1994 and 2000 presidential races.

1066 Espinoza Valle, Víctor Alejandro. Compromiso cívico y participación ciudadana en México: una perspectiva nacional y regional. (*Am. Lat. Hoy/Sala-*

manca, 48, abril 2008, p. 141–164, bibl., graphs, tables)

The author provides extensive data on Mexican political culture from three polls conducted by the Secretariat of Government in 2001, 2003, and 2005, but the conclusions and interpretations are not integrated with numerous other studies that have assessed the importance of such findings.

1067 El estado de la migración: las políticas públicas ante los retos de la migración mexicana a Estados Unidos. Coordinación de Paula Leite y Silvia E. Giorguli. México: Consejo Nacional de Población, 2009. 464 p.: bibl., ill., maps.

Some of the leading students of immigration policy have contributed to this edited collection which examines the impact of immigrants and immigration policy on both the US and Mexico, and incorporates less common topics of research including essays on AIDS and immigration, education of Mexicans in the US, and the impact of immigration on educational assistance in Mexico.

Estados y autonomías en democracias contemporáneas: Bolivia, Ecuador, España, México. See item **1314**.

Esteva, Gustavo. The Asamblea Popular de los Pueblos de Oaxaca: a chronicle of radical democracy. See *HLAS 66:930*.

1068 Estévez, Adriadna. La transición a la democracia en el TLCAN: un significante vacío. (*Perf. Latinoam.*, 14:29, enero/junio 2007, p. 187–217, bibl.)

Through extensive research, the author explores the impact of NAFTA on Mexican NGOs and social movements ideologically and organizationally. She argues that the 2000 presidential election, in spite of bringing alternation in power, did not reinforce or impact significantly the collective consolidation of these ideologies and their persistence during the Fox era.

1069 Fox, Jonathan. Accountability politics: power and voice in rural Mexico. Oxford, England; New York: Oxford Univ. Press, 2007. 438 p.: bibl., index. (Oxford studies in democratization)

Jonathan Fox, who has examined the impact of politics and policies on rural residents for decades, draws together new material and three previously published essays to test the overall thesis of the extent to which democracy has facilitated and reinforced the voices of the rural poor. Agreeing with other scholars who have examined this relationship, he concludes that while the democratic opening has facilitated the poor's efforts, they have benefited most from increased association rather than from the accountability of democratic elections.

1070 Fox Quesada, Vicente and Rob Allyn.
La revolución de la esperanza: la vida, los anhelos y los sueños de un presidente. Traducción de Juan José Utrilla. México: Aguilar, 2007. 495 p., 16 p. of plates: ill. (some col.), index.

This autobiography, also available in English as *Revolution of Hope*, provides valuable insight into those influences and experiences which gave rise to Vicente Fox's career and ultimate pursuit of the presidency. Unfortunately, it sheds little light on his actual presidency, particularly the inner workings of his office and the policy disputes and decisions of his administration.

1071 Fuentes para el estudio del sistema político, las elecciones y los partidos en México. Coordinación de Francisco Reveles Vázquez, Josafat Cortéz Salinas, y Arturo López Perdomo. México: UNAM, Facultad de Ciencias Políticas y Sociales: Ediciones Gernika, 2009. 295 p. (Col. Ciencias políticas)

The authors have organized some 2,800 sources on Mexican politics by topic and by author. Although the compilation omits numerous major sources, including many books, it is an excellent place to begin for an initial bibliography on the subject, especially of Mexican sources.

1072 García Vázquez, Nancy. Legislar para todas: mujeres en la Cámara de Diputados, 1997–2003. Zapopan, Mexico: Colegio de Jalisco, 2009. 254 p.: bibl. (Investigación)

There continues to be little serious scholarship on the impact of women in Mexican politics. This book is an excellent exception, and although the author correctly admits that she relies largely on quantitative data to paint a picture of the role of women in the legislative branch while omitting interviews with the actors themselves,

she does offer some tentative conclusions about their collective behavior in Congress, and provides a helpful place to start for anyone interested in this topic.

1073 García Zamora, Rodolfo. Desarrollo económico y migración internacional: los desafíos de las políticas públicas en México. Mexico: Doctorado en Estudios del Desarrollo, Univ. Autónoma de Zacatecas, 2009. 319 p.: bibl., ill. (Col. Ángel migrante)

All of the essays in this work are authored or co-authored by Rodolfo García Zamora and examine all the major aspects and consequences of migration, including topics on women and children in high migration communities; a comparative study of local migrant organizations and development in Michoacán, Zacatecas, and El Salvador; and remittances in Jerez, Zacatecas, within the larger Latin American context.

1074 La gerencia pública en América del Norte: tendencias actuales de la reforma administrativa en Canadá, Estados Unidos y México. Coordinación de María del Carmen Pardo y Ernesto Velasco Sánchez. México: Colegio de México; Monterrey, Mexico: Instituto de Administración Pública de Nuevo León, 2009. 582 p.: bibl., ill.

This is a rare collection of some outstanding contributions which incorporate analyses of Canadian, American, and Mexican public administrative and policymaking in comparative context. Includes essays by scholars from all three countries.

1075 Gil Mendieta, Jorge and Samuel Schmidt. Estudios sobre la red política de México. Colaboración de Alejandro Arnulfo Ruiz León. México: UNAM, Instituto de Investigaciones en Matemáticas Aplicadas y en Sistemas, 2005. 182 p.: bibl., ill.

Gil Mendieta and Schmidt, who have been working on a mathematical model of political networking for years, provide a short overview of some of their findings in this work, which focuses more on the linkages than the political consequences of those linkages.

1076 El gobierno panista de Vicente Fox: la frustración del cambio. Coordinación de Francisco Reveles Vázquez. México: UNAM, Facultad de Ciencias Políticas y

Sociales: Editores e Impresores Profesionales, 2008. 342 p.: bibl.

Other than focusing on the Fox administration and its political policy results, these essays share few common themes. However, they cover both policy and political issues; they view the Fox administration as largely not fulfilling its promises; and from a political process angle, they focus strongly on divided government and on the legislative-executive relationship.

1077 González Pérez, Marco A. México polarizado (2000–2006): estudios de psicología política. México: Tecnológico de Monterrey: Itaca, 2008. 140 p.: bibl., ill.

This short but interesting piece attempts to analyze images and media articles to establish how both conveyed stereotypes of the leading candidates and how the leading candidates did the same to their opponents.

Grammont, Hubert Carton de and **Horacio Mackinlay.** Campesino and indigenous social organizations facing democratic transition in Mexico, 1938–2006. See *HLAS 66:939.*

1078 Grayson, George W. Mexico: narco-violence and a failed state? New Brunswick, N.J.: Transaction Publishers, 2009. 339 p.: bibl., index.

Grayson, who has engaged in extensive field research on contemporary policy and electoral issues in Mexico, provides a detailed but general account of narco-violence as an excellent starting point for understanding the extent to which drug trafficking organizations are influencing state sovereignty in Mexico. The work includes considerable background on leading drug trafficking figures and their organizations.

1079 Hernández Díaz, Jorge and **Anabel López Sánchez.** La construcción de la ciudadanía en la elección de autoridades municipales: el caso de Concepción Pápalo. (*Estud. Sociol./México*, 24:71, mayo/agosto 2006, p. 363–395, bibl.)

Utilizing extensive interviews, the authors explore the issue of citizen participation in local elections in Oaxaca from 1995 to 2004, including the widespread use of "traditions and customs" (usos y costumbres) as a form of determining local leadership, through a single case study of one municipality: Concepción Pápalo. This thoughtful study, which is well-integrated into the general literature, suggests how the influx of more financial resources is having an impact on a system of local governance which was, in large part, a response to a lack of resources.

1080 Hernández Rodríguez, Rogelio. La disputa por el presupuesto federal: presidencialismo y gobiernos estatales en México. (*Foro Int./México*, 46:1, enero/marzo 2006, p. 103–121)

Hernández Rodríguez, who has enriched our knowledge of the impact of governors on Mexican politics in the last decade, focuses on their abilities and efforts to challenge the federal government's control and organization of fiscal policies. He highlights the importance of the cooperation between the governors collectively and the legislative branch to achieve their goals.

1081 Hilgers, Tina. Causes and consequences of political clientelism: Mexico's PRD in comparative perspective. (*Lat. Am. Polit. Soc.*, 50:4, Winter 2008, p. 123–153, bibl.)

One of the most important patterns that continues to characterize Mexican politics in the post-2000 era is the persistence of clientelism. Hilgers argues that the PRD has used features of clientelism in its relationship with core supporters and that scholars need to re-examine how aspects of clientelism might be appropriate and useful in explaining behavior in a democratic setting.

1082 Holzner, Claudio A. Voz y voto: participación política y calidad de la democracia en México. (*Am. Lat. Hoy/Salamanca*, 45, abril 2007, p. 69–87, bibl., graphs, table)

Holzner has contributed some of the most insightful literature on citizen participation and democracy in Mexico. In this essay, which preceded his comprehensive book, he argues that Mexico's poor, as of 2007, lack real opportunities to influence decision-makers in spite of the existence of electoral competition. He also suggests that when they do participate, it is typically in ways that do not effectively communicate their demands.

1083 Liderazgo político: teoría y procesos en el México de hoy. Coordinación de Mario Bassols Ricárdez, Alberto Escamilla Cadena y Luis Reyes García. México: Univ. Autónoma Metropolitana Iztapalapa, 2008. 296 p.: bibl., ill.

Mexican scholars have produced few books on Mexican elites, but this collection attempts to provide, in some of its chapters, an overview of the state of elite research among non-Mexicans and Mexicans alike, as well as an examination of women in Mexican politics and the leadership of political parties, among other topics.

1084 Loaeza, Soledad. La desilusión mexicana: populismo y democracia en México en el 2006. (*Foro Int./México*, 47:4, oct./dic. 2007, p. 817–838, bibl.)

Loaeza's examination of the 2006 presidential election essentially argues that the continued weakness of the state's infrastructure as Mexico attempts to achieve a democratic consolidation is a basic variable that explains Mexican political stability. Citing an incident during the Dec. 1 session of Congress, she argues that Mexican nationalism continues to be an important value—one that might substitute for the institutional weaknesses and strengthen a democratic future.

1085 Lomnitz, Larissa Adler de; Rodrigo Salazar Elena; and Ilya Adler. Symbolism and ritual in a one-party regime: unveiling Mexico's political culture. Translated by Susanne A. Wagner. Tucson: Univ. of Arizona Press, 2010. 350 p.: bibl., index.

Over the years, Larissa Adler-Lomnitz and Ilya Adler have provided much insight into the anthropological aspects of Mexican politics, especially as it applies to elections. Their original analysis of the 1988 presidential election of Carlos Salinas will be useful to those attempting to identify changes that have taken place in electoral behavior as a result of the opposition party victory in 2000.

1086 López, Jorge Alberto. 2006, ¿fraude electoral?: estudios de las anomalías de la elección presidencial. Chihuahua, Mexico: Doble Hélice, 2009. 202 p.: bibl., ill.

Although the language of this work suggests a preconceived bias about 2006 election fraud, including a role for the US,

the main text is a mathematical analysis of anomalies in the ballots which raise a number of interesting questions.

1087 López Montiel, Gustavo. Distrito Federal: realineamiento y competencia electoral. (*Iztapalapa/México*, 27:61, julio/dic. 2006, p. 93–114, bibl., tables)

López Montiel traces the explanations for the peculiar behavior of Mexico City voters, which has set them apart from the rest of Mexico. As he notes in his essay, the party that has controlled the federal government has not, for many decades, dominated voters in the capital. He examines important reasons for such a deviation from the national norm, as well as its consequences for understanding Mexican electoral behavior generally.

1088 Magaloni, Beatriz. Voting for autocracy: hegemonic party survival and its demise in Mexico. Cambridge; New York: Cambridge Univ. Press, 2006. 296 p.: bibl., ill., index. (Cambridge studies in comparative politics)

Magaloni presents a sophisticated empirical analysis using statistical models to explain what besides electoral fraud allowed the PRI to survive for so many decades. This original and deeply researched study raises new findings, from the Mexican case, to explain theories of autocratic governance.

1089 Martínez Vásquez, Víctor Raúl. Autoritarismo, movimiento popular y crisis política: Oaxaca 2006. Mexico: Consorcio para el Diálogo Parlamentario y la Equidad: Centro de Apoyo al Movimiento Popular Oaxaqueño: EDUCA—Servicios para la Educación Alternativa: Instituto de Investigaciones Sociológicas de la Univ. Benito Juárez de Oaxaca, 2007. 303 p.: bibl., col. ill.

This helpful work presents an analysis and a detailed chronology (78 p.) of the violent confrontations that took place in Oaxaca City in 2006.

Mazzei, Julie. Death squads or self-defense forces?: how paramilitary groups emerge and threaten democracy in Latin America. See item **1153**.

Medina Vidal, D. Xavier *et al.* Partisan attachment and democracy in Mexico: some cautionary observations. See *HLAS 66:962*.

1090 Méndez, José Luis. La oficina presidencial y el liderazgo político en México y Estados Unidos: ¿incertidumbre competitiva o certidumbre cooperativa? (*Foro Int./México,* 47:4, oct./dic. 2007, p. 839–867, bibl.)

In a rare comparison between Mexico and the US, the author examines the role and impact of their respective presidential staffs, focusing on the Fox administration in Mexico. He offers numerous interesting conclusions about the differences between the two countries, one of which is that Mexican presidents are viewed as depending much more heavily on cabinet members, many of whom are confidants of the president. This finding helps to explain why the presidential staff in Mexico is smaller and weaker than its US counterpart.

1091 México: democracia y participación política indígena. Coordinación de Martha Singer Sochet. México: Ediciones Gernika: UNAM, Facultad de Ciencias Políticas y Sociales, 2007. 287 p.: bibl. (Col. Ciencias políticas)

Very little scholarly work exists on indigenous political participation in Mexico, which makes this collection extremely valuable to social scientists who hope to understand the broadest picture of how all groups in civil society are being affected by the democratization process or are affecting that very process.

1092 Mexico's democratic challenges: politics, government, and society. Edited by Andrew D. Selee and Jacqueline Peschard. Washington, D.C.: Woodrow Wilson Center Press, 2010. 326 p.: index.

Selee and Peschard provide a valuable collection on democratic political change through the early years of the Calderon administration. The collection is strong in the subject matter that it covers, including important institutions and actors that are often ignored by many analysts in the democratization process, such as churches. As is the case with many collections, while several essays provide only valuable observations, most combine such observations with actual original research. The topical chapters include such appropriate subject matter as the indigenous population, civil-military relations, transparency reforms, and citizen views of democracy.

1093 Millán, Rene. Confianza y participación en México: ¿dimensiones de la cooperación social y de la valoración del gobierno? (*Opin. Públ.,* 12:2, nov. 2006, p. 211–240, bibl., graphs, tables)

In this thoroughly researched comparative study of Chilpancingo, Saltillo, and Monterrey, Millán examines the relationship between trust in governmental institutions and political participation. Surprisingly, the author discovers that no direct relationship exists between trust and governmental competence, and that other variables play a likely role.

1094 Modoux, Magali. Geografía de la gobernanza: ¿la alternancia partidaria como factor de consolidación del poder de los gobernadores en el escenario nacional mexicano? (*Foro Int./México,* 46:3, julio/sept. 2006, p. 513–532, bibl., graphs)

In her exploration of the increasing autonomy and influence of state governors, Modoux argues that the alternation in power at the federal level and the formation of the National Conference of Governors (CONAGO) in 2002 were critical in strengthening and accelerating their political influence. In contrast, she believes that the rising importance of municipalities is a counterweight to such increased influence as they too attempt to obtain greater economic resources and control over policy.

1095 Moreno, Alejandro. La decisión electoral: votantes, partidos y democracia, México. México: Estados Unidos Mexicanos, Cámara de Diputados, LX Legislatura, Consejo Editorial: Miguel Ángel Porrúa, 2009. 440 p.: bibl., ill. (Serie Las ciencias sociales) (Conocer para decidir)

Moreno, who has worked extensively on understanding Mexican voter behavior since the 1990s, uses detailed data from two NSF-funded panel surveys of the elections of 2000 and 2006 to draw important conclusions about voter attitudes and their impact on the electoral outcomes. An essential source for understanding voter behavior and presidential elections.

1096 Moreno, Alejandro. La opinión pública mexicana en el contexto postelectoral de 2006. (*Perf. Latinoam.,* 16:31, enero/junio 2008, p. 39–63, bibl., graphs, tables)

Moreno, one of Mexico's leading

public opinion pollsters and academic survey researchers, uses data from a before-and-after survey conducted by the Comparative National Election Project to analyze the relationship between elite political interpretations and ordinary citizens' views shortly after the 2006 election. Despite the fact that Mexicans reflect a variety of views similar to those expressed by political leadership, Moreno confirms that little variation existed among voters from all ideological perspectives in their confidence in the Corte Electoral after the conflictive presidential outcome.

1097 Moreno Jaimes, Carlos. Do competitive elections produce better-quality governments?: evidence from Mexican municipalities, 1990–2000. (*LARR*, 42:2, 2007, p. 136–153, tables)

Using two municipal services, water and drainage coverage, the author examines to what extent electoral competition has affected the increase in those services in various municipalities. He discovers that electoral competition, at least during the decade from 1990 to 2000, was not a significant variable in increasing municipal services; rather, other factors were more important, such as socioeconomic status, literacy, and voter participation. He also believes political clientelism remains a possible explanation for variations in improved services.

1098 Moreno Jaimes, Carlos. Gasto público y elecciones: una explicación política de la asignación de los presupuestos municipales en México. (*Foro Int./México*, 47:2, abril/junio 2007, p. 408–434, bibl., graphs, tables)

Moreno Jaimes examines a significant question in the postdemocratic era of Mexican politics: to what degree has decentralization at the local level affected municipal expenditures, especially those on public works? He offers empirical evidence to demonstrate convincingly that the alternation of political party control combined with the decentralization of policy-making has increased investment in public works since the late 1990s.

1099 Morris, Stephen D. Political corruption in Mexico: the impact of democratization. Boulder, Colo.: Lynne Rienner Publishers, 2009. 307 p.: bibl., index.

Morris, who previously published the only book which thoroughly researched contemporary political corruption in Mexico (see *HLAS 53:3368*), brings that work up to date in a new book that examines this condition in the light of Mexico's efforts to democratize its political model. Although he favors the institutional approach to curbing corruption, believing the state is still weak in the midst of its democratic transition, he also suggests that there still may be a role for culture in understanding the relationship between corruption and political change in Mexico.

1100 Muñoz Armenta, Aldo. El sindicalismo corporativo mexicano y los partidos políticos en tiempos de alternancia. (*Nueva Antropol./México*, 20:66, julio 2006, p. 133–155, bibl., table)

This well-researched essay explores the continued relationship between corporatist organizations, specifically organized labor, and political parties under democratic electoral competition. Finds that, in the case of Chihuahua, PRI, in spite of the victories of PAN and PRD, continues to provide political space to voters from many traditional organizations—including labor—a role not performed by PAN or PRD because of institutional limitations.

1101 Pacheco Méndez, Guadalupe. ¿Hacia la cuarta etapa del partido de la revolución?: la elección interna de dirigentes del PRI en febrero de 2002. (*Foro Int./México*, 46:2, abril/junio 2006, p. 303–352, bibl., tables)

Pacheco has been seriously analyzing the PRI and its internal activities for more than 20 years. Her analysis of the internal election of PRI leadership, even in 2002, is essential to understanding the trajectory of PRI candidates for the remainder of the decade, and what may happen in 2012, as the PRI positions itself strongly for presidential race. Although she recognizes a high level of uncertainty about the future, some of her predictions about internal change have taken place.

1102 Pansters, Wil and Héctor F. Castillo Berthier. Violencia e inseguridad en la ciudad de México: entre la fragmentación y la politización. (*Foro Int./México*, 47:3, julio/sept. 2007, p. 577–615, bibl., graphs, tables)

Pansters, a leading historian of regional politics in Mexico, and his co-author explore the longer-term consequences of social equality, violence, and insecurity in the nation's capital. This valuable essay provides an extensively researched argument about criminal conditions in metropolitan Mexico City prior to 2000, while concluding that the perceived levels of recent insecurity at the national level have also characterized the capital. They argue that these conditions will ultimately be solved through social justice and real democratic practices.

1103 Participación política de la mujer en México. México: Comisión Nacional de los Derechos Humanos, 2009. 287 p.: bibl., ill.

This collection on the participation of women in Mexican politics is worth consulting for the first chapter alone, a 96-p. essay on indigenous female involvement in local politics which includes extensive statistics and detailed interviews. The remaining three chapters are also carefully researched and add additional up-to-date data on women's involvement in political office.

1104 Pensar en México. Textos de José Antonio Aguilar Rivera *et al.* Introducción de Héctor Aguilar Camín. México: Consejo Nacional para la Cultura y las Artes: Fondo de Cultura Económica, 2006. 364 p.: bibl., ill. (Biblioteca mexicana. Serie Historia y antropología)

The only theme which links these essays together, one which permeates many other academic collections of this period, is pessimism about the political situation in Mexico and the disappointments of democratic consolidation. Whether economic or political, all of these contributors point to policy failures.

1105 Pérez Fernández del Castillo, Germán. Modernización y desencanto: los efectos de la modernización mexicana en la subjetividad y la gobernabilidad. México: Miguel Ángel Porrúa: UNAM, Facultad de Ciencias Políticas y Sociales, 2008. 124 p.: bibl., ill. (Las ciencias sociales. Segunda década) (Política)

Using a national survey, the author explores the potential influence of citizen attitudes, including those affected by globalization, on the governability of Mexico. He argues that objective and subjective conditions—including attitudes affecting social well-being, which are explored in this short work—are both essential for the governing process to succeed.

1106 Poder político y sociedad: diez ensayos aproximativos. Coordinación de Florencia Correas Vázquez, Carlos Figueroa Ibarra y Pedro Hernández Ornelas. México: Benemérita Univ. Autónoma de Puebla, 2006. 204 p.: bibl., ill. (Política)

Although this collection is wide-ranging and does not have a specific focus, it includes some contributions on topics rarely covered by social scientists, including Luis Ochoa Bilbao's contemporary view of intellectuals and the state, Pedro F. Hernández's examination of Church and state, and Angélica Mendieta Ramírez's survey of women and politics, which is primarily valuable for the data.

1107 Política territorial en México: hacia un modelo de desarrollo basado en el territorio. Coordinación de Javier Delgadillo Macías. Textos de Ricardo Mejía Zayas *et al.* México: Estados Unidos Mexicanos, Gobierno Federal, SEDESOL: Instituto de Investigaciones Económicas, UNAM: Plaza y Valdés, 2008. 677 p.: bibl., ill., maps.

Sponsored by the Secretaría de Desarrollo Social, this extensive collection thoroughly examines theories, practices, and conditions relevant to regional development models in Mexico, providing an excellent sampling of the views of Mexican specialists on this topic.

1108 Porras, Francisco. Rethinking local governance: hierarchies and networks in Mexican cities. (*Rev. Eur. Estud. Latinoam. Caribe*, 83, Oct. 2007, p. 43–59, bibl., tables)

This study of municipal governance, based in part on three case studies of León, Orizaba, and Zacatecas, concludes that the nonstate organizations are increasingly significant in Mexico, especially business organizations which are much more likely than civic organizations to influence local policy-making. This influence has been particularly notable in urban settings over land use.

1109 Ramos García, José María. Insegu-
ridad pública en México: una pro-
puesta de gestión de política estratégica en
gobiernos locales. Mexicali, Mexico: Univ.
Autónoma de Baja California: México:
Miguel Ángel Porrúa, 2006. 243 p.: bibl.
Conocer para decidir) (Las ciencias sociales.
Segunda década)

This excellent work on public security argues that Mexico must focus on the
relationship between citizens and their
political institutions, and not just on legal
reforms. The author offers specific recommendations for local communities.

1110 Rap, Edwin. Cultural performance,
resource flows and passion in politics:
a situational analysis of an election rally
in western Mexico. (*J. Lat. Am. Stud.*, 39:3,
August 2007, p. 595–625, maps)

This is a unique approach and analysis of "cultural performance" in local politics, a technique in which the politican uses
personal behavior to reinforce certain local
norms and enhance his ability to obtain the
support of his potential electoral clientele.
The larger issue Rap addresses—which is
essential to understanding Mexican politics
within democratic consolidation—is the
accommodation of historical and regional
behavior to the new political and economic
setting.

**1111 La reforma del estado y la calidad
de la democracia en México: una
reflexión sobre sus instituciones.** Coordinación de Óscar Ochoa González. Mexico:
Tecnológico de Monterrey, Escuela de Graduados en Administración Pública y Política
Pública: Miguel Ángel Porrúa, 2008. 222 p.:
bibl.

These authors attempt to assess the
quality of democracy through an evaluation
of institutions in Mexico. Jorge Vargas Cul-
lell offers an excellent introductory chapter
on democratization and democratic quality,
which provides the focus for the other contributors, including thoughtful essays on
federalism and transparency.

**1112 Rendición de cuentas, democracia
y sociedad civil en México.** Coordi-
nación de Henio Millán y Alejandro Natal
Martínez. Zinacantepec, Mexico: Colegio
Mexiquense, 2008. 329 p.: bibl., ill.
Stemming from a conference at the

Colegio Mexiquense, this group of scholars
examines the issue of accountability from a
wide range of perspectives, including transparency in the legal system, access to public
information, and the openness of private
welfare and nongovernmental institutions.
This is a well-focused and complementary
collection of essays.

1113 Ríos-Figueroa, Julio. Fragmentation
of power and the emergence of an effective judiciary in Mexico, 1994–2002. (*Lat.
Am. Polit. Soc.*, 49:1, Spring 2007, p. 31–57,
bibl., tables)

This early study of the changing role
of the Mexican Supreme Court provides
a now important historical examination
of how court leadership altered their behavior toward the executive branch given
the 2000 election victory of the PAN. The
author argues that it was not the institutional changes introduced by the 1994 legal
reforms, but rather the altered behavior of
the justices themselves in reaction to the
modified power structure in the chamber
of deputies. For historian's comment, see
HLAS 66:982.

**1114 Rumbo a los Pinos en el 2006: los
candidatos y los partidos en el espacio público.** Coordinación de Adrián S.
Gimate-Welsh. México: Univ. Autónoma
Metropolitana, Unidad Iztapalapa, División
de Ciencias Sociales y Humanidades: M.A.
Porrúa, 2009. 299 p.: bibl. (Serie Las ciencias
sociales)

This is the strongest, most well-
researched collection by some of Mexico's
leading scholars of the 2006 presidential
election, including chapters on parties, an
evaluation of the electronic media, the debate and TV advertisements, minorities and
communication, the legislative agenda, and
an insightful essay by Guadalupe Pacheco
Méndez on the election of Madrazo as the
PRI presidential candidate.

**1115 Las rutas de la democracia: elecciones
locales en México.** Coordinación de
Víctor Alejandro Espinoza Valle. México:
Ediciones y Gráficos Eón: Centro de Estudios de Política Comparada, 2007. 262 p.:
bibl., ill. (Eón sociales)

This collection examines regional
electoral politics, focusing on the elections
which took place locally or statewide in

2004. Among those which are particularly noteworthy for their extensive research are Luis Miguel Rionda's analysis of Durango, a state which is rarely researched; Víctor A. Espinoza Valle's contribution on Baja California; and Silvia Gómez Tagle's outstanding exploration of local and state elections in Chiapas.

1116 Sabet, Daniel M. Nonprofits and their networks: cleaning the waters along Mexico's northern border. Tucson: Univ. of Arizona Press, 2008. 292 p.: bibl., ill., index, maps.

Sabet explores the efforts of NGOs to affect water policy along the border. Not only are water issues among the most neglected policy topics in analyzing the US-Mexican relationship, but Sabet provides one of the first book-length analyses of how NGOs are actually functioning in a democratic transition. He suggests, as do other authors who explore the nonprofit sector, that despite democratic change, many behaviors which are obstacles to these organizations exercising influence continue in the present political environment.

1117 Salinas de Gortari, Carlos. La "década perdida": 1995–2006: neoliberalismo y populismo en México. México: Debate, 2008. 557 p.: bibl., indexes.

The former president offers his interpretation of the impact of neoliberal economic policies that he set in motion when he took office in 1988. This is more than a personal interpretation; it is also an analysis based on public documents and serious secondary research.

1118 Sefchovich, Sara. País de mentiras: la distancia entre el discurso y la realidad en la cultura mexicana. Mexico: Oceano, 2008. 391 p.: bibl., ill. (Con una cierta mirada) (Tiempo de México)

One of Mexico's leading commentators explores lies in the public arena, specifically comparing what public officials say versus the truth, examining the impact of those lies on culture in general and political culture specifically, and measuring the influence this activity has on Mexican behavior. This is an important topic and has received little, if any, attention in the scholarly literature.

1119 Shefner, Jon. The illusion of civil society: democratization and community mobilization in low-income Mexico. University Park: Pennsylvania State Univ. Press, 2008. 224 p.: bibl., ill., index.

Shefner skillfully uses a case study, based on extensive field research, of a popular organization in Guadalajara to illustrate the impact of the recent implementation of neoliberal policies and democratization efforts in the behavior of these types of organizations in Mexican politics generally, and specifically their impact on clientelism.

1120 Simposio Veracruzano de Otoño, 1st, 2006. La política en México. Coordinación de Enrique Florescano. Textos de Raúl Arias Lovillo *et al.* México: Taurus, 2007. 351 p.: bibl. (Taurus historia) (Col. Pasado y presente)

Although this collection is characterized by a distinguished list of Mexican contributors, many of the essays benefit largely from their observations and reflections rather than from quantitative research. Some notable exceptions include Alonso Lujambio's careful analysis of the 1977 electoral reform which he views as critical to Mexico's democratic transition, and Alberto Olvera's chapter on the changing relationship between the state and society.

1121 Sobarzo, Horacio. Esfuerzo y potencialidad fiscal de los gobiernos estatales en México: un sistema fiscal representativo. (*Trimest. Econ.*, 73:292, oct./dic. 2006, p. 809–861, bibl., graphs, tables)

At a time when there has been decentralization from federal to local control of tax revenues, thus increasing the importance of local management, relatively little is known about the impact of these changes on state fiscal policy and administration. The author provides careful evidence and arguments to support a more responsible decentralization policy and the potential for the success of such a policy on the state level, especially given the limitations of extreme economic disparities among regions.

1122 Tosoni, María Magdalena. Notas sobre el clientelismo político en la ciudad de México. (*Perf. Latinoam.*, 14:29, enero/junio 2007, p. 47–69, bibl.)

This study examines the extent to which clientelism, a significant feature of

PRI-dominated politics in Mexico for decades, continues to exert an influence over Mexican politics in spite of the democratic election of an opposition president in 2000. Based on interviews with leaders and voters in a Mexico City working class neighborhood, the author concludes that clientelism, in the form of candidates' rewards to voters in exchange for votes, is widespread and healthy, having survived democratic politics in an era of political unpredictability.

1123 Transición política, alternancia y proceso de gobierno en México, 2001–2006. Coordinación de Héctor Zamitiz Gamboa. México: UNAM, Facultad de Ciencias Políticas y Sociales: Gernika, 2008. 297 p.: bibl. (Col. Ciencias políticas)

Some of the essays in this collection are characterized by little scholarly depth, but three are particularly valuable for their research and arguments: Héctor Zamitiz Gamboa offers a criticism of the Fox transition; Francisco Reveles Vázquez, who has produced numerous studies of PRI, analyzes the political parties after 2000; and Matilde Yánez Maldonado provides insight into the Fox cabinet and good government project.

1124 Ugalde, Luis Carlos. Así lo viví: testimonio de la elección presidencial de 2006, la más competida en la historia moderna de México. México: Grijalbo, 2008. 454 p., 16 p. of plates: bibl., ill. (chiefly col.), index, col. ports.

Carlos Ugalde, president of the Instituto Federal Electoral from 2003–2006, offers one of the few first-hand accounts of the 2006 presidential election. Here he provides an inside view of the institutional controversies faced by Mexico's most important electoral agency.

1125 Uildriks, Niels A. Mexico's unrule of law: implementing human rights in police and judicial reform under democratization. Lanham, Md.: Lexington Books, 2010. 313 p.: bibl., index.

This outstanding analysis examines the needed reform to policing in Mexico and the difficulties which have been encountered in attempting to alter the behavior of actors and reforms to the justice system. The author provides much needed original

analysis based on observation, interviews, survey research, and secondary research.

1126 Universidad Nacional Autónoma de México. Seminario Académico Perspectiva Democrática. Coloquio. *1st, Instituto de Investigaciones Sociales de la Universidad Nacional Autónoma de México, 2004.* El estado actual de la democracia en México: retos, avances y retrocesos. Coordinación de Fernando Castaños, Julio Labastida Marín del Campo y Miguel Armando López Leyva. México: UNAM, Instituto de Investigaciones Sociales, 2007. 280 p.: bibl.

In this collection of essays on the vagaries of democratic consolidation, three contributions stand out: Gabriel Corona Armenta on postdemocratic presidentialism, Silvia Inclán Oseguera on judicial reform, and José Luis Velasco's case study of Fox's failed fiscal reform in the Congress.

1127 Verdugo López, Mercedes. Democratización del gobierno municipal: Culiacán, un estudio de caso, 1983–2001. Culiacán, Mexico: El Colegio de Sinaloa, 2007. 254 p.: bibl.

Verdugo López offers a case study of the important municipality of Culiacán, Sonora, to examine the impact of democratization on decision-making in the 1990s. Using archival research of city documents, he concludes, similar to other studies of local governments, that democracy's impact was limited formally as well as by traditional practices.

1128 Zamitiz Gamboa, Héctor and Irma Peña León. Una caracterización de la democracia mexicana y sus actores políticos: la elección para gobernador del estado de México, 2005. (*Rev. Mex. Cienc. Polít. Soc.,* 48:196, enero/abril 2006, p. 115–141, bibl.)

The authors provide a detailed analysis of the gubernatorial election in the state of México in 2005, suggesting that many of the weaknesses which became apparent in this election likely would have an impact on the 2006 presidential campaign. The state election may also be revealing because its victorious candidate, Enrique Peña Nieto, became the PRI presidential nominee in 2012.

CENTRAL AMERICA

CHARLES D. BROCKETT, *Professor Emeritus of Political Science, Sewanee: The University of the South*

GOVERNABILITY IS A KEY topic throughout many of the works selected for inclusion in the *HLAS 67* section on Central American Government and Politics. Conceptual issues related to the capacity of a political system to make and implement decisions is effectively explored by Artiga González in dialogue with many of the leading scholars on this theme (item **1147**); he develops numerous indicators that will be appropriate for future studies. Even the region's best performing political system, Costa Rica, continues to confront challenges in the area of legitimacy, including both vertical and horizontal distributions of power. Mora provides the rare, well-executed study of government decentralization along with measures for enhancing local government capacity (item **1143**). Several essays in the compilation *¿Hacia dónde va Costa Rica?* give close and insightful attention to executive-legislative relations with strong arguments for institutional reforms (item **1140**). Vargas Céspedes does the same for the region as a whole, centering on the difficulties inherent in the region's commonplace situation of divided government (item **1134**).

Unfortunately, democratic consolidation is reversible, as witnessed by the 2009 coup in Honduras and the continuing spectacle of Guatemala moving toward the brink. The *Journal of Democracy* features three articles by leading regional specialists in its April 2010 issue that expertly clarify the relevant dynamics. Both Ruhl for Honduras (item **1165**) and Isaacs for Guatemala (item **1158**) clarify the breakdown of minimal cooperation between elites along with their willingness to violate democratic rules, most extremely in the Honduran case by both sides. Criminality grows in both countries, most troublingly at the hands of well-organized drug trafficking gangs with complicity on the part of some public officials. Approaching the governance issue from the ground up, Mitchell Seligson and John Booth extend the analysis of their excellent 2009 book, *The Legitimacy Puzzle in Latin America: Political Support and Democracy in Eight Nations*, providing innovative measures of legitimacy. Their investigation of the relevant survey data finds the Honduran public the most permissive in all of Latin America toward nondemocratic measures, followed by Guatemalans.

Controversies concerning the significance of democratic consolidation are the predominant theme in the scholarship surveyed on El Salvador and Nicaragua. Written prior to the Frente Farabundo Martí para la Liberación Nacional's (FMLN) 2009 legislative and presidential victories, Wolf classifies El Salvador as an authoritarian government concealed behind a façade of regular elections (item **1155**). A short discussion of the 2009 elections at the end of the essay maintains the negative analysis of the two decades of Alianza Republicana Nacionalista (ARENA) dominance. In contrast, Colburn characterizes El Salvador as a robust democracy, issuing credit to both political parties for constructing a system with less corruption and better functioning than not only Honduras and Guatemala, but also Nicaragua (item **1150**).

The most frequent theme running through the works on Nicaragua is how the Frente Sandinista de Liberación Nacional (FSLN) changed from a broad-based popular movement under a collective leadership to a political party subordinated to the wishes of a single leader, Daniel Ortega, Nicaragua's president since 2007.

The broadest perspective is provided by an edited volume whose contributors highlight the consequences of the 1999 pact between Ortega and his ideological rival but collaborator in opportunism, former President Arnoldo Alemán, and their shared responsibility for Nicaragua's democratic decomposition (item **1174**). Martí i Puig offers the most in-depth treatment of the FSLN itself, focusing on its organizational apparatus and Ortega's deinstitutionalization of the party as he tightens his control (item **1172**). While Kampwirth underscores Ortega's cynicism (item **1171**), Tatar goes back three decades to uncover distortions in the Sandinistanarrative of the Monimbó insurrection in order to uphold its vanguard role (item **1173**). Standing against this perspective are two other studies indicating a vibrant grassroots movement in keeping with the more positive portrayal often presented in the past. Anderson emphasizes the positive role of a mobilized populace in providing vertical accountability to the system (item **1166**), and *Social Capital in Developing Democracies* contrasts the negative consequences of a clientilistic Peronism in Argentina with a Sandinismo that encourages horizontal ties, helping democracy to thrive (item **1167**). The contrast is well made but the thrust of the other studies would suggest a steady transformation moving the FSLN toward the Peronist party.

Still, it must be said that *Social Capital* is a model of outstanding scholarship in its combination of theoretical discussion with multidimensional research. A similar standout is a groundbreaking study of female legislators in Central America, again combining keen attention to theoretical concerns with elite interviews (item **1131**). Women and politics are central to another, well-executed empirical study focused on the relevance of gender in explaining responses to a 2006 national Salvadoran survey, while comparing the results to a similar 2003 survey (item **1146**). However, gender is found to have little impact on political conditions, participation, support, etc. More generally, sociological variables do not have much of a role in another sophisticated theoretical and empirical study of Salvadoran politics. Instead, Azpuru emphasizes the salience of ideology to the outcomes of 15 years of presidential elections (item **1148**).

The years of the region's terrible violent political conflicts continue to recede into the past and fewer works deal directly with this period than surveyed for prior volumes. Still, as Rey Tristán and Martín Álvarez point out, many important questions from this period await scholarly attention (item **1154**). One book, however, does stand out. Gustavo Porras is in a uniquely good position to explore the more than four decades of Guatemalan political turmoil following the 1954 regime change (item **1159**). The potential of what he could write from personal experience is maximized by his perspective, providing a less partisan effort at explaining motivations on all sides of the conflict than do some scholarly works.

This same period and many of the same issues have been analyzed carefully and insightfully for decades by the dean of Central American social science, Edelberto Torres-Rivas. His scholarship, mentoring, and institution-building is honored in a special volume, which has been issued as part of the prestigious Colección Pensamiento crítico latinoamericano (item **1133**).

Finally, Costa Rica once again remains in the forefront for quality when it is the subject of scholarship, usually by Costa Ricans themselves (for an example in addition to those previously mentioned, see item **1144**). For this volume, though, the gap in substantive scholarly research and publication has considerably lessened for El Salvador and Nicaragua. In contrast, scholarly attention to Honduras and Panama has been minimal.

GENERAL

Cloos, Patrick. Health inequalities in the Caribbean: increasing opportunities and resources. See item **1179.**

1129 Greentree, Todd R. Crossroads of intervention: insurgency and counter-insurgency lessons from Central America. Foreword by Robert W. Tucker. Westport, Conn.: Praeger Security International, 2008. 196 p.: bibl., ill., index, maps, plates.

Arriving in El Salvador as a young Foreign Service officer in 1981 and now professor of national security and international politics at the US Naval War College, Greentree has combined on-the-ground experience with scholarly objectives to produce a valuable assessment of US involvement in El Salvador and Nicaragua during their civil wars and of counterinsurgency and insurgency more generally.

1130 Martí i Puig, Salvador. Tiranías, rebeliones y democracia: itinerarios políticos comparados en Centroamérica. Barcelona: Edicions Bellaterra, 2004. 327 p.: bibl., maps. (Serie General universitaria; 40)

Highly competent political history—although breaks no new ground. Beginning with early colonial history, the main focus is tyrannies of the mid-20th century, processes that brought them down, and a brief analysis of the first decade of new democratic regimes. Most attention is given to Nicaragua with very little to Costa Rica, and even less to Honduras.

Palmer, Steven Paul. Launching global health: the Caribbean odyssey of the Rockefeller Foundation. See item **1184.**

1131 Saint-Germain, Michelle A. and **Cynthia Chavez Metoyer.** Women legislators in Central America: politics, democracy, and policy. Austin: Univ. of Texas Press, 2008. 338 p.: bibl., ill., index, map.

First in-depth study of women elected to national legislatures in the 1980s and 1990s, this is an impressive work of comparative analysis examining significant theoretical issues at both the individual and the national level based on interviews with almost all Central American female legislators serving during this period. Culminates with an assessment of policy consequences.

1132 Seligson, Mitchell A. and **John A. Booth.** Crime, hard times, and discontent. (*J. Democr.*, 21:2, April 2010, p. 123–135, ill., tables)

Two top regional specialists demonstrate the important utility of their recent work on measuring political legitimacy, showing with 2004 and 2008 Americas-Barometer data that among all Latin American countries, public opinion in Honduras has been most permissive of nondemocratic measures, providing a supportive climate for the 2009 coup. By their measures, Guatemala is at risk as well.

1133 Torres-Rivas, Edelberto. Centroamérica: entre revoluciones y democracia. Presentación de Jorge Rovira Mas. Buenos Aires: CLACSO: Prometeo Libros, 2009. 274 p.: bibl. (Col. Pensamiento crítico latinoamericano)

Important recognition of one of Central America's leading social scientists of recent decades. Begins with Rovira's intellectual biography of Torres-Rivas, followed by seven selections of the latter's work from 1979 to 2005 addressing major themes of his scholarship—dictatorship and democracy and underdevelopment and development—and ending with an exhaustive bibliography of his writings.

1134 Vargas Céspedes, Jean Paul. El ocaso de los presidencialismos centroamericanos. (*Anu. Estud. Centroam.*, 32, 2006, p. 37–79, bibl., tables)

Very useful comparison of executive-legislative relations grounded in the appropriate theoretical literature. Emphasizes the dimensions most relevant to the difficulty of garnering presidential support from a legislature under a divided government—the pattern prevailing in each Central American country at the time of writing (except for Panama). For book-length treatment of the topic in Costa Rica, see *HLAS 65:1509.*

BELIZE

1135 Taking stock: Belize at 25 years of independence. Vol. 1. Edited by Barbara Susan Balboni and Joseph O. Palacio. Contributions by Jaime J. Awe *et al.* Benque Viejo del Carmen, Belize: Cubola Productions, 2007. 343 p.: bibl., index, ill., maps. (Belize collection. Essay)

This collection of essays "takes stock" of Belize as it makes its way along the continuum from its first 25 years as an independent nation into the regional, international, and global arena. [C.E. Griffin]

COSTA RICA

1136 Chacón Jiménez, Luis Manuel. Un largo camino: viaje a través de la política de Costa Rica. San José: Progreso Editorial, 2009. 392 p.: appendixes, ill.

Political autobiography of a core founder of the country's major opposition political party for four decades, beginning with his successful 1966 presidential campaign. The author served what became the Partido Unidad Social Cristiana as campaign strategist, head of congressional delegation, party president, cabinet minister, and vice presidential candidate, until resigning membership in an intra-party quarrel following the disastrous showing in the 2006 elections.

1137 Cortés Ramos, Alberto. Ensayos sobre coyuntura y política en Costa Rica, 1998–2008. San José: Ediciones Perro Azul, 2009. 234 p.: bibl., ill.

Scholarly essays augmented by short opinion pieces analyzing the elections of 1998, 2002, and 2006. Volume highlights the role of controversies associated with the neoliberal transformation, such as a free trade agreement with the US and privatization, especially of the Instituto Costarricense de Electricidad, often making good use of public opinion surveys.

1138 Cubillo Paniagua, Ruth. Luisa González: el pensamiento político de una maestra costarricense comunista. (*Kañina/San José*, 32:1, 2008, p. 49–56, bibl.)

Educator, writer, and Communist Party activist, Luisa González was an important force from the early 1920s into the 1990s, as well as through her efforts to enhance the status of women. This essay briefly sketches some of her views, such as her strong anti-imperialist stand and her commitment to improving the well-being of the disadvantaged.

1139 Frajman, Eduardo. Information and values in popular protests: Costa Rica in 2000. (*Bull. Lat. Am. Res.*, 28:1, Jan. 2009, p. 44–62, bibl.)

Informative effort to explain the eruption of sustained mass protests in 2000 when a surprised government backed down on its proposed privatization of the Instituto Costarricense de Electricidad (ICE). The explanation stresses communication theory and the importance for scholars (and political actors) to consider the role of symbolic and emotion-laden issues.

1140 ¿Hacia dónde va Costa Rica?: sistema político y escenarios de gobernabilidad democrática para la próxima década 2010–2020: 5 debates sobre el futuro de Costa Rica. Edición de Jaime Ordóñez. Textos de Mylena Vega *et al.* San José: Instituto Centroamericano de Gobernabilidad: Estudios para el Futuro, 2009. 394 p.: bibl.

Well-conceived volume providing a set of essays by domestic scholars on five central issues about the Costa Rican political system. Although some contributions offer more interpretation than evidence, others are rich in evidence (especially those on recent elections and party system changes) and/or in-depth and careful analyses (especially those proposing changes in executive-legislative relations).

1141 Hernández Rodríguez, Óscar; Francisco Garro; and María Elena Rodríguez Molina. Elecciones presidenciales: inconsistencias, anomalías y otros temas. San José: Editorial UCR, 2009. 130 p.: bibl., ill. (some col.), col. maps.

Empirical examination of inconsistencies in reported election results and a call for the reform of the Tribunal Supremo de Elecciones to better minimize fraud possibilities. Focuses on 2006 but includes comparisons to other elections, especially those of 1966 and 2002. Also examines voter abstention, especially in 2006.

1142 Madrigal Nieto, Rodrigo. Escritos y ensayos. Heredia, Costa Rica: Editorial Univ. Nacional, 2008. 2 v.

Newspaper columns, essays, and speeches from 1941 to 2005 by one of Costa Rica's most distinguished public figures across this period. Successful lawyer, industrialist, and publisher, Madrigal Nieto served as president of the Chamber of Commerce, the Legislative Assembly, the Organization of American States, and the Inter American Press Association. Close to Liberationist presidents, he provides an insider view on numerous topics, especially the peace process under President Óscar Arias when he served as foreign minister.

1143 Mora A., Jorge A. El sinuoso camino a la descentralización y el necesario fortalecimiento del gobierno local. San José: FLACSO Costa Rica, 2009. 180 p.: bibl., ill.

Impressive in-depth study of governmental decentralization and its important corollary of strengthening capacity of local governments, enriched with some regional comparisons. Along with historical and legal approaches, extensive data is also provided, particularly on inequality indicators at the provincial and canton levels.

1144 Raventós Vorst, Ciska. Lo que fue ya no es y lo nuevo aún no toma forma: elecciones 2006 en perspectiva histórica. (*Am. Lat. Hoy/Salamanca*, 49, agosto 2008, p. 129–155, bibl., graphs, tables)

Informed analysis of the 2006 presidential election won by Óscar Arias, based on good use of survey data, and enhanced by grounding the account in the assessment of two major changes in election behavior in this and two prior presidential elections compared to patterns going back to the 1950s: a sharp increase in voter abstention and the deterioration of two-party dominance.

1145 Reflexiones sobre el primer decenio del siglo XXI en Costa Rica: desarrollo, cohesión social y políticas públicas en el itinerario del bienestar. Edición de Manuel Barahona Montero y Yajaira Ceciliano. Textos de Alberto Salom Echeverría *et al.* San José: Facultad Latinoamericana de Ciencias Sociales-Sede Costa Rica, 2008. 208 p.: ill.

Presentations from six forums held in Costa Rica in 2006 and 2007, along with audience questions and panelist responses. This is the third volume resulting from the Diálogos sobre el Bienestar program, sponsored by FLACSO along with Adenauer Foundation and UNICEF. Among the topics treated with the greatest depth is Costa Rica's progress toward achieving UN Millennium Development Goals. Other topics include include multiculturalism, families, and gender and lifecycle.

EL SALVADOR

1146 Arana, Rubí Esmeralda and **Jeannette Aguilar Villamariona.** La situación del país, el sistema político y la participación de la mujer en la política, desde una perspectiva de género. San Salvador: Instituto Univ. de Opinión Pública: FundaUngo, 2008. 115 p.: bibl., ill. (Col. Género; 3)

Presents the results of a large representative national survey undertaken in 2006 by the Instituto Universidad de Opinión Pública with comparisons to a similar 2003 survey. Variables other than gender explain the response variations on most questions with only about a seven-point spread when differences are found, such as support for democracy or FMLN or interest in politics.

1147 Artiga González, Álvaro. Gobernabilidad y democracia en El Salvador: bases teóricas y metodológicas para su medición. San Salvador: UCA Editores: PNUD, 2007. 505 p.: bibl.

Thorough, clear, and effective conceptual chapters on both governability (capacity of the political system to make and implement decisions) and democracy (participation of the people) constitute the first half of the volume. The second half provides equally impressive operationalization with a multitude of indicators. Although full measurement is not attempted, the study is data rich, both for El Salvador and for cross-national comparisons within the region.

1148 Azpuru, Dinorah. The salience of ideology: fifteen years of presidential elections in El Salvador. (*Lat. Am. Polit. Soc.*, 52:2, Summer 2010, p. 103–138, bibl., tables)

Sophisticated theoretical and empirical examination of the determinants of electoral support in presidential elections from 1994 through 2009 based on an analysis of individual-level data. Finds little role for sociological variables; instead, the importance of ideology and policy performance are evident. Convincingly demonstrates the utility of voting models developed for advanced industrial democracies for analyzing third wave democracies.

1149 Castellón, Ricardo and **Nicolás Doljanin.** Pakito Arriaran: de Arasate a Chalatenango. Tafalla, Spain: Txalaparta, 2008. 158 p.: ill., maps.

Tribute to one of the internationalists killed while fighting with the revolutionaries in El Salvador, in this case a member of the Basque separatist organization Euskadi Ta Askatasuna (ETA) who went into exile in late 1978, arriving in Chalatenango in Sept. 1982, dying in combat two years later. Main value to scholars is a snapshot of life in rebel territory as captured through photographs and interviews with those who knew Arriaran.

1150 Colburn, Forrest D. The turnover in El Salvador. (*J. Democr.*, 20:3, July 2009, p. 143–152)

This article praises the contributions of both major political parties in El Salvador for the creation of a better functioning and less corrupt political system—especially when compared to Guatemala, Honduras, and Nicaragua. Written following the political left's 2009 presidential victory, the essay predicts sober and responsible governance and more continuity in policy than one might expect given the ideological gap between incoming and outgoing administrations.

1151 Hume, Mo. The myths of violence: gender, conflict, and community in El Salvador. (*Lat. Am. Perspect.*, 35:5, Sept. 2008, p. 59–76, bibl.)

Drawing on the life histories of men and women in two marginal communities in Greater San Salvador and comments by men in a self-help group for those convicted of domestic violence, this article highlights the centrality of violence to masculine identity and to the continuation of male privilege. For sociologist's comment, see item **2382**.

1152 Ladutke, Lawrence Michael. Understanding terrorism charges against protesters in the context of Salvadoran history. (*Lat. Am. Perspect.*, 35:6, Nov. 2008, p. 137–150, bibl.)

Utilizes the Salvadoran case to assess the validity of Todd Landman's cross-national quantitative study of antiterrorist legislation's impact on treatment of human rights defenders ("Holding the Line: Human Rights Defenders in the Age of Terror," *British Journal of Politics & International Relations*, 8:2, May 2006, p. 123–147). Claims that the passage of the Terrorist Acts Law in 2006 has limited impact since human rights violations against protesters were already on the upswing. Good descriptive treatment but not a systematic analysis.

1153 Mazzei, Julie. Death squads or self-defense forces?: how paramilitary groups emerge and threaten democracy in Latin America. Chapel Hill: Univ. of North Carolina Press, 2009. 261 p.: bibl., graphs, index, maps.

Proposes a useful explanatory framework for paramilitary emergence, highlighting the confluence of ambivalent state officials, powerful military personnel, and privileged members of the economic elite in the face of a threat from below and human rights constraints from outside. The theory is effectively applied to case studies of El Salvador, along with Chiapas and Colombia, drawing on interviews conducted in first two.

1154 Rey Tristán, Eduardo and **Alberto Martín Álvarez.** El FMLN y la lucha revolucionaria salvadoreña: estado de la cuestión. (*ECA/San Salvador*, 63:717, julio/sept. 2008, p. 441–447, bibl.)

Despite the FMLN's centrality to the last four decades, this thorough assessment of the state of literature about the organization during the civil war years of 1980–92 notes the absence of any systematic social science or historical study. Among major gaps, the authors cite decision-making both within FMLN as well as within constituent groups, relations with mass organizations, and support from international allies.

1155 Wolf, Sonja. Subverting democracy: elite rule and the limits to political participation in post-war El Salvador. (*J. Lat. Am. Stud.*, 41:3, Aug. 2009, p. 429–465)

Characterizes ARENA's two decades of governing not as imperfect democratic consolidation but rather as regressing to "electoral authoritarianism." After a conceptual discussion, the author provides a close examination—through 2006—of electoral and media manipulation to perpetuate rule under the guise of democracy. The left's legislative and presidential victories of 2009 are briefly discussed at the end of the piece.

GUATEMALA

1156 Coloquio México-Guatemala. Estado y Ciudadanía, *San Cristóbal de Las Casas, Mexico, 2005.* México y Guatemala:

entre el liberalismo y la democracia multi-cultural: azares de una transición política inconclusa. Coordinación de Jorge Ramón González-Ponciano y Miguel Lisbona. México: UNAM, 2009. 322 p.: bibl.

Papers from a 2005 conference in Chiapas include several worthy contributions related to ethnicity in Guatemala, notably Mam agrarian struggles, Garífuna transnational citizenry, and two on continuing indigenous marginalization: Rigoberto Quemé provides the historical context for an assessment of contemporary political parties while Demetrio Cojtí utilizes a well-elaborated framework for his critical diagnosis.

1157 Díaz López, Gustavo Adolfo. Guatemala en llamas: visión política-militar del conflicto armado interno, 1960–1996: ensayo. Ciudad de Guatemala: Editorial Oscar de León Palacios, 2008. 389 p.: bibl., ill. (some col.), maps (some col).

A personal account of three and a half decades of political conflict in Guatemala from the early 1960s through 1996 by a military officer with two decades of service, beginning in 1970, including as director of the intelligence school and head of psychological operations. Little insight is provided, though, about military internal affairs, nor is much evidence or many sources presented for questionable assertions about key events.

1158 Isaacs, Anita. Guatemala on the brink. (*J. Democr.*, 21:2, April 2010, p. 108–122)

Isaacs discusses the current political climate in Guatemala including criminal violence that threatens to overwhelm the poorly performing political institutions and a substandard police force that is pervaded by its own criminality. President Álvaro Colom is given a disappointing report card at the mid-point of his tenure. This essay brings insight to the tensions between the human rights community and the rising indigenous rights movement.

Menjívar, Cecilia. Violence and women's lives in eastern Guatemala: a conceptual framework. See item **2388**.

1159 Porras Castejón, Gustavo. Las huellas de Guatemala. Ciudad de Guatemala: F&G Editores, 2010. 459 p.: bibl.

Worthwhile political memoir by a key participant in the process culminating in the Peace Accords of 1996. Porras Castejón's role was facilitated by his elite background (and childhood friendship with then President Álvaro Arzú) along with his participation in the guerrilla movements of both the 1960s and the 1970s/1980s. Additional value comes from his impressive critical self-reflection.

1160 La protesta social en época electoral, 2007. Compilación de Simona Violetta Yagenova. Asistencia de Mario Efraín Castañeda Maldonado. Ciudad de Guatemala: Área de Movimientos Sociales, FLACSO Guatemala, 2008. 68 p.: bibl., ill., maps. (Cuaderno de debate; 9)

Offers a descriptive presentation of protest data for a three-year period but most of the in-depth data refer to the 2007 election year with most attention to regional breakdowns. Ends with a case study of a conflict between protesters and local officials in one town in Alta Verapaz.

Rodríguez, Ileana. Liberalism at its limits: crime and terror in the Latin American cultural text. See item **1042**.

1161 Vela Castañeda, Manolo E. Guatemala, 1982: el corazón del orden burgués contemporáneo. (*Foro Int./México*, 47:2, abril/junio 2007, p. 369–407, bibl.)

Perhaps the most in-depth examination available of the significant 1982 coup following the fraudulent presidential election. Raises provocative issues about the usual explanations given for the plotters' motives, but falls short in substantiating the thesis that the US government played a major role in the coup.

1162 Yagenova, Simona Violetta. La protesta desde una perspectiva comparativa: el caso de las movilizaciones sociales de los médicos, maestros y personas de la tercera edad. Asistencia de Mario Efraín Castañeda Maldonado. Ciudad de Guatemala: Área de Movimientos Sociales, FLACSO Guatemala, 2008. 47 p.: bibl., ill. (Cuaderno de debate; 7)

Protest activities are compared for three sets of social actors for a two-year period beginning in late 2004, focusing on the types of demands and activities, the nature of alliances and of government response, and the degree of success, both in terms of demands and strengthening of the groups themselves.

HONDURAS

1163 Las ideas políticas en Honduras: tránsito del siglo XX al XXI. Textos de Efraín Moncada Silva *et al.* Compilación de Óscar Acosta. Tegucigalpa: Federación de Organizaciones para el Desarrollo de Honduras, 2009. 573 p.: bibl., ill.

Contrary to the title, the selections included here cover Honduran political history as far back as the 19th century, with the fullest coverage for 1948–99. The contributions are written by Honduran journalists and scholars born in the 1930s and 1940s and two European journalists from an earlier period. The most valuable chapter comes from Natalia Ajenjo Fresno, a younger Spanish scholar who analyzes the party system.

1164 Leiva Leiva, José María. Pensamiento político y realidad nacional. Tegucigalpa: Editorial Universitaria, Univ. Nacional Autónoma de Honduras, 2008. 292 p.: bibl. (Col. Realidad nacional)

Offers a series of short reflections on various political themes ("third wave of democracy," communitarism, and poverty) rather than a work of political theory, as the title suggests. One exception is the section on Christian Socialism. Includes little commentary on contemporary Honduras. Does include some good political humor. Author is law professor at the National University and a newspaper columnist.

1165 Ruhl, J. Mark. Honduras unravels. (*J. Democr.*, 21:2, April 2010, p. 108–122)

Excellent explanation of the dynamics leading up to the Aug. 2009 coup that ended the polarizing presidency of Manuel Zedillo. Opposition leader Porfirio Lobo Sosa won the subsequent contentious election of Nov. 2009. With the demonstrated willingness of civilian political elites on both sides to break democratic rules, along with the repoliticization of the military, future prospects for democracy in Honduras remain unclear.

NICARAGUA

1166 Anderson, Leslie E. The authoritarian executive?: horizontal and vertical accountability in Nicaragua. (*Lat. Am.*

Polit. Soc., 48:2, Summer 2006, p. 141–169, bibl.)

Anderson presents an effective argument, based on extensive interviews, that the delegative democracy model fits Nicaragua since 1979 poorly (despite its strong executive and legislative subordination) due to strong mechanisms of vertical accountability largely stemming from its mobilized populace. Focuses on the presidencies of Daniel Ortega (first term), Violeta Chamorro, and Arnoldo Alemán.

1167 Anderson, Leslie E. Social capital in developing democracies: Nicaragua and Argentina compared. New York: Cambridge Univ. Press, 2010. 309 p.

Outstanding effort combining a theoretical discussion of the role of social capital in democratization with an impressive research effort utilizing surveys at both neighborhood and national levels along with interviews of legislators. The work compares and contrasts the positive relationship for bridging social capital in Sandinista Nicaragua with the negative relationship for bonding social capital in Peronist Argentina. The argument is persuasive but would be stronger had more of the critical perspective utilized on the latter been applied to the former.

1168 Booth, John A. and **Patricia Bayer Richard.** Revolution's legacy: residual effects on Nicaraguan participation and attitudes in comparative context. (*Lat. Am. Polit. Soc.*, 48:2, Summer 2006, p. 117–140, bibl., tables)

Investigates the impact of revolutionary change and governance using survey data to compare Nicaragua to the rest of Central America a year and a half into the postrevolutionary period. Nicaragua is not distinctive in electoral participation, political attitudes, nor behavior, but there are differences when the comparison is restricted to countries with more comparable histories of repressive violence (such as El Salvador and Guatemala).

Cupples, Julie. Rethinking electoral geography: spaces and practices of democracy in Nicaragua. See item **775.**

1169 Guido Martínez, Clemente. Historia del poder ejecutivo de Nicaragua, 1527–2007. Managua: Lea Grupo Editorial, 2007. 197 p.: bibl., ill.

This useful handbook identifies the holders of executive power in Nicaragua, including during the colonial period. For the independent period, the volume identifies both presidents and vice presidents, as well as cabinet members since 1979. Brief discussions of presidents are grouped by regime type rather than chronology.

1170 Guzmán, Luis Humberto and **Álvaro Pinto Scholtbach.** Democracia y partidos en Nicaragua. The Hague: Netherlands Institute for Multiparty Democracy, 2008. 283 p.: bibl.

Even-handed account of a polarized party system and a political history, perhaps reflecting authors' backgrounds (leaders, respectively, in Nicaragua's Unión Demócrata Cristiana (UDC) political party and Holland's Labor Party). Along with its clear synthesis, perhaps most useful are the results of a questionnaire (even if nonrepresentative) given to activists from seven leading parties during the 2006–2007 time period.

1171 Kampwirth, Karen. Abortion, antifeminism, and the return of Daniel Ortega: in Nicaragua, leftist politics? (*Lat. Am. Perspect.*, 35:6, Nov. 2008, p. 122–136, bibl.)

Examination of the 2006 vote to prohibit therapeutic abortion in Nicaragua highlights the splits within feminist movement, the growing strength of the antifeminist movement, but most of all, the support from the Sandinista party and its successful presidential candidate that year, Daniel Ortega. Portrayed not as a shift to the right by Ortega and his party, but rather as a shift to cynicism.

1172 Martí i Puig, Salvador. The adaptation of the FSLN: Daniel Ortega's leadership and democracy in Nicaragua. Translated by Claire Wright. (*Lat. Am. Polit. Soc.*, 52:4, Winter 2010, p. 79–106, bibl., tables)

Drawing on literature about how political parties change and adapt as well as interviews across two decades, this article explains the Sandinista transformation from cadre party leading the revolutionary process to electoral party faithful to its leader. Focusing on organizational apparatus and decision-making flexibility, the article identifies Sandinista adaptation

through four stages leading to the FSLN's return to power with the 2006 elections. Argues that the key has been Ortega's deinstitutionalization and tight control of party.

1173 Tatar, Bradley. State formation and social memory in Sandinista politics. (*Lat. Am. Perspect.*, 36:5, Sept. 2009, p. 158–177, bibl.)

This theoretically rich article attempts to explain how Sandinistas changed from a popular democratic movement to a political vehicle for Daniel Ortega. Draws on Gramscian theory of popular culture to study state formation processes. The focus of this study, though, is largely a reexamination of testimonies from the crucial Monimbó insurrection of 1978 to challenge the Sandinista narrative utilized to legitimate its vanguard role.

1174 Undoing democracy: the politics of electoral caudillismo. Edited by David Close and Kalowatie Deonandan. Lanham, Md.: Lexington Books, 2004. 218 p.: bibl., ill., index.

Close examination of the Arnoldo Alemán administration (1997–2002) and the first year of his successor, Enrique Bolaños. A central theme across the contributions is the 1999 pact between the two rival caudillos, Alemán and Ortega, that remains up to today the essential driver of Nicaragua's democratic decomposition. The consequences for the economy, civil society (particularly women's groups), and relations with Catholic Church are highlighted.

PANAMA

1175 Herrera Montenegro, Luis Carlos. Políticas de control en la democracia panameña, 1994–2004. Panamá: Univ. de Panamá, Instituto de Estudios Nacionales, 2009. 195 p.: bibl., ill.

Sketches of contemporary political history, constitutional design, and a conceptual framework precede the short discussion of the book's central concern: mechanisms of horizontal control of the executive branch. Most useful is the concluding chapter's comparison of Panama to other Central American countries in terms of varying institutional features for control of the executive branch.

THE CARIBBEAN AND THE GUIANAS

CLIFFORD E. GRIFFIN, *Associate Professor, Department of Political Science, School of Public and International Affairs, North Carolina State University*

THE NEW NORMAL IN THE CARIBBEAN AND GUYANAS

CONVENTIONAL WISDOM holds that every transformative event creates a new normal as the system recalibrates by adjusting and adapting to the forces and consequences of the change. The countries of the Caribbean and Guyanas find themselves re-equilibrating as a result of the global economic transformations underway, and while all of the countries are adapting to a new normal, three are selected for analysis: Cuba, Haiti, and Guyana, all of which have long been democratically challenged.

On Friday, December 2, 2011, the leaders of 33 Latin American and Caribbean countries met in Caracas, Venezuela, to inaugurate the Community of Latin American and Caribbean States, or CELAC, a new organization that will include every country in the region with the exception of the US and Canada. The hope in some quarters is that not only will CELAC challenge US influence in the region, but that it will replace the Organization of American States (OAS), the only group open to all countries in the hemisphere. While the OAS works to promote democracy and development in the region—goals shared by all members—there are many who view this organization merely as a mechanism for pushing US interests and policies in the region.

The advent of CELAC coincided with expectations that the region would achieve approximately 5 percent economic growth in 2011 as a result of surging commodity prices, as well as attempts by a number of countries in the region to flex their muscles on the world stage. CELAC's foundation also coincides with much concern over a perceived waning of US influence in the region.

However, there is no indication that the Obama administration is worried that CELAC will someday replace the OAS. According to Dan Restrepo, President Barack Obama's senior advisor on Latin America, who spoke to the *Miami Herald* on December 1, "The notion that you can create an organization simply to be anti-American is not viable over a sustained period of time." In fact, despite the precarious state of its economy, the US is still the hemisphere's economic powerhouse and the principal destination for most the region's exports, including Venezuela's. Moreover, contends Dennis Jett, former US ambassador to Peru, CELAC's chances of flourishing rest greatly on its ability to derive solid levels of financial support from the region in much the same way that the OAS receives support from the US.

To be sure, the US remains the preponderant power in the region, and the following contrive to be among its core interests and goals: supporting democracy, trade, and sustainable economic development, and fostering cooperation on issues such as citizen safety, democratic institution-building and the rule of law, economic and social inclusion, energy, and climate change. Nonetheless, as the greater Caribbean (and the rest of the region) continues to be buffeted by the forces of globalization, interdependence, and transnationalism, at least two developments are noticeable: 1) a number of newer actors, including Brazil, China, India, Russia, and Venezuela, have been using America's distraction with two long extrahemispheric wars to position themselves to be among the leading forces in the region; and 2) Caribbean countries, having accepted and conformed to the ideology and policies associated with private-sector-led development, appear to have focused too narrowly on developing their own private sector. Their reality, therefore, suggests the need for a greater degree of economic integration. The spread of free trade and increased competition among transnational corporations continue to pose a considerable threat to these vulnerable countries that find themselves often ill-equipped to compete with and/or retaliate against more economically formidable societies (item **1187**).

Single-industry dependence has long been a feature of most Caribbean states. Initially relying on agriculture or other primary resources, these economies are now increasingly service-oriented with an emphasis on tourism (item **1183**). However, objective conditions would suggest that in order to be able to effectively adapt/adjust to the pressures, challenges, and opportunities presented by international competition, leaders throughout the region must consider—and some have indeed begun to consider—a wide range of nontraditional opportunities for development. It is for these reasons that CELAC seems attractive to countries in the region, and may be reflective of the new normal.

CUBA

There is no question that global events have forced Cuba to adjust to new realities. As Raúl Castro continues to impose his imprint on Cuba, the probing question that he must answer is this: Will he be able to manage a period of reforms in order for a new generation of leaders to recoup their dreams of socialism? As José Manuel Martín Medem argues in *Cuba: la hora de los Mamayes* (item **1226**), this is a defining moment for the country as it seeks to maintain its right and position as an independent nation (item **1220**). One important development has been the recent relaxation of restrictions against Cuban-Americans' travel to Cuba, which has, unsurprisingly, resulted in strong objections from Cuba's opponents in the US.

Supporters of this policy argue that if the embargo and the travel ban are lifted, the Cuban people will benefit economically; American companies will penetrate and influence the Cuban market; and the communist system will begin to crumble, accelerating a transition to a democratic society. However, the regime's critics disagree, contending that the travel ban and the embargo should be maintained until the Castro brothers or a successor regime is willing to provide meaningful concessions in the areas of human rights and political change. If the US were to end the embargo now, that decision would be tantamount to an undeserved gift to the Cuban leadership because of the unintended outcomes of this policy change, including enriching the coffers of the Cuban government, and providing aid—money, food, clothing—almost exclusively to white families on the island.

The Castro brothers and the Cuban leadership are neither naïve nor inexperienced, regime critics contend, and, therefore, are unlikely to allow tourists and investments from the US to subvert the revolution and influence Cuba's domestic political and economic developments. Therefore, an influx of tourists from the US is unlikely to improve the chances that Cuba will become democratic. Moreover, Cuba is unlikely to open up and allow US investments in all sectors of the economy, but instead is more likely to allow selected companies to trade and invest in the country. Rather than opening up and democratizing Cuba, they contend, these changes are likely to delay the transition to democracy and lead to greater repression and control since money will flow into businesses owned by the Cuban government, strengthening state enterprise.

On another level, regime critics point out that most Cuban-Americans who visit Cuba have contact with and bring help to their friends and family, most of whom are white Cubans, propelling a deepening economic and social divide between Cuban blacks and whites. Cuba's population is over 60 percent black or mulatto, but Afro-Cubans benefit very little from Cuban-Americans travel or remittances. Consequently, continue the critics, the Obama administration's policy of liberalizing travel to Cuba is counterproductive and benefits only a minority of Cubans. The sustained arguments that an end to the embargo will delay rather than accelerate a transition to democracy in the island, therefore, become one of the justifications for the establishment of CELAC. Others, however, examine the democratic changes that have been taking place in the country through the lenses of participation, consultation, consensus, and representation with regards to elections for the National Assembly (item **1228**).

HAITI

While the debate over the five-decade-long embargo against Cuba rages on, concerns over the state of affairs in the democracy-challenged, earthquake-ravaged Haiti continue (item **1201**), and provide yet another rationale for CELAC. Peter Roman, among others, examines the prospects for democracy in Haiti by focusing on the recent election of the national assembly's deputies from the nomination process to the campaign (item **1228**). Such investigations are important because of the circumstances surrounding the last presidential election.

Following a messy and drawn-out campaign complete with accusations of election fraud, international intervention on the part of the OAS and Western nations, and the return from exile of two former leaders, Jean-Claude "Baby Doc" Duvalier and Father Jean Bertrand Aristide, Michel "Sweet Micky" Martelly finally emerged as Haiti's newest president. During his campaign, Martelly expressed his interest in reconstituting the controversial Haitian army to help improve internal security. Historically known for its violent acts and lack of political neutrality, particularly during the Duvalier dynasty, the military was disbanded in 1995 by President Aristide after he was deposed in a coup and then restored to power with the help of UN forces. An April 2011 article in the *Washington Post* quotes Martelly as saying that "the new armed forces wouldn't be known for brutality, as their predecessors were." By signaling his desire to reconstitute Haiti's military, President Martelly appears intent on replacing MINUSTAH, which he cannot control, with local security forces sworn to comply with his orders. Martelli, therefore, is attempting to exploit the strong anti-MINUSTAH sentiments that abound in Haiti.

MINUSTAH, which was originally formed to replace the Multinational Interim Force (MIF) authorized by the UN Security Council in February 2004, after President Aristide was forced into exile, continues to operate under a mandate "to restore a secure and stable environment, to promote the political process, to strengthen Haiti's government institutions and rule-of-law structures, as well as to promote and to protect human rights." Its presence in Haiti is authorized under Chapter VII of the UN Charter, which permits the Security Council, once it has determined that a given situation constitutes a threat or breach of the peace, to impose legally enforceable measures on states without their consent. The rationale for the mission's presence in Haiti is that since 2004, violence has threatened the international community—a proposition that many question. For example, in late December 2010, the OAS Representative in Haiti, Ricardo Seitenfus of Brazil, was dismissed from his post ostensibly for his decision to publicly state the obvious—that Haiti is not an international threat, but a country whose problems are primarily socioeconomic. Similar sentiments were echoed in April 2011 by Cuba's foreign minister before the UN Security Council—that rather than an occupation army or interference and political manipulation, Haiti needs resources for rebuilding and development.

MINUSTAH includes both traditional "blue helmet" peacekeeping troops and police officers from a number of different countries. Particularly striking is the fact that very few of these forces speak Haitian Creole, the language of the island's poor. This heavily funded multinational UN peacekeeping force's remit includes performing security functions, monitoring elections, and assisting human rights groups in order to prevent Haiti from breaching international peace. The UN spent 5 billion dollars on the institution even before the earthquake hit Haiti in January 2010, and 793,517,100 dollars in 2011 thus far. In a unanimous resolution, the Security Council decided on Friday, October 14, 2011 to renew MINUSTAH's mandate for one year, reducing its numbers to pre-earthquake levels, and advocating a gradual withdrawal over time.

Calls for MINUSTAH's departure or a change in its mission are driven in part by recent accusations ranging from severe misconduct to neglect by some of the troops, including the collective rape of an 18-year-old man; and the appearance of cholera, likely an inadvertent import from Nepalese peacekeepers. Beyond these apparently isolated events, which together may have constituted the tipping point that has led to anti-MINUSTAH protests, the reality is that a supposed humanitarian group has functioned as a security force that has systematically served foreign interests over those of the Haitians. What, therefore, explains the Security Council's decision to extend MINUSTAH's mandate in the absence of any discernible international security threat?

Many Haitians and observers see MINUSTAH as an instrument of US interest in the region, and contend that these forces repeatedly have suppressed democracy, failed to address authentic humanitarian concerns, and have at times even perpetrated mass violence against Haitian citizens. That is, MINUSTAH represents one of the legs of the three-legged stool—foreign powers, the state, and the Haitian people—that is a metaphor for theorizing and explaining Haiti (item **1209**). They contend that by suppressing the Fanmi Lavalas Party and other social and political movements, MINUSTAH has actively excluded Haiti's poor majority from political participation, and has worked against the interests of Haitians fighting for progressive economic and social reform. This systematic suppression of democracy has contributed to Haiti's status as a "'leta restavek', or child servant state," acquiescent to foreign interests.

The Haitian who most closely represents the interests of the Haitian masses is the leader of Fanmi Lavalas, former President Jean Bertrand Aristide. He remains an ongoing concern for the US and other Western nations due to his unfailing popularity. Upon his return home on March 18, 2011 from his seven-year exile in South Africa, he was greeted in Port-au-Prince by hordes of journalists and thousands of cheering fans. Since then, analysts have suggested that Aristide may attempt to return to Haitian politics. Confirming claims by Aristide and his supporters as well as many observers, the Council on Hemispheric Affairs reported that the recent WikiLeaks evidence reveals that Aristide's exile in South Africa was partly organized by the US, who advocated his continued absence from Haiti. By contrast, no such concerns seem to have been raised over former President Jean-Claude "Baby Doc" Duvalier's return.

These developments notwithstanding, the earthquake-ravaged Haiti finally has something to celebrate: 44 miles of newly asphalted road, a new 605-acre industrial park in the north that will attract 65,000 jobs, and the arrival of a marquee hotel brand, the 45 million dollar, 173-room Marriott Hotel (in partnership with Digicel). On Monday, November 28, 2011, Haiti's President Michel Martelly and Luis Alberto Moreno, the head of the Inter-American Development Bank, inaugurated a newly rehabilitated Route National 1, the country's main road that connects the capital in the south to Cap-Haitien in the north. The symbolic ribbon-cutting ceremony marked the end of three years of construction by the Dominican road-building firm Estrella.

The IDB, which is investing hundreds of millions of dollars in Haiti, sponsored a two-day investment forum in Port-au-Prince beginning Tuesday, November 29, for which 1,000 people had registered, 500 of whom were business people from 29 countries. As attendees began pouring into the country and taking over every available hotel room, the IDB, President Michel Martelly, Prime Minister Garry Conille and former US President Bill Clinton spent the day spreading the news in back-to-back events across the country. Later they joined Clinton and Conille in laying the first stone of the new industrial park, an investment worth more than 300 million dollars. The park's first tenants include one of Korea's biggest clothing manufactures, Sae-A, which will eventually employ 20,000 people. About 5,000 new houses will surround the area, courtesy of the IDB and US Agency for International Development (USAID).

This good news comes in the wake of the devastating earthquake of January 2012, and a highly controversial election in a country with a long history of coups (item **1207**). "This is the kind of change we want," Martelly said. "This is what they call durable development." Nevertheless, MINUSTAH's ongoing tenure in Haiti will continue to be controversial given the negative light in which it is viewed in many circles. It will be difficult to overcome its perceived role as an interloper guzzling money that could go towards socioeconomic development; an organization whose members are seen as beach- and bar-loving, eager to exploit misery for sex; and as an occupying force whose approach to its stated role is seen as insensitive, interfering, colonialist and over-militarized.

GUYANA

Long-standing, deeply rooted, and ongoing ethnic violence has prevented Guyana from living up to its motto—One People, One Nation, One Destiny. This failure is underscored by the fact that among the things for which outgoing President Bharat Jagdeo will be remembered is the spike in violent crimes experienced throughout the country during his tenure. Jagdeo's tumultuous presidency was beset by a series of fatal bombings over the past several years, including one attack on the Ministry of Health in 2009 and two additional assaults in 2011—one at the Stabroek Market and the other at the residence of Philomena Sahoye-Shury, a leading member of President Jagdeo's People's Progressive Party (PPP) (item **1197**). As one editorial in Guyana's *Stabroek News* put it, "The security situation grows murkier by the day and it is in this milieu that there has been a rash of dangerous events."

The violence in Guyana is all the more bitter for the ethnic undertones, and there is little evidence that Jagdeo undertook any initiatives during his tenure to address this issue. Party affiliation in Guyana falls almost directly along ethnic lines. Jagdeo's PPP overwhelmingly receives the vote of the Guyanese of Indian descent, while the opposition People's National Congress (PNC) garners the support of the country's African descendants. One study of the 2001 elections called the crossover votes between ethnic groups "insubstantial" and concluded that "[PPP] is still, for all practical purposes, an Indian-dominated party." Even after the 2006 election, Jagdeo made no effort to reduce the trend. One editorial in the *Stabroek News* in 2010 commented that the two main parties still remained within their ethnic platform. The unwritten rule of Guyana's politics is that their leader must be from a particular ethnic group, and the historical evidence indicates that each party derives a high percentage of its support from a single ethnic group (item **1198**).

The country's crime data also reflects a racial coloration, as exemplified by the 2007 case of Andre Douglas, an alleged murderer of African descent, who was eventually killed by police after escaping from jail. Douglas rationalized his own crimes in the context of social marginalization and inequality, and referred to himself a freedom fighter. "Look into innocent black Guyanese problems or unrest will not finish," he said, meaning that he would continue his criminal (terror) activities until the social problems of the Afro-Guyanese were alleviated. The large turnout at Douglas' funeral showed that his frustration resonated with the country's Afro-Guyanese community.

A separate though related problem that plagued the Jagdeo administration was the number of extrajudicial killings on the part of state authorities. Since 2001, "Phantom" death squads with alleged connections to government agencies—also called the "Black Clothes Police"—have been linked to some 400 murders. According to one member of the opposition PNC, the Black Clothes Police have appointed themselves accusers, judge, jury, and executioner, and have gunned down people with impunity.

The Jagdeo administration shocked the region by rejecting a request from the US, Britain, and Canada to do an independent investigation of the repeated human rights violations. "We are very concerned about the allegations and we believe that the integrity of the government is something that is at question here," said British High Commissioner Stephen Hiscock. Amnesty International wrote an open letter to President Jagdeo in 2001 demanding prosecution of any officials involved in extrajudicial violence, and saying that the Guyanese government had "repeatedly failed to ensure the protection of the internationally recognized fundamental right to life—and to take measures to prevent such killings." Although several officers were indicted for their participation in extrajudicial killings in 2004, none were convicted. Some have responded in kind to state violence, such as in the notorious Rondell Rawlins case. Rawlins, who accused the government of kidnapping his girlfriend, waged a campaign of terror in Guyana seeking her return, resulting in 23 deaths. The future for democracy in Guyana remains uncertain; however, insights can be drawn from a comparative analysis of Guyana and Suriname, two South American countries that underwent long periods of postcolonial authoritarian rule before instituting democratic governance in the early 1990s (item **1199**).

GENERAL

1176 Amussen, Susan Dwyer. Caribbean exchanges: slavery and the transformation of English society, 1640–1700. Chapel Hill: Univ. of North Carolina Press, 2007. 302 p.: bibl., index.

Using Barbados and Jamaica, England's two most important colonies, as the units of analysis, the author examines the cultural exports that affected the development of race, gender, labor, and class as categories of legal and social identity in England. Concepts of law and punishment in the Caribbean provided a model for expanded definitions of crime in England; the organization of sugar factories served as a model for early industrialization; and the construction of the "white woman" in the Caribbean contributed to changing notions of "ladyhood." For historian's comment, see *HLAS 66:1175.*

1177 Britton, Celia. The sense of community in French Caribbean fiction. Liverpool, England: Liverpool Univ. Press, 2008. 190 p. (Contemporary French and Francophone Cultures; 10)

This book analyzes the theme of community in seven French Caribbean novels in relation to the work of the French philosopher Jean-Luc Nancy. The complex history of the islands means that community is often a central and problematic issue in their literature, underlying a range of other questions such as political agency, individual and collective subjectivity, attitudes towards the past and the future, and even the literary form itself. Here Britton studies a range of key books from the region, including Édouard Glissant's *Le Quatrième Siècle*, Patrick Chamoiseau's *Texaco*, Daniel Maximin's *L'Ile et une nuit*, and Vincent Placoly's *L'eau-de-mort guildive*, among others. Although a work of literary analysis, this book sheds light on political and social conditions and political identity in the French Caribbean.

1178 Chamberlain, Mary. Empire and nation-building in the Caribbean: Barbados, 1937–66. Manchester, England; New York, N.Y.: Manchester Univ. Press; New York, N.Y.: Palgrave Macmillan, 2010. 216 p.: bibl., index. (Studies in imperialism)

This book argues that nation-building in the Anglophone Caribbean was a more complex and messy affair, involving women and men in a range of social and cultural activities, in a variety of migratory settings, within a unique geopolitical context. Using Barbados as a case study, this author describes the messy, multiple stories of how a colony progressed to become a nation. Barbados in the 1930s was the most economically impoverished, racially divided, socially disadvantaged, and politically conservative of the British West Indian colonies.

1179 Cloos, Patrick. Health inequalities in the Caribbean: increasing opportunities and resources. (*Glob. Health Promot.,* 17:1, March 2010, p. 73–76)

This article statistically analyzes the relative impact of political institutions, economic development, economic performance, and international influences on regime change and stability in nine countries in Central America and the Caribbean basin: Mexico, Costa Rica, Honduras, El Salvador, Guatemala, Nicaragua, Panama, the Dominican Republic, and Haiti.

1180 The creolization reader: studies in mixed identities and cultures. Edited and introduced by Robin Cohen and Paola Toninato. London; New York, N.Y.: Routledge, 2010. 402 p.: bibl., ill., index. (Routledge student readers; 5)

Is President Obama black or "Creole" or neither? What does the label "Creole" mean? Is it merely another word for "mixed race" and similar to expressions used in other parts of the world such as mulatto, mestizo, métis, or colored? Is "Creole" a racial category at all, or should it be understood as a sociological, cultural, or linguistic expression? These are among some of the questions that this book attempts to answer. For sociologist's comment, see item **2419.**

1181 Forteza, Alvaro. The portability of pension rights: general principles and the Caribbean case. (*Dev. Policy Rev.,* 28:2, March 2010, p. 237–255)

This article presents a select survey of the literature on pension portability, and reviews the progress made by the Caribbean countries as well as some remaining challenges in the light of the international experience.

Glassman, Amanda et al. Confronting the chronic disease burden in Latin America and the Caribbean. See item **1039**.

1182 Hurst, Lionel. Democracy by diplomacy: Afro-Saxon Caribbean diplomats challenge the USA to improve its world leadership and expand regional freedoms. Bloomington, Ind.: AuthorHouse, 2007. 259 p.: bibl., ill.

The author makes a case for the role of diplomats—particularly diplomats from the Caribbean—in fostering a democratic culture in the Caribbean in spite of reluctance and obstruction from Great Britain and the US.

1183 Levitt, Kari. Reclaiming development: independent thought and Caribbean community. Kingston; Miami, Fla.: Ian Randle Publishers, 2005. 411 p.: bibl., index.

The author notes that whether by conviction or apparent absence of viable alternatives, Caribbean governments have been quick to implement policies of deregulation, liberalization, and privatization. She argues that it is time to reclaim the right to development and the right of nations to engage in the international economy on their own terms. She advocates an international rule-based order, which permits space for member countries to follow divergent paths to development according to their own philosophies, institutions, cultures, and societal priorities.

1184 Palmer, Steven Paul. Launching global health: the Caribbean odyssey of the Rockefeller Foundation. Ann Arbor: Univ. of Michigan Press, 2010. 301 p.: bibl., ill., index. (Conversations in medicine and society)

This book examines one of the earliest of these initiatives abroad, the Rockefeller Foundation's International Health Board. The flagship agency made its first call in British Guiana in 1914 to experiment with its new "American method" for the treatment of hookworm disease. Within months it was involved in ambitious hookworm programs in six Central American and Caribbean sites, its directors self-consciously choosing to test run the prototype for their global project in the nearest and clearest domain of American imperial influence. These efforts continued until 1930, when most of the International Health Board hookworm campaigns had evolved into public health projects of a different kind.

1185 Rudd, Alison. Postcolonial Gothic fictions from the Caribbean, Canada, Australia and New Zealand. Cardiff: Univ. of Wales Press, 2010. 233 p.: bibl., index. (Gothic literary studies)

The author provides a comparative analysis of the way the gothic has provided writers from the Caribbean, Canada, Australia, and New Zealand with a means to express the anxieties of postcolonial experience and the traumatic legacies of colonialism. She covers a diverse terrain of well-known contemporary writers, including Derek Walcott, Shani Mootoo, Margaret Atwood, Peter Carey, and Keri Hulme. Although a work of literary analysis, provides insight on political conditions in the Caribbean.

1186 Sukup, Viktor. Les Caraïbes face à l'avenir. (*Futuribles/Paris*, 360, fév. 2010, p. 21–34)

The author contends that Russia's recent rapprochement with Cuba and Venezuela, combined with the increasing engagement of China in the region, suggests that the Caribbean still has strategic importance. In this context, he ponders the future of the area, a region hit hard by the global economic crisis and threatened by the effects of climate change and recommends, among other things, that these states establish closer regional cooperation; open up to the rest of the world; diversify and upgrade their main industry, which is tourism, to exploit other areas of activity, such as craftwork, agriculture, fishing, etc.; and develop the production of renewable energy sources.

DOMINICAN REPUBLIC

1187 Cueto Villamán, Francisco. Desconfianza política, instituciones y gobernabilidad democrática en la República Dominicana. (*Cienc. Soc./Santo Domingo*, 32:2, abril/junio 2007, p. 249–280, bibl., tables)

The democratic transition in Latin American and Caribbean during the economic downturn of the 1980s ushered in a process of privatization of public companies, which was intended to reduce the level of state participation in the economy. The weak states that resulted proved incapable of sustaining economic growth, universalizing the rule of law, and implementing policies that would promote sustainable human development. This paper examines the degree of confidence that Dominican citizens felt towards the main governing institutions and the dangers that weak citizen confidence presents for democratic governance.

1188 Cueto Villamán, Francisco. Institucionalización y representación en los partidos políticos dominicanos: un estudio desde las percepciones y valoraciones de los diputados. (*Cienc. Soc./Santo Domingo*, 31:1, enero/marzo 2006, p. 23–42, bibl., tables)

The article contends that in the process of democratic transitions started in the Dominican Republic in 1978, the political parties became responsible for modifying most of rights, wishes, and hopes of the Dominican society. However, once democracy was recovered in the context of an economic crisis, citizen demands and the incapacity of the political parties to effectively manage or channel those demands produced great frustration.

1189 Derby, Lauren Hutchinson. The dictator's seduction: politics and the popular imagination in the era of Trujillo. Durham, N.C.: Duke Univ. Press, 2009. 410 p.: bibl., ill., index, map. (American encounters/global interactions)

The book is constructed around six more-or-less separate case studies, some of which have been published before. Most of the chapters are little jewels in their own right and may be read as autonomous essays on an extremely fascinating period of Dominican modern history. The author tells the story of the 1930 hurricane and its aftermath, showing how the natural disaster opened the way for Trujillo to increase his grip on Dominican society.

1190 Guedán, Manuel. Leonel Fernández, un político con iniciativa. (*Polít. Exter./Madrid*, 22:126, nov./dic. 2008, p. 115–125, photo)

This article contends that Leonel Fernández is one of the most conciliatory Latin American figures in the circle of trust among Presidents Uribe, Lula, Chávez, and Correa. During his third term as president, he set out to change the constitution, allowing the Dominican community abroad to be represented at home.

1191 Kelly, Jana Morgan; Rosario Espinal; and Jonathan Hartlyn. Diferenças de gênero na República Dominicana, 1994–2004: dois passos á frente, um passo para trás? (*Opin. Públ.*, 12:2, nov. 2006, p. 241–276, bibl., graphs, tables)

The authors assess the nature and evolution of the Dominican Republic's gender gap over the 1994–2004 period, employing data from four nationwide surveys in the Dominican Republic—the *Demos* surveys—conducted in 1994, 1997, 2001, and 2004. The indications are that what has been termed a traditional gender gap remains in place with regard to civic engagement, political interest, and attitudes toward democracy. At the same time, this gap disappeared with regard to voter participation in elections and a modern gender gap emerged for the first time with regard to attitudes about the role of women in politics.

1192 Krohn-Hansen, Christian. Political authoritarianism in the Dominican Republic. New York, N.Y.: Palgrave Macmillan, 2009. 249 p.: bibl., index.

The author advances new ways of analyzing political authoritarianism by investigating political networks and cultural ideas of power and authority in the Dominican Republic to provide insights into how authoritarian rule was created, legitimated, and embraced by various dominant and subaltern groups in Dominican society.

1193 Sandoval, Gabriel. Cigar production: how race, gender and political ideology were inscribed onto tobacco. (*Ethn. Racial Stud.*, 32:2, Feb. 2009, p. 257–277)

This paper examines the significance of race, gender, and political ideology to tobacco production in the Dominican Republic. Using the economic crisis that gripped the Dominican tobacco sector in the late 1990s as a lens, this study argues that the tobacco crisis elucidates both Dominican society's dependence upon racialized and gendered structures and the significance of racial, political, and gendered symbolism that is inscribed onto tobacco.

1194 Taylor, Erin B. Poverty as danger: fear of crime in Santo Domingo. (*Int. J. Cult. Stud.*, 12:2, March 2009, p. 131–148)

Poor urban communities throughout Latin America and the Caribbean historically have been represented as sites of physical and moral danger and have been blamed in particular for causing a surge in urban crime in recent years. This article explores how such representations are constructed through a process of engagement among many sectors of society. Argues that the poor are the victims of a class politics that is played out on designated urban spaces in which they symbolize the economic and political crises of the state and middle-class fears of loss of social status. By marginalizing the poor to bounded, powerless spaces, the middle class retain their moral right to respectability and the possibility of social ascendance.

1195 Wells, Allen. Tropical Zion: General Trujillo, FDR, and the Jews of Sosua. Durham, N.C.: Duke Univ. Press, 2009. 447 p.: bibl., index, photos, tables. (American encounters/global interactions)

The author presents Trujillo's motives towards the Jewish refugees as a political strategy designed to mollify his image and legitimize his regime in the eyes of the US government following the massacre of 15,000 Haitians a year before the Evian Conference. The study also analyzes the changes in US policy towards Trujillo during the Cold War, demonstrating that his image was subject to political interests: his atrocities were revealed when the Dominican Republic lost its relevance as a war time ally, but were covered again in view of the fear of communism.

GRENADA

1196 Sookram, Ron. East Indians and politics in Grenada, 1960–2003. (*J. Caribb. Hist.*, 41:1/2, 2007, p. 170–181)

Since 1960, politicians of East Indian descent have not only participated in every general election but have also been members of government. This article examines the involvement of East Indians in the politics of Grenada from 1960–2003 following the

constitutional reforms of 1951, which provided for the full political participation of all citizens.

GUYANA

1197 Birbalsingh, Frank. The People's Progressive Party of Guyana, 1950–1992: an oral history. London: Hansib Publications, 2007. 206 p.: bibl., ill., index, map.

This book is a collection of 27 interviews with members (and opponents) of Guyana's People's Progressive Party (PPP), as well as interviews with commentators who had long observed the PPP. These stories reveal issues of class, color, and ethnicity, which, together with Cold War factors, played critical roles in the exclusion of the PPP from political power for much of the second half of the 20th century.

1198 Misir, Prem. Racial ethnic imbalance in Guyana public bureaucracies: the tension between exclusion and representation. Foreword by Baris Karapinar. Lewiston, N.Y.: Edwin Mellen Press, 2010. 217 p.: bibl., ill., index.

Does a particular class, race, ethnicity, or gender dominate societal institutions? Is there exclusion of groups from participating at higher levels at the workplace? These two questions frame the author's effort to address the issue of ethnic participation in public service in Guyana.

1199 Singh, Chaitram. Re-democratization in Guyana and Suriname: critical comparisons. (*Rev. Eur. Estud. Latinoam. Caribe*, 84, April 2008, p. 71–85, bibl., tables)

A comparative analysis of two neighboring South American countries, both of which underwent long periods of postcolonial authoritarian rule before instituting democratic governance in the early 1990s.

HAITI

1200 Braziel, Jana Evans. Duvalier's ghosts: race, diaspora, and U.S. imperialism in Haitian literatures. Gainesville: Univ. Press of Florida, 2010. 308 p.: bibl., index.

Drawing on the diasporic cultural texts of several authors, such as Edwidge Danticat and Dany Laferrière, this book examines how writers participate in transnational movements for global social justice.

In their fictional works they discuss the many US interventionist methods in Haiti, including surveillance, foreign aid, and military assistance. Through their work, they reveal that the majority of Haitians do not welcome these intrusions and actively criticize US treatment of Haitians in both countries. For international relations specialist's comment, see item **1651**.

1201 Dumas, John Reginald P. An encounter with Haiti: notes of a special adviser. Port of Spain: Medianet Limited, 2008. 313 p.: bibl., col. ill., index, col., col. maps.

The author discusses the persistent nature and characteristics of the Haitian economic situation, the dimensions of the reconstruction task, and a certain inability of the international institutions to cope. The author claims the latter are instructive not only in terms of a study of Haiti itself, but also in terms of the international institutions—particularly the UNs' inability to come to terms with the need for innovative approaches to problem-solving.

1202 Glover, Kaiama L. Haiti unbound: a spiralist challenge to the postcolonial canon. Liverpool, England: Liverpool Univ. Press, 2010. 262 p. (Contemporary French and francophone cultures; 15)

Haiti has long been relegated to the margins of the so-called New World. Marked by exceptionalism, the voices of some of its most important writers have consequently been muted by the geopolitical realities of the nation's history. While Spiralism has been acknowledged as a crucial contribution to the French-speaking Caribbean literary tradition, it has not been given the sustained attention of a full-length study. The author offers a close look at the works of three such writers: the Haitian Spiralists Frankétienne, Jean-Claude Fignolé, and René Philoctète, and provides the first effort to consider their works individually and collectively, thereby filling an important gap in postcolonial Francophone and Caribbean studies. Although a work of literary analysis, sheds light on political conditions in Haiti.

1203 Haiti and the Haitian diaspora in the wider Caribbean. Edited by Philippe Zacaïr. Gainesville: Univ. Press of Florida, 2010. 207 p.: bibl., index. (New world diasporas)

These essays, written by historians, anthropologists, sociologists, and Francophone studies scholars, examine how Haitians interact as an immigrant group in other parts of the Caribbean as well as how they are perceived and treated, particularly in terms of ethnicity and race, in their migration experience in the broader Caribbean. By discussing the prevalence of anti-Haitianism throughout the region alongside the challenges Haitians face as immigrants, this volume completes the global view of the Haitian diaspora saga. For international relations specialist's comment, see item **1665**.

1204 Hendricks, Bracken; Aimee Christensen; and Ronald Toussaint. Green reconstruction: laying a firm foundation for Haiti's recovery. (*Innov./Cambridge*, 5:4, Oct. 2010, p. 129–141)

Arguing that the global community has an obligation to ensure that the reconstruction of Haiti's infrastructure increases economic resilience by adding value to existing assets and reducing vulnerability to external shocks, whether from natural disasters like earthquakes or man-made crises like spiking energy prices, the paper highlights a strategy for coordination across the development process, identifying the roles different partner groups can play, and identifying several priorities for that coordinated effort as the rebuilding process gets underway.

1205 James, Erica Caple. Democratic insecurities: violence, trauma, and intervention in Haiti. Berkeley: Univ. of California Press, 2010. 357 p.: bibl., index.

This text focuses on the ethics of military and humanitarian interventionism in Haiti during and after the country's 1991 coup, and explores the traumas of Haitian victims, whose experiences were denied by US officials and recognized only selectively by other humanitarian providers.

1206 Lozano, Wilfredo. La paradoja de las migraciones: el estado dominicano frente a la inmigración haitiana. Santo Domingo: Editorial UNIBE: Facultad Latinoamericana de Ciencias Sociales: Servicio Jesuita de Refugiados y Migrantes, 2008. 283 p.: bibl.

International migration in the Dominican Republic is defined as a paradox: while the economy draws Haitian workers, who work for very low wages, and are excluded from social and political life, the country sends labor forces to the US and Europe while the economy grows from remittances sent by thousands of nationals to the country. But Haitian immigration today is critical to the Dominican economy and labor market. Certainly, the Dominican Republic cannot be held accountable for the difficult situation in Haiti, but neither should it look the other way and forget internal cooperation efforts and international commitments.

1207 Marcelin, Dischler. La presse dans la gueule du loup. Port-au-Prince: Imprimerie Le Natal S.A., 2007. 271 p.: bibl., facsims., ill., ports.

This book is intended to serve as a memoir to inform current and future generations about a little slice of history. "The Press in the Lion's Den" is more precisely an attempt to provide a little information about the setback of the press during the military coup d'état of Sept. 29 and 30, 1991. It is also a document upon which journalists, press workers, intellectuals, and others can draw to provide useful information that will enrich their research agenda.

1208 Polyné, Millery. From Douglass to Duvalier: U.S. African Americans, Haiti and Pan Americanism, 1870–1964. Gainesville: Univ. Press of Florida, 2010. 292 p.: bibl., index. (New world diasporas)

This book examines the creative and critical ways African Americans and Haitians engaged the idealized tenets of Pan Americanism—mutual cooperation, egalitarianism, and nonintervention between nation-states—in order to strengthen Haiti's social, economic, and political growth and stability.

1209 Schuller, Mark. Haiti's 200-year ménage-à-trois: globalization, the state, and civil society. (*Caribb. Stud.*, 35:1, Jan./June 2007, p. 141–179, bibl.)

The author contends that a complete understanding of Haiti's history requires a tripartite framework, tracking and theorizing participation of three general sets of actors: foreign powers, the state, and Haiti's

people. In so doing, it provides a model for other scholars interested in a rich understanding of globalization and civil society by presenting a calculus that allows for a conversation between these three theoretical constructs.

1210 Ulysse, Gina Athena. Why representations of Haiti matter now more than ever. (*NACLA*, 43:4, July 2010, p. 37–40)

The author contends that because representations of Haiti and Haitians that appeared in mainstream news coverage of the disaster reproduced narratives and stereotypes dating to at least the 19th century, understanding the continuity of these representations matters more than ever today.

JAMAICA

1211 Johnson, Hume N. and Joseph L. Soeters. Jamaican dons, Italian godfathers and the chances of a "reversible destiny." (*Polit. Stud./Oxford*, 56:1, March 2008, p. 166–191)

This article hypothesizes that the so-called Jamaican "dons," who have positioned themselves as civil leaders in Jamaica, especially among the poor urban communities, resemble the Italian Mafia by virtue of their systematic, coercive organization of the ghetto community and the counterhegemonic, executive-style bureaucracy and culture. Acknowledging that the Mafia has faced considerable decline over the past 10 years, the authors seek to ascertain if the "dons" are likely to face a similar "reversible destiny."

1212 Sives, Amanda. Elections, violence, and the democratic process in Jamaica, 1944–2007. Kingston; Miami, Fla.: Ian Randle Publishers, 2010. 232 p.: bibl., ill., index.

The author posits that partisan political violence in Jamaica is not simply a fight for scarce benefits but needs to be understood as part of political identity formation and political culture. She hypothesizes that while the reformed electoral process provides an example of best practice for other developing and developed countries, until the peculiar Jamaican problem of party-controlled garrisons is addressed, the democratic process will remain flawed.

PUERTO RICO

1213 Acevedo Vilá, Aníbal. Así fue— ¿y ahora qué?: reflexiones sobre el cuatrienio 2004–2008 y sus repercusiones para el futuro. 3. ed. San Juan: Editorial Cordillera, 2009. 665 p.

This book provides an assessment of the four-year term of Puerto Rican Governor Aníbal Acevido Vilá, who, while considered by some as one of the smartest and most honest governors of the island, was indicted on 19 counts of campaign finance violations. He was subsequently found not guilty of all charges against him.

1214 García-Colón, Ismael. Land reform in Puerto Rico: modernizing the colonial state, 1941–1969. Gainesville: Univ. Press of Florida, 2009. 163 p.: bibl., ill., index. (New directions in Puerto Rican studies)

Using ethnography, political and economic theory, and primary and secondary historical sources, the author paints a compelling and human portrait of the land redistribution program by assessing not only the technical and political aspects of the program but also the ways in which the Puerto Rican people actively resisted, accommodated, and influenced the development it brought about. Considered also are the successes and failures of this historic program, which attempted in vain to reconcile the conflicting interests of planned development and free-market economics.

1215 Marsh Kennerly, Catherine. Negociaciones culturales: los intelectuales y el proyecto pedagógico del estado muñocista. San Juan: Ediciones Callejón, 2009. 276 p.: bibl., ill. (Col. En fuga. Ensayos)

In the vein of the best contemporary cultural critiques, the author introduces new and valuable perspectives in this book. The author carefully reads what constitutes a cultural and political intersection: the Division of Community Education (DIVEDCO) project, which began in Puerto Rico in the decade of the 1940s, and which coincided, not without alliances or fights, representatives of the colonial state, whether intellectuals and artists opposed in this political formation, among whom are met Réne Marqués, Pedro Juan Soto y Lorenzo Homar. In a rigorous and original manner, based on primary sources, this book investigates the tense and contradictory situation in which is discharged a series of intellectuals affiliated with DIVEDCO.

1216 Nieves, Ramón Luis. El ELA que queremos: preguntas y respuestas sobre el desarrollo del ELA. San Juan: Ediciones Puerto, 2009. 92 p.: bibl.

In this study of El ELA (Estado Libre Asociado) and the political status of Puerto Rico (free associated statehood) with the US, the author raises a number of questions, including the following: "Why is it necessary to develop along the lines of Free Associated Statehood?" "What is sovereignty?" "What does American citizenship eventuate?" "What might be done to reclaim Puerto Rico in order that it may work to solve our economic problems?" "Will development based on ELA enable us to produce riches and the thousands of jobs that we need?" "Why should the Partido Popular Democrático continue to defend development based on ELA?"

1217 Torres y Vargas, Diego de. Report on the island & Diocese of Puerto Rico (1647). Annotated translation into English by Jaime R. Vidal. Historical essays and commentary by Anthony M. Stevens-Arroyo. Scranton, Pa.: Univ. of Scranton Press, 2010. 264 p.: bibl., index, maps. (Ecos; 1)

Composed at the request of the Royal Spanish Chronicler of the Indies, Don Diego Torres y Vargas' *Report on the Island & Diocese of Puerto Rico* was the first history of Puerto Rico written by a native of the Spanish island colony. Torres y Vargas, a fourth generation Puerto Rican and descendant of Ponce de León, records here the history of the Catholic Church in Puerto Rico as well as the political, social, military, economic, and natural history of the island. This translation by Jaime R. Vidal—the first ever into English—includes three historical essays by eminent Puerto Rican and Latino Studies scholar Anthony Stevens-Arroyo and extensive translator notes to guide the reader through the realities of 17th-century Puerto Rican culture and society.

SURINAME

Singh, Chaitram. Re-democratization in Guyana and Suriname: critical comparisons. See item **1199**.

TRINIDAD AND TOBAGO

1218 Dundas, Carl W. Observing elections the Commonwealth's way: the early years. Kingston; Miami, Fla.: Ian Randle, 2007. 138 p.: bibl. (The integrationist)

This book analyzes and provides insights into lessons learned from Commonwealth election observations beginning with the observer mission to Malaysia in 1990 through the 32nd observer mission to Trinidad and Tobago in Dec. 2000.

1219 Meighoo, Kirk Peter. Democracy and constitution reform in Trinidad and Tobago. Kingston; Miami, Fla.: Ian Randle Publishers, 2008. 247 p.: bibl., ill., index.

The authors use Trinidad and Tobago as the model to determine if the countries of the Commonwealth Caribbean, which achieved independence some 40 years ago, are truly democratic, and whether the parliamentary and electoral systems they adopted are well suited to the Caribbean experience.

CUBA

1220 Bobes, Velia Cecilia. La nación inconclusa: (re)constituciones de la ciudadanía y la identidad nacional en Cuba. México: FLACSO, 2007. 188 p.: bibl. (Serie Dilemas de la política en Latinoamérica)

This book examines the development and changes the citizens of Cuba have undertaken and experienced, and seeks to explain/understand this process in relation to the symbolic definitions of the nation. The central hypothesis is that in Cuba's case, the rediscovery of the nation and the change in the model of citizenship that orients current political behavior is rooted in a long historical process and cannot be fully understood without detailed exploration of the past.

1221 Botín, Vicente. Raúl Castro: la pulga que cabalgó al tigre. Barcelona: Editorial Ariel, 2010. 301 p.: bibl., ill. (some col.), index.

The author contends that Raúl Castro thoroughly fulfilled his role as lifetime second fiddle to his brother, but behind his coarse and beardless face, behind his funny stories and bad jokes, behind his cultivated good nature hides a man with nerves of steel who has yet to disclose his true character. Without Fidel, Raúl Castro would never be known; but without Raúl, the Cuban Revolution would not have been the same.

1222 Castro, Fidel. Reflexiones de Fidel Castro. Durango, Mexico: Editorial de la Univ. Juárez del Estado de Durango, 2009. 269 p.

This collection of essays is contextualized through the person who confronted a potent imperial power—the US—and defeated it some 60 miles from the heart of the empire. How many heads of state have fallen for having attempted to confront the US? There are tens of leaders of Latin America and of the developing world, who have had neither the skill nor the intelligence to engage the "imperial giant" as Fidel Castro has done. While it may be easy to dismiss Castro as simply a dictator, the truth, and the real story of the man, and his place in history, is more nuanced and complex.

1223 Criado Alonso, Fernando. La política de democratización de la Unión Europea y el caso de Cuba. (*Rev. Estud. Polít.*, 142, oct./dic. 2008, p. 11–41, bibl.)

This work examines the main elements of the democratization policy of the European Union and analyzes how this policy has been implemented in Cuba since 1996. It contends that the combination of unanimity and lack of common will to act before the process of democratization has started holds back the development of a more activist European politics with Cuba. Moreover, the democratization policy of the EU is designed more as a policy of democratic consolidation than one of regime change.

1224 Gronbeck-Tedesco, John A. The left in transition: the Cuban revolution in US third world politics. (*J. Lat. Am. Stud.*, 40:4, Nov. 2008, p. 651–673)

This article examines the ways in which Cuba's revolution shaped the changing politics of the left in the US. Using critical strategies of transnationalism, it illustrates how a dialog developed between US activists and Cuban cultural producers, and reveals how Cuba's revolutionary discourse inflected the radical shift towards Third World nationalism.

1225 Koont, Sinan. Sustainable urban agriculture in Cuba. Gainesville: Univ. Press of Florida, 2011. 208 p.: bibl., index. (Contemporary Cuba)

Having been forced by necessity but enabled by its existing social and educational policies, Cuba in the 1990s launched the most extensive program of sustainable urban agriculture in the world. This is the first book-length investigation in either English or Spanish of this national experiment undertaken to transform the environmental, economic, and social nature of today's dominant system of producing food.

1226 Martín Medem, José Manuel. Cuba: la hora de los mameyes. Madrid: Catarata, 2008. 212 p.

The author contends that Cuba is entering a new era—the time of the Mamayes—which in Cuban means the crucial and defining moment. Raúl Castro, the new president of the Council of State announces "structural changes and concepts" albeit accompanying the Revolutionary Armed Forces that control the economy and whose priorities continue to be to defend the right of the island to be an independent nation. Among the questions posed by these new developments are: "What foreseeable impact will improved economic conditions have on the daily lives of Cubans?" "Will the party retain the capacity for intervention over the promised reforms in order to avoid a transformation of the system?" "Can the Cuban socialism be democratized?" "Will Raúl manage a period of reforms in order that a new generation of leaders recoup their dreams of socialism?"

1227 McGillivray, Gillian. Blazing cane: sugar communities, class, and state formation in Cuba, 1868/1959. Durham, N.C.: Duke Univ. Press, 2009. 386 p.: bibl., index. (American encounters/global interactions)

The author examines the development of social classes linked to sugar production, and their contribution to the formation and transformation of the state, from the first Cuban Revolution for Independence in 1868 through the Cuban Revolution of 1959. She describes how cane burning became a powerful way for farmers, workers, and revolutionaries to commit sabotage, take control of the harvest season, improve working conditions, protest political repression, attack colonialism and imperialism, nationalize sugar mills and, ultimately, acquire greater political and economic power.

1228 Roman, Peter. Electing Cuba's national assembly deputies: proposals, selections, nominations, and campaigns. (*Rev. Eur. Estud. Latinoam. Caribe*, 82, April 2007, p. 69–87, bibl.)

This article seeks to examine and evaluate Cuba's concept and practice of "democracy" based on participation, consultation, consensus, and representation by describing the way in which the Cuban National Assembly electoral process works from nominations to campaigns to elections.

1229 Routon, Kenneth. Hidden powers of state in the Cuban imagination. Gainesville: Univ. Press of Florida, 2010. 204 p.: bibl., index.

This study brings anthropology and history together by examining the relationship between ritual and state power in revolutionary Cuba, paying particular attention to the roles of memory and history in the construction and contestation of shared political imaginaries. The author describes not only how the monumentality of the state arouses magical sensibilities and popular images of its hidden powers, but he also explores the ways in which revolutionary officialdom has, in recent years, tacitly embraced and harnessed vernacular fantasies of power to the national agenda.

COLOMBIA

STEVEN L. TAYLOR, *Professor, Department of Political Science, Troy University*

THE CONSTANT THEMES in the publications on Colombian politics are democratic governance and violence. The specifics of those constants, however, vary over time. The subthemes on works of democratic governance considered here revolve around electoral reform, party behavior, and the significance of the administration of President Álvaro Uribe. Discussions of violence in recent years have shifted to include consideration of paramilitary groups as well as whether the guerrillas should be viewed as legitimate belligerents or as terrorists. Uribe's tenure in office bridges the gap between the themes of democratic governance and violence, as the administration has claimed a number of successes regarding the paramilitary forces and the guerrilla war, but these events have not been without controversy or criticism.

In regards to the topic of democratic governance, 2003 saw two important electoral reforms. With Legislative Act No. 1 of 2003, the Colombian constitution was amended to require that members of legislative bodies in Colombia be elected using the D'Hondt method (a proportional representation formula). This method replaced the quota system with largest remainders, which also had allowed for multiple lists per party and therefore a great deal of electoral fragmentation. The new system saw altered behavior by political parties; on this topic see especially Botero (item 1250), Losada and Muñoz (item 1242), and Hoyos (item 1244). Another key reform allowed for the re-election of the president, so that it became possible for Uribe to serve two terms (item 1234).

Another theme of consequence to democracy is the political party system. One of the key issues for the 2000s has been the development of the Uribe coalition, which is discussed by Olivella (1253). Likewise, the development of new parties such as the Polo Democrático Alternativo (Alternate Democratic Pole) has created interest (item 1263).

The set of works reviewed here contains a recalibration in the study of the violence (in relationship to literature discussed in recent *Handbook* volumes). While works that focus on the peace process and that provide their own peace proposals and/or are largely descriptive and documentary continue (e.g., items 1236 and 1259), two additional categories of publications in this area are noteworthy. One is the attempt at a more compressive and empirical approach to the violence. For example, Echandía's book provides a useful examination of the geography of the violence over a two decade timeframe (item 1239), and Otero's work provides a plethora of statistics and figures that brings a quantified dimension to what is typically presented primarily as a descriptive narrative (item 1254). The second example of recalibration is a burgeoning debate over how to view the violence: should it be considered, as it has in the past, an armed struggle with defined belligerents, or should it be viewed, as the Uribe administration primarily has, as the state versus terrorists (see, for example, item 1245)? This significant distinction requires further study. Another growing element in the literature on violence is attention to paramilitary groups.

A melding of the themes of democracy and the violence have resulted in a major focus on the policies of the Uribe administration, especially the Peace and Justice Law (which dealt with the demobilization of paramilitary groups) and policies that fall under the label "Democratic Security" (a topic that intersects with the above-noted question of how to address the violence from a political/policy perspective). An overview of the issue of democratic security can be found in the volume by Sánchez and Rodríguez Morales (item 1262). Focusing on Uribe's overall approach to the topic of political violence and state-building, Kline's contribution (item 1251) stands out in this set of works.

Several works that do not fall into the major themes noted above are worthy of special mention: Houghton's volume on indigenous politics (item 1266), García's study of state and civil society in Barranquilla (item **1247**), Tate's "embedded ethnography" concerning human rights and NGOs in Colombia (item **1265**), and Wills' work on women in Colombian politics (item **1269**).

Future research will continue to focus on these twin themes of violence and democratic governance (its successes and failures) and specifically on the long-term implications of the 2003 electoral reforms as they pertain to electoral and party behavior. Uribe, too, will be an object of study. Not only was he president for the longest period of time in modern Colombian history, but his influences (both positive and negative) on the quality of Colombian democracy will be studied for many years to come. Uribe's re-election and his attempt for a third term will be of particular interest to political scientists. Likewise, the question of Uribe's policies regarding paramilitary demobilization and military success against the FARC requires substantial research attention.

1230 Ayala Osorio, Germán; Oscar Duque Sandoval; and Guido Germán Hurtado Vera. Medios de comunicación y seguridad democrática: de la democracia radical al unanimismo ideológico. Cali, Colombia: Univ. Autónoma de Occidente, Grupo de Investigación en Estudios Sociopoliticos, 2006. 322 p.: bibl., ill.

This study focuses on the relationship between the media and politics, with a specific focus on newspapers, news magazines, radio, and television. The authors are critical of the media environment in Colombia as well as of the political parties, which are described as weak in their ability to adequately contribute to public discourse. Includes content analysis of major dailies and prominent columnists.

1231 Báez Pimiento, Adriana. La Alianza Nacional Popular (ANAPO) en Santander, 1962–1976. Bucaramanga, Colombia: Dirección Cultural, Univ. Industrial de Santander, 2007. 305 p.: bibl., ill. (Col. Temas y autores regionales)

Examines the entry of ANAPO into the electoral arena during the National Front, focusing on the department of Santander. Of interest to those studying the National Front period, as well as to those interested in the question of party development and electoral competition. The appendix includes a breakdown of the Anapista electoral lists and their various factions.

1232 Basset, Yann. La izquierda colombiana en tiempos de Uribe. (*Nueva Soc.*, 214, marzo/abril 2008, p. 4–13)

A long-term question in Colombian politics is that of the viability of an electoral, nonviolent left. This theme has become even more significant in the last decade given what many commentators consider a rightward turn in the general tenor of Colombian politics of the Uribe era. This piece examines the electoral fortunes of the left during the bulk of this period.

1233 Bogotá, de la construcción al deterioro 1995–2007. Textos de Alicia Eugenia Silva Nigrinis *et al.* Bogotá: Centro de Estudios Políticos e Internacionales, Facultades de Ciencia Política y Gobierno y de Relaciones Internacionales: Cámara de Comercio de Bogotá: Museo Arqueológico: Editorial Univ. del Rosario, 2009. 181 p.: bibl., ill.

Examines the politics of Bogotá during a period of significant change in Colombia's capital. Contains chapters on the tenures in office of Antanas Mockus (both terms), Enrique Peñalosa, and Luis Eduardo Garzón. The book touches on a variety of themes including the Constitution of 1991, clientelism, and local democracy.

1234 Botero, Felipe. Colombia: ¿democracia, paracracia o simplemente desgracia? (*Rev. Cienc. Polít./Santiago*, vol. 27, no. especial, 2007, p. 97–111, graphs, tables)

This article provides a description of the general political and economic context in which the 2006 elections were embedded. Includes basic electoral results for national offices and information on President Uribe's cabinet. Also includes presidential approval data going back to early 1994.

1235 Breuer, Anita. Policymaking by referendum in presidential systems: evidence from the Bolivian and Colombian cases. (*Lat. Am. Polit. Soc.*, 50:4, Winter 2008, p. 59–89, bibl.)

This article provides a framework for studying government-initiated referenda in the context of executive power. The Colombia section of the piece focuses on the set of referenda offered in 2003. The article is useful for those studying the 1991 Constitution and the Uribe administration, as well as those analyzing the general development and application of executive power in the region.

1236 Camilistas: vigencia de una tradición revolucionaria de nuestra América: entrevista a comandantes del Frente de Guerra Nororiental del Ejército de Liberación Nacional (ELN) de Colombia. Buenos Aires: América Libre: Editorial El Colectivo, 2009. 151 p.: bibl., ill.

Presents transcripts of interviews with various ELN commanders. The text is of use for those interested in this particular guerrilla group. The text also includes an introductory essay and a timeline tracing the history of the ELN as well as that of Camilo Torres, one of its more well-known members.

1237 Chernick, Marc W. Acuerdo posible: solución negociada al conflicto armado colombiano. Bogotá: Ediciones Aurora, 2008. 253 p.: bibl., ill., maps.

In this work, Chernick evaluates the possibility of a peace accord in the Colombian conflict. He addresses the question in a comparative and historical context. The primary focus is on recent violence, including the problems associated with the drug trade and paramilitarism. A main underlying theme is the stalemated nature of the conflict. The lack of a likely military victory by either side, therefore, suggests that the only way to end the conflict is via negotiation.

1238 Cogollos Amaya, Silvia and **Jaime Ramírez León.** El camino tortuoso de la participación ciudadana: una mirada al Cabildo Abierto en Bogotá. (*Univ. Humaníst.*, 63, 2007, p. 109–131, bibl.)

Examines attempts at greater citizen participation in Bogotá in the wake of the constitutional reforms of 1991 and the subsequent Participation Statute (Law 134 of 1994). The study encompasses the 1994–2004 period. The specific focus is the mechanism known as the *cabildo abierto.* Useful for those interested in the political development of Bogotá, the Constitution of 1991, decentralization, or democratization.

1239 Echandía Castilla, Camilo. Dos décadas de escalamiento del conflicto armado en Colombia, 1986–2006. Bogotá: Centro de Investigaciones y Proyectos Especiales, Línea de Negociación y Manejo de Conflictos, Univ. Externado de Colombia, 2006. 309 p.: bibl., ill., maps.

This text examines political violence over a specific 20-year period (1986–2006) and focuses heavily on the political geography of the conflict. The book contains a number of useful maps and charts that illustrate the various activities of groups like the FARC and ELN. Other topics include illicit cultivation of coca and its relationship to the violence.

1240 Ecología política en la Amazonia: las profusas y difusas redes de la gobernanza. Edición de Germán Palacio. Bogotá: Instituto Latinoamericano de Servicios Legales Alternativos: ECOFONDO: Univ. Nacional de Colombia, Sede Amazonia, 2010. 541 p.: bibl., maps. (Col. En clave de sur)

This thick tome collects essays on the politics surrounding the Amazon region of Colombia. The text contains a theoretical section followed by contributions on specific topics such as the relationship between the land and indigenous populations, conflict over land use (including the issue of natural resource exploitation), issues of the border region between Brazil and Peru, as well as the basic question of governance in the region. Of special interest to those interested in ecology/environmental policy.

1241 Edwards, Sebastian and **Roberto Steiner.** La revolución incompleta: las reformas de Gaviria. Bogotá: Grupo Editorial Norma, 2008. 300 p.: bibl., ill. (Vitral)

This book looks at the economic reforms of the César Gaviria administration (1990–94). As the authors note, they examine both the political economy of the period, but also the politics of economics at the time. The work analyzes issues such as the relevant macroeconomic indicators, political actors, and regional factors within Colombia. The conclusion touches on the longer terms implications by looking at the Samper (1994–98) and Pastrana (1998–2002) administrations.

1242 Las elecciones de 2006 en Colombia: una mirada desde la reforma política de 2003. Coordinación de Rodrigo Losada y Patricia Muñoz Yi. Bogotá: Pontificia Univ. Javeriana, 2007. 196 p.

This collection of essays by faculty of the Universidad Javeriana is focused on the outcomes of the 2006 elections in the context of the 2003 electoral reforms (the change to the D'Hondt method as well as the ability of the president to seek re-election). The work provides both a primer on the reforms as well as an analysis of the first national electoral cycle that utilized those rules.

1243 Elhawary, Samir. ¿Caminos violentos hacia la paz?: reconsiderando el nexo entre conflicto y desarrollo en Colombia. (*Colomb. Int.,* 67, enero/junio 2008, p. 84–100, bibl.)

This article criticizes the prevailing conventional wisdom that the violence in Colombia is the result of underdevelopment and that, therefore, peace will come through development. Instead, the author argues that violence and development are interconnected. The main thesis is that the exact nature of the relationship between violence and development must be understood in order to formulate appropriate policy, especially as it pertains to aid.

1244 Entre la persistencia y el cambio: reconfiguración del escenario partidista y electoral en Colombia. Edición de Diana Hoyos Gómez. Bogotá: CEPI: Univ. del Rosaio, 2007. 217 p.: bibl., ill.

Brings together a collection of articles from Colombian political scientists on the topic of party system evolution and behavior. Specifically, the volume addresses the state of the party system in advance of the 2006 elections in terms of historical context and the 2003 electoral reforms. A useful text for those interested in parties, elections, institutional reform, and the general state of Colombian politics.

1245 La estratagema terrorista: las razones del Presidente Uribe para no aceptar la existencia de un conflicto armado in- terno en Colombia. Compilación de Libardo Botero. Bogotá: Fundación Centro de Pensamiento Primero Colombia: Fundación Konrad Adenauer Stiftung, 2008. 243 p.: bibl. (Las ideas de Uribe; 2)

Brings together a collection of brief essays originally published in various places online concerning the violence. Some republished statements on the topic from the Uribe administration are also included in the volume. The focus is on the question of how to properly understand the violence in Colombia: terrorism or internal armed conflict?

Falleti, Tulia G. Una teoría secuencial de la descentralización: Argentina y Colombia en perspectiva comparada. See item **1441**.

1246 Fernández, José Antonio. "Parapolítica", el camino de la política en Colombia. (*Polít. Exter./Madrid,* 21:118, julio/agosto 2007, p. 109–120)

This relatively short article attempts to frame the basic discussion about the scandal involving Colombian politicians and their illegal dealings with paramilitary groups. It touches on the following key topics: the Peace and Justice Law, paramilitary leader Salvador Mancuso, and the Ralito Pact.

1247 García Iragorri, Alexandra. Sociedad civil y estado: del mito a la realidad: elite política, grupos e individuos en una ciudad del Caribe colombiano. Barranquilla, Colombia: Ediciones Uninorte, 2008. 285 p.: bibl., ill. (Col. Ciencia política)

A book-length case study of civil society in Barranquilla (a major city on the Caribbean coast). Themes include the role of NGOs, clientelism, and state development. Part of the analysis is based on survey research of political elites in the region. The text goes beyond description and attempts to analyze democratic development.

1248 Gómez Mejía, Santiago H. Partidos políticos, construcción nacional y conflicto armado en Colombia, 1948–2002. Barcelona: Institut de Ciències Polítiques i Socials, 2006. 122 p.: bibl. (Coll. Grana. Premis memòria doctorat; 9)

This is basically a lengthy essay (roughly 80 p.) that provides an overview of political parties and basic Colombian political history, with a primary (but not exclusive) focus on the latter half of the 20th century. Useful as a basic introduction.

1249 Gray, Vanessa Joan. The new research on civil wars: does it help us understand the Colombian conflict? (*Lat. Am. Polit. Soc.*, 50:3, Fall 2008, p. 63–91, bibl.)

Gray assesses the current literature on conflicts and applies the theories to the Colombian case. She focuses on the complexity of the case and notes the roles played by state weakness, geography, and political economy in explaining the ongoing violence.

1250 Juntos pero no revueltos?: partidos, candidatos y campañas en las elecciones legislativas de 2006 en Colombia. Compilación de Felipe Botero. Bogotá: Univ. de los Andes, Facultad de Ciencias Sociales-Ceso, Depto. de Ciencia Política, 2009. 136 p.: bibl.

A collection of essays primarily written by faculty of the Department of Political Science at the Universidad de los Andes concerning the electoral reforms of 2003 and their effects in the 2006 elections. The analysis is thorough and contains a great deal of useful data.

1251 Kline, Harvey F. Showing teeth to the dragons: state-building by Colombian President Alvaro Uribe Velez, 2002–2006. Tuscaloosa: Univ. of Alabama Press, 2009. 252 p.: bibl., index.

This book is part of Kline's ongoing analysis of state-building in Colombia. This volume focuses on the first Uribe administration (2002–2006). The text provides a very useful and succinct overview of Colombia's predicament going into the Uribe years. Further, more so than the previous works in the series, Kline offers a more complete framework for his approach to state-building in the Colombian context.

Launay, Stephen. Chávez-Uribe: deux voies pour l'Amérique latine? See item **1985**.

Mazzei, Julie. Death squads or self-defense forces?: how paramilitary groups emerge and threaten democracy in Latin America. See item **1153**.

Mejía Guinand, Luis Bernardo; Felipe Botero; and Juan Carlos Rodríguez Raga. ¿Pavimentando con votos?: apropiación

presupuestal para proyectos de infraestructura vial en Colombia, 2002–2006. See item **2022**.

1252 Nasi, Carlo. Derechización 'A la Colombiana' en tiempos confusos: un ensayo especulativo. (*Colomb. Int.*, 66, julio/dic. 2007, p. 162–183, bibl.)

Examines the question of Colombia's shift to the ideological right in recent years during a period in which many other states in the region have seen a leftward shift. Includes some discussion of Uribe, the state of the Colombian left in electoral politics (specifically the Alternative Democratic Pole), and the role of armed actors.

1253 Olivella, Santiago and **Cristina Vélez.** ¿Sobrevivirá la coalición de Uribe? (*Colomb. Int.*, 64, julio/dic. 2006, p. 194–205, tables)

Describes the basic configuration of political parties that make up the pro-Uribe coalition. The evaluation of this coalition in the article is linked to the immediate aftermath of the 2006 elections. The piece uses basic coalition theory to examine the configuration of the *uribista* bloc. Of interest to those studying the Uribe administration, but also for issues such as institutional development and party system evolution.

1254 Otero Prada, Diego Fernando. Las cifras del conflicto colombiano. 2a ed. Bogotá: INDEPAZ, 2007. 391 p.: bibl.

Most books on the subject of violence in Colombia have a tendency towards narrative description, documentation of statements made by guerrillas and government officials, or speculation about how to achieve peace. This work by Otero goes well beyond those approaches and, as the title suggests, provides a vast amount of data on the violence. The types of information are too copious to detail, but include: numbers and types of attacks, kidnapping, public and private expenditures on security, and a host of other data.

1255 Pardo Rueda, Rafael. Fin del paramilitarismo: ¿es posible su desmonte? Barcelona: Ediciones B; Bogotá: Ediciones B Colombia, 2007. 207 p.: bibl., ill. (Crónica actual)

This work provides an overview of the paramilitary phenomenon and the demobilization policies of the Uribe administration vis-à-vis the AUC (the Autodefensas Unidas de Colombia or United Self-Defense Forces of Colombia). The author has experience in the academy and in politics, including as the Liberal Party's presidential candidate in 2010. He worked in the area of peace negotiations in the Gaviria administration (1990–94). The most useful part of the work is the section that presents the descriptive background.

1256 Paz y resistencia: experiencias indígenas desde la autonomía. Edición de Mauricio Caviedes. Investigación de José Domingo Caldón *et al.* Bogotá: Centro de Cooperación al Indígena: Organización Indígena de Antioquia, 2007. 113 p.: bibl. (Col. Autonomía indígena; 1)

This edited volume examines the issue of the peace process through the lens of indigenous communities. The work is slender (roughly 100 p.) and primarily descriptive. It would be of interest for those studying differing perceptions of the peace process and the politics of indigenous groups.

1257 La penitencia del poder: lecciones de la administración del Presidente Belisario Betancur, 1982–1986. Coordinación de Diego Pizano Salazar. Bogotá: Univ. de Los Andes, Escuela de Gobierno Alberto Lleras Camargo, 2009. 576 p.: bibl., ill. (some col.), indexes.

This book examines the Belisario Betancur administration (1982–86). In this collection of essays written by a number of scholars, each chapter focuses on some aspect of public administration during the Betancur years. Topics include foreign relations, internal security, civil-military relations, the peace process, finance, and infrastructure. The approach is interdisciplinary, with contributions from political science, economics, public administration, and engineering.

1258 Los potros de bárbaros atilas: la razón de los inamovibles del Presidente Uribe en el debate sobre el llamado "Acuerdo Humanitario". Compilación de Libardo Botero. Bogotá: Fundación Centro de Pensamiento Primero Colombia, 2008. 430 p.: bibl. (Las ideas de Uribe; 3)

This collection of statements and essays addresses the topic of kidnapping and the question of how to view its usage

by armed groups, especially the FARC. The book includes statements from Uribe and the guerrillas as well as other previously published materials from scholars, activists, and politicians. The book is a companion thematically with item **1245**.

1259 Qué, cómo y cuándo negociar con las FARC. Textos de Alfredo Rangel Suarez *et al.* Bogotá: Intermedio, 2008. 331 p.: bibl.

The book consists of four long essays that propose methods of negotiating with the FARC in peace talks. The approach is academic in orientation. Thematically this is part of a broader debate about the appropriate method of dealing with armed actors in Colombia.

1260 Richani, Nazih. Caudillos and the crisis of the Colombian state: fragmented sovereignty, the war system and the privatisation of counterinsurgency in Colombia. (*Third World Q.*, 28:2, 2007, p. 403–417, graph, table)

Applies a class-based analysis of the various violent actors in the conflict in Colombia. The article is of special interest to those attempting to understand the development of the paramilitary movement in Colombia. This piece fits into Richani's ongoing work on what he calls the "war-system" in Colombia.

1261 Rodríguez Raga, Juan Carlos. Izquierdas y derechas en Colombia: una mirada rápida a los rasgos sociodemográficos del espectro ideológico del país. (*Colomb. Int.*, 66, julio/dic. 2007, p. 184–193, graphs)

A comparative look at the ideological tendencies of the populations of Latin American countries. Some regional comparisons are made, although the primary discussion compares Colombia with Uruguay and Venezuela as key cases. Examines the issue of Colombia's more rightward politics.

1262 Sánchez David, Rubén and **Federmán Antonio Rodríguez Morales.** Seguridad, democracia y seguridad democrática. Bogotá: Editorial Univ. del Rosario, 2007. 202 p.

A book-length treatment from two political scientists on the topic of conceptualizing democracy and security in the context of Uribe's "Democratic Security" policy. This is primarily a theoretical and conceptual discussion. This theme is a key one for Colombia in terms of the first decade of the 2000s.

1263 Sandoval M., Luis I. Polo Democrático Alternativo: ¿hacia dónde? ¿con quiénes? Bogotá: Centro de Pensamiento Democracia Hoy, 2009. 255 p.: bibl., ill. (some col.).

Contains background information, documents, and commentary about the Polo Democrático Alternativo (Alternative Democratic Pole or PDA), a political party of nonviolent left/center-left citizens. The volume is useful for examining the development of the party, as well as for those looking at Colombian politics of the early 2000s.

1264 Seguridades en construcción en América Latina. Vol. 1, El círculo de Colombia: Brasil, Ecuador, Panamá, Perú y Venezuela. Vol. 2, Dimensiones y enfoques de seguridad en Colombia. Edición de Manuel José Bonett Locarno. Textos de Rubén Sánchez David *et al.* Bogotá: Centro Editorial Univ. del Rosario, 2005–2008. 2 v.: bibl., ill., indexes, maps (some col.).

A collection of essay from students and faculty at the Universidad del Rosario in Bogotá. The focus is primarily on the question of the redefinition of security in the post-Cold War setting. While some of the discussion derives from international relations theory and has some comparative elements as well, the focus is primarily on the internal struggle in Colombia. Also includes discussion of military tactics. For review of vol. 1 by an international relations specialist, see *HLAS 65:2125.*

1265 Tate, Winifred. Counting the dead: the culture and politics of human rights activism in Colombia. Berkeley: Univ. of California Press, 2007. 379 p.: bibl., index, map. (California series in public anthropology; 18)

This book offers an anthropological study of the history of human rights NGOs in Colombia (or, more accurately, what the author describes as an "embedded ethnography"). The book is well-written, readable, and informative; it is both profoundly personal, but also extremely well focused on the details of the subject matter. Of general interest to those studying violence, human rights, and NGOs.

1266 La tierra contra la muerte: conflictos territoriales de los pueblos indígenas en Colombia. Edición de Juan Houghton. Bogotá: Centro de Cooperación al Indígena, 2008. 420 p.: bibl., ill., maps (some col., some folded), plates, 1 CD-ROM.

This book takes a comprehensive look at the political and social challenges facing Colombia's indigenous population. The main theme is that of indigenous territories and public policy concerning them. The essays explore linkages to economic interests in these territories and what the introduction calls a "wave of new conquistadors" pertaining to issues such as agriculture, oil, biofuels, and minerals. The book includes a great deal of data and some high-quality maps as well as a CD-ROM containing a multimedia presentation.

1267 Torrijos R., Vicente. Teoría y practica de la fertilidad revolucionaria: ¿qué tan lejos o tan cerca están las FARC de tomarse el poder en Colombia? (*Invest. Desarro./Barranquilla,* 14:1, julio 2006, p. 62–85, bibl., graphs)

This article examines the question of the conditions under which the FARC might come to power in Colombia. The author attempts to use a quasi-quantitative method, which is interesting, although the methods are questionable insofar as they are numeric, but still speculative in nature.

1268 ¿Veinte años de democracia local en Colombia?: memorias del encuentro nacional. Compilación de Luis Fernando Calderón Alvarez y Jorge Alberto Velásquez Betancur. Medellín, Colombia: Instituto Tecnológico Metropolitano, 2008. 238 p. (Col. Deliberare)

This collection publishes the proceedings from a conference on local governance. Most of the participants were politicians who had served in local capacities (e.g., mayor, governor, etc). The theme of the text is a retrospective examination of the impact of decentralization reforms of the 1980s and 1990s, especially the popular election of mayors (which started in 1988). Useful for those studying local politics and decentralization.

1269 Wills O., María Emma. Inclusión sin representación: la irrupción política de las mujeres en Colombia, 1970–2000. Bogotá: Grupo Editorial Norma, 2007. 398 p.: ill. (Col. Vitral)

This book examines the integration (and lack thereof) of women into Colombia's political democracy. The study includes a number of charts, tables, and other information about the role of women in Colombian politics and society from the mid-20th century to the early 21st (although the focus is 1970 to 2000). It will be useful not only to those interested specifically in gender politics, but also to those researching the general question of democratic development.

ECUADOR

JENNIFER N. COLLINS, *Assistant Professor of Political Science, University of Wisconsin, Stevens Point*

THE WORKS INCLUDED IN THIS SECTION were published roughly between 2006 and 2009 and correspond to a period of transition in Ecuadorian politics. The key political features of the 1990s and first couple of years of the new millennium were fragmentation and dysfunction in the political system and powerful contestatory challenges to this system by social and indigenous movements. The combination of both phenomena resulted in substantial political volatility and instability, including three presidential ousters, but also the incorporation of previously marginalized social actors into the political system, namely indigenous and popular sectors. This transition gave way, in the mid-2000s, to the decline and internal crisis of the indigenous movement and the final collapse of the party system, both of which allowed for the rise of a political outsider, Rafael Correa, to the presidency. Correa, in subsequent years, would realign social forces and the contours of Ecuadorian politics.

The bulk of recent scholarship on Ecuador's government and politics and most of the works reviewed for this *HLAS* volume fall into one of two categories: studies of political parties and formal institutions or work on social movements, particularly the indigenous movement. Theoretical differences follow the choice of subject, with the former tending to employ institutional and rational choice theories, and the latter utilizing social movement theory and qualitative methods.

Institutional reform has been a recurrent theme throughout the democratic period that began in 1978. A variety of changes to institutions and electoral law have aimed at making politicians more accountable to voters, decreasing fragmentation, avoiding gridlock, etc. The results have been disappointing. Three of the works reviewed here study the interplay between formal and informal institutions, suggesting that informal norms and practices have played a central role in the country's recurrent political instability (items **1279**, **1283**, and **1285**). While some blame a political culture characterized by a weak commitment to democracy for the failure of otherwise well-designed institutions (e.g., item **1285**), another suggests that institutional reform, in fact, undermined informal practices developed by politicians that had facilitated cooperation and lessened executive-legislative gridlock (item **1283**). One article moves beyond executive-legislative politics and analyzes problems within the judicial system (item **1279**). One book offers a new twist as it draws attention to and raises critical questions about the role played by social scientists and intellectuals in Ecuador's political debates, in particular with regard to institutional development (item **1270**). This approach could be productively applied to studying Correa's "Citizen's Revolution," given the predominance of academics in his administration and inner circle.

As has been the case since the 1990 uprising, the indigenous movement continues to be a central focus of scholarly attention. New works address important questions about how political identity has been constructed in the movement and in turn how these identities impact politics (items **1273**, **1281**, and **1284**). In contrast to much of the earlier work that focused on the ethnic character of the movement, new attention is being directed to the movement's historical connections to the left (item **1272**), as well as its contemporaneous role in left politics (item **1280** and essays in item **1273**). After two decades of organization-building and contestatory politics, the first few years of the 21st century saw the indigenous movement twice seem to nearly reach the pinnacle of political power. First was the ephemeral military-indigenous triumvirate that took power briefly on January 21, 2000, in the wake of Mahuad's ouster, and then Pachakutik's participation in Gutiérrez's government during the first half of 2002. CONAIE's participation in the triumvirate, which many classify as a coup, have led some analysts to question the assumption that the movement's impact on democracy is invariably positive, pointing to both democratic and less-than-democratic impulses within it (items **1286** and **1287**). Pachakutik's alliance with Gutiérrez proved to be disastrous and several works reviewed here shed light on the period of the alliance and its aftermath (items **1273**, **1278**, **1280**, and **1286**). The traumatic experience of this alliance forms part of a larger question scholars are beginning to grapple with: what explains the precipitous decline and internal crisis of the indigenous movement in the years following 2002 (items **1280**, **1281**, and **1286**, and an essay in item **1273**)?

Other social movements, including squatters' movements (item **1276**) and the middle class *forajido* movement that played such a key role in Gutiérrez's ouster (item **1280**), also received attention, although much less than the indigenous movement. The *forajido* movement merits more systematic scholarly inquiry, especially as it relates to Correa's eventual election. Studies of environmental organizations and their struggles also represent an area for future work, as tensions build between indigenous and environmental movements and the state over Correa's extractivist and neodevelopmentalist policies. Other noticeable gaps in the literature exist, notably the absence of work on political actors aside from social movements and politicians. The political roles and interests of the military, business, and economic elites, and the media, in particular, need to be studied. One interesting investigation of presidential assaults on the media found that it was precisely these actors who held the key to whether or not presidents were able to infringe on democratic rights (item **1271**). It would be interesting to extend this analysis and see if the same pattern holds under Correa. Finally, in contrast to the extensive work done on indigenous politics in the sierra and the Amazon, since the 1980s there has been little serious scholarship of politics in the populous coastal provinces.

Two articles on Correa (items **1274** and **1275**) signal the direction that much of the current work on Ecuador will surely be headed. While these articles focus on the ways he has concentrated power to the detriment of democracy, there will surely be lively debates on the nature and consequences for democracy under this polarizing president. For instance, there appears to be much that is innovative and progressive in his administration's social policies (item **1277**). Correa characterizes his presidency as a break with the past, and there is indeed evidence of disjuncture, such as the complete collapse of the *partidocracia,* to use Correa's term (item **1282**). The degree to which his presidency over the long-run represents a definitive break with the patterns of political fragmentation and social movement contestation that have characterized Ecuadorian politics over the last 30 years remains an outstanding question.

1270 Andrade Andrade, Pablo. Democracia y cambio político en el Ecuador: liberalismo, política de la cultura y reforma institucional. Quito: Corporación Editora Nacional: Univ. Andina Simón Bolívar, Sede Ecuador, 2009. 298 p.: bibl. (La biblioteca de ciencias sociales; 64)

A dense, but rich, political theoretical analysis of the role of ideas in democratic development and institutional change. Traces the evolution of Ecuadorian political and social thought, in particular diagnoses of political dysfunction by academics and public intellectuals in 1980s and 1990s. Demonstrates how intellectual paradigms shaped the decision to convene the 1997 Constituent Assembly and its outcome. Author is critical of the governability thesis, arguing that a narrow focus on institutions ignores structural conditions of inequality, poverty, and power relations.

1271 Barndt, William T. Executive assaults and the social foundations of democracy in Ecuador. (*Lat. Am. Polit. Soc.,* 52:1, Spring 2010, p. 121–154, appendix, bibl., tables)

This article presents a methodologically sophisticated study of publicly contested executive assaults on critical voices in the media. Utilizing a "social conflict" approach, Barndt examines 18 such "assaults" occurring between 1979 and 2004. The actors who turned out to be determinant of the outcomes of these presidential challenges to independent media were not other branches of government or popular sectors, but the security forces and business organizations. President Correa's ongoing battles with the media make this study all the more relevant.

1272 Becker, Marc. Indians and leftists in the making of Ecuador's modern indigenous movements. Durham, N.C.: Duke Univ. Press, 2008. 303 p.: bibl., ill., index, map.

Written by one of the leading historians of Ecuador's indigenous movements, this book traces the 20th-century relationship between leftists—socialists and communists—and indigenous communities and organizations. Becker challenges the widely held assumption that paternalism permeated this relationship. Instead, this sympathetic treatment of the left marshals evidence of a more positive interaction, characterized by mutual respect and influence. Coverage of historical developments previous to the 1960s, in particular, represents a crucial contribution to the history of Ecuador's indigenous movement. For sociologist's comment, see item **2495**.

1273 Coloquio Internacional "Etnicidad y Política", Quito, 2007. Los Andes en movimiento: identidad y poder en el nuevo paisaje político. Edición de Pablo Ospina, Olaf Kaltmeier y Christian Büschges. Textos de Christian Büschges *et al.* Quito: Corporación Editora Nacional: Univ. Andina Simón Bolívar, Sede Ecuador, 2009. 265 p.: bibl., ill. (Biblioteca de ciencias sociales; 65)

An essential collection of timely essays on indigenous movements, representation, and political participation by leading scholars from Ecuador, Bolivia, the US, and Europe. The opening and closing sections address broad theoretical topics such as citizenship, identity, and interculturality. Essays that make up the core of the volume are grouped in three categories—electoral participation, social movements, and symbolic representations—and are case-focused on topics such as Pachakutik and the left, local government in the Aymara community of Jesús de Machaca, and CONAIE's internal crisis.

1274 Conaghan, Catherine M. Ecuador: Correa's plebiscitary presidency. (*J. Democr.,* 19:2, April 2008, p. 46–60)

Written just one year into Correa's first term, this article characterizes his administration as a "hyper-plebiscitary presidency" in which the president "makes unmediated appeals" to the public thus bypassing other governmental actors and institutions. Correa's campaign set the stage for a head-to-head confrontation with an unpopular Congress, one that he succeeded in upending after winning the presidency. Cultivating and manipulating public support, he succeeded in rewriting the rules of the game, sidelining the opposition, and centering politics around himself.

1275 Conaghan, Catherine M. and Carlos de la Torre. The permanent campaign of Rafael Correa: making Ecuador's plebiscitary presidency. (*Int. J. Press/Polit.*, 13:3, July 2008, p. 267–284, bibl., table)

This article develops the idea that Correa used a "permanent campaign" mode not only to win the election, but subsequently to consolidate power in order to carry out far-reaching constitutional change. Media and marketing strategies by the president to increase and maintain public support are analyzed, as are his dealings with major media outlets. The polarizing nature of the permanent campaign and the use of public money creates an uneven playing field, leading to an erosion of democratic accountability.

1276 Dosh, Paul. Tactical innovation, democratic governance, and mixed motives: popular movement resilience in Peru and Ecuador. (*Lat. Am. Polit. Soc.*, 51:1, Spring 2009, p. 87–118, bibl., ill., tables)

This comparative analysis of three urban squatter movements in Quito and Lima explains the resilience of some compared with the collapse of others after the goal of titling has been achieved. Contributing to literature on social movements, this study introduces the concept of "innovator" organizations, which combine mixed motives, tactical innovation, and democratic governance to produce ongoing participation and organizational resilience. This study contributes to efforts aimed at identifying other motors of social movement involvement and activism beyond selective incentives. For Peruvian political scientist's comment, see item **1358**.

1277 Encuentro Internacional sobre Políticas Sociales y Desarrollo Institucional Público, Quito, 2008. Políticas sociales e institucionalidad pública. Quito: Instituto de la Niñez y la Familia, Ministerio de Inclusión Económica y Social: Univ. Andina Simón Bolívar: Corporación Editora Nacional, 2009. 220 p.: bibl., ill. (Biblioteca de ciencias sociales; 66)

This collection brings together presentations given at a 2008 international forum on social policy in Latin America hosted by Ecuador. The chapters are grouped into three sections: 1) broad theoretical challenges, 2) specific policy areas and country-specific programs, and 3) social policies in Ecuador. The Ecuador presentations are by ministers and appointees in Correa's government and cover all major social policy areas, thus providing an excellent overview of the administration's early initiatives.

1278 Entre la utopía y el desencanto: Pachakutik en el gobierno de Gutiérrez. Textos de Augusto Barrera *et al.* Quito: Planeta, 2004. 301 p.: bibl.

Published within a year after Pachakutik's split from President Gutiérrez, this collection of essays by key figures in Pachakutik, most of whom held high-level government positions, is a self-critical reflection on the party's passage through this administration. This excellent primary source material addresses how the alliance came to be, what led to its dissolution, and lessons for social movements and the left. Also of interest are descriptions of programs developed by Pachakutik ministries, including agriculture, tourism, oil, and education.

Estados y autonomías en democracias contemporáneas: Bolivia, Ecuador, España, México. See item **1314**.

1279 Grijalva, Agustín. Constitución, institucionalidad y derecho en Ecuador. (*Ecuad. Debate*, 71, agosto 2007, p. 31–44, tables)

Written at the start of Correa's presidency in the midst of the battle to convene a constituent assembly, this article aims to contribute to the debate over reform of Ecuador's judicial institutions, in particular those with powers of constitutional review. A key problem identified is the Constitutional Tribunal's lack of independence from

Congress, which the author argues has served to politicize it and impede its ability to act as an independent check on other branches of government.

1280 Hidalgo Flor, Francisco. Encrucijada: procesos políticos y movimientos populares en el Ecuador actual. Quito: Centro de Investigaciones para el Desarrollo; Louvain-la-Neuve, Belgium: CETRI, 2009. 121 p.: bibl., ill.

A collection of previously published essays analyzing contemporary left politics in Ecuador from 1990–2006 from a Marxist-Gramscian perspective. The author explores the possibility of leftist hegemony. The contribution and state of social movements including the indigenous, environmental, and women's movements, as well as the *forajido* uprising of 2005, are discussed. The book is useful for recalling the mood and dilemmas of the political left prior to Correa's election, as well as for its discussion of the decline of the indigenous movement.

Highland Indians and the state in modern Ecuador. See *HLAS 66:1704.*

1281 Lucero, José Antonio. Struggles of voice: the politics of indigenous representation in the Andes. Pittsburgh, Pa.: Univ. of Pittsburgh Press, 2008. 236 p.: bibl., index, maps. (Pitt Latin American series)

This important book engages in a cultural analysis of patterns of indigenous mobilization and representation, studying the "social construction of indigenous voice" through a comparison of indigenous-state relations in Ecuador and Bolivia from the mid-19th to the 21st centuries. Special attention is paid to the strategies employed by indigenous actors and how they intersect with domestic and international forces and opportunities. The focus on the multiplicity of indigenous voices, actors, and strategies is especially interesting.

1282 Machado Puertas, Juan Carlos. Ecuador: el derrumbe de los partidos tradicionales. (*Rev. Cienc. Polít./Santiago,* 27, no. especial, 2007, p. 129–147, tables)

A summary of the most important political, economic, and to a lesser extent, social trends in Ecuador during 2006. This essay offers a snapshot of the country just before the start of Correa's presidency and

therefore serves as a good benchmark for evaluating changes under Correa. It also contains useful data on the 2006 presidential and legislative elections that attest to the article's title, "the collapse of traditional parties."

1283 Mejía Acosta, Andrés. Informal coalitions and policymaking in Latin America: Ecuador in comparative perspective. New York: Routledge, 2009. 170 p.: bibl., ill., index. (Latin American studies)

This study explains how Ecuadorian presidents passed economic reforms in a fragmented legislature by forming "ghost coalitions," essentially informal, secretive agreements between party leaders and presidents. Vast amounts of quantitative data, including roll call votes, bills, and political profiles covering 25 years, dispel previously held assumptions, such as high rates of party switching and use of presidential decrees. Ghost coalitions were functional but became inoperable after political reforms in the late 1990s. The result was party system collapse and increased instability.

1284 Pajuelo Teves, Ramón. Reinventando comunidades imaginadas: movimientos indígenas, nación y procesos sociopolíticos en los países centroandinos. Lima: IFEA, Instituto Francés de Estudios Andinos: IEP, Instituto de Estudios Peruanos, 2007. 173 p.: bibl., ill. (Travaux de l'Institut francais d'études andines; 192) (América Problema; 20)

Employing Benedict Anderson's notion of "imagined communities," Pajuelo Teves analyzes the ways in which Bolivian and Ecuadorian indigenous movements have conceived of and promoted new plurinational representations of their nations. Peru is included as a contrasting case, given that no national movement has yet to emerge in that country. Case studies of map-making and the *wiphala's* symbolism illustrate this process. Ethnic politics in the Andes is deemed less divisive than in other regions because ethnic identification is embedded in this reimagining of the nation.

1285 Sánchez López, Francisco. ¿Democracia no lograda o democracia malograda?: un análisis del sistema político del Ecuador, 1979–2002. Quito: FLACSO Ecuador, 2008. 269 p.: bibl., ill. (Atrio)

This book focuses on political actors

and institutions to explain the persistent crisis of Ecuadorian democracy. Composed of stand-alone chapters on parties, the presidency, Congress, and the electoral system, this volume offers a wealth of empirical data, tables, and a summary of electoral reforms. A final chapter on the indigenous movement, while well-wrought, seems out of place. Weak commitment to the rule of law and democracy, combined with dysfunctional informal norms, undermined institutional reforms, rendering them incapable of resolving the system's problems.

Wolff, Jonas. De-idealizing the democratic civil peace: on the political economy of democratic stabilization and pacification in Argentina and Ecuador. See item **2124.**

1286 Wolff, Jonas. (De-)mobilising the marginalised: a comparison of the Argentine piqueteros and Ecuador's indigenous movement. (*J. Lat. Am. Stud.,* 39:1, Feb. 2007, p. 1–30, table)

Democratic regimes have proven surprisingly capable of "taming" social movements from below through cooptation and clientelistic integration, in this way forestalling more profound change. Internal characteristics of Argentine *piquetero* and Ecuadorian indigenous movements share commonalities that explain their strength and vulnerability. Rootedness in communities was a source of strength, while also facilitating government efforts to co-opt and divide and orient demands from national agendas to particularistic benefits. That similar dynamics were found across apparently dissimilar cases exemplifies innovative comparative research.

1287 Zamosc, Leon. The Indian movement and political democracy in Ecuador. (*Lat. Am. Polit. Soc.,* 49:3, Fall 2007, p. 1–34, table)

In 2000 the indigenous movement helped overthrow President Mahuad and participated in a brief, unconstitutional seizure of power. Characterizing this as a coup inconsistent with the broader pattern of democratic action, the author engages in a comprehensive assessment of the movement's impact on democracy. Representing new groups, wresting concessions from government, and introducing participatory practices represent significant contributions, but the coup highlights a failure to socialize a firm commitment to democracy and the complications of navigating contestation and participation.

VENEZUELA

RENÉ SALGADO, *Independent Consultant, Gaithersburg, Maryland*

THERE APPEARS TO BE a diminished international scholarly interest in Venezuelan political processes and politics, at least as reflected in the fact that the majority of books and articles included in this section were produced by academics or researchers from local universities. This finding contrasts the period between the 1960s and 1990s, when journal articles and books by American political scientists were as important as the domestic intellectual production.

With the remarkable exception of the studies by Gil Yepes (item **1294**) and Irwin and Micett (item **1297**), the arguments, discussions, and analyses found in the publications included in this section do not consistently demonstrate solid scholarship. Nonetheless, they do offer interesting insights and appraisals, worthy of being taken into consideration if for no other reason than that their authors are local academics and analysts and, thus, hold a participant-observer status.

Traditional themes of enquiry, such as political parties or electoral politics, or more generally, structural factors, no longer attract the attention of political analysts. With the exception of the analyses by Irwin and Micett—on civil-military relations—or the book by Gil Yepez—on contemporary Venezuelan political culture—nearly all of the works in this section focus on Hugo Chávez's presidential politics and style, albeit with striking differences in their perceptions and characterizations. For López Amaya , it is not clear what Chávez and Chavistas mean when they talk about "21st century socialism" (item **1296**); García Larralde does not hesitate to categorically grant the label of fascist to the regime (item **1293**); Sánchez Guerrero regards Chávez as a caudillo who exhibits a traditional authoritarian style (item **1302**); and Ramos Jiménez rejects Chávez's "populist" image and labels him instead a "personalist authoritarian" (item **1301**).

1288 Alvarez Itriago, Rosangel Mariela.
Perspectivas de la descentralización y la participación ciudadana en el Gobierno de Hugo Chávez, 1999–2009. (*Rev. Cienc. Soc./ Maracaibo*, 16:4, oct./dic. 2010, p. 665–676, bibl.)

Offers a broad exploration of tensions between central government control and decentralization. Highlights the importance of examining Chávez's Social and Economic Development Plan of 2007 to better understand the relationships between national, state, and local governments. Concludes that the Chávez regime has imposed severe limitations on regional government autonomy.

1289 Calle Lombana, Humberto de la. El día que Chávez renunció: el golpe en la intimidad de la OEA. Bogotá: Ediciones B, 2008. 350 p.: bibl., facsims. (Crónica actual)

This book is written by former Colombian Vice President Humberto de la Calle, the representative of his country to the OAS in April 2002 when Hugo Chávez was removed from power for a few hours and a government headed by businessman Pedro Carmona was installed as president. Here he offers an encompassing participant-observer discussion of the reactions of OAS country members with regard to the event.

1290 Cañizález, Andrés. Pensar la sociedad civil: actores sociales, espacio público y medios en Venezuela. Caracas: Univ. Católica Andrés Bello, 2007. 155 p.: bibl.

Author is instructor of social communication at Universidad Católica Andrés Bello, Caracas (UCAB), and is a former director of *Centro Gumilla* communication magazine. His book offers a broad discussion of the role of the media, specially the

written press and TV, in contemporary Venezuela. It also discusses how media has become particularly important for people's voicing of demands in a context of diminished representativeness of political parties.

1291 Ellner, Steve. Rethinking Venezuelan politics: class, conflict, and the Chávez phenomenon. Boulder, Colo.: Lynne Rienner, 2008. 257 p.: bibl., index.

Uses as a baseline the interesting notion that political movements should be judged by the extent to which they manage to achieve four critical objectives or substantive issues: social justice, democracy, national economic development, and economic and political nationalism. However, the book, devoted to the Chávez phenomenon, does not offer substantive empirical evidence to evaluate his regime on such counts. The first four chapters contain encompassing accounts of 19th- and 20th-century Venezuelan politics, and chapters five to seven, focusing on Chávez's domestic politics, do not offer a thorough evaluation of the performance and impact of his policies. The books suggests that social justice has improved in Venezuela because the poor are included in governmental rhetoric or have been the focus of some social programs. Yet the book does not show how and to what extent Chávez's policies have contributed to strengthen democracy or have boosted domestic economic objectives and national economic development.

1292 Fournier, Jean-Marc. L'autre Venezuela de Hugo Chavez: boom pétrolier et révolution bolivarienne à Maracaibo. Paris: Karthala, 2010. 289 p.: bibl., ill. (some col.), maps, plates. (Hommes et sociétés)

Fournier, a professor of social geography at the University de Caen in the northwest of France, offers an account of the political, economic, and social impacts of Chávez government policies. Using Maracaibo as a case study, he concludes that there has been progress but also significant limitations in quality of life. He questions the appropriateness of the use of additional oil revenues. Includes pictures of several Maracaibo neighborhoods.

1293 García Larralde, Humberto. El fascismo del siglo XXI: la amenaza totalitaria del proyecto político de Hugo Chávez Frías. Caracas: Debate, 2008. 607 p.: bibl. (Col. Actualidad)

The author is an economist and researcher of the Centro de Desarrollo CENDES, and a former member of Venezuela's Communist Youth. He is highly critical of the Chávez regime, which he characterizes as neo-fascist. The first few chapters here provide a discussion of fascism as a category of political analysis. The discussion then turns to the political mechanisms used by Chávez to keep the state and its citizens under control. The author describes his characterization of the mythologizing of Venezuelan history and the manipulation of national symbols, particularly Simón Bolívar, through the constant use of propaganda and media to legitimize a messianic leader. He also discusses the displacement of political adversaries through such mechanisms as nationalization and expropriation of their private assets; incarceration and forced exile, and the use of violence and militarization in open disregard of constitutional rights.

Gates, Leslie C. Electing Chavez: the business of anti-neoliberal politics in Venezuela. See item **1981**.

1294 Gil Yepes, José Antonio. La centro democracia. v. 1, El modelo de sociedad preferido por los venezolanos. Caracas: El Nacional, 2009. 1 v.: bibl., ill., index.

One of the most remarkable actions on the part of President Chávez has been openly disqualifying political opponents with a variety of insults and sobriquets that foster political bitterness and polarization. On the basis of systematic empirical work, this book by Gil Yepes, president of Caracas-based polling firm Datanálisis

and former professor at IESA, shows that the percentage of Venezuelans who prefer cooperative attitudes, language, and behavior has increased in recent years. The book also shows that the increasing proportion of those who reject the right-left dichotomy are in favor of private property and freedom of expression, and support the notion of public policies and practices that boost solidarity. Author shows that more than half of Venezuelans prefer tolerance, pluralism, political agreements, and more and better democracy, a set of civic attitudes that the author labels as "Center Democracy."

Guerra Britto, José. Refutación del socialismo del siglo XXI. See item **1983**.

1295 Hegemonía y control comunicacional. Edición de Marcelino Bisbal. Caracas: Editorial Alfa, 2009. 270 p.: bibl., index. (Col. Trópicos. Comunicación; 82)

Discusses the communication hegemony of the Chávez government, and Chávez's two-prong strategy of persecuting and punishing independent media critics along with the continued strengthening of pro-Chávez media, particularly TV and radio stations. Book claims that no other Latin American government has as much power over the media as Chávez does.

1296 Ideas para debatir el socialismo del siglo XXI. Edición de Margarita López Maya. Textos de Vladimir Acosta *et al.* Caracas: Editorial Alfa, 2007–2009. 2 v.: bibl. (Col. Hogueras; 40, 50)

At the beginning of his second presidential term (2007–2013), President Hugo Chávez launched his campaign for a "21st century socialism" without explaining or elaborating on its meaning. This initiative prompted a group of faculty members at the Universidad Central de Venezuela to organize a seminar with the participation of researchers, public officials, university teachers, and political activists to gain a better understanding of the novelties of Chávez's proposal. The contributions of participating panelists are offered in the book. The main conclusion of the seminar, as explained by López Maya, the coordinator of the publication, is simply that it is difficult to understand Chávez's intentions as he does not disclose or offer consistent elaboration of his political stances and visions, and governmental officials responsible for policy implementation have no understanding of the policy implications for their own bureaus. Chávez enjoys espousing policy in a spontaneous fashion in his radio programs or while writing for Twitter in such a way that his decisions often take his own ministers by surprise.

1297 Irwin G., Domingo and **Ingrid Micett.** Caudillos, militares y poder: una historia del pretorianismo en Venezuela. Caracas: Univ. Católico Andrés Bello, 2008. 336 p.: bibl.

An excellent addition to the distinguished collection of books by Irwin, which further illuminates our understanding of civil-military relations in Venezuela. The book is a useful complement to Irwin's 2008 article dealing with changes in Venezuela's military law, "Retos a la seguridad y defensa en un ambiente político complejo: cooperación y divergencia en Suramérica" (available online). This book brings together a collection of writings by the authors from 1985 until 2007 and offers serious documentary and empirical discussion of military evolution and the role of the military in politics from the beginning of the 19th century to the 21st century. Authors claim that the 19th century was that of the Venezuelan caudillo predominance, and that the military gained significant power during the 20th. They wonder if the 21st will be the century of organized and democratic civil society, and their response is full of skepticism.

Lanza, Gregorio. Bolivia y Venezuela: votos que revolucionan. See item **1325**.

Launay, Stephen. Chávez-Uribe: deux voies pour l'Amérique latine? See item **1985**.

1298 Lupu, Noam. Who votes for *chavismo*?: class voting in Hugo Chávez's Venezuela. (*LARR*, 45:1, 2010, p. 7–32, bibl., graphs, tables)

This article is based on survey data relating household income and votes between 1993 and 2006. Suggests that Chávez's support base increased mostly among the middle classes rather than the poor.

1299 Medina, Medófilo; Margarita López Maya; and **Luis E. Lander.** Chávez: una revolución sin libreto. Bogotá: Ediciones Aurora, 2007. 233 p.: bibl.

Historians Medina and López, and engineer Lander, offer an overarching descriptive view of critical milestones during Hugo Chávez's mandate, such as the failed coup of April 2002, the oil workers strike at the end of that year, and the 2006 election of Chávez.

1300 Omaña Peñaloza, Rebeca. La OEA en Venezuela: entre la democracia y el golpe de estado. Quito: Univ. Andina Simón Bolívar, Ecuador: Abya-Yala: Corporación Editora Nacional, 2008. 90 p.: bibl. (Serie Magíster; 79)

Author is a historian from the Universidad de Los Andes, Venezuela, and has been subsecretary of political affairs at the OAS. Here she discusses the background of political polarization that led to the interruption of the constitutional order in April 2002. She also offers an analysis of the role and impact of the OAS intervention to deal with the political crisis.

1301 Ramos Jiménez, Alfredo. El experimento bolivariano: liderazgo, partidos y elecciones. Mérida, Venezuela: CIPCOM, Centro de Investigaciones de Política Comparada, 2009. 292 p.: bibl.

Ramos Jiménez is a professor of political sociology at the Universidad de Los Andes, Venezuela. In this book he highlights the fact that President Chávez dislikes consensus and negotiation, thereby suggesting that his regime is "personalist authoritarian" rather than populist. He also discusses how Chávez's initial political program has been undergoing a transformation since the 2006 presidential elections, in a project that is moving in the direction of personalistic control of society as a whole, and where spaces for educational freedom, family, and personal beliefs are threatened by a singular political power. Author pinpoints this governmental conduct as the origin of Venezuela's contemporary social conflicts.

Rivas Leone, José Antonio. Las transformaciones del estado y las fuerzas armadas en la globalización: el caso de Venezuela. See item **1989**.

1302 Sánchez Guerrero, Gustavo. Caudillismo, populismo y ensoñación socialista. Madrid: Cultiva, 2008. 157 p.: bibl. (Col. Autor; 13)

Author is economist and adjunct professor at the Universidad Central de Venezuela. Suggests that Chávez is a traditional-style caudillo, with a divisive and Manichean discourse and openly authoritarian behaviors, and with the dream of imposing on Venezuelan society a destructive fantasy that the president calls "XXI century socialism."

1303 Sanoja Obediente, Mario and **Iraida Vargas Arenas.** La revolución bolivariana: historia, cultura y socialismo. Caracas: Monte Ávila, 2008. 300 p.: bibl. (Mileniolibre)

Author holds a doctoral degree in history and geography from the Universidad Complutense de Madrid, and is a retired professor of the Universidad Central de Venezuela. Suggests without sufficient elabora-

tion, that Chávez's "XXI century socialism" follows Engels' ideas, although adjusted to Venezuela's historical experience. Claims that under his leadership the country has experienced improvements in standards of living. Discusses the role of Chávez's communal councils (*consejos comunales*) as important components in the process of political socialization.

1304 Zúquete, José Pedro. The missionary politics of Hugo Chávez. (*Lat. Am. Polit. Soc.*, 50:1, Spring 2008, p. 91–121, bibl.)

Highlights religious features in Chávez's political discourse and rhetoric. Claims that interpretations of Chávez as a utilitarian or rationalistic leader are incomplete, and that understanding religious missionary dynamics on Chavista followers deserves empirical research.

BOLIVIA

JOSÉ ANTONIO LUCERO, Associate Professor of International Studies, University of Washington, Seattle

IN CONTEMPORARY LATIN AMERICA, one joke goes, dictatorship is banned, but democracy is not allowed. The region is full of countries, another joke explains, that are the countries of tomorrow, and always will be. Examining the tensions and differences that emerge in the works reviewed for the current *HLAS*, this paradoxical view of Latin American politics, stuck between democracy and dictatorship, poverty and progress, is alive and well in Bolivia. Although President Evo Morales won a landslide victory in his 2009 re-election, there continues to be significant debate about his government. For some, solid macroeconomic performance, popular support, and constitutional reform validate the "revolutionary" promises of Morales and his Movimiento al Socialismo (MAS) Party. For others, his policies signal at best modest reform and at worst dictatorial tendencies that have produced violent confrontations between state and society. The works reviewed here address the following themes: the transition from neoliberal rule, the political and economic performance of the MAS government, local and regional politics, international geopolitics, social movements and contention, and gender politics.

The 2005 election of Evo Morales serves for many as the end to a style of politics characterized by a "pact" among traditional parties and a commitment to free market reforms. Like the Hegelian owl of Minerva, several publications have emerged from the dusk of that neoliberal period that seek to explore the implosion of the status quo ante. Various works are noteworthy for providing primary and even multimedia sources—interviews with or testimonies of key actors in and analysts of the governments of Gonzalo Sánchez de Lozada and Carlos Mesa (items **1306**, **1319**, **1328**, and **1330**). Several influential analysts provide their accounts of the demise of the old political order, from different methodological and ideological perspectives (items **1312**, **1326**, **1327**, **1329**, **1344**, **1346**, and **1347**). While these works look at the old order as it was dying, other works seek to explain the rise of the new order, led by Morales and the MAS, with a similar mix of primary and secondary sources (items **1324**, **1325**, **1334**, and **1349**).

Significant scholarly debate abounds in evaluations of the Morales administration. Critical voices are many. Some are clearly associated with conservative critics of the government (item **1335**), yet many examinations of the internal tensions and shortcomings of the MAS are from leftist political or scholarly perspectives (item **1342**). Several critics of the Morales government's economic policies contribute to the scholarly debate: some caution that the government is departing from free-market policies (item **1338**), and others, perhaps more surprisingly, argue that the MAS is simply "reconstituting neoliberalism" (items **1323** and **1348**). Of course, many celebrate the revolutionary MAS goals of social justice and decolonization (items **1321** and **1340**), even while there is some doubt about how much continuity or change the new government represents (items **1322**, **1337**, **1341**, and **1347**).

One of the principal areas of research concerns local and regional politics. The legacy of Bolivian regionalism and decentralization continues to attract attention (items **1307**, **1308**, **1309**, and **1333**). Concern with the project of departmental and indigenous autonomy has also continued (items **1305**, **1307**, **1313**, **1314**, **1320**, and **1343**). Furthermore, scholars have dedicated case studies to specific local conflicts (of national and even international importance) in places like El Alto, Huanuni, Cochabamba, Santa Cruz, and Tarija (items **1310**, **1315**, **1316**, **1317**, **1331**, and **1336**). It is worthwhile to note, however, the importance of Bolivian politics not only on the subnational scale, but also globally.

Bolivia's place in international politics represents an emerging area of scholarship. Debates over (post)-neoliberalism mentioned above are inherently transnational, as crucial questions of Bolivia's development model hinge upon the terms of the country's integration with global markets, especially in strategic sectors like hydrocarbons (items **1338** and **1348**). The shadow of the US continues to fall on Bolivian politics, evidenced not only by the anti-US rhetoric of Evo Morales, who expelled the US ambassador in 2008, but also in critical analyses of US "democracy promotion" programs, which, some argue, promote empire more than democracy (item **1321**). Bolivia also occupies an important place in the geopolitics of knowledge as it has transitioned from a "poster child" of Washington-supported structural adjustment policies of the 1980s and 1990s to a part of the "Bolivarian" anti-imperial bloc along with Venezuela and Ecuador (item **1325**). The high-profile visit to Bolivia of post-Marxist intellectuals like Toni Negri and Michael Hardt (item **1321**), and the vibrant debate over the MAS's revolutionary credentials (items **1340** and **1348**), further illustrate the world-historical importance of Bolivia to global theory.

Much of Bolivia's importance to international scholarly audiences relates to the mobilization that overturned the neoliberal order. The capacity of Bolivian society to mobilize has received substantial attention in the local case studies noted above, as well as in national quantitative surveys (item **1311**). Urban social movements have received attention (items **1332** and **1336**), as have indigenous movements in the highland and lowland countryside (items **1320**, **1324**, and **1339**).

Finally, gender politics continue to receive important attention, though clearly more work is needed in this field. The Constituent Assembly of 2006–2007 represented an important space for indigenous women (item **1345**), as did mobilizations in places like El Alto as well as within the organizational process of constructing the MAS (items **1315, 1342,** and **1349**). These struggles and spaces illustrate the importance of the intersections of class, race, and gender in the remaking of contemporary Bolivia.

1305 Arnold, Denise Y. and **Víctor Villarroel.** Pueblos indígenas y originarios de Bolivia: hacia su soberanía y legitimidad electoral. La Paz: Corte Nacional Electoral, República de Bolivia, 2004. 149 p.: bibl., ill., col. maps. (Cuaderno de diálogo y deliberación; 4)

A short, impressive critique of existing electoral practices, this study pays particular attention to indigenous perspectives on elections. In addition to a solid survey of the current electoral system, through a participatory and collaborative research design, this volume offers suggestions for integrating indigenous forms of governance within the existing constitutional framework. Maps and tables also provide a helpful overview of indigenous electoral patterns.

1306 Ayo Saucedo, Diego. Democracia boliviana: un modelo para des armar: 32 entrevistas por Diego Ayo. La Paz: Oxfam: Friedrich Ebert Stiftung, ILDIS 2007. 567 p.

This collection of interviews offers a wide-ranging discussion of political parties, economic models, development, national resources, international relations, social justice, social movements, and social actors. The book provides a wonderful and varied sample of different ideological and political perspectives including (anti-MAS) opposition figures like Roberto Laserna and H.C.F. Mansilla in addition to well-known indigenous intellectuals like Silvia Rivera.

1307 Ayo Saucedo, Diego. Elementos para el debate autonómico: los consejos departamentales, el rostro oculto de la descentralización en Bolivia. La Paz: Editorial Gente Común, 2008. 141 p.: bibl., ill., tables. (Ensayo)

Examining departmental councils in Cochabamba, Oruro, and Santa Cruz, this work offers an important analysis of the "hidden face" of decentralization in Bolivia. Tracing the changing roles and functions of departmental councils since the 1990s, this political scientific essay provides a brief, careful overview of the role of councils in the wake of reforms that have created a new landscape for them between newly empowered local municipalities and departmental prefects. The author provides helpful critiques and recommendations for reforms.

1308 Barragán Romano, Rossana and **José Luis Roca.** Una historia de pactos y disputas: regiones y poder constituyente en Bolivia. Prólogo de James Dunkerley. La Paz: PNUD, 2005. 458 p.: bibl. (Cuaderno de futuro; 21)

Two leading historians offer complementary, if not necessarily well-integrated, essays on the political fact of regionalism in 19th- and 20th-century Bolivia. Roca's essay focuses largely on the long-standing rejection to federalism and has a feel of traditional political history (seen mostly from "above"). Barragán's essay is more conceptually ambitious and addresses the issues of microhistories of citizenship ("from below"). Historian Dunkerley offers a helpful prologue to these essays.

1309 Bazoberry Chali, Óscar. Participación, poder popular y desarrollo: Charagua y Moxos. La Paz: Centro de Investigación y Promoción del Campesinado: Univ. para la Investigación Estratégica en Bolivia, 2008. 192 p.: bibl., col. ill., col. map. (U-PIEB serie investigaciones; 2) (CIPCA cuadernos de investigación; 68)

This study offers a detailed examination of the process of "popular participation" in two Lowland municipalities, Charagua and Moxos. The study is valuable in noting the complexity of multi-ethnic indigenous community life and governance. Argues that national level changes shaped, but did not determine, the ways in which local actors and organizations deployed resources made available by decentralization. While more could have been done to clarify the comparison of these two cases, this volume is worth consulting as an inductive and historical study of two important local experiences.

1310 Bebbington, Denise Humphreys and **Anthony Bebbington.** Anatomy of a regional conflict: Tarija and resource grievances in Morales's Bolivia. (*Lat. Am. Perspect.*, 37:4, July 2010, p. 140–160)

Pushing against the view that antigovernment mobilization is the product of regional elite machinations, two political geographers offer an empirically and theoretically persuasive call to examine the historical and spatial patterns of resource extraction, especially as they interact with identities of place and region. This excellent article contributes to understanding the politics of resource extraction and protest in contemporary Bolivia.

Breuer, Anita. Policymaking by referendum in presidential systems: evidence from the Bolivian and Colombian cases. See item **1235**.

1311 Camacho Tuckermann, Bertha and **Cecilia Salazar de la Torre.** Civil Society Index Report: civil society in Bolivia: from mobilization to impact: country report. Translated by Alexandra Shand. Edited by Andrea Flores Ivanovic. La Paz: Centro de Investigación y Promoción del Campesinado: Catholic Relief Services Bolivia, 2005. 150 p.: bibl., ill., tables. (CIPCA cuadernos de investigación; 64)

This report is an important effort to quantify the strength of Bolivian civil society. Gathering and systematically presenting an impressive amount of data, this study provides statistical confirmation of the long-standing view that Bolivia has a strong civil society within a weak state. Examining civil society organizations throughout the country, along with media coverage of them, this study comes to the paradoxical conclusion that while Bolivian society has tremendous capacity to mobilize, it has had limited impact on public policy, due largely to the inability of weak institutions to respond to societal demands. Coming on the eve of the 2005 election of Evo Morales, this useful study provides a valuable benchmark.

Coloquio Internacional "Etnicidad y Política", Quito, 2007. Los Andes en movimiento: identidad y poder en el nuevo paisaje político. See item **1273**.

1312 Democracia en Bolivia: cinco análisis temáticos del segundo Estudio Nacional sobre Democracia y Valores Democráticos. Textos de Álvaro García Linera *et al.* La Paz: Corte Nacional Electoral, República de Bolivia, 2005. 228 p.: bibl., col. ill.

Based on data from national surveys, this volume offers various theoretical reflections on citizenship, liberalism, electoral behavior, social actors, and communication. Though it was produced before the election of Evo Morales in 2005, it remains a valuable reference for considering perennial challenges in Bolivia.

1313 Estado, identidades territoriales y autonomías en la región amazónica de Bolivia. Coordinación de Wilder Molina Argandoña. Investigación de Cynthia Vargas Melgar y Pablo Soruco Claure. La Paz: Programa de Investigación Estratégica en Bolivia, 2008. 175 p.: bibl., ill. (Investigación)

An interdisciplinary introduction to the Amazonian region of Bolivia, this work provides a geographic, cultural, and political overview of the departments of Pando and Beni. Using the concepts of territory, identity, and citizenship as analytic lenses, the authors provide a very accessible and useful survey of an often overlooked "peripheral" region and its political actors.

1314 Estados y autonomías en democracias contemporáneas: Bolivia, Ecuador, España, México. Coordinación de Natividad Gutiérrez. Colaboración de Araceli Burguete Cal y Mayor *et al.* México: UNAM, Instituto de Investigaciones Sociales: Plaza y Valdés, 2008. 367 p.: bibl.

This volume offers an excellent comparative analysis of autonomy in Spain, Mexico, Ecuador, and Bolivia. A theoretical chapter on the features of autonomy as a form of democratic governance usefully frames this collection, which includes the analysis of well-known social scientists, including Héctor Díaz-Polanco, Araceli Burgete, and 12 others.

1315 Flores Vásquez, Jesús; Iblin Herbas Cuevas; and Francisca Huanca Aliaga. Mujeres y movimientos sociales en El Alto: fronteras entre la participación política y la vida cotidiana. La Paz: PIEB, 2007. 91 p.: bibl. (Investigaciones regionales El Alto; 6)

A short, useful study of gender and social movements in El Alto, one of the more important sites of collective action in Bolivia. This study examines gender roles during times of organizational "normalcy" as well as during times of heightened conflicts. Theoretically informed and empirically engaged, it is a solid (if occasionally superficial) analysis of important themes.

1316 Foro de Análisis Político, *11th, La Paz, 2006.* Revolución democrática y cultural?: análisis y evaluación de la gestión gubernamental del MAS. Textos de Jimena Costa Benavides, Julio Aliaga Lairana y Marcelo Varnoux Garay. La Paz: Asociación Boliviana de Ciencia Política: Konrad Adenauer Stiftung, 2006. 87 p.

This volume reproduces presentations from a meeting of Bolivian political scientists in the wake of a deadly confrontation between mining organizations in Huanuni, one of the more serious challenges that the Morales government faced. The three papers included here and the summary of the debate reveal a distrust of populism generally and the governing style of Morales in particular. More essayistic than social scientific, the volume summarizes many themes of opposition which have been constant during the Morales administration.

1317 Foro de Análisis Político, *14th, Cochabamba, Bolivia, 2007.* Cochabamba 11 de enero 2007: la política como lógica de confrontación. Textos de Freddy Camacho, José Luis Gareca y Henry Pinto Dávalos. La Paz: Konrad Adenauer Stiftung: Asociación Boliviana de Ciencia Política, 2007. 105 p.: bibl., ill. (Foro de Análisis Político; 14)

Three separate essays provide commentary on the causes and consequences of the bloody clashes between government supporters and opposition forces in Cochabamba. Though the essays are sponsored by the Asociación Boliviana de Ciencia Política, they are unevenly social scientific.

They do provide interesting and contrasting accounts of who is responsible for the bloodshed on Jan. 11, 2007.

1318 Girardi, Enzo. El ejemplo aymara en Bolivia: saberes ancestrales y globalización. Buenos Aires: Capital Intelectual, 2009. 141 p.: bibl. (Claves para todos)

Relying mostly on secondary literature, this slim and breezy book makes an argument for the importance of Aymara traditions in organizing antiglobalization protests. This view is already a familiar one, and the analysis provided comes very much from the "outside" in that it lacks experience-near field research. This is a reasonable introductory text, but there are many more in-depth studies published in Spanish and English.

1319 Un gobierno de ciudadanos, 2003–2005. Coordinación de Carlos D. Mesa G. Textos de Carlos Alarcón Mondonio *et al.* La Paz: Fundación Comunidad: Plural Editores, 2008. 312 p.: bibl., ill.

This edited collection gathers a group of intellectuals and former government officials sympathetic or connected to the administration of former President Carlos Mesa, who also serves as the volume editor. While several chapters present serious and technical examination of public policy issues, including education and hydrocarbon policies, the volume reads as a somewhat self-congratulatory homage to Mesa. Despite or perhaps because of that perspective, this is a valuable collection of well-informed views on the transitional and turbulent presidency of Carlos Mesa.

1320 Gustafson, Bret Darin. When states act like movements: dismantling local power and seating sovereignty in postneoliberal Bolivia. (*Lat. Am. Perspect.*, 37:4, July 2010, p. 48–66, bibl., maps, photo)

The author offers a rich ethnographic and theoretical understanding of violence in the region of the Guarani in lowland Bolivia. Paying special attention to the ways in which indigenous activists frame violence against indigenous people and represent that violence in transnational networks, this article offers one view into changing state-society relations in Bolivia. Though subsequent episodes of government violence may challenge some of Gustafson's more optimistic conclusions, his article nevertheless provides a useful analytic framework for understanding the multiple forms of violence and demands for indigenous sovereignty in Bolivia.

1321 Imperio, multitud y sociedad abigarrada. Textos de Antonio Negri *et al.* La Paz: CLACSO: Muela del Diablo Editores: Comuna: Presidencia del H. Congreso Nacional, Vicepresidencia de la República, 2008. 145 p.: bibl., 1 CD-ROM.

This international and multimedia collection of voices conveys a conversation about the encounter between the thought of Michael Hardt and Antonio Negri and Rene Zavaleta. It brings together papers and videos of a series of presentations that brought Hardt, Negri, and other well-known international academic theorists in direct dialog with Bolivian theorists like Alvaro García Linera and Luis Tapia. Though the celebratory tone of the DVD and some papers is perhaps out of place in an increasingly conflictual Bolivia, this collection illustrates the importance of the Bolivian experience to global currents of post-Marxist and critical thought.

1322 Jeria, José de la Fuente. El difícil parto de otra democracia: la asamblea constituyente de Bolivia. (*LARR*, 45, special issue, 2010, p. 5–26)

A first-person account of Bolivia's contentious 2006–2007 Constituent Assembly (CA), this article provides a helpful and critical view of the workings of the CA. The article examines key actors (political parties, social movements, NGOs, and oppositional groups) and serious obstacles to the process (including a lack of consensus regarding goals, limited institutional capacity, and procedural rules that allowed minority veto of majority demands). The author argues that these challenges made it possible for external interests and parties, and not elected delegates, to determine the outcome of the CA.

John, S. Sándor. Bolivia's radical tradition: permanent revolution in the Andes. See *HLAS 66:1777.*

1323 Kaup, Brent Z. A neoliberal nationalization?: the constraints on natural gas-led development in Bolivia. (*Lat.*

Am. Perspect., 37:3, May 2010, p. 123–138, bibl.)

An excellent analysis of the high-profile nationalization of the hydrocarbon sector. The author argues that external and technological constraints have made this move less revolutionary than the official government rhetoric suggests. This article is an empirically and theoretically sophisticated account of the new (and not-so-new) directions of Bolivian political economy.

1324 Komadina Rimassa, Jorge and Céline Geffroy Komadina. El poder del movimiento político: estrategia, tramas organizativas e identidad del MAS en Cochabamba, 1999–2005. La Paz: CESU-UMSS: DICYT-UMSS: Fundación PIEB, 2007. 156 p.: bibl. (Investigaciones Cochabamba)

This book offers a persuasive and sociologically informed account of the rise of the Movimiento al Socialismo (MAS) as a hybrid political actor that emerges at the intersection of electoral politics and social movements. Though similar statements about MAS have been made elsewhere, this is a useful contribution for its empirical and theoretical clarity.

1325 Lanza, Gregorio. Bolivia y Venezuela: votos que revolucionan. La Paz: GCM Publicaciones, 2006. 146 p.: bibl., tables.

A useful if breezy comparison of the political trajectories of Bolivia and Venezuela, from neoliberalism to "revolutionary" presidencies. The author provides good summaries of the domestic and international factors than enabled these transitions, though is less detailed about the internal tensions of the political projects of Presidents Evo Morales and Hugo Chávez. More of a historical overview than a theoretically informed explanation of political changes.

1326 Laserna, Roberto. La democracia en el ch'enko. La Paz: Fundación Milenio, 2004. 151 p.: bibl., ill., tables.

In this work, one of the most important critics of the Morales government offers a sustained and well-informed analysis of the structural conditions that led to the crisis of the early 2000s and, implicitly, to the 2005 election of Evo Morales. Though written before the 2005 election, the study provides a useful diagnostic of political and economic tensions in contemporary Bolivia that, as the author notes in subsequent writings, have not disappeared.

1327 Lazarte, Jorge. Entre los espectros del pasado y las incertidumbres del futuro: política y democracia en Bolivia a principios del siglo XXI. La Paz: Friedrich Ebert Stiftung: ILDIS: Plural Editores, 2005. 676 p.: bibl., ill.

A leading political analyst offers a mix of theoretical essays on the end of the Sánchez de Lozada government and crisis. While these worries about governability were penned before Evo Morales became president, the study emphasizes enduring challenges that will continue to shape political life, including those related to political parties, globalization, problems of representation, and the tensions between *ethnos* and *demos* in Bolivia.

1328 Liderazgo político y oposición nacional en Bolivia: alternativas en el proceso de cambio. Edición de Diego Murillo Bernardis, Néstor Rodríguez Uriarte y Jorge Canedo Rosso. La Paz: Asociación Boliviana de Ciencia Política: Itinerario de la Coyuntura Política Boliviana, 2009. 150 p.: bibl. (Serie 15; 3)

This publication presents the proceedings of different public debates (in La Paz, Cochabamba, Santa Cruz, and Sucre) over the political leadership of President Morales and regional opposition movements. As it includes important voices like former Vice President Victor Hugo Cárdenas, as well as legislators from the MAS and academics, it provides a useful snapshot of different political positions in the political climate before the 2009 elections.

Lucero, José Antonio. Struggles of voice: the politics of indigenous representation in the Andes. See item **1281.**

1329 Mansilla, H.C.F. La crisis de la identidad nacional y la cultura política: aproximaciones a una teoría crítica de la modernización. La Paz: Producciones CIMA, 2006. 329 p.: bibl. (Col. Historias andinas y amazónicas; 7)

This book presents a collection of essays on national identity, intellectual production, and modernity (and its discontents) in the Third World, with special mention of Bolivia. Polemical and theoretically promiscuous (engaging figures as different as Freud, Tocqueville, and Juan Perón), and authored by a critic of the Morales administration, this is a suggestive text, if not always convincing.

1330 Mesa Gisbert, Carlos D. Presidencia sitiada: memorias de mi gobierno. La Paz: Fundación Comunidad: Plural Editores, 2008. 327 p.: ill. (some col.), index, 1 DVD.

This is a valuable document as a political memoir of Mesa's difficult and transitional presidency. Though the former president makes some irksome stylistic decisions (like using bold-faced names for every notable person mentioned in the book, and selecting melodramatic music and odd graphics for the accompanying DVD documentary—including the image of an eye that never leaves the screen), this is very useful set of materials for scholars.

1331 Mitre, Antonio. Nosotros que nos queremos tanto: estado, modernización y separatismo: una interpretación del proceso boliviano. Santa Cruz, Bolivia: Editorial El País, 2008. 93 p.: bibl., ill.

This essay, written by a historian, provides a helpful introduction to modernization and separatism in Bolivia, with special focus on mobilization in El Alto and Santa Cruz. Mitre finds support for the familiar view that social tensions are caused not by economic stagnation, but rather by accelerated, if uneven, economic development. While the author offers some helpful general insights, the study is not very empirically grounded.

1332 Movimientos sociales urbano-populares en Bolivia: una lucha contra la exclusión social, económica y política. Edición de Carla Espósito Guevara y Walter G. Arteaga. La Paz: Unitas, Programa Desarrollo del Poder Local, 2006. 158 p.: bibl., tables.

An ambitious but empirically thin survey of urban social movement organizations in seven cities in Bolivia, including Andean and Lowland cases. Though there are some helpful tables comparing protest activity, decision-making, and organizational strength, one wishes that more qualitative or quantitative data were included. Nevertheless, it offers many important observations of the ways in which neighborhood and local organizations have been protagonists of political change.

1333 Municipalización, diagnóstico de una década: 30 investigaciones sobre participación popular y descentralización. La Paz: Plural Editores: USAID: Friedrich Ebert Stiftung: ILDIS, 2004. 2 v.: bibl., ill. (some col.), tables.

This two-volume collection offers a set of cogent essays on the political, economic, environmental, and bureaucratic changes that were produced by the decentralization reforms. Written before the election of Evo Morales, these essays have a paradoxical quality of insightfully describing a political order in flux in ways that do not seem to anticipate the dramatic changes on the horizon.

1334 Muñoz-Pogossian, Betilde. Electoral rules and the transformation of Bolivian politics: the rise of Evo Morales. New York, N.Y.: Palgrave Macmillan, 2008. 240 p.: bibl., ill., index.

An effective institutionalist account of the rise and fall of hegemonic parties in Bolivia. Paying particular attention to the effects of electoral reforms, this book shows the unintended consequences of changes in electoral laws that created spaces for the construction of an antisystemic political party—Evo Morales' Movimiento al Socialismo (MAS)—and undermined the power of the once-hegemonic Movimiento Nacional Revolucionario. This contribution is a very efficient and theoretically informed account of recent political history up to the 2005 election of Morales.

1335 Oporto Castro, Henry. El cielo por asalto: cinco ensayos breves sobre política boliviana. Prólogo de Víctor Hugo Cárdenas. La Paz: Plural Editores, 2009. 161 p.: bibl., ill.

From the opening epigraphs (from Mario Vargas Llosa and Enrique Krauze), the neoliberal ideological leanings of the authors are clear. The prologue authored by former Vice President Cárdenas also emphasizes the critical tone of these essays, which characterize the government of Evo Morales as prone toward the concentration of political power and risky economic policies. While many criticisms are well supported,

the essays are more polemical than social scientific.

Pajuelo Teves, Ramón. Reinventando comunidades imaginadas: movimientos indígenas, nación y procesos sociopolíticos en los países centroandinos. See item **1284.**

1336 Para que no se olvide: 12–13 de febrero 2003. Textos de Carmen Beatriz Loza *et al.* La Paz: APDHU: ASOMFAMD: CBDHDD: DIAKONIA: FUNSOLON: RED-ADA, 2004. 203 p.: bibl., col. ill.

This collection offers a postmortem account of the violence of Feb. 2003. This volume looks at the role of media, youth, the state, and the police. The contributors include well-known intellectuals on the left who went on to form part of Evo Morales' administration, including Alvaro García Linera and Sacha Llorenti.

1337 Participación y representación política en el nuevo poder legislativo. Edición de Javier Palza Medina. La Paz: Ediciones fBDM, 2007. 107 p.: bibl. (Temas de reflexión y debate; 16)

This collection offers varied ideological perspectives on legislature and representation, from wonky to radical. Six essays explore familiar tensions in the literature on Bolivian representation including policy debates over efficiency and autonomy, and more philosophical debates over liberal and communitarian models of governance.

1338 El péndulo del gas: estudios comparativos de política de hidrocarburos. Edición de Fernando Candia y Napoleón Pacheco. Textos de Fernando Candia *et al.* La Paz: Fundación Milenio, 2009. 207 p.: bibl., ill.

This book offers several critical views of the political economy of the hydrocarbon sector in Bolivia, coherently presented by well-known analysts. As a whole, the work is informative and well documented, the views offered tend to converge on the skeptical end of views on nationalization and more generally reflect a critical view of the government of Evo Morales.

1339 Ponchos Rojos. Textos de Murichi Poma *et al.* La Paz: FODENPO: Plural Ediciones, 2008. 98 p.: bibl., col. ill.

This is a brief history of the "Ponchos

Rojos," an indigenous social and political organization from Omasuyos in the department of La Paz. A sympathetic portrait, meant to be a corrective to the "satanization" of Ponchos Rojos, this book offers useful historical contexts for both the origin of the Ponchos Rojos as well as their place in the large-scale social protests that set the stage for the rise of Evo Morales.

1340 Postero, Nancy Grey. Morales's MAS government: building indigenous popular hegemony in Bolivia. (*Lat. Am. Perspect.*, 37:3, May 2010, p. 18–34, bibl.)

Identifying important currents within the MAS government, focusing on indigenous rights, economic justice, and popular democracy, the author makes an argument for seeing these as "productive tensions" in the construction of popular hegemony in Bolivia. While significant challenges exist, the author suggests that the government is continuing its path to "long-term change refounding the nation and decolonizing society." Though such an optimistic conclusion is debatable, this article offers important elements for an evaluation of the agenda of the Morales administration.

1341 Postero, Nancy Grey. The struggle to create a radical democracy in Bolivia. (*LARR*, 45, special issue, 2010, p. 59–78, bibl.)

The author offers a complex and compelling account of the Evo Morales government (and a slight departure from the author's earlier views), as characterized by a profound tension between a push for social justice to overcome both colonialism and neoliberalism on the one hand, and the embrace of liberal political institutions (like elections and constitutional conventions) to do so, on the other hand. Rather than speaking of "post-neoliberal" Bolivia, the author suggests that it is more appropriate to see how liberalism is being "vernacularized" and becoming more relevant to Bolivia's indigenous peoples.

1342 Reinventando la nación en Bolivia: movimientos sociales, estado y poscolonialidad. Edición de Karin Monasterios, Pablo Stefanoni y Hervé do Alto. La Paz: CLACSO: Plural, 2007. 171 p.: bibl.

A short, excellent set of sympathetic and critical essays on the new challenges

of Bolivian politics since the election of Evo Morales. Includes a useful overview of Evismo (Stefanoni), the internal tensions of the MAS Party (Do Alto), and the challenges of decolonization (Tapia). Also adds a needed analysis of the limits and possibilities of feminist politics (Monasterios). Ends with a lively interview with Bolivian Vice President and intellectual Alvaro García Linera.

1343 Reynaga Vasquez, Walter. Bolivia al poder: recogiendo sus despojos haremos de Bolivia una verdadera nación. La Paz: Movimiento Tierra y Libertad-Tomás Katari, 2004. 189 p.: bibl.

This book offers the political platform of the Movimiento Tierra y Libertad-Tomás Katari, a political party whose ideological affinities are close to the indianismo of Fausto Reinaga and Felipe Quispe. Though it offers an analysis of economic, social, and political problems, these are best read as primary documents of MTL-TK perspectives.

1344 Rojas Ortuste, Gonzalo. Culturas política de las élites en Bolivia, 1982–2005. La Paz: Centro de Investigación y Promoción del Campesinado: Fundación Friedrich Ebert Stiftung, 2009. 270 p.: bibl.

An unorthodox and influential political scientist, the author provides a theoretically eclectic approach to the political culture of elites in Bolivia. Using historical case studies and an interpretive framework (with heavy emphasis on the hermeneutic approach of Gadamer), this volume offers a view of the colonial legacies and often antidemocratic traits of the traditional Bolivian elite class, one that was being displaced as this book was written.

1345 Rousseau, Stéphanie. Indigenous and feminist movements at the Constituent Assembly in Bolivia: locating the representation of indigenous women. (*LARR*, 46:2, 2011, p. 5–28, bibl.)

This article analyzes the different positions advanced by the indigenous movement and the feminist movement at the Constituent Assembly in Bolivia (Aug. 2006 to Dec. 2007). The success of both movements is explained through reference to the historical strength of the indigenous movement in national politics, the history of indigenous women's mobilization, and the collaboration between indigenous women and the feminist movement. The author offers a persuasive and empirically informed intersectional analysis of gender, race, and class.

1346 Toranzo Roca, Carlos F. Rostros de la democracia: una mirada mestiza. La Paz: Plural Editores: Friedrich-Ebert-Stiftung/ILDIS, 2006. 680 p.: bibl.

A series of essays (many previously published) that provides a political history of Bolivian democracy from the 1990s to the election of Evo Morales. An economist and political analyst, Toranzo is also a public intellectual; much of the analysis falls somewhere between informed journalistic analysis and social science. Perhaps the most noteworthy contribution is a sustained defense of the concepts of mestizaje and *cholificación*, concepts that according to the author offer the promise of democratic citizenship without the sins of political intolerance from either "white" or indigenous politicians.

1347 25 años construyendo democracia: visiones sobre el proceso democrá-tico en Bolivia, 1982–2007. La Paz: Vice-presidencia de la República, 2008. 226 p.: bibl., ill.

Commemorating the 25th anniversary of the return of democratic rule in Bolivia, this volume collects several papers prepared by leading Bolivian social scientists (including Luis Tapia, Xavier Albó, Roberto Laserna, George Gray Molina, and Gloria Ardaya) as well as transcripts of several regional roundtables from throughout the country. A final table attempts to pro-vide a summary of the various perspectives. With attention to themes of indigenous inclusion, political economy, and public opinion, this is a quick and useful panorama of the peaks and valleys of democratization of Bolivia since 1982.

1348 Webber, Jeffrey R. From rebellion to reform in Bolivia: class struggle, indigenous liberation, and the politics of Evo Morales. Chicago, Ill.: Haymarket Books, 2010. 281 p.: bibl., ill., index.

An important critique of Evo Morales from the left, this book suggests that Bolivia has moved to a reformist phase of "reconstituted neoliberalism." As the book is a direct challenge to the revolutionary claims of the MAS government, it has generated significant debate within and outside the country. Well-informed and well-documented, it is a valuable contribution.

1349 Zuazo Oblitas, Moira. Cómo nació el MAS?: la ruralización de la política en Bolivia: entrevistas a 85 parlamentarios del partido. La Paz: Friedrich Ebert Stiftung, 2008. 317 p.: bibl., ill., tables.

An extremely useful volume on the history of the Movimiento al Socialismo (MAS). The study offers persuasive interpretations of the institutional origins of the MAS, the role of elections in the rise of Evo Morales, and the role of protests in the MAS. Also provides a discussion of ethics and internal weaknesses in the party. Perhaps the most valuable parts of the work can be found in the included interviews with party members. Valuable as both a primary and a secondary source.

PERU

PHILIP MAUCERI, *Professor of Political Science and Dean of the College of Social and Behavioral Sciences, University of Northern Iowa*

SCHOLARSHIP ON PERUVIAN POLITICS has followed the same general themes as those in *HLAS 65*. The fragmentation of the party system, difficulties in establishing democratic norms and institutions in a society that continues to be characterized by high inequality, and the human rights legacies of the political violence and authoritarianism of the 1990s remain the focus of much of the scholarship published on Peru. A significant number of works also continues to examine innovative institutions and policies, especially at the regional and local levels.

Concerns about the stability of Peru's democracy, even as its economy has experienced an extended period of growth, were brought to the fore by the presidential runoff election of 2006, which pitted Alan García Pérez, whose previous term in office during 1985–90 was characterized by economic chaos, insecurity, and cronyism, against Ollanta Humala, a former army officer and radical nationalist who expressed admiration for Venezuela's Hugo Chávez. Both Cameron (item **1355**) and Tanaka (item **1373**) provide cogent reviews of the election's dynamics and outcomes, while *Por aquí compañeros, aprismo y neoliberalismo* (item **1368**) and Tovar (item **1374**) offer preliminary assessments of the García administration. Many wide-ranging contributions discuss the origins of democratic instability, particularly in the aftermath of the Fujimori regime. Three recent works offer historical and cultural interpretations of the difficulties in deepening democratization in Peru. Pease García suggests that while the inability to address the needs of the country's urban and rural poor have undermined confidence in democratic institutions, the country's political culture also doesn't place sufficient importance on democratic values such as deliberation and competition (item **1365**). In a similar vein, Huber examines low-level corruption in Ayacucho, focusing on the persistence of patrimonial cultures as an explanation (item **1360**). The edited volume by Pásara puts forth a range of recent experiences, including political violence, as contributing factors to the social and political instability experienced since the end of the Fujimori regime (item **1367**). Finally, a collection of writings spanning four decades by Peruvian Nobel laureate Mario Vargas Llosa offers his analysis on politics and democracy in Peru and beyond, with a strong critique of authoritarian tendencies among politicians (item **1375**). Fewer works on organized popular movements appeared relative to the recent past, perhaps a reflection of the changing organization and tactics of civil society groups. Dosh, for example, examines the complex motives of popular movements involved in illegal land invasions, teasing out the factors that contribute to sustained participation in organized movements even once land titles are acquired (item **1358**). In an examination of indigenous women's organizations, Oliart notes how women involved in these movements reinterpret discourses from external actors to meet the issues and problems they face in their daily lives (item **1363**).

The legacy of the Fujimori regime continues to garner the attention of scholars, especially as it relates to the rule of law and human rights. Burt explores the factors that led to the unprecedented trial of a former president for human rights violations, pointing to a confluence of changes in political and public opinion (item **1354**), while Root examines how Transnational Activist Networks (TANs) inserted themselves into key state and international agencies to advance a human rights agenda as the transition to democracy took place after the fall of Fujimori (item **1371**). In a similar vein, Pegram examines the extraordinary role the ombudsman's office played from within the state during the Fujimori regime as an arena for advancing the rule of law (item **1366**). A high point for the Fujimori regime was the storming of the Japanese Embassy by special commandos, in the aftermath of its takeover by members of the insurgent group Movimiento Revolucionario Tupac Amaru (MRTA). Jara offers a detailed narrative of the events, from the initial takeover of the embassy by the MRTA during an official banquet, to the killing of all insurgents in the building, raising serious questions regarding what appear to be extrajudicial killings (item **1361**). In the storming of the embassy, as in other major events of the period, presidential adviser Vladimiro Montesinos played an important role. Adding to what is already a sizable bibliography on Montesinos is a work by Rodríguez Alegre that explains his rise through the lens of weak political institutions, especially political parties, in Peru (item **1369**).

Finally, as both scholars and policymakers look to efforts at strengthening Peru's democracy, there has been a renewed examination of institutional capacity-building. For example, Dargent analyzes the current Constitutional Tribunal and problems encountered by its two predecessors (item **1357**), while Morón and Sanborn review the difficulties of concentrating policy-making almost exclusively in the presidency pose (item **1362**). Continuing a growing trend in the literature in this area of focusing on the development of local and regional institutions and policies, Rojas Rojas offers a case study of "participatory budgeting" geared to increase citizen involvement (item **1370**), while Ballón Echegaray presents a broad study of decentralization in seven of Peru's regions (item **1353**).

1350 Aguilar Cardoso, Luis Enrique.
Aproximaciones a la participación ciudadana en la región andina: el caso peruano. Lima: Comisión Andina de Juristas, 2006. 166 p.: bibl. (Serie Difusión de la Carta Democrática Interamericana; 7)

Outlines the requirements of the Inter-American Democratic Charter in the area of citizen participation and reviews Peru's adherence to these standards. Author offers an analysis of the major political, social, and institutional obstacles in achieving expectations for citizen participation.

1351 Aranda, Gilberto C.; Miguel Ángel López; and Sergio Salinas Cañas. Del regreso del Inca a Sendero Luminoso: violencia y política mesiánica en Perú. Santiago: RIL Editores, 2009. 251 p.: bibl.

Building on the ideas of Alberto Flores Galindo, the authors argue that there is a messianic tendency in Peruvian politics based on the idea of an "Andean utopia" in the collective consciousness of Andean peoples. This perception has contributed to a politics that favors charismatic leadership, which when combined with a utopian "overturning the world," has been a source of political violence. The authors' framework is applied in an examination of the guerrilla movements of the 1960s, 20th-century national-populist parties, and Sendero Luminoso.

1352 Ayacucho y la agenda wari. Edición de Rocío Romero y Carmen de los Ríos. Lima: Kantuta Editoras, 2009. 136 p.: bibl.

Authors analyze Ayacucho's current regional politics and policy-making. Regional protests in 2007 are viewed as emblematic of a more inclusive and participatory politics, as expressed in the region's "Plan Wari: Ayacucho al 2024." Social policy, education, the need for citizen participation, and the legacy of Shining Path violence are discussed.

1353 Ballón Echegaray, Eduardo. Balance del proceso peruano de descentralización desde los gobiernos regionales. Magdalena, Peru: Evangelischer Entwicklungsdienst: Grupo Propuesta Ciudadana: Escuela para el Desarrollo, Sistema de Facilitación EED-Perú, 2008. 66 p.: bibl., col. ill.

Useful overview of a broader study analyzing decentralization in seven of Peru's regions: Arequipa, Cajamarca, Cuzco, Ica, Junín, La Libertad, Piura, and San Martín. Among the issues covered are the local political context, the transfer of resources and functions from the central government, citizen participation, regional integration, and governmental transparency. Results of each regional study have been published separately.

1354 Burt, Jo-Marie. Guilty as charged: the trial of former President Alberto Fujimori for human rights violations. (*Int. J. Transit. Just.*, 3:3, Nov. 2009, p. 384–405)

An overview of the historic trial, conviction, and sentencing of former President Alberto Fujimori for human rights violations. Article examines the factors that led to the effort to hold Fujimori accountable, including changing global norms and the practice regarding the prosecution of leaders for violations, a strong and fair judicial process, and the role of public opinion.

1355 Cameron, Maxwell A. El giro a la izquierda frustrado en el Perú: el caso de Ollanta Humala. (*Convergencia/Toluca*, 16, núm. especial, 2009, p. 275–302)

An analysis of the rapid rise, and ultimate defeat, of the radical nationalist presidential candidate Ollanta Humala in the 2006 elections. Examines the advantages that Humala had as an "outsider" candidate in the Peruvian political context, but argues that a number of limitations ultimately led to his defeat in the second round of voting, including accusations of human rights abuses committed in the 1980s, the growing electoral weight of Lima, and the populist political machinery of APRA's winning candidate Alan García Pérez.

Castro Carpio, Augusto. El desafío de las diferencias: reflexiones sobre el estado moderno en el Perú. See *HLAS 66:3633.*

1356 La cuota de género en el Perú: supervisión de las elecciones regionales y municipales provinciales 2006. Lima: República del Perú, Defensoría del Pueblo, 2007. 271 p.: bibl. (Informe defensorial; 122)

A report by the Ombudsmen Office assessing the effectiveness of the law requiring that 30 percent of candidates for municipal and regional council positions must be women. Reviewing results from the 2006 elections, the report concludes that legal quotas were largely not met due to closed or blocked lists by political parties. This finding contrasts with elections to the National Congress, where the preferential voting system coupled with quotas have been largely successful. The report offers a series of recommendations, including reserving specific positions on ballot lists for women.

1357 Dargent-Chamot, Eduardo. Determinants of judicial independence: lessons from three "cases" of constitutional courts in Peru, 1982–2007. (*J. Lat. Am. Stud.*, 41:2, May 2009, p. 251–278)

A comparative analysis of the current Constitutional Tribunal and its two failed predecessor constitutional courts. In explaining previous failures, the author focuses on the existence of political pluralism as necessary to preserving the independence of the courts. However, he also notes the importance of institutional design, including the process of appointing judges and the requirements for declaring laws unconstitutional. While it is clear that inadequate safeguards in this area led the Fujimori-era court to fail, it is too early to judge whether the current court can maintain its independent role.

1358 Dosh, Paul. Tactical innovation, democratic governance, and mixed motives: popular movement resilience in Peru and Ecuador. (*Lat. Am. Polit. Soc.*, 51:1, Spring 2009, p. 87–118, bibl., ill., tables)

Examination of why some popular movements that organize illegal land invasions dissipate after acquiring land titles, while others sustain high participation. Focusing on two land invasion settlements in Peru (Oasis and Encantada in Lima) and one in Ecuador (Itchimbía), the author argues that the organizations avoided the "security trap" by being innovative and adaptive, introducing mixed motives that encompass both material and nonmaterial goals, and emphasizing democratic governance. For Ecuadorian political scientist's comment, see item **1276.**

1359 Fronteras interiores: identidad, diferencia y protagonismo de las mujeres. Edición de Maruja Barrig. Lima: IEP, Instituto de Estudios Peruanos, 2007. 380 p.: bibl. (Serie Lecturas contemporáneas; 8)

Wide-ranging collection of essays and studies focusing on women's and gender issues, with a particular concentration on Peru's Andean and Amazonian regions. A theme outlined in most essays is the formation of identities and empowerment by women in a fragmented and often violent environment. These issues are examined through the prism of a variety of topics, from gender and identity in the work of women poets to the use of sexual violence against women.

1360 Huber, Ludwig. Romper la mano: una interpretación cultural de la corrupción. Lima: IEP, Instituto de Estudios Peruanos: Proética, Consejo Nacional para la Ética Pública, 2008. 179 p.: bibl. (Serie Lecturas contemporáneas; 9)

The book offers a sociocultural interpretation of corruption in Peru. The primary focus is a case study of "small" corruption in Ayacucho, involving influence peddling, small bribes, sexual favors, nepotism, and other means used to gain advantage or favor mostly with public officials. After reviewing structural and historical explanations, Huber focuses on the persistence of neopatrimonialism, in which the patron is no longer an oligarch but a public official.

1361 Jara, Umberto. Secretos del túnel: Lima, Perú, 126 días de cautiverio en la residencia del embajador del Japón. San Isidro, Peru: Grupo Editorial Norma, 2007. 246 p.: ill. (Col. Biografías y documentos)

A well-written narration of events surrounding the capture of the Japanese Embassy in Dec. 1996 by members of the Movimiento Revolucionario Túpac Amaru (MRTA) during a banquet attended by hundreds of invited guests, including prominent social, political, and business leaders. The storming of the building by military commandos and the subsequent killing of prisoners by a secret military unit are given special attention.

1362 Morón, Eduardo and Cynthia Sanborn. Desafíos del "policymaking" en el Perú: actores, instituciones y reglas de juego. Lima: Univ. del Pacífico, Centro de Investigación, 2007. 112 p.: bibl., ill. (Documento del trabajo; 77)

A Spanish translation of an Inter-American Development Bank working paper, this short book argues that public policy-making in Peru has largely been a function of the executive, with other branches of government having a limited impact setting the policy agenda. Authors examine the causes of this imbalance including constitutional arrangements, electoral results, the weakness of political parties, and public expectations regarding executive leadership.

1363 Oliart, Patricia. Indigenous women's organizations and the political discourses of indigenous rights and gender equity in Peru. (*Lat. Am. Caribb. Ethn. Stud.*, 3:3, Nov. 2008, p. 291–308, bibl.)

Examination of how state agencies, religious groups, and NGOs have engaged with indigenous women in rural areas of the Andes and Amazon during the last three decades. Focusing on the various messages, both conventional and innovative, these groups have used in their efforts to organize indigenous women, Oliart emphasizes how the women themselves have reinterpreted these discourses in light of the everyday racism and gender inequities they face.

Pajuelo Teves, Ramón. Reinventando comunidades imaginadas: movimientos indígenas, nación y procesos sociopolíticos en los países centroandinos. See item **1284**.

1364 Palacín Quispe, Miguel. Respuesta comunitaria a la invasión minera y la crisis política: CONACAMI para el Perú y el mundo. Lima: Confederación Nacional de Comunidades del Perú Afectadas por la Minería, 2008. 272 p.: ill., map.

Useful description of the development and activities of a new indigenous organization focused on protecting the rights of indigenous peoples affected by mining operations. Provides a chronology of key conflicts involving indigenous peoples and the role that mining companies, state actors, political parties, and civil society organizations played in disputes.

1365 Pease García, Henry. Reforma política: para consolidar el régimen democrático. Lima: Fondo Editorial, Pontificia Univ. Católica del Perú, 2008. 149 p.: bibl.

A leading Peruvian social scientist and former congressman argues that public distrust of democratic institutions, including political parties, and a political culture that undervalues deliberation and competition weaken Peru's "wager on democracy." Author notes that significant political reforms are required, including altering presidential powers and finding ways for congressional representatives to better communicate and serve their constituents.

1366 Pegram, Thomas. Accountability in hostile times: the case of the Peruvian human rights ombudsman, 1996–2001. (*J. Lat. Am. Stud.*, 40:1, Feb. 2008, p. 51–82, graphs, tables)

Author argues that the position of ombudsman occupied a distinct "horizontal accountability" position in Peru during the Fujimori regime. Building on its strong foundation and professional staff, the ombudsman's office was able to build alliances and interact with numerous institutions and actors to enhance its credibility.

1367 Perú en el siglo XXI. Edición de Luis Pásara. Textos de Augusto Álvarez Rodrich *et al.* Lima: Fondo Editorial, Pontificia Univ. Católica del Perú, 2008. 439 p.: bibl., ill.

A thoughtful and wide-ranging assessment of Peru's current politics in light of historical and economic trends. A central theme of most of the chapters is the diagnosed paradox since the late 1990s of social and political instability in a period of rapid economic growth. Chapters address such issues as the impact of globalization, the continued weakness of political elites, and the ongoing impact of Peru's internal war during 1980–92.

1368 Por aquí compañeros, aprismo y neoliberalismo. Textos de Alberto Adrianzén *et al.* Compilación de Eduardo Toche. Lima: Desco, Centro de Estudios y Promoción del Desarrollo, 2008. 390 p.: bibl., ill. (some col.). (Perú hoy)

A series of essays offering an assessment of President Alan García's first two years as president in areas of democratic governance, economic and social policy, and defense and security. Overall, emphasis is on how the García administration's neoliberal economic policies, a tendency towards authoritarianism, and general inefficiency have helped undermine public confidence in the government, despite significant economic growth.

1369 Rodríguez Alegre, Iván. Vladimiro Montesinos y el poder político en el mandato del Alberto Fujimori. Lima: Editorial San Marcos, 2007. 221 p.: bibl.

The ability of presidential adviser Vladimiro Montesinos to gain power and influence in the Fujimori administration (1990–2000) is examined and explained. Author focuses the analysis on the weakness of Peru's political institutions combined with a historic bias toward the personalization of power in Peru. The insurgent violence that characterized the country during this period, it is argued, created a willingness

among both the broader population and political leaders to cede authority and trust to Montesinos.

1370 Rojas Rojas, Rolando. Poder local y participación ciudadana: la experiencia del presupuesto participativo en Villa El Salvador. (*Investig. Soc./San Marcos,* 17, dic. 2006, p. 121–158, bibl., photos)

A case study of the use of "participatory budgeting" at the local level, which lets an assembly of local leaders decide how to allocate 10 percent of the budget. Promoted as a method to involve citizens in the distribution of resources at a moment when the municipality was facing both a fragmentation of its social organizations and a leadership vacuum, the author concludes that despite the dangers of cooptation and clientelism, the model has largely been effective since its implementation in 1999 by fostering a greater role for local organizations in budgetary decision-making.

1371 Root, Rebecca K. Through the window of opportunity: the transitional justice network in Peru. (*Hum. Rights Q.,* 31:2, May 2009, p. 452–473, tables)

Examines the role that Transnational Activist Networks (TANs) played during the regime transition from the Fujimori administration to the Toledo presidency in 2000–2001. Author argues that the dramatic changes in human rights policies that took place during this period were the result of an intentional strategy carried out by the TAN to insert itself into key decision-making institutions of the state, assisted by international actors. The collapse of the Fujimori regime provided TAN an opportunity to augment its domestic influence from within the state to push for a more activist human rights agenda, including the establishment of the Truth Commission.

1372 Salvador Aroni Sulca, Renzo. "Aprendimos a convivir con los senderistas y militares": violencia política y respuesta campesina en Huamanquiquia, 1980–1993. (*Investig. Soc./San Marcos,* 17, dic. 2006, p. 261–284, bibl., maps, photos)

A useful case study of the impact of the armed conflict involving Sendero Luminoso and Peru's military on an Andean peasant community in south-central

Ayacucho. The author examines how community relationships were disrupted by the war; reviving old conflicts involving land and pasture rights and creating new intra-communal conflicts. Also argues that Sendero attempted to gain legitimacy by inserting itself into these conflicts, leading some peasants to align themselves with the military. Author emphasizes the high human cost that affected Huamanquiquia as residents were targeted by both Sendero and the military.

1373 **Tanaka, Martín and Sofía Vera.**
Perú: entre los sobresaltos electorales y la agenda pendiente de la exclusión. (*Rev. Cienc. Polít./Santiago*, 27, no. especial, 2007, p. 235–247, graphs, map, tables)
Cogent review of Peru's 2006 election results, including their impact on the country's politics. Author notes that despite changes in laws aimed at limiting the fragmentation of Peru's party system, the problem persisted in the 2006 election, with "independent" candidates at all levels doing very well. Voter support for newcomer Ollanta Humala in the presidential race suggests the persistence of deep regional cleavages.

1374 **Tovar Samanez, Teresa.** Prioridades reales: balance de los primeros meses del gobierno aprista. Magdalena del Mar, Peru: Foro Educativo, 2007. 85 p.: bibl.
Useful overview of President Alan García's education policy during late 2006 and early 2007. Examines how announced policies, including decentralizing education to provide municipal and regional governments with more authority, adding an additional hour to the school day, and eliminating illiteracy, were developed within the state bureaucracy and how they were received by social groups.

1375 **Vargas Llosa, Mario.** Sables y utopías: visiones de América Latina. Selección y prólogo de Carlos Granés. Lima: Aguilar, 2009. 460 p.: bibl., index.
A selection of previously published (mostly newspaper and magazine) articles dating from the mid-1970s onwards by Nobel Prize winning author and former presidential candidate on recent Latin American politics, emphasizing opposition to authoritarianism and critiques of nationalism, populism, and corruption. Starting with an open letter to Gen. Velasco protesting the closing of the newsweekly *Caretas*, Vargas Llosa demonstrates intolerance for violence and a passion for liberty.

CHILE

PETER M. SIAVELIS, *Professor of Political Science, Wake Forest University*

IN THE PAST SIX YEARS, numerous watershed events have occurred in Chile. In 2005, Chileans elected their first woman president—the first popular election of a Latin American woman president not related to a prominent male politician. In 2006, the death of Augusto Pinochet, who ruled Chile with an iron fist for 17 years, prompted many to proclaim the definitive end of Chile's lengthy democratic transition. The year 2010 saw the end of the center-left government that had ruled Chile for 20 years. That year Sebastián Piñera was elected president, bringing to power the first democratically elected government of the right in Chile since the election of Jorge Alessandri in 1958. Chile also celebrated its bicentennial in 2010, prompting Piñera to declare that he would oversee the consolidation of a modern and economically developed country. Because these watersheds have so deeply shaped recent research and writing on politics and government in Chile over the past few years, it is useful to organize the analysis of relevant scholarly publications along these lines.

Leading up to the 2005 presidential elections it appeared that Chile's center-left Concertación coalition was approaching exhaustion, having ruled the country for 16 years. Though at the time the coalition had won every election since the democratic transition, the Concertación was beginning to show the strains of an aging coalition. In 1999 the Concertación's socialist presidential candidate, Ricardo Lagos, came within 35,000 votes (less than one half of 1 percent) of losing the first round of the presidential election to the Unión Demócrata Independiente's (UDI) Joaquín Lavín, standard bearer of the Alianza, the coalition of parties on the right. Lavín's razor-thin loss to Lagos in the 2000 election was regarded by many as an electoral response to governing fatigue in the Concertación and the prelude to a victory in the next election.

However, the dramatic emergence of Michelle Bachelet thwarted this scenario. Her candidacy was a stroke of genius by the Concertación because her story was so compelling. The virtually unknown Bachelet began a career as a public health pediatrician, leading to her appointment by President Lagos to head the Ministerio de Salud in 2000. She went on to become the first Latin American woman minister of defense in 2002. Her family history was also very intriguing. Her father, Air Force Gen. Alberto Bachelet, died in prison after being tortured for his noncompliance with the Pinochet government. Similarly, she and her mother were imprisoned at the notorious Villa Grimaldi detention center, where they were tortured by military authorities. Despite this dramatic personal past, and expectations that she might seek vengeance, her moderate and measured performance as defense minister made her a living example of the reconciliation sought by many Chileans. Bolstering her appeal, Bachelet does not fit the mold of a traditional politician. She is a divorced single mother, an avowed agnostic, and she portrays herself as an everyday Chilean. Her uniqueness, combined with a telegenic personality, made her an ideal candidate to put a new face on an old coalition. Her personal characteristics allowed her to paint herself as the candidate of change, despite the fact that she represented a coalition that had been in power for 16 years.

Bachelet's victory over the right wing Alianza candidate came after a second round run-off election, given that no candidate had achieved an outright majority. Almost immediately upon taking office, her government was beset with crises. Transantiago, the transport plan she implemented (though it was designed by the outgoing Lagos government), was a dismal failure. Student protests over the low quality and inequity in Chile's educational system exploded unexpectedly, belying Bachelet's contention that she was in touch with ordinary people. Cabinet instability was the norm, and Bachelet's public opinion numbers plummeted. Nonetheless, her acumen in guiding Chile through the worldwide recession, with the help of Finance Minister Andrés Velasco and her wise use of rainy day funds that had been established from copper profits, allowed her to regain solid footing and leave office with an approval rating of over 70 percent.

This compelling presidency has been extensively analyzed in the scholarly literature. From the most personal perspective, Politzer provides an intimate political biography of Bachelet (item **1408**). The edited volume by Huneeus *et al.* examines the 2005–2006 elections specifically, focusing on electoral processes, the media, and the relative performance of each coalition (item **1386**). Maradones (item **1401**) and Funk (item **1390**) contribute "half-time reports" on the Bachelet government, with Maradones focusing more on the challenges she faced (that presaged many that continued to plague the Concertación) and Funk pinpointing the variables that allowed Bachelet to turn around her government. The edited volume by Borzutzky and Weeks (item **1380**) offers a comprehensive early overview of the Bachelet government in different policy areas, while Altman (item **1377**) analyzes the enduring economic challenges that the Concertación has faced—particularly inequality.

The next major milestone in Chilean politics was the death of long-time dictator Augusto Pinochet in 2006. Despite his death, the last few years have been remarkable for the notable decrease in literature dedicated to Pinochet and his legacy; although, a trickle of work on Pinochet and military politics in general continues to be published. Muñoz's personal political autobiography recounts life under Pinochet and provides a fascinating narrative of the assassination attempt on the dictator in 1986 (item **1405**). Policzer presents a long overdue, in-depth study of Chile's intelligence services during the dictatorship (item **1407**), while Fuentes recounts the variables that led the Chilean military to acquiesce to the actions of civilian authorities with relatively few destabilizing activities (item **1389**).

The end of the Concertación government that ruled Chile for over 20 years marked the next dramatic milestone. The coalition, whose success and longevity were unprecedented, presided over high levels of economic growth, impressive strides in eliminating poverty, and remarkable political stability, leading a democratic transition lauded as a model. The coalition grew from a disparate collection of center-left political parties who opposed the military government of Augusto Pinochet, defeating him in a plebiscite that he organized in 1988. The coalition devised a formula for governing based on consensus-building among its many parties and negotiation with potentially powerful veto players, including the military. Even before the coalition's 2010 defeat, a flurry of works emerged that analyze the performance of the Concertación and particular governments. In addition, some work has been dedicated to exploring the shortcomings of the Concertación and explaining how a coalition whose outgoing president left with an approval rating of over 70 percent could fall so dramatically to defeat.

Bascuñán *et al.* provide one of the most comprehensive overviews of both the rise and the performance of the Concertación (item **1402**). Angell focuses more on parties and elections (item **1378**) and the volume edited by Alcántara and Rodríguez analyzes the interaction of Chilean society and parties within the institutional structure inherited from the authoritarian regime (item **1384**). A volume edited by Funk looks at the performance of the Lagos administration and how moderate and measured it was despite stoked up fears of a return to socialism in Chile in the lead up to his election (item **1394**). More critical views of the Concertación include Alexander's analysis of how Chile's neoliberal model has limited the achievement of social justice (item **1398**) and Siavelis' account of how the model of politics employed during the democratic transition came to haunt the Concertación (item **1413**). He develops the idea that certain "enclaves of the transition" have been difficult to unseat and help to explain the defeat of the coalition.

The novel victory of the right has also been the subject of a few works, though much more remains to be done. Luna explores how the UDI was able to move from a minority party to become the party with the largest representation in Congress (item **1399**), and Moncada explores the intellectual roots of an important sector of Chile's right through an analysis of the thought of Jaime Guzmán. Political biographies of Sebastián Piñera are also many in number, the best executed of which is by Daza and Solar (item **1385**). Looking forward, there are sure to be numerous works on the Piñera government and the return of the right. Despite his government's dramatic rescue of the internationally famed miners, Piñera's longer term response to reconstruction following the devastating earthquake and tsunami of February 27, 2010, will be perhaps more important to defining the future for governments of the right. The earthquake has also reopened and widened a social fault line that has long existed in Chile and that Piñera cannot ignore. Despite high levels of growth in recent years, Chile remains one of the most unequal countries in the world. The earthquake dramatically thrust this inequality back into the limelight with graphic images of the poor and ill-housed who have suffered much more than wealthier Chileans.

The final milestone that has prompted work looking to Chile's future has been its bicentennial, celebrated in 2010. A two-volume set edited by the Universidad Católica de Chile was produced specifically to spur debate on public affairs as Chile celebrates the bicentennial, exploring reforms to enhance democracy and policy-making in a number of areas (items **1382** and **1383**). Horst's volume on decentralization, on the other hand, is a direct call to use the bicentennial as a rationale for considering a fundamental reorganization of the Chilean state in light of its excessively centralized nature (item **1410**).

Finally, a good deal of excellent literature has been produced in two areas not related to the milestones discussed here: the party system and policy-making. With respect to the evolution in the party system in general, Angell underscores the roots of its durability over many years in a pattern not often seen in Latin America (item **1379**). Fontaine *et al.* bring together a set of the most recognized experts to evaluate the current status of the party system (item **1412**). Luna and Mardones point to deterioration in support for political parties and decreases in participation, suggesting a crisis in the Chilean party system (item **1400**). Recent work has also focused on particular parties, with Luna's analysis of the electoral strategies and voter-party linkages of the UDI (item **1399**), Gamboa and Salcedo's study of factionalism within the Socialist Party and its political influences (item **1391**), and Farías' examination of the Partido Demócrata-Cristiano before the dictatorship (item **1387**).

With respect to policy-making, three recent groundbreaking works in disparate areas stand out. Haas' book analyzes the process of policy-making on women's issues, demonstrating how a women's executive agency can have the unintended consequence of working at cross purposes with reform (item **1395**). Silva explores the role of technocrats in an innovative study that moves beyond the common view that they are simply apolitical military allies in the mold of the "Chicago Boys" (see *HLAS 65:2336*). He shows instead that there is a longstanding tradition of technocrats involved in policy-making, many of whom have been drawn from the educated middle class, and that they actually have contributed to democracy in some important ways. Finally, Hilbink explores the role of judges in Chilean democracy, questioning why judges appointed during Chile's democratic regime had not taken a stand in favor of the rule of law more consistently against the illiberal policies of Pinochet (item **1396**). She finds a strong strain and tradition of apoliticism that explain this behavior. Interesting work related to the policy-making process in Congress has also appeared recently. Toro demonstrates the crucial role of the Partido Renovación Nacional (RN) in passing legislation (item **1415**). Ferraro challenges the notion that Chile's Congress has little influence on the policy process, showing the impressive informal influence it has, as well as the influence it has within the bureaucracy (see *HLAS 65:1734*). Finally, Alemán uses innovative analysis to show the continued existence of policy networks within the Chilean Congress over time, challenging the notion that their breakdown was instrumental in bringing down Chilean democracy in the 1970s (item **1376**).

1376 Alemán, Eduardo. Institutions, political conflict and the cohesion of policy networks in the Chilean Congress, 1961–2006. (*J. Lat. Am. Stud.*, 41:3, Aug. 2009, p. 467–491, graphs, tables)

Conventional wisdom is that the breakdown of Chilean democracy was caused in part by the erosion of networks of political accommodation that held together one of Latin America's strongest democracies. One of these elements was the structuring of party agreements in Congress through the use of particularistic bills. Theorists have posited that the ability to engage in particularistic horse-trading ameliorated wider ideological conflict, which extended outside of the Congress. The proposal of such bills was limited during the administration of Eduardo Frei (1964–70), leading some to argue that this mode of consensus-building had disappeared. Alemán challenges this argument through a comparison of policy networks arising from the joint sponsorship of legislation in Congress in the pre- and post-authoritarian period. Employing very innovative and interesting policy network analysis, he finds that dense policy networks continued in the past despite the outlawing of particularistic bills, and that such networks also exist in the post-authoritarian period despite similar limits on such legislation.

1377 Altman, David. Continuidades, cambios y desafíos democráticos en Chile, 2006–2009. (*Colomb. Int.*, 64, julio/dic. 2006, p. 12–33, bibl., graph, tables)

Altman is very prescient in his take on the challenges that President Michelle Bachelet and future governments in Chile are likely to face. After briefly outlining the structure of the election system and the results of the 2005 election, he goes on to provide a basic outline of the Chilean economy, pointing to four principle elements that underwrote its success: maintenance of fiscal responsibility, an open and well integrated economy, privatization of most areas of social policy, and few limits on capital investment. However, he does note some continuing challenges for the Chilean economy, the most important of which is nagging and even worsening inequality. Finally, in terms of identifying the challenges Bachelet would face (which now can be done

in hindsight, and many of the same challenges also existed for President Piñera, who took office in 2010), Altman notes maintaining party discipline in the Congress, reforming the binominal system, increasing democracy within parties, and addressing pending economic issues like inequality and the management of an economy where copper prices might not always be at the present-day high level.

1378 Angell, Alan. Democracy after Pinochet: politics, parties and elections in Chile. London: Institute for the Study of the Americas, 2007. 229 p.: bibl., index.

Angell is a long-time and respected analyst of Chilean politics. Though many of the essays in this volume have been published elsewhere before, this collection hangs very well together and presents a coherent analysis of the evolution of Chilean politics since the return of democracy. The first two chapters present his reflections on the coup and the nature of the opposition to the Pinochet dictatorship. The following four chapters present analyses of the first four presidential elections after the return of democracy, while the three subsequent chapters provide more room for Angell's excellent comparative analysis. One of the main unifying themes of the book is the evolution and transformation of the Chilean party system over time. The final chapter presents a balanced critique of government in Chile, pointing to some of the enduring challenges in enhancing the quality of democracy.

1379 Angell, Alan. The durability of the party system in Chile. (*in* Party politics in new democracies. Edited by Paul D. White and Stephen White. Oxford, England: Oxford Univ. Press, 2007, p. 275–303, bibl., tables)

Angell seeks to explain the remarkable durability of the party system in Chile in this chapter. He underscores how, with few exceptions, Chilean parties have been national, class, or sector-based and programmatic. Angell argues that a series of variables explains the durability of parties during the dictatorship. He points to strong roots, the stability of electoral blocs, a historically nonclientelistic right, and strong international support. The chapter goes on to analyze continuity within the party system as the democratic transition unfolded. As other authors have recounted, Angell points to the disturbing trend of decreasing citizen support for parties. While many causes exist for the trend, he argues that Chile's electoral system has had a negative effect on representation. He argues for efforts to make parties more inclusive and participatory.

1380 The Bachelet government: conflict and consensus in post-Pinochet Chile. Edited by Silvia Borzutzky and Gregory Bart Weeks. Gainesville: Univ. Press of Florida, 2010. 240 p.: bibl., index.

Michelle Bachelet's election as president of Chile represented a watershed in Chilean and South American politics, given her status as the first democratically elected woman head of state with no ties to a prominent male politician in South America. This edited volume evaluates the performance of Bachelet's government with an eye to several key political and economic areas. Bachelet campaigned on a promise to bring new policies and a new form of policy-making to the long-governing Concertación coalition. The chapters in the book explore her successes and failures in bringing forth a new way of doing politics in Chile. Most chapters underscore limited success, but also point to the constraints imposed by the ingrained politics of the democratic transition and the unwillingness or inability of the Concertación to fundamentally transform the economic model inherited from the Pinochet dictatorship.

1381 Boeninger, Edgardo. Políticas públicas en democracia: institucionalidad y experiencia chilena, 1990–2006. 2. ed. corr. Santiago: Uqbar Editores, 2008. 264 p.: bibl. (Col. Cieplan)

Recently deceased Boeninger (1925–2009) was one of the giants of the Chilean democratic transition, guiding political relations during the Patricio Aylwin administration from his seat as the head of the Ministerio Secretaría General de la Presidencia (i.e., Chief of Staff). From this privileged perspective, Boeninger provides an impressive and complete overview of the functioning of the Chilean political system between 1990–2006. After a brief histori-

cal overview, the book analyzes the 1980 Constitution and processes of constitutional reform, as well as the major institutions of Chilean government. Perhaps most useful is his analysis of the strategic objectives of the new democratic government in Chile. The second half of the book provides an analysis of over two dozen efforts at reform, some that were successful and others that failed. The book offers a fascinating window into the first democratic government in Chile from the point of view of an insider.

1382 Camino al bicentenario: doce propuestas para Chile: Concurso Políticas Públicas 2006. Santiago: Pontificia Univ. Católica de Chile, 2006. 387 p.: bibl., ill.

This edited volume, like item **1383**, brings together a collection of essays by university professors from across the country chosen by the Universidad Católica de Chile's Vicerrectoría de Comunicaciones y Asuntos Públicos. Both volumes comprise essays chosen in an open competition aimed at facilitating academic and public debate in the spirit of Chile's bicentennial. The essays have a clear public policy focus and should propose concrete ways to improve policy in the area dealt with in each chapter. This volume includes 12 essays under the general categories of housing, health, labor, education, defense, and public safety.

1383 Camino al bicentenario: propuestas para Chile: Concurso Políticas Públicas 2007. Edición de Ignacio Irarrázaval Llona et al. Textos de Nureya Abarca et al. Santiago: Pontificia Univ. Católica de Chile, 2007. 374 p.: bibl., ill., maps.

This edited volume, like item **1382**, is a collection of essays by Chilean university professors selected by the Universidad Católica de Chile's Vicerrectoría de Comunicaciones y Asuntos Públicos. The essays have a clear public policy focus and should propose concrete ways to improve policy in the area dealt with in the chapters. This volume includes 11 essays under the general categories of education, neighborhood courts, the environment, collective bargaining, quality of life for families, public participation, health, and regional government.

1384 Chile: política y modernización democrática. Edición de Manuel Alcántara Sáez y Leticia M. Ruiz-Rodríguez.

Barcelona: Ediciones Bellaterra, 2006. 357 p.: bibl. (Serie General universitaria; 58)

Bringing together some of the best known analysts of Chilean politics, the chapters in this volume evaluate the functioning and quality of democracy. The first section focuses on political actors, with chapters on the changing nature of Chilean society, the party system, and the logic of political learning during the democratic transition. The second section looks more closely at the concrete functioning of political institutions and processes, including analyses of the presidency, the military, human rights, and foreign relations. While many edited volumes evaluating the functioning and quality of Chilean democracy exist, the chapters of this volume distinguish themselves for the depth of the analysis and the quantity of useful and hard data brought to bear to make their arguments.

Cidadania e desenvolvimento local. See item **1509**.

1385 Daza Narbona, Loreto and **Bernardita del Solar Vera.** Piñera: historia de un ascenso. Santiago: Debate, 2010. 315 p.: bibl., index.

This is one of the first in what is sure to be a flurry of biographies of Chile's first popularly elected president from the right in over 50 years, Sebastián Piñera. This biography chronicles most of the president's life in a very personal way. It is based on a set of over 90 interviews with "friends, family and enemies." The book critically explores all facets of the president's life, from his family and family relationships, to his meteoric rise in the business world, to the series of scandals in which he was involved before assuming the presidency in March 2010.

1386 Las elecciones chilenas de 2005: partidos, coaliciones y votantes en transición. Edición de Carlos Huneeus, Fabiola Berríos y Ricardo Gamboa. Textos de Alan Angell *et al.* Santiago: Catalonia, 2007. 244 p.: bibl., ill.

The stated goal of this edited volume is to analyze the outcome of the historic 2005 election that brought Michelle Bachelet to the presidency. Chapters focus on the outcome of the election and the electoral process, the performance of parties and coalitions, and the role of the media.

The chapters examining the behavior and strategies of individual political parties are particularly interesting, with a chapter devoted to each significant party. The book also attempts to put the outcome of the 2005 election in a wider perspective, with two chapters focusing on the evolution of electoral competition and the composition of the Cámara de Diputados over the last five or six decades.

1387 Farías, Víctor. La muerte del camaleón: la Democracia Cristiana chilena y su descomposición: Jacques Maritain, Eduardo Frei Montalva y el populismo cristiano. Santiago: Editorial Maye, 2008. 260 p.: bibl., facsims.

Rather than focusing on the contemporary period, this likely-to-be-controversial history of the Chilean Partido Demócrata-Cristiano begins with its foundation and ends with the Unidad Popular government of the early 1970s. Though most Christian Democrats tie the origin of the party to the thinking of French Catholic philosopher Jacque Maritain, Farías argues convincingly that there is a much more important—and less recognized—connection between the origins of the PDC and the fascist Spanish Falange founded by José Antonio Primo de Rivera. The author posits that there was a strong tendency early on for the party to favor corporate forms of organization rather than ones based on popular democracy and market capitalism. Furthermore, he explains that after its foundation, the PDC consistently oscillated between crypto-fascism and crypto-Marxism depending on what was most expedient for the interests of the party at the time.

1388 Fuentes, Claudio. Resistencias a un cambio organizacional: el caso de la Cancillería de Chile. (*Rev. Cienc. Polít./ Santiago*, 28:2, 2008, p. 53–76)

While many governmental institutions have undergone substantial reform in Chile since the transition to democracy, the Chilean Ministerio de Relaciones Exteriores is an exception. This article argues that three variables explain this resistance to reform: 1) the many disincentives of actors to initiate reform; 2) the adaptive capacity of the ministry to develop a parallel bureaucracy; and 3) the lack of consensus within the diplomatic corps with respect to the necessary reforms.

1389 Fuentes, Claudio. La transición de los militares: relaciones civiles-militares en Chile, 1990–2006. Santiago: LOM Ediciones, 2006. 158 p.: bibl., ill. (Ciencias humanas. Gobierno y FF.AA.)

Fuentes questions why the Chilean military ultimately accepted the political transition as it played out in Chile with few destabilizing events. Most explanations for this behavior rely on a combination of one or more of three variables: the strategies of the Concertación, Augusto Pinochet's departure from the military, or the leadership of particularly influential generals. Fuentes suggests that other overlooked variables may be equally or more important. First, he argues that the parties of the right gradually distanced themselves from the old civil-military coalition that had governed Chile. Second, he underscores the role of judges as important actors who have had an impact on civil-military relations by making difficult judicial decisions.

1390 Funk, Robert L. Chile: segundo tiempo. (*Rev. Cienc. Polít./Santiago,* 29:2, 2009, p. 301–326)

This article provides a political "halftime report" on Michelle Bachelet's presidency. In essence, it responds to the reality that the Bachelet government had a very rough start and many people doubted that she could successfully implement a strategy to turn her government around. This article uses public opinion data and an analysis of government policy to argue that Bachelet was indeed able to redefine priorities and provide for a more successful second half of her term. This finding helps to explain her spectacular rebound in public opinion polls as her term in office came to a close.

1391 Gamboa, Ricardo and Rodrigo Salcedo. El faccionalismo en el partido socialista de Chile, 1990–2006: características y efectos políticos en sus procesos de toma de decisión. (*Rev. Cienc. Polít./ Santiago,* 29:3, 2009, p. 667–692)

This article analyzes factionalism within the Partido Socialista de Chile. First, it establishes the existence of factions as defined in the political science literature. Second, the article explores the relationship between the binominal electoral system and party factions, arguing that while the election system does not create factions, the logic of competition it produces does maintain them. Finally, it analyzes the role of factions in the PS decision-making process, arguing that there is a high correlation between the strength of factions and the number of legislative candidates they are able to nominate. Factional strength, they find, also plays into the relative weight of each faction within presidential cabinets.

1392 Garrido, Carolina. Subcampeones de la Concertación: la misión parlamentaria y el retorno a la labor gubernamental. (*Rev. Cienc. Polít./Santiago,* 29:1, 2009, p. 111–125, bibl., tables)

In a 2003 article, Carey and Siavelis argued that the binomial election system provided incentives for parties to reward those who assumed candidacies in risky electoral districts where the candidate was likely to lose (see *HLAS 63:2302*). They explained that these candidates, who they termed "good losers" or "subcampeones," were regularly rewarded with government positions for having assumed these risky electoral races. Here Garrido re-evaluates this supposition and argues that these candidates, for the most part, already worked for the government and simply returned to government service following their defeat.

1393 El genoma electoral chileno: dibujando el mapa genético de las preferencias políticas en Chile. Edición de Patricio Navia, Mauricio Morales Quiroga y Renato Briceño Espinoza. Santiago: Ediciones Univ. Diego Portales, 2009. 316 p.: bibl., ill. (Col. Ciencias sociales e historia)

The stated goal of this edited volume is to uncover the "genetic map" of Chile's electorate. Each of the chapters focuses on some form of voter participation and then seeks to explain it. Topics include the effect of the binominal election system, abstention, cross-ticket voting, blank and null voting, youth voting, and the ideological orientations of the Chilean electorate. Additional chapters focus more on other aspects of electoral politics, including career patterns and candidate selection. This book is essential reading for understanding the complexities of the relationships among the electoral system, voting behavior, and the party system in Chile.

1394 El gobierno de Ricardo Lagos: la nueva vía chilena hacia el socialismo. Edición de Robert L. Funk. Textos de Patricio Navia *et al.* Santiago: Ediciones Univ. Diego Portales, 2006. 168 p.: bibl., ill. (Col. Ciencias sociales e historia)

During Ricardo Lagos' campaign to become the first Socialist president to rule Chile since Salvador Allende, some on the right made dire predictions that his election would represent a return to those chaotic years. This edited volume presents a comprehensive analysis of his presidency, demonstrating that his government was actually quite moderate and measured in balancing reform with the status quo. The volume includes chapters on Lagos' popularity and its evolution, political reform, the military, social reform, economic policies, foreign policy, and international integration. The final chapter by Alan Angell sets out the challenges that Michelle Bachelet's presidency (2006–2010) inherited from Lagos. Many of these problems with the quality of representative democracy and socioeconomic inequality remain today, attesting to the incompleteness of the Concertación's reform efforts.

1395 Haas, Liesl. Feminist policymaking in Chile. University Park: Pennsylvania State Univ. Press, 2010. 225 p.: bibl., index.

This comprehensive study of feminist policy-making in Chile explores the variables that can facilitate the passage of legislation in support of women's rights. In this sense the study contributes to the literature on women and politics in Chile as well as to the literature on the legislative process in Chile more generally. The book also intersects several currents and important debates in political science. The manuscript provides a sophisticated treatment of political learning and presents the interesting puzzle that a woman's executive agency may work at cross purposes with the feminist goal of enhancing gender equality. It also provides potential comparative insights concerning when women's legislation is likely to succeed or be blocked. The book provides fascinating analysis of the general topics of

gender and legislative politics, as well as the three specific "issue" areas: domestic violence, abortion, and divorce.

1396 Hilbink, Lisa. Judges beyond politics in democracy and dictatorship: lessons from Chile. New York, N.Y.: Cambridge Univ. Press, 2007. 299 p.: bibl., index. (Cambridge studies in law and society)

Chile is notorious in Latin America for its clean government and respect for the rule of law. Nonetheless, Chilean judges who were appointed during the democratic government failed to take a stand in favor of the rule of law during the Pinochet dictatorship. This book, based on an impressive set of interviews, explores why this is the case. The point of departure for the work is that adjudication is not that different in democratic and nondemocratic regimes. However, more importantly, the long tradition of judicial apoliticism in Chile did not provide judges with the training or inclination to take more principled stands in support of democratic norms. Hilbink demonstrates this notion through an impressive longitudinal analysis that explores the social backgrounds, policy preferences, and legal philosophies of judges. She shows that the institution of apoliticisim, while not the sole explanation for judicial behavior, is more important than any other variables.

1397 Huneeus, Carlos. Hacer ciencia política en Chile y para Chile. (*Rev. Enfoques/Santiago,* 7:10, 2009, p. 391–424, bibl.)

This article, which was originally delivered as the keynote address of the first Congress of Students of Political Science in Chile, provides a wide-ranging overview of the state of politics and the study of politics in Chile. Huneeus argues that the study of political science must not simply rely on methods and literature of the US, but must also understand the particularities of the Chilean political system. He also stresses the need to study Chilean political development more carefully and to take into account more specifically the changes that have taken place in the political system since 1990. These changes include some of the problems created by the consensual political model, the dispersion of political power and the concentration of economic power, a deep crisis of representation, and the weakness of political parties.

1398 Lost in the long transition: struggles for social justice in neoliberal Chile. Edited by William L. Alexander. Lanham, Md.: Lexington Books, 2009. 208 p.: bibl., ill., index.

The richness of this edited volume dealing with those marginalized during the Chilean transition lies in its multidisciplinary focus, with authors from anthropology, history, political science, and geography. The central thesis of the book is that Chile's neoliberal model and the pact of compromise that accompanied it—with the return of democracy—had very uneven consequences, bringing extraordinary wealth to some populations and extreme poverty for others. Authors analyze labor, public health, the changing roles of unions, housing, homelessness, and the environmental impact of the economic system in a wide range of areas. The book is also unusual in its reliance on many regionally focused case studies, based on extensive fieldwork carried out by each of the authors. The book explicitly challenges Chile's status as a "model" economy in Latin America.

1399 Luna, Juan Pablo. Segmented party-voter linkages in Latin America: the case of the UDI. (*J. Lat. Am. Stud.*, 42:2, May 2010, p. 325–356, graphs)

While the parties of the center-left Concertación alliance have been well-studied, there is much less academic work on the parties of the right in Chile. In this article Luna analyzes the voter-party linkages employed by Chile's Unión Demócrata Independiente (UDI), Chile's most conservative party. Luna explores how the UDI transitioned from a relatively small party tied to the former military regime to a party with the largest contingent of representatives in Congress. In particular, he shows how the UDI employed private funds from its core constituency of upper class sectors and businesses to reach out and use "charismatic" mobilization approach to garner support in its noncore constituency (lower income voters). The party employed grassroots activists, usually upper class youths, to mobilize support in the democratic period, building upon the authoritarian clientelism it used

to cultivate support during the Pinochet dictatorship.

1400 Luna, Juan Pablo and **Rodrigo Mardones.** Chile: are the parties over? (*J. Democr.*, 21:3, July 2010, p. 107–121, graph, table)

Chile's political parties were well known in Latin America for their high levels of institutionalization and popular support. However, since the return of democracy—and despite the country's status as a "model democracy"—popular support for political parties has been decreasing steadily and voter participation rates have declined. This article traces transformations in Chile's party system, underscoring some of the reasons for the decline in support for political parties. The authors analyze internal divisions, the unfinished business of the transition, and a number of other variables that could be at the root of diminishing support. However, they conclude that the country needs better rooted parties that are more representative and provide more incentives for citizen involvement. Most importantly they underscore the need for a new social pact that will help to ameliorate the severe problems caused by Chile's socioeconomic inequality.

1401 Mardones Z., Rodrigo. Chile: todas íbamos a ser reinas. (*Rev. Cienc. Polít./Santiago*, 27, no. especial, 2007, p. 79–96, tables)

Though this piece is fundamentally a preliminary review of the early performance of President Michelle Bachelet, it goes much further in its analysis. In reviewing the early difficulties of the president, it presages the defeat of the Concertación in the elections of 2009–2010. In particular, it chronicles the difficulties that the Concertación had in arguing that it still represented the interests of Chileans after 20 years in power. Furthermore, it shows how cabinet instability, student protests, and corruption scandals undermined the continued viability of the coalition.

1402 Más acá de los sueños, más allá de lo posible: la Concertación en Chile. Edición de Carlos Bascuñán Edwards *et al.* Textos de Luis Barros *et al.* Santiago: LOM Ediciones: Corporación Justicia y Democracia: Fundación Clodomiro Almeyda, 2009.

2 v.: bibl., ill. (Ciencias humanas. Procesos políticos)

Chile's first post-authoritarian president, Patricio Aylwin, attempted to govern in his words "within the bounds of the possible" given the real constraints on his government posed by the right and the military. This two-volume set of works takes its name from Aylwin's revealing statement. The editors gather an impressive collection of academics and politicians who participated in some way in the Concertación to reflect on 20 years of democratic government in Chile. Vol. 1 focuses primarily on the foundation of the Concertación itself. It explores the alliance's history and origins, as well as the political and social pacts that were at its core. Vol. 2 takes a critical look at the actual policies of the Concertación. It includes five chapters that evaluate the ability of the Concertación to achieve its two broadest goals: democracy and growth with equity. These chapters include analyses of social change, authoritarian enclaves, reform of the state, human rights violations, and development strategy. An additional five chapters provide critical assessments in specific sectorial areas including education policy, education reform, infrastructure, foreign policy, and health. The conclusion provides statements by two illustrious members of the coalition, former President Patricio Aylwin and former Minister of Interior and Transport Germán Correa.

1403 Moncada Durruti, Belén. Jaime Guzmán: una democracia contra-rrevolucionaria: el político de 1964 a 1980. Santiago: Univ. Santo Tomás: RIL Editores, 2006. 275 p.: bibl., ill. (Serie Identikit)

Jaime Guzmán is often referred to as the "brains" behind the Pinochet dictatorship. Assassinated in 1991 by the leftist Frente Patriótico Manuel Rodríguez, Guzmán was the intellectual author of Chile's 1980 Constitution and controversial binominal legislative election system. He was also the founder of Chile's most conservative party, the Unión Demócrata Independiente (UDI). This book traces Guzmán's life, but also the influence he had in Chile in shaping the ideology of the political right and the direction of the Pinochet government. This is an excellent reference work

for those seeking to understand the institutional development of Chile as well as the evolution of the political right.

1404 Montecinos-Montecinos, Egon Elier. Limitaciones del diseño institucional para una gestión municipal participativa: el caso chileno. (*Econ. Soc. Territ.*, 6:23, enero/ abril 2007, p. 725–743, bibl.)

The return of democratic municipal government in 1992 was an important element of the full democratization of Chile. Nonetheless, citizen participation in municipal institutions has been lacking, which creates potential problems with respect to the oversight of municipal institutions. This article seeks to shed light on the reasons for the lack of participation and argues that the very institutional structures of municipal government fail to provide the incentives for voter participation in municipal management. In particular the author points to fiscal uncertainty when it comes to the funding of projects and proposals, a continuing hierarchy between the regional and municipal level where municipal authorities lack real fiscal independence, and the lack of political legitimacy of the *intendente* and regional counselors in the eyes of the public.

1405 Muñoz, Heraldo. The dictator's shadow: life under Augusto Pinochet. New York, N.Y.: Basic Books, 2008. 345 p., 16 p. of plates: bibl., ill., index.

Muñoz, a long-time political activist, government minister, and diplomat, was both a witness and protagonist in the events surrounding Chile's democratic death and resurrection. This political memoir provides readers with an intimate understanding of not just the important events in Chile's political evolution, but also the emotional significance and consequences of those events. It confirms some of what we know about the democratic breakdown and transition back to democracy by filling in crucial details from an insider's perspective. At the same time, it adds compelling new insights concerning the dictatorship and the return to democracy. Muñoz paints Pinochet as man of limited intellect who had less of a decisive plan for transforming Chile than is often depicted. Muñoz tells us how during the democratic transition the more moderate left ultimately prevailed, discussing the intricacies of opposition politics. He provides a window into the tensions and tradeoffs that the opposition faced in accepting Pinochet's plan for a return to democracy rather than elaborating its own.

1406 Navia, Patricio. El díscolo: conversaciones con Marco Enríquez-Ominami. Santiago: Debate, 2009. 231 p. (Debate. Actualidad)

Marco Enríquez-Ominami, a 36-year-old dissident candidate—or *díscolo* in Chilean political parlance—shook up the 2009 presidential race by adding a new dynamic of competition and new possibilities. Surprisingly, Enríquez-Ominami forced the election to a second round, having received 20 percent of the vote. This book presents a series of conversations between Patricio Navia, one of Chile's most influential political commentators, and the *díscolo* candidate, touching upon what is wrong and what is right with contemporary Chilean politics. Though released shortly before the elections, this is not a campaign book. The book is an exploration of the potential fault lines of Chilean democracy as the authors talk through the myriad problems facing contemporary Chilean democracy.

1407 Policzer, Pablo. The rise and fall of repression in Chile. Notre Dame, Ind.: Univ. of Notre Dame, 2009. 242 p.: appendixes, bibl., graphs, index. (From the Helen Kellogg Institute for International Studies)

Chile's notorious Dirección de Inteligencia Nacional (DINA) was known for its vicious repression and abuse of political prisoners. This book recounts the formation of the DINA and traces how it became the most powerful coercive institution in the country. Policzer also analyzes why the DINA was replaced by the Central Nacional de Informaciones (CNI) between 1977 and 1978. Though mainly a case study, this work also provides useful tools for application to other cases. In particular, Policzer draws on organizational theory to build a typology of coercive regimes based on the extent of their internal and external monitoring. He concludes with a very brief comparative discussion of organized coercion in Argentina, East Germany, and South Africa.

1408 Politzer, Patricia. Bachelet en tierra de hombres. 2. ed. Santiago: Random House Mondadori, 2010. 303 p. (Serie Debate)

Following Michelle Bachelet's historic term in office as the first female president of Chile, dozens of political biographies appeared. Nonetheless this one stands out both for its very high quality and for its completeness. Politzer takes the reader behind the scenes inside the institutions where Bachelet experienced her rise to power. She also recounts Bachelet's personal life and the challenges she faced in an extraordinarily patriarchal political system. The book explores the fresh and different leadership style that Bachelet brought to the ministries she headed as well as to the presidential palace and how she overcame the many political challenges she faced.

1409 Riesco, Manuel. Is Pinochet Dead? (*New Left Rev.*, 47, Sept./Oct. 2007, p. 5–20)

As the title implies, Riesco attempts to evaluate Chile's position with respect to the long political shadow cast by Augusto Pinochet. Many authors and works have asked how and for how long Pinochet's influence would be noticeable in Chile's political and economic models. Riesco, in his words, "cautiously" argues that Chile indeed may be in the final phases of feeling Pinochet's legacy. In particular, he points to growing activism among students and workers demanding fundamental change to the prevalent economic model. Riesco also recognizes that calls for changing the model are coming from parties within the Concertación that in the past were less vocal about the need for change, particularly the Partido Demócrata Cristiano. The author suggests that the transitional era may be over, and that Chile now has the chance to more fully democratize its political institutions and address the deep inequality that the Concertación has been unable to ameliorate.

1410 Rompiendo cadenas del centralismo en Chile. Prólogo de Ignacio Irarrázaval Llona. Edición de Bettina Horst von Thadden y Ignacio Irarrázaval Llona. Colaboracíon de Felipe del Río Goudie *et al.* Santiago: Libertad y Desarrollo: Pontificia

Univ. Católica de Chile, 2008. 201 p.: bibl., ill., maps.

Chile is known to be an extraordinarily centralized country despite efforts at decentralization beginning in 1992. This edited volume examines the current state of decentralization with special mention of the need to reconsider how the country is organized in light of the bicentennial. In addition to the introduction, the book has four chapters dedicated to municipal decentralization and four chapters dedicated to regional decentralization. As the editor notes in the introduction, there are commonalities and differences in the chapters. There is disagreement among them with respect to quality of decentralization today in Chile and how much power each level of government should have. Authors do agree, however, that subnational governments lack fiscal autonomy and have very different needs given the diversity of populations and geographies. They also agree on the importance of enhancing citizen participation (though they disagree on how to do so).

1411 Ruderer, Stephan. Das Erbe Pinochets: Vergangenheitspolitik und Demokratisierung in Chile, 1990–2006 [Pinochet's heritage: dealing with the past and democratization in Chile, 1990–2006]. Göttingen, Germany: Wallstein, 2010. 402 p.: bibl. (Diktaturen und ihre Überwindung im 20. und 21. Jahrhundert; 6)

This study examines the democratization process in Chile from 1990 until Pinochet's death in 2006. The author traces the evolution of social attitudes and legal actions from an early search for justice to prosecuting those responsible for human rights violations. Each chapter sets the historical context while also providing analysis and insight into the public debate in Chile. The concluding chapter presents the main governmental and nongovernmental (NGO) actors, mostly human rights groups, and draws comparisons to other democratized countries formerly under dictatorships and their attempts to face the past. [F. Obermeier]

1412 Seminario Internacional sobre Reforma de los Partidos Políticos en Chile, 2007. Reforma de los partidos políticos en Chile. Edición de Arturo Fontaine

Talavera *et al.* Santiago: PNUD, 2008. 448 p.: bibl., ill.

This edited volume, published by the UNDP together with a series of organizations that span the political spectrum in Chile, presents a comprehensive evaluation of the state of political parties in Chile. It brings together the foremost experts on political parties to explore their role in terms of governability, legal status, representative capacity, financing, and recruiting and selecting candidates.

1413 Siavelis, Peter. Enclaves de la transición y la democracia chilena. (*Rev. Cienc. Polít./Santiago*, 29:1, 2009, p. 3–21)

This article uses the well-known concept of "authoritarian enclaves" developed by Manuel Antonio Garretón. Just as Garretón argued that there were certain difficulties in dislodging political institutions and ways of doing things that complicated the democratic transition, this article argues there are also "enclaves of the transition" that prevented Concertación governments from developing and consolidating a high-quality representative democracy. The author argues that they include sharing political positions based on parties (or the *cuoteo*), elite control of candidate selection, domination by political party elites, elitist and extra-institutional policy-making, and an unwillingness to reform the economic model inherited from the Pinochet government. The author contends that this model of governing, while very useful in the context of a democratic transition, has outlived its usefulness and needs to be reformed if the Concertación is going to return to government.

1414 La sociedad de la opinión: reflexiones sobre encuestas y cambio político en democracia. Edición de Rodrigo Cordero. Santiago: Ediciones Univ. Diego Portales, 2009. 279 p.: bibl., ill. (Col. Ciencias sociales e historia)

In recent years the study of political opinion has been transformed in Chile, with many more institutions seeking to measure public opinion, using ever more sophisticated methods of analysis. This edited volume brings together sociologists and political scientists to analyze the connection between public opinion and the political system, primarily in Chile, but also in comparative perspective with other countries. The first section of the volume analyzes the public opinion business in Latin America and Chile. The second section focuses on the role of public opinion survey data in representation and elections. The final section explores the transformation of political opinion in Chile, with fascinating chapters on political orientations, political parties, perceptions of crime, and political opinion and the mass media.

1415 Toro Maureira, Sergio. Conducta legislativa ante las iniciativas del Ejecutivo: unidad de los bloques políticos en Chile. (*Rev. Cienc. Polít./Santiago*, 27:1, 2007, p. 23–41, bibl., graphs, tables)

While Chile's parties are usually characterized as highly disciplined, Concertación presidents have been able to legislate successfully. This article partly explains why that is. In particular, Toro provides an analysis of roll call votes that shows impressive unity on the part of the governing coalition during the presidency of Ricardo Lagos. The opposition, on the other hand, showed much more differentiation in terms of voting behavior, splitting at times to support government initiatives. Toro's analysis shows that the Partido Renovación

Nacional, in particular, was a pivotal party whose support oscillated between the government and the opposition.

1416 Vergara, Angela. Copper workers, international business, and domestic politics in Cold War Chile. University Park: Pennsylvania State Univ. Press, 2008. 222 p.: bibl., ill., index, maps.

This impressively researched book recounts the experience of copper workers in Chile. However, its contribution is much wider in scope. It shows how the demands of copper workers led to national labor reforms, but at the same time helped contribute to the radicalization of politics in the country. Vergara shows how the authoritarian government's economic model was actually a response to a much longer and wider process of economic development before the crisis of the Allende years. Indeed, she ties the ultimate emergence of the "Chicago Boys" agenda to a wider reaction to the crisis of the welfare state and import substitution industrialization of the 1950s and 1960s. This intensely personal story of workers relies on oral histories, newspapers, and archival sources to recount conditions on the ground, while at the same time placing workers within the context of larger forces like domestic Chilean politics and the country's international economic position.

ARGENTINA, PARAGUAY, AND URUGUAY

BRIAN TURNER, *Professor and Chair, Department of Political Science, Randolph-Macon College*

THE SUCCESS OF NÉSTOR AND CRISTINA KIRCHNER in re-establishing authority and in winning re-election in 2007 was the subject of much of the scholarship on Argentine politics in recent years. Volumes compiled by Cheretsky usefully analyze the 2005 and 2007 elections, in which the lack of traditional party competition itself seems to have become institutionalized (items **1465** and **1474**). Leiras also considers the provincialization of political parties (item **1452**), while two compilations theorize possible explanations for the nature of authority in the era of Kirchner from the perspective of the principal-agent problem and political psychology, respectively (items **1435** and **1440**).

A number of edited volumes focus on public administration and public policy. The shared theme of the problems of recovery of state capacity after Menem's neoliberal reforms and the crisis of 2001 is exemplified in several works (items **1430**, **1451**, and Hintze (item **1449**)). Hintze's critique of the neoliberal state's social policy focus on workforce insertion is reflected in the collection from the Ministerio de Desarrollo Social of the province of Buenos Aires (item **1439**), but here too is a marked concern for building state capacity to intervene positively. The concern for policy and participation is extended to the institutions of Mercosur in yet another edited volume (item **1470**). Several works collectively, and individual essays included in these volumes, focus on the role of civil society, most thoughtfully in *La incidencia política de la sociedad civil* (item **1450**).

Fruitful efforts to demonstrate and explain the politically discriminatory distribution of federal social programs in the 1990s are found in Nazareno, Stokes, and Brusco (item **1460**) and Giraudy (item **1444**). Institutional barriers to police reform, especially in the case of the province of Buenos Aires, are discussed in Eaton (item **1434**) and Sain (item **1467**).

Several articles address the status of women in the political process. Weathers looks at the relationship between feminist organizations and the state (item **1477**). The Law of Quotas of 1991, requiring female candidates on party electoral lists, provides data for useful analysis of the impact of various electoral arrangements on representation by Archenti and Tula at the provincial level (item **1422**) and by Alles at the federal level (item **1419**).

Several themes appear in comparative political analysis. Two studies published in Mexico productively reconsider the transitions from military regimes to democracy (items **1446** and **1466**). Two comparative studies of Argentine and Brazilian political culture (items **1453** and **1463**) are useful contributions to understanding national identity in the early 21st century and the implications of regional integration (unfortunately ignoring the smaller member countries of Mercosur). Groppo's political discourse analysis similarly finds important cultural differences in the oft-compared cases of the governments of Juan Perón and Getulio Vargas (item **1447**). Other works find that Argentina performs poorly when compared with other countries in the areas of decentralization—Colombia by Falleti (item **1441**) and Italy by Cabeza (item **1427**)—and tax structure—compared to Brazil by Melo (item **1456**). Sotomayor, however, finds that foreign peacekeeping operations have had a more positive impact on strengthening civilian supremacy over the military in Argentina than in Uruguay (item **1472**).

Two works explore contemporary Argentine political thought in depth (items **1464** and **1471**), and concern for the nature of populism in the 21st century can be found throughout the body of scholarship on Argentina (items **1454**, **1455**, and **1488**).

Political culture considerations also appear in studies of subnational politics in Trocello's analysis of San Luis province (item **1473**) and Zimerman's examination of Corrientes province (item **1478**).

The influence of political theorist Ernesto Laclau is notable in a variety of works, especially in those conducting discourse analyses. Examples include analyses of the difficult signifiers of "nunca más" (item **1458**) and "que se vayan todos" (item **1425**) to the complex discourse of Néstor Kirchner (items **1459** and **1468**).

Given the time that has passed since the 2001 crisis, recent scholarship has turned toward theorizing about its meaning and consequences. Auyero's innovative political ethnography of the 2001 lootings is an important contribution to understanding these events (item **1424**). Biglieri productively applies concepts from psychoanalysis to study the impact of the *asambleas barriales* on the political system (item **1425**); Herrera uses the idea of "protest cycles" to categorize the explosion and innovation of popular contestation during the period (item **1448**); and Carassai provides a critical analysis of other theorists' interpretations of these events (item **1431**).

For Paraguay, the landmark election of Fernando Lugo to the presidency in 2008, and the end of 61 years of continuous control of the executive by the Partido Colorado, were a focus of many publications (item **1483**; also see *HLAS 65:1806*), but analysis of the impact of alternation in political power will have to await further developments. Abente Brun (item **1479**) and Vidal Soler (item **1485**) anticipate the question with their articles published in 2007.

In the case of Uruguay, the notable election of the Frente Amplio (FA) government in 2004 provides political scientists with the opportunity to begin to assess the significance of the change in power. Several works continue to examine the rise of the left, but others begin to look at the policies and politics of the current government. The attempt to explain the causes of the FA victory continues to generate scholarly debate. Garcé and Yaffé further develop their interpretation of the evolution of the FA's internal politics (item **1493**); Luna ties that evolution to the incorporation of distinct constituencies over time (item **1494**); and Queirolo looks specifically at the determinates of voters' choices in 2004 (item **1498**). The FA's policies in its first years in office are assessed by Chasquetti (item **1492**), Armas (item **1489**), and Panizza (item **1496**). These analyses look to the FA's commitment to institutional procedures, its internal politics, and its need to reward various constituencies for an understanding of the government's policy choices.

ARGENTINA

1417 Acuña, Marcelo Luis. El corralito populista: de Perón a los Kirchner. Buenos Aires: Emecé, 2008. 239 p.: bibl.

Critical review of the history of Peronism as the dominant political force that has undermined institutionalization and opposition governments alike. The author argues that Peronism is inherently anti-democratic due to its origins in corporatist unions, its alliance with national capital, and its perception of itself as a "movement" instead of a political party.

1418 Allan, Laurence. Néstor Kirchner, Santa Cruz, and the Hielos Continentales controversy 1991–1999. (*J. Lat. Am. Stud.*, 39:4, Nov. 2007, p. 747–770, maps)

The political controversy over the boundary agreement between Chile and Argentina in the Southern Ice Fields reveals contesting perceptions of territory. President Menem promoted a "geo-economic" foreign policy of economic integration, which would be advanced by the resolution of peripheral territorial issues. However,

a tradition of geopolitical territorial nationalism was mobilized by opponents of the boundary agreement, especially in the affected province of Santa Cruz, then governed by Néstor Kirchner. The article argues that Kirchner used the controversy to oppose Menem and to enhance his political position nationally, and that his opposition to the boundary agreement foreshadowed the re-establishment of geopolitical foreign policy during his presidency.

1419 Alles, Santiago M. ¿Hacia la consolidación política?: cambios en la "estructura de oportunidades electorales" de las mujeres en Argentina. (*Am. Lat. Hoy/Salamanca*, 47, dic. 2007, p. 123–154, bibl., tables)

Through dynamic statistical analysis of national elections to the Chamber of Deputies before and after the adoption of the Law of Quotas (in 1991), the author shows the decline over time of district magnitude as an explanatory factor limiting the election of women. Also shows that more women are earning seats in the lower house. Higher levels of party fragmentation in the electoral district (the province), however, reduce the number of female candidates elected. The author argues these findings suggest women are gaining greater control of political resources and increasing their electoral competitiveness.

1420 Alvarez, Juan José. Crisis de gobernabilidad y control en Argentina: propuestas para una reforma institucional. Buenos Aires; Madrid: Ciudad Argentina, 2007. 342 p.: bibl., ill.

An interesting analysis of the problems of governing by the former minister of Justice, Security, and Human Rights under the Duhalde administration. The author argues that the institutional design of the regime produces neither governability—the capacity to effectively act—nor control—the establishment of clear limits on the power of government. The final third of the book is devoted to proposals for sweeping institutional reforms, reflecting the author's sense of the scope and nature of the problem in the institutional design.

1421 América Latina: sociedad y estado: conceptos teóricos y transformaciones históricas. Coordinación de Torcuato S. Di Tella y María Cristina Lucchini. Buenos Aires: Editorial Biblos: Fundación Simón Rodríguez, 2008. 144 p.: bibl., ill. (Estudios)

This collection of essays applies concepts of state development to the case of Argentina across its existence as an independent republic. The final essay by Juan Carlos Torre discusses the crisis of representation that has characterized the party system since 1983.

Anderson, Leslie E. Social capital in developing democracies: Nicaragua and Argentina compared. See item **1167**.

1422 Archenti, Nélida and **María Inés Tula.** Cuotas de género y tipo de lista en América Latina. (*Opin. Públ.*, 13:1, junho 2007, p. 185–218, tables)

Detailed analysis of the effects of district magnitude and preferential voting systems on the election of women to legislative bodies. Using the great variety of electoral systems at the subnational level in Argentina, the authors show that low district magnitudes and the use of preferential voting reduces women's participation in legislatures to a level below the legal quotas established for female candidacies.

1423 Auyero, Javier. The political makings of the 2001 lootings in Argentina. (*J. Lat. Am. Stud.*, 38:2, May 2006, p. 241–266)

For a book length treatment of this topic, see item **1424**.

1424 Auyero, Javier. Routine politics and violence in Argentina: the gray zone of state power. Stony Brook: State Univ. of New York, 2007. 190 p.: bibl., index. (Cambridge studies in contentious politics)

Fine study of the Dec. 2001 food riots, convincingly showing that an important measure of the riots depended on political brokers identifying targets and collaborating with state authorities to lower the risks to looters. The author's use of ethnography, interviews, and systematic review of press accounts contributes to research methods for understanding seemingly chaotic events.

1425 Biglieri, Paula. Las asambleas barriales como síntoma de la democracia representativa argentina. (*Polít. Gest.*, 9, 2006, p. 65–108, bibl.)

The appearance of "neighborhood assemblies" in the wake of the crisis of Dec. 2001 is interpreted as a "symptom" (drawing metaphorically from psychoanalysis) of the problems of democratic representation in Argentina. These assemblies based on direct democracy could not resolve the problem of representation, but by asserting democracy as their goal they affirmed the symbolic value of that regime type at a moment of profound crisis.

1426 Bonvecchi, Alejandro and **Agustina Giraudy.** Argentina: crecimiento económico y concentración del poder institucional. (*Rev. Cienc. Polít./Santiago*, 27, no. especial, 2007, p. 29–42, graph, tables)

Review of the political scene in 2006, noting especially the defeat of Kirchner allies in several provinces (especially Misiones) and the president's construction of new alliances, including with factions of the Unión Cívica Radical (UCR) political party, in anticipation of the 2007 presidential elections.

1427 Cabeza, Marta Graciela. Las capacidades internacionales de los entes subnacionales en Argentina y en

Italia: un análisis comparado. (*Am. Lat. Hoy/Salamanca*, 44, dic. 2006, p. 135–151, bibl.)

Compares the legal framework under which Italian regions and Argentine provinces may reach international agreements in areas of their competence.

1428 Canelo, Paula. Los fantasmas de la "convergencia cívico-militar": las fuerzas armadas frente a la salida política durante la última dictadura militar, Argentina, 1976–1981. (*Cuad. CISH*, 17/18, primer semestre 2005, p. 67–98, bibl.)

The author analyzes the origins and contents of various political projects from within the Proceso regime to identify the internal political structure of the military regime. She argues that internal fragmentation is one cause of the regime's inability to achieve, at a minimum, consensus regarding the forms, objectives, and time frame for a controlled transfer of power to a civilian government.

1429 Canelo, Paula. El proceso en su laberinto: la interna militar de Videla a Bignone. Buenos Aires: Prometeo Libros, 2008. 245 p.: bibl.

Argues that the "defeat of subversives," seen by the military as its one "professional achievement," has served as a source of institutional identity within the armed forces into the period of democratization.

1430 Capacidades estatales, instituciones y política social. Edición de Guillermo V. Alonso. Buenos Aires: Prometeo Libros, 2007. 266 p.: bibl., ill.

This volume assesses the state and institutional capacity to implement effective social policy in the wake of neoliberal reforms of the 1990s. Essays discussing the theory of state capacity by Alonso, Fabián Repetto, and Ana Laura Rodríguez Gustá are followed by empirical analyses organized by sector (decentralization, health, and higher education).

1431 Carassai, Sebastián. The noisy majority: an analysis of the Argentine crisis of December 2001 from the theoretical approach of Hardt & Negri, Laclau and Žižek. (*J. Lat. Am. Cult. Stud.*, 16:1, March 2007, p. 45–62)

The author reviews the treatment of the 2001 economic crisis through the lenses of political theorists and finds them only partially helpful. This result is a cautionary tale of applying abstract theory to complex specific events. Carassai interprets "que se vayan todos" not as a demand to end politics, but rather as a demand for a return to political economy and an end to widespread suffering under the state's mismanagement of "natural" economic crises.

1432 Curia, Walter. El último peronista: la cara oculta de Kirchner. Buenos Aires: Editorial Sudamericana, 2006. 309 p.: bibl., ill., index, plates.

Biography of Néstor Kirchner by the national news editor of *Clarín*. Focuses on Kirchner's personality and leadership style.

1433 Duhalde, Eduardo Alberto. Memorias del incendio: los primeros 120 días de mi presidencia. 3. ed. Buenos Aires: Sudamericana, 2007. 381 p.: bibl., ill., index. (Nuevo Rumbo; 1)

Duhalde reviews the first four months of his 17-month presidency (2002–2003), intended as the first volume of a *memoria* of the presidency. Duhalde reminds the reader of the difficult context in which he assumed the presidency, and argues that his government's policies brought the economy out of crisis. The author makes comparisons with the policies of Franklin Roosevelt.

1434 Eaton, Kent. Paradoxes of police reform: federalism, parties, and civil society in Argentina's public security crisis. (*LARR*, 43:3, 2008, p. 5–32)

In spite of "copious evidence of police involvement in crime," the author argues that police reform has been blocked by competitive pressures for control of the police force among different levels of government in the federal system, political party protection (mainly from the Peronists) for police-based criminal networks that generate campaign resources, and law-and-order movements that demand more punitive police persecution of criminals instead of stronger democratic control over police abuses. The study focuses primarily on the province of Buenos Aires.

1435 En el nombre del pueblo: la emergencia del populismo kirchnerista. Compilación de Paula Biglieri y Gloria Perelló. San Martín, Argentina: UNSAM, 2007. 166 p.: bibl. (Ciencias sociales (Univ. Nacional de General San Martín))

The essays in this volume attempt to apply political theories of hegemony, populism, and authority—especially the work of Ernesto Laclau (who provided a prologue)—to the case of the restoration of political authority under Néstor Kirchner. Several of the essays draw primarily from political psychology.

1436 Encuentro "Política y Violencia: las Construcciones de la Memoria: Génesis y Circulación de las Ideas Políticas en los Años Sesenta y Setenta", *Córdoba, Argentina, 2005.* Política, violencia, memoria: génesis y circulación de las ideas políticas en los años sesenta y setenta. Compilación de Héctor Schmucler. Textos de Raúl Burgos *et al.* La Plata, Argentina: Ediciones Al Margen, 2007. 138 p.: bibl. (Antropología y sociología)

Collection of papers presented in 2005 at a seminar organized by the Programa de Estudios sobre la Memoria of the Universidad Nacional de Córdoba. Elizabeth Jelin's essay "La conflictiva y nunca acabada mirada sobre el pasado" considers the political questions of the construction of memory after a national trauma like that of the Proceso.

1437 Encuentro Políticas Públicas en la Argentina actual, de la conceptualización a la experiencia, *Buenos Aires,* **2006.** Políticas públicas en la Argentina actual: análisis y experiencias. Compilación de María Isabel Bertolotto y María Elena Lastra. Buenos Aires: Ediciones Cooperativas, 2007. 178 p.: bibl.

Selected papers for a 2006 seminar organized by the Carrera de Trabajo Social of the Universidad de Buenos Aires. The essays are organized into three thematic groups: public policy and social movements, public policy and income distribution, and the role of social sciences in public policy. Abstracts of all 33 papers presented at the seminar are included.

1438 Estado, democracia y seguridad ciudadana: apuntes para el debate. Textos de Alejandro E. Álvarez *et al.* Buenos Aires: PNUD Argentina, 2008. 304 p.: bibl., ill.

Ten thoughtful essays review the issues of policing and police reform, subjective attitudes about insecurity and criminality, human rights, human rights education and public security, and firearms and public security.

1439 Estrategias de inclusión sociolaboral en el conurbano de la provincia de Buenos Aires. Edición y compilación de Roxana Mazzola y Diego Gojzman. Buenos Aires: Eudeba; La Plata, Argentina: Ministerio de Desarrollo Social, Provincia de Buenos Aires, 2009. 194 p.: bibl., ill., maps.

Scholars, civil society leaders, and public administrators comment on the programs for labor insertion targeted at vulnerable populations in the Conurbano Bonaerense (Buenos Aires metropolitan area). Challenges to success noted include the changing social identities of youth in the region, the need for effective state intervention to overcome discrimination against those with relatively limited cultural resources, coordination problems between programs and actors, and the political and administrative capacity of the state. The collection was brought together by the Ministerio de Desarrollo Social of Buenos Aires province.

1440 Evaluando el desempeño democrático de las instituciones políticas argentinas. Compilación de Juan Manuel Abal Medina. Prólogo de Guillermo A. O'Donnell. Textos de Juan Manuel Abal Medina *et al.* Buenos Aires: Prometeo Libros, 2007. 254 p.: bibl., ill., map. (Col. Democracia, partidos y elecciones)

Essays assess the principal-agent problem of accountability in a representative democracy. The introductory essay by Abal Medina, Martín Alessandro, and Gabriela Cheli theorizes that representatives (agents) might accept greater control by the citizenry (principals) if the perception of greater accountability strengthens leaders' effective power. The other essays are divided into considerations of electoral control and citizen control, such as through popular participation, public hearings, and social movement mobilizations.

1441 Falleti, Tulia G. Una teoría secuencial de la descentralización: Argentina y Colombia en perspectiva comparada. (*Desarro. Econ.*, 46:183, oct./dic. 2006, p. 317–351, bibl., tables)

The author explains how differentials in the increase in power of subnational governments as a result of decentralization reform depends on the sequencing of those reforms. If subnational interests prevail in the initial reforms, then political decentralization is likely to come first, creating a dynamic leading to a high degree of change in the relative power of subnational governments, as in the case of Colombia. If national interests prevail in initiating administrative decentralization, then subnational governments are unlikely to increase significantly their relative power, as in the case of Argentina.

1442 Garaño, Santiago and Werner Pertot. Detenidos-aparecidos: presas y presos políticos desde Trelew a la dictadura. Prólogo de Pilar Calveiro. Epílogo de Alcira Daroqui. Buenos Aires: Editorial Biblos, 2007. 335 p.: bibl., facsims., ill., index. (Latitud sur colección.)

Tells the stories of a small number of political prisoners who survived the dictatorship. The epilogue by Alcira Daroqui draws connections between the treatment of prisoners both during the dictatorship and in the democratic period since 1983.

1443 Gaztañaga, Julieta. Un nuevo bloque político y económico: análisis antropológico del proceso político tejido en torno a la construcción de la Región Centro de la República Argentina. Buenos Aires: Editorial Antropofagia, 2008. 141 p.: bibl., ill. (Serie Antropología política y económica)

Anthropological analysis of the political-cultural environment in which the governments of the provinces of Entre Ríos, Santa Fe, and Córdoba created the Región Centro in 2004. The author's research included interviews with federal and provincial politicians and bureaucrats, private sector professionals, and individuals active in the "Civil Society Councils" constructed as part of the political project, along with participant observation at events leading to the creation of the Región Centro. See also item **942**.

1444 Giraudy, Agustina. The distributive politics of emergency employment programs in Argentina, 1993–2002. (*LARR*, 42:2, 2007, p. 33–55, bibl., tables)

The author shows that the distortions in the distribution of emergency employment programs from a means-tested poverty formula are correlated to provincial malapportionment in the federal legislature, Peronist presidents, and piquetero mobilizations. While this finding may support arguments about the clientelist use of these programs, arguments that presidents use these programs for "vote buying" are not supported by the findings. The author suggests legislative coalition building is a more likely explanation for patterns of distribution in these programs. For political economist's comment, see item **2104**.

1445 Goebel, Michael. A movement from right to left in Argentine nationalism?: the Alianza Libertadora Nacionalista and Tacuara as stages of militancy. (*Bull. Lat. Am. Res.*, 26:3, July 2007, p. 356–377, graph)

Interesting historical work tracing the rise of 1960s leftist nationalism from roots in the right-wing nationalism of the 1930s, mediated prominently by Peronist organizations.

1446 Gómez Méndez, Myriam Jaqueline. Los caminos de la democracia en América Latina: Uruguay y Argentina. Guadalajara, Mexico: Univ. de Guadalajara, 2009. 275 p.: bibl., ill.

The author compares the way in which the two countries' political processes before the military coups of the 1970s influenced the negotiations for a return to electoral democracy in the 1980s. She finds that the military regimes' need for legality itself allowed opponents to set the stage for a return to democracy. The author concludes that the political parties had a "determinant" role in the negotiations in Uruguay, while in Argentina the military itself opened the negotiations since the political parties were unprepared and uncertain as to how to proceed.

1447 Groppo, Alejandro. Los dos príncipes: Juan D. Perón y Getulio Vargas: un estudio comparado del populismo latinoamericano. Prólogo de Ernesto Laclau. Villa

María, Argentina: Eduvim, 2009. 479 p.: bibl. (Col. Poliedros)

A careful study of the populist political discourse of Perón and Vargas that identifies the different natures of their political projects. Perón sought to embody a unified movement against internal enemies, while Vargas worked to maintain alliances across Brazil's regions in order to unify the nation.

1448 Herrera, María Rosa. La contienda política en Argentina 1997–2002: un ciclo de protesta. (*Am. Lat. Hoy/Salamanca*, 48, abril 2008, p. 165–189, bibl., graphs, tables)

The author identifies the growth in number, intensity, and diffusion of protests in Argentina, and describes the innovations in protest repertoires beginning in 1997 as markers of a "protest cycle," a classificatory concept developed by Sidney Tarrow.

1449 Hintze, Susana. Políticas sociales argentinas en el cambio de siglo: conjeturas sobre lo posible. Buenos Aires: Espacio Editorial, 2007. 155 p.: bibl. (Col. Desarrollo social y sociedad)

Analysis of the historic decline of "social protection," a type of late 20th century state welfare characterized by state support for social cooperatives, and accompanied by dramatic changes in the social structure and increases in the distribution of poverty. The state welfare model developed under the first Perón government was dismantled by the peronista government of Menem and replaced with targeted assistance connected to labor ("workfare"), but forms of "social economy" have survived and resurfaced after the crisis of 2001. The author interprets these historical processes to assess whether new forms of state welfare policy will develop.

1450 La incidencia política de la sociedad civil. Compilación de Carlos H. Acuña y Ariana Vacchieri. Buenos Aires: Siglo Veintiuno Editores Argentina, 2007. 222 p.: bibl.

This well-organized volume defines and problematizes the concepts of "civil society" and "political insertion" (in two essays by Marcelo Leiras) and considers several case studies of civil society organizations' efforts to influence public policy in the areas of reproductive health and sexual rights, environmentalism, human rights,

and fighting poverty. Acuña's concluding essay thoughtfully examines the challenges to understanding the differences between civil society organizations and the representation of interests, the problems of civil society organizations and public accountability, and the questions of whether and how civil society organizations enhance democracy.

1451 Investigaciones sobre Estado y políticas públicas: el Estado después de los 90. Textos de Gustavo Blutman *et al.* Coordinación de Gustavo Blutman. Buenos Aires: EC, Ediciones Cooperativas, 2009. 293 p.: bibl., ill.

Blutman and Patricia Catoira provide analyses of changes in organizational culture in public administration as a response to the reforms of the 1990s. Other essays focus on public administration and organizational culture at the provincial (provincia de Buenos Aires, Chubut, Salta), municipal (Rosario, municipalities of Chubut), and single institution (a public hospital in provincia de Buenos Aires) levels.

1452 Leiras, Marcelo. Todos los caballos del rey: la integración de los partidos políticos y el gobierno democrático de la Argentina, 1995–2003. Buenos Aires: Prometeo Libros: Pent, 2007. 271 p.: bibl., ill. (Col. Democracia, partidos y elecciones)

An important study of the fragmentation of the political party system and its impact on democratic governance. Fragmentation is attributed largely to the provincialization of the party system and repeated changes in the rules of the game that undermine institutionalization. Includes a comparative analysis of the party systems of the provinces of Buenos Aires and La Rioja. The author concludes with proposals for reform that would strengthen the national parties, control campaign finance, and create greater barriers to entry for alliances and new parties.

1453 Leis, Héctor and Eduardo J. Viola. América del Sur en el mundo de las democracias de mercado. Traducción de Matías Franchini. Buenos Aires: Centro para la Apertura y el Desarrollo de América Latina; Rosario, Argentina: Homo Sapiens Ediciones, 2008. 194 p.: bibl. (Col. Politeia)

A comparative study of Argentina and Brazil in the context of "the international system of the hegemony of market democracies" in the early 21st century. Both countries are characterized as "consolidating market democracies," but consolidation is not assured, and populism is an alternative model available in Latin America. Brazil is described as a "court society" (as in the court of the Monarch), which is characterized by practices of exclusion for those outside of the court in spite of the rhetoric of inclusion. Argentina is described as a "movement society" (as in the Peronist movement), characterized by "radical inclusion of those in the movement and radical exclusion of those outside of it" (p. 72). These differences in political culture are related to the patterns by which the two countries' political systems have evolved in the current global context.

1454 Lewis, Paul H. The agony of Argentine capitalism: from Menem to the Kirchners. Santa Barbara, Calif.: Praeger, 2009. 221 p.: bibl., index.

The final volume of a trilogy (*The Crisis of Argentine Capitalism*, 1990, see *HLAS 53:4109*; and *Guerrillas and Generals: The "Dirty War" in Argentina*, 2002, see *HLAS 63:2385*), in which Lewis chronicles the country's political economy finding it to be antithetical to stable capitalist development. The author reviews the failures of Menem's neoliberalism, the "crash" of 2001, and what Lewis terms the "retreat" to populism under the Kirchners, who are pursuing a statist redistributive economy similar to the policies of Perón himself.

1455 Malamud, Carlos. Perón y su vigencia en los populismos latinoamericanos actuales. (*Rev. Occidente*, 305, oct. 2006, p. 43–55, appendix)

Malamud reviews the defining criteria of Peronist populism and finds that the contemporary governments of Hugo Chávez in Venezuela and Evo Morales in Bolivia (and possibly that of Kirchner in Argentina) meet these criteria. The essay bemoans the return of populism, but does not consider the reasons for its reappearance, beyond the breakdown of party systems in certain countries in the region.

1456 Melo, Marcus André Barreto Campelo de. Institutional weakness and the puzzle of Argentina's low taxation. (*Lat.*

Am. Polit. Soc., 49:4, Winter 2007, p. 115–148, bibl., graphs, tables)

Argentina has a tax level significantly below what is predicted for a country of similar levels of economic development. Most indicators of low tax levels, such as wealth in extractive resources, do not readily apply to Argentina. The author argues that political instability, both at the national level and in intergovernmental relations, provides policymakers with few incentives to adopt policies, such as tax reforms, with medium-term returns. The only tax reform period in recent decades in Argentina was launched by Carlos Menem in the early 1990s, which corresponds with the period of lowest perceived instability. Comparisons are made with Brazil, a country with higher tax rates and greater political stability. For political economist's comment, see item **2112**.

1457 Mesyngier, Luis. La transición permanente: golpes, transiciones y alternancias en la política argentina, 1983–2007. Buenos Aires: Ediciones del Riel, 2007. 216 p.: bibl.

Argues that the inability of Argentina's political system to establish clear institutional rules creates a "permanent transition" instead of a clear consolidation of the republican and democratic regime. This "permanent transition" has become normal, but with deleterious effects on public policy and the ability of the regime to interact effectively with civil society.

1458 Mitchell, Deborah. La experiencia rupturista argentina de 1983. (*TD Temas Debates*, 10:11, oct. 2006, p. 43–65, bibl.)

Discourse analysis assessing the impossibilities of the promise—and demand—of "nunca más" to create a "radical break" making universal justice hegemonic in the discourse of the democratic regime.

Muñoz, María Antonia. Crisis política y conflicto social en Argentina: alcances y límites de un tipo de participación política no convencional. See item **2113**.

1459 Muñoz, María Antonia and **Martín Retamozo.** Hegemonía y discurso en la Argentina contemporánea: efectos políticos de los usos de "pueblo" en la retórica de Néstor Kirchner. (*Perf. Latinoam.*, 16:31, enero/junio 2008, p. 121–147, bibl.)

The authors show how Kirchner's presidential discourse was employed to identify himself—and the state—as agents of the sovereign "people," charged with repairing the "damage" inflicted by the people's enemy, "neoliberalism." They argue that this discourse strengthened Kirchner's support (he was elected with only 22 percent of the vote in 2003), and allowed him to vie for control of rhetorical spaces held by groups like the piqueteros who had confronted the state previously.

1460 Nazareno, Marcelo; Susan Stokes; and Valeria Brusco. Réditos y peligros electorales del gasto público en la Argentina. (*Desarro. Econ.*, 46:181, abril/junio 2006, p. 63–88, bibl., graphs, tables)

Noting that public spending programs were indeed used in politically discriminatory ways in the 1990s, the authors assess the ways in which this spending was targeted and whether it produced electoral benefits. Using data from 1,154 municipalities in seven provinces, the authors find that marginal voters, rather than loyal partisans, were the targets of spending, and that sometimes increased spending reduced electoral support for the party governing the municipality. Reduced electoral support was more likely to occur in municipalities governed by the Unión Cívica Radical.

1461 O'Donnell, Guillermo A. Catacumbas. Buenos Aires: Prometeo Libros, 2008. 264 p.: bibl.

Collection of essays by O'Donnell on bureaucratic-authoritarianism, written between 1975 and 1979, while he was director at the Centro de Estudios de Estado y Sociedad (CEDES) in Buenos Aires.

1462 Ollier, María Matilde. De la revolución a la democracia: cambios privados, públicos y políticos de la izquierda argentina. Buenos Aires: Siglo Veintiuno Editores, 2009. 300 p.: bibl. (Historia y cultura. Serie el pasado presente)

Study of the changes in social identity that members of the revolutionary left experienced during the transition to democracy beginning in 1983. During the period of revolutionary struggle, dissident voices within the left were suppressed, but

after 1983 these voices began to influence the identity of those who survived the military regime. Furthermore, members of the revolutionary left were transformed into subjects of human rights discourse, creating changes in their public and political identities. The revolutionary left's adaptation to and acceptance of democratic politics raises questions about the relationship between democracy and capitalism.

1463 Pasiones nacionales: política y cultura en Brasil y Argentina. Compilación de Alejandro Grimson. Textos de Mirta Amati *et al.* Supervisión de José Nun. Buenos Aires: Edhasa: UNDP Argentina, 2007. 634 p.: bibl. (Ensayo)

This volume is a single project with multiple authors that rigorously compares the national political cultures of Argentina and Brazil. Based on extensive literature reviews and 240 interviews with "sociocultural mediators" in both countries, the authors compare the two countries across five dimensions: sociopolitical divisions, concepts of social development over time (*concepciones de la temporalidad social*), ideas of justice, national sentiments, and modes of thought regarding regional integration. The implications of how each country "sees itself" and "sees its other" for regional integration are thoughtfully considered.

1464 Pensar la democracia, imaginar la transición, 1976–2006. Coordinación de Cecilia Macón. Textos de Laura Cucchi *et al.* Buenos Aires: Ladosur, 2006. 127 p.: bibl., col. ill., plates. (Col. Transformaciones; 1)

A collection of essays by philosophers and historians on the evolution of the nature of public space, collective memory, democratic legitimacy, and political attitudes about and by new generations in the democratic period since 1983.

1465 La política después de los partidos. Compilación de Isidoro Cheresky. Buenos Aires: Prometeo Libros, 2006. 437 p.: bibl., ill. (Col. Democracia, partidos y elecciones)

This volume of essays brings together several contributions analyzing the 2005 elections. Cheresky and Hugo Quiroga set the national context for these elections in separate essays, followed by eight case studies of the elections at the provincial and municipal level. The final two essays address the impact of the open primaries requirement for candidate selection (by Virginia Oliveros and Gerardo Scherlis), and an interesting "ethnographic" analysis by Daniela Slipak of the symbols of political participation and authority found in the electoral process.

1466 Russo, Juan José. Modelos de democratización: dos vías de consolidación democrática. Santiago de Querétaro, Mexico: Fundación Univ. de Derecho, Administración y Política: Instituto de Administración Pública del Estado de México: Instituto Electoral de Querétaro: Instituto de Administración Pública del Estado de Querétaro, 2007. 249 p.: bibl., ill. (Col. FUNDAp política y administración pública)

Detailed comparative study of opposition parties in Italy (Partito Comunista Italiano, 1946–56), Spain (Partido Socialista Obrero Español, 1977–82), and Argentina (Partido Justicialista, 1983–89) in the years immediately after transitions to democracy. The author argues that political conflict characterized the Italian case, while political accommodation characterized the Spanish case. Although for many, including President Alfonsín, the Spanish model has been admired as a useful model for Argentina, the author argues that political conflict may have been unavoidable, especially given the incentive structures of the opposition party. Suggests that it can also be productive for the consolidation of democracy, as was the case in Italy.

1467 Sain, Marcelo Fabián. Seguridades e inseguridades en el gran Buenos Aires. (*Foro Int./México*, 47:3, julio/sept. 2007, p. 517–534, graphs)

Critical analysis of explanations of criminality and insecurity that focus on increases in poverty. Contrary to that theory, the author connects insecurity to the politicization and corruption of police forces in Provincia Buenos Aires, and to inequality and marginalization in certain areas of the province.

1468 Segura, María Soledad. La reproducción de la exclusión en el discurso oficial: las nuevas políticas sociales en la Argentina, 2003–2005. (*TD Temas Debates*, 10:11, oct. 2006, p. 137–157, bibl.)

This essay argues that the official discourse of the Kirchner government regarding social programs is designed to position the state as the provider of goods that beneficiaries are unable to obtain in the market due to their own deficiencies of power, knowledge, and skills. This scenario effectively improves governability through control of the poor, and does not challenge the basic structure of the capitalist economic model.

1469 Seminario El Pensamiento Político, Económico y Social en la Construcción Nacional, Regional y Provincial, *Catamarca, Argentina, 2007.* Nación, región, provincia en Argentina: pensamiento político, económico y social. Edición de Mario Rapoport y Hernán Colombo. Buenos Aires: Imago Mundi, 2007. 307 p.: bibl., ill. (Col. Bitácora argentina)

Seminar papers presented in Catamarca in 2007 covering a wide range of topics, including political economy of Argentina, international and subnational regional integration, the political process, and human rights.

1470 Seminario Internacional: Políticas Públicas, Derechos y Trabajo Social en el MERCOSUR, *1st, Universidad Nacional de Córdoba, 2007.* Políticas públicas, derechos, y trabajo social en el Mercosur. Organización de Nora Aquín y Rubén Caro. Buenos Aires: Espacio Editorial, 2009. 228 p.: bibl. (Col. Ciencias sociales)

This volume includes 13 papers presented at a seminar by the same title held in Córdoba, Argentina, in 2007. Essays are grouped into three topics: public policies, which consider whether policies promote social rights, social progress, and citizen participation; democratic participation and rights in the institutions of Mercosur; and the relation of professional social work to public policy.

1471 Si éste no es el pueblo: hegemonía, populismo y democracia en Argentina. Compilación de Eduardo Rinesi, Gabriel Vommaro y Matías Muraca. Textos de Ariana Reano *et al.* Buenos Aires: IEC, Instituto de Estudios y Capacitación, Federación Nacional de Docentes Universitarios; Los Polvorines, Prov. de Buenos Aires: Univ. Nacional de General Sarmiento, 2008. 196 p.: bibl.

The authors of these essays provide a valuable contribution to the study of Argentine political thought regarding the meanings of the terms "democracy," "hegemony," and "clientelism" as they relate to the concept of "populism." As Rinesi, Vommaro, and Muraca note in their opening essay, much attention has been given to the quality of Argentina's political institutions, so this book addresses the quality of the country's citizenry as political subjects.

1472 Sotomayor, Arturo C. La participación en operaciones de paz de la ONU y el control civil de las fuerzas armadas: los casos de Argentina y Uruguay. (*Foro Int./México*, 47:1, enero/marzo 2007, p. 117–139)

Challenging the idea that participation in UN peacekeeping operations enhances civilian control over the armed forces, this comparative article shows that the outcome depends on the degree of autonomy of the armed forces in controlling peacekeeping missions and in the types of missions undertaken. The favorable impact of peacekeeping operations on civil-military relations has been much less noticeable in Uruguay than in Argentina.

1473 Trocello, Gloria. La manufactura de "ciudadanos siervos": cultura política y regímenes neopatrimonialistas. San Luis, Argentina: Nueva Editorial Universitaria: Univ. Nacional de San Luis, 2008. 418 p.: bibl., ill. (El ágora col.)

Argues that weak republican institutions and great social disparities create political cultures of dependent "servant" relations and neopatrimonial political elites who see the state as extensions of themselves. After a thorough review of theory, the author applies the analysis to the case of San Luis province under Adolfo Rodríguez Saá, 1983–2001.

1474 Las urnas y la desconfianza ciudadana en la democracia argentina. Compilación de Isidoro Cheresky. Textos de Isidoro Cheresky *et al.* Buenos Aires: Univ. de Buenos Aires, Facultad de Ciencias Sociales, Instituto de Investigaciones Gino Germani; Rosario, Argentina: Homo Sapiens Ediciones, 2009. 527 p.: bibl., ill. (Col. Politeia)

This volume of essays brings together several analyses of the 2007 elections, including nine case studies of provincial and municipal elections. In what Cheresky terms "intra-officialist" competition, fragmentation of the traditional Partido Justicialista meant that in many localities opposing lists for municipal or provincial elections supported the incumbent government at the national level.

1475 Vázquez, Daniel and **Valeria Falleti.** Política económica, deslegitimación democrática y reconstrucción social en Argentina. (*Perf. Latinoam.*, 14:29, enero/junio 2007, p. 71–109, bibl., graphs, tables)

Descriptive analysis of the relationship between measures of economic performance, public opinion about the political economy, and electoral results.

1476 Vommaro, Gabriel. Lo que quiere la gente: los sondeos de opinión y el espacio de la comunicación política en Argentina, 1983–1999. Los Polvorines, Argentina: Univ. Nacional de General Sarmiento; Buenos Aires: Prometeo Libros, 2008. 203 p.: bibl.

An innovative study of the "social technology" of public opinion and "intention to vote" surveys. The author argues that the rise of political surveys after 1983 reflects changes in the political system, not just with the return to elections but with the growing reliance of campaigns on mass media. Pollsters positioned themselves as neutral experts measuring the aggregate of individual preferences, while the media embraced polling as a means to cover campaigns like a sporting event (the familiar "horse-race" analogy in the US) rather than contests over programs and power. Thus scientific surveying has itself altered the environment for political communication, as politicians craft messages to influence their standing in the polls.

1477 Weathers, Gwyndolyn J. De la jerarquización a la transversalidad de género: feministas, tecnócratas y el estado en Argentina, 1983–2004. (*Polít. Gest.*, 10, 2007, p. 95–124, bibl.)

Insightful discussion of the paradoxical relationship that developed during the study period between the feminist movements in civil society and the state. The movements were successful in lobbying for the creation of the Consejo Nacional de la Mujer in 1992 as a state institution, but subsequently as a state institution this body became more technocratic and more closely linked to the governing party than it was to autonomous feminist movement organizations.

Wolff, Jonas. De-idealizing the democratic civil peace: on the political economy of democratic stabilization and pacification in Argentina and Ecuador. See item **2124**.

Wolff, Jonas. (De-)mobilising the marginalised: a comparison of the Argentine piqueteros and Ecuador's indigenous movement. See item **1286**.

1478 Zimerman, Héctor J. Transición democrática y nuevas formas de hacer política: Corrientes, 1987–1997. Corrientes, Argentina: Moglia Ediciones: UNNE, Facultad de Derecho y Ciencias Sociales y Políticas, 2005. 200 p.: bibl.

Study of the rise of Raúl Rolando "Tato" Romero Feris to governor of the province of Corrientes. The author places Romero in the context of neopopulism, characterized by personalist rather than programmatic appeals to voters, discretional control over public resources, and willingness to alter the political rules, all patterns identified at both the national level and in other provinces.

PARAGUAY

1479 Abente Brun, Diego. Paraguay en el umbral del cambio. (*Rev. Cienc. Polít./Santiago*, 27, núm. especial, 2007, p. 221–233, tables)

Article helpfully reviews and assesses the many political events of 2006, when Bishop Fernando Lugo rose to national political prominence.

1480 Bareiro Spaini, Luis Nicanor. Las fuerzas armadas y su profesionalidad: realidad y perspectivas: una interpretación nacional y regional. Asunción: Intercontinental Editora, 2008. 302 p.: bibl.

The book argues for professional-

ization of the armed forces, specifically through developing a stronger sense of corporate unity and efficient use of modern technology. The author sees the mission of the armed forces as "defense of the nation, its sovereignty, integrity and values," and argues that the lack of professionalization stands in the way of effective regional security integration and a credible military deterrence to aggression. The author is a retired general in the Paraguayan army, who served as minister of defense in the first years of the Lugo government.

1481 González Macchi, Luis Angel. Testimonio político: revelaciones de un presidente. Asunción: Talleres Gráficos Emasa, 2008. 348 p.: ill.

González Macchi, Paraguayan president from 1999–2003, defends his record in this publication. He illustrates the political class concepts of loyalty to the party (in this case, the Asociación Nacional Republicana-Partido Colorado), and argues that the main job of the president is managing patron-client networks through the provision of state jobs.

1482 Horst, René Harder. The Stroessner regime and indigenous resistance in Paraguay. Gainesville: Univ. Press of Florida, 2007. 224 p.: bibl., index.

Detailed study of state policy towards indigenous peoples. Describes the state's assimilationist goals under Stroessner, the opposition and at times complicity of various missionary groups and foreign actors, and the ability of indigenous peoples to utilize the growing regional discourse of indigenous rights and pan-indigenous identity to resist assimilation.

1483 Lambert, Peter and **Ricardo Medina.** Contested discourse, contested power: nationalism and the left in Paraguay. (*Bull. Lat. Am. Res.*, 26:3, July 2007, p. 339–355)

This article describes the conditions that enabled the Partido Colorado to control nationalist discourse beginning in the 1930s, with effects still apparent early in the 21st century. The political left has found it difficult to articulate a nationalist vision to compete with the "poly-classist" but conservative nationalism of the long-dominant Partido Colorado.

1484 Ortiz Sandoval, Luis. Participación directa y democratización en Paraguay. (*Estud. Parag.*, 24:1/2, dic. 2006, p. 57–74, bibl.)

Analyzes the reasons that Paraguay has yet to hold an initiative or referendum under the 1992 Constitution. The obvious reason is that both mechanisms would require action by Congress, where the political parties resist challenges to their legislative authority. The organized peasantry is identified as the most likely popular movement to force an initiative election, but the group is weakened by patterns of clientelism organized by the parties.

1485 Vidal Soler, Víctor. Rumbo a la alternancia: una oportunidad para la profundización de la participación democrática en Paraguay. (*Estud. Parag.*, 25:1/2., dic. 2007, p. 7–23, bibl.)

Detailed analysis of the conservative institutional environment that makes the use of direct measures of democracy such as initiative and referendum almost impossible. Considers the prospects for change in the use of direct democracy measures under a Lugo government.

URUGUAY

1486 Aborto en debate: dilemas y desafíos del Uruguay democrático: proceso político y social, 2001–2004. Coordinación de Lilian Abracinskas y Alejandra López Gómez. Textos de Jorge Barreiro et al. Montevideo: Mujer y Salud en Uruguay, 2007. 238 p.: bibl., ill.

A very insightful series of essays analyzing the sociopolitical environment revealed by debate in the legislature over the proposed "Law of Defense of Reproductive Health" during what Constanza Moreira terms "the last government of the traditional parties" (2000–2005).

1487 Acosta, Yamandú. Uruguay, 1985–2005: dimensiones y tensiones de la democracia. (*Cuad. Am./México*, 2:116, abril/junio 2006, p. 11–23, bibl.)

Philosophical essay about the failure of the institutions of "market democracy," limited by the imperatives of transnational capitalist interests, to provide avenues for the establishment of substantive democracy based on social inclusion.

1488 Alegre, Pablo. Matrices sociopolíticas y patrones de reforma en el Cono Sur: entre la ruta populista y autoritaria, el caso uruguayo en perspectiva comparada. (*Rev. Cienc. Polít./Santiago*, 27:2, 2007, p. 89–108, tables)

The author explains the patterns and degrees of neoliberal economic reform in the 1980s and 1990s in terms of the capacity of reformers to defeat veto coalitions defending the ISI model of development. In Chile, the authoritarian regime broke the power of unions and their party allies. In Argentina, the Menem government used clientelist control over organized sectors to prevent an effective veto coalition to arise. In Uruguay, neoliberal reforms were limited because of the capacity of the Frente Amplio to link itself to beneficiaries of ISI to veto privatizations and other reforms.

1489 Armas, Gustavo de. Sociedad y políticas sociales en Uruguay desde la transición democrática al gobierno del Frente Amplio. (*Am. Lat. Hoy/Salamanca*, 44, dic. 2006, p. 41–61, bibl., graphs, tables)

The economic crisis of 2001–2002 erased many of the impressive gains recorded since 1984 in the reduction of poverty levels, presenting the new Frente Amplio government with new challenges: poverty reduction and reallocation of priorities within social spending. The author analyzes welfare policy development in the democratic period since 1984, and describes the first steps taken by the Vázquez government to address these challenges.

1490 Buchanan, Paul G. Preauthoritarian institutions and postauthoritarian outcomes: labor politics in Chile and Uruguay. (*Lat. Am. Polit. Soc.*, 50:1, Spring 2008, p. 59–89, bibl.)

Argues that patterns of state-labor relations (strongly corporatist in Chile, more pluralist in Uruguay) that developed in the pre-authoritarian period re-emerged after the end of the dictatorships. Uruguay's independent and pluralist unions have been relatively more effective in resisting promarket reforms. For Chilean political scientist's comment, see *HLAS 65:1727*.

1491 Castells, Adolfo. Carnaval y populismo autoritario: la realidad del progresismo uruguayo. 2. ed. Montevideo: Artemisa Editores, 2007. 238 p.: bibl.

Argues that the Frente Amplio government is ideologically "authoritarian populist" and thus antithetical to the liberal democratic process. Author was an official in the Foreign Ministry in the Partido Colorado governments.

1492 Chasquetti, Daniel. Uruguay 2006: éxitos y dilemas del gobierno de izquierda. (*Rev. Cienc. Polít./Santiago*, 27, no. especial, 2007, p. 249–263, tables)

Article helpfully reviews and assesses the political events of 2006, noting the government's relative successes in economic policy, managing the conflict with Argentina over the placement of cellulose factories, and the legislative process.

1493 Garcé, Adolfo and **Jaime Yaffé.** La izquierda uruguaya, 1971–2004: ideología, estrategia y programa. (*Am. Lat. Hoy/Salamanca*, 44, dic. 2006, p. 87–114, bibl.)

A more detailed and important contribution by these two authors (see also *HLAS 63:2420, HLAS 65:1814,* and *HLAS 65:1819*) describing the evolution of the Frente Amplio into a social-democratic catch-all party by the time of its electoral victory in 2004.

1494 Luna, Juan Pablo. Frente Amplio and crafting of a social democratic alternative in Uruguay. (*Lat. Am. Polit. Soc.*, 49:4, Winter 2007, p. 1–30, bibl., tables)

An analysis of the evolution of Frente Amplio's social base, both in geographic and class terms. The author contributes to the understanding of the 2004 electoral victory in terms of the political and sociological "opportunity structures" that provided the FA a support base from two different groups: its organized historical constituency and a new group of voters who have been alienated from the traditional party system due to a lack of economic and political progress.

1495 Mallo Reynal, Susana. La concreción de un sueño anunciado: la izquierda en el Uruguay del siglo XXI. (*Cuad. Am./México*, 2:116, abril/junio 2006, p. 25–51, bibl., graphs, tables)

This article describes the ideological problems that coming to power has pre-

sented to the political left. The left has to adapt its coherent oppositional discourse to one appropriate for governing as an electoral majority, while still working towards building a substantive and participatory democracy in the era of limits imposed by globalization.

1496 Panizza, Francisco. Economic constraints and strategic choices: the case of the Frente Amplio of Uruguay's first year in office. (*Bull. Lat. Am. Res.*, 27:2, April 2008, p. 176–196)

The author describes the first year of economic policies under the Frente Amplio government as "adoption, completion, and correction" of free market reforms inherited from previous governments. The FA had to balance pressures from distinct sectors within its coalition in designing policies governing labor, debt relief (both national and sectoral), relations with the IMF and the US, social welfare, and investment. Finds that the FA did not adopt a programmatic leftist agenda, but rather worked within the constraints and opportunities of the particular political moment.

1497 Parissi, Julio. Qué fue de ellos: el enigma de los etarras en el Uruguay. Montevideo: Planeta, 2006. 251 p.: bibl.

Journalist's account of the 1992 arrest of several alleged ETA members in Uruguay and the subsequent effort by Spain to extradite various Basques accused of ETA connections. The author details how the debate over extradition or political asylum helped define the Frente Amplio in the period after this incident.

1498 Queirolo, Rosario. Las elecciones uruguayas de 2004: la izquierda como la única oposición creíble. (*Colomb. Int.*, 64, julio/dic. 2006, p. 34–49, bibl., graph, tables)

Using survey research conducted shortly before the 2004 elections in Uruguay, the author argues that risk aversion and a voter's assessment of economic conditions determine willingness to cast a vote for a party that never previously governed. In 2004, Uruguayan voters had an overwhelmingly negative assessment of economic conditions, and those who were not risk averse were most likely to vote for Frente Amplio.

1499 Rodríguez, Romero Jorge. Mbundo malungo a mundele: historia del movimiento afrouruguayo y sus alternativas de desarrollo. Montevideo: Rosebud Ediciones, 2006. 247 p.: bibl., ill.

Useful history of the Afro-Uruguayan civil rights movement, of which the author is a long-time activist and leader, in the 20th and early 21st centuries. Rodríguez chronicles resistance to a "eurocentric" vision of a homogenous society and calls instead for a multicultural and pluralist society that acknowledges and respects cultural distinctiveness. The author translates the title as "from the black person to the white man."

1500 Selios, Lucía. Los últimos diez años de la cultura política uruguaya: entre la participación y el desencanto. (*Am. Lat. Hoy/Salamanca,* 44, dic. 2006, p. 63–85, bibl., graphs, tables)

This article associates changes in Uruguayan respondents' attitudes toward political institutions and behaviors, as reported in Latinobarómetro data from 1994–2004, with the electoral calendar and with fluctuations in economic performance. The key finding is that political engagement has remained consistent and relatively high for a Latin American country, but levels of partisan identity have declined, suggesting "a moment of erosion of the parties' capacity to mediate" voter interests.

Sotomayor, Arturo C. La participación en operaciones de paz de la ONU y el control civil de las fuerzas armadas: los casos de Argentina y Uruguay. See item **1472**.

BRAZIL

ENRIQUE DESMOND ARIAS, *Associate Professor of Government, John Jay College of City University of New York (CUNY)*

IN 2005 BRAZIL WAS ROCKED by a major political scandal involving efforts of the Partido dos Trabalhadores (PT) administration of President Luis Inácio Lula da Silva to secure the votes of minor party legislators through regular under-the-table payments. Nonetheless Lula achieved a landslide general election victory in 2006, winning 60 percent of the national vote in the second round—and losing only 7 of Brazil's 27 states. He succeeded in building on his 2006 victory and managing a strong second term in which his biggest concern often appeared to be building coalitions around the country to help Dilma Roussef, his chosen successor, win the 2010 presidential election. The PT succeeded in building a broad national coalition based, in part, on deep strength in the impoverished North and Northeast as a result of its effective wealth transfer policies, such as *Bolsa Família* and *Fome Zero*, that have moderately decreased inequality in the country and provided slightly greater income security to the poorest Brazilians. The scholarly literature on Brazilian politics in this *HLAS* volume reflects these general political trends.

Consistent with intellectual developments in the US and in Brazil, the largest concentration of writing focuses on the structure, dynamics, and implications of an array of national political institutions. More than one quarter of the publications in this bibliography address the workings of national political institutions. Among these, a substantial portion focuses on elections and electoral strategies. Aline Machado in an article entitled "Minimum Winning Coalitions Under Presidentialism" takes up the important question of how Brazilian political parties build interparty electoral coalitions; she also investigates the types of coalitions that encounter the most success (item **1517**). In "Rewarding the Corrupt," Lúcio

Rennó provides evidence to support the argument that in Brazil, where the common saying *rouba mas faz* is used to justify electing corrupt politicians, politicians implicated in corruption scandals are less likely to win elections (item **1521**). Clara Araujo's interesting article shows that women have more electoral success under conditions of greater poverty and when they affiliate with smaller parties (item **1501**). Other publications on this general issue focus more specifically on the day-to-day operations of Congress and the executive branch. José Antonio Cheibub, Argelina Cheibub Figueiredo, and Fernando Limongi contribute an interesting article examining the effects of national and state political dynamics on legislative behavior (item **1508**). In addition, Figueiredo and Limongi's book entitled *Política orçamentaria no presidencialismo de coalizão* looks at how governing legislative coalitions affect federal budgeting (item **1512**). Maria Celina D'Araujo's monograph on the background and composition of high-ranking federal appointees under the recent PT administrations provides important insights into the evolving structure of Brazil's political elite (item **1502**). Similarly David Samuels' article on the "Sources of Mass Partisanship in Brazil" provides important insights into the impact of the particular structure of the PT on wider political dynamics in Brazil (item **1523**). Inácio Magna's *Democracia e referendo no Brasil* takes up the interesting story of Brazil's failed 2005 firearms control referendum, analyzing how a popular idea suffered such a resounding political defeat in a national referendum (item **1510**). Finally, Peter Kingstone and Timothy Power's edited volume *Democratic Brazil Revisited* brings together distinguished US-based Brazilianists who provide broad information on the state of the Brazilian political system (item **1511**).

Since the implementation of the Plano Real and the election of Fernando Henrique Cardoso, Brazil has experienced a degree of political and economic stability unusual in recent Brazilian history. Indeed, Cardoso was the first elected president to complete a term in office and the first president to oversee a peaceful transition of power to an opposition government since Juscelino Kubitshek did so in 1960. The relative stability and the generally well-run administrations of Cardoso and Lula, his successor, have given Brazilian policymakers at the federal, state, and municipal levels the opportunity to develop and implement an array of new and innovative policies. A considerable amount of writing listed in this bibliography reflects the rapidly developing scholarship in this area. Fernando G. Tenório's *Cidadania e desenvolvimento local* provides an interesting and detailed examination of local development policies in six Brazilian regions and two regions in Spain and Chile, offering important comparative insights into how patterns of cross-sectoral alliances support the implementation of development policies (item **1509**). Brazil has had substantial success in mitigating income inequality and achieving other policy objectives through conditional cash transfer programs. *Bolsa Família*, implemented in 2003 during the first Lula administration, is a key program for supplementing the incomes of poor families. Rosa Maria Marques takes up the question of *Bolsa Família* in her analysis of the 2006 elections, showing that the policy had a strong effect on shoring up Lula's vote that year (item **1518**). Wendy Hunter and Natasha Borges Sugiyama's article also examines the effects of Brazilian social policies, arguing that despite effective policies, the needs of many remain unmet as a result of the segmented nature of social rights and the lack of services available to much of the population (item **1514**). Finally, João Paulo dos Reis Velloso and Roberto Cavalcanti de Albuquerque have edited an interesting volume entitled *A verdadeira revolução brasileira* that brings together leading academics and policymakers analyzing and, at times, promoting, particular social policies (item **1513**). This book provides specific insights into how leading Brazilian thinkers build and debate these types of policies.

Participatory budgeting programs have been a key focus of debates on Brazilian policy over the past 10 years. In recent years this literature has moved beyond an exclusive focus on budgeting programs into other types of participatory institutions. Several solid works stand out. For example, Evelina Dagnino and Luciana Tatagiba have edited a lengthy and detailed volume on the role of participatory institutions in deepening democracy in Brazil and Latin America (item **1503**). In addition to the discussion of Brazil, some chapters examine these types of institutions in Mexico, Venezuela, and Uruguay. Leonardo Avritzer's article in *Dados* looks at the role of electoral and nonelectoral representation in Brazilian participatory institutions (item **1504**). Finally, Brian Wampler's book *Participatory Budgeting in Brazil: Contestation, Cooperation, and Accountability* offers a detailed and comprehensive analysis of participatory budgeting programs in Brazil, providing a robust theoretical discussion of the bases for why these programs succeed or fail (item **1526**).

This *HLAS* volume also contains a significant number of publications focused on Brazil's political history. Three sets of publications stand out. The first is the republication of a four-volume set of memoirs by leftist militant Paulo Cavalcanti (item **1507**). These volumes reflect on the author's experiences in politics during the 1950s through the 1970s, discussing progressive reform efforts during the period, attempts to undermine the dictatorship, and the wider political repression of the era. Similarly, Zuenir Ventura, a distinguished Rio de Janeiro journalist, has published two volumes reflecting on the year 1968, one of the most repressive periods of Brazil's 21-year military dictatorship, and its implications for today. The first volume provides a detailed discussion of events that took place that year with a particular focus on the author's home city of Rio (item **1524**). The second volume offers a readable reflection on the continuing impact of events in 1968 on contemporary Brazilian life (item **1525**). The first half of the volume is composed of journalistic essays on the different elements of Brazilian life in the 40 years since 1968. The second half of the volume contains interviews with distinguished Brazilians, including singer Caetano Veloso and former President Fernando Henrique Cardoso, about the impact of events in 1968 on their lives and on their country. Finally, Ignacy Sachs, Jorge Wilhelm, and Paulo Sérgio Pinheiro have published an edited volume that brings together prominent academics and policymakers to discuss the historical context of some of the challenges facing contemporary Brazil such as the rule of law and rural development (item **1506**).

Three books that do not fit solidly in any of the above categories stand out in this collection of publications. Emir Sader, a leading Brazilian social thinker, has published *A vingança da história*, which examines the complex political and economic terrain of contemporary Latin America and the often tense relationship between the intellectual left and the PT governments in Brazil (item **1522**). Bernd Reiter, in *Negotiating Democracy in Brazil*, has written a particularly engaging piece of political sociology based on close research of students, domestic workers, and NGOs in Salvador to develop a more robust understanding of the complex, and often unseen, processes that reproduce inequality, privilege, and dominance in Brazilian society (item **1520**). Finally, Benjamin Lessing's article entitled "As facções cariocas em perspectiva comparativa" examines the structure of criminal organization in Rio de Janeiro, São Paulo, Porto Alegre, and Recife, arguing that some aspects of how criminals have historically dominated Rio's prison system contribute to the unusual strength of criminal factions in that city and the ability of gangs affiliated with those factions to consistently dominate large shantytowns in that city (item **1515**). The well-written and researched article makes a significant and original contribution to the debate of crime and public security in Brazil.

The selected publications presented here offer a broad picture of the evolving debate on Brazilian politics. Growing focus on policy and institutional dynamics reflects the relative stability the country has experienced over the past 20 years and the opportunities that stability has presented to both policymakers seeking to develop strategies to better serve Brazil's large and growing population and scholars seeking to understand the country's complex political dynamics.

1501 Araújo, Clara and **José Eustáquio Diniz Alves.** Impactos de indicadores sociais e do sistema eleitoral sobre as chances das mulheres nas eleições e suas interações com as cotas. (*Dados/Rio de Janeiro,* 50:3, 2007, p. 535–577, bibl., graphs, tables)

This article examines the role of quotas in ensuring the equitable election of women to the Câmara dos Deputados. Overall despite quotas, Brazil lags behind other Latin American countries in the number of women holding office in this legislative house. The article indicates that women have greater success winning election in poorer states than in wealthier states and that they have greater success winning election when running on small party tickets than on the tickets of larger political parties.

1502 Araújo, Maria Celina Soares d'. A elite dirigente do governo Lula. Participação de Camila Lameirão. Rio de Janeiro: Fundação Getulio Vargas, CPDOC, 2009. 140 p.: bibl., ill.

This book provides a detailed examination of the background and training of high level government officials in the two Worker's Party administrations from 2002 through 2010. Argues that high ranking officials are well-trained professionals from an array of sectors including trade unions and the academy.

1503 Associação Latino-Americana de Ciência Política. Congresso. *3rd, Universidade Estadual de Campinas, 2006.* Democracia, sociedade civil e participação. Organização de Evelina Dagnino e Luciana Tatagiba. Chapecó, Brazil: Argos Editora

Universitária, 2007. 590 p.: bibl., ill. (Col. Debates)

A detailed examination of the role of participatory institutions in deepening democracy in Brazil and other countries in the region. Individual chapter contributions focus on Brazil for the most part, with a few looking at other Latin American examples such as Mexico, Venezuela, and Uruguay.

1504 Avritzer, Leonardo. Sociedade civil, instituições participativas e representação: da autorização à legitimidade da ação. (*Dados/Rio de Janeiro,* 50:3, 2007, p. 443–464, bibl., table)

This article explores the nature of electoral and nonelectoral representation in Brazilian participatory institutions through an examination of the theoretical bases of participation. Also develops categories of representation to understand their impact on participation.

1505 Braga, Políbio. Herança maldita: os 16 anos do PT em Porto Alegre. Porto Alegre, Brazil: s.n., 2008. 345 p.: bibl., index.

A detailed attack on 16 years of the Partido dos Trabalhadores (PT) government in the southern city of Porto Alegre. The book characterizes PT leadership in the city, perhaps with some hyperbole, as a combination of fascism and communism.

1506 Brazil: a century of change. Edited by Ignacy Sachs, Jorge Wilheim, and Paulo Sergio de Moraes Sarmento Pinheiro. Translated by Robert N. Anderson. Foreword by Jerry Dávila. Chapel Hill: Univ. of North Carolina Press, 2009. 364 p.: bibl., graphs, index, maps. (Latin America in translation/en traducción/em tradução. Brasiliana collection)

This edited volume, originally published in Portuguese as *Brasil: um século de transformações* (*HLAS 62:2187*), brings together leading Brazilian scholars and policymakers who examine the challenges confronting Brazilian democracy in a historical context. They seek to analyze how issues facing current leaders have emerged and been addressed in different ways over the last century. Includes chapters on such issues as the rule of law, rural and economic development, and international relations. For political economist's comment, see item **2142**.

1507 Cavalcanti, Paulo. O caso eu conto, como o caso foi: memórias políticas. Vol. 1, Da Coluna Prestes à queda de Arraes. Vol. 2, Fatos do meu tempo. Vol. 3, Nos tempos de Prestes. Vol. 4, A luta clandestina. 2a. ed. rev. e ampliada. Recife, Brazil: Cepe Editora, 2008. 4 v.: bibl., ill.

This is a four-volume set of the republished memoirs of a Brazilian activist and politician engaged with the peasant struggles in the state of Pernambuco. Vol. 2 focuses on the Second Republic and the dictatorship. Vol. 3 examines political repression in Pernambuco, interactions with Luis Carolos Prestes, the crisis in the Partido Comunista Brasileiro, and violence after the 1964 military coup. Vol. 4 analyzes politics in Recife before the 1964 military coup and the author's role in clandestine actions against the dictatorship. For review of the 1st ed. of Vol. 1, *Da Coluna Prestes à queda de Arraes*, see *HLAS 43:6684*.

1508 Cheibub, José Antonio; Argelina Maria Cheibub Figueiredo; and Fernando Papaterra Limongi Neto. Political parties and governors as determinants of legislative behavior in Brazil's Chamber of Deputies, 1988–2006. (*Lat. Am. Polit. Soc.*, 51:1, Spring 2009, p. 1–30, bibl., tables)

This article argues that the structure of Congress and the power of the executive to set the agenda allow federal government officials to gain the political backing of members of the Brazilian Câmara dos Deputados to support national initiatives rather than particular state or regional interests.

Article is available in Portuguese in *Dados: Revista de Ciências Sociais*, Vol. 52, No. 2, 2009, p. 263–299.

1509 Cidadania e desenvolvimento local. Organização de Fernando Guilherme Tenório. Ijuí, Brazil: Editora UNIJUI, 2007. 627 p.: bibl., maps.

This extremely detailed book examines local-level development policy in six different Brazilian regions along with regions in Spain and Chile. Argues that given changes in the historical role of the state, a more horizontal and inclusive pattern of political alliances across classes and organizations is necessary to effectively implement development policy.

1510 Democracia e referendo no Brasil. Organização de Magna Inácio, Raquel Novais e Fátima Anastasia. Belo Horizonte, Brazil: Editora UFMG, 2006. 250 p.: bibl. (Origem)

This edited volume provides an extensive set of essays on the reasons for the failure of the national referendum on the sale of arms to civilians in 2005. The book seeks to understand how the population could drastically shift from 80 percent in support of banning the sale of arms and munitions to civilians in 2003 to more than 60 percent against two years later. The authors argue that the shift emerges as a result of the ability of those in favor of the status quo to control the terms of the debate in their favor.

1511 Democratic Brazil revisited. Edited by Peter R. Kingstone and Timothy Joseph Power. Pittsburgh, Pa.: Univ. of Pittsburgh Press, 2008. 342 p.: bibl., graphs, index, tables. (Pitt Latin American series)

This book, the sequel to *Democratic Brazil* (see *HLAS 59:4031*), provides a broad analysis of an array of issues critical to understanding politics in contemporary Brazil including public safety, race, social policy, economic reform, the structure and impact of political institutions, and the role of Worker's Party power in the political system.

1512 Figueiredo, Argelina Maria Cheibub and Fernando Papaterra Limongi Neto. Política orçamentária no presidencialismo de coalizão. Rio de Janeiro: Editora FGV, 2008. 182 p.: bibl.

This book offers a detailed discussion of the budgeting process in Brazil, arguing that the relative power of political parties within the governing legislative coalition and the power of specific politicians within each of those parties affect national budgeting decisions.

1513 Fórum Especial A Verdadeira Revolução Brasileira: Integração de Desenvolvimento e Democracia, *Rio de Janeiro*, 2007. A verdadeira revolução brasileira: integração de desenvolvimento e democracia. Coordenação por João Paulo dos Reis Velloso y Roberto Cavalcanti de Albuquerque. Textos de Patrus Ananias *et al.* Rio de Janeiro: José Olympio Editora, 2008. 262 p.: bibl., ill.

This book brings together essays by leading academics, policymakers, and politicians examining and promoting social policies that seek to provide greater opportunity for the poor.

1514 Hunter, Wendy and Natasha Borges Sugiyama. Democracy and social policy in Brazil: advancing basic needs, preserving privileged interests. (*Lat. Am. Polit. Soc.*, 51:2, Summer 2009, p. 29–58, bibl., table)

This article argues that while the post-authoritarian government in Brazil has made progress in building effective social policies and addressing the needs of the poor, many important needs remain unmet as a result of the highly segmented nature of social rights and the lack of access to services for much of the population. For sociologist's comment, see item **2602**.

Leis, Héctor and Eduardo J. Viola. América del Sur en el mundo de las democracias de mercado. See item **1453**.

1515 Lessing, Benjamin. As facções cariocas em perspectiva comparativa. (*Novos Estud. CEBRAP*, 80, março 2008, p. 43–62, ill., tables)

This is a fascinating and muchneeded article on the types of criminal organization that have emerged in different cities in Brazil. The author argues that Rio's particularly well-organized criminal factions emerge as a result of the power of the gangs that run the state's prisons.

1516 Limongi Neto, Fernando Papaterra and Lara Mesquita. Estratégia partidária e preferência dos eleitores: as eleições municipais em São Paulo entre 1985 e 2004. (*Novos Estud. CEBRAP*, 81, julho 2008, p. 49–66, graphs, tables)

This analysis of municipal elections in São Paulo suggests that the Partido dos Trabalhadores (PT) had strengthened its position over time and often in confrontation with a strong right wing coalition. In more recent elections, the authors argue, centrist political parties have begun to achieve more success.

1517 Machado, Aline. Minimum winning electoral coalitions under presidentialism: reality or fiction?: the case of Brazil. (*Lat. Am. Polit. Soc.*, 51:3, Fall 2009, p. 87–110, bibl., tables)

This article finds evidence, based on data from the 1998, 2002, and 2006 Brazilian presidential elections, that parties built minimum necessary cross-party coalitions to win election. These coalitions are complicated by rules that require that coalitions be built across different levels of political competition.

1518 Marques, Rosa Maria *et al.* Discutindo o papel do Programa Bolsa Família na decisão das eleições presidenciais brasileiras de 2006. (*Rev. Econ. Polít.*, 29:1, jan/março 2009, p. 114–132, bibl., graphs, tables)

This paper provides a quantitative analysis of the role of the Bolsa Família in supporting Luis Inácio Lula da Silva's re-election in 2006 using a combination of voting data and rates of Bolsa Família in municipalities. The author argues that the Bolsa Família accounts for 45 percent of the president's vote in his re-election contest.

Pasiones nacionales: política y cultura en Brasil y Argentina. See item **1463**.

1519 Pereira, Luiz Carlos Bresser. Construindo o Estado republicano: democracia e reforma da gestão pública. Rio de Janeiro: FGV Editora, 2009. 414 p.: bibl.

This is a Portuguese translation of the English-language volume *Democracy and Public Management Reform: Building the Republican State* published by Oxford University Press in 2004 by the same author. The book focuses on the implications of state reform for building an effective "republican" state that seeks to restrict the influence of private interests on public decision-making.

1520 Reiter, Bernd. Negotiating democracy in Brazil: the politics of exclusion. Boulder, Colo.: FirstForumPress, 2009. 171 p.: bibl., index.

This book examines the practice of democracy in different sectors of Bahian society through an examination of elite students, domestic workers, and NGOs, concluding that different aspects in each of these organizations and relationships have the tendency to reproduce exclusion and privilege in Brazilian society and create challenges for efficacious democracy in Brazil.

1521 Remuzat Rennó Jr., Lúcio. Rewarding the corrupt?: reelection and scandal involvement in the Brazilian 2006 legislative elections. (*Colomb. Int.*, 68, julio/dic. 2008, p. 98–106, bibl., table)

This brief, well-researched article uses data from the 2006 Congressional election to analyze the impact of corruption on the electoral prospects of sitting deputies. This evidence gathered suggests that corruption has a significant negative effect on the chances of a member of Congress winning re-election.

1522 Sader, Emir. A vingança da história. 2a. ed. São Paulo: Boitempo Editorial, 2007. 221 p.: bibl.

This book offers an analysis of Brazil and Latin American generally in the (post?)-neoliberal era. The study focuses on the changing economic and political terrain in the region and the complex relationship between the intellectual left and the Partido dos Trabalhadores (PT) administrations of Luiz Inácio Lula da Silva.

1523 Samuels, David J. Sources of mass partisanship in Brazil. (*Lat. Am. Polit. Soc.*, 48:2, Summer 2006, p. 1–27, bibl., graphs, tables)

This article seeks to account for the relatively low levels of partisanship in Brazilian politics and to show that the only party with a mass partisan base is the Partido dos Trabalhadores (PT). Finds that

education is not strongly related to partisanship and partisan identity is related to political participation. The difference between the PT and other parties is accounted for by the PT's ability to integrate popular support on a mass institutional level, unlike other major Brazilian political parties. The author indicates that the PT lost some support as a result of the 2005 corruption scandal.

1524 Ventura, Zuenir. 1968: o ano que não terminou. Apresentação de Heloisa Buarque de Hollanda. Revised ed. São Paulo: Planeta, 2008. 284 p.: bibl., ill., index.

This book, a reprint of a previously published edition by an eminent journalist, provides a history of the political mobilization against military rule and the hardening of the dictatorship in 1968. Focuses mainly on Rio de Janeiro. For sequel to this book, see item **1525**.

1525 Ventura, Zuenir. 1968: o que fizemos de nós. São Paulo: Planeta, 2008. 221 p.: bibl., ill., index.

A sequel to Ventura's earlier book (see item **1524**), this volume reflects on the ongoing impact of the experience of 1968 on contemporary life in Brazil and especially in Rio de Janeiro. The book's first section offers a narrative journalistic account of a variety of aspects of social life that have been affected by the experience of repression in 1968. The section also examines the ways in which the country has moved on from that year. The second half of the book consists of interviews with prominent Brazilians who were living in Brazil in 1968.

1526 Wampler, Brian. Participatory budgeting in Brazil: contestation, cooperation, and accountability. University Park: Pennsylvania State Univ. Press, 2007. 312 p.: bibl., ill., index, map.

This book offers a detailed examination of participatory budgeting programs in several Brazilian cities. Argues that the variations in how citizens are empowered can be explained through an examination of the incentives for mayors to delegate authority and to control the structure of the program, along with an analysis of how community service organizations and individual citizens operate within the organization. One of the more comprehensive books on this subject.

INTERNATIONAL RELATIONS

GENERAL

MARY K. MEYER McALEESE, *Professor of Political Science, Eckerd College*

IN THE SCHOLARSHIP ON INTERNATIONAL RELATIONS reviewed for this biennium, two inter-related themes predominate: the perceived neglect of Latin America by the US due to its preoccupation with the War on Terror, and Latin American debates about the promise and problems of the region's integration efforts in the quest for development and autonomy. Interwoven with these major themes are the subthemes of the challenge of addressing growing social problems in Latin American and Caribbean countries in the context of neoliberal globalization and Latin America's deepening relations with Europe and Asia.

Three additional characteristics within this literature should be noted. The first is the relative paucity of US-based voices and the relative strength of Latin American- and European-based voices in discussing the major themes in the international relations of Latin American and Caribbean states. The second is that most of the works are edited volumes or collections of works by many different scholars, making it more difficult to highlight the specific subthemes of individual chapters from the broader focus of each compilation. The third characteristic of this scholarship is its temporal context: the vast majority (74 percent) of the works under review appeared between 2006 and 2008, during the final two years of the second George W. Bush administration and before the global financial crisis and recession became fully apparent. Nevertheless, several of the works anticipate the arrival of a new administration in Washington, and nearly all identify important policy issues facing the hemisphere.

A surprisingly small number of scholarly works directly examines US-Latin American relations. Looking back in time, Rodríguez Díaz revisits Elihu Root's ideas regarding Latin America in the early 20th century (item **1563**), while Delpar provides an interesting history of Latin Americanist scholarship in the US since 1850 (item **1538**). Grow reconsiders US presidential decisions to intervene in Latin American countries during the Cold War (item **1543**), and Hinojosa reviews the US narcotics control certification process with Colombia and Mexico during the 1990s (item **1544**). The November/December 2006 issue of *Nueva Sociedad* features essays by Abraham Lowenthal (item **1551**), Riordan Roett (item **1564**), and Roberto Russell (item **1565**) aimed at assessing the contemporary state of US-Latin American relations. Lowenthal and Roett, along with O'Neil (item **1555**), note the political costs of Washington's focus on the War on Terror to inter-American relations. They stress the changing political realities and complex socioeconomic conditions facing Latin American and Caribbean nations today which require more focused and nuanced US policy responses. They discuss the policy issues that matter most to Latin America and Caribbean states—trade, poverty and social inequality, migration, and public security—and that Washington either neglected or wrongly addressed in the framework of the War on Terror. These writers are generally skeptical about seeing much change in policy in the next president's administration (see also item **1569**), but offer thoughtful policy recommendations for resetting US policy toward the region (see especially O'Neil and item **1554**). In late 2007, a number of scholars (including Lowenthal) and 13 members of Congress discussed these various points at the Aspen Institute's Eighth Conference on US policy toward Latin America as the US prepared for an election year (item **1573**).

Impatient with Washington's inattention, Latin American scholars and policymakers contributed many worthwhile studies of the various issues shaping the politics and policy agenda of the hemisphere (e.g., item **1533**). An outstanding trilogy published in 2008 by FLACSO (Facultad Latinoamericana de Ciencias Sociales) is dedicated to contributing to hemispheric policy debates on the issues of trade, migration, and security. Each book in this trilogy offers rich empirical data and careful policy analysis from various Latin American perspectives (items **1529**, **1530**, and **1531**). Indeed, among the works under review, FLACSO published several strong collections of Latin American scholarship originally presented at its 50th anniversary congress in Quito in 2007, including (among others) Rivera Vélez's edited volume on "multidimensional" security issues (item **1567**) and Jaramillo's volume on the international relations and foreign policies of the region (item **1561**). These and other works under review take globalization as a given, employ multilevel analyses, embrace multilateralism, and tend to reject older notions of state security (e.g., item **1548**) as well as Washington's framework of security centered on the War on Terror. Instead, this scholarship seeks to redefine security issues in ways that are more relevant to Latin America's contemporary challenges.

Globalization and neoliberal reforms have entailed new transnational networks and transborder flows of goods, resources, people, and capital, leading to new political and security issues that states are hard-pressed to control effectively. Thus Alba Vega and Kruijt contribute a sobering review article on the alarming levels of social and criminal violence in the region, its transnational character, and the incapacity of governments to curb its growth (item **1527**). Salazar Medina's anthology recasts migration as a political decision by individuals disillusioned by their own government's weaknesses and calls for stronger international migration governance as part of North-South development cooperation (item **1558**). Taglioni and Théodat's anthology (item **1535**) examines licit and illicit transborder flows of people, goods, and businesses from a geo-economic perspective, underscoring the functional integration of the region beyond the control of states (see also item **1542**).

These and other issues receive sustained attention *inter alia* in various works focused on regional integration, which remains an ideal for achieving development, security, and autonomy in Latin America and the Caribbean. Reza (item **1562**) and Santana Castillo (item **1566**) contribute interesting intellectual histories of the ideals of Latin American unity and integration. Gambrill and Ruiz Nápoles provide a retrospective of Latin American and Caribbean integration experiments from the 1970s through the 1990s (item **1559**). Páez Montalbán and Vázquez Olivera present a very helpful reference work identifying the region's various integration agreements and organizations since World War II (item **1545**).

Pérez Fuentes offers a nuts-and-bolts public policy approach to regional integration as a development strategy from a Mexican perspective (item **1556**). Former Chilean President Ricardo Lagos edited an authoritative collection of papers by well-known scholars and policymakers debating the prospects for regional integration in the face of persistent poverty, regional fragmentation, and declining US power (item **1533**). FLACSO compilations by Solís and Rojas Aravena (item **1546**), Altmann and Rojas Aravena (item **1528**), and Jaramillo (item **1553**) contribute to this debate by critically evaluating the successes of and obstacles to contemporary regional integration experiments in Latin America and the Caribbean. Spain's Ministry of Defense adds an excellent anthology of Spanish scholarship that examines the UNASUR (Unión de Naciones del Sur, which replaced the Comunidad Sudamericana de Naciones in 2007), and considers its potential for addressing security challenges in South America through its Consejo Suramericano de Defensa (CSD), created in 2008 (item **1536**). Individual chapters in this anthology point to a recent regional arms race, underlying territorial disputes and bilateral tensions, and leadership rivalries that weaken the prospects for closer security cooperation in South America. Russell remains skeptical that Latin American and Caribbean countries will be able to translate their regional cooperation and integration ambitions into effective instruments for greater regional autonomy (item **1565**).

The ongoing debate within Latin America about the prospects for successful regional integration is complemented by debates about the prospects for deeper inter-regional integration between Latin America and the European Union. Trein and Guerra Cavalcanti are disappointed by the outcome of the 2006 inter-regional summit in Vienna (item **1572**). The authors are impatient with what they perceive as the EU's empty rhetoric rather than substantive progress in building a meaningful strategic partnership with Latin America and the Caribbean. However, Osterlof Obregón's collection is cautiously optimistic while examining the EU's proliferating bilateral and subregional partnership agreements in Latin America (item **1532**). The views from Spain are also diverse: Martín Arribas' anthology offers an optimistic Spanish view of cooperation between the EU and Latin American subregional organizations such as Mercosur, the Andean Community, etc. (item **1560**); however, Díaz Barrado's extensive anthology offers a more realistic assessment both of Latin American integration efforts and of EU-Latin American inter-regional cooperation (item **1557**).

A few works under review focus on Spain's bilateral relations with Latin American and Caribbean countries, including Toral's constructivist approach to examining Spanish foreign direct investment in the region (item **1571**), Noya's interesting empirical analysis of Spain's image in the region based on *Latinobarómetro* surveys (item **1552**), and Arenal's anthology on preparations for the region's bicentennial celebrations of independence from Spain (item **1534**). Looking towards Asia, China's growing economic and political relations with the region are examined by Ellis (item **1539**), who is skeptical of Latin American hopes for Beijing's promises to the region (which he dubs the "Beijing Consensus"), and by Lewis (item **1550**), who does not see China's presence as a threat to the region or to US interests there. González and Morales Muñoz's anthology introduces the general reader in Colombia to elements of Japanese culture, indicating an interest in nurturing bilateral relations with Japan (item **1549**).

The works under review signal that Latin American and Caribbean states continue to grapple with urgent problems like growing socioeconomic inequality, human insecurity, and political uncertainty. The negative effects of globalization exacerbate these problems and threaten recent progress toward democratic governance. Scholars from the region have provided some of the most salient analyses of these intermestic problems and have pointed to the ways these states might address them effectively. With policymakers in Washington distracted elsewhere, efforts toward deeper regional integration and stronger partnerships with extra-regional powers like the EU or China have been the main foreign policy focus of Latin American and Caribbean states in the period under review. While hopes for these efforts remained unfulfilled, the region anxiously awaits a new policy focus from Washington.

1527 Alba Vega, Carlos and **Dirk Kruijt.**
Viejos y nuevos actores violentos en América Latina: temas y problemas. (*Foro Int./México*, 47:3, julio/sept. 2007, p. 485–516, bibl.)

The authors present a detailed and sobering introductory essay for six articles in this issue of *Foro Internacional* focusing on the alarming increase in criminal and urban violence across Latin America in recent decades (for entries on three of the articles, see items **1102, 1467,** and **2399**). This phenomenon coincides with the transition to and consolidation of democratically elected governments along with ongoing economic crisis in the context of neoliberal globalization. Unlike the "traditional violence" of authoritarian regimes against "enemies of the state," new forms of violence emanating from criminal networks, private security forces, drug lords, and juvenile gangs have emerged. These new violent actors challenge the state's monopoly on the legitimate use of force and reveal the "empty government" of weak and perhaps failing states. In urban slums, these new violent actors often provide the only de facto form of local authority and protection as well as a sense of identity for the socially excluded, while local police and politicians are either absent or in collusion with the criminals. Reviewing case studies from major cities across the region, the authors draw general conclusions about what they see as one of the greatest challenges facing Latin American societies at the start of the 21st century.

1528 América Latina y el Caribe: ¿fragmentación o convergencia?: experiencias recientes de la integración. Edición de Josette Altmann Borbón y Francisco Rojas Aravena. Quito: FLACSO Ecuador: Ministerio de Cultura; Madrid: Fundación Carolina, 2008. 316 p.: bibl., ill. (Col. 50 años)

This strong collection of papers by Latin American scholars and policy practitioners considers whether or not the process of Latin American and Caribbean integration is advancing. Chapters include broader discussions of the meaning of regional integration for Latin America and the Caribbean as well as case studies of subregional integration. Setting this volume apart from several others under review, however, is a useful annex that includes a summary of key political events in Latin America in 2007, a bibliography of works published in that year on Latin American integration, and tables with key economic, social, and political indicators for the 2000–2007 period.

1529 América Latina y la segunda administración Bush: un debate sobre comercio. Edición de Jairo Hernández Milián y Ana Cristina Lizano Picado. San José: Editorial Juricentro: FLACSO, Secretaría General, 2008. 135 p.: bibl., ill.

This excellent trilogy seeks to contribute to a meaningful policy debate on three key issues on the agenda of US-Latin American relations: trade, migration (item **1530**), and security (item **1531**). Published with support from the Ford Foundation, the three volumes draw on Latin American scholarship from across FLACSO's various centers and present detailed analyses of the different dimensions of the issues in question. Each volume shares the same introductory chapter by the series editors providing an overview of the key findings of this project. Each volume then presents several chapters focused on one of the three issues, providing rich empirical detail and careful analysis. Each volume also includes a separate chapter offering a Brazilian perspective on the issue, and each contains numerous tables and graphs, an excellent bibliography, and an annex with the texts of speeches by Abraham Lowenthal and Mark Rosenberg advising the next US administration on how to improve US relations with Latin America and the Caribbean.

1530 América Latina y la segunda administración Bush: un debate sobre migración. Edición de Jairo Hernández Milián y Ana Cristina Lizano Picado. San José: Editorial Juricentro: FLACSO, Secretaría General, 2008. 140 p.: bibl., ill.

For review of this and another title in this series, see items **1529** and **1531**.

1531 América Latina y la segunda administración Bush: un debate sobre seguridad. Edición de Jairo Hernández Milián y Ana Cristina Lizano Picado. San José: Editorial Juricentro: FLACSO, Secretaría General, 2008. 196 p.: bibl., ill.

For review of this and another title in this series, see items **1529** and **1530**.

1532 América Latina y la Unión Europea: una integración esperanzadora pero esquiva. Edición de Doris Osterlof Obregón. Textos de Josette Altmann Borbón *et al.* San José: FLACSO, Secretaría General: Observatorio para las Relaciones Europa-América Latina, 2008. 158 p.: bibl., ill.

This clear and concise collection focuses on inter-regional integration efforts between Latin America and the European Union from a Latin American perspective. FLACSO's Secretary General Francisco Rojas Aravena provides a helpful introductory essay explaining how the vague idea in 1999 of creating a biregional "strategic partnership" has evolved into a series of subregional and bilateral Partnership Agreements between the EU and Latin America. These agreements go farther than US-sponsored free trade agreements with individual Latin American countries because the EU's partnership agreements include three fundamental "pillars": a free trade pillar, a political dialog pillar, and a development aid and cooperation pillar. Subsequent chapters by six Latin American economists and political scientists examine the partnership agreements between the EU and subregional entities including Mercosur, the

Comunidad Andino de Naciones (CAN), and Central American Common Market/SICA, as well as bilateral partnership agreements with Mexico and Chile. Individual chapters include informative tables, charts, and graphs. The book's editor has served as an international trade negotiator and diplomat for Costa Rica and teaches at the Universidad de Costa Rica specializing in trade and development issues.

1533 América Latina: ¿integración o fragmentación? Compilación de Ricardo Lagos Escobar. Textos de Eric Hobsbawm *et al.* Guadalajara, Mexico: Fundación Grupo Mayan; Buenos Aires: Edhasa, 2008. 644 p.: bibl.

Former Chilean President Ricardo Lagos brings together an impressive international team of scholars and policy practitioners who explore Latin America's place in the international system, the domestic and foreign policy challenges Latin American countries face, and how the region might strengthen its prospects for meaningful integration in an era marked by persistent regional fragmentation and emergent international power shifts. Within this broad framework, individual chapters include attention to regional security issues; Latin America's relations with the US, the European Union, and China; internal social and political conditions; and Latin America's role in the appearance of new issues on the international agenda such as the UN's Millennium Development Goals or energy politics. Contributors include Cynthia Arnson, Jorge Domínguez, Wolf Grabendorf, Monica Hirst, Eric Hobsbawm, Riordan Roett, Juan Gabriel Tokatlian, and Mario Vargas Llosa, as well as many other academic and government experts in the field who present realistic assessments and pragmatic options for the region.

1534 Arenal, Celestino del. España y América Latina 200 años después de la independencia: valoración y perspectivas. Presentación de Gustavo Suárez Pertierra. Madrid: Marcial Pons, 2009. 398 p.: bibl., ill.

This collection of articles focuses on Spain's relationship with Latin America as the bicentennial commemorations of the region's national independence movements get under way. The volume brings together

Spanish and Latin American academics to examine various aspects of contemporary Ibero-American relations with a particular focus on the identities, values, and interests shared and contested by states on both sides of the Atlantic. Chapters include general overviews of Spanish-Latin American relations since the mid-1970s; reviews of the annual Ibero-American Summits since the early 1990s and their recent institutionalization; and analyses of specific policy areas, such as Spanish aid and development cooperation policies with the region, trade and investment flows (with numerous helpful tables and graphs), migration issues and policies, and Spain's role in leading the development of EU-Latin American relations. The book closes with two chapters contemplating the plans for and meanings of the various national independence bicentennial commemorations at a time of global economic crisis and the struggle for greater social inclusion and social justice in Latin America. This collection was copublished by a Spanish think tank specializing in Spain's international relations.

1535 Coopération et intégration: perspectives panaméricaines. Sous la direction de François Taglioni et Jean Marie Dulix Théodat. Introduction par Daniel Van Eeuwen. Paris: Harmattan, 2008. 275 p.: ill., maps. (Coll. Géographie et cultures. Serie "culture et politique")

This collection takes a geographical or geo-economic approach to understanding various processes of regional and subregional integration in the Americas today. In the context of globalization and in the shadow of the US, Latin American and Caribbean countries must grapple with the fact that regional integration today means a reversal of older territorial models of the state: the national territory is no longer a fortress with consolidated borders; rather, it is a resource-space that can only serve national development if it can open itself up to neighbors and the rest of the world (p. 17–18). Individual chapters offer interesting glimpses of various kinds of cross-border flows from the microeconomic or ground level, creating a kind of functional integration beyond that foreseen or controlled by states. Pt. 2 includes several interesting chapters on licit and illicit flows of goods,

people, and production processes in Caribbean nations.

1536 La creación de UNASUR en el marco de la seguridad y la defensa. Textos de Isidro Sepúlveda Muñoz *et al.* Madrid: Ministerio de Defensa, 2010. 88 p. (Documentos de seguridad y defensa; 29)

Interesting and concise collection of papers analyzing the Unión de Naciones Suramericanas (UNASUR) in the context of new security challenges in South America and the recent "great silence" of the US regarding events in the region. Chapters examine the emergence, institutional design, tools, and goals of UNASUR and its Consejo Suramericano de Defensa (CSD), created in 2008 under the leadership of Brazil. Key issues discussed include the recent modernization of the armed forces in South America to meet new security challenges but which risks a regional arms race and threatens the delicate civil-military balance achieved with democratization; the continued relevance of older territorial disputes and bilateral tensions that may create obstacles to closer regional security cooperation; and the effectiveness of UNASUR's crisis management mechanism in response to Bolivia's 2008 political crisis while the OAS and the US sat on the sidelines. The CSD is not a military alliance, but rather only a mechanism to promote consultation on defense policy for states that continue to face important bilateral rivalries.

1537 Cueva Perus, Marcos. El nuevo mundo en la encrucijada. México: Editorial Itaca: UNAM-Instituto de Investigaciones Sociales, 2007. 318 p.: bibl.

The author takes an economic neostructuralist approach to interpret the crisis of US hegemony and its meaning for countries of Latin America and the Caribbean.

1538 Delpar, Helen. Looking South: the evolution of Latin Americanist scholarship in the United States, 1850–1975. Tuscaloosa: Univ. of Alabama Press, 2008. 241 p.: bibl., index.

Interesting history of the emergence and evolution of Latin American Area Studies as a focus of scholarship in the US. The author includes attention to challenges and controversies in the field as it emerged in the 19th century and reached its heyday in the mid-1970s, such as the uneasy relationship between academic research and government policies; the representations of "Latin America" by US scholars; the relationship between scholars based in Latin America and the US; the multidisciplinary nature of the field; and the roles of universities, foundations, and the US government in funding and framing the field in the 20th century. However, since the end of the Cold War, the processes of globalization and the rise of postmodern intellectual movements have called into question the notion of Latin America as a meaningful analytical category.

1539 Ellis, Robert Evan. China in Latin America: the whats and wherefores. Boulder, Colo.: Lynne Rienner Publishers, 2009. 329 p.: bibl., index.

Ellis is a security analyst and professor at the Center for Hemispheric Defense Studies at the National Defense University. Here he offers a highly detailed picture of China's growing presence in Latin America. Drawing from numerous press articles as well as personal interviews, government documents, and business and academic sources, Ellis examines China's economic, political, and military interests in Latin America, Latin American states' interests in cultivating relations with China, and the implications of these growing ties for the US. Descriptive case-study chapters that group countries by subregion (e.g., Southern Cone; Andean countries; and Mexico, Central America, and the Caribbean) are organized in a neat comparative framework that provides coverage of nearly every Latin American country's relationship with China along several dimensions. Ellis asserts that Latin American countries' short-term comparative advantage vis-à-vis China lies in their export of primary products, but this results in the long-term de-industrialization of the region as it imports increasingly sophisticated Chinese manufactured goods. Latin American countries are therefore misguided in believing that China provides an anti-imperialist alternative model of development and an escape from dependency (a belief Ellis dubs the "Beijing Consensus"). Ellis may at times overstate the salience of the Chinese presence in the region and its threat to US interests. For example, he suggests that long-established Chinese gangs in the triborder area of Argentina, Brazil, and Paraguay are part of a broader security threat to the US that China could someday exploit. Nevertheless, few other contemporary studies offer as detailed a picture of the Chinese presence in Latin America as this one.

1540 Emerson, R. Guy. Radical neglect?: the "War on Terror" and Latin America. (*Lat. Am. Polit. Soc.*, 52:1, Spring 2010, p. 33–62, bibl., graphs)

The rise of leftist governments in the Americas and the adoption of policy initiatives contrary to US interests highlight a disconnect in inter-American relations that cannot be understood simply as US "neglect" of Latin America. This article examines whether the War on Terror acted as a guiding paradigm for the George W. Bush administration's foreign policy toward Latin America. Opposition to this War on Terror paradigm was evident following Colombia's 2008 air strike in Ecuador and Emerson argues that this Colombia-Latin America division reflects a larger geostrategic disconnect, whereby the War on Terror is challenged, causing the increasing marginalization of Washington and resistance to US policy. [C.E. Griffin]

1541 Empire and dissent: the United States and Latin America. Edited by Fred Rosen. Durham, N.C.: Duke Univ. Press, 2008. 263 p.: bibl., index. (American encounters/global interactions)

Collection of critical interpretive essays about the relationship between the US and Latin America, edited by a NACLA (North American Congress on Latin America) contributing editor.

1542 Fronteras y globalización: Europa-Latinoamérica. Coordinación de Luis Silván Sada. Zaragoza, Spain: Prensas Univ. de Zaragoza, 2008. 272 p.: bibl., ill.

Only two chapters include attention to Latin America: one focusing on borders in the region during the Spanish colonial period and another comparing tourist sites at border areas in Europe and Latin America, including some discussion of the cosmopolitan triborder area between Argentina, Brazil, and Paraguay.

1543 Grow, Michael. U.S. presidents and Latin American interventions: pursuing regime change in the Cold War. Lawrence: Univ. Press of Kansas, 2008. 266 p.: bibl., index, map.

Grow examines eight cases of direct US intervention in Latin America during the Cold War. Rather than finding objective national security interests or economic factors as precipitating causes of these interventions, Grow identifies three different factors as having more powerful explanatory power in the decisions to intervene: presidential concerns with maintaining an image of US international credibility in the Cold War, the presidents' concerns for their own domestic political image and prestige, and the lobbying efforts of Latin American and Caribbean political actors in favor of such interventions.

1544 Hinojosa, Victor Javier. Domestic politics and international narcotics control: U.S. relations with Mexico and Colombia, 1989–2000. New York: Routledge, 2007. 122 p.: bibl., index. (Studies in international relations)

Based on the author's dissertation, this book uses narcotics control cooperation between the US and both Mexico and Colombia as test cases to investigate a number of hypotheses on the relationship between domestic and international politics (two-level games) in international bargaining. Hinojosa finds generally weak support for his various hypotheses (which relate to four domestic-level variables: electoral tests, presidential popularity, executive-legislative relations, and reputation of the Colombian president), but he provides useful descriptions of the policy shifts in the three countries on narcotics control cooperation and the disparate treatment of Mexico and Colombia by the US in its antidrug certification process.

Instituciones y procesos políticos en América Latina: siglos XIX y XX. See *HLAS 66:431.*

1545 Integración latinoamericana: organismos y acuerdos, 1948–2008. Coordinación de Rodrigo Páez Montalbán y Mario Vázquez Olivera. México: UNAM, Centro de Investigaciones sobre América Latina y el Caribe: Ediciones y Gráficos Eón, 2008. 294 p.: bibl., col. ill., col. maps.

This excellent reference book identifies and summarizes the various integration agreements and organizations produced by Latin American and Caribbean states over a 60-year period. Free trade agreements with the US and Canada are also included. For each agreement or scheme listed, the general history, characteristics, basic documents, organizational evolution and structure, membership, etc., are concisely presented. This helpful volume includes several excellent color maps illustrating the geographies of the various trade and integration schemes and their relationships to each other.

1546 La integración latinoamericana: visiones regionales y subregionales. Coordinación de Luis Guillermo Solís Rivera y Francisco Rojas Aravena. San José: Editorial Juricentro: OBREAL: FLACSO Secretaría General, 2006. 378 p.: bibl.

A joint publication of FLACSO and OBREAL (El Observatorio de las Relaciones Unión Europea-América Latina), a project created by the Director General of External Relations of the European Commission and financed through EuropeAid. This collection includes two overview chapters on regional integration, three chapters on South American (i.e., Brazilian, Chilean, and Ecuadorian) perspectives on or experiences with regional integration, and two chapters on Central American integration (with perspectives from El Salvador and Costa Rica). A penultimate chapter questions existing models of integration, particularly in light of regional fragmentation and the disappointing 2006 Vienna Summit between the European Union and Latin America and the Caribbean. A final chapter considers Cuba's development model in a regional context. The final Declaration of the Vienna Summit is included as an annex to this collection.

1547 Iran in Latin America: threat or "axis of annoyance"? Edited by Cynthia Arnson, Hālāh Isfandiyārī, and Adam Stubits. Washington, D.C.: Woodrow Wilson International Center for Scholars, 2010. 118 p.: bibl., ill. (Woodrow Wilson Center reports on the Americas; 23)

Uneven collection of essays from a 2008 conference speculating on the nature and extent of Iran's recent relations with Bolivia, Ecuador, Nicaragua, and Venezuela, and its alleged involvement in a pair of anti-Israeli bombings in Argentina in the 1990s.

1548 Kahhat, Farid. Tras la Guerra Fría: mentalidad militar y políticas de seguridad en Sudamérica. Lima: Fondo Editorial del Congreso del Perú, 2008. 227 p.: bibl.

Kahhat presents several essays on how "security" is conceived in the broader international relations literature and in the Southern Cone countries of Argentina, Brazil, Chile, and Peru. Essay topics include a consideration of older notions of state security versus newer notions of "human security" and of 19th century philosophical influences on the security discourse adopted by the region's military regimes in the 1970s and 1980s. The author also evaluates balance of power and democratic peace theories for their relevance in the Southern Cone, and concludes with a short essay on the uneasy relations between Chile and Peru.

1549 Kôten: lecturas cruzadas Japón-América Latina. Edición de Javier González y Sandra Morales Muñoz. Bogotá: Editorial Pontificia Univ. Javeriana, 2005. 305 p.: bibl., ill. (some col.), maps.

In this collection of essays on Japanese culture, the editors seek to promote a deeper appreciation for Japan while avoiding the pitfalls and stereotypes of Orientalism. Translations and discussions of Japanese poetry, religion, philosophy, art, and culture are included in this volume aimed at the general reader. The editors assert that Japan is the only "Eastern" country that makes up part of the leadership of the Western technical-financial world, and is the only non-Western country that participates in decisions taken at the highest levels of global society. As such, the evolution of the Japanese mindset is valuable to all "Others" in their cultural opposition to the West (p. 17).

1550 Lewis, Peter M. La presencia de China en América Latina: un tema controvertido. (*Estud. Int./Santiago,* 39:156, enero/marzo 2007, p. 27–53)

The author presents a realistic assessment of China's interests and behavior in Latin America and the implications for US national security interests. Contrary to some alarmist views propounded by special interests and expressed in the US Congress and the media about "the China threat," Lewis uses a rational-actor framework and calmly discusses the reasons that the PRC does not constitute a threat to US security interests in its own "backyard."

1551 Lowenthal, Abraham F. From regional hegemony to complex bilateral relations: the United States and Latin America in the early 21st century. (*Nueva Soc.,* 206, nov./dic. 2006, p. 63–77)

Lowenthal paints a clear picture of the changing economic, social, and political context of US-Latin American relations. While the "hegemonic presumption" of the US toward Latin America and the Caribbean has not been completely eclipsed, the bases, structures, and interests of US hegemony have changed significantly, as has the region itself. Latin America and the Caribbean today constitute at least five distinct subregions, each of which presents particular challenges and requires particular approaches. Moreover, in this highly differentiated landscape, nongovernmental actors of all types can influence the highly permeable US policy agenda, making it increasingly impossible for the US to develop a single policy orientation toward the region. Instead, US-Latin American relations are increasingly complex, multifaceted, and contradictory. While the US remains the most important power in the hemisphere, Lowenthal anticipates a greater leadership role for Brazil, Chile, and Argentina in forging new proposals and projects for inter-American relations. However, there is a serious need to educate the US public and members of Congress about the growing functional integration of the US with its closest neighbors and the changing broader context of inter-American relations.

Merrill, Dennis. Negotiating paradise: U.S. tourism and empire in twentieth-century Latin America. See *HLAS 66:1333.*

1552 Noya, Francisco Javier. La nueva imagen de España en América Latina. Prólogo de Felipe González. Madrid: Tecnos: Real Instituto Elcano, 2009. 547 p.: bibl., ill. (Ventana Abierta)

Noya presents an interesting and detailed empirical study of Spain's public image in Latin America based on *Latinobarómetro* surveys since 2003, the first such study of its kind. Noya notes a certain

Spanish sensitivity about Latin American criticisms of its recent foreign direct investments in the region and an awareness of renewed negative images of the Spanish conquest propounded by anti-imperialist, populist, or postcolonialist voices in the region. The prologue by González signals that Spain is eager to cultivate a more positive image and enhance its soft power in Latin America in the run-up to national independence bicentennial commemorations. The study presents numerous detailed tables and graphs that reveal a generally positive image of Spain held by ordinary citizens in Latin America and include comparisons with the EU and the US. Statistical analyses also control for country, class, ethnicity, and gender. Published by the Spanish think tank Real Instituto Elcano, which helped expand the *Latinobarómetro* survey to include questions concerning Spain's image in the region.

1553 Los nuevos enfoques de la integración: más allá del regionalismo.
Compilación de Grace Jaramillo. Quito: FLACSO Ecuador: Ministerio de Cultura del Ecuador, 2008. 280 p.: bibl., ill., maps.

Excellent collection of papers focused on integration originally presented as part of FLACSO's 50th Anniversary Congress (Quito, 2007). Theoretically and methodologically diverse chapters seek to evaluate critically the successes and challenges of regional integration experiments in Latin America following the failures of the US-sponsored Free Trade Area of the Americas (FTAA) project in 2003 and of the Doha Round of the World Trade Organization (WTO) in 2006. Chapters include attention to the Comunidad Andino de Naciones (CAN), Mercosur, and other regional integration schemes, as well as inter-regional cooperation experiments between Latin America and the EU or APEC. Common themes across several chapters include the competition between the US and the EU for market access agreements with Latin American integration organizations, the "soft hegemony" of Brazil, and the sometimes-contradictory foreign policies of Latin American states that undermine the strategic goal of regional integration. See also item **1561**.

1554 The Obama administration and the Americas: agenda for change. Edited by Abraham F. Lowenthal, Theodore J. Piccone, and Laurence Whitehead. Washington, D.C.: Brookings Institution Press, 2009. 235 p.: bibl., index.

This book grew out of a project of the Partnership for the Americas Commission, convened by the Brookings Institution, and seeks to advise the incoming Obama administration on how to improve the quality of US relations with Latin America and the Caribbean. Three introductory chapters stress overarching questions such as strengthening cooperation, building partnerships, and supporting democracy in the Americas; case study chapters focus on US bilateral relations with Bolivia, Colombia, Cuba, Haiti, Mexico, and Venezuela.

O'Brien, Thomas F. Making the Americas: the United States and Latin America from the age of revolutions to the era of globalization. See *HLAS 66:449*.

1555 O'Neil, Shannon. Las nuevas relaciones EE UU-Latinoamérica. (*Polít. Exter./Madrid*, 22:124, julio/agosto 2008, p. 95–105)

O'Neil is the Douglas Dillon Fellow at the Council on Foreign Relations and a specialist in US-Latin American relations. Writing in an election year, O'Neil surveys the challenges and options the next US president and Congress must consider to reassert leadership and ensure US interests in Latin America. Declaring decades-old policies in the areas of trade, drug trafficking, and democracy-promotion to be crumbling, O'Neil reviews important contemporary realities in Latin America and highlights their interwoven nature with realities and interests in the US. O'Neil identifies problems in four issue areas: poverty and inequality in the region, public security (particularly growing criminality and gang violence), migration movements, and energy security. She recommends that the US should help strengthen Latin American states' capacity to address these problems, undertake meaningful immigration reform that balances the needs of the US labor market with the needs of sending states and of migrants, and develop alternative and sustainable energy sources in partnership with the region. She also highlights the need for the US to reset its diplomatic relations with Brazil, Mexico, Venezuela, and Cuba.

1556 Pérez Fuentes, Judith. Integración y desarrollo: buscando alternativas para América Latina. México: Estados Unidos Mexicanos, Cámara de Diputados, LX Legislatura, Consejo Editorial: Miguel Ángel Porrúa, 2009. 363 p.: bibl., ill. (Políticas públicas serie) (Conocer para decidir)

The author presents a public policy approach to regional integration that incorporates both public and private actors in the quest for industrialization and development. After reviewing theories of economic development and integration, the role of the state and public policy in the integration process, and the Latin American experience with regional integration schemes, Pérez Fuentes calls for mechanisms that can incorporate, coordinate, and animate regional governments and businesses more effectively to create regional industrialization with stronger vertical and horizontal linkages.

1557 Perspectivas sobre las relaciones entre la Unión Europea y América Latina. Edición de Cástor Miguel Díaz Barrado, Carlos R. Fernández Liesa y Pablo Zapatero. Coordinación de Amparo Alcoceba Gallego *et al.* Madrid: Univ. Carlos III de Madrid: Boletín Oficial del Estado, 2008. 562 p.: bibl. (Col. monografías; 56)

Large collection of papers exploring various aspects of EU-Latin American relations from a primarily Spanish perspective. Chapters examine inter-regional political relations and summit meetings, inter-regional economic relations, the Latin American integration process, and new areas of inter-regional cooperation such as security, migration, organized crime, environment and natural disasters, protection of indigenous peoples, education, science and technology, and culture. An underlying theme explores the meaning of the "bi-regional strategic partnership" envisioned in the inter-regional summits since 1999 and assesses the progress, obstacles, and gaps in its development.

1558 Políticas migratorias: hacia la gobernabilidad de las migraciones transnacionales. Edición de Richard Salazar Medina. Quito: Centro Andino de Estudios Internacionales, Univ. Andina Simón Bolívar: Corporación Editora Nacional, 2009. 231 p.: bibl., ill. (Serie Estudios internacionales; 7)

Collection of papers from an international symposium on migration (Quito, June 2008). The volume seeks to begin a dialog between the Global North and the Global South in search of better governance of migration as part of a more effective development strategy. These papers move beyond traditional approaches to migration that focus on economic and social factors. Instead, they put the state and state policies, particularly those of sending countries, at the forefront of analysis and frame migration as a political act by individuals dissatisfied with their own government or its policies. Cases from Mexico, El Salvador, and Ecuador, as well as a brief overview of migration policies in other Latin American countries, are offered. Other chapters include attention to human rights and labor rights as key elements to migration governance; however, the issue of human trafficking is not addressed.

Powell, Philip Wayne. Tree of hate: propaganda and prejudices affecting United States relations with the Hispanic world. See *HLAS 66:452.*

1559 Procesos de integración en las Américas. Edición de Mónica C. Gambrill y Pablo Ruiz Nápoles. México: UNAM, Centro de Investigaciones sobre América del Norte, 2006. 181 p.: bibl.

Collection of essays reviewing old and new theories of integration, addressing certain methodological and empirical questions in the study of integration, and presenting case studies of NAFTA, CAFTA, and the Andean Community from the 1970s through the 1990s.

1560 Las relaciones entre la Unión Europea y América Latina: cooperación al desarrollo y/o asociación estratégica? Coordinación de Juan José Martín Arribas. Burgos, Spain: Univ. de Burgos, 2008. 209 p.: bibl., ill.

Martín Arribas and other Spanish scholars provide a somewhat idealized description of EU-Latin American relations in order to show the relations rest on much more than narrow development aid and cooperation mechanisms. The biregional strategic partnership rests on broader shared political interests and goals such as multilateralism in international affairs and the promotion of human rights and democratic governance. This strategic partnership has deepened the inter-regional dialog originally started with the Rio Group in 1990, and has produced a number of instruments to help institutionalize the relationship, such as development-financing mechanisms as well as "horizontal" educational, business, municipal, and environmental cooperation schemes. The last chapter focuses on Spanish trade and investment in Latin America and includes an annex with detailed tables and graphs.

1561 Relaciones internacionales: los nuevos horizontes. Compilación de Grace Jaramillo. Quito: FLACSO: Ministerio de Cultura, 2009. 270 p.: bibl.

Eclectic collection of papers focusing on international relations topics presented as part of FLACSO's 50th Anniversary Congress in 2007. The chapters in this compilation offer critical perspectives and multilevel analyses of relations between Latin American countries and the rest of the world. Topics include Latin America's relations with the US and with China, studies of the foreign policies of Ecuador and Colombia, the roles of nonstate actors and transnational networks in the region's international relations, security integration in South America, transnational human rights issues in the region, and the timid role of the OAS in responding to democratic crises in the region in 2005. Arlene Tickner contributes an interesting discourse analysis of Colombia's special "intervention by invitation" relationship with the US.

1562 Reza, Germán A. de la. La invención de la paz: de la república cristiana del duque de Sully a la sociedad de naciones de Simón Bolívar. México: Univ. Autónoma Metropolitana, Azcapotzalco: Siglo Veintiuno Editores, 2009. 170 p.: bibl., index. (Historia)

The author presents a fine intellectual history of the idea of international confederation, from the ancient Greek Delphic leagues through the writings of European Enlightenment thinkers to the Latin American Congresses of the 19th century. Extracts from the writings of the Duke of Sully, Rousseau, and Leibniz, as well as Latin American Treaties of Confederation from 1823 and 1848, are included in the annexes.

1563 Rodríguez Díaz, María del Rosario. Elihu Root y la política estadounidense en América Latina y el Caribe, 1899–1908. Morelia, Mexico: Univ. Michoacana de San Nicolás de Hidalgo, Instituto de Investigaciones Históricas, 2006. 157 p.: bibl. (Investigaciones; 3)

This slim volume traces Elihu Root's ideas and approaches to US relations with Latin America while he served as the US Secretary of War from 1899–1904 and as Secretary of State from 1904–1908. The author is an expert on Root and draws heavily from the Root Papers archive housed at New York Public Library (http://www.nypl.org/archives/1842).

1564 Roett, Riordan. Estados Unidos y América Latina: estado actual de las relaciones. (*Nueva Soc.*, 206, nov./dic. 2006, p. 110–125, ill.)

Roett identifies a number of policy challenges and failures that the George W. Bush administration faced regarding Latin America. The defeat of Bush's immigration reform bill, specifically his guest worker program, and Congress' subsequent decision to build a wall at the US-Mexican border instead, were major setbacks. Then Congress rejected the Free Trade Agreement of the Americas (FTAA). Then the Doha Round of the World Trade Organization (WTO) collapsed, with Latin American states playing an important role in those negotiations. With these domestic and international failures, the administration's focus toward Latin America became more negative and reactive. The rise of Venezuela's Chávez, the uncertainty about Cuba's future leadership, and the growing commercial and financial presence of China in Latin America provoked concerns and provided fodder for the political right in the US. These policy failures created important challenges for the next president, but Roett is skeptical about seeing a substantive policy change for the future.

1565 Russell, Roberto. América Latina para Estados Unidos: ¿especial, desdeñable, codiciada o perdida? (*Nueva Soc.*, 206, nov./dic. 2006, p. 48–62, ill., table)

Russell provides a critical review of four competing visions of inter-American relations, weighing them against contemporary political realities. The liberalist vision, summed up as the "Western Hemisphere Idea," stresses inter-American community, cooperation, harmony of interests, and mutually beneficial commercial integration. The realist vision stresses the general—and growing—irrelevance of Latin America to Washington's more global concerns and commitments. The anti-imperialist vision stresses Latin America's role as the economic base and military rearguard for US imperialist aspirations around the world. A fourth and more recent vision sees the US as a declining hegemonic power in Latin America as a result of imperial overstretch in other parts of the world. This less familiar vision stresses Latin America's moves since the 1970s and 1980s toward greater economic and political autonomy and subregional integration. Russell provides a skilled discussion and critique of each vision and concludes that Washington is actually disposed toward establishing "spheres of responsibility" in the region that provide opportunities for greater Latin American autonomy; however, Latin American countries have thus far failed to use that autonomy effectively.

1566 Santana Castillo, Joaquín. Utopía, identidad e integración: en el pensamiento latinoamericano y cubano. La Habana: Editorial de Ciencias Sociales, 2008. 306 p.: bibl. (Tesis col.)

Diverse and interesting collection of essays by a Cuban philosopher and historian. One essay focuses specifically on the history of the integrationist idea in Latin American thought and its prospects today.

1567 Seguridad multidimensional en América Latina. Edición de Fredy Rivera Vélez. Quito: FLACSO: Ministerio de Cultura, 2008. 511 p.: bibl., ill. (50 Años)

Written for FLACSO's 50th Anniversary Congress, this thoughtful collection of papers explores the various meanings and challenges of "security" across Latin America within the context of globalization. These papers are critical of neorealist definitions of "national security, " especially as conceived and applied by policymakers in Washington in the global War on Terror. Instead, the various authors apply broader notions of human security that have greater relevance for Latin American societies today. Papers are divided into five sections that examine border security and "forced" migration; the relationship of the armed forces to civil society and politics; narcotrafficking; social violence and crime; and security cooperation between states in the region. Josefina Lynn contributes a particularly interesting chapter on the myth of the terrorist threat in the so-called triborder area between Argentina, Brazil, and Paraguay, an area that caused concern for some policymakers in Washington early in the War on Terror.

1568 Shamise, Yasmine. Missed opportunity: Canada's re-engagement with Latin America and the Caribbean. (*Can. J. Lat. Am. Caribb. Stud.*, 35:69, 2010, p. 171–201)

Economic performance throughout the region during the 1980s, dubbed "the lost decade," was dismal. However, by the end of the 1990s Canada had become an important hemispheric player, a strong advocate for the Free Trade Area of the Americas (FTAA), and a respected defender of representative democracy in the region. It further boosted its profile in the region by hosting several important inter-American meetings: the FTAA Trade Ministerial on Nov. 1, 1999, the General Assembly of the OAS in June 2000, and the Quebec City Summit of the Americas in April 2001. Although the prospects for an FTAA have faded, this statement neatly encapsulates Canada's ongoing approach to hemispheric affairs. [C.E. Griffin]

1569 Smith, Peter H. Talons of the eagle: Latin America, the United States, and the world. 3rd ed. New York: Oxford Univ. Press, 2008. 438 p.: bibl., ill., index, maps.

Smith takes a historically based political science approach to understand US-Latin American relations in this widely used textbook on inter-American relations, now in its 3rd edition. He identifies four major historical periods of inter-American relations: the Imperial Era (1790s–1930s), the Cold War (1940s-80s), the Decade of Uncertainty (1990–2001), and the War on Terror (2001-present). Within each period, Smith examines the prevailing international political structures; the economic, political, and strategic interests of both the US and Latin American states; and the intellectual or ideational currents shaping the worldviews (or social constructions of reality) in both parts of the hemisphere. Smith is adept at drawing from multiple disciplines (history, economics, political science, international relations, and literature and cultural studies), integrating international and domestic levels of analysis, and incorporating Latin American perspectives to paint a nuanced picture of the patterns and paradoxes of inter-American relations. He resists predictions for the future, but sees "centrifugal political forces throughout Latin America" and rivalries for subregional leadership that make Bolivarian solidarity "more elusive than ever" (p. 414). Smith holds that as long as the US War on Terror prevails, Latin America is likely to endure neglect from its neighbor to the north. For reviews of earlier editions, see *HLAS 57:4052* and *HLAS 59:4211*.

1570 Sosa Fuentes, Samuel. Globalización y crisis de la modernidad: los cambios globales de la vida social en el sistema mundial. (*Relac. Int./México*, 98, mayo/agosto 2007, p. 35–72)

The author attempts to combine historical-structural analysis and a critical postmodern framework to understand the "instrumental logic of capitalist modernity called globalization." Extensive quotation of neo-Marxist and postmodern writers based inside and outside of Latin America may be of interest to some readers.

1571 Toral, Pablo. The foreign direct investments of Spanish multinational enterprises in Latin America, 1989–2005. (*J. Lat. Am. Stud.*, 40:3, Aug. 2008, p. 513–545, table)

Toral uses a social constructivist framework to study the significant growth of Spanish foreign direct investment in Latin America across four key industries over a 16-year period: telecommunications,

banking, oil and natural gas, and public utilities. With substantial help from the Spanish government, seven Spanish firms in these industries modernized, grew, and gained important knowledge about how to navigate privatization and liberalization policies in a national and European context in the 1980s and 1990s. That experience gave the firms' managers significant advantages while investing in Latin American markets during the region's neoliberal reform process of the 1990s and early 2000s and contributed to the resumption of economic growth in Latin America during that period. The author provides an interesting and detailed analysis of how these firms became so prominent in these key industrial sectors in Latin America. He also reveals the oligopolistic cooperation between these firms, their strong relationship with the Spanish government, and the role of the Spanish government in promoting this investment as part of its diplomatic initiatives in Latin America.

1572 Trein, Franklin and Flávia Guerra Cavalcanti. Uma análise crítica do acordo de associação estratégica entre a União Européia e a América Latina e o Caribe: a Cúpula de Viena. (*Rev. Bras. Polít. Int.*, 50:1, 2007, p. 66–85)

The authors are disappointed that the Vienna Summit of May 2006 between the European Union and Latin American and Caribbean states did not deepen the strategic partnership proposed at the first inter-regional summit held in Rio in 1999. They link the Vienna Summit's failure to incorrect European perceptions that Latin America was experiencing an "integration crisis" and even "fragmentation of the continent" at the time. These ideas were touted by the US following Venezuela's withdrawal from the CAN (Comunidad Andina de Naciones) and Bolivia's nationalization of multinational petroleum companies, including Petrobras, shortly before the Vienna Summit. The authors counter that Venezuela's action was merely a rejection of US free trade bilateralism and helped shift the axis of regional integration toward Mercosur. Moreover, as Europe's own differentiated integration experience demonstrates, Latin America's integration processes cannot be expected to be free from minor disagreements or variable speeds in moving forward. The authors trace the history of EU-Latin American relations across four phases, noting the slow but general deepening of relations between the two regions until the Vienna Summit. The authors are concerned that the biannual inter-regional summit meetings have become merely rhetorical exercises with little institutionalization occurring. An ambitious biregional strategic partnership can develop if the leaders have the political will to abandon the discourse of South American "fragmentation."

1573 U.S. policy in Latin America: eighth conference, November 27–December 2, 2007. Directed by Dick Clark. Washington, D.C.: Aspen Institute, 2008. 42 p. (Congressional program; 22)

Summary report of the Aspen Institute's Congressional Program's Eighth Conference held in Guanacaste, Costa Rica. Thirteen members of the US Congress and a number of scholars participated in this conference, with presentations by Latin America experts Pamela Starr, Javier Corrales, Abraham Lowenthal, and Peter Hakim aimed at informing members of Congress about the key issues on the regional agenda, discussing their implications, and highlighting key challenges ahead for the new presidential administration.

Which way Latin America?: hemispheric politics meets globalization. See item **1845.**

MEXICO AND CENTRAL AMERICA

ANDREW D. SELEE, *Director, Mexico Institute, Woodrow Wilson International Center for Scholars*

THE BOOKS AND ARTICLES ABOUT MEXICO in this period show an overwhelming interest in the redefinition of Mexican foreign policy vis-à-vis other countries and regions in the world. They also demonstrate a marked rise in research and writing about actors other than the federal government, including state governments, migrants, and NGOs, and about a wide range of issues from migration to trade to public security.

This shift reflects the fact that in the first years of the new millennium, Mexico's relations with the world have become more complex as the country has embraced competitive democracy and inserted itself more actively in the global arena. While issues involving NAFTA and the US are still important, they are by no means the only subject under review in this period. At the same time, Central American scholars are overwhelmingly concerned with questions of integration, primarily within the region, as these countries seek to find relevance in the international system.

Several of the works in this period focus on assessing the Fox administration's foreign policy and Mexico's major challenges in the 21st century. Noteworthy examples include the two important collections by Covarrubias on Mexican foreign policy (items **1602** and **1631**) and equally valuable efforts by Vega, Garza Elizondo, Navarrete, and Uscanga, which all take a broad look at how Mexican foreign policy has shifted with democracy and globalization. A well-written article by Velázquez does a good job making a balanced assessment of the shortcomings of the Fox administration's foreign policy (item **1635**).

There is a burgeoning literature on Mexico's principal foreign policy challenges beyond North America, including relations with Latin America and the

Caribbean (items **1595**, **1596**, **1609**, **1620**, and **1640**), Europe (item **1619**), Asia (items **1576**, **1583**, **1600**, **1614**, **1627**, and **1637**), Africa (item **1633**), and the Middle East (item **1592**). The quantity and quality of the works on Asia is particularly noticeable, reflecting the rise of Asia as a source of both diplomatic opportunity and potential economic challenge for Mexico. Several works also focus on Mexico's engagement in multilateral fora, including works on Mexico's role in the UN (item **1629**), the Organization of American States (item **1578**), international law after 9/11 (item **1616**), and cultural cooperation generally (item **1589**).

Perhaps most significantly in this period, a series of studies of public opinion on foreign policy (items **1604**, **1605**, and **1623**) highlight for the first time how average citizens view foreign policy, a testament to the democratic shift in Mexican politics. At the same time, another work (item **1636**) makes a detailed assessment of the role that state governments play in determining foreign policy.

The US and Canada continue to be an important focus of studies, including assessments of NAFTA (items **1588** and **1638**) and North America generally (items **1581**, **1585**, and **1625**), and studies that focus broadly on policy coordination between the US and Mexico (items **1577**, **1624**, and **1632**). The study by Weintraub merits particular mention as a vital re-evaluation about how asymmetry works in the relationship between Mexico and the US, suggesting that Mexico is hardly powerless in bilateral affairs (item **1639**). Ferrer Silva's study on Mexico's lobbying efforts provides interesting insights from a foreign policy professional (item **1593**).

However, increasingly, most of the Mexico-US studies focus on specific issue areas and transnational actors. There is a wealth of research on migration, for example, including a major work that assesses trends in migration and migration management by Escobar and Martin (item **1603**), a labor market analysis of the border region (item **1601**), a study of migration between Guatemala and Mexico (item **1641**), a prize for essays by migrants in the US (item **1582**), and an interesting study of the Border Patrol (item **1597**). There is also a useful study of environmental issues (item **1615**) and of the treatment of minors in the criminal justice system in the border region (item **1598**). A series of essays by Monroy on the relationship between Mexico and the US merits reading for a perceptive analysis of how the two countries are linked. Finally, an extensive study of US-Mexico security cooperation (item **1626**) sheds lights on challenges ranging from arms trafficking, money laundering, and judicial reform to a history of organized crime on both sides of the border and in Central America.

Among the most interesting works in this period is one that looks at labor insertion by women in two Mexican cities, finding greater opportunities than once believed (item **1630**), and another study (item **1587**) that finds Mexican citizens' attitudes towards economic integration with the US heavily shaped by their general assessment of the neighboring country.

The works on Central America focus overwhelmingly on issues of integration, including a broad analysis of the experience among Central American countries (item **1647**), the lessons from the European Union for the Sistema de la Integración Centroamericana (SICA) (item **1645**), and the dangers of globalization for Costa Rica (item **1642**). A historical work on Nicaragua-Japan relations (item **1644**) covers more than a century. One of the more interesting works looks specifically at the ways in which different actors shaped the labor provisions of CAFTA and the effects these are likely to have on trade and labor rights (item **1618**).

MEXICO

1574 Alanís Enciso, Fernando Saúl. Que
se queden allá: el gobierno de México
y la repatriación de mexicanos en Estados
Unidos, 1934–1940. Tijuana, Mexico: El Colegio de la Frontera Norte; San Luis Potosí,
Mexico: El Colegio de San Luis, 2007. 346 p.:
bibl., ill., maps. (El Colef)

This book offers an in-depth study of
how the Mexican government responded to
the possible and actual repatriation of Mexicans in the US during the Lázaro Cárdenas administration. The author finds that
though much planning was done, there were
relatively few new proposals and few Mexicans abroad actually returned compared
to the earlier period of forced repatriation
during the Great Depression.

**1575 Alcances y límites de la política
exterior de México ante el nuevo escenario internacional: ensayos en honor de
Mario Ojeda.** Coordinación de Gustavo Vega
Cánovas. México: Colegio de México, 2009.
398 p.: bibl., ill.

This volume honors the work of
Mario Ojeda, especially his seminal book
*Alcances y límites de la política exterior en
México* (see *HLAS 41:8638* and *42:2341* for
comments on the original publication), and
presents essays by many of Mexico's leading foreign policy thinkers about Ojeda and
about current issues in foreign policy seen
through the realist lens that he helped bring
to the study of Mexican foreign policy. The
chapters in the volume cover topics ranging
from his legacy and influences to ongoing
challenges for North American integration,
migration issues with the US, and the rise
of China.

1576 Arellano, Rogelio. Consecuencias
para América Latina del surgimiento
de China en el escenario económico mundial: el caso de México. (*Integr. Comer.*,
10:24, enero/junio 2006, p. 225–265, bibl.,
graphs, tables)

This detailed and well-documented
article suggests that Mexico faces long-
term competitiveness challenges, which
will make it difficult to adjust to China's
entry into the global economy. The article
presents crucial data on Mexico-China trade
trends and China's effect on Mexico-US
trade.

1577 Benítez Manaut, Raúl. México-
Estados Unidos: paradigmas de una
inevitable y conflictiva relación. (*Nueva
Soc.*, 206, nov./dic. 2006, p. 140–155, ill.,
tables)

The author argues that cooperation
between Mexico and the US has deepened
significantly in recent years, but that both
policy differences and public opinion make
deeper cooperation difficult. Both countries
have sectors that are deeply isolationist, and
which resist efforts at collaboration. At the
same time, the lack of progress in the immigration debate in the US has damaged that
country's image in Mexico, while Mexico's
unwillingness to pursue greater security
and defense cooperation limits a key area of
possible coordination.

Benítez Manaut, Raúl. La seguridad nacional en la indefinida transición: mitos y
realidades del sexenio de Vicente Fox. See
item **1047**.

1578 Bobadilla González, Leticia. México
y la OEA: los debates diplomáticos,
1959–1964. México: Secretaría de Relaciones
Exteriores, Dirección General del Acervo
Histórico Diplomático, 2006. 288 p.: bibl.,
ill., index, plates.

The author addresses the history of
Mexico's diplomacy in the five years from
the Cuban Revolution in 1959 to the OAS
resolution in 1964 urging member countries
to suspend their diplomatic relations with
Cuba. The book assesses both the bases
of Mexican foreign policy and Mexico's
reaction to the Cuban Revolution in this
period.

1579 Camacho Navarro, Enrique. Gilberto
Crespo y Martínez: un operador de la
diplomacia de México en la Cuba republicana, 1902–1906. (*Rev. Mex. Polít. Exter.*, 84,
julio/oct. 2008, p. 93–120)

This article presents a short biography of Gilberto Crespo y Martínez, Mexico's
first ambassador to Cuba, who served during
the presidency of Porfirio Díaz.

1580 Chacón Domínguez, Susana. México
y el escenario de América del Norte:
2000–2006. (*Foro Int./México*, 48:1/2, enero/
junio 2008, p. 123–149, bibl., tables)

This article addresses Mexico's relationship with Canada and the US. The author analyzes the failure of the Fox administration to develop a coherent strategy to promote Mexican interests within the trilateral North American relationship.

1581 Chacón Domínguez, Susana. La relación entre México y los Estados Unidos, 1940–1955: entre el conflicto y la cooperación. Prólogo de Lorenzo Meyer. México: Fondo de Cultura Económica: Instituto Tecnológico y de Estudios Superiores de Monterrey, 2008. 232 p.: bibl. (Política y derecho)

This is a groundbreaking study on the US-Mexico relationship during the WWII and its immediate aftermath (1940–55), which focuses on three episodes: military cooperation during the war, a commercial treaty, and the Bracero program. The author finds important lessons for how Mexico managed its asymmetrical relationship with the US in ways that took advantage of timing and comparative advantages. The lessons from history are quite useful for thinking through challenges in the contemporary relationship between the two countries.

1582 Concurso de Historias de Migrantes México-Estados Unidos, 1st, 2006. Historias de migrantes: México-Estados Unidos: primer concurso. Mexico: Consejo Nacional de Población: Instituto de los Mexicanos en el Exterior: Consejo Nacional para la Cultura y las Artes: Fondo de Población de las Naciones Unidas, 2006. 292 p.

This volume brings together the winners and honorary mentions from a competition of writing by Mexican migrants in the US. It is an essential volume for anyone who studies Mexican migration and wants to understand the reality through first-person accounts that illuminate the struggles and achievements of those who have migrated north.

1583 Cornejo, Romer. México y China: diplomacia, competencia económica y percepciones. (*Foro Int./México*, 48:1/2, enero/junio 2008, p. 330–351, tables)

This is a detailed study of Mexico-China relations, which suggests a lack of coherence in Mexico's objectives in a growing commercial and political relationship.

1584 Covarrubias Velasco, Ana. La política exterior "activa" una vez más. (*Foro Int./México*, 48:1/2, enero/junio 2008, p. 13–34)

The author compares the "active" foreign policy pursued by the Echeverría and Fox administrations to see if lessons can be learned from these two periods. She concludes that both sought a more engaged foreign policy based on democracy and human rights to respond to domestic political realities. However, while Echeverría's policies were driven by the need for legitimization, Fox's were driven more by changing circumstances in a democratizing country. In both cases the aims of "active" foreign policy fell short, which suggests that political leaders need to assess realistically their opportunities for success before launching an aggressive new foreign policy direction.

1585 Critical issues in the new U.S.-Mexico relations: stumbling blocks and constructive paths. Edición de Silvia Núñez García y Manuel Chavez Márquez. México: UNAM, Centro de Investigaciones sobre América del Norte; East Lansing: Michigan State Univ.: Center for Latin American and Caribbean Studies, 2008. 155 p.: bibl.

This short edited volume brings together a number of useful insights on US-Mexico relations. Perhaps most interesting is Silvia Núñez's chapter on the rise of the Hispanic Chamber of Commerce and the Institute of Mexicans Abroad as examples of new social organizations with ties to the policy establishment that are helping reshape the context of the relationship between the two countries.

1586 Cuéllar Laureano, Rubén. El petróleo y la política exterior de México: del auge petrolero a la privatización. (*Relac. Int./México*, 101/102, mayo/dic. 2008, p. 121–142, table)

The author argues, based on limited documentation, that recent "neoliberal" presidents have sought to destroy Pemex in order to privatize it. This strategy, according to the author, is centered around US attempts to ensure its energy security through Pemex.

1587 Davis, Charles L. and **Horace A. Bartilow.** Cognitive images and support for international economic agreements with the United States among Mexican citizens. (*Lat. Am. Polit. Soc.*, 49:2, Summer 2007, p. 123–148, bibl., tables)

The authors find that, for most Mexicans, public opinion of NAFTA and the Clinton-supported rescue package during the peso crisis are strongly linked to their perceptions of the US generally, rather than to strict economic considerations about whether they are winners or losers in trade. This study suggests that people's views of international cooperation depend a great deal on their opinion of the other countries involved rather than their view of the specific issue at hand.

1588 Diez años del TLCAN en México. Edición de Monica C. Gambrill. México: UNAM, Centro de Investigaciones sobre América del Norte, Instituto de Investigaciones Económicas, Facultad de Economía, 2006. 502 p.: bibl., ill., maps.

This edited volume presents a constructively critical look at the first 10 years of NAFTA. Chapters examine the lack of backward linkages in the maquiladora industry, the legal foundations of the agreement, and the effect of the agreement on wages and agriculture, among other topics. Leading scholars include the editor, Isabel Studer, Stephen Clarkson, Teresa Gutiérrez-Hacés, Sandra Polaski, and Mónica Verea.

1589 Diplomacia y cooperación cultural de México: una aproximación. Coordinación de Eduardo Cruz Vazquez. Tuxtla Gutiérrez, Mexico: Univ. de Ciencias y Artes de Chiapas; Monterrey, Mexico: Univ. Autónoma de Nuevo León, 2007. 261 p.: bibl., plate. (Col. Encrucijada)

This edited volume presents testimonies and analyses from Mexican diplomats who have been responsible for the country's cultural cooperation abroad. Contributions discuss the role that cultural diplomacy should play in Mexico's foreign policy.

1590 Dwyer, John Joseph. The agrarian dispute: the expropriation of American-owned rural land in postrevolutionary Mexico. Durham, N.C.: Duke Univ. Press, 2008. 387 p.: bibl., ill., index, map. (American encounters/global interactions)

This is an original and groundbreaking historical analysis of the way that Mexico responded to US concerns during the ex-propriation of land belonging to US citizens and companies in the 1930s. The author argues that this dispute, which preceded the expropriation of oil by three years, put the US-Mexico relationship to the test in new ways and showed how the weaker government in an asymmetrical relationship can win a series of difficult negotiations. For comment by historian, see *HLAS 66:926.*

1591 Escenarios de la política exterior de México: puntos para una reflexión. Compilación de Carlos Uscanga. México: UNAM: Plaza y Valdés, 2008. 104 p.: bibl. (Estado nación, globalización y democracia: cuadernos de trabajo)

This edited volume looks at several issues for Mexico's foreign policy in the period 2006–2012 including overarching challenges to address the changing international context; migration to the US; relations with Latin America, the Pacific, and Africa; and international cooperation.

1592 Fajer Flores, Ana Luisa. Medio Oriente: una ventana de oportunidad para México. (*Rev. Mex. Polít. Exter.,* 82, nov. 2007/feb. 2008, p. 15–34, table)

The author suggests strategies for the Mexican government to follow in order to strengthen its position with regards to foreign policy issues in the Middle East. She argues that Mexico could play a more active role, in accordance with its relative weight in global politics, and she details specific opportunities for several of Mexico's bilateral relations.

1593 Ferrer Silva, Liliana. Cabildeo en Estados Unidos: retos y oportunidades para México. (*Rev. Mex. Polít. Exter.,* 84, julio/oct. 2008, p. 9–41)

The author analyzes the recent history of lobbying in the US, especially during the NAFTA negotiations and the migration agreement discussions, and seeks to draw lessons about how Mexico can pursue a more active public relations effort in the US to advance its agenda. She concludes that there is a need to use both traditional lobbying and soft power through policy organizations and embassy/consular relationships.

1594 González García, Juan. Retrospectiva de la integración de México en la Cuenca del Pacífico. México: Univ. de

Colima: Miguel Ángel Porrúa, 2008. 270 p.: bibl., ill.

This book brings together several articles and essays written by the author from 1993 to 2005 about Mexico's integration with Asia and issues of political economy in Asia.

1595 González Navarrete, Eurídice. El sentido histórico de las relaciones Cuba-México en los últimos 50 años. (*in* América Latina: permanencia y cambio. México: UNAM, Centro Coordinador y Difusor de Estudios Latinoamericanos, 2007, p. 325–342)

The article provides a descriptive history of the Mexican government's relationship with Cuba, highlighting its support for Cuba and its right to self-determination, and later a distancing during the administration of President Fox.

1596 Guajardo Soto, Guillermo. Viejos puentes y nuevos acervos: la relación de México con América Latina y el Caribe durante el sexenio de Vicente Fox. (*Foro Int./México*, 48:1/2, enero/junio 2008, p. 268–296)

This well-argued study of Mexico's foreign policy towards Latin America and the Caribbean during the Fox administration analyzes Mexico's loss of influence in the region during this period.

1597 Hernandez, Kelly Lytle. Migra!: a history of the U.S. Border Patrol. Berkeley: Univ. of California Press, 2010. 311 p.: bibl., index. (American crossroads; 29)

This historical study seeks to understand the rise of the Border Patrol within the context of national policy priorities in the US, local economic interests and ethnic relations within border communities, and binational negotiations between the Mexican and US governments to control migration from south to north.

1598 Hernández Castro, Rocío. Menores infractores en la frontera México-Estados Unidos: cultura e identidad frente al papel de las instituciones: estudios de casos, 1996–2008. México: H. Cámara de Diputados, LX Legislatura, Consejo Editorial: UNAM, Facultad de Estudios Superiores Aragón: Miguel Ángel Porrua, 2009. 276 p.: bibl., ill. (Serie Las ciencias sociales) (Conocer para decidir)

This study focuses on the lack of adequate attention to minors in the criminal justice system in the border, especially Tijuana, Ciudad Juárez, and Matamoros. The study focuses special attention on the criminal justice system's inability to adapt to the realities of migrant youth and those of indigenous background, and it makes suggestions on how to improve the system to address their specific needs.

1599 Hernández-Vela Salgado, Edmundo. Reconstrucción de una política exterior de Estado en México: la vía nacional. (*Relac. Int./México*, 96, sept./dic. 2006, p. 151–164)

The author argues that Mexico's foreign policy has lost its ideological coherence and has been replaced by a vague set of ethical principles. He posits that Mexico's insertion into the global economy has led to a foreign policy largely driven by economic concerns and subordinated to the US. He urges educational institutions to educate a new generation of internationalists with a more nationalistic outlook.

1600 Kerber Palma, Víctor. El sol naciente de Vicente Fox: México y Japón 2000–2006. (*Foro Int./México*, 48:1/2, enero/junio 2008, p. 352–374, bibl., table)

This article describes in great detail how the Mexico-Japan Free Trade Agreement was reached, including the involvement of key nongovernmental actors.

1601 Labor market issues along the U.S.-Mexico border. Edited by Marie T. Mora and Alberto E. Davila. Tucson: Univ. of Arizona Press, 2009. 260 p.: bibl., index.

This edited volume provides a comprehensive and well-researched approach to employment issues on the US-Mexico border, including the impact of trade on wages, the impact of the growth of maquiladoras, gender differences in income, and the nature of migration to the border region vis-à-vis migration patterns broadly.

1602 México en un mundo unipolar y diverso. Compilación de Ana Covarrubias Velasco. México: Colegio de México, Centro de Estudios Internacionales, 2007. 242 p.: bibl.

This edited volume, which emerged out of a project sponsored by Oxford University, El Colegio de México, and the Mexican

Foreign Relations Secretariat, seeks to analyze major global trends and identify their effect on Mexico. The articles by leading non-Mexican scholars, including Neil MacFarlane, Laurence Whitehead, Lars Schoultz, Ken Shadlen, Robert Pastor, Jane Boulden, and Tom Farer, address the shifting structure of international relations, while the responses by leading Mexican scholars and practitioners, including Ana Covarrubias, María Celia Toro, Luis de la Calle, and Andrés Rozental, discuss Mexico's role in the changing world order. For comment on a related work, see item **1631**.

1603 Mexico-U.S. migration management: a binational approach. Edited by Agustín Escobar Latapí and Susan Forbes Martin. Lanham, Md.: Lexington Books, 2008. 291 p.: bibl., ill., index. (Program in migration and refugee studies)

This may be the single most important scholarly volume on US-Mexico migration in a decade. It includes state-of-the-art analyses of the demographics of migration, economic impacts and causes of migration, as well as the politics of reform in both countries. Leading scholars from both countries contributed to this book, which was also published in Spanish.

1604 México y el mundo 2006: líderes, opinión pública y política exterior en México, Estados Unidos y Asia: un estudio comparativo. Edición de Guadalupe González González y Susan Minushkin. México: Centro de Investigación y Docencia Económicas: Consejo Mexicano de Asuntos Internacionales, 2006. 78 p.: col. ill.

This companion volume to *Mexico y el mundo: opinión pública y política exterior en México* situates Mexican public opinion in comparison to that in China, Japan, India, and the US. For comment on companion volume, see item **1605**.

1605 México y el mundo 2006: opinión pública y política exterior en México. Edición de Guadalupe González González y Susan Minushkin. México: Centro de Investigación y Docencia Económicas: Consejo Mexicano de Asuntos Internacionales, 2006. 73 p.: col. ill.

This study by CIDE documents Mexican public opinion on a range of foreign policy issues from migration to trade to engagement in international organizations. The study looks at the divergent opinions of elite leaders and the general public on some issues and breaks down many issues along regional lines to show the similarities and differences in opinion across the country. This is an invaluable resource for anyone who wants to understand the attitudinal bases for foreign policy decision-making. For comment on companion volume, see item **1604**.

1606 Miscelánea global: tareas internacionales de México: una colección de ensayos. Coordinación de Jorge Eduardo Navarrete. Textos de Eugenio Anguiano Roch *et al.* México: UNAM, Centro de Investigaciones Interdisciplinarias en Ciencias y Humanidades, 2008. 421 p.: bibl., ill. (Col. Prospectiva global)

This edited volume with essays by distinguished Mexican scholars and practitioners of foreign policy looks at a variety of challenges facing Mexico, including UN reform, new trends in international law, human rights, disarmament, the IMF, and energy and the environment. Unlike several volumes that have taken a country and regional approach to foreign policy, this one looks at major themes emerging in the global order that Mexico will have to respond to.

1607 Monroy, Douglas. The borders within: encounters between Mexico and the U.S. Tucson: Univ. of Arizona Press, 2008. 256 p.: bibl., index.

The author weaves history and contemporary issues together to describe the way that the US and Mexico are interwoven. The stories are well worth reading and the history enlightens the challenges that the neighboring countries face today.

1608 Novelo Urdanivia, Federico. Hacia la economía política de las migraciones México-Estados Unidos. México: Univ. Autónoma Metropolitana, Unidad Xochimilco, Coordinación de Extensión Univ., 2007. 170 p.: bibl., ill.

A rough treatment of economic issues related to migration between Mexico and the US situated in a dependency framework.

1609 Ojeda, Mario. México y Cuba revolucionaria: cincuenta años de relación. México: Colegio de México, 2008. 281 p.: bibl.

This book is a well-written and documented study of the history of Mexico-Cuba relations by one of Mexico's premiere scholars of foreign policy. It covers the period from the Cuban Revolution through the Fox administration.

1610 Ojeda, Mario. Retrospección de Contadora: los esfuerzos de México para la paz en Centroamérica, 1983–1985. México: Colegio de México, Centro de Estudios Internacionales, 2007. 159 p.: bibl.

This short study of the Contadora process, and Mexico's leadership in it, contains significant detail about the negotiations themselves that will be of great value to those studying this period in Mexican and Central American history.

1611 Ojeda, Mario. Vicente Fox: el ropimiento *de facto* con Cuba. (*Foro Int./México,* 47:4, oct./dic. 2007, p. 868–894, tables)

The author chronicles the deterioration of the relationship between the Mexican and Cuban governments during the Fox administration, highlighting Fox's conservative bent as the primary driver for the change in relations.

1612 Paradigmas y paradojas de la política exterior de México: 2000–2006. Edición de Humberto Garza Elizondo. Coordinación de Jorge A. Schiavon y Rafael Velázquez Flores. México: Colegio de México: Centro de Investigación y Docencia Económicas, 2010. 472 p.: bibl., ill.

This excellent edited work analyzes Mexico's foreign policy during the Fox administration. Essays by leading Mexican scholars take a balanced approach to examining the country's progress and failures in foreign policy-making during this period, including specific topics such as the failed migration agreement, the attempt to define a national security strategy, and Mexico's participation in international organizations. The final section includes essays on Mexico's foreign policy vis-à-vis specific world regions.

1613 Peña Cid, Roberto. La fuga de cerebros en las relaciones internacionales. (*Relac. Int./México,* 101/102, mayo/dic. 2008, p. 99–120)

This article is an attempt to look at issues involved in Mexico's brain drain, although it is lacking in specific information to support the central arguments.

1614 Ramírez Bonilla, Juan José. La participación mexicana en los foros regionales del Pacífico, 2000–2006. (*Foro Int./México,* 48:1/2, enero/junio 2008, p. 375–417, tables)

The article addresses the growing importance of Asia as the new motor of the global economy and of Asian economic forums as crucial drivers in this process. The author argues that Mexico needs to be an active participant in these forums and identifies opportunities for greater insertion.

1615 Retos ambientales y desarrollo urbano en la frontera México-Estados Unidos. Textos de Christopher Brown *et al.* Tijuana, Mexico: Depto. de Estudios Urbanos y Medio Ambiente, Colegio de la Frontera Norte, 2009. 252 p.: bibl., ill., maps.

The book examines environmental challenges along the US-Mexico border region. The first section looks at urban growth and its impact on the environment, with case studies of Monterrey and the Tijuana region, as well as a study of electricity generation emissions. The second section reviews binational governance challenges, including opportunities for citizen participation and the role of the Good Neighbor Environmental Board.

1616 Reyes, Guillermo. Participación de México en el desarrollo del derecho internacional frente a los atentados del 11 de septiembre de 2001. (*Rev. Mex. Polít. Exter.,* 76/77, nov. 2005/junio 2006, p. 97–130)

Mexico has a long history of participation in strengthening international law. The author argues that Mexico has done the same after the terrorist attacks on the US in 2001 by helping to create an international legal framework for addressing terrorism. The Mexican government has been particularly active in developing an inter-American framework, but has also been active in several other international fora.

1617 Reynaga Mejía, Juan Rafael. La revolución cubana en México a través de la revista *Política:* construcción imaginaria de un discurso para América Latina. Toluca, Mexico: Univ. Autónoma del Estado de

México; México: UNAM: CCyDEL, 2007.
189 p.: bibl., ill. (Ciencias sociales. Sociología)
In this study, the author looks at how the pro-Cuban Mexican magazine *Política* contributed to an understanding of the Cuban Revolution in Mexico and a discourse of Latin American solidarity based on the ideals of the Revolution.

1618 Rodas-Martini, Pablo. El compromiso laboral del Tratado de Libre Comercio entre Estados Unidos y Centroamérica, CAFTA: una negociación no negociada. (*Integr. Comer.*, 10:25, julio/dic. 2006, p. 305–322, graph)
The author argues that Central American countries were largely forced to give in on including labor provisions within CAFTA, against their will, while US labor unions also failed to get all they wanted in the text. In the end, the labor provisions neither provide a backdoor for US protectionism, as some in Central America claim, nor will they do much to change labor standards in Central America, as unions in the US hoped.

1619 Ruano, Lorena. De la exaltación al tedio: las relaciones entre México y la Unión Europea durante el sexenio del Presidente Vicente Fox, 2000–2006. (*Foro Int./México*, 48:1/2, enero/junio 2008, p. 297–329, graphs, tables)
The author argues that although the relationship between Mexico and the European Union increased significantly during the Fox administration, the ties failed to meet the high expectations that many had at the outset. The worldwide recession, political gridlock in Mexico, and conflict within the European Union over expansion, adoption of a single currency, and the Iraq War all helped undermine the momentum for closer relations that had been generated by many European governments' excitement over Fox's election.

1620 Ruiz Guerra, Rubén. Más allá de la diplomacia: relaciones de México con Bolivia, Ecuador y Perú, 1821–1994. México: Secretaría de Relaciones Exteriores, Dirección General del Acervo Histórico Diplomático, 2007. 238 p.: bibl., ill. (some col.), index, maps (some col.). (Col. Latino-americana)
In a beautifully bound and designed volume, the author addresses the history of Mexico's relations with Bolivia, Ecuador, and Peru from independence until the mid-1990s. Although rich in specific detail on these relationships, the study also explores the larger theme of why Mexico is so close culturally to countries in South America but has never had the depth of diplomatic or economic engagements to match this.

1621 Salazar y García, José Arturo. Reseña histórica en torno al relato del general liberal Manuel Doblado, secretario de Relaciones Exteriores de la República mexicana, sobre los principios de la intervención francesa en México. Guanajuato, Mexico: Univ. de Guanajuato, 2007. 186 p.: bibl.
The author explores the role of Gen. Manuel Delgado, foreign and interior secretary under the first presidency of Benito Juárez, in negotiating with the invading European armies. Based on first-person accounts by Delgado, the work explores the dynamics of the Juárez administration's response to the invasion.

1622 Santos, Marcelo. O México como aliado dos EUA no projeto de integração das Américas. (*Rev. Bras. Polít. Int.*, 50:2, 2007, p. 146–161, bibl.)
The author argues that the US has pursued a series of agreements with Mexico, including NAFTA, the Mesoamerican Biological Corridor, and the Plan Puebla Panamá, that are designed to impose legal norms on the region that benefit large capitalists in the US. This pursuit is part of the overarching strategy to extend this model into the rest of the Americas.

1623 Schiavon, Jorge A. Opinión pública, preferencias y política exterior: México ante el mundo. (*Foro Int./México*, 48:1/2, enero/junio 2008, p. 35–65, bibl.)
The author analyzes the findings from the 2004 and 2006 public opinion surveys conducted by CIDE on foreign policy. The study shows that Mexicans are interested in foreign policy, highly pragmatic in their opinions, and have a close cultural affinity for Latin America coupled with a practical desire to engage with North America, with greater closeness to the US in the north. Overall, the author concludes that public opinion should be an important factor driving changes in foreign policy.

1624 Selee, Andrew D. More than neighbors: an overview of Mexico and U.S.-Mexican relations. Washington, D.C.: Woodrow Wilson International Center for Scholars, 2007. 43 p.: bibl., col. ill., col. maps.

The study argues that Mexico and the US are increasingly interdependent, with multiple political actors involved in the relationship, and with persistent asymmetries. This reality makes greater cooperation both necessary and difficult.

1625 Seminario Internacional "Las Políticas Exteriores de Estados Unidos, Canadá y México en el Umbral del Siglo XXI", UNAM, Centro de Investigaciones sobre América del Norte, 2000. Las políticas exteriores de Estados Unidos, Canadá y México en el umbral del siglo XXI. Coordinación de Remedios Gómez Arnau, Rosío Vargas y Julián Castro Rea. México: UNAM, Centro de Investigaciones sobre América del Norte, 2003. 303 p.: bibl.

This edited volume assesses foreign policy challenges in the three countries of North America with the participation of scholars drawn from each.

1626 Shared responsibility: U.S.-Mexico policy options for confronting organized crime. Edited by Eric L. Olson, David A. Shirk, and Andrew D. Selee. Washington, D.C.: Woodrow Wilson International Center for Scholars, Mexico Institute, 2010. 376 p.: bibl., ill. (some col.).

This study looks at the agenda set by the US and Mexican governments in 2009 to increase security cooperation and assesses the possibilities for success. Several background chapters examine the rise of organized crime in Mexico, Central America, and the US. Other authors from the two countries analyze specific policy options related to intelligence sharing, arms smuggling, money laundering, demand-reduction, judicial strengthening, police strengthening, and the protection of journalists.

1627 Shicheng, Xu. Algunas reflexiones sobre el desarrollo de las relaciones sino-mexicanas. (*Cuad. Am./México*, 3:121, julio/sept. 2007, p. 171–186)

This is a very interesting analysis by a Chinese scholar of the relationship between China and Mexico. The article chronicles the history of the relationship since the 1970s and suggests several contemporary challenges, including the current trade imbalance and illegal migration, as well as several opportunities, including education, technical research, and cooperation on major geopolitical issues.

1628 Silva Herzog Flores, Jesús. A la distancia . . . : recuerdos y testimonios. México: Editorial Oceano de México, 2007. 309 p.: ill., index. (En primera persona) (Tiempo de México)

A fascinating autobiography of Jesús Silva Herzog through his many professional adventures as secretary of the treasury, ambassador in Spain and the US, and mayoral candidate in Mexico City. His analysis of how the Mexican government needed to diversify its approach to the US by reaching out to Mexican-American leaders and regional opinion leaders is particularly instructive for those studying US-Mexico relations.

1629 Sotomayor, Arturo C. México y la ONU en tiempos de transición: entre activismo externo, parálisis interna y crisis internacional. (*Foro Int./México*, 48:1/2, enero/junio 2008, p. 238–267, tables)

This is a well-documented and theoretically solid study of Mexico's changing role in the UN under President Fox. The author argues that Mexico's new activism in multilateral affairs largely resulted from a desire to signal and lock-in internal changes related to Mexico's democratic process. However, in many cases these efforts generated internal resistance and conflict within Mexico's political elites and foreign policy establishment.

1630 Tamborini, Christopher R. Work, wages and gender in export-oriented cities: global assembly versus international tourism in Mexico. (*Bull. Lat. Am. Res.*, 26:1, Jan. 2007, p. 24–49, tables)

This is a groundbreaking study about the effect that export-oriented growth has on wages and women's insertion in the labor market. Comparing women's labor insertion in Cancún, a city dominated by tourism, and Ciudad Juárez, a city dedicated to export-oriented manufacturing, the author finds that women have carved out extensive and highly differentiated niches in both economies, with somewhat better and more diverse opportunities in Cancún's tourist industry. Contrary to studies that find aggregate impoverishment from export-led growth models, this study finds important wage gains and expanded opportunities for individual labor market insertion.

1631 Temas de política exterior. Coordinación de Ana Covarrubias Velasco. México: El Colegio de México, 2008. 486 p.: bibl.

The second of two edited volumes from a study by Oxford University, El Colegio de México, and the Mexican Foreign Relations Secretariat, this book highlights Mexico's changing foreign policy through a series of high-quality academic studies. Leading Mexican and international scholars contributed chapters to this work, which also looks at evolving international challenges for Mexico. For comment on the related volume, see item **1602**.

1632 The United States and Mexico: towards a strategic partnership: a report of four working groups on U.S.-Mexico relations. Edited by Andrew D. Selee. Washington, D.C.: Woodrow Wilson International Center for Scholars, Mexico Institute, 2009. 63 p.: bibl., ill.

This study, which involved over 100 analysts from Mexico and the US, looks at policy options for greater cooperation between the two countries in four issue areas: security cooperation, economic integration, migration, and border cooperation.

1633 Varela, Hilda. La política exterior de México hacia África subsahariana, 2000–2006. (*Foro Int./México*, 48:1/2, enero/junio 2008, p. 418–447)

The author argues that Mexico has never had a consistent foreign policy towards Africa, except in moments of crisis that allow the Mexican government to have a rhetorical position and to keep a certain presence on the continent. However, she suggests that Mexico should develop a more proactive foreign policy towards Africa that reflects Mexico's emergence as a middle power in the global system.

1634 Velázquez Elizarrarás, Juan Carlos. Problemática actual del territorio insular mexicano en el régimen convencional marítimo internacional. (*Relac. Int./México*, 98, mayo/agosto 2007, p. 11–34, table)

The author points out the lack of attention in Mexico to the strategic importance of the country's islands and the ways in which the Law of the Sea should be applied to strengthen the country's national interest.

1635 Velázquez Flores, Rafael. Balance general de la política exterior de México, 2000–2006. (*Foro Int./México*, 48:1/2, enero/junio 2008, p. 81–122, graphs, tables)

The author argues that President Fox's foreign policy failed to meet many of its objectives in large part because it was unable to react effectively to changes in the international context after 9/11. He argues that the Fox administration did not develop a coherent policy with Latin America and the Caribbean, and that it was unable to develop a new internal consensus on its goals for foreign policy. This is an excellent analysis of Fox's foreign policy goals and the reasons they did not fully advance.

1636 Velázquez Flores, Rafael. La paradiplomacia mexicana: las relaciones exteriores de las entidades federativas. (*Relac. Int./México*, 96, sept./dic. 2006, p. 123–149, tables)

This important article explores the increasing international relations efforts of Mexican states. The author lays a theoretical foundation for how subnational governments can engage in "parapolitics," and then explores both the legal faculties and the actual behavior of Mexican states in engaging in this effort.

1637 Ventura Valero, Julián. La política exterior de México en Asia-Pacífico en el periodo 2000–2006. (*Rev. Mex. Polít. Exter.*, 79/80, nov. 2006/junio 2007, p. 41–62)

Mexico has shown increasing attention to the Asia Pacific region since the 1960s. The author proposes an agenda for the Mexican government to follow in order to strengthen its relations with the countries of the region, especially China, Japan, Korea, and India.

1638 Villarreal, René. TLCAN 10 años después: experiencias de México y lecciones para América Latina: hacia una estrategia de competitividad sistémica del desarrollo. Bogotá: Norma, 2004. 415 p.: bibl., ill. (Col. Vitral)

The author argues that NAFTA was well negotiated by Mexico, except for the agricultural chapter, but that Mexico has failed to use the economic opening to develop its comparative advantages. Based in part on a comparative study of other arrangements for economic integration, the study offers valuable insights into Mexico's challenges in a globalized economy.

1639 Weintraub, Sidney. Unequal partners: the United States and Mexico. Pittsburgh, Pa.: Univ. of Pittsburgh Press, 2009. 172 p.: bibl., index. (Pitt Latin American series)

This pathbreaking book addresses the existing asymmetries between Mexico and the US through six case studies and concludes that, while the US has an asymmetry of power in its favor, Mexico has an asymmetry of attention that often favors its interest. By recognizing and accepting the impact that these differences in attention and influence have on the relationship, policymakers and citizens in both countries can learn to manage the relationship far more strategically.

CENTRAL AMERICA

1640 La construcción de una región: México y la geopolítica del Plan Puebla-Panamá. Edición de Heriberto Cairo Carou, Jaime Preciado Coronado y Alberto Rocha Valencia. Madrid: Catarata, 2007. 268 p.: ill., maps. (Serie Desarrollo y cooperación; 247)

This edited volume seeks to assess the impact of the Plan Puebla-Panamá (PPP), including understanding both the extent to which policies were implemented and how social movements reshaped the integration agenda between the south of Mexico and Central America.

1641 Encuesta sobre migración en la frontera Guatemala-México, 2005: serie histórica 2004–2005. México: Instituto Nacional de Migración: Consejo Nacional de Población; Tijuana, Mexico: Colegio de la Frontera Norte; México: Secretaría de Gobernación: Secretaría del Trabajo y Previsión Social: Secretaría de Relaciones Exteriores, 2007. 262 p.: bibl., ill., maps, 1 CD-ROM.

This is the first comprehensive study of migration from Guatemala to Mexico across the shared border, which has been constructed along the same lines (and by the same researchers) as the now well-established COLEF/INM study of Mexico-US migration. It contains a wealth of useful data, including demographic characteristics and deportations.

1642 Fumero Paniagua, Gerardo. El estado solidario frente a la globalización: debate sobre el TLC y el ICE. San José: Zeta Servicios Gráficos, 2006. 352 p.: bibl., ill.

An analysis of the dangers of free trade for Costa Rica based on a dependency framework. The author is particularly concerned with the effect of free trade on the telecommunications industry. This edited book, produced by the Universidad Autónomo de Baja California, provides students both a theoretical approach for understanding international relations (part one) and several case studies drawn primarily from Mexico's northern border. Of particular interest are chapters on student mobility, water, and public security in the border region.

1643 Granados, Carlos; Alonso Brenes; and Luis Pablo Cubero. Los riesgos de la reconversión productiva en las fronteras centroamericanas: el caso de la zona norte de Costa Rica. (*Anu. Estud. Centroam.*, 31, 2005, p. 93–113, graphs, map, tables)

The article addresses the impact of the agricultural reconversion—from traditional staples consumed domestically to export-oriented agricultural products—in the border region between Costa Rica and Nicaragua. While these efforts have successfully produced new kinds of exports, they have done so at the expense of basic foodstuffs consumed by local populations. In addition, small producers have been marginalized and local economies have been subjected to the vicissitudes of global commerce.

Greentree, Todd R. Crossroads of intervention: insurgency and counterinsurgency lessons from Central America. See item **1129.**

1644 Juárez, Orient Bolívar. Japón y Nicaragua: contribución a la historia de sus relaciones diplomáticas=Nihon

Nikaragwa. Ed. conmemorativa. Managua: Ministerio de Relaciones Exteriores de Nicaragua, 2006. 497 p.: bibl., ill.

This book covers the history of diplomatic relations between Japan and Nicaragua from the 1890s until the present day. It is primarily a diplomatic history, but does include some elements of cultural and social interrelationship between the two countries as well.

1645 Mejía Herrera, Orlando José. La Unión Europea como modelo de integración: análisis comparativo del Sistema de la Integración Centroamericana, SICA. Prólogo de Carlos Jiménez Piernas. León, Nicaragua: Editorial Univ., UNAN-León, 2008. 601 p.: bibl., indexes.

This book, drawn from the author's doctoral dissertation, seeks to shed light on the process of Central American integration in SICA by looking for lessons from the European Union. Without stating that SICA should imitate the EU, the author suggests aspects that may be applicable across the ocean.

1646 Seminario Internacional de Análisis sobre la Frontera Sur de México, *4th, San Cristóbal de Las Casas, Mexico,*

2002. El Plan Puebla-Panamá, ¿integración para el desarrollo? Compilación de Juan Pohlenz Córdova y Juan Manuel Sandoval Palacios. San Cristóbal de Las Casas, Mexico: Univ. Intercultural de Chiapas: Centro de Estudios de Fronteras y Chicanos, Sede Chiapas, 2007. 398 p.: bibl., ill., map.

This edited volume takes a dependency approach to understanding the Plan Puebla-Panamá as the linchpin of a US strategy for economic domination of Mexico and Central America.

1647 Suazo Rubí, Sergio. Concertación política e integración en Centroamérica: a veinte años de Esquípulas. Tegucigalpa: Graficentro Editores, 2008. 179 p.: bibl.

The author examines the history of Central American integration, especially since the Esquípulas peace process and through the attempts to forge economic integration in the 1990s. He proposes that the Central American governments give greater powers to the Central American Parliament and consider other measures to strengthen supranational authority that would bind the countries together.

THE CARIBBEAN AND THE GUIANAS

JACQUELINE ANNE BRAVEBOY-WAGNER, *Professor of Political Science, The City College and The Graduate School, and University Center, The City University of New York*

FOR THE FIRST TIME IN MANY YEARS, the political situation in the Caribbean has been relatively quiet, the last major event being the overthrow of Haitian President Aristide in 2004. This tranquility, coupled with the diversion of global attention and resources to the Middle East and North Africa, has shifted the attention of scholars (as well as policymakers) away from dealing with the problems of the region (except for the perennial issue of Cuba), now seen as primarily economic and financial. Most of these small developing states have been struggling to survive in a liberalized, competitive world. Moreover, they remain highly vulnerable to transnational threats of all kinds including environmental threats, narcotics trafficking, and financial crime.

Despite the threatening transnational environment, the attention of scholars working in the English-speaking Caribbean appears to be focused almost exclusively on the problems of Caribbean integration, although a few scholars do deal with drug trafficking as an incidental issue. Since the late 1990s, there has been a renewal of regionalist arrangements around the world, and the Caribbean has been no exception. Scholars therefore have expended much energy on assessing historical as well as current and potential developments in integration in the Caribbean Community (CARICOM). This voluminous and somewhat repetitive work in political economy sometimes includes contributions on economic diplomacy. However, there is little to nothing being done in traditional international relations or foreign policy; certainly there is no work employing or developing theoretical frameworks in international relations. On a more positive note, apart from the CARICOM works, there appears to be a useful mini-trend toward historical assessments of key events that interweave international and local developments. Detailed works on Associated Statehood (item **1657**) and the Caribbean labor movement (item **1667**) are representative of this genre.

With respect to Haiti, the spate of works on the 1994 intervention and its aftermath has now subsided. There were no traditional international relations contributions in this round of reviews. Instead, a sociological-anthropological-literary trend is reflected in the two contributions listed (items **1651** and **1665**).

Cuba remains the major focal point of international relations scholars of the Caribbean, offering as it does the potential for rich analyses of its problematic relations with the US and its deepening relations with Latin America and the Caribbean. The many works on Cuba's international relations continue in the public policy genre, dissecting the historical changes in US policy, and mostly offering sympathetic analyses in Cuba's favor. Among the more unusual (and therefore more interesting) studies are an excellent legal analysis of the Guantanamo lease (item **1679**) and a study of Russia-Cuba relations within a twin theoretical framework of rationalism and nationalism (item **1648**). In addition, in terms of sheer scope, Lars Schoultz's review of US-Cuba policy stands out (item **1677**).

1648 Bain, Mervyn J. Russian-Cuban relations since 1992: continuing camaraderie in a post-Soviet world. Lanham, Md.: Lexington Books, 2008. 169 p.: bibl., ill., index.

This is a good, if relatively brief, analysis of a somewhat neglected topic: Russia's legacy and its continuing, renewed relations with Cuba. The book stands out in that it goes beyond description to employ a theoretical framework based on both realism (i.e., realist pragmatism) and counterdependency (i.e., nationalism).

1649 Barfield, Scott. The eastern Caribbean: declining diplomatic influence and the banana trade dispute. (*in* Diplomacy and developing nations: post-cold war foreign policy-making structures and processes. Edited by Justin Robertson and Maurice A. East. New York, N.Y.: Routledge, 2005, p. 134–153)

The author provides details of the largely unsuccessful eastern Caribbean attempts to stave off the erosion of the EU's preferential banana regime. Beyond describing the various events and outcomes, the author's focus is on the diplomatic efforts waged by heads of government, banana-producing entities, and the resource-handicapped diplomats of these very small states.

1650 Bernal, Richard L. The dragon in the Caribbean: China-CARICOM economic relations. (*Round Table/London,* 99:408, June 2010, p. 281–302)

The author seeks to explain the expanded and intensified economic presence of China in the CARICOM region. China's motives and CARICOM's receptivity, according to the author, are influenced partly by economics and partly by politics and hence have to be understood in the global geopolitical context. [C.E. Griffin]

Bosch, Juan. Temas internacionales: ensayos y artículos. See *HLAS 66:1304.*

1651 Braziel, Jana Evans. Duvalier's ghosts: race, diaspora, and U.S. imperialism in Haitian literatures. Gainesville: Univ. Press of Florida, 2010. 308 p.: bibl., index.

The author deconstructs various literary texts reflecting Haitian political themes, including transatlantic migration/ refuge flows, capitalist development, and state violence. This is not a traditional international relations work by any means. For political scientist's comment, see item **1200**.

1652 The Caribbean Community in transition: functional cooperation as a catalyst for change. Edited by Kenneth O. Hall and Myrtle Chuck-A-Sang. Kingston: Ian Randle, 2008. 522 p.: bibl., ill.

This is one of an outpouring of books on CARICOM integration produced by scholars associated with the University of the West Indies. The book is an encyclopedic description of CARICOM functional cooperation in development, health, tourism, culture, energy, education, sport, youth, security, labor, and government sectors.

1653 CARICOM single market and economy: challenges, benefits and prospects. Edited by Kenneth O. Hall and Myrtle Chuck-A-Sang. Kingston: Ian Randle, 2007. 259 p.: bibl.

In view of the move by CARICOM toward a single market and economy, the contributors describe the main elements of the proposals for heightened integration.

1654 Castro, Fidel. Obama and the empire. Melbourne, Australia: Ocean; London: Turnaround, 2011. 134 p.

Presents Fidel Castro's thoughts and general information about US-Cuban relations. The former Cuban leader expresses his disappointment with President Obama's policies.

1655 Castro, Fidel; Olga Miranda Bravo; and Roger Ricardo Luis. Guantánamo: why the illegal US base should be returned to Cuba. Melbourne, Australia; New York, N.Y.: Ocean Press, 2011. 161 p.: bibl.

Fidel Castro fills in the background history of Guantánamo and his collaborators discuss the political and legal aspects of the controversial lease. Good basic information and a useful chronology.

1656 Confronting challenges, maximising opportunities: a new diplomacy for market access. Prepared by Joseph Farier. Kingston: Ian Randle, 2007. 186 p.: bibl. (Integrationist)

Contributions to this edition of a CARICOM journal assess and make recommendations with respect to the region's economic diplomacy and negotiations for access to northern markets in a new era of normal trade and governance-oriented conditionalities on development assistance.

Corse, Theron Edward. Protestants, revolution, and the Cuba-U.S. bond. See *HLAS 66:1310*.

1657 Cox Alomar, Rafael. Revisiting the transatlantic triangle: the constitutional decolonization of the eastern Caribbean. Kingston; Miami, Fla.: Ian Randle Publishers, 2009. 323 p.: bibl., index. (Forgotten histories of the Caribbean)

The author revisits constitutional developments in the eastern Caribbean in the 1960s, specifically the decision by the United Kingdom to grant the smaller islands Associated Statehood. The analysis benefits from archival detail and, in particular, the weaving of UK, US, and (somewhat less so) Canadian perspectives with local ones.

1658 Cuba's energy future: strategic approaches to cooperation. Edited by Jonathan Benjamin-Alvarado. Washington, D.C.: Brookings Institution Press, 2010. 143 p.: bibl., graphs, index, maps, tables.

This useful collection of papers focuses on the actual and potential state of Cuban oil, natural gas, and biofuels sectors. The contributors analyze what it will take to foster US-Cuban collaboration in the energy sector where other countries are already engaged. The prevailing assumption is that US energy independence is unattainable and Cuba needs energy for development, therefore there is room for collaboration if the embargo restrictions can be overcome.

1659 Eckstein, Susan. The personal is political: the Cuban ethnic electoral policy cycle. (*Lat. Am. Polit. Soc.*, 51:1, Spring 2009, p. 119–148, bibl., tables)

The author argues that the changes in US policy toward Cuba with respect to the embargo (in particular the personal embargo) should be viewed through the lens of an "ethnic policy electoral cycle": in election years, the Cuban vote is courted by imposing more stringent anti-Cuba policies, while with minor exceptions the easing of the embargo has tended to occur during "off" electoral years.

1660 Erikson, Daniel P. and **Paul J. Wander.** Cuba's brave new world. (*Fletcher Forum World Aff.*, 33:2, Summer/Fall 2009, p. 9–28)

Since Raúl Castro succeeded his brother Fidel, Cuba has shown the world a new, more engaging face. This paper explores the recent, and ongoing, sea change in Cuba's international relations by discussing the resurgence in Cuba's bilateral relations with the US, its engagement with neighbors in Latin America, and its leadership of the Non-Aligned Movement. Also examines Cuba's post-Cold War engagement with China on military, economic, and cultural matters, and with the EU. [C.E. Griffin]

1661 Foreign policy toward Cuba: isolation or engagement? Edited by Michele Zebich-Knos and Heather Nora Nicol. Lanham, Md.: Lexington Books, 2005. 285 p.: bibl., index. (Studies in public policy)

Good descriptive contributions on recent US, Canadian, Mexican, and CARICOM relations with Cuba, including a very good critical analysis of the role of civil society in contemporary Cuba. The contributors focus heavily on engagement with Cuba without really addressing the pros and cons as might be expected from the subtitle, "isolation or engagement."

1662 Francis, Anselm. Bridging the implementation gap in the revised Treaty of Chaguaramas. (*Iberoamericana/Stockholm*, 38:1/2, 2008, p. 103–118, bibl.)

A very readable critique and analysis of gaps in the formulation of a revised treaty of integration for CARICOM. Gaps include governance and bureaucratic and institutional limitations.

1663 Giovanni, Anania. EU economic partnership agreements and WTO negotiations: a quantitative assessment of trade preference granting and erosion in the banana market. (*Food Policy*, 35:2, April 2010, p. 140–153)

The paper seeks to provide a quantitative assessment of the impact on the banana market of the expanded trade preferences that the European Union granted Africa, Caribbean, and Pacific (ACP) countries with the Economic Partnership Agreements (EPA) and of the possible erosion of these preferences as a result of different possible conclusions, if any, of ongoing WTO negotiations. The results suggest that the impact of the EPA on production and consumption of bananas in the EU will be limited, while benefits for ACP countries will be significant (at the expense of Most Favored Nation (MFN) exporters). [C.E. Griffin]

Gronbeck-Tedesco, John A. The left in transition: the Cuban revolution in US third world politics. See item **1224**.

1664 Gros, Jean-Germain. Indigestible recipe: rice, chicken wings, and international financial institutions or hunger politics in Haiti. (*J. Black Stud.*, 40:5, May 2010, p. 974–986)

Food riots in Haiti in early April 2008 brought the plight of the Haitians to the attention of the international community. These events are neither unique to Haiti nor the product of happenstance. Instead, policies imposed on Haiti by international financial institutions (i.e., the World Bank and International Monetary Fund) since the 1980s, such as currency devaluation and trade liberalization, had a "double whammy" negative impact: they negated Haitian agricultural performance and the capacity of the Haitian state to manage the economy, thus exacerbating the current food crisis. [C.E. Griffin]

1665 Haiti and the Haitian diaspora in the wider Caribbean. Edited by Philippe Zacaïr. Gainesville: Univ. Press of Florida, 2010. 207 p.: bibl., index. (New world diasporas)

The contributors analyze various Haitian identity issues and describe instances of variable treatment (positive and negative) encountered by Haitians in the French-speaking Caribbean and Guiana as well as on the Dominican (Republic) border and in Jamaica. This is not an international relations study per se, but rather employs an anthropological-sociological approach. For political scientist's comment, see item **1203**.

1666 Hillebrink, Steven. The right to self-determination and post-colonial governance: the case of the Netherlands Antilles and Aruba. The Hague; Cambridge, Mass.: T.M.C. Asser Press, 2008. 391 p.: bibl., index.

One of the few books dealing with the Dutch Caribbean, this volume provides a legal analysis of the various options available to these small states as they seek greater independence from Holland.

1667 Horne, Gerald. Cold War in a hot zone: the United States confronts labor and independence struggles in the British West Indies. Philadelphia, Penn.: Temple Univ. Press, 2007. 262 p.: bibl., ill., index, plates.

This is an excellent resource on the Caribbean labor movement. The author details the history of the movement and its contributions to the social and political development of the West Indies in terms of Cold War divisions and the interplay of US, UK, colonial, planter, and local labor interests.

1668 Huddleston, Vicki and **Carlos Pascual.** Learning to salsa: new steps in U.S.-Cuba relations. Washington, D.C.: Brookings Institution Press, 2010. 245 p.: ill., index.

Brookings Institution (think tank) scholars offer policy proposals for the short, medium, and long term in hopeful anticipation of a US opening to Cuba. The results of six simulation exercises are reported: these include three meetings of the US National Security Council, a multilateral (foreign ministers) meeting, a meeting of Raúl Castro with his advisers, a meeting of grassroots Cuban activists, and a meeting of representatives of the Cuban-American community.

Hurst, Lionel. Democracy by diplomacy: Afro-Saxon Caribbean diplomats challenge the USA to improve its world leadership and expand regional freedoms. See item **1182**.

1669 Layne, Gordon. The concepts and activities of integration within the Caribbean Basin: is there an agenda for the

21st century. (*Iberoamericana/Stockholm*, 38:1/2, 2008, p. 119–154, bibl., tables)

This is a descriptive review of the progress made in Caribbean integration. The tone is largely positive.

Lozano, Wilfredo. La paradoja de las migraciones: el estado dominicano frente a la inmigración haitiana. See item **1206**.

1670 Mohammed, Debbie. Enhancing CARICOM competitiveness: can the Caribbean Single Market and Economy (CSME) and the EU-CARIFORUM Economic Partnership Agreement (EPA) facilitate this process? (*Iberoamericana/Stockholm*, 38:1/2, 2008, p. 81–102, bibl.)

A clearly written analysis of CARICOM's economic limitations and the problems these states face with respect to trade competitiveness. The move toward a Caribbean Single Market and Economy is seen as displaying gaps in planning. The region's partnership agreement with the EU is also seen as inadequate if agricultural competitiveness and the development of knowledge-based industries are to be achieved. See also item **1663**.

1671 Morales Dominguez, Esteban and **Gary Prevost.** United States-Cuban relations: a critical history. Lanham, Md.: Lexington Books, 2008. 166 p.: bibl., index.

The authors provide a historical review of US-Cuban relations, emphasizing that Cuba's behavior has stemmed from the desire for independence from first Spain and later US control. They discuss economic changes as well as changes in the exile community. The ability of Cuba to survive after Castro, despite the US hard line, is assessed favorably.

1672 Muggah, Robert. The effects of stabilisation on humanitarian action in Haiti. (*Disasters*, 34, special issue, Oct. 2010, p. 444–463)

This paper reviews the discourse, practice, and outcomes associated with three parallel stabilization initiatives undertaken in Haiti between 2007 and 2009. Although they shared many similar objectives, the paper describes how these separate interventions mobilized very different approaches. The specific focus is on the US, UN, and combined Brazilian, Canadian, and Norwegian stabilization efforts and their implications for humanitarian actors, including the International Committee of the Red Cross and Médecins Sans Frontières. It concludes with some reflections on the implications of stabilization before and after the country's most recent natural disaster. [C.E. Griffin]

1673 Payne, Anthony J. The political history of CARICOM. Kingston; Miami, Fla.: Ian Randle Publishers, 2008. 306 p.: bibl., index.

This is a new edition of a book written in 1980 providing useful information on the genesis and progress of the Caribbean integration movement. Updates to 2007. For comment on original edition, *The Politics of the Caribbean Community, 1961–79*, see *HLAS 45:3218.*

1674 Production integration in CARICOM: from theory to action. Edited by Denis Benn and Kenneth O. Hall. Kingston; Miami, Fla.: Ian Randle Publishers, 2006. 256 p.: bibl., index.

Presentations of a seminar on the possibilities of organizing production in regional enterprises utilizing inputs from different member states of CARICOM. This is a technical text. For political scientist's comment, see *HLAS 63:2047.*

1675 Ritter, Archibald R.M. Canada's economic relations with Cuba, 1990 to 2010 and beyond. (*Can. Foreign Policy*, 16:1, April 2010, p. 119–140)

This article seeks to analyze and explain the principal features of the economic relationship between Canada and Cuba in the decades of the 1990s and the 2000s, and to explore the major determinants and possible character of this relationship in future. Examines a range of economic dimensions, including trade in goods and services (notably tourism), direct foreign investment, international migration, and development assistance. [C.E. Griffin]

1676 Roy, Joaquín. The Cuban Revolution 1959–2009: relations with Spain, the European Union, and the United States. New York, N.Y.: Palgrave/Macmillan, 2009. 220 p.: bibl., index.

The book provides details on a topic on which there has been relatively little scholarly work: Cuban-EU relations focusing primarily on Spain. In contrast to the US, the EU policy has been one of constructive engagement but one also marred by periods of argument and insult. The author sees Spain's continued engagement with Cuba as the product of the long cultural history between them, generating a "family" style relationship. Economic and business relations, though not central to Spain's economy, underpin the relationship.

1677 Schoultz, Lars. That infernal little Cuban republic: the United States and the Cuban Revolution. Chapel Hill: Univ. of North Carolina Press, 2009. 745 p.: bibl., index.

This book can be regarded as a definitive review of US-Cuban policy from the 19th century to the 21st (that is, through the administration of George W. Bush). Written in an easily readable style, it contains a wealth of detail, including relevant historical anecdotes. The general theme is that the US has maintained a failed "realist" policy oriented toward "benevolent domination" of Cuba. The tone is decidedly sympathetic to Cuba.

1678 Spadoni, Paolo. Failed sanctions: why the U.S. embargo against Cuba could never work. Gainesville: Univ. Press of Florida, 2010. 230 p.: bibl., ill., index. (Contemporary Cuba)

How effective has the embargo been in achieving its main goal? The author dispassionately answers, "not very." By extending his analysis to nonstate actors (including multinational corporations, migrants, international travelers, indirect investors, and food exporters), the author demonstrates that the US has not only been unable to stifle the flow of foreign investment into Cuba, but has actually contributed to the recovery of the Cuban economy, particularly from the deep recession it entered following the demise of the Soviet Union. [C.E. Griffin]

1679 Strauss, Michael John. The leasing of Guantanamo Bay. Westport, Conn.: Praeger Security International, 2009. 316 p.: bibl., facsims., indexes, map.

This is a trenchant and readable analysis of the legal dimensions of the Guantánamo leasing arrangement. The author basically sees Cuban arguments as not particularly strong or sustainable. However, he also questions recent US legal decisions about the treatment of detainees, which, in rejecting the full application of US law to detainees, has created a "black hole" of uncertainty as to Guantánamo's status. See also item **1655**.

Sukup, Viktor. Les Caraïbes face à l'avenir. See item **1186**.

1680 Survival and sovereignty in the Caribbean Community. Edited by Kenneth O. Hall and Myrtle Chuck-A-Sang. Kingston; Miami, Fla.: Ian Randle Publishers, 2006. 198 p.: bibl., ill. (The integrationist)

This is an edition of a CARICOM journal covering a disparate a set of topics from abortion in Jamaica (as it relates to international law) to proposals for dealing with drug trafficking, various aspects of international economic relations, and a discussion of CARICOM applications of the eroding norm of nonintervention.

Wells, Allen. Tropical Zion: General Trujillo, FDR, and the Jews of Sosua. See item **1195**.

SOUTH AMERICA (EXCEPT BRAZIL)

ALDO C. VACS, *Professor of Government, Skidmore College*

CONTINUING A TREND started since the completion of the process of democratization in the region in the 1990s, recent publications on South American international relations reflect a sustained interest in political economic topics, such as subregional integration and economic relations, free trade agreements, relations with extrahemispheric and global organizations, and frontier area interactions and processes of integration. The impact on foreign policy of the spread and consolidation of nationalist populist and left-of-center governments in several countries has resulted in many interesting studies on the evolution of relations with the US, the emergence of intraregional tensions, and the attempts to develop common policies and establish new institutional arrangements to promote democratic stability and peaceful relations in the region. Publications focused on more traditional issues, such as territorial disputes and bilateral confrontations, are still numerous but they are generally objective and focused on analyzing and proposing negotiated solutions to the disputes. Studies of bilateral relations are predominantly focused on neighboring countries and the US, but there is a marked increase in studies addressing individual countries' relations with other developed countries and extraregional organizations. As in the past, most books and articles on international relations are produced in the largest countries in the region, but there has been an important increase in publications from smaller countries and a shift in focus from individual countries' policies to multilateral relations and international organizations. There has also been a noticeable increase in the number of publications involving experts from different South American countries, reflecting the continuous growth of academic cooperation in the region.

Among the publications devoted to international economic relations, an important number are focused on the processes of regional and subregional integration, including general studies of public opinion reaction to economic integration (item **1682**), the rise of supranationalism in the region (item **1686**), the resolution of controversies (item **1687**), the prospects of building a regional community (item **1694**), and the possibility of alternative models of integration (item **1688**). Most of the analyses of the processes of subregional integration are focused on Mercosur and the Andean Community (items **1685**, **1689**, **1690**, **1692**, and **1693**) or on contrasting the subregional processes with the proposal for a Free Trade Area of the Americas (item **1711**). Another political economic issue that has generated interest has been the signing of free trade agreements, particularly between the US and Colombia (item **1734**). Economic relations with extrahemispheric organizations such as the European Union have also resulted in interesting studies (item **1689**), while the growing importance of economic relations with China is reflected in a number of studies (items **1699**, **1717**, and **1719**). Finally, a substantial number of works have been devoted to frontier areas, concentrating on the economic, political, cultural, and social implications of the processes of integration and normalization of relations for populations living on the borders (items **1691**, **1703**, **1737**, and **1762**).

Concerning regional security problems, several important studies focus on the reverberations of Colombia's internal conflict on neighboring countries, such as Ecuador and Venezuela, including border violations, guerrilla activities, refugee flows, and other sources of tension (items **1727**, **1728**, **1731**, **1738**, **1741**, **1743**, and **1761**). In most cases these studies tend to blame the actions of the Colombian military and paramilitary groups for the deterioration of relations and call for regional initiatives to defuse tensions. Other conflictive bilateral relations involving territorial disputes and national rivalries have caught the attention of international relations experts, particularly the cases of Argentina-Chile (items **1698**, **1701**, **1705**, **1718**, **1721**, and **1726**), Chile-Peru (items **1720** and **1752**), and Ecuador-Peru (items **1739**, **1740**, **1742**, and **1744**). Most of these studies examine negotiations that in the last few years led to the resolution of these disputes and to the establishment of peaceful and more cooperative relations, while avoiding the traditional antagonistic and nationalistic approaches that characterized this kind of work in the past.

The historical evolution, current features, and future prospects of bilateral relations with the US are examined in studies focused on Argentina (item **1710**), Colombia (item **1733**), Paraguay (item **1746**), and Venezuela (item **1759**). At the same time, a number of works have been focused on relations with other extraregional actors besides those already mentioned involving China and the European Union. Among these studies are examinations of relations between Argentina and South Korea (item **1707**), Colombia and the Netherlands (item **1732**), Peru with Germany and Italy (items **1750** and **1753**), as well as analyses of the role of Chile in UN peacekeeping operations (item **1722**) and Uruguay in the Middle East (item **1756**).

Finally, a number of informative and well-researched studies examine the recent evolution and prospects of the foreign policies of most of the countries in the region, focusing on the impact of democratization and the rise of center-left and populist administrations in many of them. These studies are devoted to Argentina's foreign policies under the Kirchners (items **1704** and **1706**), Bolivia in the 2000s (items **1714** and **1715**), Chile since democratization (items **1716**, **1722**, and **1725**), Colombia in the last few years (item **1736**), Ecuador since 2006 (item **1745**), Uruguay after democratization (items **1754** and **1755**), and Venezuela under Chávez (items **1757** and **1760**).

GENERAL

1681 ALBA vs. ALCA: notas sobre política, cultura, ciudadanía e integración latinoamericanas y caribeñas. Caracas: Fundación Celarg, 2007. 301 p.: bibl. (Col. En foco; 1)

Publication of the official Rómulo Gallegos Latin American Studies Center Foundation of the Bolivarian Republic of Venezuela contains a number of articles discussing the advantages and disadvantages for the Latin American people of the Bolivarian Alternative for the Americas (ALBA) in comparison with the Free Trade Area of the Americas (FTAA). Although the contributors are unanimously in favor of ALBA and opposed to the FTAA, the volume is useful as it offers a comprehensive presentation of the economic, social, political, educational, ethical, and philosophical arguments favorable to the former while presenting a compendium of the most significant criticisms aimed at the latter in Latin America.

1682 Aragón, Jorge and **Julio César Postigo.** Integración económica regional y opinión pública en América del Sur. (*Debate Agrar.*, 40/41, julio 2006, p. 169–196, tables)

Study based on public opinion surveys conducted by *Latinobarómetro* in the Spanish-speaking South American countries and Brazil between 1997 and 2002 concludes that, despite slight fluctuations, there is majority support for and a positive attitude toward regional integration. Among other observations, the study points out that support for integration is relatively higher in the Andean countries, among the more educated, and among those who are stronger supporters of democracy in the region.

1683 Bátiz-Lazo, Bernardo; Ana Blanco Mendialdua; and **Sara Urionabarrenetxea Zabalandikoetxea.** Growth of the Spanish multinational in Latin America during the 1990s. (*Lat. Am. Bus. Rev.*, 8:1, 2007, p. 1–36, appendix, graphs, tables)

Brief but informative study of the growth of foreign direct investment by Spanish firms in Latin America during the 1990s. It includes a rapid historical review of the rise of Spanish multinationals and the evolution of the Latin American economies before focusing on the expansion of Span-

ish multinational presence in the region. It highlights that Spanish investment has been focused on the key Latin American markets (Mexico, Chile, Brazil, and Argentina) taking advantage of the processes of privatization and concentrating on demand-oriented activities such as public utilities, communications, and the financial sector rather than on creating export platform activities.

1684 Bonilla, Adrián and **Alexei Páez.** Estados Unidos y la región andina: distancia y diversidad. (*Nueva Soc.*, 206, nov./dic. 2006, p. 126–139, ill.)

Article examines the declining relations between the US and the Andean countries (Bolivia, Colombia, Ecuador, and Peru) arguing that US foreign policies toward these countries have been exclusively focused on commercial and security issues, ignoring most of the important economic, social, and political problems in the region. The Andean countries meanwhile have engaged mostly in reactive policies implemented separately without attempting to design a common policy strategy based on their shared interests in relation to the US.

1685 Castilho, Marta Reis. Acordo de Livre Comércio com a UE: a vulnerabilidade dos produtos industriais produzidos pelo Mercosul á competição européia. (*Nova Econ./Belo Horizonte*, 15:2, maio/agôsto 2005, p. 153–182, bibl., index, tables)

Well-researched paper identifies those manufactured goods produced in the Mercosur countries that could be threatened by European goods should they become more easily available as a result of a free trade agreement with the European Union. The author finds that there are more than 4,000 products vulnerable to European competition, particularly in sectors such as electrical machinery and equipment, basic metals, textiles, and transportation equipment.

La creación de UNASUR en el marco de la seguridad y la defensa. See item **1536.**

1686 Delgado, Jaime. Construcciones supranacionales e integración regional latinoamericana. San José: Editorial UCR, 2009. 288 p.: bibl.

Singular philosophical-political analysis of the rise of supranationalism in

Latin America in the context of the recent experiences of regional integration including the Andean Community, Mercosur, and the Central American process. Departing from the analysis of the state, sovereignty, and supranationalism from the Kantian and Hegelian perspectives, the author discusses the construction of supranational identities in South and Central America through economic, legal, and institutional integration, attempting to develop a philosophical foundation for the creation of a "utopian" supranational reality in a region capable of establishing a state able to protect human rights.

1687 Delich, Valentina. El intercambio comercial y la solución de controversias en América del Sur: preocupaciones y desafíos en el camino hacia el ALCA. (*Integr. Comer.*, 10:24, enero/junio 2006, p. 3–27, bibl., tables)

Informative article examining the new international legal mechanisms established to resolve commercial and economic disputes in the context of regional integration agreements in South America, particularly the Andean Community of Nations and Mercosur.

1688 Diálogo sudamericano: otra integración es posible. Edición de Richard Alan Dello Buono, Diana Avila P. y Aram Aharonian. Quito: Ediciones La Tierra; Lima: Consejería en Proyectos, 2006. 300 p.: bibl.

Collection of essays resulting from a symposium held in Quito, Ecuador, in 2005, attended by representatives of 75 regional integration organizations, political parties, NGOs, and academic institutions devoted to the discussion of South American alternative integration. The volume includes valuable essays analyzing the history of integration attempts in the region and contrasting the characteristics of the Comunidad Andina de Naciones (CAN), the Mercado Común del Sur (Mercosur), and the Alianza Bolivariana para los Pueblos de Nuestra América (ALBA). Other essays examine the challenges facing the regional civil societies in their integration attempts and the role of the mass media (including TELESUR) in this regard; the clashes between the bilateral free trade treaties promoted by the US

and the projects for regional integration; the impact of intra-regional migrations; and the possible role to be played by political parties and social movements in the context of regional integration processes.

1689 EULATIN II (Project). Jornadas Científicas. 2nd, São Paulo, 2007. MERCOSUR y Unión Europea. Textos de Manuel Cienfuegos Mateo *et al.* Coordinación de Zlata Drnas de Clément. Edición de Waldemar Hummer. Córdoba, Argentina: Lerner Editora, 2008. 343 p.: bibl.

Compendium of papers discussing different aspects of the processes of regional integration in South America and Europe delivered at the 2007 conference organized in São Paulo (Brazil) by seven European and South American universities that participate in the EULATIN II program sponsored by the European Commission. The volume contains informative analyses of the mechanisms for the settlement of controversies in Mercosur, the relations between Mercosur and the EU, the genesis and viability of UNASUR (South American Union of Nations), the incorporation of Venezuela to Mercosur, the connections with the Law of the Sea, the global free trade regime, and the role of international law.

1690 Gutiérrez Nieto, Guillermo. La Comunidad Andina: hoja de ruta hacia nuevas oportunidades. (*Rev. Mex. Polít. Exter.*, 79/80, nov. 2006/junio 2007, p. 103–127)

Critical review of the recent evolution of the Comunidad Andina (Andean Community) after negative developments such as Venezuela's departure, Bolivia's joining of the ALBA (Alianza Bolivariana para los Pueblos de Nuestra América), and the bilateral free trade agreements between the US and Peru and Colombia—as well as the incorporation of Chile as associate member, the agreements with Mexico and the EU, and the renewal by the US of the Andean Trade Promotion and Drug Eradication Act.

1691 La integración y el desarrollo social fronterizo. v. 1, Densidad, integración y conflicto en la triple frontera: Perú, Bolivia, Chile. v. 2, Cruzando la raya: dinámicas socioeducativas e integración fronteriza: el caso del Ecuador con Colombia y Perú. v. 3, La emergencia de la triple-frontera andina:

Perú, Bolivia y Chile. v. 4, Integración regional. Bogotá: Convenio Andrés Bello, 2006–2008. 4 v.: ill., maps. (Serie Integración social y fronteras; 1–4)

Valuable collection of articles published by the executive secretariat of the Convenio Andrés Bello in the series devoted to the analysis of social integration in border areas between South American countries. Departing from the premise that the relations established between neighboring national communities represent a central issue in promoting or hindering regional integration, the articles examine a number of areas and situations in which transnational cooperation and conflict have recently emerged. Among these studies, there are several focused on triple frontier cases (Peru-Bolivia-Chile; Ecuador-Colombia-Peru; Bolivia-Argentina-Paraguay) that one of the authors, Sergio González Miranda, considers "natural supranational regions"; migration flows between countries; the potential for integration among the Pacific basin countries; and the impact of border situations on the prospects of South American integration projects. In general, without ignoring the persistence of some international disputes, the authors tend to emphasize the emergence of conditions favorable to transborder economic, social, and cultural consolidation; integrative development policies; and a trend toward infrastructural, economic, educational, and environmental cooperation.

Kahhat, Farid. Tras la Guerra Fría: mentalidad militar y políticas de seguridad en Sudamérica. See item **1548.**

1692 Malamud, Andrés and **Philippe C. Schmitter.** La experiencia de integración europea y el potencial de integración del Mercosur. (*Desarro. Econ.,* 46:181, abril/junio 2006, p. 3–31, bibl., graph)

Well-researched comparative examination of the processes of integration by the EU and Mercosur analyzes them from theoretical and empirical perspectives before drawing a number of conclusions and recommendations for the future of Mercosur based on the European experience.

1693 MERCOSUR y NAFTA: instituciones y mecanismos de decisión en procesos de integración asimétricos. Edición de

Susanne Gratius. Madrid: Iberoamericana; Frankfurt, Germany: Vervuert, 2008. 371 p.: bibl.

Interesting comparative analysis of two models of integration: Mercosur—as a model of South-South integration "from above," and NAFTA—as one of North-South integration based on rules, in which the authors examine their respective institutional arrangements and decision-making processes, the mechanisms for the settlement of disputes, the power asymmetries between the participants and the possibilities of introducing reforms to reduce them, as well as the prospects for deepening the integration process in each case.

1694 Reza, Germán A. de la. Integración económica en América Latina: hacia una comunidad regional en el siglo XXI. México: Univ. Autónoma Metropolitana Azcapotzalco: Plaza y Valdés, 2006. 317 p.: bibl., ill., index.

Interesting study explores the process and mechanisms for regional integration in Latin America from the viewpoints of classical economic integration theory and the new regionalism. Concludes that it is necessary to focus on the heterodox aspects of regionalism beyond trade, to study the process from a multidisciplinary perspective (not exclusively economic), to deepen the contents of the agreements, and to expand the geographical scope of the integration accords inside and outside the region.

1695 Smith, Hugh. Terrorism in the Iguazu Falls region: $100 bills, a DIME at a time. Fort Leavenworth, Kans.: School of Advanced Military Studies, US Army Command and General Staff College, 2005. 56 p.: appendix, bibl., map.

Monograph written at the US School of Advanced Military Studies using the DIME Plus model (Diplomatic, Informational, Military, Economic, Intelligence, and Law Enforcement) to analyze the security threats present in the Tri-Border Area (joining Argentina, Brazil, and Paraguay around Iguazu Falls). The author argues that terrorist groups (particularly, Hezbollah) are present in the area taking advantage of the relative lack of control to engage in criminal activities such as drug trafficking, money laundering, and document fraud to finance and plan their actions. Most interesting is the analysis of the different interests, motivations, interpretations, and approaches held by the members of the 3+1 Group (Argentina, Brazil, Paraguay, and US) that have led to controversies and policy disagreements concerning the issue.

1696 Tello, Ángel Pablo; Jorge Claudio Szeinfeld; and Isabel Stanganelli. La política imperial: un pensamiento estratégico desde América del Sur. La Plata, Argentina: EDULP, 2007. 276 p.: bibl. (Col. Comunicaciones; 2)

Critical study of the antiterrorist strategy of the US after September 11, 2001 focused particularly on its impact on South America. The authors analyze the US "imperial actions" against the new terrorist actors from an historical and political perspective, tracing their origins back to the Roman Empire policies and discussing the current situation in South America, especially in reference to the so-called Triple Frontier (the border area shared by Argentina, Brazil, and Paraguay). The authors emphasize the need to formulate a security strategy that does not privilege military intervention in detriment to the role of the nation-state, community action, and respect for human rights, therefore resulting in an integrated space characterized by adequate development and peace.

ARGENTINA

Allan, Laurence. Néstor Kirchner, Santa Cruz, and the Hielos Continentales controversy 1991–1999. See item **1418**.

1697 Die Beziehungen zwischen Deutschland und Argentinien. Herausgegeben von Peter Birle. Frankfurt am Main: Vervuert, 2010. 380 p.: bibl., ill. (Bibliotheca Ibero-Americana; 135)

Proceedings from a conference held in Berlin in 2007 about German-Argentine relations from 1800 to the present. The work emphasizes the history of diplomatic relations, German migration to Argentina until 1945, military and economic relations in the 20th century, and cultural and literary contacts in the 20th century. Provides a good overview of some of the lesser-known aspects of German-Argentine relations. [F. Obermeier]

1698 Colacrai de Trevisan, Miryam. Las relaciones bilaterales Argentina-Chile: el impacto del contexto democrático y el incremento de contactos subnacionales. (*Estudios/Córdoba*, 18, otoño 2006, p. 57–72, bibl.)

Interesting examination of the positive evolution of Argentine-Chilean relations since the 1990s analyzes the influence of political variables, including the impact of the simultaneous processes of democratization, presidential diplomacy and the formation of a strategic alliance, and the importance of the contacts by governmental and nongovernmental subnational actors in promoting closer economic, political, and cultural relations.

1699 Galperín, Carlos; Gustavo Girado; and Eduardo Rodríguez Diez. Consecuencias para América Latina del nuevo rol de China en la economía internacional: el caso argentino. (*Integr. Comer.*, 10:24, enero/junio 2006, p. 95–127, bibl., graphs, tables)

Article examines the growing role played by China in the international economy and the new character of its relations with Argentina. It offers an informative account of the evolution of bilateral commercial relations, explores the crucial sectors for potential increase of Argentine and Chinese exports, reviews the initiatives taken by Argentina to cement these relations, and concludes with a series of recommendations aimed at strengthening the bilateral ties.

1700 García Lucero, Dafne. La política exterior argentina y su difusión en los medios gráficos de comunicación masiva: análisis de un caso: la visita del Presidente Clinton a la Argentina en el año 1997. Córdoba, Argentina: Univ. Nacional de Córdoba, Centro de Estudios Avanzados, 2007. 242 p.: ill. (Col. Tesis de maestría en relaciones internacionales; 7)

Interesting thesis addressing a relatively neglected aspect of Argentina's foreign policy: how it is presented in and influenced by the printed media. The author focuses on US President Clinton's 1997 visit to Argentina as it was reported in two of the main Argentine newspapers: *Página/12* (center-left) and *La Nación* (conservative). The content analysis indicates that both newspapers tend to rely mostly on official sources, to focus on the economic (commercial and financial) aspects of the relationship, to ignore the role of the legislators, and to present Argentina as an impoverished and strategically almost insignificant country that would be well advised to maintain a low profile. *Pagina/12* tends to take a more critical attitude concerning the US economic and diplomatic policies while *La Nación* calls for a more cooperative attitude, in both cases using Brazil as a reference to support their positions.

1701 García Romano, Martín Alejandro.
El espejismo del último conflicto: historia del límite entre Argentina y Chile, Hielos Continentales y Lago del Desierto. Santa Rosa, Argentina: Ediciones Amerindia, 2008. 421 p.: bibl., maps.

Highly critical study of the negotiations between Argentina and Chile in the 1990s that resulted in the resolution of the last remaining border dispute between both countries centered on the areas known as the Southern Patagonia Ice Field (Hielos Continentales) and Desert Lake or Lagoon (Lago del Desierto, Argentina, or Laguna del Desierto, Chile). The author severely criticizes what he interprets as the Menem administration's unjustified territorial concessions to Chile, arguing that the agreements violate Argentina's traditional rights and do not guarantee the prevention of future border disputes—thus, the title's reference to the "mirage of the last conflict." Nevertheless, the book offers an interesting and detailed survey of the negotiations, the actors involved, and the opposition of some Argentine nationalist groups to the final settlement.

1702 Giacomino, Claudio A. Cuestión de imagen: la diplomacia cultural en el siglo XXI. Buenos Aires: Editorial Biblos, 2009. 196 p.: bibl., ill. (Politeia)

One of the few studies focused on cultural foreign policy produced in Argentina. The author, a career diplomat who was cultural attaché at the Argentine embassy in Oslo, presents a comprehensive view of the importance of cultural relations before discussing its evolution and prospects from the Argentine perspective. Interesting evaluation of Argentine cultural foreign policies and useful set of policy recommendations.

1703 Grimson, Alejandro. La nación en sus límites: contrabandistas y exiliados en la frontera Argentina-Brasil. Barcelona, Spain: Gedisa Editorial, 2003. 251 p.: bibl. (Serie Culturas)

Excellent anthropological, political, and social study of the "contact culture" that has developed in the border region between Argentina and Brazil, particularly in the area of the cities of Paso de los Libres (Argentina) and Uruguaiana (Brazil) located on the Uruguay River and connected by an international bridge. The author examines the transborder networks and practices, the character and impact of the national and local identities, and the historical evolution and cycles of interaction between the Argentine and Brazilian populations. Highlights the fact that what has emerged in the area is not a homogeneous "frontier culture," but a "contact culture" in which both sides recognize themselves as having different identities, while engaging in exchanges that could result in transborder alliances and some degree of cultural hybridization.

1704 Hacia una nueva estrategia internacional: el desafío de Néstor Kirchner. Investigación de Juan Gabriel Tokatlian *et al.* Prólogo de Carlos Bruno. Buenos Aires: Grupo Editorial Norma, 2004. 214 p.: bibl. (Tiempos de cambio)

Thoughtful study of the global, regional, and national conditions in the early 2000s aimed at recommending a new international strategic approach for Argentina during the Néstor Kirchner administration (2003–2007). The first chapter analyzes the changes affecting sovereignty, power, security, and identity since the end of the Cold War in the context of globalization and democratization. The second chapter focuses on the new transnational security threats such as terrorism, drug trafficking, and organized crime, and the US approach to these threats. The third chapter discusses the problems of peace and security from the Latin American perspective, particularly after 9/11. The last chapter delineates and recommends a new Argentine grand strategy characterized as "active diversification" including promoting national identity, regional integration, and an international selective activity guided by the principles of multilateralism, peace advancement, and defense of democracy and human rights.

1705 Huneeus, Carlos. Argentina y Chile: el conflicto del gas, factores de política interna argentina. (*Estud. Int./ Santiago*, 40:158, sept./dic. 2007, p. 149–177, bibl., graphs, tables)

Critical examination of the 2004 decision by the Argentine government to reduce natural gas to Chile while increasing prices through new export taxes, leading to renewed tensions between the two countries after a period of relative calm and cooperation. The author analyzes the impact of these decisions on the Chilean economy, the crucial role played by Chile's presidents in trying to solve the problem, and the domestic political motivations of Argentine president, Néstor Kirchner, in implementing these initiatives.

1706 Lorenzini, Maria Elena. La política exterior durante la administración Kirchner entre mayo de 2003 y diciembre de 2005: ¿retórica o práctica autonomista? (*TD Temas Debates*, 10:11, oct. 2006, p. 93–113, bibl.)

Controversial article examines the Néstor Kirchner administration's foreign policy in the early part of his presidency arguing that while the rhetoric aimed at the domestic public may be autonomic, the foreign policy actions are not. Concludes that the administration assimilates confrontational discourse with autonomic practice.

1707 Mera, Carolina. Panorama general y reflexiones acerca de las relaciones entre Argentina y Corea. (*Estud. Int./Santiago*, 39:156, enero/marzo 2007, p. 67–82, bibl.)

Brief review of the evolution of the economic, political, and cultural relations between Argentina and South Korea, including an examination of Korean migration to Argentina.

1708 Rodríguez, Malvina Eugenia. La recuperación de la tercera posición como alternativa política argentina y latinoamericana. Córdoba, Argentina: Ediciones del Copista, 2006. 129 p.: bibl. (Col. "La tierra y el mar"; 5)

Informative account and positive treatment of the contents, evolution, and application of the "Third Position doctrine"

from its origins in the 1940s to the early 2000s, focusing on its application during Perón's three presidencies and Menem's administration. From a sympathetic perspective, the author discusses the possible application of the doctrine in the context of Latin American integration as a regional alternative to globalization.

1709 Russell, Roberto and **Juan Gabriel Tokatlian.** A crise na Argentina e as relações com o Brasil e os Estados Unidos: continuidade e mudança nas relações triangulares. (*Contexto Int.*, 26:1, jan./junho 2004, p. 107–148, bibl.)

Following a brief historical analysis of the relations established by Argentina with Brazil and the US from the 19th century to 2000, the authors focus on the impact of the Argentine financial-economic crisis of 2001 on the triangular relations. Concludes that Argentina would likely try to form a strategic bilateral alliance with Brazil, while developing a positive and cordial relationship with the US.

1710 Sheinin, David. Argentina and the United States: an alliance contained. Athens: Univ. of Georgia Press, 2006. 285 p.: bibl., index. (The United States and the Americas)

Historical account of the evolution of US-Argentine relations from the early 19th century until the aftermath of the Argentine crisis of 2001. Against the prevailing views, the author argues that the history of the bilateral relations—even if marked by episodic conflicts—has been characterized by cooperation based on economic ties, shared strategic interests, and strong cultural contacts. Although this interpretation could be disputed, the author's analysis and conclusions merit discussion.

1711 Simonoff, Alejandro. Los dilemas de la autonomía: la política exterior de Arturo Illia, 1963–1966. Buenos Aires: Nuevohacer, Grupo Editor Latinoamericano, 2007. 240 p.: bibl., ill.

Excellent study of a relatively neglected period in Argentina's foreign policy during the Radical administration of Arturo H. Illia (1963–66). Although emerging from vitiated elections in which Peronist participation was proscribed, the Illia administration—interrupted by the military coup of 1966—represented one of the few liberal democratic experiences in Argentina between 1930 and 1983. It attempted to implement a foreign policy that combined autonomic, nonaligned, and multipolar elements with some degree of flexibility in the application of the traditional Radical nonintervention principles. The author traces the theoretical framework of this foreign policy strategy to the ECLA and dependency perspectives, discusses the decision-making mechanisms and procedures, and analyzes the evolution of relations with the US, Western Europe, the Third World, and Latin America. He focuses on economic development, security policies, and territorial issues, and concludes by studying three cases: the Dominican Republic intervention of 1965, the annulment of oil contracts with US companies, and the Malvinas-Falklands issue.

1712 Wulffen, Bernd. Deutsche Spuren in Argentinien: zwei Jahrhunderte wechselvoller Beziehungen. Berlin: Links, 2010. 260 p.: bibl., ill., index.

Concise but useful historical overview of the last 200 years of German-Argentine relations (the earlier period is treated in a very short introduction). The presentation is centered on Germans living and working in Argentina. Includes some of the author's personal memories of working at the German Embassy in Buenos Aires. [F. Obermeier]

BOLIVIA

1713 Diálogos sobre política exterior boliviana. v. 1, La complejidad de nuestras circunstancias. v. 2, Crisis y transición: reflexiones previas al cambio, 2003–2005. Textos de Arturo de la Riva B. *et al.* La Paz: Ministerio de Relaciones Exteriores y Culto, UDAPEX: Konrad Adenauer Stiftung, 2004–2007. 2 v.: bibl.

Two volumes containing discussions among Bolivian experts, politicians, and policymakers concerning Bolivia's global insertion, international relations, and foreign policy. The first volume published in late 2004 is focused on the Bolivian foreign policy agenda; the issue of coca; relations with Peru, Chile, and the EU; frontier areas and development, the impact of the US 2004

elections; and the country's foreign policy prospects. The second volume, published in late 2007, focuses on the South American Community of Nations and the role of Bolivia, the impact of the European Generalized System of Preferences, the prospects for Bolivian relations with China, regional security, natural gas and regional relations, Bolivia's role in regional integration, and the foreign policy programs of the main political parties, including the Movimiento al Socialismo (MAS) led by Evo Morales (who was elected president in 2005). Not very well organized, but informative analysis of most aspects of Bolivia's international relations and foreign policy prospects.

1714 Fernández Saavedra, Gustavo. Bolivia in the new Latin American political scenario. (*T'inkazos*, 22, julio 2007, p. 1–11)

Article by former Bolivian minister of foreign affairs examines the political, social, and cultural transformations occurring in his country at the time of the presidential election of Evo Morales. Argues that similar developments were occurring in most of Latin America and discusses their impact on the regional integration crisis and the region's oil and gas markets in which Bolivia has an important role.

1715 Portillo, Alfredo. La nueva coyuntura geopolítica de Bolivia. (*Rev. Venez. Cienc. Polít.*, 31, enero/junio 2007, p. 75–84, bibl.)

Brief geopolitical analysis of the internal regional tensions emerging in Bolivia in the early 2000s and the possible impact on other countries, especially in terms of natural gas exports and the regional integration process.

CHILE

1716 Ampliación de las perspectivas de la política exterior chilena. (*Estud. Int./Santiago*, 39:154, julio/sept. 2006, p. 91–178)

Substantial collection of articles examining the evolution of Chile's foreign policies from the beginning of the transition to democracy in 1990 to the end of Ricardo Lagos' presidency in 2006. The collection includes articles dealing with the general evolution of Chile's regional and global policies (Joaquín Fernandois; p. 91–100), the conflictive relations with Bolivia (Oscar Fuentes Lazo; p. 101–108 and Juan I. Siles del Valle; p. 109–116), a longer account of the evolution of the bilateral relations with Brazil between 1966 and 2006 (Gelso Fonseca Jr.; p. 117–138), the agreement with India (Jorge Heine; p. 139–146), the historical evolution of relations with Japan (Roberto de Andraca Barbás; p. 147–168), and relations with China (Octavio Errázuriz Guiliasti; p. 169–178).

1717 Artaza Rouxel, Mario. Chile y Asia hoy: una mirada crítica. (*Estud. Int./ Santiago,* 39:156, enero/marzo 2007, p. 55–65)

Brief examination of the recent evolution of relations between Chile and the Asian countries concludes that despite the participation of Chile in the Asian Pacific Economic Council, the signing of a free trade agreement with China, and close relations with other Asian countries, Chile has not succeeded in becoming the "bridge" between Asia and Latin America. Chile should try to formulate a better strategy in this regard without neglecting its role in the regional integration processes.

Barton, Jonathan R.; Robert N. Gwynne; and Warwick E. Murray. Competition and co-operation in the semiperiphery: closer economic partnership and sectoral transformations in Chile and New Zealand. See item **952.**

1718 Castro Sauritain, Carlos. Las relaciones vecinales de Chile y la guerra del Atlántico Sur. Santiago: Editorial Mare Nostrum, 2006. 189 p.: bibl., map.

Interesting monograph by Chilean Air Force officer, military attaché, and specialist in international relations, that analyzes his country's position during the Falklands conflict between Argentina and the UK. Study confirms the negative attitude of the Pinochet government toward Argentina and its support for the UK, placing it into the historical context of the Argentine-Chilean territorial dispute that culminated in the 1978 Beagle Channel crisis. Written from a nationalist perspective, it justifies the Chilean position as a reaction to Argentina's aggressive policies, but does not offer new information concerning specific support for the British task force.

1719 Claro, Sebastián. Consecuencias para la región de América Latina y el Caribe de la aparición de China en el escenario económico mundial; documento informativo: el caso de Chile. (*Integr. Comer.,* 10:24, enero/junio 2006, p. 163–224, bibl., tables)

Very informative study of the recent evolution of economic relations between Chile and China including its trade composition, the competitive threat represented by Chinese products, the defensive commercial measures adopted by Chile, China's role in the world copper market, and the opportunities and problems associated with the signing of a bilateral free trade agreement.

1720 González Miranda, Sergio. La llave y el candado: el conflicto entre Perú y Chile por Tacna y Arica, 1883–1929. Santiago: LOM Ediciones: USACH, 2008. 208 p.: bibl., ill. (Historia)

Well-researched historical study of the conflict between Chile and Peru concerning the question of sovereignty over Tacna and Arica. Both the Treaty of Ancon (1883) and the later Treaty of Lima (1929) failed to resolve the territorial conflict, resulting in long-term bilateral tensions. Very interesting analyses of the role of nationalist and xenophobic groups and opinions in perpetuating the conflict and preventing a mutually beneficial resolution of the problem.

1721 Le Dantec Gallardo, Francisco. ¿Cooperación o conflicto?: relación argentino chilena. Chile: Foro Ediciones, 2008. 341 p.: bibl., ill.

Solid policy-oriented study concerning the prospects of regional security cooperation in South America focused on the Argentine-Chilean bilateral relationship. After a comprehensive discussion of recent changes in the international system and their impact on the notions of state, sovereignty, power, and identity, and the emerging concept of security involving cooperation, mutual confidence measures, and democracy, the author examines the evolution of Chilean-Argentine relations since the 1984 Treaty of Peace and Friendship and, in particular, the evolution of the bilateral security and defense relationship

that led to the formation of the Permanent
Committee on Argentine-Chilean Security
(1995). The study concludes that a flexible
system of subregional cooperative security
(including, at least, Argentina, Brazil, and
Chile) would contribute to promote regional
peace, integration, and democratic consolidation without affecting the hemispheric
security system.

1722 Le Dantec Valenzuela, Paulina. Chile
y las operaciones de paz: estudio
comparado de la política exterior de los
tres gobiernos concertacionistas: de la re-
inserción internacional a la participación en
Haití. Chile: Ministerio de Defensa Nacional, Academia Nacional de Estudios Políticos y Estratégicos, 2006. 172 p.: bibl. (Col. de
Investigationes ANEPE; 15)

Valuable study of the evolution of
Chilean participation in UN peacekeeping
operations since the transition to democracy
in 1990. The author examines the growing
participation of Chile in multilateral peace
missions against the historical background
of the country's defense and security policies since the early 20th century. Argues
that these initiatives were an integral part
of the strategy of multilateral international
reinsertion devised by the democratic administration of Presidents Aylwin, Frei, and
Lagos.

**1723 Mar de fondo: Chile y Bolivia: un
siglo de desencuentros.** Coordinación
de Loreto Correa Vera. Santiago: Instituto de Estudios Avanzados, Univ. Santiago
de Chile, 2007. 346 p.: bibl., ill. (Col. Idea.
Segunda época)

Collection of articles analyzing different historical and contemporary aspects
of the conflictive relations between Chile
and Bolivia written by authors from both
countries. The collection is very diverse and
includes valuable analyses of the security
and defense aspects of the relationship, possible ports for the export of Bolivian natural
gas, the perennial problem of Bolivia's lack
of exit to the sea, the impact of Argentina
on the bilateral treaties of 1895, and the
historical context of the Chilean-Bolivian
treaty of 1904.

1724 Rodriguez Márquez, Pablo and **Mario
Luis Puig Morales.** Chile y sus intereses en la Artártica [sic]: opciones políticas y

de seguridad frente a la escasez de recursos
hídricos. Chile: Academia Nacional de Estu-
dios Políticos y Estratégicos, Ministerio de
Defensa Nacional, 2007. 109 p.: bibl., col. ill.
(Col. Investigaciones Academia Nacional de
Estudios Políticos y Estratégicos; 18)

Monograph written by two Chilean
military officers examines the relevance
of the Antarctic continent from a Chilean
foreign policy perspective, particularly in
terms of its economic, security, and environmental interests. The authors emphasize
the importance of hydric resources present
in Antarctica and advance the hypothesis
that in the future such resources may lead
to conflicts related to global water scarcity.
They call for Chile to take the initiative to
protect its hydric resources in the context
of the Antarctic Treaty and in cooperation
with regional partners.

1725 Valdivieso, Patricio. Congreso Nacional y política exterior chilena: estado
actual y algunas propuestas. (*Estud. Int./
Santiago*, 40:158, sept./dic. 2007, p. 149–177,
bibl., tables)

Analysis of the relatively minor role
played by the Chilean Congress in the formulation of the country's foreign policy.
Recommends a number of initiatives, based
on the European experience of parliamentary activity, aimed at strengthening the
congressional role in foreign policy and
making its participation more professional,
representative, and efficient.

1726 Videla Cifuentes, Ernesto. La des-
conocida historia de la mediación
papal: diferendo austral Chile/Argentina,
1977–1985. 2. ed. Santiago: Ediciones Univ.
Católica de Chile, 2008. 709 p.: ill., indexes,
maps. (Divulgación)

Very informative chronicle of the
Beagle Channel dispute between Argentina
and Chile, the failed direct bilateral negotiations, and the Vatican mediation that
prevented armed conflict in 1978 and led to
the signing of the 1985 Treaty of Peace and
Friendship between both countries. Written by the Chilean general and former vice
minister of foreign relations who led Chile's
delegation to the negotiations, this insider's
account is objective, very detailed, and
would remain an essential source for historians, political scientists, and international
relations analysts.

COLOMBIA

1727 Colombia-Ecuador: cercanos y distantes. Edición de Socorro Ramírez y César Montúfar. Bogotá: Instituto de Estudios Políticos y Relaciones Internacionales de la Univ. Nacional de Colombia; Quito: Univ. Andina Simón Bolívar, Ecuador, 2007. 375 p.: bibl., ill.

Useful comprehensive report of the conflictive aspects and opportunities for cooperation in the relations between Colombia and Ecuador containing speeches, statements, debates, and research papers delivered by elected officials, functionaries, military officers, and experts from both countries and regional organizations at a series of bilateral meetings and workshops in 2006. The volume includes well-informed examinations and discussions of the bilateral political and diplomatic relations and the prospects for regional integration, issues of national security, particularly in the frontier areas, the problem of drug traffic and transnational crime, Colombian migration to Ecuador, border areas' integration, mutual foreign policy perceptions, the relations with the US, the impact of mass media on bilateral ties, and the cultural interactions between both countries.

1728 Colombia-Venezuela: retos de la convivencia. Coordinación de Socorro Ramírez y José María Cadenas G. Bogotá: Univ. Nacional de Colombia, Instituto de Estudios Políticos y Relaciones Internacional; Venezuela: Centro de Estudios de América de la Univ. Central de Venezuela, 2006. 413 p.: ill.

Collection of articles and statements produced by the Binational Academic Group sponsored by Colombian and Venezuelan universities after the period of heightened bilateral tensions resulting from the abduction of the FARC's Rodrigo Granda by Colombia's agents in Venezuela. The authors' explicit aim is to reduce tensions between both countries and to that end they analyze the positive economic, political, security, and cultural aspects of the relations, while recommending a number of initiatives to strengthen cooperation in frontier areas, health services, mass media, economic integration, security confidence measures, and cultural interactions.

1729 Gómez Quintero, Juan David. Las ONGD aragonesas en Colombia: ejecución y evaluación de los proyectos de desarrollo. Zaragoza, Spain: Prensas Univ. de Zaragoza, 2007. 311 p.: bibl., ill., maps. (Ciencias sociales/Prensas Univ. de Zaragoza; 64)

Interesting study of a relatively overlooked aspect of international relations in the context of globalization: the role played by NGOs in promoting development and peace in countries affected by violent internal conflicts. This sociological study delivers a useful analysis and evaluation of the activities performed by NGOs sponsored by the government of the autonomous community of Aragón (Spain) in order to encourage economic and social development and respect for human rights in the context of Colombia's armed conflict and violence.

1730 Guarnizo, Luis. Londres latina: la presencia colombiana en la capital británica. México: Univ. Autónoma de Zacatecas: Miguel Ángel Porrúa, 2008. 178 p.: bibl., ill. (América Latina y el nuevo orden mundial)

Informative examination and discussion of the relatively recent (since the 1970s) and large (between 50,000 and 70,000 people) Colombian migrant community residing in the metropolitan London area. The author analyzes the factors leading to this international migration movement, the heterogeneous characteristics of the Colombian "transnational social formation," and the impact of the relocation on sectors distinguished by different socioeconomic backgrounds, educational level, gender, linguistic skills, and regional origin.

1731 López Rojas, María Camila. Efectos de la regionalización de la política de seguridad democrática para el desplazamiento en las fronteras de Colombia. (*Colomb. Int.*, 65, enero/junio 2007, p. 136–151, bibl.)

Examination of the impact of the implementation of Plan Colombia and the Democratic Security Strategy on the displacement of Colombian populations into Ecuador, Panama, and Venezuela, as well as on the migration policies adopted by these neighboring countries. The author concludes that as a result of these approaches

"Colombian refugees do not have legal and institutional support from Colombian foreign policy that could guarantee human rights protection under its immigrant condition" in those countries.

1732 Relaciones interculturales: negociaciones entre colombianos y holandeses. Textos de Bart Van Hoof *et al.* Bogotá: Univ. de Los Andes, Facultad de Administración, 2005. 121 p.: bibl., ill. (Monografías de administración; 83. Serie Empresa, economía y sociedad)

Singular comparative study by Colombian and Dutch authors of the characteristics of both countries' negotiating styles. Based on multiple interviews, content analysis, and quantitative research, the study examines the cultural differences that affect each country's negotiating style and offers some suggestions aimed at improving the bilateral negotiation process and outcomes.

1733 Rojas, Diana Marcela. Plan Colombia II: ¿más de lo mismo? (*Colomb. Int.*, 65, enero/junio 2007, p. 14–37, bibl., graphs, tables)

Detailed analysis of the contents of the 2007–13 Strategy for the Strengthening of Democracy and Social Development adopted by the Colombian government that the author characterizes as the second phase of Plan Colombia. The article argues that the new strategy aims at gathering international support to consolidate this strategy's goals as well of those of the Policy of Democratic Security by developing a comprehensive plan that includes human rights and social and economic components that would result in a favorable response from the US and the rest of the global community.

Seguridades en construcción en América Latina. See item **1264**.

1734 Silva, Laura Cristina. El proceso de negociación del TLC Colombia y Estados Unidos. (*Colomb. Int.*, 65, enero/junio 2007, p. 112–133, bibl., graphs)

Article examines the negotiations concerning the free trade agreement between Colombia and the US, applying a two-level games model that explores the connections between domestic policy and diplomacy in international negotiations. After analyzing the actions and tactics of the actors (including policymakers, legislators, businesspeople, and civil society groups) as well as the political context, the author concludes that although President Alvaro Uribe gained adequate support from Colombia's Congress and businesspeople, his diplomatic strategy was not efficient in completing the agreement because it ignored US domestic politics as well as the activities of Peru and Ecuador.

1735 Skladowska, Bárbara. Los nombres de la patria en la Guerra de Corea, 1951–1953: ocaso de un mito. Bogotá: Univ. de los Andes, Facultad de Ciencias Sociales-CESO, Depto. de Historia, 2007. 146 p.: bibl., ill., maps. (Col. Prometeo)

Sensible study of the impact of the Colombian participation in the Korean War. Specifically, examines how the war affected the notion of "fatherland" held by Colombians in the context of the Cold War, anticommunism, and domestic violence. Interesting examination of how the war was used to construct different images of nationhood with new political and cultural meanings and social representations.

1736 Torrijos R., Vicente. Política exterior y relaciones internacionales. Bogotá: Centro de Estudios Políticos e Internacionales, Facultades de Ciencia Política y Gobierno y de Relaciones Internacionales: Editorial Univ. del Rosario, 2009. 378 p.: bibl., ill.

Collection of articles by Colombian professor and journalist analyzing different aspects of the evolution of the international system in the post-Cold War period. Those focused on Colombia's foreign policies particularly concern peace, security, and economic relations in the context of globalization. The author argues that the country's foreign policy has been erratic and requires important restructuring in order for Colombia to insert itself satisfactorily in the emerging international system.

1737 Vecindad sin límites: encuentro fronterizo colombo-venezolano, Zona de Integración Fronteriza entre el departamento de Norte de Santander y el estado Táchira. Edición de Francesca Ramos y Andrés Otálvaro. Bogotá: Editorial Univ. del Rosario, 2008. 128 p.: bibl.

Interesting contribution by Colom-

bian and Venezuelan academics and officials
to an understanding of the characteristics
and impact of the zone of frontier integration created between the neighboring department of Northern Santander (Colombia)
and Tachira state (Venezuela). Useful for
evaluating the importance of joint economic, social, and developmental interests
in neighboring areas and societies and for
promoting bilateral cooperation even in circumstances in which national governments
confront each other.

**1738 Vecindario agitado: Colombia y
Venezuela, entre la hermandad y la
conflictividad.** Edición de Eduardo Pastrana
Buelvas, Carsten Wieland y Juan Carlos
Vargas Restrepo. Bogotá: Editorial Ponti-
ficia Univ. Javeriana: Fundación Konrad
Adenauer Stiftung: Univ. del Rosario; Cali,
Colombia: Univ. Santiago de Cali, 2008.
270 p.: bibl.

Collection of articles written by Colombian academics discussing the evolution
and prospects of Colombian-Venezuelan
relations in the tense aftermath of the
March 2008 Colombian military incursion
in Ecuador. From a Colombian perspective,
the articles assess the conflicting political,
ideological, security, and economic views of
each side, as well as their negative impact
on the relationship, which they tend to
blame mainly on the positions adopted by
Hugo Chávez.

ECUADOR

1739 Ayala-Lasso, José. Así se ganó la paz.
Quito: Banco de Guayaquil, 2009.
564 p.: bibl., ill., folded col. map.

Interesting account by Ecuadorian
diplomat and former foreign minister who
conducted the negotiations resulting in the
1998 Brasília (or Itamaraty) Peace Accord.
The accord ended a secular border dispute
with Peru, which had caused periodic armed
confrontations between both countries. The
volume presents a history of the quarrel and
the negotiations from Ecuador's perspective,
and is a good source of inside information
on the political and military aspects of the
process and the importance of presidential
diplomacy.

1740 Carrión Mena, Francisco. La paz por
dentro: Ecuador-Perú: testimonio de
una negociación. Madrid: Univ. de Alcalá;

Quito: Municipio del Distrito Metropolitano de Quito: Esquel, Ecuador: FLACSO
Ecuador: Dinediciones, 2008. 615 p.: bibl.,
index, maps (some col.).

Detailed and very informative chronological account of the Ecuadorian-Peruvian
negotiations that led to the signing of the
Brasília (also called Itamaraty) Peace Accord
in 1998. Written by an Ecuadorian diplomat
and former minister of foreign relations who
participated in the negotiations, it examines the process from the failed proposal of
Vatican mediation and the Alto Cenepa War
in the early 1990s to the final agreement
in 1998, passing through the successive
rounds of negotiations set up in Argentina
and Brazil. Based on the author's personal
experience and annotations, the chronicle
provides a thorough analysis of the negotiations from Ecuador's perspective and elucidates the diplomatic steps taken to end one
of the lasting territorial conflicts in South
America.

1741 Chávez, Nashira. Cuando los mundos
convergen: terrorismo, narcotráfico y
migración post 9/11. Quito: FLACSO Ecuador: Ediciones Abya-Yala, 2008. 220 p.: bibl.
(Serie Tesis)

Interesting examination of the Ecuadorian foreign policies, particularly in reference to migration and drug traffic in the
context of the security strategy and policies
pursued by the George W. Bush administration in the aftermath of 9/11. Using a constructivist approach, the study highlights
how the US strategy has contributed to
developing a security-centered perception
of issues such as drug traffic and migration
that affected Ecuador's policies toward the
US, especially in relation to Colombian
drug and refugee problems.

**1742 Ecuador-Perú: evaluación de una
década de paz y desarrollo.** Compilación de Claudia Donoso. Quito: FLACSO
Ecuador: Corporación Andina de Fomento,
2009. 295 p.: bibl., ill., maps. (Serie Foro)

Valuable collection of articles written by Ecuadorian, Peruvian, and foreign
experts retrospectively examining the 1998
peace negotiations and agreements and their
impact on the countries and on their relationship. Comprehensive evaluation of the
role of diplomacy and the model of negotiation applied in finding a solution, as well

as the impact on economic relations, peace, and cultural identity, frontier integration, security and development policies. Reciprocal perceptions generally agree on the positive nature and effects of the agreement for both countries.

1743 Encuentro entre Dos Pueblos, *Quito*, *2007*. Encuentro entre Dos Pueblos. Edición de Erika Hanekamp y Nadesha Montalvo. Quito: Desarrollo y Paz: Comité Ecuménico de Proyectos: Ediciones Abya-Yala, 2008. 140 p.

Policy-oriented report resulting from two meetings in 2007 aimed at analyzing the question of Colombian refugees in Ecuador and making recommendations to alleviate their plight. The workshops were sponsored by Ecuadorian and Colombian religious and secular NGOs associated with the Canadian organization, Development and Peace. The first section of the book analyzes the domestic situations in both countries that resulted in growing migration from Colombia and the migrants' reception in Ecuador, while proposing the establishment of consultation mechanisms. The second section examines the conditions of the refugees and calls for the protection of their human rights, the creation of an international tribunal of opinion and reparation to sanction violations, the promotion of processes of organization, and the special protection of women and other vulnerable groups against violence.

1744 López Contreras, Jimmy. Ecuador-Perú: antagonismo, negociación e intereses nacionales. Quito: Ediciones Abya-Yala: FLACSO, Sede Ecuador, 2004. 244 p.: bibl., ill. (Tesis)

Study of the negotiation process that led to the resolution of the Ecuadorian-Peruvian border conflict framed in the context of growing interdependence. Devotes special attention to the influence of the Clinton administration's foreign policy strategy in reshaping the interests of the two countries and creating the conditions for a peaceful resolution of the dispute. Interesting attempt to analyze the issue from different international relations theoretical perspectives while placing it into the framework of global transformations, instead of the usual approach focused exclusively on domestic and bilateral circumstances.

1745 Ponce Leiva, Javier. Política exterior democrática, sociedad civil y diplomacia. (*Ecuad. Debate,* 72, dic. 2007, p. 187–203)

Examination by Ecuadorian diplomat of the general outline of the country's long-term foreign policy strategy as delineated in the Foreign Policy National Plan 2006–20 (Planex 2020) and incorporated into Ecuador's National Development Plan 2007–10. The author describes the process of elaboration of these documents, highlighting the active participation of political, bureaucratic, and civil society actors and emphasizing the autonomic and cooperative principles behind their formulation.

PARAGUAY

1746 Mora, Frank O. and **Jerry W. Cooney.** Paraguay and the United States: distant allies. Athens: Univ. of Georgia Press, 2007. 333 p.: bibl., index. (The United States and the Americas)

Valuable study of the evolution of relations between the US and an often-neglected South American country. Well-researched historical account and interpretation of Paraguayan-US relations from the 1840s to the early 2000s. Particularly interesting examination of relations during the Chaco War, the Stroessner dictatorship, and Paraguay's recent democratization. Only comprehensive source of information on the topic published in English.

PERU

1747 Couturier Mariátegui, Hernán A. Perú y Brasil: perspectivas de una nueva relación. (*Polít. Int./Lima,* 86, oct./dic. 2006, p. 69–94)

Analysis of the prospects for relations between Peru and Brazil following the 2003 joint declaration concerning a bilateral strategic alliance issued by presidents Alejandro Toledo and Luiz Inácio (Lula) da Silva. The author examines possible areas of cooperation between the countries, including bioceanic cooperation; integration along the Brazil, Paraguay, Bolivia, and Chile axis; economic and scientific-technological collaboration; development in the Amazonian region; security and defense ties; and cultural interactions.

1748 Durand, Francisco. Multinacionales españolas en el Perú: la gente que regresó con el viento. (*Estud. Geogr./Madrid*, 68:262, enero/junio 2007, p. 33–63, bibl., tables)

After a brief historical examination of Spanish-Peruvian economic relations since the 19th century, the article focuses on the growth of Spanish foreign direct investment since the early 1990s. The study argues that the rapid growth of Spanish multinational firms in Peru resulted from the sudden opening of the economy and the subsequent enjoyment of low risk/high return on investments. However, according to the author, since the early 2000s Spanish multinationals—concentrated in the banking, pension funds, gas and energy, and communications sectors—have begun to confront consumer and worker demands and a more negative public opinion that increases the likelihood of regulatory and political pressures.

1749 Morote Canales, Ricardo Estanislao. Estudio del caso de la elección del Perú al Consejo de Seguridad de las Naciones Unidas, 2006–2007. Lima: Academia Diplomática del Perú, Ministerio de Relaciones Exteriores, 2007. 97 p.: bibl.

Unique study of Peru's successful campaign to be elected as a nonpermanent member of the UN Security Council for 2006–2007. Applying a zero-sum game model and matrix analysis, the author offers a detailed study of Peru's overtures to most of the countries represented in the UN General Assembly which helped Peru secure a membership in the first round of voting by a substantial majority.

1750 Novak, Fabián. Las relaciones entre el Perú y Alemania, 1828–2003. Lima: Pontificia Univ. Católica del Perú, Instituto de Estudios Internacionales (IDEI), Fondo Editorial, 2004. 269 p.: bibl. (Serie Política exterior peruana)

Well-rounded historical study of the relations between Peru and Germany since the arrival of the first German immigrants and the establishment of diplomatic relations with pre-unification German states in the 1820s. The work offers valuable information on a relatively neglected aspect of Peruvian foreign relations, including bilateral economic ties, the German attitude during the Pacific War, the break of diplomatic relations during WWI and WWII, the intensification of cooperation during the postwar period, and the recent rise of German investment and growing bilateral cooperation in the 1990s and early 2000s.

1751 Palma, Hugo. Seguridad: alcances y desafíos. Lima: Centro Peruano de Estudios Internacionales, CEPEI, 2007. 385 p.: bibl.

Book by Peruvian diplomat discussing security issues from conceptual and empirical perspectives. Most relevant from a South American viewpoint are the chapters that focus on the Peruvian notion of security, hemispheric security, the Andean Security Network, the impact of the agreements with Ecuador, confidence-building measures and zones of peace, Peru's approach to disarmament, and the role of the armed forces.

1752 Rodríguez Cuadros, Manuel. Delimitación marítima con equidad: el caso de Perú y Chile. Lima: PEISA, 2007. 416 p.: bibl., col. maps, plates. (Ensayo)

Historical and legal study of the maritime boundary dispute between Peru and Chile by Peruvian diplomat and former minister of foreign relations. Although supportive of the Peruvian position, the work offers a detailed analysis of the origins of the controversy and the evolution of diplomatic negotiations, including arguments and proposals from both sides. The two countries were unable to reach a bilateral agreement and the dispute is currently (mid-2011) being considered by the International Court of Justice at the request of Peru.

1753 Valdez Arroyo, Flor de María. Las relaciones entre el Perú e Italia, 1821–2002. Lima: Pontificia Univ. Católica del Perú, Instituto de Estudios Internacionales (IDEI), Fondo Editorial, 2004. 206 p.: bibl. (Serie Política exterior peruana)

Comprehensive history traces the evolution of Peruvian-Italian relations from Peru's colonial period and pre-unification Italy to the early 21st century. Detailed examination of bilateral relations during the period of the War of the Pacific and its aftermath, the two World Wars, and the postwar years, including their diplomatic, economic and migration aspects.

URUGUAY

1754 Bizzozero, Lincoln. Uruguay en la
creación del Mercosur: ¿un cambio en
la política exterior? Montevideo: Univ. de
la República, Comisión Sectorial de Investigación Científica, 2008. 412 p.: bibl. (Col.
"Biblioteca plural")

Excellent study of the role played by
Uruguay as a small peripheral country in
the process that led to the creation of the
Common Market of the South (Mercosur).
The author explores the reasons that Uruguay decided to promote and participate in
this integration agreement, examining the
evolution of the regional situation in the
1990s and the challenges that it presented
for the country, the evolving regional interdependence, the impact of democratization
on regional foreign policies, and the matu-
ration of the Uruguayan decision-making
process that led to its active participation in
the creation of Mercosur.

1755 Ferro Clérico, Lilia. Democracia y
política exterior: Uruguay, 1985–2006.
(*Am. Lat. Hoy/Salamanca*, 44, dic. 2006,
p. 115–132, bibl.)

Interesting examination of the evolution of Uruguay's foreign policy from the
transition to democracy in 1985 to 2006. It
discusses the shift toward a multilateral-
ist policy under the traditional Colorado
and Blanco parties' administrations of
Julio M. Sanguinetti (1985–90; 1995–2000),
Alberto Lacalle (1990–95), and Jorge Batlle
(2000–2005), as well as the initial period of
center-left rule under Tabaré Vazquez (2005–
2010), highlighting the relative continuity
in support of regional integration as well as
the attempts to strengthen Uruguay's relative autonomy in diplomatic and economic
terms.

1756 Perazza, Federico. Uruguay y el
conflicto en Medio Oriente. (*Rev.
Mex. Polít. Exter.*, 82, nov. 2007/feb. 2008,
p. 165–204)

Historical account of a regional aspect of Latin American foreign policy that is
usually neglected examines Uruguay's role
in the UN Palestine Commission. Provides
details of the commission's elaboration of
the partition plan, its positions in the UN
concerning different problems in the Middle
East (Suez Canal and Lebanese crises, civil

war in Yemen, Yom Kippur War, and the
Iraq-Iran and Iraq-Kuwait conflicts), as well
as the participation of Uruguayan forces in
peace missions in the region.

VENEZUELA

1757 Briceño Ruiz, José. The Free Trade
Area of the Americas in the foreign
policy of Hugo Chávez. (*Unisa Lat. Am.
Rep.*, 22:1/2, 2006, p. 31–46, bibl., photo)

Article analyzes the evolution of
Hugo Chávez's policies concerning the US
proposal to create a Free Trade Area of the
Americas that moved from initial reserva-
tions, to criticism but not rejection, and
finally culminated in the total Venezuelan
rejection of the FTAA. The author argues
that Chávez's changing attitude reflected
his rejection of unipolarity, growing support
for regional integration, emergence of populist regimes in Latin America, the belief
that the US supported the 2002 failed coup,
and the perception of his role as leader in
the struggle against neoliberal globalization
and US hegemony.

1758 Jiménez M., Rafael Simón. 50 años
de política exterior de Venezuela,
1907–1958. Prólogo de Simón Alberto Con-
salvi. Caracas: El Centauro Ediciones, 2006.
334 p.: bibl.

Informative historical account of
the evolution of Venezuela's foreign policy
between the dictatorships of Juan Vicente
Gómez (1908–35) and Marcos Pérez Jiménez
(1953–58) passing through successive democratic and authoritarian periods. Interesting
examination of the growing importance of
oil in shaping the country's foreign policy.

1759 Schoen, Douglas E. and **Michael
Rowan.** Threat closer to home: Hugo
Chávez and the war against America. New
York, N.Y.: Free Press, 2009. 220 p.: bibl.

Veritable compendium of anti-Chávez
denunciations written by two political opponents of the Venezuelan president who
believe that "Chávez arguably presents a
greater threat to America than Osama bin
Laden on a day-to-day basis, and this is our
opportunity to set out the reasons why we
believe this to be the case." Many of the assertions are difficult to prove, but the book
is useful as it offers a complete summary
of the arguments used by US neoconserva-

tives and members of the Bush administration to justify their hostility toward the Venezuelan regime: the oil threat posed by Venezuela, its close ties with Iran and Cuba, military connections with Russia and China, support for the FARC, and interference in US domestic politics.

1760 Siete años de diplomacia bolivariana: discursos de los cancilleres, 1999–2005. Compilación de Iliana Gómez Tovar. Caracas: República Bolivariano de Venezuela, Ministerio de Relaciones Exteriores, 2007. 464 p.: ports. (Colección Obras del Ministerio de Relaciones Exteriores; 22)

Compilation of the most important speeches by the ministers of the Bolivarian Republic of Venezuela between 1999 and 2006, including José Vicente Rangel (1999–2000), Luis Alfonso Dávila (2001–2002), Roy Chaderton (2002–2003), Jesús A. Pérez (2004), and Alí Rodríguez (2005–2006). Useful to trace the evolution of the foreign policies of the Chávez administration, particularly before and after the failed April 2002 coup.

Suzzarini, Abdón. Venezuela ante la integración económica hemisférica: dos visiones, dos paradigmas. See item **1992.**

1761 Venezuela hoy: miradas binacionales. Coordinación de Socorro Ramírez. Bogotá: Univ. Nacional de Colombia, Instituto de Estudios Políticos y Relaciones Internacionales, 2008. 373 p.: ill., maps. (Col. Fronteras e integración)

Volume containing papers delivered at the 2007 Colombian-Venezuelan meeting sponsored by the *Cátedra Venezuela,* a group of Colombian academic experts devoted to the study of Venezuela and the relations between both countries. The book includes analyses of the possibilities of bilateral and regional integration; the different models of economic, political, and social development adopted by each country; the security policies and the role of the armed forces; frontier policies and integration; and the foreign policy strategies of both countries. Valuable set of studies that mainly clarifies the Colombian perspective on Chávez's policies and initiatives and discusses their impact on the relations with its neighbor.

1762 Zamora Cardozo, Elizabeth. Vidas de frontera: andinos y llaneros en la frontera colombo-venezolana: un estudio cualitativo. Caracas: Univ. Central de Venezuela, Facultad de Ciencias Económicas y Sociales: Fondo Editorial Tropykos, 2006. 345 p.: bibl.

Well-researched sociological study of the Colombian-Venezuelan frontier society exploring its identity and examining its cultural, social, economic, and political characteristics as well as the transnational connections and national identifications. Also studies the impact of the Colombian internal armed conflict with its correspondent regional violence, displacement, and tension.

BRAZIL

THOMAZ GUEDES DA COSTA, *Professor of International Security Affairs, College of International Security Affairs, National Defense University*

THIS BIBLIOGRAPHIC COLLECTION gathered by the Hispanic Division of the Library of Congress on Brazil's international relations permits readers to develop a comprehensive understanding of Brazil's general issues in foreign relations, especially under the administrations of Fernando Cardoso and Lula da Silva. Some specific publications address key historical eras which are crucial for diplomatic history and underlie current challenges and diplomatic culture.

The works of Cavlak (item **1774**), Machado (item **1786**), and Lopes (item **1785**) collect many primary sources for researchers. Garcia (item **1778**) provides a large set of transcripts of official documents that will facilitate the work of many interested in Brazil's diplomatic history. Costa Franco (item **1779**) assembles a more recent collection of presidential speeches, all from officials in the postmilitary regime era.

Authors provide general propositions and arguments related to Brazil's effort to position itself in the international system, both at global and regional levels, since the end of the Cold War (items **1763**, **1764**, **1772**, **1775**, **1776**, and **1796**). Many cover bilateral relations and highlight the analytical effort to understand the meteoric rise of relations with the People's Republic of China (items **1770**, **1788**, and **1789**). Works offered detailed accounts of relations with Argentina (item **1774**), Japan (item **1782**), Spain (items **1765** and **1792**), and South Africa (item **1790**). Relations with South or Latin America, in general, and within the Plata basin, in particular, continue to receive wide analytical attention as Brazilian officials focus efforts on advancing regional integration (items **1766**, **1773**, **1779**, **1783**, **1787**, and **1791**).

For those interested in US-Brazilian relations, there is a diverse menu of keen works. Spektor (item **1797**) reviewed the personality and role of Henry Kissinger in nursing bilateral relations. Moniz Bandeira (item **1769**) published the fourth edition of his perceptions of US efforts to manage Brazilian foreign policy, while Azevedo (item **1768**) rewards readers with a unique analysis of the Peace Corp's presence in Brazil, from 1961 to 1981.

A few works provide glimpses of little-visited corners of Brazilian foreign policy. Fares (item **1780**) analyzes Brazil's relations with Iraq during the oil crisis in the 1970s and the consequences for foreign policy strategy. Lopes (item **1785**) indicts Brazilian diplomacy for its accommodation to inroads of Nazi Germany at the onset of World War II. Brigagão and Proença Júnior provide a rare collection of essays on how Brazil is coping with new international conflicts that have arisen after September 11, 2001, and with its latest wave of international peacekeeping missions (item **1771**).

1763 Almeida, Paulo Roberto de. Uma nova "arquitetura" diplomática?: interpretações divergentes sobre a política externa do governo Lula, 2003–2006. (*Rev. Bras. Polít. Int.*, 49:1, 2006, p. 95–116, bibl.)

As Lula implemented Brazil's foreign policy, the author argues that his administration introduced the use of international themes in speeches and in the press to leverage the national political agenda and to secure public support of his initiatives. This approach is a remarkably different strategy than those of past administrations which rarely introduced foreign policy issues into national debates. The author suggests that foreign policy messages were presented internally by "authorized speakers," in addition to echoes from "sympathetic allies" and "independent or critical thinkers." This analysis also provides insights of bureaucratic disputes and party politics, in terms of both the clash of personalities and institutional competitions.

1764 Almeida, Paulo Roberto de. As relações econômicas internacionais do Brasil dos anos 1950 aos 80. (*Rev. Bras. Polít. Int.*, 50:2, 2007, p. 60–79, tables)

In this 30-year historical survey, the author finds that Brazil developed a defensive strategy in its international economic relations, primarily to cope with its fragility resulting from commodity exports, foreign exchange restrictions, and financial vulnerabilities of its unstable and inflationary economy until the early 1980s. To the useful aggregated data analysis, the author adds a discussion of the role of the government-led economy, exchange controls, and product substitution and exports in dominating market forces to promote internal growth and stability in foreign economic exchanges.

1765 Arahuetes García, Alfredo and **Célio Hiratuka.** Relaciones económicas entre España y Brasil = Relações econômicas entre Brasil e Espanha. Madrid: Real Instituto Elcano de Estudios Internacionales y Estratégicos, 2007. 365 p.: bibl., ill.

With Brazil's privatization and opening of markets in the 1990s, when it achieved a stable economic growth and increased participation in the global markets, Spain became an important source of direct investments for the Brazilian economy. While bilateral relations between the two countries are not the most important ones for Brazil, the authors suggest that its relations with Spain illustrate the attraction of investments that create stable growth and mutual value for both partners in a globalized economy.

1766 Araújo, Ernesto Henrique Fraga. O Mercosul: negociações extra-regionais. Brasília: Fundação Alexandre de Gusmão, 2008. 349 p.: bibl.

The author argues that in a global perspective of growing exchanges, Mercosul (the regional economic block gathering Argentina, Brazil, Uruguay, Paraguay and other associated countries) has raised its own effective identity and now serves as a platform for economic negotiations with other extraregional actors and economic blocks. This new negotiating venue is now part of the value of this regional arrangement, with potential benefits and risks in the foreseeable future. The lack of a common trade policy undermines the full utility of Mercosul's role as a negotiating unit. The author recommends that Brazil must adjust its own particular negotiating strategies to bolster, and not undermine, its own interests within the Mercosul institution, and to prevent unwanted interblock disputes or fragmentation.

1767 Arbeitsgemeinschaft Deutsche Lateinamerika-Forschung. Symposium. *Weingarten, Germany, 2005.* O Brasil na América Latina: interações, percepções, interdependências. Organização de Sérgio Costa, Hartmut Sangmeister e Sonja Steckbauer. São Paulo: Annablume; Berlin: ADLAF: Fundação Heinrich Böll, 2007. 349 p.: bibl., ill. (chiefly col.).

German scholars and Latin American colleagues assess diplomatic relations, cultural and historical ties, social and environmental sustainability, social movements, and social theory of Brazil's relations and interdependency with Latin America.

1768 Azevedo, Cecília. Em nome da América: os Corpos da Paz no Brasil. São Paulo: Alameda, 2008. 388 p.: bibl. (Série Teses)

What is the history of the Peace Corps in Brazil? This book will be of value to both academics and those members of the general public interested in the individual and collective experience of Peace Corps workers. One chapter is dedicated to the problems that arose from having volunteers in Brazil from 1961–81 and how their presence affected bilateral relations until the Peace Corps was prohibited from operating in the country. The author generally concludes that there is no public "conscious" awareness of the positive impact and benefits of the Peace Corps' experience in Brazil.

1769 Bandeira, Moniz. Presença dos Estados Unidos no Brasil. 4a ed. Rio de Janeiro: Civilização Brasileira, 2007. 682 p.: bibl., index.

This is the fourth edition of a classic work published initially in 1973. The author argues that US-Brazilian relations have been turbulent because of the effort of Washington to influence, if not dominate, Brazilian models of foreign relations and economics. Brazilian reactions to US pressures have caused bilateral tensions since WWII. Young scholars should read Moniz Bandeira to understand the perspective of this leading senior scholar who has been influential in the construction of Brazilian foreign policy under the Labor Party administrations.

1770 Becard, Danielly Silva Ramos. O Brasil e a República Popular da China: política externa comparada e relações bilaterais, 1974–2004. Porto Alegre, Brazil: Fundação Alexandre de Gusmão, 2008. 330 p.: bibl., ill.

In this survey of bilateral relations and respective approaches for national development and international politics, Becard concludes that both countries strived to advance cooperation, avoid ideological differences with pragmatic initiatives, trade, and technological and cultural exchanges. More recently, China has become one of Brazil's leading partners. The author points out that long-term challenges will affect the stability and advancement of this relation.

1771 O Brasil e os novos conflitos internacionais. Organização de Clóvis Brigagão e Domício Proença Júnior. Textos de Domício Proença Júnior *et al.* Rio de Janeiro: Gramma, 2006. 237 p.: bibl., ill., maps.

This collection gathers papers and discussion transcripts presented in academic conferences. Essays seek to understand the impact of contemporary international security issues on Brazil's interests as well as how this country responds to foreign events, policies, and interactions that affect its national security. Cases such as the strategies of the US after 9/11, the Second Gulf War with the invasion of Iraq, the Palestinian-Israeli conflict, and the problem of the Iguaçu Tri-Border Area provide assessments of how Brazil has responded to these challenges in terms of foreign and security policy initiatives.

1772 Burges, Sean W. Brazilian foreign policy after the Cold War. Gainesville: Univ. Press of Florida, 2009. 229 p.: bibl., index.

Burges proposes that Brazilian foreign policy displays a general effort to leverage political economic issues and initiatives in order to advance wide interdependence and secure regional structures with the goal of greater national autonomy in the face of global challenges. Regional projects promise to consolidate bilateral ties and exchanges. This insightful analysis shows the continuity of effort even from presidencies with different ideologies.

1773 Burges, Sean W. Without sticks or carrots: Brazilian leadership in South America during the Cardoso era, 1992–2003. (*Bull. Lat. Am. Res.*, 25:1, Jan. 2006, p. 23–42)

The author argues that as president, Fernando Henrique Cardoso pursued a policy of Brazilian leadership within South America by establishing projects for cooperation and avoiding coercive attitudes and

images. For argumentation and illustration, the author reviews the Brazilian position at the 1994 Summit of the Americas, the drive for regionalism (Mercosul and increasing ties with the Andean countries), and the implementation of Initiative for the Integration of the Regional Infrastructure of South America (IIRSA). As an added value, this article analyzes how Brazil was able to stay neutral, beyond the diplomatic discourse, within the US-led Free Trade Area of the Americas, through greater offers for investment and the exercise of smart leadership in the South American region.

1774 Cavlak, Iuri. A política externa brasileira e a Argentina peronista, 1946–1955. São Paulo: Annablume, 2008. 210 p.: bibl. (Selo univ.; 364. História)

In the traditional historical accounts of the post-WWII period, Argentina and Brazil struggled to promote respective interests in a new configuration of power. Regionally, their charismatic and authoritarian leaders, Vargas and Perón, continued to seek regional influence by balancing competing discourses and initiatives. Casting a new light with insightful considerations, Cavlak argues that internal politics and bilateral relations reveal the roots of the regional integration that emerges 40 years later. This argument is supported by documentary evidence from the Brazilian foreign ministry and sociological integration of scholarly works.

1775 Conferência Nacional de Política Externa e Política Internacional, *1st*, *Rio de Janeiro, 2006.* O Brasil no mundo que vem aí. I Conferência Nacional de Política Externa e Política Internacional, Rio de Janeiro, 6 e 7 de julho de 2006. Organização de Jeronimo Moscardo e Carlos Henrique Cardim. Brasília: Fundação Alexandre de Gusmão, 2007. 403 p.: bibl., ill.

This collection, together with item **1776**, gathers speeches and debates of leading thinkers about Brazil and tendencies in world politics after the beginning of Lula's era. The speeches were given at events organized by the Itamaraty—the Brazilian Foreign Ministry. This is a useful source for understanding how academics and government officials reason, narrate, and argue in a public forum about the future trends, perspectives, and uncertainties of Brazil's foreign policy.

1776 Conferência Nacional de Política Externa e Política Internacional, 2nd, Rio de Janeiro, 2007. II Conferência Nacional de Política Externa e Política Internacional— CNPEPI, Rio de Janeiro, 5 e 6 de novembro de 2007. Organização de Jeronimo Moscardo e Carlos Henrique Cardim. Brasília: Fundação Alexandre de Gusmão, 2008. 424 p.

See item **1775** for annotation of this volume and the volume of papers from the first CNPEPI conference in 2006.

1777 Deutsch-brasilianische Kulturbeziehungen: Bestandsaufnahme, Herausforderungen, Perspektiven. Herasugegeben von Wolfgang Bader. Frankfurt am Main: Vervuert, 2010. 351 p.: bibl., ill. (Bibliotheca Ibero-Americana, 133)

Proceedings of a symposium (São Paulo, 2008) sponsored by the Goethe Institute São Paulo and the German Ministry of Foreign Affairs. The main objective was the examination of the current relationship between the countries, particularly the reception of each other's cultural contributions. Specific topics include literature, language learning, music, theater, art and film, German and Brazilian Studies, philosophy, academic exchange, foreign policy in cultural matters, and each country's image in the media. [F. Obermeier]

1778 Diplomacia brasileira e política externa: documentos históricos, 1493–2008. Organização de Eugênio Vargas Garcia. Rio de Janeiro: Contraponto, 2008. 751 p.: bibl.

A rare, single-volume collection of official documents related to Brazilian foreign policy from a year before the Portuguese arrival in 1500 to 2008. This is a basic reference work for anyone studying Brazilian international relations.

1779 Documentos da política externa independente. Organização de Alvaro da Costa Franco. Brasília: Fundação Alexandre de Gusmão; Rio de Janeiro: Centro de História e Documentação Diplomática, 2007. 2 v.

This collection of selected official documents reveals Brazil's efforts to synthesize an independent foreign policy for the

nation during the first half of the 1960s. The book is a rich gathering of public speeches, interviews, and press releases, as well as internal documents of the Brazilian Foreign Ministry. An excellent collection of primary sources for those scholars interested in Brazil's diplomatic history.

1780 Fares, Seme Taleb. O pragmatismo do petróleo: as relações entre o Brasil e o Iraque. (*Rev. Bras. Polít. Int.*, 50:2, 2007, p. 129–145)

This is a unique article that sheds light on one of the most significant chapters of the formation of Brazil's energy and foreign policy in the latter part of the 20th century. Since the 1973 oil crisis, Brazil has sought to acquire petroleum from new and more affordable sources. Iraq became a major target in the Brazilian strategy to develop new and stable suppliers. This historical survey describes the variety of political and economic initiatives affecting Brazil's relations in the Middle East as well as with major powers, such as the US. The work is particularly useful for tracing the roots of Brazil's contemporary strategies in global politics and of its prospects for becoming an oil supplier itself in the future.

1781 Faria, Lina Rodrigues de and Maria Conceição da Costa. Cooperação científica internacional: estilos de atuação da Fundação Rockefeller e da Fundação Ford. (*Dados/Rio de Janeiro*, 49:1, 2006, p. 159–191, bibl.)

This unique work evaluates key foreign nongovernment actors that assisted in the scientific development, the education of human resources, and the establishment of science and health services in many developing countries, looking at their presence in Brazil. The analysis provides insights into how these funding foundations evolved and adjusted guidelines, partnerships, and activities in the country since the 1960s. It reveals how these foundations would adjust their narratives and attitudes and support agendas in accordance with the rise and fall of political contexts, institutions, or actors which could take advantage of or challenge their presence.

1782 Faria Nunes, Paulo Henrique. As relações Brasil-Japão e seus reflexos no processo de ocupação do território brasileiro.

(*Rev. Geogr./México*, 140, julio/dic. 2006, p. 61–77, bibl., tables)

The article proposes that Japanese capital was significant in bolstering Brazilian industrialization during the 20th century. The immigration from Japan to Brazil that started in the late 19th century did not increase the perceived value of bilateral relations. Nevertheless, the succeeding waves of Japanese arrivals gave impetus to Brazilian territorial occupation with expansion of the agriculture frontier. The value of a Japanese presence surged again in the second half of the 1990s with new investments in electronic consumer goods and automotive sectors. This study is valuable as benchmark for comparative analyses of social development during 20th-century social and demographic Brazilian experiences.

Fórum Nacional Por Que o Brasil Não é Um País de Alto Crescimento?, *BNDES, 2006.* O Brasil e a nova ordem (desordem?) mundial. See item **2163.**

1783 Fryba Christensen, Steen. The influence of nationalism in Mercosur and in South America: can the regional integration project survive? (*Rev. Bras. Polít. Int.*, 50:1, 2007, p. 139–158)

Will the discourse of nationalism and political forces of member states hinder the efforts to create regional integration blocks, such as Mercosul? The author concludes that the nationalism aspiration that one normally associates with South American international politics has not impaired the growth of regional collaboration. Nevertheless, the single opposing case is Bolivia, where the turbulent internal politics and tangled relations with Brazil have reduced the impetus for the former to join Mercosul with a sympathetic welcome from Brazilian political forces. Overall, the analysis concludes that a new sense of regional solidarity neutralizes nationalist calls against integration in most countries.

1784 Henriques Ferreira, Túlio Sérgio. A ruína do consenso: a política exterior do Brasil no governo Figueiredo de 1979 a 1985. (*Rev. Bras. Polít. Int.*, 49:2, 2006, p. 119–136, bibl.)

This analysis of foreign policy under the presidency of General João Baptista de Oliveira Figueiredo concludes that the ideological consensus that existed during previous military governments broke down. The central argument in the policy of "universalismo" stated that the international system was "unfair" to many Brazilian interests. Thus, Brazil would seek to enhance relations with countries outside the industrialized world. Yet, the author argued that this approach did not receive full support of the Foreign Ministry bureaucracy or from others that claimed that relations with key economic powers should be the priority in order to secure investors and key trading partners.

1785 Lopes, Roberto. Missão no Reich: glória e covardia dos diplomatas latino-americanos na Alemanha de Hitler. Rio de Janeiro: Odisséia Editorial, 2008. 543 p.: bibl., ill., index.

Using a journalistic approach, the author argues that leadership in Nazi Germany was very much aware of the economic value of including Latin America among its hegemonic conquests. The work further espouses that Latin American diplomats promoted economic relations with Germany based on self-interest while cowering from recognizing the Nazi aggressions. The book displays a variety of descriptive and documented accounts of routine diplomatic and economic relations related to Brazil's and neighboring countries' shameful diplomatic stands and maneuvers along with the rise of the tragic and destructive Fascist Germany.

1786 Machado, Silvio Romero Martins. Ideologia e discurso diplomático: a inserção do Brasil na ordem neoliberal, 1985–1999. Passo Fundo, Brazil: Univ. de Passo Fundo, UPF Editora, 2006. 175 p.: bibl.

This research collects diplomatic speeches of Presidents Sarney, Collor, Itamar, and Cardoso as a way to reveal messages and audiences that facilitated Brazil's presence in the prevailing neoliberal economic order of the period. The authors pose that the diplomatic discourse aimed to improve the legitimacy of Brazil as a new democracy and peaceful country, and therefore a reliable partner, and also as a promoter of multilateral approaches to solving global issues. Presidential discourse also attempted to convey that national development was the key aim of foreign policy and bilateral and multilateral strategies.

1787 Mercosul, Mercosur: estudos em homenagem a Fernando Henrique Cardoso. Organização de Maristela Basso Tamagno. Textos de Adriana Pucci *et al.* São Paulo: Atlas, 2007. 675 p.: bibl.

Fernando Henrique Cardoso, both as foreign minister and president, led Brazil in the establishment of the Common Market of the South (Mercosul). This book collects a number of essays by South American academics, diplomats, and former government officials weaving together the roles and contributions of Cardoso, the historical developments of the cooperation block, and the numerous challenges confronted by partner countries and societies in its implementation. Argues that Cardoso's political will and the effort for a constructive systematic negotiation of members' states fostered solutions that overcame mistrust and individual interests of governments, national political forces, and other nongovernment actors. The work is a valuable tool for assessing the step-by-step negotiating process, the role of leaders such as Cardoso, and the political compromises that were necessary for Mercosul to become a reality.

1788 Oliveira, Henrique Altemani de. As perspectivas de cooperação Sul-Sul no relacionamento Brasil-China. (*Nueva Soc.*, 203, mayo/junio 2006, p. 138–147)

This article seeks to identify the respective political motivations for each country to expand Brazilian-Chinese relations in the post-Cold War period. The argument compares how China and Brazil approached their cooperative efforts seeking to take advantage of disagreements among developed, industrial countries and to promote political and technological cooperation to compensate for any perceived disadvantage. The article does not foresee the massive dominance of trade exchanges as the cornerstone of post-2006 bilateral relations, overshadowing any bilateral political collaboration on global issues.

1789 Paiva Abreu, Marcelo de. La aparición de China en el escenario económico mundial: el caso de Brasil. (*Integr. Comer.*, 10:24, enero/junio 2006, p. 129–162, bibl., graph, tables)

This economic study evaluates the ties that Brazil has been creating with China during the 2000s as a means of explaining the latter's increasing economic power. On one hand, the author proposes that Brazil will play an increasing role as China's trading partner due to the expanding Chinese need for commodities and agricultural products. On the other hand, Brazil and China become both competitors and collaborators in foreign direct investments flows. Although internal and external market forces should shape the nature of the relationship, government intervention will drive initiatives and adjustments based on perceived respective interests. The article contains a wealth of statistical information.

1790 Penna Filho, Pio. O Brasil e a África do Sul: o arco atlântico da política externa brasileira, 1918–2000. Porto Alegre, Brazil: Fundação Alexandre de Gusmão, 2008. 363 p.: bibl. (Série Sul-Africana)

The study offers a historical perspective on the shifting relations between Brazil and South Africa during the past decades. The trajectory of economic exchanges and political coordination between these two Atlantic actors suffered the impact of racial and cultural relations, as well as the hidden relations of past nondemocratic regimes. The author proposes that the democratization observed on both sides of the Atlantic in the later decades of the 20th century, associated with the promotion of regional economic integration and political coordination, lays the groundwork for new engagement and legitimate collaboration. The analysis is supported by an abundance of documentation and economic data.

1791 La percepción de Brasil en el contexto internacional: perspectivas y desafíos. t. 1, América Latina. t. 2, África, Asia y Europa. Compilação de Wilhelm Hofmcister, Francisco Rojas Aravena e Luis Guillermo Solís. Rio de Janeiro: FLACSO, Secretaría General: Konrad-Adenauer-Stiftung, 2007. 2 v.: bibl., ill., maps.

This two-volume collection holds a number of essays regarding the perceptions of foreign actors about Brazil's political context, the ability of its foreign policy to uphold a leadership role in the international system, and its value as an economic and political strategic partner to other countries. While the methodology is inconsistent and most authors employed bilateral relations (numbers of agreements, economic and financial exchanges, etc.) and official declarations as proxy evidence to represent perceptions of others about Brazil, some insights do inform readers about the subject. Authors that examined the views of Brazil's neighbors posed that the expected economic benefits for countries as they increase relations with Brazil are balanced by concerns of growing political hegemony. As for distant partners such as European countries, Mexico, China, India, the US, and South Africa, the authors suggest that Brazil does not represent a distinct comparative priority even though economic relations and political dialog between Brazil and other countries has increased.

1792 Pino, Bruno Ayllón. Las relaciones hispano-brasileñas: de la mutua irrelevancia a la asociación estratégica, 1945–2005. Salamanca, Spain: Ediciones Univ. de Salamanca, 2007. 263 p.: bibl., ill. (Biblioteca de América; 34)

Assessing the bilateral engagement between Brazil and Spain since 1945, the author reveals how democratization in the 1980s, and later the opening of economic markets in the 1990s, transformed mutually irrelevant relations of the past into a strategic partnership. Trade and technological and financial exchanges offer both countries avenues for the bilateral exchanges and wider exchanges between European and South American regional economic blocs.

1793 A política externa brasileira em perspectiva: segurança, comércio e relações bilaterais. Organização de Mario Antonio Marconini. São Paulo: Lex Editora: Aduaneiras, 2006. 132 p.

Essays by leading Brazilian academics and retired diplomats assess Brazil's multilateral and bilateral relations. Authors strive to synthesize the nature of Brazil's leading approaches and dominant strategies to increase economic and security relations. The main conclusion is that state-to-state relations have started to be challenged by "societal" and nongovernmental forces and interests which are partially capturing the

national debates and influencing governmental actions in foreign relations.

1794 Ribeiro Santana, Carlos. O aprofundamento das relações do Brasil com os países do Oriente Médio durante os dois choques do petróleo de década de 1970: um exemplo de ação pragmática. (*Rev. Bras. Polít. Int.*, 49:2, 2006, p. 157–177)

The author argues that Brazil expanded its commercial relations with Middle Eastern oil suppliers to secure vital oil stocks from 1973 to the early 1990s. The pragmatic approach led to securing crude oil at the expenses of foreign reserves, while failing to expande trade as a strategy to compensate for costs during the period.

1795 Roelofse-Campbell, Zélia. Post-apartheid South Africa and Brazil: a strategic partnership. (*Unisa Lat. Am. Rep.*, 22:1/2, 2006, p. 92–107, bibl.)

Author argues that South African-Brazilian relations gained new impetus under the Lula administration. The limited mutual knowledge and history of paltry economic relations are not constraints for further development in South-South bilateral exchanges if one takes into account the desires of respective leadership.

1796 Sousa, Amaury de. A agenda internacional do Brasil: a política externa brasileira de FHC a Lula. Rio de Janeiro: Elsevier: CEBRI: Campus, 2009. 191 p.: bibl., ill., index.

The author surveys Brazilian foreign policy from the presidency of Fernando Cardoso to Luiz lnácio Lula da Silva (1994–2008). Based on extensive interviews with foreign policy practitioners and academics, the author concludes that the policy of President Lula generated significant conflicts in internal national and bureaucratic politics. Further, the work seeks to demonstrate the conflicts of principles and interests, the reduction in the bureaucratic autonomy of the Itamaraty in terms of policy implementation, and the hitherto unmatched expansion of public debates about foreign relations by internal interests and actors.

1797 Spektor, Matias. Kissinger e o Brasil. Rio de Janeiro: Zahar, 2009. 234 p.: bibl., ill. (Nova biblioteca de ciências sociais)

Spektor crafted a careful analysis of the efforts to promote the US-Brazilian rapprochement in the 1970s. While Brazil considered the US a central actor for its interests, for the latter the interest was marginal. Nevertheless, the work reveals how Henry Kissinger pursued personal and official efforts to maintain Brazil as a valuable ally in the global ideological struggle. The careful documentation supports the flamboyant display of Kissinger's personality and diplomacy matched by the unique abilities of Brazil's own foreign minister, Antonio Silveira.

POLITICAL ECONOMY

GENERAL

JONATHAN HISKEY, *Associate Professor of Political Science, Vanderbilt University*

IN THE WAKE OF THE GLOBAL FINANCIAL CRISIS OF 2008, Latin America's economies, with some notable exceptions, seem to have weathered the storm and, in some cases, performed relatively well. Countries such as Peru, Ecuador, Colombia, Brazil, and Argentina suffered economic contractions of less than 2 percent in 2009, while Uruguay, Panama, Dominican Republic, and Bolivia enjoyed positive rates of economic growth during this year of widespread global economic decline. Though much research is needed on the specific factors contributing to the region's generally positive performance, increasing ties with the Asian market, a consolidation of basic macroeconomic fundamentals, and a renewed emphasis on primary exports in many countries all played important roles in the region's relative success during a period of global economic decline.

Though largely a product of the years immediately preceding the 2008 economic downturn, research on the political economy of Latin America reviewed in this section reflects the region's experiences with the global financial crisis in many ways. Just as a diversification of export markets proved critical to surviving the 2008 crisis, recent political economy work also exhibits a marked diversification in terms of the interests and research questions when compared to research of the 1990s and early 2000s. And just as many countries in the region have put to rest debates about some of the basic economic principles of the neoliberal era, so too have many scholars arrived at an implicit, if not explicit, acceptance of the core elements of the Washington Consensus.

One key to the relative success enjoyed by some countries during the crisis years that remains underrepresented in recent work on Latin America's political economy is the increasingly prominent role of primary sector exports as an engine of development. Thus, while Bolivia, Uruguay, and Argentina, for example, were prospering during the financial crisis years due to the strength of their primary export sector, political economy scholarship in the past five years largely has remained focused on the export diversification model emphasized in the first decade or so of market-based reforms. The exception to this dearth of work on the renewed role of raw material exports in driving some Latin American economies is Dunning's work (item **1810**) that challenges in some ways the conventional understanding of the authoritarian consequences that resource abundance can have in countries such as Bolivia and Ecuador. Given the events of recent years, however, it is likely that scholars in the future will indeed focus more on the recent successes of these "economies of extraction," a model that has been dominant in the region since the colonial era, bringing with it times of tremendous economic prosperity but also a heightened vulnerability to economic crisis (to name just one of the many negative consequences that have been historically associated with economies overly reliant on primary product exports). The remainder of this essay will examine in more detail these trends in political economy research with an eye toward what we may expect to see in upcoming years as scholars begin a deeper exploration of the region's diverse experiences during the crisis years of 2008–2010.

The diversification of export markets, and specifically the heightened presence of the Asian market in Latin American export profiles, not only helped ease the path of many countries through the global financial crisis, but also has emerged as a topic of particular focus in the works reviewed here. Works by Gallagher and Porzecanski (item **1815**), Jenkins, Dussel Peters, and Moreira (item **1823**), and Mihailovic and Dantas (item **1808**) represent this growing focus on Latin America's shift away from its historical reliance on the US and European markets, with China in particular becoming a critical player in the region's trade and investment relations. And despite the financial boon provided by China's voracious export appetite during recent years, these scholars share a concern with the overall impact that China may have on the region's long-term development prospects.

Several works go beyond the case of China and explore what in some cases has been a truly watershed shift in Latin America's relations with the international community. Both Estay (item **1821**) and Cooper and Heine (item **1845**) offer edited volumes that assess the region's changing role in the international arena from various perspectives. Girón and Correa's compilation of essays (item **1800**) also examines, with a more policy-prescriptive lens, ways in which Latin America can best take advantage of its ever-changing points of intersection with the global economy. In a similar vein, Brautigam and Segarra (item **1801**) evaluate the changing role of the World Bank in countries such as Guatemala and Ecuador in an effort to understand how these and other countries can benefit from such relationships. As noted above, this emergent trend in political economy research seems likely to continue as the region's countries further diversify the number and types of economic relationships with countries around the world.

Another newly prominent theme in political economy research highlights and evaluates the impact of globalization and market-based economic reforms on an increasingly diverse range of issue areas. Though scholars have long explored the effects of neoliberalism and globalization on outcomes such as income inequality and poverty levels (items **1804**, **1805**, and **1830**), some are moving to such questions as the political economy of education in an era of globalization (items **1813** and **1838**), the impact of crime on economic development (item **1812**), the effect of globalization on tax policies in Latin America (items **1803** and **1811**), and the influence of free trade and international organizations on civil society (item **1826**). Apparent in most of these works is a far more nuanced treatment of globalization and neoliberalism as independent variables than was apparent in earlier works on similar issues.

One area of investigation that remains prevalent in political economy research, but that also reveals a more theoretically and methodologically sophisticated approach than in years past, concerns the impact of neoliberalism and globalization on Latin America's social safety nets and distributive politics more generally. Chong (item **1840**) offers an innovative assessment of the effect of privatization on these issue-areas, while Arza (item **1799**) and Brooks (item **1802**) add to the growing literature on pension reforms in the region during an era of neoliberalism. In a similar vein, Giraudy (item **2104**) contributes to the abundance of work on the "neoclientelist" bent of antipoverty programs in Latin America over the past 20 years by identifying partisan and institutional factors as additional determinants of spending patterns in Argentina's employment program.

These trends in Latin American political economy research represent a significant departure from the highly polemical work on these issues that characterized much of the scholarship in the 1990s and early 2000s. As researchers accumulate more data with which to assess the neoliberal era and its political and economic consequences, more advanced theoretical and empirical statements are being produced on this defining era in the region's political and economic development history. In summary, the works reviewed for this chapter suggest the beginning of an exciting period in research on Latin America's development experiences that will offer a more balanced and accurate sense of the challenges and opportunities the region's economies will face moving forward.

In the same vein, a parallel exists between current work on the political economy of Latin America and the region's experiences with the 2008 financial crisis. The fact that the worldwide economic collapse did not have the expected devastating effects on Latin America (with some exceptions, such as Mexico) suggests that the region's economies may have finally moved beyond the crisis-based cycle of development that characterized the 1980s and 1990s. While some warning flags should be raised with respect to the heightened reliance on raw material exports as way out of this cycle for some countries, the region as a whole has advanced from the "lost decade" of the 1980s and the self-inflicted, recessionary wounds of the 1990s. Thus it appears that similar to political economy scholarship, many of the region's countries have also entered into a post-neoliberal stage of development. On both counts, this is a welcome and long-awaited step forward.

1798 **Anner, Mark Sebastian.** Meeting the challenges of industrial restructuring: labor reform and enforcement in Latin America. (*Lat. Am. Polit. Soc.*, 50:2, Summer 2008, p. 33–65, bibl., graph, tables)

Well-executed study of labor laws and their enforcement in Latin America during the neoliberal era. The attention given to the wide variations in enforcement efforts is particularly notable, as are the discussions of these issues in the cases of Brazil and El Salvador.

1799 **Arza, Camila.** Pension reform in Latin America: distributional principles, inequalities and alternative policy options. (*J. Lat. Am. Stud.*, 40:1, Feb. 2008, p. 1–28, tables)

A highly informative review and assessment of Latin American pension reform efforts over the past 30 years, with a particular focus on the consequences of

such reforms for income inequality. In addition to including several useful tables that highlight the main elements of these reform efforts, the author also includes specific policy recommendations for pension programs to improve their distributional performance moving forward.

1800 **Asimetrías e incertidumbre: los desafíos de una estrategia económica alternativa para América Latina.** Coordinación de Alicia Girón y Eugenia Correa. México: UNAM, Instituto de Investigaciones Económicas: Plaza y Valdés, 2009. 342 p.: bibl., ill.

Driven by a view that international institutions and forces are the source of much of the economic problems of Latin America, this collection of essays offers a wide-ranging set of commentaries loosely tied together by a search for alternative strategies of development.

1801 Brautigam, Deborah A. and **Monique Segarra.** Difficult partnerships: the World Bank, states, and NGOs. (*Lat. Am. Polit. Soc.*, 49:4, Winter 2007, p. 149–181, appendix, bibl., graph)

A compelling longitudinal analysis in three countries (Guatemala, Ecuador, and the Gambia) of the impact that the World Bank's emphasis on state-NGO collaborations has had on the nature of relationships between NGOs and states in borrowing countries, the types of development projects that have emerged from these collaborations, and the evolution of this partnership agenda over the past 20 years.

1802 Brooks, Sarah M. Globalization and pension reform in Latin America. (*Lat. Am. Polit. Soc.*, 49:4, Winter 2007, p. 31–62, bibl., graphs, table)

Examines the contradictory pressures imposed by economic globalization on Latin American countries with respect to pension reforms. Though such pressures push governments to enact privatizing reforms of their pension systems in an effort to reap long-term benefits, the short-term pressures from these same international sources work against enactment of such reforms.

1803 Camargo Brito, Ricardo. Globalisation and tax policies in Latin America: an empirical assessment. (*Estud. Int./Santiago*, 40:158, sept./dic. 2007, p. 101–132, bibl., graphs, tables)

Analyzes the ways in which the general tax policies of Latin American governments have been influenced by democracy and globalization over the past three decades. Despite the inherent difficulties of measuring such multidimensional concepts as globalization and democracy, the study raises important questions regarding the intersection of global forces, particularly foreign capital and domestic policy-making.

1804 Capital, power, and inequality in Latin America and the Caribbean. Edited by Richard Legé Harris and Jorge Nef. New ed. Lanham, Md.: Rowman & Littlefield, 2008. 344 p.: bibl., index, maps. (Critical currents in Latin American perspective)

A collection of oftentimes highly critical, but convincing, assessments of the myriad development consequences of the era of market-oriented economic policies. Among the wide range of topics addressed are the impact of this era on Latin America's rural sector, social movements, and indigenous peoples.

1805 Carrera Troyano, Miguel and **José Ignacio Antón.** Las relaciones entre equidad y crecimiento y la nueva agenda para América Latina. (*Am. Lat. Hoy/Salamanca*, 48, abril 2008, p. 43–66, bibl.)

An excellent overview of the evolution of theoretical and empirical work on the "growth-equity" question. Discusses the consequent impact that the development community's understanding of this relationship has had on the development policy agenda.

1806 Chica, Ricardo. Latinoamérica frente a la globalización: una estrategia alternativa de desarrollo. Manizales, Colombia: Univ. Autónoma de Manizales, 2007. 271 p.: bibl., ill.

Moving beyond the extremes of the globalization debate, this volume sets out to articulate a realistic alternative path for developing countries to pursue to minimize what are viewed as the excessive costs of the current push for full integration with the global economy.

1807 Del sur hacia el norte: economía política del orden económico internacional emergente. Coordinación de Alicia Girón y Eugenia Correa. Buenos Aires: CLACSO, 2007. 285 p.: bibl., ill. (Col. Sur/Sur)

A series of essays that examines the nature of Latin America's connections with the global economy from various perspectives. Though addressing a variety of topics, the chapters are unified by the common notion that the key to Latin America's future prosperity lies not in changing or stopping globalization, but rather in understanding and modifying the linkages that connect Latin America to the global economy.

1808 Desarrollo e integración: la nueva geopolítica de la economía global. Coordinación de Dejan Mihailovic y Alexis Toríbio Dantas. México: Tecnológico de Monterrey, Escuela de Graduados en Administración Pública y Política Pública:

Miguel Ángel Porrúa, 2007. 235 p.: bibl., ill., maps.

As suggested by the volume's title, the contributions to this work assess the state of affairs with respect to Latin America's continuing efforts to integrate at both the regional and global level. Chapters include overviews and evaluations of Mercosur as well as the growing topic of interest among Latin American political economy scholars—China's relationship with Latin America.

1809 Deuda externa y economía ecológica: dos visiones críticas. Compilación de Fernando Martín Mayoral. Quito: FLACSO Ecuador: Ministerio de Cultura, 2009. 186 p.: bibl., ill. (Col. 50 años)

A collection of essays on two distinct but related areas of political economy viewed by the contributors as critical elements to a more complete assessment of Latin American development prospects than that offered by neoclassical economists. Pt. 1 of this volume examines the role of foreign debt in development, with a particular focus on Ecuador. Pt. 2 offers four essays on the ecological externalities and dimensions to economic development across Latin America.

1810 Dunning, Thad. Crude democracy: natural resource wealth and political regimes. Cambridge, England; New York, N.Y.: Cambridge Univ. Press, 2008. 327 p.: bibl., index. (Cambridge studies in comparative politics)

Explores the relationship between oil and other natural resources and a country's political system. Offers a more nuanced account of this relationship, adding considerably to the conventional view of the authoritarian tendencies of resource-rich countries. Cases examined include Bolivia, Chile, Ecuador, and Botswana.

1811 Echeverry Garzón, Juan Carlos et al. ¿Quién manda sobre las cuentas públicas?: inflexibilidad presupuestal en Colombia, Argentina, México y Perú. Bogotá: Univ. de los Andes, Facultad de Economía: Ediciones Uniandes, 2008. 228 p.: bibl., ill. (Col. Cede 50 años)

A multiple case study of the sources of growing budget constraints faced by developing country governments in an era of relative fiscal austerity and their consequences for the region's emerging democracies.

1812 Economía política de la seguridad ciudadana. Compilación de Fernando Carrión y Manuel Dammert Guardia. Quito: FLACSO Ecuador: Quito, Alcaldía Metropolitana, 2009. 350 p.: bibl., ill. (Serie Foro)

A timely edited volume on the critically important interrelated issues of crime, security, and economic development across Latin America. Chapters tackle the pertinent and relatively understudied question of the economic and political costs of the high levels of violence and crime that have plagued various Latin American countries. Cases examined include Chile, Peru, and the Federal District of Mexico.

1813 Espacios iberoamericanos: la economía del conocimiento. Santiago: Naciones Unidas, CEPAL: Secretaría General Iberoamericana, 2008. 135 p.: bibl., ill. (some col.), col. maps.

A study of the current state of knowledge production and attainment in Latin America that offers a rich, comparative assessment of the region's place in the world with respect to these areas. In general, the study paints a very sobering picture of the knowledge gap that exists between Latin American countries and other parts of the world with respect to such areas as higher education enrollment, patents, and scientific publications.

1814 Feinberg, Richard E. Policy issues: competitiveness and democracy. (*Lat. Am. Polit. Soc.*, 50:1, Spring 2008, p. 154–168, bibl.)

Explores the opportunities and obstacles that democracy presents for the "competitiveness agenda" in Latin America. This agenda includes institutional reforms, improvements to myriad markets (e.g., labor, credit), and progress in social service provision. Though elements of democracy work against such projects, pro-reform coalitions with quality leadership can succeed in effecting change in these areas.

1815 Gallagher, Kevin P. and Roberto Porzecanski. China matters: China's economic impact in Latin America. (*LARR*, 43:1, 2008, p. 185–200, bibl., tables)

368 / Handbook of Latin American Studies v. 67

Another recent effort to assess the growing influence of China on Latin America's trade and investment patterns over the past 15 years. The authors document the sharp and steady rise of China's trade relationship and investment presence within the region and highlight the benefits and consequences of this changing relationship.

1816 Growing pains in Latin America: an economic growth framework as applied to Brazil, Colombia, Costa Rica, Mexico, and Peru. Edited by Liliana Rojas-Suárez. Washington, D.C.: Center for Global Development, 2009. 303 p.: bibl., ill., index.

An impressive collection of essays on the long quest of Latin American countries to achieve stable, sustainable growth, and the role that economic policy reforms have had on this goal. Volume includes chapters on Mexico, Costa Rica, and Brazil, as well as a well-crafted overview of the political economy of growth in the region over the past 30 years.

1817 Guaipatín, Carlos. La cooperación público-privada como instrumento de desarrollo: lecciones de seis aglomeraciones agroindustriales en América Latina. (*Rev. Eur. Estud. Latinoam. Caribe*, 82, April 2007, p. 51–68, bibl., table)

Examines the potential benefits and problems of enhanced formal cooperation between government and the private sector in the agricultural sector. Draws from findings across a diverse set of provincial case studies in Mexico, Chile, Colombia, and Brazil, and concludes with a call for more concerted efforts to further such public-private collaborations.

1818 ¿Hacia donde va el sistema mundial?: impactos y alternativas para América Latina y el Caribe. Compilación de Julio C. Gambina y Jaime Estay Reyno. Buenos Aires: REDEM: FISYP: RLS: CLACSO, 2007. 478 p.: bibl., ill.

Lengthy and wide-ranging collection of essays examining various aspects of Latin America's place in the global economy over the past 30 years. Ranging from inquiries into the role of China in the region to a sweeping assessment of alternatives to the neoliberal model, the edited volume focuses primarily on Brazil, Chile, Mexico, and Argentina.

1819 Ideas, policies and economic development in the Americas. Edited by Esteban Pérez Caldentey and Matías Vernengo. London; New York: Routledge, 2007. 242 p.: bibl., ill., index. (Routledge studies in development economics; 56)

Collection of essays looking both forward and backward in considering the emergence of a new structuralist economic paradigm for Latin American economies in the 21st century. Many of the essays in this volume are predicated on the idea that the era of the Washington Consensus is over and the region is in need of a new economic model.

1820 Impactos de las inversiones españolas en las economías latinoamericanas. Dirección de Santos Ruesga Benito y Ramón Casilda Béjar. Madrid: Marcial Pons, 2008. 287 p.: bibl., ill. (Col. Economía/Marcial Pons)

In a highly sophisticated and sharply focused manner, addresses the impact of Spanish foreign direct investment across Latin America over the past 20 years. Using the unprecedented surge in Spanish investment in the region since the early 1990s, the volume explores in great detail the various economic consequences of flow of Spanish capital into the region.

1821 La inserción de América Latina en la economía internacional. Compilación de Jaime Estay. Textos de Orlando Caputo *et al.* Buenos Aires: CLACSO; México: Siglo Veintiuno Editores, 2008. 264 p.: bibl., ill. (Economía y demografía)

An impressive collection of essays that offer a wide range of perspectives on the various consequences of Latin America's heightened integration with the international economy. Topics include an overview of integration trends across the region over the past several decades, as well as a discussion of the region's efforts at the establishment of free trade agreements.

1822 Integración y desarrollo: una perspectiva americana. Coordinación de Saúl Macías Gamboa y Jesús Rivera de la Rosa. Puebla, Mexico: Benemérita Univ. Autónoma de Puebla, Facultad de Economía, Dirección de Fomento Editorial, 2007. 277 p.: bibl., ill. (Col. Pensamiento económico)

A refreshing collection of essays on the impact that economic integration across Latin America has had on poverty and economic development more generally. Though critical of the neoliberal project as a whole, the authors in this collection resist a call for a return to protectionist policies of the past, offering instead suggestions for modifications to the current economic model.

1823 Jenkins, Rhys; Enrique Dussel Peters; and Mauricio Mesquita Moreira. The impact of China on Latin America and the Caribbean. (*World Dev.*, 36:2, Feb. 2008, p. 235–253, bibl., graphs, tables)

As the title suggests, this article presents a well-carried out exploration of the various direct and indirect economic consequences that the growth of China's global trade profile has had on various export sectors across Latin America and the Caribbean. The authors also examine relative changes in the region's foreign direct investment flows as a consequence of China's increased investment activity in the region.

1824 Jornada de Estudios del Trabajo, 1st, Universidad del Rosario, 2007. Vías y escenarios de la transformación laboral: aproximaciones teóricas y nuevos problemas. Edición de Carmen Marina López Pino *et al.* Textos de Red de Estudios del Trabajo en Colombia. Bogotá: Editorial Univ. del Rosario, 2008. 422 p.: bibl., ill. (Col. Textos de ciencias humanas)

This edited volume of conference proceedings offers various perspectives on the transformation of the labor sector during the neoliberal era. The contributions are highly informative and cover a wide range of topics related to the struggles of the labor sector in Latin America, with a particular focus on Colombia.

1825 Lateinamerika im Wandel. Edited by Peter Birle. Baden-Baden, Germany: Nomos, 2010. 247 p.: bibl., ill. (Weltwirtschaft und internationale Zusammenarbeit; 4)

Collection of articles presenting the last 30 years of political and economic developments in selected Latin American countries. Also discusses possibilities for regional and international collaboration between Latin America and Europe on a general level. [F. Obermeier]

1826 Lazin, Olga M. La globalización se descentraliza: libre mercado, fundaciones, sociedad cívica y gobierno civil en las regiones del mundo. Prólogo de James Wallace Wilkie. Guadalajara, Mexico: Univ. de Guadalajara; Los Angeles, Calif.: UCLA Program on Mexico: PROFMEX/WORLD; México: Casa Juan Pablos Centro Cultural, 2007. 715 p.: bibl., ill., maps. (Ciclos y tendencias en el desarrollo de México; 35)

A wide-ranging, perhaps somewhat disjointed, collection of chapters on the broad topic of the impact of globalization on civil society across the developing world and international philanthropic organizations.

1827 Martínez, Gabriela. Latin American telecommunications: Telefónica's conquest. Lanham, Md.: Lexington Books, 2008. 152 p.: bibl., index.

In-depth, descriptive account of Spanish corporation Telefónica's establishment as a leading player in Latin America's telecommunications market. Also explores the implications for Latin American societies of the expanding access to communication technologies.

1828 Más allá del mercado: las políticas de servicio universal en América Latina. Edición de Joan Calzada, Antón Costas y Jacint Jordana. Barcelona: Fundació CIDOB, 2009. 410 p.: bibl., ill. (Interrogar la actualidad. Serie América Latina)

This edited volume offers a comprehensive analysis of privatization and regulatory reforms in the public utility and service sectors in selected Latin American countries. Emphasized throughout are the increasingly evident disparities in service access among urban and rural populations.

1829 Mesa-Lago, Carmelo. World crisis effects on social security in Latin America and the Caribbean: lessons and policies. London: Institute for the Study of the Americas, 2010. 111 p.: ill.

A study by one of the world's foremost experts on social security examines the initial effects of the global financial crisis on social security systems across Latin America. Offers compelling insights into the varying effects of crisis on these systems during the first year of the crisis.

1830 Milanovic, Branko and **Rafael Muñoz de Bustillo.** La desigualdad de la distribución de la renta en América Latina: situación, evolución y factores explicativos. (*Am. Lat. Hoy/Salamanca*, 48, abril 2008, p. 15–42, bibl., graphs, tables)

A comprehensive assessment of the state of research on inequality in Latin America by long-time contributors to that research. This article offers an outstanding overview of the evolution of inequality in the region, the various dimensions of inequality beyond income (e.g., education), and the wide range of causes and consequences for its persistence in the region. Includes useful tables and charts on various aspects of inequality in Latin America.

1831 Moreira, Mauricio Mesquita. Fear of China: is there a future for manufacturing in Latin America? (*World Dev.*, 35:3, March 2007, p. 355–376, bibl., graphs, tables)

Explores the various dimensions of competition between the manufacturing sectors in China and Latin America with an eye toward the question of whether Latin America's sector can remain a viable engine of development for the region in the future. Though largely descriptive, this piece highlights trends in the trade profiles of both sectors that do not bode well for Latin America moving forward.

1832 Murillo, Maria Victoria. Political competition, partisanship, and policymaking in Latin American public utilities. New York, N.Y.: Cambridge Univ. Press, 2009. 292 p.: bibl., ill., index. (Cambridge studies in comparative politics)

A compelling study of the factors that shape policies for public utilities across Latin America, with a particular focus on Argentina and Mexico. The author makes a strong case for the role of a viable electoral opposition in pushing incumbents to adopt less capital-friendly public utilities ownership and regulatory policies.

1833 Nuevas rutas para el desarrollo en América Latina: experiencias globales y locales. Compilación de Juan Maestre Alfonso, Ángel María Casas Gragea y Alba González Jácome. México: Univ. Iberoamericana, 2008. 413 p.: bibl., ill., map.

An interesting, albeit mixed, collection of essays on various topics related to the development processes of selected Latin American countries in a context of increasing international interdependence. Topics range from the global—the impact of free trade across the region—to the local—the development consequences of emigration in the state of Zacatecas, Mexico.

1834 O'Keefe, Thomas Andrew. Latin American and Caribbean trade agreements: keys to a prosperous community of the Americas. Leiden, The Netherlands: Martinus Nijhoff Publishers, 2009. 490 p.: bibl., index.

An exhaustive and highly useful volume on past, present, and what the author hopes will be future efforts at economic integration among countries of the Americas. This volume should serve as an outstanding reference on the various free trade efforts made over the years in the region. O'Keefe also makes a compelling argument for the need for future integration attempts.

1835 Parnreiter, Christof; Karin Fischer; and Karen Imhof. El enlace faltante entre cadenas globales de producción y ciudades globales: el servicio financiero en Ciudad de México y Santiago de Chile. (*EURE/Santiago*, 33:100, dic. 2007, p. 135–148, bibl., tables)

A useful comparative analysis of the global and local presence of financial service companies in Mexico City and Santiago that highlights the important role played by such companies in linking internationally oriented domestic producers with the global economy.

Pérez Fuentes, Judith. Integración y desarrollo: buscando alternativas para América Latina. See item **1556.**

1836 La pluriactividad en el campo latinoamericano. Coordinación de Hubert Carton de Grammont y Luciano Martínez Valle. Quito: FLACSO, Sede Ecuador, 2009. 307 p.: bibl., ill., maps. (Foro)

One of several volumes reviewed that examine Latin America's shrinking rural sector and the impact that market-based economic reforms have had on rural conditions. Brings together several informative chapters, including ones that focus on Peru, Ecuador, and the Dominican Republic.

1837 Podestá, Juan. Globalización, mercado, modernismo: los debates latinoamericanos. (*Rev. Eur. Estud. Latinoam. Caribe*, 83, Oct. 2007, p. 121–132, bibl.)

A brief but intriguing essay on what the author views as the four defining debates of current Latin American political economy. Though perhaps overly ambitious in attempting to delve into each of the topics, the article nicely lays out the contours of questions concerning the root causes of the region's economic development patterns, the impact of globalization on the region, the potential role of democracy in Latin American development, and the more general debate on modernity.

1838 Políticas de privatización, espacio público y educación en América Latina. Compilación de Pablo Gentili *et al.* Buenos Aires: CLACSO; Rosario, Argentina: Homo Sapiens Ediciones, 2009. 405 p.: bibl. (Serie de estudios latinoamericanos)

Interesting and well-executed collection of essays on the understudied topic of the impact of neoliberalism on public education in Latin America. Under the rubric of this broad topic, the contributions' principal concerns include the privatization of many aspects of public education in the region and the rise of the so-called transnationalization of higher education in Latin America.

1839 Porras, Francisco. Teorías de la gobernanza y estudios regionales. (*Secuencia/México*, 69, sept./dic. 2007, p. 163–185, bibl., tables)

Porras, in this imaginative article, suggests that theories about the relationship between regions and governance need to be redefined to incorporate the importance of globalization, specifically trade, on actors and regions. Using data from the European Union, he argues that relationships between public and business actors have been affected by such external (global) influences, which supports his argument favoring a change in the definition of regions. [R. Camp]

1840 Privatization for the public good?: the social effects of privatizations in Latin America. Edited by Alberto Chong. Washington, D.C.: Inter-American Development Bank, 2007. 240 p.

A welcome addition to existing work on privatization in Latin America that goes beyond the macroeconomic or sector-specific effects of privatization efforts in the regimes to examine the impact of this policy trend on the well-being of citizens themselves. Includes chapters on water service in the shantytowns of Argentina, telephone service in Peru, and water provision in Ecuador.

1841 Repensar la teoría del desarrollo en un contexto de globalización: homenaje a Celso Furtado. Coordinación de Gregorio Vidal y Arturo Guillén Romo. Buenos Aires: CLACSO; México: Red Eurolatinoamericana de Estudios sobre el Desarrollo Celso Furtado: Univ. Autónoma Metropolitana de México, 2007. 554 p.: bibl., ill. (Col. Edición y distribución cooperativa)

Outstanding collection of essays by some of the most noted development scholars of the past several decades. All, in one way or another, address the question implied in the title of the collection: "How has globalization affected the way we think about development?" Though myriad answers are offered in the volume, all pose challenges for extant work on development.

1842 Skoufias, Emmanuel; Kathy Lindert; and Joseph Shapiro. Globalization and the role of public transfers in redistributing income in Latin America and the Caribbean. (*World Dev.*, 38:6, June 2010, p. 895–907)

This paper attempts to measure the extent to which publicly subsidized transfers in Latin America and the Caribbean redistribute income. The redistributive power of 56 transfers in eight countries is measured by their simulated impacts on poverty and inequality, and by their distributional characteristic. The findings suggest that public transfers can be effective instruments to redistribute income to the poor. [C.E. Griffin]

1843 Terjesen, Siri and José Ernesto Amorós. Female entrepreneurship in Latin America and the Caribbean: characteristics, drivers and relationship to economic development. (*Eur. J. Dev. Res.*, 22:3, July 2010, p. 313–330)

This article explores female entrepreneurial activities in 13 Latin American and Caribbean countries: Argentina, Bolivia, Brazil, Chile, Colombia, Dominican

Republic, Ecuador, Jamaica, Mexico, Peru, Puerto Rico, Uruguay, and Venezuela. Among the research questions are the following: What percentage of the female and male Latin American population is involved in opportunity- and necessity-based entrepreneurial activities? And what quality of institutions is associated with female entrepreneurial activity opportunity and necessity rates? [C.E. Griffin]

1844 Torre, Augusto de la and **Sergio L. Schmukler.** Emerging capital markets and globalization: the Latin American experience. Palo Alto, Calif.: Stanford Univ. Press; Washington, D.C.: World Bank, 2007. 209 p.: bibl., ill., index. (Latin American development forum)

A detailed analysis of capital market reforms across Latin America over the past 30 years, guided by the view that these local capital markets are part and parcel of the financial globalization processes that have come to define the past three decades. Volume contains numerous useful tables and charts documenting the various implications of these trends for Latin America's economic development.

1845 Which way Latin America?: hemispheric politics meets globalization. Edited by Andrew Fenton Cooper and Jorge Heine. Tokyo; New York, N.Y.: United Na-

tions Univ. Press, 2009. 326 p.: bibl., ill., index, map.

This edited volume seeks to make collective sense of the implications of two decades of economic and political reforms implemented across the region, with a particular focus on the more recent emergence of left-of-center leaders in many countries. The collection of essays includes contributions from some of the leading scholars of Latin American politics that address a wide range of topics, from the increased presence of China in the region to the impact of Venezuelan leader Hugo Chávez.

Who decides the budget?: a political economy analysis of the budget process in Latin America. See item **2136**.

1846 Wiesner Durán, Eduardo. The political economy of macroeconomic policy reform in Latin America: the distributive and institutional context. Cheltenham, England; Northampton, Mass.: Edward Elgar, 2008. 278 p.: bibl., ill., indexes.

An ambitious analysis of the sources of macroeconomic policies across several Latin American countries during the past 30 years. A theoretical focus on effective institutions as a critical determinant of successful policy guides the analysis that includes detailed case studies of six countries, including Brazil, Colombia, and Costa Rica.

MEXICO

LAURA RANDALL, *Professor Emerita of Economics, Hunter College, City University of New York*

THE 2010 AND 2011 CONCERNS about the war on drugs and about Mexico's controversial status as a "failed state" are not reflected in the books published just a few years earlier. The focus of the books published between 2006–2009 is the impact of globalization on Mexico. The analysis of this topic became more sophisticated during these years, shifting from an examination of general complaints to a deeper evaluation of specific details. Critics condemned NAFTA for benefitting the US and offering too few advantages to Mexico. Two outstanding books indicate that NAFTA's impact on Mexico resulted from inequalities within that country. Puga (item **1885**) shows how a Mexican network of business associations, COECE, was instrumental in determining the clauses of NAFTA, benefitting the largest businesses. Rivera *et al.* (item **1876**) show how NAFTA damaged small- and medium-sized Mexican farmers. Others indicate that the lack of credit to rural areas following the shift from domestic to foreign banks severely damaged rural areas, while a study of Sinaloa indicates that foreign inputs are more important than foreign investment in agriculture (item **1891**). Bacon *et al.* (item **1853**) analyzes the impact of the world coffee market on Mexican coffee growers, and show how Mexican farmers reacted to the coffee crisis; Baklanoff and Moseley's edited volume (item **1898**) shows the impact of the crisis on Yucatan since 1982.

On the other hand, Guillermo and Tanka (item **1862**) write that opening Mexico to trade increased its manufacturing sector's productivity. Others argue that reducing the state's role in the economy, with the intention of increasing competition, led to dominance by foreign firms and a reliance on foreign finance and foreign inputs, limiting the immediate benefit to Mexico of increased economic activity. Corruption was part of the privatization process, with both corruption and theft severely weakening the oil and electricity industries.

Gerritsen and Morales Hernández (item **1889**) indicate that when some people lose their jobs, they increase production of craft goods, often because they have no cash to do anything else. Women, who are paid less, remain employed, but no longer have time to produce nutritional meals, and aid often is provided without instruction. Development on the frontier has few links to the Mexican economy as a whole.

Corrales *et al.* (item **1895**) provide a municipal development index and analysis. An edited volume by Borjas (item **1872**) finds that as Mexicans lost jobs, they migrated to the US, increasing wages in Mexico, and leading to a shortage of skilled labor within the nation. In the US, wages decreased. Social networks rather than economic considerations determined where migrants settled.

Several excellent essays on macroeconomics show that globalization's impact on the exchange rate and money supply led to the economic crisis, and the misery described above, while a weak government and fiscal evasion, as well as policies favoring bankers and the urban sector, limited government response. Loaeza (item **1870**) analyzes the political consequences of banking nationalization.

Studies published after this time period indicate that underbanking in rural areas provided the opportunity for drug organizations to offer credit to those who could no longer obtain it through regular institutional channels, and thus obtain support for their illegal operations and provide employment to some in the fragile rural areas. This contrasted with some government programs designed to improve the condition of the poorest: those based on conditionality were flawed, as in the case of many rural poor who, because they lived far from health clinics, were unable to obtain the aid they offered (item **1855**). Yet the benefits of these programs set a standard throughout the hemisphere.

Levy's (item **1869**) outstanding essay details the benefits to 5 million families of Oportunidades-Progresa; Cotler (item **1884**) shows why difficulties in registering property and obtaining loans lead to underbanking and made it difficult for the poor to help themselves. Others describe the expansion of microcredit to communal groups (item **1861**) and of credit offered by retail stores that have experience in collecting payments for items purchased on layaway. Credit previously obtained through traditional banks, is now being offered through nontraditional channels. Critics believe that providing credit should not be so profitable to the lender if it is to keep operating, arguing that the profits are too high. The key point, however, is often the availability of credit, rather than its cost. Thus, in regard to this and other aspects of the Mexican economy, there is a demand for government subsidies to ameliorate the condition of the poorest by, for example, increasing government attention to the provision of education and healthcare, enabling them to obtain acceptable living conditions within Mexico.

It is likely that water rights between the US and Mexico, and the complex topic of how this affects foreign—including non-US—investors in agriculture will spark new research and will be an important policy question in the near future. Other new research topics will likely be found in the implementation of judicial reform, as well as in the supervision of banks and other firms, and in how any changes will impact investment and doing business in Mexico. The impact of economic development on the environment, not only in regard to NAFTA provisions, but also in regard to destruction of wealth of almost 10 percent of Mexico's net ecological product—documented through Mexico's INEGI—in the course of economic development, not least of all through highly publicized oil spills and inadequate disposal of wastes in mining and other activities is a subject deserving significant research attention.

1847 El agua en México: consecuencias de las políticas de intervención en el sector. Coordinación de Hilda R. Guerrero García Rojas, Antonio Yúnez-Naude y Josué Medellín-Azuara. Textos de Musa Asad *et al.* México: Fondo de Cultura Económica, 2008. 222 p.: bibl., ill. (El trimestre económico. Lecturas)

Water and electricity subsidies and poor administration of water rights result in a misallocation of water. Reducing the amount of water supplied to agriculture, strengthening associations of local water users, placing a value-added tax on agriculture, and eliminating subsidies to agriculture would increase government income and promote more efficient use of water in agriculture.

1848 Apropiación y propiedad: un enfoque institucional de la economía mexicana. Coordinación de Fernando Jeannot. Textos de Pascual García Alba Iduñate *et al.* México: Ediciones y Gráficos Eón: Univ. Autónoma Metropolitana, Azcapotzalco, 2007. 349 p.: bibl., ill. (Eón sociales)

The Mexican economy stagnates because private property rights there, unlike those in US, Finland, and Japan, do not lead to increased productivity, but to rents requiring technological and organizational backwardness. Progress requires better definition of property rights, less corruption, improvement of the informal economy and a strengthening of the overall structure of the economy.

1849 Arés, Mathieu. El estado empresario: Nacional Financiera durante la industrialización por sustitución de importaciones, 1934–1994. (*Foro Int./México,* 47:2, abril/junio 2007, p. 201–244, bibl., tables)

Mexico's development bank gradually was accepted as the government strengthened it from 1934–47, using it to coordinate industrialization in the "stabilizing development" phase—1947–70. NAFIN lent more broadly in 1970–82; its role in the economy declined thereafter, foreign financing increased, and loans from NAFIN shifted to small and medium enterprises.

1850 Ascencio Franco, Gabriel. Regularización de la propiedad en la Selva Lacandona: cuento de nunca acabar. Tuxtla Gutiérrez, Mexico: Univ. de Ciencias y Artes de Chiapas, 2008. 192 p.: bibl., maps. (Col. Selva Negra)

Largely successful government programs to resolve disputed land titles, relocate some people, and aid those in zones of greatest poverty and conflict have not reached enough people. The militarization of the Lacandon area in response to the EZLN and to economic and political conditions explain the need for the programs.

1851 Bassols Batalla, Narciso. Las etapas de la nacionalización petrolera. México: Cámara de Diputados, LIX Legislatura: M. Á. Porrúa, 2006. 380 p.: bibl., ill. (Conocer para decidir)

Presents plentiful data for 1901–2003.

Analyzes profitability using shadow, transfer and consumer pricing for PEMEX and its four subsidiaries starting in 1993, indicating profits concentrated in crude oil operations. Explains that high petrochemical imports are the result of the small size of Mexican refineries and the lack of investment. Indicates need for ombudsman for PEMEX's contracts.

1852 Conferencia Internacional sobre Corrupción y Transparencia, 1st, UNAM, 2006. Corrupción y transparencia: debatiendo las fronteras entre estado, mercado y sociedad. Coordinación de Irma Eréndira Sandoval. Textos de Susan Rose-Ackerman *et al.* Presentación de Ricardo Pozas Horcasitas. México: UNAM, IIS: Siglo Veintiuno Editores, 2009. 503 p.: bibl., ill. (Sociología y política)

Deregulation of economy led to corruption in privatization of public goods, and transfers between levels of government. Focuses on "clientelismo," "rentismo" and "captura del estado," and lack of effective measures to protect "whistle-blowers," or effective sanctions against corrupt officials and those who corrupt them. Increasing government transparency somewhat limits corruption.

1853 Confronting the coffee crisis: fair trade, sustainable livelihoods and ecosystems in Mexico and Central America. Edited by Christopher M. Bacon *et al.* Cambridge, Mass.: MIT Press, 2008. 390 p.: bibl., ill., index. (Food, health, and the environment)

Fourteen outstanding essays analyze the world coffee market, marketing structures, and the ways in which different-sized farmers react to alternatives. Reactions depend on outlays that emphasize cash or labor; availability of technical help and credit; and certification as "social," "organic," or "ecologically friendly" by NGOs or government regulators. For geography specialist's comment, see item **790**.

1854 Desarrollo local: teoría y prácticas socioterritoriales. Coordinación de Rocío Rosales Ortega. México: Univ. Autónoma Metropolitana, Unidad Iztapalapa: Miguel Ángel Porrúa, 2007. 445 p.: bibl., ill., maps. (Las ciencias sociales)

Fifteen essays analyze local economic development regarding innovation, local government, gender and environment, and "territoriality" of local groups. Theory and methodology are explained in the first part of the book; the second part provides case studies. Aid to women often is insufficient to let them establish or expand their businesses.

Duhau, Emilio and **Angela Giglia.** Nuevas centralidades y prácticas de consumo en la Ciudad de México: del microcomercio al hipermercado. See item **793**.

1855 *Economic Development and Cultural Change*, Vol. 57, No. 3, April 2009, Symposium: Impacts of the Oportunidades Program. Chicago, Ill.: Univ. of Chicago Press.

Oportunidades, previously Progresa, provided conditional income transfers and nutritional supplements, improving nutrition and health, reducing child labor, and increasing school enrollment. Participating rural women's household income increased by about one quarter, and was used for consumption and for investment in their children and in small livestock. Greatest urban participation in the program was by the poorest with easy access to health centers.

1856 Los estudios de empresarios y empresas: una perspectiva internacional. Coordinación de Jorge Basave y Marcela A. Hernández Romo. México: UNAM, Instituto de Investigaciones Económicas: Univ. Autónoma Metropolitana, Iztapalapa, División de Ciencias Sociales y Humanidades: Plaza y Valdés, 2007. 240 p.: bibl., maps.

Brings together theories of entrepreneurship, their relationship to economic history, structure and behavior of the firm, including theories of the firm as "intrapreneur." Entrepreneurs should be studied in their daily life, including their cultural codes in specified economic, political, and social conditions whose hierarchy changes over time.

1857 Falck Reyes, Melba E. Del proteccionismo a la liberalización agrícola en Japón, Corea del Sur y Taiwán: oportunidades para México: un enfoque de economía política. México: Instituto Matías Romero, Secretaría de Relaciones Exteriores, 2006.

503 p.: bibl., ill. (Cuadernos de política internacional; nueva época)

The changes in consumer preferences among East Asian nations makes it less desirable to maintain small-scale growers for traditional markets. Author advises that Mexico diversify the nations to which it exports. It has a comparative advantage in agricultural products compared to Asian nations, and should learn how to increase its exports to them.

1858 Foro México en el Mundo: Estrategías para el Futuro, Universidad Autónoma Metropolitana, 2005. Foro México en el Mundo—Estrategías para el Futuro. Coordinación de Alejandro del Palacio. México: Univ. Autónoma Metropolitana, Unidad Iztapalapa, 2006. 424 p.: bibl., ill.

Four of five Mexicans have a relative in the US, but Mexico has little importance in US trade, and in US or world politics. NAFTA broke Mexico's internal production links. Although the state largely controls Mexican mass culture, the nation's institutions are flawed and democratic government insufficiently implemented.

1859 García de León P., Guadalupe. La inserción de México en la arquitectura cambiante de redes del suministro del vestido hacia Estados Unidos, 1985–2003. México: UNAM, Instituto de Investigaciones Económicas: Univ. de Sonora: Miguel Ángel Porrúa, 2008. 390 p.: bibl., ill. (Col. Jesús Silva Herzog)

From the mid-1980s, Mexico modernized its economy and opened its doors to international trade, especially in the clothing industry. The country shifted from dominance by maquiladoras to plants whose production began with cloth and extended through the distribution of the final product, although there were not large linkages to the domestic economy.

1860 González Chávez, Gerardo. El estado y la globalización en la industria siderúrgica mexicana. México: UNAM, Instituto de Investigaciones Económicas: Casa Juan Pablos, 2008. 373 p.: bibl., ill.

Presents the history of the Mexican steel industry, emphasizing Altos Hornos de Mexico. Initial benefits from the state during the import-substitution phase led to an oligopolistic structure and insufficient efficiency. New technology and privatization decreased employment, and led to a greater specialization of steel firms, but continuing overproduction of steel.

1861 González Núñez, José Carlos. El microcrédito de banca comunal: una alternativa de financiamiento rural en México. México: Univ. Anáhuac México Sur: Miguel Ángel Porrúa, 2008. 122 p.: bibl.

Credit to the rural poor can be effectively organized through microfinance, with loans to women's communal groups. Key factors in their success include small initial loans, a maximum placed on the size of the loan, weekly half-hour meetings, market interest rates, follow up of loans to individuals, and supply of other financial services.

1862 Guillermo, Sylvia and Beata Tanka. Measuring total factor productivity growth in Mexican manufacturing: the story before and after trade liberalization. (*Ens. Polít. Econ.*, 25:53, 2007, p. 168–219, graphs, tables)

Technical study favors the impact of NAFTA on total factor productivity. (The latter is defined as changes in output not explained by quantity or quality of factor inputs.) Trade liberalization enhanced manufacturing productivity, which fell before NAFTA, but increased after it. In contrast, the overall performance of the Mexican economy was poor from 1993–2003.

1863 Hernández, César. La reforma cautiva: inversión, trabajo y empresa en el sector eléctrico mexicano. México: CIDAC: Ventas y distribución, Co-media, 2007. 534 p.: bibl., ill.

The electric sector status quo is not sustainable. Factions fight over "dividing the loot," particularly now that there is more to gain. Subsidized tariffs, theft of electricity, high benefits to workers, and poor gas policy lead to massive losses. A belief that a reform would be "unconstitutional" impedes change. Provides useful data and statistics.

1864 Hernández Romero, Yasmín. El tejido socioeconómico y laboral en la fábrica textil La Hortensia. Toluca, Mexico: Univ. Autónoma del Estado de México, 2006.

170 p.: bibl., ill., map. (Ciencias sociales. Sociología)

Excellent history of La Hortensia (1946–94) established under a protectionist regime. It provided good labor contracts, but inadequate safety for workers. The national economic crisis and end of state subsidies led to financial problems in the 1980s. New management of La Hortensia was inadequate; strikes led to the closing of the firm.

1865 Instituciones y desarrollo: ensayos sobre la complejidad del campo mexicano. Coordinación de Raúl García Barrios, Beatriz de la Tejera y Kirsten A. de Appendini. Cuernavaca, Mexico: Centro Regional de Investigaciones Multidisciplinarias/UNAM; Chapingo, Mexico: Univ. Autónoma Chapingo; México: Colegio de México, 2008. 355 p.: bibl., ill., map. (Multidisciplina)

Ten essays explore how autonomous agents establish cooperative action, institutions, and social practices to improve their lives, guided by an ethical vision. Government subsidies do not reach small producers. Strong, complex essays urge better communication for self-sufficient agriculture, and better differentiation of high quality maiz from maiz of average quality.

1866 Internacionalización económica, historia y conflicto ambiental en la minería: el caso de Minera San Xavier. Coordinación de María Cecilia Costero Garbarino. Textos de Moisés Gámez *et al.* San Luis Potosí, Mexico: Colegio de San Luis, 2008. 213 p., 15 p. of plates: bibl., ill. (some col.), maps. (Col. Investigaciones)

Six essays indicate that the establishment of mining destroyed the historic heritage and environment of Cerro de San Pedro, in San Luis Potosí. NAFTA led to Canadian investment. Local development needs, as well as those of international investors, should be taken into account. Use of cyanide is especially damaging.

1867 Izcara Palacios, Simón Pedro. Infraclases rurales: los trabajadores eventuales agrarios de Tamaulipas, México y Andalucía, España. México: Plaza y Valdés; Madrid: Calle de la Eras,2006. 195 p.: bibl., ill.

Ethnic enclaves of casual rural labor endure discrimination and fraud. In Mexico,

orange pickers learn their trade from childhood onwards. They work harder in the US where they go for higher wages, motivated by a desire to finance their children's education. Draws a comparison with Maghrebi workers in Spain who face severe discrimination and unemployment.

1868 La lechería familiar en México. Coordinación de Alfredo Cesín Vargas, Fernando Cervantes Escoto y Adolfo Alvarez Macías. Chapingo, Mexico: Univ. Autónoma Chapingo: Centro de Investigaciones Económicas, Sociales y Tecnológicas de la Agroindustria y Agricultura Mundial, Univ. Autónomia: CONACYT: Univ. Autónoma Metropolitana, Unidad Xochimilco: Consejo Nacional de Ciencia y Tecnología: Miguel Ángel Porrúa, 2009. 291 p.: bibl., ill., maps. (Serie Las ciencias sociales. Tercera Década)

A decreasing number of young farmers are entering into family milk production in eight areas in Mexico. Milk production is less profitable than other activities. The government imported milk and dairy products to satisfy internal demand instead of developing domestic production. Twenty-eight percent of Mexican production is uncompetitive, but provides employment and nutrition in poor areas.

1869 Levy, Santiago. Progress against poverty: sustaining Mexico's Progresa-Oportunidades program. Washington, D.C.: Brookings Institution Press, 2006. 166 p.: bibl., ill., index.

Thorough analysis of technical, administrative, and political economy considerations, and evaluation of Progresa-Oportunidades from 1997 to 2005. The program reached five million families by Aug. 2003. Food consumption, health status, and education of the poor improved. Cash and in-kind transfers in 2005 were second only to those associated with social security pensions.

1870 Loaeza, Soledad. Las consecuencias políticas de la expropiación bancaria. México: El Colegio de Mexico, 2008. 182 p. (Jornadas)

The 1982 bank expropriation was carried out unilaterally, which made it impossible to foresee the consequences, which included weakening the presidency and providing an opening for a flawed democracy. Describes the uncontrolled 1970s oil boom and ensuing institutional weakness characterized by the state's insufficient communications with nonelites.

Lyon, Sarah. Coffee and community: Maya farmers and fair-trade markets. See item **483**.

1871 Mendoza Fernández, María Teresa. La industria maquiladora de exportación en el estado de Yucatán y el desarrollo regional. Mérida, Mexico: Ediciones de la Univ. Autónoma de Yucatán, 2008. 303 p.: bibl., col. ill.

Yucatán's maquiladora export industry provided only minimal backward linkages, added value, and transfer of technology. The industry created high quality, low-wage jobs whose workers, for the most part, thought the jobs were better than any other available alternative. Foreign employers provided better benefits than Mexican employers. The US economic slump starting in 2001 led to a severe decline in maquiladoras.

1872 Mexican immigration to the United States. Edited by George J. Borjas. Chicago, Ill.: Univ. of Chicago Press, 2007. 338 p.: bibl., ill., indexes. (A National Bureau of Economic Research conference report)

Excellent econometric analyses exploring why, by 2003, almost nine percent of the Mexican population had migrated to the US, decreasing wages in the US and increasing them in Mexico. Increasing skill and marriage of Mexican immigrants with nonimmigrants raised their wages. Immigration networks, more than policy reforms, explained patterns of immigration.

1873 Modelos de producción en la maquila de exportación: la crisis del toyotismo precario. Coordinación de Enrique de la Garza Toledo. México: Univ. Autónoma Metropolitana, Iztapalapa: Plaza y Valdés, 2005. 419 p.: bibl., ill.

Studies of models of maquila production and a survey in the center-southwest of Mexico indicate that aspects of the labor force and links between firms within Mexico, rather than theories of scale or the three generations of maquilas, determine maquila

production. Structural limitations prevent a change to better worker conditions.

1874 Moneda y régimen cambiario en México: contribuciones a un debate de política económica. Coordinación de Fernando Chávez. Textos de Everardo Elizondo Almaguer *et al.* México: Friedrich Ebert Stiftung: Univ. Autónoma Metropolitana Azcapotzalco, 2003. 415 p.: bibl., ill.

The impact of globalization on the exchange rate and money supply underlies Mexican economic crises. The exchange rate is "real," and not just another price. Authors present alternatives to a floating peso, including dollarization, and a monetary union with US and possibly also Canada in a context of cycles of monetary policy.

1875 La nacionalización bancaria, 25 años después: la historia contada por sus protagonistas. Edición de Amparo Espinosa Rugarcía y Enrique Cárdenas. México: Centro de Estudios Espinosa Yglesias (Mexico), 2008. 2 v.: bibl., ill., index.

President José López Portillo's 1982 nationalization of Mexico's private banks broke the ties between the private sector and government. Essays by 12 advisers and officials provide unique insights into their own theories and motivations, as well as that of the president, and into the impact of the nationalization and its aftermath.

1876 NAFTA and the campesinos: the impact of NAFTA on small-scale agricultural producers in Mexico and the prospects for change. Edited by Juan M. Rivera, Scott Whiteford, and Manuel Chávez Márquez. Scranton, Pa.: Univ. of Scranton Press, 2009. 184 p.: bibl., ill.

The Mexican government should renegotiate some clauses of NAFTA because they damaged small and medium farmers. Insufficient government credit was supplemented by private national and international suppliers and purchasers. Providing greater US than Mexican farm subsidies damages Mexico. Work includes special studies of sugar, corn, goat, and organic food farms and industries.

1877 Núñez Estrada, Héctor. Reforma y crisis del sistema bancario, 1990–2000: quiebra de Banca Serfín: enfoque organizacional. México: Plaza y Valdés, 2005. 414 p.: bibl., ill.

Explores whether rationality can be more limited if markets are imperfect and institutions change. Describes changes in laws governing Mexico's financial intermediaries, in part resulting from NAFTA. The lack of oversight of banks led to unsound loans and the financial collapse of Banca Serfin, followed by a costly banking system rescue.

1878 Ocampo Torrea, José Felipe. Pemex: mitos, realidades, testimonios y propuestas. Introducción de Ifigenia Martínez. México: Univ. Autónoma de la Ciudad de México, 2006. 312 p.: bibl., ill. (Col. Reflexiones)

Ocampo Torrea opposes the "denationalization" of Pemex, arguing that the reasons for the denationalization are based on over-aggregation, poor reasoning, and use of oil facilities at below-optimum levels. Interesting data on details of oil and petrochemical operations. Urges less foreign participation in oil industry and better rules regulating its activities.

1879 Ocegueda, Juan Manuel. La restricción externa al crecimiento económico de México: el impacto de las reformas estructurales. Mexicali, Mexico: Univ. Autónoma de Baja California, 2006. 205 p.: bibl., ill., index. (Col. tesis)

The replacement of Mexican by foreign inputs (especially chemicals, oil derivatives, rubber, plastics, metal products, machinery, and equipment) by Mexican exporters, often transnational firms, explains the shortage of foreign exchange, which restricts Mexican economic growth, consistent with Thirlwall's Law. Urges promotion of sectors with a lower propensity to import.

1880 Pacheco, Bulmaro. Los indicadores del cambio en México 1968–2000. 2da. ed. Hermosillo, Mexico: Impresos RM, 2006. 401 p.: bibl.

Presents annual changes in the world and in Mexico during three different periods of time: 1968–82; 1982–96; and 1996–2000. During the first period, there were major political reforms coupled with poor economic policy and an increase of foreign debt. The second period was characterized by a "deincorporation" of state enterprises. In the

third period, President Zedillo, (1994–2000) increased democracy, there was a takeover of bankrupt roads and toll income, but bank fraud was a problem.

1881 El papel de las ideas y las políticas en el cambio estructural en México. Coordinación de Rolando Cordera y Carlos Javier Cabrera Adame. México: UNAM: Fondo de Cultura Económica, 2008. 566 p.: bibl., ill. (El trimestre económico. Lecturas)

Seventeen essays analyze market reforms from a historical perspective; fiscal, commercial, and monetary policy; and financial challenges and future outlook. Economic growth slowdown began in 1976, share of non-oil in total exports increased starting in 1982. Human rights and poverty increased; PRI's power fell. New institutions favored privileged sectors, formal over informal labor, men over women.

1882 Política económica neoliberal y migración. Coordinación de Aurora Furlong. Textos de Aurora Furlong et al. Puebla, Mexico: Benemérita Univ. Autónoma de Puebla, Vicerrectoría de Docencia: Dirección de Fomento Editorial, 2009. 246 p.: bibl., ill.

Mexican immigrants receive 30 percent of wages compared to US counterparts. Asserts that migrant funds sent to Mexico to finance children's education is overlooked, as is the impact of migration on family relationships. Casa Puebla (New York) aids migrants. Suggests strategies to generate employment in the sending regions. Gives example of personal history.

1883 Políticas macroeconómicas para países en desarrollo. Coordinación de Guadalupe Mántey de Anguiano y Noemí Levy Orlik. México: H. Cámara de Diputados, LX Legislatura: UNAM, FES, Dirección General de Asuntos del Personal Académico: Porrúa, 2007. 526 p.: bibl., ill. (Conocer para decidir)

Presents theories explaining the behavior of the financial sector and distribution of factorial income in a market with weak money. Also examines fiscal and monetary policy in open economies, and strategies to improve economic growth in imperfect institutional global markets. Sociological factors and technological improvement supplement these explanations.

**1884 Políticas públicas para un creci-
miento incluyente.** Edición de Pablo
Cotler. México: Univ. Iberoamericana, 2007.
392 p.: bibl., ill.

Outstanding article on banking by
Cotler examines the difficulties of obtaining collateral if a loan fails, leading
to underbanking and credit restriction.
Maintains that the high cost of registering
property leads to uncertainty of ownership.
Describes bank rule changes around time of
NAFTA. Suppliers' credit often in kind and
on poor terms.

1885 Puga, Cristina. Los empresarios orga-
nizados y el Tratado de Libre Comercio de América del Norte. México: Miguel
Angel Porrúa: Facultad de Ciencias Políticas
y Sociales, UNAM, 2004. 288 p.: bibl.

COECE (Coordinadora de Organismos Empresariales de Comercio Exterior),
a unique network of business associations,
fostered consensus among them, negotiated
terms of NAFTA with the government, and
aided in the treaty's adoption. It emphasized
technical issues, and initiated large firms'
assistance to small and medium enterprises.
The government has not provided the infrastructure promised in return for business'
support of NAFTA.

**1886 Puyana de Palacios, Alicia and José
Antonio Romero Tellaeche.** México:
de la crisis de la deuda al estancamiento
económico. México: Colegio de México,
2009. 391 p.: bibl., ill.

Mexico's integration into the world
economy (1982–2006) with urban bias, over-
valued exchange rate, and decrease in bank
financing's share of GDP led to stagnation
and dispersion of average salaries and an increase in the share of capital. Overreliance
on value-added tax, fiscal evasion accompanied by insufficient investment, increased
emigration of 15–44 year olds.

1887 Ramírez Robles, Sergio. Políticas
para el mercado interno y externo en
México, 2000–2006. Guadalajara, Mexico:
Universidad de Guadalajara, 2007. 210 p.: ill.

Mexico's decelerating growth at the
beginning of the 21st century led to a reexamination of policies. The work provides
details about the shift from opening the
economy to improving competitiveness,
strengthening existing firms, inviting

new investment, and increasing bilateral
and multilateral trade treaties. Small- and
medium-sized firms benefitted from special
programs.

1888 Razo, Armando. Social foundations
of limited dictatorship: networks and
private protection during Mexico's early
industrialization. Stanford, Calif.: Stanford
Univ. Press, 2008. 246 p.: bibl., ill., index,
map. (Social science history)

Work finds that dictatorships may
promote growth. Their protection of and
support by selected social networks benefits participants at the cost of the rest of
the nation. The networks often remain in
place after regime change. Ties to bankers
are crucial, and banking and market reform benefited bankers, but did not ensure
growth.

**1889 Respuestas locales frente a la globa-
lización económica: productos regio-
nales de la Costa Sur de Jalisco, México.**
Edición de Peter R.W. Gerritsen y Jaime
Morales Hernández. Coordinación de Peter
R.W. Gerritsen *et al.* Autlán de Navarro,
Mexico: Univ. de Guadalajara; Tlaquepaque,
Jalisco: ITESO, Centro de Investigación y
Formación Social; Ixtlahuacán de los Mem-
brillos: Red de Alternativas Sustentables
Agropecuarias de Jalisco, 2007. 266 p.: bibl.,
ill., maps.

Local responses to globalization focus
on regional products, frequently produced
traditionally, if no cash is available for modern inputs. Lack of other opportunities led
campesinos to focus on artisanal products.
Aid providers frequently did not give instruction. Finds that working outside home
exhausts women, who could be better off in
traditional occupations.

Salinas de Gortari, Carlos. La "década perdida": 1995–2006: neoliberalismo y populismo en México. See item **1117.**

1890 Sánchez Bernal, Antonio. Cambio
institucional y desempeño de los
gobiernos municipales en México. México:
Academia Jalisciense de Ciencias: Plaza y
Valdés, 2008. 257 p.: bibl.

The 1983 reform of constitutional
articles 115 and 26, which increased municipal tax income, often did not have the
desired outcome. Interviews and factor

analysis indicate that municipalities lacked sufficient transformation of informal to formal regimes; could not form public policies; and could not ameliorate the impact of the economic crisis.

1891 Sinaloa en la globalización: costos ecológicos, sociales y económicos. Coordinación de Óscar Aguilar Soto y Carlos Maya. México: Plaza y Valdés, 2007. 262 p.: bibl., ill.

Sinaloa agricultural sector is more productive than average for Mexican agriculture, and produces half of Mexico's horticultural exports. Foreign inputs, not foreign investment, are important for Mexican agriculture. Seven essays discuss economic context, water scarcity, fishing—overexploitation and control, basic grains and specialization, transnational control of maíz, technology, and export dynamics under NAFTA.

Tamborini, Christopher R. Work, wages and gender in export-oriented cities: global assembly versus international tourism in Mexico. See item **1630**.

1892 Tello, Carlos. Estado y desarrollo económico: México 1920–2006. México: UNAM, Facultad de Economía, 2007. 776 p.: bibl.

Describes differing roles of the state and private enterprise in seven periods. State quality matters more than its relative size. Domestic and foreign ideas shape this quality, which should—through direct operation and regulation of the private sector—promote social justice in a democracy.

1893 Turner Barragán, Ernesto H. and Juan Froilán Martínez Pérez. El modelo de desarrollo económico de México y Taiwán. México: Ediciones y Gráficas Eón: Univ. Autónoma Metropolitana, Azcapotzalco, 2007. 317 p.: bibl., ill. (Eón sociales)

A comparison of economic models utilized in Taiwan and Mexico finds that Taiwan relied on leading edge technology, diversified its trading partners, established cooperation of domestic groups with each other and foreign firms, provided basic services, and limited inflation. Mexico increasingly polarized its economy with an informal sector that doesn't pay taxes, use enough local inputs, and is subject to criminal elements.

1894 Veinticinco años de investigación económica sobre la frontera norte de México. Textos de Valérie Berenger *et al.* San Antonio del Mar, Mexico: Colegio de la Frontera Norte, Departmento de Estudios Económicos, 2009. 535 p.: bibl., ill.

Mexican manufacturing in the northern frontier had fewer economies of scale or links to the rest of the economy. Poverty in the north is defined by income; in indigenous areas poverty is more a result of deprivations. Corruption has a small, negative, and significant impact on growth. Study includes diverse technical studies.

1895 25 años de integración económica fronteriza. Textos de Salvador C. Corrales *et al.* Tijuana, Mexico: Depto. de Estudios Económicos, Colegio de la Frontera Norte, 2009. 409 p.: bibl., ill., maps.

Eleven essays focus on northern frontier economic development, strategic sectors and industrial development, labor markets and migration, and growth and regional economic development. Introduces a municipal basic development index, incorporating socioeconomic, environmental, and institutional characteristics. Analyzes internal demand and competitiveness, and the integration of frontier with southern US.

1896 Villagómez Amezcua, Alejandro. El ahorro en México desde 1960: estructura, evolución y determinación. México: Centro de Investigación y Docencia Económicas, 2008. 164 p.: bibl., ill.

Mexican domestic savings have not increased their share of GDP since the 1980s, despite policies to increase them. There are no adequate consistent time series of savings, or of their components, especially private savings, particularly those of low-income people. Formal and informal instruments and institutions for savings should be studied.

1897 Williams, Mary and Francisco Javier Zárate Rivera. Comercio callejero en la delegación Coyoacán y microterritorios: enfoques para el desarrollo de políticas públicas. México: Gobierno del Distrito Federal, Delegación Coyoacán: Secretaría de Desarrollo Social, Dirección General de Equidad y Desarollo, Subdirección de Promoción y Fomento para la Equidad: Cenvi: Plaza y Valdés, 2006. 207 p.: bibl., ill., maps.

A study of street vendors finds that they tend to specialize, selling a narrow set of goods. Customers live closer to food than durable consumer goods stalls. Many stalls are open only on weekends, or when specific sporting or other events take place. These activities may not be covered in the census, and activities are understood as socioeconomic and politically dependent. Unions have variable quality.

1898 Yucatán in an era of globalization. Edited by Eric N. Baklanoff and Edward H. Moseley. Tuscaloosa: Univ. of Alabama Press, 2008. 192 p.: bibl., index.

Nine outstanding studies analyze the history and customs of Yucatán, and the impact of globalization since 1982. Synthetic fibers replaced henequen, whose share of production in 2000 was 2.3 percent. Favorable transport, government financing of ports, containerization, and proximity to international markets aided growth of maquiladoras, while archeological tourism boomed.

CENTRAL AMERICA AND THE CARIBBEAN (EXCEPT CUBA)

DANIEL MASÍS-IVERSON, *Scholar-In-Residence, School of International Service, American University*

THE PUBLICATIONS INCLUDED in this *HLAS* volume, broadly conceived, touch upon economic, fiscal, and monetary policy; social policy; integration into the global economy; regionalism; and governance. Taken as a whole, they could, perhaps—excepting the more historical volumes—be understood to revolve around the central question of how to achieve economic and social development in a brave new post-Cold War world of rapid technological change and shifting balances in the worldwide distribution of economic power, achieving both equity and efficiency guided by honest and democratic governance. This generalization, of course, does not indicate a consensus among the authors regarding how to arrive at this result. The authors also differ in their primary vocation: some are scholars, others are policymakers and practitioners, or community activists, and some fall into more than one classification.

Thus, for example, Rodas Martini *et al.* explore technical aspects related to monetary and trade policy, seeking to find the best fit in the process of free-market integration into the global economy (item **1900**), and the OECD examines whether the three countries it studies are pursuing policies attractive to foreign direct investors (item **1919**), while on the other hand Vargas questions the success of neoliberal economic policies in paving the way for the achievement of social development in Nicaragua (item **1917**), and other authors do the same for El Salvador, fearing, inter alia, for the survival of its agriculture.

Alongside globalization, regional integration is also a recurrent topic for the Caribbean (item **1920**), and for the free trade area comprised by the Dominican Republic, Central America, and the US (items **1911** and **1912**), and a new perspective, reflecting world economic shifts: the Pacific Rim region, centering on the Asia-Pacific Economic Cooperation (APEC) forum (item **1899**).

None of the policies proposed to advance the development of the countries of Central America and the Caribbean can be effective unless, among other conditions, there is governmental capacity to implement them. This turns on questions both general and specific such as: in what fashion and to what degree should government be decentralized, examined specifically for Central America (item **1903**); or what should be done to mend deficiencies in the political system (item **1905**); or how to deal with corruption and citizen disillusionment within the political arena (see items **1909** and **1910**).

CENTRAL AMERICA

1899 Campos, Napoleón. El Pacífico también cuenta: Centroamérica y la APEC. San Salvador: FLACSO El Salvador, 2007. 59 p.: bibl. (Debates: serie de investigación; 4)

True to its title, the author wishes to convey, in this slim but fascinating volume, that the Pacific basin does count for the Central American countries that, along with other nations in the Americas, surround it. He begins with a narration of East-West relations starting in the 13th century, then discusses permanent navigation and trade between New Spain and Asia from the 16th century, followed by Asian migration to America in the 19th century, and then on to the two world wars and the present day. The author describes the 1989 establishment and subsequent development of the Asia-Pacific Economic Cooperation forum, dedicated to the promotion of economic cooperation among the countries of the Pacific Rim, closing in 1997 at 21 members of which only five are from the Americas: Canada, Chile, Mexico, Peru, and the US (Colombia, Ecuador, and Panama remain on a waiting list). The author examines trends in Central American trade in order to respond to the question of whether the Central American countries should strive to achieve APEC membership given that they already have a free trade agreement with the US. He concludes that the existing volume of trade with APEC countries justifies the effort. He then proposes that if the countries of the isthmus do not feel ready, they should consider joining the Pacific Economic Cooperation Council as a stepping stone towards a future bid for membership.

1900 Centroamérica en la economía mundial del siglo XXI. Edición de Pablo Rodas Martini. Colaboración de David Ricardo Cristiani Flores *et al.* Guatemala: Asociación de Investigación y Estudios Sociales: Ottawa, Canada: International Development Research Centre, 2006. 4 v.: bibl., ill.

This volume includes five essays devoted to study of three cardinal issues in Central America's process of integration into the global economy: (1) exchange rate policy, including dollarization and the prospects for an optimum currency area, (2) free trade agreements and trade liberalization strategies, and (3) the linkage of labor issues to international trade negotiations. The contributions to the volume are the result of careful, detailed study and analysis and can profit both specialists and laypersons alike.

1901 Centroamérica y México: políticas de competencia a principios del siglo XXI. Coordinación de Eugenio Rivera Urrutia y Claudia Schatan. México: Naciones Unidas, CEPAL: IRDC-CRDI, 2008. 298 p.: bibl., ill. (Libros de la CEPAL; 95)

This compilation, sponsored by ECLAC, focuses on competition policy, i.e., antitrust law and the actions of competition agencies, with a special, but not exclusive, focus on telecommunications and banking in Costa Rica, El Salvador, Guatemala, Honduras, Mexico, Nicaragua, and Panama. Because of their smaller size, the Central American countries are particularly susceptible to monopolistic practices either by large firms or cartels; Mexico, historically linked to Central America, with its own legislation and agencies, has influenced the latter's competition legislation. The authors examine market distortions and the governmental responses, and then provide suggestions for improvement. (For English-language version, see Schatan, Claudia and Eugenio Rivera, eds., *Competition Policies in Emerging Economies: Lessons and Challenges from Central America and Mexico,* item **1902**).

1902 Competition policies in emerging economies: lessons and challenges from Central America and Mexico. Edited by Claudia Schatan and Eugenio Rivera Urrutia. New York: Springer, 2008. 238 p.: bibl., ill., index.

This compilation, sponsored by ECLAC, focuses on competition policy, i.e., antitrust law and the actions of competition agencies, with a special, but not exclusive, focus on telecommunications and banking in Costa Rica, El Salvador, Guatemala, Honduras, Mexico, Nicaragua, and Panama. Because of their smaller size, the Central American countries are particularly susceptible to monopolistic practices either by large firms or cartels; Mexico, historically linked to Central America, with its own legislation and agencies, has influenced the latter's competition legislation. The authors examine market distortions, the governmental responses given, and provide suggestions for improvement. (For Spanish-language version, see Rivera, Eugenio and Claudia Schatan, coordinadores, *Centroamérica y México: políticas de competencia a principios del siglo XXI,* item **1901**).

1903 Conferencia Centroamericana sobre Descentralización y Desarrollo Local. Centroamérica: hacia el desarrollo local y la descentralización del estado. Compilación de Alberto Enríquez Villacorta, Rommy Jiménez y Luís Reyes. San Salvador: Conferencia Centroamericana por la Descentralización del Estado y el Desarrollo Local, 2008. 168 p.: bibl., ill. (some col.), col. maps.

This compilation contains an interesting selection of the main conferences and papers submitted in the annual meetings of the Central American Conference for State Decentralization and Local Development [Conferencia Centroamericana por la Descentralización del Estado y el Desarrollo Local, CONFEDELCA] held from 2001 to 2006. They are organized around three main themes: (1) local development and regional integration, including the experiences of Mercosur and Europe; (2) state decentralization, governance, the construction of democracy, and the role of municipalities,

and (3) reports from Costa Rica, El Salvador, Guatemala, Honduras, Nicaragua and Panama on the current situation of their respective municipalities and process of state decentralization.

1904 El desarrollo agropecuario y rural en El Salvador: un desafío para superar la crisis: movimiento popular de resistencia 12 de Octubre-MPR12. San Salvador: Oxfam América, 2007. 126 p.: bibl., ill.

This monograph argues that between 1989 and 2005 Salvadoran agriculture deteriorated as the result of deliberate government efforts to reorient the country's economy towards trade, maquiladora production, services, and finance. The policies stemming from the "Washington Consensus" which emphasized deregulation, privatization, and structural adjustment weakened the state's capacity for intervention, leading to the deterioration of agriculture, and to the impoverishment and social exclusion of the population depending on it. To overcome the agricultural sector's crisis, a strategy is proposed that seeks the achievement of national food security and includes, inter alia, strengthening cooperatives and other small producer associations, a pardoning of farmers' debt, government support for new agricultural products, the provision of roads and other infrastructure, tax incentives for innovative farmers, farmer training and technical assistance, proper storage facilities, and special lines of credit.

1905 El Salvador por dentro: juicio al modelo, 1989–2005. San Salvador: Asociación de Mujeres por la Dignidad y la Vida: Centro para la Defensa del Consumidor: Fundación de Estudios para la Aplicación del Derecho: Instituto de Derechos Humanos de la Univ. "José Simeón Cañas", 2005. 144 p.: bibl., ill.

This short book argues that after the 1992 peace agreement ended the El Salvadoran civil war, and particularly after the departure of the UN Observer Mission in El Salvador (ONUSAL), there have been reversals in all of the topics of the peace agreement, with serious consequences for most of the population. The publication critically examines the growth of the country's economy (1989–2004), including the decline of the agricultural sector and poverty, with special attention to social inequities, including those based on gender as well as access to health, education, and housing. It argues that the nation's political system is fraught with deficiencies regarding elections and representation; that oversight of government expenditures is weak; and that central-municipal government relations are tense. The book also makes the case that the Salvadoran attorney general's office is ineffective, that the importance of the office of the human rights defender is downplayed, and that the justice system is defective. The volume concludes with a skeptical appraisal regarding the foreseeable results of the efforts of the then recently installed Saca administration (2004–09) to carry out a national dialog and arrive at concerted proposals for improved governance and change.

1906 Los estancos, las prácticas monopólicas y las rentas del Estado en El Salvador. Textos de Pedro Antonio Escalante Arce *et al.* San Salvador: Dirección de Publicaciones e Impresos, Consejo Nacional para la Cultura y el Arte, 2008. 419 p.: bibl., ill. (Biblioteca de historia salvadoreña; 20)

This volume, sponsored by the Office of the Superintendent for Competition of El Salvador, compiles the work of nine historians, and traces the evolution and change of monopolistic practices in that country from the early 16th century under the Spanish Crown, with attention to the policy shift towards promoting privatization, competition, and free trade, especially from the early 1990s, after the end of the Salvadoran civil war, and onwards to the year 2008, four years after the Salvadoran agency to foster competition was formally established. A fascinating book, and the reader will be grateful for the glossary at the end, especially for the colonial terms.

1907 González Orellana, Mauricio. El Salvador: remesas, dolarización y crecimiento. Antiguo Cuscatlán, El Salvador: Univ. "Dr. José Matías Delgado," Centro de Investigaciones en Ciencias y Humanidades: Distribución, Librería Delgado, Univ. "Dr. José Matías Delgado", 2008. 95 p.: bibl., ill.

In this provocative monograph, González Orellana examines why El Salvador's growth rate is relatively low compared to

other Latin American countries, despite a stellar performance in social and economic reforms. He argues that the country suffers from the "Dutch disease" not, as in the Netherlands, from new discoveries of natural resources, but from the flow of remittances from overseas, which causes currency appreciation and slow economic growth. He also argues that the adoption of the US dollar as El Salvador's currency has hurt growth by fixing the rate of exchange. The author advocates for abandoning the dollar and restoring currency flexibility, so as to neutralize the remittances effects, and to use devaluation as an instrument of economic growth.

1908 Gozalo Delgado, Mariola. Respuesta fiscal de los países en desarrollo a los flujos de ayuda internacional: aplicación al caso de Centroamérica. Madrid: Fundación de las Cajas de Ahorros, 2007. 512 p.: bibl., ill. (Estudios de la fundación. Serie Tesis; 26)

In this exhaustive study, the author uses econometric analysis to examine theoretically and empirically the effectiveness of foreign aid flows to improve macroeconomic indicators, reduce poverty, and promote development. Empirical research focuses on central government fiscal responses in Costa Rica and Nicaragua. In the case of Costa Rica, the author concludes that in the period of study (1970–2000) government response mostly emphasized the reduction of public debt. It also depended on the type of aid: loans had a greater impact on public debt reduction, while grants generally tended to increase expenditures in consumption, investment, and government foreign debt. In the case of Nicaragua, part of aid monies were used to pay foreign public debt, part for investment, and part for consumption; when promised aid was not delivered, public investment fell and, when the expected but not delivered aid was in the form of grants, the gap between public revenue and expenditures increased. Gozalo Delgado concludes with some valuable theoretical reflections and proposals for further research.

1909 Interrogantes sobre el rumbo del país: debates sobre economía, politica, sociedad y cultura. Vol. 1. Edición de Manuel Barahona Montero y Yajaira Ceciliano. San

José: FLACSO Costa Rica, 2007. 176 p.: bibl., ill.

This is the first of two volumes compiling the papers and proceedings of seven fora and round tables around the theme "Dialogues on Welfare" in Costa Rica, held between October 2004 and May 2006. A mix of participants, academics, government authorities, labor leaders and business people, among them, led to lively exchanges. In this volume, the topics discussed revolve around the country's development model and poverty and social policy. For comment on Vol. 2, see item **1910**.

1910 Interrogantes sobre el rumbo del país: debates sobre economía, política, sociedad y cultura. Vol. 2. Edición de Manuel Barahona Montero y Yajaira Ceciliano. San José: FLACSO Costa Rica, 2007. 180 p.: bibl., graphs, ill., tables.

This is the second of two volumes compiling the papers and proceedings of seven fora and round tables around the theme "Dialogues on Welfare" in Costa Rica, that were held between October 2004 and May 2006. In this volume, the topics discussed revolve around poverty and policy options to address it; immigration policy; culture, development and welfare; the transition from the administration of President Abel Pacheco to that of President Oscar Arias under a new, multiparty Legislative Assembly; and future challenges, including citizen disillusionment with politics; corruption; and the negotiation of a free trade agreement with the other Central American countries, the Dominican Republic, and the US. The volume concludes with some final reflections by editor Barahona and participating sociologist Carlos Sojo.

1911 Investigaciones sobre el Tratado de Libre Comercio (TLC) entre Estados Unidos, Centroamérica y República Dominicana. Vol. 1. Coordinación de Pablo Rodas Martini. Guatemala: ASIES: SEGEPLAN, 2006. 399 p.: bibl., ill., tables.

This is the first of two edited volumes published to provide a contribution to the policy debate in Guatemala over the free trade agreement signed in 2004 between the US and the Central American countries and the Dominican Republic (DR-CAFTA).

The editors and authors were aware at the time of writing that there was a clear commitment of all countries involved (with the support of their business sectors) to ratify the agreement; their analyses are intended to provide a dispassionate examination of the advantages and disadvantages of the agreement, and propose ways to optimize the benefits and minimize the costs associated with it. In this first volume, the topics addressed are agriculture, industry, services, intellectual property, labor and the environment. All issues are addressed in a manner accessible to the interested layperson.

1912 Investigaciones sobre el Tratado de Libre Comercio (TLC) entre Estados Unidos, Centroamérica y República Dominicana. Vol. 2. Coordinación de Pablo Rodas Martini. Guatemala: ASIES: SEGEPLAN, 2006. 300 p.: bibl., ill., tables.

This is the second of two edited volumes that contribute to the policy debate in Guatemala over the free trade agreement signed in 2004 between the US and the Central American countries and the Dominican Republic (DR-CAFTA). The editors and authors were aware at the time of writing that there was a clear commitment of all countries involved (with the support of their business sectors) to ratify the agreement; their analyses are intended to provide a dispassionate examination of the advantages and disadvantages of the agreement, and propose ways to optimize the benefits and minimize the costs associated with it. In this second volume, the topics addressed are investment; dispute resolution; Central American integration; implications for the political system and national security, and for national culture and the indigenous peoples; legal and institutional reforms that should accompany the FTA, and finally, alternative scenarios for Guatemala with and without the FTA. All issues are addressed in a manner accessible to the interested layperson.

1913 Martínez Peláez, Severo. La patria del criollo: an interpretation of colonial Guatemala. Translated by Susan M. Neve and W. George Lovell. Edited and introduced by W. George Lovell and Christopher H. Lutz. Durham, N.C.: Duke Univ. Press, 2009. 330 p.: bibl., index, map.

This is a remarkable edition and translation of Severo Martínez Peláez's massive book interpreting the colonial history of Guatemala and its lingering effects down to the present (1970); according to Martínez Peláez, "the history of Guatemala is best understood as one in which colonial reality remains the pivotal frame of reference" (p. 280). Lovell and Lutz provide an excellent, erudite, and critical introduction to this abridged version of a classic work of Latin American historiography as well as its author. For historian's comment, see *HLAS 66:1058*.

1914 Norori Gutiérrez, Róger. Crisis económica, bancos y reforma monetaria en Nicaragua, 1870–1926. Managua: Academia de Geografía e Historia de Nicaragua, 2008. 199 p.: bibl., ill.

Based fundamentally on primary sources and writings of the times, the author offers a fascinating look into late 19th and early 20th-century Nicaraguan monetary history. From 1870 to 1893, monetary policy was directed towards undergirding efforts to modernize the country, including the promotion of agriculture (especially coffee), attracting immigration and foreign direct investment, and building an inter-oceanic canal using the San Juan River. Following this period, under the Zelaya dictatorship, the policy of bimetallism resulted in virtually uncontrolled inflation. With the overthrow of Zelaya in 1909, the Nicaraguan córdoba was adopted as currency and the Bryan-Chamorro Treaty was signed with the US (which came into force in 1916), granting the country, inter alia, an option to build an inter-oceanic canal (which did not come to fruition as the canal route chosen by the US was Panama) in return for the sum of three million dollars, a large portion of which were applied to Nicaragua's foreign debt with US banks. For historian's comment, see *HLAS 66:1125*.

1915 Obstáculos al crecimiento económico de Costa Rica. Edición de Luis Mesalles-Jorba y Oswald Céspedes Torres. San José: Academia de Centroamérica, 2009. 295 p.: bibl., ill. (Estudio anual; 2009)

Part of an annual series of the Academia de Centroamérica, this edited volume's theme is obstacles to economic growth in Costa Rica. Four topics in as many essays are examined: the situation of the Costa Rican economy in 2008, the relationship between the country's infrastructure and economic development, the role of education in economic development, and public policy lessons gleaned from international experiences. The essays are followed by a panel discussion.

1916 Seguridad fiscal en El Salvador: medidas para fortalecer la tributación. Textos de Equipo de Macroeconomía y Desarrollo. Coordinación de Roberto Rubio Fabián y Nelson Fuentes. San Salvador: Fundación Nacional para el Desarrollo, 2008. 152 p.: bibl., ill.

This book analyzes the state of public finances in El Salvador and concludes that the country is on the path towards becoming fiscally unsustainable, unless a permanent effort is made towards the growth of revenue. Fiscal sustainability is indispensable not only to honor the country's debts, but also to comply with social commitments, such as those undertaken through the Millennium Development Goals. The authors propose a series of reforms and other measures to combat tax evasion and avoidance, and smuggling.

1917 Vargas, Oscar-René. Nicaragua 2015: los objetivos de desarrollo del milenio. Nicaragua: Centro de Estudios de la Realidad Nacional, 2006. 243 p.: bibl.

The author uses the Millennium Development Goals to assess the state of Nicaraguan development. Deploying a considerable array of facts and figures, he argues that neoliberal economic policies, applied since 1990, have completely failed in their purpose to promote growth and prosperity; to the contrary, they have contributed to greater inequality, poverty, and low growth if not stagnation. A new economic strategy is needed, where the chief goal is to achieve social progress, in particular, through an integrated set of policies to eradicate poverty, and where economic development is seen as an instrument of this goal.

CARIBBEAN

1918 Amuedo-Dorantes, Catalina; Annie Georges; and Susan Pozo. Migration, remittances, and children's schooling in Haiti. (*Ann. Am. Acad. Polit. Soc. Sci.*, 630:1, July 2010, p. 224–244)

The authors examine the impact of remittances on the schooling of children in various Haitian communities with a high incidence of out-migration. They conclude that remittances ameliorate the negative disruptive effect of household out-migration on children's schooling in some migrating communities in Haiti and, therefore, contribute to the accumulation of human capital in the midst of extreme poverty. [C.E. Griffin]

Bernal, Richard L. The dragon in the Caribbean: China-CARICOM economic relations. See item **1650**.

1919   Caribbean Rim: Costa Rica, Dominican Republic and Jamaica. Paris: Organisation for Economic Co-operation and Development, 2004. 185 p.: bibl., ill. (OECD investment policy reviews) (Emerging economies transition)

This volume contains detailed reports reviewing trends in foreign direct investment (FDI), the investment environment, and investor perceptions for Costa Rica, the Dominican Republic, and Jamaica. The reports are intended to constitute the foundation for the development of an agenda for further policy reforms to improve the attraction of FDI to the countries with the support of multilateral and bilateral organizations. The compilation is valuable not only for investors, but also for social scientists and laypersons who wish to gain insight into the development strategies and their execution in the three nations.

1920   CARICOM single market and economy: genesis and prognosis. Edited by Kenneth O. Hall and Myrtle Chuck-A-Sang. Kingston; Miami, Fla.: Ian Randle, 2007. 535 p.: bibl., ill.

This book, intended for a composite audience of students, academics, politicians, and laypersons, is a compilation of the text of the 2003 Rose Hall Declaration on Regional Governance and Integrated Development, a 1997 CARICOM Secretariat report, and 24 speeches and essays by 19 authors, on the evolution of the CARICOM Single Market and Economy (CSME) (comprising 15 Caribbean countries) since the 2001 Revised Treaty of Chaguaramas. Topics

include, regional governance; the roles of the public and private sectors, and of labor; Caribbean competitiveness; development funding; the Caribbean Court of Justice; foreign aid; labor mobility; education and gender. A detailed table reporting progress towards the CSME is included. The volume provides valuable insight into the CSME process and is very useful to the student of Caribbean integration. For political scientist's comment, see *HLAS 65:2618*.

1921   Cruz, Johannie L. James. El papel del estado en la construcción del desarrollo sostenible: el caso del turismo en El Caribe Insular. (*Cuad. Econ./Bogotá*, 28:51, 2009, p. 265–281, bibl., graphs, maps, tables)

The discussion about the relevance of state intervention in the market has been recurring in the history of economic thought. This article seeks to emphasize the implications of ignoring the role of the state in building sustainable development, with special emphasis on tourism in the insular Caribbean. [C.E. Griffin]

1922   Dookeran, Winston C. Uncertainty, stability, and challenges: economic and monetary policy, a small state perspective: excerpts from selected speeches. San Juan, Trinidad: Lexicon Trinidad, 2006. 183 p.: bibl., index.

This volume compiles speeches delivered by Dookeran during his time as governor of the Central Bank of Trinidad and Tobago. Among his topics of reflection are: the implications of increasing economic regionalization for monetary policy, the importance of monetary stability and of a sound banking system, challenges posed by e-commerce and electronic money, implications of the impending liberalization of financial services, the influence of credit rating agencies on the development of money and capital markets, the need for domestic investment in Trinidad and Tobago's energy industry, and changes in the skill-sets of "knowledge workers" as required by international markets, with special attention to the challenges posed to traditional accounting. This book is marked by its clarity and is useful to anybody interested in the development problems faced by small economies.

1923 The economy of Puerto Rico: restoring growth. Edited by Susan Margaret Collins, Barry Bosworth, and Miguel A. Soto-Class. San Juan: Center for the New Economy; Washington, D.C.: Brookings Institution Press, 2006. 607 p.: bibl., ill., index.

The result of a collaborative effort between Puerto Rico's Center for the New Economy and the Brookings Institution, this extremely well researched book of 10 essays by 15 authors, examined by another 16 discussants, centers on a paradox: Puerto Rico's economic growth is slow and approximately half of its population is under the US poverty line despite improved education, infrastructure, strong institutions, and economic openness. Topics include low employment of men, education, business climate, fiscal policy, trade, and industrial policy. A discussion of future policy options is offered in the final chapter. It could prove profitable to read this work in tandem with *Economía Política de Puerto Rico: 1950 a 2000* by Eliézer Curet (see *HLAS 65:2245*).

1924 Finance and real development in the Caribbean. Edited by Anthony Birchwood and Dave Seerattan. Saint Augustine, Trinidad and Tobago: Caribbean Centre for Monetary Studies, Univ. of the West Indies, 2006. 565 p.: bibl., ill.

This volume contains 24 papers selected from the Annual Monetary Studies Conferences hosted by the Caribbean Centre for Monetary Studies (now the Caribbean Centre for Money and Finance, of the Caricom Central Banks and the University of the West Indies) over the period 2001–2003. Major topics addressed include macroeconomics of the Caricom states, development finance, risks associated with currency crises and inflation, capital markets, trade, and economic governance. This is a useful book of mostly technical essays written for specialists interested in Caribbean monetary and financial issues as they relate to development.

Forteza, Alvaro. The portability of pension rights: general principles and the Caribbean case. See item **1181**.

Gros, Jean-Germain. Indigestible recipe: rice, chicken wings, and international financial institutions or hunger politics in Haiti. See item **1664**.

Jenkins, Rhys; Enrique Dussel Peters; and **Mauricio Mesquita Moreira.** The impact of China on Latin America and the Caribbean. See item **1823**.

1925 Lainé, Catherine. Building a better Haiti by investing in Haitians. (*Innov./ Cambridge*, 5:4, Oct. 2010, p. 37–50)

The Appropriate Infrastructure Development Group (AIDG) is one of the few small- and medium-sized enterprise (SME) financing organizations currently operating in Haiti. It hopes to incubate independent, locally owned Haitian enterprises that can serve the needs of local communities using appropriate technology. More capital is needed in the country to help establish opportunities for future private-sector investment. [C.E. Griffin]

Levitt, Kari. Reclaiming development: independent thought and Caribbean community. See item **1183**.

1926 Mottley, Wendell. Trinidad and Tobago—industrial policy 1959–2008: a historical and contemporary analysis. Foreword by Charles Rangel. Kingston; Miami, Fla.: Ian Randle Publishers, 2008. 236 p.: bibl., ill., index.

This book offers not only a well-documented, but also a fascinating account of the evolution of Trinidad and Tobago's industrial policy and its relationship to the country's development strategy over the course of nearly 50 years. The author has been a direct participant in the process and guides the reader through Trinidad and Tobago's shift from state-led to private sector-driven energy industrial policy. He examines the international context, both economic (e.g. changes in demand and prices of oil and liquefied natural gas, partnerships with multinational corporations) and political (e.g. integration of the Caribbean economies, effects of Venezuelan oil diplomacy, again partnerships with multinational corporations). A central concern of Mottley's is the marked asymmetry, in a country that has made considerable efforts to avoid the "resource curse," in the incomes of those who are linked to oil- and gas-generated wealth, and those who are not. The author concludes with thoughtful recommendations for his country's, and other countries', future development paths.

1927 **Newstead, Clare.** Regional governmentality: neoliberalization and the Caribbean Community Single Market and Economy. (*Singap. J. Trop. Geogr.*, 30:2, July 2009, p. 158–173)

Formally launched on Jan. 30, 2006, the Caribbean Community (CARICOM) Single Market and Economy (CSME) is, like many other regional economic initiatives, designed to create an economic space in which the uninhibited flow of goods, capital, and skills across the borders of member states is anticipated to generate competitive business opportunities and external investment. The author argues that such a framing of regional integration in the Caribbean misses some of the tangible ways that CARICOM works beyond the sovereign intent of member states to enable the encroachment of neoliberal-style economic orders across the region. [C.E. Griffin]

1928 **Pentecost, Eric** and **Paul Turner.** Demand and supply shocks in the Caribbean: implications for monetary union. (*World Econ.*, 33:10, Oct. 2010, p. 1325–1337)

The authors seek to determine if these economies could feasibly form part of a Caribbean monetary union. Given that correlations between the demand and supply innovations are typically low, the evidence indicates that monetary union may lead to greater stabilization problems for these economies. [C.E. Griffin]

1929 **Pichardo Muñiz, Arlette** and **Sandra Suñol Pérez.** La seguridad social en la República Dominicana. Colaboración de Juan Luis Castillo. Santo Domingo: Instituto Tecnológico de Santo Domingo, 2007. 232 p.: bibl., ill.

In this volume, the authors select the main findings of a baseline study of the Dominican social security system. It begins with a historical overview of the antecedents, which go back to the 1930s, and the birth of the modern system in 2001, with Law 87-01. In the Dominican Republic, social security comprehends not only pensions but also health care and workers' insurance. The authors provide a detailed explanation of the law, as well as of subsequently issued regulations and agencies created to carry forward its implementation, and an assessment of its actual performance, including

a study of the degree of awareness that the country's population has of the system.

1930 **Rainford, Roderick G.** Central Planning Unit to Planning Institute of Jamaica, 1955–2005: anchoring 50 years of development planning in Jamaica. Kingston: Planning Institute of Jamaica, 2006. 209 p.: bibl., ill.

This book, which recounts and commemorates 50 years of Jamaican planning experience, is especially intended for government civil servants and agencies, analysts, students, and policymakers of developing countries generally. It begins with an overview of Jamaica's development challenges and constraints, set within the country's historical context and politics, and goes on to provide a detailed institutional history of the Central Planning Unit since its creation in 1955, its transformation into the National Planning Agency in 1972, and its second transformation into the Planning Institute of Jamaica in 1984. This well-documented volume takes the reader through the interactions between development ideas, local policies, domestic inter-institutional liaisons, and relations with international bilateral and multilateral agencies. The book concludes stressing the need for political leadership in planning, and calling for the setting of long-term goals, for which an agenda of issues is suggested.

Sandoval, Gabriel. Cigar production: how race, gender and political ideology were inscribed onto tobacco. See item **1193.**

1931 **Schrank, Andrew.** Professionalization and probity in a patrimonial state: labor inspectors in the Dominican Republic. (*Lat. Am. Polit. Soc.*, 51:2, Summer 2009, p. 91–115, bibl., graph, tables)

This article argues that Dominican policymakers and bureaucrats are responding to foreign pressure by redoubling their commitment to a distinctively Franco-Iberian model of labor law enforcement, in which skilled labor inspectors use their discretion to balance society's demand for protection with the economy's need for efficiency. In so doing, they provide an alternative to traditional collective bargaining practices—which at least partly decouples both the intensity of the enforcement effort and the degree of worker protection from the level of unionization—and an example for the rest of the region. [C.E. Griffin]

1932 Tippenhauer, Hans. Freedom is not enough: Haiti's sustainability in peril. (*Local Environ.*, 15:5, May 2010, p. 493–507)

In addition to identifying the current major core conflicts of Haiti, the article also suggests solutions to various social, economic, and environmental issues. [C.E. Griffin]

1933 Tourism: the driver of change in the Jamaican economy? Edited by Kenneth O. Hall and Rheima Holding. Kingston: Ian Randle Publishers, 2006. 419 p.: bibl., ill., index.

This volume gathers papers of the 2005 Mona Academic Conference, University of the West Indies, providing a wide spectrum of topics both general (e.g., the value of tourism to the Jamaican economy, the importance of addressing social inclusion and violence in Kingston) and specific (e.g. training the tourism workforce, branding, the impact of HIV and other transportable diseases on the tourism sector). The papers, all interesting, are not overly burdened with scholarship, but they are well-documented and serious, and written in refreshingly clear English. Taken as a whole, this compilation provides considerable insight into contemporary Jamaica even beyond tourism. For political scientist's comment, see *HLAS 63:2062*.

1934 Vega, Bernardo. 60 años de política monetaria 1947–2007. Vol. 1, 1947–1965. Santo Domingo: Banco Central de la República Dominicana, 2008. 1 v.: bibl.

This slim volume is the first of three. Written in a lively essay style, it begins with a brief account of Dominican monetary history from 1905, when the country adopted the US dollar, to 1947, the year in which it abandoned the US dollar and returned to its own currency. It then goes on to study monetary policy from this year to 1965. In the author's account, from 1948–58 the country was able to maintain a single, fixed exchange rate pegged to the US dollar and to gold, with free convertibility, largely due to a stable balance of payments. The stable exchange rate was a mixed blessing: under the Trujillo dictatorship, a large number of citizens were too poor to afford imported goods. Arms purchases and capital flight following the Cuban revolution in 1959 inaugurated a period of import restrictions, diminishment of reserves, recession, and government deficits and rise in public debt. After the death of Trujillo in 1961 and the return of democracy, the economic situation improved, and the Dominican Republic was able to repay a loan to the IMF. By 1964 difficulties had returned however, due largely to considerable losses by the state-owned sugar mills and to trade deficits, leading to a new agreement with the IMF (although the IMF suggested devaluation, the government decided to adopt austerity measures instead). The author provides detailed descriptions of central bank policymaking and considerable insight regarding the relationship between economics and politics, closing with a dramatic account of monetary policy-making during the 1965 civil war.

CUBA

MARIO A. GONZÁLEZ-CORZO, *Associate Professor, Department of Economics and Business, Lehman College, City University of New York*

SINCE 2009, Cuba has confronted its most severe economic crisis since the disintegration of the socialist camp in the early 1990s. The Cuban economy grew a meager 1.4 percent in 2009 and gross domestic product (GDP) expanded just 2.1 percent in 2010; this figure was only one third the regional average reported by the Economic Commission for Latin America and the Caribbean (ECLAC) for 2010 (these and other statistics mentioned in this essay appear in item **1943**). In 2010, 65 percent of Cuba's GDP was generated by the services sector, which includes health, education, administration, defense, and trade. By contrast, the output of physical (or tangible) goods only generated 19 percent of GPD and declined 7 percent from the previous year. This was primarily the result of the decapitalization of the country's industrial (or manufacturing) sector, continuous declines in sugar production, and the contraction of the construction sector.

Gross capital formation declined to 10 percent of GDP in 2010, which was less than half the regional average. Inflation grew 1.4 percent annually, which was notably lower than the regional average, even though the money supply increased to 42 percent of GDP (double the amount reported in 1989). The fiscal deficit was reduced from 5 percent to 4 percent of GDP, but remained above the regional average of 2.4 percent, as a result of severe budget cuts initiated in 2009.

The external sector had a mixed performance from 2009–2010. Exports of goods increased (although they were still 22 percent below the level of 1989), while imports stagnated (which aggravated the severe domestic shortages in some areas of the economy) and the trade deficit decreased (still 74 percent higher than the 1989s deficit). Exports of services (payments by Cuban professionals working abroad, mostly in Venezuela, and tourism) increased and helped to offset the trade deficit. But Cuba's terms of trade deteriorated for the third consecutive year due to rising oil and food prices, external debt amounted to 20 billion US dollars (triple of 1989's) and Cuba's dependence on Venezuela grew just as the Venezuelan economy suffered the worst performance in the region.

In the social sphere there was a small nominal increase in wages and pensions in 2009 and 2010, but real values (adjusted for inflation) were respectively 73 percent and 50 percent below 1989 levels. The infant mortality rate was 4.5 per 1,000 live births; the lowest in the Western Hemisphere, after Canada, but the maternal mortality increased to levels that were notably higher than those recorded in 1989. The official unemployment rate remained unchanged at 1.6 percent, one of the lowest in the world, and the country's population decreased due to the accelerated aging process that adds to the cost of pensions and health (item **1936**).

As in the darkest hours of the "Special Period," the official response to the crisis has included a series of "structural reforms," announced by President Raúl Castro during his July 26 speech in 2007. In early 2008, Cuba implemented a series of structural changes to reactivate the economy (items **1954** and **1968**). The most notable included: the liberalization of consumption, transfers of idle state-owned land to individual farmers and cooperatives, increased labor market flexibility, and the expansion of property rights with respect to automobiles and housing. Consumption was liberalized by eliminating restrictions on the population's access to cellular phones, hotels and resorts (previously reserved for international tourists), and selected consumer products like DVDs, and home appliances.

The transfer of idle state-owned land to nonstate producers was accomplished with the approval of Decree-Law No. 259 in March 2008. By the end of 2010, close to one million hectares had been transferred and more than 130,000 applications to hold land in usufruct had been processed. However, as Nova González indicates (item **1956**), Cuba's agricultural sector remains mired in a complex web of bureaucratic constraints and onerous regulations that hinder productivity and efficient resource utilization. As one of the most significant sectors of the Cuban economy, agriculture is being prioritized, but more profound trans-formations are necessary to revitalize this sector as one of the country's principal engines of growth (item **1960**).

The approval of Resolution 9 by the Ministry of Labor and Social Security in 2008 initiated the transformation of Cuba's labor market by establishing a system that ties compensation to productivity. In 2010, the Cuban government announced its plan to transfer close to a million workers from the state sector to the emerging (nonstate) sector through the promotion of legal self-employment, the authoriza-tion of some (limited) forms of production cooperatives, and by leasing small-scale state-owned service outlets, such as barbershops and beauty salons, directly to employees organized as cooperatives or small-scale enterprises.

In addition to these structural transformations, President Raúl Castro has implemented a series of institutional changes since his official ascent to power in February 2008. The most notable include the reorganization of the administrative apparatus of the state, the consolidation of the state bureaucracy, including some important ministries like Sugar and Agriculture, and the creation of the Office of the Comptroller of the Republic (item **1966**).

The transformation of Cuba's economic model also included the implemen-tation of an austerity plan to mitigate the effects of the global financial crisis of 2008–2009. This plan included the reduction of imports, strategies to increase agricultural production and substitute agricultural imports (mainly from the US), restrictions on energy consumption by state-owned enterprises (SOEs) and the population, reductions in domestic investment, and fiscal deficit reduction mea-sures (item **1954**). As a result of these measures, imports were reduced by 37.3 per-cent and investment contracted by 16 percent in 2009, followed by lesser reduc-tions in 2010, and the fiscal deficit has been reduced (in relation to GDP).

The transformation of the Cuban economy was accelerated after the VI Con-gress of the Communist Party, which was held in April 2011. Unlike previous Congresses, the VI Party Congress was characterized by its disproportionate emphasis on economic issues. This time, however, there seems to be a wider of-ficial consensus on the importance and the need to transform Cuba's economic model by allowing nonstate actors, such as cooperatives, and individual producers and consumers, to plan a greater economy, and by creating alternative (economic) spaces to facilitate the expansion of the "emerging sector." One of the most recent effects of the VI Party Congress was the implementation of measures to further liberalize consumption after the approval of Decree-Law No. 292 in September 2011, which for the first time in five decades legalized the sale and purchase of au-tomobiles, and the approval of Decree-Law No. 288 in October 2011, which legal-ized sales of private homes (with some restrictions).

Despite these transformations, it is worth noting that under the agreements reached during the VI Party Congress, Cuba's socialist economic model is not changed substantially; instead, it has been "updated" to address existing prob-lems, in a planned and gradual manner. Central planning remains as the funda-mental mechanism of managing the economy, although with some (institutional) transformations and leaving a space for the possible role of the nonstate sector in certain areas of the economy. State-owned enterprises (SOEs) continue to be the principal productive entities in the Cuban economy, and traditional forms of decentralized management are considered as viable alternatives in some areas of the economy; these include: foreign investment (in joint ventures, but mostly with SOEs), cooperatives (e.g., existing agricultural cooperatives, and the recently authorized production and services cooperatives), small private farms, usufruct, self-employment and small-scale businesses leased by workers (organized into small production cooperatives) from the state.

Greater decentralization is prescribed in the management of SOEs, and in the future a significant number of these entities are expected to become self-financed (i.e., they will no longer receive tax subsidies); SOEs and cooperatives that default on obligations or continuously experience economic (or financial) losses will be liquidated or transferred to alternative forms of management or ownership. SOEs will be permitted to use a portion of their profits to create investment funds for the benefit of their workers and managers, and will also enjoy greater flexibility to fix prices. The agreements also contemplate allowing greater managerial autonomy when establishing various types of cooperatives and greater freedom to negotiate without state intermediaries (a consistent proposal of the majority of Cuban economists) after meeting commitments to the state; establishing tax incentives to promote private management, and developing wholesale markets that sell supplies and rent equipment to the private sector.

While the agreements drafted after the VI Party Congress in general represent a step towards the transformation of Cuba's economy from a system based on the principal tenets of classical socialism to a more flexible system, exhibiting some of the key characteristics of market socialism, there are serious limitations or constraints. First, the agreements do not really define a "model" because they do not specify the degree of participation of the plan and the market, and their interrelationships. Decentralization, self-financing, the closing of unprofitable SOEs, and the use of economic incentives were already tested several times without success in the past, and without the political will to implement these policy measures, the economic effect of the agreements can be seriously hindered. Second, according to the agreements, "the concentration of ownership will not be allowed" in the nonstate sector, and there are restrictions on the sale and transfer of property leased or sold to the cooperative sector or to individuals, which restricts the ability of these nonstate economic actors to use these assets as collateral to obtain credit financing for investments in microenterprises or any other type of economic units. Third, the agreements stipulate that price determination in selected areas of the economy will remain centralized; this limits the ability of the price system to perform its basic function of sending price signals and allocating scarce resources in a Pareto optimal fashion, leading to distortions and the inefficient allocation and utilization of resources. Fourth, foreign investment, which can serve as an engine of growth for the Cuban economy, is confined to selected activities and areas of the economy. Finally, the agreements are characterized by the pursuit of idealistic goals, such as the elimination of monetary dualism, the revival of Cuba's sugar sector, the reduction of dependence on the external sector, and the elimination of subsidies, without well-defined strategies to achieve these goals.

The complex scenarios confronted by the Cuban economy suggest that the economic reforms initiated by President Raúl Castro since 2007, and ratified by the VI Party Congress (in April 2011), represent a step towards a more flexible economic model; however, these measures face a series of obstacles and limitations and appear to be insufficient to address the complex socioeconomic problems confronting Cuba today. The effectiveness of these economic reforms and agreements is hampered by mutually conflicting or exclusive objectives. On one hand, they recognize the need to increase production, eliminate excess labor in the state sector, reduce the cost of social services, and create alternative economic spaces to facilitate the expansion of the nonstate sector. On the other hand, the agreements and policy measures set forth after the VI Party Congress emphasize the importance of central planning, economic controls, regulation, and heavy taxation of the nonstate apparatus that prevents its development and economic contributions, slowing down the country's apparent march towards market socialism.

1935 Alzugaray Treto, Carlos. Cuba cincuenta años después: continuidad y cambio político. (*Temas/Habana,* 60, oct./dic. 2009, p. 37–47, bibl.)

Discusses recent (2006 to the present) political transformations and continuity in Cuba. Argues that Cuban society is presently undergoing a process of evolution towards a new model, within the boundaries of socialism, designed to improve economic performance while retaining the principal elements of its current system.

1936 *Anuario Demográfico de Cuba.* 2010. La Habana: Dirección de Estadísticas de Población, Dirección General de Estadística, JUCEPLAN.

This comprehensive demographic yearbook is divided into six chapters. Chapter 1 provides general information about the Cuban population such as: population by age, place of residence, gender, population density by province and territory, and economically active population. Chapter 2 presents detailed fertility data by province, age of the mother, and other demographic indicators. Chapter 3 presents similar data for deaths; Chapter 4 for marriages; Chapter 5 for divorces; and Chapter 6 for domestic (internal) migration. The 2010 demographic yearbook also provides a very useful glossary of demographic terms and concepts.

1937 *Anuario Estadístico de Cuba.* 2010. La Habana: Oficina Nacional de Estadísticas.

Contains a wide range of socioeconomic statistics, mostly covering the 2005–2010 period. National account series remain questionable given recent (2001) changes in the methodology used to estimate gross domestic product (GDP) (at constant prices), and the increased role of the service sector in the Cuban economy. Coverage of external sector statistics has been expanded to include merchandise exports and imports according to their corresponding Standard International Trade Classifications (SITC), as well as balance of payments, and external debt statistics. The current (2010) version is available online through the official website of the national statistics office (http://www.one.cu).

1938 *Anuarios Estadísticos Municipales.* 2010. La Habana: Oficina Nacional de Estadísticas. (http://www.one.cu/aedm2010.htm)

Most recent volume of Cuba's (new) municipal statistical yearbook. Contains a wide range of socioeconomic statistics, mostly covering the 2005–2010 period. The data provided is similar to the data provided by the (national) *Anuario Estadístico de Cuba* (see item **1937**), and is divided into the following categories: population, national accounts, employment and wages, agriculture, energy and mining, industry, construction and investments, transport, commerce, tourism, education, health care, culture, and sports and physical education.

1939 *Anuarios Estadísticos Provinciales.* 2010. La Habana: Oficina Nacional de Estadísticas. (http://www. one. cu/aed2010.htm)

Most recent volume of Cuba's (new) statistical yearbook by province. Contains a wide range of socioeconomic statistics, covering the 2005–2010 period. The data provided is similar to the data provided by the (national) *Anuario Estadístico de Cuba* (see item **1937**), and is divided into the following categories: population, national accounts, employment and wages, agriculture, energy and mining, industry, construction and investments, transport, commerce, tourism, education, health care, culture, and sports and physical education.

1940 Cocq, Karen and David A. McDonald. Minding the undertow: assessing water "privatization" in Cuba. (*Antipode,* 42:1, Jan. 2010, p. 6–45)

The privatization and commercialization of water has proven to be one of the most controversial policy developments of the past 20 years. Largely associated with the neoliberalization of the world economy, it comes as a surprise to many that the socialist government of Cuba signed a 25-year contract with a Spanish multinational in 2000 to manage the supply of water in Havana. This paper provides an historical context for water reforms in the country and the first comprehensive study of this little-known contract. [C.E. Griffin]

1941 La condición humana en el pensamiento cubano del siglo XX: primer tercio del siglo. Tomo I. Edición de Enid Vian. La Habana: Editorial de Ciencias Sociales, 2010. 387 p.

A biographical compendium of selected Cuban intellectuals and thinkers from the first three decades of the 20th century.

1942 Cooperativas y socialismo: una mirada desde Cuba. Compilación de Camila Piñeiro Harnecker. La Habana: Editorial Caminos, 2011. 420 p.: bibl., index.

A compendium of various works on the cooperatives and cooperative experiences in different parts of the world. Pt. 1 presents an introduction to cooperatives as an alternative productive form and property type. Pt. 2 discusses the concept of cooperatives among selected socialist thinkers. Pt. 3 evaluates the cooperative experience in various countries like Spain, Uruguay, Venezuela, Argentina, and Brazil. Part four discusses the emergence of cooperatives in Cuba's transition towards socialism with a particular emphasis on the agricultural sector.

1943 Cuba: evolución económica durante 2010 y perspectivas para 2011. México: CEPAL, 2011. 51 p.: appendix, ill., tables.

Discusses the most significant trends in the Cuban economy during the 2005–2010 period, and economic prospects for 2011. The topics discussed include: recent evolution of the Cuban economy; the external sector; economic policies (e.g., fiscal policy), monetary policy, exchange rate policy, and commercial policy; output, employment and prices; and outlook for 2011.

1944 *Cuba in Transition: Papers and Proceedings of the . . . Annual Meeting of the Association for the Study of the Cuban Economy*, Vol. 20, 2010. Washington, D.C.: Assn. for the Study of the Cuban Economy.

Includes more than 30 papers and commentaries covering a wide range of topics dealing with Cuba's (future) transition to a market economy such as: Cuba's current socioeconomic situation, institutions and economic performance, agriculture, energy, real estate, tourism, the external sector, and international relations. Copies of papers and commentaries from earlier meetings of the Association are also available in both physical and electronic (pdf) format.

1945 Efectos y futuro del turismo en la economía cubana. Textos de Rogelio Quintana *et al.* La Habana: INIE, Instituto Nacional de Investigaciones Económicas; Montevideo: Depto. de Economía, Facultad de Ciencias Sociales, Univ. de la República Uruguay, 2004. 341 p.: bibl., ill. (some col.), col. map.

Examines the evolution of Cuba's tourism sector within a regional and global context. Topics discussed include: the evolution of international tourism in Cuba and in the Caribbean, the development of Cuba's tourism market in the post-Soviet era (since 1991), the economic, social, cultural, and environmental impact of international tourism, and policies and strategies to promote international tourism as one of the engines of the Cuban economy.

1946 Kath, Elizabeth. Social relations and the Cuban health miracle. New Brunswick, N.J.: Transaction Publishers, 2010. 200 p.: bibl., ill., index, tables.

Examines the principal characteristics of Cuba's health care system. Concludes that despite its developing world status and the impact of the collapse of the socialist camp and the Soviet Union in the early 1990s, Cuba's health care system continues to show impressive indicators that rival those of advanced countries. While the Cuban system is characterized by a high level of popular participation, which has been achieved through a long-standing government policy of prioritizing health care, decision-making comes from the top as political elites formulate and enforce health policy, leaving limited spaces for nonstate actors.

Koont, Sinan. Sustainable urban agriculture in Cuba. See item **1225**.

1947 León-Manríquez, José Luis. Similar policies, different outcomes: two decades of economic reforms in North Korea and Cuba. Washington, D.C.: Korea Economic Institute, 2011. 15 p.: graphs. (Academic paper series; 6:4)

Analyzes and compares the economic reforms undertaken by North Korea and Cuba since the disintegration of the socialist camp in the early 1990s. Concludes that both North Korea and Cuba have been reluctant to implement full-fledged market reforms and have followed a stop-go pattern instead by hesitantly allowing the growth of petty entrepreneurship, and retaining central planning as the principal mechanism to guide economic transactions and allocate scarce resources.

1948 Looking forward: comparative perspectives on Cuba's transition. Edited by Marifeli Pérez-Stable. Foreword by Fernando Henrique Cardoso. Notre Dame, Ind.: Univ. of Notre Dame Press, 2007. 332 p.: bibl., index.

A compendium of various works addressing a wide range of topics related to Cuba's post-socialist transition scenarios. The topics discussed include: the (possible) development and role of democracy (and democratic institutions) in Cuba, Eastern European experiences in the postsocialist transition to democratic regimes, the role of Cuba's civil society in a (possible) post-socialist transition, gender and inequality in Cuba, strategies for the transition from a planned economy to a mixed and/or market-oriented economy, social policy and social welfare, the (possible) roles of Cuban émigrés in the future of Cuba, ideology, culture, and national identity and the dilemmas of transition, and the future outlook (or possible scenarios) for relations with the US.

1949 López Segrera, Francisco. La Revolución cubana: propuestas, escenarios y alternativas. Mataró, Spain: El Viejo Topo, 2010. 158 p.: bibl., index.

Analyzes the historical roots of the Cuban Revolution (1959) and the reasons for its survival after the collapse of the socialist camp and the disintegration of the Soviet Union in the early 1990s. Examines Cuba's social and economic evolution since the 1959 revolution, and the principal challenges confronted by Cuban society during this period. Presents and compares several alternative scenarios as Cuban society continues its post-Soviet social and economic evolution, and offers a series of policy recommendations.

1950 Márquez Castro, René. Meditaciones sobre la transición socialista cubana. (*Temas/Habana*, 59, julio/sept. 2009, p. 147–156, bibl.)

Analyzes Cuba's recent socioeconomic transformations within the framework of a socialist transition. Argues that unlike the neoliberal concept of transition (from socialism to capitalism), the Cuban interpretation of this often polarizing term refers to the renovation and revitalization of the socialist experiment, rather than its replacement with capitalism.

1951 Mesa-Lago, Carmelo. Cincuenta años de servicios sociales en Cuba. (*Temas/Habana*, 64, oct./dic. 2010, p. 45–56, bibl., tables)

Presents a detailed analysis of social services in revolutionary Cuba (1959–2010), with a particular emphasis on health care, education, and social security. The topics discussed include: the evolution of social services in Cuba since 1959, state expenditures on social services (in relation to GDP), an assessment of the quality of social services in Cuba, the growing cost of pensions and social security, and Cuba's economic capacity to sustain social services in the long run.

1952 Mesa-Lago, Carmelo. El desempleo en Cuba: de oculto a visible. (*Espacio Laical*, 4, 2010, p. 59–66, bibl., graphs, tables)

Examines recent trends in Cuba's unemployment statistics, estimates the magnitude of unemployment in contemporary Cuba and its socioeconomic impact, analyzes the recent policy measures announced by the government to reduce employment in the state sector, and provides a series of policy recommendations.

1953 Mesa-Lago, Carmelo. Estructura demográfica y envejecimiento poblacional: implicaciones sociales y económicas para el sistema de seguridad social en Cuba. (*Espacio Laical,* 3, 2010, p. 87–92, bibl., tables)

Examines recent demographic trends in Cuba, and their social and economic impact on social services and the social safety net. Claims that as life expectancy increases, and the population gets older, the ratio of active workers to retirees decreases, placing a significant strain on the pension system and the social safety net. To cope with these challenges, mandatory contributions to the social security (or retirement) system are increased, the retirement age is also increased, and in some cases pensions are reduced. Cuba is currently undergoing a demographic transition resulting from three principal forces: increasing life expectancy, low birth rates, and high rates of migration. To address these challenges and to ensure higher pension payout rates and a more equitable distribution of these benefits, costs need to be reduced and pension contributions by individuals and their employers need to be increased.

1954 Mesa-Lago, Carmelo and **Pavel Vidal-Alejandro.** The impact of the global crisis on Cuba's economy and social welfare. (*J. Lat. Am. Stud.,* 42:4, Nov. 2010, p. 689–717, bibl., graphs, tables)

Analyzes the impact of the global financial crisis (2008–2009) on Cuba's economy and socioeconomic indicators. Discusses the policy measures implemented by the Cuban government as a response to the crisis, and offers policy recommendations.

1955 Miradas a la economía cubana. Textos de Omar Everleny Pérez Villanueva *et al.* La Habana: Editorial Caminos, 2009. 120 p.: bibl., col. ill., col. maps.

Includes works on the Cuban economy and Cuban society by selected Cuban scholars. The topics discussed include: recent developments in the Cuban economy, monetary policy and currency dualism, the evolution of Cuba's agricultural sector, and social and economic indicators by region.

1956 Miradas a la economía cubana II. Textos de Omar Everleny Pérez Villanueva *et al.* La Habana: Editorial Caminos: Agencia Española de Cooperación Internacional para el Desarrollo, 2009. 191 p.: bibl., graphs, col. ill., index, col. maps.

Includes works on the Cuban economy and Cuban society by selected Cuban scholars. The topics discussed include: recent developments in the Cuban economy, monetary policy and currency dualism, the evolution of Cuba's agricultural sector, social and economic indicators by region, and recent trends in Cuba's labor market by gender and race.

1957 Molina Molina, Ernesto. El pensamiento económico en la nación cubana. La Habana: Editorial de Ciencias Sociales; Panamá: Ruth Casa Editorial, 2007. 267 p.: bibl.

The author begins this history of economic ideas in Cuba studying the late 18th-century landholding criollos' advocacy for the expansion of slave-supported sugarcane production and for the lifting of some taxes and restrictions on trade. Focusing on individual thinkers and placing them in their historical and biographical context, he reviews the evolution of Cuban economic thought to the present. The complex web of relationships between Cuba and European powers and the US throughout the 19th and 20th centuries, and the problems related to maintaining economic policy independence and promoting social justice while engaging in international economic relations form a backdrop to the story. The author concludes with a call for greater Latin American integration under the Bolivarian Alternative for the Americas (ALBA). [D. Masís-Iverson]

1958 Morales Dopico, Emilio. Cuba: ¿tránsito silencioso al capitalismo? Miami, Fla.: Alexandria Library, 2009. 347 p.: bibl., ill.

Discusses the evolution of brands and brand-based marketing in Cuba since the early days of the "Special Period." The topics discussed include: the evolution of retail commerce since 1959, the impact of the policy measures implemented during the 1990s on brand awareness and loyalty, an overview of the principal state-owned enterprises (SOEs) and joint-ventures that dominate Cuba's retail network, the behavior and patterns of Cuban consumers in the post-Soviet era, the development of franchises and joint-ventures in Cuba, and the impact and role of remittances on Cuba's retail landscape.

1959 Nova González, Armando. La cadena comercializadora en el sector agropecuario cubano. (*Espacio Laical*, 2, 2010, p. 81–84, bibl., ill.)

Discusses the principal characteristics of Cuba's agricultural sector supply chain, and its agricultural markets. Outlines a series of policy measures to improve conditions in Cuba's agricultural sector by transforming its agricultural supply chain and agricultural markets.

1960 Nova González, Armando. Proyecto de lineamientos de la política económica y social, la política agroindustrial: análisis y valoración preliminar. (*Bol. Cuatrimestral*, abril 2011, p. 1–15, bibl.)

Presents the agricultural policy measures discussed during the Sixth Congress of the Partido Comunista (held in April 2011), and examines supplementary policies that could be implemented to improve this vital sector of the Cuban economy. Emphasizes the importance of implementing economic policy measures that improve linkages between Cuba's internal markets and the global economy.

1961 Panorama ambiental: Cuba 2010. La Habana: Oficina Nacional de Estadísticas, 2011. 47 p.: ill., tables.

Presents detailed environmental statistics (by province) from the 2005–2010 period. Includes data, tables, and graphs on geographical location, geographical characteristics, landmass, fauna and flora, energy consumption, weather patterns, environmental waste, investments in environmental protection, and other key indicators.

1962 Panorama demográfico: Cuba 2010. La Habana: Oficina Nacional de Estadísticas, 2011. 90 p.: ill., tables.

Presents detailed statistics (by province) such as: geographical location, geographical characteristics, and territorial surface. In terms of demographic indicators, the report includes data related to the gender composition of the population, the distribution of the population by age, and other key demographic indicators such as

rates of urbanization and population density by territory or region.

1963 Panorama económico y social: Cuba 2010. La Habana: Oficina Nacional de Estadísticas, 2011. 19 p.: ill., tables.

Summarizes and compares Cuba's principal socioeconomic indicators in 2009 and 2010. The data presented include: gross domestic product (GDP), the state budget, composition of the labor force, select tourism and physical output indicators, transportation, art and culture, education, science, technology, women in Cuban society, and a comparison between Cuba and select Latin American and Caribbean countries.

1964 Panorama territorial: Cuba 2010. La Habana: Oficina Nacional de Estadísticas, 2011. 62 p.: ill., tables.

Presents Cuba's principal socioeconomic indicators during the 2002–2010 period by province or territory. The data presented are designed to facilitate territorial comparisons, and include: demographic indicators (or statistics), physical output indicators for the nonsugar agriculture and housing sectors, investment, retail sales, human development and health indicators (e.g., live births, infant weight at birth, life expectancy, doctors per capita, dentists per capita), and educational attainment indicators (e.g., literacy rate, student-teacher ratio, school enrollment, graduates by grade and field of specialization, etc.).

1965 Pollitt, Brian H. From sugar to services: an overview of the Cuban economy. (*Int. J. Cuban Stud.*, 2:1, June 2009, p. 1–14, bibl., tables)

Presents a detailed overview of recent developments in Cuba's agricultural sector. Argues that while Cuba's "medical diplomacy" and special relationship with Venezuela have provided the island with a source of hard currency income and subsidized oil, the declining performance of its agricultural sector represents an urgent economic challenge. Cuba's agricultural sector has the potential for substantial improvements, and its revival should be a top priority as the country embarks on a far-reaching process of economic transformations. Agricultural development will allow the island to reduce its external sector dependency, particularly on Venezuela and food imports from the US, while reactivating one of the most promising sectors of its economy.

1966 Vidal Alejandro, Pavel. Los cambios estructurales e institucionales. (*Espacio Laical*, 2, 2010, p. 57–60, bibl., graphs, ill.)

Examines structural and institutional changes in the Cuban economy since 2008. Discusses four principal types of economic transformations: structural transformations, increased liberalization of consumption, and the transfer of idle state-owned lands to agricultural cooperatives and individual producers, and changes in the labor market.

1967 Vidal Alejandro, Pavel. El PIB cubano en 2009 y la crisis global. (*Econ. Press Serv.*, 9, mayo 2009, p. 1–16, graphs, tables)

Examines the structural composition of Cuba's gross domestic product (GDP) in 2009 within the context of the global financial crisis. Argues that even though the Cuban economy has been historically exposed to external shocks, which tend to have significant economic repercussions, the recent slowdown in the country's GDP has also been the result of internal structural conditions and constraints.

1968 Vidal Alejandro, Pavel and **Mario A. González Corzo.** Cuba's banking crisis: macroeconomic antecedents, principal causes, and recent policy responses. (*Int. J. Cuban Stud.*, 2:3/4, Autumn/Winter 2010, p. 201–216, bibl., graphs, tables)

Examines the macroeconomic and structural causes of Cuba's banking crisis (2008–2009). Analyzes policy responses to confront the crisis, and possible scenarios for the future of this vital sector of the Cuban economy.

1969 Vidal Alejandro, Pavel and **Omar Everleny Pérez Villanueva.** Entre el ajuste fiscal y los cambios estructurales: se extiende el cuentapropismo en Cuba. (*Espacio Laical*, 4, 2010, p. 53–58, graphs, tables)

Discusses recent reforms in Cuba's labor market, plans to expand self-employment and the possible creation of small-medium enterprises (SMEs), and the socioeconomic implications of these measures.

1970 Ward, Evan Ray. Packaged vacations: tourism development in the Spanish Caribbean. Gainesville: Univ. Press of Florida, 2008. 236 p.: bibl., ill., index, map.

Provides analytical insight into the evolution of the principal tourism destinations in the Spanish Caribbean. Examines the political and economic forces that contributed to the development of resorts in major tourist destinations such as Cuba, the Dominican Republic, Mexico, and Puerto Rico, and their social, economic, cultural, and environmental impact.

VENEZUELA

DANIEL HELLINGER, *Professor of Political Science, Webster University*

A POLARIZED COUNTRY, POLARIZED ANALYSES

MOST OF THE STUDIES reviewed here were produced in the relatively calm period between 2004, when President Hugo Chávez won a landslide re-election and claimed he would accelerate the construction of 20th-century socialism, and 2009, when the global recession called into question the continuation of high oil export earnings and the popularity of Chávez, first elected to office in 1999. The street protests and battles of 2002 to 2004 receded for a time, more likely due to the overall political dominance of the *Chavistas*, than the result of real consensus building.

The academic world, both in Venezuela and abroad, was no less divided in its opinions than were political forces in the country. Many of the works reviewed here, even some that are more empirical and cloaked in traditional academic language, reflect the polarization within the country. The dividing point could be drawn within the spectrum of intellectuals associated with social democracy. Thus, the noted economist D.F. Maza Zavala (item **1988**), known for his adhesion to the dependency school of thought, offers a harsh criticism of Chávez-style socialism. On the other hand, Jorge Giordani (item **1982**), a colleague of Maza Zavala at the Central University, argues in favor of the policies that he had a strong hand in developing as minister of planning.

Some of the literature reviewed here goes beyond harsh to extremely polemical. Valecillos goes so far as to describe Chávez's economic policies as "neofascist" (item **1993**). Corrales and Penfold-Becerra (item **1974**), though they partly abandon excess in analyzing the prospects for opposition, lay the blame for Venezuela's polarized politics at the feet of the president, with barely a nod toward the opposition's own role in fomenting extremism and confrontation. Just as worrisome in regard to the condition of democracy, but more objective and restrained, is Álvarez's analysis (item **1971**).

Several of the works included here trod a well-worn path in attributing the rise and persistence of *chavismo* to the failure in the Punto Fijo era (1958–98) to "sow the oil" in development and in the deteriorating economic and social conditions of the 1980s and 1990s. However, a stand-out contribution to our understanding of Chávez's triumph in 1998 is provided by Gates (item **1981**). Her highly creative empirical research reveals a much more complex relationship between Chávez and the private sector than we might have expected. Among the works that paint contemporary conditions with a broader brush, the most notable is El Troudi (item **1977**). His analysis is sympathetic to the Bolivarian Revolution, but he sees a transition to participatory democracy as a more realistic goal than socialism.

Some of the best work considered here has a tighter focus, with less polemical and more balanced arguments. Coing (item **1973**) looks closely at the regulation of electricity and calls for reforms less doctrinaire but closely connected to the participatory politics approach that is supposed to be at the heart of Bolivarianism. Velásquez (item **1994**) provides a ground-level vision of the impact of globalization on the state of Sucre. DiJohn (item **1976**) takes a broad look at the history of industrialization but keeps a relatively narrow focus on the influence of regulatory behavior on the development of technology and skilled labor. Rodríguez Rojas (item **1991**) focuses his lens on agriculture and the impact of subsidies. These less ambitious studies are more revealing of the contemporary political economy in Venezuela than those more prone to deviate into polemical fireworks.

1971 Álvarez, Ángel E. Venezuela 2007: los motores del socialismo se alimentan con petróleo. (*Rev. Cienc. Polít./Santiago,* vol. 27, no. especial, 2007, p. 265–289, appendices, tables)

Written shortly after the landslide reelection of President Chávez in Dec. 2006, the author reviews the prospects for the radical direction the president announced after his victory. Oil continues to be what makes the revolution run. Álvarez sees

deterioration in democratic conditions and individual rights, though he stops short of pronouncing the end of democracy.

1972 Arreaza Coll, Adriana and **Luis Enrique Pedauga.** Determinantes de los cambios en la productividad total de los factores en Venezuela. (*Ens. Polít. Econ.,* 25:53, 2007, p. 120–167, bibl., graphs, tables)

Finds that total factor accumulation and productivity have stagnated in Venezuela since the 1970s as a result of political uncertainty, institutional weakness, and macroeconomic instability. This study is based on data through 2005.

1973 Coing, Henri. Historia de la regulación eléctrica en Venezuela. Mérida, Venezuela: Centro de Investigaciones en Ciencias Humanas: Publicaciones Vicerrectorado Académico: Institut de recherche pour le développement, 2007. 197 p.: bibl., ill. (Ciencias sociales y humanidades)

The author concentrates on the low administrative capacity of the Venezuelan state to carry out effective policies in the area of electricity in the aftermath of nationalization. However, he also rejects the tendency of neoliberal policy experts to promote uniform privatization for all countries. He argues for decentralization, but under a more heterodox philosophy, characterized by and developed through a bottom-up process of discussion that will yield a new political coalition for policy in this area. Such an alliance cannot be created by decree, he warns—an obvious allusion to the nationalization process after 2004 under Chávez.

1974 Corrales, Javier and **Michael Penfold-Becerra.** Dragon in the tropics: Hugo Chávez and the political economy of revolution in Venezuela. Washington, D.C.: Brookings Institution Press, 2011. 195 p.: bibl., graphs, ill., index, map, tables.

The authors maintain that the controversial president has deliberately fomented extremism, polarization, and confrontation. Highly polemical for the most part, but the authors do present ideas on alternative paths to political development and discuss the possibilities for moderate forces to emerge.

1975 Debate por Venezuela. Edición de Gregorio Antonio Castro. Textos de Colette Capriles *et al.* Caracas: Editorial Alfa: Faces UCV, 2007. 301 p.: bibl., ill. (Col. Hogueras; 41)

This volume publishes the proceedings of a 2007 conference at the Universidad Central de Venezuela, offering highly varied viewpoints on the Bolivarian Revolution. Brings together some of the most prominent Venezuelan intellectuals with very diverse perspectives on current political and social developments in the country.

1976 DiJohn, Jonathan. From windfall to curse?: oil and industrialization in Venezuela, 1920 to the present. University Park: Pennsylvania State Univ. Press, 2009. 341 p.: bibl., index.

A refreshing departure from the usual debate of oil as either a "windfall" or a "curse." DiJohn argues that until the late 1960s, industrialization was in a relatively "easy" phase, with relatively low demands on skilled labor and technology, but that the scenario has changed with the transition to heavier industrialization. The state failed to adjust its regulatory behavior accordingly.

1977 El Troudi, Haiman. La política económica bolivariana (PEB) y los dilemas de la transición socialista en Venezuela. Caracas: Centro de Estudios Políticos Económicos y Sociales: Monte Ávila Editores, 2010. 393 p.: bibl., col. ill.

A heterodox analysis of the prospects for socialism by a sympathetic but uncompromising critic. El Troudi concludes that a transition to participatory democracy is more desirable and possible than a transition to socialism in Venezuela today.

1978 Espinasa, Ramón. El auge y el colapso de PDVSA a los treinta años de la nacionalización. (*Rev. Venez. Econ. Cienc. Soc.,* 12:1, enero/abril 2006, p. 147–182, bibl., graphs)

In the post-1975 period, PDVSA (Venezuela's state oil company) accelerated production, especially during the "opening" to foreign investment of the 1990s. PDVSA was thus a largely successful company, but it was derailed by the reforms implemented by Chávez, beginning in Nov. 2001.

1979 Freije, Samuel. Distribución y redistribución del ingreso en Venezuela. (*Am. Lat. Hoy/Salamanca,* 48, abril 2008, p. 83–107, bibl., graphs, tables)

The author finds that income became much more unequally distributed between the end of the 1970s and 2000, largely due to a decline in accumulation of capital. This decline has little to do with government policies, or with the relatively high degree of inequality at the start of the period. More recent reductions in poverty can be attributed to a redistribution of national income. Productivity and returns to labor remain low.

1980 Furtado, Celso. Ensaios sobre a
Venezuela: subdesenvolvimento
com abundância de divisas. Rio de Janeiro:
Contraponto: Centro Internacional Celso
Furtado de Políticas para o Desenvolvi-
mento, 2008. 187 p.: bibl., ill. (Arquivos
Celso Furtado; 1)

Brings together two essays written
by Furtado, the well-known structuralist
associated with Raul Prebish and the UN
Economic Commission on Latin America
(ECLAC), written in 1974 after a visit to
Venezuela, which was in the early stages of
a new boom at that time. Furtado argued
that Venezuela's oil driven economy was
a good example of the problems generated
by an outward-oriented economic development philosophy that could not overcome
the disarticulation between its domestic
structure and export sector. The essays are
supplemented with contemporary commentaries on Furtado's analysis.

1981 Gates, Leslie C. Electing Chavez: the
business of anti-neoliberal politics in
Venezuela. Pittsburgh, Pa.: Univ. of Pittsburgh Press, 2010. 195 p.: bibl., index. (Pitt
Latin american series)

Contrary to stereotypes, the Venezuelan business community was not
united against electing Chávez in 1998.
Gates uses innovative methodology to
demonstrate how corruption scandals and
dependence on state policies induced some
sectors, notably financial and media, to
hedge their bets in the election. As a result, we see a much more nuanced view
of how the 1998 election was conducted
and also of the complex interests and motives of businessmen and women in Latin
America, and we also get a sense of how
the media moguls misjudged the degree to
which their contributions to Chávez could
buy them control over government policies, especially in the area of control over
telecommunications.

1982 Giordani, Jorge. La transición venezolana, y la búsqueda de su propio
camino. Prólogo de Gastón Parra Luzardo.
Caracas: Vadell Hermanos, 2007. 150 p.: ill.

An extended explanation of the
government's strategy of development by
an academic who became the planning
minister.

1983 Guerra Britto, José. Refutación del
socialismo del siglo XXI. Caracas:
Los Libros de el Nacional, 2007. 116 p.: bibl.
(Col. Ares, Fuera de serie; 90)

A critique of the Chávez administration, arguing that "socialism of the 21st century," a term that President Chávez bor-
rowed from the work of Heinz Dietrich, is
nothing more than an effort to implant the
Cuban model in Venezuela. What could be
a useful critique based upon a comparison
between Dietrich's ideas and the Venezuelan reality too often degenerates into hyperbole, but there is some useful attention
to problems in Dietrich's notions of how to
combine market principles with socialist
ideals, a critique ironically shared by some
on the left.

1984 Hernández, Rossana. Aspectos pro-
blemáticos del excepcionalismo en
Venezuela, 1958–1989. (Rev. Venez. Cienc.
Polít., 29, enero/junio 2006, p. 153–167)

Against the argument that oil made
Venezuelan politics exceptional in this
period, the author contends that Venezuela
during the second half of the 20th century
experienced complex politics, full of contradictions, political instability, and economic
crisis not much different than the rest of
Latin America. Largely an expository essay of interpretation. See the prolific and
in-depth work of historian Steve Ellner for a
more thorough critique of the "exceptionalism" hypothesis (e.g., HLAS 63:3141).

1985 Launay, Stephen. Chávez-Uribe: deux
voies pour l'Amérique latine? Paris:
Buchet-Chastel, 2010. 258 p.: bibl.

Venezuelan President Hugo Chávez
and Colombian President Álvaro Uribe offer
conflicting views on Latin America's future,
and Uribe's vision is best, says the author.
Ultimately Brazil will have more weight in
shaping economic integration and relations
with the US.

1986 Martínez, Alberto. Microcrédito y
pobreza en Venezuela: un caso de estudio. (Rev. Mex. Cienc. Polít. Soc., 48:198,
sept./dic. 2006, p. 95–112, bibl., graphs,
tables)

A study of the government's Project
for Development of Poor Rural Communities. Sees the positive impact of the focus on
training and self-help and recommends that

these initiatives be implemented in other programs judged less successful.

1987 Mata Mollejas, Luis. Economía política y política económica para la Venezuela del siglo XXI: "el Estado fofo." (*Rev. Cienc. Soc./Maracaibo*, 12:3, set. 2006, p. 417–438, bibl., graphs, table)

The collapse of the old regime resulted in a reduction of civil society's capacity to check central government power, short-circuiting the functioning of self-correcting public choice mechanisms—especially in regard to fiscal and monetary policies, and contributing to speculation in the economy. The existence of a "black box" of funds retained by PDVSA (the state oil company) outside the control of Congress and at the disposal of the executive reinforces this weakness.

1988 Maza Zavala, Domingo Felipe. La década crítica de la economía venezolana, 1998–2007: ensayos. Caracas: Libros de El Nacional, 2009. 256 p. (Actualidad y política. Serie Ensayo)

Chávez's policies in pursuit of socialism have weakened and deformed the economic structure of the Venezuelan economy. Maza Zavala blames the use of oil revenues to overstimulate consumption without concomitant production.

1989 Rivas Leone, José Antonio. Las transformaciones del estado y las fuerzas armadas en la globalización: el caso de Venezuela. (*Relac. Int./México*, 98, mayo/agosto 2007, p. 91–111, table)

Global economic, social, and ecological changes have influenced and changed the roles and perspectives of actors, including the military, in many nation-states. While President Chávez has used the military for political ends and to advance social change, these actions do not equate to militarism.

1990 Rodríguez, Cristina. Momentos de la economía venezolana. Caracas: Banco Nacional de Crédito, 2007. 398 p.

This volume brings together 36 analytical essays, written between 1989 and 2006, with insightful reflections upon significant economic policies, presented year-by-year. Presents a useful and accessible review of the varying economic policies

pursued in the last years of the Punto Fijo era and the early years of *chavismo*.

1991 Rodríguez Rojas, José E. Lecciones de economía agraria venezolana: factores de producción y desarrollo tecnológico de la agricultura venezolana, 1945–2000. Caracas: Univ. Central de Venezuela, Consejo de Desarrollo Científico y Humanístico, 2009. 257 p.: bibl., ill. (Col. Monografías; 95)

Finds that state policies from the 1940s until the 1980s, despite the cheapening capital costs, were principally based on extensive growth that expanded land in production but not yields. Describes the impact of the 1980s crisis insofar as it cheapened labor costs, leading to the substitution of mechanized production by more labor intensive production. State subsidies continued through this time, favoring the development of an entrepreneurial middle class in the countryside.

1992 Suzzarini, Abdón. Venezuela ante la integración económica hemisférica: dos visiones, dos paradigmas. Caracas: Vadell Hnos. Editores, 2008. 252 p.: bibl.

The author takes an unabashedly neomercantile—or better put, neoliberal—perspective on Venezuelan economic policy, arguing that the goal of social justice and increasing consumption has prevailed over the need to boost productivity. He argues that the choice between protectionist versus free-market policies at home can be extended to the debate over the merits of the US-sponsored Free Trade Area of the Americas (FTAA) versus the Bolivarian Alternative for the Americas. The former, he says, is based on competition, the latter based upon social justice. He argues that the FTAA is the proper way for Venezuela to "sow the petroleum" in production.

1993 Valecillos Toro, Héctor. Crecimiento económico, mercado de trabajo y pobreza: la experiencia venezolana del siglo XX. Caracas: Ediciones Quinto Patio, 2007. 483 p.: bibl., ill.

Valecillos argues that the capacity of the state to stimulate economic development and reduce poverty terminated at the end of the last oil boom and devaluation in 1983. Failure to lay the basis for a productive economy accounts for the rise in unemployment and falling wages in the post-1983

period. The Chávez government has aggravated the problem by increasing the weight
of the state. Given this theme, one might
expect some attention to the influence of
oil exports, but Valecillos devotes no attention to this factor. Too often, his tone of
cold detachment slips, as when he classifies
Chávez's economic policies as "neo-fascist."

1994 Velásquez, Andrés. La globalización
en Venezuela y el estado Sucre. (*Tierra Firme/Caracas*, 24:94, abril/junio 2006,
p. 231–259, bibl., tables)
The author marshals data on regional
investment, including investments originat-
ing in Brazil, Asia, etc., to argue that despite
socialist rhetoric and some valuable programs under Chávez, the economy remains
capitalist and integrated globally.

1995 Venezuela, macrodinámica y política.
Coordinación de Luis Mata Mollejas.
Caracas: Comisión de Estudios de Postgrado, Facultad de Ciencias Económicas,
Univ. Central de Venezuela: Fondo Editorial
Tropykos, 2006. 376 p.: bibl.
A series of multi-authored analyses
of the course of the Venezuelan economy in
the 20th century, combined with scenarios
for the present century. The publication
commemorates the 100th birthday of the
Venezuelan intellectual, Arturo Uslar Pie-
tri, who coined the term *sembrar el petróleo*
("sow the oil"). Overall, the key task, say
the authors, is to get fiscal and monetary
policy right so that the country can finally
and effectively carry out this mandate to
use resources generated from oil exports to
create a more productive economy.

COLOMBIA AND ECUADOR

ERIC HERSHBERG, *Professor of Government and Director of the Center for Latin American and Latino Studies, American University*

RECENT RESEARCH ON THE POLITICAL ECONOMY of Colombia reflects
profound normative differences among observers of that country's affairs as well
as a range of theoretical and methodological approaches in the social sciences and
in intellectual circles more broadly. There is a substantial body of literature that
draws on neoclassical and institutionalist currents of thinking and that tends to
portray Colombia's many challenges as rooted in obstacles to the smooth functioning of markets and the inadequacies of economic and political governance
mechanisms. Prominent among such studies are treatments of fiscal imbal-
ances, labor market rigidities, and legislative processes, all of which are typically portrayed as sources of stubborn inefficiencies and suboptimal performance
(items **2001, 2002, 2003,** and **2006**). Much of this work is produced by analysts
affiliated with public agencies or nongovernmental think tanks, but there is also
considerable production by economists and political scientists based at universities both inside and outside the country. No less abundant are the writings of
Colombian analysts who are highly critical of economic orthodoxy and emphasize
both structural inequalities and struggles to overcome them, frequently situating
these in the context of endemic cycles of violence. Influenced in some instances
by Marxist analysis, and in others by currents of thinking associated with grassroots development and community autonomy, these reflections are generally
the work of academic social scientists and social justice advocates within Colombia itself (**2014**). Less numerous but noteworthy for their analytic depth and
policy ramifications are academic studies that draw on state of the art theory
and method to examine aspects of Colombian political economy that are critical

to equitable development and democratic governance. Several highly suggestive analyses trace trajectories of economic change in light of structural shifts in the Colombian economy, understood in the most sophisticated inquiries as encompassing both sectoral and territorial dimensions. Assessed overall, one encounters a heterogeneous landscape of reflection on Colombia's political economy, a metaphor, perhaps, for the diverse and conflict-ridden society from which it emerges and which it portrays.

The same degree of diversity is not evident in the far less abundant literature focused on political economy in the equally complex context of Ecuador. Foremost among the preoccupations that stand out in these writings, produced mostly by academic researchers and independent intellectuals inside the country, are phenomena of poverty, inequality, and social exclusion, as well as the injustices that perpetuate them. Colombian scholars frequently echo these themes, and like their Ecuadorian counterparts typically attribute them to the neoliberal economic models that swept most of Latin America beginning during the 1990s. Ecuador's recurrent bouts of paralyzing debt are analyzed in several studies, and the concept of "odious debt" emerges as a label for obligations that are deemed illegitimate in light of their acquisition by corrupt and rapacious ruling elites, and that consequently, by some accounts, may not merit repayment (items **2044** and **2045**).

For decades, Ecuadorian governments have resorted to the promise of revenue from petroleum exports as a means of overcoming the country's hardships, yet analysts in recent years have written widely about the limitations of petroleum-led growth, among which ecological externalities are but one of several complicating factors (item **2047**). The politics of natural resource-based development is among the topics covered in the few works under review, and echoing arguments in the literature on analogous matters in Colombia, the importance of community participation in decision-making is prominent on the agenda (item **2041**).

Whereas there is an abundance of technocratic studies focused on governance and economic management in Colombia, the studies of Ecuador included here feature only one such inquiry, on the topic of decentralization (item **2043**). This is one of three themes that emerge in the Colombian literature of a more technocratic nature. First, numerous studies lament the steady expansion of the state since enactment of the 1991 Constitution and the consequent drain on the public coffers. The state's need to finance growing expenditures is portrayed as the source of excessive rates of taxation as well as changes in tax policy that are so frequent as to suppress private investment (items **2003**, **2010**, **2013**, and **2019**). Although less ink is spilled nowadays than was the case prior to reforms that were enacted under President Álvaro Uribe's administration to rein in spending by subnational units of government, the cost of decentralization remains an important backdrop to this line of argumentation. The burden of social expenditures, principally on health and pensions, is a recurrent theme in these analyses, and while many studies argue that social expenditures are captured by relatively privileged groups—principally public sector employees (items **1997** and **2003**)—these critiques are remarkably silent regarding what alternative sort of welfare state might be constructed to ameliorate the extreme inequalities of income that motivate many of the analyses from the Colombian left.

Secondly, there is widespread concern with the impact on employment of Colombia's labor market regulations, particularly hikes in minimum wages and payroll taxes. Although econometric studies on the question differ as to the magnitude of the impact, for the most part these regulations are depicted as being responsible for the persistence of a disproportionately large informal sector and for sluggish expansion of formal employment. Finally, though again less ubiquitous than in the literature reviewed in *HLAS 63* and *65*, several recent publications cite adverse consequences of electoral rules and legislative practices that encourage undue influence of special interests and consequent distortions of public policies (items **2002** and **2038**).

Studies of Colombia emerging from a more critical vein, whether academic or activist in authorship, focus overwhelmingly on what is generally labeled as neoliberal globalization. These works are nearly unanimous in attributing Colombia's unacceptable inequalities to the deepening of a market-oriented approach to development and governance, frequently tracing the shift in that direction to policies first introduced during the 1990s by the administration of President César Gaviria (items **2005**, **2014**, **2035**, and **2037**). For some analysts, the Colombia-US free trade agreement, which at the time of this writing appeared destined for ratification by the US Congress, is emblematic of a development model that exacerbates social vulnerability, undermines local economies, jeopardizes food security and environmental sustainability, and provides incentives for land concentration, at times achieved through violence. Studies that emphasize these concerns often focus their gaze on the plight of particularly vulnerable groups and communities (items **2011**, **2025**, and **2026**).

Arguably the most valuable works on Colombian political economy to appear over the past several years have interrogated the underlying dynamics of economic transformation in the country, the constellations of interests that shape those dynamics, and the structural factors that drive logics of conflict, violence and, potentially, reconciliation. With regard to the economy, analyses of the uneven insertion of regions and sectors into competitive markets are especially worthy of mention (items **1998**, **2021**, **2024**, and **2034**). Among the most sophisticated are several studies that associate performance with technological development and capacities for productive innovation. In the realm of politics, investigations of the role of key actors in sustaining violence or creating opportunities for Colombia to benefit from an eventual peace dividend are especially insightful (items **1996**, **2017**, **2029**, and **2031**). Prominent among these are several useful inquiries into the nature and impact of narcotics trafficking and efforts to combat it. Here research highlights the degree to which external actors play as important a role as forces within the country itself. Despite some attention to disparate impacts of economic processes on different income groups, the ramifications of social class are almost entirely unexplored in this literature. A study of households and socioeconomic change in Ecuador (item **2046**), and a consideration of the frustrated aspirations of young Colombian professionals (item **2027**), are two exceptions to an otherwise disappointing gap.

To almost any rule there are exceptions, but it is fair to assert that there is a continuing dearth of cross-national comparative work that includes consideration of Colombian or Ecuadorian political economy. The focus remains predominantly, and excessively, constrained by national boundaries, even while awareness of influences beyond Colombia's borders characterizes work in that country on global neoliberalism, on trade with the US, and on drug traffic as an economic and political force. On each of these themes, as well as on a handful of others, broader regional comparisons exist but are few and far between.

COLOMBIA

1996 **Alvarez, Stephanie** and **Angélika Rettberg.** Cuantificando los efectos económicos del conflicto: una exploración de los costos y los estudios sobre los costos del conflicto armado colombiano. (*Colomb. Int.*, 67, enero/junio 2008, p. 14–37, bibl., graphs, tables)

The authors consider the direct and indirect costs of armed conflict on Colombian economy and society, highlighting measurement problems yet estimating localized impacts and the consequences of capital flight. Direct costs imposed by conflict involve infrastructure (electricity, oil/gas, telecommunications, roads), kidnappings and extortion, and cattle theft, which has become the FARC's third highest grossing illegal activity after narcotrafficking and kidnappings. The indirect costs mainly concern lost productivity, as well as high defense spending that has detracted from the government's ability to spend on education and health. The study finds that the most adversely affected sectors include hydrocarbons, electric energy, and ranching.

1997 **Arango, Carlos A.** and **Angélica Pachón.** The minimum wage in Colombia 1984–2001: favoring the middle class with a bite on the poor. (*Ens. Polít. Econ.*, 55, dic. 2007, p. 148–193, bibl., graphs, tables)

This study examines the history of the minimum wage in Colombia and evaluates its effects on the well-being of families. The authors argue that a rising minimum wage distorts market outcomes, increasing both unemployment and the hours worked by heads of households. In their view, as minimum wages rise, families with little human capital are more likely to sink to the bottom of the income distribution scale. The result is an increased gap between classes and a negative impact on living standards, as those with lower human capital remain trapped in the informal sector despite the increased formal sector wage. Conversely, families with higher human capital experience longer spells of unemployment as they seek work in a formal sector that is squeezed by the increased wage levels.

1998 **Arbeláez, María Angélica; Alexander Estacio;** and **Mauricio Olivera.** Impacto socioeconómico del sector azucarero colombiano en la economía nacional y regional. Bogotá: Fedesarrollo, 2010. 98 p.: bibl., ill., map. (Cuadernos de Fedesarrollo; 31)

This report reviews the socioeconomic impact of the sugar sector in Colombia, particularly in the region of Río Cauca. The authors attribute significant economic contributions to the sugar sector, the presence of which is correlated with positive socioeconomic indicators. Sugar refineries generate economic activity beyond the sector itself, propelling investment in related industries and boosting both tax revenues and employment. The annual aggregate effect of the refineries on the economy is estimated at US $6.3 billion. Moreover, the authors find that populations in cane-growing regions tend to have lower levels of unsatisfied basic needs and a higher quality of life index. Additionally, they exhibit higher literacy rates and better health and education indicators than their counterparts in communities with nonsugar agricultural sectors. Interestingly, data reveal that the sugar industry directs an unusually high 15 percent of its profits to Corporate Social Responsibility endeavors, exceeding the 10 percent that it contributes in taxes.

1999 **Attanasio, Orazio P.** *et al.* Children's schooling and work in the presence of a conditional cash transfer program in rural Columbia. (*Econ. Dev. Cult. Change*, 58:2, Jan. 2010, p. 181–210, bibl., tables)

This study evaluates the effect of the conditional cash transfer program Familias en Acción (FA), a program that has been operating in rural areas of Columbia since 2002, on children's school and work participation. The authors find that such programs positively impact school enrollment, negatively impact domestic work participation, and have little consequence for participation in income-generating work. Among the variables considered are childrens' ages, enrollment rates, length of time spent in school, and gender differentials.

2000 **Bucheli Gómez, Marietta.** Curas, campesinos y laicos como gerentes del desarrollo: la construcción de un modelo de desarrollo emergente en Colombia. San Gil, Colombia: Fundación Editora Social de San Gil, 2006. 280 p.: bibl., ill.

Drawing on in-depth case studies of the communities of Guanentá, Comunera, and Vélez in the southern department of Santander, this study explores how local actors negotiated paths to development over more than four decades through the *experiencia* project initiated by the Catholic Church in 1960. The transformative mechanisms of the *experiencia* included education, community organizing, and communication, but since its founding by Father Ramón González Parra in 1963, it has been continually reshaped by the community itself, without interference by traditional "development experts." The author celebrates the *experiencia's* advocacy of a holistic vision of development and distinctive emphasis on the church and local communities as agents of development, understood as a concrete dimension of Christian commitment.

2001 Caballero Argáez, Carlos; Alejandro Jadresic; and Manuel Ramírez Gómez. El marco institucional para la regulación, supervisión y control de los servicios públicos en Colombia: propuesta para su fortalecimiento. Bogotá: Fedesarrollo, 2006. 111 p. (Cuadernos de Fedesarrollo; 18)

The product of a consultancy for the Ministerio de Hacienda, this study evaluates the regulation of public services in Colombia, offering proposals for the strengthening of oversight institutions and processes. It examines the impacts of regulatory reforms enacted during the 1990s with the intention of increasing efficiency and quality of services, while reducing costs and promoting competition. Analysis of both the conceptual and legal underpinnings of the current regime is followed by a thorough review of divisions of responsibilities within the system, regulatory autonomy, and challenges of transparency and predictability. The authors lament ambiguities in the roles assigned to diverse actors and present broad outlines for reforms, emphasizing the importance of separating regulatory commissions from government ministries and moving gradually to augment their autonomy from government officials.

2002 Cadena Ortiz, Andrés Eduardo de la. Bancadas, regiones y ausentismo: el voto del congreso colombiano en el TLC con los Estados Unidos. Bogotá: Univ. de los Andes, Facultad de Ciencias Sociales-Ceso, Departamento de Ciencia Política, 2008. 90 p.: bibl., ill. (Col. Prometeo)

American political scientists have written extensively about the factors that shape legislators' votes on trade policy, and have found that public opinion in congressional districts is an important predictive factor. Yet little work has been done on the topic in Latin America. This useful contribution to the literature identifies two variables that influenced voting of Colombian legislators with regard to the free trade agreement with the US: regional public opinion concerning the likely impact of the accord, and the position adopted by a legislator's political party. Party discipline stands out as central in both chambers, and particularly in the Senate, where no members deviated from the positions of their respective parties. The author attributes the strength of party discipline to the 2005 "Ley de Bancada." Public opinion in legislators' districts was found to be insignificant in influencing member votes. Therefore, the author concludes, what most influences the economic votes of members of the Colombian Congress is the position of their party leadership, rather than the opinion of their districts, which is the most influential factor in the US. The study also analyzes absenteeism among Colombian legislators during debates about the agreement, and notes that it was overwhelmingly members of the opposition who were absent, often resulting in an inability to obtain a quorum. Absenteeism was used, at least in part, as a strategy of opposition.

2003 Cárdenas Santa-María, Mauricio and Valerie Mercer-Blackman. Análisis del sistema tributario colombiano y su impacto sobre la competitividad. Bogotá: Fedesarrollo, 2006. 157 p.: bibl., ill. (Cuadernos de Fedesarrollo; 19)

Between 1990 and 2005, government spending in Colombia nearly doubled, leading to a succession of reforms that increased tax rates across the board, relying heavily on income and value-added taxes. This study analyzes the impact of the Colombian tax system on efficiency and competitiveness, and after comparing Colombia's tax regime with other Latin American countries offers recommendations for reform. The authors contend that rate increases have suppressed private sector investment and thus reduced the supply of formal sector jobs. They maintain that businesses in Colombia are taxed more heavily than their counterparts elsewhere in the region, and particularly lament increases in employer contributions to pension and health costs. While excessive tax burden is one constraint on Colombia's economy, more important still are the complexity of the tax code, the instability caused by frequent changes to tax laws and temporary taxes, and changes in tax enforcement. The authors suggest reforms to lower tax-related administrative costs, and call for reduced fluctuation and unpredictability.

2004 Chomsky, Aviva. Linked labor histories: New England, Colombia, and the making of a global working class. Durham, N.C.: Duke Univ. Press, 2008. 397 p.: bibl., index. (American encounters/global interactions)

The field of global and transnational history is increasingly fertile terrain for historians of the Americas, and this study of labor in New England and Colombia marks a significant contribution to this body of research. As textile production in Massachusetts declined under pressure from low-cost competition from places like Colombia, where labor protections were weak or absent, the remnants of the US industry were importing immigrant workers who left places like Colombia to escape repression or to seek out dignified wages. Both industry and labor are conceived in this elegantly written study as flowing across national boundaries in ways that are mutually constitutive. The components of the book that focus on Colombia analyze the banana sector in the violence-ridden Uraba region, the coal industry that fuels power plants in places as far away as New England (and is partially controlled by US multinationals), and the role of US-based actors in suppressing labor organization in Colombia.

2005 Crisis del modelo neoliberal y desigualdad en Colombia: dos décadas de políticas públicas. Edición de Fundación Centro de Estudios Escuela para el Desarrollo, CESDE. Compilación de Ruth Quevedo, Álvaro Gallardo y Marisol Perilla.

Bogotá: Ediciones Desde Abajo, 2009. 302 p.: bibl., ill. (Biblioteca Vértices colombianos)

Attributing high rates of unemployment and unequal income distribution to a crisis of overproduction, this collection of articles by economists from the Universidad Nacional offers a Marxist analysis of the failure of a neoliberal approach to economic development, which the authors deem unsuited to Colombia's needs. Data rich sections analyze income distribution, labor markets, taxation and social policies. The former themes are framed in light of currents of *pensamiento crítico* that explicitly reject mainstream economic theories that, according to the authors, have led to the pauperization of workers in Colombia and throughout Latin America. The study concludes with brief consideration of the implications of the 2008 financial crisis for economic development in Latin America.

2006 Deuda pública territorial: conjura de banca y el gobierno central contra las regiones, propuestas para un reordenamiento financiero de Colombia. Prólogos de Angelino Garzón y Eric Toussaint. Edición de Unión Nacional de Empleados Bancarios. Bogotá: Ediciones UNEB, 2005. 215 p.: bibl., ill.

Amidst the financial liberalization and credit boom of the 1990s, subnational governments in newly decentralized Colombia incurred significant debt burdens, much of which they proved unable to pay. According to the authors of this study, inadequate regulation by the central state combined with the soaring costs of social expenditures financed at the departmental and municipal levels to bring about an urgent need for investment to restructure public debt. The main suggestions put forth in this volume include strengthening regulatory institutions and control mechanisms, and promoting public awareness of the consequences of excessive debt, especially given its consequences for inequality. A central conclusion is that the central state must retain the capacity to rein in subnational units, so as to avoid the social costs of excessive indebtedness.

2007 Dion, Michelle and Catherine Russler. Eradication efforts, the state, displacement and poverty: explaining coca cultivation in Colombia during Plan Colombia. (*J. Lat. Am. Stud.*, 40:3, Aug. 2008, p.399–419, tables)

This quantitative study addresses the effectiveness of Plan Colombia in eradicating coca and its connections to poverty. Coca cultivation is found to be most intense in regions of moderate poverty, and not in areas of extreme poverty as previously thought. The extreme poor are too resource poor to engage in cultivation, while the moderately poor lack the infrastructure (e.g. roads) to gain access to markets for legal crops. Thus, efforts to reduce coca cultivation should emphasize the development of local infrastructure and access to markets to encourage other forms of agriculture. Some funding for alternative development has been included in Plan Colombia but implementation and oversight have been flawed. The article suggests as well that where state presence is weak, guerrilla violence and corruption foster coca cultivation. Whereas aerial eradication of coca crops has been central to Plan Colombia, and coca has been reduced where this approach has been taken, that reduction is a function of population displacement rather than of fumigation per se, which suggests that fumigation contributes to the perpetuation of poverty and underdevelopment.

2008 Economía colombiana: una visión desde los sectores económicos. Compilación de Jaime Alberto Rendón Acevedo. Medellín, Colombia: Ediciones Escuela Nacional Sindical, 2005. 219 p.: bibl., ill. (Ensayos laborales; 12)

This collection of essays prepared under the auspices of the Colombian labor movement takes a sectoral approach and questions the effectiveness of the Washington Consensus development model, associating it with increased poverty and debt. This was followed by the signing of a bilateral free trade agreement with the US, the social and economic impacts of which this work analyzes from a sectoral perspective, addressing such areas as sugar, bananas, and insurance. Chapters focus on international context, macroeconomic history and labor markets, and consider microeconomic features and labor relations in these and other sectors. The objective is to assess the impact of trade policies on sectoral growth and competitiveness.

Edwards, Sebastian and **Roberto Steiner.** La revolución incompleta: las reformas de Gaviria. See item **1241**.

2009 Fukumi, Sayaka. Cocaine trafficking in Latin America: EU and US policy responses. Aldershot, England; Burlington, VT: Ashgate, 2008. 283 p.: bibl., index. (Global security in a changing world)

This book compares US and EU responses to cocaine use and trafficking within their borders, as well as their respective approaches to disrupting cocaine production and trafficking in the Andean region. Until recently, the EU classified cocaine trafficking as a social problem, whereas the military-oriented approach adopted by the US, manifested over the last 30 years in the "War on Drugs," categorizes it as a matter of national security. The author analyzes how defining the phenomenon as a social problem or a security issue informs distinctive approaches to combating cocaine trafficking internally and in the Andean region. EU policy in the Andes is primarily development-based, focused on improving economic opportunities in order to stem involvement in the drug trade. The US, in turn, relies on eradication and interdiction. These differences are evident in the conduct of Plan Colombia, the study concludes, and account for many of its flaws.

2010 Gandour Pordominsky, Miguel. Constitución fiscal y equilibrio de las finanzas públicas: efectos de la Constitución de 1991 sobre la economía política de financiamiento del gasto público en Colombia. (*Colomb. Int.*, 68, julio/dic. 2008, p. 68–97, bibl., table)

The 1991 Constitution limited the financial autonomy of the executive at the same time that it expanded space for subnational units to contract debt. This study highlights the consequences of the latter, as overall public debt expanded from around 20 percent of total GDP in 1996 to more than 50 percent of GDP a decade later. The author echoes the views of many authors in suggesting that the provisions for decentralization must be reformed in order to restore the fiscal stability of the Colombian state.

2011 Garay Salamanca, Luis Jorge; Fernando Barberi Gómez; and Iván Mauricio Cardona Landínez. La negociación agropecuaria en el TLC: alcances y consecuencias. Bogotá: Planeta Paz, 2006. 182 p.: bibl., ill., 1 CD-ROM. (Documentos de política pública para la paz)

This report estimates the likely impact on agriculture and fisheries of the free trade agreement between the US and Colombia, key provisions of which it finds more disadvantageous than those contained in the analogous US agreement with Central American countries and the Dominican Republic (CAFTA). The authors conclude that the accord is highly asymmetric, as it imposes greater tariff reductions on Colombia than on the US, excludes the sugar sector that is important for Colombia, and fails to curtail agricultural subsidies that give unfair advantages to US agrobusiness. The study predicts immediate damage to Colombian production of yellow and white corn, sorghum, soy, beans, and wheat, and sharp declines over the medium term in production of chicken meal and palm oil. For Colombian agriculture to achieve greater competitiveness a multifaceted modernization program will be required, according to the authors. Key features would include technological upgrading and reforms in land tenure. Land, they conclude, must be treated as a factor of production rather than as a resource for exercising political power and securing rents.

2012 García, Antonio. De la república señorial a la nueva sociedad: escritos económicos selectos. Edición de Luis Emiro Valencia. Bogotá: Contraloría General de la República, 2006. 443 p.: bibl., ill.

This extensive anthology of writings on Latin American and Colombian political economy by Antonio Garcia (1912–82) is prefaced by a chronology of the author's life set alongside historical events that influenced his work. The volume is divided into four sections, consisting of writings on the state and the macroeconomy, the Colombian economy, agrarian issues, and the study of economics in Colombian academe. The influence of dependency theory, and a historically informed preoccupation with the distinctiveness of Latin American intellectual perspectives on grand questions of development and democracy, are recurring topics in the works of this innovative thinker.

2013 García Molina, Mario and Ana Paola Gómez. ¿Han aumentado el recaudo las reformas tributarias en Colombia? (*Rev. Econ. Inst.*, 7:12, primer semestre 2005, p. 43–61, appendixes, bibl., graphs, tables)

This study considers the 23 tax code reforms implemented in Colombia between 1973 and 2002 to analyze their impact on tax collection and on public finance. The authors conclude that reforms in 1974 and 1990 increased tax collection substantially, but that most reforms had little to no impact and thus were an unnecessary waste of political capital. Moreover, ineffective reforms damaged economic activity by creating uncertainty. The study analyzes taxes on income, as well as tariffs and exemptions, highlighting the distribution of the tax burden, as well as the lack of public confidence in the efficient use of tax contributions and the congressional representation of different segments of the tax-paying public.

2014 Giraldo Giraldo, César. ¿Protección o desprotección social? Bogotá: Fundación Centro de Estudios Escuela para el Desarrollo, Univ. Nacional de Colombia: Ediciones Desde Abajo, 2007. 290 p.: bibl., ill., index. (Biblioteca Vértices colombianos)

This work examines social protection systems in Latin America in the context of what the author sees as increasing dominance of financial interests over economic and political affairs. As debt service has come to outweigh public welfare as the primary concern of governments, the author advocates a return to work-based rights and benefits, since those without job security or property lack access to modern social protection systems, such as pensions and health care. Drawing on a Marxist analytical framework, this study argues that fighting poverty without addressing worker rights is a recipe for continued social exclusion. Capitalism disrupts established social networks and safety nets, especially the family, underscoring the need for social protection systems. Yet even as social expenditures have risen, the state has backed away from involvement in the economy. Microcredit schemes are touted as an alternative social protection mechanism, but the author concludes that these cannot obscure the patrimonial characteristics of a state dominated by finance, which deprives workers of security and abandons individuals to seek salvation in the market.

2015 Goebertus, Juanita. Palma de aceite y desplazamiento forzado en zona bananera: "trayectorias" entre recursos naturales y conflicto. (*Colomb. Int.*, 67, enero/junio 2008, p. 152–175, bibl., map)

The transition from banana cultivation to palm oil plantations in Magdalena has had significant consequences for forced displacement in the region. Relying on insights derived from qualitative research, the author identifies several causal pathways that prompted increased displacement of rural laborers. The absence of a strong institutional presence permitted illegal armed groups to finance their activities through extortion, demand for manual labor declined through sectoral shifts in production, decreased food security prompted migration, and institutional incentives favoring palm oil extraction prompted land seizures by armed actors who provoked displacement. A persuasive case is made for a number of policy measures to decrease incentives for displacement of agricultural labor, encompassing judicial reforms as well as incentives for agricultural production emphasizing domestic food supply.

2016 Gutiérrez, Francisco and **Mauricio Barón.** Órdenes subsidiarios: coca, esmeraldas—la guerra y la paz. (*Colomb. Int.*, 67, enero/junio 2008, p. 102–129, bibl.)

This insightful article examines the relationship among extractive resources, violent conflict, and peace in Colombia, specifically contrasting the emerald and coca industries. The authors assert that in both of these sectors violent economies have been facilitated by the denial of democratic freedom, privatization of public economies, and the endorsement and strengthening of illegal or semi-legal actors. Criminal networks have an incentive for peace, as war is costly and often evokes state intervention. Whereas for emeralds, stability in transportation is valued and peace is therefore desirable, cocaine is not truly an extractive resource, a decrease in violent conflict is not as necessary for its production and circulation. The Colombian state negotiated an arrangement with the emerald industry, but owing to domestic and international factors was unable to do so with the cocaine industry.

2017 Holmes, Jennifer S.; Sheila Amin Gutiérrez de Piñeres; and **Kevin M. Curtin.** Guns, drugs, and development in Colombia. Austin: Univ. of Texas Press, 2008. 192 p.: bibl., ill., index, maps.

Drawing on insights from political science and economics, and with sensitivity to historical nuance, this study considers the impact of civil conflict and criminal violence on economic development in Colombia, emphasizing interactions among different forms of violence, coca production, and economic processes. The authors underscore the geographically uneven effects of violence, which they analyze using the best available data at the subnational level, and estimate the overall impact of violence on the economy. The final chapter offers "Four Cornerstones of Pacification," intended as a blueprint for achieving peace at a time when recent improvements in economic indicators and security have the potential to be mutually reinforcing.

2018 Jaimes, Carlos Alberto and **Luis Eduardo Rincón.** Desempeño financiero y económico de las EPS del régimen contributivo y otros actores de la seguridad social en salud en Colombia, 1993–2006. Bogotá: Univ. de Bogotá Jorge Tadeo Lozano, Facultad de Ciencias Económico Administrativas, Especialización en Economía y Gestión de la Salud, 2009. 128 p.: bibl., ill. (Informe)

Colombia's social security and health care systems have undergone important changes over the past two decades, and this empirically detailed study explores the evolution of the health insurance system between 1993 and 2006. The specific focus is on the General System of Social Security and Health (SGSSS), which was established in an effort to guarantee access to health care on the basis of universality, equality, efficiency, and quality. Micro- and macro-level data are employed to assess the strengths and weaknesses of the system, addressing its cost as well as its capacity to provide services to the population.

Jornada de Estudios del Trabajo, *1st, Universidad del Rosario, 2007.* Vías y escenarios de la transformación laboral: aproximaciones teóricas y nuevos problemas. See item **1824.**

2019 Kugler, Adriana and **Maurice Kugler.** Labor market effects of payroll taxes in developing countries: evidence from Colombia. (*Econ. Dev. Cult. Change,* 57:2, Jan. 2009, p. 335–358, graphs, tables)

Drawing on a sample of 235 Colombian firms, this article examines the impact of payroll taxes on employment and wages between 1982 and 1996. The authors find that the 1993 social security reform generated an increase in payroll taxes that was mostly directed to pensions and healthcare, and note that this increase was greater than in most countries that implement payroll tax increases. They estimate that a 10 percent increase in payroll taxes reduced formal employment by 4–5 percent, but that only a fifth of the increase in taxes was shifted to workers as lower wages. During recessions, payroll taxes provoke lower employment rates, but the negative effects of payroll taxes on employment are felt more by production than nonproduction workers, particularly in years of market expansion. The study concludes that tax subsidies for less skilled workers may be particularly effective in boosting employment, especially if applied to indirect benefits and during expansionary years.

2020 Lasso Valderrama, Francisco Javier. Impacto de los cambios de precios relativos en pobreza y desigualdad en Colombia: 1998–2007. (*Ens. Polít. Econ.,* 57, dic. 2008, p. 178–248, bibl., graphs, tables)

Written by an official of the Banco de la República in Medellín, this article examines the relationship between inflation, poverty, and inequality in Colombia between 1998 and 2007, and demonstrates the regressive character of price shifts between 1998 and 2007. The central conclusion is that inflation in food prices has an especially severe impact on the poor. The author recommends, therefore, that when inflation in food prices is relatively high in comparison to other goods and services, public policy should aim to decrease food prices by lowering barriers to imports and boosting domestic agricultural production. This policy would not only satisfy domestic demand but also, ideally, create export opportunities that might benefit agricultural producers.

2021 Macroeconomía y regiones en Colombia. Edición de Adolfo Meisel Roca. Cartagena, Colombia: Banco de la República, 2004. 333 p.: bibl., ill., maps. (Col. de economía regional)

The characteristics of the Colombian economy vary considerably across regions, and this collection of articles uses regional-level data gathered by the Central Bank through its 28 offices distributed across the country to assess that heterogeneity. The degree to which regional disparities characterize different aspects of the Colombian economy is a common concern of thematic chapters, all informed by econometric analysis. Monetary policy is found to have a uniform impact across regions, and inflation rates are shown to have gradually converged in recent decades. Yet different cities are found to have been impacted unevenly by nationwide economic trends, for example in labor markets, and processes of decentralization coincided with increasingly disparate outcomes in term of income distribution.

2022 Mejía Guinand, Luis Bernardo; Felipe Botero; and **Juan Carlos Rodríguez Raga.** ¿Pavimentando con votos?: apropiación presupuestal para proyectos de infraestructura vial en Colombia, 2002–2006. (*Colomb. Int.,* 68, julio/dic. 2008, p. 14–42, bibl., tables)

This article examines budget allocations for road infrastructure during the first Uribe administration. The authors find a statistically significant, positive relationship between the allocation of funds for roadwork and communities that hold *Consejos Comunales,* where the state commits resources to secure political support. Yet they find that areas selected for infrastructure funding frequently do not comply with the strategic plan of the administration. There is no statistically significant relationship between areas receiving budget allocations and the municipal government being Uribista. Quite the contrary, the authors find a negative relationship between communities selected to receive roadwork funds and Uribista mayorship. They conclude that the central government tries to shore up support in areas where the political leadership is affiliated with the opposition—in essence, paving with votes.

2023 Miles, William. Central bank independence, inflation and uncertainty: the case of Colombia. (*Int. Econ. J./Seoul,* 23:1, March 2009, p. 65–79)

Colombia undertook central bank reform in 1991, moving toward greater independence. Reform led to a significant decrease in the level of inflation and uncertainty, suggesting an increase in credibility. However, there has also been an increase in inflation persistence since reform. The lower mean, but greater persistence of inflation indicates that central bank independence has shifted the Phillips curve inward but also flattened it, a result that the authors deem consistent with recent research for the Euro-zone and the US. Finally, further analysis reveals that, in accordance with the Friedman-Ball hypothesis, higher inflation increases uncertainty in Colombia, but that uncertainty does not increase inflation.

2024 Moncayo Jiménez, Edgard. Impactos territoriales de la globalización: una perspectiva macro-sectorial. Bogotá: Univ. Autónoma de Colombia, Sistema Univ. de Investigación, 2007. 224 p.: bibl., ill.

This conceptually rich book analyzes the effects of the current phase of globalization on diverse territorial economies of Colombia. The study begins with the 1990s, when the Gaviria administration adopted a development strategy based on the internationalization of the economy, and examines the macroeconomic and sectoral changes that ensued. Emphasis is given to the evolution of productivity across sectors which are best understood as rooted in territorially and socially distinctive settings. The author concludes by considering how the US-Colombia Free Trade Agreement is likely to impact economies in different regions of Colombia, and presents the accord as merely another—albeit very important—episode in the ongoing process of consolidating structural reforms begun during the 1990s.

2025 Las multinacionales españolas en Colombia. Textos de Pedro Ramiro *et al.* Prólogo de Enrique Javier Diez. Bogotá: FiCa, 2008. 152 p.: bibl., ill. (Col. El pez en la red; 58)

The four articles in this accusatory collection assess the role of Spanish multinational corporations (MNCs) in Colombia. Framing their topic in the context of capitalist (neoliberal) globalization, the authors assert that the expansion of MNCs worldwide constitutes a "new era of conquest." These firms are portrayed as migrating from country to country, depending on where fiscal policies are more favorable to their interests. Spanish corporations in Colombia are blamed for an array of violations against workers, the environment and human rights, and labeled a "shadow government," influencing state policy through lobbying and other tactics.

2026 Palacio Salazar, Ivarth. Los efectos esperados del ALCA y el TLC sobre el sector agropecuario del Valle del Cauca. Investigación de Ivarth Palacio Salazar *et al.* Cali, Colombia: Univ. Autónoma de Occidente, Dirección de Investigaciones y Desarrollo Tecnológico, 2008. 193 p.: bibl., ill.

This publication analyzes the potential effects of an eventual Free Trade of the Americas Agreement (ALCA), and of the proposed Colombia-US free trade agreement, on the principal agricultural sectors in the Valle del Cauca. Reviewing the impacts of the economic opening that began in the 1990s, the authors emphasize the dramatic increase in agricultural imports alongside a sharp decline in land dedicated to crop cultivation. These twin factors are shown to have negatively affected rural investment, production, and employment, and to have eroded incomes of households involved in small- and medium-sized agricultural operations. The authors contend that the Valle del Cauca would suffer further through a hemispheric trade accord, given the ramifications of Brazilian competition in the sugarcane industry. The region's overwhelmingly smallholder-based agriculture is ill-equipped to thrive amidst economic liberalization, they conclude, and can adapt to global competition only with the support of ambitious programs of transition assistance.

2027 Peña Frade, Nayibe. Los profesionales bogotanos: precaridad económica, trashumancia y ciudadanía. Bogotá: Univ. Autónoma de Colombia, Sistema Unificado de Investigación, SUI, 2007. 298 p.: bibl.

Bogotá has undergone important social and spatial reconfigurations as a result of its integration into what economic sociologists have labeled flexible capitalism. Taking this as its point of departure, and contemplating ways that the city has "globalized," this study focuses on how changes in employment opportunities, housing patterns, and neighborhood characteristics impact professionals in Bogotá. Data from six separate surveys of recipients of professional degrees from the Universidad Autónoma between 1979 and 2003 provide the empirical foundations for the book, which highlights feelings of anguish, frustration, and vulnerability experienced by urban professionals in a generalized situation of precariousness.

2028 Pérez V., Gerson Javier. Dimensión espacial de la pobreza en Colombia. (*Ens. Polít. Econ.*, 48, junio 2005, p. 234–293, bibl.)

Poverty is not only determined by socioeconomic or environmental factors, but also by geographic location. Using data from various regions in Colombia from 1985–93, the author identifies "clusters" of poverty, and contrasts these with clusters of wealth. He finds that where poor communities are closer to rich communities, they tend to improve their lot, simply by virtue of spillovers created by geographical proximity. In turn, wealthier communities are more likely to see increased poverty if they are in proximity to poor communities. The study concludes that these patterns should inform public policies seeking to determine where to focus resources for fighting poverty.

2029 Rettberg, Angélika. Explorando el dividendo de la paz: impactos del conflicto armado en el sector privado colombiano: resultados de una encuesta nacional. Bogotá: Univ. de los Andes, Facultad de Ciencias Sociales, Departamento de Ciencia Política, 2008. 53 p.: bibl., ill.

This study by a leading Colombian political scientist draws on a national survey to examine the impact of armed conflict on the Colombian private sector. The author finds that indirect costs (transportation and distribution interruptions, lost transactions due to violence, altered consumer behavior) exceed direct costs (extortion, attacks), although costs overall were high and unequally distributed across sectors and types of enterprises. Larger firms are impacted disproportionately because they are more likely to be victims of extortion, and businesses operating on a nationwide scale suffer because transportation lines are interrupted. Although the private sector is concentrated disproportionately in Bogotá, the data indicate that the capital city remained an "oasis" from the effects of armed conflict. The author considers the business community to be a potential force for peace, and the majority of firms declare that they would boost investment and employment if not for the constraints imposed by armed conflict. Plagued by disunity, however, Colombian business has contributed little so far to resolving the country's multiple conflicts.

2030 Revéiz, Edgar. El estado lego y la fractura social. Bogotá: Academia Colombiana de Ciencias Económicas: Centro Colombiano de Responsabilidad Empresarial CCRE, 2007. 728 p.: bibl., ill., 1 CD-ROM (4 3/4 in.). (Visión de la nueva economía institucional sobre la globalización; 3)

This theoretically ambitious and thematically disparate tome is the third of three volumes in which the author seeks to explain interactions between economic institutions and performance in Colombia. Over the course of 700 pages he reflects laboriously on the emergence of a "triple society," distinguishing sectors that are co-opted, non-co-opted, and illicit, and analyzing their mutual interactions across diverse spheres of activity and territorial scales. Criticizing conventional neoliberal visions of economy and society, the author advocates a multidimensional approach to development, emphasizing the importance of institutional forms and adaptive capabilities. Separate and sometimes repetitive sections address the shortcomings of the administration of justice in Colombia, the management of risks inherent in the country's integration into a globalized economy, and the dynamics of economic change at the local level.

2031 Richani, Nazih. Colombia: predatory state and rentier political economy. (*Labour Cap. Soc.*, 43:2, 2010, p. 119–141)

This article by a leading authority on Colombia's internal conflict analyzes two interrelated factors, which the author labels "tsunamis," that have helped to make rentier capital the country's main source of accumulation and wealth. The first, spearheaded by the landed elite, which included cattle ranchers, the narco-bourgeoisie, and speculators, shifted the bulk of agricultural land from production to speculation. This was followed by a second tsunami led by a warring predatory state that is seeking natural resource rents to finance its expanding war machine. The combination of land speculators alongside a warring predatory state is found to have been transforming the rural economy, and with it Colombia's political economy, in ways that result in a diminished role for food production and for other productive sectors. The ramifications for achieving equitable development are profound and disturbing.

2032 Sabogal Salamanca, Mauricio and Luis Alberto Rodríguez Ospino. Captura y distribución de rentas en Colombia 1950–1960: una aproximación desde el Neoinstitucionalismo. (*Oikos/Medellín*, 20, nov. 2006, p. 51–64, bibl., graphs, table)

This article builds upon the work of North, Nugent and Robinson, and Coatsworth and Kalmanovitz with regards to the "institutional trajectory" of Colombia's economy in the late 19th and 20th centuries by analyzing the role of interest groups in rent-capturing and distribution in the economy from 1950 to 1960. The authors find that interest groups influenced monetary and exchange-rate policies in an effort to protect industrial and agricultural sectors, resulting in a lower cost of credit and cheaper imports, but also a sustained increase in inflation and subsequent negative impacts on various societal and export sectors. The average growth rate of certain manufacturing sectors during this time was higher than that of other sectors due to this manipulation of economic policy. The collective pressure by interest groups for resource redistribution (through rent-capturing and distribution) ultimately came at the expense of sound macroeconomic policy.

2033 Salgado R., Edgar Augusto. Nueva visión de la economía solidaria. Bogotá: Univ. La Gran Colombia, 2008. 116 p.: bibl. (Economía y administración)

This brief text envisions the "Solidarity Economy" as a means to address pressing economic and social problems such as unemployment and marginalization. Citing language contained in Law 454 of 1998, the author defines the Solidarity Economy as "a socioeconomic, cultural and environmental system defined by practices of supportive self-management." Democratic and humanistic in orientation, such an economy treats humans as subjects and agents in their work, and assigns less priority to profit-making. The book associates the Solidarity Economy with a worldwide trend towards cooperativism, and suggests that Colombia's experience can be applied internationally.

2034 Santacruz Medina, Marino. El espacio del desarrollo. Cali, Colombia: Univ. Autónoma de Occidente, Dirección de Investigaciones y Desarrollo Tecnológico, Facultad de Ciencias Económicas y Administrativas, 2009. 394 p.: bibl., ill., maps.

This book identifies geographical location as critical to understanding development outcomes, and asserts that Western models of development are inappropriate to contexts such as Colombia, given its different cultures, values, and social structures. Thus, geography matters in discerning the best development approach for any given setting, and a "reterritorialization of development" is in order. Mapping Colombia's evolution from a Fordist to a post-Fordist development model based on flexible accumulation, the author emphasizes transformations in geopolitical, regional, and urban spaces. In a concluding reflection on the current trajectory of globalization and development, he asserts that the community of nations, and US President Barack Obama in particular, must "decide" on three putatively interwoven issues that affect development, including global financial deregulation, the prohibition of psychotropic drugs, and energy.

2035 Sarmiento Palacio, Eduardo. Economía y globalización. Bogotá: Grupo Editorial Norma, 2008. 392 p.: bibl. (Col. Vitral)

This book grapples with what the author portrays as the disasters wrought by globalization as central banks have privileged control over inflation at the expense of the public interest. In the author's account, although economic deregulation opens vast opportunities for speculative profit, it exacerbates income inequality and poverty. Based on the Colombian experience and drawing on analysis of monetary and trade policy as well as income distribution, the study highlights shortcomings of theories underpinning the Washington Consensus. Reforms that could help Colombia achieve developed-country growth levels, reduce inequality, and sustain financial stability must focus on employment and industrialization, portrayed as critical foundations for a strategy that prioritizes equality.

2036 Stiglitz, Joseph E. Stiglitz en Colombia: reflexiones sobre sus planteamientos. Compilación de Cecilia López Montaño y Carlos Alberto García. Bogotá: Intermedio Editores para Círculo de Lectores, 2007. 352 p.: bibl.

A 2003 visit to Colombia by Nobel Laureate Joseph Stiglitz occasions this set of reflections on the implications of his thinking for Colombian political economy. Five authors examine aspects of the Colombian economy through the lens of Stiglitz' prescription for Latin America as a whole, and echo the Nobel Laureate's chapter criticizing the preferential treatment that has been given to the interests of finance and capital at the expense of the broader economy and social welfare. A common theme is the failure of orthodox economic policies to stimulate growth in Colombia, and the cost of excessive emphasis on taming inflation.

2037 Suárez Montoya, Aurelio. Confianza inversionista: economía colombiana, primera década del siglo XXI. Bogotá: Ediciones Aurora, 2010. 229 p.: bibl., ill.

This book argues that policies focused on the needs of international financial capital and driven by obsession with maintaining investor confidence reinforce Colombia's colonial characteristics. The study suggests that economic policies and their corollaries regarding governance and security have sought over the past decade to maximize benefits to capital, and as-

sumed that deregulation of markets would generate a "trickle down" effect to benefit society and reduce poverty. The author vehemently disagrees with this policy of privileging finance and capital over popular interests, and laments the likelihood that newly-elected President Juan Manuel Santos will continue this approach to economic management.

2038 Taylor, Steven L. Voting amid violence: electoral democracy in Colombia. Hanover, N.H.: Univ. Press of New England, 2009. 240 p.: bibl., graphs, ill., index. (Northeastern series on democratization and political development)

Colombia boasts one of the most longstanding electoral democracies in the Western hemisphere despite having suffered exceptionally persistent political violence and internal warfare. The coexistence of stability and violence is an underlying theme of this analysis of electoral and party politics over several decades. An important contribution of this study is its treatment of the impact of constitution changes on political parties and the party system. A key conclusion is that contrary to the conventional wisdom, Colombian parties are not an independent variable affecting all other aspects of the system, but rather a dependent variable reacting to the incentive structures created by electoral rules and other institutional.

2039 Trofimenko, Natalia. Learning by exporting: does it matter where one learns? Evidence from Colombian manufacturing firms. (*Econ. Dev. Cult. Change*, 56:4, July 2008, p. 871–894, tables)

A vast literature concludes that exporting may benefit businesses by providing new "learning opportunities," triggering cost-cutting strategies and improvements in product design, though some analysts argue that only those firms that are more successful in domestic markets will engage successfully in exporting. This study examines the experience of more than a thousand Colombian exporters from 1981–91, distinguishing those that trade with poor, lower-middle income, upper-middle-income, rich non-OECD, and OECD countries. Its core question is whether productivity gains are concentrated especially among firms that export to more developed markets, which demand higher standards in quality and customization. The author finds that firms with higher productivity levels reap higher returns in exporting, and particularly in exporting to advanced economy markets. Exporting alone is not sufficient for development, as only firms with high productivity can reap the benefits of exporting, even when trading with advanced economies.

2040 Varón Pulido, Orminso; Ricardo Díaz Caballero; and José Donado Ucrós. Crisis alimentaria en Colombia. Bogotá: Univ. La Gran Colombia, 2008. 207 p.: bibl., ill. (Economía y administración)

This brief report explores the consequences of a growing population, inappropriate land use, institutional shortcomings, and misguided public policies on food security in Colombia. Demand for food has increased but supply has decreased, and the authors attribute this disjuncture to the exhaustion of natural resources and the deterioration of land quality. Absent corrective measures, the study predicts that by 2020 the country will experience a severe food deficit. The solution lies in more responsible use of resources and higher productivity, without which Colombian food producers will fail to meet the challenge of global competition.

ECUADOR

2041 Aprendizaje participativo en el bosque de ceja andina, Carchi, Ecuador. Textos de Kaia Ambrose *et al.* Quito: Ecopar; Ottawa, Canada: IDRC, 2006. 300 p.: bibl., ill., maps (some col.).

This book reports on an effort, sponsored by the International Development Research Centre of Canada, to promote sustainable use of wild and cultivated biodiversity in the Ecuadorian Andes. A history of poor land use and environmental mismanagement has undermined ties between the people of the Bosque de Ceja Andina and the environment on which they depend, and the project aimed to achieve a more sustainable approach to farming and the salvation of local ecosystems. The book presents a baseline assessment of biodiversity in the zone, reviews results of an experiential learning project designed and implemented

in partnership with local farmers, and identifies participatory practices conducive to sustainable environmental management.

2042 Aviles, William. Policy coalitions, economic reform and military power in Ecuador and Venezuela. (*Third World Q.*, 30:8, 2009, p. 1539–1564)

Military coups and coup attempts, as well as the establishment or continuation of development roles for the military have been a part of civil-military relations in Ecuador and Venezuela since 1990. The author contends that the military's greater role has in part been a consequence of the failure of neoliberal policy coalitions to establish and maintain a hegemonic consensus. This failure has undermined progress in orienting the military in a "democratic" direction that prioritizes traditional security roles under the ultimate command of civilian authorities. It has also allowed for competing models of civil-military relations to emerge that draw upon nationalist or socialist models of military power and democracy.

2043 Consejo Nacional de Modernización del Estado (Ecuador). Síntesis del diagnóstico "Descentralización en Ecuador al 2006" y: "Propuesta de políticas para la descentralización fiscal." Quito: CONAM, Consejo Nacional de Modernización, 2006. 131 p.: bibl., col. ill., col. maps.

This report provides an overview of decentralization in Ecuador and then focuses on fiscal decentralization and its distributional consequences. Historically fragmented between the coastal region and the interior, efforts were made during the 1950s and 60s to unify Ecuador's administration to strengthen national unity and advance development. Decentralizing reforms of recent years reversed that dynamic, but inefficiencies in the decentralized system, particularly regarding municipal administration and tax collection, reflect ill-defined roles and responsibilities for provincial and regional levels of government. Alongside progressive taxes imposed by the central government are municipal taxes that vary dramatically, and subnational expenditures, dedicated primarily to health and education, are uneven across regions. The study concludes that efficient and equitable decentralized governance requires enhanced, horizontal coordination among different levels, more precise definition of responsibilities, and expanded space for citizen participation.

Deuda externa y economía ecológica: dos visiones críticas. See item **1809**.

2044 Ecuador en la encrucijada: abolir la deuda para liberar el desarrollo humano. Textos de Comité para la Abolición de la Deuda del Tercer Mundo. Quito: Abya-Yala, 2009. 187 p.: bibl., ill., map.

This polemical book, published by the Committee for the Abolition of Third World Debt (CADTM), lays out a blistering critique of Ecuador's debt accumulation and repayment. The authors assert that Ecuador should demand an "official and integral audit" of its internal and external public debt. This audit, they argue, would reveal the illegitimacy of Ecuador's debt, and justify its classification as "odious debt," unworthy of being repaid. Amidst a worldwide financial crisis that has damaged indebted nations and made new credit harder to come by, a review of public debt becomes all the more pressing. The volume is rife with references to the debt as a usurpation of sovereign state powers, as a form of domination and oppression, and labels it immoral to put debt service ahead of human development.

2045 Mansell, Wade. Suturing the open veins of Ecuador: debt, default and democracy. (*Law Dev. Rev.*, 2:1, 2009, p. 149–191)

In 2008 an international audit commission appointed by President Rafael Correa concluded that much of Ecuador's sovereign debt was tainted by illegality and illegitimacy, and consequently did not merit repayment. In response, the government ceased interest payments on some of its bonds and engineered a successful buyback at a large discount. Having thus reduced Ecuador's external commercial debt burden by about a third, the government is now turning to multilateral and bilateral loans also adjudged unlawful by the commission. This article examines the robust approach adopted by the Correa administration, contrasting it with previous defaults and debt workouts and situating it in the context of increasingly prominent concepts of odious and illegitimate debt.

The author observes that regardless of the provisions of international law, the underlying reality is that of an impoverished nation called upon to continue to service or redeem "debt" that brought no obvious benefit to the overwhelming majority of its people. Debt repayment, he concludes, has promoted impoverishment and also, if indirectly, facilitated devastating environmental degradation.

2046 Moser, Caroline O. N. Ordinary families, extraordinary lives: assets and poverty reduction in Guayaquil, 1978–2004. Washington, D.C.: Brookings Inst. Press, 2009. 360 p.: bibl., index.

This theoretically and empirically rich book draws elegantly on economic data and ethnographic insight to reveal complex circumstances of poverty and asset accumulation by individuals, families, and communities from Guayaquil. The book explores struggles to escape the poverty of urban slums, and finds that success entails the gradual accumulation of multiple types of assets. Its longitudinal approach enables the study to highlight the dynamic and changing nature of poverty and to explain "the underlying social, economic, and political processes in which such [asset] accumulation occurs." Contrasts are drawn between the strategies of asset accumulation pursued by the first generation of migrants to Guayaquil and those of their children, many of whom have left to seek opportunities in Spain, and the income mobility of both groups is measured empirically. An additional virtue of this remarkable volume is its consideration of how the community is affected by increasing insecurity and violence.

2047 Narváez Quiñónez, Iván. Petróleo y poder: el colapso de un lugar singular, Yasuní. Quito: FLACSO: GTZ, 2009. 584 p.: bibl. (Cuadernos de trabajo)

This lengthy volume explores the nearly 40-year history of Ecuador's Yasuní National Park in its battle against the petroleum industry, floundering state environmental policy, impotent civil society groups and the disintegration of the flora, fauna, and indigenous communities that inhabit the park. The study details the "schizophrenic" actions of both the petroleum industry and the Ecuadorian state, as they extract natural resources from the park while purporting to engage in conservation efforts. While contemplating the environmentally friendly aspects of Ecuador's 2008 constitutional reform, the author concludes that much more must be done to untangle the country's garbled approach to petroleum extraction and the protection of natural resources, specifically nature reserves.

BOLIVIA AND PERU

BARBARA KOTSCHWAR, *Research Fellow, Peterson Institute for International Economics, Adjunct Professor, Georgetown University, Robert Wood Candidate for Master of Arts, Center for Latin American Studies, Georgetown University*

TWO THEMES PREVAIL throughout the current political economies of Bolivia and Peru and are strongly reflected in the readings reviewed in this issue: decentralization and the redistribution of wealth from the nations' wealthiest to their most impoverished. Both countries have made significant strides in the past decade to move from a traditional unitary state towards greater federalism, significantly reforming the institutions of the state in a way that will have implications for economic growth, distribution, and human development.

Peru, a historically highly centralized country, has flirted with decentralization since the 1980s. Following the decade of highly centralized government that followed President Fujimori's autogolpe, the decentralization movement experienced a rebirth with Fujimori's departure. His successor, President Toledo came to power with a mandate to restore democracy, decentralize the state and transfer responsibility—as well as budgets— to subnational governments. In 2002, Peru was divided into 25 regions and elections were held. The decentralization movement experienced a setback in 2005, when voters rejected the idea of merging the 25 into smaller regions that could be more efficiently governed. However, Peruvian efforts to decentralize the federal government have continued. In Bolivia, Evo Morales' assumption of power in 2006 further encouraged the move towards a decentralized structure that first emerged in the 1990s and marked the beginning of a transition from a unitary system, governed largely from the capital, to a much more decentralized one. With devolution of power to the subnational regions, Bolivia has become one of Latin America's most decentralized states.

The June 2011 election in Peru, in which left-leaning former army officer Ollanta Humala narrowly defeated right-wing candidate Keiko Fujimori, represents, at least in part, the latest manifestation of another phenomenon that has spread through the Andean region: the electoral expression of popular dissatisfaction with the status quo. This turn is remarkable as Peru has had one of the most robust growth rates in the region over the past decade. Despite this healthy growth, dissatisfied voters have manifested their views through protests against neoliberal reforms. One of the more notable expressions of public dissatisfaction was the *Arequipazo*, a series of citizen uprisings that prevented the privatization of electricity in Arequipa. The Peruvian people have more recently expressed this sentiment by electing a a staunch critic of the recent economic policies.

A major component of Humala's presidential campaign centered on the unequal distribution of wealth, even as he has distanced himself from some of his more radical proposals of the last election, espousing pragmatism over ideology and identifying with Brazil's Lula over Venezuela's Chávez. While promising to maintain the free market economic policies that have served as an engine of growth in the Peruvian economy, he has pledged to convert Peru's economic growth into "the great motor of social inclusion Peruvians desire" and has promised the poor a greater share of the country's wealth (Bajak, Frank. "Leftist Humala wins Peru's Election," *Time.* June 6, 2011. *http://www.time.com/;* accessed June 7, 2011).

Bolivia underwent a similar and even more dramatic transition. Gonzalo Sánchez de Lozada, the main architect of Bolivia's economic reforms, was forced to resign in the wake of the Bolivian gas protests of October 2003 in which indigenous and labor protesters—among the leaders of which was current president Evo Morales—brought the Bolivian economy to a halt. Sanchez de Losada's successor, President Mesa, enacted a new hydrocarbons law, increasing state royalties from natural gas exploitation. This move was opposed by Morales and his followers who demanded full nationalization and greater participation by Bolivia's indigenous peoples in the political system and the nation's economy. As a sign of the resurgence of populism and indigenous nationalism in a much divided state, Morales was elected in December 2005 on a platform of "refounding" Bolivia.

Morales has changed the political landscape of the country, putting into place a constituent assembly and drafting a new constitution. He has largely nationalized natural resources. Morales has also severely limited departmental autonomy in the Department of Santa Cruz, the largest and one of the wealthiest regions of Bolivia, in the wake of a failed autonomy referendum effort. Business groups, international investors, academics, and policymakers will be watching Peru to see whether the Humala administration will follow the path of their neighbors in Bolivia and, of course, the Bolivarian Republic of Venezuela led by Hugo Chávez.

Peru and Bolivia share many characteristics, yet they also differ dramatically. One main difference is the status of their economies. In the latter half of the 2000s, Peru's economy grew at an average annual rate of 7.2 percent. Bolivia's, by contrast, grew at an average annual rate of 4.6 percent. Although Peru was more affected than Bolivia by the 2008–2009 world economic crisis, with growth slowing to 0.9 percent in 2009, compared to Bolivia's robust 3.4 percent, the IMF estimates have Peru's growth rebounding and sees the two economies growing by 6.1 percent and 4.5 percent per year, on average from 2011 to 2015, respectively. Another divergence is in income distribution. Bolivia ranks with Brazil and Colombia as among the countries in Latin America with the highest income inequality, while Peru ranks with Uruguay and Costa Rica as having relatively more equal income distribution.

Despite these differences, the two cases have several important commonalities, most associated with issues of wealth distribution. In the past two decades, income distribution in both countries has become less equal. A study by the Inter-American Development Bank shows that Bolivia's Gini coefficient has worsened by a score of 1.6 and Peru's by 2.0 from the early 2000s to the early 1990s. The geographical distribution of poverty is also similar in both countries: poverty is significantly more widespread in rural than in urban areas and the poverty incidence is higher among indigenous peoples than in the general population. In Bolivia, 54 percent of the total population and 76 percent of the rural population lives in poverty (2007 figures), and 31 percent of the total population and

59 percent of rural population living in extreme poverty. Nearly three-quarters of Bolivia's indigenous peoples qualify as poor. Peru's poverty rates are much less dire, but the urban/rural distribution is also stark. In Peru in 2009, 35 percent of Peruvians were poor, with rural areas seeing a poverty rate nearly twice that, at 60 percent. Poverty among indigenous peoples was at 43 percent. Peru's extreme poverty rate is 11.5 percent overall; 28 percent in rural areas. Peru's economic growth has helped mitigate poverty over the past decade: in 2001 the poverty rate was at 55 percent, with extreme poverty at 25 percent. Bolivia's strides have been smaller: national poverty has fallen from 62 percent in 2002 to 54 in 2007 and extreme poverty from 37 to 31 percent.

Adult illiteracy for the population over 15 years of age is at 9.4 percent for Bolivia and 7 percent for Peru. In both countries female illiteracy is three times male illiteracy. Bolivia still has a relatively young population, with 70 percent of the population under the age of 35 in 2010 and just 14 percent over 50. However, by 2030 this is projected to fall to 60 percent, with the over-50 population growing to 20 percent. Peru's ratio in 2010 is 65 percent under 35 and 16. 5 over 50; in 2030, 30 percent under 35 and 25 percent over 50.

Bolivia and Peru have urbanized much more slowly than most other Latin American countries. Sixty-six percent of Bolivia's population is urban; for Peru the figure is 73 percent. In comparison, 93 percent of Argentines, 85 percent of Brazilians, 78 percent of Colombians and 93 percent of Uruguayans and Venezuelans live in cities.

Given that issues of the inequality in wealth distribution stand out in the political economy of both Bolivia and Peru, it is no surprise that a firm majority of the books and article reviewed for this publication center around the issue of income distribution disparity.

Both Bolivia and Peru suffer from regional disparities. Bazzaco's article on market opening in Bolivia (item **2049**) describes how President Paz Estensorro's New Economic Policy (NEP) shifted the economic balance of power in favor of the department of Santa Cruz, which has had reverberations throughout the Bolivian economy, as well as in Bolivian politics. Arce (item **2055**) writes about the impact of increasing regional disparities within Peru: this disparity is one factor behind the repoliticization of Peruvian society in the wake of neoliberal economic reforms. Writing about the groundswell of Peruvian political activity brought about by the increased transparency and greater connectivity wrought by new social media, Arce predicts an Arab spring phenomenon. Ciquero Ibáñez and Figueroa Bello focus on the theme of decentralization by looking at ways to measure the performance of regional governments in Peru (item **2059**). This volume could be useful for policymakers aiming to maximize the results of this recent phenomenon. Rosales, Chinguel, and Siancas explore the issues of regional growth in Peru, focusing on the relationship between growth and human development in the northern regions of Peru (item **2063**). The authors look at various ways to analyze economic growth, and to mathematically assess human development and its relationship to economic growth and policy as a whole. They offer some interpretations of their data, one of which is the weak degree of correlation between economic growth and human development. Villarroel-Böhrt (item **2052**) points to the distributional impact of real exchange rate movements, particularly employment in the tradable versus nontradable sector. The distribution of funds is analyzed in Boucher *et al.'s* article on credit constraints in Peruvian agriculture (item **2057**), which focuses principally on ways to assess the effects of these constraints.

Juan Castro (item **2058**) looks at social programs in Peru during the time period 1994–2004. He finds that poor households are significantly more vulnerable to external shocks and suggests supplementing countercyclical fiscal measures with a stronger safety net. Barrantes (item **2056**) explores how wealth redistribution has occurred in Peru. She finds that the executive branch has appropriated far more resources towards redistribution than the legislature. According to her findings, Alan García during his first term and Alberto Fujimori during his 10-year rule allocated the most funding for social welfare. The author states that throughout periods in Peru's history, funds were limited by the Congress.

Intergenerational income distribution, in the form of the pension system, is the focus of several recent works on these two countries. Weyland (item **2054**) blends psychological theory, historical narrative, and economic data to explain Bolivia's lagging—and less-than-successful—privatization of its pension system, which was modeled on Chile's pension reform. The author documents the reasoning behind Bolivia's move towards privatization, explains fundamental differences between conditions in Chile and Bolivia that made the Bolivian plan less viable, and concludes with some thoughts on how pension reform in Bolivia may have been more successful. Cruz-Saco examines demographic trends in Peru (item **2060**) and describes the impact of declining fertility rates and emigration on the Peruvian population, specifically smaller pensions and a decline in the quality of health care. The author projects that over three-quarters of Peruvians over age 65 will not have a pension by 2030, and, as a result, family transfers will become more critical to the Peruvian people's financial stability. Cruz-Saco discusses the creation of social programs such as Crecer, an antihunger initiative, and EsSalud, a social security program funded by employers, employees, and the government and suggests areas for future research in this field.

The Bolivian economy is dominated by the hydrocarbons sector, particularly natural gas. Evo Morales renationalized former state-owned oil and gas assets in 2006, causing a strong reaction by private investors. Medinaceli Monrroy's book, *La nacionalización del nuevo milenio: cuando el recio fue un aliado* (item **2051**), explores the nationalization of hydrocarbons in Bolivia, weighing the advantages and disadvantages of several proposals for reform of the industry and ultimately coming down in favor of state intervention. George Gray Molina (item **2050**) looks at the nonnatural gas economy and at attempts to diversify the economy away from gas. His discussion of the Morales administration's "base estrecha" model of economic cooperation indicates the state's presence in the economy has increased. Gray Molina assesses the public policy ramifications of this economic reform, suggesting that subsidies, vertical integration, and the redistribution of markets are necessary. He outlines a plan that provides for the diversification of the Bolivian economy with a continuing role for natural gas. A specific source for Bolivia's efforts at broadening its economy is *El cacao in Bolivia: una alternativa económica de base campesina indígena.* In this volume, Bazoberry Chali and Salazar Carrasco (item **2048**), along with their collaborators, document the contribution of cacao to the Bolivian economy. They suggest that cacao is a potential export-growth crop with significant potential for economic growth.

Water, which has caused a series of violent protests since the turn of the century and has had lasting effects on both Bolivian and Peruvian politics, is the subject of a compilation of essays, edited by Miguel Solanes (item **2053**). Essays in this volume explore the issue of privatization and its relationship to the distribution of water. They also detail the history of water regulations, set out case studies of privatizations in Latin American and Asian countries, and discuss the impact of free trade agreements on the extraction and distribution of water. The in-depth exploration of these themes is highly relevant to the study of the region, due to the fact that water is one of the predominant issues of the 21st century.

These works explore each country's preoccupations with the level of distribution of power among governmental units and of resources among economic actors. A final review volume by Barrantes *et al.* examines the various facets of Peru's economic and social situation in the 2000s (item **2062**). The authors explore numerous topics, ranging from Peru's relationship with the international economy to the inequality of distribution of wealth. Each writer draws upon the investigations of prior researchers to provide the reader with a more complete picture of the many challenges and prospects associated with the Andean country.

BOLIVIA

2048 Bazoberry Chali, Óscar and **Coraly Salazar Carrasco.** El cacao en Bolivia: una alternativa económica de base campesina indígena. En colaboración con Olver Vaca *et al.* La Paz: Centro de Investigación y Promoción del Campesinado, 2008. 282 p.: bibl., col. ill., maps. (Cuadernos de investigación; 72)

Seven authors collaborated on this resource, which documents the cultivation of cacao in Bolivia and its contribution to the economy. The growth and harvest of cacao, along with its role in the market and the ways it can benefit Bolivia's indigenous communities, are explored in the book. The account illustrates a significant market potential for cacao with attention to the growth of wild cacao. It also shows how Bolivia has potential to export cacao and chocolate products but it lags behind Ecuador and Brazil in terms of production. The book offers contextual narrative with charts, graphs, and even photographs to make the case for cacao production. According to the authors, the agro-forest economy, of which cacao is a large part, is projected to have strong potential between 2011 and 2021. The authors provide a detailed exploration of the capabilities of cacao and how it has the potential to help grow Bolivia's economy.

2049 Bazzaco, Edoardo. La apertura a los mercados internacionales y la crisis de la economía regional, 1985–2005. (*Tiempos Am./Castellón*, 14, 2007, p. 89–104, graphs, photo, tables)

Bolivia, along with many other Latin American countries, passed through its worst financial crisis in recent economic history in the 1980s. This led to new President Paz Estenssoro's New Economic Policy (NEP) Washington Consensus-type economic reforms. In this article, Edoardo Bazzaco surveys the NEP reforms, which dramatically opened the Bolivian economy, and promoted exports and private investment in strategic sectors of the economy, namely hydrocarbons and agroindustry. These reforms also propelled to prominence the department of Santa Cruz as the center of economic growth. Bazzaco examines the agricultural sector in Santa Cruz, particularly the soy sector, explaining how the structure of the industry as well as its regional and international ties allowed it to disproportionately benefit from the market opening policies. Bazzaco then explores the hydrocarbons sector, the second pillar of Santa Cruz's growth. Santa Cruz controls 40 percent of Bolivia's oil production as well as significant natural gas. As foreign investment flowed in and exports grew, three phenomena resulted: first, the increased power and internationalization of the business class; second, an increase in oil and gas activities; and third, an increase in the growth of the economy. He also explores the changes that resulted in the local Santa Cruz economy, including the emergence of the services (the tertiary) sector and a shift in employment from agriculture to services. Bazzaco documents the emergence of an informal and semiformal sector and notes the significant increase in the concentration of wealth, with the top 5 percent of the income ladder increasing their share of wealth while the income of the bottom 5 percent declined even further.

2050 Gray Molina, George. La economía boliviana más allá del gas. (*Am. Lat. Hoy/Salamanca*, 43, agosto 2006, p. 63–85, bibl., graphs, table)

Gray Molina addresses the expansion of Bolivia's economy beyond the gas sector to the development of other industries and the state's role in constructing the proposed economy. The author discusses the relatively slow growth in the 20 years preceding Morales' election and the plans of the Morales administration to diversify the economy, mainly through greater state interaction in the private sector. Gray Molina provides a thorough exploration of the reasoning and impetus behind the policy transition in Bolivia. The necessity to create marketable goods and ensuring poverty are two of the many reasons cited as encouraging the "base estrecha" model. The broadened base economy model is compared with other options and is estimated to increase the economy's diversity by 53.7 percent, the highest relative margin. Gray Molina looks at the public policy ramifications of economic reform, suggesting that subsidies, vertical integration, and the redistribution of markets are necessary. The author outlines a plan which provides for the diversification of the Bolivian economy with a continuation of a role for natural gas. The election of Evo Morales was greeted with optimism by many in 2006 and while this paper raises solid suggestions and ideas about improving Bolivia's economy, it very much reflects that optimism.

Kaup, Brent Z. A neoliberal nationalization?: the constraints on natural gas-led development in Bolivia. See item **1323**.

2051 Medinaceli, Mauricio. La nacionalización del nuevo milenio: cuando el precio fue un aliado. La Paz: FUNDEMOS; Munich, Germany: Hanns Seidel Stifting, 2007. 170 p.: bibl., ill.

Medinaceli's book assesses the prospects of nationalization of hydrocarbons in Bolivia. The author's goal is to contrast the three themes associated with reforms in the hydrocarbon sector: the theoretical justification for state involvement, the laws governing hydrocarbons enacted by Jaime

Paz Zamora and Gonzalo Sanchez de Lozada, and the 2006 law decreed by the Evo Morales administration. The advantages and disadvantages of various reform proposals are weighed and measured, with detailed explanations supporting or opposing the various different taxes and measures aimed at exploiting Bolivia's vast hydrocarbon resources. Medinaceli incorporates graphs, tables, and narratives to strengthen his research and his arguments. The author has composed an argument for state intervention which drives its foundations from scientific and mathematical assessments rather than a rhetorical or moralistic argument. As Bolivia's current trajectory has been marked by greater state involvement in the energy sector, Medinaceli's analysis is useful for an understanding of the issues at hand.

El péndulo del gas: estudios comparativos de política de hidrocarburos. See item **1338**.

2052 Villarroel-Böhrt, Sergio G. Reallocation of resources within the national productive system in Bolivia: a view from the perspective of tradable and non-tradable goods. (*Econ. Mex.*, 16:1, primer semestre 2007, p. 105–149, graphs, tables)

Villaroel-Böhrt examines the unemployment situation in Bolivia, identifying the negative impacts of real exchange rate shocks as the culprit for this internal imbalance. He also looks at the impact of changes in the destination of flows of foreign direct investment. Villaroel-Böhrt constructs a model disaggregating the economy into the tradable and nontradable goods sectors and shows how real exchange rate movements shift resources either along the production possibilities frontier or into the zone of unemployment. He shows how exchange rate shifts can result in the restructuring of the economy, with unemployment as a cost. In his conclusions, Villaroel-Böhrt offers some suggestions for government policy responses, including training the labor force.

2053 Water and free trade: a social vision of water. Textos de Miguel Solanes *et al.* La Paz: Agua Sustentable: International Development Research Centre: Fundación Solón: Naciones Unidas, CEPAL, 2007. 193 p.: bibl., col. ill.

This collection of essays, compiled by four authors, explores the issue of privatization and its relationship to the distribution of water. These papers include a history of regulations and statutes regarding water, with a historical context of past privatizations, and the current status of water as determined by international organizations. Case studies in Asia and Latin America are provided, as well as discussions of Latin America's recent free trade agreements and their impact on the role of private industry in the distribution and extraction of water. The first essay, written by Miguel Solanes, explains both the historical and legal precedents for and against general privatization, noting that privatization measures succeeded in Chile, but failed in Argentina and Bolivia. He also discusses water access as both a human right and as property of investors. Howard Mann's subsequent piece discusses trade, international law, and human rights, examining the legal arguments of various sides in the debate. The final article, by Pablo Solon and Denise Rodriguez, examines both trade treaties and the case of the Bechtel water privatization that started the Bolivian Water Wars of 2000. All three essays are thorough, well-organized, and factual rather than ideological. This collection is a valuable resource for researchers wanting an in-depth exploration of water production.

2054 Weyland, Kurt. The diffusion of innovations: how cognitive heuristics shaped Bolivia's pension reform. (*Comp. Polit./New York*, 38:1, Oct. 2005, p. 21–42)

Weyland examines the reasoning behind Bolivia's adaptation of pension privatization. He specifically addresses the importance of Chile's success with its pension privatization program in the decision of Bolivia's policymakers to pursue privatization measures. The author raises a number of theories about and psychological explanations for policy decisions and choices. Weyland determines that, despite the common conception that international entities play a decisive role in the decisions made by Latin American governments in the realm of fiscal policy, Bolivia was not prodded by the IMF, the World Bank, USAID, or other organizations to privatize the pensions of its workforce. Rather, he asserts that Bolivian policymakers were motivated by an economic downturn in the mid-1980s that

seemed to endanger the state's public social security system. Widespread economic growth in Chile during the same period of time motivated Bolivia's government to adopt similar policies, and Weyland notes that the Bolivians chose to study Chile's program over Argentine, Colombian, and Peruvian policymakers' attempts to implement similar reforms, and over examples outside Latin America. The author notes that Bolivia's privatization program was less than successful, as in 1997 legislators introduced a public alternative to the privatized system which benefited seniors dependent on pensions. The author documents the reasoning behind Bolivia's move towards privatization, why it was attractive, fundamental differences between Chile and Bolivia that made the Bolivian plan less viable, and concludes with some thoughts on how pension reform in Bolivia may have been more successful. Weyland's article offers an interesting blend of psychological theory, historical narrative, and economic data that effectively informs the reader about how decisions are made and reasons for their success or failure.

PERU

2055 Arce, Moisés. The repoliticization of collective action after neoliberalism in Peru. (*Lat. Am. Polit. Soc.*, 50:3, Fall 2008, p. 37–62, bibl., graphs)

Arce seeks to explain the changing basis of collective political activity resulting from economic liberalization. The prevailing school of thought associates neoliberal economic reforms with depoliticization and claims that civil society collective action has been eroded. Arce counters this by stating that alternative forms of protest have replaced collective action by labor actors. He further asserts that in fact economic liberalization has repoliticized collective political activity. The article describes these changes, dating from the 2002 protests against the privatization of water in the town of Arequipa during the regime change from the dictatorial Fujimori to the democratic Toledo. This transition created a more conducive environment for political opposition and protest. Growing disparities among regions gave rise to increased collective political activity. Arce's central message is that national policy decisions can no longer be made without taking into account civil society views.

2056 Barrantes, Roxana. Fondos especiales: la manera económica de hacer política redistributiva en el Perú. Lima: Instituto de Estudios Peruanos, 2009. 458 p.: bibl., ill., map. (Análisis económico; 26)

Barrantes explores the ways in which wealth redistribution can occur in Peru. She utilizes a blend of historical narrative, statistical data through graphs and charts, and case studies to discuss the relationships between the state's redistribution of wealth to the poor through various means, and the ability of each branch of government to redistribute wealth effectively. She finds that the executive branch has appropriated far more resources towards redistribution than the legislature. According to her findings, the two administrations which allocated the most funding for social welfare were Alan García during his first term and Alberto Fujimori during his 10-year rule. The author states that throughout periods in Peru's history, funds were limited by the Congress. Barrantes presents a significant amount of information, but does not make overt suggestions as to how to change Peru's system of distribution. This resource is especially useful in the context of the incoming leadership in Peru: what approach will it take to reduce poverty and inequality in the country?

2057 Boucher, Stephen; Catherine Guirkinger, and **Carolina Trivelli.** Direct elicitation of credit constraints: conceptual and practical issues with an application to Peruvian agriculture. (*Econ. Dev. Cult. Change*, 57:4, July 2009, p. 609–640, bibl., tables)

Boucher, Guirkinger, and Trivelli utilize surveys and mathematical approaches to analyze the impact of credit constraints on the distribution of loans and welfare received by the Peruvian poor. The authors discuss different ways to assess the effects of these constraints, and issues associated with lack of information and enforcement and their relationship to the rationing of credit. The article describes the benefits and shortcomings of the various ways the effects can be measured. The differentiation between unconstrained and constrained households is emphasized: asymmetric information significantly impacts constrained households, but does not impact unconstrained households. Suggestions for the improvement of direct elicitation methodology (DEM) are examined in the article as the DEM is determined to have the potential to be inaccurate in assessing transaction-cost rationing. The issue of risk rationing, in the event of credits seeking to avoid risky lending, is not examined thoroughly according to the authors. However, they conclude that the DEM standard for measuring the impact of credit is generally accurate. The authors' work is laden with facts, statistics, and charts but does not provide a contextual narrative for readers, and as such is less accessible to those who are not familiar with the subject matter. On the other hand, they do provide relevant recommendations that may enable researchers to improve their assessments of the effects of credit constraints.

2058 Castro, Juan F. Política fiscal y gasto social en el Perú: ¿cuánto se ha avanzado y qué más se puede hacer para reducir la vulnerabilidad de los hogares? (*Apuntes/ Lima*, 62, primer semestre 2008, p. 55–76, bibl., graph, tables)

Castro investigates the condition of government social programs in Peru between 1994 and 2004. He finds that external shocks in international markets affect the poorest households most severely and he explores which types of policies would insulate and protect the poor from household vulnerability. Castro melds quantitative mathematical assessments with qualitative policy recommendations to provide a comprehensive analysis of the issues at hand. Using survey data, the author attempts to determine the differences between poor households, including factors such as urban or rural location, whether the household has a man or woman as head, and other factors. He finds that the susceptibility of poor households is twice as high as households which are not poor, and that poor households receiving assistance from social programs are slightly less vulnerable, but not as stable as more affluent households. He also finds that social spending for the poor falls more than 4 percent for each 1 percent reduction in per capita GDP. Thus, he suggests a countercyclical fiscal rule to help protect social expenditure coverage during recessions. This is necessary but not sufficient: Castro suggests that Peru should complement the countercyclical reforms which are in place with a stronger social safety net, and programs that increase low-income consumer access to important goods during times of economic crisis. Castro's analysis is grounded in both substance and vision, and offers the reader suggestions regarding the improvement of social welfare in Peru.

2059 Ciquero Ibáñez, Victor Raúl and Juan Pablo Figueroa Bello. Eficiencia relativa en el gasto de los gobiernos regionales: un aporte al proceso de descentralización. (*Apuntes/Lima*, 60/61, segundo semestre 2007, p. 75–128, bibl., graphs, tables)

Ciquero and Figueroa use several different ranking systems to measure the performance of regional governments in Peru. The authors bring together a series of diverse sources and methods of analyzing public efficiency. The Malmquist Index, the estimates of the government DEA, and the Spearman rank correlation are among some of the methods tested. The authors conclude that many of the barometers for measuring performance can be accurate in certain instances but have flaws. For instance, the Spearman method is cited as being reliable if one takes into account its relative lack of sophistication in measuring efficiency. The DEA method is cited as being particularly susceptible to small errors, and the efficiency indicator itself is not entirely determinant of national economic performance. The authors make several recommendations, along the lines of simplifying the methods to make them more accessible and factoring in the pressure of different industries and regional capabilities. Ciquero and Figueroa offer a thorough discussion and critique of the methods used to analyzing performance in Peru.

2060 Cruz-Saco, María Amparo. In opposite directions: demographic transition and old-age pensions in Peru. (*Apuntes/Lima*, 58/59, segundo semestre 2006, p. 5–34, bibl., graphs, tables)

Cruz-Saco accounts for the various factors that explain demographic transitions in Peru and their impact on socioeconomic conditions such as national income and healthcare. The author identifies projected changes in Peru's population as the result of declining fertility rates and emigration or out-migration of Peruvians to other countries. Cruz-Saco assesses the impact of an aging population on the availability of pensions and quality of health care, while detailing various programs enacted by the Peruvian government in the 1990s and 2000s dealing with the aforementioned issues. An aging population in Peru has its benefits, as stated in the article, as it will cause the dependency ratio to fall, opening up an opportunity for saving. Cruz-Saco discusses the creation of social programs such as Crecer, an antihunger initiative, and EsSalud, a social security program funded by employers, employees, and the government. Remittances are shown to be increasing and are suggested as a potential antidote to the inability of a less populous, younger generation in Peru to care for a large population of aging Peruvians. The author projects that more than three-quarters of Peruvians over 65 will not have a pension by 2030, and, as a result, family transfers will become more critical to the Peruvian people's financial stability. Cruz-Saco combines concise explanations of Peru's transitions with numerous charts and graphs that effectively illustrate projected trends. The author's work suggests that more research is necessary to determine how Peru's government and its people can most effectively deal with vast demographic transitions and changes in transfer of wealth between generations to ensure the sustainability of the national economy.

2061 El gobierno corporativo en el Perú: reflexiones académicas sobre su aplicación: Backus, Graña y Montero, Incasur, Profuturo AFP, Red de Energía del Perú. Edición de Pedro Franco Concha, Gina Pipoli de Azambuja y Cinthia Varela García. Textos de Elsa del Castillo Mory *et al.* Lima: Univ. del Pacífico, Centro de Investigación, 2009. 394 p.: bibl., ill.

A collection of essays discussing the multiple sectors of Peru's economy, this anthology covers a wide variety of topics. The essays focus on corporate governance and offer insights into the reasons that several private enterprises have had success. The subjects covered in the text range from common sectors discussed in the political economy field, such as banking and energy, to other sectors such as the beer industry. The authors employ charts and graphs alongside narratives to substantiate their explanations. Each author concludes their work with company assessments. Useful for researchers interested in how private sector enterprises can succeed, and for consultants or advisors to business leaders seeking to improve their business model.

2062 La investigación económica y social en el Perú, 2004–2007: balance y prioridades para el futuro. Textos de Roxana Barrantes *et al.* Lima: Consorcio de Investigación Económica y Social, 2008. 427 p.: bibl. (Diagnóstico y propuesta; 40)

The work of 10 authors emerges in this thorough investigation of the various facets of Peru's economic and social situation in the 2000s. The authors explore numerous topics, ranging from Peru's relationship with the international economy to the inequality of the distribution of wealth. Each writer draws upon the investigation of prior researchers to provide the reader with a more complete picture of the many challenges and prospects associated with the Andean country. The essayists rely primarily upon narrative and the incorporation of statistical details in a textual rather than graphical format. Recommendations and suggestions emerge in the articles, but are delivered to the reader along with precise facts supporting their arguments: for instance, a passage focused on the gathering of information related to poverty in

Peru contrasts the differences in assessing poverty reduction between 1993 and 2005. Each essay has an extensive bibliography. A useful resource for researchers interested in a comprehensive study of the many social and economic issues facing Peru in the 21st century.

2063 Rosales, Luis A.; José L. Chinguel; and Darwin A. Siancas. Convergencia económica y el desarrollo humano en el norte del Perú: influencia de la salud, la educación y las transferencias a municipios 1995–2005. Lima: Consorcio de Investigación Económica y Social; Piura, Peru: Univ. Nacional de Piura, 2008. 131 p.: bibl., ill. (Investigaciones breves; 29)

A team of three authors have collaborated to research and analyze the relationship between growth and human development in the northern regions of Peru. Luis A. Rosales, Jose L. Chinguel, and Darwin A. Siancas look at various ways to assess economic growth, mathematically assess human development and its relationship to economic growth and policy as a whole, and offer some interpretations of their data. The data utilized by the authors helps contrast the three economic approaches: the neo-classic, the endogenic, and the convergence model. They rely on highly mathematical methods to make determinations, which make the text more accessible to a researcher with a more technical background. The authors conclude that there is little correlation between economic growth and human development. The analysis is heavily detailed, but does not overtly advocate for a particular policy. The book would figure most effectively into a project analyzing economic growth from a mathematical perspective.

CHILE

MARKOS J. MAMALAKIS, *Professor Emeritus of Economics, University of Wisconsin-Milwaukee*

PART I

GOD, THE MIND, FREEDOM, KNOWLEDGE AND ETHICS are, according to James Rachels, the main problems of philosophy. It is suggested here that these also are among the main problems and issues of law, politics, and economics. There is, however, in addition to the above, one fundamental problem, which is as much philosophical as it is legal, political, and economic, that implicitly dominates, but fails to be explicitly recognized, in any field: that of markets, in particular, that of Collective Services Markets (CSM). The agora (market) below the Athenian Parthenon, where Socrates used reason and observation in addressing the fundamental aspects of a good life, remains the quintessential, terra incognita, the epitome of an enlightened collective services market where the problems of God, the mind, freedom, knowledge, and ethics inherently belong and need to be explored. Behind every philosophical, moral, and economic issue and action, there is an agora, a market, where costly ideas are created, produced (cost), exchanged (traded), and used to satisfy (utility) individual, semi- and fully collective needs. The most significant lacuna in economics, as well as in law, politics, and philosophy is the lack of recognition and understanding of these collective services markets, where existential, quintessential, issues of good or bad life are explored. Major contributions to our understanding of the long-term economic evolution of Chile, through their exploration of selected aspects of its collective services markets, were recently published (items **2065**, **2066**, **2074**, and **2080**).

ECONOMIC, POLITICAL, AND SOCIAL WELLBEING: ORIGIN, DETERMINANTS AND IMPACT OF ALTERNATIVE COLLECTIVE SERVICES MARKET STRATEGIES

Collective services markets, the pivot determining which human needs are, or are not, satisfied, undergo substantial transformations during 1910–2011 overall, and, in particular during the 1910–1970, 1970–1973, 1973–1990 and 1990–2008(11) subperiods, largely in response to diverse governmental strategies aimed at overcoming Chile's economic inferiority as described by Francisco Encina in his classic *Nuestra inferioridad economica: sus causas, sus consequencias.*

The transformative impact of government strategies, directly upon all markets and ultimately, upon economic wellbeing, is determined by the (re)actions of all institutional units (IU), i.e. households (H), financial (FC) and nonfinancial corporations (NFC), nonprofit institutions (NPI) and government units (GU), and institutional sectors (IS), i.e., H, FC, NFC, nonprofit institutions serving households (NPISH) and general government (GG).

The results of government policies are reflected in the wellbeing of all IU and IS, as measured by the degree of recognition and satisfaction, or lack thereof, of the seven enlightened, complementary collective needs for safety, security, protection of life and private property, political freedom, economic freedom(s), equal treatment by government, social harmony, and environmental protection.

Furthermore, a widely used typology postulates a choice between small and large government. However, both in Chile and elsewhere in Latin America, it is not, in principle, an issue of minimalist (presumably liberal) versus a maximalist (presumably Marxist-Leninist) government. It is more a matter of choice between architectures of mesoeconomic constitutions and collective services markets espousing notions of morality at, or between, often diametrically opposed extremes. At one end, the liberal one, morality is defined, from the perspective of the "supremacy of the individual," both procedurally (accepting the principle of) and consequentially (attaining the goal) as using the power of the state to create enlightened collective services markets (based on enlightened liberal principles), where all IUs and ISs cooperate in recognizing and satisfying the enlightened collective needs for sanctity of life, political, social, and economic freedom, sanctity of private property and the environment, equal treatment by government and social harmony. At the other pole, the Marxist-Leninist one, morality is defined, from the perspective of the "supremacy of the state," both procedurally and consequentially, as using the power of the state to create Marxist-Leninist mesoeconomic constitutions and collective services markets where all IUs and ISs are coerced to accept government controls and state property while repressing the enlightened collective needs for freedom, private property, sanctity of life, equal treatment of all, and so forth.

Liberal mesoeconomic constitutions and collective services markets, which shaped the destiny of Chile between 1910 and 1930, contribute to remarkable, though still, only partial, improvements in the degree of satisfaction of the enlightened collective needs for sanctity of life and environmental protection, political and economic freedom, equal treatment by government, social harmony, and private property. They reduce, but hardly eradicate, Chile's economic inferiority. As product, labor and financial markets reel under recurrent, relentless, external, and lagged, internal business cycle shocks, poverty persists, inequality rises, and social harmony is weakened. Increasingly, chronic economic malaise is attributed to liberal mesoeconomic constitutions and collective services markets promoting economic freedom and private property.

The cataclysmic Great Depression of the 1930s and other powerful forces, opened the door to ever more comprehensive replacement of the pre-1930 liberal by an interventionist, structuralist, Conception of God, the Mind, Freedom, Knowledge and Ethics, of related mesoeconomic constitutions and collective services markets. Liberal morality, which perceives, on the one hand, economic freedom and private property as good and right, and, on the other hand, suppression of economic freedom and private property as bad and wrong, is increasingly displaced by structuralist morality which perceives economic freedom and private property as bad and wrong, and government intervention and state property as good and right. A superb description and analysis of the powerful forces shaping the fortunes of the Chilean economy during 1910–1960 is found in item **2065**.

Blaming Chile's economic inferiority, malaise of income stagnation, uncontrollable inflation, persistent unemployment and mounting social unrest, to decadent liberal capitalism and timid structuralism, President Salvador Allende Gossens lunged into a tectonic transformation of the failing Structuralist into a full fledged Marxist-Leninist Collective Services Market.

The tectonic, mesoeconomic, plates of the collective services market of the 1970–73 era, which embody the Marxist-Leninist paradigm of "morality," including its perception of the role of the Mind, freedom, knowledge, ethics, and even God, are, the pro-Marxist morality (notion of the Right and Good) plate, on the one hand, and the antiliberal morality plate (notion of Wrong and Bad), on the other hand. The pro-Marxist-Leninist mesoeconomics promotes the (Good and Right) collective needs for government-controlled markets and collective (state, public) ownership of property. The antiliberal, Marxist-Leninist mesoeconomics unleashes a merciless persecution and repression of the liberal (Bad and Wrong) collective needs for economic freedom and private property through press restrictions, confiscation, nationalization, indiscriminate takeovers and so forth.

A Marxist perspective of the rise and fall of the Allende Presidency is articulated in item **2078**. The importance of economic forces in the ascendancy and precipitous collapse of the Allende mesoeconomic, collective services market experiment, is underscored in item **2077**. The widespread human rights violations that occurred during the violent collapse of the Allende government are described in item **2079**. Lessons learned from the Allende reign and its demise are detailed in item **2074**. The tectonic struggle and virulent clash between Allende's Marxist-Leninist and Pinochet's liberal mesoeconomic constitutions and collective services markets is portrayed in item **2066**.

Instead of ostracizing or lessening Chile's inherited economic inferiority, President Allende's Marxist-Leninist mesoeconomic constitutions and collective services market architecture unleashed centrifugal forces of a magnitude unique in Chilean history. Inflation escalated into hyperinflation. Black markets, speculation, government deficits, land and enterprise takeovers spread fear, panic, and terror, escalating into precipitous anarchy and chaos.

September 11, 1973, the day President Salvador Allende Gossens committed suicide, marks the terminus of Chile's Marxist-Leninist experiment, and the authoritarian genesis, under the military and Gen. Augusto Pinochet Ugarte, of the unique, liberal, revolutionary mesoeconomic, collective services market venture. The Marxist-Leninist moral perspective with respect to God, the mind, freedom, knowledge, and ethics, of 1970–73, is replaced by an economically liberal, but politically repressive, moral perspective of God, the mind, freedom, knowledge, and ethics during the 1973–90 Pinochet dictatorship.

An excellent description and analysis of the powerful forces that precipitated the fall of Allende and the Marxist-Leninist mesoeconomic constitutions and collective services markets, and the rise of Pinochet and the liberal mesoeconomic constitutions and the collective services markets is found in item **2066**. A superb presentation of the continuity as well as differences between the Pinochet dictatorial (1973–90) and democratic (1990–2008(11)) mesoeconomic constitutions and collective services markets is offered in item **2074**. An excellent, balanced evaluation and survey of the link between political stability, on the one hand, and economic success and/or respect of human rights, on the other hand, is presented in item **2077**. A detailed description of the extensive, brutal, human rights violations during the violent overthrow of the Allende presidency by the military and Gen. Augusto Pinochet Ugarte is provided in item **2079**. A Marxist perspective of mesoeconomic constitutions' and collective services market failure throughout 1910–2010, is advanced in item **2078**.

The 1990–2008 democratic, mesoeconomic constitutions' and collective services market restoration, propels the satisfaction of the enlightened collective need for political freedom to heights, above and beyond, most of the 1910–70 era. In addition, the Concertación fully coopts the masterfully pure, but by no means perfect, elegant, liberal economy market craftsmanship of the 1973–90 Pinochet era, thus merging the best, historically, components of the partially efficient, partially defective collective services market configurations of the 1910–70, 1970–73 and 1973–90 periods.

Encina's ghost of economic inferiority is receding but not, yet, ostracized. A dark cloud is hovered over Chile during 2011 as widespread student unrest and demonstrations, which are supported by large segments of the population, demanded changes in major segments of the liberal reforms imposed during the Pinochet presidency, especially with respect to education. It remains to be seen how, and if, Chile can manage the upheaval generated by a conflict between the morality as embodied in current institutions and that advocated by the students and their supporters.

The positive impact of free markets on property values as a result of expansion of metro lines is documented in item **2064**. The advanced level of corporate governance as a consequence of the high level of satisfaction of the enlightened collective need for political freedom is demonstrated in item **2072**. Described in item **2067** is the reciprocal strengthening of economic freedom and private public networks of loyalty and trust. A solid explanation of the high growth rate of Chile, as compared to the rest of Latin America, in terms of superior liberal mesoeconomic constitutions and collective services markets, is presented in item **2071**. The persistence of inequality in the relative distribution of income is thoroughly explored in item **2080**. Surveyed in item **2081** are the multiple policies pursued by the government aimed at improving labor market efficiency. The 1990–2008 (11) democratic collective services market is systematically explored in item **2074**.

PART II

1. THE COLLECTIVE NEED, SERVICE, MARKET AND MESOECONOMIC CONSTITUTIONS "FOR" (SAFETY, SECURITY, SANCTITY AND PROTECTION) VERSUS "AGAINST" (REPRESSION OF) HUMAN LIFE.

All IUs and ISs have been active participants in Chile's collective service market trying to promote (liberal tradition) the production of the enlightened collective service satisfying the collective need for safety, security, and sanctity of life, or to suppress it (Marxist-Leninist tradition). The 1970–90 era is marked by unprecedented metamorphoses of this market as a violent clash emerges between IUs and ISs espousing liberalism and adherents of Marxism-Leninism. The sanctity of life collective services market experiences a profound, though not necessarily immutable, renaissance upon the revival of democracy in 1990.

A balanced exposition of the revival of the collective services market of sanctity of life and the related mesoeconomic constitutions is provided in item **2074**. As documented in item **2065**, in spite of sharp, ongoing external and internal natural, economic and political jolts, the degree of satisfaction of the enlightened collective need for sanctity of life and the efficiency of the corresponding collective services submarket is increasing during the 1910–70 period.

The incredible human rights violations, and ruthless repression of the enlightened collective need for safety, security, protection of life of a large segment of Allende's Unidad Popular (Popular Unity) Extended Political Family, especially during the early phases of the Pinochet (1973–90) dictatorship, and their lasting scars etched on Chile's Collective Services Market and memory are powerfully highlighted in item **2079**. Presented in item **2079** is the thesis that the empresarial, corporate, group (both the IU and the IS) has been the most relevant actor since independence in controlling the power of the state, in using it to violate the human rights of people, in determining the nature of collective services markets and shaping the mesoeconomic constitutions.

2. THE COLLECTIVE NEED, SERVICE, MARKET AND MESOECONOMIC CONSTITUTIONS "FOR" (PROMOTION) VERSUS "AGAINST" (REPRESSION OF) POLITICAL FREEDOM.

All IUs and ISs are existential members of, and participants in each and every collective services market. Thus, they shape, and/or are affected, by the degree to which the power of the state is used to satisfy needs embodying such divergent notions of morality as the liberal and Marxist-Leninist ones. The dramatic metamorphosis of the Chilean collective service for political freedom market during 1970–2008 (11), and its tectonic impact on all other collective services markets, provides invaluable information with respect to the impact of all collective services markets, but in particular of the political and economic freedom ones, on the wellbeing of all Chilean IUs and ISs.

According to item **2077**, the stability of a political system, whether authoritarian or democratic, depends on the degree to which human rights are violated or respected and on the success or failure of economic policy. The existential complementarity between the enlightened collective services markets producing the collective services of political and economic freedom satisfying the corresponding collective needs, is documented in detail in item **2074**. As reported in item **2072**, a high level of satisfaction of the enlightened collective need for political freedom facilitates an advanced level of corporate governance.

3. THE COLLECTIVE NEED, SERVICE, MARKET AND MESOECO-NOMIC CONSTITUTIONS "FOR" (PROMOTION) VERSUS "AGAINST" (REPRESSION OF) ECONOMIC FREEDOM(S).

Never before in the history of Chile has the enlightened collective need for economic freedom been satisfied through the production of the corresponding enlightened collective service of economic freedom, as comprehensively as it has been since 1973. Never before, and maybe nowhere else, has the market of the enlightened collective service of economic freedom been as efficient as in Chile after 1973. Never before, and maybe nowhere else, has the path to economic efficiency in production, distribution and accumulation, been paved by, as painful, economic, political, and social adjustment costs, to all IUs and ISs, as those experienced in Chile, at least for a decade after 1973. Never before, in Chile, and maybe nowhere else, has the metamorphosis of the economic freedom collective services market been so intimately linked to a parallel metamorphosis of the private property collective service market. Never before, and maybe nowhere else, has it become as evident as in Chile that the path to accelerated economic growth and modernization involves enlightened metamorphoses of all seven enlightened collective services markets.

The need for continued support and efficiency of the collective service market of enlightened freedom is emphasized in item **2074**. The beneficial effects of free markets are documented in item **2064**. A detailed, comprehensive, realistic, objective account of the arduous process of creating a liberal, collective service freedom market, is presented in item **2066**. An excellent survey and analysis of the multiple forces shaping the collective service for economic freedom market and successive mesoeconomic constitutions are found in item **2065**.

In analyzing the determinants of economic wellbeing, all publications reviewed in this essay focus on the procedural and consequential role of economic freedom in its multiple incarnations within the boundary of a liberal mesoeconomic constitution, on the one hand, and complete destruction through a coercive mesoeconomic constitution, on the other hand.

There exists an almost unanimous political consensus on the acceptance, adoption, and strengthening of the liberal collective services market determining the production of the enlightened collective service satisfying the moral collective need for economic freedom in all input (labor, man-made capital, and natural resource) and output markets.

According to the Heritage Foundation and the Wall Street Journal 2011 Index of Economic Freedom, Chile's economic freedom score is 77.4, making its enlightened, collective services market economy, the 11th freest, in the 2011 index, among 179 countries. Chile enjoys the highest degree of satisfaction of its moral collective need for economic freedom in South and Central America/Caribbean region, and its ranking is higher than in the United Kingdom (16), Germany (23), Uruguay (33), Brazil (113), Argentina (138), Venezuela (175) and Cuba (177).

4. THE COLLECTIVE NEED, SERVICE, MARKET AND MESOECO-NOMIC CONSTITUTIONS "FOR" (PROMOTION) VERSUS "AGAINST" (REPRESSION OF) EQUAL TREATMENT BY GOVERNMENT.

According to the interventionist, including the Marxist-Leninist, conception of morality, government intervention, in the form of unequal treatment by government of all IUs and ISs, is necessary to overcome the extreme injustices and inequalities suffered by all IUs and ISs due to excesses unleashed by economic freedom in markets and uncontrolled private property. Unequal treatment by government through extensive controls of all markets, and restriction, if not abolition, of free markets and private property, is perceived as the only sufficient condition for advancing overall, as well as individual, wellbeing of all IUs and ISs. Since the Great Depression of the 1930s, the pendulum did increasingly swing in favor of the interventionist conception of morality and government policy, culminating in the Allende, 1970–73, Marxist-Leninist experiment, without, however, alleviating any major forces contributing to Chile's economic inferiority. According to the liberal perception of morality, the market where the moral collective service of equal treatment by government of all IUs and ISs is produced, and the corresponding moral collective need of all IUs and ISs to be treated equally by government, is satisfied, is vital in shaping the wellbeing of each and all IUs and ISs.

The mesoeconomic constitutions and collective services markets involved in the production of the collective service of equal treatment by government and the satisfaction, of the corresponding moral collective need to be treated equally, of all IUs and ISs, increase in efficiency with less government intervention and decrease in efficiency with more government intervention. Less government intervention (more economic freedom) is identified with more equal treatment, more government intervention (less economic freedom) with more unequal treatment by government. Never before in Chile and nowhere else in Latin America, has the liberal conception of "equal treatment by government" morality been implemented as forcefully as in Chile after 1973, and embraced, with modifications, after 1990 by the democratic presidencies. It has successfully overcome many, but not all, forces responsible for Chile's economic inferiority. The tectonic metamorphosis of the 1970–73 Marxist-Leninist (un)equal treatment by government market of the Allende presidency into the post-1973 liberal (un)equal one, is powerfully documented in item **2066**. An excellent survey and analysis of the multiple forces shaping the (un)equal treatment by government market and associated mesoeconomic constitutions during 1910–60 is presented in item **2065**. Extremely informative expositions of diverse aspects of the (un)equal treatment by government markets are found in item **2078** (Marxist perspective); item **2069** (international dimensions); item **2080** (unequal distribution of income); and item **2074** (broad overview).

5. THE COLLECTIVE NEED, SERVICE, MARKET AND MESOECO-NOMIC CONSTITUTIONS "FOR" (IN QUEST OF) VERSUS "AGAINST" (IN VIOLATION OF) SOCIAL HARMONY.

The degree of satisfaction of the enlightened collective need for social harmony has been highly uneven during the 1910–2011. It reached historically dismal levels during the Allende and Pinochet presidencies. The very conception of social harmony has varied reflecting, often diametrically, different interpretations of morality by liberal, Marxist-Leninist, and other perspectives. It has improved since 1990. Overcoming Encina's economic inferiority may be signaled by a rise in the satisfaction of the social harmony collective need by, and for, all IUs and ISs.

No segment of Chile's Collective Services Market has been as underdeveloped, debated, and critically important for its political, social, and economic well-being as, that of Social Harmony. This collective services market is recognized as Chile's Achilles' heel, not only during the Age of Pinochet (1973–90) and Democratic Reign (1990–2011), as documented in detail in items **2069**, **2074**, and **2080**, among others, but also during the 1910–60 period as described in item **2065** and the Marxist interregnum of Salvador Allende of 1970–73 as narrated in items **2077** and **2078**.

6. THE COLLECTIVE NEED, SERVICE, MARKET AND MESOECO-NOMIC CONSTITUTIONS "FOR" (SAFETY, SECURITY, SANCTITY AND PROTECTION) VERSUS "AGAINST" (ERADICATION OF) PRIVATE (PUBLIC) PROPERTY.

In no other Chilean collective services market have the liberal camp, which proclaims the collective need for private property to be supreme, sacrosanct, moral, right, good, and nonnegotiable, and the Marxist-Leninist camp, which declares the collective need for public property to be good, moral, right, absolute, inviolable, and unchallengeable, confronted each other as virulently as in the property market. Upon overthrowing the legitimate democracy of President Salvador Allende, and assuming the power of the state in 1973, the military and Gen. Augusto Pinochet Ugarte used the power of the state to enact a liberal mesoeconomic property constitution and create a parallel liberal collective service market. The enlightened collective need for safety, security, protection, and sanctity of private property was enshrined in the constitution as sacrosanct and irrevocable. Both procedurally (based on principle) as well as consequentially (result of action), exceptionalism may be a well-earned characterization of the liberal mesoeconomic constitution of sanctity of private property and the parallel enlightened private property collective services market. This exceptionalism continues to shine during the post-1990 Democratic presidencies of Patricio Aylwin Azócar (1990–94), Eduardo Frei Ruiz-Tagle (1994–2000), Ricardo Lagos (2000–2006), Michelle Bachelet (2006–2010), and Sebastián Piñera (2010). Although protection of private property is a necessary condition for growth and prosperity, it is by no means a sufficient one. There exists no magic wand anywhere enabling all IUs and ISs to create output, income, and wealth, and, even less so, to enable them equally. There exist, however, unlimited means, paths, and policies that can enhance the abilities of all IUs and ISs to create output, income, and wealth and minimize any negative repercussions of inequalities as a consequence of economic freedom and private property. Meeting these challenges would permit Chile to overcome many aspects of its Encina-postulated economic inferiority.

The turbulent, sometimes virulently clashing and globally pioneering, architectonics of Chile's property collective services market, during 1910–2011, are carefully explored in the following publications: The multiple forces that shape the degree of satisfaction of the, sometimes complementary, other times competitive, collective services need for private and/or public property, during 1910–60, are carefully examined in item **2065**. A prominent, firsthand documentation of the unparalleled revolutionary metamorphosis of the chaotic Marxist-Leninist collective services property market of the 1970–73 Allende presidency, to an entirely liberal, in economic terms, architecture during the Pinochet dictatorship of 1973–1990, is provided in item **2066**. A superb analysis and documentation of the flawless continuation of the liberal mesoeconomic constitution and collective services market of private property, which were created during the 1973–90 Pinochet presidency, throughout the course of the ensuing remarkable democratic presidencies is found in item **2074**. The high efficiency of capital markets as a consequence of the high degree of satisfaction of the enlightened collective need for sanctity of private property is described in item **2072**.

7. THE COLLECTIVE NEED, SERVICE, MARKET AND, ENLIGHTENED, MESOECONOMIC CONSTITUTIONS FOR (OF) ENVIRONMENTAL SAFETY, SECURITY, SANCTITY AND PROTECTION VERSUS THE PERILOUS MESO-ECONOMICS OF ENVIRONMENTAL IMPAIRMENT, DEPLETION AND DESTRUCTION.

The market where the enlightened collective need for environmental protection is satisfied, through production of the corresponding enlightened collective service, has faced numerous challenges between 1910 and 2011. Reducing Encina's economic inferiority has remained a major challenge as this market has been exposed to ever greater threats posed by national as well as global land, air, and water pollution.

Selected dimensions of the degree the enlightened collective need for environmental protection is satisfied, and thus, of the efficiency of the respective enlightened collective services market are examined in the following studies: environmental benefits and costs of major energy demand and supply components, potential energy crisis and environmental implications (item **2073**); environmental sustainability of the energy sector (item **2068**); the presumed iron grip on Chilean destiny, including its collective services market for environmental integrity, by its business elite (item **2079**); the structural damage of the environment and its implications on the future of humanity (item **2069**); the liberal collective services market economy and the environment (item **2066**).

2064 Agostini, Claudio and **Gastón Palmucci.** Capitalización anticipada del metro de Santiago en el precio de las viviendas. (*Trimest. Econ.*, 75:298, abril/junio 2008, p. 403–432, bibl., graphs, tables)

This article presents an excellent empirical analysis of the degree of capitalization in housing prices that resulted from the construction of the new line four of the metro in the Chilean city of Santiago. Authors suggest that increased property values could lead to higher property taxes. This revenue, in turn, would defray part of the metro construction costs.

2065 Almonacid Zapata, Fabián. La agricultura chilena discriminada, 1910–1960: una mirada de las políticas estatales y el desarrollo sectorial desde el Sur. Madrid: Consejo Superior de Investigaciones Científicas, 2009. 475 p.: bibl., ill. (Col. América; 16)

In this major seminal study, Almonacid Zapata makes an impressive, lasting contribution to the already rich economic historiography of Chile. The book's central objective is to provide an explanation for the generally recognized stagnation of agriculture during 1910–60. According to the dominant structuralist school largely identified with CEPAL, agricultural stagnation, both in absolute terms as well as relative to industry, was caused by the inherent backwardness of the landowners and agriculture's colonial institutions. After a detailed, balanced analysis of the writings of influential structuralist authors such as George McBride, Anibal Pinto, Jorge Ahumada, Moisés Poblete, and many others, Almonacid rejects the structuralist thesis as incompatible with the evidence. According to the dominant alternative explanation, agricultural backwardness has been the inevitable consequence of inadequate government policies promoting industry, discriminating against agriculture, and neutral with respect to construction, along the Mamalakis Theory of Sectoral Clashes and Coalitions, which is reviewed in detail, as well as advanced in the writings of Adolfo Mathei, Roberto Echeverría, Jorge Soto, and others. As the book's title suggests, Almonacid concludes, based on evidence, that negative government policies were largely responsible for agricultural stagnation, rather than the parasitic behavior of landowners tracing back to the colonial period. Thus, first, Almonacid holds that negative government policies were the fundamental cause for the poor performance of national agriculture. Second, he focuses on the permanent discrimination of agriculture in the South as a result of general agricultural discrimination aggravated by political and economic centralization. Third, he demonstrates that all power groups in the Center supported government policies favoring discrimination, while punishing the South. Fourth, the interest groups of the South were largely coopted by those of the Center. Furthermore, events in Chile were negatively affected by global forces such as the Great Depression of the 1930s, along with adverse trade agreements with Argentina and the agricultural surplus conventions with the US of the 1950s. A special bonus to the reader of this excellent study is the remarkable, comprehensive historical background information provided for the entire 1910–60 period.

2066 Büchi Buc, Hernán. La transformación económica de Chile: el modelo del progreso. Santiago: Mercurio: Aguilar, 2008. 338 p.: bibl.

Never before in the history of Chile and Latin America has a transformation in the architecture of a nation's collective services market been as radical as the one that materialized during the 1973–90 dictatorial presidency of Gen. Augusto Pinochet Ugarte. And no single individual contributed to the creation and has as intimate a knowledge of the painful, remarkable, ultimately successful process of replacing the bankrupt 1970–73 Marxist-Leninist architecture of government ownership of means of production and control over mar-

kets with an economically liberal, but ruthlessly repressive political regime as Büchi, a presidential candidate and runner-up to the triumphant Patricio Aylwin of the Concertación in 1989. Quite appropriately, the subtitle of the book's first edition, *Del estatismo a la libertad económica,* is replaced by the more teleological *El modelo del progreso* in this revised edition. As Büchi points out in his seminal, uniquely informative contribution, this "economic miracle" could never have materialized without the unwavering support of Pinochet and the military, a puritan professional team, and adherence to enlightened, fundamental economic principles.

2067 Bull, Benedicte. Policy networks and business participation in free trade negotiations in Chile. (*J. Lat. Am. Stud.,* 40:2, May 2008, p. 195–225, bibl., table)

According to this study, within Latin America, Chile is distinguished by its stable trade policies and rapid negotiation of trade agreements with countries and regions all over the world. Explanations for these phenomena often point to the stable pro-free trade coalition established in the aftermath of the shock-therapy pursued in the 1970s, and Chile's professional government bureaucracy. Although both of these elements are important, this article shows how the rapid integration of Chile into the world economy has also depended on the existence of business associations with expertise in trade issues. Through the process of integration, a close policy network has evolved between key public officials and business representatives. This finding is premised on the mutual recognition of expertise in the public and private sectors, and is held together by close personal networks of loyalty and trust across the public-private divide. However, while the development of such a policy network has been highly favorable to the process of negotiating trade agreements, it has also contributed to the de facto exclusion of societal actors that have less to contribute to trade negotiations than business sectors.

2068 Chile: energy policy review. Paris: OECD: International Energy Agency, 2009. 264 p.: bibl., col. ill., col. maps.

This excellent energy policy review

takes a comprehensive look at Chile's energy sector, including: the institutional framework, energy security, environmental sustainability, energy efficiency, as well as recent developments in subsectors such as fossil fuels, electricity, renewables, biomass, access to energy in rural areas, transport, and energy research and development. The volume provides an objective picture of the multiple energy challenges faced by Chile and makes valuable suggestions for addressing them.

2069 Fazio, Hugo. EE. UU. centro de las crisis globales: los frágiles "blindajes" de la economía chilena. Santiago: LOM Ediciones, 2008. 245 p.: bibl. (Ciencias humanas. Economía y globalización)

According to this wide-ranging monograph by Fazio, a prolific public servant, economist, and journalist, the ongoing complex process of transformation within the global economy has materialized at the cross-section of two crises: one cyclical and one structural. The cyclical, with its epicenter in the US, was transmitted to the developing world through the global capital markets. Its financial repercussions assumed an enormous relevancy and complexity as a result of the creation of sophisticated financial mechanisms. The structural crisis, then, revealed with clarity the contradictions generated by the dominant forms of the globalization process, such as the crises of the dollar and the global system of reserves, the obsolescence of the Bretton Woods institutions, the rise in unequal income distribution, the protectionist and subsidy policies of the great powers, the damage to the environment and its implications for the future of humanity, the limitations and deformities introduced by the declining role of the state, and the inroads of the emerging economies. Fazio argues that these processes and forms can be modified, with work. Worldwide globalization can acquire progressive expressions and, thus, spread its potential.

2070 García Hurtado, Álvaro. Estándares laborales y tratados de libre comercio: el caso de Chile. (*Integr. Comer.*, 10:25, julio/dic. 2006, p. 207–250, bibl., graphs, tables)

This article suggests that Chile is a good case to analyze the relationship between labor standards and commercial treaties, a result of the vast networks which Chile has signed with all countries of the Americas, with the European Union, and with various countries in Asia and Oceania. In most cases, the agreements include the labor issue. García Hurtado concludes that the basis for including labor issues in the commercial agreements is the Declaration of the International Labor Organization (ILO) of 1998. As a consequence, the commercial agreements do not impose labor obligations in addition to those Chile assumed in the ILO. Without exception, the signed agreements do not address commercial sanctions for unfulfilled labor legislation. As a result, commercial agreements, with explicit reference to fulfillment of labor standards, only reinforce the fulfillment of the standards defined and agreed upon in the ILO. Accordingly, commercial integration through free trade will not generate new labor standards. Moreover, this study demonstrates that the main challenges for the fulfillment of labor standards (high informality, low institutional capacity to prosecute the fulfillment of labor law, low levels of unionization) are not perceived as affected by the trade agreements. Any effort to overcome the difficulties of labor market implementation, within the framework of trade agreements, requires that these agreements include cooperation in informality, low productivity, and opening of markets in labor-intensive areas. This space of cooperation finds a positive precedent in NAFTA, which was not extended to the agreement signed by Chile with each NAFTA member country, nor does it form part of the framework of negotiation of the Free Trade Area of the Americas (FTAA). Any attempt to include labor standards in commercial integration will require facing the reality that at least 50 percent of the Latin American labor force is not covered by the legislation which establishes those standards.

2071 Hernández, Leonardo and **Fernando Parro.** Economic reforms, financial development and growth: lessons from the Chilean experience. (*Cuad. Econ./Santiago*, 45:131, mayo 2008, p. 59–103, appendix, graphs, tables)

According to this solid, comprehensive study, despite reform efforts, the economic performance of Latin American countries during the 1990s was disappointing—with the exception of Chile, which grew at almost seven percent per year. This paper attempts to explain this disparity. Following recent literature that highlights the role of institutions and policies on economic growth, the authors estimate a cross-section econometric model over the 1960–2005 period and find that Chile's better performance can largely be explained by a combination of better institutions and reforms that have been deeper and broader in scope than those in the rest of Latin America. In addition, they estimate that improving institutions in other Latin American countries to the Chilean Standard would have increased per-capita GDP growth rates by about 1.5 percentage points.

2072 Lefort, Fernando and **Teodoro Wigodski.** Una mirada al gobierno corporativo en Chile: casos emblemáticos. Santiago: Pontifícia Univ. Católica de Chile, Ediciones Univ. Católica de Chile, 2008. 121 p.: bibl., ill., index. (Lecciones)

In this excellent monograph, the authors provide a superb evaluation of corporate governance in Chile by examining in detail the cases of Telefónica, Soquimich, Chispas, Falabella and Almacenes París. This study reveals the challenges and solutions attained in an advanced capital market such as Chile's.

2073 Mancilla, Sergio. La crisis energética en Chile. Providencia, Chile: RiL Editores, 2009. 173 p.: bibl., ill., maps (some col.). (Bibliodiversidad) (Ensayo)

In this provocative, comprehensive study, Mancilla examines all major components of the supply and demand of energy in Chile. He concludes that the Chilean energy crisis can not be resolved unless the state assumes comprehensive ownership and control of the electric energy sector.

2074 Muñoz Gomá, Oscar. El modelo económico de la concertación, 1990–2005: reformas o cambio? Santiago: FLACSO Chile: Catalonia, 2007. 287 p.: bibl.

This seminal, balanced monograph constitutes an effort to improve the understanding of the social market economic system developed by the Concertación governments since 1990. Its central objective

is to assess the so-called market economy model as it has been adopted and adjusted by Aylwin (1990–94), Frei-Tagle (1994–99) and Lagos (2000–2006). Indirectly, it also provides an answer to the oft-raised question of the success of the transition from the liberal, free market strategy of the Pinochet dictatorship to the social market strategy of the Concertación. According to Muñoz, the free market system offers development opportunities, but by itself is not sufficient to solve all problems of economic coordination. To become more effective, equitable, and efficient, it needs to be nourished within an institutionality with a benevolent boundary shaped by, and promoting, harmonious relations among the state, society, and the private sector—thus paving the path to the social market economy. According to Muñoz, three fundamental axes have been responsible for this smooth transition: 1) the capacity of the political dialog and the center-left coalition to deliver democratic political sustainability; 2) economic policies that brought macroeconomic stability and consolidated market competitiveness, efficiency, and dynamism; and 3) the creation of a social institutionality that recognized and sought to redress such systemic iniquities as extreme poverty and social discrimination.

2075 Neilson, Christopher et al. The dynamics of poverty in Chile. (*J. Lat. Am. Stud.,* 40:2, May 2008, p. 251–274, appendix, bibl., tables)

The main objective of this well-researched paper is to study the dynamic aspects of poverty in Chile using panel (longitudinal) data from the CASEN (Encuesta National de Caracterización Socioeconómica) database from 1996 and 2001. The poverty dynamics are examined by decomposing poverty into transitory and chronic components, by identifying the direct causes of the change in poverty status and finally, by considering the factors underlying the poverty dynamics for a wide range of poverty lines. Chile has been successful in reducing poverty levels in the past. Further headway in its social policy of poverty reduction, however, will need to address the dynamic features of poverty which reveal that many more households experience transient poverty.

2076 Niño, Jorge and **Juan Pablo Romero.** How the change of CEO affects Chilean companies' stock returns. (*Lat. Am. Bus. Rev.*, 8:1, 2007, p. 37–64, graphs, tables)

In this article, the first of its kind for Chile, the authors use the event study methodology to analyze the effects on Chilean companies' stock returns that the change of CEO causes. They find that when the change occurs after a period of poor performance, it is associated with significant positive abnormal stock returns. In certain cases, the abnormal returns accumulate to six percent over the seven-day period following the announcement. The study also shows that the observed abnormal returns have increased since the market regulating agency obligated companies to communicate changes in top management within three days of their occurrence.

2077 Rosemberg Fuentes, Velvet. El desarrollo económico y los derechos humanos en la consolidación democrática de Chile. (*Cuad. Am./México*, 1:123, enero/marzo 2008, p. 73–91, bibl., tables)

In this balanced, thorough, and intrinsically interesting article, the author makes a singular contribution to our understanding of the degree of sustainability (success or failure) of authoritarianism, as compared to democracy, by focusing on the impact of two fundamental forces: the success or failure of economic policy and the promotion or violation of human rights. An additional, central contribution of this review article consists of its explicit focus on the generally underemphasized relationship between who controls the power of the state, e.g., the military (associated with authoritarianism) or the people (generally defined as democracy), and how this power is used. The extensive scholarly evidence reviewed here suggests that both authoritarianism and democracy are vulnerable to economic failure while violation of human rights during the Pinochet dictatorship led to its fall and the peaceful, electoral transition of Chile to democracy. The unique, undeniable economic torch shining in Chile during the politically repressive Pinochet era is defined by its unprecedented (in post-1930 Latin America), full-fledged choice and adoption by a military dictator of an enlightened liberal, free market economic strategy, instead of the dominant, ultimately disastrous, interventionist CEPAL approach or Cuba's Marxist economic and political totalitarianism.

2078 Taylor, Marcus. Globalization and the internalization of neoliberalism: the genesis and trajectory of societal restructuring in Chile. (*in* Internalizing globalization: the rise of neoliberalism and the decline of national varieties of capitalism. Edited by Susanne Soederberg, Georg Menz, and Philip G. Cerny. New York, N.Y.: Palgrave Macmillan, 2005, p. 183–199)

This interesting chapter examines multiple determinants of the genesis and trajectory of the unprecedented, radical, neoliberal experiment of restructuring that Chile carried out during the authoritarian Pinochet presidency (1973–80) and the democratic period of the first three Concertación governments of Aylwin (1990–94), Frei-Tagle (1994–99) and Lagos (2000–2006). The perspective, terminology, and interpretation of accurate statistics are largely Marxist. The first part describes the societal crisis and stagnation of the late 1960s and early 1970s caused by the defective, failing, structuralist development strategy and the growing tensions that precipitated the violent Pinochet dictatorship and its early monetarist and neoliberal reforms. The second part examines the era of the debt crisis and the reorientation of the neoliberal trajectory in the mid- and late 1980s. The third part describes the "growth with equity" strategy implemented by three Concertación governments upon restoration of democracy (1990–2006).

2079 Torres G., Osvaldo. La violencia de los padres fundadores: élite empresarial y las violaciones a los derechos humanos, 1973–1981. Santiago: Editorial Forja, 2008. 170 p.: bibl.

Financial and nonfinancial corporations are vital institutional units (IU) and sectors (IS) participating in all input and output markets. The relationship between corporations and collective services markets falls within two opposite patterns. At one extreme, government embraces the goal of promoting economic and universal growth and wellbeing by expanding the "state owned" segment of the corporate world through a coalition between government and state-owned enterprises. This strategy was followed, with varying degrees of intensity, during the democratic Chilean presidencies (1930–73). All enterprises located in Chile, whether state or private, Chilean or foreign-owned, were provided with extensive, sometimes absolute, protection from foreign competition. The Chilean Development Corporation (CORFO)'s Herculean effort to redress the cataclysmic impact of the depression of the 1930s permeated all economic activities, solidifying the economic foundations of modern Chile. During the 1970–73 Allende presidency, the Chilean government embarked on a unique experiment of implanting a Marxist-Leninist-Castro style collective services market. Annihilation of private enterprise through comprehensive nationalization, statization, and confiscation of all enterprises, whether Chilean or foreign-owned, emerged as the central, de facto, pillar of the Unidad Popular government, especially its uncompromising revolutionary extreme left. A historically unprecedented cloud of panic and chaos shrouded Chile as ever stronger attacks against private corporate and other ownership were carried out. A sudden, unexpected swing to the opposite, extreme liberal end of the spectrum of the collective services market paradigms materialized in 1973 as a military junta and Gen. Pinochet overthrew Allende and replaced the democratically elected Unidad Popular government with a military dictatorship.

2080 Vega Fernández, Humberto. En vez de la injusticia: un camino para el desarrollo de Chile en el siglo XXI. Santiago: Debate, 2007. 447 p.: bibl., ill. (some col.).

According to Vega Fernández, the author of this highly informative and well-documented monograph, the inequality in Chile's relative income distribution is both visible and well-documented statistically for years. However, the possibility of treating this transcendental theme as a matter of public policy is very recent as it has lost its ideological bias of the past and many members of the academic and political world agree that persistent and increasing inequality could become a great obstacle for the development of Chile. In this work, Vega presents a detailed understanding of the evolution of inequalities and injustices of the Chilean society from historical, empirical, and theoretical perspectives. He also proposes the strategies needed to overcome them, thus making the objective of increased economic, social, and cultural justice legitimate, possible, and desirable for the majority of the population and citizenship in a democratic society.

2081 Velásquez P., Mario. Chile: superando la crisis, mejorando el empleo: políticas de mercado de trabajo, 2000–2005. Santiago: Organización Internacional del Trabajo, 2006. 108 p.: bibl., ill.

Chile has developed numerous programs to satisfy the enlightened collective needs for social harmony, economic freedom, and protection of life through multiple governmental strategies aiming to improve labor market efficiency. This excellent study describes and evaluates the multiple challenges, strategies, impact, and interactions of the multifaceted labor market policies during 2000–2005 when Chile was exposed to the Asian financial crisis.

ARGENTINA, PARAGUAY, AND URUGUAY

ANA MARGHERITIS, *Professor of Political Science, University of Florida, Gainesville*

THE LITERATURE ON SOUTHERN CONE POLITICAL ECONOMY is overwhelmingly focused on the Argentine case. In particular, the concern with the implications of the 2001 crisis is evident. In the context of a wave of left-wing governments coming to office across the region in the 2000s, there has been a turn towards interventionist economic policies that has reasserted the role of the state in the regulation of socioeconomic processes and has partially rejected orthodox free market principles. Argentina under Néstor and Cristina Kirchner illustrates this point. The nationalization of the Argentine flagship airline and the pension system in the past few years (both privatized in the 1990s as per the Washington Consensus' recommendations) are paradigmatic examples of this trend. Stephen Kay's study on pension system reform offers a cautious warning against the political risks involved in those measures (item **2107**). Among others, the work by Jean Grugel and Pía Riggirozzi provides a comprehensive account of the emergence of a post-neoliberal model in the aftermath of the 2001 crisis and pays due attention to the developmental components that may affect the chances of becoming a sustainable project (item **2105**).

Along with the "return of the state," the other major concern of the literature relates to economic recovery and the sustainability of the new policy orientation. The recent performance of Southern Cone economies in general and Argentina in particular, as well as their short- and long-term prospects, is assessed in reference to the search for a better positioning in regional and global markets. In this respect, the analyses highlight continuity trends in Latin American political economy and find that the outward-oriented model is not in question. However, the impact of increasing economic ties with extrahemispheric countries (mainly, China) is proof of the recent diversification of trade partnerships and has become a recurrent theme. Some studies elaborate on the social and political implications of this trend, including the formation of new supporting coalitions for the neopopulist regimes in office today; the piece by Neal Richardson on Argentina illustrates this point (item **2119**).

Within the regional dimension, economic integration issues are particularly salient. Despite Mercosur's modest progress in the last decade, the regional trade bloc continues to be the focus of considerable scholarly attention. The volume by Jeffrey Cason, entitled *The Political Economy of Integration: The Experience of Mercosur*, stands out as a thoughtful explanation of the reasons behind the limited success of the Southern Cone integration process (item **2132**). As the bloc approaches its 20th anniversary, the author suggests a reconsideration of the factors that account for both progress and shortcomings. The comparative approach draws on the European Union experience.

The scant works on Uruguay and Paraguay take either a historical or an interdisciplinary approach to questions of development, such as population and urbanization, wealth distribution and poverty, and the impact of specific economic policies at the local level.

I am grateful to Adrian Zeh for valuable research assistance.

ARGENTINA

2082 La Argentina como geografía. Vol. 2, Políticas macroeconómicas y sistema regional, 1990–2005. Coordinación de Omar Horacio Gejo y Ana María Liberali. Textos de Ana María Liberali *et al.* Mar del Plata, Argentina: Univ. Nacional del Mar del Plata; Buenos Aires: Centro de Estudios

Alexander von Humboldt; Argentina: Unión Geográfica de América Latina: Red Latinoamericana de Estudios Gegráficos de la UGI, 2009. 2 v.: bibl., ill., maps.

The work argues that prior to 1990, Argentina adapted to world markets through a division of labor among different regions in the country. Authors examine the detrimental effects of contemporary world markets on this system, emphasizing the inter-relation of state policies, the international system, and regional consequences.

2083 Bekerman, Marta and **Santiago Rodrí-guez.** Políticas productivas para secto-res carenciados: microcréditos en Argentina. (*Desarro. Econ.*, 47:185, abril/junio 2007, p. 95–118, bibl., graphs, tables)

This article analyzes the recent ex-perience and potential of microfinance institutions in Argentina, including the role of the state; the supply and demand for the programs; their successes, impacts, and limitations; as well as differences between public and private behavior in microfinance. The authors propose recommendations for improvements to these programs and for what they believe should be the state's role in the sector.

2084 Belini, Claudio and **Marcelo Rougier.** El estado empresario en la industria argentina: conformación y crisis. Buenos Aires: Manantial, 2008. 338 p.: bibl., graphs, tables. (Cuadernos argentinos)

A historical analysis of the rise, orga-nization, evolution, and demise of several state-run industries in Argentina from 1941–81. The study focuses on the bureaucracy, ties between the state and business, and the government's role in direct intervention, and argues that the state is again becoming increasingly active in the economy.

2085 Bisang, Roberto; Guillermo Anlló; and **Mercedes Campi.** Una revolu-ción (no tan) silenciosa: claves para repen-sar el agro en Argentina. (*Desarro. Econ.*, 48:190/191, julio/dic. 2008, p. 165–207, bibl., graphs)

This article provides a historical over-view of the agricultural sector in Argentina, with a focus on its resurgence in recent de-cades. The authors analyze the many factors responsible for the revival of the industry, including modernization and mechaniza-tion of farming practices, organizational restructuring, and changes in international markets. They also make predictions for the future of the sector.

2086 Brennan, James P. Prolegomenon to neoliberalism: the political economy of populist Argentina, 1943–1976. (*Lat. Am. Perspect.*, 34:3, May 2007, p. 49–66, bibl.)

The article focuses on the economic policies of Argentine governments from 1943–76 through an analysis of the country's banking system. The author argues that there was continuity across Peronist, radi-cal, and military governments in following a model of state capitalism, with disputes primarily concerning the distribution of wealth rather than the system itself.

2087 Brenta, Noemí. Argentina atrapada: historia de las relaciones con el FMI, 1956–2006. Prólogo de Mario Rapoport. Bue-nos Aires: Ediciones Cooperativas, 2008. 590 p.: bibl., graphs, ill., tables.

A critical analysis of the role of the IMF, the US, and Argentine national govern-ments in recurrent economic crises in the country during the second half of the 20th century and in 2001, from an economic, political, and structural perspective.

Carassai, Sebastián. The noisy majority: an analysis of the Argentine crisis of December 2001 from the theoretical approach of Hardt & Negri, Laclau and Žižek. See item **1431.**

2088 Caravaca, Jimena and **Mariano Plot-kin.** Crisis, ciencias sociales y elites estatales: la constitución del campo de los economistas estatales en la Argentina, 1910–1935. (*Desarro. Econ.*, 47:187, oct./dic. 2007, p. 401–428, bibl., tables)

Despite economics only recently be-ing defined as a distinct field in many Latin American countries, the authors argue that the profession has achieved a great deal of public legitimacy in the region. Specifically, the article focuses on economists trained at the Universidad de Buenos Aires between 1914–30, when a group of these professionals would come to redefine state-society rela-tions in the country.

2089 Cayetano Olivero, Juan and **Sebastián Olivero.** Trayectoria, futuro y valor del sector rural argentino. Buenos Aires: Editorial Dunken, 2007. 135 p.: bibl., tables.

This work provides a historical over-view of the Argentine rural sector, arguing for long-term structural, rather than cycli-cal, analysis. The authors seek to under-score the value of the rural sector and call for greater civic and political involvement, as well as rapprochement between the city and countryside.

2090 Congreso de Economía, 7th, Buenos Aires, 2006. Argentina, camino al bicentenario: los desafíos de una nueva oportunidad histórica. Buenos Aires: EDICION Fondo Editorial Consejo, Consejo Profesional de Ciencias Económicas de la Ciudad Autónoma de Buenos Aires, 2007. 201 p.

A collection of essays presented at the 7th Congreso de Economía (Buenos Aires). Chapters discuss the current global economic situation and Argentina's place within the world economy, including an examination of trade agreements and blocs, as well as national strategies for development in the medium- to long-term, with chapters on fiscal policy, the labor market, and institutions.

2091 Cortés Conde, Roberto. The political economy of Argentina in the twentieth century. New York, N.Y.: Cambridge Univ. Press, 2009. 388 p.: bibl., ill., index, maps. (Cambridge Latin American studies)

A historical examination of the evolution of the Argentine economy from the 1880s to 1989 through the framework of the changing political and legal institutions of the state. The author argues that, whereas international factors had a great deal of influence on the economy during the first half of the 1900s, domestic policy decisions were largely behind the subsequent decline. For review of Spanish-language original, see *HLAS 65:2360.*

2092 Cunha, André Moreira and Andrés Ferrari. A Argentina depois da conversibilidade: um caso de novo-desenvolvimentismo? (*Rev. Econ. Polít.,* 29:1, jan/março 2009, p. 3–23, bibl.)

In contrast to the neoliberal reforms of the 1990s, the authors argue that after 2002, Argentina followed a "new" development strategy combining economic growth and an increasing state role. The article contends that Argentine society historically has been more favorable toward the liberal economic model, and raises questions about the limits, risks, and long-term viability of the current program.

2093 Da Silva, Sidney Jard. Novos modelos previdenciários na América Latina: lições da experiência Argentina. (*Rev. Econ. Polít.,* 28:2, abril/junho 2008, p. 312–330, bibl., graphs)

This article analyzes pension reforms in Argentina, beginning with a discussion of pension programs throughout Latin America and evaluating regional responses to the pension system crisis. The author then focuses on the interplay between economic imperatives and political constraints in pension reform in Argentina under the Menem government in the late 1990s, arguing that the new system has failed to deliver on many of its promises.

2094 Dagdeviren, Hulya. Political economy of contractual disputes in private water and sanitation: lessons from Argentina. (*Ann. Public Coop. Econ.,* 82:1, March 2011, p. 25–44, bibl., tables)

This article examines four cases of water and sanitation privatization in Argentina to analyze the legal, economic, political, and social problems that arose and led to the reversal of these policies. The author argues that three factors were behind disputes and renegotiations: economic viability, water quality, and the interpretation of contracts and legal rules.

2095 Datz, Giselle. What life after default?: time horizons and the outcome of the Argentine debt restructuring deal. (*Rev. Int. Polit. Econ.,* 16:3, Aug. 2009, p. 456–484, bibl.)

The author analyzes the 2005 restructuring of Argentina's sovereign debt, arguing that current models overestimate costs incurred to reputation in obtaining future loans, underestimate constraints on national governments, and overlook short-term effects. Findings imply greater flexibility for governments in taking contentious policies and that restructuring deals may be advantageous to debtors and even certain creditors.

2096 Del sistema de indicadores de desarrollo sostenible: actualización y re-lectura 2008. Coordinación de Sandra Carlino y Natalia Irurita. Buenos Aires: Instituto Di Tella: Buenos Aires Gobierno de la Ciudad: Siglo XXI, 2008. 378 p.: bibl., ill. (some col.), maps (some col.).

Following a discussion of the methodology employed, the authors examine social, environmental, economic, and institutional indicators for sustainable development, with a final section examining the interrelationships between these sectors. Authors also make recommendations for future development.

2097 Economía pública de Argentina y España. Edición de Héctor R. Gertel, Ernesto Rezk y Alejandro D. Jacobo. Buenos Aires: Fondo Editorial Consejo, 2007. 408 p.: bibl., graphs, ill., tables.

A varied analysis of the economics of the public sector in Argentina and Spain at international, regional, national, and provincial levels. Contributors on Argentina focus on the successes and failures of Mercosur, institutions, federalism and fiscal responsibility, primary education, income distribution, and the socioeconomic impacts of irrigation in arid areas.

2098 Encuentro Nacional de Economías Regionales, 7th, Santa Fe, Argentina, 2006. Plan Fénix: propuestas para el desarrollo con equidad. Santa Fe, Argentina: Univ. Nacional del Litoral; Buenos Aires: Univ. de Buenos Aires, 2007. 369 p.: bibl., ill.

A collection of lectures presented at the 7th Encuentro Nacional de Economías Regionales and the 4th Encuentro del Nodo Región Centro de Economías Regionales. Chapters take a regional perspective on economic and social development in Argentina, including discussions of desertification, the instability of the labor market, tourism, and small and medium businesses, among other topics.

2099 El estado y la reconfiguración de la protección social: asuntos pendientes. Coordinación de Marta Novick y Guillermo Pérez Sosto. Textos de Lilia M. Archaga et al. Buenos Aires: Instituto Di Tella: Siglo XXI, 2008. 542 p.: bibl., ill., index.

The authors in this volume present an analysis of the current state of social protection programs in Argentina. Essays focus on the recent restructuring of the state, the role of employment in the sector, models of development and social integration, contemporary issues, and problems specific to youth.

2100 Etchemendy, Sebastián and Ruth Berins Collier. Down but not out: union resurgence and segmented neocorporatism in Argentina, 2003–2007. (Polit. Soc./Los

Altos, 35:3, Sept. 2007, p. 363–401, graphs, tables)

The authors argue that a resurgence of a downsized labor movement has led to a form of "segmented neocorporatism" in Argentina. The work concludes that this result is due to economic and political factors in the short and long term, including the condition of the labor market, the political strategy of the government, and the institutional and structural conditions of the economy. See also item **2550**.

2101 Foros del Bicentenario, 1st, Buenos Aires, 2007 Sept. 20. Del Ford Taunus a la soja transgénica: reflexiones en torno a la transición argentina al siglo XXI. Coordinación de Jorge M. Katz et al. Buenos Aires: Edhasa, 2009. 194 p.: bibl., ill. (Foros del Bicentenario, ponencias)

A collection of essays presented at the 1st Foros del Bicentenario, analyzing the history of scientific and technological development in Argentina, with an emphasis on the negative effects of recent neoliberal policies. The book calls for long-term public policy to promote development through scientific advancement.

2102 Frid, Carina Laura and Norma S. Lanciotti. La recepción del pensamiento económico italiano en espacios académicos de la Argentina, 1914–1930. (Estud. Soc./Santa Fe, 18:34, primer semestre 2008, p. 105–119)

This article analyzes the impact of Italian economic ideas in Argentina from the 1890s to the 1930s, beginning with marginalist economic perspectives and ending with nationalist economic thought. Though both would be influential during the period, the authors argue that concepts of authoritarian leadership and corporatism would later prove incompatible with Argentine academic reformism in the early 1920s.

2103 García Heras, Raúl. El Fondo Monetario y el Banco Mundial en la Argentina: liberalismo, populismo y finanzas internacionales. Tel Aviv: Univ. de Tel Aviv, Instituto de Historia y Cultura de América Latina; Buenos Aires: Ediciones Lumiere, 2008. 222 p.: bibl. (Nuevas miradas a la Argentina del siglo XX)

The author uses sources from Argentina, England, and the US to provide a comprehensive analysis of the role of the IMF and World Bank in Argentina during the 1950s and 1960s, comparing the experience to that of other Latin American countries and helping to explain recent conflicts with these institutions.

2104 Giraudy, Agustina. The distributive politics of emergency employment programs in Argentina, 1993–2002. (*LARR*, 42:2, 2007, p. 33–55, bibl., tables)

One of a growing number of works devoted to understanding the determinants of antipoverty program spending. Here the author analyzes provincial spending patterns for Argentina's various unemployment programs implemented during the 1990s, finding that partisan and institutional factors are more important components to a fuller account of program spending than those based on a purely clientelism-driven model. For political scientist's comment, see item **1444**. [J. Hiskey]

2105 Grugel, Jean and **Pía Riggirozzi.** The return of the state in Argentina. (*Int. Aff./London*, 83:1, Jan. 2007, p. 87–107, tables)

Following the 2001 economic crisis, the authors argue that Argentine governments have rejected the neoliberal model, opting instead for a more dynamic role for the state in growth and social stability. They analyze the emergence of "neodesarrollismo" and the subsequent attempts to institutionalize the new model, concluding with an evaluation of its constraints, limits, and sustainability.

2106 Jiménez Huerta, Mariana. Neoliberal restructuring, financialisation and socio-political competition in Argentina: the Convertibility System and the contradictory outcomes of dollarisation, 1989–2001. (*Contemp. Polit./London*, 14:3, Sept. 2008, p. 335–355, bibl.)

Through an analysis of the convertibility system in Argentina, the work critiques orthodox views of monetary policy in international political economy, which assumes a process of convergence in financial markets. The author contends that outcomes are highly variable, depending on a complex set of factors including international financial flows, states, market actors, and domestic politics.

2107 Kay, Stephen J. Political risk and pension privatization: the case of Argentina, 1994–2008. (*Int. Soc. Sec. Rev./Geneva*, 62:3, July/Sept. 2009, p. 1–21, bibl., graphs)

The author examines pension privatization in Argentina in the mid-1990s and the decision to nationalize the private individual accounts system in 2008. The work argues that pension privatization does not insulate pension funds from political risk, but simply creates new forms of risk as pensions continue to be a potential financial resource for governments.

2108 Kornblihtt, Juan. Crítica del marxismo liberal: monopolio y competencia y monopolio en el capitalismo argentino. Buenos Aires: RyR, 2008. 187 p.: graphs, index, tables. (Investigaciones CEICS)

A historical analysis of the stainless steel tubing and flour mill industries in Argentina, critiquing Argentine neo-Marxists' characterization of world capitalism as entering a monopolistic stage. Instead, the author portrays Argentina's recurrent economic crises as a normal function of the capitalist world economy.

2109 López, Pablo J. Problemas de política económica en las condiciones del desarrollo desigual: industrialización y control de cambios en la Argentina entre 1931 y 1955. Buenos Aires: Ediciones Cooperativas, 2008. 203 p.: bibl. (Col. Tesis y tesinas de historia económica)

The author examines the impact of exchange rate controls in Argentina between 1931–55, with an emphasis on their impact on industrialization. The author argues that exchange rate controls formed part of the government's broader protectionist policy designed to foster development. In the end, the policy did not achieve its desired outcome.

2110 Marshall, Wesley C. Foreign banks and political sovereignty: the case of Argentina. (*Rev. Polit. Econ.*, 20:3, July 2008, p. 349–366, appendix, bibl.)

An analysis of the conflict between foreign banks and the Argentine national government in the banking crisis of 2001–2002. The article focuses on the banks' attempts to undermine the government's strategy of pesofication and argues that foreign banks come to wield a considerable amount of political strength when controlling a local market.

2111 Medio siglo de economía: conmemorativo del 50o aniversario de la Asociación Argentina de Economía Política. Edición de Alfredo M. Navarro. Prólogo de Alberto Porto. Buenos Aires: Asociación Argentina de Economía Política: TEMAS Grupo Editorial, 2007. 615 p.: bibl., ill.

An ambitious work chronicling the last 50 years of Argentine economic history, including the evolution of economic theory and methodological analysis. Contributors analyze themes including macro and microeconomics, structural inflation, the international economy, and growth to give a comprehensive view of the subject.

2112 Melo, Marcus André Barreto Campelo de. Institutional weakness and the puzzle of Argentina's low taxation. (*Lat. Am. Polit. Soc.*, 49:4, Winter 2007, p. 115–148, bibl., graphs, tables)

Using a "transaction cost politics" approach, the author seeks to explain Argentina's historically low levels of taxation. The work argues that systemic instability—caused in part by political institutions and the federalist system—has affected the tax behavior of governments in the country, leading to an incumbent preference to extract resources from society through inflation rather than taxation. For political scientist's comment, see item **1456**.

2113 Muñoz, María Antonia. Crisis política y conflicto social en Argentina: alcances y límites de un tipo de participación política no convencional. (*Rev. Eur. Estud. Latinoam. Caribe*, 87, Oct. 2009, p. 63–92, bibl.)

The author argues that the economic and political crisis of 2001–2002 in Argentina transformed the neoliberal principles of free markets and a reduced state into enemies of the "people" in the country. The work analyzes the antagonistic nature of the political conflict that emerged during the period, contrasting the reality of the situation to concepts proposed by hegemonic theories.

2114 Nállim, Jorge. Between free trade and economic dictatorship: socialists, radicals and the politics of economic liberalism in Argentina, 1930–1943. (*Can. J. Lat. Am. Caribb. Stud.*, 33:65, 2008, p. 139–175, bibl.)

The author contrasts Argentine socialist and radical party political rhetoric between 1930–43 with the groups' positions on state intervention in the economy. Despite ideological critiques of the Concordancia government to the contrary, the author argues that there was a growing consensus across party lines in favor of an increased state role in the economy.

2115 Narodowski, Patricio. La Argentina pasiva: desarrollo, subjetividad, instituciones, más allá de la modernidad: el desarrollo visto desde el margen de una periferia, de un país dependiente. Buenos Aires: Promoteo Libros, 2007. 304 p.: bibl. (Col. Ciencias sociales)

Focusing on greater Buenos Aires, the author employs theory and fieldwork to study Argentina's "passive" response to economic crisis at the local, state, and international levels, incorporating subjectivity into economic analysis. The work proposes a "plan for action" based on autonomy and micropolitics, while accounting for constraints imposed by the international system.

2116 Novaro, Marcos. Argentina en el fin de siglo: democracia, mercado y nación, 1983–2001. Buenos Aires: Paidós, 2009. 661 p.: bibl. (Historia argentina)

Ninth and final volume of the series Historia Argentina, directed by Tulio Halperin Donghi (see, for example, *HLAS 36:3176*). The work examines the establishment of democracy and the rule of law under the Alfonsín and Menem governments, highlighting the economic difficulties that prompted increasingly turbulent transformations of the political system and ultimately led to collapse in 2001.

2117 Núñez, Ana. Abrir la política urbana y las identidades sociales: ni empresarios, ni burócratas, ni vecinos: estatalizad profunda y estatilidad extensa. (*Econ. Soc. Territ.*, 9:30, mayo/agosto 2009, p. 297–347, bibl., ill.)

Through an analysis of struggles for and with water and sanitation in Mar del Plata, Argentina, the author examines social relations in urban areas. The article focuses on the construction of traditional categories of urban policy that objectify the state, business, and residents, leading to the construction of social spaces the author refers to as "deep statality" and "extense statality."

2118 Pierbattisti, Damián. La privatización de los cuerpos: la construcción de la proactividad neoliberal en el ámbito de las telecomunicaciones, 1991–2001. Buenos Aires: Prometeo Libros, 2008. 219 p.: bibl., ill.

The author examines the privatization of ENTel, the state telephone company, and its takeover by Telefónica de Argentina. The work argues that this process represented more than economic change, as the company attempted to transform workplace culture and the very identity of employees by "privatizing" individuals through the manipulation of language.

2119 Richardson, Neal P. Export-oriented populism: commodities and coalitions in Argentina. (*Stud. Comp. Int. Dev.*, 44:3, Fall 2009, p. 228–255, bibl., graphs, ill.)

An examination of the export-oriented populism that emerged under Néstor Kirchner's 2003–2007 administration. A principal difference with previous populist policies in Argentina is the base for fiscal revenue: soybeans, which are not consumed by urban workers, rather than beef or wheat.

2120 Schaumberg, Heike. In search of alternatives: the making of grassroots politics and power in Argentina. (*Bull. Lat. Am. Res.*, 27:3, July 2008, p. 368–387, bibl.)

An ethnographic analysis of the effects of recent neoliberal reforms of the Argentine state and subsequent changes in power relations within the country. Through two case studies in Argentina, the author focuses on state-subaltern relations, arguing that the national government played an important role in shaping subaltern responses to the 2001 crisis.

2121 Tommasi, Mariano. Federalism in Argentina and the reforms of the 1990s. (*in* Federalism and economic reform. Edited by Jessica S. Wallack and T.N. Srinivasan. New York: Cambridge Univ. Press, 2006, p. 25–84, bibl., graphs, tables)

Beginning with a general description of Argentine fiscal federalism, the author analyzes the relationship between federal-

ism and neoliberal reforms in the 1990s, with a focus on key "institutional" moments during the period. The chapter argues that the reforms enjoyed mixed success at best and explores connections between federalism, the 2001 crisis, and policy-making in education.

2122 Trabajo, ingresos y políticas en Argentina: contribuciones para pensar el siglo XXI. Edición de Javier Lindenboim. Textos de Luis Beccaria *et al.* Buenos Aires: Eudeba, 2008. 375 p.: bibl., ill. (Temas Economía)

A compilation of essays analyzing the recent economic recovery in Argentina and comparing this period to the 1990s and beyond. Using macroeconomic data, the authors argue that recent economic gains have not translated into improvements in overall well-being and raise questions as to how the state could promote equality while maintaining growth.

2123 Transformaciones territoriales y productivas en el mercado de trabajo litoral. Coordinación de Marta Panaia. Buenos Aires: Impresiones Buenos Aires—Editorial, 2007. 431 p.: bibl., ill., map.

The essays in this compilation focus on the Argentine provinces along the Bioceanic Corridor. Contributors discuss the effect of the construction of the roadway on regional inequality, labor markets, and the links between productive zones and technological and scientific production, including implications for regional integration, Mercosur, and international markets.

Viola, Eduardo J. and **Héctor Ricardo Leis.** Sistema internacional com hegemonia das democracias de mercado: desafios de Brasil e Argentina. See item **2210.**

2124 Wolff, Jonas. De-idealizing the democratic civil peace: on the political economy of democratic stabilization and pacification in Argentina and Ecuador. (*Democratization/London*, 16:5, Oct. 2009, p. 998–1026, bibl.)

The author argues that the procedural quality and material achievements of governments are more useful in predicting democratic stability than liberal concepts of a "democratic civil peace." The work develops a conceptual framework to analyze patterns of stabilization and pacification in Argentina and Ecuador, with a focus on explaining the viability of these regimes despite recent economic and political upheaval.

PARAGUAY

2125 Ferrer, Renée. Un siglo de expansión colonizadora: núcleo poblacional establecido en torno a la Villa Real de la Concepción: origen y desarrollo socio-económico. 2. ed. Asunción: Centro de Estudios Antropológicos de la Univ. Católica, 2008. 176 p.: bibl., ill., map. (Biblioteca de estudios paraguayos) (Col. Bicentenario)

A historical analysis of the population of Villa Real de la Concepción in northern Paraguay. The author argues that the city would become the most important social and economic center in the region in the 80 years following its establishment in 1773, highlighting criollo immigration to the city, conflict with the indigenous population, and the development of the yerba mate industry.

2126 Hetherington, Kregg. Privatizing the private in rural Paraguay: precarious lots and the materiality of rights. (*Am. Ethnol./Washington*, 36:2, May 2009, p. 224–241)

An examination of apparent contradictions in the concept of privatization among Paraguayan peasants, who oppose the process despite living on privately titled land. The author argues that this condition arises from tension in liberal theories of property rights and relationships between individuals, which have viewed property solely as an abstract right or as a right mediated by material conditions.

2127 Kleinpenning, J.M.G. Rural Paraguay 1870–1963: a geography of progress, plunder and poverty. Madrid: Iberoamericana; Frankfurt am Main, Germany: Vervuert, 2009. 2 v.: bibl., ill., indexes, maps. (Bibliotheca Ibero-americana)

The work complements a previous publication covering Paraguayan human geography from early colonization to the 19th century (see *HLAS 61:1849*). The author provides a comprehensive analysis of the Paraguayan rural economy and countryside between the end of the war with

Brazil, Argentina, and Uruguay, and the implementation of the new Agrarian Statute of 1963. For geography specialist's comment, see item **969**.

URUGUAY

2128 Calderón, César and Alberto Chong. Rent seeking and democracy: empirical evidence for Uruguay. (*Econ. Inq.*, 45:3, July 2007, p. 592–601, bibl., tables)

The authors use econometric analysis to examine the relationship between rent-seeking behavior and democracy in Uruguay. Findings support other literature on the subject, which argues that while democratic longevity may reduce rent-seeking behavior, rent-seeking behavior may undermine democracy.

2129 Goldfrank, Benjamin and Andrew Schrank. Municipal neoliberalism and municipal socialism: urban political economy in Latin America. (*Int. J. Urban Reg. Res.*, 33:2, June 2009, p. 443–462, bibl., tables)

The authors introduce concepts of "neoliberal" and "socialist" urban policy regimes in Latin America, including Uruguay, to examine how municipalities have adapted to changes in government policies and the international market. The article questions conventional views on the power of central governments and the lack of agency attributed to Latin American cities.

2130 Zurbriggen, Cristina. Estado, empresarios y redes rentistas durante el proceso sustitutivo de importaciones: las condicionantes históricas de las reformas actuales. Montevideo: Ediciones de la Banda Oriental, 2006. 193 p.: bibl., ill.

An analysis of the rentier characteristics of business-government relations in Uruguay during the period of import substitution industrialization. The author argues that these practices became institutionalized in the economy, government, and society, highlighting the difficulties in overcoming this system in the present day.

MERCOSUR

2131 Botto, Andrea Paula. ¿Quién defiende a los consumidores?: la regulación de los servicios públicos residenciales en

Argentina y en Brasil después de las privatizaciones. Buenos Aires: Prometeo Libros,
2007. 209 p.: bibl.

A comparative analysis of consumer
protection agencies in Argentina and Brazil,
including their collaboration with other
social actors, consumer mobilization, and
mechanisms adopted to ensure transparency. The author argues that while strategies in Argentina tend to be short-term and
limited in scope, in Brazil they are tied to
broader issues of public welfare, resulting in
varying outcomes.

2132 Cason, Jeffrey W. The political economy of integration: the experience
of Mercosur. New York: Routledge, 2010.
150 p.: bibl., ill., index, tables. (Routledge
Studies in the Modern World Economy)

This work examines the reasons
behind Mercosur's limited success through
a comparison with the European Union. The
author argues that Mercosur's relative "failure" is primarily due to weak domestic political institutions in the member countries,
vulnerability in the global economy, and
an imbalance in the economic and political
weight of the members.

**2133 De la tierra sin mal al tractorazo:
hacia una economía política de la
yerba mate.** Coordinación de Javier Gortari.
Posadas, Argentina: Editorial Universitaria,
Univ. Nacional de Misiones, 2007. 489 p.:
bibl., ill., map.

A compilation of academic works,
journalistic articles, and other sources
analyzing the sociopolitical and economic
history of the yerba mate industry in Argentina, Brazil, and Paraguay. Contributors focus on the negative effects the industry has
had on the Guaraní indigenous population,
proposing analytical and policy-oriented
tools to aid the struggle for social justice.

**2134 La industria automotríz en el
MERCOSUR.** Coordinación de An-
drés López. Textos de Valeria Arza *et al.*

Montevideo: Red MERCOSUR de Investigaciones Económicas, 2008. 259 p.: bibl., ill.
(Serie Red Mercosur)

Using international tendencies in the
automotive sector as a reference, contributors analyze public policy and its impact
on the automotive industry in Argentina,
Brazil, and Uruguay, and make national and
regional policy recommendations. Authors
conclude that only Brazil has come close to
meeting national objectives justifying public support for the sector.

**2135 Primos ricos y empobrecidos: creci-
miento, distribución del ingreso e
instituciones en Australia-Nueva Zelanda
vs Argentina-Uruguay.** Coordinación de
Jorge E. Álvarez Scanniello, Luis Bértola y
Gabriel Porcile. Montevideo: Editorial Fin
de Siglo, 2007. 347 p.: bibl., ill.

An analysis of differing economic
and social development in similar societies,
comparing Argentina and Uruguay to Australia and New Zealand. Compiling both
previous articles and more recent essays,
contributors examine structural, institutional, and historical changes in these countries, among other topics, and articulate
opportunities for future study.

**2136 Who decides the budget?: a politi-
cal economy analysis of the budget
process in Latin America.** Edited by Mark
Hallerberg, Carlos G. Scartascini, and
Ernesto Stein. Washington, D.C.: Inter-
American Development Bank, 2009. 300 p.:
bibl., ill.

The book points out a lack of empirical analysis of the budgetary process
in Latin America and includes chapters on
Argentina, Paraguay, and Uruguay. Authors
examine a number of topics, including relations between the executive and legislature,
the sustainability of government policies,
the quality of public provisions, and the
connection between policies and popular
preferences.

BRAZIL

MELISSA H. BIRCH, *Associate Professor, School of Business, University of Kansas*
RUSSELL E. SMITH, *Professor and Associate Dean, School of Business, Washburn University*

THE WORKS REVIEWED FOR THIS VOLUME, mostly published between 2006 and 2009, provide a window into the interests of political economists in the second half of the first decade of the 21st century. At the time of these publications, the successful implementation of the 1994 Real Plan was a full decade in the past. In the macroeconomic policy sphere, the post-Real, neoliberal stabilization policies of the first and second Cardoso administrations (1995–98 and 1999–2002) continued in the administrations of Partido dos Trabalhadores (PT) President Lula da Silva (2003–2010), although with expanded initiatives in the social sphere. Most importantly, beginning in 2004, Brazil experienced a relaxed external constraint, enjoying large inflows of foreign direct investment and an international trade surplus due to the export of primary agricultural and mineral products to China. This development greatly improved Brazil's debt and payments situation, providing the underpinning for sustained economic growth. In addition to price and political stability, the positive balance of payments, the success of social policy initiatives, and the prospect of becoming a major energy exporter (of both petroleum and ethanol) in the medium term contributed to a general climate of optimism.

As a result, the political economy literature is broadly positive concerning Brazil and its economic prospects. This sense of accomplishment is particularly salient in a growing literature on globalization (item **2140**), Brazil among the BRICS (item **2143**), and Brazil's increasing role on the world stage (item **2202**). The volumes produced by an annual forum of influential economists examine Brazil's role in the post-1989 world order and as a regional power (item **2163**), the possibility of achieving a sustained, long-run, high growth rate (item **2161**), and the strategy for a creative economy, innovation, and Brazil's global firms (item **2160**). Some (item **2151**) note that Chinese demand for Brazilian exports ended Brazil's general pattern of economic stagnation that dated from around 1975. On the other hand, some argue critically (item **2159**) that the Lula government's apparent success was the result of temporary external factors and that its social programs will not result in a meaningful, long-term improvement in income distribution. Some take a middle ground, arguing that technologies and the capacity for innovation developed during the ISI period may provide the basis for innovation, leading to new sources of competitiveness (item **2165**). Several authors (items **2171** and **2204**) are optimistic about the new industrial policy announced in 2002 and its effectiveness in spurring creative responses to global conditions.

The subjects of development, underdevelopment, and Brazil's long march toward first-world status remain constant in Brazilian economic literature. Two long-time observers of Brazil, Thomas (item **2206**) and Roett (item **2192**), have written new books that examine Brazil at this critical juncture in its path to developed country status. They emphasize the importance of appropriate policy choices at this time of opportunity. Brazil's new status in the global economy leads authors to reflect on the necessity of an explicit development policy. One collection (item **2142**) argues for a political consensus in favor of a post-neoliberal, "neo-developmentalist" vision of the state managing economic growth for greater social inclusion. Other volumes suggest components of such a strategy. Prominent in the period under review are a number of remembrances in honor of Celso Furtado, who died in 2004 (see, for example, item **2194**).

As might be expected, several volumes focus on Lula administration policies. Many authors laud the policies, while others are critical—particularly of the president's social policies. In spite of years of polemic about neoliberal reforms and their implementation, Brazilian neoliberalism was more pragmatic than an article of faith. As a result, there was a unilateral, although not complete, opening of the economy and a reduction in the size of the state under the Collor administration. These policies continued under Cardoso and included the privatization of many state firms. At the same time, Brazilian policymakers maintained a continuing belief in regulation and selective state activism. The Lula administration, despite its initial rhetoric, demonstrated the same pragmatism by continuing the Cardoso administration's cautious, if not conservative, macroeconomic fiscal, monetary, and exchange rate policies, while actively extending the scale and reach of existing social programs, such as the set of programs which provided the foundation of the Bolsa Família.

The traditional literature on various subfields within economics continued to flourish during this period. Topics in public finance, particularly the source and use of revenues, appeared with some frequency and reference the ongoing debate in Brazil on fiscal federalism. The conundrum of lingering high interest rates in Brazil gave rise to studies of banking and finance. A number of works focus on international trade and trade policy measures such as liberalization (item **2181**) and import substitution (item **2164**). While the details of specific initiatives within Mercosul no longer seem to be of interest, more abstract questions of regional integration (item **2212**, for example) and open regionalism merge into a discussion of broader trends toward globalization. Other studies look at the impact of globalization inside of Brazil, including the impact of Mercosul on economic policy in the states of Pernambuco, Bahia, São Paulo, and Rio Grande do Sul (item **2176**), the structure of production of the Brazilian economy in the 1990s as a function of trade (item **2185**), the possible short-term impact of trade liberalization on poverty and income distribution (item **2203**), and the crisis of the Fordist model of production in Brazil since the 1980s due to pressures from the readjustment of the economy promoted by the IMF (item **2193**).

Fewer publications address the economies of states and regions within Brazil and the regional focus in the current set of works centers around São Paulo and the regions most subject to its gravitational pull. One data-rich work finds that São Paulo continued as the dynamic center of the Brazilian economy, although by many measures its portion had declined with growth elsewhere in Brazil and with the economic restructuring in the period since 1980 (item **2155**). In a discussion of the structure of manufacturing in the São Paulo metropolitan region from 1970 to 2005, Campolina Diniz and Campolina find that, while São Paulo lost its polarizing role, the city, together with the adjacent cities of Campinas, São Jose dos Campos, Sorocaba, and Santos, now might form a polarizing "city-region" (item **2144**). Looking outward, the evolution of the economy of the state of Goiás is placed in the context of integration with the state of São Paulo, Brazil's march to the west, and the construction of Goiânia and Brasília (item **2198**). In Minas Gerais, outside the orbit of São Paulo, one article finds that state planning and investment had a positive impact until 1980 and that the integrated modern sector should be attractive to foreign investment (item **2169**). Several works consider appropriate policies for regional and urban development (items **2156** and **2157**).

A number of works consider the intersection of labor processes, the restructuring of production, and labor relations. Examples include an analysis of changing labor processes in manufacturing in the ABC and its impact on the organizational forms of the labor movement as Taylorist and Fordist models gave way to flexible Japanese forms of production and outsourcing (item **2201**); a selected collection on labor processes and microelectronics in modern Brazil, social organization of production and distribution of income, solidarity economy, and self-management in Brazil (item **2205**); and a collection on the organizational forms of manufacturing in new production locations between the ABC Paulista and the Fluminense South (item **2208**).

Social, wage, and labor policies maintain their place in the literature. Examples include a discussion of the early years of the Lula government's Bolsa Família program (item **2170**), income transfer programs generally (item **2199**), the role of the minimum wage as a development tool (item **2195**), work and income policies (item **2188**), the management of social services, including the debate following the 1998 reforms (item **2197**), and private retirement programs and their users (item **2186**).

With regard to the mechanics of the administration and delivery of public services, we note the presence of works that include a broad analysis of the system of employment in Brazil, placing the idea of a public employment system in historical and international context, and reviewing the Brazilian experience with labor market policies (item **2179**). A collection directed toward public managers in the state of São Paulo focuses on the general context of public policy, the public sector in São Paulo, and trends in planning (item **2207**). This topic also includes a discussion of the role of NGOs in public policy and administration (item **2172**) and a case study of the role of the participatory budget in the allocation of resources in Espírito Santo and the role of neighborhood organizations (item **2145**).

A number of outstanding studies focus on particular sectors such as energy (item **2174**), finance (items **2178** and **2211**), and manufacturing (item **2167**), as well as on some particularly well-known companies such as Vale and CSN, both formerly state-owned enterprises. In fact, the study of CSN (item **2168**) focuses more on the process of its privatization than on the company's fate thereafter. An interesting addition to the growing literature on the role of business elites and business associations in civil society is a study (item **2189**) of the Coalizão Empresarial Brasileira, its very corporatist origins, and its effective strategy for reducing "custo Brasil," that collection of small obstacles and costs that put Brazilian firms at a competitive disadvantage in global business settings.

Consistent with the new centrality of agricultural exports in Brazil's economic prospects, one notes a significant presence in the literature of studies focused on modern agriculture and agribusiness and on crops like soybeans rather than coffee. For example, Abbey, Baer, and Filizzola trace the evolution of agribusiness in Brazil and its contribution to the economy and assess the impact of agriculture on wealth and income distribution in Brazil (item **2137**). This new look at Brazilian agriculture also examines the regulatory climate for the agricultural sector and such globally topical issues as food security, environmental issues, and biotechnology.

2137 Abbey Leonard A.; Werner Baer; and Mavio Filizzola. Growth, efficiency, and equity: the impact of agribusiness and land reform in Brazil. (*Lat. Am. Bus. Rev.*, 7:2, 2006, p. 93–115, bibl., tables)

This paper traces the evolution of Brazilian agribusiness, analyzes its relative contribution to the economy and its impact on distribution of wealth and income, and examines the impact of the Brazilian government's land reform program on the concentration of property ownership. The paper also discusses the role of the MST (Movimento dos Trabalhadores Rurais Sem Terra) and its prospects in a modernizing agricultural sector.

2138 Adeus ao desenvolvimento: a opção do governo Lula. Organização de João Antonio de Paula. Textos de Leda Maria Paulani *et al.* Belo Horizonte, Brazil: Autêntica, 2005. 407 p.: bibl., ill.

Written by economists critical of the economic policies adopted by the Lula government, the chapters in this book lament the adoption of neoliberal policies that continue dependent development and omit an explicit social policy and prodevelopment economic measures. The chapters discuss the implications of measures adopted on industrial and technology policy as well as labor markets and social services.

2139 Arrecadação, de onde vem?: e gastos públicos, para onde vão? Organização de João Sicsú. Prefácio de Francisco de Oliveira. São Paulo: Boitempo Editorial: RLS, Instituto Rosa Luxemburg Stiftung, 2007. 158 p.: bibl., ill.

In the national debate in Brazil on the role of the state, and particularly its impact on development, data on the origin and destination of both revenues and expenditures are vital. These papers explore these data, especially on social spending and tax incidence, in a technical but accessible manner.

Berriel, Rosa Maria Vieira. Celso Furtado: reforma, política e ideologia (1950–1964). See *HLAS 66:3666*.

Botto, Andrea Paula. ¿Quién defiende a los consumidores?: la regulación de los servicios públicos residenciales en Argentina y en Brasil después de las privatizaciones. See item **2131**.

2140 Brasil globalizado: o Brasil em um mundo surpreendente. Organização de Octavio de Barros e Fabio Giambiagi. Prefácio de Henrique Meirelles. Textos de Fernando Henrique Cardoso *et al.* Rio de Janeiro: Elsevier: Campus, 2008. 388 p.: bibl., ill.

A collection of papers written by some of Brazil's leading economists that examines the impact of globalization on Brazil. Specifically, the papers focus on international trade and investment flows and the implications of opening markets on Brazilian economic policy, growth rate, and productivity.

2141 O Brasil sob a nova ordem: a economia brasileira contemporânea: uma análise dos governos Collor a Lula. Organização de Rosa Maria Marques e Mariana Ribeiro Jansen Ferreira. Textos de Ana Carolina Paes de Barros Boyadjian *et al.* São Paulo: Editora Saraiva, 2010. 373 p.: bibl., ill.

Written by a group of well-known economists primarily for a university audience, the chapters examine the implications of globalization and liberalization on Brazilian economic policy from 1990–2007. The highly readable chapters focus heavily on financial markets but also include labor markets, agrarian reform, privatization, public health, pension funds, education, and inequality. Numerous charts and tables give the volume a contemporary perspective.

2142 Brazil: a century of change. Edited by Ignacy Sachs, Jorge Wilheim, and Paulo Sergio de Moraes Sarmento Pinheiro. Translated by Robert N. Anderson. Foreword by Jerry Dávila. Chapel Hill: Univ. of North Carolina Press, 2009. 364 p.: bibl., graphs, index, maps. (Latin America in translation/en traducción/em tradução. Brasiliana coll.)

A collection of 13 separately authored chapters written largely by Brazilian intellectuals who have been both academics and prominent policymakers in post-military civilian governments through 2002. Reviews the Brazilian political, economic, and social development experience in the 20th century. Supports a political consensus in favor of a postneoliberal, "neodevelopmentalist" vision of the state managing economic growth including for greater social inclusion. For political scientist's comment, see item **1506**.

2143 Brazil as an economic superpower?: understanding Brazil's changing role in the global economy. Edited by Lael Brainard and Leonardo Martinez-Diaz. Washington, D.C.: Brookings Institution Press, 2009. 291 p.: bibl., ill., index, maps.

This edited volume, published by the Brookings Institution, examines Brazil's new role in the global economy as a member of the BRICs. Sections on resources (agriculture and energy), trade, technology and business (multinationals) describe Brazil's growing clout in important sectors. The book concludes with a chapter on the perpetual challenge for Brazil, income distribution. Upbeat in its outlook, the authors provide an excellent overview of the contemporary Brazilian economy.

2144 Campolina Diniz, Clélio and Bernardo Campolina. A região metropolitana de Saõ Paulo: reestruturação, re-espacialização e novas funções. (*EURE/Santiago*, 33:98, abril 2007, p. 27–43, bibl., maps, tables)

Discusses the structure of manufacturing in the São Paulo Metropolitan Region by output and by employment from 1970 to 2005. Makes comparisons with other regions and among subregions within the São Paulo regions. Finds that while during the 1970s São Paulo lost its polarizing role, now São Paulo together with the adjacent cities of Campinas, São Jose dos Campos, Sorocaba, and Santos might form a polarizing "city-region."

2145 Carlos, Euzineia. Controle social e política redistributiva no orçamento participativo. Vitória, Brazil: EDUFES, 2007. 226 p.: bibl., ill., maps.

A study of public influence over the allocation of resources by municipal governments in two cities, Vitória and Serra, in the state of Espírito Santo. Focuses on the *orçamento participativa* (participative budget) process from 1989 through 2003 in the context of the provisions of the 1988 constitution and reviews the roles of the neighborhood organizations in the preceding years.

2146 Carvalho, Carlos Eduardo. As origens e a gênese do Plano Collor. (*Nova Econ./Belo Horizonte*, 16:1, jan./abril 2006, p. 101–134, table)

The author traces the origin and development of the Collor Plan, situating its origins in academia and noting that the debate around nontraditional intervention was imposed on the presidential candidates in 1989, and was developed in discussions with advisors to several candidates including Ulysses Guimarães and Lula.

2147 Castro de Rezende, Gervásio. Políticas trabalhista, fundiária e de crédito agrícola no Brasil: uma avaliação crítica. (*Rev. Econ. Sociol. Rural*, 44:1, jan./março 2006, p. 47–78, bibl., ill.)

Discusses the highly concentrated model of agricultural production expressed in large scale, high degree of mechanization, and low labor uses. Contrasts the legacy of the latifundia and technological determinism arguments before concluding that the continued concentration stems from the regulatory reforms of the 1960s which made unviable temporary and family labor and induced mechanization and large-scale production.

2148 Conferência Internacional sobre Desenvolvimento Regional e Investimento Estrangeiro Direto, Fortaleza, Brazil, 2002. Anais. Fortaleza, Brazil: Banco do Nordeste do Brasil, 2003. 290 p.: ill. (some col.), maps (some col.).

This text is derived from presentations at a 2002 conference sponsored by the Banco do Nordeste do Brasil, the OECD and the World Bank, the first of its kind to share the experiences of regional economies in Europe and Brazil with respect to attraction of foreign direct investment. The volume concludes by suggesting the need for economic stability and perhaps a return to more long-term planning, as a precondition for FDI attraction and highlights the need for development in the Northeast of infrastructure, human capital, technological innovation, and entrepreneurship.

2149 Corazza, Gentil. O "regionalismo aberto" de CEPAL e a inserção da América Latina na globalização. (*Ensaios FEE*, 27:1, 2006, p. 135–152)

This paper discusses the evolution of CEPAL's understanding of Latin America's development challenges and its policy recommendations. It identifies CEPAL's concept of open regionalism as a departure from previous theory and seeks to analyze it in the context of globalization.

2150 Costa Neto, Yttrio Corrêa da. Bancos oficiais no Brasil: origem e aspectos de seu desenvolvimento. Brasília: Banco Central do Brasil, 2004. 156 p.: bibl.

This slim volume describes the evolution of state banks in Brazil beginning in the early 1800s, and examines their role in the conduct of economic policy. The study notes that governments of all political persuasions have created official banks to address various sectoral needs and concludes that, given Brazil's regional inequality, the shortage of national savings, and the inherent instability of foreign capital flows, there will be a continuing need for official banks.

2151 De Barrios, Luiz Carlos Mendonça. Um novo futuro. (*Novos Estud. CEBRAP*, 81, julho 2008, p. 11–20, graphs)

A discussion of Brazil's economic prospects as a result of recent growth in China and Chinese demand since 2004 for Brazilian agricultural and mineral exports. Notes that Chinese demand ended Brazil's general pattern of economic stagnation dating from around 1975. With the resulting trade surplus and the prospect for more energy exports, along with continuing Chinese presence in the market, argues that Brazil has a bright future.

2152 Desafios do federalismo fiscal. Coordenação de Fernando Rezende. Rio de Janeiro: FGV Editora, 2006. 114 p.: bibl., ill.

These papers are drawn from an international conference on the challenges posed to public finance by a federal system of government. The papers explore the competition among states and between states and municipalities for tax revenues and the pressures for decentralization, especially in the provision of social services. The challenges of tax reform in Brazil's federal system are also discussed.

2153 Dimensões do agronegócio brasileiro: políticas, instituições e perspectivas. Organização de Pedro Ramos. Textos de Antônio Márcio Buainain *et al.* Brasília: MDA, 2007. 360 p.: bibl. (NEAD estudos; 15)

This comprehensive volume provides a review of Brazilian agricultural and agribusiness policy and a discussion of the institutions and regulatory framework that have shaped rural Brazil. Includes a discus-sion of the impact of land ownership on income distribution as well as chapters on environmental policy, biotechnology, and food security.

2154 Dinâmicas regionais e questão agrária no estado de São Paulo. Coordenação de Jorge Eduardo Júlio, Leonam Bueno Pereira, e Regina Petti. 2a ed. São Paulo: INCRA-SP, 2006. 138 p.: bibl., maps.

Reports on the evolution and dynamics of the agriculture and livestock sectors in the state of São Paulo by region within the state and by nine product sectors. A diagnostic of the agrarian sector is presented and reform proposals made.

2155 Economia paulista: dinâmica socio-econômica entre 1980 e 2005. Organização de Wilson Cano *et al.* Campinas, Brazil: UNICAMP: Alínea Editora: FAPESP, 2007. 571 p.: bibl., ill., maps.

Describes and analyzes the principal economic, demographic, and social transformations of the economy of the state of São Paulo between 1980 and 2005. Its 10 data-rich chapters are organized state-wide by sector, although much of the analysis is by substate regions and jurisdictions. Finds that São Paulo continues as the dynamic center of the Brazilian economy, although its proportion by many measures has declined with growth elsewhere in Brazil and economic restructuring over most of the period.

2156 Economia regional e urbana: contribuições teóricas recentes. Organização de Clélio Campolina Diniz e Marco Crocco. Belo Horizonte, Brazil: Editora UFMG, 2006. 301 p.: bibl., ill. (População y economia)

A collection of 10 papers brought together as part of an effort to develop a national policy of regional development while self-consciously avoiding the tendency to believe that there is only one correct policy to be implemented. Theoretical and applied materials are included, among them recent historical materials and examples.

2157 Encontro de Políticas Públicas e Desenvolvimento Regional, 2nd, Fortaleza, Brazil, 2005. Distribuição de renda e políticas de desenvolvimento regional no Brasil. Organização de Ronaldo

Arraes e Klaus Hermanns. Fortaleza, Brazil: Fundação Konrad Adenauder, 2006. 322 p.: bibl., ill., maps.

A collection of 11 conference papers analyzing various aspects of public policies related to regional development. Papers consider agribusiness; clusters; the environment; income inequality; state investment funds; credit systems; local policies; regional inequality; the "fiscal war;" growth, poverty, and income distribution; and discrimination and inequality of labor income.

2158 Ensaios de história do pensamento econômico no Brasil contemporâneo. Organização de Tamás Szmrecsányi e Francisco da Silva Coelho. Textos de Amaury Patrick Gremaud *et al.* São Paulo: Editora Atlas: Ordem dos Economistas do Brasil, 2007. 464 p.: bibl., ill.

A collection of 32 original and previously published papers organized under the auspices of the Ordem dos Economistas of Brazil. This wide-ranging set of papers brings together in one place a reporting of the contributions of economists to the development of economics and to the development of Brazil.

2159 Filgueiras, Luiz Antonio Mattos and Reinaldo Gonçalves. A economia política do governo Lula. Rio de Janeiro: Contraponto, 2007. 263 p.: bibl., ill.

A critical view of the Lula government arguing that its apparent success is the result of the temporarily favorable external environment and that the shift from manufacturing to commodity and resource-intensive exports will make Brazil more vulnerable and weaker in the long run. In the social sphere, argues that programs such as Bolsa Família will not result in improvement in the distribution of income as labor's share of national output is declining.

2160 Fórum Nacional Brasil—um Novo Mundo nos Trópicos: 200 Anos de Independência Econômica e 20 Anos de Fórum Nacional, *Rio de Janeiro, 2008.* O Brasil e a economia criativa: um novo mundo nos trópicos. Coordenação de João Paulo dos Reis Velloso. Textos de Luiz Inácio Lula da Silva *et al.* Rio de Janeiro: José Olympio Editora, 2008. 599 p.: bibl., ill., maps.

Collection of 26 papers from the 2008 Fórum Nacional featuring President Lula and other high-ranking public officials in the first panel. Notable themes include the vision of the government, strategy for a creative economy, macroeconomic fundamentals, Brazil's global firms, innovation in Brazilian firms, and social development indices.

2161 Fórum Nacional Chegou a Vez do Brasil?: Oportunidade para a Geração de Brasileiros que Nunca Viu o País Crescer (PAC e "Projeto"), *Rio de Janeiro, 2007.* Chegou a vez do Brasil?: oportunidade para a geração de brasileiros que nunca viu o país crescer. Coordenação de João Paulo dos Reis Velloso e Roberto Cavalcanti de Albuquerque. Textos de Luis Alberto Moreno *et al.* Rio de Janeiro: José Olympio Editora, 2007. 741 p.: bibl., ill., maps.

Collection of 48 papers from the 2007 Fórum Nacional analyzing various aspects of opportunities for Brazil to quickly achieve a growth rate above five percent per year as well as a long-run high rate of growth. Includes several papers on the Lula administration's Programa de Aceleração do Crescimento (PAC); a long section of initiative, creativity, and the power of ideas; significant consideration of Brazil's relations with emerging economies like China and India; as well as consideration of classic topics in Brazilian economic development, including infrastructure.

2162 Fórum Nacional Na Crise Global, o Novo Papel Mundial dos BRICs (BRIMCs?) e as Oportunidades do Brasil: Crise como Oportunidade através do Plano de Ação, *Rio de Janeiro, 2009.* A crise global e o novo papel mundial dos BRICs. Coordenação de João Paulo dos Reis Velloso. Textos de Lya Fett Luft *et al.* Rio de Janeiro: José Olympio, 2009. 419 p.: bibl., ill., maps.

A collection of papers by well-known Brazilian and international economists presented at the 2009 Fórum Nacional. The papers examine the impact of the global recession on the BRICs, possibly including Mexico (the focus of the papers written by non-Brazilians) and especially on Brazil. The sections on Brazil include one on the response of Brazil, and particularly its financial institutions (BNDES, Caixa, Finep), and a second on strategies to overcome the crisis and the role of various sectors.

2163 **Fórum Nacional Por Que o Brasil Não é Um País de Alto Crescimento?, BNDES, 2006.** O Brasil e a nova ordem (desordem?) mundial. Coordenação de João Paulo dos Reis Velloso e Luciano Martins. Textos de Sergio Paulo Rouanet *et al.* Rio de Janeiro: J. Olympio Editora: Fórum Nacional, 2006. 167 p.: bibl.

Collection of 10 papers from the 2006 Fórum Nacional discussing the place and role of Brazil in the post-1989 world order when the US had become the remaining superpower. Part 1 presents seven papers including several with perspectives from the US, Europe, China, and Russia. Part 2 considers Brazil's participation in regional blocs and global insertion. After outlining the disorder and uncertainty in many parts of the world, concludes that the end of the Cold War did not bring a new world order.

2164 **Franco, Ana Maria de Paiva** and **Renato Baumann.** A substituição de importações no Brasil entre 1995 e 2000. (*Rev. Econ. Polít.*, 25:3, julho/set. 2005, p. 190–208, bibl., graphs)

This work estimates the recent import substitution process in Brazil and finds that it is driven by effective tariffs and real effective exchange rates. In 1999, after the Brazilian currency depreciation, the impact of the exchange rate variable dominates that of the effective tariffs.

2165 **Furtado, João.** Muito além da especialização regressiva e da doença holandesa. (*Novos Estud. CEBRAP*, 81, julho 2008, p. 33–46)

Analyzes, in light of Brazil's new primary products trade surplus with China and the resulting high valued exchange rate, whether Brazil faces the "Dutch disease" and the dismantling of the complex, diverse, and integrated industrial park that was built in the ISI period through 1980. Argues that many of the technologies and capacity for innovation developed in the ISI period can be the basis for innovation leading to new sources of competitiveness, even if there are some losses due to cheaper manufactured imports.

2166 **Goeschl, Timo** and **Danilo Camargo Igliori.** Property rights for biodiversity conservation and development: extractive reserves in the Brazilian Amazon. (*Dev.*

Change/Oxford, 37:2, March 2006, p. 427–451, bibl., tables)

The authors use the extractive reserves of the Brazilian Amazon to examine the relationship between property rights regimes, biodiversity, and development in the context of tropical forests. Noting the peculiar mix of public, private, and communal property rights in and around the Brazilian reserves, the authors conclude that their static nature is unlikely sustainable in the context of dynamic development. The need to maintain an ongoing revenue stream is likely to result in pressure to modify existing property rights arrangements.

2167 **Gómez Mera, Laura.** Macroeconomic concerns and intrastate bargains: explaining illiberal policies in Brazil's automobile sector. (*Lat. Am. Polit. Soc.*, 49:1, Spring 2007, p. 113–140, bibl.)

Article seeks to explain the interventionist automobile industry policy enacted in 1995, a significant departure from the neoliberal policies more favored at the time. The explanation is found in two overlapping bargains, one between business people in the auto sector and developmentalist bureaucrats in the Planning Ministry, and another between these officials and their peers in the Finance Ministry and Central Bank who were more sensitive to international financial pressures than to lobbying from the domestic auto industry.

2168 **Graciolli, Edilson José.** Privatização da CSN: da luta de classes à parceria. São Paulo: Expressão Popular, 2007. 360 p.: bibl.

A detailed study of the shifts in labor union strategies during the run-up to privatization of the Volta Redonda plant. Examines the shift from confrontation to partnership and the roles of Força Sindical to CUT at the plant level.

2169 **Haddad, Eduardo A.** *et al.* Building-up influence: post-war industrialization in the state of Minas Gerais, Brazil. (*Rev. Econ. Polít.*, 27:2, abril/junho 2007, p. 281–300, bibl., graphs, tables)

Considers the industrialization process in the state of Minas Gerais, Brazil, using data on the structure of production for 1953, 1980, and 1995. Finds positive impact of state planning and investment until 1980, as well as the influence of its cessation after 1980. Argues that the integrated modern sector should be attractive to foreign investment, but should also be a candidate for re-evaluation with time.

Hall, Anthony. Brazil's *Bolsa Família*: a double-edged sword? See item **2600**.

2170 Hall, Anthony. From Fome Zero to Bolsa Família: social policies and poverty alleviation under Lula. (*J. Lat. Am. Stud.*, 38:4, Nov. 2006, p. 689–710, table)

A discussion of the Bolsa Família, the Lula government's conditional cash transfer (CCT) program, during its first years from 2003 into 2006. The program's origins in the earlier programs like Zero Fome and those of the Cardoso government are noted. Expenditure levels, operational performance, and likely impacts on a variety of social, political, and economic variables are reviewed.

2171 Jackson, Toni de. Novos arranjos institucionais na renovação da política industrial brasileira. (*Ensaios FEE*, 28:1, 2007, p. 127–158, graph)

A new set of industrial policies announced in 2002 was crafted in the context of privatization, globalization, and a restrictive fiscal policy and resulted in the creation of the Brazilian Agency for Industrial Development in 2004. This paper traces the development of the new guidelines for industrial and technology policy and examines the effectiveness of this new agency, which it finds to be quite innovative.

2172 Jardim Pinto, Céli Regina. As ONGs e a política no Brasil: presença de novos atores. (*Dados/Rio de Janeiro*, 49:3, 2006, p. 651–670, bibl.)

Discusses the evolving role of the NGO in Brazilian society, as interlocutor of civil society, as partner of the state, and as actor recognized by the state as civil society. Notes the absence of an organized civil society in Latin America during most of the 20th century and the various links of contemporary NGOs with international organizations, social movements, and philanthropic entities.

2173 Johnson, Kenyon and **Bryan Andrew.** National exchange rate policies and international debt crisis: how Brazil did not

follow Argentina into a default in 2001–2002. (*Rev. Econ. Polít.*, 27:1, jan/março 2007, p. 60–81, bibl., graphs, tables)

Comparing the experience of Argentina and Brazil, the paper uses an econometric model to examine how exchange rate policies and IMF Stand-By Arrangements can be used to decrease the probability of a debt crisis. Results provide policymakers from developing countries with lessons that can be used to manage default risk more effectively.

2174 Leite, Antônio Dias. A energia do Brasil. 2. ed. rev. e atualizada. Rio de Janeiro: Elsevier: Campus, 2007. 658 p.: bibl., ill.

This updated edition provides two additional chapters covering 1995–2002 and 2002–2006 to an authoritative history of Brazilian energy policy that begins in the first decade of the 20th century. Well documented and data-filled, the volume provides coverage of coal, electricity, oil, gas, and alternative fuels, as well as a discussion of global strategy and growing environmental concerns.

2175 Macarini, José Pedro. A política econômica do governo Médici: 1970–1973. (*Nova Econ./Belo Horizonte*, 15:3, set./dez. 2005, p. 53–92)

Reports on the economic policy of the Medici government, 1970–73, the final period of the "miracle" boom period. Highlights the prioritization of agro-export industries in the first years and concerns about inflation in the later years. Provides a detailed discussion of the various fiscal, monetary, and taxation tools.

2176 Medeiros, Marcelo. Dinâmica subnacional e lógica centro-periferia: os impactos do Mercosul na economia política dos estados de Pernambuco, Bahia, São Paulo e Rio Grande do Sul. (*Rev. Bras. Polít. Int.*, 49:1, 2006, p. 43–67, bibl.)

Analyzes the impact of Mercosul on the economies of the Brazilian states of Rio Grande do Sul, São Paulo, Bahia, and Pernambuco, and their capitals. Questions whether the outward-looking integration of Mercosul provided additional markets for subnational regions within the trade union. Finds that the subnational regions benefitted from Mercosul, although in differing proportions and with differing impacts on the terms of trade.

2177 Mendonça, Helder Ferreira de. Efeitos da indepêndencia do banco central e da taxa de rotatividade sobre a inflação brasileira. (*Rev. Econ. Polít.*, 26:4, out./dez. 2006, p. 552563, bibl., tables)

International experience suggests that the independence of the central bank results in lower inflation and lower turnover of central bank presidents. This paper examines the experience of Brazil between 1980 and 2002 with an independent central bank and finds that inflation is unaffected but turnover is lower.

2178 Mercado de capitais e dívida pública: tributação, indexação, alongamento. Textos de Edmar Lisboa Bacha e Luiz Chrysostomo de Oliveira Filho. Apresentação de Alfredo Egydio Setubal. Prefácio de Arminio Fraga Neto. Rio de Janeiro: Contra Capa: ANBID: IEPE, CdG, 2006. 404 p.: bibl., ill., index.

The product of a second conference sponsored by the Associação Nacional dos Bancos de Investimento (ANBID) which brought together more than a dozen Brazilian economists to address financial market issues of taxation and indexation. The authors seek to explain and understand the unique aspects of Brazilian financial markets with an eye to resolving issues that inhibit the creation of deeper markets and long term economic growth.

2179 Moretto, Amilton. O sistema público de emprego no Brasil: uma construção inacabada. São Paulo: LTr Editora; Campinas, Brazil: CESIT-Centro de Estudos Sindicais e de Economia do Trabalho, IE-Instituto de Economia, Unicamp, 2009. 232 p.: bibl., ill. (Debates contemporâneos. Economia social e do trabalho; 6)

A broad analysis of the public system of employment in Brazil. Places the idea of a public employment system in historical, world context and reviews the Brazilian experience with labor market policies. Reviews the challenges of building a system with placement, labor-market information, labor market adjustment, unemployment insurance, and supply restriction functions.

2180 Musacchio, Aldo. Experiments in financial democracy: corporate governance and financial development in Brazil, 1882–1950. New York, N.Y.: Cambridge Univ. Press, 2009. 298 p.: bibl., ill., index. (Studies in macroeconomic history)

In this study of the evolution of corporate governance in Brazil from 1882–1950, the author argues that in the absence of legal regulations on ownership and voting rights, companies created regulations that protected minority shareholders in order to garner greater access to capital. The author concludes that companies are not bound by the legal environment in which they operate and that firms' financial structures respond to changes in institutions and corporate governance driven in some cases by macroeconomic shock.

2181 Nassif, André. Os impactos da liberalização comercial sobre o padrão de comércio exterior brasileiro. (*Rev. Econ. Polít.*, 25:1, jan. 2005, p. 70–93, bibl., tables)

Empirical findings suggest that the impact of commercial liberalization on international trade in the 1990s included 1) gains in labor productivity and reductions in average real costs for most manufacturers, 2) a trade pattern mostly driven by changes in imports, and 3) no gain, on average, in global competitiveness among industries with the greatest increases in technical efficiency. The author finds that those industries that made significant investments in R&D showed significant sectoral trade deficits throughout the decade.

2182 Pastoret, Corinne. Cardoso el opositor académico vs. Cardoso el político: ¿continuidad o ruptura? (*Rev. Econ. Inst.*, 8:15, segundo semestre 2006, p. 69–95, bibl.)

Analyzes the evolution of the theories of sociologist and former Brazilian President Fernando Henrique Cardoso. Compares his 1960s work as a proponent of the theory of dependent development to his work in the early 2000s when, as president, he saw liberal policies and democracy as the new utopia, arguing for policies to take advantage of the open economy and globalization.

2183 Pereira, Luiz Carlos Bresser. Macroeconomia da estagnação: crítica da ortodoxia convencional no Brasil pós-1994.

São Paulo: Editora 34, 2007. 325 p.: bibl., ill., index.

A heterodox analysis of the Brazilian economy, this volume examines the challenges that prevent more rapid economic growth in Brazil, and provides recommendations for reforms to create more inclusive growth and a more equitable distribution of income. The author's recommendations, termed *novo desenvolvimentismo*, are based on an analysis of the political and economic constraints on growth.

2184 Pereira, Luiz Carlos Bresser and **Paulo Gala.** Por que a poupança externa não promove crescimento. (*Rev. Econ. Polít.*, 27:1, jan/março 2007, p. 3–19, bibl.)

Paper provides a theoretical critique of the growth with foreign savings strategy, demonstrating that both loans and foreign direct investment will not usually increase the rate of capital accumulation since they will be offset by increased consumption spurred by the foreign exchange rate appreciation that accompanies the current account deficit. Only in the special case where expected profits are greater than the rate of interest will the marginal propensity to consume fall sufficiently to result in a net increase in savings and investment.

2185 Pereira, Wellington. A estrutura produtiva da economia brasileira na década de 90: o comércio exterior como uma lente privilegiada de análise. (*Ensaios FEE*, 28:1, 2007, p. 249–286, graph, tables)

A discussion of the changes in the productive structure of Brazil in the 1990s from the vantage point of foreign trade. Notes the general shift to a trade deficit in the decade with the opening of the economy and the relatively high value of the currency. Finds that some sectors and products were successful as exporters in the new environment, while others experienced deficits and needed attention to be more competitive.

2186 O perfil dos consumidores de planos de previdência privada no Brasil: evolução de uma demanda, 1992–2001. Textos de Kaizô Iwakami Beltrão *et al.* Rio de Janeiro: FUNENSEG, Fundação Escola Nacional de Seguros, 2004. 134 p.: bibl., ill.

Analyzes the profile of individuals and families who are consumers of private retirement programs for the purpose of assisting the strategic thinking of the providers. Reviews the development of the public and private systems and considers prospects for the development of the private system.

2187 Pinto, Celso. Os desafios do crescimento: dos militares a Lula. São Paulo: Publifolha: Valor Económico, 2007. 385 p.: ill., index.

A collection of the columns written between 1981 and 2003 by one of Brazil's leading economics and business journalists. The columns were originally published in *Folha de São Paulo, O Globo,* and *Valor Económico* and have been annotated as necessary for today's reader. Covering the Brazilian economy from the end of the military regime to the Lula administration, the columns focus on the unusual characteristics of Brazilian interest rates, debt renegotiation, stabilization plans, and relations with Argentina.

2188 Políticas públicas de trabalho e renda no Brasil contemporâneo. Organizaçao de Maria Ozanira da Silva e Silva e Maria Carmelita Yazbek. Textos de Marcio Pochmann *et al.* São Paulo: Cortez Editora, 2006. 207 p.: bibl., ill.

A collection of nine essays that analyze various aspects of policies toward work and income. Papers consider employment policy, employment and social rights, female labor and inequality, professional education, the solidarity economy, informal employment, and job training for youth.

2189 Pralon Mancuso, Wagner and **Amâncio Jorge de Oliveira.** Abertura econômica, empresariado e política: os planos domésticos e internacional. (*Lua Nova,* 69, 2006, p. 147–172, bibl.)

Article seeks to refute the idea that the Brazilian business community is incapable of taking collective action and that this failure is a result of corporatism. Analyzing the Coalizão Empresarial Brasileira (CEB), the authors argue that this organization, a creature of the corporatist Confederação Nacional da Indústria (CNI), was successful in lobbying for measures to reduce "custo Brasil," the collection of factors that prejudices the competitiveness of Brazilian firms in international markets.

2190 Relações e condições de trabalho no Brasil. São Paulo: DIEESE, 2008. 199 p.: bibl., ill.

Produced by a partnership between the Ministry of Labor and DIEESE, this volume includes chapters on wage adjustments and wage floors in collective negotiations, the impact of payroll taxes for social programs on employment, subcontracting, and length of the work day.

2191 Rocha, Rudi and André Urani. Posicionamento social e a hipótese da distribuição de renda desconhecida: Brasil, quão pobres, quão ricos e quão desiguais nos percebemos? (*Rev. Econ. Polít.*, 27:4, out./dez. 2007, p. 595–615, bibl., tables)

Provides a description of the phenomenon that Brazilians do not know the true distribution of income, although generally believe that it is seriously unequal. Discusses the causes and consequences of this gap. Based on PNAD 2001 data and social positioning analysis.

2192 Roett, Riordan. The new Brazil. Washington, D.C.: Brookings Institution Press, 2010. 178 p.: bibl., index.

The most recent in a series of volumes on Brazil written by the author over the course of more than four decades, this volume on the politics and political economy of Brazil is historical and comparative in tone. Written just prior to the 2010 elections, perhaps most interesting are the chapters covering the Cardoso and Lula governments.

2193 Schincariol, Vitor Eduardo. O Brasil sob a crise do fordismo. São Paulo: LCTE Editora, 2007. 176 p.: bibl., ill.

A review of the crisis of the Fordist model of production in Brazil during the 1980s under pressures from the readjustment of the economy promoted by the IMF as well as from the general liberalization of the economy. Separately reviews the 1985–93, 1993–98, and 1999–2002 periods.

2194 Seminário "Celso Furtado e o Século XXI", *Universidade Federal do Rio de Janeiro. Forum de Ciência e Cultura, 2005.* Celso Furtado e o século XXI. Organização de João Saboia e Fernando J. Cardim de Carvalho. Textos de Arturo Guillén R.

et al. Rio de Janeiro: MinhaEditora: UFRJ/IE; Barueri, Brazil: Manole, 2007. 445 p.: bibl.

A volume of essays in honor of Celso Furtado, this book examines current policy issues in Brazil through a developmentalist lens à la Furtado. Topics examined include economic history, regional integration, financial markets, and development policy. Like Furtado himself, these essays are often critical of policies adopted by the Lula administration for the absence of a pro-development stance.

2195 Seminário Salário Mínimo e Desenvolvimento, *Campinas, São Paulo, Brazil, 2005.* Salário mínimo e desenvolvimento. Organização de Paulo Baltar, Cláudio Dedecca, e José Dari Krein. Campinas, Brazil: Univ. Estadual de Campinas, Instituto de Economia, 2005. 228 p.: bibl., ill.

A collection of 17 papers on the role of the minimum wage in the development process. Themes include minimum wage and development; minimum wage and labor market; minimum wage, social security, and public finances; minimum wage, social policy, and income distribution; and directions for minimum wage policy.

2196 Sicsú, João; Luiz Fernando de Paula; and Renaut Michel. Por que novo-desenvolvimentismo? (*Rev. Econ. Polít.*, 27:4, out./dez. 2007, p. 507–524, bibl.)

Paper advocates the development of an alternative policy stance to neoliberalism, one that would emphasize sustained growth in order to reduce income inequality. The paper argues for the adoption of a "new developmentalism" that would focus on sustainable economic growth with social equity.

2197 Silva, Ademir Alves da. A gestão da seguridade social brasileira: entre a política pública e o mercado. São Paulo: Cortez Editora, 2004. 255 p.: bibl.

In general terms Silva reviews the management of social services in Brazil. He provides a conceptual and comparative framework in response to the neoconservative attack on the welfare state, and especially relative to Latin America, new forms of provision of services. Also discusses the debate over social security reform in Brazil since the 1998 reforms.

2198 **Silva, Eduardo Rodrigues da.** A economia goiana no contexto nacional, 1970–2000. Goiânia, Brazil: Editora da UCG, 2007. 215 p.: bibl., ill., maps.

Reports on the evolution of the economy of the state of Goiás from 1970 to 2000. Places that evolution in the context of integration with the state of São Paulo, Brazil's march to the west, and the construction of Goiânia and Brasília. Reviews the role of modernization of agriculture in the 1980s, influenced by the availability of policy support, as well as the consequences of various neoliberal policies.

2199 **Silva, Maria Ozanira da Silva e; Maria Carmelita Yazbek; and Geraldo di Giovanni.** A política social brasileira no século XXI: a prevalência dos programas de transferência de renda. São Paulo: Cortez Editora, 2004. 223 p.: bibl.

Analyzes programs of income transfer within the Brazilian social protection system, beginning with the concept of the basic citizenship income (*renda básica de cidadania*). Reports on previous pioneering efforts and the more recent nationwide efforts, as well as local initiatives. Discusses operational problems.

2200 **Silva, Marta Zorzal e.** A Vale do Rio Doce na estratégia do desenvolvimentismo brasileiro. Vitória, Brazil: Editora da Univ. Federal do Espírito Santo, 2004. 439 p.: bibl., ill., maps.

Situated in the broader discussion of the role and limits of the state, this case study traces the history of CVRD as a central feature of the developmentalist state of the 1930s to its privatization in the neoliberal 1990s and highlighting the role of state enterprise as a connection between states and markets. Based on a doctoral dissertation, the volume is well documented and contains material from the company's archives, including some photographs.

2201 **Soares, José de Lima.** Sindicalismo no ABC paulista: reestruturação produtiva e parceria. Brasília: Editora Universa, 2006. 428 p.: bibl.

Analysis of changing labor process in manufacturing in the ABC and of its impact on the organizational forms of the labor movement. With Taylorist and Fordist models giving way to flexible Japanese forms of production and outsourcing, the labor movement faces new challenges requiring new organizational forms.

2202 **Souto Maior, Luiz A.P.** O Brasil e o regionalismo continental frente a uma ordem mundial em transição. (*Rev. Bras. Polít. Int.*, 49:2, 2006, p. 42–59)

Article examines the implications of changes in the national and international arenas for Brazilian foreign policy and, in particular, the design of an emerging powers foreign policy.

2203 **Souza Ferreira Filho, Joaquim Bento de and Mark Jonathan Horridge.** Economic integration, poverty and regional inequality in Brazil. (*Rev. Bras. Econ./Rio de Janeiro*, 60:4, out./dez. 2006, p. 363–387, map, tables)

Analyzes the possible short-term impact of trade liberalization and integration on poverty and income distribution in Brazil using 2001 PNAD data. Finds that even a large shock would have a small impact on poverty, while recognizing that dynamic effects were not considered.

2204 **Suzigan, Wilson and João Furtado.** Industrial policy and development. (*CEPAL Rev.*, 89, Aug. 2006, p. 55–84, bibl.)

Using the neo-Schumpeterian/evolutionary approach, the authors analyze the success of Brazilian industrial policy until the 1970s and the unsuccessful attempts at industrial policy in the 1980s. The paper then evaluates the new industrial policy in effect in the 2002–2006 period, concluding that its new institutional organization, clear goals, and emphasis on innovation are positive, while the lack of coordination and political will and incompatibility with macroeconomic policy constitute significant weaknesses.

2205 **Tauile, José Ricardo.** Trabalho, autogestão e desenvolvimento: escritos escolhidos 1981–2005. Organização de Marcelo Paixão e Rodrigo Castelo Branco. Rio de Janeiro: Editora UFRJ, 2009. 385 p.: bibl., ill. (Col. Economia e sociedade)

A posthumous collection of 16 selected works from 1981–2005. Organized in three parts: labor processes and microelectronic technical base in modern Brazil, social organization of production and distribution of income, and solidarity economy and self-management in Brazil.

2206 Thomas, Vinod. From inside Brazil: development in a land of contrasts. Washington, D.C.: Stanford Economics and Finance: World Bank, 2006. 153 p.: bibl., ill., index, maps.

Written by the resident World Bank director for Brazil from 2001–2005, the book provides a review of contemporary Brazil from a policy perspective and through a World Bank lens with chapters on income distribution and inequality, sustainability, productivity, institutions and governance, and the quality of reforms. According to the author, Brazil's "unique human and natural assets as well as its institutional track record" make the outlook for the country among the best for developing countries. But, the author cautions, to achieve its potential, the policy reform agenda must capture the synergies among growth, distribution, and environmental protection.

2207 Tópicos de economia paulista para gestores públicos. Organização de Maria de Fátima Infante Araujo e Lígia Beira. Textos de Ana Paula Higa *et al.* São Paulo: Edições FUNDAP, 2007. 423 p.: bibl., ill., maps.

A collection of 15 densely written papers developed in the context of educational programs in the state of São Paulo for public managers. Organized in three thematic groups, including the general context of public policy (federal model, the fiscal problem, developmental trends), the public sector in the state of São Paulo, and trends in planning broadly defined.

2208 Trabalho e sindicato em antigos e novos territórios produtivos: comparações entre o ABC paulista e o sul fluminense. Organização de Iram Jácome Rodrigues e José Ricardo Ramalho. São Paulo: AnnaBlume, 2007. 364 p.: bibl., ill. (Col. Trabalho e contemporaneidade)

A collection of 13 papers on the organizational forms of manufacturing in new production locations between the ABC Paulista and the Fluminse South. Themes considered include comparisons between the regions, auto and metalworking industries, old and young workers, political articulation, sociopolitical networks and regional

development, modular and group forms of production, and labor action.

2209 Vieira, Flávio Lúcio Rodrigues. SUDENE e desenvolvimento sustentável: planejamento regional durante a década neoliberal. Prefácio de Tânia Bacelar. João Pessoa, Brazil: Editora Univ., Univ. Federal da Paraíba, 2004. 292 p.: bibl.

The volume analyzes the applied regional planning experience of Brazil's Northeast from the 1960s until the 1990s and the fundamental shift that occurred in the 1990s under pressure from international institutions. The final section of the book provides a state-by-state look at regional planning in the Northeast.

2210 Viola, Eduardo J. and **Héctor Ricardo Leis.** Sistema internacional com hegemonia das democracias de mercado: desafios de Brasil e Argentina. Florianópolis, Brazil: Editora Insular; Brasília: Santiago Dantas, 2007. 231 p.: bibl.

Written by political scientists, this book explores through a comparative lens the impact of globalization on democratic institutions in Argentina and Brazil, analyzing various globalizing processes in terms of their ability to strengthen or weaken democratic trends and institutions in each country.

2211 Von Mettenheim, Kurt. Still the century of government savings banks? The Caixa Econômica Federal. (*Rev. Econ. Polít.*, 26:1, jan./março 2006, p. 39–57, graphs, tables)

This article explores government banking, social inclusion, and democracy through a case study of the Brazilian federal government savings bank, Caixa Econômica Federal. Savings banks have expanded or contracted over time in Brazil in response to changing policy regimes and economic conditions. Since capitalization to meet Central Bank and Basel Accord guidelines in 2001, Caixa has modernized while continuing to serve as an agent of government policy, expanding both popular credit and savings activities as well as investment banking.

2212 Zambon Monte, Edson and **Erly Cardoso Teixeira.** Impactos da Área de Livre Comércio das Américas (ALCA), com gradual desgravação tarifária, na economia brasileira. (*Nova Econ./Belo Horizonte,* 17:1, jan./abril 2007, p. 37–63, bibl., graphs, tables)

Using the Global Trade Analysis Project (GTAP) general equilibrium model, the authors examine the possible impact of a Free Trade Area of the Americas on Brazil. The authors find that few agribusiness sectors and much of the manufacturing sector would not be competitive under any scenario while industries such as forestry, textiles, and footwear would undergo a significant increase in production and exports. Brazilian economic growth and welfare would increase modestly according to the model.

SOCIOLOGY

GENERAL

ENRIQUE PUMAR, *Associate Professor of Sociology, Catholic University*

THE WORKS REVIEWED for this section of *HLAS* 67 reflect the recent thematic growth of sociology in Latin America. The tone and content of this literature could not be more different than the scholarship of decades ago. For one, studies produced during the 1960 and 1970s intended, at their core, to refute vulgar interpretations of modernization theory. As such, Latin American sociologists took antithetical positions to practically every assertion proposed by aficionados of this perspective and its structural functionalist core. In no other issue is this trend more evident than with regard to the genesis and impact of development policies.

While over a decade ago a distinct Latin American sociology could be discerned rooted in the controversies of dependency and postdependency paradigms, it is clear from a reading of the entries that follow that Latin America sociology today is more globalized, comfortably inserted in continental and American perspectives, aware of the potentials and limitations of transnationalism as an analytical tool, and very attentive to other issues besides the economic ills inflicting the region.

The items reviewed here also reflect what for many may have been unforeseen years ago. Today, Latin American sociologists, following a cue from their US counterparts, dedicate an unprecedented amount of energy to exploring contemporary social problems at the expense of engaging in more reflective theorizing. Hence the entries reviewed here are organized into five practical rubrics: social inequality, politics and economics, human capital, crime and security, and religious and cultural values.

The first two topics continue to thrive despite recurrent pluralistic elections and a healthy macroeconomic performance, amidst the stubborn legacy of social inequality that plagues the region. Given this paradoxical situation, it is only fitting that the study of marginality continues to occupy center stage. Particularly noteworthy is the controversy spearheaded by Janice Perlman and her critics regarding the fruitfulness of examining the fate of the urban poor through the lenses of marginality and the mechanisms of exclusion that this literature identifies (item **2251**). It is significant that in addition to underlining how the insertion of Latin American economies into global markets is partly to blame for the despair that remains in some neighborhoods around major cities, there is the realization that poverty is multidimensional and as such there are middle-range mechanisms, such as those identified in the concepts of vulnerability and exclusion, that also provide persuasive explanations for the persistence of this pesky social ill.

Other topics that continue to attract much attention among scholars are those pertaining to religion and culture. Predominating here are concerns for how often secularization, democracy, and multiculturalism seem to accompany cosmopolitanism. Specialists have also turned their attention to the social responsibilities assumed by the Church with regards to the poor and the Church's support for national reconciliation efforts. Good illustrations of this literature are the works examining how religious norms are embedded in the proclamations issued by Truth and Reconciliation Commissions and social justice policies (for example, see item **2232**). Related to issues of human capital, many studies explore how education can empower the poor to attain a better quality of life. Although this literature calls attention to an urgent social problem, that of educational opportunities and reforms in developing societies, the analysis often falls short of the sophistication one encounters in studies produced outside Latin America. This limitation results from a lack of comprehensive data sources to support the scope of analysis that the topic of education requires.

As one may expect given the fears about crime that reign in nearly every country of the continent, research related to crime and personal insecurity has flourished of late (items **2226** and **2254**). The studies reviewed here present many valuable insights. Rather than examining crime as a mere consequence of fluctuations in domestic markets, Latin American scholars relate the flow of crime to inefficiencies in policing, infant intra-agency collaboration, and the exogenous market demand for drugs. Another provocative assertion is the one put forth by Curbet regarding the ways in which the vulnerabilities of globalization incite risk taking and deviant behaviors (item **2225**). Finally, as with many other social issues, Latin American scholars have not refrained from formulating proposals to resolve this crisis. Hence, issues such as crime prevention and the state capacity to contain organizations or even scale down the level of crime have not gone unnoticed (items **2223** and **2237**).

2213 América Latina y el Caribe: territorios religiosos y desafíos para el diálogo. Compilación de Aurelio Alonso Tejada. Buenos Aires: Consejo Latinoamericano de Ciencias Sociales, 2008. 395 p.: bibl., ill. (Grupos de Trabajo de CLACSO)

This collection of essays brings together a selection of papers presented in a 2005 workshop sponsored by the Working Group on Religion and Society in Mexico. The essays in this volume address three major concerns in the field of religion. The first is the ongoing possibilities for dialogue among different religions and denominations; the second, the intrinsic power relations embedded in religious practices and the capacity of religious movements. And the last explores how demographic changes, particularly those associated with transnationalism, have altered the territorial scope of religious practices and beliefs. Rather than approaching these ambitious topics

from the more traditional structural functional perspective, the authors in this volume investigate how dynamic social constructions impact institutional practices.

2214 Auyero, Javier; Pablo Lapegna; and Fernanda Page Poma. Patronage politics and contentious collective action: a recursive relationship. (*Lat. Am. Polit. Soc.*, 51:3, Fall 2009, p. 1–31, bibl.)

Auyero and his coauthors examine four scenarios in which patronage and collective action intersect: network breakdown, patron certification, clandestine support, and reaction to threat. Through an ethnographic examination of these instances, the authors go to great lengths to demonstrate the reciprocal connection between patronage and collective action in sparking protest movements among the urban dispossessed in Argentina today. Contrary to the conclusions reached by other scholars of contentious politics, the study concludes that more attention needs to be paid to how collective action impacts patronage arrangements.

Babb, Florence E. The tourism encounter: fashioning Latin American nations and histories. See item **435**.

2215 Barrientos, Armando and **Claudio Santibáñez.** New forms of social assistance and the evolution of social protection in Latin America. (*J. Lat. Am. Stud.*, 41:1, Feb. 2009, p. 1–26, tables)

The authors begin their study with an overview of social protection policies in Latin America, emphasizing three distinct patterns which could be roughly grouped into policies adopted prior to the crisis of the 1980s, during the structural adjustment and liberalization of the 1980s, and the more recent unconditional and conditional income transfer and antipoverty programs. The article concludes that the new forms of social protection policies throughout the region must be grounded in an understanding of the multidimensional and intergenerational nature of poverty. The emphasis of new programs, they argue, should be strengthening the capacity of the poor and enhancing their human capital potential.

2216 Barrientos, Armando; Jasmine Gideon; and **Maxine Molyneux.** New developments in Latin America's social policy. (*Dev. Change/Oxford*, 39:5, Sept. 2008, p. 759–774, bibl., graph)

The article argues that the latest wave of social policy reforms in Latin America represents a clear break from the past, showing policy innovations to respond to social protection needs. One of the distinct features of the new social policies is the use of cash transfers to incentivize the poor to participate in human capital development opportunities. To illustrate this point, the authors focus their attention on the extent of recent policy reforms in Chile, Mexico, and Bolivia. Key features of new policy programs are the emphasis on citizen rights, household capacity, and antipoverty policies. The sources of the new forms of social policy are tied to the broader perspectives of changes in models of national development.

Border crossings: transnational Americanist anthropology. See item **439**.

2217 Bülow, Marisa von. Networks of trade protest in the Americas: toward a new labor internationalism? (*Lat. Am. Polit. Soc.*, 51:2, Summer 2009, p. 1–28, bibl., graphs, tables)

Von Bülow analyzes how labor federations and their allies in civil society from Brazil, Chile, Mexico, and the US networked to articulate social clauses in trade agreements between 1990 and 2004. The author argues that to understand transnational collective action one needs to go beyond specific interests to explore how mechanisms of conflict resolution help actors overcome obstacles in order to construct shared goals. Moreover, she argues that some of the divisions among labor organizations are the legacy of ideological traditions. One way to overcome the weight of ideologies is to propose a broad base inclusive agenda that would transcend particular concerns such as the *Labor's Platform for the Americas.*

Candados y contrapesos: la protección de los programas, políticas y derechos sociales en México y América Latina. See item **1052**.

2218 Caro, Isaac. Identidades judías contemporáneas en América Latina. (*Atenea/Concepción*, 497, primer semestre 2008, p. 79–93, photos)

Caro outlines the basic principles of a new Jewish Latin American identity. This new identity is more heterogeneous today than in previous decades. The new Jewish Latin American identity is more decentralized, secular, and progressive than in the past. This new Jewish identity, moreover, celebrates delinked individual interpretations of Judaism stripped from such traditional institutions as the family and the synagogue. Caro asserts that as a reaction to this growing trend, there has also been a resurgence of orthodoxy among many Jewish families who oppose the recent trends.

2219 Congreso Latinoamericano y Caribeño de Ciencias Sociales, Quito, 2007. Mujeres y escenarios ciudadanos. Edición de Mercedes Prieto. Quito: FLACSO, Sede Ecuador: Ministerio de Cultura, 2008. 330 p.: bibl. (50 años FLACSO)

From a comparative perspective, this

volume examines the role of Latin American women in politics. One of the main goals of the book is to underline the increasing relevance of women's political participation at the same time it calls for a more inclusive political environment. The essays are organized in two sections. The first presents an overview of different conceptual issues affecting women and politics, while the second focuses on more specific case studies. As Mercedes Prieto states in the introduction, one of the innovations of this anthology is that all the contributors are women engaged in social science research.

2220 Congreso Latinoamericano y Caribeño de Ciencias Sociales, *Quito*, *2007*. Mundos del trabajo y políticas públicas en América Latina. Edición de Betty Espinosa, Ana Esteves y Marcela Alejandra Pronko. Quito: FLACSO Ecuador: Ministerio de Cultura, 2008. 324 p.: bibl., ill., maps. (Col. 50 años)

The book analyzes several employment policies designed to minimize the social effects of volatile labor markets and structural adjustment policies. Particular attention is paid to how labor market opportunities affect the youth and the different regional policies to generate employment. The first part of the book intends to provide an overview of the issue and a framework of analysis. The papers in the second section investigate employment in the rural sector. The third and last section takes a more regional approach investigating cases from the Southern Cone, Mexico, and Cuba.

2221 Consejo Latinoamericano de Ciencias Sociales. Grupo de Trabajo Pobreza y Políticas Sociales. Seminario Latinoamericano, *Buenos Aires*, *2004*. Retos para la integración social de los pobres en América Latina. Compilación de Carlos Barba Solano. Textos de Anete Brito Leal Ivo *et al.* Buenos Aires: CLACSO, 2009. 410 p.: bibl., ill. (Col. Grupos de trabajo)

This collection examines how liberal economic policies and the politics of privatization rather than generating new wealth have deepened and altered the patterns of social inequalities and created new mechanisms of social exclusion in Latin America. Using a comparative perspective, the authors in this volume propose new interdisciplinary paradigms that would enable them to examine the complexities of poverty. The book is organized in three sections. The first is comprised of five essays that discuss different conceptual aspects of poverty research and policies. The second, consisting of two papers, evaluates integration and stabilization policies. The third focuses specifically on the plight of the urban poor through an assessment of the policies of social inclusion.

2222 Creer y poder hoy. Edición de Cátedra Manuel Ancízar, Clemencia Tejeiro, Fabián Sanabria-S. y William Mauricio Beltrán Cely. Bogotá: Univ. Nacional de Colombia, Sede Bogotá, Dirección Académica, Facultad de Ciencias Humanas, 2007. 506 p.: bibl., ill. (some col.).

This diverse collection of essays originated as a series of lectures and workshops at the National University of Colombia. Unlike other volumes with a very narrow focus of analysis, this one explores the broad theme of religion in the contemporary world from interdisciplinary perspectives and theoretical orientations. One of the motivations behind this series was the effect of the events of September 11. In the case of this book, the contextual situation is important because the common theme of the book is the call for pluralism and acceptance of various religious convictions.

2223 Crimen organizado en América Latina y el Caribe. Edición de Luis Guillermo Solís Rivera y Francisco Rojas Aravena. Santiago: FLACSO, Secretaría General: Catalonia, 2008. 385 p.: bibl., ill., map.

This collection of essays reflects on the challenges faced by democratic regimes as they confront transnational organized criminal organizations. Criminal actors create two sources of difficulties for democracies. The first is internal as these regimes have a tendency to dedicate scarce resources to combating organized crime and debating the effectiveness of strategies, while simultaneously attempting to control the effects of corruption. The second set of problems arises with regard to state-society relations when organized crime challenges the rule of law and undermines confidence in the economy and governing institutions. The book concludes with a call for more international support for judicial and political reforms that would enhance the capacity of government to confront corruption.

2224 Cultural agency in the Americas. Edited by Doris Sommer. Durham, N.C.: Duke Univ. Press, 2006. 385 p.: bibl., ill., index.

This anthology consists of a compilation of essays from a 2001 conference held in Cuzco to analyze the role of cultural agency in the Americas. The essays in the collection approach this topic from a critical post-Marxist perspective. One of the basic premises of the book is that rather than being value neutral, culture constitutes a terrain of political contention and as such, culture can do damage, such as when it is envoked to legitimize acts of domination, as well as to do good through the power of oppositional discourse and resistance. The intention of these essays, as stated at the outset, is to open discursive possibilities to democratize capitalist democracy.

2225 Curbet, Jaume. Conflictos globales, violencias locales. Presentación de Paco Moncayo Gallegos y Adrián Bonilla. Prólogo de Alfredo Santillán. Quito: FLACSO, 2007. 275 p.: bibl. (Ciudadanía y violencias; 1)

This book contextualizes the roots of rising personal insecurity in Latin America within the framework of transformations brought about by globalization and the uncertainties and risk rewards inherent in contemporary capitalism. With regard to the former, Curbet asserts that the transnationalization of population movements and crime, together with increasing economic interdependence, has increased the objective and subjective sense of vulnerability among citizens. Global environmental degradation exacerbates the sense of despair and fatalism because these problems seem impossible to resolve in the short term. Finally, the increasing economic competition and risks associated with the mobility of capital seem to reward risk takers.

2226 Dammert, Lucía. Perspectivas y dilemas de la seguridad ciudadana en América Latina. Quito: FLACSO Ecuador: Quito, Alcaldía Metropolitana, 2007. 334 p.: bibl., ill. (Ciudadanía y violencias; 2)

This anthology of essays by Dammert analyzes five different aspects associated with personal insecurity in Latin America. Drawing data from the Southern Cone, particularly Argentina and Chile, the author discusses such topics as the institutional reforms spearheaded by democratic regimes to deter crime, the question of popular fear and how it determines the spatial organization of multiple Latin American cities, and the difficulties associated with the coordination of crime prevention. The first part of the book includes essays that discuss different aspects of crime prevention. The second part examines specific topics of crime in Argentina and Chile.

2227 De la Fuente, Alejandro. The new Afro-Cuban cultural movement and the debate on race in contemporary Cuba. (*J. Lat. Am. Stud.*, 40:4, Nov. 2008, p. 697–720, ill.)

In this article, De la Fuente discusses his well-known and controversial assertion that one of the effects of the so-called Special Period was to bring to the surface existing racist practices and stereotypes in Cuba. Analyzing the common grievances articulated by artists, musicians, visual artists, academics, and activists, he examines the rise of the new Afro-Cuban cultural movement. One of the peculiarities of this movement is that it does not center on a particular leader or leadership group, but rather is loosely arranged around shared concerns for racial equality. The author concludes that the movement has increased awareness of racial problems and keeps the future of race on the minds of authorities and the public alike. The movement is weakened by its failure to speak with a single voice.

2228 De los saberes de la emancipación y de la dominación. Coordinación de Ana Esther Ceceña. Textos de Ana Esther Ceceña *et al.* Buenos Aires: CLACSO, 2008. 282 p.: bibl., ill. (Col. Grupos de trabajo)

This collection of essays examines how mechanisms of power and domination are usually embedded in such cultural forms as discourse, ideology, and knowledge. A central concern of the book is understanding how different forms of cultural articulation that are intended to liberalize social actors from the pitfalls of oppression and subjugation end up encouraging us to conform to existing social orders. The essays illustrate the working of these mechanisms of conformity by examining cases from Colombia, Mexico, and the Southern Cone countries. A few chapters, including one on Bolivia and another on Colombia, discuss the resistance and emancipation attempts of popular counterhegemonic social movements.

2229 Desigualdades sociales y ciudadanía desde las culturas juveniles en América Latina. Coordinación de José Antonio Trejo Sánchez, Jorge Arzate Salgado y Alicia Itatí Palermo. México: Univ. Autónoma del Estado de México, Facultad de Ciencias Políticas y Sociales: Miguel Ángel Porrúa, 2010. 332 p.: bibl., ill. (Las ciencias sociales)

This collection analyzes the various manifestations of popular cultural expression by poor and disenfranchised youth throughout Latin America. Through a number of detailed case studies, each author explores the distinct mechanisms of cultural production among youth groups, accentuating the role of agency in creative processes which often take on political overtones as these processes become acts of identity formation and survival. The collection is organized in three sections. The first attempts to establish a distinct methodological and conceptual framework of analysis to help us understand the growing problem of urban alienation among the Latin American youth. The second examines specific impediments to social adaptation and experiences of exclusion from the point of view of youth in a handful of cities. Finally, the third section investigates different manifestations of cultural production.

2230 Dijk, Teun Adrianus van. Racism and discourse in Spain and Latin America. Amsterdam; Philadelphia, Pa.: John Benjamins Pub., 2005. 197 p.: bibl., indexes. (Discourse approaches to politics, society, and culture; 14)

In this book, van Dijk extends his approach to elite discursive racism to Spain and Latin America. Drawing from a content analysis of various media outlets and political discourse, van Dijk concludes that elites in Spain reproduce, in less dogmatic terms, the kinds of racist discourse found elsewhere throughout Europe. In Latin America, on the other hand, elite discursive racism against indigenous and African-American populations has persisted in more subtle manifestations since the end of colonialism. This continuity, van Dijk argues, is the result of elite control over institutions of cultural diffusion.

2231 Diversidad cultural y desigualdad social en América Latina y el Caribe: desafíos de la integración global. Compilación de Dana de la Fontaine y Pablo Christian Aparicio. México: Fundación Heinrich Böll, 2008. 302 p.: bibl., ill., map. (Fundación Heinrich Böll; 25)

This collection of essays published under the auspices of the Heinrich Böll Foundation, examines the cultural impact of globalization in diverse societies throughout Latin America. The book identifies three distinct patterns of cultural reaction to globalization: resistance, assimilation, and "hybridization." One of the aims of the book is to attempt to discern which segments of the population are most likely to adopt one or more of the cultural reactions since the three can coexist in one social context. Not surprisingly, those who are most likely to resist the effects of globalization are those who live at the margins of society.

2232 Dobles, Ignacio. Memorias del dolor: consideraciones acerca de las Comisiones de la Verdad en América Latina. San José: Arlekín, 2009. 345 p.: bibl.

This book presents a serious attempt to understand the sociology of memory in situations where grievous injustices have been committed by oppressive autocratic and authoritarian regimes. The aim of the book is to understand from a conceptual and philosophical position how Truth Commissions in Latin America should take into account selective memory and what should be regarded as "truth" during their deliberations. The author also makes the point that the work of these commissions constitutes a negotiated compromise of many memories. To understand this political meddling, the author anchors his interpretations on the work of Walter Benjamin. While the book does not examine in depth the empirical work of any single commission in Latin America, it provides a welcome theoretical framework for understanding how this path to reconciliation actually works.

2233 Domingues, José Maurício. Latin America and contemporary modernity: a sociological interpretation. New York, N.Y.: Routledge, 2008. 189 p.: bibl., index. (Routledge advances in sociology; 37)

This ambitious book examines the cultural and social forces by which Latin America confronts the manifestations of contemporary modernity. The book makes the point that although the region came into being as a result of the expansion of the modern world, today Latin America finds itself participating in modern ventures from a marginal position in the periphery and semiperiphery. The book follows an interdisciplinary framework of analysis mixing elements from continental and American philosophical perspectives to investigate such elements of modernity as the effects of justice and citizenship, national development, globalization, domination, and solidarity.

2234 Fernandes, Florestan. Dominación y desigualdad: el dilema social latinoamericano. Presentación de Heloísa Rodrigues Fernandes. Bogotá: Siglo del Hombre Editores; Ciudad de Buenos Aires: CLACSO, 2008. 251 p.: bibl. (Biblioteca univ. Ciencias sociales y humanidades. Col. Pensamiento crítico latinoamericano)

This anthology collects some of the most popular essays by Florestan Fernandes, a sociologist who played a key role in popularizing the critical sociological school in Brazil. The essays in the collection comprise a representative sample of his thinking from 1945 through one of his latest writings on education published in 1989. The essays are complemented by a short introduction by Heloísa Fernandes that provides an overview of Fernandes' thinking. The book closes with a bibliography of Fernandes' published books.

2235 Filgueira, Fernando. El desarrollo maniatado en América Latina: estados superficiales y desigualdades profundas. Buenos Aires: CLACSO, 2008. 196 p.: bibl., ill. (Col. CLACSO-CROP)

Latin America has reached macro levels of development that are sometimes comparable with middle-income nations around the globe. Paradoxically, the region's development path has been characterized by contradictions that manifest themselves in four areas: deepening urbanization, elevated levels of inequality, the tendency of specific demographic sectors to become vulnerable, and strangled state institutions. Filgueira explores various challenges for development while he proposes sensible policies that would transcend market arrangements and resolve these challenges.

2236 Fox, Patricia D. Being and blackness in Latin America: uprootedness and improvisation. Gainesville: Univ. Press of Florida, 2006. 207 p.: bibl., index.

Fox has produced a study of cultural context around blackness in Latin America. She examines the official print media to analyze the discourse of racial repression and apprehension and then she compares this field with the stylish presentation of black artists. What results from this analysis is a portrait of survival by African-Americans and a celebration for their many contributions. The book is organized in two parts. The first grounds African-American narratives in the values of uprootedness and improvisation. The second unbounds multiple manifestations of both these traits in many cultural experiences.

2237 Garzón Vergara, Juan Carlos. Mafia & Co.: the criminal networks in Mexico, Brazil, and Colombia. Bogotá: Editorial Planeta Colombiana, 2008. 244 p.: bibl., ill., map.

In this book Garzón studies crime organizations in Mexico, Brazil, and Colombia to understand how the transnationalization of crime affects developing societies. The book dedicates considerable attention to two aspects of this problem: first, the operational organization of criminal gangs; and second, the increasing difficulties ruling elites face when they decide to confront this problem. Part of the difficulty of controlling organized crime, especially as it relates to drug trafficking, is the sustained demand for drugs and the many opportunities for trafficking, exacerbated by interdependent global markets.

2238 Género y globalización. Coordinación de Alicia Girón. Textos de Virginia Vargas *et al.* Buenos Aires: CLACSO, 2009. 285 p.: bibl., ill. (Col. Grupos de trabajo)

This book examines the effect of globalization on gender and the role of women in society. One of the basic premises of the work is that globalization has adversely and disproportionally affected women throughout Latin America and yet the gender dimension of globalization is often overlooked among public policy circles. In addition to the usual discrimination women suffer in a patriarchal society, globalization has deepened the social inequalities. In addition, the financial instability brought about by the imposition of neoliberal policies and the increased competition in labor markets usually means fewer opportunities for women who are perceived as care takers. The book is organized in three sections. The first discusses the feminist critique of globalization. The second examines the dimensions of social inequalities affecting women. The third section analyzes the effects of privatization on women's rights.

Glassman, Amanda *et al.* Confronting the chronic disease burden in Latin America and the Caribbean. See item **1039**.

2239 Hegemonía e interculturalidad: poblaciones originarias y migrantes: la interculturalidad como uno de los desafíos del siglo XXI. Compilación de Cristina García Vázquez. Textos de Tomás Calvo Buezas *et al.* Buenos Aires: Prometeo Libros, 2009. 344 p.: bibl. (Col. Comunicación y crítica cultural)

García Vázquez and her collaborators explore how cultural connections are constructed and sustained in a globalized society. The authors discuss two features of globalization that merit further study. One is the rapid flow of people across borders and the question of whether immigrants dilute national character and social solidarity, as Huntington argued before his death. The second feature is what many have characterized as the double movement caused by globalization—the pull toward homogeneity and its counterfactual resistance. With the exception of the first chapter that draws heavily from migration data from Spain, the book is dedicated to such conceptual issues

as the mechanisms of cultural diffusion, reproduction, and mediation.

2240 Inglehart, Ronald and **Marita Carballo.** ¿Existe Latinoamérica?: un análisis global de diferencias transculturales. (*Perf. Latinoam.*, 16:31, enero/junio 2008, p. 13–38, bibl., maps, tables)

Utilizing data from the World Value Survey, Inglehart and Carballo ask two transcendental questions about how culture fosters distinct regional identities. Hence they ask, does Latin America constitute a coherent cultural region? And, does culture matter? The answers to these two questions defy conventional wisdom. First, the authors find that there is a discernable Latin American culture. More importantly, the authors conclude that within cultural zones there are discernable differences among nations, attributing these distinct identities to particular legacies of history, geography, and different levels of human capital. Economic factors alone do not determine cultural formation, the study concludes.

2241 Inmigración latinoamericana en España: el estado de la investigación. Edición de Anna Ayuso y Gemma Pinyol. Barcelona, Spain: Fundació CIDOB, 2010. 330 p.: bibl. (Interrogar la actualidad. Serie América Latina)

Analyzing sectored data from 1960 through 2005, the contributors to this collection assess the impact of Latin American migration flows to Spain. The book documents the rise of Latin American immigration to Spain, particularly after 2001 when immigrants from Latin America surpassed those from other regions. In addition, the place of origin of Latin American immigrants has also changed from the Southern Cone and the Spanish-speaking Caribbean to the Andean region. Despite this shift, the sociological composition of this migrant group has remained relatively young, with diverse migration status, and with close transnational links.

2242 Jansen, Robert S. Populist mobilization: a new theoretical approach to populism. (*Sociol. Theory*, 27:2, June 2011, p. 75–96)

In this article, Jansen proposes a new practice-based approach to populism that he calls populist mobilization. Drawing insights from the recent resurgence of populism throughout Latin America, the article first identifies the conceptual confusions and disagreements that characterized earlier stages of populist literature. For Jansen, populist mobilization is not elite-based, but instead is a political project that encourages mobilization among marginalized social sectors. Populist mobilization is often public, confrontational, and consisting of a wide array of repertoires—symbolic, rhetorical, and action-based, among others—designed to challenge established political practices.

2243 Jóvenes universitarios en latino-américa, hoy. Coordinación de María Herlinda Suárez Zozaya y José Antonio Pérez Islas. México: UNAM: Consejo Iberoamericano de Investigación en Juventud: M.A. Porrúa, 2008. 392 p.: bibl., ill. (Problemas educativos de México)

This compilation of essays assesses the state of university students. The book is roughly divided thematically into three sections. The first chapter proposes a useful historical overview of the role of the university in society and how it has changed since the end of the colonial period. The second group of essays is arranged along thematic topics such as the employability of university graduates in Latin America. The rest of the studies present empirical data related to academic attainment among university students in Colombia, Mexico, Chile, and Argentina.

2244 Kirkendall, Andrew J. Paulo Freire and the Cold War politics of literacy. Chapel Hill: Univ. of North Carolina Press, 2010. 246 p.: bibl., index.

In this book Kirkendall examines the life of Brazilian critical educator Paulo Freire. In many ways, the book is an intellectual biography since it examines Freire's critical pedagogy at length and situates his teachings as a part of the human struggle to grapple with the meanings of social conditions in specific historical contexts. According to Kirkendall, much of the controversy surrounding Freire's advocacy for literacy must be understood in the context of the Cold War. His teachings go beyond the mere acquisition of basic reading and writing skills, and he is therefore perceived to be subversive and partisan in light of the ideological dogmas of the period.

2245 Levine, Daniel H. The future of Christianity in Latin America. (*J. Lat. Am. Stud.*, 41:1, Feb. 2009, p. 121–145, photo)

After reviewing the recent history of Catholicism in Latin America, Levine makes the prediction that the region will remain Christian, but religious practices will become more pluralistic and competitive. According to Levine, recent political democratic trends have impacted not just the political arena, but also religious life. At question with regards to religiosity in Latin America today is not the predominance of Christian beliefs, but how churches and their followers will interact in less regulated, institutionalized, and more democratic environments. The biggest challenge ahead for Christianity is how to build meaningful communities in globalized, politically mobilized societies.

2246 Luchas contrahegemónicas y cambios políticos recientes de América Latina. Edición de Margarita López Maya, Nicolás Iñigo Carrera y Pilar Calveiro. Textos de Pilar Calveiro *et al.* Buenos Aires: Consejo Latinoamericano de Ciencias Sociales-CLACSO, 2008. 384 p.: bibl. (Col. Grupos de trabajo)

The book examines the fate of various counterhegemonic movements in Mexico, the Andean countries, Uruguay, and Brazil. The first part of the book is dedicated to examining conceptual theories of popular resistance movements. The essays in this section analyze how popular social movements attempt to widen democratic spaces in societies governed by left-of-center regimes. In the second part, particular case studies contextualize strategies employed by popular movements to fight social inequalities outside traditional frameworks of interest mediation.

2247 Martínez Franzoni, Juliana. Domesticar la incertidumbre en América Latina: mercado laboral, política social y familias. San José: Editorial UCR, 2008. 307 p.: bibl., ill., index, map. (Instituto de Investigaciones Sociales)

One of the central questions this book examines is how different social classes manage the mounting risks associated with labor market disequilibrium and weak social welfare policies in Latin America. Not surprisingly, the author asserts that the answer depends on the level of social stratifications and the peculiar formation of labor markets from country to country. Generally speaking, the author concludes that the risks associated with inefficient labor markets and weak welfare regimes have transformed less affluent families into units of production that exercise formal and informal economic activities. After a careful examination of welfare data, the author identifies three distinct patterns of welfare regimes: the state productive, the informal-familiar, and the state protectionist. Each of these regimes offers different levels of state-society relations and levels of social services.

2248 Molyneux, Maxine. The "neoliberal turn" and the new social policy in Latin America: how neoliberal, how new? (*Dev. Change/Oxford*, 39:5, Sept. 2008, p. 775–797, bibl.)

Molyneux examines the evolution of social protection in Latin America as it relates to "the new social policy" in the region. In particular, three policy elements are discussed—the new interpretations of neoliberalism, the role of the state, and the importance of the neoliberal reform agenda. In addition to policy evolution, the article also compares the current system of social protection with the prevailing practices and modalities associated with structural reforms in the 1960s and 1970s. The development of a new social policy is attributed to the conjunction of structural macroeconomic shocks during the 1980s and the push for policy reforms that followed. Molyneux concludes that despite political rhetoric, the state continues to be an active participant in the formulation and implementation of social safety net policies.

2249 Multiculturalismo, educación intercultural y derechos indígenas en las Américas. Edición de Gunther Dietz, Rosa Guadalupe Mendoza Zuany y Sergio Téllez Galván. Quito: Abya-Yala, 2008. 302 p.: bibl., ill.

One of the concerns that the essays in this volume share is the celebration of the multicultural essence of the Americas. Organized into four different sections, the authors analyze different aspects of the intersection between education and multiculturalism from bilingual education to the consequences of implementing a multicultural pedagogy. The volume also considers how migration and multi-ethnic societies have promoted diversity in education. Finally, part three, consisting of three essays, discusses the increasing influence that new actors—indigenous movements, refugees, and others—exercise in drafting educational policy.

2250 Pears, Angela. Doing contextual theology. London; New York: Routledge, 2010. 196 p.: bibl., index.

The book departs from the assumption that Christianity is a religion in transition and proposes to analyze its development by recognizing the contextual nature of ideas, beliefs, and theologies. In the specific case of Latin America, the author proposes an investigation of how poverty and despair drive the diffusion of justice-seeking interpretations of Christianity with specific references to the development of liberation theologies. The latter case-study is only one of six chapters in the book with particular relevance for students of Latin America. The rest of the essays take a more critical and reflective approach to a variety of justice-seeking perspectives, such as feminism and postcolonialism.

2251 Perlman, Janice E. Favela: four decades of living on the edge in Rio de Janeiro. Oxford; New York: Oxford Univ. Press, 2010. 412 p.: bibl., ill., index, maps.

After four decades of field research in the favelas of Rio, Perlman writes in this book that favelas today are an extension of urban life in mega-cities rather than exclusive zones of deprivation. Rather than characterizing residents in these neighborhoods as marginals, Perlman prefers Amartya Sen's "capability deprivation." The latter captures one of the more provocative ideas in her work, which is that the basic reasons for the existing deprivation in favelas are structural impediments and constraining mechanisms that erode the capacity of the poor to succeed, not the negative reasons associated with marginality.

2252 Personas con discapacidad y acceso a servicios educativos en Latinoamérica: análisis de situación. Dirigida por Pilar Samaniego de García. Textos de Ramón Porras Vallejo *et al.* Madrid: Ediciones CINCA, 2009. 534 p.: bibl., ill., 1 CD-ROM (3/4 in.). (Col. Cermi.es; 39)

The present volume provides a comprehensive overview of the state of students experiencing disabilities throughout Latin America. The conclusions and recommendations discussed in the book are based on empirical data up to 2008. As one might suppose, the findings analyzed in the book are both hopeful and disturbing for while the levels of illiteracy among this student population have been reduced drastically in the last decade, the levels of educational attainment continue to be well below the average student. This finding is all the more important at a time when the population of students with various types of disabilities continues to climb.

2253 Pobreza, desigualdad y exclusión social en la ciudad del siglo XXI. Coordinación de Rolando Cordera, Patricia Ramírez Kuri y Alicia Ziccardi. Colaboración de Leonardo Lomelí *et al.* México: UNAM, Seminario de la Cuestión Social: IIS: Siglo XXI Editores, 2008. 438 p.: bibl., ill. (some col.), maps (chiefly col.), plates. (Sociología y política)

The essays in this book examine the growing problem of marginality in urban areas of Latin America. Assuming that the experience of Latin America can help us understand how this phenomenon manifests itself in other cities through developing societies, the authors explore how structural factors create and perpetuate conditions of marginality. The introductory essay provides a comprehensive overview of different academic perspectives about the process of marginalization. This essay is followed by in-depth case studies from multiple cities through the region.

2254 Policing insecurity: police reform, security, and human rights in Latin America. Edited by Niels A. Uildriks. Lanham, Md.: Lexington Books, 2009. 262 p.: bibl., index.

This edited volume evaluates different attempts at law enforcement reforms in Latin America. The need for police reform is a byproduct of the post-authoritarian climate reigning throughout the region. This new political reality demands more effective police strategies to combat crime and sustain popular support for infant democratic regimes. As such, police departments have undertaken two types of reforms in recent years: operational changes, encouraging more transparency and accountability; and strategic changes such as the adoption of more community policing tactics. The impetus for many of these reforms has been driven by international actors, such as lending agencies and business interests, on the one hand, and state priorities on the other. The success of these reformist impulses varies from country to country depending on the level of corruption and other governance considerations.

2255 Producción de pobreza y desigualdad en América Latina. Coordinación de Alberto D. Cimadamore y Antonio David Cattani. Bogotá: Siglo del Hombre Editores; Ciudad Autónoma de Buenos Aires: CLACSO; Bergen, Norway: CROP, 2008. 231 p.: bibl., ill. (Biblioteca Univ. Ciencias sociales y humanidades. Temas para el diálogo y el debate) (Col. CLACSO-CROP)

This collection of essays attempts to analyze how poverty and social inequality reproduce themselves in developing societies. Analyzing the role of different institutions in Latin America, the book investigates how the constructions of such topics as the role of the state and governing regimes, labor markets, and even historic modes of appropriation have contributed to the reproduction of inequality in societies. In addition to moving beyond the thesis of the culture of poverty, the essays in this book also contribute to the sociology of knowledge of development ideas about poverty.

2256 ¿Qué hacer con las pandillas? Edición de Gino F. Costa y Carlos Romero. Textos de Carlos Mario Perea Restrepo *et al.* Miraflores, Peru: Ciudad Nuestra, 2009. 337 p.: bibl., ill.

In this book, Costa, Romero, and their collaborators are concerned with the widespread phenomena of youth gangs in multiple urban settings. The book is organized into five different parts. The first two essays assess the impact of the growth of gangs in Latin American societies in addition to providing an operational definition of the gang as a social actor. The second part discusses the development of youth gangs in Central America and Rio de Janeiro, their impact on society, and the multiple attempts to control these organizations. In the third part, three essays focus on the problem of youth gangs in the community of El Agustino in Lima. The fourth and fifth sections discuss a series of recommendations and good practices intended to control the problem of youth gangs.

2257 Race, colonialism, and social transformation in Latin America and the Caribbean. Edited by Jerome Branche. Gainesville: Univ. Press of Florida, 2008. 301 p.: bibl., ill., index, maps.

This collection of essays offers a comprehensive overview of colonial legacies of racial and social inequality in Latin America and the Caribbean. Rich in theoretical framework and close textual analysis, these essays offer new paradigms and approaches to both reading and resolving the opposing forces of race, class, and the power of states. [C.E. Griffin]

2258 Raza, etnicidad y sexualidades: ciudadanía y multiculturalismo en América Latina. Edición de Peter Wade, Fernando Urrea Giraldo y Mara Viveros. Bogotá: Univ. Nacional de Colombia, Facultad de Ciencias Humanas, Instituto CES, Escuela de Estudios de Género, 2008. 565 p.: bibl., ill., index. (Col. Lecturas CES)

This comprehensive volume investigates the intersection between citizenship and multiculturalism and how it manifests itself in particular with regard to the debate about inequality in Latin America. One innovative aspect of this book is that it considers the crucial role social class plays in shaping disparities among racial, ethnic, and gender relations. The first group of essays discusses the conceptual debate about identity and social boundaries. The second examines the role of government policies. Then the third, and more extensive, researches the social constructions of black masculinity and femininity. Lastly, the fourth section examines the political repercussions of sexism.

2259 Reconciliation, nations and churches in Latin America. Edited by Iain S. MacLean. Aldershot, England; Burlington, Vt.: Ashgate, 2006. 277 p.: bibl., index.

The volume addresses a gap in the literature of national reconciliations by exploring the role of theology, religion, and churches as political actors influencing the norms that govern reconciliation commissions in Latin America. The essays compiled in this volume are organized around three themes. The first focuses on specific case-studies regarding national and religious experiences with regard to national reconciliation. The second topic comprises two essays denoting Christian understandings of the notion of reconciliation. The final section assesses lessons from the past and future directions explored in national reconciliation literature.

2260 Redes sociales y salud pública: el apoyo social como una estrategia para enfrentar los problemas de salud, el divorcio y la violencia conyugal. Coordinación de María Zúñiga Coronado. Monterrey, Mexico: Univ. Autónoma de Nuevo León, 2007. 181 p.: bibl., ill. (Tendencias)

Focusing on Mexico as a case study, the six essays collected in this volume investigate different mechanisms of social support networks in the field of public health. The book is organized in two sections. The first explores the effectiveness of support networks in situations marked by personal illnesses. In the second part of the book, two essays examine how support networks console victims of the rising waves of divorce and domestic violence in Mexico.

2261 ¿El reino de Dios es de este mundo?: el papel ambiguo de las religiones en la lucha contra la pobreza. Compilación de Genaro Zalpa Ramírez y Hans Egil Offerdal. Bogotá: Siglo del Hombre Editores; Ciudad Autónoma de Buenos Aires: CLACSO; Bergen, Norway: CROP, 2008. 365 p.: bibl., ill. (Biblioteca univ. Ciencias sociales y humanidades. Temas para el diálogo y el debate) (Col. CLACSO-CROP)

The central focus of this collection is to analyze the relationship between Christian religions, the poor, and the Church's commitment to social justice. The essays depart from the dual interpretations of Marx on religion, whether Marxism envisions religion as "opium" or a catalyst for social justice. This paradox is evident in how the Catholic Church hierarchy has aligned itself with national elites while in the meantime grassroots voices have been more vocal advocates for social justice supporting the poor. To bridge these positions the authors underline the need to construct a dialog between religious convictions and the more empirical perspectives of social science research. The book concludes that the diversity of religious practices and concerns for the poor requires us to consider multiple approaches and perspectives.

2262 Religious pluralism, democracy, and the Catholic Church in Latin America. Edited by Frances Hagopian. Notre Dame, Ind.: Univ. of Notre Dame Press, 2009. 498 p.: bibl., ill., index.

This edited volume came about with support from the US Conference of Catholic Bishops and their concerns about the need to further study the potential challenges of secularism in Latin America. The book also discusses the eroding dominance of Catholicism as well as how religious practices have impacted democratic politics in the region. The book is organized into four sections. The first discusses Catholic institutions and beliefs in Latin America in the context of religious and social change; the second, how the Church has responded to the challenges presented by religious and political pluralism; the third, the influence of the church on public policy and democracy; and the final section touches on the past and the future of the Church in Latin America.

2263 Sánchez Serrano, Rolando. Capital social y posibilidades de desarrollo en los municipios: las condiciones socioculturales y el desempeño económico y político. Investigación de Rogelio Churata Tola *et al.* La Paz: PIEB: Plural Editores, 2007. 363 p.: bibl., ill., maps.

Through a series of in-depth interviews and focus groups, the author examines the role of municipal governments and local politics in the formation of social capital in three Bolivian communities. This book attempts to make a contribution to the literature on social capital and development with respect to Latin America. The first of the book's three parts offers a review and critique of contending theories of social capital. The second discusses the role of municipal governments in development paths and the contributions they make given the goals of diversification and decentralization of resources. And the third and final section investigates how social capital relates to the possibilities of development. The book concludes that social capital can also emerge out of the despair of the poor in working class communities and their desire to survive.

2264 Sanjinés C., Javier. Rescoldos del pasado: conflictos culturales en sociedades postcoloniales. La Paz: Programa de Investigación Estratégica en Bolivia, 2009. 233 p.: bibl.

In this book, Sanjinés contributes to the current debate regarding the state and the nation in postcolonial literature. In this highly theoretical book, Sanjinés proposes a Gramscian approach to mediate the social tensions and cleavages modernity infuses into the nation-state. In addition, he promotes a culture of integration, complementing normative and secular values, as mechanisms to promote solidarity. Although this book does not make any particular references to specific situations or countries in Latin America, it goes without saying that the conceptual framework would be most useful to students of multi-ethnic societies in the region. As with other academic essays, however, this book deprives us of a clear roadmap for fostering a culture of reciprocity and trust to cement multi-ethnic societies.

2265 Sojo, Carlos. La modernización sin estado: reflexiones en torno al desarrollo, la pobreza y la exclusión social en América Latina. San José: FLACSO Costa Rica, 2008. 252 p.: bibl., ill.

In this collection, Sojo reflects on how the role of the state could foster economic development and social well-being in Latin America. Sojo discusses the failure of the mercantilist state with regard to generating legal employment and an adequate living standard for the majority of citizens in the region. At the same time, he is skeptical about the capacities of societies to achieve these goals with minimal state intervention. The future role of the state for Sojo then is to endorse effective state institutions regardless of their size.

2266 **Stout, Noelle M.** Feminists, queers and critics: debating the Cuban sex trade. (*J. Lat. Am. Stud.*, 40:4, Nov. 2008, p. 721–742)

Following recent trends in urban anthropology, Stout challenges the tendency of contemporary of American, European feminists, and Cuban studies enthusiasts, to either conceive prostitutes as victims or demonize sex trade practices on the island, unintentionally supporting some pattern of state intervention or rehabilitation. According to Stout, the emphasis on criminalization and victimization of prostitution overlooks the particular socioeconomic conditions that fuel these practices and the advantages of perceiving sex workers as individuals responsible for their own decisions. The field research for this study was conducted between 2003 and 2004 in the city of Havana.

2267 **Tejeda, José Luis.** Latinoamérica fracturada: identidad, integración y política en América Latina. México: Centro de Cooperación Regional para la Educación de Adultos en América Latina y el Caribe: Miguel Ángel Porrúa, 2010. 176 p.: bibl. (Serie Las ciencias sociales)

The book examines the question of cultural fragmentation and how it relates to political and economic trends throughout Latin America today. Tejeda makes the point that although there has been a search for a common identity in Latin America since at least the 19th century, the process of multiculturalism accelerated by the demise of the bipolar world and the resurgence of indigenous cultures has fragmented the common identity of the region. Networks of transnational relations, economic integration regimes, and the occasional meddling of the US in the region also feed this process of fragmentation. However, rather than fostering outright confrontation, the resulting social tensions are mediated by widespread reliance on democratic and quasi-democratic mechanisms.

2268 **Toward a society under law: citizens and their police in Latin America.** Edited by Joseph S. Tulchin and Meg Ruthenburg. Washington, D.C.: Woodrow Wilson Center Press; Baltimore, Md.: Johns Hopkins Univ. Press, 2006. 342 p.: bibl., ill., index, maps.

Another study in the rapidly growing field of society studies; this book underscores the degree to which security forces, such as police forces, are becoming one of the main fault lines of governmentality throughout the region. [M. Casullo]

Wade, Peter. Race and ethnicity in Latin America. See item **713**.

2269 **Women's activism in Latin America and the Caribbean: engendering social justice, democratizing citizenship.** Edited by Elizabeth Maier and Nathalie Lebon. Foreword by Sonia E. Alvarez. New Brunswick, N.J.: Rutgers Univ. Press; Tijuana, Mexico: El Colegio de la Frontera Norte A.C., 2010. 375 p.: bibl., index.

This collection presents a comprehensive set of essays discerning feminist cultural and political interventions in Latin America and the Caribbean. Well-established upcoming scholars in the field author the essays. The heterogeneous array of essays that are part of this compendium cover a wide range of topics and perspectives in the six sections that comprise the book. However, in some form or another, they all analyze the manifestations of power relations, shifting identities, women's struggles to attain citizenship and social justice, and the transnational underpinnings of feminist activism.

MEXICO

ANTONIO UGALDE, Professor Emeritus of Sociology, The University of Texas at Austin

AS HAS BEEN THE CASE in past biennial reviews, the number of books with collected articles is copious. Some volumes contain a very large number of contributors and it is not known if the papers included have undergone a rigorous review process or were accepted with minor revisions. For this reason, and to improve the quality of materials published, it is laudable that those responsible for the new series on gender started by the prestigious Colegio de México have clarified that the articles published in the series are peer-reviewed.

Mexican sociology continues to diversify its topics of interest. Noticeable in this biennium—that includes research published mostly before 2008—is the interest in the social problems and quality of life of the elderly. In Mexico, as in all Latin American nations, reductions in the number of births and a lengthening life-span as a result of economic development have changed the shape of the demographic pyramid. Before long, in the absence of an effective safety net, the elderly are going to face nutrition and health problems, isolation, abandonment in some rural areas, and poverty. In recent years, violence has become Mexico's number one problem, with its impact touching all aspects of life: the political system, the economy, and most importantly the quality of life of each citizen. It can be said without exaggeration that every Mexican lives with fear. For the news media, the thousands of murders that are committed each year constitute a war. The government operations in different parts of the country against the drug cartels are referred to as the fronts. There are signs that the drug cartels with their immense resources and disregard for human rights have the upper hand.

It is not clear what contribution sociology can make to reduce today's war-like violence. In this biennium, sociologists continue to provide information about corruption and inefficiency within the institutions that have to fight the war: the local, state, and federal police, the army, the criminal justice system, and, in general, the institutions that should protect citizens. For example, the deplorable conditions of prisons have been well described by the surveys of inmates carried out by Azaola (item **2276**); and González Placencia *et al.* (item **2272**) have put together a collection of articles that raises questions about the trustworthiness of the official data on violence and the capabilities of law enforcement authorities. Both are good examples of solid research. Whether good research and more information about the current situation can help reduce poverty remains an open question.

More studies, from the perspective of political sociology, are needed on the possible outcomes of and opposition to decriminalizing drug use and allowing the US to resolve its own drug problem. Opinion surveys will also help to ascertain where the population stands on these issues. Interviews with opinion makers and political leaders will clarify who opposes and who favors the decriminalization option and the reasons for doing so. Other solutions, besides the incarceration of the thousands of people currently working for the cartels and committing the insidious crimes, need to be explored. Perhaps Mexico's social scientists could start doing research within the US (this will also break the myth that overseas research can only be done by scientists from wealthy countries), to determine the awareness of the US population and policymakers about the problems that US drug use creates in Mexico.

Rural sociology, which for many decades was an important field, is slowly fading. However, there are several important contributions that have assessed the impact of poverty reduction programs in rural areas and city slums. The agreement among the authors of these studies is very impressive (items **2274**, **2284**, and **2343**). Independently, they have studied the programs that have been designed and partially financed by international organizations (World Bank and Inter-American

Development Bank) and have concluded that after two decades the results are negligible. In the process, hundreds of millions of pesos have been wasted. A side comment for those interested in theory and methodology is that a few evaluations financed by the international agencies arrived at the opposite conclusion.

Studies of sexuality that began to interest sociologists not too long ago continue to grow in number. Amuchástegui and Szasz (item **2362**) have edited an excellent collection of 19 articles that advances our understanding of the influence that social and cultural variables have on our understanding of masculinity.

Migration continues to be a theme of interest. Nevertheless, the emphasis is less on demographic approaches than on understanding the consequences that migration has for those left behind, the recomposition of family roles, the interaction between migrant communities in the US and communities of origin, and the effect of return migration (see items **2306, 2331, 2357, 2358,** and **2363**).

From the beginning of this century, Mexican policymakers and academics have followed US congressional debates and presidential addresses regarding migration policies. Several contributions in this volume explain both the sense of hope that the Bush administration transmitted in its earlier years and the frustration when the hopes of an amnesty or regularization vanished.

The Mexican students of religion examine very different issues than their colleagues to the north; they continue to study the growth of evangelical and Baptist churches, the reasons behind the expansion, the consequences for the Catholic Church of the loss of religious monopoly, and the conflicts, at times violent, generated at the local level between Catholics and the followers of other churches (see, for example, items **2310, 2329,** and **2345**). Other researchers study religious traditions, such as local devotions to specific saints and virgins, and the transformation into festive events of traditions brought by migration and modernization (items **2283** and **2349**).

Mexican sociologists continue to be very productive and with scarce resources are making useful contributions to the study of migration, gender, political sociology, and into new areas such as sexuality and violence.

2270 Alarcón Olguín, Víctor. Realineamiento electoral en México: 2000–2006. (*Iztapalapa/México*, 27:61, julio/dic. 2006, p. 51–69, bibl., maps, tables)

In 1989, Mexico became a three-party system, and in 2000, after more than 70 years in power, the Partido Revolucionario Institucional (PRI) lost the national election. With three parties contending, the political realignments of the score of small parties have become politically significant. The six-year analysis forecasts what might happen in the future as representation of the three parties in the upper and lower chambers become more even.

2271 Aldana Rendón, Mario A. Zapopan: ¿una identidad guadalajarizada? (*Estud. Jalisc.*, 65, agosto 2006, p. 5–19)

Until the mid-1950s, Zapopan was a very productive agricultural municipality that had its own cultural identity. Heavy migration and natural growth made it inevitable that Guadalajara swallowed nearby towns that as a result lost their historical identity. The author explains the process of incorporation that Zapopan has experienced while maintaining its political and administrative independence.

Andrews, Abigail. Constructing mutuality: the Zapatistas transformation of transnational activist power dynamics. See *HLAS 66:900.*

2272 Aproximaciones empíricas al estudio de la inseguridad: once estudios en materia de seguridad ciudadana en México. Coordinación de Luis González Placencia, José Luis Arce Aguilar y Metztli Álvarez. México: Miguel Ángel Porrúa, 2007. 323 p.: bibl., ill. (Conocer para decidir)

This excellent collection includes articles that question the quality of official statistics on crime and the grassroots' strategies to increase security at the municipal/neighborhood level as well as the participation of civil organizations. Other articles examine views on the ability of security forces to protect citizens, their performance and abuses, and citizens' perceptions of insecurity. Some chapters use quantitative data from official sources; others use questionnaire surveys or in-depth interviews.

2273 Ariza, Marina and **Orlandina de Oliveira.** Regímenes sociodemográficos y estructura familiar: los escenarios cambiantes de los hogares mexicanos. (*Estud. Sociol./México*, 24:70, enero/abril 2006, p. 3–30, bibl., tables)

From 1959 to 2002 Mexico experienced two distinct demographic and economic periods: the first with high fertility and economic growth, followed by a second with low population growth and economic decline. The authors examine the impact of this change on household organization and women's roles. Efforts to maintain the quality of life during the second period led to the growth of nontraditional households such as those without children and those headed by women.

2274 Arzate Salgado, Jorge. Evaluación de un programa de lucha contra la pobreza extrema en México desde una perspectiva cualitativa y microsociológica. (*Fermentum/Mérida*, 16:45, enero/abril 2006, p. 138–161, bibl.)

Excellent description of Progresa, a program to fight extreme poverty in Mexico. For the Inter-American Development Bank, Progresa is the model to be followed by other Latin American countries. The author's field findings in two communities in Hidalgo show that the targeted families were low income, but not in extreme poverty. The hardcore poor were not considered appropriate targets for aid because they did not have the bare minimum to use adequately the assistance provided. By making this choice the program failed to achieve its purpose.

2275 Autonomía de las mujeres en contextos rurales. Textos de Fernando Neira Orjuela, Carolina A. Rosas y Patricia Artía.

México: El Colegio de México, Programa Interdisciplinario de Estudios de la Mujer, 2005. 125 p.: bibl., tables. (Género, cultura y sociedad: Serie de Investigaciones del PIEM; 1)

This is the first volume of the new series "Gender, Culture, and Society" issued by the Interdisciplinary Program of Women's Studies of the Colegio de Mexico. The three articles selected have been submitted to peer review. The authors study women's empowerment in the following contexts: when husbands are absent due to migration and women have to make decisions previously made by husbands; when women are working outside their households; and women's participation in the National Coordinating Association of Indigenous Women.

2276 Azaola Garrido, Elena. Las condiciones de vida en las cárceles mexicanas. (*Rev. Mex. Cienc. Polít. Soc.*, 49:200, mayo/agosto 2007, p. 87–97, bibl.)

The terrible conditions of prisons in Mexico are well known. A representative sample of inmates in two large overcrowded prisons (Mexico City and state of Mexico) provides views of the conditions. Water, food, and clothing shortages, limited medical care, improper treatment of visitors including family members, lack of personal security, and lack of knowledge of their rights as prisoners are some of the critical comments provided in the survey.

2277 Azaola Garrido, Elena. Imagen y auto-imagen de la policía de la Ciudad de México. México: Ediciones Coyoacán, 2006. 168 p.: bibl. (Alter libros; 3)

There are about 80,000 police officers in Mexico City. Their corruption has been documented in reports, books, and mass media. Based on responses to a questionnaire administered to 170 police officers and on 110 autobiographies by police, the author offers an interesting account of how the police force views its working conditions, causes of corruption, and potential solutions.

2278 Blancarte, Roberto. Sexo, religión, y democracia. México: Editorial Planeta, 2008. 262 p.: bibl. (Temas de Hoy)

Written for a general public, this essay is a critique of the Catholic hierarchy's disconnection with contemporary society and secularization trends. While the criticisms end up pointing towards Rome as ultimately responsible, the volume contains a wealth of information about the Church in Mexico. Blancarte claims that the Church hierarchy is obsessed with moralizing and controlling sexual behavior and provides Mexican examples to prove this point.

2279 Bokser de Liwerant, Judit. El lugar cambiante de Israel en la comunidad judía de México: centralidad y procesos de globalización. (*in* Identidades judías, modernidad y globalización. Edición de Paul Mendes-Flohr, Yom Tov Assis, y Leonardo Senkman. Buenos Aires: Ediciones Lilmod, 2007, p. 455–480)

This chapter provides a history of the relationship between Israel's foreign policy and assistance for the development of the Zionist community in Mexico. Mexico's vote at the UN has consistently opposed Israel's treatment of Palestinians creating tension among Jewish immigrants in Mexico. Author's views of news media that criticizes Israel's retaliation against Palestinians could be interpreted as biased in an otherwise informative paper.

2280 Bokser de Liwerant, Judit. Reflexiones sobre un "fenómeno difuso" a partir de la Primera Encuesta Nacional sobre discriminación en México. (*Rev. Mex. Cienc. Polít. Soc.*, 49:200, mayo/agosto 2007, p. 71–85, bibl.)

The 2005 National Survey on Discrimination includes the following groups that could be the subject of discrimination in Mexico: the elderly, indigenous populations, religious minorities, the disabled, and homosexuals. Not enough information is provided about the survey to judge the validity of the responses. Most minorities do experience discrimination (90 percent), and respondents are not willing to live near homosexuals (48 percent), foreigners (38 percent), or those with different religious or political beliefs (36 and 38 percent, respectively).

2281 Bustamante, Juan José and Carlos Alemán. Perpetuating split-household families: the case of Mexican sojourners in mid-Michigan and their transnational fatherhood practices. (*Migr. Int.*, 4:1, enero/junio 2007, p. 65–86, bibl.)

A critical analysis of the 1997 temporary visas program for agricultural workers in the US. According to the authors, the program benefits US agricultural businesses that can obtain cheap labor as needed. The income offered attracts Mexican workers—not necessarily peasants—who are willing to quit their jobs and move north. The possibility of working extra hours—frequently needed in agricultural jobs—is an additional attraction. For Mexican families left behind and for migrants themselves, separation becomes a heavy burden. Giving up the responsibilities of fatherhood creates anguish and remorse for male migrants. This paper explores how migrants face and resolve this seldom-researched problem.

2282 El Campo no Aguanta Más. Coordinación de Armando Sánchez Albarrán. México: Univ. Autónoma Metropolitana, Unidad Azcapotzalco: Miguel Angel Porrúa, 2007. 297 p.: bibl. (Ciencias sociales. Segunda década)

The title of the book is the name of a social movement that in 2002 brought together 12 well-recognized peasant organizations. Its objective was to oppose neoliberal agricultural policies and their implementation through NAFTA. The nine chapters examine the nature, temporary successes, and ultimate failure of the movement. The outcome of the official discussions that took place during Feb. and March 2003 between leaders of the movement and the government are also studied. It is a useful collection for understanding Mexico's agricultural policies and limited power of the peasantry.

2283 Campos Moreno, Araceli and Louis Cardaillac. Indios y cristianos: cómo en México el Santiago español se hizo indio. Zapopan, Mexico: Colegio de Jalisco; México: UNAM: Editorial Itaca, 2007. 457 p., 32 p. of plates: bibl., col. ill.

In Mexico, the devotion to the apostle Saint James is second only to the veneration of Our Lady of Guadalupe. The authors have researched the origins of the tradition from the colonial era to the present. They gathered information from towns and villages where the saint is venerated and studied the iconography, legends, dances, and festivities that take place during the apostle saint's day. The result is a study of religious syncretism and of the interrelations between religion and culture.

2284 Cardozo Brum, Myriam. Políticas de lucha contra la pobreza en México: principales resultados y limitaciones. (*Fermentum/Mérida*, 16:45, enero/abril 2006, p. 15–56, bibl.)

A solid critical assessment of programs to fight poverty from the mid-1970s to 2006 shows the limited impact that they have had in reducing income inequalities and helping the poorest of the poor. The World Bank recommended and financed several of these programs. The author suggests that any improvements of conditions among the poor are the results of remittances.

2285 Cartografías del feminismo mexicano, 1970–2000. Coordinación de Nora Nínive García, Márgara Millán y Cynthia Pech. México: Univ. Autónoma de la Ciudad de México, 2007. 432 p.: bibl. (Pensamiento crítico; 4)

A collection of very diverse papers that reflects the plurality of women movements and the different legal approaches utilized to reduce discrimination and violence. After a chapter explaining the plurality, there are chapters on the lesbian movement, the movement against violence toward women, the role of the Zapatista Army of National Liberation (EZLN) in reducing gender inequalities among ethnic minorities, and the contribution of women's journals. The last part includes chapters on the presence of women in the arts. The book ends with a 1970–2000 chronology detailing all events, meetings, and publications that should be noted by students of women's movements.

2286 Caso Raphael, Agustín; Maria José González del Cojo; and Miguel Mejía Sánchez. Migración y repatriaciones: México en la encrucijada norte-sur. México: Rosa Ma Porrúa, 2006. 222 p.: bibl., ill., col. maps.

From a legal point of view, the meanings of repatriation, expulsion, deportation, and extradition are very different. Author clarifies the differences and explains the repatriation that took place after September 11, 2001. Explains the programs created by the Mexican government to assist migrants who need to return to their home countries and programs to help minors. Also discusses the repatriation of Central American migrants from Mexico.

2287 Castillón Quintero, Anabel. Un proceso identitario en San Luis Potosí: el navismo. (*Estud. Jalisc.*, 65, agosto 2006, p. 20–33)

This is an interesting historical study of the end of bossism (*caziquismo*) in San Luis Potosí in the early 1960s. The fight between the city's independent, conservative but prodemocratic forces and the heavily centralized PRI that supported the state's all powerful *cazique* during more than 20 years provides useful information for understanding Mexico's political history at the state level.

2288 Chávez Gutiérrez, María Antonia. Acercamiento a la explotación sexual y comercial de niños, niñas y adolescentes en Jalisco. Guadalajara, Mexico: Univ. de Guadalajara, 2006. 115 p.: bibl.

Little is known about the number of children that are exploited in Mexico and the consequences and effectiveness of the few social services available to them. This report includes findings from interviews in Guadalajara with a person responsible for assisting street children, and from in-depth interviews with five boys and seven girls who earn money through prostitution.

2289 Coloquio Desarrollo y Cultura: Perspectivas desde el Campo Mexicano, *San Cristóbal de Las Casas, Mexico, 2006.* La dimensión cultural en procesos de desarrollo rural regional: casos del campo mexicano. Coordinación de Tim Trench y Artemio Cruz León. Chapingo, Mexico: Univ. Autónoma Chapingo, 2008. 322 p.: bibl., ill.

Most of the 10 articles included in this volume discuss the power structures and the need to find ways to transform them as a prerequisite for achieving change in rural areas. Authors also stress the necessity of taking into account the qualitative dimensions of the rural development processes. The importance of finding ways of incorporating the culture of the agricultural workers into strategies for improving land use and quality of life is the central theme of the contributions.

2290 Coloquio Internacional XX Años de Ciencias Sociales, *Colegio Mexiquense, 2006.* Memorias. Compilación de Cecilia Cadena Inostroza. Zinacantepec,

Mexico: Colegio Mexiquense, 2008. 359 p.: bibl., ill.

The 12 articles explore the role of social science in society and the limitations imposed by the nature of current methodologies. The articles included in the first part examine the need to make social science meaningful in the resolution of today's problems. Articles in the second part explore difficulties of social science multidisciplinary research, recognizing that without collaborative research it is difficult to influence social policies. Chapters in the third section incorporate history as a social science apart from historiography and present examples in the field of education and economics. The final part includes articles that examine theoretical approaches to Third World development, specifically structural and neoliberal theories and their limitations.

2291 Córdova Plaza, Rosío. El difícil tránsito de "hechiza" a "hechicera": construcción de la subjetividad entre sexoservidores transgénero de Xalapa, Veracruz. (*Secuencia/México*, 66, sept./dic. 2006, p. 91–110, bibl.)

For the author, Mexico's social norms dichotomize sexual behavior. According to norms, transvestites are abnormal, perverts, and dangerous. Normative transgression attracts some of them to the practice of prostitution. By breaking the norms, transvestites create an "acceptable" behavioral category for their actions. Based on in-depth interviews of 50 transvestites and of two users of their services.

2292 Cuando el trabajo nos castiga: debates sobre el mobbing en México. Coordinación de Florencia Peña, Patricia Ravelo Blancas y Sergio G. Guadalupe Sánchez. México: Eón: Servico Europeo de Información sobre el Mobbing: Univ. Autónoma Metropolitana—Azcapotzalco, 2007. 293 p.: bibl., ill. (Eón sociales)

The first nine chapters deal with different theoretical and applied aspects of mobbing. Institutional conflicts between groups and the use of mobbing by those who control or achieve the control of the institutions are described in the last six chapters. Mobbing is seen as an instrument to impose behaviors or expel those who do not comply.

2293 Cuando la democracia nos alcance: sistemas de cuotas y agendas de género en Baja California Sur, Coahuila, Colima, Durango, Guerrero, Jalisco y Nayarit. Coordinación de Lourdes C. Pacheco Ladrón de Guevara. Textos de Blanca Olivia Peña Molina *et al.* Tepic, Mexico: Univ. Autónoma de Nayarit; México: Casa Juan Pablos, 2007. 379 p.: bibl.

Very detailed information about the role of women in politics in each Mexican state. The information provided includes the number and names of women elected by party, by year, in some cases by municipality; the quota system by parties; committees headed by women and other positions occupied by women within the legislature; and barriers to political access. Also includes legislative changes regarding women's participation and quota systems. The number of elections studied differs from state to state.

2294 Denman, Catalina A. Mujeres, maquila y embarazo: prácticas de atención de madres-trabajadoras en Nogales, Sonora, México. Hermosillo, Mexico: Colegio de Sonora, 2008. 455 p.: bibl., ill., index, maps.

Using in-depth interviews with women workers, managers, and physicians, and a questionnaire administered to a representative random sample of workers in a large factory, the author addresses in this lengthy monograph women's reasons for working in maquilas and for deciding to have children and their management of pregnancy while working. Public health insurance limitations have an influence on the way pregnant women seek health care and self-imposed health behaviors during pregnancy. Of significance also is the information regarding strategies used by pregnant women to continue working in jobs that could threaten the health of the fetus and their own employment.

2295 Díaz Polanco, Héctor. El laberinto de la identidad. México: UNAM, 2006. 317 p.: bibl. (Col. La pluralidad cultural en México; 12)

As nation-states attempt to modernize, the identity of minority ethnic groups is a common topic of interest. The author has selected two cases that he considers emblematic in order to analyze the complexity of cultural maintenance in the midst of socioeconomic development: the experience of indigenous populations of Chiapas and those of ethnic communities in the Atlantic Coast of Nicaragua under the Sandinistas.

2296 Educación, sindicalismo y gobernabilidad en Oaxaca. Coordinación de Joel Vicente Cortés. Textos de Isidoro Yescas Martínez *et al.* México: SNTE, 2006. 248 p.: bibl.

In Oaxaca, for more than two decades, teachers held yearly strikes to obtain better labor conditions. In 2006, the strike lasted a good part of the year and became very violent. The nine authors of the chapters in this work are all local social scientists who document critically—before the strike was over—the reasons for the violence, the extreme authoritarian nature of the union leadership, and the strike's consequences for the state and the students.

2297 Encuesta sobre migración en la frontera norte de México, 2005. México: Secretaría del Trabajo y Previsión Social, 2007. 224 p.: ill.

The Migration Surveys of Mexico's Northern Border (EMIF) began in 1993. The surveys include persons who have stayed over one month and return voluntarily (including tourists) and those returned by US authorities. It also includes migration from other parts of Mexico to the eight border cities where the survey takes place. The volume includes methodology and results of the 2005 survey.

Enríquez Acosta, Jesús Ángel. Ciudad de muros: socialización y tipología de las urbanizaciones cerradas en Tijuana. See item **795.**

2298 Envejeciendo en la pobreza: género, salud y calidad de vida. Edición de V. Nelly Salgado de Snyder y Rebeca Wong. Cuernavaca, Mexico: Instituto Nacional de Salud Pública, 2003. 211 p.: bibl., ill.

The eight chapters approach the volume's theme from different methodological perspectives: some are ethnographic, some are essays, and others are quantitative based on surveys and census data. The conclusion is clear: the aging poor lack the social and health services needed. Unfortunately, this problem is not high on the political agenda.

2299 Erviti, Joaquina. El aborto entre mujeres pobres: sociología de la experiencia. Cuernavaca, Mexico: UNAM, Centro Regional de Investigaciones Multidisciplinarias, 2005. 420 p.: bibl., ill., index.

There have been very few monographs on abortion, and therefore this is a most welcome volume. Based on in-depth interviews of 34 women at a public hospital and four who chose private centers. The presentation of the social, political, and family contexts assists in making the monograph an important contribution.

2300 Escalante Gonzalbo, María de la Paloma. Violencia, vergüenza, violación: ¿cómo se construye el miedo en la ciudad? México: Instituto Nacional del Antropología e Historia, 2007. 115 p.: bibl. (Col. Científica; 513. Serie Antropología)

For this ethnography, the author uses a variety of methods including participant observation, three questionnaires given to a total 185 men and women in two districts of Mexico City, 10 life histories, two large focal groups, and interviews. In addition to study of self-perceived fears of the city's crime and violence, the author explores the long-lasting impact of sexual abuse and rape.

2301 Estrella Castillo, Damaris and José Armando López Manrique. Estamos contentos—pero no tanto: una aproximación etnográfica a la ancianidad en Yucatán. Mérida, Mexico: Ediciones de la Univ. Autónoma de Yucatán, 2006. 250 p.: bibl., ill. (Tratados; 26)

A descriptive study of how the elderly understand aging, their role in society, and their awareness of services available to them. Rural indigenous persons and those in low income urban barrios offer contrasting views. In traditional societies, the elderly continue to have an authoritative role and receive more respect than their urban counterparts.

2302 Familias mexicanas en transición: unas miradas antropológicas. Compilación de David Robichaux. México: Univ. Iberoamericana, 2007. 399 p.: bibl., map. (Unas miradas antropológicas; 3)

The title "Families in Transition" does not refer to generational changes, but to factors that transform or create new types of family organization and also impact behaviors. The purpose of the 14 chapters is to offer examples of those factors. International and rural-to-urban migration, shifts of labor employment and unemployment, the increasing participation of women in the labor force, and even marital unions of youth who live on the streets are topics included in this volume.

2303 Feliciano, Cynthia. Gendered selectivity: U.S. Mexican immigrants and Mexican non-migrants, 1960–2000. (*LARR*, 43:1, 2008, p. 139–160, appendix, bibl., graphs, tables)

Using US and Mexican census data from 1960 to 2000, the author compares the educational attainment of recent Mexican immigrants to nonmigrants. Both male and female immigrants are more educated than nonmigrants, and that gap increased from 1960 to 2000. Women have been consistently better educated than men throughout the past four decades, but earlier female migrants tended to have more education than more recent ones.

2304 Foro de Reflexión Binacional, 1st, México, 2004. Los mexicanos de aquí y de allá: ¿perspectivas comunes?: memoria del primer Foro de Reflexión Binacional. Compilación de Roger Díaz de Cossío. México: Senado de la República: Fundación Solidaridad Mexicano Americana, 2004. 470 p.: bibl., ill.

The Mexican Senate and one US private foundation organized a forum in 2004 to examine the status of US migration reform, voting patterns of Mexicans in the US, social consequences of migration, and Chicano literature. The proceedings include 25 speeches by well-known celebrities and congressmen, and academic presentations by recognized faculty from both sides of the border.

2305 Foro de Reflexión Binacional, 2nd, México, 2005. Los mexicanos de aquí y de allá, problemas comunes: memoria del segundo Foro de Reflexión Binacional. México: Fundación Solidaridad Mexicano Americana: Senado de la República, LIX Legislatura, 2006. 243 p.: bibl., ill., map.

Sponsored by the same groups as the first forum (see item **2304**), the authors of this volume include Mexican senators, faculty, and members of research and nonprofit

NGOs from both sides of the border. This combination offers complementary views of migration that have consequences for both countries. Topics discussed include US migratory reform, education and health services available to migrants, and the cultural and educational role of mass media.

2306 Foro "Migración: Reconfiguración Transnacional y Flujos de Población," Universidad Iberoamericana Puebla, 2005. Migración: reconfiguración transnacional y flujos de población. Coordinación de Marcela Ibarra Mateos. Textos de Luis Guarnizo *et al.* Puebla, Mexico: Univ. Iberoamericana Puebla, 2007. 350 p.: bibl. (Col. Separata; 8)

Several of the 16 chapters in the volume were presented at a migration forum at the Universidad Iberoamericana-Puebla. Some discuss aspects of Mexican migration to the US, such as remittances or interactions between migrants and those left behind. Others examine theoretical aspects or deal with a variety of international topics, for example migration flows or the impact of wars on migration. The quality, methodology, and length of contributions are quite varied; some are based on empirical data and fieldwork while others are more speculative essays.

2307 Fortalezas y desafíos de las familias en dos contextos: Estados Unidos de América y México. Edición de Rosario Esteinou. México: CIESAS: DIF, Sistema Nacional para el Desarrollo Integral de la Familia, 2006. 517 p.: bibl., ill. (Publicaciones de la Casa Chata) (Antropologías)

A cultural approach to understanding the challenges and risks that families encounter in the US, Mexico, and among Mexican families in the US. The first part deals with aspects of stress and the process of socialization and the second provides more specific case studies of the role of the family in offering assistance to overcome difficulties. The role of the extended family and the cultural influence given to the family in Mexico is contrasted with the importance of individualism promoted in American families.

2308 Franco Solís, Guillermo A. ¡Que se estén quietecitos!: movimientos sociales en el oriente de Morelos. Cuernavaca,

Mexico: Editorial La Rana del Sur, 2006. 190 p.: bibl.

A fight and confrontation with political authorities in a traditionally forgotten part of a Morelos municipality were able to achieve the creation of three teachers' schools and a new municipality. The detailed narration of events is a mine of information for understanding Mexican politics at the grassroots level in the 1970s.

2309 García Luna, Genaro. ¿Por qué 1,661 corporaciones de policía no bastan?: pasado, presente y futuro de la policía en México. Mexico: s.n., 2006. 186 p.: bibl., ill.

The head of the Agencia Federal de Investigación, the investigative arm of the federal police, offers a candid account of the changes that he had to make in order to modernize, fight against corruption, and make the agency more efficient. In the process, he provides useful crime statistics, discusses issues of police corruption, and offers an overall view of the organization of law enforcement in the country.

2310 Garma Navarro, Carlos. Buscando el espíritu: pentecostalismo en Iztapalapa y la ciudad de México. Ixtapalapa, Mexico: Univ. Autónoma Metropolitana-Unidad Iztapalapa, División de Ciencias Sociales y Humanidades; México: Plaza y Valdés, 2004. 324 p.: bibl. (Col. Antropología)

Grounded in the classics (Weber, Durkheim, Eliade, Lévi-Strauss) and other well-recognized scholars of sociology and anthropology of religion, this volume is the result of years of fieldwork that includes participant observation and in-depth interviews with members and leaders of the Pentecostal church. The author explains the belief system; organizational structures, including leadership patterns, rituals, and the role of women; and variations that exist among Pentecostal congregations. Frequent comparisons with other religious groups make this monograph a valuable contribution to our knowledge of Christian fundamentalism in Mexico.

2311 El género y sus ámbitos de expresión en lo cultural, económico y ambiental. Coordinación de María Luisa Quintero Soto y Carlos Fonseca. México: Cámara de Diputados, LIX Legislatura: Miguel Ángel Porrúa, 2006. 322 p.: bibl., maps, tables. (Conocer para decidir) (Las Ciencias sociales. Estudios de género)

An uneven collection of 11 articles grouped under themes such as labor participation, gender, marriage, sexuality, and the role of women in protecting the environment. Of significance is the chapter that discusses the high positive correlation between levels of education and the transformation of gender roles, and between low education and household violence. The chapter on the changes in rural households between 1994 and 2002 shows only a moderate increase of female participation in the labor force, but more significant changes in educational levels.

2312 Guadarrama, Gloria. Tiempo, circunstancia y particularidades de la asistencia privada en el Estado de México. Zinacantepec, Mexico: Colegio Mexiquense, 2007. 236 p.: bibl., ill., maps.

A comprehensive historical account of private and public institutions organized to assist those in need including the poor, the elderly, invalids and the sick, unemployed, orphans, etc. From colonial days to the present, the author explains the shifting approaches from charity to solidarity and human rights. A list of registered organizations from 1998 to 2006 is included.

2313 Guevara Zárraga, María Estela. Procesos de socialización de los inmigrantes latinoamericanos en Guadalajara. Tepatitlán de Morelos, Mexico: Univ. de Guadalajara, Centro Univ. de Los Altos, 2007. 141 p.: bibl. (Cuadernos de los Altos. Col. Antropología)

Middle- and upper-class international Latin American migrants to Mexico have not been frequently studied. Marriage, violence at home, education, and employer or business needs are the common reasons for migration. Through in-depth interviews of Peruvians and Central Americans, the author examines the process of adaptation and acculturation and the degree of acceptance by natives.

2314 Gutiérrez Castorena, Daniel and **Jesús Ramírez Ramírez.** Corporativismo y contratos de protección en Aguascalientes. Aguascalientes, Mexico: Univ. Autónoma de Aguascalientes, 2006. 182 p.:

bibl. (Ciencias sociales y humanidades. Sociología)

Protection contracts are contracts prepared by lawyers of corporations and signed by union leader without the workers' knowledge. The contracts are typically signed before the factory or work site starts production, so the workers remain unaware that they are unionized. The monograph provides a wealth of information about how the deception is legalized and examines the characteristics of union leaders who betray workers. According to the authors, protection contracts are common in maquila industries.

2315 Hacer política desde la sociedad. Coordinación de Jorge Regalado Santillán y José Gómez Valle. Guadalajara, Mexico: Univ. de Guadalajara, 2006. 208 p.: bibl.

The chapters in this book result from the awareness that the end of militarism and the beginning of a party system has not brought democracy to Latin America and Mexico. New communication technologies and the growth of civil organizations are creating new actors and new forms of participation in the political system. Articles also study the responses by international organizations and public institutions to the demands made by the new actors.

2316 Hernández, Sarah. Democratizando a la jerarquía: relaciones en la producción y la división del trabajo en una cooperativa mexicana. (*Nueva Antropol./México*, 20:66, julio 2006, p. 61–85, bibl.)

Workers of the large soft drink and juice firm, Pascual, took over the firm and organized the Cooperativa Trabajadores de Pascual. Study analyzes the transformation and the workers' success in maintaining vertical lines of authority for reasons of efficiency. Observations at one of the plants and 45 in-depth interviews of workers were conducted in 1991–92. A good contribution to the literature on cooperatives.

2317 Hernández Baqueiro, Alberto. Características y contribuciones de las organizaciones civiles del VIH-SIDA en la ciudad de México. (*Perf. Latinoam.*, 15:30, julio/dic. 2007, p. 39–78, appendixes, bibl., graphs, tables)

Based on a survey, this paper provides descriptive information about the size; year of foundation; the characteristics of the staff, users, and volunteers; and activities and services provided by organizations that care for HIV-AIDS patients. Most of the organizations are very small, and most volunteers work for the few larger ones.

2318 Hernández Lomelí, Francisco and Guillermo Orozco Gómez. Televisiones en México: un recuento histórico. Guadalajara, Mexico: Univ. de Guadalajara, 2007. 184 p.: bibl.

The introduction and the four chapters were previously published in other volumes or journals. The chapters center on the history and consequences of the intense private-public relations that characterize the television industry in Mexico, and the oligopolistic powers that private TV has achieved by satisfying the demands of political leaders.

2319 Hernández Vega, Leticia. ¿De aquí p'a allá o de allá p'a acá?: clubes de migrantes jaliscienses, promoción estratégica de capital social y desarrollo. (*Migr. Int.*, 3:4, julio/dic. 2006, p. 60–84, bibl., graphs, maps, tables)

In the late 1990s and early 2000s, a number of Mexican migrants to the US organized social clubs that brought together migrants from the same communities for the purpose of helping each other and newcomers. The author looks at leadership characteristics, objectives, and other variables of two organizations and their communities of origin in Jalisco (historical, political, and economic) to explain differences in social capital production.

2320 Hoffmann, Odile. Negros y afromestizos en México: viejas y nuevas lecturas de un mundo olvidado. (*Rev. Mex. Sociol.*, 68:1, enero/marzo 2006, p. 103–135, bibl.)

A critical review of the scant literature written about the Afro-Mexican minority. The author explains why the study of the black population in Mexico must be approached differently than in the US and other Latin American countries. The self-identity of Afro-Mexicans is not uniform and varies by location based on different historical experiences, political interests, processes of assimilation, and other social and cultural variables.

2321 In God We Trust: del campo mexicano al sueño americano. Compilación de Rosío Córdova Plaza, María Cristina Núñez Madrazo y David Skerritt Gardner. Xalapa, Mexico: Univ. de Veracruz; México: Plaza y Valdés, 2007. 257 p.: bibl., ill.

Most of the 11 chapters in this volume study international migration from two states: Veracruz and Michoacán. Until recently, the number of migrants from these states to the US was small. The authors explain reasons for the rapid migration growth, characteristics of the flow, place of origin by municipalities, the impact on families left behind, and other variables that are commonly included in migration studies.

2322 ¿Invisibles?: migrantes internacionales en la escena política. Coordinación de Cecilia Imaz. México: UNAM, 2007. 343 p.: bibl., ill., map.

Several of the 15 articles examine US migration policies and national and state policies in Mexico to assist migrants. Two articles discuss German migrant policies, while another two look at Latin American migrant organizations—one for Peruvian migrants in Chile and the other for Mexicans in New York. Another article studies the results of extending migrants the right to vote in Mexican elections. The abuses of Central American transit migrants in Mexico are well known; a chapter in the volume documents the abuses committed by gangs (*maras*) in the state of Veracruz, where Central Americans on their way to the US arrive by riding on top of trains from the southern border.

2323 Los jóvenes ante el siglo XXI. Coordinación de Emma Liliana Navarrete. Zinacantepec, Mexico: El Colegio Mexiquense, 2004. 193 p.: bibl., tables.

The seven articles can be grouped in two categories. Those in the first one study sexual and reproductive behavior and teenage pregnancy and maternity, while those in the second are centered around labor force participation and education. By and large contributions to the first part are more solid. Sources of data and analysis vary: regression analysis using national surveys, cross tabulations from national health and education surveys, and focus groups and interviews.

2324 León Zermeño, María de Jesús. La representación social del trabajo doméstico: un problema en la construcción de la identidad femenina. Puebla, Mexico: Benemérita Univ. Autónoma de Puebla, Instituto de Ciencias Sociales y Humanidades, Maestría en Psicología Social: Dirección General de Fomento Editorial, 2003. 294 p.: bibl., ill.

Examines data from 40 life histories of low-income women (mothers and daughters) in which they offer their subjective understanding of women's domestic roles. This information is enriched by interviews with men. By looking at two generations, the author is able to reach conclusions about the transformations that have taken place and their causes.

2325 Leyva Piña, Marco Antonio and Javier Rodriguez Lagunas. El sindicalismo mexicano en el gobierno de Fox (corporativismo, democracia y sindicatos). (*Trabajo/México*, 3:4, enero/junio 2007, p. 181–216, bibl.)

Historically, Mexican labor unions have been allied with the PRI, the dominant party. In 2000, the conservative PAN won the national election for the first time, and the unions had to adjust to new political realities. Authors examine the unions' new political and ideological realignments. Several powerful unions decided to support the PAN. According to authors, there was no change in the unions' authoritarian and corporative organizational behavior, which might have been expected as the Mexican political system moved from an authoritarian one-party system to a more open two-party system.

Lomnitz, Larissa Adler de; Rodrigo Salazar Elena; and Ilya Adler. Symbolism and ritual in a one-party regime: unveiling Mexico's political culture. See item **1085**.

2326 López, Silvia and Gerardo Manuel Ordóñez Barba. Pobreza, familia y políticas de género: el Programa Jefas de Familia en Tijuana. México: CONACYT; Tijuana, Mexico: El Colegio de la Frontera

Norte; San José: Instituto Nacional de las Mujeres, 2006. 375 p.: bibl., ill., map.

Authors examine the implementation of the Female Head of Households Program through a representative survey of 173 participants; more than 40 percent of the recipients were not qualified to be enrolled because they were above the poverty level. Interviews of 39 mothers whose houses were used as Centers for Child Care and 52 whose children were attending those centers were used to assess the impact of CCC. The study also examined the empowerment of women teachers at the CCC, the performance of three NGOs that participated in the implementation of the program, and the impact of a reproductive health program.

2327 Loza Torres, Mariela *et al.* Jefaturas de hogar: el desafío femenino ante la migración transnacional masculina en el sur del Estado de México. (*Migr. Int.*, 4:2, julio/dic. 2007, p. 33–59, bibl.)

Examines social relations and gender changes that take place in three communities in the state of Mexico when male heads of households migrate to the US. The autonomy and new roles that women assume are a response to the absence of their spouses and not to the freedom that they now have to spend remittances. Women are very aware of the sacrifices that their spouses are making while working abroad, and as a result carefully manage the remittances.

2328 Macías-Macías, Alejandro. La identidad colectiva en el sur de Jalisco. (*Econ. Soc. Territ.*, 6:24, mayo/agosto 2007, p. 1025–1069, bibl.)

Explains the resilience of Jalisco's southern towns in maintaining a local identity. Geographical isolation, historical events, and ethnic and socioeconomic barriers to integration have contributed to the distance between communities and the maintenance of different cultural traditions. Ironically, global social and economic changes, and the resultant collapse of traditional economies, have further contributed to the gap between modern and traditional cultures.

2329 Marroquín, Enrique. El conflicto religioso Oaxaca, 1976–1992. México: UNAM, Centro de Investigaciones Interdisciplinarias en Ciencias y Humanidades, Coordinación de Humanidades; Oaxaca, Mexico: Univ. Autónoma "Benito Juárez" de Oaxaca, Instituto de Investigaciones Sociológicas, 2007. 236 p.: bibl., ill. (Col. Alternativas)

Using case studies, the author provides examples of different types of rural religious conflicts. Conflicts between religions, mostly Catholicism and Protestant Evangelicalism, show the difficulties that new sects have in adhering to ethnic traditions such as *tequio*, or the cargo system, leading to community infighting. The Catholic lower clergy's support of the rights of indigenous groups led to internal conflicts within the Catholic Church when the Church hierarchy saw the ghost of communism in the attempts to emancipate the poor. Religion was also drawn into land tenure conflicts as each side turned to its religious leaders for support.

2330 Más allá del combate a la pobreza: visiones sociales e institucionales de la política social. Compilación de Eugenio Arriaga Cordero y José Sosa. Guadalajara, Mexico: Ayuntamiento de Guadalajara: Instituto Tecnológico y de Estudios Superiores de Occidente: Univ. de Guadalajara, 2005. 227 p.: bibl., ill., maps.

Professional staff from the municipality of Guadalajara's social services discusses the difficulties of providing services to the entire population at the time of budgetary reductions. A literature review of the influence of ideological positions on the role of the state and the public sector is followed by a chapter about the city's poor perception of the causes of poverty and consequences.

2331 Massey, Douglas S.; Jorge Durand; and Fernando Riosmena. Capital social, política social y migración desde comunidades tradicionales y nuevas comunidades de origen en México. (*Rev. Esp. Invest. Sociol.*, 116, oct./dic. 2006, p. 97–121, bibl., tables)

Compares the likelihood of first migration departures and returns from traditional communities with new migration communities (southern and northern-border states). Independent variables include having migrant relatives (social capital), needing documents, the intended length of the first trip (human capital), ownership of properties and businesses in the US and/or Mexico, age, education, marital status, size of community, and employment. Social capital raises the odds of a first migration for both communities, but not for later trips, which are influenced more by human capital. Data come from surveys done before 2002.

2332 Mexico. Secretaría de Desarrollo Social. Innovación y responsabilidad en la política social. México: Fondo de Cultura Económica: Secretaría de Desarrollo Social, 2005. 279 p.: bibl., ill. (Col. editorial del gobierno del cambio)

A report of activities by SEDESOL, Mexico's social development agency. The report assesses many programs, such as Oportunidades, nutrition interventions, employment assistance, migrant assistance, credit programs, and more. It also includes legal and administrative changes during the Fox presidency. As expected, the self-evaluation is positive and contrasts with that of independent researchers. Nevertheless, it is useful to understand the myriad of social assistance programs and their transformation with changes of administrations.

2333 Mexico-United States migration: regional and state overview. Texts by Elena Zúñiga Herrera, Paula Leite, and Luis Acevedo Prieto. México: Consejo Nacional de Población, 2006. 233 p.: col. ill., col. maps.

The purpose of this quantitative demographic study is to analyze the contemporary characteristics of the Mexico-US migratory process. It examines at the regional and national level the origin and destination of migrants, reasons for migration, household composition, occupation, and income of Mexicans residing in the US. Graphs and tables cover different periods, some from 1970 to 2000, others cover shorter spans. Data come from a variety of US and Mexican sources, such as censuses and migration surveys. Includes an annex with 132 pages of tables.

2334 La migración a Estados Unidos y la frontera noreste de México. Coordinación de Socorro Arzaluz Solano. Tijuana, Mexico: El Colegio de la Frontera Norte, 2007. 245 p.: bibl., ill., maps.

One chapter presents demographic information about the migration flows from the three Northeastern Mexican states, and another offers a historical account of migration from Monterrey to San Antonio. The impact on migration caused by the employment situation in Mexico is the topic of a third chapter. The role of the contracted persons, *coyotes*, who transport migrants to the US, and the complexities of their interactions with migrants are explained in another chapter. The final contribution is a historical report of policies designed to attract migrants to Honduras at the beginning of the 20th century, followed by statistics and causes explaining the large migration to the US beginning in the 1970s.

2335 Miradas sobre la vejez: un enfoque antropológico. Textos de Imelda Orozco Mares *et al.* Tijuana, Mexico: El Colegio de la Frontera del Norte; México: Plaza y Valdés, 2006. 313 p.: bibl. (Antropología)

Based on 101 interviews of elderly poor in Chiapas, Guanajuato, Jalisco, and Veracruz conducted in rural and urban areas. The average number of children alive at the time of the study was 5.8, a number that suggests the availability of family support. Worth reading for understanding the elderly's role in the family and community, their social status, the meaning that religion has at this time of their lives, and dependency issues.

2336 Moloeznik, Marcos Pablo. Public security and police reform in Mexico. (*in* Public security and police reform in the Americas. Edited by John Bailey and Lucía Dammert. Pittsburgh, Pa.: Univ. of Pittsburgh Press, 2006, p. 169–186)

The chapter describes changes within law enforcement organizations and the creation of new police organizations up to 2004. The analysis may seem obsolete because brutal cartel-related violence has escalated exponentially since then. Nevertheless, the chapter provides useful information about the successes and failures of the public security system changes that took place since 1990. Author concludes that in spite of changes, public security continues to be a major unresolved issue and the policies implemented were contrary to those recommended by the UN.

2337 Núñez Noriega, Guillermo. Masculinidad e intimidad: identidad, sexualidad y SIDA. México: Programa Univ. de Estudios de Género: Colegio de Sonora: Miguel Ángel Porrúa, 2007. 386 p.: bibl., ill. (Las ciencias sociales. Estudios de género)

Ethnographic data from rural and urban Sonora allows the author to examine the diversity of meanings of masculinity. For him, to be a man is a historical, but also a daily social construction that is in constant dispute. He also studies homophobia and sexual relations between men, and criticizes the predominant model of explaining the homoerotic experience in Mexico. Contrary to what the title suggests, little attention is given to HIV/SIDA.

2338 Ortiz Guitart, Anna and **Cristóbal Mendoza.** Vivir (en) la Ciudad de México: espacio vivido e imaginarios espaciales de un grupo de migrantes de alta calificación. (*LARR*, 43:1, 2008, p. 113–138, bibl., ill., map, tables)

In-depth interviews with 20 expatriates from Spain who reside in Mexico City and work for transnational corporations, NGOs, or international agencies. New technologies, including internet, and frequent trips home keep expatriates in close contact with Spain. For many, the temporary nature of their residency contributes to a weak feeling of belonging to Mexico.

2339 Pacheco Castro, Jorge Atocha. Cambio y continuidad sociocultural en la región sur del campo yucateco. México: Plaza y Valdés: Univ. Autónoma de Yucatán, 2007. 355 p.: bibl., ill., maps.

Between 1952 and 1964, the public sector launched a modernization program, improved the infrastructure, and introduced new crops in southern Yucatán, the region studied. The purpose of the research was to assess the acculturation of the population and the socioeconomic benefits of the development program after 40 years.

Pansters, Wil and **Héctor F. Castillo Berthier.** Violencia e inseguridad en la ciudad de México: entre la fragmentación y la politización. See item **1102.**

2340 Parrini Roses, Rodrigo. Panópticos y laberintos: subjetivación, deseo, y corporalidad en una cárcel de hombres.

México: El Colegio de México, 2007. 277 p.: bibl.

A prison is a complex organization with rules imposed by authorities and by the prisoners themselves. Fifteen in-depth interviews of inmates in a prison that houses twice as many persons as it was designed to hold gives the reader an account of the prisoners' organization, their leadership patterns, and use of power. Of main concern to the author is the arbitration of conflict and satisfaction of sexual needs.

2341 Perfiles de la masculinidad. Coordinación de Rafael Montesinos. México: Univ. Autónoma Metropolitana, Unidad Iztapalapa: Plaza y Váldes, 2007. 317 p.: bibl., ill.

The eight chapters present alternative views of masculinity to the traditional feminist discourse. Claiming that sociocultural changes are occurring, authors use in-depth interviews, focal groups, life histories, and gender relations to find a more complex reality. Masculinity is not a social construct that is imposed from the outside but rather discourses that organize and coordinate social relations.

2342 Política, etnicidad e inclusión digital en los albores del milenio. Coordinación de Scott S. Robinson, Héctor Tejera Gaona y Laura R. Valladares de la Cruz. México: Univ. Autónoma Metropolitana, Unidad Iztapalapa: Miguel Ángel Porrúa, 2007. 429 p.: bibl., ill., maps. (Las ciencias sociales)

The articles are grouped under three themes: politics, culture, and citizenship (four chapters); studies of political sociology and of gender of ethnic minorities—more than half of the book (six chapters); and a very short section on the role of new technologies of communication (three chapters). Topics, methodology, and length are as varied as the quality of the contributions.

2343 La política social en México: tendencias y perspectivas. Coordinación de Rolando Cordera y Carlos Javier Cabrera Adame. México: UNAM, Facultad de Economía, 2007. 401 p.: bibl., ill.

Authors analyze social programs implemented during the last 20 years and the changes that took place with each new government. All the significant programs, except the Seguro Popular (The People's

Health Insurance of 2004), are reviewed. In spite of huge budget allocations, authors conclude that an unacceptably large number of Mexicans continue to live in poverty because programs have not targeted the causes.

2344 Quintero Ramírez, Cirila. El sindicalismo en las maquiladoras: la persistencia de lo local en la globalización. (*Desacatos*, 21, mayo/agosto 2006, p. 11–28, bibl., photos, tables)

The paper examines the impact on labor organization of the threats of closing down maquila factories along the US-Mexico border. Moving factories to other countries with lower salaries is a common threat. Pressures from the public sector and employers have weakened the ability of labor leaders to demand salary increases and improved labor conditions.

2345 Religión y cultura: crisol de transformaciones. Edición de Miguel J. Hernández Madrid y Elisabeth Juárez Cerdi. Zamora, Mexico: El Colegio de Michoacán; México: Consejo Nacional de Ciencia y Tecnología, 2003. 317 p.: bibl., index, maps. (Col. Debates)

This collection of 14 articles will be of interest to sociologists of religion who are interested in the transformation that the Catholic Church is experiencing in Mexico. Also of interest to those who follow the presence and growth of Protestant, Pentecostal, and Mormon churches in the country. The chapters are by and large analytical, regarding issues of adaptation to belief and moral systems, proselytism, and diversity in religions that by nature are authoritarian.

2346 Reyes Parra, Elvira. Gritos en el silencio: niñas y mujeres frente a redes de prostitución: un revés para los derechos humanos. México: Miguel Ángel Porrúa, 2007. 461 p.: bibl. (Conocer para decidir)

The author explains her work at the Centro de Atención Integral y Servicios created by the Federal District Commission on Human Rights. The Center's objective is to protect the human rights of prostitutes, including those under age. From her clinical practice at the Center, in addition to describing the life experience, abuses, and violence suffered by prostitutes, she provides a devastating account of corruption at all levels including law enforcement agents and NGOs. The Human Rights Commission's complacency and acquiescence does not help to change the abuses.

2347 Rivera Farfán, Carolina. Acción política de organizaciones evangélicas en los Altos de Chiapas. (*Iztapalapa/México*, 28:62/63, 2007, p. 15–27, bibl., graph)

Evangelical groups have been rapidly expanding in Mexico. This paper examines their organizational responses in a Chiapas region where members suffered violence such as evictions, kidnappings, the closing and destruction of temples and personal property, physical assaults, and even homicides at the hands of Catholics. The exodus of evangelicals to San Cristóbal, the capital of Chiapas, to escape violence facilitated the organization of associations. These associations responded to the abuses with legal and political interventions, and promoted religious freedom and human rights.

2348 Rivera Navarro, Jesús and Sandra Mancinas Espinoza. El anciano ante la muerte: análisis del discurso en el noreste de México. (*Estud. Sociol./México*, 25:74, mayo/agosto 2007, p. 341–367, bibl., tables)

The purpose of the article is to understand the place where the elderly would want to die, rituals they would want to have performed after their death, the perceptions they have regarding euthanasia, the impact that the death of relatives has on them, and the meaning of death. Five small discussion groups organized in Ciudad Victoria (Tamaulipas) with a total of 32 elderly participants are the data sources. As expected, Catholic beliefs influence participants' perceptions, although the idea of ending life by passive euthanasia was accepted by the majority.

2349 Rivera Sánchez, Liliana. Cuando los santos también migran: conflictos transnacionales por el espacio y la pertenencia. (*Migr. Int.*, 3:4, julio/dic. 2006, p. 35–59, bibl.)

Author describes the celebration of St. James in one village in Puebla that has many migrants in New York. Each year, the *mayordomo* is elected to organize and pay the expenses of the village festivities that could reach 20,000 US dollars. To be the *mayordomo* is highly coveted and most *mayordomos* have been migrants who travelled back to the village for the celebration. Internal village conflicts and problems between migrants and nonmigrants began when the parish priest travelled to New York with the statue of St. James to celebrate the festivity there.

2350 Román Pérez, Rosario and **Zonia Sotomayor Peterson.** Masculinidad y violencia homicida. México: Plaza y Valdés, 2007. 260 p.: bibl.

To understand the reasons why men commit violence against women, authors interview four convicted prisoners. One had committed physical violence and two had assassinated their female companions. The fourth one sexually abused his eight-year old niece. Their stories and a review of the literature allowed authors to offer their interpretation of male criminal violence.

2351 Román Sánchez, Yuliana and **Martha Suárez García.** Adultos mayores: mortalidad y morbilidad en el Valle de Toluca, 1980–2030. Toluca, Mexico: Consejo Estatal de Población, 2008. 173 p.: bibl., ill., maps.

For the purpose of this demographic study, the Metropolitan Area of Toluca includes only six municipalities. Data are from the National Council of Population and the National Institute of Statistics, Geography, and Informatics. Older people are those 60 and above. The report examines specific mortality rates by gender and municipality, and offers projections of shifts in mortality causes.

2352 Romero Melgarejo, Osvaldo. La violencia como fenómeno social: el linchamiento en San Miguel Canoa, Puebla. México: Jorale: Colegio de Tlaxcala, 2006. 367 p.: bibl., maps. (Col. Historia rescatada)

In 1968, in Canoa, a town near Puebla, a group of six excursionists and a peasant who housed them were lynched; four of them died at the scene and three were rescued by the Puebla police. Based on the event, three commercial movies have been produced. Years later, Romero, a social anthropologist, reconstructed the lynching and has provided an insightful study of the systematic use of violence by the caciques and allies, among them the Catholic Church and the ultra-conservative regional leaders. The victims were employees of the Autono-

mous University of Puebla, which had been portrayed by the extreme right as the cradle of communism. According to findings, the Canoa priest mobilized the local population against the communists.

2353 Ronquillo, Víctor. Migrantes de la pobreza. Tlalnepantla, Mexico: Grupo Editorial Norma, 2007. 169 p.

Written by an investigative reporter, the book narrates the experiences of the author's process of migration. In addition to the difficulties and exploitation that migrants encounter during their journey to the US, the author also writes about the violence that migrants from Guatemala find when crossing into Mexico.

2354 Rostros de una infancia vulnerada. Coordinación de Claudia Ávila González. Guadalajara, Mexico: Univ. de Guadalajara, Centro Universitario de Ciencias Sociales y Humanidades, 2006. 193 p.: bibl., ill.

Social workers study street children and children in institutional settings in Guadalajara. After an assessment of the legislation and programs to reduce abuses and provide assistance to children in need, fieldwork provides information for three chapters on the conditions of children housed in a religious center, the abuse of those working in supermarkets, and the exploitation of children through prostitution in a variety of locales, such as schools, homes, and streets.

2355 El Santo Juan Diego: historia y contexto de una canonización polémica. Compilación de Lourdes Celina Vázquez, Juan Diego Ortiz Acosta y Luis Rodolfo Morán Quiroz. Guadalajara, Mexico: Univ. de Guadalajara, 2006. 171 p.: bibl., ill.

In 2002, the pope canonized the first American Indian who, according to some historians, including the Church's own historians, was never born. For them, folklore created the humble Indian who had a vision of Mary, giving rise to the cult of Our Lady of Guadalupe, the most powerful political and religious icon of Mexicanism. The book includes a historical review of the myth, characteristics of the debate that followed the canonization, political manipulations of the Guadalupana symbol, and an overview of other Mexican saints.

2356 La seguridad pública local: inseguridad, delincuencia y participación ciudadana en Ciudad Juárez. Coordinación de José Alfredo Zavaleta Betancourt. Ciudad Juárez, Mexico: Univ. Autónoma de Ciudad Juárez: Consejo Nacional de Ciencia y Tecnología, 2007. 217 p.: bibl., ill.

Written before the explosion of drug-cartel-related homicides that began in 2007, the first chapter discusses the citizens' sense of insecurity caused by the lack of resolution of the many femicides committed in the city during the previous several years. The second chapter examines critically the security resources available in the city and their utilization to overcome crime and the estimated 4,000 points of retail drug distribution also known as *narcotiendidas*. The final chapter offers findings from a 730-page survey of citizens (ages 15 to 64) and 14 focal groups regarding issues and perception of security.

2357 Serrano Avilés, Tomás. Y, se fue: los municipios hidalguenses de muy alta migración internacional. Pachuca, Mexico: Univ. Autónoma del Estado de Hidalgo, 2006. 156 p.: bibl., ill., map.

A demographic study of four municipalities in Hidalgo that have very high rates of migration compared to others in Mexico. Sources of information include the 1990 and 2000 population census, the international migration questionnaire applied to a subsample of the 2000 census, and qualitative data (interviews and focus groups) from CONAPO. Causes and consequences of migration confirm findings from other studies.

2358 Serrano Avilés, Tomás and María Félix Quezada Ramírez. Indocumentado: sabe a mentira tu verdad: los municipios hidalguenses de alta migración internacional. Pachuca, Mexico: Univ. Autónoma del Estado de Hidalgo, 2007. 275 p.: bibl., ill., index, maps.

The 16 municipalities with the highest international migration are selected for the study. In each chapter the socioeconomic and demographic data of one municipality is presented with extensive quotes from migrants regarding their crossing experience and work in the US.

2359 Un siglo de sindicalismo en México: los desafíos del movimiento obrero vistos a través de su historia. Coordinación de Alejandro Covarrubias V. y Vicente Solís Granados. Hermosillo, Mexico: Univ. de Sonora: Colegio de Sonora: Univ. Autónoma de Querétaro, 2007. 240 p.: bibl., ill.

The year 2006 marked the 100th anniversary of a landmark in Mexico's labor history: the first mining strike in Sonora that cost the life of most workers. The 12 articles collected as a remembrance of this episode are divided among the three parts of this work. The first part discusses the history and nature of the labor movement, obstacles encountered, and transformations since earlier days. It is the most significant part of the volume. The second section contains articles that address specific issues such as responses to flexibility, labor demands that emerged with neoliberal economics, and technological changes. The final section examines problems facing labor unions in the era of globalization.

Stahler-Sholk, Richard. Resisting neoliberal homogenization: the Zapatista Autonomy Movement. See *HLAS 66:1007.*

2360 Staudt, Kathleen A. Violence and activism at the border: gender, fear, and everyday life in Ciudad Juárez. Austin: Univ. of Texas Press, 2008. 184 p.: bibl., index. (Inter-American series)

Between 1993 and 2003, more than 370 women were murdered and their bodies dumped in Ciudad Juárez, a sister city of El Paso, Texas. Based on in-depth interviews with activists, authorities, and law enforcement officers, and on observations from both sides of the US-Mexico border, the author provides insights into the several theories that try to explain the intensity and brutality of violence against women in Ciudad Juárez.

2361 Staudt, Kathleen A. and Irasema Coronado. Fronteras no más: toward social justice at the U.S.-Mexico border. New York, N.Y.: Palgrave Macmillan, 2002. 204 p.: bibl., ill., index, map.

Authors studied cross-border cooperation or its lack, the social and institutional networks and NGOs working at the almost 2.5 million urban population conglomerate of Ciudad Juárez-El Paso. Key issues examined are those that transcend the border: environment, business and labor, and human rights.

2362 Sucede que me canso de ser hombre: relatos y reflexiones sobre hombres y masculinidades en México. Coordinación de Ana Amuchástegui y Ivonne Szasz Pianta. México: Colegio de México, 2007. 681 p.: bibl.

The first part of the volume theorizes about the difficulties of universalizing the concept of masculinity. The themes of the rest of the 19 articles include the differences that social class and rural-urban locations have on men's heterosexual experiences; the impact that international migration has in transforming the concept of masculinity in rural areas; and accounts by youth (13 years and older) of their perception of sexuality and initiation on sexual relations according to social class. The last part explores the social construction of the male body and the concept of sexual desire and practices among homosexuals in Mexico City. Based on qualitative methods.

2363 Talamantes Gómez, Héctor Manuel. Radiografía de la migración y las remesas en el Estado de Durango. Durango, Mexico: Univ. Juárez del Estado de Durango, Instituto de Ciencias Sociales: COC y TED, Consejo de Ciencia y Tecnología, 2006. 218 p.: bibl., ill., maps.

Using the population census of 2000, data from the National Population Council, the author studies Durango's internal and international migration flows, the economic characteristics of migrants, and other demographic variables. A survey of 2,870 households in the state of Durango looks at the economic impact of remittances on the economy of the families and on regional development.

2364 Tamayo Flores-Alatorre, Sergio. Crítica de la ciudadanía y la democracia sin adjetivos: ocho escenas de un conflicto ciudadano en la ciudad de México. (Secuencia/México, 66, sept./dic. 2006, p. 113–142, bibl., tables)

The central argument here is that democracy and citizenship must be understood as practices and not as predetermined attributes. Using the mega-march against violence of 2004 in Mexico City organized by rightist business groups, the author criticizes Sartori's understanding of democracy without adjectives. The selective definitions of terms such as violence, human rights, justice and others by organizers of the march is viewed by the author as a mechanism to advance their own political and economic interests. Organizers ignored violence by police, by unscrupulous employers, by men against women, white collar crimes, etc., and limited their discourse to robberies and street and gang violence.

2365 Torre, Renée de la. La Ecclesia Nostra: el catolicismo desde la perspectiva de los laicos: el caso de Guadalajara. México: Fondo de Cultura Económica: Centro de Investigaciones y Estudios Superiores en Antropología Social, 2006. 439 p. (Sección de Obras de Sociología)

This monograph is an in-depth study of Guadalajara, a city known by its conservative ideology. The author looks at the influence that the archdiocese exercises on powerholders within the city and outside its boundaries in Mexico and other parts of Latin America. Also examines tensions and conflicts that exist between various lay groups and the Church hierarchy in Guadalajara regarding pastoral and doctrinal issues, and the celebration of the sacraments.

2366 Valdéz-Gardea, Gloria Ciria. "Soy pescadora de almejas": respuestas a la marginación en el Alto Golfo de California. Hermosillo, Mexico: El Colegio de Sonora, 2007. 248 p.: ill.

Fieldwork for this ethnography took place in the mid-1990s. The small fishing village located at the delta of the Colorado River in the Sea of Cortés had to confront an economic crisis as shrimp and fish captures dwindle in the nineties. The author looks into the survival strategies including migration to the US and drug trafficking.

2367 Vargas González, Pablo E. Estado y movimientos sociales en Hidalgo. Colaboración de Armando Azpeitia Díaz y Irma Eugenia Gutiérrez M. Puebla, Mexico: Red Nacional de Investigación Urbana; Pachua, Mexico: Univ. Autónoma del Estado de Hidalgo, 2005. 205 p.: bibl.

In the 1980s, leading Mexican sociologist González Casanova began a project to promote the study of social movements. Following his call, authors of the three chapters began collecting information. Here they present their findings collected over 30 years about the efforts of social movements to democratize two labor unions (teachers and miners), and to overcome municipal bossism in the state of Hidalgo.

2368 Villagómez Valdés, Gina I. Familia y violencia: políticas de atención a la violencia doméstica en Mérida. Mérida, Mexico: Ayuntamiento de Mérida, 2005. 294 p.: bibl.

Provides a wealth of information about the characteristics of home violence suffered mostly by children and women. Types of violence (physical, psychological, sexual, and economic) and statistics, characteristics of perpetrators and causes are well presented. Programs to educate and alert potential victims, to assist victims, and to change behaviors are also discussed. About 50 pages of testimonials are included. Data sources are from three assistance programs and records of the State Attorney's Office.

CENTRAL AMERICA

CECILIA MENJÍVAR, *Professor of Sociology, Arizona State University*

SEVERAL INTERRELATED CENTRAL AMERICAN social currents are reflected in the research production of the past few years. First, the rapid socioeconomic transformations, informed by neoliberal reforms and the shrinking of the state, are evident in the preoccupation of researchers in and of the region. Second, the region continues to be one of the most active in terms of migratory movements in the world today, some of which are related to the political and economic convulsions in the recent history of the region. Third, Central America—at least its "northern triangle," composed of El Salvador, Guatemala, and Honduras—has sustained some of the highest rates of violent deaths in the world in the past few years; thus it is not surprising to see substantial research attention to this area. A theme that binds these social dynamics is that of youth violence, or gangs, as this phenomenon has been linked to migratory flows and often identified as a root cause for the high rates of violence seen in the region today. Several themes related to these currents will be highlighted in this review.

A major theme in the works reviewed deals with violence in its various forms. Some scholars locate its root causes in internal as well as external forces (item **2379**), while others focus on "post-conflict" violence, providing interpretive accounts of the experiences and perspectives of individuals in violent situations (item **2390**) and the sense of insecurity that they regularly experience (item **2400**). A related current of scholarship continues the strong trend in the region of examining youth violence, or gangs, presenting more nuanced understandings of the root causes of this phenomenon, of the views of the youth who join gangs, and discussing alternative models and options as responses to the "strong hand" approaches of local governments (items **2384, 2399, 2403,** and **2409**). Within the theme of violence, scholars have started to concentrate on specific forms of violence that women endure, which researchers conceptualize as encompassing direct physical violence, as well as structural and symbolic violence, and feminicide (items **2369, 2372, 2382, 2387, 2388,** and **2407**).

The political conflicts have ended, but the transformations they ushered in have forever changed the region. There remain questions about the legacy of the conflicts, the changes that occurred, and those that did not materialize. Identity politics plays an important role. Recent works have examined post-conflict projects that sought to redefine social, in particular, ethnic, relations (item **2370**). Related to the legacy of the conflicts, there is work that concentrates on lessons learned about the effectiveness of social movements (item **2375**) and the varied motivations and methods informing combatants' decisions and strategies (item **2408**). The former studies offer potential lessons for other cases and contexts. The legacy of the conflicts can be complex, filled with both disillusionment *and* joy (item **2401**). An important development for women has been a new gendered consciousness embodied in the growth of the women's movement, with partially kept promises that continue to be fulfilled (item **2386**). Assessments of the evolution of these movements and their accomplishments are the focus of much attention (items **2392** and **2402**). Following a long-standing trend in the region, the questions of ethnic identity and race continue to be examined, particularly in regard to the impact of political conflicts on identity and identity formation. Some researchers focus on the potential effects of ethnic redefinitions (item **2370**), while others examine how popular language and images serve to solidify inequalities and sustain racism and discrimination (items **2378** and **2396**).

The works reviewed reveal attention to additional research themes related to the region's rapid socioeconomic transformations, initiated, exacerbated, or accelerated by neoliberal reforms. Some of the most notable works look at the impact of neoliberal policies and a globalized economy on work and the labor force. Among the topics studied are the increased precariousness of workers (item **2373**), the increased competition for markets in a highly unequal global economy (items **2376**, **2391**, and **2397**), and consequences for the workers' well-being (item **2385**). But not all research related to labor force participation is cast in a negative light, as some argue that even in precarious work arrangements workers can find ways to advance and succeed (item **2394**). Special attention is given to the situation of maquila workers in the region (items **2376** and **2383**), and to the conditions for women workers in general (item **2404**). Within the general theme of neoliberal reforms, there has been attention to the effects of privatization of social services and education (items **2374** and **2381**), as well as on the effects of neoliberal reforms on economic production, as, for example, in a study on agricultural workers' engagement in risky enterprises geared to satisfy global demands (item **2377**).

Another continued theme of focus is that of migrations within the region and from the region to the US. Transnational links between migrants and their origin communities (item **2371**), as well as those connections that refugees construct within experiences of disruption and displacement (item **2393**), and the effects of remittances on the families and communities that receive them (items **2405** and **2406**) continue to produce important studies, but attention to the demographic profiles and aggregate descriptions of the flows have also generated interesting work (items **2389** and **2395**). Scholars also paid attention to the migrants' human rights and to the violence they face as they journey north (item **2389**).

In addition to the major themes above, valuable publications on the family should be noted here, particularly studies of the various modalities of patriarchy (item **2380**) and the understandings that young individuals have of this concept (item **2398**).

2369 Araque G., Gloria María and **Adriana Ospina Vélez.** La violencia económica hacia las mujeres en El Salvador: aproximaciones a un problema social invisibilizado. San Salvador: Progressio, 2008. 110 p.: bibl., ill.

This very informative and solid report uses the term "economic violence" to refer to all the unequal relations and naturalized practices through which women do almost all domestic chores, earn less than men do, and take care of dependents without any recognition. The report seeks to demonstrate that these are forms of violence because of the harm done to women's health and to their development as human beings.

2370 Bastos, Santiago. La construcción de la identidad Maya en Guatemala: historia e implicaciones de un proceso político. (*Desacatos*, 24, mayo/agosto 2007, p. 197–214, bibl., photos)

The postconflict projects that seek to redefine political and social relations and the violent political context in Guatemala serve as a backdrop for this examination that traces the development of a "Maya" identity. Examines a wide variety of experiences, the transformations to the meaning of Maya identity, and the potential of these transformations for ethnic constructions in Guatemala and Latin America.

2371 Caamaño Morúa, Carmen. Espacio trasnacional e identidad de los Ticos entre "Arriba" y "Abajo". (*Veredas*, 8:15, segundo semestre 2007, p. 31–51, bibl.)

Based on fieldwork in Costa Rica, the author examines the transnational links that Costa Rican migrants create between their sending community and their destination point in New Jersey. Through the active deployment of ties across borders, migrants challenge borders and notions of sovereignty, but it is due to the existence of these limitations that transnational ties develop.

2372 Carey, David and **M. Gabriela Torres.** Precursors to femicide: Guatemalan women in a vortex of violence. (*LARR*, 45:3, 2010, p. 142–164)

The authors argue that rather than an exceptional phenomenon, femicide in Guatemala today reflects a trend in the normalization of gender-based violence over the

course of the 20th century. This examination shows that structures that historically have sustained impunity, reinscribed patriarchal relations, and maintained cultural practices of violence are central to understanding postwar violence against women.

2373 Castillo Fernández, Dídimo. Los nuevos trabajadores precarios. México: UNAM, Facultad de Ciencias Políticas y Sociales: Miguel Ángel Porrúa, 2009. 283 p.: bibl., ill. (Serie Las ciencias sociales)

Based on aggregate national data and quantitative analysis, this study analyzes work force dynamics in Panama in light of the economic restructuring of the 1980s, labor reforms, and major demographic shifts in the population. Focuses on the increased precariousness of labor conditions, particularly in urban jobs in the private sector.

2374 Castro V., Carlos *et al.* Transformaciones en la estructura social en Costa Rica: estratos sociooand cupacionales, educación y trabajo. San José: Instituto de Investigaciones Sociales: Editorial UCR, 2007. 281 p.: bibl., ill.

The privatization of education, social services, and banking, together with economic models that position Costa Rica as more dependent on tourism in the global economy, have contributed to the shrinking of the middle class and to gaps in the country's social development. These authors argue that "socio-occupational stratification" is a more practical analytic concept than social classes, a term they consider irrelevant for today's social reality.

2375 Darling, Juanita. Latin America, media, and revolution: communication in modern Mesoamerica. New York, N.Y.: Palgrave Macmillan, 2008. 226 p.: bibl., index, map. (Palgrave Macmillan series in international political communication)

Combining historical research with anthropological techniques, this author compares the media that rebels in El Salvador, Nicaragua, and Chiapas used to transmit their messages about an alternative system and to create imagined communities to network and support their vision. The choice of medium, which is influenced by history, tradition, and availability, can shape the way a particular movement develops.

2376 Esbenshade, Jill. The process of exporting neoliberal development: the consequences of the growth of export processing zones in El Salvador. (*in* Wages of empire: neoliberal policies, repression, and women's poverty. Edited by Amalia L. Cabezas, Ellen Reese, and Marguerite Waller. Boulder, Colo.: Paradigm Publishers, 2007, p. 152–165)

Based on field research and 54 in-depth interviews with workers, factory owners, government officials, and NGO staff members in El Salvador, this chapter describes the development of Export Processing Zones (EPZs), documents working conditions in these factories, and discusses potential effects of new strategies (like lowering the minimum wage) that aim to keep Salvadoran EPZs competitive, particularly in relation to China and the Philippines.

2377 Fischer, Edward F. and Peter Blair Benson. Broccoli and desire: global connections and Maya struggles in postwar Guatemala. Stanford, Calif.: Stanford Univ. Press, 2006. 212 p.: bibl., ill., index, map.

This ethnography highlights the confluence of needs and aspirations that connect producers of nontraditional export crops in rural Guatemala to middle class consumers in the US. In tracing this commodity chain, the authors focus on moral experiences, power differentials, and collective processes that entangle the two ends of the chain. The work is set within the context of neoliberal policies that shape what Maya farmers do and what US consumers desire.

2378 González Ponciano, Jorge Ramón. Blancura, cosmopolitismo y representación en Guatemala. (*Estud. Cult. Maya,* 27, 2006, p. 125–147, bibl.)

This examination focuses on the ideological dynamics behind racist and classist frameworks that are used to exclude both indigenous peoples and ladinos who come from lower and popular classes. The analysis uses ethnic and socioracial categories and terms that come from popular culture and the media. Such frameworks and language serve to place individuals in a strict social hierarchy and reproduce servile relations and symbolic violence.

2379 Guatemala: violencias desbordadas. Edición de Julián López García, Santiago Bastos y Manuela Camus. Córdoba, Spain: Servicio de Publicaciones de la Univ. de Córdoba, 2009. 415 p.: bibl., ill., maps.

This impressive collection of essays seeks to take a critical look at the roots and production of violence. As they identify sources of violence today, the authors shift the angle of vision from external forces to internal roots, focusing on how local actors operate in conjunction with outside forces. They point to the depolitization of violence in official discourse as an ineffective course to understand and address this issue.

2380 Hagene, Turid. Negotiating love in post-revolutionary Nicaragua: the role of love in the reproduction of gender asymmetry. Oxford, England: Peter Lang, 2008. 340 p.: bibl., index. (Hispanic studies: culture and ideas)

In this qualitative study of women's lives—focused on the spheres of religion, work, and gender relations—the author argues that relations with men, especially romantic relations, in a social order she calls "absentee patriarchy," reproduce existing gender hierarchies. In this context, love and gendered emotions play a central role in the reproduction of gender inequality. The study has potential relevance for other contexts and cases beyond Nicaragua.

2381 Haglund, LaDawn. Limiting resources: market-led reform and the transformation of public goods. University Park: Pennsylvania State Univ. Press, 2010. 238 p.: bibl., ill., index.

This book focuses on the conflicting paths that some countries have taken, between the privatization and marketization of public goods and state-led development, by comparing the approaches of Costa Rica and El Salvador regarding electricity and water provision. The author highlights the difficulties for states to act within neoliberal frameworks that do not promote justice, human rights, and sustainability in developing countries.

2382 Hume, Mo. The myths of violence: gender, conflict, and community in El Salvador. (*Lat. Am. Perspect.,* 35:5, Sept. 2008, p. 59–76, bibl.)

In postwar El Salvador violence has been normalized within the context of masculine domination, gender inequality, symbolic structures of violence (especially in the family and the state) and the community. An exploration from a feminist perspective helps to reveal how violence is normalized and legitimized and deeply embedded in ideologies that preceded the civil war. For political scientist's comment, see item **1151**.

2383 López de Cáceres, Carmen. Sólo pedimos que nos traten como humanas: discriminación laboral femenina, por razones de género con énfasis en las empresas textiles y/o maquiladoras de Guatemala. Edición de María Leitón Barquero. Elaborado por Carmen López de Cáceres, Lucrecia López López y María Eugenia Díaz Díaz. San José: Fundación para la Paz y la Democracia, 2007. 165 p.: col. ill.

Based on a survey of 516 maquila workers, this report provides information about labor conditions in this sector. Even though there have been serious labor rights violations among the women workers, there also have been some positive changes for the workers due to investigations, monitoring, complaints filed, and so forth, especially by organizations working for human rights.

Martí i Puig, Salvador. Tiranías, rebeliones y democracia: itinerarios políticos comparados en Centroamérica. See item **1130**.

2384 Martín Álvarez, Alberto; Ana Fernández Zubieta; and Karla Villarreal Sotelo. Difusión transnacional de identidades juveniles en la expansión de las maras centroamericanas. (*Perf. Latinoam.*, 15:30, julio/dic. 2007, p. 101–122, bibl., table)

This review essay focuses on the mechanisms (not just the causes) that have facilitated the expansion of *maras* (gangs) in Central America and the US. It argues that the *maras'* ability to create an appealing identity framework that resonates culturally with youth, together with new repressive government policies, explains their expansion throughout the region.

2385 Martínez Franzoni, Juliana. ¿Arañando bienestar?: trabajo remunerado, protección social y familias en América

Central. Buenos Aires: CLACSO, 2008. 192 p.: ill., map. (Col. CLACSO-CROP)

This book focuses on social transitions and examines welfare regimes in Guatemala, Honduras, El Salvador, and Nicaragua. Each country is classified according to how it prioritizes human capital. Argues that these countries have similar regimes, but El Salvador differs from the others due to variations in its occupational structure and how it manages migrant remittances.

2386 Méndez Gutiérrez, Luz and Walda Barrios-Klee. Caminos recorridos: luchas y situación de las mujeres a trece años de los Acuerdos de Paz. Ciudad de Guatemala: Unión Nacional de Mujeres Guatemaltecas, 2010. 121 p.: table.

This evaluation of Guatemalan women's conditions is based on a similar report published in 2004. Using a mixed methods approach, the study notes that significant advancements have been the development of a gendered consciousness, the expansion of the women's movement, and women's concerted objectives to fight for their human rights and liberation. Despite progress, much remains to be done.

2387 Menjívar, Cecilia. Enduring violence: Ladina women's lives in Guatemala. Berkeley: Univ. of California Press, 2011. 288 p.: bibl., index.

Based on longitudinal fieldwork, this book examines how the confluence of various forms of violence—structural, political, symbolic, everyday, gender, and gendered—are normalized and misrecognized in the quotidian lives of Ladinas in eastern Guatemala and Maya women in the Altiplano, and how this situation can set conditions for more open and egregious expressions of violence against women.

2388 Menjívar, Cecilia. Violence and women's lives in eastern Guatemala: a conceptual framework. (*LARR*, 43:3, 2008, p. 109–136)

Most of the article outlines a useful framework of different forms of violence—structural, political, symbolic, and interpersonal. The framework then is utilized to examine the pervasive violence in everyday lives of Ladina women in a small eastern town. Based on fieldwork conducted in the last half of the 1990s. [C. Brockett]

2389 Migraciones en el sur de México y Centroamérica. Edición de Daniel Villafuerte Solís y María del Carmen García Aguilar. México: UNICACH: Miguel Ángel Porrúa, 2008. 398 p.: bibl., ill., maps.

This comprehensive volume explores the different migratory movements taking place today within the Central American region and southern Mexico from various perspectives and disciplines, from general presentations to specific case studies. It examines this phenomenon from a viewpoint that entwines migratory dynamics, development, and human rights, and highlights the migrants' vulnerability and the violence that they face.

2390 Moodie, Ellen. El Salvador in the aftermath of peace: crime, uncertainty, and the transition to democracy. Philadelphia: Univ. of Pennsylvania Press, 2010. 294 p.: bibl., index. (The ethnography of political violence)

This carefully crafted ethnography of postconflict violence examines the varying perceptions and interpretations of violence and crime that "ordinary" individuals have, without reifying images of the country as dangerous and violent. Indeed, the book is more about shedding light on changes in state and social structures in this postwar society than on criminogenic aspects per se.

2391 Mora S., Minor and Juan Pablo Pérez Sáinz. Se acabó la pura vida: amenazas y desafíos sociales en la Costa Rica del siglo XXI. San José: FLACSO Costa Rica, 2009. 176 p.: bibl., ill.

Using the concept of social exclusion, the authors examine the relationship between social inequality and the risk of poverty in the context of globalization, and propose a framework that highlights power relations for understanding persistent market inequalities. The Costa Rican era of social inclusion seems to have ended with the adoption of new economic models in the context of global processes of accumulation.

2392 Movimiento de mujeres en El Salvador 1995–2006: estrategias y miradas desde el feminismo. Edición de Morena Soledad Herrera. Textos de Morena Soledad Herrera *et al.* San Salvador: Fundación Nacional para el Desarrollo, 2008. 816 p.: bibl., col. maps.

This comprehensive volume reflects on the forms of collective action and on the representation of women's interests in the current women's movement in El Salvador. It seeks to define the movement and its objectives, while critically examining its persistent battles for basic services. The work takes an inclusive view that incorporates different positions and perspectives of feminism.

2393 Nolin, Catherine. Transnational ruptures: gender and forced migration. Aldershot, England: Ashgate, 2006. 246 p.: bibl., ill., index, maps. (Gender in a global/local world)

Based on a multi-sited, transnational ethnography in Guatemala and Canada, this book focuses on the transnational ties that Guatemalan refugees living in Canada have forged, and exposes their experiences of displacement, political violence, the destruction of communities, identity construction and transformation, the obstacles that disrupt as well as factors that facilitate settlement, and the gendered angles embedded in these processes.

2394 Offit, Thomas A. Conquistadores de la calle: child street labor in Guatemala City. Austin: Univ. of Texas Press, 2008. 228 p.: bibl., index, map, photos, table.

This ethnography of child street laborers argues that although these youths are deprived of formal education, they acquire informal education and skills in the street that hold promise for their futures. Far from dead-end jobs, the various jobs they do present opportunities for advancement and to overcome the poverty that brought them to the street in the first place.

2395 Paredes Orozco, Guillermo. Migración de guatemaltecos a México y Estados Unidos a partir de la *Encuesta sobre migración en la frontera Guatemala-México 2004*: un análisis de estrategias migratorias. (*Migr. Int.*, 5:1, enero/junio 2009, p. 93–124, bibl., tables)

Using data from the Emif Gua-Mex survey collected among returning migrants in two towns at the Guatemala-Mexico border in 2004, this article compares quantitatively Guatemalan migration to Mexico and to the US. The authors note that Guatemalan migratory flows to Mexico and to the

US are demographically different, including along the lines of gender and educational level.

2396 Las políticas del reconocimiento: una mirada al quehacer institucional y organizacional sobre racismo y discriminación en Guatemala. Ciudad de Guatemala: Asociación para el Avance de las Ciencias Sociales en Guatemala, 2008. 107 p.: bibl., ill. (some col.). (Texto para debate)

Based on a survey conducted among governmental entities and community organizations to explore contemporary practices of racism and discrimination, the authors observe that both bodies have made efforts to recognize the rights of indigenous peoples. However, this recognition is focused on cultural aspects, without identifying fundamental social and economic causes, a shift that would require the implementation of major redistributive policies.

La protesta social en época electoral, 2007. See item **1160**.

2397 Rivers-Moore, Megan. No artificial ingredients?: gender, race and nation in Costa Rica's international tourism campaign. (*J. Lat. Am. Cult. Stud.*, 16:3, Dec. 2007, p. 341–357)

This article critically examines popular images about Costa Rica's exceptionalism and national imagery that often is conveyed to potential tourists. The constructed narrative places indigeneity away from the major tourist centers and interweaves whiteness, modernity, and development as the official tourist discourse so as to keep Costa Rica competitive in the international market for tourism.

2398 Rosés, Patricia. Algunos elementos para la construcción de tipos de paternidad a partir de casos de padres jóvenes costarricenses. (*Anu. Estud. Centroam.*, 31, 2005, p. 137–165, bibl., tables)

Based on a study of motherhood and fatherhood among 15- to 25-year-olds in a low-income community in San José, this article examines various aspects of fatherhood, including authority, material support, and affective links. It proposes various Weberian-like ideal types of fatherhood and points to important changes in family

dynamics in Costa Rica that need further exploration.

2399 Savenije, Wim. Las pandillas transnacionales o "maras": violencia urbana en Centroamérica. (*Foro Int./México*, 47:3, julio/sept. 2007, p. 637–659, bibl.)

This article questions whether the phenomenon of *maras* (gangs) is truly foreign to the region, notes the critical link between the *maras'* expansion and the socialization of the street, and discusses the limitations of current government strategies that focus on enforcement. It argues that the Nicaraguan case might hold important answers for dealing with this situation in the rest of the region.

2400 Securing the city: neoliberalism, space, and insecurity in postwar Guatemala. Edited by Kevin Lewis O'Neill and Kedron Thomas. Durham, N.C.: Duke Univ. Press, 2011. 220 p.: bibl., index, table.

Each chapter in this timely volume explores ethnographically how individuals in Guatemala City are experiencing increased levels of "postconflict" violence and insecurity of life, how they internalize it, and how they respond to this collective insecurity. Some people hire private security services, others become more religious, and others engage in urban renewal projects.

2401 Silber, Irina Carlota. Everyday revolutionaries: gender, violence, and disillusionment in postwar El Salvador. New Brunswick, N.J.: Rutgers Univ. Press, 2011. 238 p.: bibl., ill., index, map. (Genocide, political violence, human rights series)

This book explores the complexity of the postwar lives of former revolutionaries in El Salvador in the context of neoliberal reform. The author focuses on how these individuals craft new identities and what democracy means for them. Though there is disillusion, there are also moments of joy and satisfaction. The challenges of mending the social fabric of the war-torn country weave through the narrative.

2402 Silber, Irina Carlota and Jocelyn Viterna. Women in El Salvador: continuing the struggle. (*in* Women and politics around the world: a comparative history and survey. Edited by Joyce Gelb and Marian

Lief Palley. Santa Barbara, Calif.: ABC-CLIO, 2009, p. 329–351, bibl.)

Salvadoran women's critical participation in political parties, collective action, grassroots groups, and community organizations, through which women's groups seek to address the shortcomings created by neoliberal reforms and the retrenching of the Salvadoran state, are the focus of this piece. The article also notes the importance of the Salvadoran diaspora in these efforts.

2403 Tobar Estrada, Anneliza. Entre mundos ajenos: encuentro de percepciones de jóvenes pandilleros, ex pandilleros y acompañantes sobre la sociedad guatemalteca. Ciudad de Guatemala: Facultad Latinoamericana de Ciencias Sociales, FLACSO-Guatemala, 2007. 103 p.: bibl. (Serie Estudios sobre pobreza)

Centered in a framework of poverty and social exclusion, this qualitative study avoids simplistic explanations and presents a holistic view of questions about gangs, including their development within a context of poverty, the views the youth involved have of themselves, and those the broader society has of them. Critiques of the negative effects of governmental policies that focus on punitive measures are included, as well as media representations of these youths as criminals.

2404 Trabajo reproductivo: debates para un nuevo contrato social en El Salvador. San Salvador: Unidad de Investigaciones, Organización de Mujeres Salvadoreñas por la Paz, 2008. 119 p.: bibl., ill. (Mujer y mercado laboral, El Salvador)

This publication is part of the series, started in 2006, on the women's labor market and once again places emphasis on remunerated work. It presents historical trends demonstrating how women's participation in the labor force has been shaped and the impact of the civil war on those trends. The work seeks to highlight women's economic contributions, which continue to be invisible.

2405 Velásquez, José Humberto; Tito Elmer Crespín Menjívar; and José Alejandro Sosa Cortez. Identidad rural: educación, familia y migración en El Salvador. San Salvador: Univ. Pedagógica de El Salvador, Dirección de Investigación Científica y Transferencia Tecnológica, 2006. 240 p.: bibl., ill., maps.

This social anthropological study examines the lives of individuals in a rural village and focuses on the effects of remittances on the families' social and material conditions. Importantly, the findings of this work do not support previous studies or public discourse, as the authors note that nonmigrant family members continue to work and the cultural effect of migration on the families who remain in El Salvador is minimal.

2406 Villacrés, Daniela N. A view from the inside: grounding the remittance-development link. (*Migr. Int.*, 5:2, julio/dic. 2009, p. 39–73, bibl.)

This study conducted in Intipucá, El Salvador, shows that though remittances help to raise living standards in sending communities, those who receive them do not see them as significantly altering their communities' development path. Family and collective remittances have different effects on development, shaped by contextual factors and the degree of control of their investment.

2407 Violencia de género contra las mujeres y feminicidio: un reto para el Estado salvadoreño. San Salvador: Organización de Mujeres Salvadoreñas por la Paz, 2008. 127 p.: bibl.

This inclusive interdisciplinary report on violence and its social, cultural, and economic implications for women's lives includes up-to-date statistics on the various forms of violence against women. Poverty and a history of political violence might play a role, but the report also highlights the state's responsibility for this violence, as well as the media's role.

2408 Viterna, Jocelyn. Pulled, pushed, and persuaded: explaining women's mobilization into the Salvadoran guerrilla army. (*Am. J. Sociol.*, 112:1, July 2006, p. 1–45, map, tables)

Using a representative sample of grassroots activists and nonactivists, this study identifies three mobilization patterns among Salvadoran women combatants—politicized, recruited, and reluctant guerrillas. It highlights heterogeneity of motives, biographies, and social location of the combatants, and it underscores important points useful for theorizing about mobilization beyond the Salvadoran case.

Wittman, Hannah and **Charles Geisler.** Negotiating locality: decentralization and communal forest management in the Guatemalan highlands. See item **761.**

2409 Wolseth, Jon. Jesus and the gang: youth violence and Christianity in urban Honduras. Tucson: Univ. of Arizona Press, 2011. 156 p.: bibl., index, photos.

This ethnographic study argues that the structural violence that comes from neoliberal reforms and recent gun violence creates highly constrained choices for poor Honduran youth who respond by joining either gangs or religious movements. Their bodies are proof of the state's failure to provide for them. Catholic and Pentecostal churches present alternatives, each with a different approach and set of options.

THE CARIBBEAN AND THE GUIANAS

BENIGNO E. AGUIRRE-LÓPEZ, *Professor of Sociology, Department of Sociology and Criminal Justice, University of Delaware*

HOW TO MAKE SENSE of the Caribbean? What rhetorical device or master metaphor provides the necessary insight to understand the complexity and mystery of the region? These are the central, if at times implicit, questions asked by the authors of a number of recent monographs in the field of sociology. It is worthwhile to review the variety and significance of some of the arguments expressed in this literature, for each gives important insights.

For authors Ho and Nurse (item **2429**), the Caribbean must be understood from the perspective of long-term globalization. Societies in the region are both diasporic and global; their popular culture is the site of identity contestation. Theirs is an important statement challenging many of the assumptions that are made nowadays about globalization, which in their view is not primarily economic, but instead represents the interface of culture, society, and political economy; is a secular trend in historical capitalism; is marked by the increasing importance of cultural transnationalism and deterritorialization that render less useful standard concepts such as national boundaries and identities. Their emphasis is on exploring the often-unacknowledged South-to-North penetration in which the Caribbean is not a passive victim but a producer and exporter of cultural objects. The monograph has sections on Caribbean cultural identity, carnivals, music, cinema, and popular culture. Plaza and Henry (item **2445**) argue that it is the movement of people, or more specifically the return migration of Caribbean people, that is the defining process for the Caribbean. They point out that travel—departure and return—has been a constant in Caribbean history, during the colonial and postcolonial periods, and now including the diaspora experience. They also acknowledge that return migration has increased dramatically since the 1990s. Their introductory chapter includes a useful review of theories of return migration, transnationalism, literature, factors involving the decision to return, and a useful theory map outlining a model of return migration.

Caribbean transnationalism is also the main theme of Gowricharn's monograph (item **2430**). Its chapters are divided into sections exploring the nature of the Caribbean, regional transnationalism, and the social cohesion of old and emerging

Caribbean societies. The chapters in the book come from papers presented during a conference on Globalization, Diaspora, and Identity that took place at the University of Suriname in February 2004. He argues that Caribbean societies are the result of different diasporas, or communities formed by the forced dispersion of people; that the displaced people's identities are often linked to their places of origin; and that such communities are transnational communities linking the Caribbean to the former colonial metropolis and to the US. Other worthwhile texts are by Cohen and Toninato with its emphasis on creolization (item **2419**), Bashi's emphasis on familial and other types of networks (item **2413**), Henke and Magister's collection of articles on Caribbean diasporas throughout the world (item **2417**), Levy's monograph on the importance of African worldviews for Caribbean culture and society (item **2410**), and Curbelo *et al.*'s important monograph on the new religious movements that are active in the countries in the region (item **2434**). Perhaps one of the best monographs that has been published on religion and development in Cuba is by Hearn (item **2432**). It examines the life options of poor families, many of them black, living in a "solar" or housing complex with very limited resources and services. It analyzes the inability of the state to help these families in conjunction with the presence of NGOs and informal groups trying to offer assistance. The emphasis is on the grassroots initiatives and the efforts of the state to incorporate them into government programs. Finally, Padilla's monograph on the role that unemployment plays in the creation of a sex trade offers a novel approach to the study of the Caribbean (item **2441**). He uses data from the Dominican Republic on the exchanges between gay male tourists and male sex workers to show how patterns of economic development that have limited employment opportunities create structural conditions that encourage illicit sex exchanges, even if such practices are widely condemned on the island. Padilla's is a nuanced analysis of a problem that exists elsewhere in the Caribbean due to the economic choices and policies in many countries in the region.

The recently published material on Cuba includes a number of excellent monographs. Ochoa (item **2439**) examines the Quita Manaquita and the Palo Alto Praise, secretive religious practices that have a large following inside and outside Cuba. He attempts to convey in words the experiences he had while learning their secrets, which apparently are so subtle as to perhaps defy understanding in the absence of personal experience. It is nevertheless a worthwhile challenge. Hernández Fox (item **2433**) examines the use of ecclesiastical juridical procedures governing divorce in Cuba during 1763–1878 that favored men but that often were used by wives to protect their interests. The book includes a description of the family institution in Cuba; a review of canonical and civil law governing marriage and divorce; as well as interesting analyses of cases.

Arguably the most important recent trends in writings about Cuba are the analyses of Cuban culture and the problem of racism in Cuba. Both of these themes are very important and both have been the objects of excellent scholarship. Fernández Robaina's monograph examines racism in Cuba during the revolutionary period (item **2427**). With unusual courage, he examines the period of 1959–84 as one of lost opportunities. While Fidel Castro condemned racism in his speeches, his government wiped out the island's voluntary associations of black people, which might have been capable of sustaining affirmative action programs against racism. He identifies Gustavo E. Urrutia and Juan René Betancourt as early intellectual figures of the black community who spoke and wrote about the need to resocialize the Cuban people on the matter of racism, and also mentions the most important writers of the 1970s, 80s, and 90s who tried to create a movement against racism in Cuba, including Natalia Bolívar, Carlos Moore, Gabino La Rosa, Pedro Serviat, and Jesús Guanche. Fernández Robaina examines the most recent "Special Period," from 1990 until the present, listing with remarkable candor the efforts that have taken place in Cuba to eradicate racism, the extraordinary support that the Biblioteca Nacional José Martí and the Fundación Fernando Ortiz have given to this effort in cultural and social change, and the continued challenges still ahead, such as preventing the exclusion of black Cubans from the tourism industry, the main source of dollars on the island. A propos, Pérez and Lueiro (item **2444**) have compiled a very important collection of original writings on the problem of racism in Cuba and how to ameliorate or eliminate it, and Fernández Robaina (item **2426**) has also compiled a parallel collection of documents that could be of great importance to anyone with an interest in understanding what has been done to change the racism that is endemic in so much of the culture. Lest the problem of racism be considered unimportant, Hansing (item **2431**) documents the discrimination and racism encountered by blacks who join the Rastafari movement in Cuba, a movement that has gone unstudied until now. The monograph includes a chapter on the real situation in contemporary Cuba in which material and spiritual difficulties abound. The work includes a description of how race is understood in Cuba and how the government's efforts to deal with the economic crisis of the 1990s impacted black people most severely. Another chapter describes the emergence and development of the Rastafari movement in Cuba. It points out that the popularity of reggae music and its presence on radio programs facilitated the spread of the movement, which occurred alongside an upsurge of students from the English-speaking Caribbean who went to study in Cuba. Unsurprisingly, the generalized negative attitude towards the Rastas has encouraged an ideology of resistance among the mostly black youth who are members of the movement.

Cuban culture is the other area that has received quite a bit of scholarly attention, with substantial edited volumes on a variety of topics. Tinajero offers a collection of writings on Cuban culture during the 21st century (item **2421**). Hernandez-Reguant's emphasis is on the Special Period and how it has transformed Cuban culture (item **2420**). Finally Almazán del Olmo and Moré's (item **2443**) volume is perhaps the most comprehensive collection, attempting to offer a panorama of Cuban culture that includes the "official" position, such as writings on culture by Fidel Castro, Ernesto Che Guevara, and some of their acolytes. Hernandez-Reguant's chapter on multi-Cubanness (*multicubanidad*) in her volume is very good. She points out that exile and diaspora, concepts previously not spoken in the same breath, are now being considered together as crucial elements of the emerging notion of Cuban identity. While it is not possible to comment on all of these contributions, it is necessary to point out that this emphasis on culture is of fundamental importance to understanding the Cuban Revolution and the future of the country. One of the most important and obscure achievements of the Cuban government has been the systematic transformation of all aspects of Cuban culture to dovetail with the political needs of the regime. We have only a limited understanding of how this transformation has taken place during more than half a century of state domination by the present government. Perez Malo and Legra's chapter in item **2443** gives an account of the cultural policy of the regime, but still our knowledge of cultural transformation in Cuba remains scant.

Obviously, to understand what has transpired in Cuba, it is important to recognize how social control is used to keep things flowing in the direction the regime finds appropriate. In this context, two chapters merit comment. The first, a chapter by Roberto Zurbano included in Hernandez-Reguant's volume (item **2420**), explains how the rap movement was introduced in Cuba. He points out that the artists who wanted to introduce it in Cuba needed the initial sponsorship of Hermanos Saiz Association. Initially, the idea received a cold reception from the Ministry of Culture. Nevertheless, the artists continued their efforts to institutionalize rap as an accepted style of music. Rap music is seen as confrontational to those in power throughout the world, and this is no less true in Cuba where artists have used music to address the problem of racism. Zurbano points out that after more than a decade, rap is in a precarious situation; as a music style it is accepted by most youths, but despite the efforts of many it has not been institutionalized. The second is a chapter by Diane Soles in Tinajero's volume (item **2421**) examining the response of the regime to three films: *Fresa y chocolate, Alicia en el pueblo de las maravillas,* and *Guantanamera.* She asks how the filmmakers in Cuba were able to resist censorship of their works. The first film, on homophobia and the rights of homosexuals, did not cause much reaction from the censors presumably since it was introduced at the height of the crisis and the government was too busy to worry about it. The second film, *Alicia,* caused widespread negative reaction from the Partido Comunista de Cuba. The filmmakers appealed to Castro even as they made it clear that they were not developing a political criticism of the regime. Eventually Castro agreed with them and the censure ended. Castro himself spoke out against *Guantanamera,* and started a public reaction against the film. In this case, the filmmakers appealed to international associations of filmmakers who contacted Castro to plead for the film. Eventually he agreed to stop the censure of the film on the island. Soles concludes sagely that filmmakers are an important constituency of the Cuban state. They offer the state legitimacy as well as an important source of income. This example, very rare in the literature on Cuban culture, shows the limits of power of a totalitarian state faced with mobilized national and international associations and interest groups that maintain ongoing relations with the regime.

Recent publications on the Dominican Republic include an excellent compendium on carnivals in the island by Dagoberto Tejeda Ortiz (item **2450**). It is without doubt an exhaustive description of the cultural practice, written under the auspices of the National Dominican Section of the Pan American Institute of Geography and History. In 10 chapters the volume covers all historical periods, from the colonial era, to the period of North American intervention 1916–24, the dictatorship of Trujillo, and the post-Trujillo period. Other chapters examine the various personal stereotypes in the figures represented in the carnival, the characteristics of the groups participating in it, and the masks used in the different carnivals in the country. Chapter 7 describes the different local carnivals throughout the country. Chapter 8 examines Cimarron Carnival, which is less well known than some other types of carnivals. The last two chapters examine the role of carnival and its likely development in the future, as well as the relationship between carnival and national identity. It is hoped that the book will be translated into the English language so that tourists and others with limited knowledge of the Spanish language and customs of the Dominican Republic can benefit from reading it.

Recent scholarship has also examined the importance of emigration to the lifestyle of the population of the Valle de Neiba, Dominican Republic, through the conduit of remittances. Gonzalo Ramírez de Haro *et al.* (item **2425**) studied the impact of remittances on the town of Vicente Noble. They find that the bulk of the émigrés in the town went to Barcelona, Spain. They also find that the extended family is used to spread the resources that are sent from Spain when people do not have close family members participating in the emigration. Remittances have diminished the condition of poverty and improved the quality of the urban environment of the town, particularly the materials used in the building of houses. Cement blocks nowadays predominate in construction. Furthermore, there are more businesses in the town and fewer cases of severe malnutrition among infants. On the negative side there is greater socioeconomic inequality, and the leadership of the community has suffered since many of the local leaders have emigrated. This is an excellent study of an important process that is transforming the entire Caribbean; remittances are one of the most important sources of hard currency in every country in the region.

Two other monographs that deserve mention are the study by Simmons of Dominican racial identity (item **2449**) and the study of female emigration by Antonio Méndez (item **2436**). Méndez's monograph is a thorough study of the situation of women in the Dominican Republic. He offers statistics to show that women have had to struggle against discriminatory practices and prejudices that have excluded them from participating in the political system and in the workforce, are much more likely to be victims of domestic violence and to be infected with AIDS, and are much less likely to receive medical and public health services. He documents the importance of Dominican women in the transnational community in four states in the US: Florida, New York, New Jersey, and Massachusetts. The book concludes with a series of recommendations to improve the life chances of Dominican women in the US and in their country of birth. It is very rare to find a study such as this one, in which the factors pushing women into the emigration stream are presented together with their subsequent experience in their place of destination. It is a comprehensive methodology worth emulating. The monograph by Simmons explores the meaning of African roots for Dominicans both in the Dominican Republic and in the US. The last two of five chapters deal with the change in self-identification that has occurred among Dominican immigrants in the US; from their use of the term *indio* (mixed), the word *mulatto* as a new Dominican identity more accepting of its African origins emerges. The concluding chapter examines how many Dominicans are embracing their African origins in a collective reaffirmation of self that reverses the rejection of the African past that is so common in their country of birth.

The published material from Puerto Rico is extensive, covering a number of important topics. One monograph offers a sociological analysis of the nationwide effort by social movements during the second half of the 20th century to take over land and buildings—the "rescates"—for the use of the poor (item **2418**). A second monograph presents the nationalist writings of the essayist and intellectual Julio A. Muriente Pérez on Vieques (item **2438**). A third monograph (item **2435**) presents the findings of a national study of the experience of violence by young people, including violence in their homes, schools, and neighborhoods. It concludes with a number of recommendations that would prove very useful not only for Puerto Rican society, but also for the entire Caribbean and other parts of Latin America. A monograph by Vélez Camacho (item **2453**) offers a history of feminist groups in Puerto Rico. It includes a chapter on the origin of feminism on the island. A chapter in the book describes the most important feminist groups in the 1970s.

Subsequent chapters describe the feminist organizations active during the 1980s, 1990s, and during 2000–2006. It concludes with a useful bibliography on the topic of feminism.

Jorge Duany, the well-known Cuban-born Puerto Rican anthropologist, has published (item **2424**) a compendium of his articles that appeared in Puerto Rican newspapers and mass media journals, in what he calls an effort in cultural journalism. The book includes many of the island's cultural practices and serves as an excellent introduction for anyone who wishes to understand the intricacies of the society. An equally worthwhile introduction to Puerto Rican culture is the monograph by Fiet (item **2428**) describing the town of Loíza and the celebration of Santiago Apóstol. The monograph includes a number of photos of the celebration. One of the chapters in the book describes the practice of male crossdressing, conventional role-playing by women, and the importance of the elderly in the ceremonies associated with the saint.

Soberal edited an important interdisciplinary collection of scholarly articles on Puerto Rican social and cultural diversity (item **2422**). The book is divided into sections on various dimensions of diversity; the institutional context of diversity; genre and sexuality; and a final section on emergent aspects of diversity. To her credit, she has been able to include the work of well-known scholars and writers, such as Duany, who writes on the discrimination and prejudice that Dominicans suffer in Puerto Rico; Ramos Rodríguez's review of the challenges faced by the transgender and transsexual communities on the island; Rivera Ortiz who writes about the importance of tolerance of different political viewpoints for a working democracy; and Valle Ferrer who examines domestic violence and the responses to it by its victims, among a number of other collaborators.

The challenges faced by queer minorities on the island are the topic of a monograph that emerged out of a 2008 national colloquium held at the Universidad de Puerto Rico in Mayaguez in protest of Resolution 99 (item **2416**). The latter was a proposed referendum in 2008 that sought to amend Puerto Rico's constitution to define marriage as a union between a man and a woman and ban same-sex marriages, civil unions, and domestic partnership benefits. Nothing came of it. In what is arguably the best statement condemning the narrow-mindedness and hypocrisy of Caribbean culture when it comes to the topic of homosexuality, Rolón Collazo wrote an astute analysis of the homophobia that must be defeated for sexual diversity to have a chance to thrive.

Two books are devoted to the racial question. Rivero (item **2447**) examines how race and ethnicity are presented in television programs in Puerto Rico, centering on the influence of Cubans in the industry, and Ortiz García writes a history of blacks in Puerto Rico (item **2440**). Rivero attempts to show the way that blackness has been represented in Puerto Rico's commercial media entertainment programming, discussing an initial historical period in which it was assumed, however incorrectly, that race had no discernible effects on life chances in the island. The work includes a very interesting chapter on the television program "Mi Familia," in which racial differences were clearly articulated.

Ortiz García's monograph is an ambitious project, combining coverage of many subjects that are usually not included together in one book. His work reviews the origin of European colonialism and its nefarious impacts on Africa and traces the African origins and religions of black slaves. Ortiz García then looks specifically at Puerto Rico, speculating on the African origins and ethnicities of the slaves who were brought to the island to work on land estates devoted to sugar and in the sugar mills. He describes the society of the Taínos, the indigenous peoples whose population was completely decimated by the European conquest. He then describes contemporary African religions in Puerto Rico and the discrimination and prejudices their followers suffer. The final chapters discuss the cultural contributions of black people to contemporary Puerto Rican society. Throughout his work, Ortiz García offers suggestions for the best ways to educate Puerto Ricans about the contributions of African people to contemporary Puerto Rican society and culture. These are some, but not all, of the topics covered in this monograph.

Three monographs represent the English-speaking Caribbean. One of them is by the well-known anthropologist Barry Chevannes (item **2415**). He presents a comprehensive analysis of Jamaican society. The book has chapters on the impact of Africa on Jamaican identity; the Rastafari movement; fatherhood; cosmological reproduction; law and the African Caribbean family; crime and ganja; and the problem of social integration. Another monograph is by Green and Scher (item **2451**), who write about carnival in Trinidad, or the cultural politics of a transnational festival. Their book has nine chapters, including chapters on the Calypso craze of 1957; steel band music; carnival in Aruba; Caribana 1997; returning transnational in the carnival of Trinidad and Tobago; the conflict between authenticity and commerce in the Trinidad Carnival; a long disquisition by an anthropologist about the ethical issues surrounding the study of carnival; the global context of the Trinidad Carnival; and the impact of the increasing participation of women on the esthetics of Trinidad Carnival.

A third important monograph is by Morgan and Youssef (item **2437**). They use linguistic and discourse analysis to study violence in Caribbean society. Their analysis examines the presence of violence in fictional and nonfictional discourse. They discuss how globalization and the worldwide flow of people to and from the Caribbean contribute to violence in the region. They also examine how depictions of violence in the media and in the workings of the institutions of Caribbean societies contribute to the normalization and increase of violence in Caribbean societies. The book also explores the connection between male marginalization and violence, and the relation between violent encounters involving race, nation, ideologies, and ethnic differences and male-female acts of violence. The book sees the family as the primary locus of violence and also as the place where human support and caring can, and often do, occur.

2410 The African-Caribbean worldview and the making of Caribbean society.
Edited by Horace Levy. Kingston: Univ. of West Indies Press, 2009. 248 p.: bibl.

Papers from a 2006 conference celebrating the work of Professor Barry Chevannes describe the impact of African worldviews on Caribbean culture and society. Contributions include examinations of the Rastafari movement, the colonial legacy in the Caribbean, race relations, and Creoles and national identity. The volume concludes with a note by Chevannes himself.

2411 Alcázar Campos, Ana. "Jineterismo": turismo sexual o uso táctico del sexo? (*Rev. Antropol. Soc.,* 19, 2010, p. 307–337)

This paper deals with the relationships between tourists and Cubans at the beginning of the 21st century. It seeks to portray "sexual tourism" as a perspective— whether local or global—from which to investigate the (re)production of the inequalities of gender, race, class, and nationality. "Jineterismo" is seen as a Cuban phenomenon characterized by the overlapping relationship between sexuality and tourism, and involving relations of domination of gender, class, and historical-political position. [C.E. Griffin]

2412 Anderson, Thomas F. Carnival and national identity in the poetry of Afrocubanismo. Gainesville: Univ. Press of Florida, 2011. 341 p.: bibl., ill., index, photos.

This volume is the first to examine, from a literary perspective, the long-running debate between the proponents of Afro-Cuban cultural manifestations and the predominantly white Cuban intelligentsia who viewed these traditions as "backward" and counter to the interests of the young republic. Including analyses of the work of Felipe Pichardo Moya, Alejo Carpentier, Nicolás Guillén, Emilio Ballagas, José Zacarías Tallet, Felix B. Caignet, Marcelino Arozarena, and Alfonso Camín, this rigorous, interdisciplinary volume offers a fresh look at the canon of Afrocubanismo with surprising insights into Cuban culture during the early years of the Republic. [C.E. Griffin]

2413 Bashi, Vilna. Survival of the knitted: immigrant social networks in a stratified world. Stanford, Calif.: Stanford Univ. Press, 2007. 319 p.: bibl., ill., index.

In this ethnography of West Indian social networks, Bashi emphasizes familial and other types of networks that connect migrant life in the Caribbean. She develops an important model of a transnational immigrant network organization, in which seasoned migrants (hubs) act as migration experts and send repeatedly for newcomers (spokes). She argues that geographic mobility is a vehicle for socioeconomic and cultural mobility.

2414 Cabrera, Ángel; Frank Neville; and Samantha Novick. Harnessing human potential in Haiti. (*Innovations/Cambridge,* 5:4, Oct. 2010, p. 143–149)

Rebuilding a better Haiti will require a radically different approach to education. A combination of improved funding, smart allocation of resources, and use of low-cost modern technology may allow Haiti to leapfrog to significantly higher performance levels. Part of a special journal issue dedicated to strategies for societal renewal in Haiti. [C.E. Griffin]

2415 Chevannes, Barry. Betwixt and between: explorations in an African-Caribbean mindscape. Kingston; Miami, Fla.: Ian Randle Publishers, 2006. 245 p.: bibl., index.

Well-known anthropologist Chevannes presents a comprehensive analysis of Jamaican society. Chapters include examinations of the impact of Africa on Jamaican identity, the Rastafari movement, fatherhood, cosmological reproduction, law and the African-Caribbean family, crime and ganja, and the problem of social integration.

2416 Coloquio ¿Del Otro La'o? Perspectivas sobre Sexualidades "Queer", 2nd, *Universidad de Puerto Rico, Recinto de Mayagüez, 2008.* Actas. Recopilación de Lissette Rolón Collazo. Mayagüez, P.R.: Centro de Publicaciones Académicas, Facultad de Artes y Ciencias, UPR-RUM, 2010. 154 p.: bibl., ill.

Papers from a conference on sexuality and queer minorities in Puerto Rico address the challenges that queer minorities face in the island. The conference was organized to protest Resolution 99, a referendum proposed in 2008 to amend the Puerto Rican constitution to define marriage as a union between a man and a woman, and to ban same-sex marriages, civil unions, and domestic partnership benefits. The referendum never passed. Rolón Collazo contributes a powerful statement condemning the narrow-mindedness of Caribbean culture regarding homosexuality by analyzing homophobia and arging that it must be defeated for sexual diversity to succeed and thrive in the region.

2417 Constructing vernacular culture in the trans-Caribbean. Edited by Holger Henke and Karl-Heinz Magister. Lanham, Md.: Lexington Books, 2008. 407 p.: bibl., index. (Caribbean studies)

This compilation brings together several papers on Caribbean diasporas throughout the world. Transnational identity, music, rituals, feminism, and sexual identity are among the topics discussed.

2418 Cotto Morales, Liliana. Desalambrar: orígenes de los rescates de terreno en Puerto Rico y su pertinencia en los movimientos sociales contemporáneos. San

Juan: Editorial Tal Cual, 2006. 253 p.: bibl., ill.

Presents a sociological analysis of the nationwide social movements during the second half of the 20th century that attempted to take over land and buildings and make them available to the poor for housing (*rescates*).

2419 The creolization reader: studies in mixed identities and cultures. Edited and introduced by Robin Cohen and Paola Toninato. London; New York, N.Y.: Routledge, 2010. 402 p.: bibl., ill., index. (Routledge student readers; 5)

Almost 30 contributions discuss the meaning of Creole identity and what it means to have a mixed cultural background. Topics such as politics, religion, identity, and transnationalism are addressed. For Caribbean political scientist's comment, see item **1180**.

2420 Cuba in the Special Period: culture and ideology in the 1990s. Edited by Ariana Hernandez-Reguant. New York, N.Y.: Palgrave Macmillan, 2009. 226 p.: bibl., ill., index. (New concepts in Latino American cultures)

Chapters in this important compilation discuss the Special Period and how it transformed Cuban culture. Careful attention is paid to literature, music (rap), film, art, and santería.

2421 Cultura y letras cubanas en el siglo XXI. Recopilación de Araceli Tinajero. Madrid: Iberoamericana; Frankfurt am Main: Vervuert, 2010. 299 p.: bibl., ill.

Brings together a multidisciplinary collection of writing by intellectuals on Cuban culture at the beginning of the 21st century. Topics include politics, culture, society, and contemporary art.

2422 La diversidad cultural: reflexión crítica desde un acercamiento interdisciplinario. Recopilación de Rosalie Rosa Soberal. Hato Rey, P.R.: Publicaciones Puertorriqueñas, 2007. 413 p.: bibl., ill.

A compilation of scholarly articles on Puerto Rican social and cultural diversity constitutes an important interdisciplinary effort. Sections include dimensions of diversity; the institutional context of diversity, genre, and sexuality; and emerging aspects

of diversity. Brings together the work of well-known intellectuals such as Jorge Duany, Virgen Ramos Rodríguez, Angel Israel Rivera Ortiz, and Diana Valle Ferrer, among others.

2423 Duany, Jorge. Blurred borders: transnational migration between the Hispanic Caribbean and the United States. Chapel Hill: Univ. of North Carolina Press, 2011. 284 p.: bibl., index.

Blending extensive ethnographic, archival, and survey research, the author contends that migration challenges the traditional concept of the nation-state as increasing numbers of immigrants and their descendants lead "bifocal" lives, bridging two or more states, markets, languages, and cultures throughout their lives. Even as nations attempt to draw their boundaries more clearly, the ceaseless movement of transnational migrants requires the rethinking of conventional equations between birthplace and residence, identity and citizenship, and borders and boundaries. [C.E. Griffin]

2424 Duany, Jorge. La nación en vaivén: identidad, migración y cultura popular en Puerto Rico. San Juan: Callejón, 2010. 251 p.: index. (Col. en fuga. Ensayos)

This publication brings together a selection of newspaper columns that, according to the author, represent "cultural journalism." An excellent starting point for learning about the intricacies of Puerto Rican society.

2425 Efectos de la migración internacional en las comunidades de origen del suroeste de la República Dominicana. Dirección de Gonzalo Ramírez de Haro. Textos de Dolores Brandis *et al.* Dominican Republic: Instituto Panamericano de Geografía e Historia, Sección Nacional de República Dominicana, 2009. 258 p.: bibl., ill. (some col.), maps.

Studies the effects of remittances on the town of Vicente Noble. Finds that most emigrants had gone to Barcelona. Describes a situation in which one extended family shares the resources sent from Spain when no close family members are directly involved in the migration. Finds that remittances have diminished poverty and severe malnutrition among infants and improved the quality of life and economic diversity in the small Dominican town. However, socioeconomic inequality has risen and the community lacks leadership since many local leaders have emigrated.

2426 Fernández Robaina, Tomás. Cuba, personalidades en el debate racial: conferencias y ensayos. La Habana: Editorial de Ciencias Sociales, 2007. 202 p.: bibl. (Etnología)

The author compiles a collection of documents that are important for understanding efforts to combat racism in Cuban culture.

2427 Fernández Robaina, Tomás. Identidad afrocubana, cultura y nacionalidad. Santiago, Cuba: Editorial Oriente, 2009. 126 p.: bibl.

Examines racism in Cuba during the revolutionary period. Sees the 1959–84 period as one of missed opportunities for racial harmony. Describes the scenario in which Castro condemned racism in public speeches, but at the same time his government disbanded the voluntary Afro-Cuban associations. Identifies intellectual leaders of the black community who spoke out against racism and advocated for resocializing the Cuban people on matters of race and race relations. Also highlights efforts since 1990 to eliminate racism, noting the support of the Biblioteca Nacional José Martí and the Fundación Fernando Ortiz in this endeavor. Mentions continued challenges for eradicating racism, such as ending the exclusion of blacks from the tourism industry.

2428 Fiet, Lowell. Caballeros, vejigantes, locas y viejos: Santiago Apóstol y los performeros afropuertorriqueños. Viejo San Juan, P.R.: Terranova Editores, 2007. 156 p.: bibl., ill. (some col.).

This worthwhile introduction to Puerto Rican culture describes the town of Loíza Aldea and the celebration of Santiago Apóstol. Includes a number of photographs of the celebration. One chapter describes the practice of male cross-dressing, conventional role-playing by women, and the importance of the elderly in ceremonies associated with St. James.

2429 Globalisation, diaspora and Caribbean popular culture. Edited by Christine G.T. Ho and Keith Nurse. Kingston; Miami, Fla.: Ian Randle, 2005. 375 p.: bibl., ill., index.

This volume looks at globalization from a long-term perspective. Rather than strictly discussing the economic impact of globalization, the chapters here look at the intersection of culture, society, and political economy. Popular culture emerges as the site of identity contestation.

2430 Gowricharn, Ruben S. et al. Caribbean transnationalism: migration, pluralization, and social cohesion. Lanham, Md.: Lexington Books, 2006. 253 p.: bibl., index.

Chapters in this volume on Caribbean transnationalism are divided into sections that explore the nature of the Caribbean, regional and global transnationalism, and the social cohesion of old and emerging Caribbean societies. Gowricharn argues that Caribbean societies are the result of different diasporas or communities formed by the forced dispersion of people. He also suggests that the displaced peoples' identities are often linked to their places of origin and that such communities are transnational in that they link the Caribbean to former colonizers and to the US. Contributions were prepared for an international conference on Globalisation, Diaspora, and Identity Formation organized by the University of Suriname in 2004.

2431 Hansing, Katrin. Rasta, race and revolution: the emergence and development of the Rastafari movement in socialist Cuba. Münster, Germany: Lit, 2006. 264 p.: bibl. (Beiträge zur Afrikaforschung; 28)

Documents the discrimination and racism encountered by blacks who join the Rastafari movement in Cuba, a movement that has gone mostly unstudied until now. Includes a chapter on contemporary Cuba in which material and spiritual challenges abound. Describes how race is understood in Cuba and how the government's efforts to deal with the 1990s economic crisis affected black Cubans most severely. Another chapter describes the emergence and development of the Cuban Rastafari movement, noting that the popularity of reggae music facilitated its spread throughout the island—which occurred at the same time that students from the English-speaking Caribbean came to study in Cuba.

2432 Hearn, Adrian H. Cuba: religion, social capital, and development. Durham, N.C.: Duke Univ. Press, 2008. 220 p.: bibl., ill., index, maps.

Excellent contribution to the discussion of religion and development in Cuba. Examines the life options of poor families, many of them black, living in a *solar* (housing complex) with limited resources and services. Analyzes the inability of the state to help these people alongside civil society associations—NGOs and informal groups—trying to provide assistance. Emphasizes grassroots initiatives and state efforts to incorporate the poor into government programs.

2433 Hernández Fox, Leonor Arlen. El divorcio en la sociedad cubana, 1763–1878. La Habana: Editorial de Ciencias Sociales, 2007. 80 p.: bibl. (Pinos nuevos. Ensayo)

Examines the use of ecclesiastical juridical procedures governing divorce in Cuba during 1763–1878. The laws favored husbands, but were used by wives to protect their interests. Includes a description of the family institution in Cuba, a review of canonical and civil law governing marriage and divorce, and an interesting analysis of historical cases.

Johnson, Hume N. and **Joseph L. Soeters.** Jamaican dons, Italian godfathers and the chances of a "reversible destiny." See item **1211**.

Kelly, Jana Morgan; Rosario Espinal; and **Jonathan Hartlyn.** Diferenças de gênero na República Dominicana, 1994–2004: dois passos á frente, um passo para trás? See item **1191**.

2434 Los llamados nuevos movimientos religiosos en el Gran Caribe: reflexiones sobre un problema contemporáneo. Textos de Juana Berges Curbelo *et al.* La Habana: Ediciones CEA, 2006. 256 p.: bibl.

Important contribution on new religious movements that are active in Latin America and the Caribbean.

2435 Lucca Irizarry, Nydia and **Juanita Rodríguez Colón.** Violencia y juventud en Puerto Rico: una perspectiva ecológica y fenomenológica. Hato Rey, P.R.: Publicaciones Puertorriqueñas, 2008. 146 p.: bibl., ill.

Presents the findings of a national study of violence and young people in Puerto Rico, including violence in their homes, schools, and neighborhoods. Concludes with a number of recommendations that would benefit Puerto Rico as well as the Caribbean region and other parts of Latin America.

2436 Méndez, Antonio A. La mujer dominicana: inmigrante en busca de la igualdad. Santo Domingo: Secretaría de Estado de Cultura, Editora Nacional, 2009. 220 p.: bibl., ill. (Col. Ultramar)

Presents a thorough study of female migration in the Dominican Republic. Cites statistics to show that women have struggled against discriminatory practices and prejudices that have prevented them from participating in the political process and in the workforce; that they are much more likely to be victims of domestic violence and be infected with AIDS; and that they are much less likely to receive medical and public health services. Concludes with recommendations to improve the life chances of Dominican women in the US and in the Dominican Republic. This rare, comprehensive study looks at factors that push women to migrate and also reflects on their experiences in their destination countries.

2437 Morgan, Paula and **Valerie Youssef.** Writing rage: unmasking violence through Caribbean discourse. Kingston: Univ. of the West Indies Press, 2006. 268 p.: bibl., index.

Presents a study of violence in Caribbean society using linguistic and discourse analysis. Looks at the presence of violence in literature and mass media and examines how globalization and the worldwide flow of peoples contributes to the presence of violence. Explores the connection between male marginalization and violence and discusses the relationship between violent encounters involving race, nation, ideology, and ethnic differences and male-female acts of violence. Notes the irony in the notion that the family is both the primary locus of violence and the place for human support and caring.

2438 Muriente Pérez, Julio A. Isla Nena: queda mucho por hacer. Río Piedras, Puerto Rico: Publicaciones Gaviota, 2009. 243 p.

Brings together the nationalist writings on Vieques by Muriente Pérez, an essayist and intellectual.

2439 Ochoa, Todd Ramón. Society of the dead: Quita Manaquita and Palo Praise in Cuba. Berkeley: Univ. of California, 2010. 313 p.: bibl., index.

Examines the Quita Manaquita and Palo Praise, secretive religious practices that have a large following inside and outside Cuba. The author attempts to convey his experience of learning the cults' secrets, although their subtleties may defy understanding in the absence of personal experience.

2440 Ortiz García, Angel L. Afropuertorriqueño(a). Río Piedras, P.R.: Editorial Edil, 2006. 281 p.: bibl., ill.

An ambitious project to record the history of blacks in Puerto Rico and to offer suggestions regarding the best way to educate Puerto Ricans about the contributions of people of African descent to contemporary Puerto Rican culture and society. Reviews the origin of European colonization and its nefarious impact on Africa; traces the African origins of black slaves; and describes the African origins, ethnicity, and religions of slaves who were brought to Puerto Rico to work in sugar mills and land estates devoted to sugar. Also discusses the fate of the Taino indigenous peoples who were decimated by European conquest.

2441 Padilla, Mark. Caribbean pleasure industry: tourism, sexuality, and AIDS in the Dominican Republic. Chicago, Ill.: The Univ. of Chicago Press, 2007. 294 p.: bibl., ill., index, map. (Worlds of desire)

In recent years, the economy of the Caribbean has become almost completely dependent on international tourism. One of the main ways that foreign visitors to the region seek pleasure is through the services of prostitutes. While much has been written on the female sex workers who service these tourists, the focus of this work is on male sex workers. Drawing on his groundbreaking ethnographic research in the Dominican Republic, the author discovers a complex world in which the global political and economic impact of tourism has led to shifting cultural and sexual politics. He examines bisexuality and tourism as much-neglected

contributing factors to the HIV/AIDS epidemic. [C.E. Griffin]

2442 Padilla, Mark. The embodiment of tourism among bisexually-behaving Dominican male sex workers. (*Arch. Sex. Behav.*, 37:5, Oct. 2008, p. 783–793)

This article examines how the growth of the tourism industry in the Dominican Republic has produced sexual practices and identities that reflect both the influence of large-scale structural processes and the resistant responses of local individuals. It draws on long-term ethnographic research with bisexually behaving male sex workers in two cities in the Dominican Republic, including participant observation, in-depth interviews, focus groups, and surveys. [C.E. Griffin]

2443 Panorama de la cultura cubana: antología. Recopilación de Sonia Almazán del Olmo y Pedro Torres Moré. La Habana: F. Varela, 2007. 462 p.: bibl.

This anthology attempts to offer a panorama of Cuban culture, including the "official" position (writings by Fidel Castro, Che Guevara, etc.). One chapter by Perez Malo and Legra provides an account of the cultural policy of the regime.

Pedraza, Silvia. Political disaffection in Cuba's revolution and exodus. See *HLAS 66:1339.*

Race, colonialism, and social transformation in Latin America and the Caribbean. See item **2257.**

2444 Raza y racismo. Compilación de Esther Pérez y Marcel Lueiro Reyes. La Habana: Editorial Caminos, 2009. 388 p.: bibl., ill. (Antología de Caminos)

Very important collection of original writings, previously published in the journal *Caminos* between 1998–2008, on the problem of racism in Cuba. Offers suggestions on how to reduce or eliminate it.

2445 Returning to the source: the final stage of the Caribbean migration circuit. Edited by Dwaine Plaza and Frances Henry. Trinidad and Tobago; Jamaica; Barbados: Univ. of the West Indies Press, 2006. 263 p.: bibl.

Collection of papers on the experience of return migration in several Caribbean nations. In the introductory piece, Plaza and Henry argue that the movement of the people is a defining process for the region. They note that travel has been a constant in the history of the Caribbean, throughout colonial, postcolonial, and diaspora eras. They review theories of return migration and transnationalism and present a theory map outlining a model of return migration. They find that return migration has increased since the 1990s.

2446 Richman, Karen E. A more powerful sorcerer: conversion, capital, and Haitian transnational migration. (*NWIG*, 82:1/2, 2008, p. 3–45, bibl.)

The author argues that poor Haitian migrants construe religious conversion as a rhetoric and set of behaviors for mastering the US model of individual, social, and economic success. The rhetoric and behaviors practiced in Haitian Protestant evangelical congregations offer an escape route from the fetters of obligation and interdependence that undergird their transnational domestic and ritual ties. Haitian pastors help fit migrants with the religious armor to resist the spiritual and magical enforcement of those moral obligations by modeling for their flock the assertive, separatist disposition which, according to Weber, was central to the religion's appeal and initial success in Europe four centuries ago. [C.E. Griffin]

2447 Rivero, Yeidy M. Tuning out blackness: race and nation in the history of Puerto Rican television. Durham, N.C.: Duke Univ. Press, 2005. 264 p.: bibl., ill., index. (Console-ing passions)

Examines the racial and ethnic dimensions of television programs in Puerto Rico, focusing on Cubans in the industry.

2448 Rivke, Jaffe. Tourism, sexuality and power in the Spanish Caribbean. (*Rev. Eur. Estud. Latinoam. Caribe*, 88, April 2010, p. 111–116)

A review essay on books by Amalia L. Cabezas, *Economies of Desire: Sex and Tourism in Cuba and the Dominican Republic* (2009); Steven Gregory, *The Devil behind the Mirror: Globalization and Politics in the Dominican Republic* (2007; see *HLAS* 65:2067); and Mark Padilla, *Caribbean Pleasure Industry: Tourism, Sexuality and AIDS in the Dominican Republic* (2007; see item **2441**). [C.E. Griffin]

Routon, Kenneth. Hidden powers of state in the Cuban imagination. See item **1229**.

2449 Simmons, Kimberly Eison. Reconstructing racial identity and the African past in the Dominican Republic. Gainesville: Univ. Press of Florida, 2009. 148 p.: bibl., ill., index, map. (New World diasporas)

This examination of racial identity in the Dominican Republic explores the meaning of African roots for Dominicans both in the Dominican Republic and in the US. Chapters address the change in self-identification that has occurred among Dominican immigrants in the US, from their previous use of the term *indio* (mixed) to current use of mulatto, as a new Dominican identity more accepting of its African origins emerges. Concludes with a discussion of the notion that many Dominicans are embracing their African origins in a collective reaffirmation of self that reverses the rejection of the African past that is so common in their country of birth.

Stout, Noelle M. Feminists, queers and critics: debating the Cuban sex trade. See item **2266**.

Taylor, Erin B. Poverty as danger: fear of crime in Santo Domingo. See item **1194**.

2450 Tejeda Ortiz, Juan Dagoberto. El carnaval dominicano: antecedentes, tendencias y perspectivas. Dominican Republic: Instituto Panamericano de Geografía e Historia, Sección Nacional de Dominicana, 2008. 608, 26 p.: bibl., col. ill.

This excellent compendium of carnivals in the Dominican Republic includes an exhaustive description of the cultural practice on the island. Covers all historical periods from colonization to North American intervention (1916–24), through the Trujillo dictatorship and the post-Trujillo period. Examines the personal stereotypes in the figures represented in the carnival, the characteristics of the groups participating in it, and the masks used in different carnivals. Final chapters look at the role of carnival and its likely development in the future, as well as the relationship between carnival and national identity. An English translation would greatly enhance the reach of this worthwhile contribution to the scholarly literature on carnival.

2451 Trinidad carnival: the cultural politics of a transnational festival. Edited by Garth L. Green and Philip W. Scher. Bloomington: Indiana Univ. Press, 2007. 254 p.: bibl., ill., index.

Nine chapters describe and discuss the cultural politics of a transnational festival by analyzing various aspects of carnival in Trinidad. Topics include the calypso craze of 1957 in the US, steelband music, carnival in Aruba, returning transnationals and carnival in Trinidad and Tobago, the conflict between authenticity and commerce in Trinidad, the global context of Trinidad's carnival, and the impact of the increasing participation of women on Trinidad's carnival.

2452 Ulysse, Gina Athena. Downtown ladies: informal commercial importers, a Haitian anthropologist, and self-making in Jamaica. Chicago, Ill.: Univ. of Chicago Press, 2007. 333 p.: bibl., index, maps. (Women in culture and society)

The Caribbean "market woman" is ingrained in the popular imagination as the archetype of black womanhood in countries throughout the region. Challenging this stereotype and other outdated images of black women, *Downtown Ladies* offers a more complex picture by documenting the history of independent international traders—known as informal commercial importers, or ICIs—who travel abroad to import and export a vast array of consumer goods sold in the public markets of Kings-

ton. Both by-products of and participants in globalization, ICIs operate on multiple levels and, since their emergence in the 1970s, have made significant contributions to the regional, national, and global economies. [C.E. Griffin]

2453 Vélez Camacho, Myrna Iris. Grupos femenistas en Puerto Rico: luchas y logros en busca de la equidad del género, 1971–2006. Hato Rey, P.R.: Publicaciones Puertorriqueños, 2008. 180 p.: bibl.

Provides a history of feminist groups in Puerto Rico. Describes the origin of feminism in the island, highlighting the most important feminist groups in the 1970s. Discusses feminist organizations active throughout the time period and concludes with a valuable bibliography on the topic.

2454 Weinreb, Amelia Rosenberg. Cuba in the shadow of change: daily life in the twilight of the revolution. Gainesville: Univ. Press of Florida, 2009. 254 p.: bibl., ill., index. (Contemporary Cuba)

The political and economic systems of Cuba in the post-Soviet period pose ongoing challenges to ordinary Cubans as they struggle in the waning years of the Castro regime. The author takes readers deep inside the everyday life of middle-class Cubans— arguably the majority of citizens on the island. Untheorized and underdescribed, the book demonstrates that the major reason this group has been ignored in the scholarly literature is because remaining obscure is one of their strategies for coping with these challenges. [C.E. Griffin]

COLOMBIA AND VENEZUELA

WILLIAM L. CANAK, *Professor of Sociology, Middle Tennessee State University*

COLOMBIA

CONTEMPORARY COLOMBIAN SOCIOLOGISTS continue to live in the era of Orlando Fals Borda and his students. That written, the several generations of sociologists whose work finds review in this report have built a strong intellectual culture and institutional infrastructure for research, training, and civic engagement. A cosmopolitan discipline with strong ties to both Europe and North America, its practioners have charted a distinctly Colombian path while contributing to sociology well beyond their border.

Over the past three decades, some themes remain central, most notably the body of empirical studies focusing on various dimensions of organized regional violence and insurgent struggles. Demographic research has developed new insights and relevance to social policy through a focus on displaced populations. Studies of rural and urban political economy define a core theme for Colombian sociologists, but the incorporation of gender, racial, and ethnic dimensions of social movements, political organizations, and economic inequality mark important extensions of research to address Colombia's changing social structure. One must note an increasing interest in religion and ethnicity tied to religion, again recognizing profound changes in the cultural landscape of Colombia as a result of migration and proselytizing.

Research reviewed in this section includes several studies of rapidly changing religious identities, markets, and organizational forms (items **2457**, **2458**, and **2468**). Continuing the growth of interest in racial and ethnic identity, especially consideration of Afro-Colombians, recent publications demonstrate the impact of a set of well-funded and well-led university programs that have focused on Colombia's Pacific region (items **2455**, **2464**, **2475**, and **2477**). These studies examine community resources, social mobilization, conflict, and cultural aspects of Colombia's Afro-Colombians and link these studies to related research on demographic trends, such as displaced peoples and patterns of violence. Recent political economy research uses empirical methods, both field research and analysis of aggregate public data files, to provide a richly detailed profile of Colombia's population, especially the poor but also including the political economy of Colombia's drug economy (items **2459**, **2461**, **2463**, **2465**, and **2475**). Reflecting decades of regional violence, but also public policy and economic restructuring, Colombian demographers have contributed to our understanding of displaced populations (items **2460**, **2472**, and **2479**). Sociological research into the structure, causes, and consequences of violence remains strong (items **2459**, **2469**, **2471**, **2474**, **2476**, **2477**, **2478**, **2479**, **2480**, and **2481**).

VENEZUELA

Venezuela's sociologists traditionally have had strong ties to the intellectual themes and methodological strategies that characterize North American sociology. Under the Chávez government, recent years have seen a drift from mainstream analyses of culture, crime, health, and demography. More critical studies of social psychology, race, poverty, violence, and community have emerged, but so have critical studies of public policy and programs. Thus one may characterize much of current Venezuelan sociology as "social problems" research, as opposed to the social identity, demography, professionalization, and popular culture focus that dominated much of Venezuelan production in past years. Now we find research into cultures of fear (item **2487**) and cultural polarization (items **2486**). Policy analysis and program evaluation research (items **2490**, **2491**, and **2492**) considers the impact of government on community and class structure. Research on topics of class, race, ethnicity, and gender systematically evaluate the impact of economic change and public policy on these core structures of civil society (items **2482**, **2483**, **2485**, and **2492**). The background for much of this work may be expressed in a 2004 conference (item **2489**) devoted to Venezuelan political, military, and popular institutions and their relations. Richly endowed with natural resources, Venezuela's continuing social, economic, and political decline seems to be motivating sociological research to shift focus and concentrate on these crisis points of contemporary social order.

COLOMBIA

2455 Asher, Kiran. Black and green: Afro-Colombians, development, and nature in the Pacific lowlands. Durham, N.C.: Duke Univ. Press, 2009. 247 p.: bibl., ill., index, maps.

A significant contribution to the scholarship addressing race, ethnicity, gender, and social movements in Colombia's western region where Afro-Colombian communities are concentrated. Two decades of research on Afro-Colombian identity, culture, economic status, and political mobilization provide a foundation for this political economic study of environment, gender, racial identity, and social movement organization. A good starting point for anyone seeking to explore these topics in the Colombian context.

2456 Beltrán, Isaac de León and **Eduardo Salcedo Albarán.** El crimen como oficio: ensayos sobre economía del crimen en Colombia. Bogotá: Univ. Externado de Colombia, 2007. 396 p.: bibl., ill.

A quantitative and historical study of homicide in Bogotá during the last quarter of the 20th century, using data from various agencies, including forensic data, to explore the relationship of such societal considerations as spatial patterns, inequality and unemployment, youth gangs, types of weapons, and drug trafficking. A compelling and competent addition to Colombian criminology.

2457 Beltrán Cely, William Mauricio. De microempresas religiosas a multinacionales de la fe: la diversificación del cristianismo en Bogotá. Bogotá: Bonaventurana, 2006. 338 p.: bibl., col. ill. (Serie Religión, sociedad y politica; 1)

Describes the rapidly changing religious reality of Bogotá, as new and old religious organizations and communities vie in the marketplace for members, economic activity, and political influence. Includes consideration of new mega-churches, Mormons, and Protestant congregations.

2458 Beltrán Cely, William Mauricio. Pentecostales y neopentecostales: lógicas de mercado y consumo cultural. Bogotá: Univ. Nacional de Colombia, 2006. 119 p.: bibl. (Cuadernos de Trabajo del GESREC; 4)

An empirical study of Pentecostals in Bogotá, describing the historical context and organizational structure of this Protestant church, including its "informal" grassroots initiatives in neighborhoods, the role of women, and factors related to the rapid growth of Pentecostal congregations. A useful contribution to the growing body of research focused on Protestants in Latin America.

2459 Brittain, James Jeremiah. Revolutionary social change in Colombia: the origin and direction of the FARC-EP. Foreword by James Petras. London; New York, N.Y.: Pluto Press, 2010. 336 p.: bibl., ill., index, maps.

A remarkable and compelling account of insurgent organizations and zones of Colombia by a sociologist whose fieldwork included interviews with FARC supporters, leaders, and rural peoples in order to describe the links among a complex drug economy, government institutions—including the military, and a global political economy that directs earnings from the drug trade to political parties, military officials, politicians, and multinational banks.

2460 Cabrera Suárez, Lizandro Alfonso. Una mirada integral al desplazado en Colombia. Cali, Colombia: Univ. Santiago de Cali Editorial, 2009. 278 p.: bibl., ill.

Recognizing the extensive and profound impact of violence and displaced peoples on Colombian society, this study examines the structural causes of displacement, which has impacted approximately three million Colombians in the past 20 years. Using multiple data sources, the review describes important organizations and political actors influencing displacement, especially those from rural areas, the government's role, and organizational initiatives for dealing with displaced populations, including links to international NGOs.

2461 Cárdenas, Juan Camilo. Dilemas de lo colectivo: instituciones, pobreza y cooperación en el manejo local de los recursos de uso común. Bogotá: Univ. de Los Andes, Facultad de Economía, 2009. 312 p.: bibl., ill., map. (Col. CEDE 50 años)

Compilation of previously published high-quality articles focusing on Colombian community development corporations and local government. Includes chapters describing incentives, limits, regulations, and disincentives to forming cooperative local organizations. Additional studies evaluate organizations that address poverty, public/private experiments, asymmetries, and inequality in use of common resources.

2462 Coloquio Colombiano de Sociología, 9th, Departamento de Ciencias Sociales de la Univ. del Valle, 2005. La sociología en Colombia: balance y perspectivas. Compilación de Pedro Quintín Quílez. Cali, Colombia: Programa Editorial, Univ. del Valle, 2007. 219 p.: ill. (Col. Ciencias sociales)

Provides a useful guide to contemporary Colombian sociology through a series of chapters organized into three thematic sections. The first section reviews Colombian sociology's development over 40 years in three chapters that emphasize the critical political economy methods and theory. A second set of contributions reviews the teaching of sociology as a discipline, with a special focus on Colombia's contributions to urban studies. A third part profiles Colombian sociology's role in the life of the larger society. The role of two universities, Universidad Nacional and Universidad del Valle, gets special attention.

2463 Empleo, pobreza y desigualdad: una mirada desde la investigación universitaria. Compilación de Luis Fernando Ramírez Hernández y Jairo Guillermo Isaza Castro. Bogotá: Centro de Investigaciones de Economía Social, Grupo de Investigaciones de Economía Laboral, Facultad de Economía, Univ. de La Salle, 2007. 251 p.: bibl., ill., col. maps.

Seven chapters provide a quantitative and theoretically informed assessment of poverty and inequality in urban Colombia, including urban wages, internal migration, wage discrimination, labor markets, violence, and comparisons with Latin American health systems. In sum, these studies offer a sound foundation for considering poverty in Colombia's urban contexts.

2464 Escobar, Arturo. Territories of difference: place, movements, life, *redes*. Durham, N.C.: Duke Univ. Press, 2008. 435 p.: bibl., ill., index, maps. (New ecologies for the twenty-first century)

A valuable addition to two decades of research on black communities in Colombia's Pacific region by the author and related scholars. This book realizes a set of methodological strategies and theoretical frameworks derived from that experience, building an analysis that combines political ecology, social movements, political economy, and cultural politics, and identifies social and organizational networks and more. If you want to understand race, place, space, and community in Colombia's Pacific region, start here.

2465 Estudios de género en el DANE. Textos de Claudia Carolina Córdoba Currea *et al.* Bogotá: Pontificia Univ. Javeriana, 2007. 149 p.: bibl., ill.

Using data from Colombia's federal statistics agency to examine labor markets, the authors focus on discrimination and segregation processes that influence and shape women's work and economic resources. These data and analyses define the foundation for anyone seeking a gendered insight into Colombian social mobility, work, and economic resources.

2466 Las familias en Bogotá: realidades y diversidad. Edición de Martha Lucía Gutiérrez Bonilla. Textos de Ana Isabel Aguilar Rugeles *et al.* Bogotá: Pontificia Univ. Javeriana, Facultad de Ciencia Política y Relaciones Internacionales, 2008. 250 p.: bibl., ill.

A series of empirical studies profiling dimensions of family structure and relations in Bogotá. Separate chapters investigate measures of family well-being, characteristics of poverty, violence, survival strategies, and indigenous families. Provides useful data for social programs and urban planning.

2467 Garcés Montoya, Ángela Piedad; Carlos Darío Patiño Gaviria; and Juan José Torres Ramírez. Juventud, investigación y saberes: estado del arte de las investigaciones sobre la realidad juvenil en Medellín 2004–2006. Medellín, Colombia: Univ. de Medellín, 2008. 204: bibl., ill. (some col.), plate.

An excellent integrative overview of multiple research topics profiling adolescents in Medellín. Chapters include reviews of education, health, employment, culture, family, well-being, ethnicity and race, and more.

2468 García, María del Rosario. Identidad y minorías musulmanas en Colombia. Bogotá: Centro de Estudios Políticos e Internacionales, Facultades de Ciencia Política y Gobierno y de Relaciones Internacionales, Editorial Univ. del Rosario, 2007. 118 p.: bibl., ill.

Adds to the body of Colombian ethnic community studies with a brief description of the history, subcommunities, ethnic identity, and political life of Muslims. A refreshing addition to the intensive focus on Protestant communities that dominates scholarship on religious communities.

Gill, Lesley. The limits of solidarity: labor and transnational organizing against Coca-Cola. See item **644.**

2469 Guerra y violencias en Colombia: herramientas e interpretaciones. Edición de Jorge Restrepo y David Aponte Castro. Bogotá: Pontificia Univ. Javeriana-Bogotá, 2009. 604 p.: bibl., ill. (some col.), maps (some col.).

Series of 12 chapters by scholars associated with the Resource Center for Analysis of Conflicts. Four chapters in Pt. 1 review themes of state policy, urban insecurity, information controls, and organized forces, while eight chapters in Pt. 2 focus on distinct regions of Colombia. An important contribution to Colombia's extensive literature on civil violence.

2470 Machado C., Absalón and **Carlos Salgado.** Academia, actores sociales y políticas en el sector rural. Bogotá: Univ. Nacional de Colombia, Facultad de Investigaciones para el Desarollo, Centro de Investigaciones para el Desarrollo, 2006. 201 p.: bibl., ill. (La academia y el sector rural; 6)

Colombia's rich scholarship on the political economy of rural development continues to produce insightful studies. This book offers a multi-thematic review of the relationship between academic scholarship and rural and agrarian development and comprises a final report resulting from a long-term multi-institutional set of studies funded by domestic and international (Canadian) agencies. An important reflection on the definition and redefinition of rural/

agrarian relations and academic studies over recent decades.

2471 Madariaga, Patricia. Matan y matan y uno sigue ahí: control paramilitar y vida cotidiana en un pueblo de Urabá. Bogotá: Univ. de los Andes, Facultad de Ciencias Sociales—CESO, Depto. de Antropología, 2006. 106 p.: bibl. (Col. Prometeo)

Ethnographic case study of a village that for three decades was confronted by a variety of armed groups aiming to control the region. Madariaga presents the adaptations, justice, identity, and survival strategies of the village's inhabitants. She insightfully considers the impact on residents' emotional lives.

2472 Martínez Gómez, Ciro. Las migraciones internas en Colombia: análisis territorial y demográfico según los censos de 1973 y 1993. Bogotá: Univ. Externado de Colombia, 2006. 469 p.: bibl., graphs, maps.

A thorough representation of Colombian migration patterns and the characteristics of migrants. Attracted from traditional and rural areas, migrants concentrate near large cities, particularly close to petro-chemical industries and illicit drug markets. Detailed analysis of gender, age, and economic status provides practical insights to these fundamental societal trends.

2473 Mejía Ochoa, William. Presencia embera en el Área Metropolitana Centro Occidente. Pereira, Colombia: Fundación Cultural Germinando; Holanda: Fundación Bernard Van Leer; Pereira, Risaralda, Colombia: Red de Universidades Públicas del Eje Cafetero ALMA MATER; Colombia: C. Uribe Ediciones, 2007. 255 p.: bibl., ill. (some col.), map.

Following Colombia's 1993 census, increasing attention to the status of indigenous peoples has produced empirical studies of distinct populations in Colombia's various regions. This empirical study focuses on indigenous peoples from one subregion and provides a detailed summary of migration, health, socioeconomic conditions, and cultural images of organizational dimensions of "the Emberas."

2474 Novoa Torres, Edgar Alberto. Luchas cívicas, trayectorias geopolíticas en Colombia: Movimiento Cívico del Oriente

Antioqueño, Movimiento Popular Los Inconformes y Comité de Integración del Macizo Colombiano CIMA. Bogotá: Univ. Nacional de Colombia-Sede Bogotá, Facultad de Derecho, Ciencias Políticas y Sociales, Depto. Ciencia Política, Instituto Unidad de Investigaciones Jurídico-Sociales Gerardo Molina, 2009. 232 p.: bibl., maps.

Antioquia's history as the early engine of Colombian industry and its coffee economy is combined with its concentration of violence, social movements, and popular struggle. This book explores the multifactorial aspects of local resistance strategies, organizations of popular mobilization, and violent struggles for control of resources between politically defined groups and against government control. Civic groups bridge urban and rural environments, but their changing dynamics never led to a coherent national project.

2475 Posso Quiceno, Jeanny Lucero. La inserción laboral de las mujeres inmigrantes negras en el servicio doméstico de la ciudad de Cali. Cali, Colombia: Programa Editorial Univ. del Valle, 2008. 397 p.: bibl., ill., maps. (Col. Libros de investigación)

A multi-method empirical analysis of low-income female domestic workers in Cali. Based on fieldwork completed in the 1990s, Posso follows three paths. The first draws on a survey of women's motives, decisions to emigrate, and the role of employment agencies. A second path contrasts the informal character of domestic labor relations with the norms and regulations governing other forms of labor. A third approach presents intensive case studies of four women's experiences of gender, racial, and class discrimination, thus reinforcing their impoverished status.

Ramírez, María Clemencia. Between the guerrillas and the state: the cocalero movement, citizenship, and identity in the Colombian Amazon. See item **574.**

2476 Riaño Alcalá, Pilar. Dwellers of memory: youth and violence in Medellín, Colombia. New Brunswick, N.J.: Transaction Publishers, 2006. 220 p.: bibl., ill., index, maps. (Memory and narrative series)

Using intensive ethnographic methods and a symbolic interaction perspective, the author reconstructs youth perceptions and idea maps and techniques for constructing a narrative account of their violent experiences, the social and spatial map of an urban environment, and the impact of widespread violence on subjective accounts of identity.

2477 Rodríguez Garavito, César A.; Tatiana Alfonso Sierra; and Isabel Cavelier Adarve. El desplazamiento afro: tierra, violencia y derechos de las comunidades negras en Colombia. Bogotá: Univ. de los Andes, Facultad de Derecho, CIJUS: Ediciones Uniandes, 2009. 271 p.: bibl. (Col. Estudios CIJUS)

A scholarly contribution to Colombia's displaced population research that extends analysis to the Afro-Colombian population and communities. This relatively brief volume applies the insights of displaced population studies, including government policies, racism, and more. Incorporates data from multiple public databases (surveys) from 2001–2007. Includes policy recommendations.

2478 Salazar Cruz, Luz María. Las viudas de la violencia política: trayectorias de vida y estrategias de sobrevivencia en Colombia. Zinacantepec, Mexico: Colegio Mexiquense, 2008. 490 p.: bibl., ill., col. maps.

Adds to the substantial literature on Colombian violence through a focus on the status of women as widows. Describes socioeconomic and demographic contexts and characteristics of these widows, then expands the analysis to detail residential, employment, and survival strategies through personal and collective organizations of Colombian widows. Thorough, scholarly, and deeply moving.

2479 Salazar T., Boris; María del Pilar Castillo; and Federico Pinzón. ¿A dónde ir?: un análisis sobre el desplazamiento forzado. Cali, Colombia: Programa Editorial, Univ. del Valle, 2008. 102 p.: bibl., ill. (Col. Ciencias sociales)

Colombia's rich body of research on two themes—violence and displaced populations—finds new focus on "forced migration" populations, concluding that they have gone to the same locations as other populations fleeing violence, the largest cities, where they renew a population of severely impoverished and marginal residents.

2480 Sánchez, Fabio. Las cuentas de la violencia: ensayos económicos sobre el conflicto y el crimen en Colombia. Textos de Mario Chacón B. *et al.* Bogotá: Grupo Editorial Norma: Univ. de los Andes, Facultad de Economía, 2007. 485 p.: bibl., ill., maps. (Col. Vitral)

A set of eight important contributions to Colombian criminology focusing on themes of violence, but also noting recent significant declines in violence. A good start for those seeking an overview of the origins, history, and dimensions of Colombia's remarkably high levels of violence over many decades, but also the profound changes in policy, culture, economic relations, and organizational relations that are associated with dramatic shifts toward a more peaceful society.

2481 Seminario Internacional "La Violencia en la Sociedad Actual: Contextos, Impactos y Respuestas", *Bogotá, 2008.* La violencia en la sociedad actual: contextos, impactos y respuestas. Compilación de Saúl Agudelo Franco, Decssy Cuspoca y Clara Suárez. Bogotá: Univ. Nacional de Colombia, Sede Bogotá: Programa Interfacultades, Doctorado en Salud Pública, 2009. 438 p.: bibl., ill.

The product of a 2008 symposium on Colombia's history of violence, contributions are grouped into historical analyses, war and terrorism, and the impact of violence on social institutions such as art and social groups. Chapters consider violence as it relates to gender, families, public health, patterns of suicide, and more. While other comprehensive and integrative reviews of *La Violencia* exist, this most current volume is a good place to start.

VENEZUELA

2482 Bermúdez S., Mailyng. Silencio y exclusión: la afrovenezolanidad tras la sombra: una perspectiva desde la enseñanza de la historia. Caracas: Fundación Editorial el Perro y la Rana, 2009. 157 p.: bibl.

Useful introduction to considerations of Venezuela's population of African descent, exploring four themes: the socioeconomic history of Afro-Venezuelans and their manipulation and control by elites; the evolution of a self-identity in Afro-Venezuelan culture; racial discrimination and ethnicity, including residential segregation; and the falsification of Venezuelan history through misrepresentation of Afro-Venezuelans.

2483 Castellanos, Ana Carolina; María Victoria Canino; and Hebe Vessuri. Mujeres pobres en el torbellino del cambio social: un estudio de case de la dinámica privado/público. (*Rev. Venez. Econ. Cienc. Soc.*, 13:1, enero/abril 2007, bibl., tables)

Feminist theory-informed analysis of women's survival strategies using intensive field interviews to determine means that poor women employ to engage a public and social context distinct from their private family world.

2484 España, Luis Pedro. Detrás de la pobreza: diez años después. Caracas: Asociación Civil para la Promoción de Estudios Sociales: Univ. Católica Andrés Bello, 2009. 470 p.: bibl., ill.

Based on a series of surveys during the 1997–2008 period, examines changes in poverty and the impact of social policies, particularly after the 2002–03 protests and mobilizations and the 2004–07 economic boom linked to global petroleum prices. Over 6,000 households, stratified by region and size, rural and urban, modern and traditional, were the focus of these surveys. An essential starting point for understanding the extent, variations, causes, and consequences of contemporary poverty in Venezuela.

2485 García, Jesús. Caribeñidad: afroespiritualidad y afroepistemología. Caracas: Ministerio de la Cultura, Fundación Editorial el Perro y la Rana, 2006. 117 p.: bibl., ill., maps. (Col. Alfredo Maneiro. Política y sociedad. Serie Identidades)

Brief introduction to the Afro-Caribbean culture's history and contemporary dimensions, including religion, music, and spirituality, with reference to recent trends reconnecting Caribbean culture with Sub-Saharan Africa.

2486 Gómez Calcaño, Luis. La disolución de las fronteras: sociedad civil, representación y política en Venezuela. Caracas:

Centro de Estudios del Desarrollo, Univ. Central de Venezuela, 2009. 142 p.: bibl.

Presents a conceptual overview for social transitions and systematically examines 1990s organizations linked to assertions of civil rights and political rights within a system dominated by clientelism. Includes case studies of organizations within an increasingly diverse, but also polarized, Venezuelan society.

2487 Guardia Rolando, Inés Margarita and Adlin de Jesús Prieto Rodríguez. La construcción del miedo en la Revolución Bolivariana, 1998–2007. (*Rev. Venez. Cienc. Polít.*, 32, julio/dic. 2007, p. 75–91, bibl.)

Since Guillermo O'Donnell's seminal work in the 1960s, sociologists have studied how cultures of fear are used to control and marginalize civil society's grassroots democratic institutions. This study of President Chávez's speeches describes the social construction of fear in Venezuela, including analysis of news media.

2488 Inseguridad y violencia en Venezuela: informe 2008. Edición de Roberto Briceño-León, Olga Ávila y Alberto Camardiel. Caracas: Editorial Alfa: LACSO, 2009. 414 p.: bibl., ill. (Col. Hogueras; 48)

Drawing together contributors from multiple leading research institutes and universities in Venezuela and using multiple investigation methods, including a 2008 survey of adults, focus groups in seven cities, and case studies, 30 chapters review many dimensions of Venezuela's increasingly violent society. The chapters include quantitative studies of victims, perpetrators' cultures of fear, and perceptions of the justice system.

2489 Una lectura sociológica de la Venezuela actual V. Caracas: Konrad Adenauer-Stiftung: Univ. Católica Andrés Bello, 2009. 152 p.: bibl., index, table.

Includes three studies presented at the 2004 conference for which this book is named. The fifth edition studies begin with a profile of Venezuelan political institutions; a second study focuses on relations between Venezuela's military and civil society; a third study describes Venezuelan

populist movements and their relationship to political regimes, especially that of the Chávez government.

2490 Ramírez, Luis Alfredo. La participación en el contexto comunitario. Mesa técnica de agua del barrio Brisas del Paraíso en Caracas. (*Espac. Abierto*, 16:4, oct./dic. 2007, p. 669–687, bibl., tables)

Explores the relationship of urban infrastructure resources, in this case water, to urban planning, community organization, participation, and well-being. Concludes that noncontrolled development threatens physical, mental, and collective health for local communities in Caracas.

2491 Rodríguez, Francisco and Daniel Ortega. Freed from illiteracy?: a closer look at Venezuela's *Misión Robinson* literacy campaign. (*Econ. Dev. Cult. Change*, 57:1, Oct. 2008, p. 1–30, graphs, tables)

A program evaluation measuring the cost-benefit outputs and outcomes of Venezuela's well-funded and well-publicized national literacy campaign. Concludes that some minor advances in literacy are linked to the campaign, but that the program's actual size was more modest than claimed and content of the program was misdirected to political support. In addition, the program failed to incorporate established models of cognitive design common to successful programs elsewhere.

2492 Stephany, Keta. Políticas de ajuste y protesta popular en Venezuela: 1989 y 1996. Caracas: Ediciones Facultad de Ciencias Económicas y Sociales, Vicerrectorado Académico, Univ. Central de Venezuela, 2006. 252 p.: bibl.

Reviews 1989–96 economic adjustment policies and their impact on Venezuelan society, including popular mobilizations and protests. Throughout Latin America, the "debt crisis" of the 1980s resulted in IMF, World Bank, and international-banking institution mandated policies that restructured governments and negatively impacted standards of living for middle class and working class populations. This study provides a quick summary of policies, protests, and resulting social restructuring.

ECUADOR

NICHOLAS RATTRAY, *Researcher, School of Anthropology, University of Arizona*

THE SOCIOLOGICAL LITERATURE published during this biennium continues to address important concerns about ethnic politics, development, gender, and migration, placing them in the context of political volatility and economic restructuring. Under the leadership of Rafael Correa, voters approved Ecuador's 20th constitution in 2008. For some analysts, the consolidation of Correa's power and the new constitution signal a new era shifting Ecuador away from neoliberal tendencies and political instability. Ecuador's purposeful default on foreign commercial debts in 2008 was based not on an inability to pay, but on moral grounds. For others, the promise of a citizen's revolution has given way to policies that have undermined the power of popular movements. Tensions between the Correa administration and grassroots organizations active in environmental protection, indigenous politics, and women's rights have deepened. The wide scope of the new constitution has impacted nearly every sector of civil society. As struggles over Ecuador's cultural imaginaries play out through the politics of the "plurinational" and "intercultural society," scholars like Walsh (item **2511**) trace cleavages between competing visions of modernity, such as collective and individualistic approaches to development.

Social scientists have expanded their documentation and analysis of indigenous movements and the politics of race and ethnicity. An innovative book written in collaboration by Andolina, Laurie, and Radcliffe draws from poststructuralist theory to show how "ethnodevelopment" is both enabled and constrained by indigenous politics and transnational networks in Ecuador and Bolivia (item **2493**). Becker (item **2495**) offers a meticulous account of the enduring links between leftist politics and indigenous activism. With its timelines and photographs, his work serves as an invaluable bibliographic resource. Martínez Valle and North seek to reformulate models of social capital by demonstrating how family businesses in Highland communities find new ways to adapt to international economic pressures (item **2503**).

Scholars have deepened our understanding of gender as a social category by drawing upon feminist theory in a number of important contributions. In many of these studies, ethnographic approaches are used to link narratives of identity to broader global processes. Several works examine the construction of gender identities, including Torres' sensitive ethnographic work with imprisoned *"mulas"* (mules) who worked in the transnational drug trade (item **2509**) and Silva's attempt to bring attention to the marginality of Afro-Ecuadorian women in Esmeraldas (item **2508**). Villacres (item **2510**) adroitly situates immigration by Colombian sex workers within cultural representations and local economic demand in Quito.

Research on migration continues to be an active area. Increased attention has been given to new immigrant communities in Ecuador and the long-term impacts of multigenerational transnational migration. Spurred in part by international conferences, new works, such as a collection of papers on citizenship and identity produced by Spanish and Ecuadorian scholars (item **2499**), track social transformations taking place in destination communities as Ecuadorians move into segmented labor markets and face new forms of social exclusion. A book that deserves particular attention is Pribilsky's monograph on the social and economic costs of transnational migration between Highland Ecuador and New York City (item **2505**). This ethnography offers unique insights into the everyday lives of Ecuadorians profoundly affected by global processes. Priblisky examines how the restructuring of family roles and gender identities of migrant households relates to changing dynamics in sending communities. In addition, Pedone considers how the transmission of remittances is structured by household gender dynamics (item **2504**). Shifting migration patterns suggest new areas of inquiry as the Ecuadorian state continues to search for ways to draw investment back into the domestic economy.

Innovative research is also being done on geopolitics, discourses of ethnicity, and youth issues. Lauret (item **2502**) incorporates a sociocultural perspective on borders (*la frontera periférica*) that stresses the interdependence of communities within the Ecuador-Colombia border zone. Based on interviews with urban elites, Roitman's (item **2507**) monograph investigates how ethnic discourse circulating within Ecuador's upper classes sustains the privilege associated with the analytically broad category of mestizaje. Another topic that has piqued the interest of academics and policymakers is the growing importance of issues affecting Ecuadorian *jóvenes* (item **2498**). Students will be especially interested in *The Ecuador Reader* (item **2501**), an anthology that covers key cultural, political, and historical topics from conquest to the 20th century through a broad selection of essays, original texts, and creative works. Compared to recent *HLAS* volumes, research into urbanization has received less attention.

Ecuador's 2008 constitution has suggested to some the advent of a "biocentric" turn whereby environmental rights will become paramount, as has been evidenced by the opposition of indigenous communities to extractive industries. As the consequences of the constitution become more pronounced, academics and practitioners will likely pay greater attention to environmental concerns and conflicts over citizen participation. From a comparative perspective, we can expect to see new investigations of the impacts of Correa's *revolución ciudadana* (citizens' revolution) within the broader context of post-neoliberal politics throughout Latin America.

2493 Andolina, Robert; Nina Laurie; and Sarah A. Radcliffe. Indigenous development in the Andes: culture, power, and transnationalism. Durham, N.C.: Duke Univ. Press, 2009. 345 p.: bibl., index.

This valuable and ambitious contribution to studies of indigenous development in the Andes examines the often contradictory interactions between transnational development organizations and local actors in Ecuador and Bolivia. Through multisited ethnographic methods and an interdisciplinary orientation, the book builds on poststructuralist approaches by theorizing "ethnodevelopment" as a specific form of "social neoliberalism" that incorporates indigenous groups into development. Case studies on topics such as community, water, and education interrogate the role that gender, cultural identity, race, place, and space play in development. Concludes by laying out how discourses of development and culture constrain and enable indigenous politics, and makes recommendations for policy and practice. For geographer's comment, see item **822**.

2494 Arias, Custodio. Ascenso y crisis del movimiento indígena ecuatoriano: 1990–2006. (*Investig. Soc./San Marcos*, 17, dic. 2006, p. 217–234, bibl.)

This article traces the emergence and subsequent fractures within Ecuador's indigenous social movement. As CONAIE (Confederación de Nacionalidades Indígenas

del Ecuador) rose to prominence by linking indigenous politics to class struggle
through agrarian reform and education, its
fragile alliance with the Gutiérrez government collapsed after the implementation
of neoliberal policies. Suggests that the
rapid development of Ecuador's indigenous
movement in the 1990s has shifted to more
deliberate strategies aimed at establishing a
pluricultural state.

2495 Becker, Marc. Indians and leftists
in the making of Ecuador's modern
indigenous movements. Durham, N.C.:
Duke Univ. Press, 2008. 303 p.: bibl., ill.,
index, map.

This engaging study of Latin American indigenous movements rejects prevailing approaches toward indigenous resistance
that focus on the late 20th century and
privilege ethnic consciousness over class
interests. Through methodical historical and ethnographic documentation, the
author argues that Ecuador's indigenous
movements have long-standing ties to leftist
politics dating to the 1940s. The book traces
how divergent forces have shaped the way
that indigenous activists negotiate gender,
class, and ethnicity within the context of
agrarian reform, urban and rural alliances,
and other key historical events. Accessibly
written and includes noteworthy photographs. For political scientist's comment,
see item **1272.**

2496 Camacho Zambrano, Margarita.
Diversidades sexuales y de género:
exclusión social e inserción laboral en
Quito. Quito: Centro de Vida y Crecimiento
Personal, 2009. 187 p.: bibl., ill.

The author documents social exclusion and the consequences of heteronorma-
tivity through qualitative and quantitative
research with people who identify as lesbian, gay, bisexual, transgendered, and inter-
sexual TLBGI people in Quito. Argues that
members of these communities are funneled
into specific urban spaces, face unstable job
markets, and have limited educational opportunities. Concludes that recognition of
rights around gender identity, as well as the
right to work and education, will improve
conditions for members of Quito's TLBGI
community seeking employment in formal
and informal labor markets.

**2497 Celi, Carla; Camilo Molina; and
Gabriela Weber.** Cooperación al desarrollo en la frontera norte: una mirada
desde Sucumbíos 2000–2007. Quito: Centro
de Investigaciones Ciudad: Observatorio de
la Cooperación al Desarrollo en el Ecuador,
2009. 188 p.: bibl., ill. (some col.), maps
(some col.).

Report compiles geographic, health,
economic, and demographic data relevant
to development efforts in the northern
province of Sucumbios. Useful statistics,
colorful maps, and additional resources
accompany the discussion of Colombian
refugees, geopolitical conflict, and environmental consequences of border policies.
This study highlights the impacts of a wide
array of international development projects
in the context of Plan Colombia and ongoing economic restructuring.

2498 Cevallos, Chrystiam. Los jóvenes en
el Ecuador. (*Ecuad. Debate*, 68, agosto
2006, p. 51–76, graphs, tables)
Filling an important gap on the sociology of *jóvenes* (ages 15–29), this article
summarizes key issues facing a demographic group that, since 2010, has become
Ecuador's largest. The author reports on
levels of poverty and single mothers, education, housing, literacy, employment, health,
and income. Concludes by discussing the
ramifications of limited academic research
and suggests that future work should attend
to diverse "social imaginaries" and particularly the inclusion of *jóvenes* in research
and planning.

**2499 Ciudadanía y exclusión: Ecuador y Es-
paña frente al espejo.** Textos de Víctor
Bretón *et al.* Madrid: Catarata, 2007. 303 p.:
bibl., ill. (Col. Investigación y debate; 7)
Based on papers from an international conference in Spain cosponsored
by FLACSO, this edited volume offers a
number of high-quality chapters focused
on citizenship and exclusion in Spain and
Ecuador. The three sections focus on historical constructions of citizenship and
identity, Andean perspectives on social
movements and incorporation in Ecuador,
and the social impacts of Ecuadorians working in Spain. The earlier chapters focus on
historical constructions of modernity, race,
and citizenship in Ecuador, and the latter

chapters reflect on cultural and political transformations in Spain on axes of gender and ethnicity.

2500 Ecuador: la migración internacional en cifras. Quito: FLACSO Ecuador: UNFPA, 2008. 93 p.: bibl., col. ill., col. maps.

Presents a statistical overview of immigration and migration trends. Based on a variety of census and employment surveys, the first section documents rates of poverty, household dynamics, sending and receiving regions, gender, remittances, and occupation. While a majority of Ecuadorian migrants move to Spain, an increasing number are settling in the US and Italy. The study indicates that in 2007, 1.5 million Ecuadorians (10 percent) continue to reside overseas and contribute over three billion dollars, or 7 percent, of GDP.

2501 The Ecuador reader: history, culture, politics. Edited by Carlos de la Torre and Steve Striffler. Durham, N.C.: Duke Univ. Press, 2008. 437 p.: bibl., ill., index, map. (The Latin America readers)

This useful anthology brings together a broad range of essays and original texts designed to introduce readers to key political and cultural issues and intellectual debates in Ecuador from the conquest to the 20th century. The volume is divided into six sections that include the consequences of colonial rule, struggles for sovereignty, popular movements, transnational linkages, tensions between democracy and capitalism, and cultural identity. The wide range of genres (poems, edited essays, interviews, and primary texts) and crossdisciplinary orientation make this compilation valuable for university classrooms or readers seeking information on issues of culture, society, and politics in Ecuador.

2502 Lauret, Sander. La frontera norte ecuatoriana ante la influencia del conflicto colombiano: las sorprendentes dimensiones de la dinámica transfronteriza entre la provincia de Carchi y el departamento de Nariño. Quito: Abya-Yala, 2009. 214 p.: bibl., maps.

Ethnographic inquiry into the local consequences of conflict in Colombia on the northern border of Ecuador. Emphasizing the theoretical importance of sociocultural and economic interdependence across borders, the book explores how communities in Carchi and Nariño are linked through health initiatives, economic transformations, and cultural ties in the context of drug trafficking, armed conflict, and broader geopolitical relations. Stresses the importance of public policies that are sensitive to the persistent fear of violence, the need for economic development, and transborder linkages.

2503 Martínez Valle, Luciano and Liisa North. Vamos dando la vuelta: iniciativas endógenas de desarrollo local en la Sierra ecuatoriana. Quito: FLACSO Ecuador, 2009. 116 p.: bibl., ill. (Atrio)

Presents evidence from a case study of garment producers from the canton of Pelileo (Tungurahua) who have built cultural capital through dynamic, family-based economic strategies. Combines previously published research and new qualitative data in analyzing development strategies that do not focus solely on agriculture. Argues for new models of "social capital" that capture the interplay of family businesses, regional social networks, and global linkages, as well as public policies that support local firms as diverse sectors of sustainable economic development.

2504 Pedone, Claudia. Estrategias migratorias y poder: tu siempre jalas a los tuyos. Quito: Abya-Yala: AECI: Plan Migración, Comunicación y Desarrollo, 2006. 438 p.: bibl., ill., maps.

Examines movement of Ecuadorian families to Spain since mid-1990s through extensive, multisited qualitative and spatial analysis. The author draws linkages between migration as a response to fears of economic insecurity and as a response to political transformations in Europe and Ecuador that affect social imaginaries. Notable for making visible how an increasing proportion of women migrants have altered gender relations and for specifying the restructuring of labor market niches in Spain. Concludes by stressing a diachronic approach that relates the flows of remittances to the livelihood strategies of transnational households.

2505 Pribilsky, Jason. La chulla vida: gender, migration, and the family in Andean Ecuador and New York City.

Syracuse, N.Y.: Syracuse Univ. Press, 2007.
336 p.: bibl., ill., index, maps. (Gender and
globalization)

This richly textured book investigates
the consequences of transnational labor
migration on Ecuadorian families. Based
on multisited ethnographic narratives from
Cañar, Ecuador, and New York City, the
author chronicles cultural transformations
that have accompanied what has become
a rite of passage symbolizing modernity as
male migrants seek work in the US. Careful
analysis offers theoretical insights into how
masculinities are reshaped by the challenges of establishing a life in Queens, NY,
and earning enough to send remittances.
Concludes by stressing the importance of
linking gender identities to the increasing
social and economic costs of the transnational migrant experience.

**2506 Las propias y los ajenos: miradas
críticas sobre los discursos del movimiento de mujeres del Ecuador.** Edición de
Raquel Rodas. Quito: Fondo para la Igualdad de Género, Agencia Canadiense para el
Desarrollo Internacional: Consejo Nacional
de las Mujeres, CONAMU: Ediciones Abya-
Yala, 2007. 248 p.: bibl., ill.

A collection of five essays that trace
the shifting politics of the women's movement in Ecuador. Analyzes discourses of
subjectivity and identity from data collected
from business elites, women's movement
leaders, youth, and progressive members of
the Catholic Church. Includes photographs
depicting social activism from the 1970s to
the present. Framed by a useful introductory
essay, suggests that the women's movement
has lost its critical voice as it has developed
new relationships with state actors.

2507 Roitman, Karem. Race, ethnicity, and
power in Ecuador: the manipulation
of "mestizaje." Boulder, Colo.: FirstForum-
Press, 2009. 317 p.: bibl., index.

This ambitious study uses a mixed-
methods approach to examine the way that
urban elites take advantage of existing narratives about ethnicity in Ecuador. Drawing
on poststructuralist theories of power, the
author compares ethnic discourses among
elites in Guayaquil and Quito to demonstrate how mestizaje retains exclusionary
dimensions that shroud privilege associated

with "white mestizos" and marginalizes
others (such as *montubios* or *cholos*), who
cannot access "ethnic capital." Noteworthy
for methodological reflections on studying
elites (including four ex-presidents) as a native researcher.

2508 Silva, Erika. Feminidad y masculinidad en la cultura afroecuatoriana: el
caso del norte de Esmeraldas. Quito: Abya-
Yala: Agence canadienne de développement
international, 2010. 436 p.: bibl., maps.

This dense book investigates the
construction of ethnic and gender identities
in Esmeraldas through analysis of historical, geographic, and ethnographic material.
Supported by the Fondo para la Igualdad de
Género (FIG), a program of the Canadian
Agency for International Development, addresses the previously undocumented role
played by women within Afro-Ecuadorian
culture by drawing on a wide range of feminist theory. Concluding chapters situate the
empowerment of women within tension
between local kinship structures and complex ethnic formations.

2509 Torres Angarita, Andreina. Drogas,
cárcel y género en Ecuador: la experiencia de mujeres "mulas". Quito: ABYA
YALA: FLACSO Ecuador, 2008. 198 p.: bibl.
(Serie Tesis)

Innovative and timely ethnography
of experiences of women incarcerated for
transporting drugs as mules. Discusses the
historical shift in the incarceration of Ecuadorian women and geopolitical policing, and
how discursive themes of injustice and deception mediate the livelihoods of "mules"
working in the transnational drug trade.
Includes insightful reflections on fieldwork
in prisons. Deftly situates the hidden lives
of women mules—losses, sacrifice, love—
within the logic of global networks and the
construction of gender identities.

2510 Villacres Manzano, Pamela. La industria del sexo en Quito: representaciones sobre las trabajadoras sexuales colom-
bianas. Quito: Abya Yala, Univ. Politécnica
Salesiana: FLACSO Ecuador, 2009. 154 p.:
bibl., ill., index. (Serie Tesis)

This concise book examines the
experiences of Colombian women who have
migrated to Quito as sex workers in increasing numbers since the 1990s. Ethnographic

and archival evidence situates sex work by immigrants within broader transnational economic incentives, state regulation, and cultural representations that exoticize Colombian women within local notions of masculinity and sexuality. Concludes by emphasizing how the agency of sex workers is mediated by structural violence, forced migration, and persistent economic demand.

2511 Walsh, Catherine E. Interculturalidad, estado, sociedad: luchas (de)-coloniales de nuestra época. Quito: Univ. Andina Simón Bolívar, Ecuador: Abya-Yala, 2009. 252 p.: bibl.

Important book that reflects on dynamic shifts in discourses constructed around national identity in Ecuador and Bolivia. Situates "interculturality" as a concept based on dialog and knowledge developed out of indigenous and Afro-Ecuadorian movements in opposition to colonialist legacies of mestizaje and more recent state projects of pluriculturalism and multiculturalism. Concludes by suggesting that the full potential of intercultural politics depends upon an explicit "decolonial" shift based on principles of coexistence and understanding of historically subordinated groups.

PERU

KEITH JAMTGAARD, *Research Assistant Professor, Department of Rural Sociology & Office of Social and Economic Data Analysis, University of Missouri System*

ONE OF THE PRINCIPAL THEMES in the recent sociological literature of Peru is the construction of identity. Additional work was published in the areas of women's studies, issues related to children, social movements, geospatial relationships, and poverty.

Several studies considered various aspects of the ways in which Peruvian identities were constructed. A number of publications looked at identity from a historical perspective. One study examined the lasting influence of the colonial period on the formation of self-image (item **2527**), arguing that the manner in which the conquest and subsequent Spanish occupation of Peru took place has had a lasting impact on the identity of Peruvians today. Another study focused on the early republican period and in particular on the democratizing role of the press in creating a Republican identity (item **2533**). Also using printed works as the source for insight, we see autobiographies from the early 20th century used to understand the development of the individual (item **2513**). Another study looks to the future with this topic, asking the question of how, following the upheavals at the end of the 20th century, Peru can create a more constructive national identity (item **2516**).

A number of studies explore the diversity of identities in Peru. Two studies focus on the creation of Afro-Peruvian culture (items **2525** and **2534**). Others look at the wide diversity of collective identities created in Peru (item **2535**), investigating cases such as that of Palestinian migration to Peru. An analysis of rural development from a feminist perspective explores the topic of heterosexuality as a social construction among rural Andean women (item **2528**).

A number of studies examine important societal issues from the standpoint of women. One study examines the emergence and eventual institutionalization of the feminist movement in Peru. The study describes how the movement negotiated the difficult period between 1980 and 2000 (item **2536**). Also reflecting on the aftermath of the 1980–2000 period, another study ponders the best ways to help women recover from the social conflicts that took place during that period (item **2526**). One compilation (item **2528**) offers a feminist perspective on rural development, emphasizing the importance of multidisciplinary approaches. The 10-year history of a project that helps women access credit through microcredit financing is explored in item **2531**. An underappreciated issue that disproportionately affects the ability of women to fully participate in society is their difficulty in obtaining identity documents, and the difficulties of living as undocumented individuals in their own country (item **2512**). Prison is not experienced equally by men and women. The lives of women in prison and their subsequent struggles to reintegrate into society are explored in two studies (items **2514** and **2530**).

Peru's children are the focus of several studies. One concerns the case of children who are living on the streets, and the efforts of a project that tries to help them (item **2518**). Another describes a larger population that it calls "invisible children" (item **2537**), which includes children with disabilities, children with HIV, the child victims of terrorism, child laborers, as well as children living on the street. Two studies look at issues related to the education of children. One focuses on cognitive and affective development in Andean children, using a multidisciplinary approach (item **2532**). Another brings together contributions emphasizing the importance of understanding cultural processes in education (item **2528**).

A number of social movements emerged in response to state and corporate interventions in recent years. One area in particular is mining and extractive industries and the response of local communities to these through social movements (item **2529**). Another study commissioned by Peru's Congress examines socioenvironmental conflicts related to extractive activities in Peru (item **2520**). This study was particularly concerned with the concerns as perceived by local residents and the impact on residents following the conflicts. A series of recommendations are offered for reducing the scale of such conflicts. One study gauges the success of democratic institutions in responding to the social dissatisfaction widely felt throughout society following the 1980–2000 period, and more specifically their success in dealing with more recent social movements related to mining activities (item **2524**). One study explores whether or not the protests that began in 2003 by coca growers constituted a social movement (item **2523**). The book also contains a history of coca growing in Peru and describes the recent radicalization of the growers.

The impact of globalization on the structuring of geographic space is examined in item **2521**. The book provides an overall theoretical framework, and then explores how it works with a number of case studies from Peru. The ways in which development is taking place in the peri-urban areas of Lima are explored in item **2522**. The study explores three peri-urban areas in the north of Lima.

A number of important studies on crime and migration were published during this period. One recent publication is part of an ongoing series studying crime and its victims (item **2515**). This volume contains the results from a victimization survey which shows some of the perceptions of crime in Peru and offers a comparative context with neighboring countries. Another study looks at an instance of internal migration flow from Puno to Huancayo (item **2519**). The origin of poverty in Peru is the topic of item **2538**, where the causes of recent poverty are distinguished from those of persistent poverty. Following a series of earlier publications, a new study looks at agricultural development and its relationship to malnutrition (item **2517**), and the role of multinational corporations in this dynamic.

2512 Alianza por el derecho a la identidad de todas las peruanas y los peruanos: los obstáculos en el acceso al Sistema de Identificación Nacional. Lima: Estudio para la Defensa de los Derechos de la Mujer: Ministerio Británico para el Desarrollo Internacional, 2004. 80 p.: map.

The difficulties associated with obtaining legal identity documents is a serious problem for many in Peru, particularly for rural women. This edited volume of six articles details the obstacles that many face in trying to obtain their identity documents, and their resulting inability to participate fully in civil society. Five of the articles describe the difficulties in obtaining the Documento Nacional de Identidad (DNI). One article examines the problem from a broader judicial level, another looks at the problem of rural women in general, and three examine the problem in Ayacucho, Huánuco, and Cajamarca, respectively. One article provides a summary of the overarching problems faced by those trying to obtain identity documents in Peru.

2513 Araujo, Kathya. Dignos de su arte: sujeto y lazo social en el Perú de las primeras décadas del siglo XX. Madrid: Iberoamericana; Frankfurt am Main: Vervuert: Santiago: Univ. de Santiago de Chile, 2009. 258 p.: bibl. (Nuevos hispanismos; 4)

The focus of this work is individual identity formation in the early decades of the 20th century in Peru. Through the use of autobiographies as primary evidence, the author explores the development of the individual in Peru. Concepts such as skin color or place of residence that were useful in explaining identity formation in other colonial settings lack explanatory power in Lima. More useful for distinguishing individuals was their capacity to engage in consumption, or certain types of consumption—such as travel to Europe as opposed to the interior of the country.

2514 Avilés, Marco. Día de visita: confesiones de mujeres desde el penal Santa Mónica. Santiago de Surco, Lima, Peru: AGUILAR, 2007. 212 p.: ill.

This book offers a window into the lives of women prisoners in the Santa Mónica prison in Chorillos. Presented here is a series of narratives about the previous lives of these women, their crimes, their lives in the prison, and their plans for the future. The data were collected through an "innovative" strategy: the author presents himself on visitation day to selected women, obtaining introductions through other contacts in the prison. In exchange for small gifts, he is given an opportunity to visit with the women and talk about their lives.

2515 Basombrío Iglesias, Carlos. Delito e inseguridad ciudadana: Lima y otras ciudades del Perú comparadas con América Latina. Lima: Instituto de Defensa Legal, Área de Seguridad Ciudadana, 2007. 79 p.

Little systematic information exists regarding popular perceptions of crime in Peru. This is one of a series of publications that attempts to address the issue of crime, and it does so in a comparative international context. As in previous volumes, this study uses survey results (principally for Lima) conducted by an independent organization. Results from a victimization survey conducted by the Interior Ministry at the end of 2005 are also included. The latter survey had a broader coverage and included Peru's other principal cities. The discussion also extends to a comparison of indicators of victimization and perceptions of crime for Mexico, Venezuela, Colombia, Ecuador, Bolivia, Chile, Argentina, Uruguay, and Brazil. Other topics include analysis of the perception that crime is worsening; an examination of law enforcement institutions, the reasons that citizens mistrust the police, and citizen self-protection; and an exploration of alternative solutions.

2516 Batallas por la memoria: antagonismos de la promesa peruana. Edición de Marita Hamann *et al.* Lima: Pontificia Univ. Católica del Perú: Univ. del Pacífico, Centro de Investigación: Instituto de Estudios Peruanos, 2003. 462 p.: bibl., ill. (some col.).

This edited collection of essays is the result of a seminar on the process of healing and learning from the tumultuous events of the late 20th century in Peru, in particular, figuring out how to manage the countless injustices and unbearable memories from that period. Although desirable, society faces difficulties attempting to use this history to create a more constructive national identity due to the persistence of societal fragmentation that helped to bring about the conflict in the first place. The 19 articles are accompanied by several commentaries.

2517 Caballero Armas, Wilfredo and **Alfonso Flores Mere.** Pobreza, hambre y desnutrición: Perú en el contexto mundial. Lima: Ediciones AGRUM, Univ. Nacional Agraria La Molina, 2008. 231 p.: bibl., ill. (some col.), maps.

The fourth in a series of books related to the role of agriculture in Peru's development, this work provides a history of the food production system as it has developed in Peru, and examines its relationship to poverty and malnutrition during the last 40 years. The analysis involves examining food staples that have become increasingly important in the diets of Peruvians such as rice, barley, maize, wheat, tubers & root crops, meat, fish, milk, and oils. Particular attention is given to Peru's rural poverty and nutrition, and the role of multinational corporations in magnifying the problem. Where possible, the authors locate Peru in a comparative international context. The study uses secondary sources of information to reach its conclusions.

2518 Casquero Mayuntupa, Roberto. La realidad sobre los niños, niñas y adolescentes en situación de calle: Programa Casas Hogares. Miraflores, Peru: CEDRO, 2006. 142 p.: bibl., ill.

This study presents an updated description of the situation of street children in Peru. Particular attention is given to a program known as "Las Casas Hogares" that provides group homes for children, sponsored by CEDRO and the Instituto Generación. The primary tool used to collect information was a focus group. The information that was collected was related to the factors that led to the children leaving their families, their experiences on the street, and experiences with drugs and sex. A total of 33 children participated in the study.

2519 Condori Apaza, Marisol. La migración puneña en Huancayo. Huancayo, Peru: Centro de Capacitación J.M. Arguedia-

nos: Univ. Alas Peruanas, Filial Huancayos, 2008. 156 p.: bibl., ill.

This study describes a case of internal migration from Puno to Huancayo. The author is from a family that was originally from Puno and moved to Huancayo. The study describes the factors that led to emigration from Puno: the scarcity of land, unequal land distribution, and racial and ethnic discrimination against indigenous peoples. Describes the migration process, along with the networks, institutions, traditions, and strategies used by the Puneños to make the journey possible.

2520 Los conflictos socioambientales por actividades extractivas en el Perú. Lima: República del Perú, Defensoría del Pueblo, 2007. 186 p.: bibl., ill. (some col.), map. (Serie Informes extraordinarios; 2)

The Peruvian Defensoría del Pueblo, or "ombudsman," prepared this study of social-environmental conflicts related to extractive activities at the request of the Peruvian Congress. The study examines the causes and consequences of the conflicts, as well as the impacts on the rights of the persons and organizations involved. Concerns about the potential for environmental contamination and the state's inability to prevent such contamination were frequently cited as a causes of conflicts. Another category of concern was related to extractive activities taking place in areas where the residents have been historically excluded and discriminated against, and where fears were great that outsiders were taking advantage of their ancestral resources. The report includes a series of recommendations for reducing the scale of the conflicts.

2521 Dammert, Manuel. Dialéctica del territorio/esquizofrenia del lugar: Perú y Suramérica ante los desafíos de la globalización. Lima: Univ. Nacional Mayor de San Marcos, 2008. 303 p.: ill. (some col.), maps (some col.).

The author describes some of theories regarding geographic space, power, and development. Challenged by globalization and a new global division of labor, South America is undergoing a process of integration. The author presents five case studies that explore the significance of these trends:

the role of South America's "mega-regions" in the new global configuration; one of the challenges facing Peru—the relationship between spatial development and decentralization; Peru's National Development Plan for the country's public ports; the plan for the spatial use of the Machu-Picchu National Sanctuary; and Peru's land-use plan for local economic development, using as a case study the most populous district in the country—San Juan de Lurigancho in metropolitan Lima.

2522 Diagnóstico situacional y ejes de desarrollo de Cajamarquilla, Jicamarca y Nieveria: la "pobreza" como factor de desarrollo en áreas peri-urbanas de Lima Metropolitana. Coordinación de Guido Maggi. Lima: Observatorio Socio Económico Laboral de Lima Norte: Univ. Católica Sedes Sapientiae, 2008. 189 p.: bibl., col. ill., maps. (Col. Investigación y desarrollo)

This publication is a synthesis of two efforts: a descriptive study of a number of the peri-urban areas of Lima, and a development plan for these same areas. The peri-urban areas studied include Cajamarquilla, Jicamarca, and Nieveria. The descriptive study focuses on the current situation of the three areas regarding housing, social capital, family relationships, health, education, and employment. The development plan seeks to support a process of integrated local development that would be participatory, sustainable, and consistent with local values.

2523 Durand Ochoa, Ursula. Coca o muerte: la radicalización del movimiento cocalero. Lima: Centro de Estudios y Promoción del Desarrollo, 2008. 177 p.: bibl. (En blanco y negro)

Addresses the question of whether or not the organized protests by coca growers that began in 2003 in Peru constituted a social movement. Alternative interpretations state that the protests were more closely related to subversive activities and that there were no social demands associated with these groups. The book discusses the history of coca production in Peru following the arrival of the Spanish; the emergence of organizations representing coca growers; the relationships of the coca organizations with the guerrillas and with the state during the 1980–2000 period of violence; the

events that led to the first national confederation of coca growers in 2003; and the subsequent radicalization of the coca growers movement.

2524 Entre el crecimiento económico y la insatisfacción social: las protestas sociales en el Perú actual. Edición de Romeo Grompone y Martín Tanaka. Lima: Instituto de Estudios Peruanos, 2009. 415 p.: bibl., ill. (Serie Ideología y política; 32)

In the aftermath of the upheavals between 1980–2000, and during the current period of rapid economic growth, a question arises as to how democratic institutions in Peru have responded to social dissatisfaction in the most affected regions. This collection of articles examines the response, using as illustrations the municipal workers in Puno, coca growers in the Apurímac and Ene river valleys, dissident factions in the teachers union in Ayacucho, and groups affected by mining activities in Cajamarca. The authors use an analysis of social movements to understand these conflicts.

2525 "Escribir" la identidad: creación cultural y negritud en el Perú. Compilación de Mbaré Ngom. Lima: Univ. Ricardo Palma, Editorial Univ., 2008. 381 p.: bibl., ill.

The creation of Afro-Peruvian culture has not been adequately appreciated by the intellectual community. This collection of studies attempts to address this oversight by contributing perspectives regarding the creation of the culture of Peruvians of African descent and the contribution of Afro-Peruvians to the national identity. The primary focus is on literature, but music, dance, theater, and popular song are also discussed. A few illustrations: the "cumanana" a popular poetic form originally from the North of Peru, and associated with the Afro-Peruvian population; the contributions of Afro-Peruvians to "La Marinera"— a popular dance form; and a number of novels written by Peruvian authors that contain African characters and analyses of the communities and times in which they lived.

2526 Guillerot, Julie. Para no olvidarlas más: mujeres y reparaciones en el Perú. Jesús María, Peru: Asociación Pro Derechos Humanos: Consejería en Proyectos; Miraflores, Peru: Estudio para la

Defensa de los Derechos de la Mujer, 2007. 109 p.: bibl., ill.

In the aftermath of the years of conflict and authoritarianism in Peru from 1980 to 2000, it became clear that the horror experienced by citizens varied according to gender. This book describes the effects of the violence experienced by women, and proposes the development of social programs to address damages to the social structure, women's health, education, human rights, economic reparations, and damage to communities. The programs would undertake actions ranging from public recognition of the harm done to women by both the insurgents and the government forces, to helping those affected restore their mental and physical health, to providing pensions and economic settlements to allow individuals and communities to rebuild.

2527 **León, Ramón; Bernardo Ahlborn Alvarado; and Javier Villanueva.** España y el Perú: cómo valoramos los peruanos la herencia colonial? Lima: Univ. Ricardo Palma, Depto. Académico de Psicología: Editorial Hozlo, 2008. 255 p.: bibl.

Explores the legacy of Spanish culture in Peru following 300 years of colonization, including the impact on Peruvians' perception of their heritage, the impact of the conquest on self image, trade relations, and migratory patterns. Modern Peru traces its origins to a moment of deception and profound injustice: the encounter between Atahualpa and Pizarro at Cajamarca in 1532. Spain's conquest and domination of Peru continues to influence contemporary Peruvian culture. According to the authors, the list of inherited cultural characteristics is long and mostly negative.

2528 **Mannarelli, María Emma et al.** Desarrollo rural y sexualidad: reflexiones comparativas. Lima: Univ. Nacional Mayor de San Marcos; British Council Peru; Newcastle upon Tyne, England: Newcastle Univ., 2008. 153 p.: bibl. (Serie Coediciones)

This collection of articles explores the concept of rural development from a feminist perspective. One chapter examines how a feminist geography would differ from traditional approaches, and sets out an agenda for a more complete understanding of development. Another looks at the impor-

tance of a multidisciplinary approach when studying health and education in rural Peru where cultural processes are especially important. Another article examines rural society, women, and sexuality in the Peruvian context. The book concludes with a discussion of heterosexuality as an example of a social construction.

2529 **Minería, movimientos sociales y respuestas campesinas: una ecología política de transformaciones territoriales.** Edición de Anthony Bebbington. Lima: IEP, Instituto de Estudios Peruanos: CEPES, Centro Peruano de Estudios Sociales, 2007. 349 p.: bibl., ill., maps. (Serie Minería y sociedad; 2)

This edited collection is concerned with the relationships among mining, democracy, and development in the Highlands of Latin America, and in the Andes in particular—with one chapter focusing on Guatemala. The chapters use a conceptual framework based on political ecology to explore these relationships. Mining represents an example of modern capitalistic activity as experienced in Latin America today, but it is not all-powerful. The response of communities and individuals can be decisive in changing the impact of the mining activities. State and global entities also play a role in the interaction between capital and communities.

2530 **La mujer en el sistema penitenciario peruano: estudio sobre las condiciones de vida en el Establecimiento Penitenciario de Mujeres de Chorrillos y el Establecimiento Penitenciario de Régimen Cerrado Especial de Mujeres de Chorrillos.** Coordinación de Borja Mapelli Caffarena. Lima: Junta de Andalucía: IDEMSA, 2006. 338 p.: bibl., ill.

This study takes place in two prisons for women in Chorrillos, Lima: the Chorrillos Women's Penitentiary and the Chorrillos Special Women's High Security Penitentiary. The research team made extensive use of a questionnaire instrument as its data gathering tool. The authors conclude that women endure greater suffering in prison due, among other reasons, to their inability to exercise their roles as mother or spouse and to see their families split up because of their inability to act as the integrating force.

Factors such as these caused the nature of their existence in prison to be different from men. The authors have elaborated a set of recommendations to address the diverse situations of the women in these institutions.

2531 Pait Volstein, Sara. Alcancías comunales, una experiencia de crédito, ahorro y capacitación con mujeres de Lima, EDAPROSPO 1997–2006. Jesús María, Peru: Edaprospo, 2007. 149 p.: bibl., ill. (some col.).

This case study examines a microfinance project in Peru over a 10-year period. The project worked primarily with low income women in the poorer neighborhoods of Lima and the central sierra, helping them to develop a culture of savings by granting them access to credit and helping them develop plans and complete training to attain their goals. The book also provides a history of communal banks over the past 30 years and a summary of lessons learned and best practices. In assessing the impact of the project, the book presents brief reviews of the cases of nine women participants and how their lives were affected by the project.

2532 Reátegui Colareta, Norma. Niños rurales andinos: condiciones de aprendizaje y desarrollo cognitivo-afectivo. Lima: Foro Educativo, 2008. 139 p.: bibl., ill. (some col.).

Empirical analysis of the cognitive and affective development of rural Andean children, using an interdisciplinary approach from three perspectives: cultural anthropology, psychology, and education. Ten rural communities in the departments of Apurímac, Ayacucho, Cuzco, and Huancavelica were included in the study, which examined parents, children, and teachers in each community using a number of different methodologies.

2533 La república de papel: política e imaginación social en la prensa peruana del siglo XIX. Compilación de Marcel Velázquez Castro. Lima: Univ. de Ciencias y Humanidades, Fondo Editorial, 2009. 341 p.: bibl., ill. (Serie Comunicación y sociedad)

This edited collection of 12 articles explores the role of the press in the modernization of 19th-century Peru, and in the creation of a republican culture. The experience was a democratizing one, with magazines and newspapers making their way to all levels of urban society. The drawings and numerous images that were displayed on the printed page during this time were powerful tools for the formation of a community that experienced the world in a similar way. The articles include analyses of specific newspapers and themes, such as the use of satiric poetry to maintain racial barriers. Another article reviews the use of the word "nation" during the late colonial and early republic period as a device for understanding political concepts of the time. One article reviews the perspective of the North American press on the war in South America, between Peru, Chile, and Bolivia during the later 19th century, where notions of manifest destiny were found to apply.

2534 Rodríguez Pastor, Humberto. Negritud: afroperuanos, resistencia y existencia. Lima: Centro de Desarrollo Étnico 2008. 460 p.: bibl., ill. (Serie Mano negra; 1)

A history of persons of African descent in Peru, this work begins with the period of slavery, discussing communities of escaped slaves and slave revolts during the colonial and republican periods. The work also addresses the abolition of slavery in Dec. 1854, and the subsequent demands for indemnization by the former slaveholders, which resulted in compensation to these claiments by the Peruvian government, made possible by revenues generated by guano exports. The book contains a selection of newspaper reports concerning the post-abolition Afro-Peruvian population. One chapter discusses the culinary traditions and contributions of the Afro-Peruvians. The book contains a comparative analysis of Asian and African immigration, and the relationships between the two immigrant populations, for example the increased immigration of peoples from Asia following the abolition of slavery. An Afro-Peruvian tradition in verse, the "Decima" is the topic of another chapter. The experience of Afro-Peruvians in the Andes is also considered. The book also pays tribute to other authors who have contributed to Afro-Peruvian studies and describes efforts to organize Afro-Peruvian populations socially and politically.

2535 Sentido de pertenencia: construcción de las identidades en la sociedad peruana. Edición de Américo Meza Salcedo y

Ricardo Soto Sulca. Huancayo, Peru: Taller de Estudios Sociológicos: Centro de Capacitación J.M. Arguedianos, 2008. 197 p.: bibl.

This is a collection of eight articles related to the development of social identity in Peru. Presents life stories of different groups and individuals, such as Palestinian immigrants in Huancayo. Another chapter describes the Sunday market in Huancayo of the 1950s, the characters that inhabited the market, the products they sold, and the connections they had with the goods they sold and the people who purchased them. Peruvian popular music as a social construction and a means of building a collective identity is also studied.

2536 Vargas, Virginia. Feminismos en América Latina: su aporte a la política y a la democracia. Lima: Univ. Nacional Mayor de San Marcos, Fondo Editorial de la Facultad de Ciencias Sociales: Programa Democracia y Transformación Global: Flora Tristán, Centro de la Mujer Peruana, 2008. 374 p.: bibl. (Col. Transformación global)

This collection of some 20 articles spanning several decades describes the development and growth of the Peruvian feminist movement. The articles document the history of the relationships between feminist groups and insurgent parties on the left during the 1980s, followed by the authoritarianism of the Fujimori decade of the 1990s and their impact on the movement. There is a summary of the impacts of these two decades on the feminist movement, the decreasing militancy and increased trends toward institutionalization of the movement. Then the frame of reference shifts

to the entire region with a summary of the trends in feminist movements across Latin America, and then across the globe.

2537 Vásquez, Enrique. Los niños no visibles para el Estado. Lima: Save the Children: Univ. del Pacífico, Centro de Investigación, 2007. 211 p.: bibl.

Based on a variety of statistical sources, this publication seeks to characterize in a descriptive, factual manner, the situation of marginalized children in Peru: the disabled, HIV-positive, victims of terrorism, child laborers, and street children. Examines the psychological impact of marginalization on children; investigates the relationship between teenage mothers and poverty; and describes the heads of households with at-risk children.

2538 Verdera, Francisco. La pobreza en el Perú: un análisis de sus causas y de las políticas para enfrentarla. Lima: IEP: Fondo Editorial de la Pontificia Universidad Católica del Peru; Buenos Aires: CLACSO, 2007. 304 p.: bibl., ill. (Análisis económico; 24)

An analysis of poverty in Peru that examines permanent and more recent poverty, as well as policies designed to combat poverty. The study includes a review of the literature regarding measurement of the presence of poverty and income distribution inequality. Pays particular attention to the quality of data used. Distinguishes between the causes of rural versus urban poverty. Traces recent poverty to macroeconomic policies intended to stabilize the economy, which disproportionately affect lower-income families.

ARGENTINA, CHILE, AND URUGUAY

MARÍA ESPERANZA CASULLO, *Professor, Universidad Torcuato Di Tella, Argentina*

A REVIEW OF THE MOST RECENT SOCIOLOGICAL production in Argentina, Chile, and Uruguay reveals some interesting trends. On the one hand, sociologists in the Southern Cone are expanding the scope of their research into previously unexplored territories, such as the sociology of daily life, issues of crime and public security, and the study of global phenomena including global migrations or global cities. On the other hand, however, we find a renewed interest in "old" topics. Notable, for instance, is the remarkable amount of work dedicated to the discussion of the political events of the 1960s and 1970s in the region—that is, the wave of leftist political activism that arose at that time and the repressive regimes that ensued. Finally, there is one glaring absence: there is very little debate about the transformations that have taken place during the 1980s and 1990s, as well as the new places in which the countries of the region are bound to occupy in the global order.

We find, then, a new salience in what might be called the "sociology of the private life." This broad body of literature deals with issues such as changes in family structures, youth behavior, the life of the elderly, the life of groups with diverse sexualities, etc. (see items **2541**, **2542**, **2544**, and **2556**, among others). The subfield of gay rights, queer identities, and more broadly, diverse sexuality studies (sometimes articulated with gender studies) has advanced dramatically in recent years, as the struggle for gay rights in the Southern Cone gained momentum (items **2553** and **2554**). (The most notable victory in this fight was the recent passing by the Argentine Congress of a bill legalizing egalitarian marriage; similar bills are being advanced in Brazil and Uruguay.)

The rise of a type of sociological production that focuses on minority lifestyles and other "private" matters is accompanied by a certain loss of interest in the more "classic" sociological topics such as social movements, labor unions, and class relations in general. This literature is by no means absent, but it does not enjoy the preeminence that it once had (item **2560**).

In parallel, it is interesting that this very modern sociological literature seems to be competing for preeminence—at least from a quantitative point of view—with another literature that is almost completely historical in scope. There seems to be an overwhelming interest in the political events of the sixties and seventies. Roughly half of the works surveyed for this piece deal with the history of the political movements of the 60s and 70s, their origins, their models of organization, the life-stories of the people that participated in them, and the way in which they impacted public life. There is also a tremendous interest in the history of the dictatorships that ensued, of the terrible repression that they unleashed over the body politic, and, after democratization, of the almost heroic struggle of human rights organizations to bring the perpetrators to justice in the years that followed (for example, see items **2539**, **2547**, **2550**, **2552**, and **2564**).

The continued interest in the history of the seventies in the region is not accompanied, however, by a parallel interest in the history of the 1980s and 1990s. This finding is puzzling, for the 1980s and 1990s were times of deep and lasting change for the region; arguably the transformations that the region underwent during that time—the debt crisis, the "twin transitions" to democracy and an open market economy, the processes of structural reform and privatizations—are as deep as those caused by the events of the 1970s. However, sociologists are less interested in understanding them and their legacies. There is a lack of works that deal with the changes in labor structures, the role of financial elites in the shaping of public policy, and the transformation in the state capacities that were then put in place.

The economic, political, and social transformations brought about by the crises of the neoliberal regimes that were prevalent in the 1990s and the rise of left-of-center governments in the region are tremendous social shifts that require exploration and explanation. It is crucial to understand these changes given that the region's place in the global arena is changing rapidly, thanks to several years of economic growth and the so-called rise of the BRICs (Brazil, India, and China). It is now more necessary than ever to comprehend the economic, social, and political transformations that are currently taking place, in order to have a better sense of direction on the road to the future.

ARGENTINA

2539 Adamovsky, Ezequiel. Historia de la clase media argentina: apogeo y decadencia de una ilusión, 1919–2003. Buenos Aires: Planeta, 2009. 538 p.: bibl., ill.

This book is a welcome addition to the historiography of a commonly overlooked subject: the Argentine middle class. It describes the ascendancy of a thriving middle class from 1919 to the 1970s, and the way in which the collusion of economic crisis and political repression threatened the very existence of this class from the 1970s to 2003.

Auyero, Javier. Routine politics and violence in Argentina: the gray zone of state power. See item **1424**.

2540 Bergman, Marcelo S. and **Gabriel Kessler.** Vulnerabilidad al delito y sentimiento de inseguridad en Buenos Aires: determinantes y consecuencias. (*Desarro. Econ.*, 48:190/191, julio/dic. 2008, p. 209–234, bibl., graphs, tables)

This paper seeks to describe and explain the relationship between crime, perceived insecurity, and urban space in the city of Buenos Aires, given the changes in the use of public space brought about by the (real and perceived) rise of crime rates.

2541 Blofield, Merike Helena. The politics of moral sin: abortion and divorce in Spain, Chile and Argentina. New York, N.Y.: Routledge, 2006. 245 p.: bibl., ill., index. (Latin American studies)

Blofield's book attempts to answer the question of why the European countries were able to limit the power and influence of Catholic organizations on issues such as abortion and divorce while Latin American countries have been less successful in doing so.

2542 Budassi, Sonia. Mujeres de Dios: cómo viven hoy las monjas y religiosas en la Argentina. Prólogo por María

Moreno. Buenos Aires: Editorial Sudamericana, 2008. 252 p.

A sociological study on an unusual subject: the daily life of Catholic nuns in Argentina.

2543 Burocracias penales, administración institucional de conflictos y ciudadanía: experiencia comparada entre Brasil y Argentina. Organización de Sofia Tiscornia, Roberto Kant de Lima y Lucía Eilbaum. Buenos Aires: EA, 2009. 279 p.: bibl.

This book reviews the relationships between some aspects of the penal justice system and social control, broadly understood. It belongs to the relatively recent subfield of anthropology of the law.

2544 Cabello, Roxana. Las redes del juego. Los Polvorines, Argentina: Univ. Nacional de General Sarmiento; Buenos Aires: Prometeo Libros, 2008. 181 p.: bibl. (Col. Comunicación y crítica cultural)

An original account of an uncharted social world: the *locutorios* (internet cafés) in which teenage boys play first-person, Internet-based video games for hours on end, and the socialization networks that are created in them.

2545 Caldo, Paula. Mujeres cocineras: hacia una historia sociocultural de la cocina argentina a fines del siglo XIX y primera mitad del XX. Rosario, Argentina: Prohistoria, 2009. 180 p.: bibl. (Col. Historia & cultura; 1)

A sociocultural history of the female world centered around cooking, focused on the turn of the last century.

Capacidades estatales, instituciones y política social. See item **1430**.

2546 Construcción estatal, orden oligárquico y respuestas sociales: Argentina y Chile, 1840–1930. Edición de Ernesto Lázaro Bohoslavsky y Milton Godoy Orellana. Textos de Rodrigo Araya Gómez *et al.* Buenos Aires: Prometeo Libros; Santiago:

Univ. Academia de Humanismo Cristiano; Los Polvorines, Argentina: Univ. Nacional de General Sarmiento, 2010. 335 p.: bibl. (Col. Humanidades)

Bohoslavsky and Godoy Orellana have compiled a selection of works by Argentine and Chilean authors who seek to shed light on the ways in which subaltern groups and classes were able to influence the state-building processes of the late 19th century in those two countries.

2547 Crenzel, Emilio. Las resignificaciones del *Nunca Más*: releyendo la violencia política en Argentina. (*Secuencia/México*, 73, enero/abril 2009, p. 107–138, bibl.)

This article follows the changes in the ways in which Argentine society has used and interpreted the *Nunca Más*, the report issued by the special commission that President Raul Alfonsín appointed to gather testimonies about the acts of state terrorism committed by members of the last dictatorship.

2548 Cultures of legality: judicialization and political activism in Latin America. Edited by Javier Couso, Alexandra Huneeus, and Rachel Sieder. Cambridge, England; New York, N.Y.: Cambridge Univ. Press, 2010. 287 p.: bibl., ill., index. (Cambridge studies in law and society)

This book provides groundbreaking comparative evidence on the ever-growing role that courts play in Latin American democracies, and the way in which civil society activists use them.

2549 Enforcing the rule of law: social accountability in the new Latin American democracies. Edited by Enrique Peruzzotti and Catalina Smulovitz. Pittsburgh, Pa.: Univ. of Pittsburgh Press, 2006. 362 p.: bibl., ill., index. (Pitt Latin American series)

This books presents interesting evidence on the way in which civil society organizations and public activists make use of the media to fight corruption and hold public officials accountable. For political scientist's comment, see *HLAS 63:1857*.

2550 Etchemendy, Sebastián. Tras las huellas del "clasismo": el sindicalismo revolucionario en Argentina. (*Lucha Armada Argent.*, 2010, p. 4–17)

This article seeks to shed light on a poorly researched topic: the action of revolutionary, or "classist," labor unions in the Argentine 70s, as opposed to the mainstream Peronist unions. See also item **2100**.

2551 Galindo, María and **Sonia Sánchez.** Ninguna mujer nace para puta. Buenos Aires: Lavaca Editora, 2007. 220 p.: ill. (some col.).

A feminist view of the world of prostitution, from the point of view of the women involved, told in their own words.

2552 Gandsman, Ari. "Do you know who you are?": radical existential doubt and scientific certainty in the search for the kidnapped children of the disappeared in Argentina. (*Ethos/Arlington*, 37:4, Dec. 2009, p. 441–465, bibl., photos)

The Argentine dictatorship known as "Proceso de Reorganización Nacional" committed, among a host of crimes, an especially hideous one by stealing the children of "desaparecidas" (they waited until pregnant imprisoned women gave birth, kept the babies, and then killed the mothers) and raising them as their own. The Abuelas de Plaza de Mayo (Grandmothers of Plaza de Mayo) continue to search for almost 400 *nietos* (grandchildren) who they believe are still alive. This book provides an account of their struggle.

2553 Género y trabajo: asimetrías intergéneros e intragéneros: áreas metropolitanas de la Argentina, 1992–2002. Compilación de Amalia Eguía, Juan Ignacio Piovani y Agustín Salvia. Buenos Aires: Editorial de la Univ. Nacional de Tres de Febrero, 2007. 256 p.: bibl., ill.

This book analyzes the intersection of labor and gender, in its inter- and intra-gender dimensions.

2554 La gesta del nombre propio: informe sobre la situación de la comunidad travesti en la Argentina. Coordinación de Lohana Berkins y Josefina Fernández. Buenos Aires: Madres de Plaza de Mayo, 2005. 142 p.: bibl., ill.

This study, co-edited by Lohana Berkins, a transgendered activist, presents an evaluation of the situation of one of the most discriminated minorities in Argentina.

Herrera, María Rosa. La contienda política en Argentina 1997–2002: un ciclo de protesta. See item **1448**.

2555 Infeld, Ana. Pobres y prostitutas: políticas sociales, control social y ciudadanía en Comodoro Rivadavia, 1929–1944. Rosario, Argentina: Prohistoria Ediciones, 2009. 125 p.: bibl., ill. (Col. Crónicas urbanas, 8)

This book delves into the relationships among poverty, social control, and prostitution in a city in Southern Patagonia, a region in which, due to its unique demographic characteristics, prostitution has historically been a salient public issue.

2556 Informe sobre género y derechos humanos: vigencia y respeto de los derechos de las mujeres en Argentina. Buenos Aires: Equipo Latinoamericano de Justicia y Género: Editorial Biblos, 2005–2009. 2 v.: bibl., ill.

This work provides one of the most thorough assessments of the situation of gender and human rights in Argentina. It contains a revision of legal norms and public policies that impact gender equality, a diagnosis of the areas in which action is necessary, and a treasure trove of up-to-date data.

2557 Martínez, Paola. Género, política y revolución en los años setenta: las mujeres del PRT-ERP. Buenos Aires: Imago Mundi, 2009. 181 p.: bibl. (Col. Bitácora argentina) (Serie Historia)

A fascinating entry into the gender structures of the armed guerrilla Partido Revolucionario de los Trabajadores and Ejército Revolucionario del Pueblo ("PRT-ERP") in the 1970s.

2558 Maternidades en el siglo XXI. Organización de Mónica Tarducci. Buenos Aires: Espacio Editorial, 2008. 191 p.: bibl. (Col. Desarrollo social y sociedad)

This book reviews the way in which the meaning of the concept of motherhood is evolving due to the current social, cultural, and technological changes, such as single parenting, adoption, and in vitro fertilization.

2559 La migración boliviana en el Partido de Villarino, Prov. de Buenos Aires: transformaciones socioculturales. Coordinación de Alicia Pérez y María Elena Gino-

bili. Bahía Blanca, Argentina: Editorial de la Univ. Nacional del Sur, 2008. 159 p.: bibl., ill., maps.

Bolivian immigrants have always chosen to live in Argentina, but in the last two decades this immigration is both larger in numbers and more extended geographically. Bolivian families are moving into areas in which they were largely absent before (such as Northern Patagonia, where Villarino is located) and changing their social landscape. This study reconstructs the social and cultural implications of this phenomenon from the point of view of the immigrants.

2560 Minería transnacional, narrativas del desarrollo y resistencias sociales. Edición de Maristella Svampa y Mirta Antonelli. Textos de Mirta Antonelli *et al.* Buenos Aires: Editorial Biblos, 2009. 319 p.: bibl., map. (Sociedad)

Svampa and Antonelli give an account of the ways in which spontaneous social movements are fighting against the expansion of industrial mining practices, such as mountain-top mining, in Argentina.

2561 Occhipinti, Laurie A. Acting on faith: religious development organizations in Northwestern Argentina. Lanham, Md.: Lexington Books, 2005. 211 p.: bibl., index.

This book seeks to map out the impact of small, Catholic NGOs on the development of poor indigenous communities in Northern Argentina.

2562 Políticas sobre la discapacidad en la Argentina: el desafío de hacer realidad derechos. Compilación de Carlos H. Acuña y Luis G. Bulit Goñi. Buenos Aires: Siglo Veintiuno Editores: Univ. de San Andrés: Asociación Síndrome de Down de la República Argentina, 2010. 382 p.: bibl., ill.

This book thoroughly assesses the strengths and weaknesses of the policies of the Argentine state that have been designed to advance the inclusion of people with disabilities. It includes an analysis of the legal and constitutional framework and a discussion of the performance of the relevant offices within the national state.

2563 Los programas sociales en Argentina hacia el bicentenario: visiones y perspectivas. Textos de Guillermo Cruces *et al.* Edición de Eduardo Amadeo *et al.* Buenos Aires: Banco Mundial, 2008. 349 p.: bibl., ill.

This collective study commissioned by the World Bank offers an assessment of the performance of national social programs in Argentina, a survey that presents data from the program's beneficiaries and policy recommendations for future welfare investments. It is notable in that it advocates for universal social policies, reversing a 20-year commitment to targeted social expenditures on the part of the World Bank.

2564 Rein, Raanan and **Efraim Davidi.**
Deporte, política y exilio: protestas en Israel durante la Copa Mundial de Fútbol, Argentina, 1978. (*Estud. Soc./Santa Fe,* 18:35, segundo semestre 2008, p. 169–198)

During the Soccer World Cup of 1978, Argentine exiles organized protests against the dictatorship in countries such as France and Italy. This article chronicles the protests that took place in Israel.

2565 Las relaciones de género en la prostitución: construcción social de nuevas subjetividades. Textos de Nora Das Biaggio *et al.* Concepción del Uruguay, Argentina: Univ. Nacional de Entre Ríos, 2008. 148 p.: bibl. (Seria Académica)

Another work that seeks to give voice to women who are in a state of prostitution, and to reconstruct the power strategies that they employ to fight patriarchal oppression.

2566 Rivero, Cynthia. Entre la "comunidad del acero" y la "comunidad de María": un análisis antropológico sobre los avatares sociopolíticos de San Nicolás. Buenos Aires: Editorial Antropofagia, 2008. 140 p.: bibl. (Serie Antropología política y económica)

The city of San Nicolás grew as a typical industrial city, its whole life organized around the steel mill that was its heart. The steel mill was privatized during the 90s, yet the struggling city encountered an unexpected boom, when a group of women claimed to have been visited by the Virgin Mary in the city's cathedral. Today, the yearly celebrations of the sighting are an important source of income for the town. The book gives an ethnological account of the "two cities": the "city of steel" and the "city of the Virgin."

2567 Saintout, Florencia. Jóvenes, el futuro llegó hace rato: percepciones de un tiempo de cambios: familia, escuela, trabajo y política. Buenos Aires: Prometeo Libros, 2009. 211 p.: bibl.

This book depicts the strategies that Argentine youth used to cope with the lack of opportunities and shifting social ground of the decade of the 90s.

2568 Sarlo, Beatriz. La ciudad vista: mercancías y cultura urbana. Buenos Aires: Siglo Veintiuno Editores, 2009. 231 p.: bibl., ill. (Sociología y política)

Beatriz Sarlo, one of Argentina's most well-known cultural essayists, has taken hundreds of photos of the city of Buenos Aires through the years. Now, she has compiled the photos and uses them as a device with which to open a dialogue about the urban transformations, consumption, and cultural life.

2569 Seguridad ciudadana en las Américas: proyecto de investigación activa. Textos de Carlos Basombrío Iglesias *et al.* Compilado por Jessica Varat. Washington, D.C.: Woodrow Wilson International Center for Scholars, 2007. 190 p.: bibl., ill. (Woodrow Wilson Center reports on the Americas; 18)

This study seeks to answer two simple yet powerful questions: whether civic participation can help improve public safety policies throughout Latin America, and whether such participation has a positive effect on broad societal perceptions of insecurity and crime.

2570 Smulovitz, Catalina. La política por otros medios: judicialización y movilización legal en Argentina. (*Desarro. Econ.,* 48:190/191, julio/dic. 2008, p. 287–305, tables)

In this article, Smulovitz offers some insight about the way in which Argentine civil society activists make use of the court system to advance rights-based claims.

Toward a society under law: citizens and their police in Latin America. See item **2268.**

CHILE

2571 El arte de clasificar a los chilenos: enfoques sobre los modelos de estratificación en Chile. Coordinación de Alfredo

Joignant y Pedro Güell. Santiago: Ediciones Univ. Diego Portales, 2009. 153 p.: bibl., ill. (Serie Políticas públicas)

This is a review and discussion of the transformation of the ways in which demographic and socioeconomic changes are measured in Chile.

2572 Domedel, Andrea and **Macarena Peña y Lillo.** El mayo de los pingüinos. Santiago: Ediciones Radio Univ. de Chile: Univ. de Chile, Instituto de la Comunicación e Imagen, Escuela de Periodismo, 2008. 217 p.: bibl.

This book is a journalistic chronicle of the first rebellion of high school students against the educational policies of the national state. This rebellion, which rages on at the time of the publication of this piece, has become Chile's foremost current political issue.

2573 Grasmück, Oliver. Eine Marienerscheinung in Zeiten der Diktatur: der Konflikt um Penablanca, Chile; Religion und Manipulation unter Pinochet. Berlin: De Gruyter, 2009. 709 p.: bibl., ill. (Religionsgeschichtliche Versuche und Vorarbeiten; 56)

Study about a supposed apparition, not recognized by the Catholic Church, of Saint Mary in Peñablanca (near Valparaíso) in the years 1983–88. Rumors existed about a (never-proven) manipulation by the Chilean dictator Augusto Pinochet. Even if the focus is the social context of this religious episode, the study gives as introduction a general overview about popular religious folklore in Chile. [F. Obermeier]

2574 Joignant Rondón, Alfredo. Un día distinto: memorias festivas y batallas conmemorativas en torno al 11 de septiembre en Chile, 1974–2006. Santiago: Editorial Universidad: Depto. de Ciencia Política, Univ. de Chile, 2007. 173 p.: bibl., ill. (some col.). (Los sentidos de la política)

The author describes the ways in which the celebration of "11 de septiembre" (September 11), that is, the day of Augusto Pinochet's coup against President Allende, has changed from 1974 to today, from the celebratory parades of Pinochet's dictatorship to the emergence of a counterculture of resistance and protest.

2575 León León, Marco Antonio. La cultura de la muerte en Chiloé. 2. ed. Providencia, Chile: RIL, 2007. 236 p.: bibl., ill., map. (Ensayos & estudios)

León León gives a description of the fascinating and unique culture of the Isla Grande de Chiloé (Big Island of Chiloé) and the role that rituals of death play in it.

2576 Libertad sindical y derechos humanos: análisis de los informes del Comité de Libertad Sindical de la O.I.T., 1973–1990. Edición de Elizabeth Lira y Hugo Rojas. Santiago: LOM: Univ. Alberto Hurtado: Centro de Investigaciones Diego Barros Arana, Dirección Bibliotecas, Archivos y Museos, 2009. 235 p.: bibl., 1 CD-ROM (4 3/4 in.). (Ciencias humanas. Derechos humanos)

This book gives a historical account of the evolution of labor rights and labor activism in Chile from the onset of Pinochet's dictatorship to 1990. Labor was one of the primary targets of Pinochet's repression.

Lost in the long transition: struggles for social justice in neoliberal Chile. See item **1398.**

Mooney, Jadwiga E. Pieper. The politics of motherhood: maternity and women's rights in twentieth-century Chile. See *HLAS 66:1388.*

2577 Robles, Víctor Hugo. Bandera hueca: historia del movimiento homosexual de Chile. Santiago: Editorial Arcis: Cuarto propio, 2008. 215 p.: bibl. (Memorias sociales)

Robles, an active Chilean gay rights organizer, compiles a history of the gay movement in Chile, whose identity has been ignored and made invisible by mainstream 20th-century social thinking.

2578 Varas, Augusto; Claudio Fuentes; and **Felipe Agüero.** Instituciones cautivas: opinión pública y nueva legitimidad social de las fuerzas armadas. Santiago: FLACSO-CHILE, Catalonia, 2008. 199 p.: bibl., ill.

This book compares the results of two public opinion surveys that sought to gauge social perceptions about the Chilean armed forces; the first was done in 1990 and the second one after the death of Augusto Pinochet in 2006.

URUGUAY

Aborto en debate: dilemas y desafíos del Uruguay democrático: proceso político y social, 2001–2004. See item **1486**.

2579 Demografía de una sociedad en transición: la población uruguaya a inicios del siglo XXI. Coordinación de Carmen Varela Petito. Montevideo: Programa de Población, Facultad de Ciencias Sociales, Univ. de la República: UNFPA: Ediciones Trilce, 2008. 173 p.: bibl., ill., maps.

Presents a demographic description of Uruguay's current population structures.

2580 Derechos humanos en Uruguay: informe. Compilación de Servicio Paz y Justicia. Montevideo: El Servicio, 2005. 1 v.: ill.

An updated report on the human rights situation in Uruguay by the prestigious civil society organization, Servicio de Paz y Justicia.

2581 Falero, Alfredo. Las batallas por la subjetividad: luchas sociales y construcción de derechos en Uruguay: una aproximación desde la teoría sociológica. Montevideo: CSIC, Univ. de la República: FANELCOR Editorial, 2008. 268 p.: bibl.

This book analyzes the ways in which social movements have influenced the political process and the definition of new rights in Uruguay.

2582 Migración uruguaya: un enfoque antropológico. Compilación de Beatriz Diconca y Gabriela Campodónico. Montevideo: Facultad de Humandidades y Ciencias de la Educación, Univ. de la República: Organización Internacional para las Migraciones, OIM, 2007. 189 p.: bibl.

Uruguay has been a country with high out-bound migration rates throughout history; it is thought that today approximately 16 percent of the country's population lives abroad. This book seeks to understand the patterns and causes of Uruguayan migration to Spain.

2583 Multiculturalismo en Uruguay: ensayo y entrevistas a once comunidades culturales. Edición de Felipe Arocena y Sebastián Aguiar. Montevideo: Ediciones Trilce, 2007. 230 p.: bibl., ill.

This book presents interviews with representatives from 11 cultural communities that form Uruguay's multicultural society: descendants from Native American nations, people of European origins, migrants from Latin America, and so on.

Rodríguez, Romero Jorge. Mbundo malungo a mundele: historia del movimiento afrouruguayo y sus alternativas de desarrollo. See item **1499**.

BRAZIL

DANIEL HILLIARD, *Executive Director, Zoo Conservation Outreach Group @ Audubon Nature Institute*
MEREDITH DUDLEY, *Adjunct Assistant Professor, Tulane University*
XELA KORDA, *Doctoral Candidate, Tulane University*

DESPITE ACHIEVING SIGNIFICANT SOCIAL, economic, and political gains during the first decade of the 21st century, Brazil continues to face ongoing challenges, including racism, sexism, extreme economic inequality, poverty, rapid urbanization, and the degradation of rural environments, among others. Sociologists and social scientists continue to explore the historical roots of these problems while documenting situated realities and larger social trends. Likewise, as continued economic growth and a deepening of representative democracy help transform Brazilian society, some studies have begun to more thoroughly reevaluate many of the myths that once served as foundations of Brazil's national identity. Brazil's rich cultural heritage continues to provide opportunities for more nuanced interpretations of overlapping dimensions of identity, including ethnicity, race, gender, sexuality, religion, and class. These varied research interests are reflected in the large number of recent social science publications on Brazil, many of which document the significant contributions of Afro-Brazilian culture to the country's national identity. As such, Brazilian sociology and social sciences play an important role in emergent scholarship on processes of identity formation, social transformation, and local-global articulations of change.

The sociology of Brazil also continues to be enriched by contributions from both Brazilian and non-Brazilian scholars and a robust selection of Brazilian publications in Portuguese. Even so, there remains a schism between English-language publications and researchers and many of their Brazilian counterparts. To address the growing dialogue among Brazilian scholars, a number of important Brazilian publications have been republished in English and other European languages over the past few years (items **2584**, **2592**, and **2608**). The studies reviewed here represent only a small sample of a much larger body of sociological research published over the past five years.

Processes of racial and ethnic identity formation continue to provide fertile ground for social science research in Brazil, even as social scientists continue to deconstruct essentialist notions of race. Recent regulatory debates over quotas and affirmative action in Brazil have brought academic and activist discussions of race into popular discourse, as has the 2003 Law 10.639, which requires the inclusion of Afro-Brazilian history and culture in school curriculums (items **2585** and **2614**). The salience of race is reflected in several themes within Brazilian sociology, including the persistence of racism, inequality, and segregation; the relationship between race and Brazilian national identity; racial identity formation and cultural performance; and race-based social movements.

Recent sociological research on race relations in Brazil continues to challenge the conventionally held "myth of racial democracy" by documenting both the historical roots of discrimination and the ongoing exclusion experienced by nonwhite Brazilians (items **2584**, **2587**, **2595**, **2596**, **2609**, **2612**, **2616**, and **2621**). For instance, Santos (item **2616**) provides a historical account of race relations and racial inequality in Brazil from the 19th century until the present and utilizes social, economic, and political analysis to deconstruct the myth of racial harmony. Santos demonstrates the ways in which racial inequality is structurally perpetuated in Brazilian society at the same time as the concept of miscegenation, which is central to Brazilian national identity, works to hide racial prejudice. Fernandes (item **2606**), in an updated version of his 1972 publication *O Negro no mundo dos brancos*, explores race relations in the city of São Paulo and arrives at a similar conclusion. According to Fernandes, Brazilian national identity reflects a "white ethic" that sought to position blacks and mulattos at the margin of the new social order established during the consolidation of the country's industrial complex.

In another updated classic, Costa (item **2595**) presents testimonials from black Brazilians from different economic, social, and cultural backgrounds to examine issues of racism in Brazil. Unlike the 1982 edition, which documented disillusionment with social and economic exclusion, the discourse of individuals interviewed in Costa's 2009 edition demonstrates increasing confidence among Brazilians of African descent. Brazilian sociologists have also utilized secondary data sources to document larger trends in race relations. For instance, Garcia (item **2598**) analyzes IBGE and AED census data to document demographic change, racial inequalities, and urban segregation in Salvador and Rio de Janeiro. Other scholars have examined expressions of race in popular culture, including literature, music, cinema, and carnival traditions in order to highlight the tension between Brazil's official position of racial democracy and the reality of marginalization experienced by many Afro-Brazilians (items **2584, 2609, 2612,** and **2621**). In a synthesis of his research, Afolabi (item **2584**) explores the tension between racial rhetoric and praxis among a wide range of genres, including music, literature, film, and dance, and brings diverse voices into his analysis. Afolabi argues that Afro-Brazilian cultural productions address conflicting issues of identity and racism through a variety of "veils" that ridicule, provoke, protest, or create demand for change.

The scholarly debate about Brazil's "myth of racial democracy" is directly addressed by Bailey (item **2587**) in his book *Legacies of Race: Identities, Attitudes, and Politics in Brazil,* which provides an empirically grounded examination of Brazilian public opinion in order to analyze racial identities, attitudes, and politics. Bailey reviews the development of Freyre's myth and subsequent challenges by both social scientists and leaders of the black movement, and questions the "thesis of Brazilian ignorance" implied by these newer characterizations of the myth. By drawing on representative data sets and public opinion research, Bailey's book departs from other studies about racial attitudes which have been more local or ethnographic in origin. Finally, both Bailey and Risério (item **2612**) discuss how conceptualizations of race and racism in the US and Brazil emerged from different historical contexts, although Bailey points out that these two framings of race are beginning to converge and discusses possible meanings for race-targeted policy initiatives in both countries.

Afro-Brazilian identities have attracted growing interest among scholars of race and racial identity formation, reflecting a broader interest in Latin Americans of African descent (item **2625**). In his 2006 review article of Afro-Latin studies (item **2625**), Wade highlights the significant contribution of Afro-Brazilian scholarship and places Brazilian research within larger trends in the field. Wade summarizes three broad topics that continue to frame research: comparative studies of slavery and race relations in the Americas; issues of racism, with a strong comparative focus on racial classification in Brazil and the US; and the role of Africa in the construction of black identities. As predicted by Wade, an important emerging theme is the complex interplay among conceptualizations of Africa, black diaspora culture, globalization, and social change in the formation of black identities in Brazil (items **2585, 2608, 2614,** and **2625**).

In a four-volume set of collected works that explores the African matrix in Brazil (item **2614**), various authors present political, historical, and cultural perspectives on the contributions of African heritage to national identity and Brazilian popular culture. Alberti and Pereira (item **2585**) likewise discuss how Afro-Brazilian culture is part of the cultural heritage of all Brazilians, not just those who are of African descent. Other scholars have focused their research on Afro-Brazilians and the construction of black identities, taking an anthropological approach to the study of "African derived" cultural performances, rituals, and religion (items **2584, 2597, 2604, 2608, 2617, 2619,** and **2625**). Pinho (item **2608**) explores the centrality of cultural conceptions of Africa in cultural productions and constructions of blackness by elaborating her concept of the "myth of Mama Africa." Although an essentialized myth of Africa may appear static, Pinho's research shows that notions of Africanness and blackness are dynamically constructed by Afro-Bahian cultural groups in dialectic with black diaspora culture.

A growing body of research is focused on the relevance of cultural constructions of Africa to the emerging black movement in Brazil (items **2584, 2585, 2608, 2612,** and **2613**). For instance, Alberti and Pereira (item **2585**) argue that the concept of Africa has played a critical role in the construction and consolidation of a militant black identity. However, Pinho (item **2608**) argues that the myth of Africa provides an inspiration for black resistance on the one hand, while leaving black culture vulnerable to exploitation by state and commercial interests related to tourism. Several studies have examined the relationship between Afro-Brazilian identities, politics, and religion, particularly within the context of Afro-Brazilian religions such as Candomblé (items **2592, 2615, 2617,** and **2623**). Selka's ethnographic study of the relationship between religion, identity, and the black movement in Bahia provides a more nuanced discussion of how deeply these intertwine in Northeastern Brazil (item **2617**). By documenting how Evangelical Protestantism, Catholicism, and Candomblé figure into political resistance and the construction of Afro-Brazilian identities, Selka provides a more nuanced discussion of the deep interconnections among religion, identity, and the black movement in Northeastern Brazil.

Although classic studies of Brazilian national identity highlight the mixture of European, African, and indigenous cultural heritage, more sociological research has been devoted to African or mixed African-European heritage than mixed African-indigenous heritage (item **2625**). An important exception is research conducted by Jan French (item **2597**). In *Legalizing Identities: Becoming Black or Indian in Brazil's Northeast,* French provides an ethnographic and legal analysis of two neighboring communities in Northeastern Brazil that have constructed different collective identities: one indigenous and the other black or Quilombo (descendants of a fugitive slave community). This book bridges research on Afro-Brazilian and indigenous identities, which tend to be treated as separate subjects, and discusses how mixed race identities are negotiated within legal parameters that provide changing opportunities and constraints. While most studies of Afro-Brazilian identities have focused on the northeastern region of Brazil, Rodrigues (item **2613**) represents a growing number of scholars who study Quilombo communities in southern Brazil and elsewhere, and analyze the complex relationships among territorial land claims, the black movement, and government agents in the remaking of ethnic and collective identities.

Another major avenue of research is an exploration of gender and sexuality, and the ways in which gendered experiences cross-cut other aspects of identity. A continued trend in Brazilian sociology and social sciences is an expanded interest in discussing citizenship and human rights issues, especially as they pertain to gender and nonheteronormative sexualites. Many of the reviewed works examine women's rights, scrutinizing gender-based violence (item **2601**), gender hegemony (items **2618** and **2624**), the politics of representation (item **2588**), and plastic surgery and beauty (item **2593**). Most of these authors weave calls for activism (transparent political agendas) into their research, asserting that both knowledge of and active engagement with inequalities is essential to their work. Other studies of gender have focused on the construction of masculinity in Brazilian society (items **2601** and **2611**).

Studies that document the history of the gay and LGBT movement in Brazil continue to receive research attention (item **2620**). Meanwhile, an important emerging theme—nonheteronormative sexualities and the politics of partnership and parenthood (item **2590**)—demonstrates that sex and sexuality inhabit contentious terrain in Brazil, and that determinative battles continue to be fought over what is "moral, healthy, legitimate, and legal" in Brazilian society. Unfortunately, works on both lesbian rights and institution-building continue to be underrepresented in Brazilian sociology.

Research on Brazil's religious institutions is well represented in recent social science literature. Many of the reviewed publications examine both the history of religion in Brazil, as well the manner in which traditional religious institutions have attempted to adapt to the political and socioeconomic transformations taking place in contemporary Brazilian society. Souza and Otto describe the changing nature of Catholicism in Brazil (item **2594**) and reveal the Catholic Church to be a multifaceted system of power that has undergone a series of mutations throughout the development of the Brazilian Republic. A historiography of the Catholic Church in Brazil's center-west region (item **2591**) offers unique insights into the "Christian experience" in central Brazil; a significant void in the research literature on the history of Protestantism in Brazil is filled by a collection of interdisciplinary articles organized by Ferreira (item **2606**); and Liliana Porto (item **2610**) documents the complex interactions of race, religion, and identity formation in a rich and detailed ethnographic work on the role of Catholicism and nontraditional spirituality in the daily lives of residents of a small, rural community in Brazil.

Urbanization and urban conditions remain a central area of focus of social science research in Brazil. Demographic changes, segregation, and persistent inequality in urban areas are explored in detail in Garcia's work (item **2598**), which describes how modern metropolises recreate racial hierarchies in Brazil. Likewise, Rejane Penna's examination of interurban migration in the city of Canoas, Rio Grande do Sul (item **2607**) demonstrates how migrants frequently transfer to their new localities many of the same social constraints present in their former communities. Oftentimes, these social constraints manifest themselves in poor communities in the form of violence and crime, which, according to Desmond Arias and Davis Rodrigues, continue to define daily life in Rio de Janeiro's *favelas* (item **2586**). Other researchers have documented how inequality and social constraints are also manifested as violence against other oppressed populations, such as women (item **2624**).

Sociologists and social science researchers continue to examine the government policies meant to address persistent socioeconomic and political inequality in Brazil. Kerstenetzky (item **2603**) argues that principles of social justice must be included in targeted or universal social sector policies that seek to improve the inequitable distribution of income in Brazil. Others, like Hunter and Borges Sugiyama (item **2602**) contend that the lobbying power of entrenched economic interests must be confronted in order for social sector reforms to go beyond raising basic standards of living for Brazil's poor and indigent classes. Finally, Hall (item **2600**) suggests that programs like the *Bolsa Família*—a conditional cash transfer program that provides targeted government assistance to over 44 million Brazilians—may threaten Brazil's future economic development, despite providing much-needed, short-term relief to some of the country's most impoverished groups.

Clearly, the persistent racial and socioeconomic inequalities that characterize contemporary Brazil continue to engage social science scholarship. Documenting and exploring the fundamental forces driving socioeconomic disparity in Brazil therefore remains a top research priority and much of the resulting scholarship is dedicated to developing a more nuanced understanding of the relationship between economic and political opportunity and aspects of identity such as class, race, gender, and sexuality. Likewise, more recent social science research has focused on the intersection of Brazil's changing social conditions, and has described new social sector programs that seek to remove some of the most persistent exclusionary barriers present in Brazilian society. As Brazil attempts to secure its most recent economic and political advances, sociologists and social scientists will continue to focus research attention on issues of social transformation, inequality, and exclusion, particularly as they relate to the overlapping dimensions of national identity in an increasingly globalized Brazil.

2584 Afolabi, Niyi. Afro-Brazilians: cultural production in a racial democracy. Rochester, N.Y.: Univ. of Rochester Press, 2009. 429 p.: bibl., index. (Rochester studies in African history and the diaspora)

This book provides a synthesis of years of research by Brazilian scholar Niyi Afolabi on the challenges faced by Afro-Brazilians over the past two centuries. In particular, Afolabi analyzes the tensions between the official position of Brazil's "racial democracy" and the reality of marginalization experienced by many Afro-Brazilians. The tension between racial rhetoric and praxis is explored across an impressive range of topics, including literature, music, film, carnival traditions, and history, and, in doing so, Afolabi brings diverse voices into his analysis. Afolabi argues that diverse contributions to Afro-Brazilian cultural production address conflicting issues of identity and racism though a variety of "veils" that ridicule, provoke, protest, or create demand for change.

2585 Alberti, Verena and Amilcar Araujo Pereira. Qual África?: significados da África para o movimento negro no Brasil. (*Estud. Hist./Rio de Janeiro,* 39, jan./junho 2007, p. 25–56, bibl.)

This article gives a historical overview of the meanings of Africa for the black movement in Brazil. The goal of the text is to examine how Africa appears in Brazil's black movement, especially from 1970 on. The authors reference Law 10.639, which was passed in 2003 and mandates that the

study of the history and culture of Africa and Afro-Brazilians must be included in Brazilian school curricula. The authors contend that including these topics of study is important for both white people and people of color, especially in a country where over half the population is of African descent. The authors contend that all groups involved in the black movement had as goals the combating of racism and fighting for improvements in the living conditions of the black population. In this fight, the discovery of Africa had an important function in constructing and consolidating a militant black identity. It increased consciousness about their roots of origin and opened possibilities for action.

2586 Arias, Enrique Desmond and Corinne Davis Rodrigues. The myth of personal security: criminal gangs, dispute resolution, and identity in Rio de Janeiro's favelas. (*Lat. Am. Polit. Soc.,* 48:4, Winter 2006, p. 53–81, bibl.)

This article examines the politics of dispute resolution used by drug traffickers to maintain order in the favelas of Rio de Janeiro. The authors develop a theory of the "myth of personal security" to describe the sense of safety that some members of the local community feel despite high levels of violence, and examine how this myth is maintained through interactions between traffickers and residents. By conforming to certain norms, well-connected community members can negotiate inclusion in groups that enjoy a right to security. Furthermore,

the authors argue that these political negotiations in favelas mirror broader strategies
for securing safety in social contexts of
inequality and oppression that define many
parts of Brazil.

2587 Bailey, Stanley R. Legacies of race:
identities, attitudes, and politics in
Brazil. Stanford, Calif.: Stanford Univ. Press,
2009. 294 p.: bibl., ill., index.

This book provides an empirically
grounded examination of Brazilian public
opinion to understand racial identities,
attitudes, and politics, particularly as these
vary between elite and popular classes.
Bailey reviews Freyre's "myth of racial
democracy" and subsequent challenges by
social scientists and the black movement,
and questions the "thesis of Brazilian ignorance" implied by these newer characterizations of the myth. Rather than assuming
that the majority of Brazilians are in denial
regarding the existence of racism, Bailey
set out to test whether the myth, invented
by intellectuals and appropriated by the
government, actually reflects common
sense about race in Brazil. By drawing on
large-sample attitudinal surveys and public
opinion research, this book departs from
most studies about racial attitudes, which
are more local and ethnographic in orientation. Analyzing representative data across
the Brazilian population, Bailey reveals
attitudes about racial group boundaries,
racial discrimination, the black movement,
and race-targeted policy initiatives. Finally,
Bailey compares changing framings of race
in the US and Brazil, and the possible meanings of convergence between the two.

2588 Buitoni, Dulcília Helena Schroeder.
Mulher de papel: a representação da
mulher pela imprensa feminina brasileira.
2a. ed. rev., atualizada e ampliada. São
Paulo: Summus Editorial, 2009. 239 p.:
bibl., ill.

In this revised and updated 2nd
edition of her text exploring gender and
the media, journalist Buitoni examines
representations of women in the Brazilian
female press from the mid-19th century
(~1850s) to the beginning of the 21st century (2001). The primary goal of this work
is to look at the impact of the female press
in cultural context—to research the im-

ages of women that are transmitted by the
media and that target a female audience.
Analyzing representations and models of
the feminine that exist in the media, Buitoni finds that there is and has been a lack
of what she considers to be "real" (rather
than idealized) women in the pages of the
female press. She contends that the ideal
"woman" is reflected in the press according
to the expectations of society, and thus, in
a society driven by men, representations of
women are based on what men want to see.
Given that women, youth, and adults are
under the powerful influence of the media
she argues that women still have a lot to do
to stop being represented in mythical forms
and to become real.

2589 Cardoso, Adalberto Moreira. Escra-
vidão e sociabilidade capitalista.
(*Novos Estud. CEBRAP*, 80, março 2008,
p. 71–88)

This article draws on historiographi-
cal studies of the social history of labor in
Brazil in order to analyze the relationship
between slavery and capitalism. In particular, Cardoso describes how structural features of former slavery practices informed
the emergence of capitalist sociability and
led to social inertia. According to the author, this framework of structural inertia
provided the general parameters for the
reproduction of free labor in the beginning
of the capitalist order in Brazil. The article
also examines how rigid social hierarchies
and attitudes about manual labor, race, and
poverty reflect this legacy.

**2590 Conjugalidades, parentalidades e
identidades lésbicas, gays e travestis.**
Organização de Miriam Grossi, Anna Paula
Uziel e Luiz Mello. Rio de Janeiro: Editora
Garamond, 2007. 429 p.: bibl., ill. (Garamond univ.) (Col. Sexualidade, gênero e
sociedade. Homossexualidade e cultura)

This edited volume of 20 chapters,
with two chapters in Spanish and 18 in
Portuguese, seeks to expand an emerging
field of study: lesbian, bisexual, gay, and
transvestite (LBGT) marriage, parenthood,
and identity. The chapters discuss aspects
of these themes as they occur in Brazil,
Argentina, Chile, Spain, and France. Topics
considered include media representations of
nonheterosexual unions; modes of interac-

tion between gay male couples; the meaning and importance of a gay or lesbian identity; the role of the state and legal system in shaping marriages and people's relationships; adoption, families, and access to rights; and political and intellectual debates about gay marriage, among others. The volume is motivated by an integrationist perspective that seeks to secure the same rights for gays, lesbians, and transvestites that are already enjoyed by heterosexual citizens, and to disrupt hegemonic notions of marriage, family, parenthood, and identity.

2591 Cristianismos no Brasil central: história e historiografia. Organização de Eduardo Gusmão de Quadros, Maria da Conceição Silva e Sônia Maria de Magalhães. Goiânia, Brazil: Editora da UCG, 2008. 315 p.: bibl., ill.

Compilation of research presented at the III Regional Symposium of the Centro de Estudos da Historia da Igreja na América Latina in Goiás, Brazil (Aug. 2006). The book helps advance the historiography of the Catholic Church in Brazil's Center-West region. All of the texts express a common preoccupation with developing a better understanding of the experience of Christianity in Central Brazil, especially the devotional practices of the poor.

2592 Dantas, Beatriz Góis. Nagô Grandma and White Papa: Candomblé and the creation of Afro-Brazilian identity. Translated by Stephen Berg. Chapel Hill: Univ. of North Carolina Press, 2009. 198 p.: bibl., index. (Translation of the books in the series Latin America in translation)

An English-language translation of Beatriz Góis Dantas' original historico-ethnographic study that compares the formation of Yoruba (Nago) religious traditions and ethnic identities in the Brazilian states of Sergipe and Bahia. Dantas reveals how religious traditions and ethnic identities diverge from each other due to differing social and political contexts. Originally published in Brazil, the work is an important case study of social identity formation as a relational process involving the political mobilization of cultural markers to define group differences. Dantas' close examination of the roles played by insiders and outsiders in the process of social identity formation situ-

ates *Nagô Grandma and White Papa* within a dialog set forth by a new generation of scholars that are examining the creation and recreation of cultural, religious, and ethnic identity in the Brazilian Northeast.

2593 Edmonds, Alexander. Pretty modern: beauty, sex, and plastic surgery in Brazil. Durham, N.C.: Duke Univ. Press, 2010. 297 p.: bibl., ill. (some col.), index, plates.

In this ethnography, anthropologist Alexander Edmonds explores the development and popularization of plastic surgery in Rio de Janeiro city among rich and poor alike, in the context of a modernizing Brazil. Edmonds argues that beauty is a distinct form of modern capital that cannot be reduced to other forms of inequality or capital. Brazil's relationship to plastic surgery, gender, sexuality, race, beauty, and class are all highlighted in this ethnography, as are the paradoxes that emerge from contradictions between modernity and global capitalism, and the simultaneously emancipatory and restrictive power of capital.

2594 Faces do catolicismo. Organização de Rogério Luiz de Souza e Clarícia Otto. Florianópolis, Brazil: Editora Insular, 2008. 374 p.: bibl., ill.

A collection of academic reflections on the history and changing nature of Catholicism in Brazil from the late 19th through the early 21st century. Seventeen chapters focus their analyses on the Catholic Church in the state of Santa Catarina, but nevertheless demonstrate the plurality of Catholicism in Brazil by outlining its diverse customs, forms, and historical dynamics. Breaks with the traditional linear and monolithic vision of the history of the Catholic Church in Brazil to reveal Brazilian Catholicism as a multifaceted system of power in constant mutation throughout the development of the Brazilian Republic. Describes the historical processes that characterize the customs, organization, and expansion of the Catholic Church in Brazil, as well as its relationship to the development of the Brazilian Republic.

2595 Fala, crioulo: o que é ser negro no Brasil. Organização de Haroldo Costa. Ed. rev. e ampliada. Rio de Janeiro: Editora Record, 2009. 333 p.

Updated version of the 1982 book. Presents testimonials and interviews of black Brazilians from different economic, social, and cultural backgrounds to examine issues of racism and racial prejudice in Brazil. Unlike the first edition, which focused on black Brazilians' disillusionment with their lack of economic and social advancement, the discourse of those interviewed in the updated volume demonstrates a growing social and economic self-confidence of Brazilians of African descent, as well as a belief in the country's ability to overcome issues of racial prejudice.

2596 Fernandes, Florestan. O negro no mundo dos brancos. Apresentação de Lilia Moritz Schwarcz. 2a. ed. rev. São Paulo: Global Editora, 2007. 313 p.: bibl. (Col. Florestan Fernandes)

Updated version of the 1972 edition. (See *HLAS 35:8490* for comment on original edition.) A diverse collection of 14 essays that uses the city of São Paulo as a vantage point from which to explore the complex issues of race relations and social formation in Brazil. Contends that the development of a Brazilian national identity was regulated by a white ethic that sought to position blacks and mulattos at the margins of the new social order established during the consolidation of the country's industrial complex. Argues persuasively that stereotyping, the accommodation of prejudice, and racial inequality persist in contemporary Brazilian society.

Fórum Especial A Verdadeira Revolução Brasileira: Integração de Desenvolvimento e Democracia, *Rio de Janeiro, 2007.* A verdadeira revolução brasileira: integração de desenvolvimento e democracia. See item **1513**.

2597 French, Jan Hoffman. Legalizing identities: becoming Black or Indian in Brazil's northeast. Chapel Hill: Univ. of North Carolina Press, 2009. 247 p.: bibl., index, photos.

An ethnographic, historical, and legal analysis of two neighboring communities in Northeastern Brazil that have constructed different collective identities: one indigenous (Xocó Indian) and the other black or *quilombo* (descendants of a fugitive African slave community). French demon-

strates how these two community identities emerged in response to legal reforms that provided opportunities for government recognition and land rights, and which eventually were gained by both communities. The book bridges research on Afro-Brazilian and indigenous identities, which tend to be treated as separate subjects, and discusses how mixed race identities are negotiated within legal parameters that provide changing opportunities and constraints. French concludes that acknowledging the constructed nature of collective identities should not undermine "authenticity"; instead, processes of construction form the basis of all identities.

2598 Garcia, Antonia dos Santos. Desigualdades raciais e segregação urbana em antigas capitais: Salvador, cidade D'Oxum e Rio de Janeiro, cidade de Ogum. Rio de Janeiro: Garamond, 2009. 543 p.: bibl., ill, maps.

This comparative case study uses Instituto Brasileiro de Geografia e Estatística (IBGE) and Análise do Direito (AED) census data to analyze demographic changes, racial inequalities, and urban segregation in the former colonial capital cities of Salvador and Rio de Janeiro. Using race as a central variable, the author examines the spatial distribution of individuals and households and describes how modern metropolises recreate racial hierarchies in Brazil. Results demonstrate significant social and racial stratification in both cities, especially in Salvador. Garcia concludes that urban segregation in Brazil is significant with regard to race, yet not entirely self-evident, and that the traditional polarization of favela-barrio does not reveal the full extent of racial inequalities in Brazilian cities.

2599 Hale, Lindsay. Hearing the mermaid's song: the Umbanda religion in Rio de Janeiro. Albuquerque: Univ. of New Mexico Press, 2009. 192 p.: bibl., index.

Ethnographic account of the religious practices, beliefs, and experiences of Umbanda practitioners in Rio de Janeiro. Based on a decade of research and immersion in the religious world of Umbanda, Hale offers detailed descriptions of lived experiences and intimate practices, and analyzes this emergent religion in the broader context of Brazilian history and culture. In doing so, Hale provides insights into the growing popularity of this religion across diverse sectors of the Brazilian population, and how it serves different personal needs. For comment by ethnologist, see item **557**.

2600 Hall, Anthony. Brazil's *Bolsa Família*: a double-edged sword? (*Dev. Change/ Oxford*, 39:5, Sept. 2008, p. 799–822, bibl., graphs, table)

An insightful review and evaluation of Brazil's *Bolsa Família*, a conditional cash transfer program that provides targeted government assistance in education, health, and nutrition to over 44 million Brazilians. Suggests that the program's initial effectiveness in providing short-term relief to some of the most deprived groups in Brazil could ultimately be negated by increased levels of dependence on government patronage, long-term reductions in social spending, and an undermining of the country's future economic development.

Hall, Anthony. From Fome Zero to Bolsa Familia: social policies and poverty alleviation under Lula. See item **2170**.

2601 Hautzinger, Sarah J. Violence in the city of women: police and batterers in Bahia, Brazil. Berkeley: Univ. of California Press, 2007. 342 p.: bibl., ill., index, maps.

Focusing on a 20-year span beginning with the end of the military dictatorship in 1987, anthropologist Sarah J. Hautzinger explores gender-based violence and the construction of women's police stations in this ethnography based in Salvador da Bahia, Brazil. The work analyzes the shifts in constructions of masculinity that emerge when men's violence against women becomes criminal as well as socially unacceptable. Hautzinger argues that high rates of violence in Salvador are not simply a reflection of female subjugation but in fact evidence of women's resistance to male domination, and symptomatic of changing gender norms. Although the ethnography is not focused on religion, its title references the seminal 1947 text published by anthropologist Ruth Landes, *The City of Women* (see *HLAS 13:322*), about women in Candomblé in Salvador da Bahia, as well as J. Lorand Matory's chapter "Man in the City of Women" in his book *Black Atlantic Religion: Tradition, Trans-*

nationalism, and Matriarchy in the Afro-Brazilian Candomblé (2005).

2602 Hunter, Wendy and **Natasha Borges Sugiyama.** Democracy and social policy in Brazil: advancing basic needs, preserving privileged interests. (*Lat. Am. Polit. Soc.*, 51:2, Summer 2009, p. 29–58, bibl., table)

This article examines the impact of progressive political reforms designed to alleviate poverty and promote greater socioeconomic equality in Brazil. The authors argue that these factors have been counterbalanced by strong political influence and the lobbying power of organized interests, which have a stake in maintaining existing arrangements of privilege. To illustrate the challenges for social sector reforms, the article provides an analysis of four key sectors of the federal government: social security, education, health care, and public assistance. The authors conclude that entrenched interests and inequalities will need to be confronted for social sector reforms to go beyond raising basic standards of living. For political scientist's comment, see item **1514**.

2603 Lessa Kerstenetzky, Celia. Políticas sociais: focalização ou universalização? (*Rev. Econ. Polít.*, 26:4, out./dez. 2006, p. 564–574, bibl.)

This article describes social policies in Brazil and public debate focusing on the choice between targeted and universal programs. The author argues that this choice is misleading unless principles of social justice are examined. The article looks at different social justice connotations of targeting policies and universal policies, and elaborates a number of neglected policy options for improving distributive justice.

2604 Lima, Ivaldo Marciano de França and **Isabel Cristina Martins Guillen.** Cultura afro-descendente no Recife: maracatus, valentes e catimbós. Recife, Brazil: Edições Bagaço, 2007. 250 p.: bibl.

This volume takes an anthropological and historical approach to African-descended culture in the city of Recife in Pernambuco state, Brazil, and is based on five years of research and over 20 years of active contact with local *maracatuzeiros* and *maratacuzeiras* (performers of the *maracatu* genre). The work is a social and cultural reflection on the history of Recife with a focus on the diverse manifestations of Afro-descended religions and rituals. The essays in this collection seek to privilege the historic experience of Afro-descendants and to understand those who make popular culture as the subjects of a rich and diverse history.

2605 Moreira, Roberto José. Terra, poder e território. São Paulo: Editora Expressão Popular, 2007. 360 p.: bibl.

A collection of interdisciplinary works that provides insight into agrarian cultural dynamics, social identity formation, and Brazilian national character. Divided into ten chapters, the book explores the social determinants of asymmetrical power relationships in Brazil. For geography specialist's comment, see *HLAS 65:1359.*

2606 Novas perspectivas sobre o protestantismo brasileiro. Organização de João Cesário Leonel Ferreira. Textos de Breno Martins Campos *et al.* São Paulo: Fonte Editorial: Paulinas, 2009. 424 p.: bibl., ill.

Eleven authors offer an interdisciplinary panorama of contemporary Brazilian Protestantism, with studies about rural Protestantism, religious practices, and the role of the media in religion. The collective effort considers the new wave of fundamentalism to be in direct conflict with the more enlightened Protestant tradition and its diverse interpretations of biblical texts. Analyzes the Protestant movement in Brazil from new thematic and theoretical perspectives and fills a void in the research literature on the history of Protestantism in Brazil.

2607 Penna, Rejane. Deslocamentos e adaptações: uma proposta de interpretação das narrativas de migrantes, unindo elementos da hermenêutica e da análise de discurso. (*Estud. Ibero-Am./Porto Alegre,* 32:1, junho 2006, p. 99–115, bibl., tables)

Uses subject interviews and oral history narratives to examine the displacement and insertion of inter-urban migrants into the industrial city of Canoas, Rio Grande do Sul. Findings indicate that migrants did not effectively integrate into their new metropolitan area. Instead, the research subjects attempted to reconstruct their new neighborhood environments in the image of their former localities by transferring social and religious customs as well as some of the same social constraints present in their former communities.

2608 Pinho, Patricia de Santana. Mama Africa: reinventing blackness in Bahia. Original edition translated by Elena Langdon. Durham, N.C.: Duke Univ. Press, 2010. 266 p.: bibl., index.

The first English-language translation of Pinho's 2004 acclaimed book *Reinvenções da Africa na Bahia,* Mama Africa is an expanded and updated edition of the original publication. In this edition, Pinho elaborates her concept of the "myth of Mama Africa," or the centrality of cultural conceptions of Africa in Bahian constructions of blackness. Research focuses on the cultural production of Afro-Bahian cultural groups, known as *blocos afro,* and how Bahian notions of Africanness and blackness influence, and are influenced by, black diasporic culture. Pinho argues that the essentializing myth of Africa provides an inspiration for black resistance, while leaving black culture vulnerable to exploitation by state and commercial interests related to tourism. Updated for an Anglophone readership, the book provides a more nuanced comparison of Brazilian and North American models of race relations, and an analysis of how the latter are reconceptualized by black activists in Brazil.

2609 Por que "raça"?: reflexões sobre "questão racial" no cinema e na antropologia. Organização de Maria Catarina Chitolina Zanini. Santa Maria, Brazil: Editora UFSM, 2007. 275 p.: bibl., ill.

A collection of texts that reflect on the language of Brazilian cinema and its relation to race relations in Brazil. The publication, which developed from an anthropology and cinema project in a social science course at the Universidade Federal de Santa Maria, adds to the rich debate about the nature and persistence of racial inequality in Brazil. Particularly relevant to those interested in understanding more about expressions of race and race relations in Brazilian popular culture.

2610 Porto, Liliana. A ameaça do outro: magia e religiosidade no Vale do Jequitinhonha MG. São Paulo: Attar Editorial, 2007. 262 p.: bibl., map. (Col. de antropologia. Movimentos religiosos no mundo contemporâneo)

A rich and detailed ethnographic work that uses oral testimonies and historical data to describe and analyze religious life in the small town of Vale do Jequitinhonha. Highlights the centrality of Catholicism in the region's religious life, while documenting the significant presence of witchcraft and other magical beliefs within this spiritual worldview. Central to Porto's analysis is the interaction of race, religion, and collective memory. The author therefore proposes that witchcraft is strongly connected with local and regional racial conflict, and is used by outsiders to racially stigmatize the predominantly black town. A welcome addition to the literature on the anthropology of religion in Brazil.

2611 Representações do masculino: mídia, literatura e sociedade. Organização de Maria Inês Ghilardi-Lucena e Francisco de Oliveira. Campinas, Brazil: Alínea Editora, 2008. 292 p.: bibl., ill.

This edited volume presents a range of research on constructions of masculinity in Brazilian society. The organizers offer the chapters as an invitation to reflect on what it means to be a man in today's postmodern society, and how these experiences may conflict with gender roles and experiences rooted in classical Western traditions. The book is divided into three sections: the first on masculinity and the media, including magazines, product ads, and telenovelas; the second on masculinity and literature; and the final on masculinity in society, including issues of social hierarchies, gaucho traditions, and paternity.

2612 Risério, Antonio. A utopia brasileira e os movimentos negros. São Paulo: Editora 34, 2007. 438 p.: bibl.

A broad examination of race relations, racial inequality, and the black movement in Brazil. Highlights the African influence on areas of Brazilian culture, such as including language, literature, music, and cinema and evaluates the contributions of black movements in the history of Brazilian race relations, from the fight against slavery to the current debates about quotas and affirmative action. An ambitious work directed more toward broader public audiences than traditional academic circles.

2613 Rodrigues, Vera. "¡Vio cómo el negro tiene derecho!": el debate etno-racial y político de las comunidades quilombolas en el sur del Brasil. (*Investig. Soc./San Marcos*, 17, dic. 2006, p. 19–40, bibl., photos)

Spanish translation of an anthropological analysis of identity politics that characterize *quilombo* communities in Brazil, and the relation of these conflicts to similar experiences throughout Latin America. In particular, Rodriques outlines the conflictive history of a territorial land claim by the Anastácia Quilombo in southern Brazil, and the ethnic and racial debates and politics that characterize the dispute. The author also examines the role of the black movement and government agents in the remaking of ethnic and collective identities in Afro-Brazilian communities of southern Brazil.

2614 Sankofa: matrizes africanas da cultura brasileira. v. 1, A matriz africana no mundo. v. 2, Cultura em movimento: matrizes africanas e ativismo negro no Brasil. v. 3, Guerreiras de natureza: mulher negra, religiosidade e ambiente. v. 4, Afrocentricidade: uma bordagem epistemológica inovadora. Organização de Elisa Larkin Nascimento. São Paulo: Selo Negro Edições, 2008–2009. 4 v.: bibl., ill., maps.

This four-volume set of collected works explores the global African matrix, including colonial legacies and relationships between Africa and its diaspora, with a focus on Brazil and pan-Africanism. The works seek to valorize an identity that reflects Brazil's culture, acknowledging that the entire population (whether Afro-descended or not) inherited traditions from Africa. The authors discuss diverse themes from political, historical, and social perspectives. The first volume is focused on understanding why Africa is considered the cradle of civilization, ancient and modern. The second and third volumes deal with basic aspects of how the African matrix is a fundamental part of Brazilian culture and how important the fight against racism is for Brazilian history. Both volumes also highlight the fundamental role of black women, Afro-descended religiosity, and the environment. The fourth volume explores contributions of African intellectuals to the development and knowledge of the contemporary world.

2615 Santos, Edmar Ferreira. O poder dos candomblés: perseguição e resistência no Recôncavo da Bahia. Salvador, Brazil: EDUFBA, 2009. 209 p.: bibl., ill.

This book analyzes the sociopolitical history of Candomblé in Cachoeira, Bahia. Deconstructs the myth of a systematic political repression of Candomblé congregations by demonstrating the nuanced and interdependent relationships between politics and Afro-Brazilian religiosity throughout the history of Bahia. Based on the author's 2007 Master's thesis.

2616 Santos, Gevanilda. Relações raciais e desigualdade no Brasil. São Paulo: Selo Negro Edições, 2009. 94 p.: bibl., ill. (Consciência em debate)

A historical account of race relations and racial inequality in Brazil from the 19th century until current times. Six chapters explore themes such as race relations during the Old Republic; the Vargas Era and the myth of racial democracy; postwar race relations; the military dictatorship; and the black protest movement. Uses social, economic, political, and cultural analysis to deconstruct the myth of racial democracy in Brazil, document the exclusion of blacks throughout Brazilian history, and demonstrate how racial inequality is structured and perpetuated in Brazilian society. Contends that the concept of racial harmony and lack of racial inequality in Brazil is a stereotype that hides deep-seated Brazilian racial prejudice. Santos highlights the real and symbolic changes that have occurred in Brazilian race relations since the end of the 19th century and offers education-based public policy prescriptions as a means of promoting the equality of race relations, political awareness of historical diversity, and respect for differences.

2617 Selka, Stephen. Religion and the politics of ethnic identity in Bahia, Brazil. Gainesville: Univ. Press of Florida, 2007. 175 p.: bibl., ill., index. (New World diasporas)

A multilocal ethnographic study of the relationship between religion, identity, and the black movement in Brazil. Examines how Evangelical Protestantism, Catholicism, and traditional Afro-Brazilian religions, such as Candomblé, are deployed in discursive struggles concerning racism and identity in Brazil. Outlines how Brazilians of African descent draw upon both Christian and African diasporic religions to construct their racial identities and discusses the ways in which Catholicism, Candomblé, and Evangelical Protestantism figure into resistance, struggle, and the construction of Afro-Brazilian identity. Demonstrates how deeply religion and race intertwine in Brazil despite attempts by some religious practitioners to keep them discursively separate. Based on the author's fieldwork in the Bahian cities of Cachoeira and Salvador.

2618 Seminário Internacional Fazendo Gênero, 7th, Universidad Federal de Santa Catarina, 2006. A construção dos corpos: perspectivas feministas. Organização de Cristina Maria Teixeira Stevens e Tania Navarro Swain. Ilha de Santa Catarina, Brazil: Mulheres, 2008. 308 p.: bibl., ill. (chiefly col.). (Série Ensaios)

A contemporary feminist collection based on the 2006 symposium "Fazendo Gênero" (Making Gender), and organized around the subtheme, "The Construction of Bodies: Material and Symbolic Violence." The authors contend that bodies are constructed through violence, that bodies are not passive, and that women resist domination. The volume is multidisciplinary in terms of both contributors and subjects, and the discussions it presents bring feminist perspectives and analyses to diverse topics in history, literature, education, psychology, sociology, and physical education. In addition to an academic agenda, the authors in this collection promulgate a political agenda of female liberation and resistance through an examination of the relationships between sex and gender and bodies and sexuality.

2619 Silva, Ana van Meegen. Kalunga. Goiânia, Brazil: Editora da UCG, 2007. 115 p.: bibl.

An ethnographic study of the Kalunga —a community of black subsistence agriculturalists and commercial traders that live in the rural northeastern zone of Goiás state. Reviews the historical, cultural, socioeconomic, and religious factors that contributed to the ethnic identity formation of the Kalunga community.

2620 Simões, Júlio Assis and Regina Facchini. Na trilha do arco-íris: do movimento homossexual ao LGBT. São Paulo: Editora Fundação Perseu Abramo, 2009. 191 p.: bibl., ill. (História do povo brasileiro)

Adopting terminology previously used by US historian James Green and anthropologist Regina Facchini, this ambitious book covers the chronology of the homosexual/LGBT movement in Brazil by organizing it into three phases or "waves." The first wave corresponds to the "political opening" of 1978, the second corresponds to the 1980s when the movement is institutionalized and the AIDS epidemic begins, and the third corresponds to the mid-1990s forward and is characterized by a multiplication of activist groups, a diversification of the movement, the emergence of the term LGBT, the formation of regional and nation networks, the consecration of Gay and LGBT Pride parades, and the growth of markets around homosexuality. This volume brings together diverse and wide-ranging data and research on the politicization of sexual and gender identities in last several decades in Brazil and traces how these identities and roles are continually redefined, most recently with a focus on sexuality. The book ends with a discussion of the "LGBT citizen" as an individual with rights and a multiplication of identities.

2621 Sovik, Liv Rebecca. Aqui ninguém é branco. Rio de Janeiro: Aeroplano Editora, 2009. 175 p.: bibl.

A critical treatise on the "myth of Brazilian racial democracy." Essays on popular music explore the topic of race relations and racial hierachies in Brazil. Contends that long-held beliefs in Brazilian racial democracy and miscegenation as a "national emblem" have acted to conceal white hegemony, social hierachies, and racial exclusion. Presents a critical, and sometimes dissonant, reinterpretation of traditional elements of Brazilian culture in an attempt to develop a new understanding of the complexity of race relations in Brazil. An interesting point of departure from

which to explore issues of race and race relations in Brazil.

2622 Ulyssea, Gabriel. Informalidade no mercado de trabalho brasileiro: uma resenha da literatura. (*Rev. Econ. Polít.*, 26:4, out./dez. 2006, p. 596–618, bibl., tables)

A well-organized and systematic review of the literature on the Brazilian informal labor market. Includes works related to wage differentials between formal and informal workers, labor market segmentation, and the effect of institutions on the informal sector.

2623 Vallado, Armando. Lei do Santo: poder e conflito no candomblé. Rio de Janeiro: Pallas, 2010. 156 p.: bibl.

A sociohistorical examination of the themes of power and conflict in the Candomblé religion. The book weaves together empirical research with personal narrative to offer interpretations of the internal organization of Candomblé shrines. Likewise, it examines the rules and customs governing Candomblé sects and describes the hierarchical arrangements that help define power and mediate conflict within this Afro-Brazilian religion. Vallado offers unique insights regarding the effects of slavery on the transatlantic transfer of Candomblé from Africa to Brazil, and suggests that it possesses the ability to compete as a sacred alternative in the panoply of Brazil's "religious market." Based on the author's doctoral dissertation.

2624 Violências esculpidas: notas para reflexão, ação e políticas de gênero. Coordenação de Eline Jonas. Goiânia, Brazil: Editora da UCG, 2007. 210 p.: bibl.

Organized by feminist sociologist Eline Jonas, this edited volume consists of 12 chapters that are written in both Spanish (2) and Portuguese (10). The collection starts from the premise that violence is an expression of the unequal distribution of power in society and that inequality manifests itself most clearly in oppressed populations, such as women. Following the volume's title, the authors contend that violence is "carved" into the bodies and emotions of women in multiple ways. While touching on some more commonly discussed themes, such as legitimate versus illegitimate use of force, the banality of violence, and old and new forms of interpersonal and domestic violence, the text adds gender as a factor, and has as its focus violent actions perpetrated against women. The volume also examines attitudes and practices of resistance and describes how reactions to the advances of women often manifest in violent practices.

2625 Wade, Peter. Afro-Latin studies: reflections on the field. (*Lat. Am. Caribb. Ethn. Stud.*, 1:1, April 2006, p. 105–124, bibl.)

In this 2006 review article, Wade evaluates both the state of Afro-Latin studies and significant contributions to the field made over the past few decades. Given the predominance of Afro-Brazilian research, much of the reviewed content refers to Brazil. However, Wade's treatment of broader themes helps place the contribution of recent Afro-Brazilian studies within larger trends in the field of Afro-Latin studies. He summarizes three broad topics that continue to frame the field: comparative studies of slavery and race relations in the Americas; issues of racism, with a strong comparative focus on racial classification in Brazil and the US; and the role of Africa in the construction of black identities. The article concludes with a discussion of future directions, including the dynamics of the Atlantic diaspora and globalization.

ABBREVIATIONS AND ACRONYMS

Except for journal abbreviations which are listed: 1) after each journal title in the *Title List of Journals Indexed* (p. 575); and 2) in the *Abbreviation List of Journals Indexed* (p. 585).

ALADI	Asociación Latinoamericana de Integración
a.	annual
ABC	Argentina, Brazil, Chile
A.C.	antes de Cristo
ACAR	Associação de Crédito e Assistência Rural, Brazil
AD	Anno Domini
A.D.	Acción Democrática, Venezuela
ADESG	Associação dos Diplomados de Escola Superior de Guerra, Brazil
AGI	Archivo General de Indias, Sevilla
AGN	Archivo General de la Nación
AID	Agency for International Development
a.k.a.	also known as
Ala.	Alabama
ALALC	Asociación Latinoamericana de Libre Comercio
ALEC	*Atlas lingüístico etnográfico de Colombia*
ANAPO	Alianza Nacional Popular, Colombia
ANCARSE	Associação Nordestina de Crédito e Assistência Rural de Sergipe, Brazil
ANCOM	Andean Common Market
ANDI	Asociación Nacional de Industriales, Colombia
ANPOCS	Associação Nacional de Pós-Graduação e Pesquisa em Ciências Sociais, São Paulo
ANUC	Asociación Nacional de Usuarios Campesinos, Colombia
ANUIES	Asociación Nacional de Universidades e Institutos de Enseñanza Superior, Mexico
AP	Acción Popular
APRA	Alianza Popular Revolucionaria Americana, Peru
ARENA	Aliança Renovadora Nacional, Brazil
Ariz.	Arizona
Ark.	Arkansas
ASA	Association of Social Anthropologists of the Commonwealth, London
ASSEPLAN	Assessoria de Planejamento e Acompanhamento, Recife
Assn.	Association
Aufl.	Auflage (edition, edición)
AUFS	American Universities Field Staff Reports, Hanover, N.H.
Aug.	August, Augustan
aum.	aumentada
b.	born (nació)
B.A.R.	British Archaeological Reports
BBE	Bibliografia Brasileira de Educação
b.c.	indicates dates obtained by radiocarbon methods
BC	Before Christ

bibl(s).	bibliography(ies)
BID	Banco Interamericano de Desarrollo
BNDE	Banco Nacional de Desenvolvimento Econômico, Brazil
BNH	Banco Nacional de Habitação, Brazil
BP	before present
b/w	black and white
C14	Carbon 14
ca.	*circa* (about)
CACM	Central American Common Market
CADE	Conferencia Anual de Ejecutivos de Empresas, Peru
CAEM	Centro de Altos Estudios Militares, Peru
Calif.	California
Cap.	Capítulo
CARC	Centro de Arte y Comunicación, Buenos Aires
CARICOM	Caribbean Common Market
CARIFTA	Caribbean Free Trade Association
CBC	Christian base communities
CBD	central business district
CBI	Caribbean Basin Initiative
CD	Christian Democrats, Chile
CDHES	Comisión de Derechos Humanos de El Salvador
CDI	Conselho de Desenvolvimento Industrial, Brasília
CEB	comunidades eclesiásticas de base
CEBRAP	Centro Brasileiro de Análise e Planejamento, São Paulo
CECORA	Centro de Cooperativas de la Reforma Agraria, Colombia
CEDAL	Centro de Estudios Democráticos de América Latina, Costa Rica
CEDE	Centro de Estudios sobre Desarrollo Económico, Univ. de los Andes, Bogotá
CEDEPLAR	Centro de Desenvolvimento e Planejamento Regional, Belo Horizonte
CEDES	Centro de Estudios de Estado y Sociedad, Buenos Aires; Centro de Estudos de Educação e Sociedade, São Paulo
CEDI	Centro Ecumênico de Documentos e Informação, São Paulo
CEDLA	Centro de Estudios y Documentación Latinoamericanos, Amsterdam
CEESTEM	Centro de Estudios Económicos y Sociales del Tercer Mundo, México
CELADE	Centro Latinoamericano de Demografía
CELADEC	Comisión Evangélica Latinoamericana de Educación Cristiana
CELAM	Consejo Episcopal Latinoamericano
CEMLA	Centro de Estudios Monetarios Latinoamericanos, Mexico
CENDES	Centro de Estudios del Desarrollo, Venezuela
CENIDIM	Centro Nacional de Información, Documentación e Investigación Musicales, Mexico
CENIET	Centro Nacional de Información y Estadísticas del Trabajo, Mexico
CEOSL	Confederación Ecuatoriana de Organizaciones Sindicales Libres
CEPADE	Centro Paraguayo de Estudios de Desarrollo Económico y Social
CEPA-SE	Comissão Estadual de Planejamento Agrícola, Sergipe
CEPAL	Comisión Económica para América Latina y el Caribe
CEPLAES	Centro de Planificación y Estudios Sociales, Quito
CERES	Centro de Estudios de la Realidad Económica y Social, Bolivia
CES	constant elasticity of substitution
cf.	compare
CFI	Consejo Federal de Inversiones, Buenos Aires
CGE	Confederación General Económica, Argentina
CGTP	Confederación General de Trabajadores del Perú
chap(s).	chapter(s)
CHEAR	Council on Higher Education in the American Republics

Cía.	Compañía
CIA	Central Intelligence Agency
CIDA	Comité Interamericano de Desarrollo Agrícola
CIDE	Centro de Investigación y Desarrollo de la Educación, Chile; Centro de Investigación y Docencias Económicas, Mexico
CIDIAG	Centro de Información y Desarrollo Internacional de Autogestión, Lima
CIE	Centro de Investigaciones Económicas, Buenos Aires
CIEDLA	Centro Interdisciplinario de Estudios sobre el Desarrollo Latinoamericano, Buenos Aires
CIEDUR	Centro Interdisciplinario de Estudios sobre el Desarrollo Uruguay, Montevideo
CIEPLAN	Corporación de Investigaciones Económicas para América Latina, Santiago
CIESE	Centro de Investigaciones y Estudios Socioeconómicos, Quito
CIMI	Conselho Indigenista Missionário, Brazil
CINTERFOR	Centro Interamericano de Investigación y Documentación sobre Formación Profesional
CINVE	Centro de Investigaciones Económicas, Montevideo
CIP	Conselho Interministerial de Preços, Brazil
CIPCA	Centro de Investigación y Promoción del Campesinado, Bolivia
CIPEC	Consejo Intergubernamental de Países Exportadores de Cobre, Santiago
CLACSO	Consejo Latinoamericano de Ciencias Sociales, Secretaría Ejecutiva, Buenos Aires
CLASC	Confederación Latinoamericana Sindical Cristiana
CLE	Comunidad Latinoamericana de Escritores, Mexico
cm	centimeter
CNI	Confederação Nacional da Indústria, Brazil
CNPq	Conselho Nacional de Pesquisas, Brazil
Co.	Company
COB	Central Obrera Boliviana
COBAL	Companhia Brasileira de Alimentos
CODEHUCA	Comisión para la Defensa de los Derechos Humanos en Centroamérica
Col.	Collection, Colección, Coleção
col.	colored, coloured
Colo.	Colorado
COMCORDE	Comisión Coordinadora para el Desarrollo Económico, Uruguay
comp(s).	compiler(s), compilador(es)
CONCLAT	Congresso Nacional das Classes Trabalhadoras, Brazil
CONCYTEC	Consejo Nacional de Ciencia y Tecnología (Peru)
CONDESE	Conselho de Desenvolvimento Econômico de Sergipe
Conn.	Connecticut
COPEI	Comité Organizador Pro-Elecciones Independientes, Venezuela
CORFO	Corporación de Fomento de la Producción, Chile
CORP	Corporación para el Fomento de Investigaciones Económicas, Colombia
Corp.	Corporation, Corporación
corr.	corrected, corregida
CP	Communist Party
CPDOC	Centro de Pesquisa e Documentação, Brazil
CRIC	Consejo Regional Indígena del Cauca, Colombia
CSUTCB	Confederación Sindical Unica de Trabajadores Campesinos de Bolivia
CTM	Confederación de Trabajadores de México
CUNY	City University of New York
CUT	Central Unica de Trabajadores (Mexico); Central Unica dos Trabalhadores (Brazil); Central Unitaria de Trabajadores (Chile; Colombia); Confederación Unitaria de Trabajadores (Costa Rica)

CVG	Corporación Venezolana de Guayana
d.	died (murió)
DANE	Departamento Nacional de Estadística, Colombia
DC	developed country; Demócratas Cristianos, Chile
d.C.	después de Cristo
Dec./déc.	December, décembre
Del.	Delaware
dept.	department
depto.	departamento
DESCO	Centro de Estudios y Promoción del Desarrollo, Lima
Dez./dez.	Dezember, dezembro
dic.	diciembre, dicembre
disc.	discography
DNOCS	Departamento Nacional de Obras Contra as Secas, Brazil
doc.	document, documento
Dr.	Doctor
Dra.	Doctora
DRAE	*Diccionario de la Real Academia Española*
ECLAC	UN Economic Commision for Latin America and the Caribbean, New York and Santiago
ECOSOC	UN Economic and Social Council
ed./éd.(s)	edition(s), édition(s), edición(es), editor(s), redactor(es), director(es)
EDEME	Editora Emprendimentos Educacionais, Florianópolis
Edo.	Estado
EEC	European Economic Community
EE.UU.	Estados Unidos de América
EFTA	European Free Trade Association
e.g.	*exempio gratia* (for example, por ejemplo)
ELN	Ejército de Liberación Nacional, Colombia
ENDEF	Estudo Nacional da Despesa Familiar, Brazil
ERP	Ejército Revolucionario del Pueblo, El Salvador
ESG	Escola Superior de Guerra, Brazil
estr.	estrenado
et al.	*et alia* (and others)
ETENE	Escritório Técnico de Estudos Econômicos do Nordeste, Brazil
ETEPE	Escritório Técnico de Planejamento, Brazil
EUDEBA	Editorial Universitaria de Buenos Aires
EWG	Europaische Wirtschaftsgemeinschaft. *See* EEC.
facsim(s).	facsimile(s)
FAO	Food and Agriculture Organization of the United Nations
FDR	Frente Democrático Revolucionario, El Salvador
FEB	Força Expedicionária Brasileira
Feb./feb.	February, Februar, febrero, febbraio
FEDECAFE	Federación Nacional de Cafeteros, Colombia
FEDESARROLLO	Fundación para la Educación Superior y el Desarrollo
fev./fév.	fevereiro, février
ff.	following
FGTS	Fundo de Garantia do Tempo de Serviço, Brazil
FGV	Fundação Getúlio Vargas
FIEL	Fundación de Investigaciones Económicas Latinoamericanas, Argentina
film.	filmography
fl.	flourished
Fla.	Florida
FLACSO	Facultad Latinoamericana de Ciencias Sociales
FMI	Fondo Monetario Internacional

FMLN	Frente Farabundo Martí de Liberación Nacional, El Salvador
fold.	folded
fol(s).	folio(s)
FPL	Fuerzas Populares de Liberación Farabundo Marti, El Salvador
FRG	Federal Republic of Germany
FSLN	Frente Sandinista de Liberación Nacional, Nicaragua
ft.	foot, feet
FUAR	Frente Unido de Acción Revolucionaria, Colombia
FUCVAM	Federación Unificadora de Cooperativas de Vivienda por Ayuda Mutua, Uruguay
FUNAI	Fundação Nacional do Indio, Brazil
FUNARTE	Fundação Nacional de Arte, Brazil
FURN	Fundação Universidade Regional do Nordeste
Ga.	Georgia
GAO	General Accounting Office, Wahington
GATT	General Agreement on Tariffs and Trade
GDP	gross domestic product
GDR	German Democratic Republic
GEIDA	Grupo Executivo de Irrigação para o Desenvolvimento Agrícola, Brazil
gen.	gennaio
Gen.	General
GMT	Greenwich Mean Time
GPA	grade point average
GPO	Government Printing Office, Washington
h.	hijo
ha.	hectares, hectáreas
HLAS	*Handbook of Latin American Studies*
HMAI	*Handbook of Middle American Indians*
Hnos.	hermanos
HRAF	Human Relations Area Files, Inc., New Haven, Conn.
IBBD	Instituto Brasileiro de Bibliografia e Documentação
IBGE	Instituto Brasileiro de Geografia e Estatística, Rio de Janeiro
IBRD	International Bank for Reconstruction and Development (World Bank)
ICA	Instituto Colombiano Agropecuario
ICAIC	Instituto Cubano de Arte e Industria Cinematográfica
ICCE	Instituto Colombiano de Construcción Escolar
ICE	International Cultural Exchange
ICSS	Instituto Colombiano de Seguridad Social
ICT	Instituto de Crédito Territorial, Colombia
id.	*idem* (the same as previously mentioned or given)
IDB	Inter-American Development Bank
i.e.	*id est* (that is, o sea)
IEL	Instituto Euvaldo Lodi, Brazil
IEP	Instituto de Estudios Peruanos
IERAC	Instituto Ecuatoriano de Reforma Agraria y Colonización
IFAD	International Fund for Agricultural Development
IICA	Instituto Interamericano de Ciencias Agrícolas, San José
III	Instituto Indigenista Interamericana, Mexico
IIN	Instituto Indigenista Nacional, Guatemala
ILDIS	Instituto Latinoamericano de Investigaciones Sociales
ill.	illustration(s)
Ill.	Illinois
ILO	International Labour Organization, Geneva
IMES	Instituto Mexicano de Estudios Sociales
IMF	International Monetary Fund

Impr.	Imprenta, Imprimérie
in.	inches
INAH	Instituto Nacional de Antropología e Historia, Mexico
INBA	Instituto Nacional de Bellas Artes, Mexico
Inc.	Incorporated
INCORA	Instituto Colombiano de Reforma Agraria
Ind.	Indiana
INEP	Instituto Nacional de Estudios Pedagógicos, Brazil
INI	Instituto Nacional Indigenista, Mexico
INIT	Instituto Nacional de Industria Turística, Cuba
INPES/IPEA	Instituto de Planejamento Econômico e Social, Brazil
INTAL	Instituto para la Integración de América Latina
IPA	Instituto de Pastoral Andina, Univ. de San Antonio de Abad, Seminario de Antropología, Cusco, Peru
IPEA	Instituto de Pesquisa Econômica Aplicada, Brazil
IPES/GB	Instituto de Pesquisas e Estudos Sociais, Guanabara, Brazil
IPHAN	Instituto de Patrimônio Histórico e Artístico Nacional, Brazil
ir.	irregular
IS	Internacional Socialista
ITESM	Instituto Tecnológico y de Estudios Superiores de Monterrey
ITT	International Telephone and Telegraph
Jan./jan.	January, Januar, janeiro, janvier
JLP	Jamaican Labour Party
Jr.	Junior, Júnior
JUC	Juventude Universitária Católica, Brazil
JUCEPLAN	Junta Central de Planificación, Cuba
Kan.	Kansas
KITLV	Koninklijk Instituut voor Tall-, Land- en Volkenkunde (Royal Institute of Linguistics and Anthropology)
km	kilometers, kilómetros
Ky.	Kentucky
La.	Louisiana
LASA	Latin American Studies Association
LDC	less developed country(ies)
LP	long-playing record
Ltd(a).	Limited, Limitada
m	meters, metros
m.	murió (died)
M	mille, mil, thousand
M.A.	Master of Arts
MACLAS	Middle Atlantic Council of Latin American Studies
MAPU	Movimiento de Acción Popular Unitario, Chile
MARI	Middle American Research Institute, Tulane University, New Orleans
MAS	Movimiento al Socialismo, Venezuela
Mass.	Massachusetts
MCC	Mercado Común Centro-Americano
Md.	Maryland
MDB	Movimiento Democrático Brasileiro
MDC	more developed countries
Me.	Maine
MEC	Ministério de Educação e Cultura, Brazil
Mich.	Michigan
mimeo	mimeographed, mimeografiado
min.	minutes, minutos

Minn.	Minnesota
MIR	Movimiento de Izquierda Revolucionaria, Chile and Venezuela
Miss.	Mississippi
MIT	Massachusetts Institute of Technology
ml	milliliter
MLN	Movimiento de Liberación Nacional
mm.	millimeter
MNC	multinational corporation
MNI	minimum number of individuals
MNR	Movimiento Nacionalista Revolucionario, Bolivia
Mo.	Missouri
MOBRAL	Movimento Brasileiro de Alfabetização
MOIR	Movimiento Obrero Independiente y Revolucionario, Colombia
Mont.	Montana
MRL	Movimiento Revolucionario Liberal, Colombia
ms.	manuscript
M.S.	Master of Science
msl	mean sea level
n.	nació (born)
NBER	National Bureau of Economic Research, Cambridge, Massachusetts
N.C.	North Carolina
N.D.	North Dakota
NE	Northeast
Neb.	Nebraska
neubearb.	neubearbeitet (revised, corregida)
Nev.	Nevada
n.f.	neue Folge (new series)
NGO	nongovernmental organization
NGDO	nongovernmental development organization
N.H.	New Hampshire
NIEO	New International Economic Order
NIH	National Institutes of Health, Washington
N.J.	New Jersey
NJM	New Jewel Movement, Grenada
N.M.	New Mexico
no(s).	number(s), número(s)
NOEI	Nuevo Orden Económico Internacional
NOSALF	Scandinavian Committee for Research in Latin America
Nov./nov.	November, noviembre, novembre, novembro
NSF	National Science Foundation
NW	Northwest
N.Y.	New York
OAB	Ordem dos Advogados do Brasil
OAS	Organization of American States
OCLC	Online Computer Library Center
Oct./oct.	October, octubre, octobre
ODEPLAN	Oficina de Planificación Nacional, Chile
OEA	Organización de los Estados Americanos
OECD	Organisation for Economic Cooperation and Development
OIT	Organización Internacional del Trabajo
Okla.	Oklahoma
Okt.	Oktober
ONUSAL	United Nations Observer Mission in El Salvador
op.	opus

OPANAL	Organismo para la Proscripción de las Armas Nucleares en América Latina
OPEC	Organization of Petroleum Exporting Countries
OPEP	Organización de Países Exportadores de Petróleo
OPIC	Overseas Private Investment Corporation, Washington
Or.	Oregon
OREALC	Oficina Regional de Educación para América Latina y el Caribe
ORIT	Organización Regional Interamericana del Trabajo
ORSTOM	Office de la recherche scientifique et technique outre-mer (France)
ott.	ottobre
out.	outubro
p.	page(s)
Pa.	Pennsylvania
PAN	Partido Acción Nacional, Mexico
PC	Partido Comunista
PCCLAS	Pacific Coast Council on Latin American Studies
PCN	Partido de Conciliación Nacional, El Salvador
PCP	Partido Comunista del Perú
PCR	Partido Comunista Revolucionario, Chile and Argentina
PCV	Partido Comunista de Venezuela
PD	Partido Democrático
PDC	Partido Demócrata Cristiano, Chile
PDS	Partido Democrático Social, Brazil
PDT	Partido Democrático Trabalhista, Brazil
PDVSA	Petróleos de Venezuela S.A.
PEMEX	Petróleos Mexicanos
PETROBRAS	Petróleo Brasileiro
PIMES	Programa Integrado de Mestrado em Economia e Sociologia, Brazil
PIP	Partido Independiente de Puerto Rico
PLN	Partido Liberación Nacional, Costa Rica
PMDB	Partido do Movimento Democrático Brasileiro
PNAD	Pesquisa Nacional por Amostra Domiciliar, Brazil
PNC	People's National Congress, Guyana
PNM	People's National Movement, Trinidad and Tobago
PNP	People's National Party, Jamaica
pop.	population
port(s).	portrait(s)
PPP	purchasing power parities; People's Progressive Party of Guyana
PRD	Partido Revolucionario Dominicano
PREALC	Programa Regional del Empleo para América Latina y el Caribe, Organización Internacional del Trabajo, Santiago
PRI	Partido Revolucionario Institucional, Mexico
Prof.	Professor, Profesor(a)
PRONAPA	Programa Nacional de Pesquisas Arqueológicas, Brazil
PRONASOL	Programa Nacional de Solidaridad, Mexico
prov.	province, provincia
PS	Partido Socialista, Chile
PSD	Partido Social Democrático, Brazil
pseud.	pseudonym, pseudónimo
PT	Partido dos Trabalhadores, Brazil
pt(s).	part(s), parte(s)
PTB	Partido Trabalhista Brasileiro
pub.	published, publisher
PUC	Pontifícia Universidade Católica

PURSC	Partido Unido de la Revolución Socialista de Cuba
q.	quarterly
rev.	revisada, revista, revised
R.I.	Rhode Island
s.a.	semiannual
SALALM	Seminar on the Acquisition of Latin American Library Materials
SATB	soprano, alto, tenor, bass
sd.	sound
s.d.	*sine datum* (no date, sin fecha)
S.D.	South Dakota
SDR	special drawing rights
SE	Southeast
SELA	Sistema Económico Latinoamericano
SEMARNAP	Secretaria de Medio Ambiente, Recursos Naturales y Pesca, Mexico
SENAC	Serviço Nacional de Aprendizagem Comercial, Rio de Janeiro
SENAI	Serviço Nacional de Aprendizagem Industrial, São Paulo
SEP	Secretaría de Educación Pública, Mexico
SEPLA	Seminario Permanente sobre Latinoamérica, Mexico
Sept./sept.	September, septiembre, septembre
SES	socioeconomic status
SESI	Serviço Social da Indústria, Brazil
set.	setembro, settembre
SI	Socialist International
SIECA	Secretaría Permanente del Tratado General de Integración Económica Centroamericana
SIL	Summer Institute of Linguistics (Instituto Lingüístico de Verano)
SINAMOS	Sistema Nacional de Apoyo a la Movilización Social, Peru
S.J.	Society of Jesus
s.l.	*sine loco* (place of publication unknown)
s.n.	*sine nomine* (publisher unknown)
SNA	Sociedad Nacional de Agricultura, Chile
SPP	Secretaría de Programación y Presupuesto, Mexico
SPVEA	Superintendência do Plano de Valorização Econômica da Amazônia, Brazil
sq.	square
SSRC	Social Sciences Research Council, New York
STENEE	Empresa Nacional de Energía Eléctrica. Sindicato de Trabajadores, Honduras
SUDAM	Superintendência de Desenvolvimento da Amazônia, Brazil
SUDENE	Superintendência de Desenvolvimento do Nordeste, Brazil
SUFRAMA	Superintendência da Zona Franca de Manaus, Brazil
SUNY	State University of New York
SW	Southwest
t.	tomo(s), tome(s)
TAT	Thematic Apperception Test
TB	tuberculosis
Tenn.	Tennessee
Tex.	Texas
TG	transformational generative
TL	Thermoluminescent
TNE	Transnational enterprise
TNP	Tratado de No Proliferación
trans.	translator
UABC	Universidad Autónoma de Baja California

UCA	Universidad Centroamericana José Simeón Cañas, San Salvador
UCLA	University of California, Los Angeles
UDN	União Democrática Nacional, Brazil
UFG	Universidade Federal de Goiás
UFPb	Universidade Federal de Paraíba
UFSC	Universidade Federal de Santa Catarina
UK	United Kingdom
UN	United Nations
UNAM	Universidad Nacional Autónoma de México
UNCTAD	United Nations Conference on Trade and Development
UNDP	United Nations Development Programme
UNEAC	Unión de Escritores y Artistas de Cuba
UNESCO	United Nations Educational, Scientific and Cultural Organization
UNI/UNIND	União das Nações Indígenas
UNICEF	United Nations International Children's Emergency Fund
Univ(s).	university(ies), universidad(es), universidade(s), université(s), universität(s), universitá(s)
uniw.	uniwersytet (university)
Unltd.	Unlimited
UP	Unidad Popular, Chile
URD	Unidad Revolucionaria Democrática
URSS	Unión de Repúblicas Soviéticas Socialistas
UNISA	University of South Africa
US	United States
USAID	*See* AID.
USIA	United States Information Agency
USSR	Union of Soviet Socialist Republics
UTM	Universal Transverse Mercator
UWI	Univ. of the West Indies
v.	volume(s), volumen (volúmenes)
Va.	Virginia
V.I.	Virgin Islands
viz.	*videlicet* (that is, namely)
vol(s).	volume(s), volumen (volúmenes)
vs.	versus
Vt.	Vermont
W.Va.	West Virginia
Wash.	Washington
Wis.	Wisconsin
WPA	Working People's Alliance, Guyana
WWI	World War I
WWII	World War II
Wyo.	Wyoming
yr(s).	year(s)

TITLE LIST OF JOURNALS INDEXED

For journal titles listed by abbreviation, see *Abbreviation List of Journals Indexed*, p. 585.

Amazônica: Revista de Antropologia. Univ. Federal do Pará, Instituto de Filosofia e Ciências Humanas. Belem, Brazil. (Amazôn. Rev. Antropol.)

Ambio. Royal Swedish Academy of Sciences. Stockholm. (Ambio/Stockholm)

América Latina Hoy: Revista de Ciencias Sociales. Univ. de Salamanca, Instituto de Estudios de Iberoamérica y Portugal. Salamanca, Spain. (Am. Lat. Hoy/Salamanca)

American Anthropologist. American Anthropological Assn. Washington, D.C. (Am. Anthropol.)

American Antiquity. Society for American Archaeology. Washington, D.C. (Am. Antiq.)

American Ethnologist. American Anthropological Assn., American Ethnological Society. Washington, D.C. (Am. Ethnol./Washington)

American Journal of Sociology. Univ. of Chicago Press. Chicago, Ill. (Am. J. Sociol.)

Anales de Arqueología y Etnología. Univ. Nacional de Cuyo, Facultad de Filosofía y Letras. Mendoza, Argentina. (An. Arqueol. Etnol.)

Anales de Geografía de la Universidad Complutense. Univ. Complutense de Madrid, Facultad de Geografía e Historia, Depto. de Geografia Humana. Madrid. (An. Geogr. Univ. Complut.)

Ancient Mesoamerica. Cambridge Univ. Press. Cambridge, England; New York. (Anc. Mesoam.)

Annals of Public and Cooperative Economics. Blackwell Publishers. Oxford, England. (Ann. Public Coop. Econ.)

The Annals of the American Academy of Political and Social Science. American Academy of Political and Social Science. Philadelphia, Pa. (Ann. Am. Acad. Polit. Soc. Sci.)

Annals of the Association of American Geographers. Blackwell Publishers. Oxford, England; Malden, Mass. (Ann. Assoc. Am. Geogr.)

Annals of the Missouri Botanical Garden. Missouri Botanical Garden Press. St. Louis, Mo. (Ann. Mo. Bot. Gard.)

Annual Review of Anthropology. Annual Reviews, Inc. Palo Alto, Calif. (Annu. Rev. Anthropol.)

Anthropologica del Departamento de Ciencias Sociales. Pontificia Univ. Católica del Perú, Depto. de Ciencias Sociales. Lima. (Anthropol. Dep. Cienc. Soc.)

Anthropological Notebooks. Drustvo antropologov Slovenije. Ljubljana, Slovenia. (Anthropol. Noteb.)

Antípoda: Revista de Antropología y Arqueología. Depto. de Antropología, Facultad de Ciencias Sociales, Univ. de los Andes. Bogotá. (Antípoda)

Antipode. Basil Blackwell. Oxford, England; Cambridge, Mass. (Antipode)

Antiquity. Antiquity Publications Ltd. Cambridge, England. (Antiquity/Cambridge)

Anuario de Estudios Centroamericanos. Univ. de Costa Rica. San José. (Anu. Estud. Centroam.)

Anuario Demográfico de Cuba. Dirección de Estadísticas de Población, Dirección General de Estadística, JUCEPLAN. La Habana. (Anu. Demogr. Cuba)

Anuario Estadístico de Cuba. Dirección General de Estadística. La Habana. (Anu. Estad. Cuba)

Anuarios Estadísticos Municipales. Oficina Nacional de Estadísticas. La Habana. (Anu. Estad. Munic.)

Anuarios Estadísticos Provinciales. Oficina Nacional de Estadísticas. La Habana. (Anu. Estad. Provinc.)

Applied Geography. Butterworths. Sevenoaks, England. (Appl. Geogr.)

Apuntes: Revista de Ciencias Sociales.
Univ. del Pacífico, Centro de Investigación. Lima. (Apuntes/Lima)

Archaeology and Anthropology. Walter Roth Museum of Anthropology, Ministry of Culture. Georgetown, Guyana. (Archaeol. Anthropol.)

Archives of Sexual Behavior. Plenum Press. New York, N.Y. (Arch. Sex. Behav.)

Area. Institute of British Geographers. London. (Area/London)

Arqueologia. Univ. Federal do Paraná, Centro de Estudos e Pesquisas Arqueológicas (CEPA). Curitiba, Brazil. (Arqueologia/Curitiba)

Arqueologia do Rio Grande do Sul, Brasil. Instituto Anchietano de Pesquisas. São Leopoldo, Brazil. (Arqueol. Rio Gd. Sul)

Astronomiche Nachrichten. Wiley-VCH. Berlin. (Astron. Nachr.)

Atenea. Univ. de Concepción. Concepción, Chile. (Atenea/Concepción)

Belgeo. KUL (Katholieke Univ. Leuven). Leuven, Belgium. (Belgeo/Leuven)

Belizean Studies. Belizean Institute of Social Research and Action; St. John's College. Belize City. (Belizean Stud.)

Boletim do Museu Paraense Emílio Goeldi Série Ciências Humanas. Museu Paraense Emílio Goeldi. Belém, Brazil. (Bol. Mus. Para. Emílio Goeldi Sér. Ciênc. Hum.)

Boletín Cuatrimestral. Centro de Estudios de la Economía Cubana (CEEC). La Habana. (Bol. Cuatrimestral)

Boletín del Museo Chileno de Arte Precolombino. Santiago, Chile. (Bol. Mus. Chil. Arte Precolomb.)

Bulletin de l'Institut français d'études andines. Lima. (Bull. Inst. fr. étud. andin.)

Bulletin of Latin American Research. Blackwell Publishers. Oxford, England; Malden, Mass. (Bull. Lat. Am. Res.)

Bulletin of the Peabody Museum of Natural History. Peabody Museum of Natural History. New Haven, Conn. (Bull. Peabody Mus. Nat. Hist.)

Cambridge Archaeological Journal. Cambridge Univ. Press. Cambridge, England. (Camb. Archaeol. J.)

Canadian Foreign Policy. Canadian Foreign Policy Publishing Group. Ottawa, Canada. (Can. Foreign Policy)

Canadian Journal of Latin American and Caribbean Studies = Revue canadienne des études latino-américaines et caraïbes. Univ. of Calgary Press. Calgary, Canada. (Can. J. Lat. Am. Caribb. Stud.)

Caribbean Geography. Univ. of the West Indies, Dept. of Geography. Kingston. (Caribb. Geogr.)

Caribbean Studies. Univ. de Puerto Rico, Instituto de Estudios del Caribe. Río Piedras, Puerto Rico. (Caribb. Stud.)

Catauro: Revista Cubana de Antropología. Fundación Fernando Ortiz. La Habana. (Catauro/Habana)

CEPAL Review. UN, Comisión Económica para América Latina (CEPAL). Santiago, Chile. (CEPAL Rev.)

Children's Geographies. Taylor and Francis. Abingdon, England. (Child. Geogr.)

Ciencia y Sociedad. Instituto Tecnológico de Santo Domingo. Santo Domingo. (Cienc. Soc./Santo Domingo)

Climatic Change. Reidel Publishers. Boston, Mass. (Clim. Change)

Colombia Internacional. Univ. de los Andes, Centro de Estudios Internacionales. Bogotá. (Colomb. Int.)

Comparative Politics. City Univ. of New York, Political Science Program. New York. (Comp. Polit./New York)

Competition & Change. Harwood Academic Publishers. Newark, N.J. (Compet. Change)

Contemporary Politics. South Bank Univ. London. (Contemp. Polit./London)

Contexto Internacional. Pontifícia Univ. Católica, Instituto de Relações Internacionais. Rio de Janeiro. (Contexto Int.)

Contributions to Mineralogy and Petrology. Springer. Berlin. (Contrib. Mineral. Petrol.)

Convergencia: Revista de Ciencias Sociales. Univ. Autónoma del Estado de México, Facultad de Ciencias Políticas y Administración Pública. Toluca, Mexico. (Convergencia/Toluca)

Cuadernos Americanos. UNAM. México. (Cuad. Am./México)

Cuadernos de Economía. Univ. Nacional de Colombia, Facultad de Ciencias Económicas, Centro de Investigaciones para el Desarrollo. Bogotá. (Cuad. Econ./Bogotá)

Cuadernos de Economía: Latin American Journal of Economics. Pontificia Univ.

Católica de Chile, Facultad de Ciencias Económicas y Administrativas, Instituto de Economía. Santiago. (Cuad. Econ./Santiago)

Cuadernos del CISH. Univ. Nacional de La Plata, Facultad de Humanidades y Ciencias de la Educación, Centro de Investigaciones Socio Históricas. La Plata, Argentina. (Cuad. CISH)

Cuba in Transition: Papers and Proceedings of the . . . Annual Meeting of the Association for the Study of the Cuban Economy. Assn. for the Study of the Cuban Economy. Washington, D.C. (Cuba Transit.)

Cultural Anthropology: Journal of the Society for Cultural Anthropology. American Anthropological Assn., Society for Cultural Anthropology. Washington, D.C. (Cult. Anthropol.)

Cultural Geographies. Arnold. London. (Cult. Geogr./London)

Current Anthropology. Univ. of Chicago Press. Chicago, Ill. (Curr. Anthropol.)

Current Issues in Tourism. Channel View Books. Clevedon, England; Routledge. Abingdon, England. (Curr. Issues Tour.)

Dados. Instituto Universitário de Pesquisas do Rio de Janeiro. Rio de Janeiro. (Dados/ Rio de Janeiro)

Debate Agrario. Centro Peruano de Estudios Sociales. Lima. (Debate Agrar.)

Democratization. Frank Cass. London. (Democratization/London)

Demography. Population Assn. of America. Washington, D.C. (Demography/Washington)

Desacatos. CIESAS, Centro de Investigaciones y Estudios Superiores en Antropología Social. México. (Desacatos)

Desarrollo Económico: Revista de Ciencias Sociales. Instituto de Desarrollo Económico y Social. Buenos Aires. (Desarro. Econ.)

Development and Change. Blackwell Publishers. Oxford, England; Malden, Mass. (Dev. Change/Oxford)

Development Policy Review. Sage. London. (Dev. Policy Rev.)

Disasters. Blackwell Publishers. Oxford, England. (Disasters)

Diversity. MDPI (Molecular Diversity Preservation International). Basel, Switzerland. (Diversity/Basel)

ECA. Univ. Centroamericana José Simeón Cañas. San Salvador. (ECA/San Salvador)

Ecological Economics: The Journal of the International Society for Ecological Economics. Elsevier. Amsterdam. (Ecol. Econ./Amsterdam)

Economía, Sociedad y Territorio. El Colegio Mexiquense. Toluca, Mexico. (Econ. Soc. Territ.)

Economía Mexicana. Centro de Investigación y Docencia Económicas. México. (Econ. Mex.)

Economic Development and Cultural Change. Univ. of Chicago Press. Chicago, Ill. (Econ. Dev. Cult. Change)

Economic Inquiry. Western Economic Assn. International. Huntington Beach, Calif. (Econ. Inq.)

Economics Press Service. Havana Inter Press Service Tercer Mundo. La Habana. (Econ. Press Serv.)

Ecuador Debate. Centro Andino de Acción Popular. Quito. (Ecuad. Debate)

Ensaios FEE. Governo do Rio Grande do Sul, Secretaria de Coordenação e Planejamento, Fundação de Economia e Estatística Siegfried Emanuel Heuser. Porto Alegre, Brazil. (Ensaios FEE)

Ensayos sobre Política Económica. Banco de la República, Subgerencia de Estudios Económicos. Bogotá. (Ens. Polít. Econ.)

Environmental Conservation. Cambridge Univ. Press. Cambridge, England. (Environ. Conserv./Cambridge)

Environmental Politics. Frank Cass. London. (Environ. Polit.)

Die Erde. W. de Gruyter. Berlin. (Erde/Berlin)

Espacio Abierto: Cuaderno Venezolano de Sociología. Asociación Venezolana de Sociología. Maracaibo, Venezuela; International Sociological Assn. Madrid. (Espac. Abierto)

Espacio Laical. Consejo Arquidiocesano de Laicos de La Habana. La Habana. (Espacio Laical)

Estudios Atacameños. Univ. del Norte, Museo de Arqueología. San Pedro de Atacama, Chile. (Estud. Atacameños)

Estudios de Cultura Maya. UNAM, Instituto de Investigaciones Filológicas, Centro de Estudios Mayas. México. (Estud. Cult. Maya)

Estudios de Cultura Náhuatl. UNAM, Instituto de Investigaciones Históricas. México. (Estud. Cult. Náhuatl)

Estudios Geográficos. Instituto de Economía y Geografía Aplicadas. Madrid. (Estud. Geogr./Madrid)

Estudios Internacionales. Univ. de Chile, Instituto de Estudios Internacionales. Santiago. (Estud. Int./Santiago)

Estudios Jaliscienses. El Colegio de Jalisco. Zapopan, Mexico. (Estud. Jalisc.)

Estudios Migratorios Latinoamericanos. Centro de Estudios Migratorios Latinoamericanos. Buenos Aires. (Estud. Migr. Latinoam.)

Estudios Paraguayos. Univ. Católica Nuestra Señora de la Asunción. Asunción. (Estud. Parag.)

Estudios: Revista del Centro de Estudios Avanzados. Univ. Nacional de Córdoba, Centro de Estudios Avanzados. Córdoba, Argentina. (Estudios/Córdoba)

Estudios Sociales: Revista Universitaria Semestral. Univ. Nacional del Litoral, Secretaría de Extensión, Centro de Publicaciones. Santa Fe, Argentina. (Estud. Soc./Santa Fe)

Estudios Sociológicos. El Colegio de México, Centro de Estudios Sociológicos. México. (Estud. Sociol./México)

Estudios y Perspectivas en Turismo. Centro de Investigaciones y Estudios Turísticos. Buenos Aires. (Estud. Perspect. Turismo)

Estudos Avançados. Univ. de São Paulo, Instituto de Estudos Avançados. São Paulo. (Estud. Av.)

Estudos Históricos. Fundação Getulio Vargas, Centro de Pesquisa e Documentação de História Contemporânea do Brasil. Rio de Janeiro. (Estud. Hist./Rio de Janeiro)

Estudos Ibero-Americanos. Pontificia Univ. Católica do Rio Grande do Sul, Faculdade de Filosofia e Ciências Humanas, Depto. de História, Programa Pós-Graduação em História. Porto Alegre, Brazil. (Estud. Ibero-Am./Porto Alegre)

Ethnic and Racial Studies. Routledge & Kegan Paul. London. (Ethn. Racial Stud.)

Ethnohistory: The Bulletin of the Ohio Valley Historic Indian Conference. American Society for Ethnohistory. Columbus, Ohio. (Ethnohistory/Columbus)

Ethos. Society for Psychological Anthropology; American Anthropological Assn. Arlington, Va. (Ethos/Arlington)

EURE: Revista Latinoamericana de Estudios Urbano Regionales. Pontificia Univ. Católica de Chile, Facultad de Arquitectura y Bellas Artes, Instituto de Estudios Urbanos. Santiago. (EURE/Santiago)

The European Journal of Development Research. Frank Cass. London. (Eur. J. Dev. Res.)

Fermentum: Revista Venezolana de Sociología y Antropología. Univ. de los Andes. Depto. de Humanidades y Educación, Centro e Investigación en Ciencias Humanas. Mérida, Venezuela. (Fermentum/Mérida)

The Fletcher Forum of World Affairs. Fletcher School of Law and Diplomacy. Medford, Mass. (Fletcher Forum World Aff.)

Food Policy. IPC Science and Technology Press. Guilford, England. (Food Policy)

Foro Internacional. El Colegio de México, Centro de Estudios Internacionales. México. (Foro Int./México)

Frontera Norte. El Colegio de la Frontera Norte. Tijuana, Mexico. (Front. Norte)

Futuribles. Association Internationale Futuribles. Paris. (Futuribles/Paris)

Geoarchaeology. John Wiley. New York. (Geoarchaeology/New York)

Geoforum. Pergamon Press. New York; Oxford, England. (Geoforum/New York)

The Geographical Journal. The Royal Geographical Society. London; Institute of British Geographers. Cambridge, England. (Geogr. J./London)

Geographical Review. American Geographical Society. New York. (Geogr. Rev.)

GeoJournal. D. Reidel Publishing Co. Boston, Mass. (GeoJournal/Boston)

Global and Planetary Change. Elsevier. Amsterdam. (Glob. Planet. Change)

Global Health Promotion. Sage. London. (Glob. Health Promot.)

Health Affairs. Project Hope. Millwood, Va. (Health Aff.)

Historia. Pontificia Univ. Católica de Chile, Facultad de Historia, Geografía y Ciencia Política, Instituto de Historia. Santiago. (Historia/Santiago)

Historia Mexicana. El Colegio de México, Centro de Estudios Históricos. México. (Hist. Mex./México)

Historical Methods. Heldref Publications. Washington, D.C. (Hist. Methods)

The Holocene. Edward Arnold. Sevenoaks, England. (Holocene/Sevenoaks)
Human Ecology. Kluwer Academic Publishers. Dordrecht, N.Y. (Hum. Ecol.)
Human Organization. Society for Applied Anthropology. Washington, D.C. (Hum. Organ.)
Human Rights Quarterly. Johns Hopkins Univ. Press. Baltimore, Md. (Hum. Rights Q.)

Iberoamericana: Nordic Journal of Latin American Studies/Revista Nórdica de Estudios Latinoamericanos. Stockholm Univ., Institute of Latin American Studies. Stockholm. (Iberoamericana/Stockholm)
Indiana. Gebr. Mann Verlag. Berlin. (Indiana/Berlin)
Innovations. MIT Press. Cambridge, Mass. (Innovations/Cambridge)
Integración & Comercio. Instituto para la Integración de América Latina, Depto. de Integración y Programas Regionales, Banco Interamericano de Desarrollo = Inter-American Development Bank. Buenos Aires. (Integr. Comer.)
International Affairs. Royal Institute of International Affairs. London. (Int. Aff./London)
International Economic Journal. Korea International Economic Association. Seoul. (Int. Econ. J./Seoul)
International Journal of Cuban Studies. International Institute for the Study of Cuba, London Metropolitan Univ. London. (Int. J. Cuban Stud.)
International Journal of Cultural Studies. Sage. London. (Int. J. Cult. Stud.)
The International Journal of Press/Politics. Sage Publications. Thousand Oaks, Calif. (Int. J. Press/Polit.)
International Journal of Transitional Justice. Oxford Univ. Press. Oxford, England. (Int. J. Transit. Just.)
International Journal of Urban and Regional Research. E. Arnold. London. (Int. J. Urban Reg. Res.)
International Social Security Review. International Security Assn. Geneva. (Int. Soc. Sec. Rev./Geneva)
Investigación & Desarrollo. Univ. del Norte, Dirección de Investigaciones y Proyectos, División de Humanidades y Ciencias Sociales, Centro de Investigaciones en

Desarrollo Humano. Barranquilla, Colombia. (Invest. Desarro./Barranquilla)
Investigaciones Geográficas: Boletín del Instituto de Geografía. UNAM, Instituto de Geografía. México. (Invest. Geogr./México)
Investigaciones Sociales: Revista del Instituto de Investigaciones Histórico Sociales. Univ. Nacional Mayor de San Marcos, Facultad de Ciencias Sociales. Lima. (Investig. Soc./San Marcos)
Irish Studies Review. Irish Studies Review. Newton Park, England. (Ir. Stud. Rev.)
Iztapalapa. Univ. Autónoma Metropolitana—Unidad Iztapalapa, División de Ciencias Sociales y Humanidades. México. (Iztapalapa/México)

Journal for the Study of Religion, Nature and Culture. Equinox Publishing. London. (J. Stud. Relig. Nat. Cult.)
Journal of Agrarian Change. Blackwell Publishers. Oxford, England; Malden, Mass. (J. Agrarian Change)
Journal of Anthropological Archaeology. Academic Press. New York. (J. Anthropol. Archaeol.)
Journal of Archaeological Method and Theory. Plenum Pub. Corp. New York. (J. Archaeol. Method Theory)
Journal of Archaeological Science. Academic Press. New York. (J. Archaeol. Sci.)
Journal of Arid Environments. Academic Press. London. (J. Arid Environ.)
Journal of Black Studies. Sage. Newbury Park, Calif. (J. Black Stud.)
Journal of Caribbean Archaeology. Univ. of Florida, Florida Museum of Natural History. Gainesville. (J. Caribb. Archaeol.)
The Journal of Caribbean History. Univ. of the West Indies Press; Univ. of the West Indies, Dept. of History. Mona, Jamaica. (J. Caribb. Hist.)
Journal of Church and State. Baylor Univ., J.M. Dawson Studies in Church and State. Waco, Tex. (J. Church State)
Journal of Cultural Geography. Popular Culture Assn.; American Culture Assn.; Popular Press, Bowling Green State Univ. Bowling Green, Ohio. (J. Cult. Geogr.)
Journal of Democracy. National Endowment for Democracy, International Forum for Democratic Studies. Washington, D.C.; Johns Hopkins Univ. Press. Baltimore, Md. (J. Democr.)

Journal of Environmental Management. Elsevier. Oxford, England. (J. Environ. Manag.)

Journal of Environmental Planning and Management. Carfax. Abingdon, England. (J. Environ. Plann. Manag.)

Journal of Ethnobiology and Ethnomedicine. Biomed Central. London. (J. Ethnobiol. Ethnomed.)

Journal of Field Archaeology. Boston Univ. Boston, Mass. (J. Field Archaeol.)

Journal of Historical Geography. Academic Press. London; New York. (J. Hist. Geogr.)

Journal of Island & Coastal Archaeology. Taylor & Francis Group. Philadelphia, Pa. (J. Island Coastal Archaeol.)

Journal of Land Use Science. Taylor & Francis. Abingdon, England. (J. Land Use Sci.)

The Journal of Latin American and Caribbean Anthropology. Univ. of California Press, Journals Division. Berkeley. (J. Lat. Am. Caribb. Anthropol.)

Journal of Latin American Cultural Studies. Carfax Publishing. Abingdon, England. (J. Lat. Am. Cult. Stud.)

Journal of Latin American Geography. Conference of Latin Americanist Geographers. Tucson, Ariz. (J. Lat. Am. Geogr.)

Journal of Latin American Studies. Cambridge Univ. Press. Cambridge, England. (J. Lat. Am. Stud.)

The Journal of Peasant Studies. Frank Cass & Co. London. (J. Peasant Stud.)

The Journal of the Royal Anthropological Institute. London. (J. Royal Anthropol. Inst.)

JQS: Journal of Quaternary Science. Quaternary Research Association. Harlow, England. (JQS)

Kañína. Univ. de Costa Rica. San José. (Kañína/San José)

Labour Capital and Society. Centre for Developing-Area Studies, McGill Univ. Montreal, Canada. (Labour Cap. Soc.)

Land Use Policy. Butterworths. Guildford, England. (Land Use Policy)

Latin American and Caribbean Ethnic Studies. Taylor & Francis. Colchester, England. (Lat. Am. Caribb. Ethn. Stud.)

Latin American Antiquity. Society for American Archaeology. Washington, D.C. (Lat. Am. Antiq.)

Latin American Business Review. Business Assn. of Latin American Studies; International Business Press. Binghamton, N.Y. (Lat. Am. Bus. Rev.)

Latin American Perspectives. Sage Publications, Inc. Thousand Oaks, Calif. (Lat. Am. Perspect.)

Latin American Politics and Society. Univ. of Miami, School of Interamerican Studies. Coral Gables, Fla. (Lat. Am. Polit. Soc.)

Latin American Research Review. Latin American Studies Assn.; Univ. of Texas Press. Austin. (LARR)

The Law and Development Review. Berkeley Electronic Press. Berkeley, Calif. (Law Dev. Rev.)

Local Environment. Carfax Pub. Co. Abingdon, England. (Local Environ.)

Lua Nova. Centro de Estudos de Cultura Contemporânea. São Paulo. (Lua Nova)

Lucha Armada en la Argentina. S. Bufano; G. Rot. Buenos Aires. (Lucha Armada Argent.)

Magallania. Instituto de la Patagonia, Univ. de Magallanes. Punta Arenas, Chile. (Magallania/Punta Arenas)

Mayab. Sociedad Española de Estudios Mayas. Madrid. (Mayab/Madrid)

Mesoamérica. Plumsock Mesoamerican Studies. South Woodstock, Vt.; Centro de Investigaciones Regionales de Mesoamérica. Antigua, Guatemala. (Mesoamérica/Antigua)

Mexicon. Verlag Anton Saurwein. Markt Schwaben, Germany. (Mexicon/Germany)

Migraciones Internacionales. El Colegio de la Frontera Norte. Tijuana, Mexico. (Migr. Int.)

NACLA: Report on the Americas. North American Congress on Latin America (NACLA). New York. (NACLA)

Natural Hazards. Kluwer Academic Publishers. Dordrecht, The Netherlands. (Nat. Haz.)

New Left Review. New Left Review, Ltd. London. (New Left Rev.)

Nova Economia. Univ. Federal de Minas Gerais, Faculdade de Ciências Econômicas, Depto. de Ciências Econômicas. Belo Horizonte, Brazil. (Nova Econ./Belo Horizonte)

Novos Estudos CEBRAP. Centro Brasileiro de Análise e Planejamento. São Paulo. (Novos Estud. CEBRAP)
Nueva Antropología. Escuela Nacional de Antropología e Historia. México. (Nueva Antropol./México)
Nueva Sociedad. Fundación Friedrich Ebert. Caracas. (Nueva Soc.)
NWIG: New West Indian Guide/Nieuwe West Indische Gids. Royal Institute of Linguistics and Anthropology, KITLV Press. Leiden, The Netherlands. (NWIG)

Oikos. Editorial Univ. de Antioquia, Programa de Economía. Medellín, Colombia. (Oikos/Medellín)
The Open Area Studies Journal. Bentham Science Publishers. Hilversum, The Netherlands. (Open Area Stud. J.)
Opinião Pública. Univ. Estadual de Campinas, Centro de Estudos de Opinião Pública. Campinas, Brazil. (Opin. Públ.)

Papeles de Geografía. Univ. de Murcia, Facultad de Letras, Depto. de Geografía Física, Humana y Análisis Regional. Murcia, Spain. (Pap. Geogr.)
Papers from the Institute of Archaeology. Institute of Archaeology. London. (Pap. Inst. Archaeol.)
Perfiles Latinoamericanos. Facultad Latinoamericana de Ciencias Sociales (FLACSO). México. (Perf. Latinoam.)
Pesquisas Antropologia. Instituto Anchietano de Pesquisas. São Leopoldo, Brazil. (Pesqui. Antropol.)
Política Exterior. Estudios de Política Exterior S.A. Madrid. (Polít. Exter./Madrid)
Política Internacional. Academia Diplomática del Peru. Lima. (Polít. Int./Lima)
Política y Gestión. Univ. Nacional de General San Martín. Rosario, Argentina. (Polít. Gest.)
Political Geography. Butterworth-Heinemann. Oxford, England. (Polit. Geogr.)
Political Studies. Blackwell Publishers. Oxford, England; Malden, Mass. (Polit. Stud./Oxford)
Politics & Society. Geron-X, Inc. Los Altos, Calif. (Polit. Soc./Los Altos)
Population and Environment. Human Sciences Press. New York. (Popul. Environ.)

Proceedings of the National Academy of Sciences of the United States of America. Washington, D.C. (Proc. Natl. Acad. Sci. U.S.A.)
Procesos. Corporación Editora Nacional. Quito. (Procesos/Quito)
The Professional Geographer. Assn. of American Geographers. Washington, D.C.; Blackwell Publishers. Abindgon, England; Williston, Vt. (Prof. Geogr.)

Región y Sociedad: Revista de El Colegio de Sonora. El Colegio de Sonora. Hermosillo, Mexico. (Reg. Soc./Hermosillo)
Regional Environmental Change. Springer. New York, N.Y. (Reg. Environ. Change)
REIS: Revista Española de Investigaciones Sociológicas. Centro de Investigaciones Sociológicas. Madrid. (Rev. Esp. Invest. Sociol.)
Relaciones Internacionales. UNAM, Facultad de Ciencias Políticas y Sociales, Coordinación de Relaciones Internacionales. México. (Relac. Int./México)
Review of International Political Economy: RIPE. Routledge. London. (Rev. Int. Polit. Econ.)
Review of Political Economy. Edward Arnold. London. (Rev. Polit. Econ.)
The Review of Radical Political Economies. Sage Publications for the Union for Radical Political Economics. Thousand Oaks, Calif. (Rev. Radic. Polit. Econ.)
Revista Brasileira de Economia. Fundação Getúlio Vargas, Escola de Pós-Graduação em Economia. Rio de Janeiro. (Rev. Bras. Econ./Rio de Janeiro)
Revista Brasileira de História. Associação Nacional de História. São Paulo. (Rev. Bras. Hist./São Paulo)
Revista Brasileira de Linguística de Antropólogica. Univ. de Brasília, Laboratório de Línguas Indígenas. Brasília. (Rev. Bras. Linguíst. Antropol.)
Revista Brasileira de Política Internacional: RBPI. Instituto Brasileiro de Relações Internacionais. Brasília. (Rev. Bras. Polít. Int.)
Revista de Antropología Social. Editorial Complutense. Madrid. (Rev. Antropol. Soc.)
Revista de Arqueología Americana. Instituto Panamericano de Geografía e Historia. México. (Rev. Arqueol. Am./México)

Revista de Ciencia Política. Pontificia Univ. Católica de Chile, Instituto de Ciencia Política. Santiago. (Rev. Cienc. Polít./Santiago)

Revista de Ciencias Sociales: RCS. Univ. de Zulia, Facultad de Ciencias Económicas y Sociales, Instituto de Investigaciones. Maracaibo, Venezuela. (Rev. Cienc. Soc./ Maracaibo)

Revista de Economia e Sociologia Rural = Brazilian Review of Agricultural Economics and Rural Sociology. Sociedade Brasileira de Economia e Sociologia Rural = Brazilian Society of Agricultural Economics and Rural Sociology. Brasília. (Rev. Econ. Sociol. Rural)

Revista de Economía Institucional. Univ. Externado de Colombia, Facultad de Economía. Bogotá. (Rev. Econ. Inst.)

Revista de Economia Política = Brazilian Journal of Political Economy. Centro de Economia Política. São Paulo. (Rev. Econ. Polít.)

Revista de Estudios Políticos. Centro de Estudios Políticos y Constitucionales. Madrid. (Rev. Estud. Polít.)

Revista de Geografía Norte Grande. Pontificia Univ. Católica de Chile, Facultad de Historia, Geografía y Ciencia Política, Instituto de Geografía. Santiago. (Rev. Geogr. Norte Gd.)

Revista de Occidente. Fundación José Ortega y Gasset. Madrid. (Rev. Occidente)

Revista do Museu de Arqueologia e Etnologia. Univ. de São Paulo, Museu de Arqueologia e Etnologia. São Paulo. (Rev. Mus. Arqueol. Etnol.)

Revista Enfoques. Facultad de Ciencia Política y Administración Pública, Univ. Central de Chile. Santiago. (Rev. Enfoques/Santiago)

Revista Española de Antropología Americana. Univ. Complutense de Madrid, Facultad de Geografía e Historia, Depto. de Historia de América II (Antropología de América). Madrid. (Rev. Esp. Antropol. Am.)

Revista Europea de Estudios Latinoamericanos y del Caribe = European Review of Latin American and Caribbean Studies. Center for Latin American Research and Documentation = Centro de Estudios y Documentación Latinoamericanos. Amsterdam. (Rev. Eur. Estud. Latinoam. Caribe)

Revista Geofísica. Instituto Panamericano de Geografía e Historia, Comisión de Geofísica. México. (Rev. Geofís.)

Revista Geográfica. Instituto Panamericano de Geografía e Historia. México. (Rev. Geogr./México)

Revista Mexicana de Ciencias Políticas y Sociales. UNAM, Facultad de Ciencias Políticas y Sociales. México. (Rev. Mex. Cienc. Polít. Soc.)

Revista Mexicana de Política Exterior. Instituto Matías Romero de Estudios Diplomáticos. México. (Rev. Mex. Polít. Exter.)

Revista Mexicana de Sociología. UNAM, Instituto de Investigaciones Sociales. México. (Rev. Mex. Sociol.)

Revista Reflexiones. Univ. de Costa Rica, Facultad de Ciencias Sociales. San José. (Rev. Reflex./San José)

Revista Venezolana de Ciencia Política. Univ. de Los Andes, Facultad de Ciencias Jurídicas y Políticas, Centro de Estudios Políticos y Sociales de América Latina. Mérida, Venezuela. (Rev. Venez. Cienc. Polít.)

Revista Venezolana de Economía y Ciencias Sociales. Univ. Central de Venezuela, Facultad de Ciencias Económicas y Sociales, Instituto de Investigaciones Económicas y Sociales Dr. Rodolfo Quintero. Caracas. (Rev. Venez. Econ. Cienc. Soc.)

Revue de géographie alpine. Univ. de Grenoble, Institute de géographie alpine. Grenoble, France. (Rev. géogr. alp.)

The Round Table. Routledge Journals. Abingdon, England. (Round Table/London)

Secuencia: Revista de Historia y Ciencias Sociales. Instituto de Investigaciones Dr. José María Luis Mora. México. (Secuencia/México)

Singapore Journal of Tropical Geography. Blackwell Publishers. Oxford, England; Malden, Mass. (Singap. J. Trop. Geogr.)

Social & Cultural Geography. Routledge Journals. Basingstoke, England. (Soc. Cult. Geogr.)

Social Identities. Taylor and Francis. Abingdon, England. (Soc. Identities)

The Social Science Journal. Elsevier Science, Inc. New York. (Soc. Sci. J./New York)

Socialismo y Participación. Centro de Estudios para el Desarrollo y Participación. Lima. (Social. Particip.)

Sociological Theory. Jossey-Bass. San Francisco, Calif. (Sociol. Theory)

Studies in Comparative International Development. Transaction Publishers. Somerset, N.J. (Stud. Comp. Int. Dev.)

Suplemento Antropológico. Univ. Católica de Nuestra Señora de la Asunción, Centro de Estudios Antropológicos. Asunción. (Supl. Antropol.)

Td: Temas y Debates. Univ. Nacional de Rosario, Facultad de Ciencia Política y Relaciones Internacionales. Rosario, Argentina. (Td Temas Debates)

Temas: Cultura, Ideología, Sociedad. Instituto Cubano del Libro. La Habana; Univ. of New Mexico, Latin American Institute, Cuban Project. Albuquerque, N.M. (Temas/Habana)

Temas de Historia Argentina y Americana. Pontificia Univ. Católica Argentina, Facultad de Filosofía y Letras, Centro de Historia Argentina y Americana. Buenos Aires. (Temas Hist. Argent. Am.)

Third World Quarterly. Taylor & Francis Group, Carfax Publishing. London; New York. (Third World Q.)

Tiempos de América. Univ. Jaume I—Campus de Borriol, Centros de Investigación de América Latina. Castellón, Spain. (Tiempos Am./Castellón)

Tierra Firme. Editorial Tierra Firme. Caracas. (Tierra Firme/Caracas)

T'inkazos: Revista Boliviana de Ciencias Sociales. Programa de Investigación Estratégica en Bolivia. La Paz. (T'inkazos)

Tipití: Journal of the Society for the Anthropology of Lowland South America. Society for the Anthropology of Lowland South America (SALSA). New Orleans, La. (Tipití)

Tourism and Hospitality Research. Sage Publications. Thousand Oaks, Calif. (Tour. Hosp. Res.)

Tourism Geographies. Routledge. London. (Tour. Geogr.)

Trabajo. Centro de Análisis del Trabajo. México. (Trabajo/México)

Transactions—Institute of British Geographers. Institute of British Geographers. Oxford, England. (Trans. Inst. Br. Geogr.)

Transport Reviews. Taylor and Francis. London. (Transp. Rev.)

El Trimestre Económico. Fondo de Cultura Económica. México. (Trimest. Econ.)

Unisa Latin American Report. Univ. of South Africa, Centre for Latin American Studies. Pretoria. (Unisa Lat. Am. Rep.)

Universitas Humanística. Pontificia Univ. Javeriana, Facultad de Filosofía y Letras. Bogotá. (Univ. Humaníst.)

Universum. Univ. de Talca. Talca, Chile. (Universum/Talca)

Urban Geography. V.H. Winston. Silver Spring, Md. (Urban Geogr.)

Urban Studies. Oliver & Boyd. Edinburgh, Scotland. (Urban Stud./Harlow)

Veredas: Revista del Pensamiento Sociológico. Univ. Autónoma Metropolitana. México. (Veredas)

Water Alternatives. Water Alternatives. Montpelier, France. (Water Altern.)

Wayeb Notes. Association européenne de Mayanistes. Bruxelles. (Wayeb Notes)

World Archaeology. Routledge & Kegan Paul. London. (World Archaeol.)

World Development. Elsevier Science; Pergamon Press. Oxford, England. (World Dev.)

The World Economy. Blackwell Publishers. Abingdon, England; Williston, Vt. (World Econ.)

Yaxkin. Instituto Hondureño de Antropología e Historia. Tegucigalpa. (Yaxkin/Tegucigalpa)

Yearbook of the Association of Pacific Coast Geographers. Univ. of Hawaii Press. Honolulu. (Yearb. Assoc. Pac. Coast Geogr.)

ABBREVIATION LIST OF JOURNALS INDEXED

For journal titles listed by full title, see *Title List of Journals Indexed*, p. 575.

Am. Anthropol.   American Anthropologist. American Anthropological Assn. Washington, D.C.

Am. Antiq.   American Antiquity. Society for American Archaeology. Washington, D.C.

Am. Ethnol./Washington.   American Ethnologist. American Anthropological Assn., American Ethnological Society. Washington, D.C.

Am. J. Sociol.   American Journal of Sociology. Univ. of Chicago Press. Chicago, Ill.

Am. Lat. Hoy/Salamanca.   América Latina Hoy: Revista de Ciencias Sociales. Univ. de Salamanca, Instituto de Estudios de Iberoamérica y Portugal. Salamanca, Spain.

Amazôn. Rev. Antropol.   Amazônica: Revista de Antropologia. Univ. Federal do Pará, Instituto de Filosofia e Ciências Humanas. Belem, Brazil.

Ambio/Stockholm.   Ambio. Royal Swedish Academy of Sciences. Stockholm.

An. Arqueol. Etnol.   Anales de Arqueología y Etnología. Univ. Nacional de Cuyo, Facultad de Filosofía y Letras. Mendoza, Argentina.

An. Geogr. Univ. Complut.   Anales de Geografía de la Universidad Complutense. Univ. Complutense de Madrid, Facultad de Geografía e Historia, Depto. de Geografía Humana. Madrid.

Anc. Mesoam.   Ancient Mesoamerica. Cambridge Univ. Press. Cambridge, England; New York.

Ann. Am. Acad. Polit. Soc. Sci.   The Annals of the American Academy of Political and Social Science. American Academy of Political and Social Science. Philadelphia, Pa.

Ann. Assoc. Am. Geogr.   Annals of the Association of American Geographers. Blackwell Publishers. Oxford, England; Malden, Mass.

Ann. Mo. Bot. Gard.   Annals of the Missouri Botanical Garden. Missouri Botanical Garden Press. St. Louis, Mo.

Ann. Public Coop. Econ.   Annals of Public and Cooperative Economics. Blackwell Publishers. Oxford, England.

Annu. Rev. Anthropol.   Annual Review of Anthropology. Annual Reviews, Inc. Palo Alto, Calif.

Anthropol. Dep. Cienc. Soc.   Anthropologica del Departamento de Ciencias Sociales. Pontificia Univ. Católica del Perú, Depto. de Ciencias Sociales. Lima.

Anthropol. Noteb.   Anthropological Notebooks. Drustvo antropologov Slovenije. Ljubljana, Slovenia.

Antípoda.   Antípoda: Revista de Antropología y Arqueología. Depto. de Antropología, Facultad de Ciencias Sociales, Univ. de los Andes. Bogotá.

Antipode. Antipode. Basil Blackwell. Oxford, England; Cambridge, Mass.

Antiquity/Cambridge. Antiquity. Antiquity Publications Ltd. Cambridge, England.

Anu. Demogr. Cuba. Anuario Demográfico de Cuba. Dirección de Estadísticas de Población, Dirección General de Estadística, JUCEPLAN. La Habana.

Anu. Estad. Cuba. Anuario Estadístico de Cuba. Dirección General de Estadística. La Habana.

Anu. Estad. Munic. Anuarios Estadísticos Municipales. Oficina Nacional de Estadísticas. La Habana.

Anu. Estad. Provinc. Anuarios Estadísticos Provinciales. Oficina Nacional de Estadísticas. La Habana.

Anu. Estud. Centroam. Anuario de Estudios Centroamericanos. Univ. de Costa Rica. San José.

Appl. Geogr. Applied Geography. Butterworths. Sevenoaks, England.

Apuntes/Lima. Apuntes: Revista de Ciencias Sociales. Univ. del Pacífico, Centro de Investigación. Lima.

Arch. Sex. Behav. Archives of Sexual Behavior. Plenum Press. New York, N.Y.

Archaeol. Anthropol. Archaeology and Anthropology. Walter Roth Museum of Anthropology, Ministry of Culture. Georgetown, Guyana.

Area/London. Area. Institute of British Geographers. London.

Arqueol. Rio Gd. Sul. Arqueologia do Rio Grande do Sul, Brasil. Instituto Anchietano de Pesquisas. São Leopoldo, Brazil.

Arqueologia/Curitiba. Arqueologia. Univ. Federal do Paraná, Centro de Estudos e Pesquisas Arqueológicas (CEPA). Curitiba, Brazil.

Astron. Nachr. Astronomiche Nachrichten. Wiley-VCH. Berlin.

Atenea/Concepción. Atenea. Univ. de Concepción. Concepción, Chile.

Belgeo/Leuven. Belgeo. KUL (Katholieke Univ. Leuven). Leuven, Belgium.

Belizean Stud. Belizean Studies. Belizean Institute of Social Research and Action; St. John's College. Belize City.

Bol. Cuatrimestral. Boletín Cuatrimestral. Centro de Estudios de la Economía Cubana (CEEC). La Habana.

Bol. Mus. Chil. Arte Precolomb. Boletín del Museo Chileno de Arte Precolombino. Santiago, Chile.

Bol. Mus. Para. Emílio Goeldi Sér. Ciênc. Hum. Boletim do Museu Paraense Emílio Goeldi Série Ciências Humanas. Museu Paraense Emílio Goeldi. Belém, Brazil.

Bull. Inst. fr. étud. andin. Bulletin de l'Institut français d'études andines. Lima.

Bull. Lat. Am. Res. Bulletin of Latin American Research. Blackwell Publishers. Oxford, England; Malden, Mass.

Bull. Peabody Mus. Nat. Hist. Bulletin of the Peabody Museum of Natural History. Peabody Museum of Natural History. New Haven, Conn.

Camb. Archaeol. J. Cambridge Archaeological Journal. Cambridge Univ. Press. Cambridge, England.

Can. Foreign Policy. Canadian Foreign Policy. Canadian Foreign Policy Publishing Group. Ottawa, Canada.

Can. J. Lat. Am. Caribb. Stud. Canadian Journal of Latin American and Caribbean Studies = Revue canadienne des études latino-américaines et caraïbes. Univ. of Calgary Press. Calgary, Canada.

Caribb. Geogr. Caribbean Geography. Univ. of the West Indies, Dept. of Geography. Kingston.

Caribb. Stud. Caribbean Studies. Univ. de Puerto Rico, Instituto de Estudios del Caribe. Río Piedras, Puerto Rico.

Catauro/Habana. Catauro: Revista Cubana de Antropología. Fundación Fernando Ortiz. La Habana.

CEPAL Rev. CEPAL Review. UN, Comisión Económica para América Latina (CEPAL). Santiago, Chile.

Child. Geogr. Children's Geographies. Taylor and Francis. Abingdon, England.

Cienc. Soc./Santo Domingo. Ciencia y Sociedad. Instituto Tecnológico de Santo Domingo. Santo Domingo.

Clim. Change. Climatic Change. Reidel Publishers. Boston, Mass.

Colomb. Int. Colombia Internacional. Univ. de los Andes, Centro de Estudios Internacionales. Bogotá.

Comp. Polit./New York. Comparative Politics. City Univ. of New York, Political Science Program. New York.

Compet. Change. Competition & Change. Harwood Academic Publishers. Newark, N.J.

Contemp. Polit./London. Contemporary Politics. South Bank Univ. London.

Contexto Int. Contexto Internacional. Pontifícia Univ. Católica, Instituto de Relações Internacionais. Rio de Janeiro.

Contrib. Mineral. Petrol. Contributions to Mineralogy and Petrology. Springer. Berlin.

Convergencia/Toluca. Convergencia: Revista de Ciencias Sociales. Univ. Autónoma del Estado de México, Facultad de Ciencias Políticas y Administración Pública. Toluca, Mexico.

Cuad. Am./México. Cuadernos Americanos. UNAM. México.

Cuad. CISH. Cuadernos del CISH. Univ. Nacional de La Plata, Facultad de Humani-dades y Ciencias de la Educación, Centro de Investigaciones Socio Históricas. La Plata, Argentina.

Cuad. Econ./Bogotá. Cuadernos de Economía. Univ. Nacional de Colombia, Facultad de Ciencias Económicas, Centro de Investigaciones para el Desarrollo. Bogotá.

Cuad. Econ./Santiago. Cuadernos de Economía: Latin American Journal of Economics. Pontificia Univ. Católica de Chile, Facultad de Ciencias Económicas y Administrativas, Instituto de Economía. Santiago.

Cuba Transit. Cuba in Transition: Papers and Proceedings of the . . . Annual Meeting of the Association for the Study of the Cuban Economy. Assn. for the Study of the Cuban Economy. Washington, D.C.

Cult. Anthropol. Cultural Anthropology: Journal of the Society for Cultural Anthropology. American Anthropological Assn., Society for Cultural Anthropology. Washington, D.C.

Cult. Geogr./London. Cultural Geographies. Arnold. London.

Curr. Anthropol. Current Anthropology. Univ. of Chicago Press. Chicago, Ill.

Curr. Issues Tour. Current Issues in Tourism. Channel View Books. Clevedon, England; Routledge. Abingdon, England.

Dados/Rio de Janeiro. Dados. Instituto Universitário de Pesquisas do Rio de Janeiro. Rio de Janeiro.

Debate Agrar. Debate Agrario. Centro Peruano de Estudios Sociales. Lima.

Democratization/London. Democratization. Frank Cass. London.

Demography/Washington. Demography. Population Assn. of America. Washington, D.C.

Desacatos. Desacatos. CIESAS, Centro de Investigaciones y Estudios Superiores en Antropología Social. México.

Desarro. Econ. Desarrollo Económico: Revista de Ciencias Sociales. Instituto de Desarrollo Económico y Social. Buenos Aires.

Dev. Change/Oxford. Development and Change. Blackwell Publishers. Oxford, England; Malden, Mass.

Dev. Policy Rev. Development Policy Review. Sage. London.

Disasters. Disasters. Blackwell Publishers. Oxford, England.

Diversity/Basel. Diversity. MDPI (Molecular Diversity Preservation International). Basel, Switzerland.

ECA/San Salvador. ECA. Univ. Centroamericana José Simeón Cañas. San Salvador.

Ecol. Econ./Amsterdam. Ecological Economics: The Journal of the International Society for Ecological Economics. Elsevier. Amsterdam.

Econ. Dev. Cult. Change. Economic Development and Cultural Change. Univ. of Chicago Press. Chicago, Ill.

Econ. Inq. Economic Inquiry. Western Economic Assn. International. Huntington Beach, Calif.

Econ. Mex. Economía Mexicana. Centro de Investigación y Docencia Económicas. México.

Econ. Press Serv. Economics Press Service. Havana Inter Press Service Tercer Mundo. La Habana.

Econ. Soc. Territ. Economía, Sociedad y Territorio. El Colegio Mexiquense. Toluca, Mexico.

Ecuad. Debate. Ecuador Debate. Centro Andino de Acción Popular. Quito.

Ens. Polít. Econ. Ensayos sobre Política Económica. Banco de la República, Subgerencia de Estudios Económicos. Bogotá.

Ensaios FEE. Ensaios FEE. Governo do Rio Grande do Sul, Secretaria de Coordenação e Planejamento, Fundação de Economia e Estatística Siegfried Emanuel Heuser. Porto Alegre, Brazil.

Environ. Conserv./Cambridge. Environmental Conservation. Cambridge Univ. Press. Cambridge, England.

Environ. Polit. Environmental Politics. Frank Cass. London.

Erde/Berlin. Die Erde. W. de Gruyter. Berlin.

Espac. Abierto. Espacio Abierto: Cuaderno Venezolano de Sociología. Asociación Venezolana de Sociología. Maracaibo, Venezuela; International Sociological Assn. Madrid.

Espacio Laical. Espacio Laical. Consejo Arquidiocesano de Laicos de La Habana. La Habana.

Estud. Atacameños. Estudios Atacameños. Univ. del Norte, Museo de Arqueología. San Pedro de Atacama, Chile.

Estud. Av. Estudos Avançados. Univ. de São Paulo, Instituto de Estudos Avançados. São Paulo.

Estud. Cult. Maya. Estudios de Cultura Maya. UNAM, Instituto de Investigaciones Filológicas, Centro de Estudios Mayas. México.

Estud. Cult. Náhuatl. Estudios de Cultura Náhuatl. UNAM, Instituto de Investigaciones Históricas. México.

Estud. Geogr./Madrid. Estudios Geográficos. Instituto de Economía y Geografía Aplicadas. Madrid.

Estud. Hist./Rio de Janeiro. Estudos Históricos. Fundação Getulio Vargas, Centro de Pesquisa e Documentação de História Contemporânea do Brasil. Rio de Janeiro.

Estud. Ibero-Am./Porto Alegre. Estudos Ibero-Americanos. Pontificia Univ. Católica do Rio Grande do Sul, Faculdade de Filosofia e Ciências Humanas, Depto. de História, Programa Pós-Graduação em História. Porto Alegre, Brazil.

Estud. Int./Santiago. Estudios Internacionales. Univ. de Chile, Instituto de Estudios Internacionales. Santiago.

Estud. Jalisc. Estudios Jaliscienses. El Colegio de Jalisco. Zapopan, Mexico.

Estud. Migr. Latinoam. Estudios Migratorios Latinoamericanos. Centro de Estudios Migratorios Latinoamericanos. Buenos Aires.

Estud. Parag. Estudios Paraguayos. Univ. Católica Nuestra Señora de la Asunción. Asunción.

Estud. Perspect. Turismo. Estudios y Perspectivas en Turismo. Centro de Investigaciones y Estudios Turísticos. Buenos Aires.

Estud. Soc./Santa Fe. Estudios Sociales: Revista Universitaria Semestral. Univ. Nacional del Litoral, Secretaría de Extensión, Centro de Publicaciones. Santa Fe, Argentina.

Estud. Sociol./México. Estudios Sociológicos. El Colegio de México, Centro de Estudios Sociológicos. México.

Estudios/Córdoba. Estudios: Revista del Centro de Estudios Avanzados. Univ. Nacional de Córdoba, Centro de Estudios Avanzados. Córdoba, Argentina.

Ethn. Racial Stud. Ethnic and Racial Studies. Routledge & Kegan Paul. London.

Ethnohistory/Columbus. Ethnohistory: The Bulletin of the Ohio Valley Historic Indian Conference. American Society for Ethnohistory. Columbus, Ohio.

Ethos/Arlington. Ethos. Society for Psychological Anthropology; American Anthropological Assn. Arlington, Va.

Eur. J. Dev. Res. The European Journal of Development Research. Frank Cass. London.

EURE/Santiago. EURE: Revista Latinoamericana de Estudios Urbano Regionales. Pontificia Univ. Católica de Chile, Facultad de Arquitectura y Bellas Artes, Instituto de Estudios Urbanos. Santiago.

Fermentum/Mérida. Fermentum: Revista Venezolana de Sociología y Antropología. Univ. de los Andes. Depto. de Humanidades y Educación, Centro e Investigación en Ciencias Humanas. Mérida, Venezuela.

Fletcher Forum World Aff. The Fletcher Forum of World Affairs. Fletcher School of Law and Diplomacy. Medford, Mass.

Food Policy. Food Policy. IPC Science and Technology Press. Guilford, England.

Foro Int./México. Foro Internacional. El Colegio de México, Centro de Estudios Internacionales. México.

Front. Norte. Frontera Norte. El Colegio de la Frontera Norte. Tijuana, Mexico.

Futuribles/Paris. Futuribles. Association Internationale Futuribles. Paris.

Geoarchaeology/New York. Geoarchaeology. John Wiley. New York.

Geoforum/New York. Geoforum. Pergamon Press. New York; Oxford, England.

Geogr. J./London. The Geographical Journal. The Royal Geographical Society. London; Institute of British Geographers. Cambridge, England.

Geogr. Rev. Geographical Review. American Geographical Society. New York.

GeoJournal/Boston. GeoJournal. D. Reidel Publishing Co. Boston, Mass.

Glob. Health Promot. Global Health Promotion. Sage. London.

Glob. Planet. Change. Global and Planetary Change. Elsevier. Amsterdam.

Health Aff. Health Affairs. Project Hope. Millwood, Va.

Hist. Methods. Historical Methods. Heldref Publications. Washington, D.C.

Hist. Mex./México. Historia Mexicana. El Colegio de México, Centro de Estudios Históricos. México.

Historia/Santiago. Historia. Pontificia Univ. Católica de Chile, Facultad de Historia, Geografía y Ciencia Política, Instituto de Historia. Santiago.

Holocene/Sevenoaks. The Holocene. Edward Arnold. Sevenoaks, England.

Hum. Ecol. Human Ecology. Kluwer Academic Publishers. Dordrecht, N.Y.

Hum. Organ. Human Organization. Society for Applied Anthropology. Washington, D.C.

Hum. Rights Q. Human Rights Quarterly. Johns Hopkins Univ. Press. Baltimore, Md.

Iberoamericana/Stockholm. Iberoamericana: Nordic Journal of Latin American Studies/Revista Nórdica de Estudios Latinoamericanos. Stockholm Univ., Institute of Latin American Studies. Stockholm.

Indiana/Berlin. Indiana. Gebr. Mann Verlag. Berlin.

Innovations/Cambridge. Innovations. MIT Press. Cambridge, Mass.

Int. Aff./London. International Affairs. Royal Institute of International Affairs. London.

Int. Econ. J./Seoul. International Economic Journal. Korea International Economic Association. Seoul.

Int. J. Cuban Stud. International Journal of Cuban Studies. International Institute for the Study of Cuba, London Metropolitan Univ. London.

Int. J. Cult. Stud. International Journal of Cultural Studies. Sage. London.

Int. J. Press/Polit. The International Journal of Press/Politics. Sage Publications. Thousand Oaks, Calif.

Int. J. Transit. Just. International Journal of Transitional Justice. Oxford Univ. Press. Oxford, England.

Int. J. Urban Reg. Res. International Journal of Urban and Regional Research. E. Arnold. London.

Int. Soc. Sec. Rev./Geneva. International Social Security Review. International Security Assn. Geneva.

Integr. Comer. Integración & Comercio. Instituto para la Integración de América Latina, Depto. de Integración y Programas Regionales, Banco Interamericano de Desarrollo = Inter-American Development Bank. Buenos Aires.

Invest. Desarro./Barranquilla. Investigación & Desarrollo. Univ. del Norte, Dirección de Investigaciones y Proyectos, División de Humanidades y Ciencias Sociales, Centro de Investigaciones en Desarrollo Humano. Barranquilla, Colombia.

Invest. Geogr./México. Investigaciones Geográficas: Boletín del Instituto de Geografía. UNAM, Instituto de Geografía. México.

Investig. Soc./San Marcos. Investigaciones Sociales: Revista del Instituto de Investigaciones Histórico Sociales. Univ. Nacional Mayor de San Marcos, Facultad de Ciencias Sociales. Lima.

Ir. Stud. Rev. Irish Studies Review. Irish Studies Review. Newton Park, England.

Iztapalapa/México. Iztapalapa. Univ. Autónoma Metropolitana—Unidad Iztapalapa, División de Ciencias Sociales y Humanidades. México.

J. Agrarian Change. Journal of Agrarian Change. Blackwell Publishers. Oxford, England; Malden, Mass.

J. Anthropol. Archaeol. Journal of Anthropological Archaeology. Academic Press. New York.

J. Archaeol. Method Theory. Journal of Archaeological Method and Theory. Plenum Pub. Corp. New York.

J. Archaeol. Sci. Journal of Archaeological Science. Academic Press. New York.

J. Arid Environ. Journal of Arid Environments. Academic Press. London.

J. Black Stud. Journal of Black Studies. Sage. Newbury Park, Calif.

J. Caribb. Archaeol. Journal of Caribbean Archaeology. Univ. of Florida, Florida Museum of Natural History. Gainesville.

J. Caribb. Hist. The Journal of Caribbean History. Univ. of the West Indies Press; Univ. of the West Indies, Dept. of History. Mona, Jamaica.

J. Church State. Journal of Church and State. Baylor Univ., J.M. Dawson Studies in Church and State. Waco, Tex.

J. Cult. Geogr. Journal of Cultural Geography. Popular Culture Assn.; American Culture Assn.; Popular Press, Bowling Green State Univ. Bowling Green, Ohio.

J. Democr. Journal of Democracy. National Endowment for Democracy, International Forum for Democratic Studies. Washington, D.C.; Johns Hopkins Univ. Press. Baltimore, Md.

J. Environ. Manag. Journal of Environmental Management. Elsevier. Oxford, England.

J. Environ. Plann. Manag. Journal of Environmental Planning and Management. Carfax. Abingdon, England.

J. Ethnobiol. Ethnomed. Journal of Ethnobiology and Ethnomedicine. Biomed Central. London.

J. Field Archaeol. Journal of Field Archaeology. Boston Univ. Boston, Mass.

J. Hist. Geogr. Journal of Historical Geography. Academic Press. London; New York.

J. Island Coastal Archaeol. Journal of Island & Coastal Archaeology. Taylor & Francis Group. Philadelphia, Pa.

J. Land Use Sci. Journal of Land Use Science. Taylor & Francis. Abingdon, England.

J. Lat. Am. Caribb. Anthropol. The Journal of Latin American and Caribbean Anthropology. Univ. of California Press, Journals Division. Berkeley.

J. Lat. Am. Cult. Stud. Journal of Latin American Cultural Studies. Carfax Publishing. Abingdon, England.

J. Lat. Am. Geogr. Journal of Latin American Geography. Conference of Latin Americanist Geographers. Tucson, Ariz.

J. Lat. Am. Stud. Journal of Latin American Studies. Cambridge Univ. Press. Cambridge, England.

J. Peasant Stud. The Journal of Peasant Studies. Frank Cass & Co. London.

J. Royal Anthropol. Inst. The Journal of the Royal Anthropological Institute. London.

J. Stud. Relig. Nat. Cult. Journal for the Study of Religion, Nature and Culture. Equinox Publishing. London.

JQS. JQS: Journal of Quaternary Science. Quaternary Research Association. Harlow, England.

Kañína/San José. Kañína. Univ. de Costa Rica. San José.

Labour Cap. Soc. Labour Capital and Society. Centre for Developing-Area Studies, McGill Univ. Montreal, Canada.

Land Use Policy. Land Use Policy. Butterworths. Guildford, England.

LARR. Latin American Research Review. Latin American Studies Assn.; Univ. of Texas Press. Austin.

Lat. Am. Antiq. Latin American Antiquity. Society for American Archaeology. Washington, D.C.

Lat. Am. Bus. Rev. Latin American Business Review. Business Assn. of Latin American Studies; International Business Press. Binghamton, N.Y.

Lat. Am. Caribb. Ethn. Stud. Latin American and Caribbean Ethnic Studies. Taylor & Francis. Colchester, England.

Lat. Am. Perspect. Latin American Perspectives. Sage Publications, Inc. Thousand Oaks, Calif.

Lat. Am. Polit. Soc. Latin American Politics and Society. Univ. of Miami, School of Interamerican Studies. Coral Gables, Fla.

Law Dev. Rev. The Law and Development Review. Berkeley Electronic Press. Berkeley, Calif.

Local Environ. Local Environment. Carfax Pub. Co. Abingdon, England.

Lua Nova. Lua Nova. Centro de Estudos de Cultura Contemporânea. São Paulo.

Lucha Armada Argent. Lucha Armada en la Argentina. S. Bufano; G. Rot. Buenos Aires.

Magallania/Punta Arenas. Magallania. Instituto de la Patagonia, Univ. de Magallanes. Punta Arenas, Chile.

Mayab/Madrid. Mayab. Sociedad Española de Estudios Mayas. Madrid.

Mesoamérica/Antigua. Mesoamérica. Plumsock Mesoamerican Studies. South Woodstock, Vt.; Centro de Investigaciones Regionales de Mesoamérica. Antigua, Guatemala.

Mexicon/Germany. Mexicon. Verlag Anton Saurwein. Markt Schwaben, Germany.

Migr. Int. Migraciones Internacionales. El Colegio de la Frontera Norte. Tijuana, Mexico.

NACLA. NACLA: Report on the Americas. North American Congress on Latin America (NACLA). New York.

Nat. Haz. Natural Hazards. Kluwer Academic Publishers. Dordrecht, The Netherlands.

New Left Rev. New Left Review. New Left Review, Ltd. London.

Nova Econ./Belo Horizonte. Nova Economia. Univ. Federal de Minas Gerais, Faculdade de Ciências Econômicas, Depto. de Ciências Econômicas. Belo Horizonte, Brazil.

Novos Estud. CEBRAP. Novos Estudos CEBRAP. Centro Brasileiro de Análise e Planejamento. São Paulo.

Nueva Antropol./México. Nueva Antropología. Escuela Nacional de Antropología e Historia. México.

Nueva Soc. Nueva Sociedad. Fundación Friedrich Ebert. Caracas.

NWIG. NWIG: New West Indian Guide/Nieuwe West Indische Gids. Royal Institute of Linguistics and Anthropology, KITLV Press. Leiden, The Netherlands.

Oikos/Medellín. Oikos. Editorial Univ. de Antioquia, Programa de Economía. Medellín, Colombia.

Open Area Stud. J. The Open Area Studies Journal. Bentham Science Publishers. Hilversum, The Netherlands.

Opin. Públ. Opinião Pública. Univ. Estadual de Campinas, Centro de Estudos de Opinião Pública. Campinas, Brazil.

Pap. Geogr. Papeles de Geografía. Univ. de Murcia, Facultad de Letras, Depto. de Geografía Física, Humana y Análisis Regional. Murcia, Spain.

Pap. Inst. Archaeol. Papers from the Institute of Archaeology. Institute of Archaeology. London.

Perf. Latinoam. Perfiles Latinoamericanos. Facultad Latinoamericana de Ciencias Sociales (FLACSO). México.

Pesqui. Antropol. Pesquisas Antropologia. Instituto Anchietano de Pesquisas. São Leopoldo, Brazil.

Polít. Exter./Madrid. Política Exterior. Estudios de Política Exterior S.A. Madrid.

Polit. Geogr. Political Geography. Butter-worth-Heinemann. Oxford, England.

Polít. Gest. Política y Gestión. Univ. Nacional de General San Martín. Rosario, Argentina.

Polít. Int./Lima. Política Internacional. Academia Diplomática del Peru. Lima.

Polit. Soc./Los Altos. Politics & Society. Geron-X, Inc. Los Altos, Calif.

Polit. Stud./Oxford. Political Studies. Blackwell Publishers. Oxford, England; Malden, Mass.

Popul. Environ. Population and Environment. Human Sciences Press. New York.

Proc. Natl. Acad. Sci. U.S.A. Proceedings of the National Academy of Sciences of the United States of America. Washington, D.C.

Procesos/Quito. Procesos. Corporación Editora Nacional. Quito.

Prof. Geogr. The Professional Geographer. Assn. of American Geographers. Washington, D.C.; Blackwell Publishers. Abindgon, England; Williston, Vt.

Reg. Environ. Change. Regional Environmental Change. Springer. New York, N.Y.

Reg. Soc./Hermosillo. Región y Sociedad: Revista de El Colegio de Sonora. El Colegio de Sonora. Hermosillo, Mexico.

Relac. Int./México. Relaciones Internacionales. UNAM, Facultad de Ciencias Políticas y Sociales, Coordinación de Relaciones Internacionales. México.

Rev. Antropol. Soc. Revista de Antropología Social. Editorial Complutense. Madrid.

Rev. Arqueol. Am./México. Revista de Arqueología Americana. Instituto Panamericano de Geografía e Historia. México.

Rev. Bras. Econ./Rio de Janeiro. Revista Brasileira de Economia. Fundação Getúlio Vargas, Escola de Pós-Graduação em Economia. Rio de Janeiro.

Rev. Bras. Hist./São Paulo. Revista Brasileira de História. Associação Nacional de História. São Paulo.

Rev. Bras. Linguíst. Antropol. Revista Brasileira de Linguística de Antropólogica. Univ. de Brasilia, Laboratório de Línguas Indígenas. Brasilia.

Rev. Bras. Polít. Int. Revista Brasileira de Política Internacional: RBPI. Instituto Brasileiro de Relações Internacionais. Brasília.

Rev. Cienc. Polít./Santiago. Revista de Ciencia Política. Pontificia Univ. Católica de Chile, Instituto de Ciencia Política. Santiago.

Rev. Cienc. Soc./Maracaibo. Revista de Ciencias Sociales: RCS. Univ. de Zulia, Facultad de Ciencias Económicas y Sociales, Instituto de Investigaciones. Maracaibo, Venezuela.

Rev. Econ. Inst. Revista de Economía Institucional. Univ. Externado de Colombia, Facultad de Economía. Bogotá.

Rev. Econ. Polít. Revista de Economia Política = Brazilian Journal of Political Economy. Centro de Economia Política. São Paulo.

Rev. Econ. Sociol. Rural. Revista de Economia e Sociologia Rural = Brazilian Review of Agricultural Economics and Rural Sociology. Sociedade Brasileira de Economia e Sociologia Rural = Brazilian Society of Agricultural Economics and Rural Sociology. Brasília.

Rev. Enfoques/Santiago. Revista Enfoques. Facultad de Ciencia Política y Administración Pública, Univ. Central de Chile. Santiago.

Rev. Esp. Antropol. Am. Revista Española de Antropología Americana. Univ. Complutense de Madrid, Facultad de Geografía e Historia, Depto. de Historia de América II (Antropología de América). Madrid.

Rev. Esp. Invest. Sociol. REIS: Revista Española de Investigaciones Sociológicas.

Centro de Investigaciones Sociológicas. Madrid.

Rev. Estud. Polít. Revista de Estudios Políticos. Centro de Estudios Políticos y Constitucionales. Madrid.

Rev. Eur. Estud. Latinoam. Caribe. Revista Europea de Estudios Latinoamericanos y del Caribe = European Review of Latin American and Caribbean Studies. Center for Latin American Research and Documentation = Centro de Estudios y Documentación Latinoamericanos. Amsterdam.

Rev. Geofís. Revista Geofísica. Instituto Panamericano de Geografía e Historia, Comisión de Geofísica. México.

Rev. géogr. alp. Revue de géographie alpine. Univ. de Grenoble, Institute de géographie alpine. Grenoble, France.

Rev. Geogr./México. Revista Geográfica. Instituto Panamericano de Geografía e Historia. México.

Rev. Geogr. Norte Gd. Revista de Geografía Norte Grande. Pontificia Univ. Católica de Chile, Facultad de Historia, Geografía y Ciencia Política, Instituto de Geografía. Santiago.

Rev. Int. Polit. Econ. Review of International Political Economy: RIPE. Routledge. London.

Rev. Mex. Cienc. Polít. Soc. Revista Mexicana de Ciencias Políticas y Sociales. UNAM, Facultad de Ciencias Políticas y Sociales. México.

Rev. Mex. Polít. Exter. Revista Mexicana de Política Exterior. Instituto Matías Romero de Estudios Diplomáticos. México.

Rev. Mex. Sociol. Revista Mexicana de Sociología. UNAM, Instituto de Investigaciones Sociales. México.

Rev. Mus. Arqueol. Etnol. Revista do Museu de Arqueologia e Etnologia. Univ. de São Paulo, Museu de Arqueologia e Etnologia. São Paulo.

Rev. Occidente. Revista de Occidente. Fundación José Ortega y Gasset. Madrid.

Rev. Polit. Econ. Review of Political Economy. Edward Arnold. London.

Rev. Radic. Polit. Econ. The Review of Radical Political Economies. Sage Publications for the Union for Radical Political Economics. Thousand Oaks, Calif.

Rev. Reflex./San José. Revista Reflexiones. Univ. de Costa Rica, Facultad de Ciencias Sociales. San José.

Rev. Venez. Cienc. Polít. Revista Venezolana de Ciencia Política. Univ. de Los Andes, Facultad de Ciencias Jurídicas y Políticas, Centro de Estudios Políticos y Sociales de América Latina. Mérida, Venezuela.

Rev. Venez. Econ. Cienc. Soc. Revista Venezolana de Economía y Ciencias Sociales. Univ. Central de Venezuela, Facultad de Ciencias Económicas y Sociales, Instituto de Investigaciones Económicas y Sociales Dr. Rodolfo Quintero. Caracas.

Round Table/London. The Round Table. Routledge Journals. Abingdon, England.

Secuencia/México. Secuencia: Revista de Historia y Ciencias Sociales. Instituto de Investigaciones Dr. José María Luis Mora. México.

Singap. J. Trop. Geogr. Singapore Journal of Tropical Geography. Blackwell Publishers. Oxford, England; Malden, Mass.

Soc. Cult. Geogr. Social & Cultural Geography. Routledge Journals. Basingstoke, England.

Soc. Identities. Social Identities. Taylor and Francis. Abingdon, England.

Soc. Sci. J./New York. The Social Science Journal. Elsevier Science, Inc. New York.

Social. Particip. Socialismo y Participación. Centro de Estudios para el Desarrollo y Participación. Lima.

Sociol. Theory. Sociological Theory. Jossey-Bass. San Francisco, Calif.

Stud. Comp. Int. Dev. Studies in Comparative International Development. Transaction Publishers. Somerset, N.J.

Supl. Antropol. Suplemento Antropológico. Univ. Católica de Nuestra Señora de la Asunción, Centro de Estudios Antropológicos. Asunción.

Td Temas Debates. Td: Temas y Debates. Univ. Nacional de Rosario, Facultad de Ciencia Política y Relaciones Internacionales. Rosario, Argentina.

Temas/Habana. Temas: Cultura, Ideología, Sociedad. Instituto Cubano del Libro. La Habana; Univ. of New Mexico, Latin American Institute, Cuban Project. Albuquerque, N.M.

Temas Hist. Argent. Am. Temas de Historia Argentina y Americana. Pontificia Univ. Católica Argentina, Facultad de Filosofía y Letras, Centro de Historia Argentina y Americana. Buenos Aires.

Third World Q. Third World Quarterly. Taylor & Francis Group, Carfax Publishing. London; New York.

Tiempos Am./Castellón. Tiempos de América. Univ. Jaume I—Campus de Borriol, Centros de Investigación de América Latina. Castellón, Spain.

Tierra Firme/Caracas. Tierra Firme. Editorial Tierra Firme. Caracas.

T'inkazos. T'inkazos: Revista Boliviana de Ciencias Sociales. Programa de Investigación Estratégica en Bolivia. La Paz.

Tipití. Tipití: Journal of the Society for the Anthropology of Lowland South America. Society for the Anthropology of Lowland South America (SALSA). New Orleans, La.

Tour. Geogr. Tourism Geographies. Routledge. London.

Tour. Hosp. Res. Tourism and Hospitality Research. Sage Publications. Thousand Oaks, Calif.

Trabajo/México. Trabajo. Centro de Análisis del Trabajo. México.

Trans. Inst. Br. Geogr. Transactions—Institute of British Geographers. Institute of British Geographers. Oxford, England.

Transp. Rev. Transport Reviews. Taylor and Francis. London.

Trimest. Econ. El Trimestre Económico. Fondo de Cultura Económica. México.

Unisa Lat. Am. Rep. Unisa Latin American Report. Univ. of South Africa, Centre for Latin American Studies. Pretoria.

Univ. Humaníst. Universitas Humanística. Pontificia Univ. Javeriana, Facultad de Filosofía y Letras. Bogotá.

Universum/Talca. Universum. Univ. de Talca. Talca, Chile.

Urban Geogr. Urban Geography. V.H. Winston. Silver Spring, Md.

Urban Stud./Harlow. Urban Studies. Oliver & Boyd. Edinburgh, Scotland.

Veredas. Veredas: Revista del Pensamiento Sociológico. Univ. Autónoma Metropolitana. México.

Water Altern. Water Alternatives. Water Alternatives. Montpelier, France.

Wayeb Notes. Wayeb Notes. Association européenne de Mayanistes. Bruxelles.

World Archaeol. World Archaeology. Routledge & Kegan Paul. London.

World Dev. World Development. Elsevier Science; Pergamon Press. Oxford, England.

World Econ. The World Economy. Blackwell Publishers. Abingdon, England; Williston, Vt.

Yaxkin/Tegucigalpa. Yaxkin. Instituto Hondureño de Antropología e Historia. Tegucigalpa.

Yearb. Assoc. Pac. Coast Geogr. Yearbook of the Association of Pacific Coast Geographers. Univ. of Hawaii Press. Honolulu.

SUBJECT INDEX

Chomsky, Noam, 496
Choquequirao Site (Peru), 409
Chorti (indigenous group). Ethnic Identity, 170, 493. Language and Languages, 170, 493. Social Conditions, 170, 493
Christianity, 2245, 2250, 2259, 2261. Bolivia, 633. Brazil, 2591. Colombia, 2457. Guatemala, 494, 521. Historiography, 2591. Indigenous Peoples, 545. Mexico, 473, 2283, 2355. *See Also* Religious Life and Customs.
Chupicuaro Site (Mexico), 19
Church-State Relations. Mexico, 1063, 1106
Cihuatán Site (El Salvador), 100
Cinema. *See* Film.
Cities and Towns, 685, 691, 700, 704, 2253. Amazon Basin, 1032. Andean Region, 288. Argentina, 939. Caribbean Area, 720. Mesoamerica, 7, 288. Mexico, 815
Citizenship, 1040, 2258. Bolivia, 625, 1312. Caribbean Area, 2423. Cuba, 1220. Ecuador, 578, 2499. Guatemala, 1156. Mexico, 1057, 1156, 2364. Spain, 2499
City Planning, 685. Argentina, 926, 939. Brazil, 981, 1028, 2156. Chile, 960. Colombia, 840, 849, 852, 1233. Ecuador, 861. Mexico, 807, 813. Venezuela, 833, 2490. *See Also* Cities and Towns; Urbanization.
Ciudad Juárez, Mexico (city). Crime, 2356. Police, 2356. Violence, 2360. Women, 2360
Civil-Military Relations, 1567. Argentina, 1428, 1446, 1472. Chile, 1389, 2578. Ecuador, 2042. Honduras, 1165. Peru, 1372. South America, 1536. Uruguay, 1446, 1472. Venezuela, 1297, 1989, 2042, 2489
Civil Rights, 1558, 2233. Argentina, 1470, 2543. Bolivia, 1305. Brazil, 2543. Chile, 2079. Colombia, 2455. Uruguay, 1499, 2580. Venezuela, 2486. *See Also* Human Rights.
Civil Service. Guyana, 1198
Civil Society, 616, 1042, 1688, 2268, 2548–2549, 2569. Argentina, 1450, 1477, 2570. Bolivia, 1311. Brazil, 1503–1504, 2172. Colombia, 1247. Cuba, 1661, 1948, 2432. Globalization, 1826. Haiti, 1209. Honduras, 1166. Mexico, 1049, 1057, 1069, 1091–1092, 1112, 1119. Peru, 2535. Venezuela, 1290, 1987, 2486–2487
Civil War. Colombia, 1245, 1249. Guatemala, 477, 490, 1157, 1159
Civilization, 694. Brazil, 1506, 2142. Jamaica, 2415

Class Conflict. *See* Social Classes. *See* Social Conflict.
Clientelism. Argentina, 1444, 1471, 2104. Indigenous Peoples, 596. Mexico, 1081, 1122. Venezuela, 2486
Climate Change, 670, 678, 692–693, 705. Andean Region, 829–830. Brazil, 356. Caribbean Area, 733, 737. Chile, 368. Migration, 733. Tourism, 737
Climatology, 675. Mexican-American Border Region, 820. Peru, 884, 888, 895
Clothing Industry. Mexico, 88, 1859, 1864
Coal Mining. *See* Minerals and Mining Industry.
Coalitions. Argentina, 1452. Brazil, 1512, 1517. Chile, 1386, 1402, 1415. Colombia, 1253. Ecuador, 1283. *See Also* Political Parties.
Coastal Areas. Cuba, 739
Coastal Ecology. Chile, 371
Cobá Site (Mexico). Precolumbian Architecture, 126
Coca. Colombia, 574, 2007. Peru, 580, 2523. *See Also* Cocaine.
Cocaine, 2009. Colombia, 2016–2017. Peru, 580. *See Also* Coca.
Cochabamba, Bolivia (dept.). Biodiversity, 915. Emigrant Remittances, 913. Land Use, 899. Political Violence, 1317. Social Conflict, 1317. Social Movements, 1324
Codices. Borbonicus, 222. Mesoamerica, 241
Coffee Industry and Trade, 696. Central America, 790, 1853. Competition, 483. Guatemala, 483. Mexico, 790, 1853. Sustainable Development, 790, 1853
Colca Valley (Peru). Food Supply, 897. Land Settlement, 896
Colla (indigenous group). Contact with Incas, 420
Collective Bargaining. Chile, 1383. *See Also* Negotiation.
Collective Memory, 435, 2232. Argentina, 1436, 1464, 2547. Colombia, 2476. Guatemala, 758. Peru, 580, 2516
Colom, Álvaro, 440, 1158
Colombians. United Kingdom, 1730
Colonia, Uruguay (dept.). Excavations, 425
Colonial History. Guatemala, 1913
Colonization. Caribbean Area, 258. Peru, 2527
Coluna Prestes (revolutionary movement), 1507. *See Also* Revolutions and Revolutionary Movements.
Commerce, 1819. Brazil, 1765, 2176. Colom-

2462. *See Also* Bilingual Education;
Elementary Education.
Education and State. *See* Educational Policy.
Educational Policy, 1838, 2249. Argentina,
2121. Chile, 1382–1383, 2572. Mexico,
432. Peru, 1374. Puerto Rico, 1215
Ejército de Liberación Nacional (Colombia),
1236
Ejército Guerrillero de los Pobres (Guate-
mala), 1159
Ejército Revolucionario del Pueblo (Argen-
tina), 2557
Ejército Zapatista de Liberación Nacional
(Mexico), 487, 499
El Alto, Bolivia (city). Demography, 904.
Gender Roles, 1315. Political Conditions,
1331. Social Movements, 1315
El Bajío, Mexico (region). *See* Bajío, Mexico
(region).
El Beni, Bolivia (dept.). Autonomy, 1313
El Niño Current, 678. Peru, 888
Elderly Persons. *See* Aged.
Election Fraud. Mexico, 1086, 1088
Elections. Argentina, 1419, 1426, 1460, 1465,
1474–1476. Brazil, 1501, 1516–1518, 1521.
British Caribbean, 1218. Chile, 1377–
1378, 1386, 1391–1392, 1406. Colombia,
1234, 1242, 1244, 1250, 2038. Costa
Rica, 1137, 1140–1141, 1144. Ecuador,
1274–1275, 1282. El Salvador, 1148, 1150,
1155. Guatemala, 1160. Jamaica, 1212.
Law and Legislation, 1356. Mexico, 1044–
1045, 1048, 1055–1056, 1058, 1063, 1065,
1068, 1071, 1077, 1085–1086, 1095–1096,
1100–1101, 1114, 1124. Peru, 1355–1356,
1373. Trinidad and Tobago, 1219. Uruguay, 1498. Venezuela, 1299, 1301, 1981.
Women, 1046, 1419. *See Also* Campaign
Funds; Voting.
Electric Industries. Mexico, 1863. Nationalization, 1973. Venezuela, 1973. *See Also*
Microelectronics Industry.
Electricity. Costa Rica, 1139, 2381. El Salva-
dor, 2381. Privatization, 1139
Elementary Education. Brazil, 984
Elites, 2230. Argentina, 1473. Bolivia, 1344.
Brazil, 1502. Colombia, 1247. Ecuador,
2507. El Salvador, 1155. Mexico, 1043,
1075, 1083, 1604. Peru, 1367. Uruguay,
2128
Embera (indigenous group). Colombia, 2473
Emigrant Remittances, 664. Bolivia, 913.
Brazil, 1007. Costa Rica, 2371. Cuba,
1958. Dominican Republic, 2425. El
Salvador, 1907, 2405–2406. Haiti, 1918.

Mexico, 1073, 1882, 2284, 2306, 2327,
2363
Emigration and Immigration. *See* Migra-
tion. *See* Return Migration.
Employment, 1836, 2220. Argentina, 1439,
1444, 2099, 2104. Brazil, 2179, 2188, 2190.
Colombia, 859, 2019, 2475. El Salvador,
2404. Mexico, 799, 2292. Women, 2553
Empresa Nacional de Telecomunicaciones
(Argentina), 2118
Energy Consumption. Chile, 2068, 2073
Energy Policy, 1832. Bolivia, 2051. Brazil,
989, 1012, 1035, 1780, 2174. Chile, 2068,
2073. Cuba, 1658. Panama, 780–781. US,
1586
Energy Supply. Bolivia, 2051. Brazil, 2174
Enríquez-Ominami, Marco, 1406
Entrepreneurs, 452. Mexico, 1856, 1981.
Women, 1843
Entrepreneurship. Mexico, 1856. Women,
1843. *See Also* Small Business.
Environmental Degradation, 681, 705. Ar-
gentina, 922–923, 925, 940, 943. Brazil,
973, 1027. Colombia, 850, 854, 858. Ecua-
dor, 871. Mexico, 215, 788, 796, 801–802,
815, 1891. Peru, 406, 418, 893
Environmental History, 687. Brazil, 997
Environmental Policy, 663, 710. Amazon
Basin, 547, 1033, 1240. Bolivia, 906–907,
911, 914. Brazil, 997–999, 1005. Caribbean
Area, 726–727, 744. Chile, 951, 956, 967.
Colombia, 850. Cuba, 740, 1961. Ecuador,
878, 2047. Mexico, 791. Peru, 884, 888
Environmental Pollution. Brazil, 1030.
Mexican-American Border Region, 1116.
Mexico, 1866
Environmental Protection, 663, 679, 699,
716. Brazil, 976, 1025. Caribbean Area,
726, 744. Chile, 951, 961. Cuba, 1961.
Ecuador, 878. Mexico, 818. Paraguay, 968.
Peru, 894, 2520. *See Also* Conservation
(environment).
Environmental Sustainability. *See* Sustain-
able Development.
Epigraphy. Mesoamerica, 39
Erosion. *See* Soil Erosion.
Escuela Internacional de Arqueología y
Etnología Americanas (Mexico), 70
Esequiba Region (Guyana and Venezuela).
See Essequibo Region (Guyana and
Venezuela).
Esmeraldas, Ecuador (prov.). Ethnic Identity,
2508. Gender Roles, 2508
Espírito Santo, Brazil (state). Folklore, 564.
Social Life and Customs, 564

610/ Handbook of Latin American Studies v. 67

Participation, 429, 462, 475, 512, 578, 596, 613, 1091. Property, 581. Public Opinion, 458, 530. Puerto Rico, 271. Religious Life and Customs, 471, 518, 601. Rites and Ceremonies, 540, 565. Sex and Sexual Relations, 546. Social Conditions, 489, 567, 875. Social Life and Customs, 464, 497. Traditional Medicine, 491. Views of, 554, 561. Voting, 1305. Women, 454, 459, 465, 518, 538, 567, 1363. Women's Rights, 529

Indigenous Policy. Guatemala, 440

Indigenous Resistance. Aztecs, 23. Bolivia, 1281. Chile, 642. Ecuador, 1272, 1281, 2495. Mayas, 124, 228, 476

Industrial Development Projects. *See* Development Projects.

Industrial Policy. Brazil, 2171, 2204. Mexico, 1887. Trinidad and Tobago, 1926. Uruguay, 2130

Industrial Productivity. Venezuela, 1972

Industrial Relations, 1824. Colombia, 1824, 2004. Mexico, 2314. US, 2004

Industrialization. *See* Industry and Industrialization.

Industry and Industrialization, 1685. Argentina, 1421, 2084, 2109, 2115. Brazil, 1782, 2169. Colombia, 2008. Mexico, 1849, 1888. Venezuela, 1976

Inflation. Argentina, 2111. Brazil, 2175, 2177. Colombia, 2020, 2023

Informal Labor. *See* Informal Sector.

Informal Sector. Argentina, 947. Brazil, 2622. Ecuador, 647. Jamaica, 2452. Mexico, 793, 1897

Instituto Federal Electoral (Mexico), 1044, 1046, 1058, 1124

Instituto Nacional de Pesquisas da Amazônia, 976

Insurance. Colombia, 2018

Insurgency. *See* Insurrections.

Insurrections. Central America, 1129. Colombia, 1239, 1259, 2016, 2029, 2459. El Salvador, 1149. Nicaragua, 1173. Peru, 580, 1361, 1372

Intellectual History. Cuba, 2443. Mexico, 504

Intellectuals. Cuba, 1941, 2412. Mexico, 1106

Interest Groups. *See* Pressure Groups.

Internal Migration. *See* Migration.

Internal Stability. *See* Political Stability.

International Bank for Reconstruction and Development. *See* World Bank.

International Economic Relations, 1528–1529, 1553, 1694, 1807–1808, 1813, 1818,

1821, 2225. Argentina/Chile, 1705. Argentina/China, 1699. Brazil, 1764, 1787, 1791, 1793, 2140, 2162–2163, 2192. Brazil/China, 1789. Brazil/South Africa, 1790, 1795. Brazil/Spain, 1765, 1792. Caribbean Area, 1652–1653, 1670, 1680, 1927–1928. Caribbean Area/China, 1650. Caribbean Area/European Union, 1572. Caribbean Area/US, 1535, 1537. Central America, 1900. Central America/Mexico, 1646. Central America/Pacific Area, 1899. Chile, 2069. Chile/China, 1719. Chile/New Zealand, 952. Chile/Pacific Area, 1717. Colombia/US, 2002, 2024. Colombia/Venezuela, 1737. Cuba/Canada, 1675. Cuba/US, 1658, 1678. Dominican Republic/Haiti, 723. Ecuador/Peru, 1744. Germany, 1785. Haiti, 1664. Latin America/China, 1539, 1831. Latin America/European Union, 1532, 1560, 1572. Latin America/Spain, 1571, 1820. Latin America/US, 1535, 1537, 1541, 1564. Mexico, 1631, 1638. Mexico/Pacific Area, 1594, 1614. Mexico/US, 1587, 1639, 1858–1859. Peru/Spain, 1748. South America, 1691. South America/Europe, 1689. Uruguay, 1754. Venezuela, 1992

International Labour Organisation, 2576

International Law. Caribbean Area, 1680. Mexico, 1616

International Migration. *See* Migration.

International Monetary Fund (IMF), 2087. Argentina, 2103

International Relations. Argentina/Brazil, 1774. Argentina/Chile, 1418, 1698, 1721. Argentina/Germany, 1697. Argentina/Italy, 1427. Argentina/South Korea, 1707. Argentina/Uruguay, 1492. Argentina/US, 1710. Barbados/Great Britain, 1178. Bolivia/Chile, 1716, 1723. Bolivia/Mexico, 1620. Brazil, 1775–1776. Brazil/Chile, 1716, 1788. Brazil/China, 1770. Brazil/Germany, 1777. Brazil/Iraq, 1780. Brazil/Peru, 1747. Brazil/US, 1768, 1797. British Caribbean/UK, 1657. British Caribbean/US, 1667. Caribbean Area, 1186. Caribbean Area/US, 1182, 1563. Central America/US, 1129. Chile/Pacific Area, 1716. Colombia, 1264. Colombia/Ecuador, 1727. Colombia/Venezuela, 1728, 1738, 1761. Costa Rica, 1142. Cuba/Mexico, 1595, 1609, 1611. Cuba/Russia, 1648. Cuba/Spain, 1676. Cuba/US, 1222, 1654–1655, 1659–1661, 1668, 1671, 1677, 1679, 1948. Dominican Republic/US,

1195. Ecuador/Mexico, 1620. Haiti/US, 1200, 1208, 1651. Latin America/Canada, 1568. Latin America/China, 1539, 1550, 1561, 1808. Latin America/Europe, 1542, 1825. Latin America/European Union, 1557, 1560. Latin America/Iran, 1547. Latin America/Spain, 1534, 1552. Latin America/US, 1540, 1551, 1554–1555, 1561, 1563, 1565, 1569, 1573, 1696. Mexico/Africa, 1633. Mexico/Canada, 1580. Mexico/China, 1583, 1627. Mexico/ European Union, 1619. Mexico/Pacific Area, 1637. Mexico/Peru, 1620. Mexico/US, 1580, 1624, 1626, 1632, 1858. Paraguay/US, 1746. Peru/Germany, 1750. Peru/Italy, 1753. Political Thought, 1562, 1565–1566. Puerto Rico/US, 1216. Uruguay/Middle East, 1756. Uruguay/Spain, 1497

International Trade, 1529, 1821. Brazil, 2140, 2165, 2181. Jamaica, 2452. Mexico, 1876
International Trade Relations, 1834. Brazil, 1794. Brazil/China, 2151. Caribbean Area, 1649, 1663. Central America, 1900. Central America/US, 1911–1912. Chile/New Zealand, 952. Colombia/US, 1734. Cuba/ Canada, 1675. Dominican Republic/US, 1911–1912. Latin America/China, 1815, 1823. Mexico/China, 1576. Mexico/Japan, 1600

Internet, 714. Argentina, 2544. Mexico, 817
Intervention. *See* Foreign Intervention.
Investment. *See* Investments. *See* Saving and Investment.
Investments, 1805. Chile, 2076
Irrigation. Andean Region, 824. Ecuador, 867
ISI. *See* Import Substitution.
Italian Influences. Argentina, 2102
Jade. Caribbean Area, 254
Jalisco, Mexico (state). Children, 2288. Cultural Identity, 2328. Economic Conditions, 1889. Economic Policy, 1889. Social Life and Customs, 481
Japanese. Brazil, 1014
Jesuits. Southern Cone, 612
Jews, 2218. Cultural Identity, 2218. Dominican Republic, 1195. Mexico, 2279
Jiménez, Marcos Pérez. *See* Pérez Jiménez, Marcos.
Jobs. *See* Employment.
Journalism. Colombia, 1230. Political Culture, 2533. *See Also* Mass Media; Newspapers.
Journalists. Haiti, 1207

Juárez, Benito, 1621
Juárez, Mexico (city). *See* Ciudad Juárez, Mexico (city).
Judges. Chile, 1396
Judicial Power. Chile, 1396. Ecuador, 1279. History, 1396. Mexico, 1113, 1126. Peru, 1357
Judicial Process. Ecuador, 1279. Mexico, 1113. Peru, 1357
Jujuy, Argentina (prov.). Rock Art, 306
Juvenile Literature. *See* Children's Literature.
Kaminaljuyu Site (Guatemala), 85, 217
Kasapata Site (Peru), 415
Kings and Rulers. Andean Region, 284. *See Also* Chiefdoms.
Kinship. Argentina, 600
Kirchner, Néstor, 1426, 1432, 1435, 1459, 1704, 1706
Kissinger, Henry, 1797
Kuelap Site (Peru), 421
La Blanca Site (Guatemala). Excavations, 152
La Habana, Cuba (city). Economic Development, 738. Land Use, 738
La Hortensia S.A., 1864
La Ligua, Chile (city). Water Resources Development, 956
La Paz, Bolivia (dept.). Natural Resources, 912
La Plata, Argentina (city). Floods, 924
La Unión, El Salvador (dept.). Emigrant Remittances, 2406
La Violencia (Colombia). *See* Violencia, La (Colombia).
Labor and Laboring Classes, 1798. Andean Region, 823. Brazil, 980, 1019, 1022, 2190. Chile, 1416, 1490. Colombia, 644, 2004. Dominican Republic, 1931. El Salvador, 2376. Guatemala, 2383. Maquiladoras, 2344. Mexico, 1864, 1867, 2344. Panama, 2373. Uruguay, 1490. US, 2004. Venezuela, 1993. Women, 2311. *See Also* Labor Market; Labor Supply; Migrant Labor.
Labor Market, 1799, 1814, 1824, 2220, 2247. Argentina, 2090, 2098, 2100, 2122–2123, 2550, 2553. Brazil, 2179, 2205, 2622. Chile, 2070, 2081. Colombia, 1824, 2019, 2463, 2465. Cuba, 1956, 1969. El Salvador, 2404. Mexican-American Border Region, 1601. Mexico, 1630, 1873. Venezuela, 1993. *See Also* Labor and Laboring Classes.
Labor Movement, 1490. Argentina, 2100, 2550. Brazil, 2201. Caribbean Area, 1667.

Malaria. Argentina, 929

Malnutrition. *See* Nutrition.

Maltrata Site (Mexico), 159

Mam (indigenous group). Religious Life and Customs, 521. Social Conditions, 521

Manufactures, 1685, 1831. Mexico, 1862

Maps and Cartography, 688, 697. Argentina, 930. Belize, 749. Chile, 965. Dominican Republic, 732. Honduras, 764, 767. Mexico, 448. Natural Resources, 902. Nicaragua, 749

Mapuche (indigenous group). Indigenous/Non-Indigenous Relations, 643. Indigenous Resistance, 642. Land Tenure, 961. Religious Life and Customs, 640. Rites and Ceremonies, 640. Social Movements, 641

Maquiladoras. Guatemala, 2383. Labor Market, 1873. Mexican-American Border Region, 2344. Mexico, 1873, 2294. Pregnancy, 2294. Women, 2383

Maquilas. *See* Maquiladoras.

Mar del Plata, Argentina (city). Public Works, 2117

Maracaibo, Venezuela (city). Housing, 838. Petroleum Industry and Trade, 1292. Slums, 1292

Marajó Island (Brazil). Archeological Surveys, 324. Archeology, 352–353, 355. Precolumbian Pottery, 335. Shells and Shell Middens, 335. Stone Implements, 335

Marcaya Site (Peru), 424

Marginalization. *See* Social Marginality.

Marine Resources. Caribbean Area, 728. Honduras, 768. Mexico, 215

Maritain, Jacques, 1387

Maritime Policy. Mexico, 1634

Marketing. Cuba, 1958

Markets, 1837, 1844. Argentina, 2082, 2106. Brazil, 975, 2176, 2178, 2194. Chile, 2072

Mary, *Blessed Virgin, Saint*, 2566

MAS. *See* Movimiento al Socialismo (Bolivia).

Masculinity. Brazil, 2611

Masks. Puerto Rico, 2428

Mass Media, 1688, 2549. Argentina, 1476. Central America, 2375. Colombia, 1230. Ecuador, 648, 1271, 1275. Elections, 1065. Haiti, 1207. Mexico, 1617. Peru, 2533. Political Culture, 1230, 1271, 1290, 1295, 1386, 1476, 2375. Venezuela, 1290, 1295. *See Also* Journalism.

Mataco (indigenous group), 603. Argentina, 607, 619

Matagalpa, Nicaragua (dept.). Cultural Identity, 779. Local History, 779

Mate (tea), 2133

Material Culture, 301. Amazon Region, 565. Andean Region, 293. Argentina, 603. Ecuador, 385. Mesoamerica, 42. Mexico, 459. Paraguay, 589. Precolumbian Civilizations, 342. Puerto Rico, 272

Mato Grosso, Brazil (state). Excavations, 338. Land Use, 1000. Museums, 563

Mato Grosso do Sul, Brazil (state). Indigenous Peoples, 339

Mayas. Agricultural Ecology, 75. Agricultural Systems, 75. Archeology, 21. Artifacts, 185. Artisanry, 162. Astronomy, 206, 219–220, 224, 227. Biography, 434. Calendrics, 30, 206, 220, 224, 227, 230. Caves, 33, 173. Ceramics, 162. Cities and Towns, 26, 187, 235. City Planning, 126. Civil Rights, 526. Coffee Industry and Trade, 483. Commerce, 187. Cosmology, 30, 219, 228, 230, 433, 476. Cultural History, 81. Cultural Identity, 81, 482, 2370. Dance, 43, 484. Death, 25. Economic Conditions, 48, 470. Economic Geography, 74. Economic History, 48. Economic Models, 74. Education, 461. Ethnic Identity, 151, 467, 482, 536. Folklore, 533. Food, 216–217. Food Supply, 169. Guatemala, 81, 2370. Historiography, 15. Human Ecology, 130. Human Geography, 22, 52. Human Remains, 217. Iconography, 35, 144, 433. Income Distribution, 67. Indigenous Literature, 531, 533, 536. Kings and Rulers, 25, 184. Language and Languages, 84, 467, 473. Linguistics, 239. Migration, 22. Mortuary Customs, 25. Murals, 233. Music, 484. Myths and Mythology, 22, 24, 68, 228, 230, 474, 476. Nutrition, 216–217. Painting, 35. Philosophy, 47. Political Conditions, 536. Political Economy, 67. Political Geography, 235. Political Participation, 440. Political Systems, 52. Precolumbian Architecture, 152, 171, 191, 198, 200. Precolumbian Land Settlement Patterns, 130, 160, 200. Precolumbian Pottery, 198. Religion, 474. Religious Life and Customs, 32, 47, 68, 79, 473, 494, 525, 532. Research, 15, 21, 32. Rites and Ceremonies, 47, 79, 140, 173, 185, 219, 433, 474, 525. Science, 84. Sculpture, 24, 192. Social Conditions, 49. Social Life and Customs, 43, 49, 52, 79, 141, 145, 482, 525, 532. Social Movements, 477. Social Structure, 32. Stone Implements, 121, 205, 214. Symbolism, 144, 191, 212, 433. Urban Planning, 206. Water Distribution, 127. Water Supply, 127, 204. Writing, 224, 226, 230, 233, 239, 531

Mayors. Colombia, 1233

Mbya (indigenous group). Beekeeping, 591. Migration, 566. Religion, 560. Religious Life and Customs, 559, 566. Science, 560. Social Life and Customs, 559, 566, 591

Meat Industry. Brazil, 1012. *See Also* Cattle Raising and Trade.

Meco Site (Mexico), 177

Medellín, Colombia (city). Center/Periphery Relations, 840. City Planning, 840, 849. Housing, 849, 856. Urban History, 847. Urbanization, 847. Violence, 2476. Youth, 2467, 2476

Media. *See* Mass Media.

Medical Anthropology. Mexico, 431, 443

Medical Care, 1039, 1179. Colombia, 2018, 2463. Costa Rica, 755. Cuba, 1946, 1951. Mexico, 431, 443. *See Also* Medicine.

Medical Policy. Colombia, 2018

Medicinal Plants. Mexico, 491

Medicine. Peru, 579. *See Also* Medical Care.

Mendoza, Argentina (prov.). Wine and Wine Making, 936

Mercado Común del Sur. *See* Mercosur.

Mercosul. *See* Mercosur.

Mercosur, 1470, 1685, 1689, 1692–1693, 1754, 1766, 1783, 1787, 2132, 2134, 2176

Mérida, Mexico (city). Ethnology, 450. Family and Family Relations, 2368. Urban Sociology, 450. Violence, 2368

Mérida, Venezuela (city). City Planning, 833. Public Spaces, 833. Sustainable Development, 837. Urban Policy, 837

Mesa Gisbert, Carlos D., 1319, 1330

Mestizos and Mestizaje, 1180, 2419. Bolivia, 1346

Metal-Work. Brazil, 2208

Metallurgy. Ecuador, 386. Mexico, 237

Metropolitan Areas. *See* Cities and Towns.

Mexica. *See* Aztecs.

Mexican-American Border Region, 1632, 1639. Climatology, 820. Ecology, 786. Economic Conditions, 1894. Economic Development, 1895. Economic Integration, 1895. Environmental Policy, 1615. Illegal Aliens, 1597. Migration, 1597. Migration Policy, 1597. Urbanization, 1615. *See Also* Borderlands.

Mexican Americans, 1585. Acculturation, 2304–2305. Economic Conditions, 2305,

2333. Employment, 1574. Social Conditions, 2304–2305, 2333

Mexicans. US, 1582, 2304–2305, 2307, 2319, 2333

México, Mexico (city). AIDS, 2317. Banking and Financial Institutions, 1835. Citizenship, 2364. Commerce, 793. Crime and Criminals, 819, 1102. Democracy, 2364. Democratization, 1061. Fear, 2300. Internet, 817. Migration, 2338. Pentecostalism, 2310. Police, 2277. Political Conditions, 1087. Political Culture, 1059. Political Participation, 1061. Prisons, 2276. Religious Life and Customs, 520. Spaniards, 2338. Violence, 1102, 2300. Voting, 1087. Water Distribution, 784. Water Supply, 784

México, Mexico (state). Corn, 803. Elections, 1128. Indigenous Peoples, 511. Municipal Government, 1128. Political Conditions, 1043. Prisons, 2276. Social Conditions, 511. Women, 2327

Mexico. Congreso. Comisión de Concordia y Pacificación, 487

Michoacán, Mexico (state). Migration, 2321

Michoacán de Ocampo, Mexico (region). Ethnology, 522. Ranchers, 522

Microcredit. *See* Microfinance.

Microelectronics Industry. Brazil, 2205. *See Also* Electric Industries.

Microfinance. Argentina, 2083. Mexico, 1861. Peru, 2531. Venezuela, 1986. *See Also* Credit.

Middle Classes. Argentina, 2539

Migrant Labor. Argentina, 636. Ecuador, 2505. Mexican-American Border Region, 2297. Mexico, 527, 1582, 1603. US, 653, 1582, 1603, 2505. *See Also* Agricultural Labor.

Migrant Labor, Haitian. Dominican Republic, 1206

Migrant Labor, Mexican. US, 1608, 2281

Migration, 439, 664, 673, 682, 712, 1530, 1558, 1688, 2239. Amazon Basin, 544. Argentina, 920, 2559. Bolivia, 913. Brazil, 1018. Caribbean Area, 725, 733–734, 2413, 2423, 2430, 2445. Central America, 2389. Colombia, 1730–1731, 2510. Cuba, 256, 1936, 1948. Dominican Republic, 1206, 2425, 2436. Ecuador, 1741, 2500, 2504, 2510. Education, 1067, 2303. El Salvador, 2405–2406. Guatemala, 760, 1641. Haiti, 1203, 1206, 1665, 1918, 2446. Mexican-American Border Region, 1598, 1601, 2297. Mexico, 454, 524, 796, 798,

Movimiento de Unidad Plurinacional
Pachakutik-Nuevo País (Ecuador), 1278
Movimiento Revolucionario Túpac Amaru
(Peru), 1361
Movimiento Tierra y Libertad—Tomás
Katari (Bolivia), 1343
Multiculturalism, 673, 2231, 2239, 2249,
2258, 2264, 2267. Bolivia, 630, 2511.
Chile, 643. Colombia, 514, 575. Ecuador,
2511. Guatemala, 494, 1156. Mexico, 27,
437, 447, 462, 475, 514, 1156. Puerto Rico,
2422. Uruguay, 2583
Multinational Corporations. Colombia,
2025. Peru, 1748
Multinational Corporations, Spanish, 1571,
1683
Municipal Government. Bolivia, 634, 1307,
1309, 1333, 2263. Brazil, 1516, 1526, 2145.
Central America, 1903. Chile, 1404, 1410.
Colombia, 1233, 1268, 2461. Costa Rica,
1143. Elections, 1110. Mexico, 1080, 1094,
1097–1098, 1108–1109, 1121, 1890, 2293.
Peru, 1370. Uruguay, 2129
Municipal Services. Mexico, 1097
Mural Painting. Mexico, 98, 103
Murals. Mayas, 123, 190
Museu Paraense Emílio Goeldi, 343
Museu Rondon, 563
Museums. Brazil, 343
Muslims. Colombia, 2468
Myths and Mythology. Mayas, 28. Meso-
america, 17. Taino, 276
NAFTA. See North American Free Trade
Agreement (NAFTA).
Nahuas (indigenous group). Christianity,
528. Cultural Identity, 455. Government
Relations, 506. Political Conditions, 506.
Rites and Ceremonies, 436, 528. Social
Life and Customs, 436, 455
Nahuatl (language), 444–445
Narcotics Policy. Colombia, 574. Mexico,
1078. US, 574, 1544
Nation-Building. See State-Building.
National Autonomy. See Autonomy.
National Characteristics, 1329, 1566, 2257,
2267. Argentina, 1463, 1703. Bolivia,
1329. Brazil, 1463, 1703. Caribbean
Area, 2257. Colombia, 1732. Dominican
Republic, 2449. Mexico, 1607. Puerto
Rico, 2424. US, 1607. See Also National
Identity.
National Defense. See National Security.
National Identity, 435, 694, 707. Bolivia,
2511. Brazil, 2596. Caribbean Area,
2429. Costa Rica, 2397. Cuba, 2412. Do-

minican Republic, 2450. Ecuador, 2511.
Guatemala, 81. Haiti, 1210. Mexico,
27. Peru, 2516, 2527. See Also National
Characteristics.
National Parks. See Parks and Reserves.
National Patrimony. Mexico, 447
National Security, 1531, 1567, 1695–1696,
2009, 2225, 2254. Argentina, 1438, 1721.
Brazil, 1771. Chile, 1721. Colombia, 1262,
1264. Ecuador, 1741. Mexico, 1047, 1060,
1109, 1612, 1626, 1632. Peru, 1751. South
America, 1536. Southern Cone, 1548. US,
1550, 1578, 1626, 1632, 1679, 1759
Nationalism. Argentina, 1445. Brazil, 1783.
Colombia, 2468. Cuba, 1220. Mexico,
1084. Paraguay, 1483
Nationalization. Bolivia, 1323, 1338, 2051.
Mexico, 1851, 1870, 1875, 1878. Petroleum
Industry and Trade, 1851, 1878. Venezu-
ela, 1973, 1978
Natural Disasters, 678, 687, 918. Guatemala,
757. Haiti, 1672. Peru, 884, 892. See Also
Hurricanes.
Natural Gas. Andean Region, 828. Argen-
tina, 1705. Bolivia, 1323, 2050. Cuba,
1658
Natural History. Brazil, 1017. Caribbean
Area, 262
Natural Resources, 663, 679, 919, 1810.
Argentina, 922, 925–926, 933–934, 942.
Bolivia, 631, 902, 907, 912, 1310. Brazil,
997. Colombia, 854. Ecuador, 2047. Mex-
ico, 798. Nicaragua, 777. Peru, 583, 895.
Venezuela, 834
Nature, 698. Ecuador, 869. Jamaica, 729
Nayarit, Mexico (state). Social Life and
Customs, 481
Nazca Culture, 424
Negotiation. Colombia, 1237, 1255, 1259,
1732. Ecuador/Peru, 1742, 1744. See Also
Collective Bargaining.
Neighborhood Government. Argentina,
1425
Neoliberalism, 616, 1804, 1822, 1838, 2248.
Agricultural Development, 2377. Argen-
tina, 621, 1430, 2106, 2120–2121. Bolivia,
1323. Brazil, 1522, 1786, 2138. Chile, 641,
967, 1398, 2078. Colombia, 2004–2005.
Costa Rica, 1137. Ecuador, 648. Guate-
mala, 2400. Mexico, 1117, 1882. Peru,
1368. Uruguay, 1488, 2129. Venezuela,
1981. See Also Economic Liberalization.
Neuquén, Argentina (prov.). Human Geography, 941
Newspapers. Argentina, 1700

Soil Erosion. Cuba, 739. Mexico, 802
Soils. Brazil, 313, 316–317, 327, 329, 355, 357–358, 974
Soldiers. Colombia, 1735
Sonora, Mexico (state). Agricultural Geography, 787. Cattle Raising and Trade, 808. Economic History, 805. Gender Roles, 2337. Indigenous Peoples, 441. Ranchers, 808. Social History, 805
Sovereignty. Bolivia, 1320. Dutch Caribbean, 1666. Puerto Rico, 1216. *See Also* Autonomy.
Soybeans. Argentina, 944
Spaniards. Honduras, 770
Spanish Conquest. Mexico, 90, 193
Spanish Influences. Public Opinion, 1552
Squatter Settlements. Ecuador, 1276, 1358. Jamaica, 743. Peru, 1276, 1358. Puerto Rico, 2418. *See Also* Slums.
Standard of Living. *See* Cost and Standard of Living.
State, The, 1461, 2265. Argentina, 1421, 1430, 1459, 2084, 2105. Brazil, 1519, 2172. Colombia, 1249. Haiti, 1209. Mexico, 1120. Venezuela, 1987
State-Building. Argentina, 2546. Barbados, 1178. Colombia, 1251. Nicaragua, 1173
State Enterprises. *See* Public Enterprises.
State Reform. Argentina, 1420. Brazil, 1519. *See Also* Political Reform.
Statesmen, US, 1563
Statistics. Cuba, 1937–1939, 1961–1962
Steel Industry and Trade. Brazil, 2168. Mexico, 1860
Stone Implements. Argentina, 304. Belize, 214. Brazil, 314, 320, 326, 335, 347–348, 350, 360–361. Caribbean Area, 263. French Guiana, 394. Guatemala, 85. Guyana, 392. Mesoamerica, 20, 139. Mexico, 128, 150, 164, 175, 188, 193
Street Children. Mexico, 2354. Peru, 2518, 2537
Strikes and Lockouts. Mexico, 1089
Structural Adjustment. Mexico, 1881. Venezuela, 1980, 2492
Student Movements. Chile, 2572
Students, 2243, 2252. Political Participation, 2572
Sucre, Bolivia (city). Historical Geography, 905. Phenomenology, 905
Sucre, Venezuela (state). Agriculture, 835. Development Projects, 835. Economic Conditions, 1994
Sucumbíos, Ecuador (prov.). Development, 2497

Sugar Industry and Trade. Colombia, 1998. Cuba, 1227
Sustainable Agriculture. Amazon Basin, 1002. Caribbean Area, 742. Cuba, 740. Ecuador, 873, 2041
Sustainable Development, 662, 677, 716, 1809. Amazon Basin, 975. Argentina, 942, 2096. Bolivia, 907. Brazil, 1031, 1767, 2209. Caribbean Area, 721, 734–735, 741, 1921. Central America, 790, 1853. Chile, 953. Colombia, 857. Cuba, 740. Ecuador, 862, 865–866. Jamaica, 729. Mexico, 790, 813, 1853. Paraguay, 588. Patagonia, 916. Peru, 880, 890. Venezuela, 837
Symbolism. Andean Region, 284. Architecture, 428. Mexico, 69, 237
Symbolism (art). Incas, 407. Mayas, 68. Mesoamerica, 42. Peru, 413
Syncretism. Mexico, 473, 528
Taino (indigenous group). Artifacts, 262. Indigenous/Non-Indigenous Relations, 262. Myths and Mythology, 276. Sculpture, 274. Social Life and Customs, 262. West Indies, 266
Tajín Site (Mexico), 55
Tamaulipas, Mexico (state). Agricultural Labor, 1867. Excavations, 65
Tapajó (indigenous group). Land Settlement, 329
Tapiete (indigenous group). Ethnic Identity, 592
Tarahumara (indigenous group). Education, 432. Ethnography, 523. Political Participation, 492. Religious Life and Customs, 523. Rites and Ceremonies, 498. Social Life and Customs, 523
Tariffs. Brazil, 2164
Tarija, Bolivia (dept.). Natural Resources, 1310
Tawahka (indigenous group). Land Tenure, 771
Tax Reform. Colombia, 2003, 2013
Taxation, 1803. Argentina, 1456, 2112. Brazil, 2177–2178. Colombia, 2003, 2019. Ecuador, 2043. El Salvador, 1916
Taxes. *See* Taxation.
Technical Assistance, US. Brazil, 1768
Technological Development. Argentina, 2101. Brazil, 2171
Technological Innovations, 1827. Argentina, 2101
Telecommunication, 1827, 1832. Argentina, 2118. Central America, 1901–1902. Costa Rica, 1642. Privatization, 1828, 2118
Telefónica S.A., 1827

Ucayali, Peru (dept.). Environmental Degradation, 886
Umbanda (cult). Brazil, 557, 2599. *See Also* African Influences.
UN. *See* United Nations.
Underwater Archeology. Brazil, 346, 350–351. Guyana, 390
Unemployment. Bolivia, 2052. Cuba, 1952
Unión de Colonos Independientes (Guadalajara, Mexico), 1119
Unión de Naciones Suramericanas, 1536
Unión Demócrata Independiente (Chile), 1399
United Nations, 1472, 1629, 1722, 1749, 1756
Urarina (indigenous group). Material Culture, 650. Social Life and Customs, 650
Urban Areas. Argentina, 935, 941, 943. Brazil, 2598. Mesoamerica, 38, 64. Venezuela, 836
Urban History. Colombia, 847, 853, 860
Urban Planning. *See* City Planning.
Urban Policy, 676, 685, 691, 704, 2129. Argentina, 2117. Brazil, 981, 1028, 1030. Chile, 960, 2064. Colombia, 857. Jamaica, 743. Mexico, 807. Peru, 887. Uruguay, 2129. Venezuela, 837
Urban Sociology, 704. Argentina, 945, 2568. Chile, 949. Colombia, 852, 860. Mexico, 450
Urbanization, 671, 700. Argentina, 928, 935. Brazil, 981, 1032. Caribbean Area, 720. Colombia, 847, 853, 857, 860
Uribe Vélez, Álvaro, 1232, 1234–1235, 1245, 1251, 1253, 1258, 1985
Urubu Kaapor (indigenous group). Religious Life and Customs, 553. Social Life and Customs, 553
Uruguayans. Spain, 2582
Valle del Cauca, Colombia (dept.). Agriculture, 2026
Varal Site (Mexico), 157
Vargas, Getúlio, 1018, 1447
Veracruz, Mexico (state). Human Geography, 510. Indigenous Peoples, 510. Migration, 2321
Veracruz-Llave, Mexico (state). Ethnography, 539
Vernacular Architecture. Mexico, 428
Vieques, Puerto Rico (island). History, 2438
Violence, 1042, 1527, 2226. Argentina, 607, 1424. Bolivia, 626. Brazil, 2251, 2601, 2624. Caribbean Area, 2437. Central

America, 2384, 2399. Colombia, 1243, 1249, 1260, 1743, 1996, 2466, 2476, 2480. Economic Conditions, 1812, 2036. Ecuador, 648. El Salvador, 1151, 2382, 2390, 2407. Guatemala, 1158, 2372, 2379, 2387–2388, 2400. Honduras, 2409. Mexico, 1078, 2292, 2350, 2364. Migration, 2353. Puerto Rico, 2435. Statistics, 1254. Venezuela, 2488. Women, 2346, 2350, 2360, 2368–2369, 2526. Youth, 2435. *See Also* Abused Women; Political Violence.
Violencia, La (Colombia), 2481
Virginity. *See* Sex and Sexual Relations.
Vitória, Brazil (city). Municipal Government, 2145. Political Participation, 2145
Voting. Argentina, 1422, 1476. Bolivia, 1305. Chile, 1393, 1399, 1415. Colombia, 2002. Costa Rica, 1144. El Salvador, 1148. Mexico, 1062, 1095, 1122. Nicaragua, 775. Uruguay, 1498. *See Also* Elections.
Wages. Brazil, 2188, 2190, 2195, 2622. Colombia, 1997, 2463. Mexico, 1630
Waorani (indigenous group). *See* Huao (indigenous group).
Wari (indigenous group). *See* Huari (indigenous group).
Water Distribution. Andean Region, 824. Mesoamerica, 69. Mexico, 783–784, 1847
Water Resources Development, 662, 684. Andean Region, 827. Bolivia, 715, 906. Brazil, 998–999. Chile, 715, 956. Costa Rica, 2381. Ecuador, 876–877. El Salvador, 2381. Mexico, 715, 783
Water Rights, 684. Andean Region, 821, 824, 827. Bolivia, 715, 903, 910, 2053. Chile, 715. Ecuador, 867, 876. Mexico, 715, 1847
Water Supply, 662, 684. Andean Region, 827. Argentina, 2094, 2117. Bolivia, 903, 910, 2053. Brazil, 997–999. Chile, 956, 1724. Cuba, 1940. Ecuador, 876. Mesoamerica, 69, 501. Mexico, 783–784, 1847. Peru, 887, 889. Privatization, 1840
Waterways. Ecuador, 867
Wealth. Brazil, 1013. *See Also* Capital.
Welfare. *See* Social Welfare.
Wichí (indigenous group). *See* Mataco (indigenous group).
Wildlife Refuges. *See* Parks and Reserves.
Wine and Wine Making. Argentina, 921, 936. Chile, 921
Women, 2238, 2269. Argentina, 1419, 1422, 2545, 2551, 2565. Blacks, 2475. Bolivia, 635, 1315, 1345. Brazil, 1501, 2624. Carib-

AUTHOR INDEX

Guevara Gil, Jorge Armando, 827
Guevara Sánchez, Arturo, 515
Guevara Zárraga, María Estela, 2313
Guffroy, J., 295
Guido Martínez, Clemente, 1169
Guillen, Isabel Cristina Martins, 2604
Guillén Romo, Arturo, 1841, 2194
Guillermo, Sylvia, 1862
Guillerot, Julie, 2526
Guinea, Mercedes, 385
Guirkinger, Catherine, 2057
Guiteras Mombiola, Anna, 629
Gustafson, Bret Darin, 1320
Gutiérrez, Francisco, 2016
Gutiérrez, Horácio, 1768
Gutiérrez, Natividad, 1314
Gutiérrez Bonilla, Martha Lucía, 2466
Gutiérrez Castañeda, Griselda, 1057
Gutiérrez Castorena, Daniel, 2314
Gutiérrez Estévez, Manuel, 429
Gutiérrez Flórez, Felipe, 848
Gutiérrez M., Irma Eugenia, 2367
Gutiérrez Nieto, Guillermo, 1690
Gutiérrez Sánchez, Javier, 508
Guyot, Sylvain, 937
Guzmán, Luis Humberto, 1170
Guzmán Mejía, Rafael, 472
Gwynne, Robert N., 952–953
Haas, Jonathan, 422
Haas, Liesl, 1395
Hacer política desde la sociedad, 2315
¿Hacia dónde va Costa Rica?: sistema político y escenarios de gobernabilidad democrática para la próxima década 2010–2020: 5 debates sobre el futuro de Costa Rica, 1140
¿Hacia donde va el sistema mundial?: impactos y alternativas para América Latina y el Caribe, 1818
Hacia una nueva carta étnica del Gran Chaco VII, 597
Hacia una nueva estrategia internacional: el desafío de Néstor Kirchner, 1704
Haddad, Eduardo A., 2169
Hagene, Turid, 2380
Haglund, LaDawn, 2381
Hagopian, Frances, 2262
Haiti and the Haitian diaspora in the wider Caribbean, 1203, 1665
Hale, Lindsay, 557, 2599
Hall, Anthony, 2170, 2600
Hall, Kenneth O., 1652–1653, 1674, 1680, 1920, 1933
Hallerberg, Mark, 2136
Halperin, Christina T., 138, 168

Hamann, Marita, 2516
Hanekamp, Erika, 1743
Hanks, William F., 473
Hansen, Richard D., 206
Hansing, Katrin, 2431
Harner, John P., 799–800
Harris, Mary Hill, 251
Harris, Richard Legé, 1804
Hart, Thomas, 474
Hartlyn, Jonathan, 1191
Hartog, Thierry, 734
Hastorf, Christine Ann, 284
Haughney, Diane, 641
Hausler, Elizabeth, 731
Hautzinger, Sarah J., 2601
Hayward, Michele H., 270
Healan, Dan M., 139
Hearn, Adrian H., 2432
Heckenberger, Michael J., 331, 358
Hegemonía e interculturalidad: poblaciones originarias y migrantes: la interculturalidad como uno de los desafíos del siglo XXI, 2239
Hegemonía y control comunicacional, 1295
Heine, Jorge, 1845
Heinrich-Böll-Stiftung. Oficina Regional para Centroamérica, México y Cuba, 2231
Helen Kellogg Institute for International Studies, 1948, 2262
Hellin, Jonathan, 803
Helmke, Christophe, 140
Henderson, John S., 163
Henderson, Lucia, 225
Hendon, Julia A., 141
Hendricks, Bracken, 1204
Henke, Holger W., 2417
Henriques Ferreira, Túlio Sérgio, 1784
Henry, Frances, 2445
Herbas Cuevas, Iblin, 1315
Heredia Espinoza, Verenice Y., 23
Herlihy, Peter H., 804
Hermanns, Klaus, 2157
Hernández, César, 1863
Hernández, Christine L., 219
Hernández, Felipe, 704
Hernandez, Kelly Lytle, 1597
Hernández, Leonardo, 2071
Hernández, Rossana, 1984
Hernández, Sarah, 2316
Hernández Alarcón, Rosalinda, 490
Hernández Baqueiro, Alberto, 2317
Hernández Castillo, Rosalva Aída, 465
Hernández Castro, Rocío, 1598
Hernández Díaz, Jorge, 1079
Hernández Fox, Leonor Arlen, 2433

Iran in Latin America: threat or "axis of
annoyance"?, 1547
Irarrázaval Llona, Ignacio, 1383, 1410
Irurita, Natalia, 2096
Irwin G., Domingo, 1297
Isaacs, Anita, 1158
Isaza Castro, Jairo Guillermo, 2463
Isch L., Edgar, 821
Isfandiyārī, Hālāh, 1547
Ishihara, Reiko, 148
Island shores, distant pasts: archaeological
and biological approaches to the pre-
Columbian settlement of the Caribbean,
259
Istituto italo-latino americano, 322
Isunza Vera, Ernesto, 1045
Itatí Palermo, Alicia, 2229
Itier, César, 652
Itinerario de la Coyuntura Politica Boli-
viana, 1328
Ivo, Anete Brito Leal, 2221
Izcara Palacios, Simón Pedro, 1867
Jackson, Margaret Ann, 413
Jackson, Sarah E., 35
Jackson, Stephen T., 690
Jackson, Toni de, 2171
Jackson-Smith, Douglas, 669
Jacobo, Alejandro D., 2097
Jadresic, Alejandro, 2001
Jaffe, Rivke, 720
Jaime-Riverón, Olaf, 149
Jaimes, Carlos Alberto, 2018
Jaksic, Fabián, 959
Jamadar, Peter A., 1219
James, Erica Caple, 1205
Jamin, Thierry, 414
Jansen, Robert S., 2242
Jara, Umberto, 1361
Jaramillo, Grace, 1553, 1561
Jaramillo E., Luis Gonzalo, 294, 373
Jaramillo G., Lino, 859
Jardim Pinto, Céli Regina, 2172
Jeannot, Fernando, 1848
Jenkins, Rhys, 1823
Jepson, Wendy E., 1000
Jeria, José de la Fuente, 1322
Jernigan, Kevin A., 579
Jiménez, Edith, 800
Jimenez, Maren Andrea, 984
Jiménez, Rommy, 1903
Jiménez Badillo, Margarita, 1055
Jiménez Basco, Beatriz, 665
Jiménez Díaz, Luis, 889
Jiménez Huerta, Mariana, 2106
Jiménez López, José Concepción, 78

Jiménez M., Rafael Simón, 1758
Jiménez Piernas, Carlos, 1645
Johnson, Hume N., 1211
Johnson, Kenyon, 2173
Johnson, Lyman L., 661
Joignant Rondón, Alfredo, 2571, 2574
Jonas, Eline, 2624
Jones, Julie, 1
Jordán, Valeria, 1813
Jordana, Jacint, 1828
Jorge, Janes, 1001
Jornada Ariovaldo Umbelino de Oliveira,
Presidente Prudente, Brazil, 2005, 995
Jornada de Estudios del Trabajo, *1st, Univer-
sidad del Rosario, 2007*, 1824
Jornadas de Arqueología (Mexico), *Escuela
Nacional de Antropología e Historia*, 36
Jornadas de Investigadores en Arqueología
y Etnohistoria del Centro-oeste del País,
5th, Río Cuarto, Argentina, 2003, 289
Jornadas de Investigadores en Arqueología
y Etnohistoria del Centro-oeste del País,
6th, Río Cuarto, Argentina, 2005, 289
Jornadas Interdisciplinarias del Sudoeste
Bonaerense, *5th, Bahía Blanca, Argen-
tina, 2008*, 934
Journal of Caribbean Archaeology, 260
Los jóvenes ante el siglo XXI, 2323
Jóvenes universitarios en latinoamérica,
hoy, 2243
Joyce, Arthur A., 37–38
Juárez, Orient Bolívar, 1644
Juárez Cerdi, Elizabeth, 2345
Juárez Silva, Ranferi, 113
Julca, Alex, 733
Júlio, Jorge Eduardo, 2154
Jung, Courtney, 475
Juntos pero no revueltos?: partidos, candida-
tos y campañas en las elecciones legislati-
vas de 2006 en Colombia, 1250
Justeson, John, 39
Kahhat, Farid, 1548
Kaltmeier, Olaf, 1273
Kampwirth, Karen, 1171
Kane, Adrian Taylor, 698
Kanitscheider, Sigrun, 935
Karasik, Carol, 534–535
Karper, Jes, 747
Karsh, Marianne B., 692
Kasapata and the Archaic period of the
Cuzco Valley, 415
Kath, Elizabeth, 1946
Katz, Jorge M., 2101
Kaufman, Terrence, 39
Kaup, Brent Z., 1323